THE ROYAL AIR
1930 TO 193

At the Jubilee Review of 1935, King George V was shown an air force of biplanes. By the time that war broke out in 1939 the RAF had been transformed. Fixed undercarriages, fixed-pitch propellers, twin Vickers guns in fighters, bombs slung beneath the wings, open cockpits and fabric-covered fuselages were on their way out. Eight Browning guns buried in the wings of monoplane fighters, bombers with bomb-bays in the fuselage, retractable undercarriages, variable-pitch propellers and power-operated gun turrets were on the way in.

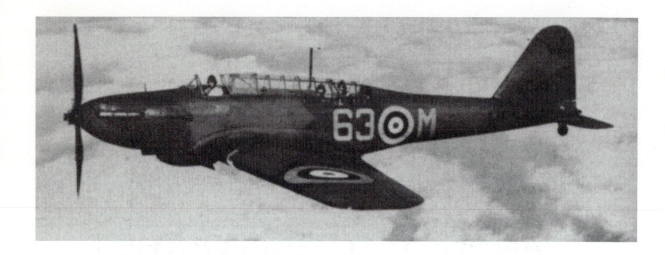

THE ROYAL AIR FORCE
1930 TO 1939

AN ENCYCLOPEDIA OF THE INTER-WAR YEARS

VOLUME II – REARMAMENT 1930 TO 1939

By Wing Commander
I.M. Philpott RAF (Retd)

First published in Great Britain in 2008 by
Pen & Sword Aviation
an imprint of
Pen & Sword Books Ltd
47 Church Street
Barnsley
South Yorkshire
S70 2AS

ISBN 978-1-84415-391-6

A CIP catalogue record for this book is available from the British Library

Volume I of this work 'The Trenchard Years 1918 to 1929' was published in 2005 and is available from
Pen and Sword Books, ISBN 1 84415 154 9.

Typeset in 9/11pt Palatino by
Mac Style, Nafferton, E. Yorkshire

Printed and bound in the UK by
CPI

Pen & Sword Books Ltd incorporates the Imprints of Pen & Sword Aviation, Pen & Sword Maritime, Pen & Sword
Military, Wharncliffe Local History, Pen and Sword Select, Pen and Sword Military Classics and Leo Cooper.

For a complete list of Pen & Sword titles please contact
PEN & SWORD BOOKS LIMITED
47 Church Street, Barnsley, South Yorkshire, S70 2AS, England
E-mail: enquiries@pen-and-sword.co.uk
Website: www.pen-and-sword.co.uk

Contents

Author's Foreword

This second volume of my inter-war history follows the same format as Volume I. What is different is the emphasis because this volume is about rearmament. Examples of the different treatment can be found in the chapter on Air Control operations in the 1930s. These operations differed little from those carried out in the 1920s, so the arrangement of Chapter 4 gives a different emphasis. The same applies to Chapter 6. The RAF's participation in Fleet Air Arm operations and training in the 1930s differed little from those of the 1920s. Chapter 6 in this volume concentrates on the changes in the policy of the employment of airpower at sea with the approach of war.

Apart from the chapter on Air Control operations overseas, the book is not about war but about the preparations for war. I am reminded of my old music master at school who introduced us to the *Planets* Suite by Gustav Holst. It was Mars that always impressed me. Mars was the bringer of war. It is the growing menace that Holst so brilliantly puts to music. Or it is like those passages from Shakespeare's *Henry V* before the battle of Agincourt: the hammer of the smithies preparing the arms and armour for battle. This is the essence of the 1930s after the failure of disarmament and the coming to power of Adolf Hitler in Germany.

Recently I was discussing the presentation of my work with an established author of RAF history. He was worried that putting photographs or images of aircraft so often in among the narrative might patronize the reader. While I respect his work I chose to differ. Placing diagrams and photographs among a closely argued narrative in no way detracts from the quality of an argument or discussion. Recently I read a history of the Russian army's advance on Berlin in 1945. It was a very detailed account of battles and the disposition of German and Russian units at different stages of the campaign. But I never knew who was where at different stages of the battle. For me the enjoyment of a book on military campaigns is derived from having maps and other illustrations in among the narrative so that I know exactly who is where, even at the end of every day in a short campaign. For those like me there are plenty of illustrations built into the subject paragraphs. For any reader who might feel patronized, he or she has only to ignore the visual material.

As with Volume I, so with this volume: nearly all paragraphs have headings in heavy type. This is for ease of reference. There are no footnotes, since this is meant to be a comprehensive account of the period. A specific source may often be quoted alongside a heading. There is a reference to books that have been consulted in compiling this history so that those who may wish to undertake further study may know where to turn. Most of the information gathered which is included here has been found at the National Archives at Kew and the reading room of the RAF Museum, Hendon. The squadron histories can be found on microfilm, and details of the week-to-week activities of the RAF during the inter-war period from Air Ministry weekly orders. There are literally hundreds of weekly orders that provide a detailed picture of the RAF. I had to choose those that would provide a mixture of activities. I chose some orders for their unusual content, like the forerunner of the modern wet suit, which appears in Volume I, and the flying-boat that took off in a circular clockwise pattern. Others provide a comparison between aircraft movements in and out of a modern RAF airfield on paved runways with air traffic control and movements in the 1930s, when a pilot had to keep a good lookout for other aircraft approaching the grass airfield, take account of the wind direction in making an approach and report his arrival at the watch office after touch-down.

It is hoped that this work fills a gap in the market in studies of the development of airpower in those critical inter-war years.

Wing Commander I.M. Philpott MSocSc, BSc (Econ), MCMI, RAF (Retd)

Acknowledgements

To Mr Peter Elliott and to his research staff of the RAF Museum, Hendon, for their untiring efforts in producing photographs and source material for the compilation of the encyclopedia.

To Group Captain D.E. Larkin RAF (Retd) at RAF Halton, who provided expert knowledge of the Boy Apprentice scheme in the 1930s.

To Wing Commander C.G. Jefford RAF (Retd) whose book *RAF Squadrons* has been a constant companion and source for tracing the movement of RAF squadrons in the 1930s.

To the staff of the National Archives, Kew, who have been most helpful during my many visits there over the past five years, and for the provision of photographic material.

To the author John W.R. Taylor and the publishers Ian Allen for a *Pictorial History of the RAF 1918 to 1939 Vol. 1.* This publication provided a wealth of useful photographs of the period.

To the publishers of the *Aeroplane* for the use of photographic material.

To the Putnam Press and HMSO for the most useful accounts of the development of the aircraft industry during the 1930s as seen through the eyes of Harald Penrose, the chief test pilot of Westland Aircraft during the 1930s.

To the publishers and authors of the 'Action Stations' series of books, which give details of squadron movements at airfields in the United Kingdom and overseas and other pertinent information about the development of these airfields. Information was extracted from these publications as they applied to the period 1 January 1930 to 3 September 1939, saving months of research.

To the Imperial War Museum for the use of photographic material.

To the authors and publishers of books listed in the bibliography who are not already mentioned.

Preface

British Air Policy from 1918 to 1939

With the memory of the 1999 Balkan air campaign fresh in the mind, it is fair to conclude that airpower alone forced President Milosevic of Serbia to withdraw his forces from Kosovo to let in the NATO-led troops. On the other hand it may be argued that it was the threat of a land invasion that tipped the scales in NATO's favour. Whichever view is taken, it cannot be denied that NATO aircraft inflicted unacceptable damage to Serbian military, industrial, communications and transport targets. Moreover, in spite of the Serbs having a sizeable air force, little or no attempt was made to defend the country against NATO bombardment. Can it therefore now be claimed that, with the sophistication of modern strike-aircraft armed with laser-guided weapons, the employment of airpower alone can result in a belligerent nation suing for peace without even putting up a fight? This question is very relevant to this history since the Air Staff's argument in the early 1920s in fighting for the survival of the RAF as an independent service was based upon the doctrine of the offensive use of airpower independent of the other two services. Chapter 10 critically examines the RAF's bombing doctrine, or lack of it, in the inter-war years.

In 1918, the year the Great War ended, the Independent Bomber Force (IBF) of the Royal Air Force was formed. It was to operate independently of the battlefield, unlike the many Allied squadrons operating in direct support of the land and naval forces, i.e. the strategic rather than the tactical use of airpower. The IBF was tasked to attack industrial targets and so weaken the enemy's will and ability to continue with the war. The Germans for their part had employed Zeppelin airships and Gotha bombers to attack targets in England. Strategic bombing became a possibility when bomber aircraft and airships had the range and bomb-carrying capacity to take the war to the enemy's homeland. As the war ended there was already speculation that the employment of airpower alone had the potential to bring victory. It was said that the bomber would always get through and that the effect on the morale of the civil population at the prospect of air bombardment could itself be decisive. Among exponents of the offensive use of airpower were Major-General Hugh Trenchard, later appointed to the post of Chief of the Air Staff, of the RAF, the American Colonel Billy Mitchell and the Italian Douhet. Trenchard was quite clear about the importance of maintaining a strong offensive bomber force. Even after his retirement from the RAF in 1930 he continued to press the case for bombers, seeing little need for fighters if the war was taken to the enemy. In retrospect, claims made for the effectiveness of the bombers were perhaps premature. Strategic bombing in the Great War was in its infancy. Some of the units of heavy bombers, such as the HP V/1500 were only working up as the war ended, and Berlin was not bombed. The claims made for the effectiveness of bombing was based more on its perceived potential to bring an enemy to sue for peace rather than experience gained in war. For all the talk of heavy bombing, small two-man biplane bombers, almost indistinguishable from the fighters, continued in service until the mid-1930s.

In the event, the formulation of air policy in 1919 and the years that followed was not so straightforward. In general terms air policy is determined by a mix of factors. Firstly there is the foreign policy stance of a nation, i.e. does it stand alone, is it neutral like Switzerland or Sweden, or is it a partner in a military alliance when friendly countries may be expected to provide military support in the event of an attack by a country or countries outside the alliance? Countries in an alliance may also be able to reduce the burden of defence expenditure through collaborative efforts in weapon design, development and procurement, contingency planning and joint exercises. Secondly, there is the willingness of governments, and indirectly electorates, to spend money on defence rather than on hospitals and schools. Thirdly, there is the industrial capacity of a nation to produce aircraft and weapons at home. The alternative is to import, but countries then run the risk that foreign sources of supply might dry up in the event of war. Finally, and perhaps most importantly is the need to maintain national security. By this is not meant the use of aircraft against the civilian populations, which is internal security, but defence against attack by a belligerent nation. This can extend to the oceans, since the protection of maritime trade can be vital to a country such as Britain.

The First World War, or the Great War, as it was then known, ended on 11 November 1918. In order to understand how British air policy was formulated on cessation of hostilities, and how it developed in succeeding years, one has to consider the situation faced by the British government of the day and the British people. To begin with there were the memories of the slaughter of millions of men in the bloody trench warfare in Flanders and beyond, which created war weariness. This had to be the war to end all wars, and Britain was to be 'a land fit for heroes'. Then there was the League of Nations, which would be a world forum to which nations could appeal if a dispute looked likely to lead to conflict, and naturally hopes were pinned on the League to avert war. Finally there was the 'Ten-Year Rule'. This was national defence policy framed in the belief that Britain would not be involved in a major conflict for at least ten years. For all these reasons defence expenditure would be low on a list of priorities for public expenditure.

In these circumstances there was no need for 184 operational squadrons backed by training units at home and abroad, and a period of rapid disbandment followed, so that the number of operational squadrons was reduced, by March 1921, to a mere twenty-eight fully formed squadrons; and of these, twenty-one were abroad and three in Ireland. The RAF also gave up 149 airfields, 122 landing grounds and 2,240 hirings (land and buildings). Of the three remaining squadrons three were with the Royal Navy. This left one RAF squadron in England, giving refresher training to pilots. To make matters worse, the Admirals and Generals saw little reason for the maintenance of a separate air force, and argued for the return of squadrons to their respective services whence they had come on 1 April 1918, the day the RAF was officially formed from units of the Royal Naval Air Service and the Royal Flying Corps. It was argued that the expense of maintaining an Air Ministry alone was unacceptable in the prevailing financial climate.

On 11 January 1919 Hugh Trenchard was reappointed to the post of Chief of the Air Staff (CAS) in succession to Major-General Sykes. Trenchard had resigned as the RAF's first CAS following differences with Lord Rothermere over policy. For his part Sykes sought to secure the future of the RAF as an independent force by advocating an imperial service involving the Dominions of Canada, Australia and New Zealand, the Union of South Africa and India. At that time neither the Westminster Parliament nor the Dominions were ready for such a grandiose plan of expansion. Trenchard, on the other hand, it was said, 'was prepared to make do with a little and would not have to be carried'. This made him much more appealing to a cost-conscious government. And so it fell to Trenchard to fight the battle for survival. He was fortunate in having the sympathetic ear of Winston Churchill, who was Secretary of State for War and the Air. Churchill had no intention of returning the RAF to the Royal Navy or the Army, and, instead, asked Trenchard to put in writing his own ideas for the new service. This was to be the Trenchard Memorandum, which laid down the foundations of the independent air force. Its publication was followed by the granting of new RAF rank titles, which served to emphasize a separate identity. Once the Memorandum was accepted, the RAF moved forward, even though attempts by the Royal Navy and Army to reclaim what they regarded as their air components continued for some years to come. It was not until 1937 that the Royal Navy took complete control of the Fleet Air Arm, but by that time the RAF was firmly established as the third armed service. Another factor that helped to sustain the RAF in the face of inter-service rivalry and government cut-backs was air control. At the Cairo Conference in March 1921 it was accepted that the RAF should replace the Army as the primary force in maintaining order in the Middle East. Trenchard had shown that it was possible for a few aircraft, with a minimum of air-transportable land forces, to suppress revolts by dissident tribesmen when the 'Mad Mullah' was defeated in the protectorate of British Somaliland in 1920. Formerly large Army garrisons had been necessary to maintain order. Aircraft were much quicker in nipping incipient trouble in the bud. By the time Army troops arrived on the scene it was more likely that the trouble would have escalated, resulting in heavier casualties on both sides. As a consequence air control was much more economical in money and lives than in those operations where only land forces were used. This was bound to be attractive to a government seeking economies. Air control, then, gave the RAF an operational raison d'être, and was used in Mesopotamia (Iraq) and India, followed later by Transjordan and Palestine.

The next development in air policy was for the Conservative Government to recognize the need for the RAF to contribute to national security. By now the nation realized that the Royal Navy could no longer guarantee that the territory of the British Isles would not be violated by an enemy. It was agreed that the RAF could expand to fifty-two squadrons, seventeen fighter and thirty-five bomber, but that in the prevailing economic climate this would not happen immediately. It would be phased in over a minimum of five years. Add to this the Ten-Year Rule, the hope that the League of Nations would prove effective in preventing conflict on a large scale and the declared pacifism of a number of MPs, and it may be understood that the Westminster Parliament would not wish to be seen sending signals to the rest of the world that it was rearming Britain. Strange, then, that the preponderance of squadrons from the fifty-two would be bomber, but this was the very essence of Air Staff thinking at the time, i.e. offensive defence. The number of squadrons needed to defend Britain would be that necessary to defeat an aerial assault by any power within striking distance of its shores. It may seem bizarre to have seen France as a potential aggressor in the early 1920s, but this was not the intention. It was that France had, at that time, the largest air force in Europe. This was to be the yardstick. Therefore, by the end of 1923, British air policy provided for the continued existence of the RAF as a separate service, air control in India and the Middle East and the gradual expansion in an unspecified number of years to fifty-two squadrons for national defence, plus a continuation of the Ten-Year Rule.

It would seem strange today if civil aviation comprising commercial airlines came under the control of a ministry of defence. But this was the situation after the Great War. Even the Air Estimates, the money voted annually by Parliament for expenditure on the RAF, contained an element for civil aviation. This might seem all the more perplexing since the government's attitude was that the airlines should 'sink or swim', so to speak, in the market place. The explanation for public expenditure on civil aviation lies in the overlap between the development of military and civil flying, and the great reliance that the struggling firms in the aircraft and aero-engine manufacturing industry placed on aircraft orders. The aircraft industry badly needed contracts for both civil and military types to survive, and there was little to choose between the design of both. Indeed, a civil airliner could always be adapted for military use. Therefore the larger the civil air fleet, the larger the nation's war potential. Both civil and military aircraft prototypes went to the RAF's experimental establishment at Martlesham Heath in Suffolk for airworthiness tests and evaluation, if landplanes, and to the Marine Experimental Establishment, Felixstowe, if they were flying-boats or floatplanes. If found satisfactory by the RAF test pilots, they could then enter service or receive modifications. To have required the nascent aircraft industry to set up its own parallel organization would have been too costly. As it was, the French were prepared to subsidize their airlines, and for a while in 1921 only foreign aircraft touched down at Croydon. In the end the British government relented and granted a modest subsidy of £60,000 to help the airlines. And because the costs of civil aircraft development were met in part from public funds, the airline and aircraft industries were given time to get on their feet, if one will forgive the allegory. Indeed, at a time when the RAF was unable to place orders for new military aircraft, Trenchard sensibly awarded contracts for prototypes so that firms manufacturing aircraft could at least keep their core staff of designers and builders in employment until better days came along. Each year's specifications for military aircraft were sent out to aircraft manufacturers numbered sequentially throughout the year, e.g. Specification 16/22 called for a long-distance coastal-defence biplane. Finally, it should be remembered that most of the pilots of both civil aircraft and airships were ex-service pilots who flew in their retired ranks, thus emphasizing the parallel development of military and civil flying.

The development of airships was very prominent during the inter-war years. Owing to their low speed and poor manoeuvrability relative to aircraft, however, airships were not considered a serious rival in combat, although they were admirably suited to reconnaissance, particularly maritime reconnaissance. Where the airship could score over the aircraft of the day was in long-distance flying, and the idea of linking the far-flung Dominions of Canada and Australia with the Mother country was appealing. Indeed the necessary airship sheds and mooring masts for berthing airships were built in such places as India in preparation for Imperial air routes. But the inter-war years are best, if sadly, remembered, for the catastrophes befalling airships, although British enthusiasts like Commander Burney remained undaunted. It was not until the tragic loss of the R101 at Beauvais in northern France on a flight to

India in 1930 that the policy was virtually to abandon further airship development. Only a small staff was kept on at Cardington in Bedfordshire for work on balloons, and the latter were to feature as part of aerial defence during the Second World War. Until the loss of the R101, governments had been equivocal in giving support to airship development. On the one hand there was the feeling that since airships were to be used commercially then the private sector should bear the cost of development, but on the other hand the government had a part to play to give British airships a fighting chance in the developing international airline market. After all, the Germans were successfully using airships on long-haul civil flights. The result was that two large airships were built in the late 1920s. One, the so-called 'capitalist' airship, was a private venture titled R100, and the other, the so-called 'socialist' airship, was state funded and titled the R101. As has been said, the loss of the R101 spelled the end of serious airship development in Britain, but in Germany too the end was not far off. The tragic loss of the German airship Hindenburg at Lakehurst, New Jersey, in 1937 sealed the fate of lighter-than-air machines for all practical purposes.

In the early 1930s successive British governments saw the need to strengthen the RAF in an uncertain world, at the same time wishing to be seen to play their full part in general disarmament. The League of Nations had been successful in averting conflict involving smaller countries, but was unable to prevent a determined major power from acting aggressively. First it was Japanese expansionism in the Far East, when, in 1932, Manchuria became Manchukuo. This was followed by the Nazis coming to power in Germany to create the Third Reich in 1933, and lastly there was Italian aggression against Abyssinia in 1935. When the League sought to admonish Mussolini it only threw the latter into the arms of the German dictator, Adolf Hitler, so creating the Rome–Berlin axis. Since neither leader ran a democracy they could spend money on armaments pretty well at will. As the Disarmament Talks at Geneva got bogged down in endless bickering over the details of disarmament, they eventually ran into the sands. Hitler could conveniently see no reason why the the major powers should not come down to the arms limits imposed upon his country at Versailles in 1919. Of course Hitler would be happy not to see arms limitations adopted that might limit his own freedom to act. When he withdrew Germany from membership of the League of Nations, the time had come for Britain to look to its defences. No longer would she look at France's air capability, but at that of the Third Reich.

So began the policy of rearmament and expansion. More squadrons with up-to-date aircraft and new airfields were going to be needed. Now it was not the funds made available by the Treasury that was to be the constraint, but the ability of the RAF and the aircraft industry to cope with the demands made upon them.

Trenchard had built 'his cottage'. He had built an air force that placed quality before quantity, and his successors were initially loath to water down a highly professional force through too fast an expansion. Fortunately the opening of reserve and auxiliary squadrons from 1925 onwards, and the introduction of short-service commissions in 1923, meant that there was a pool of reserve and ex-service pilots in civilian jobs who could be called on to serve. For the aircraft industry the answer lay in the contracting-out of work to 'shadow' factories. Motor car firms were involved in building engines and airframes to designs and specifications put out by the aircraft industry.

As the inevitability of a second world war became clear for all to see, the fear grew that Britain was dropping behind Germany in the production of military aircraft and the forming of air units, and so criticism fell on His Majesty's Government that not enough was being done. Winston Churchill, then on the back-benches of the House of Commons, and thus out of government, was loudest in voicing his discontent. The British Prime Minister in 1938, Mr Neville Chamberlain, did not succeed in persuading Hitler to abandon his territorial ambitions. Having already absorbed Austria into the Third Reich and brought about the dismemberment of Czechoslovakia, Hitler had eyes on Poland, and there was added fear that Britain would not be ready if war came in 1938. If not successful in bringing 'peace in our time', which Chamberlain had declared on his return from the Munich Conference, having signed away Czechoslovakian independence, he did at least give the RAF and the aircraft industry a breathing space, so that when war did come in 1939, there was an effective radar-based fighter control system in place, and Spitfires and Hurricanes were coming off the production lines to provide defence. But except for the Battle light bombers sent to France with the Advanced Air-Striking Force in September 1939, the heavy bombers needed to carry the war to the enemy were still to come.

This book goes into detail to explain how air policy was applied in the years between 1930 and 1939 by dealing with all the major events in this context. It tells of the famous and the not-so-famous, the successes and the failures and the advances made in aircraft and air weapon design over the first ten years in Volume I, and between 1930 and 1939 in this, Volume II.

Part I
Operations and Training

Chapter 1
The Failure of Disarmament, 1930 to 1932

RAF Order of Battle, 1 January 1930 – The end of airships – Disarmament talks – RAF displays – 1931 Schneider Trophy race – Flying and operational – A & AEE Martlesham Heath and MAEE Felixstowe

INTRODUCTION

The decade started with hope that international agreement could be secured to a programme of disarmament, but the success of such talks depended critically on qualitative as well as quantitative agreement, that is to say that reductions in armaments cannot be based simply on a battleship for a battleship or a fighter aircraft for a fighter aircraft, since the quality of units of weaponry can vary enormously. On mainland Europe, France had most to lose, having a substantial army and the largest air force. On the other hand, Germany had been limited by the Versailles Treaty, being permitted no air force, no submarines, no warships with a displacement exceeding 10,000 tons and an army sufficient in size for defence purposes only. Even that force of 100,000 men could not station any units west of the River Rhine for fear that France could be again threatened by a German army.

The League of Nations had been successful in dealing with threats to peace in the 1920s when disputes affected the interests of smaller states. No one knew what would happen if a major power was involved. The League had no armed forces at its disposal, and aggressor states might be condemned and at worst subjected to economic sanctions. To make matters worse, the Unites States had retreated into post-war isolationism, leaving Britain and France as the main guarantors of international peace. The Locarno and Kellogg/Briand Pacts showed a willingness on the part of the major powers to use all peaceful means to settle disputes, and there was hope that this could lead to major disarmament. This led to the Geneva Conference on disarmament in 1932. In 1930 Italy had a fascist dictator, although Mussolini had not at that time threatened military action against another state. Hitler had not come to power in Germany and Japan had not invaded Manchuria, but all was about to change.

For her part, Britain had the outposts of her Empire to defend, and responsibilities as a mandated power under the League of Nations, in addition to homeland defence. Even in a programme of international disarmament, nation-states would retain the right to maintain armed forces for purely defensive purposes. In the period after the First World War the British government was committed to a 'Ten-Year Rule', which, for the purposes of defence policy, ruled out the possibility of Britain becoming involved in a major war for at least ten years. This period was simply carried forward, year on year, for as long as the rule remained part of government policy. HM Government was not keen, therefore, to be seen to build up the country's armed forces, but was, nevertheless, persuaded in 1923 to approve a modest expansion of British airpower to guard against any violation of national territory. Before the Great War the Royal Navy provided the defence against such violations, but the attacks upon Britain by German Zeppelins and Gotha bombers showed that the Royal Navy alone could no longer guarantee to protect the country from attack. The need for strong air defences was clear for all to see, and hence the modest expansion of airpower.

In 1923, when the expansion began, the Chief of the Air Staff (CAS), Air Chief Marshal Hugh Trenchard, had persuaded the government that the best way of ensuring homeland security was, at the outset, to carry the war to the enemy and destroy the industries that produced weapons of war, as well as attacking the bases from which attacks against Britain might be launched. Therefore, of the fifty-two planned RAF squadrons the majority were to be bomber squadrons. No time limit was put on completion of the expansion plan, since the Ten-Year Rule removed the urgency. In 1930 Marshal of the Royal Air Force Lord Trenchard handed over as CAS to his successor, Air Chief Marshal Sir John Salmond. The order of battle that the latter inherited is shown on the following pages.

ORDER OF BATTLE OF THE ROYAL AIR FORCE ON 1 JANUARY 1930

UNITED KINGDOM

Heavy-Bomber Squadrons
No. 7 Squadron, Worthy Down
No. 9 Squadron, Manston
No. 58 Squadron, Worthy Down

Virginia

No. 10 Squadron, Upper Heyford
No. 502 (Special Reserve) Squadron, Aldergove
No. 503 (Special Reserve) Squadron, Waddington

Hyderabad

No. 99 Squadron, Upper Heyford

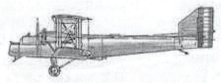

Hinaidi

No. 101 Squadron, Andover

Sidestrand

Light-Bomber Squadrons
No. 12 Squadron, Andover

Fox

No. 35 Squadron, Bircham Newton

DH9A and Fairey III

No. 600 (Auxiliary) Squadron, Hendon
No. 601 (Auxiliary) Squadron, Hendon
No. 602 (Auxiliary) Squadron, Renfrew

Wapiti

No. 501 (Special Reserve) Squadron, Filton
No. 603 (Auxiliary) Squadron, Turnhouse
No. 605 (Auxiliary) Squadron, Castle Bromwich

DH9A

Torpedo-Bomber Squadrons
No. 33 Squadron, Eastchurch
No. 100 Squadron, Bicester
No. 504 (Special Reserve) Squadron, Hucknall

Horsley

Fighter Squadrons
No. 3 Squadron, Upavon
No. 17 Squadron, Upavon

Bulldog

No. 23 Squadron, Kenley

Gamecock

No. 1 Squadron, Tangmere
No. 19 Squadron, Duxford
No. 25 Squadron, Hawkinge
No. 29 Squadron, North Weald
No. 32 Squadron, Kenley
No. 41 Squadron, Northolt
No. 43 Squadron, Tangmere
No. 56 Squadron, North Weald
No. 111 Squadron, Hornchurch

Siskin

Maritime Reconnaissance Squadrons
No. 201 Squadron, Calshot
No. 204 Squadron, Mountbatten

Southampton

No. 207 Squadron, Bircham Newton

Fairey IIIF

Army-Cooperation Squadrons
No. 2 Squadron, Manston
No. 4 Squadron, Farnborough
No. 13 Squadron, Netheravon
No. 26 Squadron, Catterick

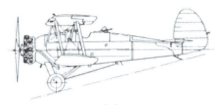

Atlas

No. 16 Squadron, Bicester

Bristol F2B

OVERSEAS SQUADRONS

Palestine
No. 6 Squadron, Ismailia – **Bristol F2B**
No. 14 Squadron, Amman – **Fairey IIIF**

Iraq and Aden
No. 8 Squadron, Khormaksar – **Fairey IIIF**
No. 30 Squadron, Mosul – **Wapiti**
No. 55 Squadron, Hinaidi – **DH9A**
No. 70 Squadron, Hinaidi – **Victoria**
No. 84 Squadron, Shaibah – **Wapiti**
No. 203 Squadron, Basrah – **Southampton II**

Egypt
No. 45 Squadron, Helwan – **Fairey IIIF**
No. 208 Squadron, Heliopolis – **Bristol F2B**
No. 216 Squadron, Heliopolis – **Victoria I, IV, V**

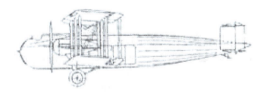

Victoria

India
No. 5 Squadron, Quetta – **Bristol F2B**
No. 11 Squadron, Risalpur – **Wapiti**
No. 20 Squadron, Peshawar – **Bristol F2B**
No. 27 Squadron, Kohat – **DH9A**
No. 28 Squadron Ambala – **Bristol F2B**
No. 31 Squadron, Quetta – **Bristol F2B**
No. 39 Squadron, Risalpur – **Wapiti**
No. 60 Squadron, Kohat – **DH9A**

Miscellaneous Units
No. 15 Squadron, Martlesham
No. 22 Squadron, Martlesham
These two units had various aircraft for testing, but also had a war role if required

No. 24 Squadron
Air Ministry Communications, various aircraft

Flying Training Schools
No. 1 FTS Netheravon
No. 2 FTS Digby
No. 4 FTS Abu Sueir
No. 5 FTS Sealand

TRENCHARD'S AIR FORCE

The RAF of 1930 was very much Trenchard's creation. Volume I explains why he chose to concentrate on quality and not quantity, and why he was determined to create a very professional base for later expansion should a major war come again. Looking at the order of battle, one can see an air force wedded to biplanes with open cockpits and armed with Vickers and Lewis guns, just as they had been in November 1918. There are several explanations for retaining aircraft that actually flew operationally during the Great War (Bristol Fighter and DH9A) and later aircraft that were little improved in speed and performance over the 1920s. One was the severe financial constraints imposed upon the Air Ministry. Then there was the Ten-Year Rule, which meant that there was little urgency in developing aircraft for a major war. The only pressing operational requirement was for a general-purpose aircraft. This would be one that would not encounter air opposition, was rugged, easy to maintain and was effective in dealing with tribal unrest in remote and often inhospitable regions of Empire. The Bristol F2B, the DH9A, and later the Wapiti, were ideally suited to this role, known as air control.

The senior commanders of the RAF had all started life as Army or Naval officers, but Trenchard had been determined at the outset to create an 'air force spirit', an air force that was independent of the Army and the Navy. He had fought off several attempts by these sister services to reclaim their air components, and had succeeded. To ensure that his officers and men were trained in the skills and arts of air warfare there was a staff college, an RAF cadet college and an apprentice school that would ensure a thorough professionalism throughout the service. He had also created an Auxiliary Air Force and instituted short-service commissions. When it came to aircraft types and numbers the aim was for the RAF to be able to defend the United Kingdom against air attack by any continental power within striking range of these islands, with a policy of offensive defence. For this purpose France was to be the yardstick.

Trenchard was to stay in post far longer than any of his successors, but this illustrates his determination to put the service on a secure footing before going into retirement.

It is easy with hindsight to see that the RAF had to be designed to be capable of the substantial expansion that was to commence in 1934, but in 1930 a major war was still a long way off. The RAF's order of battle met the requirements of the Air Staff and the government still hoped to achieve a measure of disarmament. This volume will chart the enormous strides that were made in aircraft design and weapon development.

THE END OF THE AIRSHIP

Introduction

One might wonder what airships are doing in a book about the RAF between the two world wars. They did not equip any RAF or FAA units, but they had been used extensively in the Great War, on both maritime reconnaissance and anti-submarine duties. The Germans had used them successfully in bombing England. When the war ended all the airships and mooring stations were decommissioned. All that survived was an experimental establishment at Howden to see if airships and balloons would have any future military use. From the very tight budget upon which Trenchard had to manage it was all that could be afforded. There were enthusiasts, however, who were determined to keep alive the dream of international air travel that could link the Mother country with the far-flung Dominions. Such men were Commander Dennistoun Burney and Dr Barnes Wallis.

The military use of airships was questionable. They were slow relative to aircraft and presented huge tempting targets for fighter aircraft, which had the speed and height to ensure interception. Perhaps as a troop transport or long-range reconnaissance vehicles over the sea, where land-based aircraft could not catch them, the airship might have a role. And so it was that in the late 1920s the government was prepared to fund the construction of a large airship, the R101, which was then dubbed the 'socialist' airship. This may be understood because at the same time the private sector was embarking on an equally large airship, the R100, which was dubbed the 'capitalist' airship. Britain seemed to be staking everything on these two projects as the decade came to a close. The government had in mind the requisitioning of the R101 in time of war for maritime reconnaissance, but this only started yet another row between the Air Ministry and the Admiralty, this time over who was going to man it, naval or air force personnel.

The Germans continued to develop the airship after the Great War, and since they were denied an air force under the Versailles Treaty, they had necessarily to devote their energies to designing civilian aircraft. In the field of international air travel their *Graf Zeppelin* airships were very successful. For their part the Americans were building airships for military use with the United States Navy, and Britain was pinning its hopes on the R100 and R101 to stay in the airship race. The numbering of the two airships is significant: the R100 was supposed to indicate the last of the old, and the R101 the first of the new. But things were not going to turn out the way the rival concerns perhaps anticipated.

The Secretary of State for Air, Lord Thomson, announced that the total expenditure of the airship programme since 1924 had been £2 million. He said that by early 1930, of 427 people who had flown the Atlantic, 402 had crossed in airships. He added that, given a good skipper and crew, the R101 was strong enough to stand any gale and that he would go out in her in any weather.

THE ANATOMY OF AN AIRSHIP

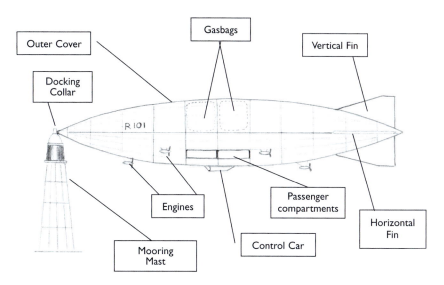

These are only the basic features of an airship. They differed in detail; for example, the Graf Zeppelin had its control cabin right forward under the nose. The gas bags were held in position by longitudinal, lateral and angled girders. It was critically important that the buoyancy was distributed along the length of the hull so that the frame was not subjected to undue stresses. As the airship moved through the air the hull flexed causing chafing of the bags against the girders. This in turn cause leakages which were acceptable to a degree.

The successful commercial operations of the Zeppelins were not marred by leakages. The leakages which were found in the R101 were potentially serious.

Rolling motion

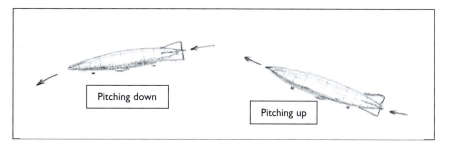

Pitching down

Pitching up

The R100.

The R101.

He was as good as his word, even if it later cost him his life. In presenting the Air Estimates for 1930/1, Lord Thomson devoted much of the White Paper to airships. He said that the R100 and R101 were adequately stable and easy to control, and he made much of the use being made of the first heavy oil compression-ignition engines to be used in a British aircraft. Actually, his claim was not, strictly speaking, correct, for Typhoon engines had been used in an Avro Aldershot IV testbed.

Construction and flight testing
The construction and powering of these airships differed in several important respects. With regard to lift it had been announced that the Air Ministry designers at Cardington would increase the lift of R101 by inserting a new mid-section. This was in December 1929. The R101, which was being constructed at Cardington in

Bedfordshire, would have diesel engines. Since it was intended to fly over hot countries *en route* to Egypt, India and the Far East, the fire risk would be less using diesel fuel. The R100, on the other hand, would work the north transatlantic route using petrol engines. In Parliament there was some disquiet that the latter could would have to be confined to routes in northern latitudes. The reason given for this restriction to the employment of R100 was that the compression-ignition (diesel) engines were still in an experimental stage.

Both airships were under the supervision of Wing Commander R.B.B. Colmore, who had been promoted to the post of Director of Airship Development on 1 January 1930. On the 16th of that month, the R100 made her third flight, largely to investigate a rippling pulsation of the fabric outer cover. A new method of securing it was devised and deemed an improvement when tested on the 22nd. Five days later final acceptance trials were completed in a flight of fifty-four hours, during which the airship attained a speed of 81 mph. The speed required in the contract was the lesser speed of 70 mph, which was faster than that of her rival. The controls were satisfactory, but longitudinally she had a long, slow, pitching motion of about five degrees each way. This was within acceptable limits, and the airship was handed over to the Air Ministry at Cardington, the home of the R101, for acceptance trials.

On 21 May the R100 was brought out of her hangar under the command of Squadron Leader R.S. Booth, with Squadron Leader E.L. Johnston acting as navigator. On board were Sir Dennistoun Burney, Nevil Shute Norway, the Under-Secretary of State for Air, Frederick Montague and Sir Harry Britain MP. The purpose of this particular flight was to test the petrol engines prior to the proposed Atlantic flight. The engines performed well, but the tailpiece, intended to improve the airflow over the rear end of the ship, had buckled. There was also damage caused by the slipstream to one of the bays behind a power car. The cover, securing wires and tapes had suffered. The test run had been conducted at 80 mph, and it was found necessary to build the tailpiece from a heavier-gauge metal, and intermediate girders were fitted where there was damage to the bay. The repairs took longer than anticipated as new material had to be manufactured, and this necessitated a postponement of the flight to Canada to the end of June or beginning of July. Modifications were carried out by Cardington personnel, and not members of the design staff from Howden, where the R100 had been built. The pointed tail of the original airship had been replaced by one of a more rounded shape, which made her slower than her competitor.

The rising costs of building and testing the R101 were causing some anxiety in the House of Commons. The expenditure on the airship between the time she left her shed for her first flight trials and 31 March 1930 was

£34,000, of which £21,000 had been for modifications alone. In order to improve the airship's performance it was deemed necessary to discard all non-essential equipment, including control servo-motors, to save weight, and transverse wiring was altered to increase the gas volume in the ballonets. In early June, after preliminary flight trials were carried out, the airship was left to ride at her mooring mast until the new midship section was ready. At the time of mooring the wind was light, but it soon rose, resulting in a longitudinal split of 140 ft, and the wind strength was, by then, too great to permit the manhandling of the airship into her hangar. There was nothing for it but to patch her up at the mast, and when another split developed the following day the inner cover was reinforced with doped-on tapes after repairs had been effected. The airship was due to be demonstrated at the forthcoming RAF Display, Hendon, even though she was losing buoyancy from leaks caused by the gas valves chattering on their seatings. Nothing was done to remedy this fault, and she crossed over Hendon at 1,000 ft, which impressed the crowd, unaware that all the time gas was escaping. The AID (Aeronautical Inspection Directorate) inspector on board noted the leaks in his report, stating that he could not grant an extension of the Permit to Fly until remedial action had been taken. On returning to Cardington the R101 was put into her shed for the insertion of the new bay amidships designed to improve her buoyancy.

The Flight of R100 to Canada

Aboard the R100 on her flight to Canada were Sir Dennistoun Burney and Nevil Shute Norway from Vickers, the builders, but the brains behind the project, Sir Barnes Wallis, was not invited. As it happens, Barnes Wallis and Dennistoun Burney were not temperamentally suited. The former was in any case busy at that time working on a replacement torpedo-bomber to Air Ministry specifications at Weybridge. Dennistoun Burney, the entrepreneur and showman, was an entirely different character, wishing to show off 'his airship'.

The modified R100 departed from Cardington, bound for Canada, on 29 July 1930. She left her moorings at 03.50 hrs in the chilly dawn, which gave the airship the advantage of unexpanded gas. She carried 34.5 tons of fuel for the 3,360-mile flight. It took three days to cross the Atlantic, and at 02.00 hrs on 1 August the crew could see the lights of Montreal. The crossing had been made at an average speed of 42 mph, and she arrived with just 5 tons of fuel remaining.

The airship had not completed the crossing unscathed. While in flight, the long slow lateral roll of the R100, through a twenty-degree arc, caused a fraying and leakage from the gasbags. There had also been a near-disaster as the airship approached the mile-high mountain ranges on the north shore of the St Lawrence river. There the R100 was caught in the tremendous turbulence produced by the north wind swirling over the mountain tops, and she bucked violently, resulting in both a pitching and a rolling motion. Alarm bells rang from the starboard and aft cars. The triangular starboard tailplane had a big tear in the under-surface where the lower fin joined the hull, and the fabric hung in rags. An earlier passage described how the Cardington engineers had blunted the tail, and this must have affected the pressure distribution of the tailfins. The top fin, however, remained sound.

The airship captain, Squadron Leader Booth, with Major Scott at the controls, decided to wait for dawn before attempting a mooring. Scott hovered the R100 for two hours to allow the repair crew to get inside the long 4 ft fin and tail. They stood on the wires linking the leading edge and spar girders to sew and lash the fabric together. They succeeded in securing a great sheet of cotton fabric over most of the 15 ft hole. The airship then got under way and was proceeding at reduced speed when a violent gust lifted her. The elevators were pushed hard down, causing the craft to assume a thirty-degree nose-down angle. She was then swept upwards some 4,500 ft, swinging through ninety degrees, and torrential rain flooded the ship. This time two 12 ft tears appeared in the starboard tailplane, and the lights were out for ten minutes. After repairs were effected to the fabric, the R100 was at last attached to the mooring mast. A 200 sq. ft canvas had to be delivered by Canadian Vickers to effect the repairs to the horizontal fin, which were delayed due to strong winds.

Before returning to the United Kingdom the R100 made a goodwill flight over Ottawa, Toronto and Niagara Falls, watched by half a million people. This was on 10 August. The troubles were not over even then, for as the airship returned to Montreal in the late afternoon the reduction gear of one of the three starboard engines failed. The metal sheathing on the propeller flew off and penetrated the hull, which caused slight damage to the girders. Since no one had thought fit to send the special engine-lifting derrick to Canada, it was decided to fly home on the remaining five engines. It was in any case normal practice for airships to shut down engines while cruising, particularly if there was a following wind. This would be the case on the return of R100 to England, and she arrived back at Cardington on Saturday morning, 16 August.

The last flight of the R101

In telling the story of the loss of the R101, the author is reminded of the tragic loss of the American spacecraft Challenger. The rocket engines were known to have faulty '0' rings, which acted as seals. The mixed crew of people from different professions meant that the flight was deemed to have to go ahead for political reasons. The spacecraft engines blew up shortly after take-off and the entire crew perished. So, too, the R101 suffered from reported known defects, which included leaking and chafing gasbags, serious trouble with the outer cover and limited lift. She was now overweight following the insertion of a new centre section. Be that as it may, Lord Thomson, the Secretary of State for Air, seemed not to have understood the implications of these defects on the handling of the airship in flight. He insisted that the flight to India was to go ahead as scheduled, again for political reasons. The national publicity engendered by the proposed flight was important, and Lord Thomson wanted to reach Karachi on 9 October 1930 and return in time for the Imperial Conference in London on the 20th of that month.

Hurried preparations were made for the flight, and the lengthened airship was flown on 1 October in perfect weather, which meant that the defects were unlikely to cause any problems. Accompanying Lord Thomson on the flight was Sir Sefton Brancker, who was bold enough to advise the Secretary of State that the R101 was not fit for the long flight. This only invited a taunt that he was 'showing the white feather', so he thereafter kept his peace. Even the Certificate of Airworthiness had been falsified, because the trials were supposed to have included a full-speed run and some abrupt manoeuvres following the modifications made to the hull, and these were not done.

At 18.30 hrs on 4 October the airship left Cardington. The route would take the airship over Paris, Toulouse and Narbonne, and thence to the Mediterranean. The R101 passed over Beauvais at approximately 02.00 hrs. The weather was bad with heavy rain and a strong south-easterly wind. The airship was not behaving abnormally as one of the mechanics, a Mr Binks, went to the aft engine car just before 02.00 hrs to relieve the mechanic on duty, and checked the oil pressure, cooling and number of engine revolutions. Suddenly the ship went into a dive, and as she dipped a signal came from the control car to reduce speed, but before he could react the airship crashed into the hillside. Mr Binks and his colleagues found themselves trapped in their engine car by flames when the overhead service water tank burst. For a moment the flames cleared, and wrapping their heads in wet cloths they smashed their way out, to find themselves in bracken and bushes. Mr Disley, a wireless operator, also escaped with his life. When the gong sounded to slow the engines he made for the switchboard. No sooner had he thrown one switch than the airship went into a dive. He heard a series of crashes and explosions, and the next thing he knew was that the ship was on fire. It flared up in an instant from stem to stern, and Mr Disley's instinct was to escape the mass of flames around him. He threw himself at the fabric cover, trying to break through, but was unsuccessful. Seconds later he was to find himself sitting on wet grass. It was all over in a minute.

The Commission of Inquiry into the disaster

A Commission was immediately established into the cause of the disaster. With the exception of Barnes Wallis, Norway and Squadron Leader Booth, the experts in this field of aeronautics perished in the inferno, as did the Secretary of State for Air, Lord Thomson, and Sir Sefton Brancker, head of civil aviation. Sir Sefton had long been associated with both military and civil flying. These two men were a loss to the nation as well as to flying.

There were many theories as to how this crash occurred. There were the problems with lift, chafing gasbags and the overweight of the craft. Then there was the weather. The R101 had been nosing into a gale for seven and a half hours, covering only 220 miles, when the accident happened, an average of a mere 29.3 mph. The Beauvais ridge was known to pilots for catching out the unwary. In the earliest days of flying those making for Paris who had tried getting through under low cloud and did not succeed added to the litter of wrecks. With a gale blowing on that Saturday night the R101 would have been subjected to a terrific down-draught on the leeward side of the ridge. It has been reported that the R100 had been caught in a violent up-draught as she approached the mooring mast at Montreal. Caught in a violent up-draught or down-draught, airship crews would experience difficulty trying to regain control. Perhaps the R101 should have been flying higher, but there was the loss of lift created by escaping gas.

In the course of many weeks the Inquiry Commission, headed by the Liberal lawyer Sir John Simon, assisted by Lieutenant Colonel J.T.C. Moore-Brabazon and Professor C.E. Inglis as assessors, investigated every aspect of the construction and loss of the R101. The economic consequences alone were devastating to the lives of those involved in the construction of the airship. All employees of the Royal Airship Works, Cardington, were discharged, and the only entitlement they had under the Unemployment Insurance Act was, in the present decimal currency, 90p per man per week, with 75p for a wife and 20p for a child.

Sir John Simon concentrated his inquiry on the airworthiness of the R101 for the long-haul flight to India. One witness was Air Marshal Sir John Higgins, who had been virtually responsible for the airship programme as Air Member for Supply and Research. At the time of the inquiry he had just resigned to become chairman of Armstrong Whitworth, the aircraft manufacturer. He had not been an engineer, but an administrator of both airship and aeroplane development, nominally responsible for ensuring that all safety precautions had been taken. The chairman wanted to know how far technical matters had been brought to the attention of the Air Ministry. After the flight over the Hendon air display it had been

The skeletal remains of the R101 on the hillside near Beauvais.

reported that the loss of gas would not account for the heaviness of the airship. Was there a responsible official at the Air Ministry who could act on the report? Higgins replied that the designer had studied the report and talked it over with Wing Commander Colmore. He made it quite clear to the Inquiry that Colmore was the responsible officer and the sole judge of whether reports of the behaviour of the ship in flight were of sufficient importance to pass to the Air Ministry. This situation is rather akin to that of ministerial responsibility in government when a civil servant makes a mistake. It used to be the case that the Minister would resign over a serious matter, though that convention no longer seems to apply to British governments in the first decade of the twenty-first century.

Higgins was making the point that he delegated his responsibilities to Colmore, but the latter had died in the crash, as indeed had many others from the design team. This meant that Sir John Simon was obliged to question one of the few members of the Royal Airship Works who was not killed in the crash and who might have had something to do with the airworthiness of R101. But Mr F.M. McWade, the Inspector-in-Charge at Cardington, refused to be made a scapegoat for the disaster. He referred to his letter of July in which he declined a Permit to Fly until the gasbag leakage had been rectified. Lieutenant Colonel H.W.S Outram, Director of the AID, had not submitted McWade's report because, after consulting Colmore, he was satisfied that the leakage holes were so small that the loss of gas would not have been important. Sir John countered that the designer had given evidence to the effect that the loss could be four or five tons of lift in twelve hours. McWade then said that as the ship set out for India things were still the same as they had been when he wrote his July letter, except for some added padding,

which, he complained, was ineffective since it could be rubbed off with the hand. If it had been left to him a Certificate of Airworthiness would not have been issued. No satisfactory reason for its issue could be ascertained.

Even Dr Eckener, the designer of the *Graf Zeppelin*, came from Germany to try to throw some light on the causes of the crash. Following the loss of the R101 he had become convinced that helium gas should be substituted for the combustible hydrogen. Helium gas, however, was heavier, and it would mean redesigning the new Zeppelin, LZ 128, to give it greater gas capacity. Professor Bairstow made statements based upon wind-tunnel tests that he had carried out. The tests showed that if one assumed certain losses of gas it would have been impossible to prevent the airship from stranding in a trimmed and loaded condition. The Professor agreed that the elevator was ineffective when the airship attained a certain out-of-horizontal position, and that a heaviness of 13–15 tons was the maximum that could be carried dynamically. A leakage of 50,000 cu. ft of gas per day from the R101 was utterly abnormal. In contrast, the *Graf Zeppelin* would not lose more than 7,000–8,000 cu. ft, and after the trip round the world the leakage was no greater than it was at the start of the voyage. Moreover she could remain in her shed for four months without the need for reflation.

After the foregoing discussion of the probable cause of the accident, the conclusion of the Inquiry may come as a surprise. Sir John Simon held that there had been a large rent that suddenly occurred in the forward gasbag due to the outer cover failing in its vicinity. He said that this would have exposed the gasbag to a rupturing air flow of 54 knots. There was no criticism of individuals. Dr Barnes Wallis has his own ideas, but the question marks remained. The outcome was predictable: this was the end of the great airships as far as Britain was concerned, and the R100 was broken up and sold for scrap. The only military use that the RAF would have for anything remotely resembling an airship was the barrage balloon. Barrage balloons were deployed in large numbers as static point defences against low-flying enemy aircraft during the Second World War. As a postscript, Lord Amulree was appointed as the new Secretary of State for Air on 14 October 1930 following the death of Lord Thomson. He was a complete stranger to everyone in aviation, and had not shown any active interest in the subject.

THE GENEVA DISARMAMENT CONFERENCE
(Source: National Archive document Air 41/8)

Introduction
In this chapter the disarmament talks that took place in Geneva are considered only as they affected the RAF.

That said, aerial bombardment was a new and frightening prospect for civilian populations, and so disarmament in the air was in any case of paramount importance at the conference. The talks were bedevilled from the beginning because there were so many ways of approaching the problem. Countries wanted different things. Were the forces of the member countries to be reduced to nothing? Should disarmament affect land, sea and air forces, or just bomber forces? Should the reduction of armaments be measured in terms of quantity, quality or both. Germany had no air force so why should other European nations? Would German security be assured only when there was parity with other European nations? If so, should there be parity with the European nation that had the largest army, navy or air force? Britain had used the strength of the French air force as a basis for the moderate increase in the number of fighter and bomber squadrons in 1923. And a final question guaranteed to cause His Majesty's Government some heart searching was the use of aerial bombardment in internal security operations in the Middle East and India. If aerial bombardment was going to be banned in war should it not apply to Empire policing in peacetime?

The Geneva Hares

A number of hares were started at Geneva. There were at least four, and the hunting of each had its ardent advocates in the United Kingdom. The first was the real and primary quarry of the conference, namely the limitation and reduction of armaments, and this was urged by the Air Ministry. Secondly, there was restriction of bombing within reasonable limits. Here the British Foreign Office and other countries regarded this as of primary, not secondary, concern. At the conference the matter of bombing threatened to assume greater importance than the general reduction in armaments. Others wished to see all national air forces disbanded. But even if total disbandment of national air forces was achieved, there was always the potential threat from countries that might use civil aircraft modified to carry bombs and or guns. To deal with that possibility it was proposed that civil aviation be internationalized. These various hares caused a great deal of complication at Geneva. Chasing these various hares resulted in no single hare being chased to an agreed end.

The effect on rearmament

Air armaments would have disappeared altogether if the most far-reaching proposals had been accepted. Countries intent on pursuing programmes of rearmament would find that the various proposals discussed in the preceding chapter would affect those programmes in different ways. Some countries might find themselves simply with an air force reduced in size, others with an air force devoid of bombers.

Bearing in mind that Trenchard and his successors argued for offensive defence, which depended critically upon the RAF having more bombers than fighters, Britain had most to lose from any reduction in bomber numbers.

Perhaps too much time at the conference was taken up with the question of bombing. It may be argued that had the conference stuck to the primary aim, the limitation and reduction of armaments, more might have been achieved. Delegates were not so concerned about air combat that did not affect civilian populations. Examples were aerial dog-fighting and maritime operations. What worried them most was aerial bombardment, and the banning of the bomber had to be dealt with before there could be an agreement on general air disarmament, let alone a general reduction and limitation of armaments.

The Leeper Plan

On 19 March 1932, Sir John Simon, the Foreign Secretary, circulated to his colleagues in the Cabinet a paper entitled 'Suggested lines of Policy in the Disarmament Conference'. This paper was the work of Mr A.W.A. Leeper, and became known as the Leeper Plan. The main thrust of the argument in this paper was that public opinion throughout the world paid the greatest attention to aerial bombardment, and the complete prohibition of bombing by aircraft of the territory and shipping of another sovereign state should be the policy of HMG.

As may be expected, the Air Staff vigorously opposed the Leeper Plan. On 26 March, Lord Londonderry submitted a note to the Ministerial Committee on Disarmament, pointing out that if the plan was to be accepted government policy Britain could not attack enemy warships from the air that were bombarding our coastline from outside territorial waters. In the days of ships' cannon, the extent of territorial waters was determined by how far a cannon ball could reach from a shore battery, for there was little point in having a limit beyond three miles that could not be enforced. By 1932 the range of a battleship's armament was such that a vessel with 15 in. guns could do considerable damage to coastal towns, as the inhabitants of a most unlikely target, the seaside town of Scarborough, found out during the Great War. A further interesting point is that the Leeper proposals would permit Britain to continue to bomb her own subjects during air control operations in the Empire while forbidding the RAF or FAA to attack an enemy. Lord Londonderry therefore concluded in his note to the Ministerial Committee that the Leeper proposals were impracticable and would do nothing to solve the major problem of reducing air armaments, which he presumed was the real objective.

Both the Admiralty and the War Office stepped in with their respective views of the Leeper Plan. The

Admiralty believed that all our bombers and bombing from the air should be abolished. The War Office, for its part, supported the Admiralty view and added submarines and heavy guns as candidates for abolition. This must have gone down very well with their Lordships in the Admiralty, and it does illustrate the temptation for the three British service departments to resurrect old conflicts and rivalries, given half the chance.

The Leeper Plan was then considered by a sub-committee of the Committee of Imperial Defence presided over by the Prime Minister, Mr Baldwin. The sub-committee concluded that the proposed prohibition of aerial bombing on the territory and shipping of another sovereign state possessed considerable disadvantages both for Imperial defence generally and for the defence of London and other objectives of air attack in the UK in particular. The view of the Air Staff prevailed, and it was agreed that a counter-offensive strategy was vital to the defence of London and the country as a whole. This had been Trenchard's view consistently held during the inter-war years. To believe that a prohibitory convention on air bombardment would remove the danger to Britain in a war was to nurse a dangerous illusion.

That said, it was Mr Baldwin himself who put forward a revolutionary suggestion for further consideration. He wanted to investigate the possibility of achieving the entire prohibition, not only of bombing, but of air warfare itself. All military and naval aircraft would disappear, and civil aviation would be placed under international control, for the possibility of converting civil aircraft to military use had been considered by Major-General Sir Frederick Sykes, the Chief of the Air Staff, immediately after the Great War. Mr Baldwin had long entertained this idea, and expressed his conviction to the House of Commons on 10 November 1932. The House listened to his impassioned appeal to the young men of Britain to save civilization by ridding the world of the menace from the air. This the Members did with evident sympathy and respect.

Draft Convention for the abolition of military aircraft

The Draft Convention for the Abolition of Military Aircraft and the Internationalization of Civil Aviation was in fact prepared by the Foreign Office in London in May 1932. Having successfully opposed the Leeper Plan, the Air Staff were also opposed to this more far-reaching proposal. The Chief of the Imperial General Staff held the opinion that the abolition of naval and military aircraft would be advantageous to Britain as 'tending to restore to us the sea as our first line of defence and as removing the danger of an attack on London'. The First Sea Lord added his opinion that 'aircraft contribute more towards attacks upon surface shipping than towards their defence'. Both service departments supported the abolition of naval and military aircraft. Whether this was a symptom of inter-service rivalry or a genuine attempt to make the world a safer place is open to debate.

Although thus strongly supported by the Admiralty and the War Office with the recommendation of a Cabinet Committee, HMG did not proceed with the draft convention at this time. Exploratory enquiries made at Geneva in June 1932 showed that the French ministers were not in favour. The French, with the largest air force in Europe, were not eager to lose a vital shield in the defence of their territory without corresponding cuts in the air forces of other countries. The British draft convention was to be revived at a later date, apparently in the hope that it might save the moribund conference from dissolution.

BRITISH DISARMAMENT POLICY
Introduction

The official British government policy on disarmament was published in a White Paper on 7 July 1932. The programme for consideration at Geneva contained the following main proposals, that there should be:

1. A complete prohibition of all bombing from the air save within limits laid down as precisely as possible by an international convention, which would also prohibit entirely attacks upon the civilian population.
2. Strict limitation of unladen weight of military and naval aircraft.
3. A restriction in numbers of military and naval aircraft.

The policy document consisted mainly of proposals made by the Air Ministry, but at the insistence of the Foreign Office, there was to be a qualified prohibition of bombing. The British representative at the conference went further still by assenting to the 'Benes Resolution' of 23 July 1932, which provided that the High Contracting Parties should agree as between themselves that all bombardment from the air should be abolished, subject to agreement with regard to the means of observing the effectiveness of this rule. This, however, simply highlighted another problem in securing international agreement on disarmament, and that was verification. It is one thing to agree on limits to armaments but it is another to make sure that signatory countries honour commitments made. Even in these days of spy satellites one could not be absolutely sure whether or not Saddam Hussein had weapons of mass destruction hidden in Iraq.

The White Paper of November 1932

Lord Londonderry was quick to point out the disparity between the government's disarmament policy and the 'Benes Resolution' He warned the Ministerial

Committee on Disarmament that the adoption of the latter would gravely endanger the defence of the country and the Empire if bombing was prohibited in all circumstances. But the Air Ministry's view had to be reconciled with that of the Foreign Office. Accordingly the Ministerial Committee asked the Air Ministry to submit concrete proposals for disarmament if only to allow the Geneva Conference to get on with the business of disarming. The Air Ministry's proposals were eminently practical, but an acceptance of them would have resulted in smallish national air forces with a limited capacity:

1. The French air force should be cut by one-third, with other countries' air forces being fixed to the reduced figure.
2. No military aircraft except a flying-boat or a troop carrier should be of a greater unladen weight than three tons.
3. Air attacks should be confined to military objectives and completely prohibited against the civilian population.

The simplicity of an absolute approach to disarmament had its appeal, but was never going to be acceptable to countries with established air forces, but then neither were the compromise proposals above. Once the delegates got enmeshed in the 'nitty-gritty' detail of weights, limits and what constituted a troop carrier as opposed to a bomber, like the Vickers Vernons of No. 45 Squadron in Iraq, the whole disarmament project was almost bound to end in tears. It is interesting to note that the attempts to limit nuclear delivery vehicles after the Second World War, as between the USA and USSR, were always overtaken by technical advances in aircraft, delivery systems and static defences.

His Majesty's Government's Declaration of Disarmament Policy

A new White Paper was then issued on 17 November 1932 with the title shown above. The government tried to satisfy both the Air Ministry and the Foreign Office. Accordingly the new White Paper embodied the Air Staff proposals already outlined in the preceding paragraph, but it also included prominently the proposal for an inquiry into the practicability of abolishing military and naval aircraft altogether. It thus represented an amalgam of the views of the Air Ministry, the Prime Minister and the Foreign Office.

Sir John Simon submitted this proposal for 'air disarmament down to zero' to the Bureau of the Geneva Conference. He left the conference in no doubt that the British government was intent on the abolition of air forces, and aerial bombing in particular, for which there was always the danger that civil aircraft might be used. He added that HMG was anxious to cooperate with the

other 'chief powers' in a thorough examination into the practicability of so extensive a scheme. The examination of this scheme was entrusted to an air committee set up by the General Commission of the Conference on 16 February 1933. The Air Committee was not composed of the representatives of the 'chief powers' but of representatives of no fewer than twenty states. The terms of reference were those suggested by the UK delegation, namely:

To examine the possibility of the entire abolition of military and naval machines and of bombing from the air, combined with an effective international control of civil aviation.

The Air Committee met for the first time on 20 February 1933, and Lord Londonderry said that his government was prepared to subscribe to the idea of the proposed abolition of air forces and bombing except 'police bombing'. This was a reference to the policy of air control operations carried out in India and Iraq, etc. Understandably this drew the attention of other countries to the methods used by Britain to maintain internal security in her possessions, but in the event any 'finger wagging' was of little consequence.

The work of the Air Committee met with no successes. The stumbling block was the near-impossibility of ensuring that civil aircraft could not be used for bombing, albeit unlawfully, by a state determined to circumvent any agreement. At home in the United Kingdom the Ministerial Committee of the Cabinet was also unable to come up with a solution to this problem, and concluded that the total abolition of military air forces was impracticable and that other methods had to be considered. This was the recommendation made to the Cabinet and approved by that body on 8 March. Meanwhile, even as the Air Committee and the British Cabinet's Ministerial Committee deliberated upon the practicability of total air disarmament, Adolf Hitler had just been installed as the Chancellor of Germany. Whatever agreement might have been achieved at Geneva, the work of the conference was already doomed to ultimate failure, and during the six years that followed there was to be an arms race akin to that which preceded the Great War in the building of Dreadnought battleships.

The British Draft Convention

In the spring of 1933 the world had yet to grasp the significance of Hitler's rise to power, and so HMG plodded on in a vain attempt to achieve disarmament. The abolition of military and naval aircraft was again inserted into the British Draft Convention submitted to the Geneva Conference on 16 March 1933. This was in spite of the Cabinet agreement that total abolition was impracticable. In what may now be regarded as a forlorn attempt to at least appear to be genuinely seeking total air disarmament, HMG proposed the setting up of a Permanent Disarmament Commission to work out the best possible scheme for abolition of military and naval aircraft, coupled with the effective control of civil aviation. Almost as if HMG knew that the above proposals stood little chance of acceptance, an alternative scheme was also proposed, that such a disarmament commission should attempt to fix a minimum number of machines required by each of the participating states. Tentatively a table annexed to the Air Clauses assigned an establishment of 500 aircraft to each of the principal air powers, and proportionately lower numbers for the other states. No mention was made of Nazi Germany, still at that time bound by the Versailles Treaty, which prohibited a German air force. A 'let-out' clause to cover British air control operations was couched in the following diplomatic language. There would be:

'the complete prohibition of bombing, except for police purposes in certain outlying regions'.

This reservation, as has already been pointed out, drew criticism when it was inserted in the draft convention. It was criticized both in Parliament and the Press, and had to be defended in the House of Commons by Anthony Eden on 13 June and again on 5 July 1933. His response was that the matter of imperial policing was a small issue compared with the great political questions, which were holding up the work of the conference. Indeed the work of the conference did not founder on the matter of imperial policing, but rather the impossibility of reconciling French demands for security with the German demands for equality of rights.

The French government had always been nervous that a reduction in the size of the French air force would not be matched by reductions of the air forces of other powers. The French sought security in alliances, which bound powers to act together. In a sense Hitler was demanding the same thing. With what some may regard as righteous indignation, Hitler was claiming that Germany would be insecure unless all other countries reduced their air forces to zero, like Germany. But the methods used by Hitler to come to power in Germany meant that his words could not be taken at face value, and the French and the Poles were suspicious. Hitler had spelt out the direction that foreign policy would take, should he become the leader of Germany, in *Mein Kampf*, written while he was in Landsberg prison in 1924. He had no intention of being bound by the shackles of any disarmament convention. He had always made it clear in many speeches that he would repudiate the Versailles Treaty and avenge Germany's defeat in 1918. He constantly blamed the

'November criminals', the socialist government of Germany in 1919, for accepting the limits imposed on Germany's armed forces. It is little wonder that some were alarmed at his coming to power. Following a Polish military demonstration in Danzig in March 1933, Marshal Pilsudski suggested to the French the desirability of a joint preventative war against Germany.

Once it became clear that Hitler was determined on rearmament, the British and French governments had to decide whether to use military force to ensure that the provisions of the Versailles Treaty were being upheld. It was either that or come to some accommodation with Germany, for public opinion in both countries was in no mood for renewed conflict after the ghastly casualty figures for the Great War. Thus began the period of appeasement, for Hitler could see how reluctant were the two governments to take any action, and he would exploit this lack of resolve time and again in the late 1930s.

The End of the Geneva Conference

The British Draft Convention was brought forward as a 'last-ditch' attempt to save the conference. The German delegation had already withdrawn from the conference in September 1932, and finally walked out on 14 October 1933, complaining of the 'humiliating exactions of other powers'. For all practical purposes the conference was at an end, although it lingered on into 1934. The reasons for the failure cannot be laid solely at the door of Nazi Germany. The conference would probably have failed in any event. The issues that divided Europe were too fundamental to be settled by way of discussion and protocol. Something worthwhile might have been achieved had less ambitious aims been set.

Measures of limitation and restriction might have been acceptable to the Air Ministry and the French air force, whereas total abolition of military and naval aircraft was a step too far. Cluttering up the conference with side issues served only to make attainment of the main issues more difficult. One might argue that attempts by the major powers after the Second World War, to achieve even some incremental measures of disarmament, have not met with success either. The SALT I and SALT II talks (Strategic Arms Limitation Treaty) are two examples. Technical developments in weapons and their delivery systems have to be addressed as they occur. This was not quite the case in the 1930s. The League of Nations performed effectively in the 1920s, when minor powers were being reprimanded, but could not cope in the face of German, Italian and Japanese aggression. The end of the conference was shortly followed by the British government's decision to rearm, and for the remainder of the decade the various RAF expansion plans were put into operation.

RAF DISPLAYS

1930 Display

On 28 June the eleventh RAF Display took place at Hendon. It was a day of summer sunshine with light cloud. Everything went like clockwork, but the RAF pilots knew their machines from previous years, and at long last the DH9A had been dropped from the Display. The Army Cooperation squadrons were equipped with the Atlas, and were able to demonstrate accurate pick-ups, and a spirited attack was made on some lorries by an Atlas flown by Flight Lieutenant Schofield.

In the New Types Park there was an assortment of sixteen types, ranging from the Vickers twin-engined night-bomber to the tailless Pterodactyl. The new Vickers bomber looked a great deal cleaner in appearance compared with the largest RAF heavy bomber, the Vickers Virginia. In a static exhibition were the beautiful Schneider Competition floatplane, the Supermarine S6 and the Gloster VI. It is perhaps strange to consider that in 1930 the Schneider floatplanes were considered an abnormality. Among the fighters was the Fairey Firefly II, contrasted with the Hart day-bomber, for there was little difference in external appearance between the fighters and light day-bombers of the day. The Hornet was deemed too secret to put on display, but visitors could see the Blackburn Lincock fighter, the much-publicized Handley Page Gugnunc and the Army Cooperation version of the well-proved Wapiti. Since the Prince of Wales had ordered a DH Puss Moth, there was considerable interest in this aircraft. Some interesting features to see included the Townend circular-slot, drag-reducing ring around the Siskin IIIB fighter, and the deflector box-tail of the C19 Autogiro, which relied upon aircraft-type ailerons, elevator and rudder.

C19 Autogiro.

Westland Pterodactyl.

The flying display included the volunteer pilots of the Auxiliary Air Force, who flew beautifully sequenced manoeuvres in their Wapitis. RAF Bulldogs fought an aerial battle with Horsleys, and RAF pilots serving with the FAA flew their ageing Flycatchers. A formation of Siskins, Foxes and Fairey IIIFs flew in salute to the King, who was the only representative of the Royal Family at the 1930 Display. Then in the distance there appeared the monstrous shape of the R101 airship, and it crossed the airfield at 1,000 ft. One flyer of note who flew in the display was Flying Officer Frank Whittle, who would go down in history as the inventor of the jet engine. Together with Flying Officer G.E. Campbell, he flew a Lynx-powered Avro.

The display came to its usual spectacular end. A Siskin attacked a Kite balloon and there was a set-piece battle between the 'good guys' and the 'bad guys'. Pirates, flying the skull-and-crossbones flag, landed in what was portrayed as British Colonial Territory. They installed themselves in the building of a planter, whom they hanged. When an RAF day-bomber appeared, the pirates fired at it with anti-aircraft guns, but when they brought in reinforcements they were attacked by two squadrons of RAF fighters. The estate was then finished off by day-bombers.

1931 Display

Just before the 1931 Display it had been wet and stormy, but the display organizers' fears were put to rest when 27 June turned out to be a glorious sunny day with a cloudless sky. The Duke of Gloucester was there, accompanied by Lord Amulree, the Secretary of State for Air, and Air Chief Marshal Sir John Salmond, the Chief of the Air Staff.

There were the usual thrilling displays of airmanship, including aerobatics by Central Flying

School Gypsy Moths led by Flight Lieutenant B.E. Embry. The scarlet Grebes trailed smoke and there were parachute descents from a Vimy bomber. There were also two interesting demonstrations, namely in-flight refuelling with a Virginia, and the launching of an aircraft by catapult. In-flight refuelling opened up the possibility of reaching the air bases in the Empire without having to land in unfriendly countries. The catapult was designed by a Mr P. Salmon of the Royal Aeronautical Establishment. As things stood, the foldable cordite-fired unit, like that aboard the battle cruiser HMS *Hood*, could launch a 7,000 lb aircraft at 60 mph with an acceleration of 2.36 G. Mr Salmon's catapult was a windlass, gear-driven by two swash-plate compressed-air engines operating at 400 lb/sq. in. Developing 4,000 hp, it could launch an aircraft of 18,000 lb at 60 mph in 100 yards with an acceleration of 1 G. This might make it possible to launch a heavy land-bomber with sufficient acceleration to take off with even heavier bomb loads.

The journalists present noted the significant advance made in the RAF's equipment. This was the Hawker Fury. As it had been in squadron service for only a matter of weeks, the squadron pilots might have been forgiven for not being ready for the display. The Fury was fast but easy to handle, and three pilots gave a good account of themselves in an aerobatic display. The Navy was also impressed with this aircraft, and it was ordered as a fleet fighter and renamed the Nimrod.

1932 Display

The thirteenth annual display was held on 26 June, again in glorious weather. Present with Air Vice-Marshal HRH the Duke of York were Sir Philip Sassoon, Air Chief Marshal Sir John Salmond and Air Marshal Sir Edward Ellington. The superstitious worried that there might be a major accident at the thirteenth display, but this did not happen. Another much smaller peril lay in the habit of some visitors who dropped their glass bottles in the exclusive ten-shilling (50p) enclosure. The broken glass punctured the tyres of the cars belonging to the wealthy.

The formation flying, aerobatics and battle sequences were all there, and still continued to thrill the crowds. There was, however, a novel event, and this was a competition for the slowest circuit of the aerodrome by Tiger Moths of No. 3 FTS. This meant flying at or near the point of stall, when the nose was well up, but every time a stall was saved by the leading-edge slots. Tiger Moths were also engaged in multi-glider towing, when three of these aircraft simultaneously released their gliders in line astern.

The Pterodactyl at the display was painted as a fearsome sharp-toothed monster. This aircraft attracted considerable interest since it seemed to point the way to the future. The editor of the *Aeroplane*, C.G. Grey, believed that a larger version could provide the solution to ocean-going flying-boats. He felt that the simple body could become an extremely efficient hull that eliminated the need for the long turned-up tail associated with conventional flying-boats. The absence of the tail would reduce weight and drag. With the wings so swept back and outward, comparatively small wingtip floats would give perfect three-point water support. Big engines could be installed high at the back so that the propeller blades would be clear of the spray thrown up by the bows. In fact models of such a craft were already being tested in the Westland wind tunnel and the water tank at the National Physical Laboratory. There was also design work on a two-seat tailless fighter with a tractor propeller and metal sesquiplane structure meeting the necessarily high load factors, and Air Ministry Specification F3/32 was being written to embrace these proposals.

The year 1932 was the first in which the New Types Park was open on the Monday following the display, and on 27 June overseas visitors and special guests were invited to view the aircraft. In 1931 manufacturers had been allowed to show such aircraft to a limited number of visitors, but the new arrangement permitted the Society of British Aircraft Constructors (SBAC) to have its own display, with static exhibits in the morning and a flying display in the afternoon. One newspaper reporter gave it as his opinion that the public were not invited on the occasion of the first SBAC display, which was only an experiment. However, the event might be a public affair in 1933 or 1934 if the Air Ministry would be willing to lend Hendon for that purpose.

THE SCHNEIDER TROPHY COMPETITION OF 1931

Introduction

The RAF Schneider team had won the 1927 contest in Venice and, as the winner of the competition, would host the following contest, which did not take place until September 1929 in the Solent. As the winner a second time, the RAF team would again host the competition in the Solent, and it was to take place in 1931. Given the economic situation in 1929, the government was cautious on matters of public expenditure, and within a few weeks of the 1929 competition it put under review future policy regarding the contest. Then it was decided that an RAF team would not be entered again It was accepted that the RAF entry in 1927 and 1929 had given impetus to the development of high-speed aircraft, but the government believed that sufficient data had been collected in this respect and that any further involvement was unnecessary. When strong representations were made to the government it was decided to reconsider the situation, but the expenditure of £80,000 in the prevailing economic climate could not be justified, and the government stuck to its previous decision. If public money was not to be forthcoming, only private enterprise, in the form of the Royal Aero Club, could save the British entry.

Pressure on Government

The Government and the Royal Aero Club The Press headlined the government decision, and the general feeling expressed was one of anger since it was felt that a great international sporting event was sacrosanct. There were pointed questions in the House of Commons, and the Royal Aero Club (RAeC) offered to raise the necessary funds by the end of the month. The Under-Secretary of State for Air, Frederick Montague, said that the decision not to enter an RAF team had been taken, not simply on financial grounds, but for reasons of policy and principle. The RAeC pointed out that the RAF floatplanes were government property, and no British pilots, other than the RAF pilots, had been trained to fly them; moreover the French and Italian governments had built their Schneider aircraft for the races. The Society of British Aircraft Constructors (SBAC) added their voice to the pleas, and the London Chamber of Commerce pointed out that if Britain won the trophy outright it would give a tremendous boost to the marketing of British aircraft abroad.

The Prime Minister's response to the criticisms of the Government's policy was that he had not promised support but expressed hope that a British entry would, nevertheless, come to pass. However, a year passed and the RAeC was unable to raise the necessary funds, but the government still felt unable to reverse its decision not to support an official entry. A Liberal, Leslie Hoare-Belisha, asked if the government would reconsider the matter if the House of Commons voted for entry. Ramsay MacDonald replied that he was as keen as any man to see a British entry, but it was not the government's fault that there would not be a British team. After further Parliamentary lobbying the government made it clear that it was against a competition between rival government teams, but was prepared to assist with entry provided there was a definite undertaking from private donors to provide the necessary funds. The RaeC was informed that it would have to find £100,000 or the RAF machines and pilots would not be loaned to the club for the races.

Lady Houston to the rescue

Three days elapsed and the RAeC was able to announce that a telegram had been received from Lady Houston that she would guarantee the full amount required by the government. This, however, gave rise to a war of words between members of the government and Lady Houston. Sir Philip Sassoon, the chairman of the club, was invited to her yacht to discuss the offer. She expressed irritation with the government's attitude by saying that she was 'utterly weary of the lie-down-and-kick-me attitude of the Socialist government'. She objected to the continual pleading of poverty and objections made to entry for a race against teams supplied by nations much less wealthy than Britain. She was further angered by a telegram from the government insisting that a banker's guarantee was required by the Thursday of the week in question. To the Press Association she communicated her feeling of being insulted by the government, but she went ahead and complied with the demand. Mr Montague, speaking in Reading, said that he regarded Lady Houston's attitude as proof that rich people regarded Labour governments as a hateful interlude during which there was only the barest pretence of social decency. Finally, Lady Houston's offer left Reginald Mitchell and Ernest Hives (Supermarine aircraft designer and Rolls-Royce engineer) with the urgent need to give the aircraft, the S6 and the R-engine, a new lease of life.

Preparations

The High-Speed Flight Squadron Leader A.H. Orlebar was the commanding officer of the new High-Speed Flight (HSF) at Calshot. Orlebar had led the successful 1929 Schneider team, and after that contest he had broken the world's speed record with 357.7 mph. Since then he had been Officer Commanding the Flying-boat Development Flight at RAF Felixstowe. The pilots were drawn from the Aircraft and Armament Experimental Establishment (*A & AEE*) and the Marine Aircraft Experimental Flight (MAEE):

1931 Schneider Trophy Team		
High-Speed Flight	Squadron Leader Orlebar*	Officer Commanding
	Flight Lieutenant W.F. Drury	Engineering Officer
	Flight Lieutenant E.J.L. Hope	Pilot
	Flight Lieutenant F.W. Long	Pilot
	Flight Lieutenant J.N. Boothman	Pilot
	Flight Lieutenant G.H. Stainforth*	Pilot
	Flying Officer H.H. Leech	Pilot
	Flying Officer L.S. Snaith	Pilot

* Previous Schneider experience

Practice for the 1931 contest began as soon as the initial reconditioned S6 floatplane, N247, was received. Orlebar had flown this aircraft when he broke the world speed record. N248 was the next aircraft to be received, but was written off. This is service parlance for being struck off stock record, i.e. the seaplane had been lost. A piece of cowling had come adrift and struck Flight Lieutenant Hope's head during a flight test. He had to attempt an immediate landing, and touched down smoothly on the water, but unfortunately the wash from a passing liner caused the S6 to ricochet into the air, and as it hit the water it promptly turned over and sank in fifty feet of water. Fortunately Hope managed to extricate himself from the S6 before she sank. His convalescence would be too long, given the time constraint in preparing the team, and sadly he had to be replaced by a naval officer, Lieutenant G.L. Brinton.

Technical Problems

The French team was also in trouble with the engines for their wire-based low-wing aircraft. On the other hand the Italians were practising hard and in great secrecy. Their faith was pinned on a tandem Fiat-powered Macchi monoplane, which was said to be capable of 440 mph. At Rolls-Royce Hives was working with Ellor. Both men were busy with Rodwell Banks of the Ethyl Corporation on last-minute problems with the 1929 R engine. A higher supercharger gear ratio was being used, and this meant that the engine would have to have the power equivalent of the 360 hp Eagle engine used in the Great War. Supercharging means that the fuel is forced into the cylinders so that it develops greater power, but this could only be achieved by making changes to the parts of the engine that would be under greater stress, for the centre main bearing of the engine was loaded to 9 tons. The blade and fork connecting rods were replaced by articulated rods, salt-cooled exhaust valves became necessary and induction passages had to be enlarged, but greater power and higher revolutions with an engine running for an hour meant changes to the fuel. Rodwell Banks had devised a new fuel by mixing benzol, alcohol and tetra-ethyl-lead in proportions, which would give sufficient cooling and minimum detonation.

Hollis Williams at Fairey Aviation was responsible for propeller design for the Schneider aircraft, but when tasked to produce a design he did not then know what power the R engine would develop. He had to make some 'guesstimates'. The twisted design made from duralumin blanks was not acceptable for even the 1929 aircraft, and so it was decided to sculpt the propellers from thicker blanks, in which the helix was continued right into the integral boss. This permitted a smaller spinner to fair into the lines of the racing aircraft. In the end it looked more like a marine propeller than one

fitted to an aircraft. As the race date approached, three propellers had been completed and the rest were in an advanced state of machining.

At the end of May the two S6B floatplanes being built at the Supermarine seemed far from completion. The problem for Mitchell was in dealing with the additional heat from the engine, which had to be dissipated through the almost dragless surface radiators of two 24-gauge sheets of duralumin $1/8$ in. apart that formed the skin of otherwise conventional wings of simple pressed ribs with flanges flush with the top of the two duralumin spars. There was the danger that there might be leakage due to the wire-braced wings bending in flight. In addition to the water radiators built into the wings, further engine cooling was achieved by having water radiators covering the floats above the chine line. The floats also contained tinned-steel fuel tanks in the midship sections. The fuselage was of duralumin monocoque construction. The engine bearers ran from the nose to Frame No. 40 and were its only longitudinal members. The fin and most of the top fairing of the aircraft formed the oil tank, and additional coolers ran along the sides and the belly of the aircraft in the form of shallow channels attached to the skin and internally fitted with copper-foil tongues athwart the flow to aid heat dispersion. Reginald Mitchell was using his experience with metal hulls by using single curvatures except for the cowling; indeed, skinning a fuselage was still a novel art.

The secret of success was to get the R engine into the lowest-possible-drag airframe. The engines used in the previous competition in 1929 had been cleared to run at 3,000 rpm, and this was to be raised to more than 3,600 rpm for the 1931 event. But the R engine, which was a modified Buzzard, ran at a maximum of 2,200 rpm, and so a great deal of work was going to be required to be ready in time for the competition. For its part, Rolls-Royce was busier than at any time since the Great War with the contract to build the Kestrel engine for the RAF's Fury and Hart aircraft then in production. It was then being asked to assign the task of uprating the R engine to its experimental department. The way this was done was gradually to increase the power, step by step, until various components, like the valve springs or connecting rods, failed. After an engine failure, undamaged parts would be built into another engine where failed parts had been strengthened. These were then tested to destruction. This went on, day after day, but every morning the rebuilt engine was ready for retesting. The roar of the open exhausts coming from the test sheds, day and night, was indescribable. One person working on the project said that his whole body seemed to be in a state of high-frequency vibration. In spite of the disturbance to the local residents, there seems to have been an acceptance that the noise was all in a good cause. It was essential that the engine should run for an hour.

On one test the engine ran for thirty-four minutes before the crankshaft failed from fatigue. The engine had previously been run at full throttle for nine hours! A new crankshaft was fitted, but the engine ran for only two minutes short of the hour when there was a loud bang. This time the carburettor air pipe split and the engine stopped dead as aluminium rivets flew in all directions. And so it went on until 12 August, a month before the contest. The much-modified R engine was at last run for an hour at 3,200 rpm, giving 2,350 bhp, which was nearly 200 hp per cylinder, yet the total weight of the engine was only 1,630 lb.

In spite of all the exhaustive tests to which the engine had been subjected, it was again stripped and each component was again inspected and tested before the engine was cleaned and dispatched to Calshot. There the original S6 floatplanes and the Napier-powered Gloster VI were being worked hard. The Rolls-Royce engines in the S6s were only cleared for an hour's running, so there had to be an engine replacement after almost every flight, and teams of Rolls-Royce engineers had to work day and night modifying the installation. Indeed, the foregoing passages serve to show the degree of dedication and teamwork required to enter the RAF High-Speed Flight for this competition.

Final preparations, the Italian and French withdrawal and the death of Lieutenant Brinton

Training was often hampered by heat haze and the constant passage of ships in the Solent. The ideal weather condition was a gentle breeze that would ruffle the surface of the lake. The tragic death of Captain Monti (see next paragraph) showed only too clearly what can happen if the height of the aircraft above the water cannot be judged accurately. The aircraft is either flown in or it bounces off the surface if there are waves. With these hazards in mind, the OC, Squadron Leader Orlebar, would check wind and water in his Firefly seaplane, which meant that he, and not the flight pilots with their precious competition machines, would suffer any mishap that arose. But then he was the most experienced pilot and most capable of recovering from difficulty. On 18 August he signalled to the pilots waiting on the water that conditions were suitable for practice, but on alighting he almost capsized his seaplane when he was caught in the wash of a passing steamer. Perhaps a pilot with less experience might have come to grief. However, at 20.00 hrs it was Lieutenant Brinton's turn for take-off. Brinton, it will be remembered, was the naval officer who replaced the injured Flight Lieutenant Hope in the team. As he began his take-off in the Supermarine 6A, his machine bounced, dropped back, bounced again and stalled its starboard wing, tilted steeply and hit the water hard, ripping off the floats. The machine turned over and there was silence. By the time the rescue launch reached the overturned seaplane, Brinton, who was trapped in the fuselage, had drowned. In spite of this tragic accident, it was in the RAF tradition that practice flights simply carried on as planned.

The French and Italian teams Britain's competitors were Italy and France. If neither of these countries could prevent Britain from winning for a third time, the trophy would be won by the RAF for all time. It is therefore sad to recount that both teams lost good pilots, both killed during practice flights. On 2 August the Italian team was practising at Lake Garda in northern Italy when the pilot, Captain Monti, misjudged his height above the surface of the lake. It was deduced that as he turned the new Macchi floatplane over the lake he must have been dazzled by the sun's reflection and he slanted in and was killed. The French team had only one pilot with high-speed experience, Lieutenant de Vassai Bougault. On 30 July he was flying one of the Bernard training floatplanes from the Etang de Berre when the propeller broke, causing a fatal crash. Whether there would be rival contestants was in doubt. Be that as it may, the Italian Air Attaché in London, Colonel Bitossi, announced that an advance party of the Italian team would arrive in England on 22 August and that the main body with the racing machines would follow shortly thereafter. All that was known of the French team was that their high-speed flight had been dispersed because neither the Nieuport-Delage nor Bernard racing machines were ready. If the Italians dropped out there would be a walkover.

On 3 September the RAeC received submissions through both the Italian and the French Air Attachés that the 1931 contest be cancelled and rearranged for 1932. If not, both teams would be withdrawn. This placed the British team in a very difficult position, for it was only with Lady Houston's help that the RAF had been entered for the 1931 contest. The Americans had sportingly postponed the 1924 contest when the British team was not ready. The RAeC wrote to both the Italian and French aero clubs after consulting the Air Ministry. It was advised that, according to the rules, the contest could only be postponed on a day-to-day basis if the stewards ruled that the weather conditions were not satisfactory. Britain argued that to agree to a postponement would be to admit that the RAF team was not ready, which was not the case. Large expenditure had been incurred, and local authorities and private interests had provided accommodation for the public to witness the contest. With only nine days remaining, argued the RAeC, it was too late to undo these elaborate arrangements, and regret was expressed by the host country that the 1931 competition must go ahead as planned. There was a last-minute attempt by the Fiat company to assume full responsibility for funding an

Refuelling the racers could take a long time!

Italian entry if the government would send Lieutenant Neri and Warrant Officer Agello to join the three racers already packed. The Italian government refused, and both the French and Italian teams were subsequently withdrawn. The British team was to go ahead by simply aiming to break the 1929 record for the 100 km. With that the public interest in the competition was understandably affected.

The 1931 Competition
(See Appendix E for the administrative arrangements.)
Practice continued with the Schneider machines. Stainforth, Long, Boothman and Snaith flew them in succession, and on 7 September the S6Bs were withdrawn to have their engines fitted. The strain on all involved in preparing the racers was beginning to show. Major G.P. Bulman walked with Mitchell from the RAF mess to see the new engines having their final run the night before the contest. There was a last-minute panic when Jimmy Ellor from the Rolls team ran up to the two men to report that the wing radiators were stone cold and not working. The panic in the man's voice sounded a note of despair in Mitchell's mind, and he declared that he should never have gone along with the idea of wing radiators and that the design team would be the laughing stock of the world. But it was all a false alarm, for by the time Mitchell and Bulman got to the seaplanes, gleaming under the floodlights, the radiators were working well.

On the 12th there were crowds at every vantage point, but there was a squally wind and rain. The sea had a nasty lop, and as the rain grew heavier and the sea rougher the guardship HMS *Medea* slipped back to her anchorage as if the race had been cancelled. The RAeC immediately queried the decision, and at 11.30 hrs the

Clerk of the Course, Colonel Bristow, climbed into the rear cockpit of the Armstrong Whitworth Atlas, with its stainless-steel floats, and was taken round the harbour for half an hour assessing the weather conditions, before being carried ashore by one of the landing party. There he met Orlebar to agree that the races would have to be postponed.

Fortunately the weather on the 13th was almost perfect for racing conditions. The visibility was 12 miles and a few scattered clouds floated high in a blue sky. Orlebar checked with the Atlas before Boothman and Snaith went round the course in the seaplane. Long carried out his practice circuit in the Fairey Firefly. As the blue and silver S6Bs were towed to the start line, the plan was that Boothman should fly the course with S1595. If he should fail to complete the course, Snaith would follow with the S6A, and should he fail then Long would try with the second S6B. Boothman took off and was soon climbing in a wide turn above Cowes before slanting down to alight in slowly diminishing hops, accompanied by spray.

After the take-off and landing there were the required two minutes while the seaplane was taxied. Then there was a roar as the engine was opened up, and Boothman's racer was silhouetted against the sky as it made a climbing turn before diving past the *Medea*. This marked the beginning of the timed circuits, and he was soon heading towards St Helen's and on to Wittering. It was not long before the stream of black smoke, with the S6B at its head, could be seen approaching, then flashing past to begin the second of seven circuits. Although the lap speeds were slowly decreasing, the average of 340 mph was very satisfactory. After completing the final lap Boothman made a climbing turn above Cowes before making a very smooth landing. John Boothman had achieved a Schneider victory.

Flight Lieutenant J.N. Boothman in S1595.

Stainforth's attempts at the World Speed Record At 16.00 hrs on 13 September, after Boothman's success, Stainforth was going to attempt a world speed record in the second S6B. The course was from Spithead Fort in mid-Solent, up Southampton Water to Hythe Pier. The measured 3 km run was midway between Lee-on-Solent Pier and Hillhead at Titchfield Harbour. Four runs were measured, averaging 379 mph. Three days after this attempt he capsized in Southampton Water in the same seaplane, and his aircraft sank in 50 feet of water. It was recovered by a naval vessel and towed ashore. Further attempts were postponed until a specially tuned engine and a different propeller were fitted.

It was not until 29 September that a further attempt at the world speed record was attempted, and this time Stainforth used the ultimate R engine. He averaged 407.5 mph on the four measured runs. His report of the flight was recorded as follows:

Opened up quickly and got nearly full revs very soon, but did not get full power during take-off. Swung too much to the left but brought her back before porpoise could develop. Slight porpoise damped out after throttling slightly. Felt fore and aft instability a little just after getting into air. Machine accelerated slowly and was tail heavy. Engine got really going after ASI [Air Speed Indicator] read 200 mph, and tail heaviness disappeared. Started runs at Warner Lightship at one end and Hythe Pier at the other. Visibility not good, but kept line by use of clouds. Landing OK except for slight swinging from side to side.

And that was it! From Calshot he was posted to Farnborough, where he began testing the Westland Pterodactyl IV, though not at speeds in excess of 400 mph.

FLYING AND OPERATIONAL
(Source: Air Ministry Weekly Orders A & N)

Introduction
The section entitled 'Flying and Operational' appears in this chapter and Chapters 2 and 3 containing both permanent (A Orders) and temporary (N Orders) orders issued by the Air Ministry to units of the RAF. They are a sample of the many orders issued during the 1930s and are intended to provide a snapshot of regulations applying to service flying in this period.

N.74 GOSPORT AERODROME – OBSTRUCTION
1. Deck landing practice is periodically carried out in the centre of the aerodrome at Gosport.
2. Pilots arriving at Gosport by air should therefore keep a sharp lookout for aeroplanes carrying out these practices, and should, in that event, land at the extreme north end of the aerodrome. If it is evident that no deck-landing practices are in progress, landings may be made in the centre of the aerodrome. (AMWO 281/1925 cancelled)

Author's note: Instructions to pilots, such as N.74, were given in the days when there were no talk-downs from air traffic control nor did the aircraft land on a metalled runway. It was up to the pilot of a visiting aircraft to search the air for other possible aircraft attempting to land, and to observe conditions on the ground which might be spelt out using ground signals (see A.249). It was then up to the pilot to make a judgement on landing, taking into consideration wind speed and direction and high-rise obstacles on the glide path, given his approach. The aircraft in question, which would almost certainly be a biplane, would have a low landing speed, which is why a pilot did not need the whole field to land. On his arrival the pilot would report to a watch office, where he might say how long he was staying and request fuel and possible long-term-stay parking. In this case visiting pilots who would normally land in the middle of an airfield were to know that the landing area was being temporarily restricted, hence the N Order.

N.139 LONDON–BRUSSELS AIR ROUTE – EMPLOYMENT OF FLASHING NAVIGATION LIGHTS (90333/31)
1. A three-engined Fokker F.VII aircraft operating on the London–Brussels night air service has been fitted for experimental purposes with flashing side lights. The red and green side lights on this aircraft will each exhibit sixty flashes a minute.
2. The timetable for this service is as follows, Saturday and Sunday nights being excluded:

Leaves		*Arrives*	
Brussels	23.30 hours	Croydon	02.00 hours
Croydon	02.30 hours	Brussels	05.00 hours

3. RAF pilots, flying at night, who sight this aircraft are invited to report on the efficiency of the new type of navigation lights. Information is required on the following points:

(i) Are the lights visible at the required ranges (e.g. five miles for side lights and three miles for a tail lamp)?
(ii) Do the flashing lights attract the attention of the observer more readily than fixed lights?

4. Reports on this subject are to be forwarded to the Secretary, Air Ministry, through the usual channels, as and when information is obtained.

A.196 FORMATION OF ICE ON AIRCRAFT – WARNING TO PILOTS (28.7.32)

1. The attention of all pilots is drawn to the dangerous conditions which may arise from the formation of ice on aircraft flying in clouds or under other conditions favourable to ice formation.
2. The ice deposited may make the loads differ widely from those for which the aircraft was designed, and steep dives or aerobatics should be avoided on aircraft on which any considerable ice has formed.
3. Experiments in this direction have shown that there is a risk of the structure being damaged or the pilot incapacitated during the thawing-out period, these risks increasing with the speed of the aircraft. This is particularly so in regard to the formation of ice on the airscrew, firstly, because of the vibration set up, and secondly, because of the danger to the personnel and material from flying ice fragments.
4. According to present information, the worst conditions for ice formation exist in cloud when the temperature is between zero and –4°C, or when, owing to temperature inversion, rain is falling into the stratum, the temperature of which is below freezing point.
5. Pilots are to avoid conditions likely to cause the formation of ice on aircraft, except when they are required to do otherwise for experimental purposes. When deposits of ice are observed, the pilot is to endeavour to thaw out the aircraft by gliding below the cloud layer or by climbing above it, whichever is desirable.

A.241 FLYING BY THE AID OF INSTRUMENTS – ISSUE OF PAMPHLETS (144130/31)

1. A pilot requires considerable training before he can maintain accurate flight, in conditions of indifferent or total lack of visibility, using instruments. Arrangements have been made accordingly to train a number of pilots at the Central Flying School.
2. These arrangements will not provide for all pilots who will be required to use turn indicators. A pamphlet has been prepared, therefore, giving a simple guide to a course of self-instruction in flying by the aid of instruments. Sufficient copies are being issued to supply one to each pilot in units which have been or are about to be supplied with turn indicators.
3. A further pamphlet, covering the subject in greater detail, which has been prepared for the use of instructors after completing a course of instruction, is also being sent to units for reference purposes.
4. Complete distribution will be made in the immediate future, and no further demands should be submitted.

A.249 AERODROME AND CIRCUIT RULES (38991/30 DATED 8 SEPTEMBER 1932)

1. After experience with the working of the rules for circuits at RAF aerodromes introduced by AMOs A.66/31 and A.67/31, it has been decided that the following procedure shall be adopted at all RAF aerodromes.
2. Aircraft flying by day in the immediate vicinity of RAF aerodromes are to adopt a definite circuit. At all RAF aerodromes, other than those indicated in para. 3 below, a permanent direction of circuit is to be established. This may be either **RIGHT-HAND** or **LEFT-HAND** as decided by the Command concerned and will be indicated as follows:

Circuit	Signal		Remarks
	To Ground Personnel	To Personnel in the Air	
Left Hand	Red Flag	Letter "L"	The latter "L" or "R" is to be situated in the aerodrome circle and is to be constructed of similar material to the circle. The letter is to be 30ft. long.
Right Hand	Green Flag	Letter "R"	

3. Exceptions to the above rule will occur only in the cases of:

    (i) Cranwell
    (ii) Halton
    (iii) Flying Training Schools.

At these stations the direction of the circuit may vary from time to time, according to local conditions and requirements, and will be decided by the station commander or his representative. In order to indicate that the circuit is variable, the aerodrome circle will be left blank. The direction of the circuit will be indicated as follows:

Circuit	Signal		Remarks
	To Ground Personnel	To Personnel in the Air	
Left Hand	Red Flag	Letter "L"	The signal to personnel in the air is to be constructed and exhibited in the manner described in para. 4 below.
Right Hand	Green Flag	Letter "R"	

A.161 CONSERVATION OF PETROL IN AIRCRAFT IN FLIGHT (SEE AMO E.477/1931)

The attention of all COs is directed to the need for economy in the consumption of fuel while aircraft are in the air. It is considered that a considerable saving of petrol could be effected by correct manipulation of the altitude control, resulting, not only in a saving of money, but in an increased operational range of the aircraft.

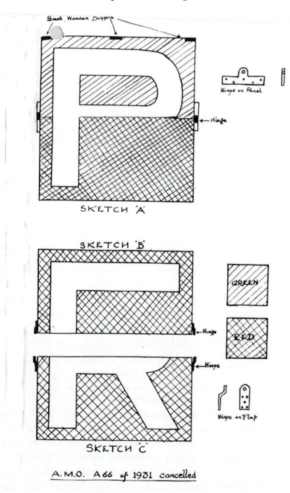

Ground Signals relating to AMWO. A.249

AIRCRAFT TEST FLYING – A & AEE MARTLESHAM AND MAEE FELIXSTOWE

Introduction

Test flying at the Aircraft and Armament Experimental Establishment at Martlesham Heath and the Marine Aircraft Experimental Establishment at Felixstowe is described in this section and in corresponding sections of Chapters 2 and 3. Also involved are the test-firing ranges at Orfordness. Both establishments were geographically very close, lying only a few miles either side of Ipswich. All civil and military types were test-flown at both establishments in the inter-war years, for at that time civil aviation came under the Air Ministry. Certificates of airworthiness were then issued to all aircraft that passed the tests satisfactorily. At Martlesham there were two squadrons: No. 15 Squadron tested armament and No. 22 Squadron tested aircraft. This was a hazardous business for all those involved in test-flying, since, certainly in the 1920s, so much was still to be learned about aerodynamics. Even as war approached in the late 1930s, lives were still being lost in test-flying. At the outbreak of war both establishments were deemed to be too close to the threat of enemy air action and were moved, the A & AEE going to Boscombe Down and the MAEE to Helensburgh on the Clyde.

In this chapter are three trials carried out at Martlesham Heath that are representative of the test work of the establishment during this period. The first is a trial on a bomb used frequently in air policing overseas during the inter-war period. This was the 230 lb bomb. The second involves trials on a Gloster fighter that was not in fact adopted by the RAF, which was built to AM Spec. F10/27. The third involves tests on the Hinaidi bomber, the first to be built all in metal.

TRIALS OF 230 LB BOMBS REPORT M/ARM/356 DATED 15 SEPTEMBER 1932

1. **Introductory** In accordance with Air Ministry letter dated 11 July 1932, thirty-three 230 lb bombs have been dropped from heights of up to 10,000 ft on to representative types of surfaces, to ascertain whether the bomb breaks up on impact, before the tail fuzing

has had time to detonate the filling. The programme originally proposed in the Air Ministry letter was modified, as no detonation failures occurred.

2. **Method of Fuzing** Two methods of fuzing were used, viz:

    (a) Instantaneous.

    (b) Fifteen-second delay

The components laid down in AP.1243, Plate XII, were used, except that a No. 4, Mark I Detonator AB (Instantaneous) was substituted for the Detonator AB, Mark I, one-second delay.

3. **Trials and Results** Twenty-six bombs were dropped at Orfordness, Seven bombs which had been reported on by the Superintendent of Experiments were dropped on to sand at Shoeburyness. All the bombs detonated with good fragmentation and were fairly stable in flight. Details regarding height of release, type of surface, and size of crater, for the bombs dropped at Orfordness, are tabulated below:

INSTANTANEOUS ACTION

Height of Release in feet	Surface	Crater Depth ft. ins.		Diameter ft. ins.		Remarks
2,000	Mud and shingle	5	8	17	0	
2,000	Shingle	3	0	17	4	
3,000	Shingle	2	8	16	5	
3,000	Mud and Shingle	6	0	18	9	
3,000	Shingle	2	6	16	5	
4,000	Shingle	2	8	17	3	
4,000	Shingle	2	5	18	5	
6,000	Shingle and Sand	3	0	17	0	
6,000	Shingle and Sand	2	9	16	9	
6,000	Shingle	3	7	16	0	
6,000	Shingle	3	4	17	0	
6,000	Water	–		–		could not be measured
6,000	Soft Mud	–		–		
6,000	Shingle and Sand	2	8	17	3	
6,000	Shingle and Sand	2	11	18	0	
8,000	Shingle	4	0	18	9	
8,000	Soft Mud	–		–		could not be measured
8,000	Mixture of shingle and Clay	3	4	18	6	
8,000	Grass with under surface of Clay	5	6	22	10	
8,000	Shingle	3	0	19	0	
8,000	Shingle	2	11	18	2	

DELAY ACTION

9,500	Shingle	7	0	37	0	
9,500	Shingle	10	0	40	0	fell into an old crater
9,500	Shingle	6	6	34	0	
9,500	Very soft mud with layer of water	–		–		could not be measured
10,000	Shingle	8	6	40	6	fell into an old crater

4. **Conclusions**   The trials confirm that 230 lb bombs do not break up when dropped from heights up to 10,000 ft on to surfaces such as shingle, sand and mud, and that satisfactory crater effects are obtained, the average crater being approximately 17 ft in diameter and of 3 ft depth when the bombs are fuzed for instantaneous action.

TRIALS WITH THE GLOSTER J.9125 AM SPEC. F10/27
A & AEE Report No. M/572/Int.1, January 1931

1. **Flying Qualities**   The controls are considered very good all round and well harmonized. All aerobatic manoeuvres can consequently be carried out with great ease. The view is good all round except forward where it is obstructed by the Townend ring. The take-off is easy with no vices. The landing is easy in spite of the flat glide in, owing to the excellent control at low speeds. The aircraft does not swing on landing but brakes have to be used for taxiing in a high wind. The general arrangement of the cockpit and controls is very good with the exception of the following points:

   (a)   The throttle control is not robust enough.
   (b)   The lever catch on the seat adjustment catches up at times and could be improved.
   (c)   The backward adjustment of the rudder bar is not sufficient for a short pilot.
   (d)   The compass cannot be seen unless the seat is in the bottom position.
   (e)   The seat could be made more comfortable by bringing the back further forward.
   (f)   The cockpit is considered rather draughty and could be improved by alteration suggested in e. above.

The gravity petrol tank has had to be removed on one occasion for repair. A good deal of trouble was experienced in removing it, it being necessary to dismantle the air cooler. Generally speaking this aircraft while on test has caused very little trouble. The

engine has stood up extremely well. Some trouble has been experienced with the Townend ring anchorages breaking, these were strengthened and they have since stood up to their job. To begin with much trouble was experienced with the rudder, and considerable 'hunting' directionally was experienced in diving tests. Three different rudders were fitted. The last fitted is completely satisfactory and the aircraft can now be dived to very high speeds and is beautifully steady. Alterations were necessary, to begin with, in the petrol system and even at present it is far from satisfactory. The engine has cut out on one or two occasions when running on Pump and Gravity. This appears to occur on the change over from main to gravity, the main tank having been emptied. The aircraft is considered entirely satisfactory for spinning and diving.

2. **Conclusion**   Considering the load carried and the very high degree of manoeuvrability, this aircraft is considered an excellent General Purpose fighter. It is a steady gun platform up to very high speeds. The aircraft lands fairly fast but has very good control and should be reasonably easy to force land. The forward view, however, might be improved.

HINAIDI J.9478 FAILURE OF TAIL SKID SHOE
(Source: A & AEE Report No. M/490c/F.1, dated 4 January 1930)

One cannot imagine today that a bombing aircraft would not have a tailwheel. Tail skids were used throughout the Great War and the 1920s. With aircraft landing on grass the wear on a metal skid was not as great as it would have been on tarmac. If skids wore out they could be easily and cheaply replaced. In this case, however, a failure of the skid could have been serious. During tests on the above-mentioned aircraft, the skid pan fractured and dropped off during the flight over the aerodrome. The fracture was caused by the base of the plate wearing away in the normal manner. The part which fell off weighs 5 lb 10 oz. This is being reported owing to the danger of the pan falling off during flight when the skid pan wears through. It is practically impossible for the mechanic to observe the wear that has taken place without dismantling the skid, and taking fairly accurate measurements. It is suggested therefore that this type of pan is replaced as soon as

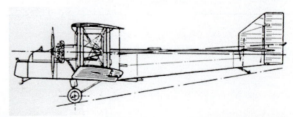

possible by a modified pan having web casts at the points shown on the diagram below. Modified in this manner the danger of the pan falling off in the air will be obviated.

COMPARATIVE PERFORMANCE TRIALS AND VIBRATION TESTS ON HANDLEY PAGE J.9301. JUPITER VIII ENGINES FITTED WITH SMALL-DIAMETER AIRSCREWS)

(Source: A & AEE Report M/490d/Int.1. dated 10 May 1930)

Introductory

In accordance with Air Ministry letter reference 890301/28/RDA1/FEC dated 7 April 1930, comparative performance trials have been carried out on Handley Page 'Hinaidi' J.9301 fitted with Jupiter VIII engines. The aircraft is fitted with a modified CSBS mounting a modified compass mounting and a pair of airscrews of reduced diameter. The aircraft in this state has been tested at Upper Heyford and reported satisfactory from a vibration point of view. Further vibration tests have been carried out at this establishment and a report on this subject is included with the present one.

Loading a centre of gravity

The aircraft has been loaded to Weight Sheet Summary Serial No. 97 Issue No. 1. The details of load are given in the next paragraph, which also shows the all-up weight to be 13,120 lb. The all-up weight of Hinaidi J.9033 with which comparison is made with respect to performance was 13,100 lb. Report M/490b/A.2./Spec. 14/28 dated 1 May 1929.

Tare Weight	8,136 lb
Military Load 'F'	445 lb
Military Load 'R'	2,383 lb
Fuel (300 Gallons)	2,310 lb
Oil (30 Gallons)	291 lb
Flying weight	13,120 lb

With this condition of loading, the centre of gravity position is 44.0 inches aft of the leading edge of the bottom plane, centre section, measured parallel to the chord.

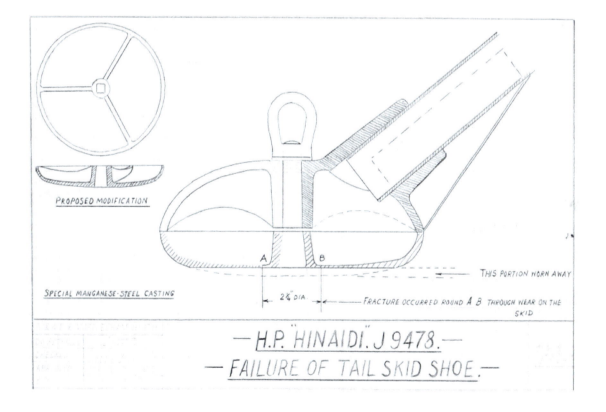

PROPOSED MODIFICATION

SPECIAL MANGANESE-STEEL CASTING

A   B

2¼" DIA

THIS PORTION WORN AWAY

FRACTURE OCCURRED ROUND A B THROUGH WEAR ON THE SKID

— H.P. "HINAIDI". J 9478.—
— FAILURE OF TAIL SKID SHOE.—

DETAILS OF THE POWER UNIT AND AIRCRAFT:

Engine

Maker's No.	J.8110	RAF No. 104591	
	J.8111	104592	
Normal r.p.m.	2,000	Maximum permissible r.p.m. 2,200	
Normal B.HP	440 @ 4,000'	Maximum B.HP. 563	
Gear Reduction.	0.5 to 1		

Aircraft

Span	75'4"
Height	17'6"
Length	59'11"
Surface Area of main planes	1476.5 sq.ft
Surface Loading	8.9 lbs per sq.ft.
Power loading	14.9
Tail Volume Coefficient.	= 0.387
Rudder Volume Coefficient.	= 0.050

Airscrew Details

	Port	Starboard
Markings	Drg.No.Z.201	Drg.No.Z.201
	A.992	A.993
	Diameter 3355	
	Pitch 3200	

Measurements

Diameter.	Port. 3355	Stbd. 3355
Pitch	Port. 3224	Stbd. 3251
Weight	97 lbs	93½ lbs.

PERFORMANCE

Climb

Standard Height Feet	Time in mins.	Rate of Climb ft/mins	RPM		A.S.I. M.P.H.	A.S.I. corrected
			Port	Stbd		
0	0	485	1905	1905	72.0	73.2
1,000	2.15	440	1900	1895	71.0	72.3
2,500	6.00	370	1890	1890	69.0	70.5
3,000	7.40	350	1890	1885	68.5	70.1
5,000	12.10	540	2030	2020	71.0	72.3
6,500	15.10	475	2020	2010	69.0	70.5
10,000	23.80	335	2000	1995	65.0	67.0
13,000	35.00	210	1985	1980	61.5	63.9
15,000	47.20	120	1975	1970	59.5	62.1

Estimated absolute ceiling.	17,100 ft.
Estimated service ceiling.	15,400 ft.
Maximum height reached	16,100 ft in 58.5 mins.

The Rate of Climb at this height being 60ft/min.

Airscrew r.p.m. aircraft stationary on ground	L.1780 r.p.m.
	R.1780 r.p.m.

Full speed trials

Standard Error Height Feet	R.P.M. Port	Stbd	True Air Speed m.p.h.	A.S.I. m.p.h.	Correction for Position m.p.h.
5,000*	2190	2190	110.5	105.0	−2.5
6,500*	2190	2190	110.0	102.0	−2.2
10,000*	2190	2190	108.5	95.0	−1.5
13,000	2175	2175	105.6	87.0	−0.5
15,000	2125	2125	99.5	78.5	plus 0.4

* Engines throttled so as not to exceed maximum permissible r.p.m. 2,200

True landing speed	52m.p.h. (approx)
Landing Run	265 yards)
Time of run	$25^1/_5$ secs) Wind 5 m.p.h.
Take-off run	236 yards)
Time of run	$14^2/_5$ secs)
Run to clear 0ft screen = 413 yards	

Comparison of Airscrews – all four bladed wood aircrews

	Hinaidi J.9301 Drg.No.Z.201		Hinaidi J.9033 Drg.No. 129/2	
	Port	Stbd	Port	Stbd
Mean Diameter	3355m.m.	3355m.m.	3511m.m.	3512m.m.
Pitch	3224m.m.	3251m.m.	2824m.m.	2824m.m.
Weight	97 lbs	$93^1/_2$ lbs	100lbs.	100lbs.

Comparison of Hinaidi's J.9033 and J.9301

Climb

Standard Height.Feet	Time Mins. J.9033	J.9301	R/C ft/mins J.9033	J.9301	R.P.M(mean) on climb. J.9033	J.9301
0	0	0	375	485	1810	1905
1,000	2.8	2.15	335	440	1805	1895
2,500	7.75	6.00	275	370	1795	1890
3,000	9.70	7.40	255	350	1790	1885
5,000	15.30	12.10	615	540	2045	2025
6,500	18.00	15.10	540	475	2030	2015
10,000	25.90	23.80	370	335	2010	2000
13,000	36.20	35.00	225	210	1985	1985
15,000	47.60	47.20	130	120	1965	1975

Speeds

Standard Height Feet	T.A.S(True Air Speed) m.p.h.		Mean R.P.M.	
	J.9033	J.9301	J.9033	J.9301
5,000	112.0	110.5	2200	2190*
6,500	111.5	110.0	2200	2190*
10,000	110.5	108.5	2200	2190*
13,000	106.0	105.6	2165	2175
15,000	100.0	99.5	2100	2125

* Engines throttled so as not to exceed maximum permissible R.P.M. (2200)

	J.9033	J.9301
Estimated absolute ceiling (feet)	17,700	17,100
Estimated service ceiling	15,600	15,400
Airscrew r.p.m.stationary on ground	1,790	1,780

Attention has already been drawn in a letter reference AM15/6 dated 6 May 1930 to the fact that the airscrews are over-revving. The RPM at 6,000 ft at full, level speed are about 2,250. The level speeds quoted in the present report were obtained with the engines throttled so as not to exceed the maximum permissible rpm of 2,200. The normal rpm for the Jupiter VIII engine are 2,000 and this figure is slightly exceeded in the neighbourhood of 5,000 ft on the climb. Comparing the performances of J.9301 and J.9033 it will be seen that there is very little to choose between them. J.9301 is very slightly poorer in performance as regards level speed when the figured obtained on J.9033 are reduced to the same condition of throttling to maximum permissible rpm.

Vibration
It is considered that the reduced diameter airscrews definitely obviates all abnormal vibration and J.9301 in comparison with J.9478 (the all-metal Hinaidi at present at this Establishment) is superior in this direction even though the latter was considered quite reasonable. With regard to the compass bowl vibration this is now considered to have been practically eliminated and the behaviour in flight satisfactory. The vibration on the Course Setting Bomb sight mounting is also considered as having been considerably improved.

Suitability of bomb-sighting arrangements
From the bombing point of view the bomb sight raises the following points:

(a) When the bomb sight is lowered to its fullest extent it is considered difficult to read the compass bowl on the bomb sight owing to the bad lighting of the top of the bowl. This is probably due to the underside of the fuselage preventing light shining on the compass bowl.

(b) The present stiffening struts to the bomb sight pillar are pivoted to clamping brackets fixed round the bottom longeron on one side and the bombing aperture stiffening beam on the other. As the sliding panel, covering the aperture, runs in grooves cut in these two members, it is impossible with the present anti-vibration struts, to close this panel in the bottom of the fuselage.

(c) The sight must be in the bottom position on the bracket for the height bar to clear the leads to the ASI.

(d) The wind screening is very bad and the position is very draughty.

THE MARITIME AIRCRAFT EXPERIMENTAL ESTABLISHMENT, FELIXSTOWE
The MAEE tests selected for inclusion in this and succeeding chapters serve to remind the reader that flying-boats were important aircraft in the RAF inventory in the inter-war years, and the peculiarities of operation as compared with landplanes are significant. Except for major servicing, when a flying-boat would be brought ashore using a slipway, routine servicing, refuelling and crew embarkation and disembarkation had to be carried out using various craft. Tenders were used, which had to manoeuvre alongside the flying-boat, and care had to be

taken not to cause hull damage, for these aircraft remained at their moorings when not airborne. In these circumstances it was imperative that flying-boat hulls did not leak.

WATER HANDLING AND TAKE-OFF AND LANDING TESTS OF FLYCATCHER S.1418 WITH METAL FLOATS FITTED WITH CHINE STRIPS
(Source: MAEE Report F/A/243 dated 7 September 1931)
Introduction
In Felixstowe Report F/A/241 the take-off and water-handling qualities of Flycatcher S.1418 when fitted with vee-bottom metal floats were described. These floats were considered to be an improvement over the flat-bottom wooden floats previously fitted as regards take-off and landing, but water was thrown onto the airscrew disc during the early stages of take-off even under fairly calm sea conditions. The replacement of the wooded airscrew on this aircraft by one of metal was recommended. The manoeuvrability of the aircraft was fair, but it was thought that the absence of water rudders would cause difficulty in winds of 15 mph or more.

After these tests the aircraft was sent to Messrs Fairey, who fitted chine strips to the floats in an endeavour to prevent water being thrown into the airscrew disc. The present report describes tests made after the fitting of these strips.

Description of chine strips
The aircraft has not been to the MAEE since the chine strips have been fitted but the photograph, taken by RAF Lee-on-Solent, shows their general arrangement. They consist of angle strips of duralumin about 1½″

deep riveted to the float bottoms near and parallel to the chine lines on the inner sides of the floats. They extend from near the bow to the first transverse bulkhead forward of the step on each float. Their location is such that they should not be easily susceptible to damage in service.

Handling in calm water
The aircraft was flown from Messrs Fairey at Hamble to Lee-on-Solent by the same pilot who had made the tests described in Report F/A/241, and take-offs and landings were made. The sea was calm and the surface wind about 5 mph. Some of the take-offs were made in the wash of passing boats but no spray was thrown up into the airscrew disc. A wooden airscrew was fitted as before.

The manoeuvrability of the aircraft on the water was not so good as before the chine strips were fitted. When previously tested the aircraft could be turned completely round in winds up to 8 mph with the engine throttled back, but in the present tests use of the engine was required to keep the aircraft on a straight course out of wind.

Water handling under rough conditions
Shortly after the above tests had been made it was reported by the School of Naval Cooperation, Lee-on-Solent, that water was thrown onto the airscrew of this aircraft when taking-off and taxiing in rough water, and that several (wooden) airscrews had been damaged in consequence. A further visit was therefore made to Lee-on-Solent by the same MAEE pilot. On the day of the tests the surface wind was 16 mph and the sea was so rough that normally flying on this aircraft would not be attempted. The aircraft on this occasion was fitted with a metal airscrew. Three take-offs and landings were made and the pilot reported that the aircraft handled very well. The average time on take-off was 7 seconds. No water was thrown into the airscrew disc during any of these take-offs and landings. It was found that spray was thrown up when the aircraft was being taxied slowly

The Flycatcher floatplane.

across wind, but if the control column was held right back the quantity entering the airscrew disc was negligible. If, however, the control column is pushed forward when taxiing slowly, a considerable amount of water is thrown into the airscrew disc. When taking-off in rough water the control column should be pushed forward gradually and a normal take-off made. If this is done no water is thrown onto the airscrew.

Conclusions

The chine strips appear to be effective in preventing water being thrown into the airscrew disc of this aircraft under normal conditions, but they hamper manoeuvrability on the water. Care must be exercised when taxiing slowly in rough water, and water will be thrown up unless the control column is held back. It is considered that the provision of water rudders and a metal airscrew is desirable for this aircraft.

DAMAGE TO HULL OF IRIS III, N.238, DURING CRUISE TO MALTA

(Source: MAEE Report F/A/188 dated March 1930)

Damage occurred to the hull of Iris III, N.238, during the recent cruise to Malta. This damage was discovered after two unsuccessful attempts to take off at Malta. These take-offs were attempted in conditions of bad swell, and the first attempt was abandoned after a two-minute run

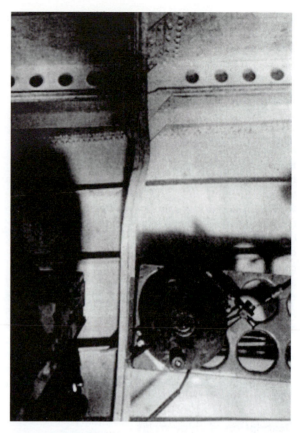

and the second after a one-minute run. The all-up load of the aircraft at the time was 31,000 lb. No leaks were found in the hull as a consequence of this damage, and, although bad take-off conditions were encountered at Naples on the return, the aircraft was flown back to Felixstowe without any repairs being carried out and without any leaks developing.

The damage occurred to Bulkheads 8, 9, 10 and 11, just aft of the navigator's position, and was mainly concentrated on the port side, although there were indications that similar failures were commencing on the starboard side.

The condition of the bulkhead that received the most injury is shown in the attached photograph. A full description of the take-off difficulties encountered by Iris III on this cruise will be given in the full report on the cruise which is now being prepared. The damaged portions of the hull are now being removed and replaced by new plates and bulkheads by Messrs Blackburn. This work is being carried out at Felixstowe.

FAILURE OF STANDARD 'SOUTHAMPTON' WOOD AIRSCREWS BY SPLITTING ALONG LAMINATIONS

(Source: MAEE Report F/A/236 dated 1 April 1931)

A standard 'Southampton' airscrew made to Drawing No. 3868 was recently discovered on inspection to have a bad crack along one of the laminations. The extent and

DAMAGE TO HULL OF SAUNDERS-ROE R.4/27 FLYING-BOAT CAUSED BY DINGHIES
(Source: MAEE Report F/A/238 dated 29 May 1931)

Damage has occurred to the Saunders-Roe R.4/27 in the neighbourhood of the rear cockpits due to contact of dinghies with the sides of the hull in the normal course of operation of the aircraft. None of this damage has been caused by misuse or careless handling of the dinghies but has gradually occurred during normal use of the aircraft. The condition of the hull on the port side is shown on the attached photographs, but the condition of the starboard, while not at present so bad, is similar.

The plating of the hull of this aircraft is stiffened throughout the longitudinal corrugations pitched about 9 inches apart, the corrugations being $1\frac{1}{2}$ inches wide by $\frac{1}{2}$ inch deep. These projecting corrugations form the only protection of the hull against damage from dinghies or other craft, and already they have suffered considerable damage although the aircraft has so far done only 70 hours' flying. So far the aircraft has no doubt been subjected to much more careful handling than it might normally be expected to receive in service, particularly when operating away from home waters.

It is considered that some modification to the hull in the neighbourhood of the rear cockpit will be necessary in order to give effective protection against damage before the aircraft is suitable for service use.

position of the crack is shown in the attached photograph.

The airscrew had been in use for a total of $18\frac{1}{2}$ hours' flying prior to the time on failure. During this time the aircraft had been subjected to normal use only and has not been landed, taken off or taxied in water conditions sufficiently rough to cause damage to the airscrew.

The failure has occurred along the glue joint between the two laminations and this, in an airscrew which is in otherwise good condition, suggests that the failure is due to faulty manufacture.

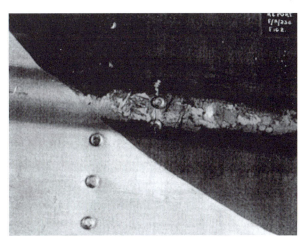

Chapter 2
The Rise of the Dictators, 1933 to 1936

Major changes in the organization of the RAF – Flying training – Flying and operational – The expansion schemes and shadow factories – The threat from Nazi Germany – RAF displays – A & AEE Martlesham and MAEE Felixstowe – The Abyssinian crisis

Introduction

The three years from 1933 to 1936 were going to witness the beginnings of a massive expansion of the RAF following the failure of the disarmament talks at Geneva described in the last chapter. In the League of Nations there was no real determination to succeed in addressing the threat to peace that came from Japan and then Nazi Germany and Mussolini's Italy. The League was to be as effective in keeping the peace as the resolve of the powers capable of confronting the dictators. With the United States in splendid isolation, it was up to Britain and France to show leadership in taking steps to keep the peace. At the beginning of 1933 Japan had already invaded Manchuria, renamed Manchukuo, but was to get bogged down in a war in China. Italy was still to transgress and Hitler had still to start on his territorial quests. Those who understood Fascism knew that violence was an essential part of the ideology and that war was going to come again to Europe unless something was done to nip that violence in the bud. It was not to happen, and the territorial designs of both Fascist dictators were to be met with inaction on the part of the British and French governments. There are reasons for this that can be studied in the wealth of historical works on this period. In the context of the growth of British airpower in the late 1930s it is sufficient alone to state that the National Government in Britain did take the Nazi threat seriously.

It was the realization that Hitler's Germany posed a threat that would have to be confronted. The German army had yet to be expanded from its Versailles strength of 100,000 men. The German Navy was also small, and at the height of its expansion its surface fleet would never rival the combined tonnage of the capital ships of the Royal Navy. The German submarine arm was, of course, a different matter. It was in the air that the major threat would come. Once the reborn *Luftwaffe* was unveiled to the world in 1935, the race was on to ensure that the RAF maintained parity with the monthly growth in German squadrons. And so began the move from a peacetime air force to one that would confront Germany in 1939. Some of the schemes of expansion did not see the light of day because the Air Ministry was overtaken by events and rapid reappraisals had to be made. Throughout the period the government was loath to move to a war footing in either the mobilization of fighting men and women or industrial productive resources. This contrasted sharply with Nazi Germany, where a nation could be mobilized under a Fascist dictator who embodied the will of the nation.

Both German and Italian forces were to join the Spanish Civil War in 1936 in support of the Nationalists under the command of Generals Mola and Franco. This was important because this three-year war between the Republicans and Nationalists turned out to be a German dress rehearsal for the major European conflict that was to come. In particular it would provide the *Luftwaffe* with the opportunity to develop the tactics of the *Blitzkrieg*, or 'lightning war', which is described in the section of this chapter dealing with the German threat. The RAF, on the other hand, was not to experience a contested air war, only the continuing operations known as air control, chiefly against troublesome local tribes in the Empire.

CHANGES IN THE ORGANIZATION OF THE RAF
NEW HOME COMMANDS

The expansion of the RAF meant an enormous increase in the size of the service, which was growing ever more technically complex. The specialization of function that had accompanied that increase required a redistribution of responsibilities. The development in operational techniques and methods necessarily involved some changes in the organization of the service. The most important of these was the creation in 1936 of three new operational commands, Bomber, Fighter and Coastal, which replaced the old command entitled the Air Defence of Great Britain. A Training Command was established at the same time, which was subdivided into Flying Training and Technical Training Commands. In 1938 three further Commands were added, namely Maintenance, Balloon and Reserve. Maintenance Command was made responsible for the administration of all storage units and depots, and Reserve Command for the training of the Volunteer Reserve and the control of the Elementary Flying Training Schools (EFTSs). The initial training of Regular personnel was carried out at the EFTSs before the trainees moved on to the Flying Training Schools (FTSs). A further formation, Army Cooperation Command, was not established until after the war had started. Before the Second World War, units intended for duty with the Army were organized in a group under Fighter Command.

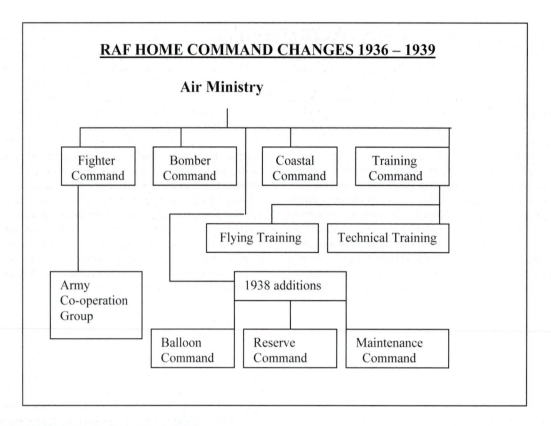

FLYING TRAINING BETWEEN 1933 AND 1936

(Source: National Archives document AIR 32/14)

Introduction

During the 1920s aircraft were for the most part single-engined biplanes manned by one or two men. The requirement was for a 'universal' pilot who could fly any service type both in peace and in combat. Pilot navigation was the business of the pilot, who could also shoot a fixed forward-firing machine-gun, drop bombs and observe. If there was a second crew member he would either observe or fire a Lewis gun mounted on a Scarff ring. In fact during the Great War air gunners were known as air observers, but the tradesmen's title reverted to air gunner at the end of the war. The pilot would have to be able to handle his aircraft in all conditions of weather, both day and night, over fairly short distances, and shoot with a reasonable degree of accuracy. The exception was the maritime patrol aircraft, where reasonably long-distance flights might be undertaken over water. In these circumstances navigational ability would be important.

This was the situation that prevailed until 1934. The RAF trained approximately 300 pilots a year at the bare minimum of schools. Air gunners were recruited from squadron ground personnel and locally trained. The officers recruited for a permanent career were given *ab initio* pilot training at RAF Cranwell, those on short-service commissions were trained at one of a number of flying training schools, one of which was situated in Egypt. The problem was that the pilots were given little more than a brief introduction to the military aspects of flying, so that they arrived on their operational squadrons with the ability to fly an aeroplane and little more. This would mean that squadrons would have to undertake the continuation training of new pilots until the latter were operationally fit to fly. The arrival of newly trained pilots on a squadron would therefore diminish the operational readiness of the unit until such pilots had been trained. This had the effect of turning squadrons into miniature training units. In peacetime squadrons trained for war, but on a unit basis. The operational training of individual pilots, it was argued, should not be the responsibility of squadrons, particularly during war when the experienced pilots could not possibly spare time from operations to train any newcomers.

To add to the problems facing a squadron having to undertake the operational training of its pilots was the growing complexity of aircraft during the mid- to late 1930s. These were progressively equipped with retractable undercarriages, variable-pitch propellers, radios, sophisticated navigation and bomb-aiming equipment and power-operated gun turrets. Moreover the aircraft would be single, twin and four engined. A solitary pilot and perhaps an air gunner alone could not manage a multi-engined aircraft in combat. Crew numbers would mount and individual crew members would be required to specialize in navigation, air signalling, bomb aiming and firing the turret guns. Single-seat fighters excepted, the pilot would have to become an aircraft commander, and new aircrew categories would have to be created.

Finally, the mid- to late 1930s would be characterized by a succession of expansion plans. The number of operational squadrons would rise and with it the number of aircrew required. Not only would training have to cater for the new aircrew categories, but the existing flying training schools could not possibly cope with the numbers both of regular and reserve pilots and other aircrew categories needing to be trained. Then there were arguments over who should be responsible for navigating an aircraft, since some believed that this should not be delegated by an aircraft commander to another crew member. This dispute alone would tax the minds of training planning staffs.

Flying Training Capacity in 1933

Flying training schools taught *ab initio* pupil pilots on a ten-month course. The flying was carried out entirely on single-engined aircraft, training on twin-engined aircraft having been discontinued in 1931. It was felt that if pilot training was given on a Vimy immediately after the completion of basic training on an Avro the pupil would not be sound on aircraft with light, accurate and even controls. At the FTSs pilot navigation or air pilotage was taught. Armament instruction was theoretical and ground instruction was concerned with basic all-round training. The flying training schools of the RAF before expansion were:

Ab Initio Training
RAF Cranwell (cadet officers)
No. 2 FTS – Digby (closed in December 1933)
No. 3 FTS – Grantham
No. 4 FTS – Abu Sueir, Egypt
No. 5 FTS – Sealand

Secondary Specialist Training
School of Army Cooperation – Old Sarum
School of Naval Cooperation – Lee on Solent
Air Pilotage School – Andover
Flying-boat Training Squadron – Calshot (29-week course)
Navigation Course – Calshot (7-month course)
Coast Defence Training Unit – Gosport

Instructor Training
Central Flying School – Upavon

Reserve Training
Four civil schools at Hatfield, Filton, Hamble and Brough.

There was also the training base at Leuchars, where officers from the Navy and the Army were given flying training and the special requirements of pilots of carrier-borne aircraft was catered for. RAF Cranwell trained a small number of cadets in practical flying during a two-year course, and each FTS turned out about eighty pilots a year. Except for those going on specialist training, the newly trained pilot would proceed from FTS direct to a squadron, and it would be a year or more before a man became a fully competent military pilot. While this might be satisfactory for a peacetime air force of the size of the RAF in 1930, it would not do during a period of rapid expansion or war. A squadron's combat efficiency was reduced according to the number of new pilots needing to be trained to an operational standard. In addition to the FTSs there were various specialist schools, listed above, giving instruction in navigation and conversion courses for pilots destined for Army and Naval Cooperation squadrons.

Flying training on squadrons

The tendency to pass the responsibility for training on to squadrons had reached its peak in 1927. The squadron was responsible for continuation training in navigation, except for flying-boat pilots, and this was given by pilots who had attended a course in air pilotage at Andover. Then there was practical armament training, when annual visits were made to practice training camps for practical experience. Thirdly, there was conversion to the squadron's type of aircraft, and finally night-flying training. Each flight of a twin-engined squadron was supposed to have a flying instructor trained at the Central Flying School (CFS). The amount of individual training required to be given to the FTS-trained pilot differed according to the squadron's role. Fighter and short-range day-bomber squadrons would need considerably less individual pilot training than flying-boat and night-bomber squadrons. Flying-boat pilots had to learn to handle their type of aircraft, undertake long-distance navigation over expanses of water and be captain of the crew. Night-bomber pilots had to have much the same. Individual training by squadrons had to be dealt with before the squadron's corporate training as a fighting unit could begin. In general the types of aircraft in service use made comparatively light demands on pilots. Elaborate cockpit drills were still in the future, no squadrons were equipped with monoplanes and there was little call for instrument and bad-weather flying. Night-flying and long-distance navigation were needed only by five bomber squadrons and the crews of twenty-four flying-boats.

THE NEED FOR A REORGANIZATION OF FLYING TRAINING
Introduction
The training organization that had existed since the 1920s had been adequate. The quality of recruits

presented few problems. The numbers required were small and pilots could be chosen with care from either civil life or serving airmen. Specialist matters such as armament and navigation were regarded as particular aspects of a pilot's general equipment, and the specialist officers concerned with them were junior and only advisory to the main trend of policy of both operational requirements and training. This then was the training organization in 1934. The Ten-Year Rule had been official government policy, i.e. no major war involving the UK within ten years, so there was no set date for squadrons to be operationally ready for war. It therefore followed that there was no urgency in bringing individual pilots up to an operational standard, and since the continuation training of pilots was the responsibility of squadrons, it cost the RAF less than it would if the capacity of the flying training schools was expanded to take over this work. As it was, experienced squadron officers were both teachers of young pilots and mainstays in war. Fifteen Regular squadrons had been chosen to give *ab initio* training to pilots in order not to have to enlarge the flying training organization. But they were teachers without the specialized equipment of schools.

Review of flying training in 1934

The four civil schools were already carrying out *ab initio* training of Reservists, and this training substantially covered the first stage of training at the service FTSs. In July 1934 Air Marshal Sir John Higgins was chairman of Armstrong Whitworth Aircraft Ltd and A.V. Roe and Co. Ltd. To Air Marshal Bowhill, Air Member for Personnel, he put forward the suggestion that Air Service Training Ltd, a company with which he was associated, should undertake preliminary training and pre-selection of pilots before they entered the service. He had made a similar suggestion ten years earlier but had been turned down. Air Service Training Ltd could not be the chosen instrument, for it did not satisfy service requirements. Savings could only be achieved by cutting the time spent at the FTSs, for using civil schools would mean extra cost. In any event FTS training was already below squadron requirements. But in October 1934 Air Commodore Tedder was Director of Training, and he brought the possibility of using civil schools into his review of flying training in both peace and war. He initiated a review that contemplated the complete reorientation of the training system. This review had two main aims:

1. Establishing a training system in peacetime that would not require radical alteration in wartime.
2. Reorganizing the existing system to relieve the squadrons of basic individual training and so allow them to give attention to collective flight and squadron training.

The civil schools' course lasted about seventy days and provided fifty hours of flying on an elementary type, whereas the FTS course lasted a year and consisted of three stages:

1. Flying training on an elementary type.
2. Flying training on a service type.
3. Service training in air warfare.

The proposal

The proposal was that *ab initio* flying training should be carried out by civil schools and applied flying on service types at the existing FTSs. The new pupil entries would go to a civil school for an *ab initio* flying course corresponding to the courses given to the Class AA Reserve and which would lead to training on a service type. The course content would include fifty hours' flying, including cross-country and instrument flying on a seventy-day course. On successful completion of this *ab initio* course the trainees would be posted to the RAF Depot at Uxbridge, where they would receive disciplinary and administrative training. Those being awarded a short-service commission would be kitted out in uniform. From Uxbridge, pupils would go to an FTS for a ten-month training course, the first term being of five months, which would involve flying training on a service type of aircraft, while the second term was directed to applied flying. On the FTS course pilots would be taught navigation, instrument flying, air gunnery and bombing.

Disadvantages of the proposal

The civil school/FTS course scheme increased the total period of training before the pilot reached his squadron, and so not only reduced the length of his service career on a squadron but also meant that slightly more pilots would have to be trained. Another difficulty was the status of personnel, both commissioned and airmen pilots, while at the civil schools. The financial increase was also heavy, with the annual increase in costs estimated to be £110,000:

Cost of old FTS scheme	£552,000 p.a.
Cost of civil school course	{ £134,000 p.a.
Plus FTS course	{ £672,000 p.a. +
Total	£806,000 p.a.
Extra cost	£254,000 p.a.

Against this one additional FTS was saved, that is to say, the construction and equipping of a new FTS:

Annual saving, Equipment,	£140,000
Construction	£300,000
Annual estimated extra cost	£110,000 with an offset of £300,000 on capital cost.

THE NEW SCHEME OF FLYING TRAINING

Introduction

The reorganization of flying training was introduced by AMO A135/35. This order stated that the reorganization was intended

> by accelerating the elementary stage of flying and ground instruction, to carry service training to a materially higher level than can at present be obtained. This could be achieved without, however, increasing the total length of training and consequently reducing the period of service by short-service officers and airmen pilots in squadrons.

The extended syllabus was intended to eliminate a considerable part of the individual training given to a pilot in his first year in a squadron and thus render him fit to take part in flight training immediately on posting to a squadron. The new scheme commenced in August 1935, when the trainee stayed two months at the civil school before spending nine months at an FTS. Just as the scheme was being put into operation, plans had been laid for the expansion of the RAF. Previously there had been a gradual expansion to fifty-two service squadrons, but the expansion proposed was of a new order and a larger training organization was going to be needed. The four years 1935 to 1939 would witness the rapid expansion of facilities for pilot training both at home and overseas, and the growth of the Reserve would follow a parallel course. Details of this expansion appear in Chapter 3

Training requirements under Expansion Plan A

Expansion of the RAF began in February 1934 with the scheme to bring the home defence squadrons from forty-two up to fifty-two squadrons, which was in the 1923 plan. Expansion Scheme A was approved in July 1934 and called for 1,000 additional pilots over and above the normal flow of replacements to be trained in the four years 1935 to 1939. It involved the formation of two new FTSs to bring the total number of schools up to six. The training base at Leuchars was renamed No. 1 FTS, but continued with its specialist work. In January 1935 the number of pilots required was found to have been underestimated. It would have been difficult to open up a new school at short notice because aircraft and instructors could not be provided quickly. It was decided to increase the number of pupils per course from forty to forty-eight at all schools except RAF Sealand, for bad weather and congestion made an increase there inadvisable. The larger courses started in the early summer of 1935, but it was necessary to transfer 10% of the instructional staff of front-line squadrons to man the FTSs. This would be 40% to meet Scheme C. By August 1935 the trainee population of the schools was as follows:

No. 1 FTS Leuchars (Opened 1/4/35)	Population 80	Aircraft Establishment
No. 2 FTS Digby (Re-formed 1/10/34)	Population 96	62 service aircraft
No. 3 FTS Grantham	Population 96	3 elementary aircraft
No. 4 FTS Abu Sueir	Population 96	
No. 5 FTS Sealand	Population 80	Audax, Hart and Fury
No. 6 FTS Netheravon (Re-formed 1/4/35)	Population 96	

Note: The service types were, notably, the Hart, Audax and Fury. The elementary types were retained for instrument training.

Training requirements under Expansion Plan C

A considerably larger and quicker increase was approved in May 1935. The target was a metropolitan air force of 123 squadrons with 1,512 first-line aircraft by April 1937. This meant that another 2,000 pilots had to be found in rather less than two years. To achieve this programme a total of eleven flying training schools was required, and five new schools were opened between October 1935 and March 1936:

No. 7 FTS Peterborough (Westwood)	Opened 2/12/35	Aircraft Establishment
No. 8 FTS Montrose	1/1/36	as above
No. 9 FTS Thornaby	2/3/36	
No. 10 FTS Tern Hill	15/12/35	
No. 11 FTS Wittering	1/10/35	

These five new FTSs started on the new training system as they opened. The existing schools, with the exception of No. 1 FTS, changed over as they re-equipped with service aircraft. Leuchars stayed with the *ab initio* system. The FTSs were divided into intermediate and advanced training squadrons in 1937.

Effect of expansion schemes on the front-line squadrons

These expansion schemes had an increased effect on the front line. In order to provide instructors, pilots had to be withdrawn from the squadrons. If the sequence and length of training remained unchanged, 40% of the front line would have been needed to act as instructors to the new pilots. This would have had a serious effect on the squadrons, not only in their readiness for war, but also on the amount of post-FTS-school training, which at that time was an essential part of the pilot's training. By the time Scheme C was put into effect, however, the vast reorganization in the training of service pilots that had taken place relieved the situation to a certain extent. Even so, the shortage of instructors and the shortage of training aircraft did restrict the number of pilots trained to the barest minimum. Their training syllabus, too, was limited due to these considerations. Under the new training scheme the ideal length of the pilot's training course was estimated to be thirteen to fourteen months. This was later cut to twelve and then nine months.

The training at civil schools

The new system of training was introduced at the four civil schools in August 1935, and during the next six months nine new schools were opened:

Hatfield	Tiger Moth
Filton	Tiger Moth
Hamble	Tiger Moth
Brough	Blackburn B2

New Schools with opening dates

Ansley 6/1/36		Tiger Moth
Desford 21/11/35		Tiger Moth
Hanworth 10/6/35		Blackburn B2
Perth 27/1/36		Tiger Moth
Prestwick 17/2/36		Tiger Moth
Reading 21/11/35		Tiger Moth
Sywell 10/6/35		Tiger Moth
White Waltham 8/11/35		Tiger Moth
Yatesbury 6/1/36		Tiger Moth

The new courses

Pupils spent one term of thirteen weeks (fifteen in the summer) and did about fifty hours' flying in each. A new course was accepted every three months and the size of each intake remained as before, i.e. forty-eight pupils. The thirteen civil schools were affiliated to the FTSs and supplied the pupil pilots. The affiliation was for liaison purposes and to ensure continuity of instruction. The course for regular personnel at the civil schools lasted normally for eight weeks, although in the winter it was ten weeks to allow for bad weather. During this period the pupils carried out a minimum of twenty-five hours' dual and twenty-five hours' solo flying. Throughout the course these pilots, who were candidates for short-service commissions, were civilian, although they were paid by the Air Ministry. The serving airmen wore plain clothes, were given allowances and lived out under their own arrangements.

On completion of the civil flying course the pupil pilots were sent to the RAF Depot, Uxbridge, for two weeks' discipline training before being sent to their FTSs. The aims of the first stage of the FTS was to bring the pupils up to a standard when handling the aircraft was a means to an end, not an end in itself. Navigation training included map reading, elementary direction finding and elementary DR (dead reckoning), which was practised on a 200-mile cross-country flight. Some instrument flying was also carried out. The advanced training was largely devoted to armament training; cine camera guns and camera obscura were also used and the work culminated in a month's attachment to an Armament Training Camp. In addition the FTS course covered photography, reconnaissance and formation flying. New features such as night-flying and twin-engined training at the FTSs were quickly introduced in the months following the reorganization. By the summer of 1936 there were thirty Elementary and Reserve Flying Training Schools (E & RFTSs), as the civil schools were called, feeding ten FTSs.

Pilot position on 1 July 1936

The number of trained pilots on 1 July 1936 is shown opposite. The changes to training and the opening of new schools would not have had much impact by this time, but they do indicate the mountain still to be climbed to find 2,000 extra pilots:

Regular Air Force Qualified Pilots	Permanent Officers-----------------------------1676
	Short and medium service personnel----------781
	Airmen pilots ------------------------------592
	Attached or seconded from other services----171
	3220

Pilots under Training	Cranwell Cadets --------------------------------135
	Short/Medium service personnel---------------718
	Airmen Pilots --------------------------------- 108
	Attached or seconded from other services------37
	998

Reserve Forces Qualified Pilots	Class A & AA ----------------------------------888
	Class C --348
	Class E ---54
	Class F --------------------------------------- 403
	1693

| Auxiliary Air Force Qualified Pilots & Special Reserve | Auxiliary Air Force ----------------------------142 |
| | Special Reserve---------------------------------34 |

| Pilots under training | ---16 |

| Grand Total Qualified Pilots --5089 |
| Pilots under training ---1014 |

Conclusion

The new system of training still did not turn out pilots up to first-line standard. It was certainly better than the old system, indeed as far as it went it was excellent, but it did not go far enough, being limited to a year due to financial constraints. It was then cut down to nine months when Expansion Plan C called for so many pilot instructors. It was the FTSs that suffered. Training was further reduced to six months in late 1935 when the proper duration was ten. There was support for the reduction in training times since it was thought that to open more than the bare number of schools that might only be needed for a few years was extravagant. Thirdly, the shortcomings of the scheme were accentuated by the increased complexity of the new types of aircraft with which squadrons were being equipped. Soon after the new system of training was introduced other steps were being taken to improve the training of pilots. Night-flying was given a greater part in the system of training. Later in 1936 twin-engined aircraft were being introduced to the FTSs. The following three years saw the rapid expansion of the training machine. Courses were reduced in length and the capacities at schools were increased to meet the various expansion schemes. The annual output of an FTS had risen from eighty in 1934 to 140 two years later. Between April 1935 and May 1938, 4,500 pilots were trained. This shows an annual average of 1,500, compared with 300 per year in 1934. Although there were thoughts about establishing more FTSs, nothing happened, and No. 4 FTS Abu Sueir remained the sole FTS outside the United Kingdom.

NIGHT-FLYING TRAINING

Introduction

Before 1934 night-flying was one of the Cinderellas of training. Being neglected by the FTSs, it was left to squadrons to teach the necessary skills. Even the CFS training given to instructors was not coordinated. However, in August 1935 a policy for night-flying training was decided upon whose basic features were as follows:

1. Flying is an art in itself which can be either taught or practised under conditions of daylight, cloud or darkness. The application of this art is taught or practised as service training in the form of day-bombing, night reconnaissance, the use of clouds for cover, etc. It is clear that night-flying falls, as regards instruction, under the category of the art of flying under conditions of darkness.

2. Night-flying instruction should be given, as in day- and instrument-flying, during the flying training school course. The application of night-flying to service training, e.g. night navigation and

reconnaissance if taught at the schools, should occur during the second term.

3. The CFS, being the establishment responsible for formulating the methods of flying training, should issue the instructions for night-flying instruction.

There was considerable delay, however, in providing night-flying equipment for FTSs. It was not until the middle of 1936 that CFS staff began night-flying training. The aim was limited. It was recognized that the time available during the course would not produce enough practice to produce experienced night-flying pilots, and so the purpose of the FTSs' night-flying training was defined as:

Ensuring that every service pilot had flown at night, keeping instructors in night-flying practice and destroying the theory that night-flying practice required some special technique and skill.

The Brooke-Popham Report

The syllabus aim was to provide pupils with six hours of flying at night, all on circuits and landing, except for one out-and-back flight of twenty miles. In April 1934 Air Marshal Brooke-Popham asked for some special provision to be made for training night-bomber pilots. He maintained that the preliminary training on twin-engined aircraft and in night-flying, which had to be carried out on squadrons, was really only basic flying training. He pointed out that the requirements of night-bombers were comparable with those of flying-boats, with which it had been found necessary to set up a special training unit, and he suggested four ways of providing the necessary training:

1. By putting a service squadron exclusively on training.
2. By creating an advanced training school to specialize in night- and twin-engined flying.
3. By creating a special *ab initio* school.
4. By creating training nuclei that could be expanded in time of war either to schools or service squadrons.

He concluded his report by saying that it was inevitable that night-flying and multi-engined flying must ultimately be in the curriculum of FTSs. This night-flying problem was held in abeyance for nearly a year, and even when the new system of training was introduced it went only a little way to meeting the difficulties. It did include some night-flying, but no twin-engined training. In fact night-flying training was introduced in the *ab initio* training of pilots in 1935 and was carried out on Moths and Tutors.

TWIN-ENGINED TRAINING
The problem

On 15 March 1933 an advanced training squadron was formed at No. 2 FTS Digby to provide twin-engined

training, but this school closed in December 1935. In June of that year the Director of Training examined the whole problem of twin-engined training. He came up with the conclusion that training on twin-engined aircraft at the FTSs would be useful only if suitable light twin-engined trainers could be produced and if the FTS course was of the length originally designed, i.e. nine months. The only other way of providing this training outside the squadrons was a special twin-engined school. This school could either deal merely with twin-engined conversion, in which case three weeks would be long enough, or take three months and tackle the problem fully. The short course was dismissed as having insufficient value to justify a special school. A three-month course could not be managed with the numbers and dates set by the expansion programme. It was therefore agreed by the Chief of the Air Staff (CAS) in July 1935 that no special twin-engined training would be possible during the expansion period, and squadrons would have to go on giving basic preliminary training. The ultimate solution of a special twin-engined school was left to a more distant future when the pressure of expansion would be relaxed. Two months later he proposed to ease the transition from school to squadron by giving advanced training on the twin-engined aircraft of the FTSs. This was the only improvement possible under the existing conditions. There was no intention of relieving the squadrons of any major burden, and only conversion to twin-engined flying would be carried out. The training given would remain substantially the same as that for single-engined training. After some discussion this scheme was finally agreed by the CAS.

The appropriate aircraft

The next difficulty was aircraft. Obsolete aircraft such as the Virginia were quite unsuitable for training. There were so many various types of multi-engined aircraft in service that it was quite impossible to give each school specimens of every type. What was needed was a twin-engined trainer that had the general characteristics of the various service types. The other requirement would be the speed of production. The aircraft question came

Vickers Virginia.

down to whether Avro Ansons or modified Envoys could be produced earlier in the numbers needed. Air Marshal Newall investigated and found that Ansons could be so produced. The CAS then approved their use in the FTSs.

Introduction of twin-engined flying training

Twin-engined training was eventually introduced into the FTSs in late 1936 in order to meet the growing demand for twin-engined pilots and to relieve the service squadrons of the responsibility of providing conversion training. One-third of the pupils from each course, those destined for heavy-bomber, general reconnaissance and flying-boat squadrons, would be trained on twin-engined aircraft. It was laid down that:

> In the first instance it is essential to provide all pupils, irrespective of what type they are to fly later, with single-engined training. Pilots destined for twin-engined aircraft would therefore be required to fly single-engined aircraft in the first six weeks of their term at the FTSs when it is hoped that they will complete twenty-five hours dual and solo flying. Thereafter pilot training in the first and second terms will be carried out on twin-engined aircraft.

The equipment of FTSs

The first schools to be equipped with Ansons were No. 3 FTS at Grantham, No. 6 at Netheravon in November 1936 and No. 9 at Thornaby in the December. The aircraft establishments were altered to sixty-nine aircraft at each school, twelve single-engined aircraft being withdrawn and sixteen Ansons added. A difficulty came with the introduction of twin-engined training. The policy requiring pupils to fly Harts during their first six months at the FTS meant that the first term tended to degenerate into a conversion course to the service types, with navigation, instrument-flying and night-flying receiving less attention. In November 1936 No. 23 Group proposed that twin-engined pupils should be trained throughout

Hawker Hart.

Avro Anson.

on Ansons. This proposal was turned down, and the policy of commencing training on single-engined aircraft was reaffirmed by the Air Ministry. The proposal was again put forward in July 1937. Aggravation of the already difficult problem of getting all pupils off solo at night was given as the chief reason. The scheme was tried experimentally, found successful and approved in November 1937. Four more Ansons were allotted to the FTSs involved (Nos 3, 6 and 9) and four Harts were withdrawn.

FLYING AND OPERATIONAL

Circuit rules

The circuit rules at RAF aerodromes were intended before the days of metalled runways and air traffic control towers, when aircraft could land in any direction onto the grass. Of course the wind direction would determine the approach to the airfield, and the prevailing wind would mean that pilots would land and take off in the same direction. Nevertheless it was essential to keep a good lookout for other aircraft in the vicinity and to know of any restrictions or special rules that applied to particular airfields like Gosport, described in Chapter 1.

A.50 – Circuit Rules – RAF Aerodromes (38991/30 – 22.2.34)

1. At certain RAF stations, special flying regulations in force are designed to minimize the risk of collision. Pilots proceeding to aerodromes with whose local flying rules they are unfamiliar should observe the following procedure:

    (i) They should not fly within 1 mile of the aerodrome when they are below 2,000 ft, except for the purposes of landing or taking off, and they should not remain in this area longer than necessary.
    (ii) They should enter this area at a low speed and should on no account dive into it from a height or out of clouds.
    (iii) Unless it is intended to land in formation, aircraft in company should 'break up' outside the area.
    (iv) Aerobatics should not be practised within 2 miles of the aerodrome.

2. The rules constitute no more than reasonable precautions for flying near a strange aerodrome and all pilots should be trained to observe them.

Spinning of a Fairey IIIF and floatplanes

During the 1920s fatal flying accidents due to spinning were a serious matter for the Air Ministry. The size of the fin and rudder was important in this respect. A 1933 AMWO is a case in point. This is followed by another order relating to floatplanes:

A.61 – Spinning of the IIIF (GP, FAA and T) aircraft

[GP means General Purpose and FAA denotes that this aircraft was used aboard aircraft-carriers.]

1. In the spinning of the above types, when the centre of gravity is in the forward part of its range, the character of the spin may change after a few turns, the nose coming up and the spin becoming faster. Recovery is then difficult. Full opposite rudder is essential and should be maintained until recovery is effected, as directed in para. 253A of AP.129 (Flying Training Manual, Part 1). Special care is necessary in these circumstances, because the force required to apply full rudder is abnormally large, and if the rudder is not held fully on, recovery may not be possible. The elevator control is also extremely heavy, and both hands are required to move the control lever fully forward in a spin, and a short pilot is liable to relax his pressure on the rudder in his attempt to do so. The aircraft emerges in a steep dive, and the loss of height may be as much as 2,500 ft from the time of setting the controls correctly for the recovery.

2. The centre-of-gravity range to which the above particulars apply is from 19 in. to 23 in. aft of the leading edge of the lower plane, and corresponds to the state of any of the above aircraft when flown without equipment although complying with the instruction plates in the aircraft with regard to ballast.

A.114   Spinning of Aircraft (5567/30 – 20.4.33)

1. Spinning of aircraft.
   (i) Subject to para. 2 below, the spinning of aircraft, the maximum permissible weight of which, for all forms of flying exceeds 6,000 lb, is prohibited unless specially authorized by the Air Ministry.
   (ii) The spinning of aircraft when carrying bombs, torpedoes or smoke floats is prohibited.
   (iii) KR [King's Regulations] & ACI [Air Council Instructions] will be amended in due course.

2. Spinning and rolling of floatplanes.

   Pending the results of investigation into their peculiarities, the spinning and rolling of all types of floatplanes is prohibited except for experimental purposes under the orders of the Air Ministry.

3. If an involuntary spin occurs while the aircraft is carrying bombs, torpedoes, or other detachable loads, the loads should not be dropped during the spin as they would be likely to strike and wreck the structure of the aircraft.

Cloud-flying control

This AMWO is included because it again illustrates the problems of flying without radio and air traffic control centres, which can keep aircraft flying with the necessary horizontal and vertical separation to avoid collisions. Civil aircraft movements are also catered for in this order.

A.353 – Regulations for cloud-flying control (28.12.33)

1. In order to minimize the risk of collision between aircraft flying in clouds, the following regulations are to be brought into force forthwith.

2. No cloud flying is to take place below 2,000 ft above ground level except by service aircraft practising cross-country flying in accordance with para. 3, or in cases of emergency owing to stress of weather or other cause.

3. Cross-country cloud-flying training may be practised on Mondays, Wednesdays (until 12.00 hours) and Fridays by certain squadrons as laid down by the AOC-in-C, ADGB. For this purpose England has been divided into the following areas:

   (i) North of a straight line joining Southwold to Chester.
   (ii) Bounded by a line joining Overton (Flintshire), Old Newton (8 miles east of Bury St Edmunds), Bury St Edmunds, Colchester, Bicester, Reading, England–Wales boundary 7 miles north of Abergavenny, thence England–Wales boundary northwards to Overton.

(iii) Bounded by a line joining Avonmouth, Andover, Dorchester, Portisham, thence westwards along the coast to Avonmouth.

(iv) Point 4 miles NE of Hartley Row, Aldershot, Burwash (Sussex), Hastings, westward along coast to Portsmouth, Havant, point 4 miles west of Ringwood, Basingstoke, point 4 miles NE of Hartley Row.

The use of these areas is subject to restrictions and is to the proviso that if it is intended to route a cross-country cloud flight through an area allotted to civil flying club or school the CO of the squadron is responsible that prior safety arrangements are made with the club or school concerned (who will in all cases have prior right to the area).

4. The following area has been allotted to civil air lines – bounded on the north by the north bank of the River Thames, to Southend then by straight line to North Foreland, continuing in a south and west direction along the coastline via Dungeness to Bexhill, thence by straight lines joining Gatwick, Dorking and Kingston-on-Thames. No cloud-flying by service aircraft except battle flight climbs by units stationed at Kenley and Biggin Hill is to take place in this area. Such battle flight climbs are only to be performed after consultation with the Chief Aerodrome Officer, Croydon Airport.

NAMING OF COCKPITS IN AN AIRCAFT

The following AMWO was published to standardized references to the cockpits and other positions in an aircraft. There had to be a common way of referring to aircraft and equipments so that no confusion arises, which is akin to standardizing the way letters or reports are written to ensure that they are readily understood by all service personnel:

A.207 Nomenclature of Cockpits of Aircraft (224512/32 – 16.8.34)

1. With a view to securing uniformity of practice in regard to the naming of cockpits (other than the pilot's cockpit) of aircraft, it has been decided that:

   (i) cockpits are to be named according to their location in the aircraft;

   (ii) the openings in the underside of the fuselage are to be called 'positions' to distinguish them from cockpits.

2. The accompanying drawing illustrates this and the nomenclature explained therein is to be used on all occasions.

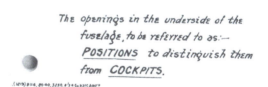

THE EXPANSION SCHEMES

(Source: National Archives Document AIR41/8) (References to government Expansion Progress Meetings appear in the texts as EPMs.)

INTRODUCTION

The RAF expansion schemes that were embarked upon by the Air Ministry during the years leading up to the Second World War were designed to meet the growing threat from Nazi Germany, where the newly formed

Luftwaffe was unveiled to the world in 1935. The official records on the expansion plans, which provide the source material for much of this text, concentrate almost entirely on comparative strengths of the different aircraft types. Little attention is paid to the quality of the new German aircraft types, nor are strategy and tactics discussed. For a consideration of these matters reference should be made to the relevant sections of this chapter and Chapter 3 dealing with the growing German threat, and Chapter 10, which deals with strategy and tactics.

The RAF peacetime strength on 1 January 1930 is laid out in Chapter 1 and was the product of the Trenchard years reflecting the needs of Empire defence together with an ongoing expansion of the Metropolitan Air Force to fifty-two home-based squadrons. It was a force of landplanes, floatplanes and flying-boats, all of biplane construction with open cockpits. It was this small force that was expanded during the second half of the decade to the strengths not seen since November 1918. Trenchard had built a 'cottage' on the foundations that could accommodate a 'castle'; in other words an RAF that could be rapidly expanded without sacrificing the quality that Trenchard had striven so hard to achieve.

Such was the rate of expansion that the British aircraft industry alone could not produce the required numbers of aircraft and engines to meet the ever-changing plans to the timescale laid down. There were two ways of dealing with the shortfall, and those were to buy abroad and/or to use productive resources in the United Kingdom not hitherto used to build aircraft or engines. Buying from Italy was considered, but in the event HMG bought from the United States of America. The use of indigenous productive resources was considered and came to fruition as the 'Shadow Factory' scheme. Firms that made motor cars and engines, including leading brand names such as Austin, Morris, Standard, Rootes, and Rover, were pressed into service to produce aircraft and engines to the designs of the professional aircraft builders such as Avro, Supermarine, Fairey, Hawker and Vickers. These professional aircraft builders would oversee the work of the 'shadow' firms to ensure the required quality of output. The shadow scheme would eventually embrace a large number of other manufacturing firms brought in to produce a huge range of accessories and aircraft components.

As it happens, there was a sort of precedent for this overlap between the production of motor vehicles and aircraft. On cessation of hostilities in 1918 the dearth of orders for aircraft from the established firms in the industry forced the aircraft producers to turn to vehicle production simply to survive: Short Brothers and Martinsyde come to mind in this context. But the rate of expansion and the growing sophistication of aircraft in the 1930s meant that moving from one industry to work in another could only be accomplished with a great deal of careful planning and supervision.

THE EXPANSION SCHEMES

The expansion plans from 1935 to the outbreak of war in 1939 and beyond are described in this and Chapter 3. They were lettered from A to M. They are listed below, and the omitted letters reflect abandoned schemes overtaken by events. The expansion programme, as one can tell from the accompanying table, was subject to constant revision in the light of the estimates of German air strength. Although Italy did in fact fight alongside the Germans in 1940, Mussolini's air force, the *Regia Aeronautica*, was not included in the enemy threat since it was not known which side Mussolini would take until the very last moment (in spite of the Rome–Berlin Axis.) In any event the threat posed by Italian airpower would be felt principally in the Mediterranean, and not against the Metropolitan Air Force but the Middle East Air Force. Similarly the threat that came from Japan affected the Far East Air Force.

Of course the expansion plans had to cater for the needs of the RAF abroad, and RAF formations in those theatres had to be reinforced. The factors that affected the rate of expansion and further details of each scheme are listed below for those initiated during the period 1933–6, and in Chapter 3 for those initiated during the period 1937–9.

Scheme A

This was designed to give a maximum first-line strength and therefore lacked adequate reserves. The scheme's aim was primarily political in scope, and the scheme was meant to 'deter' Germany and to impress public opinion at home. No advanced types of service aircraft were included in the programme. The provision of reserves was to be catered for up to 1938/9 at an estimated cost of £1,200,000, but reserves beyond that date were deferred since it was assumed that the RAF was not required to be ready for war until 1942. The Interim Report of the Ministerial Committee on Disarmament pointed out that the Reserve must be provided before an outbreak of war became imminent. In addition to the eighty-four metropolitan squadrons shown in the table, there would be twenty-seven squadrons overseas comprising 292 aircraft and 16 ½ squadrons for the Fleet Air Arm. It was not until 1938 that the FAA was transferred in its entirety to the Admiralty.

Scheme C

This was the first scheme designed to achieve parity with the German Air Force in accordance with Mr Baldwin's pledge of 8 March 1934. When Sir John Simon and Mr Eden met Adolf Hitler in Berlin on 26 March 1935, their conversation resulted in the implementation of the scheme. Hitler had informed the two men that Germany had already reached parity with the UK in the air and that it was his intention to move on to build up to parity with the French Air Force in France and North

RAF EXPANSION SCHEMES A to M
TOTAL FORCE FIGURES

Scheme	Bomber Sqns A/C	Fighter Sqns A/C	Coastal Sqns A/C	Army Co op Sqns A/C	Total * Sqns A/C	Completion Date
A	43(8)** 500	28(5) 336	8 64	5 60	84 960	31.3.39
C	70(11) 840	35(5) 420	13 162	5 90	123 1512	31.3.37
F	70(11) 1022	30(5) 420	13 162	11(4) 132	124 1736	31.3.39
H	87(7) 1631	34(9) 476	13 183	11(4) 132	145 2422	31.3.39
J	90(7) 1442	38(9) 532	19*** 281	11(4) 132	158 2387	Summer 41
K	77(3) 1360	38(9) 532	19(4) 281	11(4) 132	145 2305	31.3.41
L	73(3) 1352	38(9) 608	19(4) 281	11(4) 132	141 2373	31.3.40
M	85 1360	50(14) 800	19(4) 281	9(2) 108	163 2549	31.3.42

Notes   *   **Totals for the Metropolitan Air Force**

      **   **Figures in brackets are for non-regular squadrons**

      *** **Includes 4 Trade Defence squadrons (56 aircraft) location unspecified**

AIR STAFF ESTIMATES OF GERMAN AIR STRENGTHS

To Correspond with RAF Expansion Scheme	Total German Air Estimates A/C	Total German Bomber Force A/C
Scheme C	1512	800/950
F	1572	840/972
H	2500	1700
J	3240*	1458*
K	2700	1350
L	4400	1950

Note   *   **Excluding Naval Co-operation Types**

Africa. This, he assessed, gave the French a total of 2,000 first-line aircraft. The Air Staff regarded this figure as an exaggeration. It was estimated that Germany would achieve a first-line strength of only 126 squadrons of 1,512 aircraft by the spring of 1937. It was intended that Scheme C should provide for parity with German estimates on a purely numerical basis, to include all first-line aircraft of the Metropolitan Air Force, both regular and non-regular, but excluding the FAA. It was, in fact, realized that Scheme C would not give true parity with Germany, but the programme was accepted as the best that industry could achieve by 31 March 1937 under peacetime conditions of production. The shadow factory scheme was to provide the answer to the need for rapid expansion of RAF strength, of which more later in this chapter. Like Scheme A, it was still hoped at this stage that the expansion programme would act as a deterrent to Hitler.

Scheme F

Cabinet approval was given to Scheme F on 25 February 1936, and provided for 124 squadrons at home and thirty-seven squadrons overseas, with twenty-six squadrons for the FAA (forty squadrons by 1942). Scheme F was initiated against a background of the Italo-Abyssinian war and continuing German rearmament, for Schemes A and C had not had the desired deterrent effect. This was therefore the occasion not only to meet the increased threat but to provide for adequate war reserves. On 10 February 1935 the Secretary of State for Air proposed a reorganization of the Air Striking Force to improve its offensive power. With this object in view the scheme proposed to rearm all the light-bomber squadrons with medium bombers, and to increase the establishment of these nineteen regular squadrons from twelve to eighteen aircraft. Similarly, ten of the medium-bomber squadrons formed under Scheme C would have their establishments increased by the same number. The remaining eight medium-bomber squadrons formed under Scheme C would be equipped each with twelve Vickers medium bombers, and the establishment of the torpedo-bomber squadrons would be raised from twelve to sixteen aircraft. The original calculation of the basis of war reserves, for which £50,000,000 was allocated, was that they should be sufficient to cover the first four months' wastage, after which it was thought war potential would be adequate to cover aircraft losses month by month. The figure of 150% of first-line strength represented the reserves considered necessary to cover the average anticipated wastage rates among various types of home-based squadrons during the first three months of the war. The fourth month's wastage was to be met from the immediate reserves, and workshop (maintenance) reserves from Scheme F (stored immediate and workshops) totalled 225% of first-line strength. There was provision for Army Cooperation squadrons to accompany the Field Force. For this commitment five regular Army Cooperation squadrons of this scheme were to be reorganized to provide seven under Scheme F. Ten squadrons were to be added to the RAF in the Far East to meet the growing threat of Japanese imperialism. Finally, the first-line strength of the FAA was to be raised to 504 aircraft by 1942 to correspond with the naval programme.

AN ASSESSMENT OF THE THREE SCHEMES

It has been stated that the principal purpose of Schemes A and C was to act as a deterrence to Hitler, but it had become clear that the German Chancellor had no intention of slackening the pace of rearmament. In the event of a European war Britain would stand alongside France and place an expeditionary force on the continent. The air component, which was to become the Advanced Air Striking Force, would need to be equipped with bombers that could cause the maximum damage to enemy ground forces, rear areas and lines of communication. The light-bomber squadrons were equipped with Hart, Hind and Gordon light biplane bombers, hardly the aircraft to create havoc among the enemy forces. The Air Staff submitted three schemes aimed at re-equipping the regular light-bomber squadrons with medium bombers (Schemes D, E and E1). Advances in aircraft and engine design meant that the biplanes could be replaced by more powerful monoplane medium bombers. Under Scheme F all of the thirty light-bomber squadrons were to be re-equipped with the new medium bombers, the Blenheim and the Battle.

In the case of the heavy bombers, the new Heyford, Whitley, Harrow and Wellington bombers would replace the remaining biplane bombers, and it is almost incredible that the Virginia, which would not have been out of place in the period immediately after the First World War, was not finally pensioned off until 1937.

As for the fighters, in Scheme F the strength of the force was left at a total of 420. At the launch of the scheme the new eight-gun monoplane fighter was still in the development stage, and it was not until the last year of peace that the Furies, Gladiators, Gauntlets and Demons were replaced in quantity by the Spitfire, Hurricane and Defiant.

Aircraft in other roles included those for Army Cooperation, maritime and general reconnaissance, as well as those in the various roles overseas. The Army Cooperation squadrons were raised from five to eleven, of which four would be auxiliary squadrons assigned for work with the TA, but with a unit establishment of aircraft lowered from sixteen to twelve aircraft. To meet the growing threat posed by the Italians in the Mediterranean and the growing expansionist activities of Japan in the Pacific, HMG saw fit to reinforce overseas commands by ten new squadrons. There would be thirty-seven squadrons of 468 aircraft.

To meet the needs of the Royal Navy to combat the submarine menace and to undertake maritime reconnaissance there would be a force of thirty-six flying-boats. The Fleet Air Arm was still the responsibility of the Air Ministry, and it was planned that by 1939 there would be twenty-six squadrons of 213 aircraft.

With this planned expansion of air forces, reorganization at Air Ministry departments and an increase in productive capacity was vital. In 1935 supply and research was divided into separate departments, namely Research and Development and Supply and Organization, each being under the charge of a member of the Air Council. The Air Member for Research and Development was Air Marshal Sir Hugh Dowding and that for Supply and Organization was Air Marshal Sir Cyril Newall. To meet the requirements of the shadow factory scheme that was necessary to implement Scheme F, a new directorate was formed. This was the Directorate of Aeronautical Production, which came into existence in March 1936 under Lieutenant-Colonel H.A.P. Disney, whose responsibility was the production of airframes and engines, as well as the manufacture of associated equipment and armaments.

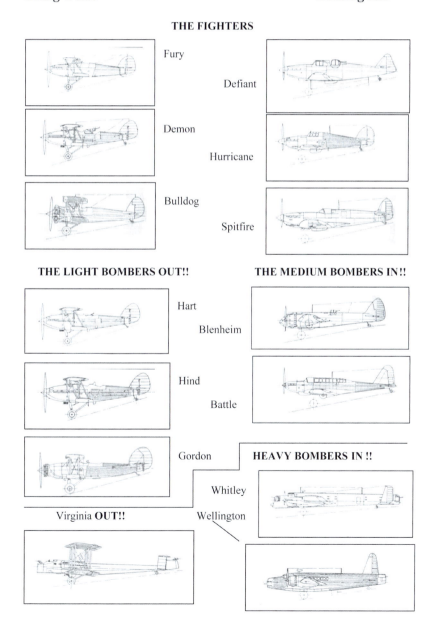

Going Out!!

Coming in!!

THE FIGHTERS

Fury

Defiant

Demon

Hurricane

Bulldog

Spitfire

THE LIGHT BOMBERS OUT!!

THE MEDIUM BOMBERS IN!!

Hart

Blenheim

Hind

Battle

Gordon

HEAVY BOMBERS IN!!

Whitley

Virginia **OUT!!**

Wellington

PURCHASE OF US AIRCRAFT

The suggestion that HM Government might purchase military aircraft from the United States was made by Lord Swinton at an EPM on 29 September 1936. He stated that he had asked the Chief of the Air Staff to produce a plan for two or three squadrons each of bomber and fighter aircraft within a few months. This was to be based on the hypothesis that the first-line strength of the RAF might have to be increased very rapidly within fifteen months of that date, i.e. September 1936, before the shadow factories had got into full production. After some discussion at that meeting it was decided that the Douglas DBI bomber and the Seversky P35 fighter would be the best types to order, and that discreet enquiries should be made about the possible purchase of them.

Later, however, it was decided to order other types, and in June 1938 the Air Ministry placed contracts in the USA for 200 North American Harvard training machines and 200 Lockheed Hudson reconnaissance aircraft, these numbers being subsequently increased to 400 and 250 respectively. This increase was announced by Sir Kingsley Wood in the House of Commons on 9 March 1939. There was a certain amount of criticism of the government action in going abroad for its purchases of aircraft. On 15 June 1938 one Member of Parliament was to suggest that Britain should place an order with a German aircraft manufacturer. When Sir Kingsley Wood replied that the government had no more orders in contemplation, the member asked, 'Is Germany considered an enemy country, then?'

THE SHADOW FACTORY SCHEME

(Source: AIR41/8)

INTRODUCTION

The shadow factory scheme was devised by His Majesty's Government in 1935 to meet the requirements of a rapidly expanding RAF that was being prepared to meet the threat posed by the German dictator, Adolf Hitler. Even if the aircraft and aero-engine industries worked to the limits of their capacities, it would not have been possible to produce military aircraft in sufficient numbers to equip the rapidly expanding number of RAF squadrons, let alone build up a war reserve. It was decided that the motor car industry, if given the plans and the tools, would be capable of producing airframes and engines to the requisite high standard. The firms that built airframes for civil aviation could also be pressed into service. Thus it was that the household names of the period – Austin, Standard, Daimler, Rootes (Humber, Hillman, Commer), Wolseley, Rover and Singer – were selected to undertake this work. Lord Nuffield was the exception in withholding permission for the Morris works to take part in the scheme at its inauguration, although he did join at a later date.

The Secretary of State for Air, Lord Swinton, presented a White Paper to Parliament in October 1936 entitled 'On the policies of His Majesty's Government in relation to the production of aero-engines. Command Paper 3295'. The main purpose of the White Paper was to defend the principle of the scheme as adopted in the face of opposition to the scheme by Lord Nuffield. In fact Lord Nuffield did not assist in the expansion of the RAF until after Sir Kingsley Wood had become Air Secretary in May 1938. He then agreed to organize a factory for the production of Spitfires at Castle Bromwich. It was envisaged that the companies taking part in the scheme would not be required to go on producing aircraft and engines once the expansion plans were completed. It was made clear to them that they would not receive any orders from the Air Ministry for any units produced, once the scheme was ended. The White Paper stated that it was essential that the factories producing engines should be established in closest possible association with the works of the managing firms, which would, in the event of war, turn their main factories over to war production. The associated shadow factory could then be put on a war footing.

The siting of shadow factories, and firms selected

The siting of the new factories in close proximity to the parent works had both advantages and disadvantages. It enabled the managing firm to undertake the supervision of the new factory with the minimum of interference with its own business, but it was open to the objection that it would involve risks in wartime. Coventry and Birmingham, near which most of the shadow factories were established, were already centres of war production and obvious targets for air attack. Decentralization, it seems, was not then

Fairey Battle.

Bristol Blenheim.

considered as important as it was at a later date. In a speech in the House of Commons on 15 March 1937, Lieutenant-Colonel Moore-Brabazon pointed to the danger of having all Britain's aero-engine 'eggs' in one basket.

The firms selected are listed above, but of these, Singer and Wolseley fell out of the scheme before it was inaugurated. The place of these two firms was taken by the Bristol Aeroplane Company and the Austin Motor Company. The latter agreed to share the work of engine assembly for which the parts had been made by the participating firms. The Austin company thus had a double role: it manufactured crankshafts and some other parts as one of a team making Mercury engines. The Austin company was also responsible for airframe construction in one of two factories established to produce Fairey Battle and Bristol Blenheim bombers. Indeed, the Battle factory was erected close to the Austin motor works at Longbridge, Birmingham, as was the new engine factory. The airframe factory for the construction of Blenheims was situated at Speke in Lancashire, and was managed by Rootes Securities Ltd, which was also responsible for one of the engine factories under the scheme. This was situated at Coventry.

The Battle light bomber
On looking back, one has the benefit of hindsight, and in the case of the Battle bomber it was a mistake to build this aircraft under the shadow factory scheme. The matter was discussed at the Secretary of State's EPM No. 25, held on 6 February 1936. The Chief of the Air Staff declared himself in favour of letting a shadow factory manufacture Battles. He said that it was a type that motor car firms could perfectly turn out, and as it already existed, the firms involved could inspect it before committing themselves. Lord Weir suggested that it might be best if one shadow firm undertook to manufacture medium bombers and another the heavy bombers, but the Secretary of State felt that the heavy bombers should be built by the professional aircraft constructors. The shadow firms were best suited to smaller aircraft that would be required in large numbers. It was felt that the construction of heavy bombers presented special problems and that their construction by shadow firms could be very costly. Indeed, at an expansion progress meeting of 5 January 1937 it was suggested that the Austin shadow factory should produce the B12/36 heavy bomber with six other firms, but the idea was later dropped.

It was decided to have 900 Battles produced in shadow factories, for it was felt that it was a more suitable machine than other possible aircraft for construction by firms not previously engaged in aircraft construction. From that point of view the Battle was a good choice, but by 1936 other medium bombers were being designed that had greater endurance, speed and carrying capacity. In other words, as the order went out to have these aircraft constructed, the Battle was already being overtaken by aircraft with superior qualities. It was a single-engined aircraft and could not carry a navigator, which was necessary in a medium bomber. On 21 December 1936, the Chief of the Air Staff, Sir Edward Ellington, directed that no more Battles were to be ordered. This decision followed EPM No. 60 held on 24 November 1936, when Ellington had declared that types like the Battle were not acceptable. When there was a set-back in the delivery programme in 1937 it was clear that by the time many of the Battles came off the production line they would already be obsolescent. It is sad to say that when they went to France with the Advanced Air Striking Force they were no match for enemy fighters, and there were heavy losses. Soon afterwards they were withdrawn and used only for training. When an offer was made to the French to sell them the Battle, the offer was declined. Looking back, one can only conclude that the Battle had never been a suitable machine for the purpose for which it was intended. The Air Member for Research and Development, Sir Wilfred Freeman, at an EPM held on 16 November 1937, declared his belief that the decision to go ahead with its production had been a blunder.

Other shadow factories
In addition to the airframe and engine factories, others were established for the manufacture of airscrews, carburettors and magnetos. They were all turning out their products by the end of 1938, some indeed by the end of 1937. In the House of Commons on 9 March 1939 the Air Secretary, Sir Kingsley Wood, was able to report that, of the eleven established under the expansion scheme, all were in production. One very large factory that was not in the original eleven was that erected by Lord Nuffield at Castle Bromwich in 1938 for the production of Spitfires. The factory covered $2\frac{1}{2}$ million square feet of floor space and cost about £$4\frac{1}{2}$ million to construct. Lord Nuffield objected to the word 'Shadow', so this factory did not join the official list of eleven.

There were two outlying factories built at Crewe and Glasgow building Merlin engines, which went into the Spitfires. The supply of guns, aviation fuel, etc. went hand-in-hand with the production of airframes and engines, and the output soon surpassed that required to sustain a peacetime air force. A huge variety of spare parts, accessories and instruments was required, and some of the items had not been previously used by the RAF. The cannon-gun was an example, for throughout the inter-war years there had only been Vickers and Lewis guns mounted in aircraft. Although eight 0.303 in. Browning guns had been incorporated into the design of the Spitfire and Hurricane, something bigger than the Vickers 'K' gun and the 0.303 in. Browning would be

Browning guns being loaded with 0.303 in. ammunition.

20 mm cannon guns.

required. The cannon selected was the 20 mm Hispano/Suiza, and it required protracted negotiations with Prince Poniatowski, the agent for the French firm that produced it, to obtain the licence to build the cannon in Britain. The weapon was produced in a factory in Grantham. The intention was for it to be installed in the Westland Whirlwind, and not in the Spitfire and Hurricane. As it was, the cannon was fitted to the latter in 1940, although machine-guns continued to be carried as standard armament.

Another question that involved lengthy negotiations was that of the supply of high-octane petrol. By the use of 100 octane rather that 87 octane fuel, the horsepower, both for take-off and for cruising, was increased by 25%. A commercial supply of petrol of such an octane value, however, was inadequate, and it became necessary to enter into contracts with three of the largest oil producers for a large increase in their capacity for production of it and the tetra-ethyl lead that is an ingredient. The three companies were Imperial Chemical Industries, Trinidad Leaseholds and Shell International. The provision of tankage for the fuel when delivered was another matter for which special arrangements had to be made with the oil companies.

To equip this burgeoning number of aircraft it was necessary to arrange for extra supplies of gun turrets, retractable undercarriages, bomb carriers and bomb-sights, bomb cases, optical glass and DF loops. Then there were tubes and extrusions, extrusion presses, machine-tools, light alloys and other kinds of materials.

THE OUTSIDE FIRMS

There were firms in the aircraft industry that could contribute output as part of the shadow factory scheme but were not approved by the government. This was one of the criticisms levelled at the shadow factory scheme: the government was turning its back on a preferable plan of bringing the whole of the aircraft industry into the expansion effort. This view was put forward by Lord Sempill in a speech in the House of Lords on 17 December 1936. He explained that, since 1920, the Air Ministry's policy had been to divide the aircraft-producing facilities in the country into two distinct categories, the 'approved' and 'unapproved' firms. By a coincidence there were sixteen in each of these two categories. Lord Sempill's contention was that the Air Ministry, in failing to make use of the unapproved firms, was neglecting a valuable source of supply and had been left out in the cold. He believed that all of the aircraft industry should be invited to participate. He believed that, with the exception of a few orders for training machines, a substantial part of the aircraft industry, the unapproved firms with an adequate capital of £5 million, were being thwarted in their efforts to get work from the Air Ministry (House of Lords Debates, Vol. 103 Cols 975–82). Lord Swinton rejected Lord Sempill's assertions. The former believed that the shadow factory scheme was all right as it was having the support of the great industrialists like Lord Weir and Lord Hirst, whose advice had to be set against the views of Lord Sempill. He went on to dismiss the need for the plan of action proposed by Lord Sempill, adding that small firms were hardly likely to have greater production experience than the approved firms such as Austin, Standard, Daimler and Humber. Other voices were to be added to those of Lord Sempill the following year.

THE AIR THREAT FROM NAZI GERMANY
INTRODUCTION

The preceding sections of this chapter have dealt almost exclusively with numbers, but numbers alone revealed very little about the actual threat, as opposed to the perceived air threat to Great Britain in the mid-1930s. For example, the enemy might possess 1,500 bombers, but was there a sufficient spares back-up to keep those aircraft in the air for an appreciable length of time, and were there the crews trained to a high standard to fly the aircraft operationally? From the foregoing sections of this chapter and in studying Chapter 11, it is clear that the government of this country was concerned very much with raw numbers by type, e.g. bomber, fighter, etc. To assess the actual rather than the perceived threat to Britain from the *Luftwaffe*, other factors must be considered:

1. The political imperatives of the leadership in Germany.
2. The development of air doctrine.
3. The qualities of military leadership in the Third Reich.
4. The qualities of aircraft and crews.

(Germany's military involvement in the Spanish Civil War from 1936 to 1939 will have had a bearing on these factors.)

THE POLITICAL IMPERATIVES OF THE LEADERSHIP IN NAZI GERMANY
The characteristics of Fascist rule
Germany in 1934 had become a totalitarian state. It was a National Socialist regime that was in power, which means that it exhibited the characteristics of the racist form of Fascism. Fascist regimes are characterized by *Fuhrerprinzip*, which means that an all-powerful leader embodies the will of the nation and is, by definition, the nation personified. He is infallible and not subject to the will of the electorate, once in power. By 1 July 1934 Hitler had consolidated his power by purging the Nazi Party of the last vestiges of dissent to his rule, in the infamous 'Night of the Long Knives'. Once President Hindenburg died in the following month, all hope of dissent to Hitler's rule was extinguished.

Another characteristic of Fascism is irrationality. The essence of the ideology is that it must appeal to the heart and not the head. Flags and uniforms are essential in the mystification process if the 'masses' are to be kept in awe. Charisma rather than intellect is what matters in a Fascist leader. This may also mean that irrational behaviour is exhibited by Fascist leaders. Such generals as Rommel and Von Runstedt may have always had their feet on the ground, but others, like Keitel and Jodl, did not. Their response to a war situation may be dictated by ideology or blind adherence to the will of the leader rather than pragmatism. Hitler's insistence that his 6th Army was not to retreat one inch in the battle for Stalingrad, when a tactical withdrawal would have made sense, is a case in point. In 1940, maddened by the RAF bombing of Berlin in 1940, Hitler flew into a rage, and Goering, eager to please his master, switched bombing attacks from the fighter airfields to London as a reprisal. This move undoubtedly cost the Germans the battle and saved Britain from invasion. Of course these defects in a Fascist system did not come to light until war began, but none the less, they existed in the 1930s.

Given the absolutist nature of Fascist rule, decision making may consist of the leader acting on prejudices, and in Hitler's case a reported adherence to astrology. Add to this the hatred he had of the Jews and an abnormal amount of money that could have been spent on armaments was spent on the intended extinction of an entire race. His aversion to Communism and his determination that Jews and Bolsheviks were hand in glove to exploit mankind meant that, above all, Russia had to be defeated. This would also give him the *Lebensraum* he needed to settle the surplus population. All this was forecast in *Mein Kampf*, the turgid pages of which were ignored by European heads of state. In these circumstances the military leadership of the Third Reich did not dictate the thrust of grand military strategy – it might only modify it. Could the British governments of Baldwin and Chamberlain have known what the real threat would be in the event of war? Hitler did not regard Britain as a natural enemy, and he believed that this country could be persuaded to remain neutral, leaving him a free hand in Europe, if he left Britain and her trade with the Empire alone. Only when Neville Chamberlain at last realized, after Czechoslovakia, that Britain would have to confront Germany over Poland, did the perceived threat become a real threat.

The political imperatives
It was important that Germany did not find itself fighting on two fronts, as it had from 1914 to 1917. This meant having a temporary or permanent alliance with countries on either side with a commitment not to go to war. This happened in 1939 between Russia and Germany. In the case of Nazi Germany it meant eventually going to war with Russia, but first eliminating the threat to Germany's rear when the invasion was launched. A prior attack upon France and the Low Countries would be made before turning East. Hitler's determined nationalism meant absorbing Austria and the Sudetenland Germans into the Third Reich, followed by the Polish Corridor. And his resentment of the Treaty of Versailles dictated his own political imperatives, that he must reclaim territory lost in the Great War and shake off the shackles imposed by the Versailles Treaty, which limited Germany's armed forces. In one sense, therefore, given the nature of Fascist rule, one needed to look no further than the leader to determine the actual threat. One last factor under this heading, which is not confined to Fascist regimes, is the necessity to be prepared to go to war on the ground at very short notice. A country that has contiguous borders with her continental neighbours can find itself embroiled in a ground war very soon after the commencement of hostilities. France's answer to this possibility was the demilitarization of the Rhineland after the Great War, followed by the building of the Maginot Line. In these circumstances there may be a political imperative to form defensive alliances.

THE DEVELOPMENT OF GERMAN AIR DOCTRINE
Failure to create a strategic bombing force

From the foregoing it may be deduced that Nazi Germany needed a strategic air doctrine. Given the theories of the employment of airpower handed down from Trenchard, Mitchell and Douhet, German security could be achieved by taking the war to the enemy to break his will to resist, and by destroying military and economic targets through a bomber offensive. If there is going to be a considerable war at sea it might also require having the means of deploying naval airpower. In this last respect Germany differed markedly from Britain. Being the leader of a continental power, military objectives could well be accomplished by the use, primarily, of ground forces. Both corporals who ended up as their country's leaders, Hitler and the Emperor Napoleon, failed to take proper account of British sea power. If Hitler was going to invade Britain he would first have to cross the English Channel. Hitler's naval commander-in-chief, Admiral Erich Raeder, had his Z plan for a substantial German fleet, equipped with aircraft-carriers, but it was not due for completion until 1945, too late for Hitler's timetable for war. To defeat Britain without a seaborne invasion would require a sustained strategic air offensive against vital military and economic targets as far north and west as Liverpool and Belfast. Unless German air bases could move forward into France or the Low Countries, their bombers would have to have the range and bomb-carrying capacity to reach their targets from Germany. The Germans could not cross the airspace of these countries to reach Britain unless there was a state of war between them. They would be restricted to flying from bases in northern Germany, taking them over the North Sea. It might well not be possible for fighters to accompany the bombers to their targets, making the latter a prey to British fighters. If Germany was to be able to mount a strategic offensive against Britain from France or the Low Countries, the *Luftwaffe* would still need heavy, long-range, four-engined bombers, and possibly long-range fighter escorts. These were not being constructed by Germany in the late 1930s. But it was not simply the fact that Germany did not possess strategic bombers as she went to war; even if they had been in existence there was still the problem of finding and hitting targets with accuracy at night and in bad weather.

The failure to create a strategic bombing force before the outbreak of war cannot be blamed entirely on the German Air Staff. There were plenty who believed it was in Germany's interest to possess heavy bombers. After all the Gotha bombers and Zeppelins had been used aggressively against targets in Britain during the Great War. In 1934, when British air expansion began, the *Luftwaffe* was an infant service, since the Versailles Treaty had forbidden Germany to possess an air force. Inevitably the officers of the *Luftwaffe* had to come from the small German Army and Navy. Their thinking about the strategic employment of airpower would be affected by their previous military experience. But again one is drawn back to the realities of a Fascist regime. With Goering as their new commander-in-chief, decisions were made about the structure of the new service that were dictated by a man who had been a squadron pilot in the Great War flying in direct support of the ground war. He became a commander-in-chief because of his position in the Nazi hierarchy, and not because of what he knew about air warfare. To add to the difficulties of those in the senior ranks of the *Luftwaffe* who were trying to put together a sensible and balanced air doctrine, the entire Nazi system of government was riven with petty jealousies. Hitler loved to play one of his underlings off against the other in a policy of 'divide and rule'. This could easily result in the most capable men not getting important posts in the *Luftwaffe* because they were out of favour, like Wolfram von Richthofen when he left for Spain to join the Condor Legion in 1936. Add to this a lazy commander-in-chief who only attended to his air force duties when it suited him, and was ignorant of strategy, supply, technology, aircraft engineering and aircraft capabilities, one must conclude that at the highest levels of command there was poor leadership.

In spite of these deficiencies inherent in a totalitarian system, the German high command did consider what role the *Luftwaffe* should play as part of overall strategy. Erhard Milch was one of those who had responsibility for the organization and development of the *Luftwaffe* during the period 1933 to 1936, and he began his work in May 1933, only five months after Hitler had been installed as Chancellor. The Douhet 'strategic bombing' theories were considered together with Tirpitz's 'risk theory', a theory of deterrence. If Germany was to be restored as a great power in Europe it must face the possibility that France would feel immediately threatened, and Germany would have to fight a preventative war. The conclusion was that Germany would have to create a strong air force rapidly, and present France, and possibly Poland, with a *fait accompli*. A force of some 400 four-engined bombers would be required. When it came to the morale effect of bombing it was argued that the morale of a highly disciplined society like Nazi Germany would not be the first to break down. Building a bombing fleet would have a greater deterrent effect than forming an army of 100 divisions. Naturally the Army rejected the idea that the *Luftwaffe* could usurp its role, a situation akin to the hornet's nest that Trenchard stirred up when he seemed to suggest that the RAF could win a war without the help of the other two services. It was even suggested by opponents of airpower that the creation of air forces so devastating might create a situation where war was an impossible means of pursuing foreign policy by other means, as Clauswitz famously said. Mussolini said that a country should go to war at least once every twenty-five years as an act of national cleansing. The pacifism, which might result in the democracies, from creating air forces with devastating might would then be attractive to Fascist regimes.

Another factor that contributed to the *Luftwaffe* not developing a strategic bomber was, surprisingly, the inability of the German aircraft industry to produce one. They had no experience in building a strategic bombing fleet and lacked the designers and industrial capacity. At that time the industry was lucky to produce 1,000 aircraft in the first production programme. Milch himself was the prime mover in the early development of the service, and must be credited with dealing efficiently with the administrative and logistical problems. Most of the effort in the first building programme was devoted, not to combat aircraft, but training aircraft for the *Luftwaffe* to have sufficient pilots to fly the combat aircraft as they came off the production line, a point made in the opening paragraph of this section. From January 1933 the industrial base of only 4,000 workers was expanded to 16,870 workers in 1934, and 204,100 in the autumn of 1938.

General Wever was the other important figure in the attempt to create a strategic bomber force. He was no great advocate of a strategic force; rather he favoured a balanced approach with regard to air doctrine. The creation of an independent air force did not mean that the *Luftwaffe* should not work with the other two services. The war role of the air force should include attacks on the enemy air forces, his army, his fleet and economic resources, including the armaments industries. Fighter defences would be important, but the bombing campaign could be decisive. Wever set down his thinking on German air doctrine in his work of 1935, *Die Luftkriegführung*, 'The Conduct of Air War'. The aim was not to put German air commanders in a strait-jacket, but to give them latitude in their thinking and encourage flexibility. A very pragmatic approach was adopted in declaring that the way airpower was employed should depend on such things as the topography, the time of year, which would affect weather, and the character of an enemy, as well as Germany's own capabilities. The achievement of air superiority could be elusive and air resources should not be employed piecemeal. One had to consider calls for direct help to the Army in the field and the Fleet, and weigh these against the strategic bombing commitments. Wever was concerned that the strategic bombing offensive would take so long to achieve its objectives that it would be at the expense of help to the Army and Navy. Cooperation between all three services would be the best means of achieving the objectives of grand national strategy. Wever's death in the spring of 1936 undoubtedly had an effect upon the formulation of a strategic doctrine in the next three years, the three years of the Spanish Civil War. The

further developments in Air Staff thinking in Germany, and the impact of the *Luftwaffe*'s involvement in Spain on that thinking, are further considered in Chapter 3, dealing with the years 1936 to 1939.

THE QUALITIES OF THE MILITARY LEADERSHIP IN THE THIRD REICH
Introducing the commanders
Before being officially unveiled to the world, the *Luftwaffe* had to be organized secretly. All the senior commanders would have to come from either the Army or the Navy. Actually this is not as absurd as it might sound, since the RAF in April 1918 had to be commanded by officers who had spent their entire careers in one or the other of the sister services. The major difference was that the RAF commanders had much more recent combat experience in the 1920s. The new commanders of the *Luftwaffe* had to look back to the Great War some sixteen years earlier. The following list is by no means exhaustive. Their names have been chosen as persons intimately involved in the foundation of the new service.

Hermann Goering It was precisely this combat experience that qualified Hermann Goering to command the *Luftwaffe*. Goering had been a fighter pilot and a decorated flying ace, but that does not, of itself, equip a man to command an air force. His appointment as the commander of the *Luftwaffe* had everything to do with his becoming one of the earliest members of the Nazi Party and a close friend of Hitler. Compared with the very professional leadership of the RAF, Goering was an amateur. Hitler always maintained an ill-defined chain of command during his period as leader. The very way in which the Nazi hierarchy operated would eventually lead to the regime's downfall. Hitler's immediate subordinates were always trying to curry favour with him, and ended up fighting each other, which is fine if one is operating a 'divide and rule' policy but is hardly conducive to the taking of rational decisions. As an example, Hitler had appointed Werner von Blomberg as Minister of War with overall responsibility for the three services. This did not prevent Goering from going behind Blomberg's back to ensure a privileged status for his *Luftwaffe*, particularly when it came to allocating scarce resources.

Ernst Udet and Erhard Milch Like Goering, Udet had served with distinction during the Great War and had been credited with sixty-two kills, second only to Baron Manfred von Richthofen, who had eighty kills to his credit. Goering appointed Udet to be the Technical Director of the *Luftwaffe*, although the latter had little or no experience of the aircraft industry. In consequence, German aircraft production continued on a peacetime basis, even after the war began. With the opening of the second front against Russia in 1941, German losses mounted, and the pressure on Udet proved too much and he committed suicide. On the other hand, Erhard Milch did have a sound knowledge of the German aircraft industry, knowing its managers and designers, but he was appointed Secretary of State for the new Air Ministry.

Walther Wever Goering appointed Wever to the post of Chief of the Air Staff. Wever was responsible for formulating the service's doctrine and strategy. He maintained a balanced approach in the employment of air forces in war and adopted the view that Trenchard was obliged, in the end, to accept. An air force on its own could not win a war, but could do so only by cooperating with its sister services. Be that as it may, he did advocate the primacy of the bomber as the decisive weapon of air warfare. Had he not been killed in a flying accident in 1936, the *Luftwaffe* might have had a heavy strategic bomber.

Wolfram von Richthofen Wolfram was the cousin of the famous Baron Manfred, of Great War fame. He went to Spain as Chief of Staff of the Condor Legion. This was a force assigned to aid the Nationalist forces fighting in the Civil War. Both Mussolini and Hitler provided military support to Generals Mola and Franco. Following Mola's death in an aircraft accident, Franco assumed overall command, to become the third European Fascist dictator in 1939. Richthofen was to develop a new type of warfare, which became known as the *Blitzkrieg*, or 'lightning war'. This may be described as fast-moving armoured warfare with dive-bombers providing close air support. This involved having air officers with the ground troops who could talk to the pilots and direct their fire onto enemy battlefield targets. This new form of warfare was not in the *Luftwaffe* book of tactics at the time, but it was to prove decisive against Poland, the Low Countries and France during 1939 and 1940.

HENDON RAF AND SBAC DISPLAYS, EMPIRE AIR DAYS

1933
RAF Display

The 1933 Annual Display was held on 24 June in the pouring rain. The clouds were low and the visibility nil. In spite of this, only one event failed to materialize. The leader of a wing of three squadrons took off but soon disappeared from the view of the spectators. He wisely led his formation off to another landing ground. The low cloud made low bombing by nine aircraft hazardous, and could so easily have resulted in a collision as each in turn appeared out of the cloud, only to disappear as quickly. A team of test pilots from Martlesham had to

abandon an aerobatic display with Bulldogs. Instead they performed a display using coloured smoke trails They wove a pattern of orange and green smoke around a white one. Those involved were Flight Lieutenant J.F. Moir, Flying Officer H.H. Leech and Flying Officer A.J. Pegg. There was a fly-past of flying-boats and amphibians, which came up from Felixstowe in extremely bad weather. They cruised around Hendon aerodrome awaiting their turn to come in. Initially one could see their grey shapes as they approached the railway embankment before the spectators saw the recognizeable shapes of the Short Singapore II, the Sarafand and Supermarine Southampton emerge from the overcast.

From the New Types Park came the C.30 Autogiro and the Hawker 'Super Fury'. It was incredibly fast, and the effectiveness of lateral control was probably enhanced by the tapered wings. The day- and night-fighters followed, namely the Bristol Bulldog IV, the Armstrong Whitworth AV XVI and the Gloster SS 19B. There then followed the Vickers M1/30 and the Blackburn torpedo-bomber, the Vickers Vespa high-altitude and a very quiet Fairey IIIF, which was taking part in silencing research. Eleventh out of the Park was the Wapiti, with a new Bristol Phoenix compression-ignition engine, and a Hawker Horsley, also with a similar engine made by Rolls. The largest aircraft, which towered above the rest in the Park, was the Handley Page HP43 bomber-transport. It took off after a very short run, to be followed by the Blackburn Commercial monoplane. The prototype HP43 had been flown by the Martlesham test pilots. It was a maze of interplane struts resembling, as one RAF man was heard to remark, 'a bit like Bournemouth Pier'! The controls were heavy and badly harmonized, and the performance was poor. There was little prospect that the HP43 would go into production. The only hope was that the Air Ministry might find that a monoplane version would be acceptable.

1934
RAF Display

The 1934 RAF Display took place on 30 June. It was a beautiful day but marred by a tragic flying accident. It was also a sad day for another reason, of which the watching crowd was oblivious, for Hitler was to eliminate all those members of his own Nazi Party who posed a threat to him and this would allow him to consolidate power in his own hands. This consolidation of absolute power would eventually lead to war, where British airpower would be tested to the limit and aircraft like the 'New Types' on display that day were going to be needed in the coming conflict.

The aerobatic display that day would result in the death of the Lord Mayor's son, Squadron Leader Collet, who was the Commanding Officer of No. 600 (City of London) Bomber Squadron. The Hawker Hart in which he was flying was piloted by Flying Officer R.F.G. Leigh, part of a four-squadron display. These four squadrons were undertaking synchronized aerobatics, looping in line astern and changing into echelon while coming off the top. The aircraft dived in echelon before changing into line astern. They then broke away to left and right of the Royal Box with a half roll outwards. At the last moment the aircraft dived in salute to the Prince of Wales. As Leigh's machine was about to salute the Royal visitor, there was a sudden engine failure and the aircraft undershot. There was a hollow thud as the aircraft disappeared from view, but the black column of smoke and the flames spelled disaster. Although Leigh himself was only slightly injured, Collet did not survive.

But 'the show has to go on', as they say in the theatre, and ten events followed. Although the crowd was enthralled by the airmanship of the RAF pilots, the 'New Types' were of the greatest interest to the enthusiasts. Among them was the high-speed Fury with a spatted undercarriage and N-strutted wings, of which only the lower were tapered. Fighters built to Air Ministry Specification F7/30 were the Private Venture Hawker 3 fighter, the Westland biplane and the Supermarine Type 224. Westland showed off its P7 monoplane, which seemed very advanced compared with the Fairey and Armstrong Whitworth biplanes. The Boulton & Paul Overstrand was significant in that it had a new rotating gunner's turret in the nose. This could be rotated through a full 360 degrees to permit the guns to be fired backwards over the mid-section of the upper wing (see the section of this chapter on aircraft testing at the A & AEE Martlesham) The Handley Page Heyford came last. In the 1920s RAF pilots prefered to fly in open cockpits, but the Heyford's was enclosed, and its engine nacelles were higher, slimmer and streamlined. The finale was the time-honoured display of an attack on a fort or similar building. When this one exploded it did so with the usual display of pyrotechnics.

SBAC Show

The display was followed by the now-established SBAC Display, the third to be precise. There were some 1,500 guests to witness the flying display of forty aircraft built by eighteen British firms.

Military aircraft predominated, but all the aircraft demonstrated had been seen before, excepting the AW35 Scimitar. Flown by Turner Hughes, this aircraft made some spectacular vertical climbs from left to right. Cyril Uwins flew the Gloster Gauntlet, Turner flew the Pegasus Bulldog IV and Gerry Sayer flew the Gloster Gauntlet. Mr Sayer then handled test flying for that company on behalf of its new owner, Hawker. George Bulman with the Fury Mk II, together with Lucas flying the Pegasus-powered Hart and Sayer in the Kestrel-powered Hart, finished the demonstration with a formation known as 'The Prince of Wales's Feathers'.

The Westland F7/30 had to be flown cautiously, as stretch in the cables had caused overbalance in the ailerons.

1935
RAF Display
The 1935 Display was held on 29 June. Since 1930 Air Commodore B.C.H. Drew had been the secretary of the display and everything went like clockwork, but with the usual known aircraft, the Harts, Audaxes, Demons, Ospreys and the Autogiro. A novelty event was a demonstration by an instructor and pupil flying an Avro Tutor in crazily clambering flight, ending in sudden impact with the ground. The machine collapsed with drooping wings, but a fire tender was at hand in seconds and covered the aircraft in foam. The crew was rescued uninjured.

By 1935 the display had settled down to a well-rehearsed spectacular, if somewhat routine, performance. To report the event would be to repeat reports of previous years if one excepts the novel ones just described. Only seven of the fourteen aircraft in the New Types Park were flown. They were the Gloster Gladiator, Hawker Pegasus-powered G.4/31, the Handley Page HP47and the Vickers GP biplane carrying a torpedo. Then there was the Avro 652, which was being produced as the Avro Anson, the massive AW23 bomber-transport that first flew on 4 June, and the Supermarine Seagull, renamed the Walrus. The Vickers GP monoplane did not fly, nor did the Bristol Type 130 twin-engined high-wing bomber-transport. The latter had only had its maiden flight a week earlier, piloted by Uwins. There should have been a radio-controlled version of the Tiger Moth called the Queen Bee developed by the RAE as a flying target for naval gunnery. Some wag remarked that someone at Farnborough must have pushed the right buttons for it to taxi out of the 'New Types' park on its own to fly away. Another aircraft that should have been there was the Pterodactyl V, but both its test pilot and Flight Lieutenant Stainforth, of Schneider Trophy fame, succumbed to influenza. But at least the hitherto scarlet-painted Comet was there in silver and RAF tricolour.

SBAC Show

On 1 July numerous demonstration aircraft and several prototypes arrived at Hendon for the SBAC Show. Chris Staniland flew the Fairey multi-gun Fantome with his usual high artistry and verve. The fuel system for the Hawker Super Fury, flown by George Bulman, had been arranged for inverted flying, which allowed him to make upward rolls and steep inverted climbs. Among the civilian aircraft displayed was British Aircraft's Eagle cabin monoplane, which had a retractable undercarriage. This was a significant development, since the drag created by a fixed undercarriage would be eliminated and streamlining of aircraft would take on a new meaning. There was also the twin-engined Short Scion with Pobjoy engines, the Saunders-Roe Cloud amphibian, the Airspeed Envoy and Courier, the new Monospar ST-25, the Percival Gull and the latest version of the Mew Gull, which had landing flaps and a longer fuselage. Representatives from forty-seven countries were also able to witness displays of British equipment in one of the hangars, some of whom commented on the absence of Miles aircraft. Miles was, in 1935, the second largest producer of light aircraft in the country. The explanation given was that the strict rules of the Society of British Aircraft Constructors forbade companies that were not members to take part.

1936
RAF Display
The 1936 Display featured a 'live' exhibition of historic aircraft, which began with a replica of the 'Wright Flyer' under power. It had to be mounted on a tricycle trolley to enable the aircraft to be taxied. There was a graceful Antoinette, which had to be towed because of an unserviceable engine, an Anzani-powered Blériot XI that taxied under power but was not fully airworthy, and a khaki-painted 'Horace' Farman flown by Squadron Leader D.V. Carnegie. An Anzani-powered white Caudron was flown by Squadron Leader H.A. Hamersley of Avro fame, and a Clergy engine powered a Sopwith triplane flown by Flight Lieutenant N.R. Buckle, who was the event organizer. There was a halo of blue smoke surrounding a Camel flown by its owner, R.O. Shuttleworth, an SE5A with the wartime markings of No. 60 Squadron was flown by Flight Lieutenant J. Hawtrey and a Bristol Fighter was flown by its owner, Flying Officer N. Tangye, RAFO.

The whole episode almost overshadowed the main event from the New Types Park, the pale-coloured ice-smooth Spitfire. Its elliptical wings were in sharp contrast to the square wing-tips of the vicious-looking Vickers Venom that followed. While the Spitfire had a fixed-pitch wooden propeller, the radial-engined Venom had a two-speed DH Hamilton, thanks to the persuasion of Roy Fedden. There was a spectacular slow roll of a Heyford bomber after its pilot had carried out a mock bombing attack, three Gauntlets carried out an aerobatic display tied together, while Flight Lieutenant Harry Broadhurst carried out aerobatics with his voice being broadcast as he described to the crowd each manoeuvre in turn. There was the usual end-of-display climax, this time involving a power station. This went up with a bang, leaving a huge column of smoke

SBAC Display
The SBAC Display, which took place on Monday 29 June 1936, was attended by foreign diplomats and technicians. The Blenheim had had its maiden flight on 25 June and was still too secret to show. The Wellington did not turn

up, but the Spitfire, flown by Mutt Summers, did. The qualities of the Blackburn Shark were shown off by Flight Lieutenant A.M. Blake and the agility of the Whitley bomber was demonstrated by Mr C.K. Turner-Hughes. To the amusement of visitors the Battle was announced as the only Fairey aircraft that could fly, when what the announcer really meant was that it would not be accompanied by the other Fairey biplanes. The Hurricane, flown by George Bulman, performed rolls and loops, and a Gladiator fighter with enclosed cockpit put on an excellent aerobatic display. While the new Lysander Army Cooperation aircraft did not perform aerobatics, it did impress the crowd with its ability to slot hang and take off and land in a space the size of a football pitch.

EMPIRE AIR DAYS
The RAF Displays had been such a success in the inter-war years because they kept the RAF in the forefront of the public mind, but they also kept the public abreast of developments in aircraft design, construction and performance. Be that as it may, the RAF Display had served its purpose, and the Display of 1937 was to be the last. From 1934, running in tandem with the Display, would be the Empire Air Days. These were inspired by the new Chairman of the Air League, Air Commodore Chamier. Having the one annual display at Hendon tended to restrict the number to people within easy reach of London, and there was, in any case, an absolute limit to the number of people who could gain admission to the airfield. Having both military and civilian airfields open to the public around the country vastly increased the number of people who could enjoy the spectacle of aerobatics and see military and civil aircraft, hangars, workshops and barracks at close quarters. The King and Queen, who might have gone to Hendon, were thus able to travel the short distance from Sandringham to Bircham Newton in Norfolk to visit Nos 35 and 207 Bomber Squadrons. The commanding officer of Bircham Newton at the time was Wing Commander Raymond Collishaw, the wartime air ace and squadron commander in southern Russia during their civil war.

In all, 82,000 people visited thirty-nine RAF and FAA aerodromes and maritime bases on 24 May 1934. Among the civil aerodromes Croydon was successful in attracting 4,000 visitors, and there was very good attendance at other civil fields. There were plenty of joy riders and every type of civil aircraft was on display. There were those who were afraid that international spies would take advantage of these air days to find out vital things about the RAF that should remain secret, but it was the Pacifists who created a stir by distributing leaflets asserting that the RAF was promoted by capitalists whose money was invested in the production of armaments. By attending the various displays, they said, the public were helping to destroy disarmament and peace.

The Jubilee Review – Mildenhall, Suffolk

The Silver Jubilee of the reign of King George V was celebrated in many ways. The Royal Air Force marked the occasion with a review of the service on 6 July at RAF Mildenhall in Suffolk. His Majesty arrived by road at 11.20 hours, accompanied by Air Chief Marshal the Prince of Wales, Air Vice-Marshal the Duke of York and Sir Philip Cunliffe-Lister. The Royal party was received by the Lord Lieutenant of Suffolk. After the King had inspected a guard of honour, he toured the ranks of aeroplanes in an open Rolls-Royce. Three hundred and fifty aircraft were marshalled in a huge eight-rank chevron, but it was a display of obsolete aeroplanes. Only four years were to elapse before the commencement of the Second World War, yet not one monoplane fighter was on show. In fact there was still a biplane fighter to come that was too late for the show, and that was the Gloster Gauntlet, with a top speed of 231 mph. When the massed squadrons flew over the airfield it was a stately procession, with the Heyfords flying at 98 mph, and the Harts and eighty-one mixed fighters passing at a slightly higher speed of 115 mph.

AIRCRAFT TEST FLYING – A & AEE MARTLESHAM AND MAEE FELIXSTOWE
AIRCRAFT AND ARMAMENT EXPERIMENTAL ESTABLISHMENT
Armament testing

Armament testing during the 1920s concentrated on the two standard aircraft weapons of the RAF, the Vickers and Lewis guns. As it happens, neither was British. Two Americans, Colonel Lewis and Hiram Maxim, designer of the Vickers gun, gave us these weapons. There were also some experiments with the Coventry Ordnance Weapon, which fired a 37 mm round, but it was not adopted by the RAF. During a decade when economy was the watch-word it made sense to arm prototypes with 'left-over' stocks of weapons from the Great War. The problem was that because these two guns, shown in the accompanying photographs, were originally army weapons, the rounds fired from the aircraft were slowed down in the slipstream of the aircraft and slimmer rounds had to be produced.

The gun that would be fitted to the eight-gun fighter was to be the 0.303 in. Browning, but, as described in

The Lewis gun.

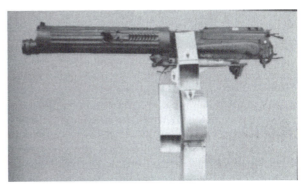

The Vickers machine-gun.

Chapter 5, these had to be mounted in the wings. Until 1935 a fighter's guns were mounted on the fuselage either side of the centre line. A light bomber of the period would have an additional gun, the Lewis gun mounted on a Scarff ring. Pilots both in the years of the Great War and in the 1920s, wanted to be able to clear a stoppage in their guns, which were fired by means of a Bowden cable. What the designers had to come up with was a gun with a high rate of fire and one that was going to have to be sited well away from the pilot's cockpit. Three things were required of the Browning: one was proved reliability to allay the fears of fighter pilots who could no longer clear stoppages in flight; two was storage for a great deal of ammunition in a manner that would not give rise to stoppages when the rounds were fed into the breech; and three was a means of firing the weapon when cables could no longer be fed from the cockpit to the firing mechanism on the weapon.

It fell to No. 15 Squadron at Martlesham to test a new pneumatic firing gear devised by engineers from Messrs Dunlop. The following is a test of this device with the Browning guns fitted to the Gauntlet fighter. Of equal importance in the development of bombers was the necessity of providing turrets to protect gunners from the slipstream in faster aircraft. The second test in this section relates to the testing of a rotating gun turret fitted to an Overstrand bomber.

PNEUMATIC FIRING GEAR (REPORT NO. M/ARM/449/1 DATED DECEMBER 1935)
Introduction

Tests with pneumatic firing controls in a Gauntlet aircraft equipped with two Browning guns have been conducted in accordance with Air Ministry letter 365941/34/R.Arm.1 HSVT dated 30 September 1935. Three trials were undertaken before the Air Staff requirements concerning the duration of fire were received, but the last two trials were made in accordance with these requirements, which demanded an average of seven bursts in seven seconds.

Description

The aircraft is equipped with a standard compressor driven by the engine which supplies air to two bottles. One bottle is coupled to the pneumatic firing gear and the wheel brakes, the other is used for engine starting. The two bottles can be interconnected by opening a hand valve which is accessible to the pilot, but throughout these trials the air for the firing gear was drawn from one bottle only. A pipe-line of $1/8''$ internal diameter runs from the air bottle to a firing button on the ring-handle of the control column. A similar pipe-line runs from the firing button to a box from which it branches to the reservoir base of the synchronizing gear and to each gun. At the reservoir base two spring-loaded plungers are fitted which operate the ball valves. Under each gun a spring-loaded plunger operates a sear in the bolt frame which holds the bolt to the rear. Although the actual firing of the gun by means of the synchronizing gear is done when the breech is fully closed, it has been found necessary to retain the bolt to the rear when firing is not in progress in order to accelerate cooling. The firing button has a knurled ring by means of which the button can be locked in the 'safe' position when not required for firing.

Operation

When the gun is not being fired, the pipe-lines to the synchronizing gear and sear-plungers are at atmospheric pressure. On pressing the button, these pipe-lines are connected with the compressed air system and the plungers are operated. On releasing the button, the compressed air in these pipe-lines returns to normal atmospheric pressure through exhaust holes in the plunger of the button itself. When the system is put under pressure, the bolt is released and travels forward to close the breech. During this period, the synchronizing gear is stopped, owing to its operating plunger having the stronger return spring. This action ensures that the bolt is held in the rear position with the breech open.

Trials and results

Tests were carried out at heights above 30,000 ft at temperatures between –40°C and –52°C. In addition to these tests, fourteen flights were carried out at low altitudes during trials of the Browning gun installation in the aircraft. The firing gear worked satisfactorily in all instances. During the initial trials it was found most difficult to read the air pressure gauge as positioned by the aircraft manufacturers. This feature was represented to Messrs Dunlop, who with the approval of R.D.Arm.1 arranged for the supply of an additional pressure gauge which was conveniently situated. After the first trial it was suspected that the spring of the sear-plunger was too strong and so reduced the number of successive bursts. The firm supplied a weaker spring, which was fitted for the last two tests and proved satisfactory. It was noticed during trials that unless the press button was rapidly operated, a leak occurred from the bottles through the 'atmospheric return holes'. As the tendency of any pilot is to take the first pressure of his trigger when he is bringing his sights on to the target, and to apply the second pressure of his trigger when his sights are properly aligned, this tendency to leak an application of first pressure may considerably deplete the supply of air. It is understood that the makers (Messrs Dunlop) are already considering the design of this button to overcome this handicap. The U-packing washers on the plungers operating the gun sears are located by means of a nut and spring-washer, and it was found that this nut slackened, causing leakage. A locking device is therefore required in addition to, or in lieu of, the spring-washer supplied. The comparative failure of the first test led to the supposition, based on experience with the automatic pilot, that snow and ice might be forming in the air system and so choking the pipe-lines. No further instances of this nature occurred although on the last test the bottle was deliberately filled with damp air during a fog and the test subsequently done at 32,000 ft, when the equipment worked satisfactorily. It is considered, however, that prolonged service trials will be necessary to establish freedom from such possibility. It was discovered that, although the air pressure on the ground was 200 lb per sq. in., this pressure had dropped considerably at the test height due to contraction. The compressor was unable to restore it. The loss of pressure depended on the time which elapsed between taking aim and firing, as well as on the decrease in temperature. Although this loss did not affect the operation of the gear, it is a feature which should be kept under observation during service trials. All pilots reported favourably on the instantaneous response of this system of firing and its definite superiority over the Bowden wire method.

Conclusions

The pneumatic firing installation as installed in the Gauntlet will fulfil the Air Staff requirements in that particular aircraft and its adoption for service trials is recommended. During such trials the following points should receive special attention:

(a) Possibility of freezing of the pipe lines.
(b) Pressure drop due to contraction of the air in the bottle.
(c) Recuperation from this loss by the compressor.

An improved locking device is necessary on the nut of the plunger which operates the rear sear.

INTERIM REPORT ON THE POWER-OPERATED FRONT GUN TURRET OF THE OVERSTRAND BOMBER

(Source: A & AEE Report No. M/Arm/387/1/Int.1, dated February 1934)

This report has been prepared in response to RDAI letter 239030/33 dated 24.1.34. While the tests so far made are not sufficiently extensive for a final report to be rendered, the following information can be given.

1. *Turret rotating mechanism* Difficulty has been experienced due to the reducing valve sticking. A new type of valve has been provided by the makers but has not yet been tested. The period of continuous operation of the turret is considered insufficient. It is probable that an increase of this period will be recommended after further experience has been obtained. No great difficulty is anticipated in achieving this by increasing the capacity of the compressed air reservoirs and/or adding a second compressor. The speed of rotation from ahead to the beam is much greater than vice versa. It is probable that the provision of a means for maintaining a constant speed of rotation in both directions will be recommended.

2. *Elevating arm mechanism* This has been improved by modifications made by the makers. It is desirable that the range of upward and downward travel of the seat should be increased in order to permit the gunner to fire at greater angles of depression and elevation without unfastening his thigh straps. Alternatively the requirement might be met by increasing the radius of the elevating arm if and when the diameter of the turret is increased.

3. *Free secondary traverse* The amount of free secondary traverse of the gun before the operating valves start to open has been increased from 7 deg. to 9 deg. on each side of the central. A cinema camera has been fitted to the gun and the optimum amount of free traverse and the degree of sensitivity required of the valves is being investigated.

4. *Visibility and comfort* On first experience gunners complain of a confined feeling and distraction of the eye by the turret framework, but soon become accustomed to these conditions. Visibility is satisfactory except under ice-forming conditions. The turret is cramped for gunners of average size. An increase in the size of the turret is most desirable, particularly at its mid-height.

5. *Field of fire* Drawing No. EA.316 shows the field of fire in Sidestrand J.9186. Drawing No. EA.317 shows the field of fire from a ring-mounting in Sidestrand J.7938. It is emphasized that both these drawings show the theoretical fields and that practically the whole of the theoretical field of fire is realized in practice with the turret due to screening, whereas effective fire cannot be brought to bear to the beam and downwards from the ring-mounting at fighting speed due to air pressure. It is suggested that any comparison should be made on this basis. Drawing No. EA.318 shows the field of fire in Sidestrands J.9186 and J.7938 from the rear cockpit, and indicates that a larger screen provided in J.9186 does not reduce the field of fire.

6. *Gun sights and sighting* No mechanical sight has been supplied, but promising scores have been obtained with a Norman vane sight when firing under favourable conditions. It is impossible to use the sight as the gun approaches maximum elevation as the gunner cannot get his head back far enough while still strapped to the seat to align his eye with the sights. This is not considered to be a serious disadvantage as it is improbable that it will be necessary to use the gun near the maximum elevation and because this area can be commanded by the rear gun.

7. *Screening and gun fumes* The screening is now satisfactory and represents a decided advance on the protection obtained with the open ring. The 'Zipp' cover of the slot has been extended upward about 12" and the top of the turret has been closed for the reason stated in paragraph 5. above. No discomfort is experienced from gun fumes.

8. *Azimuth and bomb-release control* The means provided for withdrawing the flexible azimuth from the turret to the stowed position must be improved. The layout of the electrical bomb-release gear will probably require modification. The electrical bomb-release and inter-communication brush contacts on the slip-ring at the base of the turret have given trouble. The makers proposed to increase the force of the springs

on these contacts. The jettison switch performs two functions:

(a) To enable all bombs to be jettisoned in case of emergency.
(b) Provides an indicating light which shows when the bomb selector switch is operated and goes out when the bomb leaves the carrier.

As regards (a), it is considered unnecessary to place the jettison switch inside the turret provided that it is duplicated in the pilot's cockpit and efficient inter-communication is provided between the bomb aimer and pilot. As regards (b), it is considered most desirable for the indicating light to be situated within the bomb aimer's field of view when actually using the bomb-sight. In order to achieve this, it will be necessary to place the indicating light inside the turret.

8. *Maintenance, gun stoppages and parachutes* The turret has required very little maintenance during the trials so far made. It is desirable that the turret entrance doors should be redesigned to make them more accessible. The gun magazine fouls the vertical members on either side of the gun slot, causing stoppages when firing just below the horizontal and utilizing the free movement allowed by the gun mounting in the vertical plane and when using the secondary traverse to operate the valves. This is considered to be the most serious defect so far detected as it cannot be overcome by mounting the gun further inboard. As far as can be seen the only means of overcoming this difficulty is by fitting an alternative type of gun or increasing the diameter of the turret at its mid-height. It is considered that stowage for the gunner's parachute should be provided in the turret, as the quickest means of exit in emergency would be to rotate the entrance door forward and drop through the doors. The screening of the pilot and rear gunner is satisfactory except that sludge forms on the screens under ice-forming conditions.

9. *Conclusions* This is the first power-operated turret to undergo tests at this Establishment. As an initial design it is considered to be so promising that it should be developed. Gunners quickly become accustomed to the controls and can do good shooting from the turret. The results of tests to date indicate all criticisms can be met by modifications which can be incorporated easily except in regard to the increase of the diameter of the turret at its mid-height to prevent gun stoppages. This, or another solution of the problem, is considered to be essential. An increase in the size of the turret is also considered desirable in order to provide greater freedom for the gunner, stowage for the gunner's oxygen equipment and stowage for the gunner's parachute.

TRIALS ON THE WESTLAND TYPE A.39/34 K.6127 WESTLAND LYSANDER

(Source: A & AEE Reference M/4497/15 – AT.114 Report No. M/694/Int.1, dated July 1936)

This trial relates to one of the most famous aircraft of the Second World War, test-flown by the chief test pilot of Westland Aircraft, Harald Penrose, whose published works of the aircraft industry during the inter-war years have been so valuable in the compilation of this encyclopedia. The Lysander had a short landing and take-off capability, which made it eminently suited for Army Cooperation work and for the landing and retrieval of British agents working in occupied Europe during World War II.

Test flying by pilots of No. 22 Squadron was a hazardous business when aircraft handling often disclosed defects for which company modifications would be required. The risk for the company test pilots, like Penrose, was in fact that much greater, since they had to make that maiden flight, placing complete trust in the designers. Volume I, for example, tells of the maiden flight of the Westland Dreadnought, which cost the test pilot, Stuart Keep, the loss of his legs when the aircraft crashed on take-off. The following paragraph illustrates the potential hazards encountered on that first flight.

Penrose began taxiing trials on 10 June 1936 before the wings were removed from the aircraft for transit by road to the grass airfield at Boscombe Down. There, on 15 June, he made the maiden flight. He recalls the first take-off . . . 'heading into a gentle west wind, the throttle was steadily opened; already the tip slats were fully out and within the first few yards the root slats pulled forward and partly lowered the interconnecting flaps. In less than 150 yards the machine was climbing away.' During the flight Penrose found the controls a little heavy and that the aircraft was unstable. On landing he ran out of elevator ten feet above the ground. Since the tailplane was not adjustable Penrose had to use the engine to help flatten out the glide. Back in the workshop a wide strip had to be added to the trailing edge of the elevator to increase the chord, but this made little difference to the handling characteristics. Even the wind-tunnel tests did

Prototype Lysander 6127.

not predict the excessive nose-down trim with the slats and flaps fully deployed.

The problems with the tailplane persisted, and Penrose wanted a variable-incidence tailplane, but this introduced the danger that when full throttle was applied in an overshoot the aircraft pitched upwards. He had to use minimum power to maintain flying speed, and only by resetting the tailplane to neutral could an overshoot be accomplished without fear of stalling. These matters were of considerable concern to Penrose, and he was loath to send it to Martlesham in that condition, but was overruled by Westland's boss Petter and the production staff. Further modification would delay production by six months, and the firm needed the contract to build the Lysander; handing over a prototype to the A & AEE was a vital first step. It was felt that a notice in the cockpit warning pilots of this hazard when overshooting should suffice. These problems may be compared with the test flying in the report that follows:

MARTLESHAM TRIALS REPORT ON THE LYSANDER
Introduction
Brief handling and performance trials have been done on the above. Owing to the short time available these results are provisional and subject to confirmation in the final report. The trials have been done at the following loadings and position of centre of gravity:

Weight	Centre of Gravity Position
5,731 lb	9.7" forward of datum
5,663 lb	8.5" forward of datum
5,440 lb	12.2" forward of datum

Ailerons
On the ground the aileron control works freely and full movement of the control column can be obtained when the pilot is in the cockpit. There is slight but not excessive play. In the air the aileron control is light under all conditions of flight up to maximum level speed. The response is quick and the control is most effective. Heaviness of control increases very slightly with the increase of speed. In general the aileron control is extremely pleasant to handle and no improvement can be suggested. No aileron bias gear was fitted.

Rudder
On the ground the rudder control works freely and without play. Full movement of the rudder bar, which is adjustable, can be obtained by all pilots. In the air the rudder is light under all conditions of flight, especially at high speeds. The response is very quick at high speeds, becoming slightly slower as speed is decreased down to the stall. Under all conditions the rudder is effective. Although the heaviness of the rudder control does increase slightly with the increase in speed, it is remarkably light at high speed, and would be improved if it were made slightly heavier to harmonize with the other controls. Rudder bias control was not fitted, and although the rudder control is extremely light such a fitting is considered desirable as the aircraft has a consistent tendency to swing to the right.

Elevators
On the ground the elevator control operates freely and allows full movement of the control column and there is only very slight play. In the air at slow speeds, that is on the glide below 70 mph, at the stall and when landing the elevator control is heavy. Response is slow and is not very effective. Under all conditions of flight, above 70 mph the control is light and effective with a quick response, and at maximum level speed the control is almost too effective. Heaviness of control increases slightly with increase of speed. There is rocking of the control column fore and aft at cruising speed and up to maximum level speed, this is also noticeable in tight turns. Steps should be taken to eliminate this. There does not seem to be quite enough fore and aft range on the control column. When landing, the control column is always in the fully back position before touching down when the aircraft is trimmed fully aft, and although it is easy to do three-point landings, the pilot has the impression that it would be better if there were a little more movement allowed for the control column. The elevator control is not sufficiently powerful to keep the nose down if the engine is opened up fully with the aircraft trimmed for landing. The fact that the control column is hard up against the forward stop if the engine is opened up with the aircraft trimmed for landing, indicates the need for more forward movement of the control column.

Tail trimming gear
The tail trimming gear does not slip and is reasonably effective. However it is rather stiff and takes a long time (about 13 seconds) to get full movement. The range of the tail trimming gear is insufficient both forward and aft to trim 'hands off' over the whole centre of gravity range.

TAIL SETTING

Loading	Engine on			Engine off
	Climbing at best speed	Maximum level flight	Specification cruising speed	Best approach speed
Full Load with				
Corresponding CG	2	$1^1/_2$	2	14 (Max)
CG Forward	4	2	$2^1/_2$	14 (Max)
CG Aft	Forward 0	4	6	13

Engine and flap controls and brakes

The engine controls are quite satisfactory and work easily without play or slip. The flap gear is automatic and not controlled by the pilot. The flaps are effective and their automatic operation is a great advantage. A simple device operated by the pilot is fitted for locking the flaps and inner slots in any position on this experimental aircraft, but it is not considered to be necessary in this particular case and could be deleted. The brakes work on the Dunlop system, being hand operated with a differential action on the rudder bar. They are easy to operate and very effective, and they give a smooth and progressive action. No improvement can be suggested.

FLYING QUALITIES OF THE LYSANDER
Lateral stability

Laterally the aeroplane is neutrally stable under all conditions of flight. It has been put through the tests laid down in ADM.293 with the following results:

(a) *At most aft position of centre of gravity at full typical service loading* Under the first test at 55mph the aeroplane sinks, with the speed decreasing until 38mph when the nose appears to remain steady. The speed then increases slightly to 42mph and the aeroplane remains in a stalled glide, and it is always controllable with no tendency to spin. Under the second test when the aileron is applied to unbank, the wing comes up and the aeroplane assumes an even keel – both to the left and right. There is no tendency to spin or spiral. Under the third test both to left and to right the aeroplane goes into a slow shallow spiral with the speed increasing to approximately 78mph.

(b) *Loading for centre of gravity at forward limit and flaps down* Under the first test the ASI [Air Speed Indicator] settles down to a reading of 40 mph and the aeroplane sinks very slightly right wing low. There is no tendency to flick into a spin. Considerable force has to be used to keep the control column fully back and it is doubtful whether a fully stalled condition is ever reached. Under a second test the ASI was gradually reduced to 42 mph and when the control column was moved to unbank the

aeroplane levelled up at once and there was no tendency to spin or spiral. Under the third test no spin develops and the aeroplane was not thought to be fully stalled, this manoeuvre was repeated the nose being thrown up by pulling back the control at an ASI well above normal gliding speed. Full rudder was then applied at an ASI reading of approximately 30 mph. The aeroplane responded as before. On repeating this test with the tail adjusting gear set for maximum level flight, a spiral developed with the ASI rising to 80 mph.

(c) *Loading for centre of gravity at aft limit* The results for all three tests at this loading were identical to those obtained when the aeroplane was loaded at normal centre of gravity.

Directional stability

Directional stability is not easy to assess as no rudder bias is fitted, and the aeroplane has a tendency to swing to starboard under all conditions of flight, but if left rudder is applied and then released, the aeroplane will return fairly rapidly to a straight flight path, and then swing round to the right. The directional stability is the same with the engine on or off.

Longitudinal stability, slots and characteristics at the stall

There is slight hunting which involves corresponding movement of the control column at speeds of 130 mph and above, but the aeroplane may be said to be reasonably stable in this plane. If the control column is pushed forward and then released the aircraft will return to a straight flight path but rather slowly. On the glide there is no hunting and the return to straight flight path after disturbances of the control column is approximately the same as when the engine is on. The longitudinal stability is the same for all loadings, the centre of gravity range being small. The slots are effective and give good lateral control at the stall. The outer slots start to open at 90 mph and the inner slots at 80 mph. The outer slots are fully open at 60 mph and the inner slots at 38 mph. The aircraft can be held in a stalled glide at any loading down to 40 mph ASI. It is exceptionally free from any vice at the stall or at the minimum speed at which it can be flown.

Landings and take-offs

Take-off at all loads is simple and straightforward and there is no tendency to swing. As mentioned above, three-point landings can be made with ease but the elevator control feels insufficient. If the engine is opened up full with the aeroplane trimmed for landing, it will stall even with the control column hard up against the forward stop, unless the trim is corrected on the tail-adjusting gear.

Sideslipping and ground handling

The aeroplane is easy to sideslip at small angles, but if a steep sideslip is attempted the control column comes up against the forward stop. The aeroplane is easy to handle on the ground in winds up to 30 mph.

The undercarriage

The undercarriage is of the internally sprung wheel type and the shock-absorbing qualities are excellent. There is

The characteristic fixed undercarriage with spatted wheels and Dowty internally sprung wheel. This was connected to the fuselage by a single cantilever undercarriage. The photograph below shows the square-section 'hairpin' extrusion, its attachment stirrups and the wing strut attachment.

too much recoil on the tail wheel which causes tail bouncing. The tail wheel is friction damped and it is possible that the bouncing may be cured by fitting oleo damping.

Flying view and cockpit comfort

Flying view is very good forward and sideways. Neither engine of variable-pitch airscrew has been throwing oil onto the windscreen during tests. In rain vision was still good. The view backwards is slightly obstructed. There is plenty of room in the cockpit but it is difficult to enter and leave. A ladder has to be used as a safety precaution against entering between the airscrew and the cockpit. It is understood that the firm are modifying the method of entry to avoid this. Both cockpits [Prototypes K.6127 and 6128] are somewhat noisy, probably owing to drumming inside the cockpit covers. The cockpit is very warm, no heating being required at a temperature of 22°C.

Instruments and intercommunication

The compass is clearly visible, but the needle is unstable in flight. All flying and engine instruments are well arranged and easily read by the pilot. In the rear [observer's] cockpit, intercommunication is good at all speeds being better with the hood closed. In the front [pilot's] cockpit intercommunication is poor below 120 mph and impossible above that speed with the hood either open or closed. A greatly improved audibility in the pilot's cockpit is essential. It is considered that the rear cockpit would be good for the reception of either R/T or W/T.

Lysander contract and hot weather trials

The Air Ministry issued a production contract for 169 Lysander Mk Is to AM Spec. A36/36, and this paved the way for the largest and longest-running production programme of any fixed-wing Westland-designed aircraft. Development flying continued with the two prototypes, and the A & AEE pilots accepted the aircraft

K.6128 at Miranshah.

in spite of the problems with the unmodified tail units. In service there would be scores of crashes, but the other outstanding qualities of this aircraft meant that this was something that pilots would have to live with. There were other outstanding military aircraft that had potentially hazardous attributes; the German Me109 could kill the unwary pilot. Squadron Leader Collings, a Martlesham test pilot who flew K.6128, was awarded the Air Force Cross for not abandoning the aircraft when all the fabric on the top surface of the wing began to rip and tear off in the slipstream after pulling out of a high-speed dive. During early 1938, K.6128 was flown out to the base of No. 5 Squadron at Miranshah in Waziristan for some successful tropical and general field trials. Deliveries to RAF squadrons began on 15 May 1938 when the Lysander I replaced the Atlas and Audax aircraft on No. 16 Squadron at Old Sarum.

MARINE AIRCAFT EXPERIMENTAL ESTABLISHMENT

Introduction

The first example of the work of the MAEE, Felixstowe, for the period 1933 to 1936 has been chosen because of its unusual character. The circular take-off pattern for a flying-boat has had its land-based counterpart when, some years ago in the United States, trials were made with a circular runway that would provide aircraft, both landing and taking off, with an infinite runway. There are obvious advantages to be gained from circular patterns, but equally obvious disadvantages, for an aircraft approaching a conventional runway has a flare-path and gooseneck, which is very important in judging height and correct rate of descent to remain on the correct glide-path. A fixed runway also keeps the aircraft pointed into the prevailing wind. Both the land and maritime versions of circular take-off and landing patterns were not, in the end, adopted. Such experiments are nevertheless of interest for the thinking of the time, since in this case it was anticipated that take-offs and landings might have to be made by flying-boats in restricted waters.

CIRCULAR TAKE-OFF RUNS ON A FLYING-BOAT, MAEE
Report F/Res/97, dated August 1936

Purpose of the tests

The Air Staff required the MAEE to investigate the possibility of take-offs of flying-boats on an approximately circular path. These tests were to be carried out on a Scapa and a Stranraer flying-boat, with further tests to follow if the original ones bore fruit.

Operational requirements

Since flying-boats might, sometimes, be required to take off in restricted waters, the length of the normal take-off run might exceed the length of run available. If this was practicable it was necessary to know what differences there would be in length of the take-off run given different aircraft loads.

Conduct of tests

The tests on the Scapa were made at two weights, 14,000 and 17,600 lb, and the Stranraer tests at a weight of 15,300 lb. The Stranraer was to have undertaken tests at a greater weight, but the aircraft was allotted to other duties before tests were complete. Runs were to alternate at the different weights, i.e. circular and linear take-offs and a series of tests comprised eight runs. The path of the flying-boats was measured from shore stations and photographed from the air. Cinema pictures of the Scapa take-offs were also taken from the shore to illustrate the manoeuvre pictorially. Finally the tests were made on a calm sea in light winds parallel to the shore. Both flying-boats were unequal-span biplanes with wingtip floats and hulls of a conventional design. Each was powered by two engines, the Scapa with the Kestrel III.MS and the Stranraer with the Pegasus III, and they were mounted immediately below the top wings and disposed on either side of the plane of symmetry.

A number of pictures were taken of three stages in the take-off run, and these are shown in the diagrams on the next page. In the accompanying diagram the time and speeds reached at each stage are shown. The take-off was started beam to the wind, and the pilot opened the throttle on the outer (port) engine to half throttle and turned into wind using the ailerons to hold down the inner (starboard) wingtip as much as possible. The turn was continued using the rudder and the throttle controls, the starboard engine running considerably more slowly than the port engine. As the speed increased, the centrifugal forces caused the boat to skid outwards and to roll over on to the wingtip float. The most difficult stage was when the flying-boat reached Point C on the diagram. The centrifugal force was considerable and a wall of water had built up. The conditions remained nearly the same until just Stage D was reached, when both engines were opened up to full throttle, the rudder was centralized and the path straightened. The air speed was measured by a sensitive low-reading air speed indicator connected to a pressure head mounted on an outrigger fitted to the bow of the flying-boat. The total time and take-off speeds only were recorded on the other tests.

The normal straight take-offs were made by first turning the flying-boat into wind with engines fully throttled, then opening up as quickly as possible to full throttle and taking off on a straight path. The path was obtained by taking plane table bearings from two shore stations 375 yards apart. The bearings were taken at the start and the finish of each run and tangentially to the flying-boat's course when describing the curved course. The bearings so obtained were plotted, thus giving the start and finish of the runs. The path described by the flying-boat during the complete manoeuvre was then drawn with the assistance of the tangential bearings. A similar shore method was adopted for measuring the normal straight take-offs, plane table bearings being

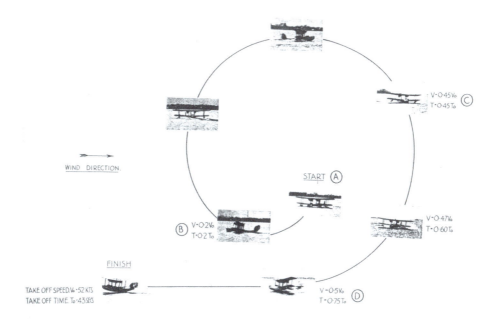

WIND DIRECTION.

START Ⓐ

Ⓒ V·0·45V₀
T·0·45T₀

Ⓑ V·0·2V₀
T·0·2T₀

V·0·47V₀
T·0·60T₀

FINISH

TAKE OFF SPEED V₀ ·52 KTS
TAKE OFF TIME T₀ ·43 SECS

V·0·5V₀
T·0·75T₀ Ⓓ

PICTORIAL REPRESENTATION OF A CIRCULAR TAKE OFF.
SCAPA — 14000 LB.

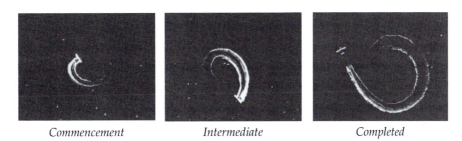

Commencement   *Intermediate*   *Completed*

Circular take-offs with Scapa flying-boat.

taken at the start and finish of the runs. The take-off time and air speed were observed from the flying-boats.

Results of the tests

The mean of the results are given in the table below. Two distances were taken for the circular take-offs, one the overall distance measured parallel to the wind direction and the other the maximum ordinate. These are referred to as distances A and B in Table I.

Considering the light-load take-offs of both flying-boats, the percentage reduction in distances A and B compared with straight-line take-offs is about 40% and 25% respectively. These values are approximately halved for the results obtained on the Scapa with the weight increased by 25.7%.

TABLE I

Scapa. (Kestrel III.M.S. engines)
Wind Speed: (Mean) 5 Knots   Sea Calm

Weight Lb	Wing Loading	Straight Take-offs		Circular Take-offs				
		Distance Yards (X)	Total Time Secs	Distance Yds (A)	Distance for max.ordinate Yds (B)	Total Time Time Secs	Percentage reduction in distance compared with straight take-off	
							X – A	X - B
14,000	10.87	275	15	163	209	43	41%	24%
17,600	13.65	600	33	462	522	73	23%	13%

<u>TABLE II</u>

Stranraer (Pegasus III. Engines)
Wind Speed: 4 Knots   Sea Calm

15,300	10.50	240	15	149	173	38	38%	28%

Conclusions

The maximum projected distance to take-off by the circular method is not that measured parallel to the wind direction, but is given by an ordinate which makes an angle of about 45% to that line. Taking this distance as the criterion for the run required, the results show that a reduction in take-off run of about 25% can be achieved on the Scapa and Stranraer at light loads, while the tests at heavier load on the Scapa show a reduction of only 13%. The reduction obtainable is limited by the severe loads imposed on the structure during that part of the turn made at about half the take-off speed. Similar tests on other flying-boats are proposed to be done as the opportunity occurs.

THE ABYSSINIAN CRISIS

On 3 October 1935 Mussolini ordered his armed forces to invade Abyssinia. He had made no secret of his determination to expand into Africa with dreams of a revived Italian empire to match that of Imperial Rome. For several years he had been sending labourers to Eritrea and Italian Somaliland, along Abyssinia's southern and north-eastern borders. Hangars, roads and docks had been built in readiness for invasion. On the 10 October a vote was taken in the Assembly of the League of Nations, with fifty nations to one voting to take collective measures against Italy for her aggression. The problem for the League was that anything less than the sternest of measures against Italy would be a signal to Hitler that the organization was not prepared to confront aggression. On the other hand, if the League condemned Italy's actions and used force to evict her armies from Abyssinia Mussolini would be driven into the arms of the German dictator. In the event, only economic sanctions were applied, and Mussolini still allied himself with Hitler in what became known as the Rome–Berlin Axis.

The supplies for the Italian armies had to pass through the Suez Canal to reach Eritrea and Italian Somaliland, so the British government could have denied Italian supply ships passage through the canal. But to have done this would have been tantamount to an act of war, since Italy and Great Britain were not, at that time, belligerent nations. The episode nevertheless created international tension in the region and it was felt sensible to reinforce the RAF presence in the area above the sole squadron at Khormaksar in Aden and the squadrons in Egypt and Palestine. Light-bomber and fighter squadrons were ordered to the region. Some of these aircraft were dismantled and crated and departed Liverpool on 4 October, the day after the Italian invasion, for mobilization had been anticipated. Later three flying-boat squadrons and units of the Fleet Air Arm were added to the British air reinforcement.

Clearly the Air Ministry had covered the entire Mediterranean from Gibraltar to Alexandria. The units in Hal Far, Malta, were only minutes' flying time from Sicily. The Demons of No. 74 Squadron would provide an element of air defence and the torpedo-bomber squadron could intercept shipping leaving the Italian peninsula. The Bulldogs of No. 3 Squadron went to the Sudan to join No. 47, the resident squadron. No. 8 Squadron at Khormaksar was closest to the scene of operations and was joined by one fighter and light-bomber squadron. The Chief of the Air Staff, Sir Edward Ellington, suggested bombing targets in northern Italy from bases in southern France, but no military action was taken. The reinforcing units were nevertheless kept in the area as a precaution, and were not finally stood down until the late summer of 1936. If nothing else, the whole episode was a valuable exercise in rapid reinforcement.

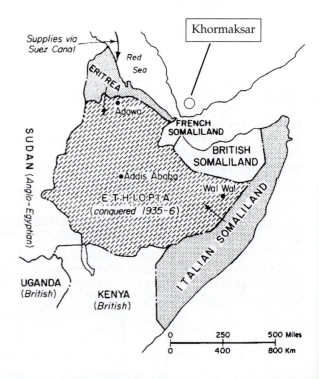

Sqn No./Type/Aircraft	Departed	For	Remarks
3 (F) Bulldog	Kenley 18/10/35	Port Sudan	Returned 28/8/36
12 (LB) Hart	Andover 4/10/35	Khormaksar	" 11/8/36
22 (TB) Vildebeest	Donibristle 10/10/35	Hal Far	" 29/8/36
29 (F) Demon	North Weald 31/10/35	Amiriya	" 12/9/36
33 (LB) Hart	Upper Heyford 4/10/35	Mersah Matruh	Remained in Middle East
35 (LB) Gordon	Bircham Newton 4/10/35	Ed Damar	Return Worthy Down 26/8/36
41 (F) Demon	Northolt 4/10/35	Khormaksar	" Catterick 25/9/36
74 (F) Demon	Formed on board H.M.T. *Neuralia* 3/9/35	Hal Far	" Hornchurch 21/9/36
204 (FB) Scapa	Mount Batten 27/9/35	Aboukir	Returned 5/8/36
210 (FB) London II Stranraer	Felixstowe 28/9/35	Gibraltar	Return Pembroke Dock 7/8/36
230 (FB) Singapore III	Pembroke Dock 24/10/35	Alexandria	Returned 3/8/36

Note: Squadrons departing 4/10/35 are from Liverpool.

A Hart of No. 33 Squadron flying over its home station of Bicester in 1934. The following year the squadron's aircraft moved to Upper Heyford before they were dismantled and crated for shipping from Liverpool on 4 October 1935 to join the other units in the area for reinforcement during the Abyssinian crisis.

Chapter 3
The Prelude to War – 1937 to 1939

Expansion Schemes – The Shadow Factory Scheme – flying training – high altitude flights – RAF Display and Empire Air Days – flying experiences from home RAF Stations – flying and operational – Air Staff management of Expansion - A&AEE Martlesham & MAEE Felixstowe - the threat from Nazi Germany – the Munich crisis – the approach of war -Order of Battle 3rd September 1939.

INTRODUCTION
In recalling historical events there are often popular conceptions and popular misconceptions. It is generally believed that the Munich crisis, of September 1938, gave Britain the year it needed to be ready to meet Hitler's armed forces in battle. In some respects this is true in others it is not. The *Kreigsmarine* was no match for the Royal Navy in capital ships and aircraft carriers. Whilst the German Navy was to enjoy some small success with their surface raiders the capital ships fought an unequal war. Admiral Raeder had planned a sizeable navy for 1945 so it was the Germans who needed the extra preparation time. The U-boats, on the other hand would become a real threat. The Army was preparing to fight a war but it was not the sort of land war that the Germans had in mind. The 'steamroller' of the *Blitzkrieg* was to push the British Expeditionary Force back to the beaches of Dunkirk. The British Army would not enjoy the support of a tactical air force in Europe until 1944 that would be part of the Allied *Blitzkrieg* as the Germans fell back on their own country.

Did the RAF need the extra year? The RAF had begun to rearm in 1934 as soon as it was realised that Hitler posed a real threat so it cannot be said that successive governments in the 1930s had not done all that could be expected. But chasing numbers would not be enough. The mix of aircraft types was important. Given the Air Staff determination to fight an air war of offensive defence there might be enough bombers but would there be enough fighters? If the enemy was to do to Britain what Britain intended to do to the enemy, Britain would need strong fighter defences equal to the threat. If Britain's bomber forces were not to produce an early victory then there might well be a war of attrition. This would mean reserves. The RAF cannot be accused of not providing for reserves both in aircraft and aircrew but when it came to repair and maintenance Chapter 8 will show that the policy was still being worked out as the RAF went to war.

The growing threat from Nazi Germany is examined further. The *Luftwaffe* was sharpening its talons in Spain and the Italian dictator, Mussolini had shown that he could cause trouble in the Mediterranean. For both Britain and France with its far-flung colonial possessions it was not simply a matter of securing the home base but

of allocating air, sea and land forces accordingly. The threat was measured in numbers. Historians have the luxury of knowing what happened when war came and of the fatal flaws in Hitler's personality which led him and his country to defeat. It is easy now to say, as the author does at times, that the German air force was simply not equipped to deal a 'knock out blow' in 1940 but at the time the perceived threat was very real.

As war approached the numbers game became ever more pressing and one expansion scheme followed another as the international situation deteriorated. The lack of readiness of Bomber Command for an offensive strategy was by 1938 only too apparent, not only in not having the right aircraft but in the lack of training of the aircrews on the squadrons and of operational training units for newcomers. The fighter squadrons were only just beginning to receive the Hurricanes in numbers and the Spitfires were to follow. Air Marshal Freeman would use the remaining months of peace to ensure that, not only was the aircraft industry doing all it could to keep up with the *Luftwaffe* in the arms race, but that the right aircraft were being developed to take the war to the enemy. France, Britain's ally in the forthcoming war, was a formidable fighting force on land and at sea, but the French Air Force which had emerged from the Great War as the largest and most powerful in Europe, was to be found wanting when war came. What was not expected, however, was the rapid collapse of the French, which would leave Britain alone to fight Nazi Germany in 1940.

THE EXPANSION SCHEMES
(Source National Archive Document AIR41/8)

Introduction
Expansion plans A & C had been implemented principally as a deterrent to Hitler who was visibly arming Germany. Having shaken off the shackles of the Versailles Treaty, Hitler had made it quite clear that it was unreasonable to expect Germany to be inferior in military strength. He could point to the fact that neither Britain nor France had been prepared to come down to German force levels during the talks at the Geneva Disarmament Conference and so Germany needed parity with the two foremost European powers for the purposes of national security. Hitler had made it clear to

HMG, therefore, that he sought not just parity with Britain but also with France.

Britain's response went beyond deterrence since, by this time, Germany was pulling ahead in numerical terms. France had a first-line strength of some 3,400 aircraft and the RAF had to be expanded significantly just to keep pace with German rearmament, hence Scheme F which was described in Chapter 2. In the wake of Scheme F came the shadow factory scheme. This chapter explores the expansion schemes which followed in the years leading up to the outbreak of World War II. These were Schemes H,J,K,L & M.

There was not simply a need to keep pace with a potential enemy's first-line strength. It was vital to build up an adequate reserve. In air warfare the clash would be immediate, intensive and sustained and the losses heavy. With high expected wastage the Air Staff knew that reserves must be drastically enlarged. It was estimated that a period of several months would elapse before full war production would be possible. When Scheme C was initiated this gap could only be filled by building up reserves sufficient to enable the operational squadrons to sustain their effort until new production had reached the required level. Hence Scheme F which with the shadow factory scheme, permitted not only a substantial increase in first-line strength but also the building up of reserves. The intention had been that the shadow factories should only be utilised when war had actually begun, but by bringing the scheme into operation in peace did permit the building up of reserves before war began. Thus the use of the shadow factories for this purpose was not inconsistent the original intention. Looking back one can see that this was a wise move since, during the Battle of Britain it was not the shortage of aircraft that worried Air Marshal Dowding but the shortage of pilots.

EXPANSION SCHEME H

Lord Swinton preparing to fly with No. 24 Communications Squadron, RAF Hendon.

Both schemes H & J are noteworthy because neither of them actually came into operation. It is useful, nonetheless, to see the thinking that went behind them and the reasons for their replacement with Scheme K. Scheme H of January 1937, was inspired by a speeding up of German rearmament. It was yet another deterrent scheme and a makeshift one. First proposed in an Air Staff Memorandum of 14th January 1937, Scheme H was submitted by Lord Swinton to the Cabinet on the same day. He stated that Britain should not have a striking force inferior to Germany's and that there should be a fighter force capable of meeting a probable attack by that force. Lord Swinton's concern was that possessing a striking force of only 1022 first-line bombers by 1939 was not a sufficient deterrent since Germany's bomber force would by then consist of 1700 machines. He advised that the number of squadrons be increased from 124 (Scheme F) go 145 bringing the number of aircraft up to 2422. But this was to be achieved by a manipulation of the reserves. Scheme H provided for 87 bomber squadrons with 1631 aircraft but 150 of these were to be obtained by drawing, from the reserves, three aircraft for each of the fifty squadrons on the outbreak of war. This meant that the peace-time strength of the bomber force would be only 1481 aircraft. A further 180 aircraft would be obtained by retaining at home, ten of the twelve squadrons which were to form overseas by April 1939. The first-line establishment of these squadrons was raised from 12 to 18 aircraft which was a true increase in strength. But although 198 more bomber aircraft would be added to Britain's first-line strength with the proposal to form eleven new squadrons, this was only to be achieved by robbing the commands abroad of ten squadrons.

The Air Staff was not happy with this situation due to the risks involved and said so in a memorandum. Putting a larger force into the air on the outbreak of hostilities whilst not having the capacity for sustained operations was acceptable only if an early victory over the enemy air forced was achieved. It was much more likely that a war of attrition would ensue when reserves count! As it was the strike force of 1631 aircraft would be inferior to the estimated bomber force of 1700 aircraft. What Scheme H should provide was a British strike force of a size sufficient to deter Germany in 1939. By that time it was expected that, in respect of experienced personnel, Germany would be in a position inferior to Britain. At best Scheme H was temporary expedient to meet a transient situation. Not surprisingly the Cabinet found the Scheme H proposals unacceptable except for the recommendation that thirty new operational stations be acquired.

EXPANSION SCHEME J

Scheme J was proposed in October 1937. It was perhaps the best of schemes put forward but it would have

Hurricane production at Kingston-on-Thames.

involved a forced draft and the mobilisation of industry. The Air Staff had made an appreciation of German intentions and a strengthening of first-line strength to meet operational requirements, both at home and overseas as well as adding to the reserves was part of the plan. It was intended that the RAF at home be increased by thirty squadrons bringing the strength up to 2331 aircraft. The overseas establishment would be 644 aircraft following the addition of seven squadrons. There would also be four additional squadrons totalling 56 aircraft for trade defence. Had this scheme come to fruition there would have been 20 more bomber squadrons than with Scheme F . Unlike Scheme H there would not be any juggling with reserves.

Only the method of calculating the reserves was open to criticism. Reserves on an all-rounded basis would amount to 150% of first-line strength. This was the percentage applied to Scheme F and carried over to Schemes H and J and was based upon the varying rates of wastage for the different types of aircraft e.g., 210% for medium bombers and 110% for fighters. But the overall percentage applied to a force of a certain composition and it had not been reviewed when the ratio of heavy to medium bombers had been altered. The intention was to provide, in peace, a reserve for wastage during the first three months of the war. In a fourth month the Immediate and Workshop Reserve would cover wastage amounting to 75% of first-line strength at home at home and 100% overseas. For the fifth and sixth months of the war wastage would be met from the accumulating output of industry. If a time factor had thus been taken into account a figure of nearly 200% would have been applicable to Scheme J.

With the benefit of hindsight Scheme J, with its forced draft and mobilisation of industry, would have provided a force in substantially better shape to meet German aggression in 1939. But in October 1937 ministers were not to know that war would be less than two years away and Scheme J was not due for completion until the summer of 1941. To have advanced the scheme to achieve parity at an earlier date would have meant resorting to industrial measures in peace time that would have had an effect upon the other service industries and on trade and industry generally.

And so Scheme J did not become operative. In overall cost terms alone £650,000,000 would have had to have come from an overall defence budget of £1500 million for the five years 1937 – 1941 as set out in the White Paper, 'Statement relating to Defence Expenditure', dated 16th September 1937. The scheme was opposed by Sir Thomas Inskip, the Minister for the Co-ordination of Defence, and was referred back to the Air Ministry for revision. A less ambitious scheme was called for but a new figure of £607 million was still unsatisfactory from the Treasury's point of view. Further cuts had to be made which affected war potential and the war reserve and after effecting some other economies, the Air Ministry ended up with a figure of £567 million.. Thus modified Scheme J became Scheme K.

EXPANSION SCHEME K

Scheme K was viewed by the Air Staff as a solution motivated by politics and money. The forced reductions of Air Staff requirements were regarded as temporary with shortages made good as soon as financial constraints were lifted. In other words Scheme K was the best that could be hoped for but did not represent even the minimum insurance that the Air Staff considered necessary in the Metropolitan force. Scheme K cut the striking force from 90 bomber squadrons of 1442 bombers in Scheme J to 77 squadrons of 1360 bombers. The Metropolitan force of 158 squadrons in Scheme J was reduced in numbers of aircraft from 2387(158 squadron) to 2305 (145 squadrons). The four trade defence squadrons were part of the higher figure.

Like Scheme J, it was due for completion in 1941 but by 31st March of that year and not the summer. Another drawback was that the estimates of German bomber strength was based, in framing Scheme K, on the figures for mid 1938 whereas Scheme J's estimates of enemy strength were for December 1939 i.e., the Air Staff were aiming for a lower figure. A third drawback was the provision, or purported provision made for reserves. The programme, stated by the Air Staff in January 1938, provided for the completion of first-line requirements with part reserves by the end of the financial year 1940/1, with the remainder of the reserves becoming available with a few exceptions about mid way through 1942. In other words, given the expected wastage during a war, the full replacement of losses could not occur until then. This would have meant either the laying off of some of the squadrons or the operational employment of all squadrons at less than full strength. In the event it was for neither of these reasons that Scheme K was not adopted. The scheme had been declared just before the Anschluss or the forcible absorption of Austria into the Reich by the Nazi regime. Although the Government excused its inaction on the questionable grounds that Austria was a German speaking nation and willingly accepted the annexation of the country, the truth was that the episode exposed Hitler's territorial ambitions. The Anschluss only served to emphasise the need to accelerate the expansion programme and at a Cabinet meeting of 14th March 1938 it was decided to send Scheme K back to the Air Ministry for revision.

SCHEME L

It may come as no surprise to learn that Scheme L was an accelerated version of Scheme K. It was approved by the Cabinet on 27th April 1938 and was announced to Parliament on 12th May. There would be a Metropolitan air force of 141 squadrons equipped with approximately 2370 first-line aircraft by 31st March 1940. The Fleet Air Arm and overseas establishments of first–line aircraft would be raised to 500 and 490 respectively. But the execution of the plan depended critically upon the capacity of the aircraft industry to 'deliver the goods'. The Cabinet was giving final approval for the construction of some 4,000 machines in the first year of the Scheme's operation and 8,000 in the second, a total of 12,000 machines in the two years ended 31st March 1940.

Whitleys being produced at Coventry.

In Scheme L there were in fact to be four fewer squadrons than in Scheme K. This can be deceiving in terms of strike power since unit establishment of aircraft can be raised. Scheme L, for example, had raised the initial equipment for fighter squadrons from 14 to 16 machines and provided for a large number of medium bomber squadrons, with an initial equipment of 24 machines while reducing the number of heavy bomber squadrons which each had 16 aircraft. Be that as it may the Air Staff had not been happy with Scheme K and were even less happy with Scheme L since it was believed that it fell below the level of safety considered necessary. It was felt that the Metropolitan air force should include a strike force at least equal in strength, at any given time to the Germans. The fighter force should also be adequate enough to deal with the enemy bomber force, having regard to any reduction in the scale of enemy attacks consequent upon the success or otherwise of British and allied air attacks upon enemy airfields, factories and aircraft storage parks.

The Air Staff's other concerns were the reserves and static defences. They reiterated the need for an adequate war reserve of aircraft, equipment and trained personnel, backed by the necessary production and training capacity. The first-line units had to be able to continue operations on the required scale of intensity. The need for a secure base was also emphasised with anti-aircraft guns and searchlights supplemented by a thorough ARP (Air Raid Warning Police.) organization. Scheme J fulfilled these requirements but neither 'K', nor L did. Even Scheme J involved an element of risk in that it could not be completed *parri pasu*, with the German Programme.

The Air Staff observed that Britain was endeavouring to compete with a nation of 40 million people who had been mobilised in peacetime as if it was wartime. The

Fascist state is a corporate state where the entire nation answers to the will of the leader. From 1934 Hitler had been able to command the unquestioning obedience of his people. Not only could he command industry to provide the weaponry but he could also recruit the required manpower into the armed forces. Britain's air expansion was based upon a voluntary system and the non-interference with the normal flow of trade. It was not until 22nd March 1938 that the Cabinet decided that double shifts could be worked in industry and peacetime factories diverted to war requirements but six months later men of the aircraft firms were working neither night shifts nor overtime. At an EPM held on 14th September 1938 it was decided to press them to do so.

The necessity for national mobilisation was still far from realisation in 1938. In the spring of that year there were some 90,000 people working in the aircraft industry as against 347,000 at the peak of the British war effort in the Great War when the building of an aircraft involving only 1/10th of the man hours involved twenty years later. Sir John Simon, speaking in the House of Commons on 21st September 1939 stated that even in the May of that year the labour force in the aircraft industry had only reached 128,000, 97,000 working on airframes and 21,000 on engines. The output was then 178 aircraft per week. On the outbreak of war the number of workers had risen to 350,000. It was only after war began that there was a great expansion to a point in 1944 when the numbers so employed was estimated to be 1,821,000.

EXPANSION SCHEME M

Scheme M may be regarded as a "mopping up" scheme. It was framed so as to incorporate all outstanding items from previous expansion schemes. The date for completion was 31st March 1942, that is to say two years after completion of Scheme L. The distinguishing feature of Scheme M was the increased emphasis placed on the fighter arm. (Air Staff doctrine of the period is discussed in Chapter 10.) It is significant that in spite of all the teaching of Trenchard and his successors, that the best way to defend Britain was to go straight on to the offensive, the need for strong fighter defences was recognized. Sir Kingsley Wood said as much in a meeting of the Cabinet on 25th October 1938. He was concerned that Britain might have to go to war before completion of the expansion plans. The Munich crisis had put the country almost on a war footing but thankfully the crisis passed without the country going to war. This gave the government another year to be better prepared than it was in the autumn of 1938. He said that static defences, that is the anti aircraft guns, barrage balloons and searchlights, were not ready. Also passive defence measures, including the wearing of gas masks, were not ready. The only way of stopping formations of

enemy bombers entering British air space, was strong fighter defences.

Sir Kingsley requested immediate authority for the placing of such orders as would enable the first-line fighter force to be built up to 640 aircraft backed by substantial reserves to be ready by 1st April 1940 and to 800 by the Spring of 1941. The requirement for trained personnel and accommodation was also taken into account.

THE END OF PRE-WAR EXPANSION

Scheme M was the last of the pre-war expansion schemes. The completion date for this scheme was 31st March 1942 by which time the Metropolitan air force would have a strength of 2549aircraft. But the Air Staff estimated that the Germans had more than that number at the time the scheme was proposed. As it was, the outbreak of war overtook both Britain and Germany. From 3rd September 1939 and beyond all programmes of armament expansion were framed against a backdrop of general mobilisation. Indeed, only three months after the outbreak of World War II, Britain was engaged on a programme of expansion that would double aircraft production since the beginning of the war. The Government envisaged an output of 2,000 aircraft per month within 18 months from the outbreak of war. At one stage there was a proposal to increase this figure to 3,000 a month but in the event HMG settled for a more modest figure of 2,550. On the outbreak of war there were orders outstanding for 18,000 aircraft.

THE SHADOW FACTORY SCHEME

Problems with sub-contracting

Other voices were added to those pressing the case for small firms to be admitted. Mr Oliver Simmonds suggested that one reason for the small firms not being treated fairly was definitely jealously between the old and the new industry. Through the lean years of the early 1920s the established firms had struggled against adversity, some facing bankruptcy with too many years of low incomes and low dividends. Trenchard had given these firms contracts for prototypes if only to keep them from liquidation. Then came rearmament and the growth in orders could give established firms a real boost only to find that they would have to share orders with these new firms. Ever mindful that the established firms had sunk a lot of capital into aircraft manufacture over the years, the Air Ministry was standing by the old industries. Be that as it may, a year later one finds Mr Garro Jones MP, in the House of Commons, charging the 'old gang' with harbouring a selfish and, in the circumstances, an unpatriotic opposition to newcomers. These new firms were described as young and enterprising yet had been denied a chance to participate.

The old firms had been successful in freezing out the new.

At an EPM of 21st November 1936 , a further difficulty arose in the matter of sub-contracting. Some of the established firms, which had been awarded Air Ministry contracts, were disinclined to allow outside firms to assist them. At the meeting Lord Swinton referred to a satisfactory state of affairs in the industry in the matter of subcontracting insofar as the established firms were not resorting to it to the fullest possible extent. The Secretary, Sir Donald Banks, expressed the view that the 'family' and 'non-family' issue constituted a very real danger and exposed the Air Ministry to serious criticism if it came out that a single 'non family' firm had to stand off 200 men (as General Aircraft had) because a single 'family firm' in the same neighbourhood would not sub contract.

It is difficult to see why these outside firms could not be associated with those employed in the construction programme. It was only when Sir Kingsley Wood succeeded Lord Swinton as the Secretary of State for Air that things began to change. In the House of Commons on 7th March 1940 Sir Kingsley was able to claim that the great increase in production which had been achieved was due in no small measure to our having sought eighteen months or more ago the assistance of thousands of small firms with a considerable amount of plant and labour that could be brought into the expansion scheme. How widely the net was cast during his administration is shown in an informative memorandum, which he submitted to the Cabinet in October 1938. It is clear from what he said in it that he did not share his predecessor's view of the ability of the professional industry reinforced by the shadow factories to meet the increased demands for air equipment.

Dispersal of Manufacturing Units
In the memorandum accompanying the Air Estimates for 1938/9 Lord Swinton had spoken of the shadow factory scheme in enthusiastic terms. Sir Kingsley was less so, pointing out that labour was the limiting factor at a time when production was being accelerated. The professional industry was unable to meet its own forecasts capable though it may be in its own judgement. He enumerated the measures, which had been instituted to supplement the efforts of the aircraft industry and the shadow factories. It was impractical to concentrate the whole of the required labour force at the assembly shops. Lord Weir had expressed the view that it was better to take the labour to the work not the other way round. Sir Kingsley prevailed and the principle was adopted that work be taken to the supply of labour by means of sub-contracting. Aircraft firms had been instructed to put out 35% of their production, as measured in man-hours, to sub-contractors. Wherever possible components would be made by sub-contracting firm and brought to assembly shops. New firms like Metropolitan Vickers, Vickers Armstrong and English Electric would provide central assembly shops. The very great dispersal of firms contributing to aircraft production reduced the vulnerability of the organisation to enemy air attack. Indeed the extension of the works of the English Electric Company to produce Handley Page aircraft was justified at an Expansion Progress Meeting on 11th January 1939 on the grounds that an alternative source of supply could be provided in a safer area than Cricklewood. The memorandum also referred to increases in the productive capacity of the aircraft industry itself. Extension of the works at Bristols, Glosters, Avro, Faireys and Shorts were reported and there were instances of associations of these firms with principle engineering organizations. Examples were Blackburn with Denny, Westlands with John Brown and Short Brothers with Harland.

Concurrently with the extension of airframe production, steps had been taken to extend the capacity for the manufacture of engines, various components and accessories and armament equipment. The erection of new engine works to supplement the capacity of Rolls Royce and for the factory for the production of carburettors and airscrews, the organization of quantity production of automatic pilots by Metropolitan Vickers and of the Browning Machine Guns by BSA are examples of what was done. Similar action was taken to provide capacity for the production of materials with a view to securing additional sources of supply and fabrication.

The Group System
The purpose of the Group System was to associate firms into a number of 'production groups' :-

Group A The production of Manchester bombers. The principal firms would be Avro, Fairey, Rootes and Metropolitan Vickers with associated groups of sub contractors in the Liverpool-Manchester – Crewe area. Capital Cost £7.75 million

Group B The manufacture of Stirling bombers. Capital Cost £11.75 million

Group C The production of Halifaxes. Capital Cost £0.75 million

Group D The production of fighters. The firms involved were Hawker (including Glosters), Supermarine, Westland and Nuffield organizations in the South of England and Midlands. Capital Cost £0.75 million for Westland Group and £3.5 million for Hawker/Gloster Group.

Smaller groups would be created to undertake other types of aircraft. Firms which would not be brought into the 'group' form of organization would continue, with other sub contractors as separate manufacturing units. Sir Kingsley gave some further particulars about the 'group' system of production in a speech introducing the Air Estimates in the House of Commons on 9th March 1939. He said that the objects of the system were to reduce the number of designs in service and to facilitate economical and rapid production. He believed that system would facilitate large scale planning and ordering. The volume of technical work would be reduced through all the stages of design, maintenance, store holding and equipment throughout the service. The group system would also reduce distortion, which might result in wartime if, for any reason, one of the manufacturing units was unable to continue in production. Sir Kingsley went on to say that the system would embrace, not only the firms in the aircraft industry but the 'government' factories and the new factories which were being created by such firms as Metropolitan Vickers.

The question of mass production
The policy of the government had been to diffuse rather than concentrate manufacture. It was a wise policy given the threat posed by enemy bombers, although with the benefit of hindsight the *Luftwaffe* did not possess a strategic bombing force. Attacks were made by the tactical units of *Luftflotten* 2 and 3 in the summer of 1940, on known industrial targets like the Supermarine works in the south of England. Such targets were within range of the *Luftwaffe* units based in Northern France. When German attacks were launched against the Coventry and Birmingham areas during 1940 – 1941 some material damage was inflicted but Lord Beaverbrook had only to institute a greater measure of dispersal. Decentralisation in the British Isles was dictated by geography unlike the USA where huge centralised plants were possible since there was little or no threat of air attack. This is just as well given that the tendency of American industry is always to the colossal such as the works erected by Henry Ford at Willow Run near Detroit.

Given the constraints within which the British aircraft industry had to operate the adoption of mass production methods was considered with the placing of an expert in mass production techniques in the Air Ministry. The motor car industry, by then involved in aircraft production, had long adopted the production line to turn out cars for the mass market. (As a matter of interest Henry Ford was not the first to introduce this method of production. Several centuries had elapsed since the Venetians had produced galleons by having pre-fabricated parts added as the hulls moved down a canal.) Aircraft, however, had not reached the stage of technical development of design that would justify anything like the full adoption of mass production methods and processes. The real foundation for really large scale production methods does not lie so much in

the methods themselves but in the extent to which production possibilities are embodied in the design of the product itself. It was felt that when aircraft design became more conventional and progress in performance became less marked, then production methods may approximate more closely to those of the motor car industry.

FLYING TRAINING 1937–1939
National Archive document AIR 32/14

NAVIGATION TRAINING
Introduction of new multi-engined aircraft In April 1936 the crewing of aircraft was laid down by the C.A.S. as one pilot and one observer plus wireless operators and air gunners where necessary for bomber and two-seat fighter aircraft. For GR aircraft the crewing was laid down as one pilot and one navigator, who was a pilot. The introduction of newer types of aircraft i.e., Blenheim, Whitley, Hampden, Battle and Wellesley, made it increasingly difficult both to fly and navigate the aircraft. Consequently the crewing of aircraft was revised in 1937.Whenever possible bombers were given two pilots and special provision was made with regard to navigation for those bombers which could not carry two pilots i.e., Blenheim, Wellesley and Battle. For medium bombers which could not carry two pilots, observers were specially trained. The course at the Air Observers' School, North Coates was extended from two to three months and navigation training similar to that given to pilots at the FTSs was added to the syllabus.

The effects of the change in policy This two-pilot decision increased the pilot output required from the FTSs and the amount of squadron navigation officers' training needed but no more schools were opened and the six month course was retained. Then the capacity of the School of Air Navigation was increased and the course for squadron navigators went from twelve pupils on a thirteen week course to twenty-two pupils on a ten week course. The increased rate at Manston was not however enough and it was necessary to find other means of producing squadron navigation officers. Eventually it was decided to train pilots at two civil schools on a three month course in navigation. These schools were at the Imperial School of Air Navigation, London which took its first 47 pilots in April 1937, and Air Service Training Ltd, Hamble which took 20 pilots in July. These courses included no practical work on flying. In January 1938 another batch of 67 students was sent to the school for training. It was agreed in 1937 to give pilots more navigation training than given on the FTS course. There was to be a separate navigation course that would follow a pilot's FTS training. It was to last ten weeks and produce the squadron navigation standards to which only squadron navigation officers had previously been trained. In addition half the pilots destined for long range aircraft would have a four-week course in astronomical navigation. The numbers to be dealt with were formidable. Plans were being made to give 1500 pilots navigation training in 1938/9. The capacity of the School of Navigation was increased by transferring the navigation reconnaissance training for pilots of GR squadrons to a new school of general reconnaissance training at Thorney Island in April 1938. Even so Manston could not handle all the training. Six civil schools were to used for the remainder, working to the Manston syllabus and including air experience and air instruction. Some pilots had taken courses at civil schools at their own expense and obtained second class navigator's licences. This led to temporary acceptance by the Air Ministry with their order 1/36 with the licence as a qualification for squadron navigation officers.

Observer Training It was felt that training pilots in navigation by means of the ten week course would be impractical in war. The most that could be done would be to teach basic DR navigation so that pilots could supervise navigation after some experience as second pilots. A conference was then held on training and establishment of air observers, for the feeling was growing that in wartime the observer and not the pilots should be responsible for navigation of the aircraft. The change of policy from pilot responsibility for navigation to the observer on the outbreak of war was fundamental. The corollary of this new policy was the need to add observers to peace-time crews and train them in peace otherwise there would be a reliance on the Volunteer Reserve for observers on the outbreak of war. But in April 1938 there was a lack of trained observers which was seen to be serious and a further four civil schools had been approached to do the training. These four schools were meant to raise their observer training, thus the requirement for observer training went up sharply and by the middle of 1938 a very rapid and considerable development had taken place. The navigation training for observers was carried out at:-

No.7 EFTS Desford commencing 9/8/38
No.9 EFTS Anstey commencing 17/8/38
No.10 EFTS Yatesbury commencing 9/38
No.12 EFTS Prestwick commencing 9/8/38

The Macworth proposal And so after May 1938 all pilots and observers were trained on a ten week course up to squadron navigation standard. But in February 1939 Wing Commander Macworth, Department OR3 pointed out that this seemed to involve a disproportionately large amount of training in flying to ensure that aircraft were safely navigated. Three men were being fully trained for every large aircraft and two for every smaller bomber. To cut down the amount of

training effort devoted to navigation he proposed that navigation become the observer's responsibility both in peace and war. The pilot should be given sufficient training to get them across country or bring the aircraft back in an emergency. The observer would be given a ten week course up to squadron navigation standard plus an astronomical navigation course in the case of long-range aircraft. Air Marshal Ludlow-Hewitt objected strongly to the idea of making the observer responsible for navigation, arguing that the aircraft captain should be both competent and responsible and should then delegate navigation to the observer. If the observer should be made responsible, the pilot would wash his hands of navigation. Air Vice Marshal Sholto-Douglas, however, saw no difficulty in the Captain being less than fully competent than the observer provided that the pilot's basic grounding was good enough to enable him to appreciate the problems of navigation.

Introduction of new policy The policy of observer responsibility for navigation was introduced in May 1939. It was acknowledged that the previous aim of training all pilots and observers on a ten week course had never been realised in practice. In future all pilots would be given basic training beginning at the FTS and continuing with a six week course at navigation school. Observers would be trained to the high standard required and were therefore to be given the ten week course (twelve weeks at the civil schools) and a four week astronomical course if it was needed. Pilots were to be capable of bringing back the aircraft in an emergency and supervising navigation. Squadron leaders were to have a six week course in advanced navigation to that they could give adequate supervision to squadron training. To ensure that pilots were trained to the required standard the FTS syllabus was re-written so that it and the six week course covered the same ground as the ten week course. These courses however had not commenced by the outbreak of war and a revised war-time training syllabus was put into effect. It was recognized that the courses at Manston were better than those at civil schools and therefore observers should be trained there. The capacity of the schools and the numbers involved, however, made this difficult to put into practice and it was decided to keep pilot training at Manston and continue observer training at the civil schools.

OPERATION OF FLYING TRAINING SCHOOLS
Introduction Throughout the expansion period flying training schools were working under heavy pressure which was due, in considerable degree to their organization. Maintenance was done in flights and the instructors had to deal with ground instruction, maintenance and administration as well as flying instruction. In spite of the fact that everyone did a little

bit of everything flying training schools worked satisfactorily only because the organization was extravagant. It was clear that this system, which was working with difficulty in peace, would break down under war time pressure.

The Tedder proposals Air Commodore Tedder wrote a paper on the organization of FTSs in June 1936 in which he compared the flight system of maintenance with civil operations and found the service system uneconomical. Of course a direct comparison was not possible but service economies in war and civil economies in peace were very much akin. There had to be efficient working with the strictest economies while preserving the ability to expand. He applied these principles to a flying training school and deduced that there should be a functional organization by which technical maintenance was delegated in its entirety to one group containing all the technical personnel under an officer in charge of maintenance. In war these would need for strict economy in the employment of men because there would be competition for trained technicians between the RAF and industry. Similarly there should be the administrative organization to relieve the instructional staff and maintenance personnel of all administrative work. The FTSs should therefore have three distinct divisions. Tedder described this as 'an office, a garage and a school.'

Miles Master training aircraft.

No.2FTS Harvards.

Reorganization of 1937 The flight system of maintenance ended in May 1937 when maintenance was centralised for each squadron. 1936 and 1937 were therefore years of considerable activity and reorganization The RAF was starting to expand and expansion was dependent on the efficiency and capacity of the training schools but at the same time new factors had to be considered. Squadrons were being re-equipped with heavier and faster aircraft and the monoplane was replacing the biplane. This meant that the gap between the training and operational aircraft widened considerably. Originally the aircraft of the FTSs were themselves service types, e.g. Harts, Audaxes etc., but special training aircraft had to be introduced into the FTSs in November 1936 in the shape of twin-engined trainers. Plans were also being laid for the introduction of a single-engined training aircraft called the Don. This aircraft, however, proved to be a failure and Masters and Harvards were eventually to equip the schools. But there was considerable delay in the production of the new trainers and at the outbreak of war most schools were still equipped with biplanes.

Expansion Plan L In spite of problems the training was improved. Night flying and navigation training was introduced and the distinction between the training of fighter and bomber pilots instituted in 1935 resulted in the training syllabuses being altered. During 1937 some of the stations used by flying training schools were also required by operational units as the expansion developed. No.9 FTS moved from Thornaby to Hullavington in July, No.3 FTS from Grantham to South Cerney in August and No.2 FTS from Digby to Brize Norton in September. In May 1938 Expansion Plan L was approved. Since 1935 the annual output of pilots from schools had been about 1500 but to provide pilots for Scheme L by April 1940 an annual rate of 2500 was needed in 1939. Eight more FTSs over and above the eleven already at work were going to be required. Of these eight, only three would be required for peace time, the other five being needed to for the one year spurt in 1939. To man these eight schools some 300 officers and 4000 airmen were needed and practically all would have to be drawn from first line squadrons. Squadrons were already considerably light of experienced men. To take away a large number of experienced pilots and skilled maintenance staff for employment in FTSs was likely to wreck their efficiency. Air Vice Marshal Sholto-Douglas wrote, ' As a result of intensive efforts during the past two years the squadrons are just beginning to obtain some sort of operational efficiency. I feel that we should do everything in our power to maintain and improve that standard.' Air Vice Marshal Peirse was 'seriously concerned about the effect on the first-line squadrons'. A comparatively small nucleus of experienced pilots was in fact wanted for three distinct purposes:

(a) As a backbone on squadrons for war readiness.
(b) For training new pilots on squadrons as they worked up.
(c) As instructors in schools.

The nucleus was not sufficient to serve all three purposes fully so the number of extra FTSs to be opened was cut to four. A suggestion by Air Commodore Leckie that some pilots straight from the FTS should be trained and employed as instructors was not considered likely to make a substantial reduction in the number of experienced men wanted. The suggestion was acted on, however, with the result that an appreciable though not catastrophic lowering of the standard of FTS instruction was observed.

FTS situation 1938/39 Four FTSs rather than eight would result in a deficiency of 720 pilots in April 1940, It had however been planned to offset the shortage of Reserves to some extent by providing spare pilots from squadrons. And the deficiency of 720 meant only that spare pilots would be lacking in April 1940. The deficiency would be overtaken in the following September and the addition of the four additional schools was approved in April 1938:

No.12 FTS opened at Grantham on 1st December 1939
No.13 FTS opened at Drem on 17th March 1939
No.14 FTS opened at Kinloss on 1st April 1939
No.15 FTS opened at Lossiemouth on 1st May 1939

During this period other moves and changes took place:

No.11 FTS moved from Wittering to Shawbury in May 1938.
No.6 FTS moved from Netheravon to Little Rissington in August 1938.

No.1 FTS changed from *ab initio* training to the re-organized system of intermediate and advanced training squadrons. The pupils came from the elementary civil schools in May 1938 and its output continued to go to the Fleet Air Arm and it moved from Leuchars to Netheravon in August 1938. In May 1939 No.7 FTS Peterborough also began to train for the Fleet Air Arm its twin-engined aircraft being replaced by single-engined aircraft during the summer of that year.

Extra Civil flying schools To feed the four extra FTSs new civil schools had to be utilised and additional regular courses were allocated to seven other civil schools towards the end of 1938.

E&RFTS – Elementary and Reserve Flying Training School
No. 7 E&RFTS Desford commenced on 13th March 1939

An Audax and a Fury of No.3 FTS South Cerney (Glos.) during a gunnery affiliation exercise.

No. 9 E&RFTS Anstey commenced on 6th February 1939
No.11 E&RFTS Perth commencing of 13th March 1939
No.12 E&RFTS Prestwick commenced on 6th October 1938
No.19 E&RFTS Gatwick commenced on 6th October 1938
No.22 E&RFTS Cambridge commenced on 27th March 1939
No.30 E&RFTS Derby commenced on 27th March 1939

All but three of these schools were already carrying out training for Regular RAF personnel. The remaining schools were carrying out reserve training only.

The standard of FTS training 1938/39 The length of training at the FTSs remained unchanged at six months. The mounting demand for pilots and the inability to open more than the minimum of additional schools made the originally planned course of nine months' duration more remote than ever. The organized system was held however to be successful. To have raised the standard at which pilots left schools and to have relieved squadrons of the responsibility for much individual training was an achievement and the FTS training system was confirmed as the permanent system of pilot training in June 1938. Nevertheless it was necessary for Air Marshal Newall to write in May 1938 :

There is no doubt that the standard of training obtained by pilots where they joined service units is higher now than it has been before, but at the same time there has been a great increase in the complexity of modern bomber aircraft and also the responsibility of the captain of the aircraft, having regard to the size of the crew and the cost of the aircraft. The improvement in the standard of training, although very considerable, has not kept pace with the increased demands placed on the fully trained pilot.

There is therefore a gap, which we must fill between the time the pilot leaves the FTS and the time when he is fit to assume the responsibilities of the captain of an aircraft. In addition there is a consideration that during the period following the arrival of a pilot at a service unit he is in what we have called the *accident prone zone*. It is therefore desirable that he should be trained to fly the big expensive types by the interim stage rather than flying them immediately after leaving the FTS. In my opinion there should be an interim stage after leaving the FTS when a pilot should concentrate on getting in air hours. He would not go up with a full crew and would fly the lighter type of modern aircraft. The idea is to give him air hours in an aircraft with all the modern characteristics such as a retractable undercarriage, variable pitch airscrews etc. But in the meantime we must make do with the aircraft which are available. The several pilots within squadrons will allow this training to be given without appreciably interfering with operational training.

The above passage was a reference only to Bomber Command. Air Chief Marshal Newall continued:

Some time ago it was decided that even for initial training it was desirable that the aircraft used for this purpose should have, as far as possible, the characteristics of a modern service aircraft ie. a low wing monoplane which has inherent disadvantages particularly in regard to spinning and it seems clear that it is more difficult to recover from a spin in an aircraft of modern characteristics then it used to be in the older biplane types. I do not consider that it is in any way necessary that the ab initio training should be carried out on an aircraft with modern characteristics. What is required is a simple aircraft, free from vice, easy to maintain and easy to fly. We should give the pilot confidence in himself and in flying generally. It will be easy to extricate from a difficult position should it, for instance, inadvertently put in a spin. I have therefore decided that we will abandon our present ideas at the earliest possible date and revert to an older type such as the Moth for the ab initio training school. Both these decisions are, I think, desirable in order to avoid accidents particularly under the stress of rapid and extension of expansion.

The development of the modern trainers had been going on and the Airspeed Envoy had eventually been modified into a twin-engined trainers known as the Oxford which was brought into service at No.3 FTS South Cerney, No 5FTS Sealand and No.7 FTS Peterborough in June 1938. The single-engined training aircraft was to be the Don but when it was found to be unsuitable a decision was made to continue to use the Hart for single-engined training until the North

Airspeed Oxford.

American Harvard was available and the Miles Master produced but the point has already been made that the latter were late in arriving. The first Harvards were used at No.12 FTS Grantham in January 1939 and the Master followed in 1940.

Details of Pilot and Non Pilot training courses at the Elementary and Reserve Flying Training Schools may be found at Appendices C and D respectively.

NIGHT AND ALL-WEATHER-FLYING POLICY

Introduction There were differences in night flying policy between RAF Commands. The standard policy for night-lights and night flying was worked out in 1937 and 1938. FTSs continued to do little more than ensure that every pilot had flown at night. The use of Tutors for instrument flying was discontinued in 1937, the Harts taking their place. In general it was considered at this time desirable to give as much instruction as possible in the air but this proved so difficult that Link Trainers were installed at the FTSs early in 1938. These were the forerunners of today's sophisticated flight simulator.

Bad weather and instrument flying In February 1939 Air Vice Marshal Pattison, AOC No.23 Group pointed out that bad weather training, for which Bomber Command had asked, was virtually impossible at the FTSs for their aircraft carried no radios and it was therefore essential that pupils should keep in sight of the ground on cross-country flights. Instrument flying could only be practiced under the 'hood'. The FTSs could

Instrument flying hood on an Avro 504N aircraft.

The Link Trainer.

provide five hours under the hood together with ten hours in the Link trainer. Air Marshal Burnett the C-in-C Training Command added an argument that there was no time in the FTS course to make additional bad-weather practice possible. He also considered that no time could be found for it in the pilot-navigation course and it could not therefore be done until pilots went to 'Group Pools'. The formation of group pools for Bomber and Coastal Commands had, however, been postponed and Air Vice Marshal Sholto-Douglas insisted that pilots should be given best grounding in instrument flying possible at the FTS. The syllabus requirement nevertheless remained unchanged and the impossibility of FTS practice in cloud and bad visibility was agreed. For the same fundamental reason lack of wireless facilities only added to the problem. With regard to a flying exercise in March 1939 Air Marshal Bennett said,

> When this exercise was introduced it was considered that it could give the young pilots confidence in their ability to fly by night out of sight of the aerodrome lights and it would relieve the air congestion in the vicinity of the aerodrome. The experience now indicates that the risk involved in sending pupils on cross country flights by night with no proper navigation facilities or wireless aids particularly in multi-engined types where the view to starboard is poor, is such that these flights have to be almost entirely confined to nights when the visibility was sufficiently good to enable the pupil to see his own aerodrome's beacon throughout the flight. It will be appreciated that under such conditions there will be little to be gained by this exercise whilst any sudden or unexpected deterioration of weather conditions was likely to result in pupil's getting lost with serious results.

It was recognized that these shortcomings with night and bad weather training that the FTS training should be carried out to the stage where the pupils will have completed his individual training and have had some experience of flight training. But pressure of time and lack of facilities made it inevitable that night cross country and bad weather training would be left to a later stage of a pilot's career.

The training given to Fairey Battle pilots The training of Fairey Battle pilots came under review later in 1938. It was laid down by the Air Ministry that they should be trained on single-engined aircraft and given a limited amount of bomb-aiming practice on twin-engined aircraft. Under a suggestion from Training Command that it would be better to teach them on twin-engined aircraft so that they got more training in piloting for precision bombing and photography was turned down. In February 1939 it was decided to standardise the training for all single-engined pupils at FTSs, there being no special bombing instruction except those destined for single-engined bombing squadrons. This reduced the different types of pilot to be trained to single-engined or Group 1 and twin-engined or Group 2. In May 1939 the proportion of pupils to be trained to Group 2 was two thirds, reflecting the greater number of multi-engined aircraft planned for Schemes L and M. But some schools continued to train only one third of the intake as Group 2 because they had insufficient twin-engined training aircraft.

TRAINING ON THE APPROACH OF WAR

Training for war The full war training was not considered practical in peace time but the possibilities of either increasing the number of pupils or shortening courses were considered. There were a number of difficulties. The extra wear and tear of more intensive work would need runways and relief landing grounds but FTS airfields were grassed and the schools had only four relief landing grounds suitable for the new types of training aircraft when there was a requirement for twenty relief landing grounds. Then there was the familiar problem of finding enough instructors. The most serious difficulty turned out to be the lack of training aircraft. Additional Ansons, Oxfords and Harvards would not begin to be available until late in 1939 while the Master trainers would be later still. In the end it was decided to adopt a plan suggested by Air Vice Marshal Pattison. The size of the FTS courses was to be increased from forty-eight to sixty. Beginning in September each school was to be given eleven extra aircraft, five single-engined and six twin-engined. There were to be additional maintenance staff, an increased flow of spares, one additional staff pilot and instructor strength was to be kept up to establishment. The plan was to apply to all schools except Nos. 1 and 7 FTS. It was estimated that this would produce extra 468 pilots a year. Increased intakes at the civil schools began in June but war broke out before they passed on to the FTSs.

The training of pilots after leaving the FTSs On 18th May 1938 a minute was written by the Chief of the Air Staff regarding the training of pupil pilots after leaving the FTSs. The full text of this minute appears on pages 78 and 79 in which Air Chief Marshal Newall spoke of an *accident prone zone'* after a pilot leaves the FTS and advocating an interim training stage between that time and time a pilot reaches his operational squadron. The ultimate organization for the interim stage was agreed to be *Group Pools* (originally called advanced flying centres) which were to be equipped with Oxfords or Ansons, but in June 1938 it was realised that the possibility of doing any form of intermediate training depended upon the supply of these aircraft and there would be some time, perhaps more than a year, before they were available. Be that as it may it was decided in November 1938 that Group Pools should be established for each fighter and bomber group and one for Coastal Command making ten in all.

  6 Bomber Pools for 73 bomber squadrons.
  3 Fighter Pools for 36 fighter squadrons.
  1 Coastal Pool for 19 coastal squadrons.

These units were to act as reserves of trained pilots and crews from which replacements could be drawn in addition to carrying out interim training and advanced training for Reservists. Their functions were defined as follows:

IN WAR: 1 To provide each operational group with a 'reservoir pool' from which replacement crews could be drawn.
         2. To train the output of FTSs up to an operational standard before moving to squadrons.

IN PEACE: 1. To provide intermediate training and practice for regular pilots after leaving the FTS and before passing to squadrons.
          2. To act as advanced training centres for flying personnel of the RAFVR and thus fit them to take their places in operational units as soon after the outbreak of war as they are required.

During October and November 1938 two conferences emphasised that group pools were urgently needed both as a measure of war readiness and for the training of reservists. Only one was selected before the outbreak of war. This was No.11 Group Pool, Fighter Command. In Bomber Command there was a number of non mobilisable squadrons that could give intermediate training as a temporary measure. These squadrons retained a nucleus of their more experienced pilots to act as instructors and half the operational types of aircraft

were replaced by Ansons. Thus by the outbreak of war considerable expansion had taken place. There were then 15 FTSs fed by 16 civil schools. In addition a large volunteer training organization had been established and more than 40 civil schools were giving part-time instruction to volunteer pilots. Further discussions were taking place regarding the possibility of establishing more schools overseas but the only results achieved were to plan to establish an FTS in Kenya and permission to form a school in France.

HIGH ALTITUDE FLIGHTS

In September 1936 Squadron Leader F.R.Swain gained the world height record in a Bristol 138, reaching 49,967 feet. In May the following year the record was broken by

The Bristol 138.

an Italian pilot taking the record to 51,362 feet but in the following month Britain regained the record when Flight Lieutenant M.J.Adam of the Royal Aircraft Establishment took a Bristol 138 to 53,937 feet.

This monoplane was made of wood and had a special Bristol Pegasus engine with a two-stage supercharger. The weight is saved by having a fixed undercarriage and very small wheels. By modern standards the pressure suit and helmet seem very crude.

Achieving long-distance and height records was an important aspect of RAF policy during the inter-war years. Apart from the kudos there was a more serious intent which was to develop the airframes and engines that would place Britain in the forefront of aeronautical development.

RAF DISPLAYS AND EMPIRE AIR DAYS

1937
On Saturday 29th May 1937 Empire Air Days were held at 53 RAF stations and some civil aerodromes. The twin purposes were to show RAF squadrons operating and to raise money for the RAF Benevolent Fund. It was a sunny day and crowds turned up in their hundred thousands. On display, however, it was almost entirely an obsolescent biplane affair if one excludes the Handley Page Harrow and Fairey Hendon.

The 1937 RAF Display took place on 26th June. There were Germans at the Display, no doubt assessing British air strength. In this they were misled because the new generation of monoplanes were still to be seen. Most of the participating aircraft were biplanes like the Hector and the Gauntlet. In terms of numbers this was the most successful of the 18 Displays since the Great War as 200,000 people paid for admission. A formation of 260 aircraft in five columns flew over the crowd and gave the spectators a taste of what it might be like if massed formations of bombers flew over Britain in a future war. This marked the end of the RAF Displays which had been so successful in promoting the RAF and advances in technology. Only the Empire Air Days would continue and then only for 1938.

1938
EMPIRE AIR DAY AND SBAC DISPLAY
There was no SBAC display in 1938. The organizers said that trade flying of the latest types of aircraft and engines would not be in the public interest given imminence of war. The aircraft industry was in any case far too busy to think about diverting resources to put on a display.

The Empire Air Day would also be the last before the war. Post war there would be the Farnborough Air Show and RAF stations have put on air days to raise money for the RAF Benevolent Fund so the pre war events have been carried on in spirit. The 1938 Empire Air Day was held on Saturday 28th May accompanied by rain. In the days before the event there were massed formations of aircraft flown over 170 cities and towns using ten routes twice daily so that the largest number of people could see them. In spite of the rain crowds poured into the RAF stations in their hundred thousands and Cardington put on a display of barrage balloons. There were 15,000 visitors to Martlesham and at Felixstowe spectators arrived by excursion train and bus to see the Fairey Sea Fox, Short Singapore, Supermarine Stranraer, Saro London, Mayo Composite and Blackburn Perth. The Secretary of State for Air, Sir Charles Kingsley Wood flew in the Air Council De Havilland Rapide to visit Halton, Odiham, Farnborough, Kenley and Biggin Hill.

FLYING EXPERIENCES FROM HOME RAF STATIONS IN THE 1930S

Introduction
Chapter 4 is devoted to the operational flying of RAF squadrons abroad. At home squadrons were also busy particularly when the expansion got under way. Squadrons were being re-formed which had not seen the light of day since the massive run down of the RAF during the years 1919 to 1923. The usual practice was to take B Fight of an established squadron to form the basis of a new squadron. Both squadrons would then be brought up to full strength. The following accounts give a picture of squadron training during the 1930s.

A pilot's flying training
One trainee pilot recounts that he had attended one of the elementary flying training schools prior to enlistment in the RAF. This was at Sywell, Northampton and the school was run by Brooklands Aviation. Officer training was carried out at Uxbridge before being turned out as an Acting Pilot Officer. In the New Year of 1937 he went to No.10 FTS at Tern Hill in Shropshire. On arrival he could see the enormous 'C' Type hangars being erected as part of the expansion plan. Some additional building was going to be required to replace the Officers Mess that had been burned down a few months before. He and the other students were to fly Harts, which had a top speed of 184 mph and that was ten miles an hour faster than the Bulldog fighter. Later in the term this student was graded as 'exceptional' before passing out to gain his wings.

After a spot of leave the student returned to undertake applied flying on the Audax with occasional trips on a dual control Hart when the instructor could check progress. The Audax carried full military equipment, which included bombs, guns and cameras. Students would take it in turn to fly in the pilot's cockpit or gunner's position when carrying out exercises. This student remembers passing out with a New Zealander. He also remembers at the time of his pass-out, the loss of the airship, the Hindenburg at Lakehurst, New Jersey. He also recalls Flight Lieutenant Adam breaking the world height record in the Bristol 138 monoplane and the Short-Mayo composite aircraft both described in this volume.

He was destined for twin-engined aircraft and he progressed to the Senior Team where trainee pilots were able to fire the guns and drop $11^1/_2$lb bombs and was taught to clear a stoppage in a Vickers gun. This was carried out at the Armament Practice Camp, Sutton Bridge on the Wash in Lincolnshire. Some of the ordnance that was dropped was left over from the Great War.

SQUADRON SERVICE

No.233 Squadron was a reconnaissance squadron in Coastal Command whose motto was *Fortis Fidelis*. This unit had been last equipped with the DH4 when it was disbanded in May 1919. Having been re-formed at Upper Heyford on the 18th May the squadron was equipped with Ansons before being sent to Thornaby on 9th July 1937. The Anson was a modified civil airliner and was acceptable to the RAF because it was economical but by the time it had been loaded with guns and military equipment it could only carry a bomb weight of 280lb. It did have a retractable undercarriage, an artificial horizon and a gyro direction indicator. If the pilot forgot to wind down the undercarriage on landing a loud Klaxon would sound. Only the CO and OC A Flight were experienced officers but this was inevitable given the rate of expansion in the 1930s. All-in-all the bulk of the squadron personnel were 150 very inexperienced men. In his opinion it was a good job the RAF had two years before having to go to war.

The station was shared with No. 224 Squadron also equipped with Ansons. The navigation training was over the North Sea but the wireless sets rarely worked and the wireless operators were inexperienced hence radio bearings could often not be obtained. He recounts how thirteen squadron personnel were killed in crashes including the Adjutant and OC 'A' Flight. This left the CO without any officer above the rank of Pilot Officer. Later another CO took over who was ex Navy. (The scheme which allowed Naval Officers to fly wearing an RAF equivalent rank had existed from the early 1920s. Inevitably some officers transferred to the RAF.) There followed an exercise around the shores of Great Britain involving all twelve squadron aircraft. They called through Abbotsinch, the home of No.269 Squadron thence to the air firing range. On down to Manston they went and on to Hacks Lightship off the Dutch coast. No aircraft had gone unserviceable during the exercise.

On 1st September 1938 both Nos. 224 and 233 Squadrons were sent to Leuchars. A week after the Czech crisis 233 Squadron flew further up the coast to Montrose, the squadron's war station also the home of 8 FTS. Messing was in field kitchens and the aircraft were doped in camouflage. Vickers and Lewis guns were fitted together with cameras. Squadron personnel were permitted to go home on leave using squadron aircraft by treating the flights as navigation training. The London airports were popular.

War games became increasingly common as war approached and the Navy's Spring Cruise involved all Coastal Command squadrons, both land planes and flying boats. A fighter affiliation exercise was carried out between No.233 Squadron and the Fury IIs up from Catterick. The exercise with the Furies resulted in aircraft losses. On the second morning of the exercise one of the Fury fighters overturned on take-off and the pilot could not give an adequate explanation for the accident. Since the Furies were being phased out with the arrival of the Spitfire I in the January of 1939, there were no replacement aircraft. Then, in the afternoon, there was a similar accident with another Fury. The only thing that the pilot could say was that he felt the aircraft decelerate and swing to the left. The propeller had smashed as the tail rose and the nose dug in. Flying had to be cancelled for the day and the CO had a conference with squadron pilots and technical personnel to try to ascertain the causes of these accidents but without success. When the CO himself also experienced the same accident the following day, it was discovered that it was due to the boggy conditions on grass airfields that can follow periods of bad weather. A 'mole drainage' system had been installed at Leuchars and steel blades had been sunk into the ground at six-foot intervals creating three inch wide trenches into which gravel had been poured. Whilst this drainage system had proved effective, grass had since grown to hide the gravel. The Ansons with their broad tyres bridged these narrow gravel runs but the Furies, with their narrow wheels, sunk into the gravel troughs causing the loss of three aircraft.

There were also anti-shipping exercises using armoured speedboats with decks strengthened to withstand $11^1/_2$lb bombs. These boats were normally moored in the River Tay but would wait off the Bishop Rock lighthouse for exercises. An exercise against the Hurricanes from Wittering gave experience for the gunners to lay their guns on these fast moving, weaving targets. The drill was that if an Anson was set upon by a fighter the pilot would take immediate evasive action. The problem for the gunner was in keeping the enemy in his sights when this happened. Even if the gun was not laid precisely on the enemy aircraft it was important to fire bursts in his direction if only to cause the enemy to take evasive action.

NIGHT FLYING

One of the instructors on a station undertaking night flying in 1937 was appointed OC Night Flying and an hour before flying was about to start some twenty assorted ranks assembled under his supervision. Also present were six trainee pilots, an electrician, fire fighters, an engine fitter and a tractor driver who moved the floodlights into position. The Duty Pilot in the control tower would check the airfield for obstructions or other hazards. Red lamps would have been positioned on the airfield to mark hazards and the marshalling point for the aircraft would have been marked with a battery-operated electric signpost. Aircraft would taxi to this signpost waiting for the signal to take-off. The flare path will have been laid to take account of the wind direction forecast by the Met Office. The goose-neck flares will have been lit and if the smoke indicated a wind direction different to that forecast the floodlight would have to be relocated. Across the top of the flare path two other flares would then be laid form a letter 'T'.

When dusk was falling the least experienced pilots would attempt take-offs before it was fully dark. All the aircraft carried a red light on the port wing and a green one on the starboard plus a white recognition light in the centre of the top wing. The experienced eye could tell from this the direction in which the aircraft was travelling. Finally call signs were tapped out in Morse code to draw attention to the fact that a pilot was ready to take-off or land as the case may be.

The drill on take-off was to line up on the right of the flare path and when given the green light the throttles would be opened and the aircraft would disappear into the darkness. On the approach one could see the red and green lights on the wing tips seem to grow further apart as the aircraft drew nearer. As it sank lower and lower the floodlight would be switched on and a yellow or silver Hart would appear for a touch down in the light-soaked area. The throttle was cut as soon as the aircraft touched down and the searchlight would be immediately switched off. Meanwhile the flares were being checked by ground crew to check the paraffin levels and top up if necessary. If there was a change in the wind direction the aircraft in the circuit would have to be brought down before the flarepath was changed. This would take some twenty minutes and if aircraft on a cross country flight arrived over the airfield a red lamp was used to warn them not to land until the floodlight and flare path had been repositioned. Since radios were not carried there was no means of knowing how much fuel remained in the tanks of aircraft circling the airfield. Such were the hazards of night flying at this time.

FLYING AND OPERATIONAL
(Source: Air Ministry Weekly Orders 'A' and 'N')

Use of Gosport Airfield

Chapter 1 described temporary restrictions at Gosport airfield. It was a grass airfield used, from time to time, for practising carrier take-offs and landings with FAA aircraft. It is therefore of interest to note the changes made to the operation of the airfield once it had paved runways.

The date of the following order is January 1938 when the FAA and Gosport was still administered by the Air Ministry. The interesting point is that pilots could ignore the paved runways unless the weather put the grass out of use. In the days before paved runways pilots would have to put down on the grass, whatever the weather.

A.3. Use of Permanent Runways and Taxiing Tracks - Gosport

1. The following instructions are issued concerning the use of the new permanent runways and taxying tracks at the RAF Station, Gosport.
2. The runways may be ignored by aircraft taking-off or landing unless the state of the aerodrome renders the exclusive use of the runways necessary.
3. When the aerodrome is unserviceable owing to wet weather, the following regulations for the landing and taking-off of aircraft will be in force.
   (i) Only one runway will be used at any one time.
   (ii) The runway to be used will be indicated to aircraft on the ground by an "E" or "W" flag.(Naval Code). (See accompanying diagram) hoisted as inferior to the Affirmative flag (Naval Code). The "E"flag denotes the eastern runway. The "W" flag denotes the western runway.
   (iii) The runway that is not in use will be marked at each end by a white cross of the dimensions shown on the diagram. The existence of the

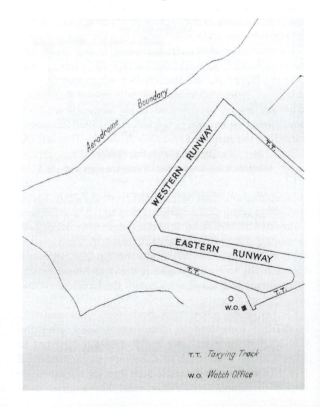

T.T. *Taxying Track*

W.O. *Watch Office*

runways may be ignored when neither an "E" nor a "W" flag is hoisted and no white crosses are shown on either runway.

(iv)   After landing on a runway , aircraft are to proceed in the direction of landing to the end of that runway and return to the hangar *via* the taxiing track. If it is desired to take-off again, aircraft are to continue taxiing to the end of the runway and return to the take-off end of the runway *via* the taxiing track.

(v)   Aircraft are not to turn round on a runway under any circumstances; the invariable rule being to continue taxiing in the direction of landing and return to the hangar or take-off end of the runway *via* the taxiing tracks.

(vi)   Aircraft are not to enter a runway prior to taking-off until it is ascertained that no aircraft are approaching the runway to land.

(vii)   When the runways are in use, landing or taking-off in formation is prohibited.

FLYING HIGH PERFORMANCE AIRCRAFT

In 2004 the flying of high performance aircraft by service pilots is taken for granted but in 1938 fast monoplane fighters were only just entering squadron service. For years pilots had flown biplanes with their light wing loading and senior officers of the Air Staff had not known anything else. One can therefore understand the caution with which these senior officers approached the matter of handling aircraft like the Hurricane and the Spitfire. Not only did they not want these new 'toys' to be prematurely written off but also they did not want their young pilots to black out with high 'g' forces. Reference to the operation of the controls 'gently' sounds particularly quaint. It is altogether the sort of care one takes when one has brought a new car !

A.15. New types of Fighter Aircraft – Restriction of Aerobatics (666817/37. – 20.1.38)

1. In view of the high performance and controllability of new types of fighter aircraft, special care is needed to avoid accelerations dangerous to personnel. For this reason, and on account of increased weight and wing loading, it is necessary to supplement the instructions contained in K.R. & A.C.I., para.717, as follows, in respect of the Hurricane and Spitfire aircraft:

   (i)   Aerobatics may be carried out only by pilots who have at least 50 hours flying experience of the particular type of aircraft, and who have received written authority from their squadron commander to perform aerobatics in that type.

   (ii)   Aerobatics are prohibited below 5,000 feet.

   (iii)   Spinning is prohibited.

   (iv)   The aeroplane controls are to be operated gently, and high accelerations are to be avoided.

2. Squadron commanders are to report to their group headquarters, through the normal channels, the names of those pilots to whom they have given written authority referred to in para. 1 (i), stating the type of new fighter aircraft to which it applies.

3. The above regulations will not apply to specific experiments at experimental establishments which are ordered by the Director of Technical Development.

Swordfish Aircraft

The next order applies to the handling of the Swordfish aircraft. It was this aircraft that played a major role in dispatching the Italian fleet in Taranto harbour in 1940 and in the following year they disabled the German battleship, the *Bismarck*. Clearly this order was, with hindsight, of particular importance for its operational role.

A.337 Swordfish – Use of Rudder at High Speeds (687537/37. – 14.10.37)

1. The rudder of a Swordfish has failed owing to its hard application at about 200 mph (A.S.I.) in a torpedo-attack practice dive. A strength test of an identical rudder has shown that it has greater strength than has normally been required in aeroplanes of this class. The failure appears to have followed an oscillation of the rudder. Such oscillation may occur at high speeds, at large rudder angles, on rudders with "horn" balance. (an area ahead of the hinge line, above the top hinge).

2. The design requirements for rudders are being revised, but it is not possible to design for the increased load which may come from extreme use of rudder at maximum diving speed.

3. All pilots are to be instructed that just as care is necessary in the use of the elevator and aileron controls at high speeds, the rudder also should not be applied violently when the aeroplane's speed if high.

AIR STAFF MANAGEMENT OF THE EXPANSION

Introduction

On 1st April 1938 Air Marshal Freeman was appointed to the post of Air Member for Development and Production. By combining development and production into one department the Air Council was, in a sense, streamlining the process for bringing aircraft to the front-line squadrons. Freeman appointed Ernest Lemon from the LMS railway to be his Director General of Production. He had to oversee the shadow factory scheme which included a host of subcontracting firms that were feeding parts to the motor car companies which were assembling airframes and engines. Eight new directorates had to be created to deal with jurisdiction over:

1. Airframes
2. Aero engines
3. Subcontracting
4. Statistics and planning
5. Materials
6. Factory construction
7. Equipment
8. War production planning

Airframes

By September 1938 it was evident that aircraft deliveries were not matching forecasts due to shortages in skilled labour. To complete the current programme the labour force would need to rise from just over 60,000 in September 1938 to a figure in excess of 180,000 by January 1939. The problem was that the industry could only recruit and train new labour at a rate of little more than 10% a month. Since sub contracting appeared to be the only answer, general engineering firms, which had previously had little or nothing to do with aircraft production, would have to be pressed into service. Under Freeman's leadership the scheme was put into practice and by July 1939 more than 1,200 firms were engaged in airframe subcontracts. To handle the research side of his large department he brought in Arthur Tedder. Tedder would take much of the work off his Master permitting Freeman to concentrate on production.

With the Sudetan crisis in the late summer of 1938 there were renewed fears that the country would not be ready to go to war and Freeman was recalled from leave, Kingsley Wood, who had taken over as the Secretary of State for Air, asked him what more could be done to accelerate aircraft production. Freeman responded with one or two ideas one of which was to take the Speke shadow factory from the management of the Rootes Group and hand it to Bristols or Avro, even though this would involve considerable compensation to Rootes. This, he said could be justified if production could reach 15 to 20 a week instead of the present 10. Another solution was to increase the production of existing types like the Battle or Blenheim but this would only be at the expense of newer more modern types. Indeed the Battle of France would expose the obsolescence of the Battle. Thirdly relaxation of inspection regulations and the cessation of the anodic treatment of metal could bring incremental savings in time.

Freeman had direct access to the Cabinet and once the Munich crisis had passed he asked for a decision on whether the RAF should plan for a war in 1939 or continue with scheme L which was due for completion in March 1940. (Refer to Pages 86 & 87 for Scheme L). In 1938 there was a shift of production to fighters and Spitfires were being produced in preference to Battles. In the short term the production of long-range bombers could reach only two-thirds of the number of German

Spitfire production at Woolston.

bombers by April 1940 but less than half the number of fighters. Freeman was not heralding a predominantly defensive posture but simply recognising the reality of the situation facing the country. Fighter defence took priority without losing sight of the need for heavy bombers, in keeping with long term policy. The adoption of the heavy bomber could result in savings. Fewer newer aircraft carrying a much larger bomb load was preferable to a large number of smaller older types. The requirements for a heavy and medium bomber were spelt out in a memorandum from Tedder to Freeman:

	Heavy Bomber	Medium Bomber
Average bomb load in lb	10,000	2,500
Number of aircraft required	896	3,584
Cost (£ Millions)	47	79
Number of engines needed	3,584	7,168
Flying personnel (Aircrew)	6,720	22,400
Flying Schools ratio	1	4
Labour units	1,926	3,584
Maintenance personnel	14,000	42,000

The figures spoke for themselves but Chamberlain clung to the hope that war could still be avoided and the Treasury hesitated to come to a decision and ordered a further 3,700 fighters instead. The Wellington bomber was in production and one solution was to increase the output of this aircraft but Vickers were unable to supply the completed production drawings to the other firms and Freeman realised that there would be a long delay in producing the design. Until the production of heavy

Wellington Production at Weybridge.

bombers could begin Armstrong Whitworth and Austin would continue to produce Battles and Whitleys. Sir Charles Craven, the managing director of Vickers Armstrong was approached to see what could be done to speed up production of Wellingtons from the parent company's factories. Freeman's advice was acted upon and during the last year of peace a network of sub contractors was established in the north west of England to supply components to the Wellington assembly plant in Chester followed by another network centred on Blackpool.

In December 1938 the creation of several other group schemes for the manufacture of heavy bombers and fighters was proposed by Freeman. The details of this group scheme may be found on page 89. The Group system was devised to produce the latest types but since these were ordered from the drawing board there was always the possibility that one or the other would prove to be unsuitable like the Manchester two-engined bomber. The Group system provided the flexibility needed to switch production to other, hopefully more successful designs. The geographical spread also ensured that sub contractors in one part of the country would not be swamped with orders.

Freeman had to turn his attention to other aircraft types such as aircraft for training and the FAA. Some aircraft were imported saving time all round and the Lockheed Hudson fell into this category. Miles, De Havilland and Airspeed produced training aircraft with an additional import in the form of the North American Harvard. For the FAA Faireys and Blackburns could be relied upon.

When Hitler seized the rump of Czechoslovakia in March 1939, Chamberlain gave his pledge to come to the aid of Poland and it would prove to be the last bloodless coup before war. The Cabinet lost any illusions that war could be avoided. Normal procedures for ordering aircraft and engines were abandoned. Freeman now had direct access to the Treasury and it was then a matter of 'action first and paper later'. Freeman asked for stop-gap orders for another 1,000 aircraft at a cost of £12.5 million which would allow him to put in hand the production of the heavy bombers.

Engines

The heavy bombers had four engines so that immediately increased the demand for aircraft engines which, in turn, meant increasing production capacity if there was not to be a shortage of engines. The shadow factories producing engines would need machine tools which had to be purchased and Freeman recommended a third section of the Rolls Royce engine plant at Crewe. Then there was the further capacity to produce the Mercury and Pegasus engines costing £300,000 and even higher levels of output would be needed when war came. With 24,000 airframes being required in 1940 there would be a huge additional demand for carburettors, airscrews, armament, turrets and raw materials. The output of Merlin engines, which went into the Spitfire, would have to rise to 1,000 per month and that of Bristol engines to 800 per month. 600 of these would be the Taurus and Hercules two-row sleeve-valve engines. When Hitler seized Czechoslovakia the German aircraft industry had an immediate increase in capacity and Freeman felt bound to match it by asking for a further £30 million for engines and ancillary equipment. Given Chamberlain's continuing reluctance to sanction even more expenditure in the forlorn hope that Hitler would make no more territorial demands, Freeman had to ask for the money in instalments, asking only for £9.45 million immediately. The Chancellor of the Exchequer let it be known that an additional £30 million could not be found at this stage, but whatever sum was made available for engines, turrets and ancillary equipment Freeman knew that it had to produce complete units. Freeman needed £4.5 million immediately for the new

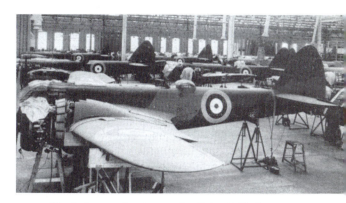

Blenheim production at the Bristol Works.

Rolls Royce factory alone, with a balance of £2 million to come later.

For his part the Chancellor was prepared to finance the extra engine production capacity in 1939 but could give no guarantee for funding in later years. Given that much of the extra labour coming on-stream was unskilled it was necessary to purchase more expensive automatic machine tools. There were also problems with mass producing the Hercules engine needed for the four-engined Stirling. Faced with a possibility of delay in turning out the new heavy bombers Freeman would have to continue with the production of Blenheims, Wellingtons and Hampdens which in turn would mean keeping the Mercury and Pegasus engine production lines going when they should be turning out the Hercules. It was a viscous circle but mass production of the Hercules could not be guaranteed and he considered using the Vulture engine. The Vulture was being fitted to the twin-engined Manchester but with war only one month away both the airframe and the engine were found to be too heavy. An alternative was the 36 litre V-12 Griffon engine and Rolls Royce were asked to consider developing this engine in lieu.

What may be so easily forgotten in the frenetic pace of events involving the shadow factories is that firms like Austin, Morris and Rootes could not simply stop producing motor vehicles because Air Marshal Freeman was breathing down their necks. He planned to produce complete Rolls Royce engines in the Austin and Humber works but production in the Austin factory could not go ahead when their management wished to accept a contract from the War Office for cars. Be that as it may Freeman did not wish to lose access to the skilled labour. He did however obtain agreement that Austins would work as subcontractors to Rolls Royce in war time. Standard and Jaguars would produce the Armstrong Siddeley engines leaving the factories of Rootes and Rover to repair Rolls Royce aero engines.

Ancillary equipment and materials
The Director of War Production Planning prepared a series of war programmes and airframe production was placed at the centre. The requirement for such items as gun turrets, magnetos, airscrews, aircraft instruments and carburettors was carefully analysed. Then there was the production of barrage balloons, high explosives and incendiary bombs, to name but a few of the things that had to be catered for in addition to airframes and engines which was taking most of Freeman's time. The business of repair is covered in detail in Chapter 8.

With the production of the heavy bombers would come the requirement for greater quantities of light alloys but the capacity to produce them in the UK in the quantities required was out of the question. Even after importation and domestic factory extensions the supply fell far short of what would be required in war time and

it would need £4.6 million to add to the UK capacity. Freeman had got used to asking the Treasury for cash in instalments and persuaded them that he would only need a fraction of that sum to begin with. It was calculated that the expansion scheme would result in the demand for 90,000 tons of raw aluminium per annum but there would be a shortfall of 60,000 tons. UK production could be increased to 41,000 tons and the rest would have to be imported, from Canada as it happened.

AIRCRAFT TEST FLYING – A&AEE MARTLESHAM AND MAEE FELIXSTOWE

AIRCRAFT AND ARMAMENT EXPERIMENTAL ESTABLISHMENT
Introduction Of the many aircraft that were sent to Martlesham for testing during the Expansion period there is only space here for one. An entire book could be devoted to the tests carried out on them all. In the last chapter the Lysander was selected and the author feels that he might not be forgiven if he did not find room for either the Spitfire or the Hurricane. The choice was made during the author's visit to the National Archive for the appropriate records only to discover that the Spitfire trial reports had been taken out for the day by another reader. In that sense the choice had been made. Strictly speaking the trials on the Hurricane belong to Chapter 2 but the trial reports have been placed in this chapter because they are associated with the gun operation reports following the failure of the guns above a certain altitude due to freezing.

The side elevation shows how the Hurricane was modern at the front end but retained the features of the 'old' at the rear. The rear fuselage like those of the Hart

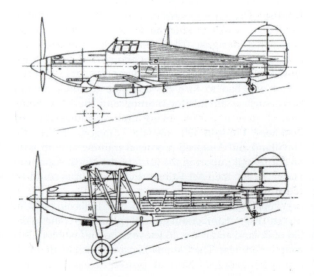

derivatives shares the same construction of wooden stringers covered in fabric. The Spitfire was of an all-metal construction. Both aircraft would, however, share the Merlin engine and both be equipped with eight Browning .303in machine guns and, in later marks, cannons. It has already been mentioned that, of the two fighters, the Hurricane provided a more stable gun platform.

HANDLING TRIALS ON HAWKER HURRICANE FIGHTER K.5083
A&AEE Report No.M/689 dated April 1936

Hurricane Prototype – K.5083.

The handling trials were made with the aircraft loaded to a total weight of 5672lb, the position of the centre of gravity at the start of the flight being 51.2ins aft of the datum point. As the present Centre of Gravity range of movement is very small, and is only representative of the change as fuel and oil are consumed, no attempt was made to test the aircraft loaded for the start of its flight at any other Centre of Gravity position than that quoted above.

Controls
Ailerons The aileron controls operate freely and without play when the aircraft is on the ground and full sideways movement of the control column can be obtained when the pilot is in the cockpit. In the air the ailerons are light to handle at low speed when climbing and on the glide, but increase in speed results in a steady increase in heaviness; and at maximum level speed and in a dive the aileron control is heavy for a fighting aircraft. A small peculiarity in the control is that, at moderate speeds only, when the starboard aileron is raised the feel suddenly becomes slightly lighter and the control is more effective. The response to the ailerons is rapid and they are effective under all normal manoeuvres in flight. During landing , take-off and at the stall the response is less rapid and the ailerons less effective but both remain satisfactory. In general it is

This frontal view of the Hurricane shows the depth of the wings which will each have to house four Browning .303in machine guns.

considered that the aileron control is satisfactory for a fighting aircraft. If it could be made lighter at high speed without over-balancing it would be improved.

Rudder and rudder bias gear On the ground the rudder control operates freely and without undue play. In the air it is light at low speeds with engine on and on the glide. With engine on heaviness increases considerably with increase of speed and in the dive it is extremely heavy. Response is quick and the control is effective at all speeds and under all conditions of flight. In general it is considered that the rudder control is adequate but would be considerably improved if it could be made lighter at speeds over 150mph. The rudder bias control is quick and easy to operate and effective. The range of controls is just adequate when the trimming strip on the rudder has been correctly adjusted.

Elevators On the ground full movement of the elevators can be obtained without undue friction or play. In the air the elevator controls are light and effective. They give a quick response under all conditions of flight from the stall to diving speeds. The control is quite satisfactory and suitable.

Tail trimming gear and tail setting The tail trimming gear is easy and rapid in operation and has no tendency to slip. Range control is not quite adequate to trim the aircraft for every condition of flight. A slight increase in the range at both ends of the scale may prove necessary to allow for change in the centre of gravity position. The operating cables are inclined to stretch, allowing some free movement to the trimming tabs and giving an unpleasant effect of fore and aft instability.

TAIL SETTING

Loading	Engine on		Engine off	
	Climbing at Best speed	Maximum level flight	Specification Cruising speed	Best approach Speed
Full load with Corresponding C.G.	Full forward	Not quite full forward	Not quite full forward	Fully back
C.G. Forward	Not tested			
C.G. Aft	Not tested			

Engine controls, flaps and brakes The engine controls are well placed in the cockpit and operate without play or tendency to slip. The flap control gear is well placed in the cockpit, is easy to operate and takes 10 – 15 seconds to move over the full range. Although there is a noticeable change of trim with the flaps down, the tail trimming gear need not be adjusted until the flaps are fully down as the elevator control is powerful enough to counteract the change in trim. The flaps are very effective and, when down, give improved aileron control. Use of the flaps make the approach very simple and reduces flatness of glide. If the throttle is opened when the flaps are lowered the aeroplane will maintain height. The brakes are smooth, progressive, effective and easy to operate; but care must be exercised towards the end of the landing run to avoid tipping the aircraft on its nose.

Flying Qualities

Stability Laterally the aircraft is stable. It tends to fly left wing down on the climb and right wing down at top speed. Directionally the aircraft is stable under all conditions of flight with engines on and off. Longitudinally the aircraft is neutrally stable with engine off for the centre of gravity position tested. The stall is normal with no vice nor any snatching.

Aerobatics Loops, half rolls off loops and stalled turns have been carried out. The aircraft handles well at moderate and slow speeds, but at high speeds the aerobatic handling would be improved by a lighter rudder and ailerons.

Landing and Take off The aircraft is easy and normal to take-off and to land. There is a tendency to swing to the left when taking off but this can easily be counteracted by the rudder. There is no swing on landing. If the engine is opened up with the undercarriage down and with tail trimming gear and flaps set for landing the aircraft can still be held by the elevator control.

Side slipping and ground handling The aircraft is difficult to sideslip and cannot be held in sustained sideslip beyond about 10deg. The aircraft is easy to handle on the ground and stable in winds up to 30mph.

Undercarriage The undercarriage is very satisfactory having good shock absorbing qualities and good rebound damping. The retracting gear is simple and easy to operate. The undercarriage can be restricted in about 45 seconds without undue exertion by the pilot, and it can be lowered in about 20 seconds. The indicator works satisfactorily and the wheels themselves can be seen, when up or down, through small windows in the floor. This latter is an excellent feature.

Flying View The view forward and around the upper hemisphere is good except that there is one small blind spot aft which obscures the tail and rudder. In a fighting aircraft view in this direction may be important, though for Home Defence purposes less important, and if this blind spot could be eliminated for fighting, view would much improved. View downwards is largely blanked by the wings, but the view for take-off and landing is good. The covered cockpit enables the pilot to look aft without the risk of having his goggles blown off.

Cockpit comfort The cockpit is extremely roomy and comfortable and keeps warm even down to –50deg.C. It is not unduly noisy and the layout of instruments and controls is satisfactory. The cockpit is easy to enter and leave when the aircraft is on the ground and the roof fully open. It was found that at speeds above approximately 150mph it was impossible to slide the cockpit roof to the open position and at these speeds the air pressure will slide the cockpit roof from the open to the closed position. Consequently it is quite impossible for the pilot to make an emergency exit at any speed above 150mph, and it is submitted that this is a defect unacceptable in a high speed fighting aircraft. Modification is required to the cockpit roof so that it can be opened at any speed.

Interim Report on the barrel flow, gun temperature and other tests.
Report No. M/689/2/Arm/Int.3. dated 28th September 1937

The tests on which this report is based were made between 15th June and 19th August 1937

Introduction
1. In accordance with the verbal instructions received from the Air Ministry, certain tests of the Hurricane gun installations have been carried out in addition to the normal gunnery trials. Although the full series of tests have not been completed, information upon some of the points is now available and is submitted in this interim report.

Object of the trials
2. (a) To determine the speed and direction of airflow in the gun barrels.
   (b) To find the difference in temperature in the gun body when the breech block is back and when it is forward.
   (c) To test the functioning of guns after, firstly a climb with the breech open followed by a climb with the breech closed.
   (d) To ascertain the effect of the condensation in the guns after firing.
   (e) To determine whether the air bottle capacity and speed of recuperation of air pressure are satisfactory.
   (f) To investigate the possibility of the wings being deflected under load (torsion and sweep-back) and so altering the angles of guns to the line of sight.
   (g) To find out whether one or two rounds of tracer inserted towards the end of each belt give visible warning that ammunition is nearly expended.

Trials and Results
3. (a) **Barrel Flow** Two lightly fitting plugs of cotton wool were inserted into the barrels of two guns before flight. In one gun the plug was fitted about 2″ from the muzzle, and in the other the

same distance from the chamber. After flight both plugs had disappeared and were subsequently found inside the wing in the gun bay. Small pressure and static heads supplied by the Royal Aircraft Establishment were fitted to one gun and connected to an accurate air-speed indicator in the cockpit. The readings obtained with and without flash eliminators fitted are plotted against the aircraft speed.

(b) **Gun Temperature** Climbs to 33,000 feet were made with Distant Reading thermometers strapped to the bodies of the two guns; one had its breech open and the other closed. Figures II and III show the differences in temperature experienced. Both the gun temperatures continued to drop below that recorded at 33,000ft. In one instance the temperature of the breech open gun was –7 deg.C at 33,000ft. and six minutes later when the aircraft had descended to 11,000ft it was –10 deg.C. It is thought that this may possibly be due to the absence on the glide and presence on the climb of hot exhaust gases from the engine heating the wing root and so warming the whole volume of air within the wing; the lag of the thermometers is not great enough to explain such large differences in temperature. These tests will be repeated and outside air temperatures recorded.

(c) **Effect of breech block position on functioning** The first test was inconclusive as only one gun fired. Two guns were set with breechblocks open Neither of the breech open guns fired any rounds and, although they each had a round in the chamber, the caps were not struck – this shows that the rear sear pneumatic units functioned, but the fire and safe units did not function. Of the breech-closed guns one fired all its rounds in the normal way after the first round had been fired by use of the fire and safe valve; the other gun did not fire; the cap was very lightly struck and no recoil took place. This gun subsequently functioned perfectly at low altitude. All these tests were done at 33,000ft with a recorded gun temperature of –7deg.C. At low altitude in a subsequent test, after the pneumatic gear had been considerably improved, all four guns worked satisfactorily except for normal stoppages not due to the installation (mis-feed and separated case.)

Climb No.4 – 2 scoops fitted – breeches open – figures in degrees Celsius

Height	Temp. Near gun Port 4	Temp Near gun Starboard 4	Radiator inlet	Outside Air Temp
Ground	12½	21	105	9
5,000ft	24	27	100	6½
10,000ft	27	27	110	−2
15,000ft	23	24	115	−10
20,000ft	18	18	115	−22
25,000ft	13	12	120	−35
30,000ft	2	–	110	−48

Wait at 30,000ft

1 minute	−3	105	
2 minutes	−2	−4	105
3 minutes	−3	−4	100
4 minutes	−5	−6	95
5 minutes	−7	−7	95
6 minutes	−8	−8	100
7 minutes	−8	−8	100
8 minutes	−8	−8	100
9 minutes	−8	−8	100
10 minutes	−8	−8	100

It is interesting to note how the gun temperatures settled down after six minutes with a continuing outside air temperature of −48deg.C. and a stabilised radiator inlet temperature of 100deg.C.

(d) **Gun functioning** 5,831 rounds were fired at high altitude with gun temperatures as shown. Twenty-seven stoppages occurred of which the details are as follows:

Seventeen due to lack of air pressure or leaks and consequent failure of the rear sear to operate.

Four due to the inability of the breech block to complete the recoil stroke, this resulted in the empty cartridge case not being ejected. A possible reason for this type of stoppage is that the links employed had already been used once, an adequate supply of new links not being available. Slightly damaged or distorted links might account for the recoil movement not being completed. The fact that the guns were new and therefore rather tight may be a contributory cause. It was also noted that the feed block slides of some guns were fouling the feed necks and this might slow the recoil.

Three lightly struck caps were found. These were due to traces of mineral jelly, which had not been properly removed from the new guns, obstructing the forward movement of the firing pin.

Two misfires

One failure of a fire and safe unit owing to low air pressure.

(e) Pneumatic system and Compressor

(f) Pneumatic system and compressor

The following figures were recorded:-

Climb No	Air Bottle Pressure at Take-off before firing	At 30,000ft	At 30,000ft	No. of bursts
2	185	175	130	10
3	185	170	120	18

During Climb No.4 detailed figures were taken and these were:

Height	Pressure	At 30,000ft during wait	
		Minutes	Pressure
Ground	190	1	170
5,000ft	200	3	165
10,000ft	205	7	160
15,000ft	205	10	155
20,000ft	200	13	150
25,000ft	190		
30,000ft	175		

At 30,000ft after firing		
1 burst	pressure 145	
2 bursts	130	
3 bursts	120	
4 bursts	115	
5 bursts	100	

On descent which included a wait of six minutes at 20,000ft, the pressure at 10,000ft was only 130.

Conclusions and Recommendations The radiator suitability has been retested as it was considered it might be affected by the scoops fitted to the hot air inlet pipes. It was found to be satisfactory and will be made the subject of a separate report to this establishment. It is recommended that the heating system should be applied to production Hurricane aircraft.

HURRICANE L.1562 – GUN HEATING AND HIGH ALTITUDE FIRING
Report No. M/689/2 dated 23rd March 1938

The trials upon which these reports were based were carried out between 2nd March and 14th March 1938.

Introduction
1. In accordance with Air Ministry letter No.S.38267/ 36/R.D.Arm.1(a)/W.R.H. dated 14th February 1938 tests have been completed at this Establishment on a production Hurricane aircraft in which both gun bays are heated by hot air. The heating system is similar to that described in the last of the reports quoted above except that the diameter of the hot air pipes leading from the radiator to gun departments has been increased to 2″. High altitude flying and air compressor tests were combined with the gun heating trials.

Object of the trials
2. (a) To find the temperature within the port and starboard gun bays under the worst possible conditions and to compare these with the outside air temperature.
   (b) To test the functioning of the guns at high altitude.
   (c) To obtain data on the performance of the pneumatic firing system and air compressor.

Trials
3. (a) **Temperatures** Distant reading thermometers were installed in the aircraft with the elements as far as possible from the hot air inlet pipe, that is outboard of No.4 gun on each side. Eight climbs to 30,000ft were made and periods of from 10 to 15 minutes were spent at this height to allow the gun bay temperatures to become steady. The gun temperatures and radiator inlet temperatures were recorded at intervals on the climb, during the wait at 30,000ft and in some instances on the descent. The outside air temperatures were obtained from another aircraft using a strut thermometer. The guns were fired in the majority of the tests but when this was not done the installation was arranged as it would have been if firing had been intended (e.g., all ejection apertures were open, feed necks etc., in position.) In order to increase the flow of hot air, two scoops were constructed at this Establishment and were attached to the pipes which had been fitted behind the radiator by the makers. These pipes were cut at an angle of 45deg. to the radiator surface as in the original heating system applied to the prototype Hurricane. The scoops are somewhat similar to ship ventilators: the bell-mouthed part is just clear of the radiator honeycomb and has a diameter of some $3\frac{1}{2}$″. Their length was originally such that the point of intake was rather more than half way down the radiator. At the request of Messrs. Hawkers the scoops were shortened for the last trial so that their mouths were a little above the middle of the radiator.
   (b) **Gun functioning** The guns were fired at 30,000ft usually after climbs with the breech open. The guns were Browning Mk.II and they were fitted with the bellows type fire and safe unit and the rear sear units of the latest pattern.
   (c) **Pneumatic gear and compressor** Air bottle pressures were recorded during the climb, the wait at 30,000ft and the descent. The fall of the pressure for the different number of operations of the pneumatic firing gear was also noted.

Results
4. During the firing of 5,831 rounds at high altitude with gun temperatures as shown:

Port Gun 4 from 24deg.C at 5,000ft to –8deg.C after 10 minutes at 30,000ft.
Starboard Gun 4 from 27deg.C at 5,000ft to –8deg.C after 10 minutes at 30,000ft.

Seventeen stoppages were due to lack of air pressure of leaks and consequent failure of the rear sears to operate.

Four stoppages were due to the inability of the breech block to complete the recoil stroke. This resulted in the empty cases not being ejected. A possible reason for this type of stoppage is that the links employed had already been used once.

MARINE AIRCRAFT EXPERIMENTAL ESTABLISHMENT
LANDING TESTS OF A WALRUS IN A SIDE WIND
A.M. Ref: 320511/34/ 399511/35/R.D.A.2
MAEE Ref: T.116.

Introductory Landing tests were required to determine the worst wind and sea conditions in which a Walrus could be landed at angles up to 90° to a wind.

Tests Made Tests were first made in winds up to 14–16 mph. and these were continued as opportunity offered until tests were made in side winds of 20mph. Finally a series of five cross wind landings were made in a 20mph wind at 20°, 45°, 70° and 90° to the wind. The tests were made between March and July 1938

Results of Test No difficulty was experienced in making a landing in a side wind of 14 to 16 mph. There was a tendency for the aircraft to swing into the wind towards the end of the run but this was easily controlled by the rudder. The Walrus was in no way severely strained during these trials and there appears to be little danger of damage occurring in these conditions. A side load on the leeward float was naturally experienced but examination of the float bracing after five landings revealed no damage. Tests were made in a wind of 20mph with a swell of about 1½ft. the crests of which were at right angles to the wind. When landed across

wind at angles up to about 70° the aircraft tended to bounce off the swell in a stalled condition. This tendency was less pronounced at 90°. During the landings at 90° to the wind there was a tendency for the aircraft to drop the leeward wing during the holding-off period. This could be corrected by the use of ailerons. After the aircraft touched the water the leeward float showed a tendency to submerge and this caused the aircraft to turn into the down-wind direction. This turn could not be entirely prevented by rudder and ailerons. There was considerable strain on the aircraft during these landings but examination showed no damage whatever after five landings.

Conclusions It is concluded from the above tests that the Walrus can be safely landed across wind at angles up to 90° in side winds up to 20mph. It is, however, considered that if the height of the waves exceeds about 1½ ft. there would be risk of damage to the structure. The conditions stated are therefore regarded as limiting conditions for the aircraft.

AN INVESTIGATION OF THE WATER PERFORMANCE OF THE SUNDERLAND FLYING BOAT
M.A.E.E. Ref: R.68 Report issued on 8th January 1940

Introduction This test does not fit, strictly speaking into a history of the inter-war years, since it takes place in 1940, furthermore the test does not take place at Felixstowe. It is therefore one of the first tests to be carried out at Helensburgh and is a reminder that the Suffolk base was too exposed to probable action for experimental work and so Clydeside was considered more secure come the war. This particular test was carried out on a Sunderland flying boat. Tests had been made at M.A.E.E. to investigate the water performance to provide full-scale data for comparison with tank tests on the model.

Range of investigation Measurements of attitude, acceleration and speed have been made in take-offs, landings, accelerated and steady taxiing runs.

Conclusions The mean altitudes for elevator neutral have been obtained and these show that the attitude at the hump and higher speeds is 3½ lower during take-off than in landing. The steady run attitudes are intermediate. Flaps have little effect on attitude but the control available by the use of elevator during take-off is considerable, amounting to 3½ at the hump and three times this at 50kts. The effect of wind is to reduce the hump attitude both in take-off and landing by about 1½" for a 10kt wind. Porpoising occurs with extreme stick positions at the hump speed and above but it has not been found dangerous.

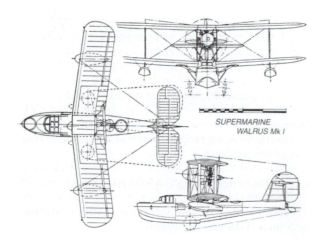

SUPERMARINE
WALRUS Mk I

The drag of the Sunderland has been calculated from the observed accelerations and an estimate of the thrust has found to be less in landings than in take-off at the same attitude. The difference is greatest at the hump where the drag accelerating in the take-off is 60% greater than the drag decelerating in the landing. The differences diminish at higher speeds until there is substantial agreement at 65 kts. Corrections for slipstream effects are not sufficient to explain the differences so that it appears that acceleration itself increases the drag.

Further developments

Check tests will be made in winds of less than 5 kts and in these tests the effect of a known applied moment on the attitude in steady runs will be tried. The effect of acceleration on drag will be investigated in the tests of the Scion which has been fitted with a model of the Sunderland hull and a force recording undercarriage.

Discrepancies in attitude during take-off have been noted with several seaplanes when the full scale results have been compared with the results of tank tests on the corresponding models. Comprehensive tests to investigate the water performance of the Sunderland were therefore made in such a form that they could be readily compared with the results of model tests to be made in the seaplane testing tank at the Royal Aircraft Establishment, Farnborough. The tests described in the present report were made at Felixstowe over the period from November 1938 to August 1939.

THE THREAT FROM NAZI GERMANY

THE IMPACT OF THE SPANISH CIVIL WAR ON THE DEVELOPMENT OF THE LUFTWAFFE

The air war fought by the Condor Legion

It may be fairly said that German air doctrine was a by-product of the prosecution of the air war against Republican forces. The latter were being aided by the Soviets and so Russian types were met in combat. Early in the conflict two lessons were learned:

1. The JU 52, which turned out to be a very successful transport, was of limited use as a bomber.
2. The He51 biplane was inferior to the Russian fighters supplied to the Republic.

The Ju. 52

The He. 51

Me. 109

He. 111

Ju.87

Do.17

Notice the distinctive markings of the aircraft which belonged to the Condor Legion and compare them with the operational markings of German aircraft in World War II which follow.

It is interesting to see that Germany, like Britain, were using biplane fighters in the mid to late 1930's

By 1939 the Germans had produced the very successful Me 109, the Heinkel III, the Dornier 17 and the JU.87 dive bomber:

On the ground the 88mm flak-gun proved itself effective against aircraft and ground targets.

The doctrine of close air support

As chief of staff of the Condor Legion, Richthofen was well aware of the theories of air power championed by Trenchard, Mitchell and Douhet but these did not provide an answer to the stalemate on the ground. Trying to fight a strategic air campaign met with very little success. There was a lack of strategic targets in Spain with few armament factories to target and bombing the cities did not contribute to a lowering of the morale and discipline of the working classes. In any case this was not a war between two combatant countries but a civil war. The Condor Legion had to adopt different tactics. Against considerable opposition and without official sanction Richthofen went on to develop the doctrine of close air support to the ground forces. For this to be successful the ground forces had to be in radio communication with the aircraft. It helped also to assign *Luftwaffe* officers to work on the ground with Army units to talk to pilots in their own language. The Stuka Ju.87s would dive on enemy ground forces to disperse them and break their morale making it easier for the friendly ground force below to advance.

The *Luftwaffe* had experienced difficulty in hitting targets accurately from a high altitude. This was not a problem with dive bombers and Udet came to the extravagant conclusion that every bomber should be a dive bomber. With a low production rate of bombs in the late 1930s the *Luftwaffe* could ill afford to waste bombs. When the Ju.88 prototype was flown Udet demanded that this aircraft have a dive-bombing capability. This, together with other design changes, resulted in a five ton increase in unladen weight with a consequent sacrifice in speed. To attempt to give a dive-bombing capability to a Ju.88 was bad enough, the attempt to do so with the He177 bordered on the ridiculous. The He 177 was a long range strategic bomber which was then in the

middle of a development programme. There were already problems with the engine design and trying to include in its role dive bombing and anti-shipping, as well, only served to ensure that the aircraft would not evolve into an effective strategic bomber. The wish to reduce drag by using coupled pairs of engines was mistaken. The engines caught fire in flight too often, six of the eight prototypes crashed and many of the 35 pre production aircraft were either written off through in-flight fires or swinging on take-off. A few were sent to bomb Britain in 400mph shallow dives without proper aiming equipment. So much for strategic bombing! It also underscored the muddled thinking that went into German bomber development at a critical moment and would result in German aircraft industry churning out various marks of the He.111 which, by 1944 was an outdated aircraft.

THE EFFECTS OF GERMAN REARMAMENT ON FRANCE AND BRITAIN

It cannot be denied that the *Luftwaffe*, in the support of land forces, was extremely successful in prosecuting the war against Poland, the Low Countries, France and initially the Soviet Union. Even as the war progressed German industry would produce the Me.262 jet fighter, the FW190 and the V1 and V2 rockets. The reasons for Germany's collapse lies as much in the political leadership of the Third Reich as it does in the growing strength of the Allied land, sea and air forces ranged against it. In the period 1938/9 all this was to come and the fears engendered by Germany's rearmament were very real. America was maintaining its isolation so it was up to Britain and France to thwart Hitler's ambitions.

What impressed governments most was the numbers, particularly the British government. Insufficient attention was paid to the quality of political leadership in Germany and the lack of strategic direction with Göring at the helm. Göring had neither the training nor the understanding to sustain the success of the German forces in the early years of the war. The numbers game was played by Hitler who wanted to quintuple the size of the *Luftwaffe* by 1942. This megalomania was common to both fascist dictators. Mussolini boasted of an air force that would blot out the sun but neither dictator had the economic resources to realise their dreams. Göring, ever eager to give his master the numbers of aircraft he wanted, ignored advice on the necessity to devote between 20 and 30% of output on spares needed to keep his aircraft in the air. The *Luftwaffe* would later find that cannibalisation was the only way operational aircraft would be returned to combat readiness.

The French appeared to be mired in their Maginot Line mentality. They believed that if the *Luftwaffe* crossed the French frontier it could not survive the forest of anti aircraft guns and could not therefore influence the land battle in France. On the other hand the British

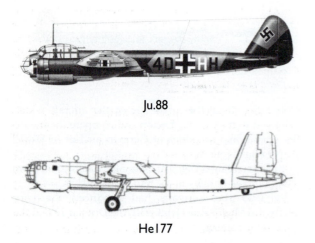

Ju.88

He177

government, in the words of the Prime Minister, Mr Baldwin, believed that 'the bomber will always get through'. The British chiefs of staff had warned successive governments about the German air threat. At Munich in 1938 it was apparent that both the British and French governments were reluctant to push Hitler into a war believing that a military confrontation over Czechoslovakia would come at a time when Germany would dominate the skies. It was just before the Munich crisis, however, that French morale suffered a collapse. In mid August 1938 the French chief of the Air Staff visited Germany to be shown an example of aerial might. This led the French government into believing that their air force would survive for only two months against the *Luftwaffe*. Georges Bonnet, the French foreign minister, warned the German ambassador that an attack upon Czechoslovakia would lead to war, at the same time fearing that France might actually be forced to honour her obligation to defend Czech independence. The belief that the Maginot line alone could defeat the *Luftwaffe* evaporated and there was a real fear that French cities would be laid waste. France, it appeared, was paying the price for neglect of its air force.

Both countries may have feared the threat of aerial bombardment but in 1938 the German high command had no plans to conduct a strategic air campaign against the British Isles. On the section of this chapter dealing with the deployment of fighter squadrons in the UK, it was emphasised that German aircraft would have to cross the North Sea to attack Britain. The attacks on Britain during the late summer of 1940 and the Blitz which followed were possible due to the collapse of France not to any war plans devised in the pre-war period. General Felmy, commander of the Second Air Force, warned the High Command that a war of destruction against England was not possible given the means at his disposal. The lack of a strategic bomber has already been mentioned. A staff officer of *Luftflotten* 2 had also advised that Germany's capability to attack Britain would amount only to pin pricks. The German air force was committed to assisting the Army in prosecuting a ground war and in providing fighter defence of Germany not in prosecuting a strategic air war. For one thing the Germans had made little or no attempt at solving the problem of finding and attacking targets at night or in bad weather. This left them with no other option but to tie in their war plans to those of the Army which would involve close air support. In this their experience of the Spanish civil war would prove invaluable.

In saying that the *Luftwaffe* had no other option but to support the land forces may seem to discount the naval option. Hitler, like Napoleon Boneparte before him was the leader of a continental power where the threat on land was much more immediate. Germany was no different from France and any other European country in

that land forces could cross their borders within hours. Both leaders had land-locked minds. Admittedly Napoleon had a fleet which could rival that of Britain. So also did the Kaiser in the Great War when it was 'dreadnought for dreadnought' but the latter were not decisive in the outcome of hostilities. The British Admiralty clung to its belief in the battleship as the capital ship of the fleet and Hitler wished to build up a German surface fleet albeit belatedly. The Anglo German Naval Agreement did give the German dictator the 'go ahead' to launch two battle cruisers but a war at sea was not high on the list of Hitler's priorities. Like the strategic bomber there was no sense of direction and only half-hearted attempts were made to extend German air power over the sea. Where were the aircraft carriers? One was laid but not completed. Where were the long-rang maritime attack aircraft? The FW 200 Condor was a four-engined reconnaissance aircraft which began life in the late 1930s, but there was no shipping attack version until the last production variant, the FW 200C-8 which was based at Bordeaux-Marignac, France in 1944. This variant met with little success and the type reverted to its original role. The lack of strategic direction is self evident.

THE MUNICH CRISIS

The details of the international crisis of September 1938, concerning the future of the Sudetan Germans, when the Prime Minister, Mr Chamberlain, went to Munich to meet Adolf Hitler has been well chronicled. It is of interest in this narrative principally because it was feared that a second world war was imminent. The fact that war did not begin for another year gave the country a breathing space in which to make final preparations. This section will look at the deficiencies that had to be tackled with so little time to spare. The Expansion Plans have been fully described and the aircraft industry together with the shadow factories were busy producing aircraft of all types for the impending conflict and the nation's manpower was to be mobilised as never before. In and out of uniform were members of the RAF, RAFVR, AAF, WAAF and the Civil Air Guard. In the streets the Army were assisting with the filling of sandbags and the placing of same round public buildings. Meanwhile the Air Staff considered the matters requiring their urgent attention

The Readiness of Bomber Command This has been considered in some detail in Chapter 10 in the matter of strategic air doctrine. In terms of the number of bomber squadrons ready for war the Mobilisation Committee looked at the figures. There were, in September 1938, 32 squadrons available with 372 aircraft, Of these 22 squadrons were equipped with medium bombers, Wellesleys, Battles and Blenheims and 10 heavy bomber squadrons had Whitleys and Harrows totalling some 120 aircraft. This figure is misleading since a further 15 squadrons were either being re-equipped with new types or had obsolete aircraft like Heyfords, Hinds and Hendons. The Air Staff regarded these as reserves. There was a shortage of up-to-date aircraft and some squadrons had had to hang on to outdated types for far too long, like the venerable Virginia. There was also a shortage of aircraft crews and spares. Even the squadrons which were regarded as ready for mobilisation were not all fully operational. Ten squadrons had possessed their aircraft for less than five months. No.21 Squadron, for example, had had Blenheims for only one month. In short, if Bomber Command had had to go to war in September 1938, the air effort would have declined rapidly. There were 2,500 reserve pilots at the time of Munich but only some 200 were ready to go to war. Taking the example of Coastal Command 3 of its 15 squadrons were training. If a squadron was ready to go to war it had to deploy to its war station. In some cases squadrons did not reach their war station until after the crisis was over.

The Readiness of Fighter Command In September 1938 there were 29 squadrons, comprising 406 aircraft, ready for war and of these only five squadrons (70 aircraft) had the Hurricane and one squadron had the Spitfire I (No.19 at Duxford). Fighter Command would have had to go to war with Gauntlets and Gladiators. These had little or no margin of speed over the German bombers and to make matters worse Fighter Command needed 688 fighters not 406, to defend the British Isles. The Hurricanes could not fire its Browning guns above 15,000ft since the modification required to heat the guns what not then available.(Trials on the guns of a Hurricane are described earlier in the chapter) Four of these squadrons were set to accompany the Field Force which would go to the Continent on mobilisation. Of those left at Home 238 fighters were either obsolete of obsolescent. The extra year to prepare for the war when it came was vital in getting Fighter Command equipped with 8-gun monoplane fighters. If one adds the extra months of the 'phoney war', it is significant that the Battle of Britain was fought almost entirely with Spitfires and Hurricanes.

Overall situation During the Munich crisis Herman Goering was overheard to say that the RAF could not have taken on the *Luftwaffe* had he ordered his air force to attack Britain at that time. Since at that time France had not been defeated one must suppose that he meant a strategic bombing offensive mounted from German airfields. With nothing heavier than HE.111s it is doubtful if Germany would have been able to deliver a 'knock out' blow. Be that as it may a senior politician, working for Sir Thomas Inskip delivered a gloomy forecast to match Goering's optimism. He gave the RAF

only three weeks with RAF pilots going to a certain death whilst the Air Member for Supply and Organization expressed the opinion that what the RAF had been building up during the Expansion period was nothing but a facade. He feared that there was nothing in the way of reserves or organization behind the front line with which to maintain it.

Remedial Steps
As a direct consequence of the Munich crisis all Air Ministry departments and RAF Commands were required to write a report on the shortcomings of each. When these had been received they disclosed not problems peculiar to one command but general shortcomings. Trenchard had said at the outset that he would build a cottage on the foundations of a castle, but it was not that simple given the massive expansion that took place from 1934 onwards. It was not simply the RAF that was finding it difficult to cope, manufacturing industry was not equipped for wartime production. Organizationally the RAF Commands which had come into existence in 1935 were not well equipped for war. The Group headquarters were supposed to do little more than control the operations of their constituent squadrons. They were kept largely free of administrative and supply matters. Group HQs had only a small administrative staff and no technical staff. Speaking for Bomber Command, Air Marshal Sir Edgar Ludlow-Hewitt proposed that whilst Command HQ should deal with personnel administration, Group HQ should have engineering, signals, medical and equipment staffs with an organization staff officer to co-ordinate their work.

Some latitude in financial management was also proposed. It was proposed that Command and Group commanders should be able to authorise expenditure for measures of an extraordinary nature and this resulted in sums of up to £25,000 being made available to each C-in-C. This together with the other reforms would increase the efficiency of Groups. Of course, intention was one thing implementation was another. The shortage of suitable specialist officers would mean delay before Ludlow-Hewitt's reforms could take effect.

Indeed the quality of existing staff officers was called into question by Sir Warren Fisher at the Treasury. He had written a minute to the Prime Minister criticising the Air Staff. He accused them of displaying a lack of imagination and foresight and incompetence in practical matters including strategic policy. He inferred that the Air Staff continually misled the government and the only hope for the country was thoroughly to reform the Air Staff including selection of the right men. Fisher took the view that the Air Staff were mistaken in believing that the early expansion schemes would act as a deterrent to Hitler. The only enemy that Britain had to fear was Germany and that technological development of air warfare made this country particularly vulnerable to air attack.

Sir Kingsley Wood naturally rebutted these views. Fisher's assertion that the Air Staff had been disingenuous was wounding. The Air Minister could point to the difficulty in obtaining intelligence from a totalitarian regime which reduced the value of Air Attachés and military missions in this respect. The *Luftwaffe* had been built up in an atmosphere of great secrecy and reliance had to be placed on reports from British agents who had managed to obtain a copy of the 1934 plan for the *Luftwaffe*. This and other intelligence matters relating to the threat from Germany had been correlated and passed periodically to the Cabinet and the Committee of Imperial Defence. It had been shown that the Army had not been neglected but preference for resources had been given to the *Luftwaffe*. The Air Ministry therefore considered that the threat which underpinned the Expansion Schemes was based on the best intelligence available. Kingsley Wood could also remind the Prime Minister that it was the Treasury that opposed the acceleration of Scheme A albeit unsuccessfully and that financial limitations were imposed on Scheme J by the Cabinet in December 1937 resulting in its rejection.

Whether or not Fisher's views were in any way justified it was a bit late in the day to undertake a root and branch overhaul of the Air Ministry. Kingsley Wood had immediately to set about remedying the deficiencies in the RAF. In October 1938 he wrote in a Cabinet Paper that every effort had to be made to escape from the position in which the Air Ministry had found itself during the recent crisis when squadrons had less than one week's reserves particularly the fighter squadrons. Slessor had warned that operations that were not vital to the security of the country should be avoided to conserve strength. The series of conferences that took place during October resulted in Scheme M. This supplemented Scheme L by increasing the first line fighter strength to about 30 per cent above the figure in the existing scheme. Scheme M would, in fact, mop up all outstanding items from previous schemes and was set for completion by 31st March 1942.

Kingsley Wood had to show that the RAF was maintaining parity with Germany but he sought to show that parity could be measured in the number of bombs that could be dropped in a given period. In this respect he favoured the heavy bomber. The heavy bomber had a longer range and bomb load and could carry the amount of defensive armament required to enhance the prospects of reaching the target intact. He added that it also meant economy in flying time, in maintenance personnel and accessories. He regarded parity with the *Luftwaffe* in number was always going to be difficult given the unlimited effort the Germany was prepared to put into armaments.

THE APPROACH OF WAR

AIR RAID PRECAUTIONS AND DEFENCES

The Air Raid Precautions Act of 1937 became law on 1st January 1938 and volunteers were called for to become wardens. The business of organizing the air raid precautions for the British Isles fell to Mr E.J. Hodsoll who headed a special department in the Home Office and financial responsibility was shared between central and local government. In the event there was an overestimate of the number of human casualties due to enemy bombing. On the other hand the damage to houses and public buildings was underestimated and virtually no preparations were made to repair housing stock nor to rehouse those who had lost their homes. Furthermore the volunteers were often untrained in air raid precautions and fire emergency.

Under Civil Defence Emergency Scheme Y the country was divided into regions for ARP purposes, each with a regional commissioner. Specific measures were put into place to mitigate the effects of bombing, not simply with high explosives but also incendiary and gas. Plans were laid for children who lived in the areas considered most likely to be subjected to serious and prolonged bombing attacks, to be evacuated to the country. This actually happened and the author remembers arriving home from school one day to find a strange child seated on the floor playing with his toys. Some ruffled feathers had to be smoothed!! Then there was the problem of survival during bombing attacks. Here there was a choice. For those with gardens, an Anderson Shelter could be constructed. These were named after Sir John Anderson who joined the Cabinet in late 1938 as Lord Privy Seal with special responsibility for civil defence. For those who had no garden and would therefore have to take refuge in the home there was the Morrison shelter, again named after a prominent Labour politician, Herbert Morrison. This took the form of a steel box covered with a steel mesh. The occupants of a house were meant to place the shelter against a wall, preferably in the corner of a room where falling ceilings are less likely to come crashing down on the cage. By April 1939 nearly 300,000 Anderson shelters had been distributed from a total order for $2^1/_2$ million. Local authorities were also empowered to grant loans to households to enable people to make their own shelters. Public shelters were also built in towns and other places where the civil population would congregate when they could not use their own shelters. Finally gas masks for adults and children were issued and these were regularly tested with gas vans visiting localities to ensure a good respirator fit. Babies were placed in a respirator, which enclosed the entire body.

Air raid warnings would prove to be vital, not only for scrambling the necessary fighter squadrons to intercept enemy bombers but also to permit the population, in the areas likely to be subject to attack, to take cover. In this respect the British public were well served. Under Air Marshal Dowding's leadership the chain of radar stations would be ready and these would be linked to the Sector Operations Rooms of Fighter Command with information going to the affected civil defence region for the purpose of giving either the air raid warning or the 'all clear' signifying the departure of attacking enemy aircraft. By the summer of 1939 there were 20 RDF stations in operation. The Royal Observer Corps, which had been formed in 1925, was to play a vital role in the forthcoming conflict. It was a civilian manned organization commanded by a retired RAF officer. Recruited locally and controlled by the Home Office through Chief Constables in the Counties , the observers were able to supplement the information gained from the radar stations in that the actual strength of enemy formations and aircraft types could be ascertained as they crossed the coast.

A further measure designed to protect industrial targets and conurbations from air attack was the use of barrage balloons. RAF Balloon Command had been formed to provide barrages and more than 1,000 balloons were produced. Although the balloons remained substantially the same as those used in the Great War the cables had been redesigned, to part when struck by an aircraft. Its weight and inertia would cripple an aircraft. The barrages extended upwards to a height of 5,000 ft and London alone was defended by 142 balloons, although 450 had been planned. Each balloon was 63ft long and 31ft high and filled with hydrogen. A handling crew of ten was required for each balloon so a simple arithmetical calculation will show the manpower required just to protect London. As war approached the British public grew used to the sight of crews inflating their balloons in public parks or other open spaces.

MILITARY PREPARATIONS
Introduction
Everyone who has studied the history of the period knows that the French armed forces succumbed to the Nazi onslaught in just two short months in the summer of 1940 but it should be borne in mind that such a sudden collapse, leaving Britain alone to face the Germans, was not visualised in the period leading up to the war. The plans provided for the dispatch of an expeditionary force (British Expeditionary Force or B.E.F.) to go to France to fight alongside the French Army and for an air striking force (Advance Air Striking Force or AASF) to accompany the B.E.F. The AASF was to be comprise ten squadrons of Battles and Blenheims for attacks upon enemy columns and four squadrons of Hurricanes for fighter defence. In theory Fighter Command and Bomber Command were prepared to send additional forces if required but, in the event, Dowding refused to commit any more fighters to France

in a vain attempt to stem the advance of German forces across France and Belgium for fear that it would deplete the squadrons needed for home defence.

The French had a well-equipped army but it was believed that air action would precede a ground war. They did not have a highly developed radar network and it was relatively easy for the Germans to penetrate French air space in 1940 and when they did there was not the efficient fighter control system that would put French fighters into the air to meet their adversaries. Nor did they possess many high performance fighters, which would make the contribution of the AASF all the more important. The French were only just beginning to re-equip their squadrons with more up-to-date fighters whereas the Germans had done so in 1937/8 and Britain in 1938/9. Both countries had territories overseas to protect which would affect the disposition of their forces. At home RAF Coastal and Fighter Commands, in October 1938, did not between them have enough aircraft to provide for offensive operations as well as reconnaissance patrols. Coastal Command therefore decided to concentrate its limited resources on reconnaissance and interception in the North Sea and the sea areas which might be used by enemy warships attempting to break out into the North Atlantic.

LATE 1938/ EARLY 1939
A good example of the preparations for mobilisation was an Air Ministry order which went out to fighter squadrons concerning the setting of gun sights. The scale at the base of the reflector sights had a rotating mark which was to be set to correspond to the wingspan of target aircraft, ie., the wing span dimensions of German aircraft were to be used for range estimation. This was vital in view of the introduction of the 8-gun fighters where the four guns in each wing were set so that the cone of fire would meet at a predetermined distance in front of the aircraft. This would provide the lethal concentration of rounds on the target aircraft which was the whole raison d'être of the 8-gun fighter. In addition Blenheim squadrons were ordered to make medium range sorties across the North Sea to test full fuel load consumption. At the same time these bombers could simulate air attacks on the mainland on their return to exercise the personnel in the radar stations and observer posts.

The Munich crisis highlighted the lack of suitably equipped fighters manned by appropriately trained pilots to operate against enemy bombers flying at night nor was there a long range fighter capable of penetrating German air space. The lack of an effective night fighting force in Fighter Command was evident in the fact that that there was no effective system of finding a target at night. The Tangmere based squadrons did not have fighters with navigation lights. Eventually these Fury biplanes would be equipped with a lighting system adapted from bicycle lamps.

When Germany seized Czechoslovakia in March 1939 the radar stations were put on a 24 hour watch. They looked out to sea for 120 miles over arcs of 120 degrees. That same month squadron identification markings were painted out and national markings made less conspicuous. Hangars and buildings were covered with netting to break up their outline and aircraft were dispersed to parts of airfields well away from buildings that might be the subject of attack. Meanwhile Fairey Battles dropped live bombs during close-support exercises. Each aircraft released two 500 lb bombs or four 250 lb bombs but poor weather forced unit commanders to reduce the size of formations in order to reduce the prospect of collisions. In some areas the weather prevented pilots from finding their targets.

The summer months of 1939

In July the Wellingtons on No.149 Squadron simulated a daylight raid on Marseilles. The aim was to practice the defensive formation flying to enhance the effectiveness of the bombers' guns when attacked by fighters. (Refer to Chapter 10 for detailed illustrations and explanation). In this the bombers were required to fly in 'vics' of three, the aircraft rotating their positions to confuse enemy fighters. This was a questionable tactic however if, during a rotating manoeuvre, the gunner's aim was disturbed at a critical moment and it actually led to a loss of two Wellington bombers on 18th September 1939. The port propeller of the right-hand aircraft of the vic cut through the fuselage of the lead aircraft. The tail-less aircraft then collided with the first aircraft with the consequent loss of both. These aircraft belonged to No.9 Squadron which, in the immediate pre-war period, was practising formation flying which culminated in a fly-past over the 25th International Aviation Exhibition in Brussels. The same month saw interception exercises when RAF fighters were scrambled to counter RAF bombers acting as enemy intruders. No.11 Group controllers achieved an interception rate of 60% but this was often against lone aircraft and Fighter Command complained that Bomber Command did not send formations of bombers. Lone aircraft picked up on radar could be civil aircraft or RAF aircraft from other Commands. Eventually Bomber Command responded to the complaints from Dowding and his staff at Bentley Priory and formations of bombers were sent. There was a problem for single-engined bombers, which did not venture more than ten miles off shore before trying to simulate an attack. This was not very realistic but flying over the water for long periods invited the possibility of having to ditch in the event of single-engined failure. Higher navigation skills were also required. July also saw the issuing of Syko encrypting machines to provide greater security of signals' traffic. Letters and numbers were substituted with characters from a Syko card. These were random characters and the cards were

changed every twelve hours making it extremely difficult if not impossible to break the code before the cards were changed again.

The summer of 1939 was also important for the crop of new aircraft that were to move the RAF significantly from a biplane to a monoplane force. Late in the day as these arrivals might have been they were soon to enter service. The first of these, the production Defiant, flew for the first time in July. In the event these were not to be a success in action. The pilot had no fixed forward firing machine guns and therefore relied entirely on the gunner behind him in a power-operated turret. Initially the Germans may have been unpleasantly surprised in a tail chase but it did not take them long to work out how to approach one of these fighters. On 7th July the Beaufighter made its maiden flight. This would prove to be a highly successful night fighter. The Avro Manchester flew for the first time on 25th July. This aircraft was not a success but when Roy Chadwick lengthened the wings and added another two engines to produce the Lancaster he produced a heavy bomber which was the mainstay of the strategic bomber force in the Second World War.

Mobilization

Bomber Command was mobilized a month before war began. On 1st August war establishment exercises began and Wellington squadrons simulated enemy attacks in a full scale home defence exercise. As before Fighter Command complained about the way the bomber squadrons were playing their part in the exercise but, sadly, two of these aircraft were lost over the North Sea. The French air force also took part and the formations of fighters, bombers and reconnaissance aircraft raided Harwich. Targets in the Midlands, the West Country and London were also attacked.

On 3rd August the *Graf Zeppelin* airship crossed the North Sea to record the high frequency transmissions from suspected coastal radar stations. It approached the coast at Bawdsey before flying the length of Britain's east coast all the way to Scapa Flow in the Orkneys. No transmissions were picked up. This seemed to indicate that its presence had not been detected even though fighter squadrons were scrambled to make visual contact. In fact in May 1939 the *Graf Zeppelin* had been detected by the CH stations, the Germans concluded otherwise. When the Battle of Britain began it was all too clear to German pilots that they always seemed to be expected but the *Luftwaffe* did not seem to have appreciated the link between detection of aircraft and the prompt scrambling of fighters to meet them. The word 'seemed' is used by Willamson Murray in his book on the *Luftwaffe* from 1933 to 1945. Both he and Denis Richards, in his contribution to Purnell's History of the Second World War, believe that the pilots of the *Luftwaffe* found the radar masts difficult to attack and found No.11

Group's airfields in the south east of England more profitable targets. A more plausible explanation is provided by Sir Edward Fenessy who was closely involved in the early development of radar. He too was surprised that the German pilots did not single out the radar masts and it was only after the war when he met General Martini at the Farnborough Air Show that he learned more about the visit by the *Graf Zeppelin* in 1939. General Martini had been the Chief Signals Officer of the *Luftwaffe* and he held the belief that British radar had not tracked the airship. When he was assured that the *Graf Zeppelin* had been tracked he put in hand some research which provided an interesting example of mirror imaging. Because the Germans used a much higher frequency in their naval radars they expected that the British scientists would do the same. Consequently they were not looking for the British on metric frequencies when in fact the entire RDF chain was locked on to a fifty-cycle grid. A giant airship like the *Graf Zeppelin* had thousands of rivets and her bulk was being bombarded with heavy power radar. With radiations going off in all directions the radar stations were simply being confused. The German scientists on board the airship concluded that they were not being picked up by the radars but that the signals they were receiving were the flashing over of power. It may be concluded that the *Luftwaffe*'s intelligence simply did not know enough about the British system neither did they appreciate the sophistication of the RAF's fighter control system. One postscript to this sorry saga is that, during the Battle of Britain, Göring was asked for permission to make a concerted attack on the radar masts but only one day was allowed. What could have crippled the RDF system was simply not followed through like the attacks on 11 Group's airfields during the battle.

During the month civilian airlines operated as normal in spite of the imminence of war and both sides used the opportunity to indulge in a bit of intelligence gathering. The German airline, Deutsche Lufthansa was also engaged in covert intelligence gathering and their service to Croydon was more than a commercial flight, but then RAF pilots had been taken on board British airliners as supernumerary crew, ostensibly to gain experience in long range high speed flight. Whenever the opportunity presented itself to observe aircraft movements on German airfields, or spy on industrial or communications centres, that opportunity was taken. The number of civil flights doubled in the few remaining weeks of peace, including night flights, ostensibly carrying freight and the RAF crews being carried would say, if questioned, that they were on route familiarization trips.

German forces crossed into Poland on 31st August and fighting began on 1st September. Britain and France were pledged to come to the aid of Poland but that did not mean actually sending armed forces into that country to fight alongside the Poles. Instead an ultimatum was passed to Berlin that, unless German forces were at once withdrawn from Poland, a state of war would exist between Britain and Germany. With the Second World War only hours away general mobilization was ordered for all RAF Commands. The BBC television transmitter at Alexandra Palace was closed down in case it became a radio navigational beacon along with the RAF's teleprinters. Radio transmissions continued normally however since they came from a number of locations. It was well within the capability of even an amateur spy to work out which squadrons were located at which airfields, and the scatter plan was put into operation. This not only put all the German knowledge of the whereabouts of RAF squadrons back to square one, it also prevented a successful single 'knock out' blow by the enemy. In fact such an outcome was unlikely in 1939 since German aircraft would have had to launch attacks from German airfields and whilst the bombers may have reached Britain they would have done so without fighter escorts. It is nevertheless illustrative of the thinking amongst British politicians during the pre-war period to be prepared for the worst. There was some probing of British air defences during the autumn of 1939, like that over the Firth of Forth in October, but such forays could be carried out over the North Sea which did not mean crossing the airspace of non-belligerent countries. There was no aerial onslaught until the late summer of 1940, only the 'phoney war'.

THE RAF'S ORDER OF BATTLE FACING GERMANY – 3RD SEPTEMBER 1939

NOTE: A detailed Order of Battle for all theatres may be found in Appendix F.

Introduction

War was declared on Germany at 11.00hrs on Sunday 3rd September 1939. This final section dealing with the inter-war years places precisely the location of all RAF squadrons, both at home and overseas, at that time. The locations maps which follow show the whereabouts of squadrons by type, eg., fighter, bomber etc., and these will be accompanied by a short account of the nature of the war each was expected to fight, given the perceived threats. The reader must put out of his or her mind that Britain would shortly be fighting Germany alone. In 1939 a powerful ally, France, stood with a large army, a substantial navy including capital ships and a large air force. As soon as war was declared the BEF and the AASF would go forward prepared to fight on French soil and in the air above France and units of the French navy would co-operate with the Royal Navy to try to keep German naval units bottled up in port where Bomber

Command could attack them at their moorings.

The Benelux countries were neutral so attacks upon Germany from Britain would have to be made across the North Sea. Attacks from France would have to be made across the Maginot Line.

On 3rd September the RAF strength numbered 157 squadrons as follows:

Metropolitan Air Force	113 squadrons
AASF	9 squadrons
	(All Battle squadrons)
Overseas	35 squadrons

These dispositions were for 3rd September and disguise the fact that the AASF would comprise two Blenheim squadrons. (Nos. 59 and 139) and six Hurricane squadrons (Nos. 1,56,73, 85,87 and 151) in addition to the Battles squadrons. These units joined later, from 4th September up to February 1940.

DEPLOYMENT OF SQUADRONS OF BOMBER COMMAND

The Western Air Plans The formulation of the Western Air Plans is described in Chapter 10. They were produced by the Air Staff in the pre-war period and included draft operational orders that would be constantly reviewed and amended as necessary so that, in the event of war, these orders could be signed and sent to operational Commands, thence to Groups and squadrons. The Air Plans included a wide range of targets agreed between the Air Staff and their political masters. Between them the British and French had some 3,400 first line aircraft and 3,800 in reserve for operations in Europe. On the outbreak of war the RAF had two primary aims, the first was to be prepared to defend British air space to ensure that the Germans did not achieve a 'knock out blow'. Secondly, at the insistence of the Admiralty, there was to be a search for the main German fleet. (Two pocket battleships, *Graf Spee* and the *Deutchsland*, were already at sea and had been since August).

Bomber Command and Coastal Command went to war with attacks on the German Navy. Coastal Command would mount patrols and Bomber Command's No. 3 Group was to make daylight sorties in formation to attack German warships. At this very early stage of the war the Government was hopeful that Hitler would negotiate with the Allies. Care was to be taken to avoid casualties amongst the German civilian population and damage to industrial buildings. The last thing the Government wanted was to enrage Hitler which might unleash a savage reprisal. German ships were not to be attacked if they were in or close to the territorial waters of Holland, Belgium and Denmark. Finally, if the targets were not reached before dusk an aircraft's bombs were to be dropped into the sea, indeed

three Wellingtons jettisoned their bombs into the North Sea on the first day of the war.

Whilst the squadrons of Bomber Command were positioned and equipped to bomb targets in Germany it was clear that HMG did not wish to appear provocative. The French particularly did not want to invite German air raids on the eastern departments of France since the French air defence system was not in a fit state to prevent serious damage and casualties should cities be attacked. The British government had agreed with the French to drop nothing more lethal than leaflets intended to persuade the German population to overthrow the Nazi government and end the war. In the meantime the Wellington and Whitley squadrons could reconnoitre potential targets and test the German air defences.

DEPLOYMENT OF SQUADRONS OF FIGHTER COMMAND

The map which follows shows precisely the dividing lines between the Group areas and the squadrons deployed to each group. It is difficult not to think of the Battle of Britain when describing the fighter defence of the British Isles. By July 1940 there were two German air fleets in Belgium and Northern France (*Luftflotten* II and III) and a third air fleet in Norway (*Luftflotten* V). In August 1939, however, all German air fleets were on German soil. The Benelux countries were neutral and so the only approach to the British Isles would have been across the North Sea. Clearly No.10 Group was unlikely to have any unwelcome visitors and there was but one Hurricane squadron at Filton. That would all change when the *Luftwaffe* was based in the Channel Islands. As long as the *Luftwaffe* operated only from Germany No.12 Group could expect to be busy protecting the industry of east and west Midlands and the north west. No.11 Group could always expect to be busy protecting the

Air Vice-Marshal Sir Quintin Brand AOC No. 10 Group.

Air Vice-Marshal Sir Trafford Leigh-Mallory AOC No. 12 Group.

SQUADRONS OF BOMBER COMMAND – 3 SEPTEMBER 1939

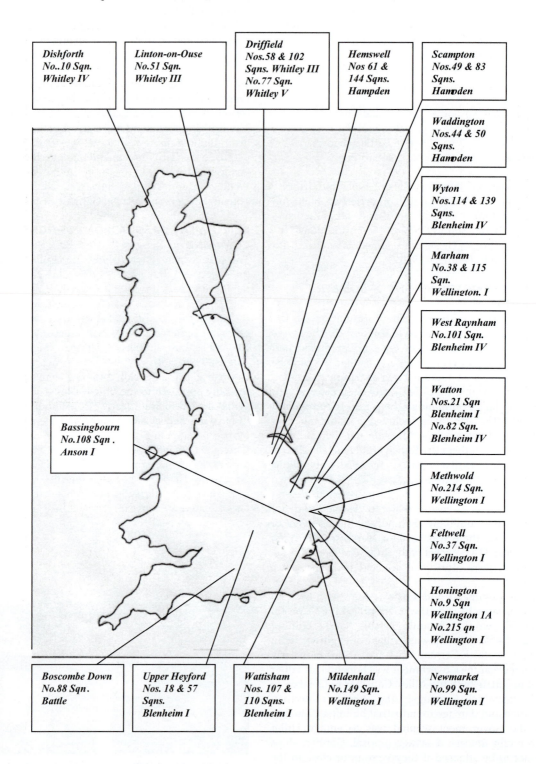

Dishforth
No..10 Sqn.
Whitley IV

Linton-on-Ouse
No.51 Sqn.
Whitley III

Driffield
Nos.58 & 102
Sqns. Whitley III
No.77 Sqn.
Whitley V

Hemswell
Nos 61 &
144 Sqns.
Hampden

Scampton
Nos.49 & 83
Sqns.
Hampden

Waddington
Nos.44 & 50
Sqns.
Hampden

Wyton
Nos.114 & 139
Sqns.
Blenheim IV

Marham
No.38 & 115
Sqn.
Wellington. I

West Raynham
No.101 Sqn.
Blenheim IV

Watton
Nos.21 Sqn
Blenheim I
No.82 Sqn.
Blenheim IV

Bassingbourn
No.108 Sqn .
Anson I

Methwold
No.214 Sqn.
Wellington I

Feltwell
No.37 Sqn.
Wellington I

Honington
No.9 Sqn
Wellington 1A
No.215 qn
Wellington I

Boscombe Down
No.88 Sqn .
Battle

Upper Heyford
Nos. 18 & 57
Sqns.
Blenheim I

Wattisham
Nos. 107 &
110 Sqns.
Blenheim I

Mildenhall
No.149 Sqn.
Wellington I

Newmarket
No.99 Sqn.
Wellington I

SQUADRONS OF FIGHTER COMMAND – 3 SEPTEMBER 1939

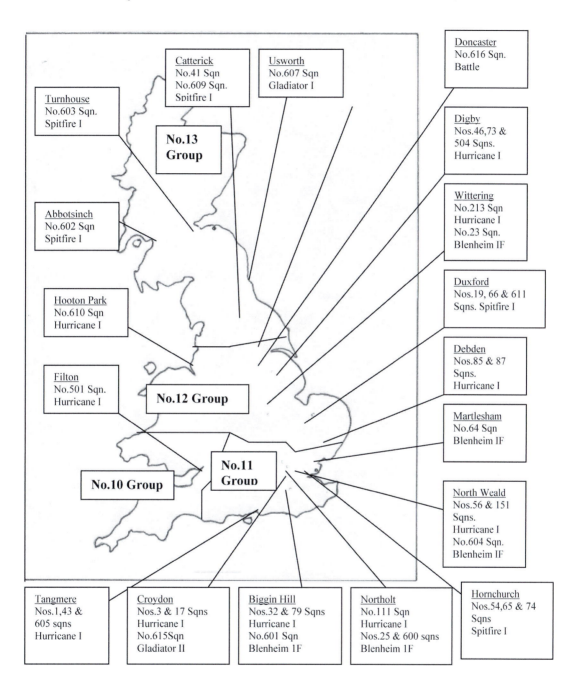

Turnhouse
No.603 Sqn.
Spitfire I

Abbotsinch
No.602 Sqn
Spitfire I

Hooton Park
No.610 Sqn
Hurricane I

Filton
No.501 Sqn.
Hurricane I

Catterick
No.41 Sqn
No.609 Sqn.
Spitfire I

Usworth
No.607 Sqn
Gladiator I

No.13 Group

No.12 Group

No.10 Group

No.11 Group

Doncaster
No.616 Sqn.
Battle

Digby
Nos.46,73 &
504 Sqns.
Hurricane I

Wittering
No.213 Sqn
Hurricane I
No.23 Sqn.
Blenheim IF

Duxford
Nos.19, 66 & 611
Sqns. Spitfire I

Debden
Nos.85 & 87
Sqns.
Hurricane I

Martlesham
No.64 Sqn
Blenheim IF

North Weald
Nos.56 & 151
Sqns.
Hurricane I
No.604 Sqn.
Blenheim IF

Tangmere
Nos.1,43 &
605 sqns
Hurricane I

Croydon
Nos.3 & 17 Sqns
Hurricane I
No.615Sqn
Gladiator II

Biggin Hill
Nos.32 & 79 Sqns
Hurricane I
No.601 Sqn
Blenheim 1F

Northolt
No.111 Sqn
Hurricane I
Nos.25 & 600 sqns
Blenheim 1F

Hornchurch
Nos.54,65 & 74
Sqns
Spitfire I

Air Vice-Marshal Saul AOC No. 13 Group.

capital and the map discloses deployments around the capital all excepting Tangmere. Units would be moved forward to West Malling, Manston and Lympne once the Germans were sitting on the Channel coast. No.13 Group had only five squadrons to protect the industries of the north east and Scotland from bombing raids from across the North Sea. German occupation of Norway in April 1940 would increase the threat to Saul's Group.

Flexibility was built into the system and units could be deployed to meet changing threats. The battle was meant to be fought by the Group Commanders, as indeed it was, but from his operations room at Bentley Priory near Stanmore, Dowding had an overview of the war as it affected the entire United Kingdom and when the Battle came units could be withdrawn from No.11 Group to rest up in the North of England. This was an entirely integrated system and the operational procedures were thoroughly rehearsed. Air Vice-

Air Vice-Marshal Sir Keith Park AOC No.11 Group.

Marshal Saul had been Senior Air Staff Officer at fighter Command HQ and it was his organizational ability that had ensured that the Command was an effective fighting force by the outbreak of war. The responsibility for the air defence of the United Kingdom was delegated to Dowding and his subordinate Group commanders.

Of course Park took the brunt of the battle with responsibility for No.11 Group covering the South East and his pilots had to be able to be airborne in two minutes if they were to intercept the enemy before they crossed the coast. In the latter part of the Battle of Britain when Goering had switched targets from Park's airfields to London, No.12 Group could be brought into the battle. Leigh Mallory believed in the ' big wing' when three squadrons of fighters would be assembled at altitude over East Anglia before intercepting the enemy even if it meant shooting down enemy aircraft returning to France after attacking their targets. Park left it to his squadron commanders to engage the enemy, being directed to their targets by the fighter controllers. Saul's squadrons did come into the battle briefly when Bombers of *Luftflotten* V, based in Norway, launched an attack on the North East of England. It was not possible to provide the bombers with fighter escort over such a range and the He.111s and Me.110s fell easy prey to Saul's fighters. The war would eventually come to the South West of England once the Channel Islands fell and hit and run raids could be made along the coasts of Devon, Cornwall and Somerset.

DEPLOYMENT OF SQUADRONS OF COASTAL COMMAND

The Ansons of the Command were tasked to keep watch over the North Sea and the English Channel and, in co-operation with Bomber Command, were in a position to attack German surface vessels. It was the larger flying boat squadrons and the Lockheed Hudsons that had the range to cover the ocean approaches to the British Isles. The flying boat squadrons at Invergordon and Scapa Flow were positioned to patrol the seas north of the mainland to spot any attempted break out of Germany's surface raiders into the North Atlantic. The squadrons at Aldergrove (Ulster), Pembroke Dock (West Wales) Falmouth and Mount Batten (The West Country) covered the approaches to Liverpool and the Clyde in the north and the Western Approaches to the Bristol and English Channels. There were two anti-shipping squadrons that could mount attacks on enemy shipping once sighted

It would be two American aircraft that would have the greatest impact on the war at sea, when it came. The Catalina and the Lockheed Hudson were to prove very effective, not only in the war against the surface ships' such as the *Bismarck*, but on the U-boats. The Saro Lerwick was a failure and, in spite of modifications to its structure, had eventually to be withdrawn from service.

SQUADRONS OF COASTAL COMMAND – 3 SEPTEMBER 1939

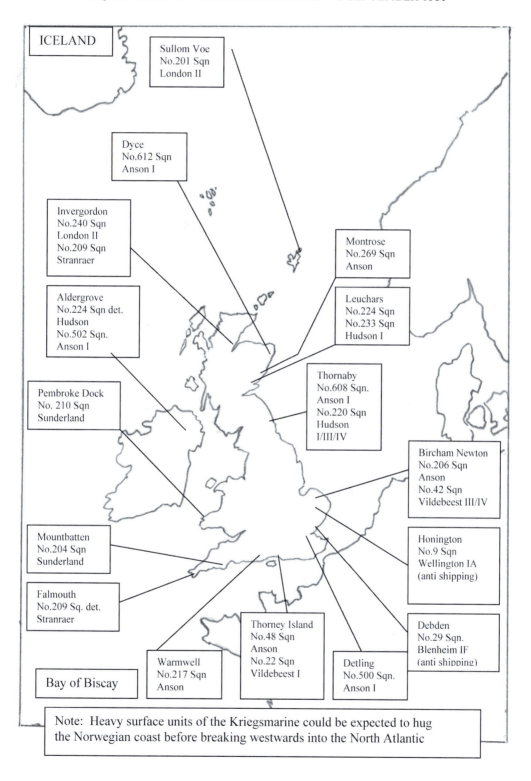

ICELAND

Sullom Voe
No.201 Sqn
London II

Dyce
No.612 Sqn
Anson I

Invergordon
No.240 Sqn
London II
No.209 Sqn
Stranraer

Montrose
No.269 Sqn
Anson

Aldergrove
No.224 Sqn det.
Hudson
No.502 Sqn.
Anson I

Leuchars
No.224 Sqn
No.233 Sqn
Hudson I

Pembroke Dock
No. 210 Sqn
Sunderland

Thornaby
No.608 Sqn.
Anson I
No.220 Sqn
Hudson
I/III/IV

Bircham Newton
No.206 Sqn
Anson
No.42 Sqn
Vildebeest III/IV

Mountbatten
No.204 Sqn
Sunderland

Honington
No.9 Sqn
Wellington IA
(anti shipping)

Falmouth
No.209 Sq. det.
Stranraer

Bay of Biscay

Warmwell
No.217 Sqn
Anson

Thorney Island
No.48 Sqn
Anson
No.22 Sqn
Vildebeest I

Detling
No.500 Sqn.
Anson I

Debden
No.29 Sqn.
Blenheim IF
(anti shipping)

Note: Heavy surface units of the Kriegsmarine could be expected to hug
the Norwegian coast before breaking westwards into the North Atlantic

The biplane flying boats which were a left-over from the 1930s, such as the Stranraer and London were phased out early in the war.

DEPLOYMENT OF ARMY CO-OPERATION AND TACTICAL RECONNAISSANCE SQUADRONS

These units were situated in close proximity with the Army Commands, with whom much of their training was carried out. They would be the eyes and ears of the artillery and infantry units and carry out battlefield communications. The Hector squadron would provide target towing aircraft for practice shoots. Squadrons, like Nos. 4 and 13 Squadron had been assigned to work with the Army ever since the 1920s and both would move to France with the AASF in September 1939 to work with the British Expeditionary Force.

DEPLOYMENT OF THE ADVANCED AIR STRIKING FORCE IN FRANCE

Initially the Advanced Air Striking Force consisted of nine Fairey Battle squadrons which were in place on the day war broke out. These were later reinforced by Hurricane and Lysander squadrons to provide fighter protection and give close support to the army. No Spitfire squadrons were sent. The Battles fared badly once the Battle for France got underway since they were no match for Me.109s. They were soon withdrawn from operations being relegated to training duties. It will be noticed from the map that the AASF was positioned facing the Belgian frontier and the Ardennes forest, the path that the German armoured formations would take in May 1940.

ARMY CO-OPERATION AND TACTICAL RECONNAISSANCE SQUADRONS – 3 SEPTEMBER 1939

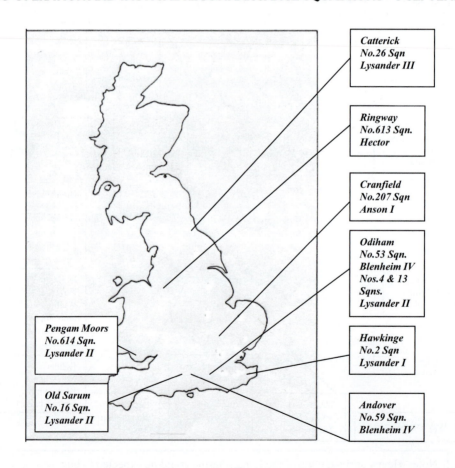

Catterick
No.26 Sqn
Lysander III

Ringway
No.613 Sqn.
Hector

Cranfield
No.207 Sqn
Anson I

Odiham
No.53 Sqn.
Blenheim IV
Nos.4 & 13
Sqns.
Lysander II

Pengam Moors
No.614 Sqn.
Lysander II

Hawkinge
No.2 Sqn
Lysander I

Old Sarum
No.16 Sqn.
Lysander II

Andover
No.59 Sqn.
Blenheim IV

SQUADRONS OF THE ADVANCED AIR STRIKING FORCE IN FRANCE – 3 SEPTEMBER 1939

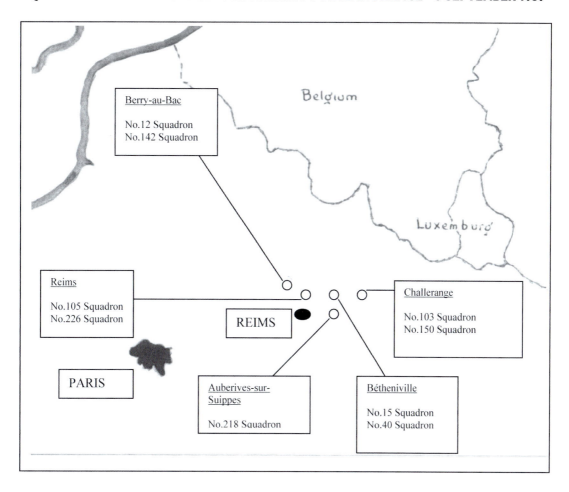

Berry-au-Bac

No.12 Squadron
No.142 Squadron

Belgium

Luxemburg

Reims

No.105 Squadron
No.226 Squadron

REIMS

Challerange

No.103 Squadron
No.150 Squadron

PARIS

Auberives-sur-
Suippes

No.218 Squadron

Bétheniville

No.15 Squadron
No.40 Squadron

Chapter 4
RAF Operations – 1930 to 1939

Introduction – An outline of air-control operations by theatre – Operations by RAF squadrons in Iraq, Palestine, India, Aden and the Sudan, as recorded in operations record books

ABOUT THIS CHAPTER

The corresponding Chapter 4 in Volume I dealt with the nature of air-control operations, which encompassed political, technical and geographical limitations, the attitude of air commanders and the reaction of tribesmen on the receiving end of RAF operations. These passages are not repeated in this volume. Tactics employed in air-control operations in the 1930s were broadly the same as they had been in the 1920s. The squadron operations record books do report a preference for units bombing in formation in the 1930s, and the approach to the target area might be by echelon, with aircraft bombing in a circle over the target. What did change was the aircraft, as more modern types replaced the venerable DH9A and Bristol Fighter. This did not, however, significantly reduce deaths due to flying accidents, and these sad events appear all too often in the various squadron records. There was also, during the 1930s, increasing use made of wireless/telegraphy communication, which facilitated cooperation between air and ground units. Then there are the extremely amusing happenings in the air, like the air gunner who fell through the floor of his Wapiti, and another air gunner who was about to bale out of his aircraft but climbed back in again to retrieve his packet of cigarettes, since he was unlikely to be able to purchase any in the jungle.

As far as possible the words used in the extracts from the operations record books are those actually used by the various squadron adjutants who wrote them. All the records have been put into the past tense, and as far as possible the actual accounts have been reproduced as they were written. They have only been changed if, for example, the sense is not clear. Any comments by the author appear in square brackets.

INTRODUCTION

By 1930, air-control operations were well established in the outposts of the Empire. With the exception of Palestine these operations were directed chiefly against tribesmen who were either acting unlawfully against the state or were at war with each other. The British Army or Levy forces were tasked to deal with outbreaks of local unrest, but from 1922 a new policy had been put into force whereby airpower would be used to deal with threats to internal security, with the Army in support. In Iraq an Air Officer Commanding had taken over from a General Officer Commanding, in command of all land

and air forces. While the Army had maintained overall control in India, the RAF was given considerable freedom to initiate air operations on the North-West Frontier, with notable success in what became known as 'Pink's War', named after the local air commander, Wing Commander R.C.M. Pink.

The *modus operandi* in most cases of tribal unrest was for the local air commander to act in close cooperation with the Political Officer. If military action seemed appropriate in dealing with the situation, warnings were given to the appropriate tribes giving the latest date for compliance. This might be the surrender of hostages, sometimes captured servicemen, or the cessation of hostile activities against other tribes. The whole point of using aircraft was that, with their speed and flexibility, unrest could be 'nipped in the bud', whereas the Army might take days to reach the area of operations, by which time the situation could have deteriorated. If the tribesmen who had received the warnings had not met the conditions stipulated by the local political officer, air action would commence. Tribal areas were bombed and cattle killed. Some tribesmen might take to caves, but without their animals they could not survive. Experience gained in air-control operations showed that these methods sooner or later met with success. The punishment would nearly always involve a fine, which meant the tribal leaders surrendering what mattered most to them, weapons or animals.

Where air-control operations of the sort described were inappropriate was in Palestine. The intercommunal violence between Arab and Jew often took place in built-up areas, and aircrews could not distinguish between warring factions in the streets below. In these circumstances the deployment of ground troops was far more effective. Aircraft were still very useful, however, in the reconnaissance and communications roles.

Most of the squadrons employed on these duties were still equipped with aircraft that had seen operational service during the Great War, namely the DH9A and Bristol F2B, affectionately known as the 'Ninak' and the 'Brisfit'. As the 1920s drew to a close the Westland Wapiti was just beginning to reach overseas squadrons. All three aircraft were workhorses. What was required was an aircraft of sturdy construction, easy to maintain and capable of dropping small bombs. The DH9A could carry a heavier bomb load than the Bristol Fighter. The Wapiti's performance was not a great improvement on that of its older sisters, but it was a newer aircraft and paved the way for the final pensioning-off of the Ninak and Brisfit. What was not required was a fighter aircraft, for at no time between the wars did aircraft employed on air-control operations encounter air opposition. Nos 1 and 3 Squadrons, which had Snipes in Iraq, were redeployed. Air Marshal Trenchard, ever eager to exploit any chance of employing RAF squadrons in operations overseas, also contributed air units in the war against piracy.

There have been outspoken critics of air control. Some have argued that it was unselective in its employment, in that a whole mountain tribe might be punished for the actions of a few. The power that tribal leaders had over certain sections of a tribe was questionable, particularly on the North-West Frontier, yet the whole tribe might be punished. If troublemakers were young then they might be even less inclined to follow the word of a tribal chief. This could result in a tribal chief declaring his loyalty to the government yet finding that certain sections of his tribe would receive punishment. The killing of animals and the destruction of all means of sustaining livelihood in tribal areas was seen as inhumane, but since these tribes could be nomadic, the normal rules of society, whereby those who break the law are arrested, tried and, if found guilty, sent to prison could not realistically be applied.

Another criticism stems from the assertion that His Majesty's Government was doing whatever was necessary to maintain control over the subjects of its Imperial territories. Some of the language used by the squadron adjutants in the operations record books betrays a certain dismissiveness of tribal peoples, describing them as 'natives'. There was a belief that the awesome sight of aeroplanes would itself be sufficient to cow the tribesmen into submission. Demonstration flights were made over villages to act as a warning of bombing attacks to come, or, as in the Sudan, tribal chiefs would be taken up for a flight or given demonstrations of the destructive powers of the aeroplane. These measures could often achieve compliance with government demands, but then the aeroplane was still a relatively new weapon, and colonial governors would not hesitate to use airpower if it could achieve quick results with economy. Comparisons have been made with the use of air control in the British Isles, during the struggle for home rule in Ireland, where bombing of villages would have been politically unacceptable because the RAF would not be dealing with uncivilized members of tribal peoples. In other words, successive British governments applied a double standard.

Finally there is the assertion that air control was a function of inter-service rivalry. Volume I deals exhaustively with the efforts made by Air Marshal Trenchard to sustain the RAF in the face of threats from its sister services to bring about its extinction. There is no doubt that the Air Marshal would do everything in his power to prove the efficacy of airpower. This he did by persuading the Colonial Secretary in 1920 to permit the use of aeroplanes to contain tribal unrest in British Somaliland. And in Iraq in 1922 an Air Officer Commanding superseded a General Officer Commanding in overall command of both land and air forces. While the Army retained overall control of internal security operations in India, the usefulness of aeroplanes was readily understood. Some individual commanders, like Arthur Harris, have been blamed for putting the efficacy of the employment of airpower above any consideration of the effects it might have upon innocent tribal peoples. All of this was in the name of Imperial domination of its subjects outside the United Kingdom.

There is no denying that Britain was an Imperial power. It was not the first and will assuredly not be the last. It may be argued that Britain had to be shamed by Ghandi to leave India. On the other hand, the British Prime Minister, Harold Macmillan, recognized the need for Britain to hasten the self-determination of African subjects in his 'winds of change' speech during a visit to that continent. Be that as it may, while Britain was the Imperial power, successive British governments did have the responsibility to maintain order in the countries of the Empire until those countries achieved self-determination. Whether air control was less humane than security maintained by land forces is arguable. Faced with the needs for economy, HMG found air control preferable to the alternatives. In Palestine the responsibility for internal security was placed upon the British government by a League of Nations mandate, so HMG had an inescapable responsibility to keep order in a steadily worsening situation as Arab confronted Jew. And in that situation of urban unrest airpower was of little use.

With the approach of war the RAF squadrons that had been employed on air-control duties had to prepare for operations that were expected to come from Germany's ally, Italy. Mussolini did belatedly join the conflict and wage war in the Western Desert, and it was only later that German forces entered the Middle-East theatre of operations. Of course trouble from the hill tribesmen did not simply evaporate, but the Indian and Iraqi air forces were able to take on operations of an internal security nature to release RAF squadrons preparing for war. For some years RAF squadrons in the Middle East and India had been engaged in reinforcement flights to Singapore, not simply to ascertain that entire squadrons could reach their destination intact, but to take part in combined-service exercises before returning to their home stations.

Critics of the use of airpower often gloss over the difficulties facing the RAF pilots, air gunners and ground crews in maintaining and flying the aircraft in inhospitable climates, with obsolete aircraft and lack of spares, particularly in India in the early 1920s. The war was certainly not one sided. The tribesmen could prove resourceful in deceiving pilots by moving ground signals pointing to their positions. Some of them were also very good riflemen, particularly the Afridis, and aircraft would often be on the receiving end of well-aimed shots, resulting in forced landings or crashes, with injury and death among crew members. RAF pilots were flying in some of the most inhospitable mountainous regions of the earth, where engine failure would result in a fatal crash. The operations record books, the extracts of which follow, show just how many men died in operations and through engine failures and aircraft accidents. And flying aside, tropical diseases would take their toll. One final thought may serve to show that the RAF did not cow their tribal adversaries into submission. Most of the air-control operations only brought about a temporary peace during the inter-war years, and it was often not long before sections of tribes would renew their hostilities. While the author would not wish to imply that the confrontation between the tribesman and the aeroplane took on the nature of an annual sport, he is reminded of his meeting with an officer of the Trucial Oman Scouts in 1970: 'I must be off now, old chap,' he said, as he got into his Landrover, 'it's the "open season" for shooting the British.'

The 1930s ended with the squadrons in India and the Middle East being equipped with Blenheim Mk Is, in the case of bomber squadrons, and Lysanders for Army Cooperation work. There was a very well-organized procedure for re-equipping the overseas squadrons with the light bombers, with a Blenheim Delivery Flight ferrying the aircraft to the respective theatre aircraft depots. Dual-control aircraft were produced to permit pilots of the various squadrons to convert to the new types. For most of them this was their first experience of flying in aircraft with an enclosed cockpit with a much-enhanced performance. The conversion was most often completed for all squadron pilots in the shortest possible time. Of course we shall never know how effective Blenheims might have been in the air-control role, for war soon followed their introduction into service. After the war Britain would quit India and Palestine.

AN OUTLINE OF AIR-CONTROL OPERATIONS BY THEATRE

The following is a brief outline of the conduct of operations in each theatre during the 1930s. The detail may be found in the excerpts from the various squadron operational records, unit diaries or, in the case of No. 60 Squadron, the unit history.

Fairey IIIF

Hawker Hart

Hawker Demon

Vickers Vincent

Vickers Wellesley

Hawker Audax

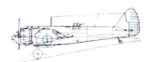

Bristol Blenheim

THE SQUADRONS EMPLOYED, THEIR AIRCRAFT AND THEATRES

Squadron	Aircraft throughout the 1930s in theatre

Aden

No. 8 Squadron	Fairey IIIF, Vincent, Demon, Blenheim

Palestine and Transjordan

No. 6 Squadron	Bristol F2B, Gordon, Hart, Demon, Hardy, Gauntlet I & II
No. 14 Squadron	Fairey IIIF, Gordon, Wellesley
No. 208 Squadron	Bristol F2B, Atlas, Audax, Demon, Lysander I & II

Iraq

No. 30 Squadron	Wapiti, Hardy, Blenheim I
No. 45 Squadron	Fairey IIIF, Hart, Vincent, Gordon, Wellesley, Blenheim I
No. 55 Squadron	Wapiti, Vincent, Blenheim I
No. 70 Squadron	Victoria IV, V & VI, Valentia
No. 84 Squadron	DH9A, Wapiti, Vincent, Blenheim

North-West Frontier

No. 5 Squadron	Bristol F2B, Wapiti
No. 11 Squadron	Wapiti, Hart, Blenheim I
No. 20 Squadron	Bristol F2B, Wapiti, Audax
No. 27 Squadron	DH9A, Wapiti
No. 28 Squadron	Bristol F2B, Wapiti, Audax

No. 31 Squadron	Bristol F2B, Wapiti, Valentia
No. 39 Squadron	Wapiti, Hart, Blenheim I
No. 60 Squadron	DH9A, Wapiti, Blenheim I

The Sudan

No. 47 Squadron	Fairey IIIF, Gordon, Vincent, Wellesley

ADEN

Air-control operations did not feature greatly in the maintenance of order in the British Protectorate of Aden during the 1930s. Except for the arrival of RAF squadrons brought into RAF Khormaksar in response to the Abysinnian crisis of 1935/6, only one squadron was in permanent residence. This was No. 8 Squadron, which was transferred from Iraq to Aden in 1927 to resist the encroachment of Zeidi tribesmen into the colony. The Imam of the Yemen was head of the Zeidi Sect of Islam and opposed the British occupation of Aden. After a long struggle for independence from Turkish rule, the Imam refused to recognize the boundaries of the Protectorate agreed between Britain and Turkey in 1905. Indeed, he claimed the entire protectorate, and used force against the territory of sheikhs who were under British protection. In 1922 Trenchard, ever eager to show that his aeroplanes could replace some of the Army units in Aden, proposed sending a flight of aircraft, and so it was decided to withdraw one Indian battalion and the Yemen infantry battalion was disbanded. This flight acted not only against Zeidi raiders but also Protectorate

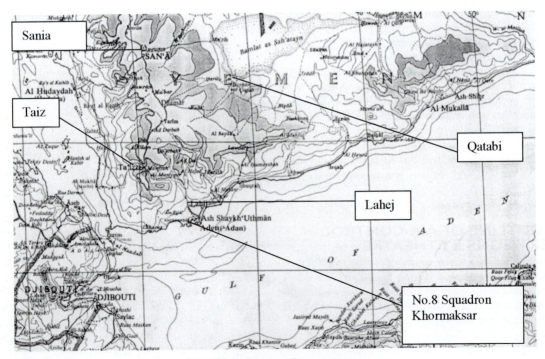

The Aden theatre of operations.

tribes who obstructed trade routes. There were no aerodromes forward of Khormaksar that could be used, and the Bristol Fighter did not have the range and bomb capacity to be really effective in operations far from the home base. And so in the late 1920s it was decided that a more effective modern-day bomber was required in squadron strength. When No. 8 Squadron moved to Aden it still had its DH9As, but these were soon replaced by the Fairey IIIF. During the period between 1928 and 1930 the Cabinet decided to withdraw the two infantry battalions and rely for the defence of the Protectorate on No. 8 Squadron, some armoured cars and the Aden Protectorate Levies.

PALESTINE AND TRANSJORDAN

To understand the part played by the RAF in Palestine in the period between the wars one must first understand the progressively deteriorating internal security situation. There are not many clues from the squadron diary of No. 6 Squadron, which follows. Frequent references are made to attacks upon groups of armed Arabs, but little or no mention is made of the Jewish population. Britain had a mandate from the League of Nations to govern Palestine until, at some future date, it would be possible for the inhabitants of the region to achieve self-determination. The problem confronting the British authorities was Jewish immigration, which

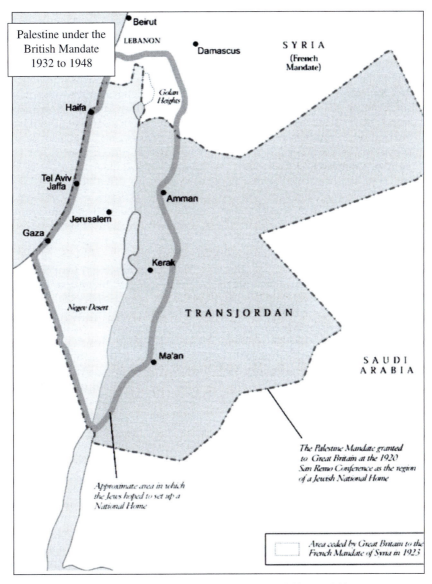

Palestine under the British Mandate, 1932 to 1948.

resulted in the immigrants obtaining increasing amounts of land. There was a political purpose in all of this, which was headed by the Zionist movement. The Zionists wanted a national home for the Jewish people in Palestine. In 1922 the Jewish residents in Palestine represented 11% of the population. By 1931 that figure had risen to 17% and by 1945 to 31%. Two things angered the Palestinian Arabs: they were threatened with marginalization within their own land; and secondly, the Arabs were being progressively dispossessed of their own land. Whereas the Muslim Arabs had not resented Jewish immigration at the outset, the mood soon changed to one of anger and resentment. This led to intercommunal conflict in 1929, which is described in Volume I as it affected RAF operations. When the Arabs attacked Jewish communities the Jews formed terrorist groups and retaliated. The British authorities were in a 'no win' situation. If they helped either side they risked being on the receiving end of violence. Indeed both Arab and Jewish groups attacked all the symbols of British authority in the area. Thus Jew attacked Arab and vice versa, and both attacked the British. The Jewish terrorist groups wanted the British forces out of the way so that they could settle matters directly with the Arabs, once and for all, which they did when the British Mandate ended in 1948 and the state of Israel was born.

In the meantime the Army and the RAF had to hold the ring. The situation faced by the security forces in Palestine was markedly different from that experienced on the North-West Frontier, Iraq or Aden. The trouble did not simply come from hostile tribesmen, as today there were and remain two irreconcilable races, Arabs and Jews. There was also the problem of taking air action against hostile groups in built-up areas. This made the task of supporting the Army and Police in keeping order in Palestine much more difficult than it had been for the RAF in operating against hill tribes. From 1936 to 1939 the Arab Revolt meant a campaign against Jews and their property, and the violence that erupted in 1936 continued for almost a year. After a lull, the violence resumed in September 1937. The diary of No. 6 Squadron has little to say about operations during the late 1930s because to do so would have been very repetitious. It was very much business as usual, with the RAF giving direct support to the Army, either escorting convoys or acting in cooperation with Army patrols in a never-ending attritional war. Urban violence had to be contained by the Army and Police, and from time to time the RAF issued orders limiting air attacks on built-up areas. The most the RAF could usefully do in the towns was to reconnoitre and report to the forces on the ground.

IRAQ

The problems confronting the British government in Iraq during the inter-war years were encountered in its attempts to create in the country an independent sovereign state. The end of the Great War had seen the end also of the Ottoman Empire, but it did not stop the modern state of Turkey from entertaining territorial ambitions in the oil-rich areas of northern Iraq. The situation was further aggravated by demands for Kurdish autonomy voiced by Sheikh Mahmoud, who hoped to be King of Kurdistan. As a result of the Anglo-Iraqi Treaty of June 1930, full independence was promised to Iraq in September 1932, and it was agreed that the RAF would withdraw from Hinaidi and Mosul to a new base at Habbaniya, approximately fifty miles west of Baghdad, within five years of Iraqi independence. In the meantime the RAF could assist by helping to foil any attempts to create a separate Kurdish state in the north, and countering Turkish encroachment in the area.

Sheikh Mahmoud was a constant source of trouble in Iraq. He was intent on establishing a Kurdish kingdom, and relying upon disturbances among the tribes around Sulaimania would gather forces along the border with Iran. The Sheikh's men would move from village to village exacting dues and inciting the villagers to rebellion. When ordered to withdraw his forces from Iraq he refused, and it fell to the Iraqi Army to take action against him. If need be the RAF could be called upon to support the Army, and Nos 30 and 55 Squadrons were on hand if the need arose. The difficulty for the government was that many of these tribal communities professed allegiance to the government. Bombing their villages, because it was believed that they were harbouring Mahmoud's men, could change that allegiance.

Mahmoud suffered a temporary setback at Surdash, for he reappeared in January 1931 with a small force of rebels. By ambushing government troops he could acquire arms and ammunition. Concerted action by the Army and the two RAF squadrons drove his men from the Halebja Plain on 1 February, but he returned again moving towards the Qara Dagh. Again concerted action by Nos 30 and 55 Squadrons resulted in a severe mauling of the Sheikh's forces, and the Sheikh was on the run. When he failed to gain the support of the tribes for further action, he escaped to Iran on 23 April, and sought to surrender in a letter to the Oriental Secretary to the High Commissioner the following day. This brought to an end a sixteen-year fight against the Iraqi government.

Another troublesome Sheikh was Ahmed of Barzan. He had considerable influence in a large area north-east of the Greater Zob river stretching to the Turkish border. One solution was for the Army to move into the area from a firm base that would support armed posts at strategic points. There was a landing strip at Diana that could accommodate a flight of No. 30 Squadron. There was also the embryonic Iraqi Air Force, which could gain valuable experience in peace-keeping. Just as in India,

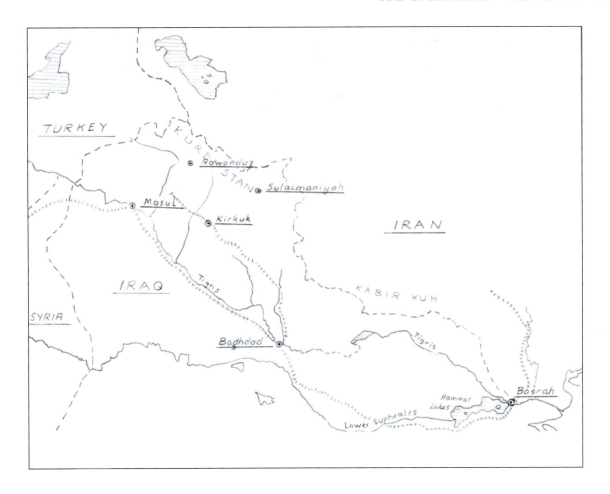

there would be periodic Army relief columns, and No. 70 Squadron's Victorias would prove extremely useful for supply, convoy protection and casualty evacuation. In 1932, in response to enemy activity, an RAF strike force was formed comprising all of No. 55 Squadron, most of No. 30 Squadron and a flight of No. 70 Squadron. Faced with this new force, Sheikh Ahmed was eventually driven to the Turkish border, where he surrendered himself to the Turkish authorities. The RAF squadrons in Iraq duly moved to Habbaniya/Dhibban before the outbreak of war in 1939. Nos 30 and 55 Squadrons were active in Iraq in the 1930s, but in contrast to the 1920s No. 84 Squadron had little to do in the air-control role.

THE SUDAN

The Sudan did not present the RAF with a tribal problem in the classic air-control mode. Except for the period of the Abysinnian crisis, only No. 47 Squadron operated along the Nile. During the 1920s only a flight was

stationed at Khartoum. This was increased to squadron strength, and there was a modest reduction in the strength of the Army garrison. The tribal problems in the Upper Nile Province were almost always dealt with by the Sudan Defence Force without the necessity for RAF assistance. Apart from squadron training, the authorities did call upon No. 47 Squadron to carry out a number of aerial surveys. The pilots were also called upon to report the whereabouts of elephant poachers. The upper reaches of the Nile provided the squadron with the valuable opportunities for cruises by their floatplanes. One of the tasks of the squadron was to reconnoitre for sites for landing grounds, but the floatplanes could land on the tributaries that extended into the Province.

No. 47 Squadron was joined by reinforcements during the Abysinnian crisis of October 1935, and these units remained until well into 1936. Three other airfields were then brought into use, namely Port Sudan, Gebeit and Ed Damur.

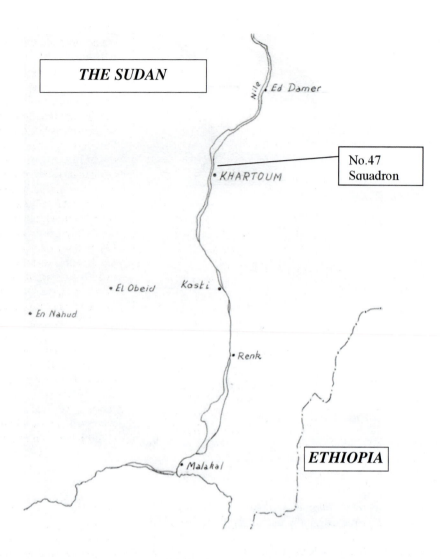

THE NORTH-WEST FRONTIER

Air-control operations in India during the 1930s did not differ substantially from those of the previous decade. There were the usual periodic bouts of unrest, sometimes affecting whole tribes, but often sub-sections of tribes. The tactics used were broadly the same, but the unrest was sometimes part of regional tension. In India it was pretention to the Afghan throne. In Iraq it could be Turkish territorial ambitions or Kurdish autonomy when it proved useful to be able to exploit tribal unrest. In India, however, there was a new threat to the peace, and this was from Mahatma Ghandi, who had organized a campaign of civil disobedience. He gave inspiration to the Indian National Congress, and as part of the national campaign the North-West Frontier became involved. A Frontier Youth League was formed in March 1930, and members who were enrolled began to be identified by the red uniforms they wore. These 'Redshirts' were able to exploit differences between the tribes and the government, and although Ghandi may have preached non-violence the often young members of tribes were only too happy to create mayhem, and soon unrest spread to the Vale of Peshawar. The younger members were often unwilling to listen to older, wiser counsels, and although tribal leaders at times accepted government terms to end bouts of unrest they were unable to rein in the young men. There were prolonged periods of unrest in the 1930s, not simply due to Redshirt activity, but also because of the activities of one particular faqir, the elusive Faqir of Ipi, and to a lesser extent the Faqir of Alingar. The former was almost a 1930s version of the Al Q'aeda leader Osama Bin Laden. The history of No. 60 Squadron alone gives a detailed account of the air-control operations of the period. And understanding of the territories occupied by the various tribes may help the reader in understanding the

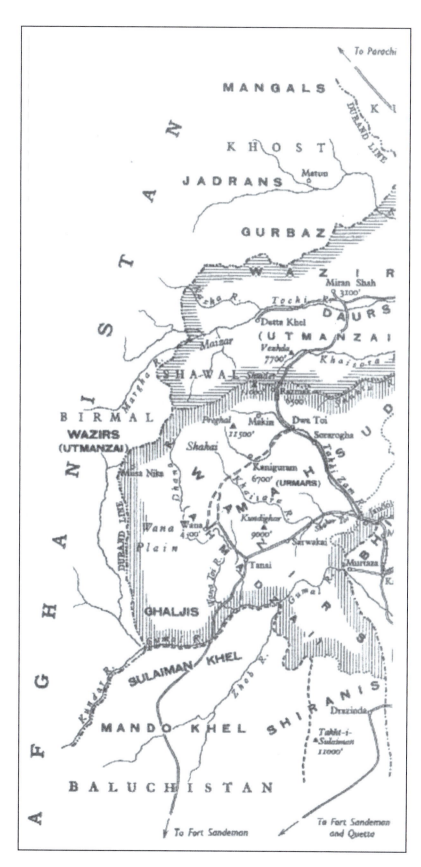

accounts of operations in the various squadron operations record books, or Forms 540.

There was a high level of activity on the North-West Frontier at the beginning of the decade. Bombing in the Mohmand country commenced on 11 May 1930 and continued until the end of the month, when the disturbances moved north into Utman Khel territory. Bombing was carried out in both areas from 30 May, lasting until 11 June, when operations were confined to Utman Khel country. On 7 July operations commenced in Waziristan, which lasted until the 22nd of that month. After a break of over a fortnight, operations were again undertaken, this time in the Tirah, where they were concluded on 15 August. A feature of these operations was the continual changing of bomb racks on a daily basis. Very often bomb racks had to be changed several times between raids. The adjutant of No. 39 Squadron commented that considerable strain was thus put on all personnel, which could have been avoided if universal adjustable racks had been in use.

During the period January to December 1931, in order to gain and maintain the acquiescence of of tribes in the passage of aircraft over their territory and to acquire useful information of the lives of the tribesmen, regular reconnaissances were ordered to be made of Mohmand territory. Attention was to be paid to the following points:

1. Gatherings or movements of personnel and animals.
2. The state of crops and fields.
3. The presence of water.
4. The presence of snow during winter.
5. Weather and visibility.

This, then, was the activity at the beginning of the decade. Operations continued as the RAF went to war in 1939, and can be followed in the record books of the squadrons listed below.

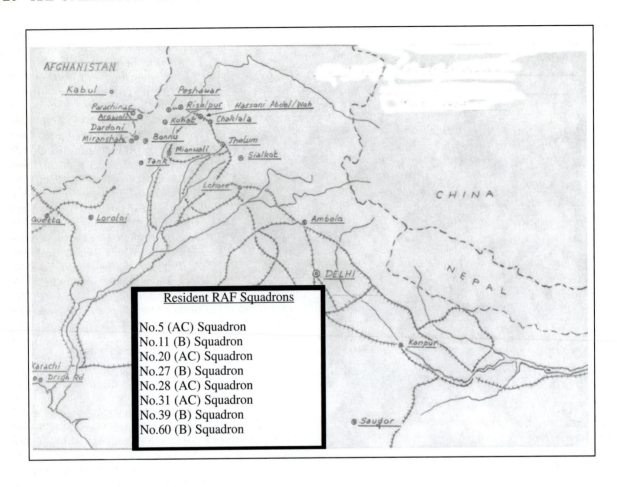

Resident RAF Squadrons

No.5 (AC) Squadron
No.11 (B) Squadron
No.20 (AC) Squadron
No.27 (B) Squadron
No.28 (AC) Squadron
No.31 (AC) Squadron
No.39 (B) Squadron
No.60 (B) Squadron

AUTHOR'S NOTE ON CONTENTS OF THE SQUADRON DIARIES

Before commencing to read extracts from the diaries of units that were employed on operations overseas, it is pointed out that they are essentially in the form that they appear in them. The words are those used by the various unit adjutants tasked with maintaining these unit records. The style and content vary considerably between individual adjutants and units. What follows are extracts, for the author could not include literally everything that was set down. There would be enough material to fill this entire volume. Since much that was written was pure routine administration, it would not be of great interest. What has been selected is often items that throw light on operational procedures and the nature of operations and qualities of aircraft and aircrews. There may be years about which little or nothing is recorded in this work. This will be because there is nothing of significance to report or where the records themselves are illegible. The choice of what has been selected for inclusion is entirely that of the author.

NO. 5 SQUADRON

Frangas non flectas
(Thou mayest break but shall not bend me)

1930

The squadron moved from Quetta to Kohat in connection with operations against the Mohmands and the Afridis on 16 May and returned to Quetta on 15 March 1931. During this period detachments were made to Poona, Secunderabad, Jubbulpore and Fort Sandeman.

1931

In May the squadron's Bristol Fighters, which had been the standard equipment since the squadron was re-formed on 1 April 1920, were exchanged for Westland Wapitis. All the Brisfits were flown to Karachi for disposal. In October Squadron Leader Bryson MC, DFC

AIRCRAFT
Bristol F2B
Westland Wapiti

was relieved by Squadron Leader W.K. Mercer and returned to Home Establishment. The AOC India, Sir John Miles Steel KBE, CB, CMG carried out his annual inspection of the Squadron on 13 October. Between 9 and 14 November the AGG, the Hon. Mr A.M.L. Cater, was flown on a tour of Kalat province. He viewed Banjur, Turbar, Disparom, Kappiparom and Sohtagam. This tour carried out by road would have taken 14 days as some roads in these parts were practically impassable. A Flight was detached to Lahore for cooperation with Northern Command between 2 and 21 December and C Flight at Secunderabad, Poona and Ahmad Magar for cooperation with Southern Command between 2 January and 10 February 1932.

1932

On 16 May operations were carried out against the Mohmands, a tribe living in the hills due north of Shabkadar. Led by the Haji of Turangzai, the tribe was again threatening disorder in the locality. A bombing raid using 20 lb Cooper bombs was ordered for 18 May but was cancelled. Instead, the squadron carried out a reconnaissance of the country by flights, enabling the pilots to become acquainted with the main items of interest. On 19 May constant surveillance was kept up, aircraft relieving each other in the air. Small parties of men were seen and about nine 20 lb Coopers were dropped. After two days standing by at two hours' notice, a similar reconnaissance using two-way radio was carried out on 22 May.

The next day the squadron proceeded to Peshawar to report to Group for orders. A raid using 20 lb Coopers, carried out by flights in line astern, was carried out against a nullah 4 miles NNW of Matta Mughal Khel, then the aircraft returned to Peshawar to refuel. The next day bombing was carried out by a single aircraft using 'bombing circles'. The Haji was given 24 hours to come in, later extended to 48 hours. This did not elicit a response and on 28 May the squadron made another raid with Nos 27, 60, 39 and 11 Squadrons on detailed targets. On 29 May there was another raid on a nullah near Hafiz Kor. On the 31st the squadron, in company with Nos 1 and 2 Wings, carried out a raid on the village of Sultana. The bombing was successful. Operations were resumed against the Afridis in the Tirah on 2 June preceded by reconnaissances using 2-way WT, and 700 men were seen. Later reconnaissances revealed 1,500 men advancing ten miles from Peshawar. The squadron was put on stand-by but no orders were received. Night bombing on the villages on 5 June was followed by raids on the following day. It was apparent that the Afridis had suffered heavy casualties and the Tirah quietened down. Commencing on 15 June, A Flight, commanded by Flight Lieutenant J. Warburton, started a two-month detachment to Miranshah, but the Flight remained there until 13 September. This was due to the ongoing

commitments cooperating with the Wana Patrol and the Razmak column in providing air cover against hostile lashkars. RT and message dropping were employed in keeping contact with the ground forces. Operations against various hostile lashkars were continued and after suffering casualties they became quiet. In July a lashkar of approximately 500 men attacked a Khassadar post at Shamak destroying the road bridge above the village. The lashkar then endeavoured to attack another village but met with opposition from the women of the village. The Tochi Scouts went into operation in cooperation with the detached flight. On 7 July Squadron Leader Bryson with three machines of B Flight and one machine of C Flight joined with the detached flight at Miranshah. Targets were attacked in the Sararogha area, machines being directed towards targets by arrows. During the night of 9 July the lashkars left. Three men were found dead in a tree. During October reconnaissances were kept up and the year ended with the squadron operating with the Army on artillery shoots. There were scattered groups of tribesmen but only a few bombs were dropped on these groups and their animals.

1933

In January there were reconnaissances over the Tirah and a few successful operations in conjunction with 31st and 58th Field Batteries. A lot of low cloud and rain during the month made low flying very difficult and February was much the same. A close reconnaisance was carried out with the 2nd Brigade on 23 February and a reconnaissance of Chasadda was made on the 22nd in connection with the 'Red Shirt' movement, and considerable movement was observed. Nine machines flew to Delhi for the Delhi Air Display. The route was via Rawalpindi and Lahore where the night was spent before proceeding to Bala and Delhi. On 20 February, the Hon. Mr Carter, the AAG for Baluchistan, was flown from Fort Sandeman to Quetta and on the 22nd was flown from Quetta to Gohan and back. On the 22nd and 25th there were three close reconnaissance sorties with the 1st Devonshires. One message was picked up and seventeen dropped. On the 22nd a topographical reconnaissance was carried out by three students of the Staff College near Pichin, two of the three being flown by Wing Commander D'Albiac DSO.

In May a demonstration was given in supply dropping and message pick up/drop at Pichin, and tank positions were indicated by stannic chloride. There was cooperation with Signals and RT working was very satisfactory. The Junior Division of the Staff College was attached to the RAF from the 29th to the 31st for studies in connection with their work. Lectures were given and also short descriptions of the section's equipment. The officers were taken up for a reconnaissance on the 30th and 31st, together with demonstrations of R/T and W/T.

In June there was an Army Cooperation night exercise during Divisional night manoeuvres on the 17th. On the 17th, 23rd, 24th and 30th cooperation was carried out with a platoon of the Chagai Levy Corps at Nurgamma and Ghandawa (Sind). Of eleven flights undertaken four had to be abandoned due to weather. All flying was carried out from Quetta and 2-way W/T and situation reports were sent. During the months July to September Army Cooperation continued and there were inter-brigade exercises. In November and December, at Zhob militia posts, trials were carried out with a new Stannic release for simulating tank attack.

1934

In March the squadron won the Salmond Bombing Cup. The following month there were R/T practices. This was followed by bombing and air firing practices and 16,000 rounds were fired by pilots and air gunners. On 28 July the squadron came of age and a day's holiday was granted with dinner in the officers' mess. During the remaining months of the year the training routine was maintained.

1935

In March there were a number of personnel movements:

Arrivals
6th	Flight Lieutenant W.A. Opie
	Pilot Officer Alloway
	Pilot Officer Paylor
	Pilot Officer D.G.M. Spencer
9th	Pilot Officer J.E. Kirk

Departures
14th	Flight Lieutenant R.C. Hancock
	Flying Officer R.B. Wardman
	Flying Officer H.B. Horner
	Flying Officer J.H. Kirkparick
	Pilot Officer G.A. Bartlett

On 31 May the Baluchistan earthquake began. The first shock was felt at 03.06 hrs. The night was fine but dark and there was no moon. The main tremors were south to north and the westward effect was limited to a great extent in the Quetta cantonment by a deep nullah called the Turanni Nullah, which ran from north to south through the cantonment immediately east of the fort. Though many buildings west of this line were damaged none were wrecked in the way that those east of the line suffered. The RAF lines, comprising No. 3 (India) Wing and No. 5 (AC) Squadron, were in the direct line of the earthquake. The single officers' quarters and some married quarters were situated about a mile and a half from the airmen's barracks. Owing to the fact that they had comparatively small rooms they withstood the quake long enough for the airmen to escape before they collapsed. The majority of the occupants were partially buried or slightly injured, only one was so seriously injured that he could not go to the less fortunate families in the lower quarters. These bungalows were situated south of Quetta near the Pishin railway line about three-quarters of a mile from the airmen's barracks. All suffered very badly. The inside walls and ceilings collapsed, with the first shock jamming all the doors. Those which were usually left open at night were covered with strong extended steel netting to keep out thieves and proved just as effective in keeping the occupants in. Some time was spent releasing these families and making the injured as comfortable as possible. The greatest shock awaited the rescue party when it reached the airmen's lines. What had once been the airmen's barracks was nothing more than a series of detached heaps of brick rubble with the tin roofs torn off and twisted, resting on top. A few survivors were wandering among the ruins in a stunned condition calling to trapped inmates. A few were desperately digging down with their bare hands trying to release their buried friends. In all not more than fifty men were clear of the wreckage and most of these were injured. The rescuers started work with three great handicaps. Firstly, there was no light, and great clouds of dust cut out what little light there might have been from the stars. All electric light cables were down and it was not light until 06.30 hrs. Secondly, they had nothing to dig with but their bare hands and most were dressed in their pyjamas. Few had shoes and all had been cut or bruised by broken glass and falling bricks. Thirdly, the work was continually being undone by further quakes which occurred at frequent intervals during the first few hours often reburying victims who had just been on the point of release, causing the workers to vacate hurriedly the neighbourhood of any wall or roof. Many of the men could only be reached by crawling under roof trusses through torn corrugated sheeting into positions from which rapid exit was impossible. Rescue work was very dangerous, and the courage of men who had only just been dug out and who had then to return in pitch dark to these dangerous positions was beyond question.

Immediately before dawn a battalion of Punjabis, who had been on a night march, came to the assistance of the rescuers. With their entrenching tools it greatly speeded up the work. At about 08.00 hrs a section of light tanks arrived and were at once set to work pulling off heavy roofs from the ruins. This was also of great value, enabling the workers to get into the centre of the wreckage. The last survivor was extracted at noon. The last body was removed at 16.00 hrs. A bull terrier was found alive and uninjured 36 hours after the disaster when search was being made for kit and personal belongings. It was found that many victims had died from suffocation. The ceilings of the bungalows were made of mutty, nearly one foot thick, held in position by wire netting. This mutty caused a great cloud of dust, and many of the men who were under mosquito nets were unable to breathe owing to dust and tightness of the nets over their faces. Wire netting and mosquito nets also hampered the rescue workers who, having no cutting equipment, had to tear them away using brute force. It was possible that the building was occupied by the Indian Air Force personnel, and their families were in even worse conditions than those of the British airmen. Not a single man escaped uninjured owing to the fact that many of the followers had entire families sleeping in the quarters. The death toll was enormous. It is impossible to give an accurate assessment of casualties in this part of the camp. The only officer killed was the Orderly Officer, Pilot Officer Charles R Taylor, who had joined the squadron only two months earlier. He was sleeping in No. 3 (India) Wing Orderly Room when he died. The total Air Force dead were:

1 Officer
53 British other ranks
2 children (of Flight Sergeant Higgs and Captain Byles).

During the following few days every squadron in India sent aircraft to Quetta laden with doctors, nurses and medical supplies. They returned carrying injured women and children. The Officer Commanding No. 3 (Indian) Wing then arranged for the evacuation of the remnants of the wing, and during June the entire RAF personnel plus a small salvage party were moved to the RAF Depot, Karachi. Eighteen aircraft were flown down and six more were sent by rail. From Karachi a small number of injured men and a majority of the married families were sent back to the United Kingdom. Early in June the AOC RAF India inspected those members of the wing who were fit to parade. This totalled about seventy-five. The following day His Excellency the Viceroy, Lord Willington, inspected the wing and congratulated them on their courage and endurance after the earthquakes. Early the following year a certificate was signed by the Viceroy and presented to each member of the wing.

The arrivals and departures for July 1935 were as follows:

Arrivals
Squadron Leader P.F. Fullard DSO, MC, DFC posted in to command the squadron.
Flight Lieutenant R.K. Hambling for signals duties.

Departures
Squadron Leader C.N. Ellen DFC to Home Establishment.
Flight Lieutenant W.A. Opie invalided to Home Establishment.
Flight Lieutenant T.W. Hodgson invalided to Home Establishment.

On 8 July a conference was held at the Aircraft Depot, Drigh Road, opened by the Officer Commanding No. 3 (India) Wing. He said that the AOC required the squadron, consisting of the HQ and two flights, to be at Risalpur on 1 August. Arrangements for the issue of equipment was discussed. It was decided that nine serviceable aircraft should be picked, as far as possible, from the aircraft of No. 5 (AC) Squadron and the number was to be made up by aircraft of No. 31 (AC) Squadron and No. 3 (Indian) Wing. It was proposed to form an advanced party to be at Risalpur at least seven days before the squadron arrived.

On 5 September an aircraft of the Abbotabad Flight landed from dusk patrol with all bombs still on the racks. The pilot taxied into the space between two other aircraft and switched off. The armoury sergeant commenced to look at the safety wires on the bombs. A few minutes later there was an explosion and a flash in front of the sergeant, who was reported to have had one of the 20 lb bombs in his arms. The aircraft at once burst into flames and petrol poured from the holed tanks. Many bodies were lying in the vicinity of the fire with the exception of two. These were all carried to a safe distance. The two bodies not recovered until the following morning were those of Sergeant Brereton, the armoury sergeant, and LAC Ayres. The latter was sitting in the aircraft cockpit at the moment of the explosion but had not been seen there before the accident. During the fire it was impossible to see into the cockpit due to the flames and smoke. A clerk, Private Brown of the South Wales Borderers, who was working in an office tent 75 yards away, was killed outright by shrapnel. It was considered that the remaining bombs, which could be seen in the flames, could go off. As a safety precaution against heavy loss of life, no firelighting was allowed. Of the two adjacent aircraft, one was bombed up with sixteen 20 lb bombs, and in order to lessen the danger of further explosions this aircraft was dragged away from the scene of the fire and did not catch light. By this time the third aircraft was burning at the wingtip and might have been saved, but the danger to salvage personnel was considered too great for an attempt to be made and they were ordered to a safe distance of 200 yards. A crowd of hundreds had collected and stood only yards from the burning wreckage, from which Very lights and 0.303 in. ammunition was spurting in all directions. A platoon of the South Wales Borderers arrived and forced the spectators to retire to a safe distance. Fortunately none of the remaining bombs exploded. The names of Pilot Officer M.V. Alloway, the pilot of the aircraft, and Flight Sergeant Harrison were brought to the notice of the Air Council for gallantry and devotion to duty between the rescue and the salvage work. In all, the casualties killed were Sergeant Brereton, LAC Ayres, Private Brown, Coolie Faquir and Coolie Mohameddin. Injured were Corporal Fraser, Corporal Frost, LAC Tyler, LAC Burton and LAC Johnson.

During August the Mohmand tribes deliberately damaged the Gandab Road and they encouraged others to use their territory for operations against the government. A lashkar of about 1,500 men, of whom approximately half were members of two tribes, including Safis, assembled in the hills along this road and attempted to destroy it. The government therefore sanctioned air action against these two tribes to force them to accept its terms. A report of the Hazara operations between 22 August and 23 September spoke of unrest in the Hazara, Black Mountains and the Allai area owing to the Shahidganj disturbances in Lahore. The Governor, North-West Frontier province, called for the deployment of troops to assist the civil power in protecting the administrative frontier of the Hazara District. It was necessary to stop any possible incursions by hostile lashkars of tribesmen. The RAF squadrons involved included elements of No. 5 (AC) Squadron – 4 officers, 25 airmen and 3 aircraft located at the Abbotabad landing ground where they were encamped.

1936

February In February normal training was carried out during the month. One officer was attached to India Wing HQ for a ten-day course in blind flying. As an ex-CFS instructor he was able to return and give blind-flying instruction to all pilots. This was a sphere of training that, up to this time, was neglected in India. Two pilots on the squadron had done no blind flying since their *ab initio* course and more senior pilots had had none at all. From the 23rd of the month Squadron Leader McLaren-Reid DFC took over the command of the Squadron from Flight Lieutenant A.F. Hutton DFC, who returned to his flight. Arrivals and Departures in the month were as follows:

Arrivals
24th   Flying Officer R.F. Smith
25th   Pilot Officer Delaboeur-Beresford
        Pilot Officer D.C. Smith.

Departures
26th   Flying Officer C.M. Stewart
29th   Flying Officer E.B. Waddy.

109 hours were flown during the month since flying was greatly limited. The aerodrome was unserviceable during half of the month following exceptionally heavy rain.

March On 5 March four Wapitis were flown up from the Aircraft Park at Lahore and C Flight was re-formed, the first time the squadron had been composed of three flights since the Quetta earthquake. The flights were still not up to full strength in officers and men. Four more canvas hangars were erected but a fourth was not constructed as it was considered likely that three flights would not long be together at Chaklala. On the 23rd a composite flight went to Kohat for air firing and bombing tests. The objects of these tests was to get all air gunners qualified for the year so that they could be put on air gunner establishment. The flight returned on the 28th, all air gunners having passed. Normal training was again hampered due to the airfield being rendered unserviceable after heavy rain. Arrivals for the month of March were:

4 March   Pilot Officer Lees
            Pilot Officer Surplice.
5 March   Pilot Officer Holmes.

April At the beginning of the month it was decided that the squadron should take over Miranshah Fort and Waziristan from Kohat. The RAF maintained a permanent detachment at the fort for security purposes. Flights would remain at the fort for two months at a time, meaning that each individual could spend four months in the place. As these four months were not continuous no extra leave or allowance could be drawn. On the 14th of the month A Flight took over the RAF section at the fort from No. 1 (India) Wing, Kohat. Improvements had been made since the previous occupation of the districts by No. 5 Squadron. Old Dardoni Camp had been razed to the ground and additions to the Tochi Scout Post had been made to accommodate the RAF.

July During the month normal flying training was carried out and some pilots completed a short instrument-flying course carried out on the squadron. On officer attended the mountain warfare course at Abbatobad and the Northern Command Intelligence Course at Muree.

November B Flight moved to Risalpur for night-flying practice for four days. A Flight at Miranshah were involved in minor operations consisting of rounding up Zilli Khel sheep which were being grazed in the blockaded area. The sheep were finally returned to the tribe at a price of 2s. per head. From the 4th to the 8th pilots cooperated with the District at Lahore. Between the 26th and 27th there was stubborn fighting by the Tori Khel and the fact that both columns were retiring. Wing Commander Lees and one further flight of No. 27 (B) Squadron arrived at 08.00. The Wing Commander took charge of the operations and No. 5 (AC) Squadron carried out four reconnaissance sorties and one photographic flight. Twelve 20 lb bombs were dropped and 1,700 rounds of SAA were fired. No. 27 Squadron flew six close-support sorties, one supply-drop sortie and one road-reconnaissance sortie. Fifty-nine 20 lb bombs were dropped and seventy rounds of SAA were expended. During November reconnaissances were carried out over Mahsud, Mada Khel and Tori Khel country. Reconnaissances of the area continued throughout December 1936.

1937

January   Cooperation continued throughout the month covering such areas as Datta Khel and Arsal tribal areas, followed by offensive patrols.

February   At 10.30 hrs on 7 February a car carrying the Khassadars' pay was ambushed and looted. All the occupants of the car were wounded. One British officer, one Tochi Scout orderly and two Mada Khel Khassadars were fatally wounded. The Officer Commanding, Tochi Scouts, asked for an aircraft to try to locate the murderers. Two sorties were carried out without result. On the 17th a column was sniped at from the time that it left camp until it was clear of the Wchobii Lakai Ridge. The column was to march from Obasa to Wana in one day but owing to the persistent nature of the sniping they were unable to complete march and camped the night on the line of march. Air action was taken against the snipers, with twenty-four 20 lb bombs being dropped.

March   Owing to the disturbed state of the tribes in Waziristan, Headquarters called for reconnaissances over the convoys using the roads. Two reconnaissances were provided. This was followed by a pamphlet drop on Arsal Kot warning of the commencement of bombing. On the 29th the 1st Infantry Brigade was in action when it was attacked by a lashkar of unknown strength. The brigade suffered seventy-four casualties while seventy of the tribesmen were killed, with an unknown number wounded in the hills north of Damdil Bosdli Road.

April   Action against local tribesmen continued with blockade sorties flown particularly over the Shinki area where bombs were dropped. One flight of No. 28 Squadron arrived to take over the fort at Miranshah. On the 20th of the month the squadron left for Risalpur. The total flying hours flown since the beginning of the Waziristan operations was 1,807 hrs 35 mins. It was reported that, owing to the concentration of the RAF in Waziristan, the RAF Hill Depot at Lower Topa would not be run on normal lines. In order to leave as much room as possible for the last party who had spent the first half of the hot weather on the plains it was decided to send the squadron up in two parties.

Arrivals and Departures – March to July

to Home Establishment
14/3   Flight Lieutenant Harvey.
17/3   Flight Lieutenant Tuttle
         Flying Officer Chacksfield

Flying Officer Watson
Flying Officer Becker
Pilot Officer R.F. Smith.
17/4   Squadron Leader McLaren Reid to No. 20 Squadron.
31/3   Flight Lieutenant Daubnui to No. 28 Squadron.
1/5   Flight Lieutenant Seymour to HQ RAF India.
16/5   Flying Officer Spencer
         to No. 5 Squadron
         Pilot Officer W.O.L. Smith
         Pilot Officer O'Grady.
16/6   Pilot Officer Blomfield
31/7   Squadron Leader Cannon (to command)
         Pilot Officer Close
         Pilot Officer Weston.

Death

11/3   Flying Officer K.N. Rees as a result of injuries in an aircraft accident when his machine struck telegraph wires on the Wana/Manzai road.

September   On the 6th one aircraft went to Razmak and took Captain Symons and Colonel Henderson on a reconnaissance over the Wazdiv. Another aircraft flew to Wana to take Colonel Heath on a reconnaissance over the Kaniguram area. Two of the usual road reconnaissances were carried out and one tactical reconnaissance in the Drazinda area, the aircraft stopping at Manzai for instructions.

October   Three road and photo reconnaissances were carried out during the month, followed by close support sorties. On return the aircraft were fired at from the ground. 184 rounds were fired in retaliation.

1938

February   Continuing support for ground forces working for Tochi Scouts.

March   On the 29th the following officers were posted in to the squadron:

Pilot Officer Fowler
Pilot Officer Fairnbairn
Pilot Officer Adamson.

By the end of the month the majority of the aircraft of the squadron had been re-equipped with wireless, the new set being the TR 1091.

April   The squadron move to Risalpur, originally planned for 24 April, was brought forward to the 21st. With the squadron's departure a guest night was held in the Rawalpindi Club. With eighty guests present the evening was a great success. On the 9th Pilot Officer Holmes was detailed for operations over the

Wana/Manzai convoy. He took off in a Wapiti J.9482 at 13.15 hrs with AC1 Higgins as air gunner. The convoy had been held up by hostile tribesmen in Shahurtangi since 07.40 hrs. Holmes arrived overhead at 13.35 hrs to find a situation that had become very grave and he was instructed to attack any hostiles that could be seen within range of the convoy. The main opposition was being experienced on the north side of the road and this was passed to Holmes by W/T, but from a height of 2,300 ft he was unable to see the enemy so he came down to 1,000 ft in order to search broken ground in more detail. He saw twenty men on a peak about 700 yards north of the road and climbed 2,500 ft preparatory to delivering his attack. When coming out of his dive in his second attack a bullet struck his boot and went through the main petrol tank. Petrol poured freely into the cockpit and he decided to turn off the main petrol cock and switched off the engine. He landed on the road about three-quarters of a mile east of the Chagmali Post and at the end of the run was pulled off the road by a bush. The undercarriage collapsed sideways and the aircraft tipped gently onto its nose. Army vehicles which were available in South Waziristan were not suitable for conveying the aircraft for repair without doing it further damage, and a Crossley crane lorry, *en route* to Manzai on the 17th, was the first vehicle that was able to effect a recovery. A flight sergeant Fitter was flown to Manzai to join the crane lorry, which then went under Army protection to the Chagmali Post.

May A wing parade was held on the 7th when the Group Commander, Group Captain C.C. Darley CBE, presented the DFC to Flying Officer F.A. Holmes for his flying in connection with the Shahurtangi ambush which took place on 9 April. An OBE was presented to No. 515747 LAC Woodcock for gallantry displayed at Miranshah in April 1937 in attempting to rescue the crew of a blazing aircraft loaded with bombs and small-arms ammunition.

1939

January to March Tactical reconnaissances and photographic sorties were still the order of the day.

April On the 1st the coming of age of the RAF was marked with a Ladies' Guest Night in the Officers' Mess. Meanwhile bombing sorties continued. On the 5th Group Captain Glenny carried out an inspection of the station and a refuelling and rearming exercise was carried out. Owing to operational commitments the remaining aircraft of C Flight did not take part.

August Close air support continued with the Wana convoy and total flying time for the month was 302 hours.

September Germany invaded Poland on the 1st and the squadron was reduced to one flight and moved from Risalpur to Fort Sandeman and close support against tribesmen continued after war was declared.

NO. 6 SQUADRON
Oculi exercitus
(The eyes of the Army)

1930

January Three aircraft landed and inspected the Beersheba landing ground. One aircraft carried out a reconnaissance between Ramleh and Maan before dark and returned to Amman lasting up to 2 hours 5 minutes. The aircraft left Ramleh for Gaza and Maan but could not reach Maan before dark and so returned to Amman. Two aircraft left Ramleh to cooperate with the Transjordan Frontier Force and remained at Semakh landing ground overnight to return on 25 January.

AIRCRAFT
Bristol F2B
Fairey Gordon
Hawker Hart
Hawker Demon

February On the 3rd two aircraft preceded to Haifa and Acre to take photographs, the flight lasting two hours. Reconnaissances and photographing continued until the 11th. On that day two aircraft searched for houses in villages to the north-east of Jaffa with three blue circles on their roofs. These houses were to be used for concentration of villagers in case of attack. On the 23rd Captain Miller of the Palestine Police Corps was flown as a passenger when two aircraft visited the Beersheba, Wadi Aqaba district in search of police wanted as witnesses at a trial at Beersheba. Squadron Leader C.R. Cox was posted to command No. 6 Squadron on the 28th of the month.

March On the 1st of the month three active operations with armoured cars carried out over the Bair and Imshah district. The following day Flying Officer Spaight was posted in the unit. From the 2nd to the 11th reconnaissances were carried out daily over Bair, Camp B, Imshah and Black Rock district. Tribes were located at Imshah on the 6th and this was reported. On the 7th a message was dropped on a tribe at Imshah telling them to move to the west of Bair Wells. On the 9th of the month the tribe was located 10 miles west of Bair Wells and was visited by Flight Lieutenant Swain in an armoured car who instructed them not to wander east of Bair. On the 12th Flight Lieutenant C.F. Strafford was posted to No. 6 Squadron. On the same day armoured cars were working with the Transjordon frontier Force (TFF) between Azrak and Landing Ground D. Tribes were located 20 miles east of Landing Ground D and aircraft carried out reconnaissances over the tribes while arrests were being made. On the 13th three aircraft working with armoured cars and the TFF located a police car and led it to the armoured cars. The aircraft then led the TFF on to good tracks for their return to Zerka. On the 16th Squadron Leader C.H. Keith was posted from the squadron. On the same day four aircraft were ordered to take air action by HQ Palestine and Transjordan on Azrak Castle. The raiding tribe, on seeing the aircraft, left quietly. During the month of March four forced landings were made, two aircraft were written off and two repaired and flown back to Ramleh. Two aircraft from B Flight and two from A Flight flew to Amman the same day and gunnery practice took place over the sea in the absence of a range. 23 hours 25 minutes were devoted to photography during March.

April   On 1 April Flight Lieutenant R.W.B. Bryant was posted to No. 6 Squadron. The same day the following Army personnel were taken on a reconnaissance: Lt Street of the 3rd South Staffordshire Regiment was taken up by Flying Officer Parkin. Captain Gordon of the same Regiment was taken up by Sergeant Keens. Flying Officer Parkin had to make a forced landing, and two other aircraft that also force-landed were so badly damaged that they had to be written off. Gunnery tests were carried out by all squadron aircraft over the sea and orders were received from HQ Air Palestine to photograph ten strips of country each 2 miles long and overlap runs were made of each strip and supplied to Sir John Hope-Simpson in connection with the Lands Commission. Flying Officer Fairhead and Flight Lieutenant Howard were posted from No. 6 Squadron to Home Establishment.

June   The Bristol Fighter J.4362 crashed owing to a wheel sinking into the ground on landing. Flying Officer Parkinson was posted from No. 6 Squadron on the 16th. One aircraft carried out a reconnaissance of areas likely to see civil disturbances at a time when death sentences were due to be carried out on three Arabs the following day, 17 June. No unusual gatherings were noticed. On the 21st three Bristol Fighters and one Avro proceeded to Beersheba to take part in celebrations in the conclusion of the Locust Campaign. Total flying for the month was 367 hours.

July   On the 25th C Flight proceeded to Ramleh to relieve A Flight. Two Victoria aircraft conveyed personnel and stores. Approximately 11 miles east of El Arish one Victoria force landed owing to a broken connecting rod. A new engine was flown out from No. 216 Squadron, Heliopolis and this Victoria proceeded to Ramleh the next day.

August   On the 14th a ground party consisting of Flight Lieutenant Strafford and Flying Officer Sprague proceeded by surface transport to Hebron where a search was made with police officers to find a more suitable message picking-up site. On the 16th Bristol Fighter JR.6635 made a successful forced landing on Gaza landing ground due to engine trouble. The exhaust valve stem had broken and fallen into a cylinder, breaking the piston. On the 28th the same aircraft crashed while landing at Kolundia landing ground. The pilot, Flight Lieutenant Strafford, with no air gunner, sustained a fractured humerus and abrasions and was admitted to the Government General Hospital, Jerusalem. The airframe was written off and the Court of Inquiry was held at Ramleh on the 30th.

September   B Flight replaced C Flight at Ramleh with effect from the 8th of the month. Major Smithers and Major Anstruther were flown over the Suez Canal for survey purposes.

November   Stand-by order was received for two flights to hold themselves at readiness to proceed to Ramleh at 24 hours' notice. Orders for one flight and Advanced Headquarters to proceed forthwith to Ramleh were received at 09.30 hrs, and the move was completed by 14.30 hrs on 15 November. A reconnaissance on the 19th was made of certain Jewish areas to spot for markings on Jewish concentrations, buildings and posts.

December   On the 5th a Bristol Fighter J.6798 struck the chimney of the incinerator at Ramleh aerodrome. The pilot, Flying Officer Richards, and his passenger, Squadron Leader the Reverend J.C. Thomas, were removed to the Palestine General Hospital and the aircraft was written off.

1931

January   331 hours were flown. The flights cooperated with No. 2 Armoured Car Company [the author's old unit] and photographic mosaics were carried out of Lake Timsah and the Bitter Lakes.

February   On the 1st Squadron Leader J.P. Coleman AFC assumed command of No. 6 Squadron and Squadron Leader Cox left on posting to Air Headquarters Palestine/Transjordan. On the 11th Bristol Fighter J.8284 hit a bush on taking off at Ainhosb and the engine and airframe were burned in situ. The pilot, Flying Officer R. Jones, and passenger were uninjured. On the 20th there was a flying display when unit aircraft demonstrated message picking up and formation flying with wingtips tied together. On the 24th Bristol Fighter J.8274 force landed at Abu Zabul. The airframe and engine were destroyed *in situ*. The pilot and passenger were uninjured.

March   On the 27th No. 363026 LAC Smith W.H., a Fitter (Aircraft and Engines) was killed and No. 363139 LAC Luck R.G., also a Fitter AE, was seriously injured swinging the propeller of Bristol Fighter H.1483.

April   On the 1st, the squadron designation was changed from Army Cooperation to Bomber. The attached flight at Ramleh was ordered to stand by at 30 minutes' notice during daylight hours for the Nebi Musa Festival. On the 4th Fairey IIIF S.1143, from the Heliopolis Communications Flight, lost flying speed when turning into land at Ismailia and crashed. The pilot, Squadron Leader Waugh, died from his injuries on the 7th, and his crewmen, AC1 Goldphin and AC1 Thomas were seriously injured. On the 9th the Chief of the Air Staff, Air Chief Marshal Sir John Salmond, and the AOC, Air Vice-Marshal F.R. Scarlett visited Ismailia. The CAS arrived by air from Amman and the AOC from Heliopolis. The CAS left in an Iris flying-boat from Lake Timsah and the AOC by air to Heliopolis. Flying hours for April were 323, with 325 flights being made.

June   On the 10th conversion training began on the Fairey Gordons K.1729 and K1730 when they were delivered to the squadron.

July   On the 27th Flying Officer Stephenson was posted to Home Establishment for a Long Signals Course. Flying hours to July were 397, with 373 flights.

October   On the 1st Atlas. J.9960 of No. 208 Squadron, crashed on take-off from Ismailia. The pilot, Flying Officer F.E. Adult and his passenger, Lieutenant-Colonel Rowan, commanding the 1st Wiltshire Regiment, Alexandria, were killed. On the 2nd the body of Colonel Rowan was taken to Aboukir for burial. Also on the 2nd Flying Officer Howell was posted from the RAF Depot and Flight Lieutenant J. Freeman-Fowler to No. 6 from Home Establishment as the Accountant Officer. On the 7th Air Vice-Marshal Cyril Newall assumed command of the RAF Middle East. A Short Rangoon flying-boat landed on Lake Timsah from Lake Tiberius. The flying hours for the month were 392, with 431 flights.

December   On the 9th the Air Officer Commanding visited Ramleh to inspect No. 2 Armoured Car Company. On the 20th a French Potez aircraft of the 39th Regiment flew in from Royak, Syria, piloted by Adjutant Chef Guilliottau, and carrying as passenger Colonel Antoinet, commanding the French Air Force in Syria. Both men returned to Royak on the 22nd. Flying hours

for the month were 337, with 319 flights.

1932

January   A roundup of squadron personnel at the beginning of the year shows the following in post:

Squadron Leader J.P. Coleman	Squadron Commander
Flight Lieutenant Burton	A Flight Commander
Flight Lieutenant Swain	B Flight Commander
Flight Lieutenant Sanderson AFC	C Flight Commander
Flying Officer Pritchards	Pilot
Flying Officer Connelly	Pilot
Flying Officer Cass	Pilot
Flying Officer Martin	Pilot
Flying Officer Sprague	Pilot
Flying Officer Lewis	Pilot
Flying Officer Maclellan	Pilot
Flying Office Cave	Pilot (attached from HQ Middle East)
Flight Lieutenant Cottle	Pilot (not filling a vacancy on establishment)
Flight Lieutenant Attwood	OC Wireless Telegraphy Station
Warrant Officer Bird	Armament Officer
Warrant Livingstone	Engineering Officer
Warrant Officer Patterson	Discipline
Warrant Officer Farmer	Signals.

Squadron Leader Coleman proceeded on leave and Flight Lieutenant Cottle took over temporary command. The flying hours for January were 318, with 368 flights.

February   On the 9th five Bristol Fighters proceeded from Ismailia to assist in a search for a missing Wapiti aircraft of No. 55 Bomber Squadron. Six out of twelve had force-landed in a snow storm while *en route* from Cairo to Baghdad for display duties. On the 23rd Flight Sergeant Cooper, piloting a Bristol Fighter C.4683, carrying ballast, crashed while landing on a night-flying practice. The aircraft was a write off. The pilot was slightly injured. Flying hours for the month were 337, with 353 flights.

March   On the 8th Squadron Leader Coleman returned from leave. On the 17th the AOC carried out his annual inspection. Flying hours for the month were 326, with 410 flights.

June   On the 1st re-equipment of the squadron with Fairey Gordons was commenced and four Bristol fighters were flown to the depot at Aboukir.

September to November   Routine duties.

December   Flying hours for the month were 443, with 380 flights. The changes to squadron personnel listed for January:

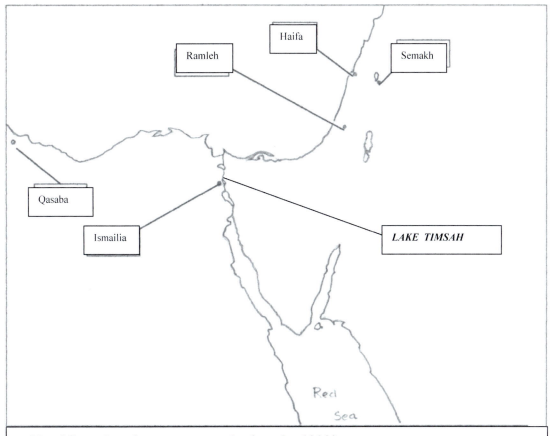

No. 6 Squadron's movements during the 1930's :-

Base Station	From	To	Detachments
Ismailia	28.10.29	29.5.36	Semakh, Ramleh, Haifa and Qasaba
Ramleh	29.5.36	19.11.36	Semakh
Ismailia	19.11.36	22.11.37	
Ramleh	22.11.37	17.2.41	Haifa and Ismailia

Pilots: Flying Officer Milson
Flying Officer Alvey
Flying Officer Sabine
Flying Officer Richards
Flying Officer Hammel
Flying Officer Greigson
Flying Officer Reid
Flying Officers R.E. Barnett and H.M. Middleton
(Not filling vacancies on establishment)
Signals Warrant Officers Allerston and Wendon.

1933

February   On the 20th six squadron aircraft proceeded on a training flight to Khartoum. All returned safely by the 28th, with the exception of Sergeant Poltock who had engine trouble at Aswan and Flying Officer Cass at Wadi Halfa. These pilots returned on 4 and 5 March respectively.

March   On the 31st there was a Cairo/Rhodesia flight which left Ismailia, and the following officers comprised the flight: Flight Lieutenant Swain, Flying Officer Alvey (navigation officer), Flying Officers Richards, Lewis and Sabine. Group Captain Pulford, who was the AOC's representative, also took part in the flight. A spare aircraft accompanied the flight as far as Khartoum. The route taken was from Wadi Halfa, Khartoum, Malakal, Juba, Entebbe, Tabora, Abercorn, Broken Hill,

Livingstone, Bulawayo to Salisbury. Flying hours were 677, with 622 flights.

June   On the 13th there was a loss of a Gordon when Flight Lieutenant Swain crashed in aircraft No. K.6244 twenty miles south of Juba. It was burned *in situ* after all instruments and articles of value had been salvaged. Flying Officer Alvey (passenger) was slightly injured.

1934

January   A Flight flew to Ramleh and was joined by B Flight as a precautionary measure against demonstrations by the Arabs on the occasion of Ramadan. On the 22nd Squadron Leader H.M. Massey MC arrived from the UK to take command of No. 6 (Bomber) Squadron, vice Squadron Leader Coleman. Flight Lieutenant Hyden arrived from the UK on posting in as Medical Officer. On the 27th the Annual Athletics Sports Day was held. On the 31st Flying Officer Sabine was posted to No. 47 (B) Squadron.

April   On the 4th five aircraft provided an escort at Port Said on the occasion of the Chief of the Air Staff's arrival in Egypt.

June   On the 5th the Target Towing Flight was formed at Ismailia and two Gordon aircraft were allotted to this flight. By the end of the month there were 14.2 effective pilots, 5 airman pilots, 1.2 reserve pilots and 0.9 non-effective pilots. During the month 567 hours were flown, with 525 flights.

December   On the 20th instructions were received for the squadron to assist in a search for a missing KLM airliner last seen passing Landing Ground No. 13 flying on an easterly course. Two flights of eight aircraft were put on a state of readiness to proceed at one hour's notice during daylight and two hours' notice on the night of the 20th/21st. Then information was received on the morning of the 21st that the missing aircraft had been found. Squadron personnel at the end of the year was as follows:

Squadron Leader Massey	Squadron Commander
Flight Lieutenant Tighe	A Flight Commander
Flight Lieutenant Tattersall	B Flight Commander
Flight Lieutenant Mc Reynolds	C Flight Commander
Flight Lieutenant Hyden	Medical Officer
Flying Officer Sims	Squadron Pilot
Flying Officer Sutton	Squadron Pilot
Flying Officer Harris	Squadron Pilot
Flying Officer Theed	Squadron Pilot
Flying Officer Withy	Squadron Pilot
Flying Officer Hunter	Squadron Pilot
Flying Officer Greigson	Squadron Pilot
Flying Officer Howell	Squadron Pilot
Flying Officer Judge	Not filling establishment post
Warrant Officer Bird	Armament Officer
Warrant Officer Drinkwater	Engineering Officer
Warrant Officer Patterson	Discipline
Warrant Officer Macario	Signals Officer
Flight Lieutenant Cherhill	OC Wireless Telegraphy Station
Warrant Officer Wenden	Signals
Warrant Officer Lindsay	Signals

1935

January   On the 31st was the squadron's 21st Anniversary but the unit was away, taking part in the Middle East Air Display on the day, so the celebrations had to take place on 8 February. The station was thrown open to personnel from other units who inspected the aircraft and general equipment of the squadron. Station Headquarters played the squadron at both association football and hockey, resulting in a win for the Station Headquarters' teams in both games. This was followed by an anniversary ball.

August   There was a serious curtailment of flying hours. The aircraft were taken out of service to have fins strengthened and the Panther II engines' unserviceability was due to anticipated failure of the master connecting rod assembly.

September   An extra flight was added to the squadron. This was D Flight and was part of the Expansion Programme and personnel for this flight began to arrive on the unit. On the 30th information was received that the squadron was about to be re-equipped with the Hawker Hart light bomber. D Flight was to be equipped with the Hawker Demon.

October   On the 14th Flying Officer F.W.C. Shute was in Demon, Serial No. K.5049, when he taxied into a patch of soft sand on the aerodrome, causing the aircraft to tip onto its nose. No damage was done except to its airscrew. By now the number of effective officers was 14.6 with 9.8 airman pilots and 2 Reserve pilots plus 1.5 non-effective officers and 2.2 non-effective airman pilots. Flying hours for the month were 825, with 622 flights.

November   On the 30th the squadron pilots had a lecture on dive bombing given by Squadron Leader G. Hallawell from HQ Middle East.

1936

February   On the 8th there was a practise move of the squadron. Orders were received at 15.00 hrs on the 5th for the immediate move of the squadron to the Qasaba landing ground, a temporary location, due to the situation in the Western Desert. Three bomber/transport aircraft, conveying the advance maintenance party, left for Qasaba at 08.30 hrs the following morning. On the 14th practise bombing raids were carried out at targets in the Brownsbottom air firing and bombing ranges in Sanai. Air-to-ground firing was carried out by the pilots and air gunners of A Flight. B, C and D Flights carried out high-altitude bombing.

May There was a deterioration in the general security situation. On the orders of HQ Palestine and Transjordan, the following duties were allocated to the squadron. The unit was to maintain:

(a) One aircraft standing by at 30 minutes' notice at the disposal of the Officers Commanding each of the four areas – Nablus, Jerusalem, Saffrea and Haifa.
(b) One aircraft standing by at the disposal of Officer Commanding, Armoured Car Detachment, Auga.
(c) One striking force of three aircraft standing by at 45 minutes' notice to operate in any area.

A hangar was allotted to the squadron to house two additional flights, A and B, and an operations room was established. In general the constant tension between Arab and Jew during the month led to the commencement of serious rioting in Palestine, and a General Strike was called by the Arab party. The cases of murder, sabotage, arson and the destruction of crops was reported over a wide area, and it was considered necessary to reinforce the Palestine garrison. Orders were issued to the effect that machine-gun fire from the air may be used without previous authority only in the following circumstances:

(a) When persons are caught flagrantly committing acts of violence, e.g. looting or incendiarism.
(b) When an officer commanding a body of troops engaged with tribesmen asks for assistance to extricate him from a difficult position.
(c) Against armed bands of tribesmen which, by reason of their numbers, appearance and movements are known to be intent upon acts of aggression or about to be or have been engaged in such aggression.
(d) Against that house or those houses in villages, not towns or main centres, from which hostile rifle fire has been directed against aircraft of security forces.

In fact no air action was taken that month.

June On the 4th a quantity of 5,000 leaflets was received for dropping on Arab villages. On the 9th it was arranged that a wireless tender should accompany the Cameron Highlanders who were patrolling the

Jerusalem to Ramleh road in case air cover was required. On the 10th the operational commitments for the squadron were similar to those above, for May. The two areas to be covered by one aircraft standing by at 30 minutes' notice were for Northern Brigade and Southern Brigade Areas. There was an additional requirement to that listed for May, namely one aircraft standing by for cooperation with the troops patrolling the Jerusalem to Ramleh Road trying to locate snipers. When thirty armed Arabs did attack the convoy the aircraft that arrived at the scene could not take air action since the Arabs had dispersed and taken refuge in caves. During the month that followed there were several changes made to the squadron's operational tasks. On the 25th restrictions which existed on bombing in Palestine were reduced and conditions for the different forms of attack were laid down. No bombing was, however, to take place within 500 yards of any town, village or buildings. The armament section was moved to Ramleh and all aircraft on duty in the bombing areas were equipped with four 20 lb HE bombs. On the 26th one of the pilots observed six Arabs carrying a coffin. This they threw to the ground and opened fire on the aircraft. Fire was returned and three Arabs were killed. The aircraft was hit once but there were no casualties to squadron personnel. There was reinforcement in the form of six Hart aircraft from No. 33 Squadron, which arrived from Mersah Matruh on the 29th of the month. Meanwhile pamphlets continued to be dropped on the population. A new system was inaugurated for emergency calls by wireless telegraphy to call up air support during the month. Under this scheme road patrols and convoy escorts were in direct communication with the squadron. This enabled aircraft to reach the scene of an action more quickly than before and consequently assistance given by aircraft was more effective.

July Convoys continued to be fired upon. In spite of dropping pamphlets, casualties were eventually sustained. On the 26th emergency calls were received from the officer i/c road patrol on the Jaffa to Jerusalem road. Pilots flew to the scene, one to the north and one to the south of the road. The one to the north of the road saw armed Arabs retreating northwards and inflicted casualties among them using bombs and guns.

August On the 21st a new trick was discovered, played by the Arabs. An aircraft proceeded on call-out to the Musmus Pass and contacted the armoured cars and troops. Armed Arabs were located and air action was taken. Six Arab casualties were seen. The aircraft were hit twice with negligible damage when a new Arab trick was discovered. On one occasion an Arab lying on his back fired up at an aircraft as it passed over, only to roll onto his face concealing his rifle. The country was heavily wooded and casualties were hard to estimate.

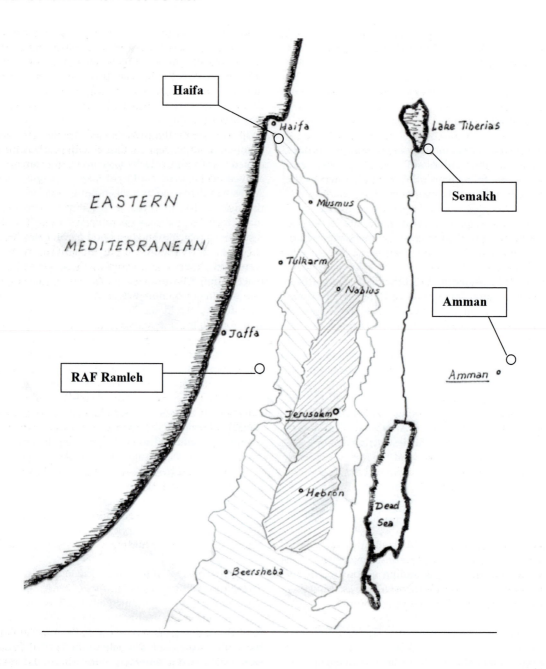

Arab strikes were threatened, and Nuri Pasha, the Foreign Minister of Iraq, was now in Palestine making attempts to induce Arab leaders to call off the strike and disorder. So on the 25th His Excellency, the Governor of Palestine, considered that the following three to four days should be as free as possible of air action. At the end of the month Palestine was divided into four emergency call zones. The squadron at Ramleh was responsible for answering emergency calls in the Middle Aircraft Zone. The most important development in the operations was that the squadron operated independently of the ground forces and far away from the roads. On these occasions information was received in the form of immediate messages that the enemy were reported to be in a certain vicinity. Aircraft proceeded to reconnoitre and located the enemy on two occasions when air action took place and casualties were inflicted. The total casualties inflicted for the month were 84 from air action. From then onwards there was to be economy in the words used for signalling emergency calls. Certain routes were given letters, e.g. Route A was the Jerusalem to Jaffa road and Route B was that from Jerusalem to Hebron and Beersheba.

September   There were thirteen emergency calls received during the month. On the 3rd the squadron sustained casualties when Squadron Leader Massey was shot in the knee and forced to land at Tulkarm. At the end of that day troops reached a crashed aircraft and reported that Pilot Officer Hunter and his air gunner, AC1 Lincoln, were dead. Flight Lieutenant Tighe had to assume command of the squadron. The squadron then received orders that it could fire at houses in villages from which hostile rifle fire was seen to come. At the end of the month fewer emergency calls for air action were received than during the preceding two months although requests for immediate reconnaissances had increased. This seemed to indicate that the enemy were working on a more organized basis. Secondly, enemy attacks were less sporadic than before. This created a force more concentrated in numbers as our increased efficiency in intelligence showed. On the 7th His Majesty the King had graciously approved the following awards:

Squadron Leader Massey	DSO
Flight Lieutenant Clarke	DFC
Pilot Officer Burns	DFC
Sergeant Dale	DFM

December   Training was considerably interfered with due to an outbreak of Scarlet Fever. This reduced flying hours to 198. The diary talks about returning to Palestine.

1937

February   On the 20th the squadron badge was approved. This was a black falcon perched inside the loop of the numeral '6' [see squadron badge on p. 126] with the motto 'oculi exercitus'. When the badge did not receive the approval of the Inspector of RAF Badges it

Hawker Hart K.4468 of No. 6 Squadron displaying the unit's pre-1936 emblem on its fin.

had to be changed. After much machination it was decided to replace the squadron number with a snake in the shape of a figure '6'. The objection to the original design was that the badge rather conflicted with that of No. 1 Fighter Squadron. It was against the rules to feature a squadron's number in the design. That went on the border.

The actions of the Arabs had once again become sporadic and the year continued with much of the same, i.e. the location of the enemy and the firing on small armed bands.

1938

February   On the 2nd the AOC Palestine/Transjordan carried out his annual inspection. On the 21st Squadron Leader Hobson, who had taken command of the unit, attended a conference at the RAF Station Ismailia on the rearming of the squadron with the Hardy aircraft, of which 79 were held at that station.

April   On the 9th Squadron Leader Hobson died suddenly, and command of the squadron was temporarily taken over by Squadron Leader Selway. Posthumously Squadron Leader Hobson was awarded a DSO. At the same time a DFM was awarded to Sergeant George Kennedy. Some airmen were also given awards by the GOC British Forces in Palestine/Transjordan for distinguished conduct displayed in action against armed bandits:

Sergeant Stubbs, Corporal Bain, AC1 Askey, AC1 Haxton and AC1 Tudor

December   Air operations during the remainder of the year continue as an ongoing attritional war. As the year drew to a close the following awards were granted:

Flying Officer Amlot	DFC
Sergeants Coggins and Stubbs	DFM
AC1 Tudor	DFM

On the 11th of the month one aircraft from Ramleh took part in a search for a Blenheim of No. 30 Squadron. [Blenheims had just arrived in the Middle East.] On the 20th Flight Lieutenant was awarded a DFC and Sergeant Onions a DFM.

1939

January to September   Operations against armed bands of Arabs continued right up to the declaration of war. The manning of the squadron on 3 September was:

Squadron Commander	Squadron Leader Singer DSO
A Flight	Acting Flight Lieutenant Brown
	Flying Officer Dawes
	Flying Officer Saunders

Flying Officer Field
Pilot Officer Scott
Sergeant Donaldson
Sergeant Mc Loughlin

B Flight
Flying Officer Wood
Flying Officer Langlois
Pilot Officer McFall DFC
Pilot Officer Fletcher
Pilot Officer Macrobert Bart.
(Sir Macrobert)
Sergeant Jarvis

C Flight
Acting Flight Lieutenant Ley DFC
Flying Officer Williams
Pilot Officer Hammerbeck
Pilot Officer Roberts
Flight Sergeant Stubbs
Sergeant Smallwood.

NO. 8 SQUADRON

Uspiam et passim
(Everywhere unbounded)

AIRCRAFT
Fairey IIIF
Vickers Vincent
Hawker Demon
Bristol Blenheim I

1930

January During the early part of the month two machines flew to Somaliland to lay seaplane moorings. While there they proceeded to Berber and visited the Survey Flight. Owing to exceptionally heavy rain at the end of January the landing ground had been flooded and greatly interfered with the squadron training. It also interfered with recreational activities as most of the sports ground was washed away. The landing ground was reported on two occasions to be unsafe for aircraft to land.

February On the 1st the Annual Inspection took place. Owing to the flooded state of the parade ground the full parade could not be carried out. Group Captain T.C. MacLean carried out the inspection. On the 7th the Survey Flight dispatched the first completed batch of prints and negatives to the Air Ministry. Having completed the first half of the survey, the flight was in the process of moving its base to Halin for which an advance party of one officer and five left Barran on the 15th.

March On the 30th the squadron carried out reconnaissances for the construction of landing grounds.

April The flight left Salalah on the 3rd and spent the night at Mukala and went on to Aden the next day. The landing grounds at Amasuda and Dhala were re-marked. The previous markings had got worn out. Due to the few demands for aircraft for other purposes during the month, good progress had been made on training. Instruction comprised a series of lectures on bombing, air pilotage, signals and engines. Lectures were also given on the work of coastal defence, artillery and the work of the RAF in India. During the month seaplane training had continued and several pilots had carried out their landing tests. On the 12th orders were given from the Air Ministry for the withdrawal of the SOA Flight from British Somaliland on completion of the photography.

June On the 6th certain flights started night-flying, which was continued on the 10th, 11th and 13th, by which date all pilots in that flight had passed their tests, with one flight left to test.

July On the 6th at 07.20 hrs a crash occurred in the vicinity of the camp. It was a Fairey III machine No. J.9143, resulting in the death of Flying Officer Pilcher and his passenger 507565 LAC Laidler. The funeral of the victims of the crash took place at the Services cemetary Ma'ala, and was attended by the officers, NCOs and all the men of the squadron. On the 31st Wing Commander J.L. Vachell MC assumed command of the British forces in Aden, vice Group Captain MacLean DSO, MC.

August On the 6th all flights of the squadron were qualified in night-flying.

October On the 18th Wing Commander Vachell resumed command of the squadron.

1931

January On the 26th Squadron Leader R.F. Sorley DSC, AFC assumed command of the squadron.

1932

November On the 14th Flight Lieutenant A.E. Beilby assumed command of the Squadron, vice Squadron Leader Sorley.

1933

January On the 6th Squadron Leader H.B. Russell AFC assumed command of the squadron, vice Flight Lieutenant Beilby.

March On the 31st at Sheikh Othman the defence scheme was successfully carried out by the squadron. The alarm was received by runner from Aden at 04.05 hrs and tenders were dispatched to Levy lines.

1934

March On the 22nd raids were carried out over the Qatabi area. The first of these raids was carried out by two machines of C Flight. Weather conditions were very bumpy so salvo bombing was the method applied. A photographic machine accompanied the machines of C Flight, taking pictures of the bomb bursts. These raids continued on the 23rd and 24th, still using the salvo method. On the 28th Sergeant Ower carried out the last raid of the day.

April A mosaic was put together of the bombed area. On the 7th rear guns were used against goats and cattle, but there were still no signs of the tribes coming to terms. The targets on the 10th was Quarite, Wahida and Dar Wahida, Geran and Jidera. Operations continued, and on the 24th Group Captain Portal carried out a reconnaissance over Qatabi, the main object of which was to see if the aeroplane was fired upon. No fires were observed and a large amount of stock, cows, camels and goats were seen in the Dar Nassir and Wadi Nisrah.

May On the 24th Sergeant Landry carried out a night-bombing raid and gunfire was used along the Wadi. Group Captain Portal joined in the night raids himself. On the 21st two machines took Colonel Lake and a native to As Sauda for a conference with the leaders of the Qatabis. Terms of peace were arranged and Colonel Lake returned to Aden with the Amir of Dhala, and a draft treaty was drawn up to bring an end to the 1934 operations.

July/August Routine squadron training was carried out.

1935

January On the 9th four Fairey III aircraft, led by Squadron Leader H.B. Russell, flew to Freetown in Sierra Leone and back on a training flight, returning on 10 February. Awards were given to members of the squadron for services rendered during operations in the Aden Protectorate between 22 March and 21 May 1934:

Squadron Leader Russell AFC DFC
Flight Lieutenant D Mc Fadyen Mentioned in Dispatches
No. 345044 Corporal Stokes Mentioned in Dispatches
No. 506822 Corporal Stack Mentioned in Dispatches

February During February the first flight was equipped with the Vickers Vincent aircraft powered by a Bristol Pegasus 2NIII engine. On the 23rd Squadron Leader H.S.B. Walmesly MC, DFC arrived to take command of the squadron.

June On the 3rd No. 386338 Sergeant (Pilot) Mandrey was awarded the AFM for outstanding general service in the Aden Protectorate, British Somaliland and with the West African Flight.

October During the Italo-Ethiopian dispute, the organization and the duties of the squadron were considerably affected. No. 203 (FB) Squadron flew in and a flight of six Hawker Demon two-seater fighter aircraft formed a fourth flight of the squadron. On the 13th there was a special detachment to British Somaliland to cooperate with the Somaliland Camel Corps patrolling the frontier between Italian Ethiopian border with British Somaliland. The detachment also maintained all W/T communications between the Camel Corps HQ and the Company HQ on the frontier.

November On the 1st the Demon Flight was transferred to No. 41 Squadron. On the 5th Khormaksar became a station headquarters. [This means that it has the status and title of RAF Station and is commanded by a Commanding Officer and not an Officer Commanding. The distinction is important, because a Commanding Officer has certain financial and disciplinary powers not enjoyed by an Officer Commanding.] No. 8 Squadron's commander was appointed station commander, and Khormaksar administered Nos 8, 12 and 41 Squadrons. The station carried out major overhauls of aircraft, engines and MT [motor transport], pay and accounting, and photographic work. During the early period of the crisis all three squadrons were accommodated at Khormaksar and 500 tons of bombs were transported to and stored on the station. Four Bessoneaux hangars were erected and used for the storage of aircraft. Three new bomb stores were built at Khormaksar and one at Perim. On the 19th Nos 8, 12 and 41 Squadrons cooperated in a brief bombing operation at Al Asala against the Marqshai, sub-section of the Fadhli tribe. On the 25th No. 12 Squadron moved to a semi-permanent station at Robat and the squadron moved between Khormaksar and Robat until it was time to go home in 1936.

December Cooperation exercises were carried out with the Navy, the Royal Artillery and Royal Engineers by day and night during November and December.

1936

March On the 18th No. 41 Squadron moved to a semi-permanent station at Bir Fadhl. Cooperation exercises with the other services continued to occupy most of the squadron's training until July, when the state of emergency was announced to be over.

August On the 5th a fourth flight of Vincents was formed from personnel of the Emergency Squadrons and reserve aircraft held at Khormaksar. The establishment of personnel was raised from 190 to 230 and of aircraft from 13 IE and 12 reserve to 19 IE and 18 reserve. On the 11th personnel of Nos 12 and 41 Squadrons left for England. On the 13th air action started against a section of the Aulaqi tribe in an area 150 miles north-east of

Aden. The tribesmen refused to provide an escort for a political officer passing through their territory in June and had not paid a fine of rifles and money which was due on 10 August. The bombing by flight salvos using instantaneous and delayed-action munitions continued until the 21st, when the fine was paid in full. The air action was therefore entirely successful and had the knock-on effect on tribes in the surrounding countryside that had not experienced bombing.

December On the 4th the detachment returned from British Somaliland after 14 months' service. The establishment of the squadron reverted to the three flights of four aircraft as it had been before the emergency.

1937

April On the 1st operations were commenced against the Shairi tribe in the Dhala area when they refused to work on road repairs in the Khoteiba Pass. The tribe had offered armed resistance to the political officer. During the operations, which lasted until p.m. on 2 April, 12½ tons of bombs were dropped. On the 13th two aircraft proceeded to Burao in British Somaliland to watch for movements of Abyssinnian refugees over the border. The aircraft operated from Aurano and carried out reconnaissance patrols along the border. The aircraft returned to Aden on the 16th. On the 23rd five Vincent aircraft, led by Flight Lieutenant W.G.H. Ewing, made a long-distance flight to Khartoum, returning via Egypt, Palestine, Iraq and the Hadramout Coast, a total distance of 6,074 miles. The flight was treated as training and a reinforcement, which was accomplished without incident.

September More operations were carried out against tribes attacking trade routes.

1938

January Officers of the squadron at the beginning of the year were as follows:

Squadron Commander	Squadron Leader J.F.T. Barrett DSO, DFC
Adjutant	Flying Officer J.W. Bayley
Equipment Officer	Flight Lieutenant H.M.S. Dawes
Medical Officer	Flight Lieutenant D.G. Smith MB, ChB
Accountant Officer	Flight Lieutenant J.E. Horsfield
Pilots	Flight Lieutenants W.D. Butler, Glencross and Farnhill Flying Officers R.I.K. Edwards, F.W. Flood, R.E. Carey and C.E.R. Tail Pilot Officers M.A. Goodwin, S.A.F. Robertson, H. St.G.

Turner and W. Morello Acting Pilot Officers M.H.B. Davies, G.C. Gauthier, P.A. Nicholas and F.C. Bowles.

On the 11th a Moth aircraft of the squadron crashed at Dar Mansur near Sheikh Othman. The pilot, Acting Pilot Officer M.H.B. Davies, and his passenger, 516857 LAC Campbell, were killed. The funeral took place with full military honours at Maalla Cemetery on 12 January. On the 17th the Inspector-General of the RAF, Marshal of the Royal Air Force Sir Edward Ellington, inspected the station.

March On the 3rd an impressive surrender ceremony was held at Shihr when the guilty section of the Hamemi tribe publicly surrendered. The personnel of the detached flight were present when the criminals, hostages and looted property were handed over.

June On the 14th a Vincent aircraft K.4148 crashed on the edge of the aerodrome. The pilot, Sergeant Franks, and his passenger, AC1 Wilson, were only slightly injured.

July On the 1st Squadron Leader J.F.T. Barrett was promoted to the rank of wing commander. Also, operations were now against the Mansuri section of the Subeihi tribe who had held up and looted lorries and caravans on the main trade routes. After that they were heavily escorted by aircraft when they both took place on Mondays, Wednesdays and Saturdays, and this was the only traffic permitted on that section of the road where the Mansuri section had looted lorries and caravans.

1939

March On the 5th a number of Yemeni forces crossed the border into the Protectorate then returned to the correct side of the boundary, but it strained relations. From the 5th to the 20th daily reconnaissance patrols were carried out by aircraft along the border. In connection with operations against the Mansuri operations the following awards were made:

A bar to his DSO	Wing Commander J.F.T. Barrett DSO, DFC
A DFC	Flying Officer R.I.K Edwards
A DFM	No. 564500 AC1 Shaw
Mentioned in Dispatches	Flight Lieutenant A.R. Glencross No. 560354 Sergeant Buswell H.D. No. 516191 Corporal Bruce W.D. No. 523900 Corporal Chap W.E. No. 523942 AC1 Derace R.S.

On the 30th an engineer specialist, Flying Officer J. Barnard, at the Air Ministry, arrived to instruct on and assist with the maintenance of Blenheim aircraft and to ensure the completeness of the equipment. During his stay in Aden his award of an MBE was announced.

May   On the 10th Squadron Leader I.L. Phillips was posted to command No. 8 (B) Squadron from SHQ Khormaksar. On the 20th six of the new aircraft were delivered to the squadron by air. They had been ferried from Thorney Island to Ismailia by pilots of Coastal Command.

July   On the 7th two Blenheim aircraft, one taking off and one landing, collided on the aerodrome and both machines were completely wrecked. One of the pilots, Pilot Officer M.D. Howell was only slightly injured.

August   On the 19th two Blenheim aircraft set out for Salalah but owing to thick low cloud were unable to find the landing ground and it was decided to return to Reida, but on the way one aircraft was forced to land near Sharkhat owing to lack of petrol. The other aircraft reached Reida successfully, refuelled and conveyed petrol to the force-landed aircraft. Both aircraft then returned to Reida for the night.

September   Due to the increased seriousness of the international situation it was decided to move to their dispersal points. On the 3rd the adjutant wrote in the operations record book that, due to the hostilities, the ORB was closed forthwith.

NO. 11 SQUADRON

Ociores acrioresque aquilis
(Swifter and keener than eagles)

AIRCRAFT
Westland Wapiti
Hawker Hart
Bristol Blenheim I

1930

March   On the 13th Flying Officer P.G.J. Atkinson was posted to Home Establishment on medical grounds following a flying accident causing slight injuries to the head. Flight Lieutenant C. Feather was posted to the squadron as Flight Commander of B Flight on the 25th.

April   Air firing and bomb classification for the training season 1929/30 were completed. There was a Viceroy's tour of India, and six machines of the squadron escorted the Hinaidi in which His Excellency was flown from Arawali to Miranshah. On the 12th three machines escorted him from Miranshah to Wana. On the 14th six machines escorted him to Chaktara. On the 18th Pilot Officer Millar was posted to the squadron from No. 4 FTS.

May   On the 7th there were operations against the Haji of Turagzai. On the 17th Flying Officer R.W.A. Stroud was killed in action on a bombing raid and No. 364367 AC1 Wiltshire, the air gunner, flew the machine back to Risalpur but was killed in the crash on landing.

August   Air operations against the Afridis. There were punitive raids on two Tirah villages in the Bara valley following an Afridi attack on Peshawar.

September   On the 26th Sergeant O.C. Clarke and AC1 Valentine were killed in a flying accident in the Lowarai Pass operating with the column.

December   On the 10th Flying Officer P.W. Lowe-Holmes was posted to the United Kingdom for the Long Armament Course at Eastchurch.

1931

February   On the 27th Air Marshal Sir Geoffrey H. Salmond KCB, KCMG, DSO vacated the post of Commander RAF India to be replaced by Air Marshal Sir John Miles Steel KBE, CBE, CMG.

March   Air Firing and Bombing Competition for the year 1930/1 completed.

May   Air Marshal Steel visited the squadron.

July   A demonstration flight of four machines including three from No. 11 Squadron carried out a flight over the Kal Kot district. This proved a flight of great importance over a section of very mountainous country. The chief object was to demonstrate over a jirgah at Barbusaa. A height demonstration in conjunction with the Ghurka Regiment was given at Attock.

December   Squadron Leader Cummings was posted to the Aircraft Depot, Karachi, with effect from 1 December 1931, and Flight Lieutenant F.H. Isaac of No. 39 Squadron took part in the Red Shirt operations following unrest in the area. The squadron offered valuable assistance to Army columns operating in this part of the Frontier Province.

1932

January   On the 18th the squadron strength was as follows:

Squadron Commander	Squadron Leader R.T.B. Houghton AFC
A Flight Commander	Flight Lieutenant R.E. Hall

B Flight Commander	Flight Lieutenant McKinley-Hay
C Flight Commander	Flight Lieutenant B.W.T. Hare
Adjutant	Flying Officer G.N. Roberts
Armament	Flying Officer A.O. Molesworth
Air Pilotage	Flying Officer L.W.C. Bower
Pilots	Flying Officer F.G. Ferrier
	Flying Officer T.W. Hoyle
	Flying Officer M.J. Adam
	Flying Officer R.B. Abraham
	Flying Officer J.C. Adkins
	Pilot Officer C.L. Monckton.

In anticipation of the re-equipment of the squadron with the Hawker Hart aircraft a series of lectures was given by Mr Finch, a factory representative from Rolls-Royce.

February   The re-equipment of the squadron with the Hawker Hart aircraft commenced on the 26th, A Flight receiving four aircraft. The squadron combined with the civil and military authorities in maintaning order during polling and the visit of His Excellency the Viceroy to the North-West Frontier Province. Several reconnaissances were carried out and the combined effort was often a very effective blockade of the north bank of the Kabul, thus preventing an influx of 'Red Shirt' elements into Peshawar. The general internal security situation then grew quieter.

August   The re-equipment of the squadron with Hart aircraft was complete.

September   The squadron was engaged in the relief of the Chitral column. When this happened, the relief of the garrison was accompanied by considerable tribal interference.

October   see photograph caption.

November   Two officers of the Afghan air force visited the station on the 23rd, and a small flying display was given for their benefit.

1933
April   Squadron Leader S.D. Culley DSO gave a lecture on the Northern Frontier tribes of India, their customs, etc.

August   At the start of the month the presence of an Afghan 'pretender' to the throne was instrumental in getting a bombing order issued on the 1st. It was feared that the unrest the 'pretender' was fomenting would cause diplomatic problems with Afghanistan. Throughout August, although the Army was busy on the ground, the bombing squadrons were simply kept on stand-by.

October   C Flight was busy preparing for a long-distance flight to Singapore, which they expect to undertake in January 1934.

November   On the 8th B Flight set off on 14 days' detachment to Delhi. This was the result of a new scheme to give flights on the station experience of working on their own. In Delhi they did air surveys, Army Cooperation and normal squadron training.

Nos 11 and 39 Squadron Harts of No. 2 (Indian) Wing flying from Risalpur to Gilgit on 17 October 1932.

The Gilgit river.

1934

February   On the 1st C Flight, consisting of four machines with Flight Lieutenant MacKay as their leader, left Risalpur. Flight Lieutenant Lindley, Pilot Officer Brotherhood and Sergeant Price made up the quartet. They proceeded according to plan until they reached Rangoon on the 5th, when Sergeant Price damaged the wingtip of his aircraft while atttempting to land. He had to wait there for repairs, but these were effected in time for him to rejoin the flight on the return journey. On the 7th Pilot Officer Brotherhood crashed on landing at Mergui. Neither he nor his passenger was injured, but his aircraft was damaged beyond repair and had to be shipped to Calcutta and thence by rail to Karachi, where the appropriate repair facilities were available. Thus only two aircraft of the flight completed the journey to Singapore and back.

December   The officers on the strength of the squadron at the end of the year were as follows:

Squadron Leader C.F. Poer-Trench
Flight Lieutenant M.B. MacKay
Flight Lieutenant W.J.H. Lindley
Flight Lieutenant Barett
Flying Officer D. Barclay
Flying Officer H.M. Bowes-Lyon
Flying Officer W.L. Stedman
Flying Officer C. Broughton
Pilot Officer W.R. Brotherhood
Pilot Officer N.C. Jones
Pilot Officer M.C. Corelli
Pilot Officer C.C. House.
Pilot Officer R.P.H. Carew.

1935

January   The whole squadron went to Singapore on a long-distance training flight. The only pilot not to get there was Flying Officer Broughton, who damaged a wingtip on landing at Dacca and had to be left behind. [Damaging wingtips seems to have been an occupational hazard.] The eleven remaining aircraft arrived safely in Singapore on 8 January and left on the 15th for the return flight. This was apparently the first time that a complete squadron of RAF landplanes had attempted a long-distance flight.

February   On the 21st nine aircraft of the squadron took part in a large-scale demonstration of five squadrons flying in line astern. This was intended to impress the Faqir of Alingar, who had raised a lashkar which was causing considerable unrest among the tribes on the west side of the Swat river.

March   No. 100 (Torpedo-Bomber) Squadron from Singapore made a long-distance training flight to Risalpur.

April   On the 16th nine aircraft of the squadron took part in an interception exercise designed to practise interception methods in the air and to exercise squadrons in methods of surprise and concealment in bombing attacks. Two bombing raids were carried out by the squadron and a Kohat squadron attempted interception.

May   On the 2nd the officers received a lecture with the title, 'Assuming the Government of India Bill becomes law discuss the future of India in relation to the Empire'. [That sounds like an examination question, not the title of a lecture, but that is what is written in the squadron diary.] All officers present in the squadron that day attended.

June   On the 1st Flight Lieutenant Mullet and Flying Officer Jones flew to Quetta, taking with them a W/T pack set in order to assist in establishing communications after the disastrous Quetta earthquake which took place at approximately 03.00 hrs that day.

July   On the 31st Flying Officer Corelli was transferred from the British Military Hospital Rawalpindi to the Central Hospital for Mental Diseases, Yaravda; on information received this officer had been declared insane. Nos 11 and 39 Squadrons were involved in disturbances brought about by the Haji of Turangai and his sons. A lashkar began to attack the Gandab Road. On the 17th the lashkar had grown to 2,000 men. On the 16th the government sanctioned an air blockade of the villages Burhan and Isakhel in order to force them to withdraw their lashkars. Bombs were dropped on the

23rd, the day operations commenced. It had the desired effect and the lashkar gradually reduced in size to approximately 800 men.

September Operations were carried out in Mohmand country. The role of the squadron remained unchanged. As a result of the squadron's actions two of the sub-tribes submitted to the government and were fined ten rifles or one hostage in lieu of each rifle deficient.

1936

January to November Nothing of significance to report.

December The officers of the squadron at the end of the year were as follows:

Squadron Leader R.O. Jones	Squadron Commander
Flying Officer M.C. Jones	A Flight Commander
Flight Lieutenant R.S. Howe	B Flight Commander
Flying Officer D.W.H. Gardner	C Flight Commander
Pilot Officer A.G. Dudgeon	Adjutant
Flying Officer J.W. Buchanan	Pilots
Flying Officer MR.H.P. Carew	Pilots
Pilot Officer M.P.C. Corkery	Pilots
Pilot Officer T.S. Jameson	Pilots
Pilot Officer A.G.C. Baird	Pilots
Pilot Officer W.L. Rowbottom	Pilots.

1937

January There was another long-distance flight to Singapore.

February From the 1st to the 4th the squadron took part in Far East Combined Exercises.

April Operations in Waziristan showed no signs of diminishing. Plans were prepared for the move of the squadron to Arawali so that relief could be afforded to Nos 27 and 60 Squadrons which were bearing the brunt of the work. It was not found necessary to put these plans into effect.

1938

January On the 6th, 7th and 8th flying tests of long-range fuel tanks and equipment on K.3921 were carried out. This aircraft had been camouflaged and fitted with two auxiliary tanks holding 23 gallons each mounted on the universal bomb racks under the wings. Petrol from these tanks was pumped to 'auxiliary gravity' tanks by the air gunner, using a Vickers pump in the rear cockpit.

February On the 2nd the squadron carried out a bombing, refuelling and rearming exercise.

March On the 1st the squadron was ordered to Miranshah to carry out punitive bombing against the Madda Khel tribes in the Tochi valley. The road convoy left Risalpur on the 1st for Miranshah. During the latter part of March long-range fuel and oil tanks were fitted to all aircraft of the squadron preparatory to carrying out a reinforcement flight to Egypt.

April On the 9th twelve aircraft of the squadron and one Valentia from the Bomber Transport Flight, India, formed an echelon V Eleven on the reinforcement flight to Egypt.

July On the 20th ten aircraft of the squadron took part in a Group search for a lost aircraft. The wreckage of an aircraft was subsequently located near Knumdian by police. Both occupants were killed. On the 23rd Flying Officer W.L. Rowbottom was killed as a result of a flying accident near Mardan.

August On the 31st Pilot Officer Richardson died in the British Military Hospital, Nowshera, as a result of injuries sustained in a car accident.

September On the 28th the squadron was ready to move to Iraq at 48 hours' notice. This was part of a possible mobilization following the Munich Crisis.

November On the 6th the squadron moved to Miranshah to take part in operations against certain tribes in north Waziristan.

1939

March On the 21st all flying ceased except for absolute necessities, and preparations were made to move the squadron to Singapore on a war basis on account of the critical political situation prevailing in Europe.

April Flying is being reduced to a minimum in order to reserve flying hours for any possible reinforcement flight in the event of war. Consequently practically no training has been done.

May Flying was restricted throughout the month by HQ orders to a maximum of one hour per aircraft per day.

June On the 13th a party consisting of Squadron Leader Spendlove, who was by then squadron commander, Flight Lieutenant Dudgeon, Flying Officer Ellaby and eight airmen left Ambala to go on a conversion course to twin-engined machines prior to embarking for Egypt. The purpose was collecting Blenheims, the new machine with which the squadron was to be equipped.

July The first Blenheim aircraft left Heliopolis for Risalpur. The remainder followed a few days later. All Blenheims belonging to the squadron were at Risalpur on the 28th, having been flown to Ambala in ones and twos.

August   On the 7th the squadron was redeployed to Tengah in the Far East.

September   On the 3rd war was declared.

NO. 14 SQUADRON

I spread my wings and keep my promise

1930

January   on the 1st the officers of the squadron were as follows:

AIRCRAFT
Fairey IIIF
Fairey Gordon
Vickers Wellesley

Squadron Commander	
Squadron Leader Soden DFC	
A Flight Commander	Flight Lieutenant Williams
B Flight Commander	Flight Lieutenant Greet
C Flight Commander	Flight Lieutenant Storrie
Adjutant	Flight Lieutenant Sutherland DFC
Pilots	Flying Office Moore
	Flying Officer Hutchings
	Flying Officer Wayte
	Flying Officer Robertson
	Pilot Officer Franks
	Pilot Officer Field
	+ 6 sergeant pilots
Medical Officer	Flying Officer Crowley
Stores	Flying Office Smith
Accounts	Flying Officer Cave.

On the 6th the 'Cape Flight' set out from Amman for Heliopolis. One aircraft force-landed at El Arish and only Abu Sueir was made that night, with the flight continuing to Heliopolis the following day. Here the flight was joined by Air Commodore A.C. Board, who was the senior officer selected to travel with the flight. On the 11th the flight to Cape Town commenced from Heliopolis. The route taken was Cairo–Wadi Halfa–Khartoum–Ongalla–Entebbe–Nairobi–Tabora–Abercorn–Broken Hill–Livingstone–Bulawayo–Pretoria–Bloemfontein–Beaufort West–Cape Town. There was one forced landing near Salisbury due to a fractured petrol pipe, and a landing was successfully carried out on long grass three to four feet high. A special runway was cut for the subsequent take-off. On the return journey the flight was accompanied by a flight of the South African Air Force. Fairey IIIFs were given to the squadron in order to carry out this flight, not the usual DH9As.

May   Activities of the desert tribes for the summer period began for the year in real earnest. The flights that operated from Amman found that by the time they got to the affected area the raiders had disappeared so it was decided to place armoured car detachments on guard permanently at all the watering places at which raiders, either from our own tribes or from beyond the border, must water on the inward and outward journey. The plan, therefore, was to have an aircraft patrolling the area, to be relieved by another, to direct dawn and dusk patrols keeping station over any observed raiders until the arrival of armoured cars and the relieving aircraft. On the 9th, using these procedures, it was possible to stop a raid in the Nedj country, and when the armoured cars arrived they were able to arrest the leading tribesmen and the camels were confiscated.

July   On the 28th the Transjordan Frontier Force aided by aircraft of the squadron managed to forestall an operation.

December   Periodical reconnaissances were carried out, to impress the tribes, of the Haifa to Baghdad Road. Continuous watch of the movements of the tribes in the Transjordan had been kept throughout the month.

1931

January   The policy of the squadron in January 1931 was to leave control of the Transjordan tribes to the Tribal Control Officer, Captain Glubb, but at the same time to offer sufficient forces in immediate reserve to assist him, if and when necessary.

February   On the 11th a special flight involving Flying Officer Jarman was made to test the upper air temperature in connection with a meteorological scheme from 10,000 to 15,000 feet, the temperature being 14 °C at 1,000 ft above sea level and -15 °C at 15,000 ft. During the latter period of February the situation in northern and southern deserts and the Jordan valley had been normal. The two aircraft attached at Amman could alone be employed in operations. This enabled the remainder of the squadron to devote more time to squadron training.

December   At the end of the year Squadron Leader F. Soden was still the squadron commander.

Squadron Commander	Squadron Leader F. Soden DFC
A Flight Commander	Flight Lieutenant B Atcherley
B Flight Commander	Flight Lieutenant Ronkeley
C Flight Commander	Flight Lieutenant Dale
Adjutant	Flying Officer Hewitt
Pilots	Flying Officer Halahan
	Flying Officer Binley
	Flying Officer Smith
	Flying Officer Charman
	Flying Officer Bramley
	Flying Officer Hole
Medical Officer	Squadron Leader Atteridal
Stores Officer	Flight Lieutenant Young
Accounting Officer	Flight Lieutenant Donkin.

1932

January Squadron Leader Soden arrived from leave in the UK in his own aircraft, a DH Pussmoth.

April The Iraq/Egypt air mail was conveyed weekly from Amman to Rutbah and return. Cooperation with the Transjordan Frontier Force continued.

October On the 29th Squadron Leader Cockey assumed command of the squadron, vice Squadron Leader Soden.

December There were reports of tribesmen being determined to attack either the Transjordan tribes, Aqabar, Ma'an or Amman.

1933

January A visit by the Secretary of State for Air, the Marquess of Londonderry.

1934

December On the 21st ten Gordons carried out a search for a KLM Douglas airliner which had been reported missing. The airliner was found crashed in the Wadi Hauram, 50 miles south-west of Rutbah. All persons on board had been killed.

1935

July On the 2nd Squadron Leader Cockey was promoted to the rank of wing commander.

August On the 6th Squadron Leader Traill DFC arrived and took over the command of the squadron.

1936

April On the 22nd two aircraft were sent to Jisr Mejamie in connection with recent troubles. Constant reconnaisances were carried out but no large movements of Arabs occurred in the Jordan area. Nothing of interest was seen. Reconnaisances were also made to discourage crop burning.

1937

January The officers on the squadron were:

Squadron Commander	Squadron Leader Traill DFC
Adjutant	Flying Officer Aylmer
A Flight	Flight Lieutenant Grace
	Flying Officer Grace
	Flying Officer Seys
	Pilot Officer Cruikshanks
	Sergeant Hefey
	Sergeant O'Brien
	Sergeant Chick
B Flight	Flight Lieutenant Sims
	Pilot Officer Cooke
	Pilot Office Bell
	Sergeant Tremeer
	Sergeant Morison
	Sergeant May
C Flight	Flight Lieutenant Howes
	Pilot Officer Fenwick-Wilson
	Pilot Officer Lunn
	Sergeant Sooley
	Sergeant Birt.

April On the 29th two officers were taking part in endurance tests with long-range fuel tanks.

August After much correspondence with the Chester Herald, the squadron badge was approved by His Majesty and presented to the squadron on a ceremonial parade by Air Vice-Marshal C.T. MacLean CBE, DSO, MC. On the 12th the squadron had been forced to accept a winged plate on the squadron crest in place of the old winged shield, in spite of the fact that No. 14 was one of the oldest squadrons in the service.

1938

February It is interesting to note that a section of armoured cars *en route* from Maan to Amman was snowed in for three days. Supplies were flown out to them and dropped on two occasions. The training programme was greatly curtailed during the month due to adverse weather conditions.

March The squadron establishment was increased, the total rising to 27 aircraft, each flight had six aircraft plus 2 reserve and 3 squadron reserve. Personnel were increased accordingly, with 5 extra flying officers or pilot officers, 6 NCO pilots, 22 corporals and 47 other ranks. The new establishment ME/E/106 dated 14 February 1938 was as follows:

Squadron Leader	1
Flight Lieutenant	3
Flying Officer/Pilot Officer	12
NCO Pilots	12
Warrant Officer Armament	1
Flight Sergeant (Fitter 1)	3
Sergeant	4
Sergeant Observer	3
Corporal Air Observer	20
Corporal	18
Aircraftmen	86
Civilians	12
Total	175

The squadron was re-equipped with Vickers Wellesley aircraft, commencing with an allotment of two on the 19th. The Gordons were withdrawn as the new types were received. Thirteen pilots flew the new aircraft successfully, there being no dual aircraft available.

April   On the 13th six aircraft of No. 11 Squadron, flying through from India, overshot the Amman in a thick dusk haze. A Gordon was dispatched at 12.30 hours and located the missing aircraft, which had landed safely at four different places in the Jordan valley, north of the Dead Sea. At the end of April all pilots had flown the Wellesley aircraft. Two pilots had flown them at night.

June   The squadron is entirely equipped with Wellesley aircraft.

August   The situation in Palestine continued to deteriorate, and night reconnaisance flights over the northern Palestine curfew area were carried out on a further ten occasions during the month. All aircraft dropped flares but it was discovered that it was practically impossible to detect the movement of Arab gangs from the air at night. Two Wellesley aircraft crashed at Zerka on the 8th while carrying out air-to-ground firing. Sergeant Sweeting, the pilot, and AC2 Crofts, the air gunner, were killed instantaneously.

September   Reconnaissance flights of the Palestine northern frontier carried out on fourteen nights owing to the situation in Palestine. Pilots then carried revolvers and the aircraft contained a rifle and ammunition when flying over Palestine.

October   The Palestine situation continued to deteriorate and active operations continued. Night action in Ar Rama area caused great morale effect and terror among the villagers, who did not know aircraft could fly at night. The main difficulty experienced was in dropping bombs with accuracy from 600 feet on a moonlit night.

1939
January to March   In the early months the squadron was busy carrying out reconnaissance flights.

April   Frequent reconnaissance flights were carried out over northern Transjordan with the object of locating armed bands reported in the vicinity. Cooperation was maintained with the Transjordan Frontier Force and the Arab Legion during this period.

August   On the 19th coastal and seaward reconnaissances were carried out by day and by night to locate ships attempting to land illegal immigrants into Palestine. On the 20th a signal was received telling the squadron to be prepared to move to its war station. On the 24th the squadron moved to Ismailia. The strength of the unit was 30 officers and 146 other ranks. The squadron was joined by 30 and 55 Squadrons to form No. 1 Bomber Wing. On the 28th flight routine was resumed. As far as possible flying was carried out by all new pilots. On the 30th a Blackout of the Canal Zone was witnessed by Squadron Leader Selway and Flight Lieutenant McNab between the hours of 23.30 and 00.30.

September   On the 3rd was the declaration of war with Germany.

NO. 20 SQUADRON
Facta non verba
(Deeds not words)

AIRCRAFT
Bristol F2B
Westland Wapiti
Hawker Audax

1930
April   On the 7th Squadron Leader L.L. Brown DFC, AFC assumed command of the squadron, vice Flight Lieutenant W.K. Turner. Reconnaissance flights carried out almost daily with five on the 26th. Gatherings of between 150 and 200 men were reported in Charsadda and Shabkadar. Congressmen were conspicuous in all gatherings. On the 28th parties of Congressmen were reported in Mohmand country. This was very special activity.

May   On the 3rd the internal boundaries of technical areas of camp protected by barbed wire. Two platoons of airmen formed to provide piquets and patrols of the cantonment under orders of the Kings Own Yorkshire Light Infantry. On the 10th a conference of the wing's squadron commanders was held at Group Headquarters and the question of bombing operations was discussed.

On the 11th five Bristol Fighters of the squadron left on a bombing raid of tribesmen in a nullah and 20 lb bombs were dropped in flight formations at 4,000 ft. On the 12th a column entered the city to arrest Congress leaders at 05.00 hrs. Continuous reconnaissance carried out over Peshawar and Mohmand country. The visibility was poor and two photographic aircraft accompanied this raid to record bursts on target at Reference R.1988, for while the nullah was being bombed the tribesmen would shelter in the caves. On the 13th bombing attacks were therefore made on those caves. On the 14th an aircraft crashed in the Khyber Pass, killing Flight Lieutenant Tavendale and LAC Chappel. The following day Flying Officer Hawke died at Jhelum as a result of an accident. His funeral was held on the following day. For the rest of May continuous reconnaissance patrols were carried out over Mohmand country. Occasionally the aircraft were shot at.

June   The Afridi tribesmen were creating trouble, and night-bombing attacks were carried out on them. On one of the attacks, on 5 June, when attacks were inflicted on some Afridis in the nullah, one aeroplane was badly hit by rifle fire. On the 18th an aircraft was forced down at Shabkadar landing ground. The trouble was rectified and the aircraft was returned to base. On the 23rd one aircraft was shot through a longeron and a bullet was embedded in the control column. The aeroplane landed at Shabkadar owing to restricted elevator control. On another aircraft the control wire and actuating gear was shot away.

August   Throughout the month reconnaissance flights and offensive patrols continued during daylight hours in Mohmand country. Army officers were taken over the area to look for themselves. On the 31st two reconnaissances were carried out and small parties of tribesmen were seen in the area. A party of 12 tribesmen fired at an aeroplane from Reference B8066, and three 20 lb bombs were dropped on them. Operations over the Kajuri plain were postponed until further notice.

October   On the 14th a close reconnaissance was carried out with the 2nd and 9th Brigades, mostly the 9th Brigade.

December   The year ends with continued reconnaissance flights over the area [Mohmand country].

1931

April   On the 24th it was reported by Khassadars, sent out by the political agent, that an aircraft had crashed near Shin Kamer, both occupants being dead. The bodies of the pilot, Flying Officer D.H.G. Wood, and the air gunner, AC1 Ring, were brought into Peshawar during the night of 25/26 April and they were buried with full

Air Force honours at 08.30 hours on Sunday 26 April. There were no signs of mutilation or bullet wounds in either case.

June   On the 27th reconnaissance flights were carried out in connection with Red Shirt activities.

August   Much reconnaissance activity was carried out but without result. Reconnaissance was carried out within a ten-mile radius of Peshawar for Red Shirt activity, but none was seen.

October   On the 20th special reconnaissance was carried out over Peshawar disrict in search of Red Shirts. About 2,000 men in Red Shirts and 1,500 men in white were seen at Autmanzai led by a man on horseback with a white, green and red flag. Later this concentration of approximately 3,500 men were seen in a tightly packed circle listening to speakers. Photographs were taken at various altitudes.

December   Owing to Red Shirt rumours spreading throughout Peshawar, special reconnaissances flights were carried out on Christmas Day by the Peshawar Brigade. Using W/T contact was maintained with police and troops. Parties of Red Shirts varying between 30 and 60 were seen in Charsadda, some of whom were drilling while others were holding meetings. Other parties of men in both Red shirts and White were seen in Nisatta, Rajjar and Taingi. Two vertical photographs were taken to check movement.

1932

January   Activity still going on with Red Shirts. On the 26th the Walai Post was burned down but movement was seen within three miles of the post. Villagers fired about 30 to 40 shots at aircraft. Four Bristol Fighters were flown to Lahore to be changed for Wapitis.

February   An aircraft was fired on by villagers. On the 11th in the Mohmand area, small-arms ammunition (SAA) was fired at an aircraft by men at Chingai and 197 rounds were fired back. Groups of tribesmen were scattered around the vicinity and these returned the fire. When the aeroplane was examined bullet holes were found in the front main spar, starboard lower plane, the port bottom aileron, in the exhaust pipe cowling, in the port top plane and one in the port elevator. Obviously the pilot was lucky to get away with it. On the 12th a gathering of 250 tribesmen was seen, the aeroplanes being targets for very heavy fire. Aircraft retaliated with bombs and rear guns. A total of two 112 lb bombs, twenty-four 20 lb bombs and 1,089 rounds of ammunition being expended. A patrol was carried out at a height of only 100 feet and many tribesmen appeared to have been killed or wounded. Very few shots were fired. Aircraft C.9752 had a hole in the starboard bottom plane and No. 6 camber rib. Aircraft H.9753 had a hole in the propeller, another in the starboard bottom aileron and one hole in the port elevator.

March   On the 13th a flight of five Bristol Fighters was flown to Lahore to be exchanged for Wapitis, and on the 14th a third flight of three Wapitis arrived at Peshawar. The re-equipment of the squadron was complete.

April   Retaliatory action seemed to be dropping 20 lb bombs or 112 lb bombs on the villages of tribesmen, as well as firing SAA from the forward gun. On the 19th LAC East was wounded by a Daur Khel tribesman while travelling from Miranshah to Peshawar accompanied by LAC James, who was uninjured. The tribes appeared to be under the influence of drugs, and LAC East died in Bannu hospital that day.

June   On the 18th notification was received that the assassin of LAC East had been sentenced to death.

November   On the 9th Squadron Leader L.N. Hollingsworth OBE, DFC. assumed command of No. 20 Squadron, vice Squadron Leader L.L. Brown DFC, AFC, who was posted to the Aircraft Depot, Karachi.

1933

August   Continual attacks and damage to aircraft were being sustained. On the 18th there was considerable damage to an aircraft before it dropped its bombs, but by that time most of the enemy had taken shelter in the village.

1935

June   On the 3rd nine aircraft flew to Quetta for relief work in connection with the earthquake.

September   On the 29th tribesmen had been driven off the crest of a hill and were not seen on the first sortie. They had taken cover from air observation by taking to the western slopes, which were in deep shadow. However, the bombers were able to hit targets that were in dead ground to army artillery.

December   The squadron converted from Wapitis to Audaxes.

1936

March   On the 17th and 18th Air Marshal Sir Edgar Ludlow Hewitt, the Air Officer Commanding, inspected the station.

September   On the 10th the squadron was involved in the Chitral relief.

1937

January   The Khaisora Operations 2nd Phase took place. On this occasion there was little opposition to air operations and there was no opposition between the 12th and the 14th. On the 20th was the first armament training camp to be held in the country.

April   On the 7th the squadron was inspected by Air Marshal Sir Edgar Ludlow Hewitt.

August   Convoy protection duties were carried out during the month.

September to November   Close-reconnaissance patrols were maintained.

1938

March   On the 28th the new AOC, Air Marshal Joubert-de-la-Ferté, carried out an inspection. There was a modified parade because most of the officers were disabled following innoculation against rabies. This difficulty lasted about a fortnight. The AOC presented the DFM to LAC Springett for his valuable services in the 1937 Waziristan operations.

May   On the 13th two squadrons were stationed at Miranshah. They were No. 20 Squadron and No. 39 Squadron detached from Rislapur. The role of B and C Flights of No. 20 Squadron was that of a bomber squadron over two proscribed areas of south Waziristan. A Flight was there to provide Army Cooperation sorties.

June   During May and June leaflets were dropped on Mahsud country warning tribes not to support a Shampir, or Holy Man, from Syria who had settled in the country and was seeking the support for an Afghan revolution. So leaflets were dropped on the locals telling them not to support him. On the 24th and the 25th increased enemy activity was reported, with considerable fire on aircraft. Continued close support was given.

August   At Miranshah close support was given, particularly to the Tochi Scouts over the road to Razmak.

September   On the 29th Squadron Leader Embry DSO, DFC relinquished command of the squadron on posting to the flying training school in Delhi. Squadron Leader R.C. Mead assumed command of the squadron on posting from No. 28 Squadron.

November   There was very little operational flying.

December   The month was very quiet and there were only blockade sorties.

1939

January There was only sporadic activity.

February On the 6th air action resulted in killed and wounded among the enemy. Thanks were received from the Officer Commanding Tochi Scouts at Datta Khel. On the 27th Squadron Leader Mead was awarded the DFC for night-flying operations from Miranshah on the nights of the 5th, 6th, 7th and 8th of the month. This was the eighth decoration received by members of the squadron in the last year.

August Proscriptions were continually carried out.

September War was declared on the 3rd.

NO. 27 SQUADRON

Quam celerrime ad astra
(With all speed to the stars)

AIRCRAFT
DH9A
Westland Wapiti

1930

May On the 27th at 17.00 hrs propaganda was being widely circulated among the tribes along the North-West Frontier due to the recent political unrest. There was a demonstration flight of ten machines of this squadron. Combined with squadron formations of Nos 11, 39 and 60 Squadrons and No. 20 (AC) Squadron, flights were carried out over Shabkadar and Mohmand country, dispelling rumours that the British Raj had ceased to exist, with the hope that the tribes that were gathering would return to their villages. A travelling flight of two machines was carried out to Bannu to pick up the Assistant Commissioner of Bannu and to take him to Peshawar for a conference regarding the political situation of the North-West Frontier Province. Much trouble was being caused along the whole of the frontier by Congressmen spreading unfair rumours. The Assistant Commissioner was flown back to Bannu from Peshawar, returning to Kohat the same evening. On the 10th verbal orders were received for five machines to proceed to Peshawar at dawn on the 11th to collect orders for a proposed bomb raid at the time stated. Five DH9As of C Flight carried out a formation flight to Peshawar. One machine also left Kohat at the same time to carry out a reconnaissance over the hostile area to obtain wind speed and direction for the proposed raid. This information was conveyed by signal to Peshawar. Instructions were issued to the flight commander in charge of the five DH9As by District HQ to carry out a bombing raid over the Mohmand country in

order to disperse a lashkar which was forming in the caves in the area. A total of eighty 20 lb bombs were dropped at various intervals on various gatherings. The machines returned direct to Kohat on completion of the raid. No further raids were required on this day, but this flight remained on stand-by at two hours' notice. On the 12th Congressmen were again carrying out propaganda. It was widely believed by the tribes, whose object was to follow, as they thought, the British down the line and loot each place which was supposed to have been evacuated. Immediately they discovered that they had, in some way, been betrayed. Many of the parties were split up when tribesmen tried to return to their homes. This was unfortunately not so among the younger member of the tribes who, having hungered after power, were more on pretext than sympathy staying in the valleys and caves with a view to causing future trouble. And if defeat placed their leaders in shame, the younger men could take over their reins in the various villages. The Congressmen they employed in this area were acquainted with the idiosyncracies of the tribes with which they dealt and were easily able to sway them with fictitious promises. At 19.10 hours on 12 May a formation bomb raid by two machines was carried out over a lashkar besieging Datta Khel Fort, a total of thirty-two 20 lb bombs being dropped. There was much firing by the natives of the lashkar at the fort. On the 13th a Wapiti was flown to Peshawar to collect orders for the extensive bombing of the same day. At 08.30 hours a formation bomb raid was carried out over the tribesmen besieging the Datta Khel Fort, a total of sixty-four 20 lb bombs being dropped and 300 rounds of SAA being fired by the rear gunners on tribesmen in reply to their desultory fire. At 17.30 hours Captain Taylor of the Tochi Scouts was flown to Sararogah for duty with the column, which was employed on operational duties against hostile tribes in the area. The machine returned the same day. Much of the same activity continued on the 14th and 15th. On the 14th eighty 20 lb bombs were dropped when bombing formations were flown over the Madda Khel tribes in Mazir country. At 08.30 hours on the 23rd C Flight proceeded to Karachi with the last of the DH9As, comprising a formation of five machines. One of the pilots, Flight Lieutenant A.C. Delamain MC, who was one of the first to fly DH9As in India, was specially selected to lead the last of the DH9As on the final flight. One of the machines, F.1098, held the record for a climb and had been chosen for the photograph which appeared on the handbook for this type. On the 27th this flight returned from Karachi with five Wapiti aircraft, thus completing the full re-equipment of the squadron, exclusive of reserve machines. By the end of the month the security situation was under control, with tribesmen waiting to return to their villages.

June On the 4th the squadron continued to carry out formation bombing, dropping quantities of 112 and 20 lb bombs. Also during this period of 5/6 June, incendiary bombs were dropped. Still at the end of the month the squadron was trying to stop the build-up of the gatherings of natives. On the 21st the intention was to destroy a complete village. Altogether 400 incendiaries were dropped, together with forty 20 lb and twelve 230 lb bombs. The area of Waziristan was Sultana. Three machines took part in the raid. Many direct hits were observed and many buildings were seen to be in flames on completion of the raid.

July   On the 8th more attacks were made on villages, the idea being to break up gatherings of youths in the villages in the area.

August   On the 8th gatherings of natives were still being reported, and extensive bombing operations were again ordered with flight formation raids. A total of eighteen 230 lb, two 112 lb and two 20 lb bombs were dropped. Many direct hits were observed on the gatherings located that day. On the 10th the entry in the operations record book discloses that the purpose of the raids was to destroy as much property as possible in the hope of driving the tribesmen gathering in this area back to their villages.

September   On the 19th bombing raids on that day brought operations for 1930 to a successful conclusion. Sometime later a complimentary letter was received by No. 1 (India) Wing from the Chief Commissioner, thanking all ranks for the very great assistance in helping to subdue the tribes.

1931

August   On the 14th Squadron Leader T.M. Bryer OBE, DFC assumed command of the squadron, vice Squadron Leader F.W. Trott OBE, MC.

1932

January   On the 7th and 8th, Operation Orders 816, 817 and 818 being issued, all aircraft were fitted with bomb racks, except aircraft M, which had photographic facilities fitted instead.

February   On the 22nd at 11.30 hours was the commencement of the Ellington Bombing Competition. Meanwhile bombing operations continued.

March   Bombing operations were suspended on the 10th due to low cloud and poor visibility. On the 12th and 13th there were only records of take-off and landings with the number of bombs dropped. The operations had become almost routine.

July   On the 12th A and B Flights carried out a refuelling exercise. From the 14th to the 22nd there were no

operations which permitted normal training. Squadron Leader Bryer dropped supplies in parachute containers, with an error of 35 yards. There was cooperation with the 2nd Gurkhas and the Punjab Regiment.

September   A warning order for bombing operations on the Shamozai villages in Arang area. On the 15th there were various attacks upon Chingai. Tactics used were the burning of crops using incendiaries.

October   No operations meant a return to normal working routine. The tribes submitted to government terms.

1933

March   The Pretender to the Afghan throne had been causing trouble on the border of Afghanistan in the North-West Frontier Province. The Mahsuds and Wazirs were giving assistance to the Pretender. A government order was issued to the tribes to return to their homes and a Jirgah was held at Wurzhagai to impose terms on the tribes. A composite squadron consisting of A and C Flights and machines from No. 60 Squadron was ordered to carry out a demonstration flight over Wurzhagai. Having carried out a demonstration flight the aircraft returned to Kohat, but over the R/T it was ordered to return and make a further demonstration over the same area, finally landing back at 18.30 hours. A message was received from the political agent that the demonstration was very accurately timed and had greatly improved the situation among the tribesmen. Two machines left Kohat for the Datta Khel area on the 14th to pick out villages as 'example' targets should it become necessary. Those machines returned at 18.20 hours.

May   The Pretender was trying to stir up trouble again to get these tribes on his side by saying he would pay them. It turned out that this so-called Pretender had no connection with the Amanullahs.

July   It was reported that he was most probably the son of Mohammed Khan, uncle of the Ammanullah. On the 29th it was reported that notices were dropped over the Bajour territory ordering the Pretender at Kotkai to be handed over to the government. This was not complied with so it was decided to punish the Khan of Khar and Tilawar Khan of Kotkai with bombing raids. The Khan of Khar protested his loyalty to the government, and it was decided not to bomb his village, so attacks continued against Tilawar Khan. These attacks were carried out on his house, and a few direct hits were registered using 30 lb bombs.

August   No bombing raids were carried out on the 5th. A composite squadron consisting of five aircraft of the squadron and four aircraft from No. 60 Squadron carried out demonstration flights in the Bajour district.

December On the 1st A Flight, consisting of two Wapiti IIA aircraft with Jupiter VIIIF engines, accompanied by a Clive aircraft belonging to the Bomber/Transport Flight from Lahore, left to go on a long-distance flight to Rangoon. The particulars of the personnel who took part in this flight were:

Wapiti J.9724	Flight Lieutenant J.W. Nissett (Flight Commander)
	Corporal Green (364812) Air Gunner/Wireless Operator
Wapiti J.9483	Sergeant Pilot Daly J.A. (561100)
	LAC Coveney G (365707) Air Gunner/Carpenter/Rigger
Wapiti J.9708	Pilot Officer R.A.C. Carter
	LAC Gill G (364006)
Wapiti J.9745	Flying Officer H.G.M. Ramsbottom-Isherwood
	Corporal Burns A.E. (328222)
Clive Transport	Sergeant Stewart I.G. (365815) Pilot
	Flight Sergeant Robertson R.S. (242557) Metal Rigger
	Corporal Berry W.S. (157978) Rigger Aero
	LAC Cunday A. (509369) Wireless Mechanic
	AC1 Neve R (365488) Fitter Aero Engines
	AC Reys M.E. (364204) Fitter A.

While on this flight the Wapiti aircraft were authorized to carry a load which was not to exceed a total weight of 5,700 lb per aircraft. They were to carry sufficient spares in the Clive to maintain the aircraft for 14 days. In the Wapiti the following items of equipment could be carried:

1 Set – Light series 20 lb bomb carriers
1 Set – 230 lb bomb carriers
1 Vickers gun
1 Lewis gun + 4 magazines
1 F8 camera (per flight)
1 W/T 2-way wireless (per flight)
4 Cross-country equipments
60 lb Officer's kit
40 lb Other ranks' kit.

If the 20 lb bomb carriers and Lewis gun were not to be carried, then the kit of officers could be increased to 115 lb and that of other ranks to 60 lb, in addition to the spares. The presence of the Clive aircraft and its personnel was considered to be a luxury. It helped make the flight more pleasant. By way of preparation, orders were received that each aircraft had to have a minimum of 60 hours to fly before being due for a 120-hour airframe inspection. The overhaul of engines entailed two 120-hour inspections and a change of three engines. Each aircraft was fitted with an underside locker for the stowage of the aircraft chocks, and small articles of equipment were stowed behind the W/T locker. There was stowage for the starting handles between the front and rear cockpit. These aircraft were fitted with 3-ply floors in the W/T locker to act as a shelf for the equipment and a special fitting to take a spare airscrew.

These preparations were carried out in normal working hours, and one month's notice was given for the date of the commencement of the flight. The undermentioned route and timetable were to be adhered to as far as possible. RF in brackets is for refuelling and NS for night stop:

To Lahore (RF)–Ambala (NS)– Delhi (RF)–Allahabad (NS)–Goya (RF)–Dacca (NS)– Akyab (RF)–Chittagong (NS)–Sandaway (RF)–Bassein (NS) and Rangoon.

The flight was uneventful except that the Clive experienced engine trouble between Kohat and Lahore. It was rectified at Lahore. Just after leaving Dacca the Clive again experienced engine trouble and returned. The Wapitis picked up the W/T message that the Clive was returning to Dacca and returned themselves. The trouble was not rectified until 16.30 hrs, when it was too late to proceed on the journey that day. There was not a telephone on the landing ground at Dacca and no wireless, so it was very difficult to send messages quickly. The nearest post office was two miles away and there was no one available to run messages other than rather indolent natives. A guard of the 1st Norfolks was left on the airfield as the personnel spent a second night at Dacca. The Commissioner at Dacca was very kind and invited the flight commander and Flight Lieutenant Downes, the first pilot of the Clive, to stay with him. No trouble was experienced with the Wapitis throughout the journey and no parts were required for them. The weather throughout the whole journey was excellent and the met. stations fed the Wapitis with met. information.

1934

January On the 16th the Most Hon. Marquess of Londonderry, Secretary of State for Air, visited the squadron during his tour of India.

October On the 20th the Under-Secretary of State for Air, the Rt Hon. Sir Philip Sassoon Bart, GBE, CMG, MBE inspected the squadron.

1935

June On the 1st a replica of the squadron crest, in the form of a large silver trophy, was purchased from Messrs

Gieves Ltd. On this trophy was engraved the names of all the flying officers, places at which the squadron had been stationed and the aircraft with which it had been equipped. Captain R.M. Bacon, the political agent at Kurram, was carried as an observer on a reconnaissance of the Chamkamni country. In an earthquake at Quetta enormous loss of life was reported and the squadron was called upon to fly relief work in flying medical personnel and stores to the district and distressed area. Four IMS personnel were carried to Quetta in connection with this work. Five aircraft took part in this flight.

July   On the 9th at Gandab, a party of approximately 100 tribesmen, drawn from the Durhan and the Isa Khel, fired on the Frontier constabulary and the Khassadars covering repair parties on the Gandab Road. Although the situation was restored by the local military, the Haji of Turangzai seized upon the occasion to harass the government. When a large lashkar was gathered together, they also continued to damage the Gandab Road. Bombing was obviously going to be required again, and it was considered necessary to blockade the area, particularly the tribes of the Safi area. Due to the blockade of the district it meant that the number of people joining the lashkar was reduced to only 800 men, and the squadron's involvement in these particular operations was confined to the Safi and Kamari areas, where the blockade was maintained (a) by attacking any movements in the area and (b) by the destruction of certain key villages (which had been reconnoitred).

September   Operations did not cease until 26 September, and only after a considerable dropping of bombs. The purpose of the operations was to disrupt the domestic life of the tribes rather than to destroy. The success of this method was particularly marked in the Kamari area.

1936

January   Long-distance navigation exercises were carried out by the squadron, involving A and B Flights respectively. [For the remainder of the year the diary is almost illegible. Some adjutants have typed their operations' records, others have not. There are columns of figures showing tons of bombs dropped but without explanation.]

1937

January   Further action has been taken against Razin village. Bombs were dropped in flight formation. There was also the dropping of pamphlets. The year 1937 is characterized by more reconnaissance flights and blockades of villages.

August   On the 2nd blockade action was taken and pamphlets were dropped. This continued throughout the month.

November   On the 11th was Poppy Day and the squadron gave a demonstration of formation flying for ex-servicemen on the aerodrome.

1938

March   An inspection of the squadron was carried out by the AOC, Air Marshal P.V. Joubert de-la-Ferté.

April   On the 28th all ranks of the British in India were immunized against Cholera, following an epidemic.

July   On the 18th three sorties were carried out on the first and subsequent days. The special correspondent of the *Manchester Guardian* was flown from Wana to Razmak via the Madda Khel country. The blockade was lifted on the 19th. Brigadier Maynard, commander of Waziristan, was conveyed from Miranshah to Razmak in an aircraft of this squadron.

1939

January   Continuation of sorties against local tribesmen continued as per previous years.

April   Normal squadron training. [The operations record book then becomes illegible.]

May   Normal training of air gunners took place. On the 1st a full programme of low-level bombing was completed and the results were considered. The majority of pilots were inexperienced and the squadron was very short of qualified air gunners. A full programme of high-level bombing was then completed. One aircraft of the squadron was provided to act as a W/T escort for His Excellency the Governor of the North-West Frontier Province, who was conveyed in a wing aircraft from Peshawar to Rangu and return. On the 6th Squadron Leader A.H. Fear assumed command of the squadron, vice Squadron Leader H. McKechnie, who was proceeding to Egypt on posting. A Flight completed a normal central reconnaissance, new pilots being carried as passengers to enable them to obtain first-hand information of the Frontier Province. The remainder of the squadron was on training, map reading, photography, instrument flying, etc. One aircraft carried out a successful 4½-hour air survey mosaic at 15,000 ft over the Karesti Algad area. On the 19th air gunner training continued. Night-flying was carried out on the night of the 17th/18th and was successful, followed by a further mosaic of 4½ hours of the same area. On the 26th Squadron Leader Fear, one other officer and five airmen pilots proceeded to Ambala for Blenheim conversion training prior to going to Egypt on the second Blenheim collection party, henceforth known as the Blenheim Collection Party. In the absence of Squadron Leader Fear, Flight Lieutenant Selkirk assumed command of the squadron. Owing to a severe dust haze for the remainder of the month, flying had to be considerably curtailed, especially night-flying. On the 19th the aircraft detached to Risalpur were returned for 60-hour inspections. The first hill depot party returned on the 31st, the second party left the same night. From 20 to 30 May a personnel draft, including two NCOs and three LACs and AC1 fitters, were sent to Karachi for Blenheim fitting and rigging training. On their return they were to act as instructors for the remainder of the squadron personnel. Also at the end of May the air gunners were being trained in the timing bead method of WS amd D finding. The complete squadron remained at Kohat for the month of May, with the exception of one aircraft, and one crew was detached to Risalpur for D/F-testing duties.

June   Training continued as the new aircraft were arriving on the squadron.

August   Due to the severe shortage of personnel very little flying training was done. Bad weather restricted training to formation practice and forced landings. One officer was attached to No. 1 (Indian) Group for cypher duties. One officer and five airmen left for Blenheim conversion training and BCPs. That left one officer at the Hill Depot on sick leave. The squadron received orders from the HQ, ordering one flight to proceed to Madras and one flight to Bombay for coastal defence duties. By this time the squadron boasted one officer and very few airmen. All pilots and crews, where possible, were recalled, and Squadron Leader H.F. Jenkins was attached to take over command of the coastal defence flights. All personnel worked night and day, preparing the aircraft and fitted long-range tanks, etc., and packing up flight stores and personal kit. The aircraft were tested and kit for both road and rail parties were ready by 22.00 hrs on the 27th. Pilots and crews had returned in ones and twos and all was in readiness for the move. At 07.00 hrs on the 28th Squadron Leader Jenkins and the air party of A Flight, consisting of four Wapiti aircraft, left for Bombay at 07.15 hrs, arriving intact at 17.30 hrs. The road party left by special train at 09.00 hrs, arriving intact at 10.00 hrs on the 30th. Mobilization took place on 30 August. Squadron Leader Fear, who had gone to Egypt, was kept there in charge of servicing and the dispatch of Blenheims.

September   When war was declared on the 3rd the squadron was prepared for any eventuality.

NO. 28 SQUADRON

Quicquid agas age
(Whatsoever you may do, do)

AIRCRAFT
Bristol F2B
Westand Wapiti
Hawker Audax

Note The operations record book commences with entries for 1932

1932

March   to   August   The supplementary summary of operations from 29 March to 18 August 1932: the squadron provided escorts to Their Excellencies the Viceroy and the Countess of Willington The duty of the escort aeroplanes was chiefly wireless. A listening watch was maintained in the event of failure occurring in the Avro X wireless set. The escort aeroplane was responsible for transmitting position messages at fifteen-minute intervals.

April   On the 16th three aircraft of A Flight escorted Their Excellencies the Viceroy and the Countess of Willington from Lahore to Rawalpindi. Their Excellencies were flown in their own aircraft, an Avro 10, and were proceeding on a tour of inspection of the North-West Frontier Province and Baluchistan. Escort duties were handed over to a flight of No. 11 (Bomber) Squadron in the air at Rawalpindi.

May   On the 11th pamphlets were dropped from aircraft on the villages in the vicinity of Rupar, promising a reward of 3,000 Rupees for the arrest of criminals who escaped from a train while on their way to Lahore.

November   On the 18th B Flight proceeded to Patiala to cooperate with detachments from State forces of the Punjab Circle. The programme included field exercises, Army Cooperation demonstrations and lectures spread over four days. Three aircraft, six officers and twenty airmen joined detachments from State forces numbering 200 officers and 2,000 Indian other ranks. For accommodation and messing the RAF officers and airmen were the guests of the State forces. At the end of November A Flight proceeded with an artillery practice camp, when live shoots were carried out with various brigades of the Army.

1933

January   On the 1st the squadron, less C Flight, with the majority of section personnel moved to Jhansi, by air, rail and road to take part in the Eastern Command Exercises and manoeuvres. On the 2nd the Ambala–Singapore flight left with the following pilots participating:

Flight Lieutenant Groom DFC
Flying Officer Carey
Flying Officer Sandeman
Flying Officer Watson

The flight arrived at 16.35 hrs on 11 January (local time), two days having been lost due to bad weather.

March   On the 16th Pilot Officer R. Young crashed while carrying out an air-to-ground camera gun practice. The aircraft dived into the ground, and it was found that Young had attempted to make three exposures in one dive. The air gunner escaped with minor injuries.

June   On the 30th Pilot Officer D.H. Furze and his air gunner were killed on the racecourse. The cause of the accident was obscure, but it was thought that the pilot was turning too near the ground.

August   On the 15th three orders were received for C Flight to move on the 18th and arrive at Risalpur for operations. The aircraft left Ambala on the 18th and on arrival the pilots were required to make themselves thoroughly familiar with Mohmand and Bajour territory.

December   The squadron was involved in artillery cooperation with gun practices. Shoots of this nature were carried out as follows: The pilot called for fire on the pinpoint of the 'puff trailer' to the artillery, and the battery fired blank ammunition. After a lapse of time, to allow for the flight of a shell, a puff was detonated. The pilot transmitted a correction which was then applied to the guns. This range was not entirely satisfactory, and was abandoned after a few attempts. All pilots visited batteries while shoots were in progress and watched them from a splinter-proof shelter.

1934
January   Exercises continued with the Army, and 34 shoots of all types were carried out. On the 12th the Secretary of State for Air, the Marquess of Londonderry, arrived by air at 10.30 hrs. His arrival had been delayed by adverse weather conditions. He inspected the station during the morning and lunched with the officers. [Little reference is made to operations in the record book.]

February to November   Continued cooperation with the Army.

1935
January   Army-Cooperation work continued.

March On the 12th, at Ambala, Air Marshal Sir J.M. Steel KCB, CBE, CMG, the AOC India, paid a farewell visit to the squadron. The incoming AOC was Air Marshal Sir Edgar Ludlow-Hewitt.

June   On the 1st was the Quetta earthquake. Fourteen flights were carried out by officers of this squadron, flying a total of 126 hours and 55 minutes. Gas courses were attended by officers of the squadron.

December   Army Cooperation during exercises.

1936
January   On the 11th A Flight, under the command of Flight Lieutenant J. Norwood, proceeded on detachment to Lucknow. Cooperation with No. 6th Infantry Brigade was carried out and the flight returned on the 23rd. On the 22nd Pilot Officer D.M. Newman, on returning from artillery reconnaisance, collided with two other Wapiti aircraft after landing on the aerodrome.

March Close reconnaissance carried out for the artillery was followed by long-distance bombing exercises, demonstrations of supply dropping and R/T. On the 24th Air Marshal Sir Edgar Ludlow-Hewitt inspected the station.

April   On the 2nd Pilot Officers P.H.R. Saunders, J.C. Miller, E.P.T. Nelson and A.S. Downley were posted to the squadron. On the 17th Flight Lieutenant R.J. Carvell proceeded to the United Kingdom on 91 days' leave.

June   The squadron was re-equipped with Hawker Audax aircraft. The first five Wapitis left Ambala for Karachi on the 22nd. Flying training on the Audax was carried out by C Flight at Karachi up to the 30th. On the return to Ambala, Pilot Officer Downley crashed one mile short of Jodhpur aerodrome after running out of petrol. The pilot sustained minor injuries, the air gunner was unhurt. The aircraft was a complete write-off. Pilot Officer Stickley proceeded to Lower Topa as officer in charge of the Hill Depot. [This was usually a squadron leader.]

July   On the 1st Squadron Leader Dearlove proceeded to England on posting to Home Establishment. Further replacement Audax aircraft were received.

October   On the 1st Flight Lieutenant A.F. Hutton DFC was promoted to the rank of squadron leader.

1937
March   On the 8th at Peshawar, the squadron participated in No. 1 (India) Wing's collective training exercise, which lasted until the 10th. The unit acted throughout as a bomber squadron. On the 14th/15th a change of medical officer occurred. Flying Officer V.D. Jones left for the United Kingdom and Flight Lieutenant V.H. Tomkins was posted in. On the 24th one aircraft gave a demonstration of communications between ground and the air to cadets of the Indian Military Academy.

April On the 13th a verbal warning order was received for the squadron to be prepared to take part in the Waziristan operations. The operations record book was therefore closed and a war diary maintained. On the same day Squadron Leader A.F. Hutton DFC received verbal orders from the HQ RAF India to prepare the squadron immediately to take part in those operations. The flights were to consist of four aircraft each, the remaining aircraft to be flown to and left at Peshawar to act as a reserve. On the 24th the squadron pilots were cooperating with the Razmak column. Intelligence reported 1,000 tribesmen in the Shatkau valley. The orders were to give close support to the armoured cars and road convoys. A conference took place between Group Captain Bottomley, the Officer Commanding No. 1 (India) Group, and Squadron Leader Barnes, a staff officer who arrived by air. The conference was also attended by Major Skrene of the South Waziristan Scouts. They discussed, among other things, communications between aircraft and the scout posts. In their intelligence summary they said that the Mahsuds were a powerful tribe officially at peace but in fact reinforcing lashkars, and the Faqir of Ipi had their moral support. Lashkars in the field totalled about 3,000 men. Close support of convoys, improvement of signals and signals testing were also discussed. This was important since reception by aircraft tended to deteriorate in the hilly areas.

May On the 28th reports of bad visibility through a dust haze were received. A lashkar was gathering in the vicinity of Manzai. One hundred men and twenty camels had been seen in the Shaza valley. No air action was taken. On the 27th there was a report of heavy oil consumption by the Audax aircraft. In the worst cases machines had been changed but the new engines were giving carburation trouble. Orders were sent out to change the oil every fifteen hours. In the summer heat very high temperatures were being experienced and engines were overheating abnormally quickly.

June Close support was given to the Waziristan Scouts. On the 8th close support was given to the Razmak Column proceeding from Razmak to Sorarogha. One sortie was flown to locate a lashkar reported in the Pezu Pass area. For the first time during current operations the Army commander gave orders that any gang over 25 in number might be attacked on sight in British India. The pilot could not locate the lashkar, but close support was given to a train in the pass. Four airmen were hospitalized through heat, for the maximum temperature was 114°F. Sandfly fever was also a problem, and the condition of one of the men admitted to hospital was very serious. Visibility during the previous week was poor due to a dust haze. With effect from the 8th of the month the squadron came under the orders of the Waziristan Division. On the 13th the adjutant recorded that operational requirements were nil and the airmen earned a well-deserved rest. Fight Lieutenant Mead and Flying Officer Franklin were in sick quarters with tonsilitis and a poisoned foot, respectively. On the 27th air action was taken. Weather impeded flying but one aircraft managed to attack tribesmen who were about to attack a Scout post. Casualties were inflicted but numbers were not known.

July On the 3rd close support was given to Waziristan units. On the 10th the move back to Ambala commenced. Close support was given to convoys from Miranshah. Mr Wilson, an Education Officer Grade III, was posted to the unit from Home Establishment.

November On the 6th the test mobilization scheme was carried out. From the 6th to the 15th all sections were packed and stores crated and were ready to move. MT vehicles were loaded onto the railway trucks to test railway loading arrangements. The results were entirely satisfactory.

1938

January On the 11th Squadron Leader Hutton left for the United Kingdom on posting to Home Establishment. On the 13th Squadron Leader F.L.S. Ward assumed command of the squadron.

March On the 25th the AOC inspected the unit. On the 31st Squadron Leader Ward and ten aircraft of the squadron proceeded to Risalpur to take part in the Ellington Trophy Competition.

April On the 1st a RAF station headquarters was formed at Ambala and was commanded by Squadron Leader Maude until the 11th, when Wing Commander Horsley MC took command of the station, having been Senior Personnel Staff Officer at Headquarters RAF India.

July The squadron received instructions on the 18th to take part in a search for an aircraft. Flight Lieutenant Nelson from HQ RAF India was reported missing between Lahore and Miranshah. Five aircraft led by Wing Commander Horsley took off late in the evening and flew to Lahore. The flight was carried out in very bad weather, landing at Lahore in a blinding rainstorm. One aircraft was damaged. Between the 19th and the 20th aircraft split up and went either side of the River Indus. There was no trace of the downed pilot. The aircraft was eventually found by the police embedded in the River Indus 14 miles south of Mianwali on the morning of the 20th. The pilot was missing, later reported killed. The air gunner was seriously injured and died a few days later.

September   On the 7th Pilot Officer A.K. Byrne died in the British Military Hospital from acute anterior poliomyelitis. He was buried with full military honours in the British Military Cemetary, Ambala. At RAF Ambala all cinemas, cafes, public and private buildings in the Ambala cantonment were placed out of bounds to all officers and airmen from the 7th to the 24th. All training ceased with effect from the 19th due to the European [Munich] crisis, to bring all aircraft up to a state of readiness for a move overseas. The squadron was on the point of moving according to Plan Y, being all packed up and ready to go, but the crisis passed and the personnel resumed normal work.

December   On the 22nd Squadron Leader Ward was posted to the Staff College, Quetta, and was succeeded in command of the squadron by Squadron Leader H.G. Blair. Flying for the month of December was by day 6 hours 40 minutes and by night 2 hours 45 minutes.

1939

January   Infantry Brigade exercises went on throughout the month.

February   The squadron moved from its permanent station at Ambala to Kohat. The squadron had been at Ambala since 1 February 1920. [In fact No. 28 Squadron was No. 114 Squadron renumbered and re-formed at Ambala on 1 April 1920, and had changed its base station several times during the inter-war years. Refer to No. 28 Squadron in Appendix B.] One flight was detached from Kohat to Miranshah. This was followed by a second flight as soon as the move had been effected. In spite of this imminent move, some commitments could not be moved, and all three flights had to proceed to the Armament Training Camp practice. A crash occurred on the 18th. Flying Officer W.A. Harris, with No. 566423 LAC Strickland as passenger, crashed on the aerodrome while testing one of the command reserve aircraft. He and his passenger were both seriously injured but subsequently recovered. The accident was due to negligent flying on the part of the pilot, and he was summarily punished, being given a severe reprimand by his CO and a loss of three months' seniority.

March   The squadron was then at Kohat. On the 3rd A Flight left Kohat for Miranshah by road and air for operational duties with C Flight, which was already there. On the 21st due to the situation in Europe instructions were received that the flights at Miranshah, consisting of eight aircraft, eleven officers and seventy airmen, were moved to Kohat. The squadron was to be prepared to move overseas if required. The air party left on the 24th and the ground party the following day. The squadron then carried out a full mobilization.

July   On the 8th at Miranshah, while carrying out proscription duties, Pilot Officer W.C. Duncan with his passenger, 523893 AC1 Baxter J.B., crashed 1½ miles west of Miranshah in Audax K.5566. Pilot Officer Duncan was seriously injured and AC1 Baxter was killed. The accident was due to a bullet fired accidentally by AC Baxter while he was endeavouring to clear a stoppage in his Lewis gun. This bullet severed the rudder cable. The restriction did not become apparent until Pilot Officer Duncan attempted to land. The final strands of the cable then parted and the aircraft crashed out of control.

September   On the 3rd, war was declared and the squadron was restricted to essential flying only.

NO. 30 SQUADRON

Ventre a terre
(All out)

AIRCRAFT
Westland Wapiti
Hawker Hardy
Bristol Blenheim I

1930

January   On the 1st Squadron Leader H.B. Hale was promoted wing commander.

February   On the 11th Squadron Leader Goddard assumed command. On the 28th three French aircraft arrived from Dur-ez-Zur conveying a colonel of the French Army and a French intelligence officer for a conference with the Administrative Inspector. The aircraft returned on 1 March.

October   On the 27th A Flight (4 Wapitis) moved to Sulaimania for cooperation with the Iraqi Army, and this operation became known as 'Fulfly'. Reconnaissance of the district was carried out before landing.

November   On the 26th the flying hours logged by the squadron were as follows: By flights at Sulaimania 246 hrs 55 min, by flights at Kirkuk 209 hrs 35 min.

1931

February   On the 23rd the operational area of the squadron was reduced by the exclusion of Sulaimania and Kirkuk and increased by the addition of a desert area north-west of a line joining the junction of the River Tigris and the Lesser Zab with the junction of the Euphrates and the Syrian border.

April   On the 11th it was reported that the gales, storms and heavy rain had hampered work and flooded the landing ground in camp.

Iraqi operations, 1932 (for use with the accompanying texts).

July   On the 9th Squadron Leader Johnstone arrived to take over command of the squadron. On the 27th and 28th at Mosul the Iraqi Army took over Billeh, marching from Aqra on the 27th and camping the night at Dinatra. Next day they marched over the Piris Dagh to Billeh. Air cooperation was provided morning and evening. No hostile elements were seen.

August   Between the 4th and the 7th the AOC was on a trek in the mountain district, north-east of Diana, and was visited daily by aircraft. Letters were dropped to the party at Beri Birdan.

September   On the 22nd/23rd aircraft patrolling Barzan district during police operations and Herin and Bira Kipra. Certain parties of men observed but the police had the situation in hand.

October   On the 5th the AOC arrived by air to carry out his annual inspection.

December   On the afternoon of the 9th the Iraqi column was forced back from Barzan by unexpectedly strong forces and lost forty men during the retreat. Instructions were received at midnight from Air Headquarters to bomb Barzan and other suitable targets in the immediate vicinity. Accordingly eighteen 112 lb bombs, sixty-four 20 lb bombs and eight cases of incendiaries were dropped. All were dropped on Barzan itself as being the most satisfactory target. Warning notices in Kurdish were dropped half an hour before bombing commenced. AC1 Gilroy fell through the floor of his Wapiti. His parachute opened and he reached the ground on the south-east side of Barzan. Later he arrived safely in Bileh camp, showing considerable presence of mind in so doing. No serious damage was observed in Barzan, and the incendiaries did not set fire to any buildings. [It is not clear whether the adjutant is expressing relief that none of the enemy's property suffered serious damage or commenting on the ineffectiveness of his unit's bombing!] On the 11th certain men were observed in Barzan wearing the uniforms of captured Iraqi Army troops. All appeared quiet with the Chiashirin. Preceded by a Wapiti with 'balloon' tyres, two Victorias landed at Billeh and brought away several wounded.

1932

March   On the 7th operations commenced against Sheikh Ahmed of Barzan. No. 30 Squadron provided reconnaissance on the 6th and 7th on the approaches of the flanks to the Rowanduz gorge. On the 12th an ultimatum was dropped to Sheikh Ahmed via the police post at Bileh for transmission to its destination. C Flight moved to Diana to cooperate with the Iraqi Army column moving up from Balikian towards Mergasor. Squadron Leader Frew from Air Headquarters took command of all the aircraft at Diana and Mosul. On the 19th there was a night attack by a party of Kurds on the Iraqi Army camp at Mergasor. Seven were killed and fourteen were wounded among the troops. C Flight was sent out after daybreak to search for the raiders, who had, by then, disappeared to the west. On the 24th a flight of No. 55 Squadron arrived at Mosul to act as a reserve or reinforcement in case of extensive bombing being required.

April   During operations on the 2nd in the afternoon Sergeant Waylen's engine stopped over Aqra Dagh, and the crew jumped, landing uninjured. Bombing was carried out from 6,000 ft above Raizan and in pairs. On the 3rd there was further bombing of Raizan and sixteen 250 lb bombs and eight 112 lb bombs were dropped by aircraft from Mosul. The Diana Column left Zazhok, and while moving down a valley the transport column was attacked by the Kurds from the ridge on the west, and

confusion broke out. The main body of troops was out of effective range and made no serious attempt to get back. Henceforward the fate of the column rested with the aircraft of C Flight, which repeatedly attacked the Kurds with bombs and machine-guns until dusk, by which time the enemy had been driven off. All five aircraft were hit. When releasing his last bomb, Sergeant Hudson was shot in the lung and subsequently died. AC1 Thomas was hit in the foot. Sergeant Hudson's aircraft was handed over to Flight Lieutenant Bradbury, who went up with the flight commander, the latter acting as air gunner. On the 17th three Iraqi Moths arrived to operate with No. 30 Squadron. On the 18th the Bileh Column moved to Barzan and encamped. One flight worked from Bileh, the other with the two Moths, but there was no opposition. A Moth crashed in the afternoon and the crew was killed. On the 25th seven aircraft from Mosul dropped 400 proclamations on 35 villages in the area bounded by the Shensdinan River, to the south-west by the crest of the Chiashinin, to the south-east by the Rukuchuk and to the north-east by a line from Zaita to Hiruz. The opportunity was taken to complete a set of photographs of the villages in this area. No. 55 Squadron and half of No. 70 Squadron arrived to make an air striking force, but on the 28th it was reported that in view of the trouble with the Jupiter FVIII engines in the aircraft of No. 55 Squadron it was decided that the latter would be temporarily withdrawn from the air striking force and replaced by No. 30 Squadron. The Army's requirements were reduced to a minimum. The troops, however, had been stationary for a long time and their requirements were unlikely to be great.

May   On the 6th the Diana Column was moving again. Three battalions with 900 men under command had proceeded to Birisia, supported by seven Wapitis from Diana. There was no fighting. On the 11th it was reported that the activities of the RAF air striking force were confined to the south-east side of the Rukuchuk. Pending discussions with Sheikh Ahmed on the 23rd, A Flight relieved B Flight at Diana for Army Cooperation duties. On the 25th, Sheikh Ahmed having refused to comply with government terms, the striking force launched an attack against him. No. 55 Squadron, one flight of No. 70 Squadron and two flights from Mosul attacked specific targets in the Mazuri Bala. Offensive patrols took place every day until the 14th except for one or two Sundays. Operations were directed by Group Captain Breese, the Commander of Erbil.

June   On the 11th the Diana Column crossed the Rukuchuk above Chama on or about this date. Sheikh Ahmed was driven from his hiding place on the Kur-E-Hore. On the 19th the Sheikh was reported to be at Zaita, but he had crossed the frontier and given himself up to the Turks. Bombing therefore ceased.

August   On the 4th Squadron Leader Johnstone handed over command to Squadron Leader Chamberlayne AFC. On the 30th two flights of five Atlas aircraft from No. 4 FTS visited Mosul.

1933/4

For the rest of 1932 and into 1933 and 1934 there was nothing of significance to report.

1935

March   On the 26th Squadron Leader A.L. Fiddament DFC took over command of No. 30 Squadron from Squadron Leader R.D.J.M.I.C. Chamberlayne AFC. [These are the initials that appear in the operations record book, but was the adjutant pulling our legs?] The flight commanders on this date were as follows: A Flight – Flight Lieutenant R.J. Legg, B Flight – Flight Lieutenant T.B. Prickman, and C Flight – Flight Lieutenant A.F. Scroggs.

April   On the 30th the re-equipment of the squadron with Hawker Hardy aircraft began with A Flight. C Flight was equipped on 8 May and B Flight on the 14th.

1936

February to June   At the end of 1935, the flight commanders had changed. On 22 February Flight Lieutenant Dicken took over C Flight and Flight Lieutenant B.D. Nicholas took over B Flight. On 6 June Flight Lieutenant H.J. Walker arrived to take over command of A Flight.

October   On the 19th No. 30 Squadron moved from Mosul to Dhibban, the advance party consisting of C Flight and representatives of the other sections under the command of Flight Lieutenant Nicholas in their Hardy aircraft and the Valentias. [Dhibban/Habbaniya was the new RAF base in Iraq.]

November   On the 7th Squadron Leader A.J. Rankin AFC arrived from Home Establishment to assume command of the squadron and RAF Station Dhibban from Wing Commander Fiddament.

1937

July   On the 26th a flight of four Hardy aircraft under the command of Flight Lieutenant A.G. Dicken undertook a training flight to Egypt. Various landing grounds and RAF aerodromes were visited and the flight returned to Dhibban on the 31st.

August   On the 25th Squadron Leader G.H. Stainforth AFC took over command of the squadron from Wing Commander A.J. Rankin OBE AFC. In view of the situation in Palestine, arrangements were made for the complete mobilization of the squadron in the event of

further reinforcement of RAF squadrons. The situation improved as the existing arrangements were considered adequate, and the move was cancelled.

September   From the 13th to the 19th a flight of four Hardy aircraft flew to Syria on a training flight for the purposes of liaison with the French Air Force, visiting stations at Demas, Rayak, Aled, Ain-Prous, Deir-ez-Sor and Beyrouth, HQ of the French Air Force in Syria.

1938

January to April   Re-equipment of the squadron with Blenheim Is, shipped from England to Alexandria and assembled at the RAF Depot, Aboukir, whence they were flown to Dhibban in batches of two or three at a time, in all cases non-stop in about 3¼ hours. The first Blenheim arrived at Dhibban on the 13th. Completion of conversion courses of all pilots in the squadron, i.e. 15 + 2 others occupied about 38 flying days, all dual instruction being carried out by one instructor. None failed to qualify.

June   A flying accident occurred at Habbaniya [note the adjutant's use of the new name in the record book]. This resulted in the death of Pilot Officer C.A. Stephen and AC1 Davies. As far as can be ascertained, one engine of the Blenheim failed shortly after take-off. The machine hit the ground with great violence and caught fire. The two occupants were killed instantaneously.

September   There was the Munich Crisis and the great possibility of a European conflict. Later on in the month the situation deteriorated and the squadron was ordered to prepare for complete mobilization, which took place on the 29th, and the air and ground echelons left Habbaniya on the 30th. The air echelon arrived at Heliopolis the same day. The ground echelon arrived at Landing Ground No. 5, where it halted pending further instructions. Later it was ordered to return. The air echelon remained in Egypt for twelve days, during which time demonstration flights were carried out over various cities and towns with the object of impressing the inhabitants with the speed and mobility of the squadron.

October   By the 14th all the air echelon had returned to Habbaniya.

November   On the 3rd Squadron Leader U.Y. Shannon took over command of the squadron from Squadron Leader G.H. Stainforth AFC.

December   On the 10th a Blenheim aircraft on a flight from Habbaniya to Ismailia was reported missing. An extensive search was organized but no trace was found of the missing aircraft. The search was abandoned after seven days. On the 20th a native tribesman reported finding aircraft wreckage forty miles WSW of Ramadi. A ground party left for the spot indicated and identified the wreckage as that of the missing aircraft. The aircraft had flown into the side of a hill and all six occupants were dead. They were Squadron Leader D. Kinsey, the Command Signals Officer; Captain J.P. Harvey from the Argyll and Sutherland Highlanders, attached to the Iraq Levies; Sergeant Garside, the pilot; and Aircraftmen Gamble, Cooper and Carpenter.

1939

June On the 19th three Blenheim aircraft proceeded on the first long-distance bombing exercise between Iraq and Egypt.

July With the imminence of war there was an increase in the number of reconnaissance flights looking for landing grounds in the Western Desert near Sidi Barrani and Sollum.

August On the 25th twelve aircraft with Squadron Leader Shannon as leader left Habbaniya and transferred to their war station at Ismailia. As Flight Lieutenant Phillips was sick and Pilot Officer Lydall was attached to No. 4 FTS for navigation training, one aircraft was flown by Squadron Leader Brookes of the Air Staff No. 1 Bomb Wing. On the 28th the aircraft on the aerodrome were dispersed to various parts of the aerodrome. At 14.00 hrs on the 29th the twelve aircraft were picketed out at dispersal positions. Squadron guards were mounted out of working hours.

September On the 3rd, with the declaration of war, the squadron was put onto stand-by at two hours' notice. [Italy posed the threat to the United Kingdom in that theatre.]

NO. 31 SQUADRON

In caelum indicum primus
(First into Indian skies)

AIRCRAFT
Bristol F2B
Westland Wapiti
Vickers Valentia

[This record is characterized by almost incessant changes of command of the unit. These record books disclose a variety of ways in which the different adjutants maintained them. Some, for example, placed operational matters in appendices. In this case the writer clearly wants to record for posterity the comings and goings of the squadron and flight commanders without always accounting for the changes.]

1930

February On the 18th Flight Lieutenant Strudwick assumed command, vice Squadron Leader Gordon, who proceeded to Mhow on an inspection of the Southern Flight (B)

March On the 20th Flight Lieutenant Rodgers assumed command, vice Flight Lieutenant Strudwick. On 30 March Squadron Leader Gordon resumed command, vice Flight Lieutenant Strudwick [Not Rodgers]. On 24 March Flight Lieutenant Rodgers assumed command of the squadron. On the 28th A Flight, under Flight Lieutenant McRoberts, proceeded to Fort Sandeman to cooperate with the 6th Mountain Battery Royal Artillery.

April On the 1st Flight Lieutenants Strudwick and Cross were posted to Home Establishment. On the 3rd Squadron Leader Gordon resumed command of the squadron, vice Flight Lieutenant Rodgers.

June On the 4th a raiding party crossed the border and abducted two officers and a lady on the Chaman–Quetta Road. Flying Officer Monro-Higgs made a reconnaissance of the road to report movements of the raiders. A squadron of the Scind Horse was ordered to the area and the squadron continued to cooperate with the Scind Horse. These operations were close to the Afghan border. [No mention is made of the outcome.]

July On the 1st Flight Lieutenant Rodgers assumed command of the squadron, vice Squadron Leader Gordon, who had assumed command of No. 3 (Indian) Wing. On the 13th Flight Lieutenant Ackerman assumed command of the squadron, vice Flight Lieutenant Rodgers, who proceeded on leave.

August On the 11th Squadron Leader Gordon resumed command of the squadron, vice Flight Lieutenant Rodgers [who was supposed to be on leave, leaving Ackerman in command]. [Throughout the rest of the month the flights were carrying out mail-carrying duties to Jerusalem.]

November/December Throughout the whole of these two months there were constant changes of command.

1931

February On the 13th the first Wapiti Mk IIA, powered by a Jupiter VIIIF engine, arrived at Quetta, and re-equipment of the squadron commenced. On the 20th Squadron Leader Gordon resumed command of the squadron, yet again.

June On the 30th Flight Lieutenant D. Ankers DCM was promoted to squadron leader.

September   On the 15th Squadron Leader Gordon was absorbed into Home Establishment.

October   On the 19th Squadron Leader Ankers proceeded to Lahore, attending the AOC's economy conference, and returned on the 21st.

1932

There is nothing significant to report for the year, only routine postings and other administrative happenings.

1933

November   On the 20th a demonstration was given to the Mekhram Levy Corps, which involved Popham Panels, message picking-up and supply dropping. There was also a short scheme involving reconnaissance and a low-flying attack against an irregular force, flour bags being used as bombs.

1934

January   On the 21st the Secretary of State for Air, the Marquess of Londonderry, arrived by air with the AOC, Sir John Steel, and escorted by an aircraft of No. 20 (AC) Squadron. The Secretary of State inspected the station in the afternoon of the 23rd and visited the Khajaj Pass.

March   On the 12th Squadron Leader C.J.S. Dearlove was posted in to assume command of the squadron, vice Squadron Leader Ankers.

April   On the 16th three aircraft of the squadron took part in the fly-past on the occasion of the installation of the Durbar of HM the Khan of Kohat. On the 22nd Squadron Leader Dearlove and Flight Lieutenant Addams proceeded to Fort Sandeman for a conference with the Zhob Militia and an inspection of the detached flight there.

May to December   Cooperation with the military field batteries.

1935

May   On the 31st a severe earthquake occurred which destroyed practically all the buildings in the RAF Camp, Quetta. The barrack blocks were completely destroyed, the majority of the airmen being buried under the debris. Rescue work continued throughout the day. Reconnaissance flights were carried out by Flight Lieutenants Long, Thompson and Holmes, of Sibi, Loralai and Chamon to ascertain the extent of the earthquake area and to establish communications with

The bomb dump at Miranshah.

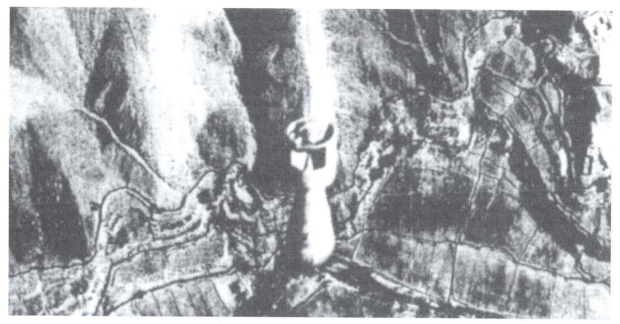

It's 'bomb away', from an aircraft of No. 31 Squadron.

Simla. Flight Lieutenant Long crashed at Sibi without injury to himself or his air gunner. The latter returned to Quetta by rail and Flight Lieutenant Long was retained at Sibi to assist with control work at the Sibi railway station.

June On the 1st work on repair of aircraft that were damaged in the hangars began, together with general reorganization. All personnel were accommodated under canvas. On the 2nd Flight Lieutenant Huxham reconnoitred the local village of Mas Tung and the Bolan Pass to ascertain the damage. All personnel were moved up to the lines of the 1st Battalion, the Queen's Royal Regiment. Another severe shock occurred at 15.10 hrs. On the 3rd work on the aircraft and salvage continued. When all aircraft were serviceable Flight Lieutenant Yale, Flying Officer Wilkins and Pilot Officer Gillman ferried aircraft to Drigh Road. All the families were evacuated to the Aircraft Depot, to be housed with Depot married personnel. On the 7th salvage continued.

July On the 6th the AOC, Sir Edgar Ludlow Hewitt, inspected the area. The military division of the Most Excellent Order of the British Empire was awarded to No. 511822 LAC Wickenden J.J. for meritorious service rendered in connection with the Baluchistan earthquake. [It must be assumed that this entry refers to a presentation made during the AOC's inspection.] On the 7th His Excellency the Viceroy made an address to No. 3 (Indian) Wing of the RAF at Karachi on that Sunday. Wing Commander Slessor, officers and airmen of No. 3

(Indian) Wing were praised for the way they carried out their duties and recovered their aircraft quickly, and he was very sad about the parting of families from the husbands of those that survived. He said that he would do everything possible to reunite families again.

1936
Cooperation with the Army and routine training.

1937
March On the 19th three aircraft flew from Quetta to Fort Sandeman, whence a formation of seven aircraft carried out a demonstration over the northern Zhob area. No concentration of tribesmen was reported.

April/May Reconnaissance flights and exercises but nothing to report.

June On the 16th Squadron Leader Hammond MM, OND assumed command of the unit, vice Squadron Leader J. Lairey DFC. On the 30th Flying Officer W.J. King died in the British Military Hospital Karachi.

1938
March On the 19th Pilot Officer Grant was transferred to Home Establishment for medical reasons. [No cause was entered in the record.]

June On the 30th a Westland Lysander was taken on inventory for service trials in India. Trials were carried out by Flight Lieutenant Widdowson and Flying Officer Warse.

July On the 1st Squadron Leader Hammond and Flight Lieutenant Wicks DFC were selected for Andover Staff College course commencing in January 1939.

August On the 1st, Flight Lieutenant F.F. Wicks DFC was promoted to the rank of squadron leader.

October On the 9th Squadron Leader F.F. Wicks DFC assumed command of the squadron, vice Squadron Leader Hammond, who had returned to Home Establishment. On the 18th the squadron advance party left for Lahore on the change of station. On the 19th A Flight moved from Risalpur to Lahore when the international crisis became less acute. Pilot Officer Stevens crashed on landing at Nushki. Pilot and passenger were unhurt and they returned to Lahore by rail on the 27th. The aircraft was salvaged by a party from Fort Sandeman and dispatched to the aircraft depot by rail.

December On the 28th the remainder of the Southern Flight commitments of the squadron were taken over by No. 5 (AC) Squadron pending the rearming of the squadron with bomber/transport aircraft. Certain details of B Flight's ground party remaining at Hakimpet were given. [There is no squadron record for 1939, nor the period from September 1939 to March 1942.]

NO. 39 SQUADRON

Die noctuque
(By day and night)

AIRCRAFT
Westland Wapiti
Hawker Hart
Bristol Blenheim I

1930

January On the 1st Squadron Leader V.G.H de Crespigny MC, DFC was promoted to wing commander, and on the 25th was posted to command No. 2 (Indian) Wing at Risalpur.

April On the 4th Squadron Leader S.B. Harris DFC, AFC was posted from HQ (RAF) India to command the squadron.

May On the 2nd the squadron was called hurriedly and ordered to bomb up with 20 lb bombs on every serviceable aircraft, to stand by for active operations against the Mohmand tribes about eighty miles NW of Peshawar and four miles west of Abaxai. There was no action on that day nor 3 May. On the 12th B Flight of the squadron carried out the first raid, dropping 56 bombs in all. C Flight did the second raid but no bombs were

dropped. When the flight landed it was discovered that Flight Lieutenant McKeever had received a bullet in the protection plate to the rudder controls in the tail of the aircraft. Flying Officer Wheeler's aircraft was also damaged in the tailplane. On the 7th the squadron carried out a demonstration flight over Mohmand country about eighty miles north of Peshawar, as disturbances has been reported from there. This flight was followed by several bombing raids. On the 20th the situation in Mohmand territory had considerably improved, so much so that the day was inactive as far as air work was concerned. But on the 21st the squadron was again in action and the Battle Flight was standing by from 05.00 hrs. Eight 112 lb bombs and twenty-eight 20 lb bombs were dropped on R.1988. All aircraft returned safely. On the 24th the bombing was done by formation, followed by bombing by single aircraft. At 14.30 hrs on the 27th verbal orders were received by A Flight to take off as soon as possible and locate and bomb 2,000 tribesmen who were reported as having been seen between Abazai and Tangi. The next bombing raid was designated against R.0878, which amounted to two large red boulders which they were ordered to bomb. For the rest of May the squadron continued to bomb in the Mohmand country. On the 30th the flights received orders to reconnoitre an area bounded to the east by the River Swat, and to the west by a line joining D.9735, Khaurai and Khaudara. A bridge at D.9735 was to be bombed, and this was carried out from a height of 5,500 feet. Three 112 lb and forty 20 lb bombs were dropped on and around the bridge. One direct hit was scored with a salvo of 112 and 20 lb bombs. One salvo hit the west end of the bridge and two salvos were within twenty yards of the bridge. It appeared to be still intact but no movement was observed in the area.

June On the 2nd the tactics were changed. No. 2 (Indian) Wing was ordered to bomb villages, and the objectives and types of bombs to be used were stated. The villages to be bombed were Nave and Dhand. On the 3rd information was issued by No. 2 (Indian) Wing that a demonstration flight was to be carried out on 4 June over the Kajuri Plain. Photographic aircraft were to accompany the bombers to take photographs of bombing strikes. On the 5th formation bombing was carried out with aircraft bombing in a circle. They approached in a V formation then bombed in a circle. On the 7th orders were received from Wing that one aeroplane, loaded with 20 lb bombs, had to carry out a reconnaissance over the Mohmand territory and bomb any persons seen to the north of Gandera, but not Palli. On the 8th flights were ordered to bomb any activity seen to the right of the Swat river. On the 13th night bombing was carried out. On the 14th the bombing was against the village of Kala Kalai. The squadron carried out the raids from 4,000 ft. The results were bad owing to disturbed weather conditions

The Swat river.

at that height. They then bombed from 2,000 ft, and the results achieved were excellent, all bombs landing in the village, with fires being started by incendiaries. On the 17th between 10.00 and 11.20 hrs Flying Officer Collings had to return to Risalpur with engine trouble. On the 18th aircraft kept up a constant patrol of the unrestricted bombing areas. No bombs were dropped and back guns were not used. One pilot, Flying Officer Blain, on his first patrol, observed four Red Shirts at L.2301 working in a field. No action was taken. Later he observed two Red Shirts armed with rifles at L.4606 walking north-west along a canal bank. No action was taken as they appeared to be peaceful. Intensive bombing continued with day and night bombing for the remainder of the month. [The results achieved were more or less the same as described above, yet there is nothing in the diary that indicates that the tribal leaders had given in to the government's terms.]

July Bombing in Waziristan appeared to be good. The aircraft were operating from Bannu, where the machines were armed and refuelled. Flying Officer Collings, having dropped all of his bombs, was forced to land at Razmak on the landing ground with engine trouble. Later, an aeroplane belonging to No. 11 Squadron force-landed at Razmak, turned over and caught fire, causing one bomb to explode, which damaged the tail unit of Flying Officer Collings's aeroplane. Spare parts were sent out from Miranshah at dawn the next day. Flying Officer Pearson force-landed at Miranshah in the afternoon of the 10th with rocker gear trouble on No. 3 cylinder. On the 14th Flying Officer Collings returned to the aerodrome without dropping any bombs on account of engine trouble. On the 17th the squadron was ordered to carry out two raids in Utman Khel country. The first was done in squadron strength of eight aircraft, one

having force-landed on the aerodrome. The second raid was done by flights at short intervals. The bombing was accurate. On the same day Flying Officer Collings landed at Miranshah with engine trouble yet again, and Flight Lieutenant Lea-Cox landed at Miranshah with plug trouble, but the bombing was accurate. The bombing raids on the 17th were carried out against the villages in the Arang valley in Utman Khel country. This time Flying Officer Wheeler returned from that raid with engine trouble. [The squadron had had Wapitis for little more than one year.]

August On the 12th A and B Flights were ordered to Peshawar armed for attacking personnel, i.e. carrying rear guns and light bombs. Tribesmen who were observed in caves were either bombed or fired at. The results could not be ascertained.

September On the 5th, at 14.30 hrs individual aircraft dropped supplies to the Chitral relief column at Kajr. Seven aircraft were employed.

1931

June On the 26th the following awards to personnel of the RAF were published in the *London Gazette*. These were in recognition of gallant and distinguished conduct in operations on the North-West Frontier of India between 23 April and 4 September 1930:

> Squadron Leader S. Berkeley-Harris DFC, AFC – Bar to his DFC
> Flight Lieutenant S. McKeever – DFC
> No. 345850 Sergeant James E.W. (since deceased) – DFM
> No. 363389 LAC (now Corporal) Ellis R.W. – DFM

The following were mentioned in dispatches:

> Flight Lieutenant C.L. Lea-Cox
> No. 342688 Sergeant Addis T.H.
> No. 361607 Corporal Oldfield H.A.
> No. 352675 LAC (now Corporal) Lee A.W.
> No. 358923 AC1 Rootes J.T.

September On the 4th and 6th of the month the squadron carried out two evening reconnaissance flights of the Tirah on account of possible Afridi trouble. Aircraft operated directly on the orders of Group HQ. On the 7th A and B Flights stood by for operations, armed with 20 lb bombs, from 16.30 hrs until 18.30 hrs. At 18.30 hrs a starting-up test was carried out, six engines being started in 4½ minutes.

November/December The squadron was re-equipped with the Hawker Hart aircraft powered by a 480 hp Rolls-Royce Kestrel engine. During December serious trouble developed in connection with the Red Shirt movement in the province. The squadron had previously carried out two reconnaissances on 16 and 30 October and had take a number of photographs for military operations. On 29 December, as soon as re-equipment of the squadron allowed, the unit took part in a series of daily reconnaissance flights of Red Shirt villages in the district surrounding Mardan, Swabi and Nowshera. These reconnaissance flights were carried out in cooperation with ground forces for the purpose of reporting movements and gatherings to the various columns operating in the same area, to give warnings of any indication that processions were converging on Mardan. Patrolling aircraft were in constant W/T communications with Risalpur and the HQ Nowshera Brigade. Information was conveyed to ground forces by means of message dropping.

1932

January From the end of December until the middle of February, sorties were effected, much activity being reported and a considerable amount of propaganda being dropped. On one occasion propaganda took the form of small dolls dressed in Red Shirt uniforms, labelled 'Red Shirt'. During this period the following two wireless operators were specially commended for their work:

No. 363282 Corporal Wright R. (air gunner) During the period 29 December 1931 to 12 February 1932 he flew 38 flights, with a total time of 83 hours.

No. 364812 LAC Green K.A. (wireless operator) During the period 29 December 1931 to 9 January 1932 he flew 49 flights, with a total time of 95 hours.

On two occasions an aircraft was sent to Jhelum to work under the Jhelum Brigade for the purposes of reconnaissance over the Mirpur and the Punch areas in connection with violent communal disturbances in the state of Kashmir. A total of twelve reconnaissance flights were carried out, some in cooperation with the Kashmir State troops. A large number of burning villages were observed.

March Over Mohmand country the fear with the political authorities was that there would be Red Shirt activity immediately before or during the visit of the Viceroy to Peshawar on the 16th. It was considered necessary to prevent rowdy elements from districts north of the Kabul river from entering Peshawar and inducing the Red Shirts of Peshawar City and the Sadr Tehsil to cooperate with them. Accordingly all ferry boats were recalled to the right bank of the river on the 15th. It was proved that with aerial cooperation it was possible to control a waterway more than eighty miles in length. Certain sections of the Mohmand tribe were trying to raise a lashkar to attack villages on this side of the administrative border, the adjutant reported, but they ignored the warnings of the political authorities on the 8th, that punitive measures would be taken against them unless they dispersed. These sections of the tribe were therefore bombed on that day, but they refused to comply with terms, so bombing continued. In particular the house of the Haji of Turangzai at Dagh was singled out, and the squadron commander himself made four raids on the house, dropping two 230 lb bombs, and flight attacks were made by diving down the hillside onto the house and sighting on the front gunsights. By the 14th the situation in the Bajour appeared to be restored, but the Utmanzai Mohmands appeared still to be out, so the squadron carried out bombing on their villages in the Yakh Dand area. When more lashkars were raised orders were given to the squadron to arm up with anti-personnel loading. On the 19th there was no trace of the lashkars observed from the air. It was thought that they had dispersed due to the bombing on the 18th. The operations in March 1932 can be summarized as follows:

During these operations the squadron carried out a total of 2 squadron and 36 flight raids with 9 raids by single aircraft dropping a total of $20^3/_4$ tons of bombs and 20 petrol bombs, of which 13 tons of HE bombs and 13 petrol bombs were direct hits. The operations record book then lists all the individual bombing raids, with tonnages carried out during the period.

April On the 12th the squadron took part in a refuelling and rearming exercise at Arawali. All four bomber squadrons in the command participated. Squadrons arrived at Arawali at intervals with empty bomb racks (tribal loading) and Lewis gun magazines and oil and fuel tanks empty to represent the flying involved in a raid of two hours' duration. All aircraft were rearmed and reloaded by personnel of No. 2 (Indian) Wing. Bombs and ammunition were then removed by their respective stations within an hour of being on the ground. The flights in connection with this exercise were carried out in squadron formation, and landings were made at Arawali in flight formation. On the 23rd a display was given for Indian Army pensioners at Risalpur in which the squadron took part. About two hundred pensioners attended.

May to December The operations record book records a considerable amount of work carried out in cooperation with the Army. On 6 October the squadron carried out a reconnaissance with the 1st Risalpur Cavalry Brigade. Photographic exposures were made with an F8 camera.

1933

March   On the 9th nine aircraft of the squadron carried out two demonstration flights, one over a jirgah at Adwana and one over a jirgah at Sararogha which were being held by His Excellency the Governor of the North-West Frontier Province in connection with the unrest in the Khost district of Afghanistan. These aircraft also escorted the aircraft in which His Excellency was flying, in company with other squadrons of the Command. On the 14th Squadron Leader Culley DSO took over command of the squadron, vice Squadron Leader S.B. Harris DFC, AFC, on the latter's return to the United Kingdom. Demonstrations were carried out late in the month on the Datt Khel and over the Wuzh Gai. This demonstration was in support of a jirgah held by the political authorities in connection with the unrest in the Khost area.

May   On the 15th Flight Lieutenant G.R. O'Sullivan assumed command of the squadron while Squadron Leader Culley was sent to command the RAF Hill Depot, Lower Topa.

June to August   The squadron was involved in bombing from 18 July until 4 August. On that day aircraft in formation dropped a total of twelve 112 lb bombs and four 20 lb bombs on Kotkai, followed on the 5th by a demonstration over Bajour country. On the 30th Squadron Leader Culley resumed command of the squadron.

1934

January   On the 17th a visit by the Secretary of State for Air, Lord Londonderry, was made. He visited Risalpur and No. 39 Squadron, except one flight, which was detached to Delhi, and was inspected by him.

April   On the 12th the C-in C, Field Marshal Sir Philip Chetwode Bart, GCB, GCSI, KCMG, DSO made a short inspection of the squadron. This was followed three days later by the AOC, Air Marshal Sir John Steel KBE, CB, CMG. He inspected the station and departed on the 18th. The same day two aircraft of the squadron and one of No. 11 Squadron flew to Chilas with two surgeons for attendance on Captain A.W. Best and returned to Risalpur on the 20th. Three aircraft of the squadron flew to Chilas to collect the two surgeons, who were then flown to Peshawar.

September/October   Between 15 September and 14 October the squadron was engaged in the relief of the Chitral garrison. Unless the weather prevented it, the mail used to be dropped by air on the column except on 10 October when a mailbag hung up on the tail of the aircraft and could not therefore be delivered. During the relief of the garrison the enemy casualties were

estimated by the political agent at Malakand to be eighty killed and wounded. Reports have been received that the Faqir of Alingar was among the wounded.

November   From the 5th to the 8th a flight of five aircraft flew to Gilgit by the Indus valley route. Mr A.J. Hopkinson ICS, Chief Secretary to the Governor of the North-West Frontier Province, was carried as a passenger by Flying Officer R.G.E. Catt.

1935

February   On the 21st information was received that the Faqir of Alingar had crossed the Swat river with 800 followers and was causing considerable unrest among the tribes on the west side of the Swat, particularly in Darang. A demonstration flight of nine aircraft from each squadron in No. 1 (Indian) Wing was ordered, and these flew over the disturbed area by squadron in line astern.

March   On the 6th Vildebeest aircraft of No. 100 (TB) Squadron arrived at Risalpur from Singapore. They left for the return flight on the 12th. On the 14th Air Marshal Steel paid a farewell visit to the station and gave a congratulatory letter to the squadron for services rendered.

April   On the 12th a visit was made by the incoming AOC, Air Marshal Edgar Ludlow Hewitt.

August   The Mohmand operations of 1935 came about as a result of a quarrel between the Burajm and Isa Khel over the distribution of moneys received from contracts for the Gandab Road. About 100 members of these tribes moved to the vicinity of the road at the end of July, and a repair party, protected by Khasssadars, was fired at by these tribesmen. Batshah Gul moved down to the Pindiali area with a force of Safis and the outlaw Chinnai's gang. On the night of the 7th and 8th a party of Burhan and Isa Khel pulled down telephone lines on the main road south of Abazai and attacked a frontier post, but were driven off. On 14 August Batshah Gul issued instructions for the destruction of the Gandab road. A lashkar of about 200 arrived near Dand and began to damage the road and burn some of the Khassadars' shelters. The Haji of Turangzai and his two sons, Batshah Gul II and III, left Lakarai for Baezai and Kandahard country to raise the Upper Mohmands. A lashkar rapidly formed, and on 17 August numbered approximately 2,000, being distributed on both sides of the road between Dand and the Nahakki Pass. They consisted mainly of the Burhan Khel, Isa Khel and Safis. The numerous bad characters and adventurers from other sections of the Mohmands and Anbahar were among them, and the Baezai and Khawalzai, from across the presumptive border, were also well represented. The leaders of the lashkar were the three Batshah Guls, the Faqir of Alingar and the murderer and outlaw Chinnai. Continuous patrols were ordered by No. 2 (Indian) Wing and were carried out by Nos 11 and 39 Squadrons, all aircraft being armed with four 112 lb Mk VI bombs, but no SAA. Any movement on the road was to be attacked on sight. On the 16th at 07.35 hrs the squadron began the first of three patrols that were made during the day. The first was abandoned due to low cloud. The other two patrols each dropped four bombs on or near the road. Four demonstration flights were carried out, and bombing attacks continued into the 17th. Warning notices were dropped and the Burhan and Isa Khels were warned that their country would be bombed from the 19th onwards until further notice. A blockade of their country would also be enforced until there was compliance with the government's demands. On 18 August intelligence reports were received that casualties had been inflicted on the anti-road lashkar. On the 19th a new operation was ordered:

Phase I (06.00 hrs) The inhabitants of the affected villages would be forced to evacuate their homes. Preliminary bombing with practice bombs would be followed by 20 lb and 112 lb bombs.

Phase II Following the bombing a blockade would be enforced, the object of which was to prevent the inhabitants from moving into the open, tending their cattle or ploughing their fields. A continuous two-hour patrol was to be maintained by a single aircraft over the Burhan Khel throughout the day.

Phase II operations continued to the 20th. There were continuous attacks upon the tribes until the end of the month, with no apparent end in sight.

September Five patrols were carried out, particular attention being paid to the watershed west of the Swat river and Danish Kol. On the 10th, owing to the small movement being observed in the operational area, the system of attack was changed. Special bombing attacks were allotted to certain patrols in addition to their normal patrol work. On the 14th control of all operations against the Mohmand were passed to the GOC Northern Command. At this stage a large force comprising four brigades of Army units had assembled in the Gandab valley. Orders were received for a change in certain respects, in the use of the RAF during the advance of the Army to attack and capture the Nahakki Pass and village. This stage did not, however, affect the blockade

of Burhan and Isa Khel territory by air, but increased, temporarily, the area allotted to No. 1 (Indian) Wing by adding the area lettered D from Nash Khakhwar and the Nahakki bridge. It was not until the 23rd, at 17.30 hrs, that the Burhan and Isa Khels had come in to agree to the government's terms. Air action was stopped that day and congratulatory messages were sent to all units from Group HQ.

October On the 15th a jirgah of all Upper Mohmands was held at Wuchajawar. HE the Governor of the North-West Frontier Province addressed the gathering and stipulated the government's terms, all of which were accepted.

1936

January The Singapore reinforcement programme training began, and all twelve aircraft of the squadron were flown there and returned by the same route as the outward journey. Squadron Leader J.H. Butler was in command.

February Normal routine was observed. There were more refuelling and rearming exercises at Arawali.

March On the 16th a composite flight of four aircraft, three from the squadron and one from No. 11 Squadron, led by Flight Lieutenant G.H. Shaw, proceeded to Drosh to carry out the quarterly inspection of the landing ground and to convey stores to the garrison there. Major F.N. Clifton, Royal Engineers, was carried as a passenger. On the return flight severe snow storms were encountered after crossing the Lowarai Pass. Owing to the freezing up of the air intakes on all aircraft, great difficulty was experienced in maintaining engine revolutions. One aircraft, K.1417, piloted by Flight Lieutenant Shaw with No. 515284 LAC Germain C. as the wireless operator, was forced down and crashed on landing at Krappa on the Bin river approximately west of Dir. When his engine failed, thick cloud totally obscured the ground and Flight Lieutenant Shaw instructed Germain to use his parachute, but it deployed before the air gunner left the aircraft and it became entangled in the empenage of the machine. Shaw managed to get his machine to the ground, but owing to the rocks and snow, the aircraft was completely wrecked, the crew being slightly injured. Major H.H. Johnston CIE, MM, the political agent of Dir, Swat and Chitral, and the Nawat of Dir rendered every assistance. An assistant surgeon was sent out to attend to the crew, and on the following day Flight Lieutenant Carslaw, the medical officer at Risalpur, proceeded by car to Robat to collect the two injured men. The aircraft was salvaged by a party under the command of Flying Officer W.G. Devas. The complete engine and dismantled airframe were conveyed by coolies over difficult country from

Krappa to Dir, a distance of approximately eighteen miles. On the 20th the AOC, Air Marshal Edgar Ludlow Hewitt, carried out his annual inspection.

September On the 21st at Peshawar, while carrying out air-to-ground firing, the pilot of Hart aircraft K.2110 declared that his aircraft was on fire and ordered his air gunner, No. 560553 LAC Bunyan J.L., to leave the aircraft. LAC Bunyan made a parachute descent but injured his foot on landing. The aircraft dived into the ground from a height of 200 feet, and shortly afterwards the air firing-range party arrived to find the pilot, Flying Officer Charles Henry Thornton Warner, dead in his cockpit. An investigation by a court of inquiry could find nothing which could have caused the pilot to smell burning, and the body was conveyed to Peshawar, thence to Risalpur for burial on the 22nd.

1937

March On the 11th Squadron Leader S.H.B. Harris was posted from HQ RAF India to command the squadron.

April On the 8th owing to the dissatisfaction in Waziristan spreading to Mahsud country, the squadron took part in a demonstration flight over the Razmak area. It was due to this that the AOC abbreviated his tour of inspections to a considerable extent. At this time raids were being carried out on Datta Khel. On the 12th, to complete the destruction of the village, three aircraft each carried out one raid with incendiary and petrol bombs.

September Between the 1st and the 30th a great deal of work was carried out by the squadron in connection with the scheme which entailed preparation of the squadron to move in any direction at short notice. While at Lower Topa the squadron took part in the Boxing Cup, Shooting Cup, the Rifle Shooting Cup, the Association Football Cup, the Long-Distance Athletic Cup and the Durston Cup.

October/November From 9 October to 6 November one aircraft was flown to Karachi to assist in the training of air gunners on the air gunner qualifying course.

1938

January From the 1st to the 10th squadron preparations were in hand for the long-distance training flight. All other activities were suspended to enable inspections to be carried out on the aircraft. The squadron departed on the 10th for Seletar, thence to Tengah.

February On the 1st all pilots and air gunners of the squadron attended an explanatory conference on the coming of combined operations at Seletar. Personnel

were flown over to Seletar and back to Tengah by aircraft of No. 70 (B/T) Squadron.

April Operations occurred in Baddar Algad and Maintoi river valleys. The events leading up to the employment of the squadron in these areas began with a jirgah attended by the Bahlozai tribe. The political agent ordered the expulsion of Mullah Sher Ali from all of the Mahsud country, but the latter chose to ignore these orders, and after a visit by the Faqir of Ipi at Darra Khela, Sher Ali collected a gang of about 150 men. These included many from the Bahlozai tribe, and they moved towards Dargaisar, where they threatened both the Jandola/Razmak amd Jandola/Wana roads. To counteract this, two units of the South Waziristan Scouts moved to Dargaisar on the 13th. The next day an engagement was fought. The Scouts were outnumbered and the two units decided to withdraw, which was accomplished by midday on the 15th. The casualties to the South Waziristan Scouts numbered one British officer and three Indian other ranks, and ten Indian other ranks wounded, as opposed to eighteen enemy killed and fifteen wounded, including some well-known hostile leaders of Sher Ali's gang. In consequence it was decided to punish the Bahlozai Mahsuds living in the Split Toi valley, who were not only territorially responsible but supplied many followers to Sher Ali's gang. The inhabitants of the Baddar Algad and Mantoi river valleys were also to be punished for harbouring Sher Ali and his followers during the preceding four months and for supplying him with men to carry out the attacks upon the Scouts. Notices were therefore dropped on these areas on the 16th and 17th. The squadron was ordered to move to Miranshah for operations against these tribes. As a result of reconnaissance flights carried out, orders were issued to destroy the villages by air bombardment. On the 19th intensive bombing was carried out by fighters in formation. On the 20th bombing continued and a blockade was imposed on the proscribed area. [The operations record book then goes on to describe the damage inflicted on the various villages.] On the 24th nine individual bombing raids were carried out on the three sub-tribes, and the next day it was ordered that offensive bombing of the proscribed areas was to discontinue and only blockade operations were to be carried out. For these sorties the armament carried comprised two 20 lb bombs and two 112 lb bombs, and the front and rear guns were only to be used if movement was actually seen. Delayed-action bombs were dropped on anyone working in the fields. This blockading by aircraft showed that, in many cases, normal routine was being observed by the inhabitants of the area, in spite of the fact that the pamphlets originally dropped warned all against living in the area. Flocks of sheep and cattle were general over the area. On the 26th the blockade continued, but it was found that in the village of Abdur Rahman Khel, which was just inside the proscribed area, the inhabitants were living complete with their children and cattle as normal, and this village had been attacked heavily by anti-personnel bombs. It was not until the 30th that it was noticed that the number of personnel moving and the numbers of cattle seen were appreciably lower in the area, so the bombing was taking a long time to have any effect.

May On the 2nd Group Captain C.C. Darley CBE, AM interviewed all ranks to explain the reasons for the operations, their course and the probable turn of events in the near future. By the 10th it could be seen that the tribal elders seemed to have lost control of their younger members. They refused to come to the jirgah at Ladha, to discuss terms. On the 11th another jirgah was held at Razmak. The inhabitants of the Mantoi and Baddar Algad refused to comply with demands of the government, and in consequence pamphlets were dropped that evening over the whole of these areas, giving forty-eight hours' warning of the opening of destructive bombing. These operations tied in with the operations of other squadrons, and involved the Faqir of Ipi, who was causing a great deal of trouble in the area. During this time the squadron was operating in both the Baddar Algad and the Mintoi river valley and in the Splitoi area. Punitive bombing of the Madda Khel began. Four squadrons were chosen to do the destructive bombing in the area, namely No. 11 (B) Squadron operating from Risalpur, 39 (B) Squadron from Miranshah and Nos 27 and 60 Squadrons from Kohat. No. 5 (AC) Squadron based at Arawali carried out blockade duties of the areas proscribed. On the 16th the squadron carried out five flight raids and one squadron raid, while one flight dropped delayed-action HE bombs, 112 lb Mk VII, over the Splitoi area. Operations in the Baddar Algad and Mintoi river valleys were suspended from the 15th. Bombing then continued the next day, and by the end of the 17th the damage to Sherani was considerable. The bombing programme on this day was similar to the previous day. Nine flight raids were made over Madda Khel country, with one flight dropping long-delay bombs over the Splitoi area. Bombing raids continued and on the 22nd only three flight raids were put in against Janbe Khel because the squadron was getting ready to a move to Risalpur the following day. No. 1 (Indian) Wing had been ordered to relieve the squadron of operational duties so that on the 23rd the aircraft could return, followed by the ground party the following day.

July On the 1st Air Commodore R.H. Peck OBE, the Air Officer Commanding RAF India, visited the squadron during his visit to the Wing stations. The rest of July was spent in exercises, long-distance flights and reconnaissance flights over tribal areas. The events

leading up to the employment of the squadron in Ahmedzai country west of the Kurram river are described in the operations record book.

Disturbances in the Bannu district revealed persons of a hostile lashkar in Ahmedzai Wazir territory, and the government is of the opinion that this tribal area is guilty of harbouring the lashkar and supporting it. These disturbances consist of raiding and kidnapping, raids against villages in the Administrated Territory that have been particularly prominent in the Bannu area. This is chiefly the work of the Tori Khel and the Bhattani tribes. A Frontier Constabulary lorry was recently held up by a gang. Those responsible were pursued by a Frontier Constabulary patrol, but a village inside the Bannu civil district turned out in force and the raiders made their escape. The government has therefore decided that air action should be taken.

August Operations commenced on the 2nd, and ten raids were carried out against Tarkhe Oba and Larkarrai. Pilots were ordered to remain over the Admedzai area and take action against movments seen. If no movment was seen, 112 lb bombs carried by the aircraft were to be dropped on one of the villages. In all, twelve 112 lb bombs and fifty-three 20 lb bombs were dropped. Some movement was still noticed in the area and air action was taken, but little damage was recorded against the villages of Tarkhe Oba and Larkarrai. Raids continued throughout August and into September, and the squadron alternated day and day about between operations and routine squadron training.

September On the 20th Squadron Leader W.M. McKechnie was posted from No. 1 Group. This was an emergency posting to command the squadron. On the 29th a warning order was received by the squadron to be ready to move to Singapore withing forty-eight hours' notice. Accordingly preparations were made covering such items as the issue of indentity discs, censorship of letters and next-of-kin details. Having taken all the necessary steps, the unit returned to normal routine.

October On the 9th Squadron Leader McKechnie was posted to command No. 27 (B) Squadron at Kohat.

November On the 7th the squadron proceeded to Drigh Road for an armament training camp. On the 8th all pilots received a lecture on range regulations, and personnel who had not previously visited Karachi were shown over the range at Manora. Air firing commenced at 10.00 hrs and from the 11th to the 22nd bombing was carried out. Thirteen pilots and sixteen air gunners were involved and the following squadron averages were achieved:

The Vickers quarter test – 33.8
The Lewis quarter test – 76.8
The Vickers astern test – 12

The Vickers astern test was carried out on the new 3 ft towed drogue. The average shown in the Vickers quarter test was nearly double that of 1937 and four times as great as that of 1936. In carrying out the bombing they managed to hit the armoured motor boat twice. In fact the dive-bombing results were extremely good, the average error, while attacking the motor boat on a straight course, being 32.6 yards. Attacking a 'jinking' boat resulted in an error of 21.6 yards, with a percentage of 62.4 hits.

December On the 9th Squadron Leader A.F. McKenna was posted in From No. 1 (Indian) Wing to command the squadron. For some time past the Faqir of Ipi had been living in the Madda Khel country in the Shawaltangi Algad. This harbouring of Ipi in the territory was directly against the terms of the Madda Khel Agreement of June 1938, but punishments were deferred to allow the tribe to persuade the Faqir to come forward to discuss peace terms. When no response was forthcoming it was decided to punish the Madda Khel by air action. The remainder of the month was characterized by ongoing air operations.

[For some inexplicable reason the operations record book is maintained to 31 December 1938 and is not resumed until 1940.]

1939

June The squadron is equipped with Blenheim I aircraft.

August The squadron moves from Risalpur to Tengah in the Far East.

September War is declared on the 3rd.

NO. 47 SQUADRON

Nili nomen roboris omen
(The name of the Nile is an omen of our strength)

AIRCRAFT
Fairey IIIF
Fairey Gordon
Vickers Vincent
Vickers Wellesley

1930

January On the 1st reconnaissance and bombing raids were carried out, and this day saw the collapse of the Nuba operations. On the 3rd an unfortunate accident occurred at Jebel Eliri. A dud 112 lb bomb was found by a native and brought towards a party of RAF personnel. At about 30 yards' range it exploded,

seriously wounding Dr Hall of the Sudan Defence Force medical services and Mr Opie, the District Commissioner. No. 335889 LAC Purse was luckily the only RAF casualty. Three native soldiers were killed. [Two points arise from this report. Firstly, one must not construe from the Adjutant's words that Purse was lucky to be a casualty, and secondly, by describing the bomb as dud meant that it did not explode on impact when dropped.] On the 4th, 6th and 17th reconnaissance flights were carried out at the request of the Governor of the Nile Province in connection with the Nuer Settlement Scheme. On the 17th demonstration flights were carried out at the request of the Sudan government. A number of sheikhs and notables of the various provinces were given short flights.

February On the 8th Squadron Leader E.L. Howard-Williams MC arrived and assumed command of the squadron, vice Squadron Leader C.R. Cox AFC.

May On the 12th two aircraft proceeded to Malakal, one machine conveying a nurse to an urgent case of typhoid. On the 30th the squadron had taken a lioness called Belinda on squadron strength as a mascot. The squadron was still taking local chiefs for flights. Inspection of landing grounds continued.

June The squadron was looking for suitable floatplane moorings. Very bad weather can be experienced in the area. At least a floatplane can put down on the water where a landplane cannot for fear of being bogged down when aerodromes get swampy.

July From the 7th to the 16th three floatplanes carried out a cruise of the waters of the Nile and its tributaries and swamps in southern Sudan. The following task was undertaken for the Civil Administration: Reconnaissance of Zeraf island was carried out at the request of the Governor of the Upper Nile Province. The purpose of the reconnaissance was to search for recalcitrant Gaweir Nuers that had taken refuge on the island to see if they were still there. They had, however, departed as a result of a demonstration carried out by two aircraft in April.

August From the 18th to the 22nd two floatplanes carried out a reconnaissance of the Southern Sudan and Uganda in order to locate poachers who had crossed the Ugandan/Abyssinian border and taken nine elephants. The poachers were reputed to be about fifty strong and armed with nine rifles. According to an expedition of the Sudan Defence Force, they were operating near Opirpari. A simple code was prepared and dropped on a punitive expedition, which put out various signals that the poachers had recrossed the border to Uganda and were probably 40 miles away in any given direction. The country was searched high and low but no evidence was obtained of any wayward party in the vicinity.

September   From the 22nd to the 29th three floatplanes carried out a flight of 110 hours in twelve days to investigate the water and meteorological conditions that existed in the areas covered by the rivers of the Southern Sudan during the floods. Experience using floatplanes showed that the squadron could get airborne off a flat calm or a heavily sudden river with two passengers, kit for three crew for twelve days and all the tools and spares and 100 lb of stores. The adjutant said that the trick in the squadron was to ensure that all squadron pilots were trained in watermanship. Anchor drill was particularly important, together with hoisting in and hoisting out drill, and the means by which we have found these essentials best taught.

October to December   Exercises continued to ensure that the best use was made of floatplanes in the Sudan.

1933

January   On the 17th there was a change of command of No. 47 (Bomber) Squadron. Wing Commander W.R. Howard MC handed over to Squadron Leader A MacGregor MBE, DFC.

April   The Akobo incident happended when the squadron was patrolling the frontier. The Governor of the Upper Nile reported that a critical situation existed, arising out of an inter-sectional dispute among the local Dinka. An anti-government attitude was being manifested. The security of Bor was at stake, and the governor, who had taken responsibility, instructed Captain Coriat, the District Commissioner, to proceed with a pilot to Bor, to investigate and report on the situation. Air reconnaissance of the disturbed area was carried out and the aircraft returned to Malakal. The situation became easier when police detachments from the Equatorial Corps, Torit, arrived on the 30th, by which time the thought of an attack on the government headquarters had subsided. The aircraft therefore returned to Malakal. An exercise took them to Cyprus, working with the Cyprus Military Police, using the T Panel Code. The aircraft also flew round the island visiting Paphos, Limassol and Larnaca, when landings were made at these points.

1934

February   On the 22nd there was a reconnaissance in consequence of certain disorders on the French Equatorial frontier in the Western Darfur and the fear that the Sudan territory might be infringed. Two aircraft fitted with machine-guns and 20 lb bomb racks were ordered to proceed from Khartoum to El Fasher. The two aircraft proceeded to Jeneina on the 24th to operate in

conjunction with the Sudan Defence Force. The situation eased, however, and the aircraft were withdrawn to El Fasher on the 25th and to Khartoum on the 27th. Army Cooperation followed, with a flight of four aircraft taking part in Camel Corps exercises at Ginan. Between the 3rd and the 9th there was an air reconnaissance of the Jebel in which the exercises were to be carried out. Thereafter aircraft were employed on reconnaissance during the exercises and in bomb attacks on the enemy on the caves of the Jebel.

June/July   There was more familiarization with the use of floatplanes. The record book simply records the flights undertaken in achieving familiarization.

1935

January   While engaged in cooperation duties at Kolaji Springs, Darfur Province, on the morning of the 24th, the fitter of one of the aircraft, No. 563149 LAC Harffey, jumped out of the back cockpit at 200 feet and was killed! The funeral took place with military honours.

April   Camel Corps exercises continued.

September   Squadon Leader A.P. Ritchie AFC was appointed to command No. 47 (Bomber) Squadron, vice Squadron Leader G.E. Gibbs MC.

October   The RAF in the Sudan was reinforced under the emergency measures taken by the government during the Italian campaign in Abyssinia. No. 3 (Fighter) Squadron arrived at Khartoum on 22 October and remained there until January 1936, when it returned to Port Sudan. No. 35 (Bomber) Squadron arrived from Bircham Newton on 18 October and was located at Ed Damur. No. 207 (Bomber) Squadron also came to Ed Damur on the 28th. The two bomber squadrons were then located at Gebeit, and No. 5 Wing was at Khartoum to administer all the units located in the Sudan. An aircraft park was established at Berbara.

1936

August   On cessation of the League of Nations sanctions against Italy, all emergency units were withdrawn to the United Kingdom, and the stations at Berbara, Gebeit and Port Sudan were closed down. There was a reconnaissance of the Boma Plateau and surrounding countryside involving four Fairey Gordons leaving Khartoum on the 3rd. Working from a base in Kapoeta, three Vincents left the following day carrying spares and extra personnel for a detachment. It became apparent that the landing ground at Kapoeta was far too far away from the Boma plain, and it was decided to move the detachment forward if a suitable landing ground could be found. An excellent site was found by the Sudan Defence Force on the Kuran river, and the first flight moved forward on the 15th. The new landing ground was 75 miles nearer the area of operations. It was also possible to observe the weather conditions over the plateau. There was a reconnaissance of the frontier because of troubles in Abysinnia, and refugees were thought to be crossing the border into Sudan.

September New information was received that the Dinka and two clans of the Alaib tribe had been fighting at Papiirrol District of the Upper Nile and had killed the native police who had been sent to restore order. Two Vincents and two Gordons were sent and messages were dropped at the police post. But the District Commissioner then reported that since things were quiet he did not require the aircraft any more.

1937

April On the 25th information was received from the Governor of the Upper Nile Province that inter-tribal disturbances had broken out at Khorteri, south-west of Akobo, between the Nuer and the Beir tribes. Consequently on the 27th four Vincents proceeded to Malakal to stand by for operations if required. However, the District Commissioner rounded up the miscreants satisfactorily and the aircraft returned to base. During the remainder of 1937 aircraft demonstrations succeeded in acting as a deterrent. Appalling weather conditions in the Sudan and extremes of temperature also made flying extremely difficult in the wet months.

1939

July On the 23rd the squadron was equipped with Wellesley aircraft.

September On the 3rd war is declared on Germany.

NO. 55 SQUADRON

Nil nos tremefacit
(Nothing shakes us)

1930

February On the 7th Squadron Leader J.W Woodhouse DSO, MC assumed command of the squadron, vice Wing Commander C.H. Elliot-Smith AFC. B Flight was equipped with Westland Wapiti aircraft powered by Bristol Jupiter VIIIF engines.

March On the 15th three aircraft of A Flight, led by Flight Lieutenant Freehill DFC, left for Rutbah carrying a full operational load. Reconnaissance flights were carried out daily carrying the SSO. On the 17th, while cooperating with the police cars south of Rutbah, effective front-gun action was taken against a band of horsemen. On the 21st demonstration and reconnaissance flights were carried out along the Iraq/Nejd border.

May On the 1st Flight Lieutenant M. Freel DFC assumed command of the squadron, vice Squadron Leader Woodhouse.

July On the 21st a flight of five aircraft, led by Flight Lieutenant Taaffe, left Hinaidi on a liaison visit to the French in Syria.

September On the 2nd Squadron Leader Woodhouse resumed command of the squadron.

November On the 4th three aircraft left for Penjwin with thirty 20 lb bombs, and reconnaissance flights were carried out over the Sulaimania–Kirkuk road in the afternoon. On the 11th an Armistice parade was held and on the same day Flying Officer A.L.T. Naish was evacuated by Victoria aircraft to the RAF Hospital, Hinaidi. On the afternoon of the same day a football match was played between the resident armoured car company and A Flight.

1931

January On the 31st Squadron Leader George Cecil Gardiner DFC assumed command of the squadron, vice Squadron Leader J.W. Woodhouse DSO, MC.

March On the 7th Flight Lieutenant Wright and Sergeant Stafford, with Flight Lieutenant Mumford SSO as passenger, flew on a reconnaissance of Penjwin, Khuniana, Nazara, Qizilja and Saliawa. The aircraft landed at Penjwin. Twenty armed horsemen were seen at Nubuk but the rebels did not fire so no action was taken other than to direct them. They dismounted and fled into the watercourse. A reconnaissance flight on the 8th reported no activity, and during most of March 1931 there was much reconnaissance activity but nothing to report in the Qara Dagh valley. [For the end of March 1931 the adjutant had written in large letters, 'Dust Storm', and nothing more.] On the 19th Squadron Leader Gardiner and Pilot Officer Carr left on a reconnaissance flight of the Muan Plain. On the 20th Flying Officer Naish and Pilot Officer Earle left for Hinaidi. Sergeant Chudley, 2nd Lieutenant N.H. Janabi of the Iraqi Air Force and Sergeant Stafford arrived from Hinaidi. A message was picked up which stated that the police reported that Mahmoud was back at Tatltatakia and probably moving to Jaafaran that night. Another pilot was gaining height to drop a message on the Baikuli police post when he observed what appeared to be sheep moving towards Sivisinan. It was noticed that they were horsemen, estimated to be around 150, galloping for cover in the village. It was then too late to attack for fear of hitting the village, but about 20 horesmen and 40 men on foot were attacked near a watercourse. One bomb was dropped and the bomb-release handle broke away. [five bomb-release handles broke off during the operation.] A message was dropped at Paikuli, and Sivisinan was again visitied. A majority of horses were in the village, and about 20 were under cover. The pilot stated that he was fired upon from the village, and a message to that effect was dropped on Shalcol. Total flying hours for the day was 6 hrs 30 mins. On the 22nd the wind was blowing at gale force and no flying was carried out until 15.00 hrs. Flying Officer Carr left with secret mail for the SSO at Qala Shiwana. Messages were dropped and picked up from the column at Qara Dagh. Flying Officer Carr landed at Qala Shirwana at 16.10 hrs. On the 23rd Sergeant Anthony, with AC Nicholas, left to drop and pick up messages from the column at Qara Dagh. Flying Officer Carr landed at Qala Shirwana at 16.10 hrs. On the 23rd Sergeant Anthony with AC Nicholas left to drop and pick up messages from the column at Qara Dagh. While endeavouring to pick up a message the pilot struck a tree with his wing. The machine crashed and caught fire, exploding the four bombs which were carried and killing the crew. On the 29th Flight Lieutenant Wright and Flying Officer Eady of No. 84 Squadron left on a reconnaissance and bombed some caves at Shawzi. Two incendiaries were dropped, which had practically no effect on the mud houses. Houses nearby which had straw and matting were completely burned. By late morning Squadron Leader Gardiner, with Major Roberts as passenger, and Flying Officer Carr arrived and saw rebels entering Qala Dagh and Shiwdaz. As these villages had already had special proclamations dropped on them they were attacked with bombs and machine-guns. While the squadron pilots were bombing, the villagers took refuge in watercourses and caves, but it was almost impossible to say whether or not they were peaceful inhabitants or rebels.

April On the 1st Pilot Officer L'Estrange and Flying Officer Carr of No. 84 Squadron left on a reconnaissance in cooperation with the police. The area was quiet and messages were picked up by Pilot Officer L'Estrange. Each aircraft flew for four hours. On the 5th at 09.55 hrs a striking force under the command of Squadron Leader Gardiner took off to locate the enemy and the column. After contact with the column the area was thoroughly combed and the enemy were found in the Karam Basan and Birika. Approximately 50 rebels were seen in a large wadi, and there were a large number of saddled horses in and around the village. After the usual warnings the squadron leader gave the signal to attack, and started by

dropping the first bomb of the day. Flying Officer Carr dropped two 112 lb bombs but was then signalled by Squadron Leader Gardiner to return for more bombs and reinforcements. Meanwhile Gardiner flew around the village machine-gunning anyone who tried to break away. [By this means the adjutant says the the squadron leader was able to keep the rebels centralized.] When Flying Officer Carr returned, Squadron Leader Gardiner signalled that he was in difficulties, dropped a bomb to indicate 'carry on bombing', fired a Very light and made for the nearest landing ground, having been badly shot about.The main petrol tank was pierced and the carburettor hit. Sergeant Koch with LAC Cargill and Sergeant Stafford with AC Durham arrived to keep up a continuous bombardment. At 10.15 hrs Pilot Officer L'Estrange with LAC Morse left to do a medium-contact W/T reconnaissance and returned to Sulaimania at 14.05 hrs. Flying Officer Carr had orders to wait for the arrival of Victorias to indicate bombing targets to them, in the village of Arika. When the Victorias did not arrive, Flying Officer Carr flew to Sulaiman Beg, it being too dark to return to Sulaimania, landing there at 18.55 hrs. [It was the opinion of two of the pilots of the strike force that Sheikh Mahmoud's followers were equipped with machine-guns. This would not be an unrealistic assumption, and would certainly shorten the odds for the vulnerability of the aircrew.] There was no action on the 6th, only patrolling. On the 7th Squadron Leader Gardiner and Flying Officer Carr left on receipt of a message to carry out a reconnaissance of the caves and villages along the Gilazada Range, returning at 13.05 hrs. Flying Officer Carr was left to carry out the same task again, but during the afternoon the wind grew to gale force so little was accomplished. On the 9th the only attack was on the village of Bani Banok. The usual warnings were given before the dropping of bombs, and the village appeared to suffer considerable damage. On the 17th Squadron Leader Gardiner's aircraft was again attacked, and the petrol tank and a flying wire were struck. On the 21st it was reported that Sheikh Mahmoud had crossed the border. It was anticipated that very little flying would then be done. The last flight of the day was by Flight Lieutenant Freehill, who flew to Sivisinan to try to find a suitable landing ground so that help could be given to a Victoria that had force-landed earlier. After an unsuccessful attempt he returned to Sulaimania, landing at 10.45hrs. [The operations record book then reports a temporary cessation of hostilities.] Between 23 and 25 April there were no operations, and all aircraft were stood down and returned to Hinaidi. On the 28th Air Marshal Ludlow Hewitt inspected the squadron and watched B and C Flight bombing.

June On the 23rd a DSO was awarded to Squadron Leader Gardiner, and a DFC went to Flying Officer Sydney Joseph Horace Carr.

September On the 14th an aircraft proceeded to photograph the Euphrates near Fallujah, and another aircraft with W/T cooperated with two sections of armoured cars in a tactical scheme. The rest of 1931 was then characterized by surveys, exercises, message picking up, photography and practising formation flying.

1932

January On the 5th of the month the squadron was inspected by the Under-Secretary of State for Air, Sir Philip Sassoon. On the 8th a Puss Moth, flown by Squadron Leader Warburton, who was attached to the Iraqi government, force-landed in the afternoon. On the 9th the squadron was ordered to search for the lost aircraft between Landing Grounds R and P. Flight Lieutenant Freehill with a W/T set, Flying Officers Lowe and Earl and Sergeant Baker arrived at Rutbah at 15.20 hrs and proceeded on a reconnaissance of El Gid and the area around Rutbah, without success. The search continued on the 11th and the 12th. Then in the afternoon of the 12th information had been received from a camel rider that Squadron Leader Warburton was safe and just south of the area swept by the CO's flight. In fact Squadron Leader Warburton had seen Flight Lieutenant Freehill's flight during the first reconnaissance of 10 January.

February The annual dinner of the Squadron Old Boys' Association was held on the 6th, and a report of the squadron's work was sent to the association.

April On the 26th six aircraft left Erbil at 08.00 hrs on a reconnaissance of the operational areas, and seven umounted horses had been seen, believed to belong to the rebels. Six aircraft left on a second reconnaissance, but one of them, flown by Flying Officer Wells with LAC Evans, failed to return. When aircraft of the squadron did eventually locate the aircraft there was nowhere other aircraft could land alongside. Flying over the crashed aircraft, Flight Lieutenant Carruthers said that the crash was a bad one. He could not land but could not see any sign of the crew. The airframe was upside down and the gunner's platform was open to give a clear view through the Scarff ring to the ground. The crash gave the impression of having been the result of a spin. A search was then made of the surrounding countryside, but there were no ground strips nor were parachutes seen. [The operations record book makes no further references to the missing crew.]

May On the 2nd a flight of five aircraft left Erbil at 12.30 hrs GMT to bomb specified villages south-east of the Rukuchuk, followed by more bombing raids the following day. The results were observed to be very good, and the police posts in the area put up a 'Y' signal,

indicating that all was well. On the 24th the pilots could see a signal indicating that the post had been attacked, but no firing was heard nor were the enemy seen. Group Captain Breese was the operational commander at Erbil.

August to December The 1932 campaign proved to be inconclusive since Mahmoud was reported to be over the border yet hostile acts continued. Since these did not require air action the squadron returned to training routine.

1933

January Only formation flying this month.

February On the 26th the Iraq Command Rifle Meeting was held and the squadron took part. [A slight misnomer here, for the meet was for other weapons in addition to rifles.] Squadron results were:

> Falling Plate – the squadron was beaten in the semi-finals
> Lewis Gun Competition – the squadron came third
> Revolver – the squadron came fourth
> Open Revolver – No. 357922 Corporal Stonier was 4th
> Open Rifle – Flying Officer Nixon was 9th
> RAF Rifle Championships – Corporal Stonier was 6th
> The squadron was 5th out of 12 teams

[Perhaps the squadron spent too much time on formation flying rather than musketry practice, but then a retired RAF Regiment officer would say that, wouldn't he?]

June/July Air firing, included front and rear gunner practices, was carried out during the months.

November Air training and ground maintenance, photography and special flights, which included fitting aircraft with long-distance tanks and flying to Karachi.

1934

January to November Routine squadron training.

December On the 13th four aircraft were fitted with long-distance tanks and led by Flight Lieutenant Gemmel proceeded to Heliopolis. The flight landed at Rutbah for fuel and flew to Heliopolis non-stop. The total flying time was 8 hrs 35 mins.

1935/6

Routine squadron training.

1937

February The squadron equipped with the Vincent aircraft.

April   On the 14th the River Tigris burst its banks at Daudiyah, 16 miles north of Baghdad. The river was by then well above flood level and still rising. In addition to the normal flood precautions the squadron carried out three visual and photographic reconnaissance flights each day, and others were ordered to take up various officials concerned with preventing flood damage.

May   Early in the month a structural defect was found in the Vincent, and all the aircraft were placed unserviceable, but the squadron did produce nine serviceable aircraft to take part in the fly-past at the conclusion of the ceremonial parade to mark the Coronation of Their Majesties King George VI and Queen Elizabeth.

September   The squadron left Hinaidi on the 14th to take up permanent residence at Dhibban, on the west bank of the River Euphrates. The move was completed in nine days.

November   Remanning of the squadron continued, and a second flight was organized completely on a Fitter II/Mate basis. [See Chapters 8 and 9 for a full explanation of the thinking behind this scheme.]

1938
March   On the 23rd Squadron Leader R.A.T Stowell assumed command of the squadron, vice Squadron Leader G.W. Hayes.

June   No. 516362 AC1 Holden F.W., wireless operator of this squadron, was awarded a medal of the Military Division of the Most Excellent Order of the British Empire for meritorious service. This award was published in a special supplement to the *London Gazette*.

December   As many aircraft of the squadron as were available took part in an extensive search for a missing Blenheim aircraft of No. 30 (B) Squadron. The search commenced on the 11th and was finally abandoned on the 19th. The squadron's aircraft were based at Rutbah at this time.

1939
February   On the 24th one Blenheim aircraft fitted with a dual conversion set was issued on loan to the squadron for the pilots to undergo conversion courses in preparation for the rearming with Blenheim aircraft.

March   On the 29th the squadron commenced rearming with Blenheims when the first aircraft was delivered by the Blenheim Delivery Flight.

August   On the 20th information was received that the squadron might have to move to its war station owing to

the delicacy of the international situation. Consequently all aircraft were made serviceable and the entire mobilization equipment was packed up in readiness for the move. On the 25th twelve Blenheim aircraft and three Valentias of No. 70 Squadron, carrying additional equipment and personnel, flew to Ismailia, arriving on the same day. The squadron's ground convoy of 24 MT vehicles left Habbaniya on the 25th of the month, arriving at Ismailia on 1 September.

September   Together Nos 14, 30 and 55 (Bomber) Squadrons formed No. 1(Bomber) Wing, with its headquarters at Ismailia. The wing was under the operational command of Egypt Group. [This would change on the 21st of the month when No. 1 (Bomber) Wing became No. 250 Wing and Egypt Group became No. 202 Group.] On the 2nd the squadron was placed on two hours' notice for operations. On the 3rd war was declared.

NO. 60 SQUADRON
Per ardua ad aethera tendo
(I strive through difficulties to the sky)

AIRCRAFT
DH9A
Westland Wapiti
Bristol Blenheim I

Introduction
The history of No. 60 Squadron is carried forward from Volume I, and is different from the histories of the other squadrons depicted in this chapter in that it is not derived from squadron operational record books or unit diaries. The operational activities of No. 60 Squadron are taken from the squadron history. The operational record books and unit diaries in the National Archives are sometimes incomplete or illegible, and so No. 60 Squadron's history has been selected to give a very detailed picture of operations on the North-West Frontier.

1930
On 8 March 1930 the squadron's DH9As were at last replaced by the Westland Wapiti. The Wapiti was a 1926 design, which saved the Air Ministry money by using up spare DH9A wings. In the event these were not satisfactory and were replaced by wings with metal spars and ribs. Most importantly the Bristol Jupiter VIIIF engine was a vast improvement of the Liberty engine of the DH9A. The Wapiti was not as easy to control on the ground in the wind, nor did it have wheel brakes, but in the air the Wapiti was vastly superior. For example it took only four hours to reach Kohat from Karachi, as

against nine hours in the DH9A. Although other squadrons were to receive new types of aircraft during the decade, No. 60 Squadron would retain its Wapitis until the outbreak of war. By May 1930 the squadron was fully operational with its new aircraft.

Inspired by Mahatma Ghandi and the all-Indian Congress, members of the Frontier Youth League began to wear red uniforms. On 20 April the leader of the 'Red Shirts', Abdul Ghaffar Khan, held a large meeting of members of the league at Utmanzai near Charsadda, where a highly seditious drama was performed by boys of the Azad school. This led to the arrest of Ghaffar Khan and nine other leaders, and widespread rioting followed. An armoured car was burned out and Peshawar native city was in the hands of Congress volunteers for ten days. As agitation spread, more volunteers joined the Red Shirts, and trouble broke out in Kohat, which was eventually contained by the authorities. However, in Waziristan trouble flared up involving the Madda Khel tribe, which invested the Datta Khel Tochi Scout Post near the headwaters of the Tochi river. On 12 May five aircraft were detached from Kohat to Miranshah. The lashkars around Datta Khel Post were bombed, and demonstration flights were made over Kaniguram as a warning to the Mahsuds. On 14 May warnings were issued to the Madda Khel and Kiddar Khel. When these warnings went unheeded the villages of these tribes were promptly bombed by aircraft of Nos 27 and 60 Squadrons. Thirty houses and seven tribesmen were killed. Due to this prompt air action Tochi valley remained quiet for the rest of the year.

Unrest in the Vale of Peshawar spread to Bajour, north of Peshawar, the Red Shirts having stirred up the Mohmand tribe, and it was necessary, on 9 June, to bomb a lashkar of 1,000 tribesmen, as well as their villages north of the Swat river, on 16 May. The trouble in early June was even more serious when reconnaissance disclosed approximately 2,000 men advancing on the outskirts of Peshawar. They were repulsed by the Army and harried from the air as they retreated across the Khajori Plain on 6 June.

Accurate bombing of tribesmen moving up precipitous valleys, particularly with the bombsights and equipment then available, was difficult. In wooded country they could be seen only directly from above the trees. The bomb aimer then had to estimate the height before the bomb run was commenced, then the pilot would have to go round again to observe the results, unless his aircraft was being followed by another that could make observations instead, but without an intercom corrections could not be communicated to the bomb aimer. The tribesmen did not sit passively and take punishment. The Afridis on hill outposts, equipped with modern rifles, could hit a pilot or air gunner if the aircraft was not flying across their front, requiring a deflecting shot from them. Flying Officer Stroud, from Risalpur, was killed by a shot from behind while the bomb aimer lay prone at the bombsight, and the latter succeeded in getting the aircraft with the dead pilot back to base. He had no rudder pedals, only a detachable control column to bring the aircraft down to a safe landing, and he was justly awarded a DFM.

The Mahsuds were active again in July, when a lashkar of 3,000 tribesmen invested a post of the South Waziristan Scouts on the 6th. From inside the Sorarogha Post a 'director arrow' was used to signal to Army Cooperation aircraft. From 7 to 9 July attacks on the post continued, when the tribesmen were witnessed using an ancient cannon. On 12 July the Shabi Khel surrendered, but the Badinszai were still active, and four squadrons were involved in bombing their villages on the 14th. Eventually this sub-tribe surrendered, followed by the Nazar Khel on 27 July. B Flight of the squadron alone carried out thirty-six attacks between 14 May and 24 July.

The troubles continued into August, and martial law had to be declared on the 15th in the Peshawar District, and remained in force until 24 January 1931. It is a tribute to one of the squadron's airmen that the George Cross was awarded for gallantry during the operations described above. The actual citation that appears in the squadron history is quoted in full here:

262370 Leading Aircraftman Robert Ewing DOUGLAS, Royal Air Force. For conspicous gallantry displayed in an attempt to save the lives of two fellow airmen at Kohat, India, on 13 June 1930. An aeroplane proceeding on patrol with a crew of two and a load of live bombs stalled shortly after leaving the ground and crashed on the edge of the aerodrome, immediately bursting into flames. Leading Aircraftman Douglas, who witnessed the crash, was the first to arrive on the scene of the accident and found the air gunner lying two yards from the wreckage, his clothes burning badly. These flames Douglas quenched with a hand extinguisher, and, after disentangling part of the gun equipment from the injured man's person, dragged him clear of the machine with the assistance of another airman who had arrived on the scene, and, after subduing a renewed burst of flames in his clothing, got him on board the ambulance. He then turned his attention to the pilot in the burning machine and had approached to within twelve yards of the wreckage when the first of the bombs exploded. Realizing that there was no hope of finding the pilot alive, he started to get clear and was thirty yards away when a second bomb exploded. In advancing so close to the flames this airman took a grave risk, as he was fully aware that the aircraft contained live bombs of a powerful type.

1931

Air Marshal Sir John Steel KBE, CB, CMG relieved Sir Geoffrey Salmond as AOC India in February. Salmond had been in post for five years, the longest to serve in that capacity, and he was able to witness the Delhi Air Display before his departure. He had organized this event, which celebrated the official opening of New Delhi, and No. 60 Squadron took part. The display featured formation cross-overs, which were difficult without radio contact between formation leaders.

Routine duties during this period included inspections of landing grounds, daily meteorological flights and refuelling exercises at Arawali. Liaison was maintained with the Tochi Scouts during the two months' detachment made each year to Miranshah by each flight, and the Resident in Waziristan was flown there frequently. His name was Mr Gould, later Sir Basil Gould. Finally, air experience was given, not only to Army personnel but also to headmen and maliks on the recommendation of the District Commissioner. The hillmen were much better than plainsmen in adapting themselves once airborne, and they could point out their villages from the air.

As the cold weather period approached, Flight Lieutenant McBain and Flight Lieutenant Lart, commanding B and C Flights respectively, were posted after a long spell with the squadron. Flight Lieutenant Britton DFC and Flight Lieutenant Stemp took over their posts. The latter had given flying instruction to the Prince of Wales, who would become Edward VIII, and his brother, who would become George VI. One of the sergeant pilots was R.A. Falcolner, who retired as a squadron leader with an OBE and a DFM.

1932

The squadron's commander, Squadron Leader Neville, departed the squadron on 20 February, to be replaced by Squadron Leader K.M.St.C.G. Leask MC at the end of a 4½-year tour, an exceptionally long tour served with distinction. He returned to command the fighter station at North Weald in the rank of wing commander. Leask had come from the Aircraft Depot, where he had been employed in an engineering capacity. He had been an outstanding fighter pilot during the Great War, when he achieved fifteen victories in action, flying SE5A Scouts. [As Air Vice-Marshal Leask he claimed a few balloons in addition to the enemy aircraft shot down.] Pilot Officer M.W.S. Robinson, who joined No. 60 Squadron in March, was also to reach high rank.

No sooner had Squadron Leader Leask assumed command than the squadron was involved in minor operations over Mohmand country, commencing 8 March. In the absence of accurate maps, villages had to be identified from air photographs, and operations continued until 30 May without casualties. There was some feudal infighting between the Upper and Lower Mohmands, and in July the Halimzai Mohmands had to appeal for help against the Upper Mohmands, whose lashkars dispersed when the government acceded to their request. Refuelling exercises on 23 August disclosed water contamination of the petrol, probably as a result of repairs to the pipelines in the bulk fuel installation. It was thought that this had been rectified until Flight Lieutenant Britton, Flying Officer Robinson and Sergeant Parks took off. Britton's and Robinson's engines both cut out and they crashed in the bed of the Kurram River. Sergeant Parks had refuelled from an uncontaminated source and landed safely. Fortunately only minor injuries were sustained by both pilots and air gunners. It is interesting to note how an element in the design of the Wapiti aircraft contributed to these crashes. The high undercarriages of these aircraft gave them a high ground angle. Since the petrol tank was mounted in front of the pilot, the feed pipe to the carburettor was attached to the bottom of the tank. When the water was drained away by disconnecting the pipe, a small reservoir of water was retained between the pipe union and the back of the tank.

There was a new development in the last quarter of 1932. The overland march to relieve Chitral was always a trial, when the tribesmen would do their best to lay

The road to Chitral – ideal country for ambushing the relief column, and the aircraft must avoid flying into the mountainside, sometimes in appalling weather.

ambushes, and the resident squadrons were always busy bombing until the various tribes submitted. The latest example of operations to keep open the route took place between 17 and 23 September against the Shamozai Mohmands. Bombing had to continue until 16 October before the tribe submitted and withdrew from the Relief Column's line of march. The Kabul rescue had shown what could be done by bomber/transports, and a bomber transport flight had been formed. This unit was equipped with four Vickers Valentias, which could transport twenty-two fully armed soldiers. Even with full throttle it required great pilot skill to negotiate a heavily laden aircraft through valleys with precipitous mountain passes at 11,000 ft altitude, but once the flight was in business, Chitral and Gilgit could be relieved without the recurring problem of keeping open the line of march.

1933

After only eleven months in command, Squadron Leader Leask was on his way again. His engineering skills were in demand and he went to Delhi in January to Air Headquarters as Senior Engineering Staff Officer. Squadron Leader A.D. Pryor came from the Aircraft Park, Lahore, on 10 January to take over command. He too would have only eleven months in command of the squadron, but during that time he made his mark in a domestic way. As President of the Mess Committee he developed the garden of the officers' mess, and came up with the idea of a swimming pool, which was built with the help of the Kohat Garrison Engineer at a much smaller cost than expected. On the airfield all-weather metalled runways were built. One ran from east to west parallel with the hangars, and a second, shorter strip was laid north to south on the west side of the airfield. This was an essential improvement due to the monsoons and winter rains, when the grassed areas of the airfield were unusable.

There were some minor operations in March when supporters of the ex-Amir Amanullah tried to restore him in Kabul, and tribal lashkars had to be broken up by air action. Two operations then began simultaneously, namely the Bajour and Mohmand. In the first of these, RAF operations alone were sufficient to achieve success. It was May, and the Khan of Khotkai, together with the Khan of Khar, tried to raise a rebellion against Nadir Shah, Amir of Afghanistan. The Khan of Khotkai was sheltering a pretender to the Afghan throne, and political measures and leaflet drops had proved ineffective, for, unlike the Khan of Khar, he would not submit. When RAF operations commenced it was again found that the maps were inaccurate, and photographs had to be relied upon. This came to light when Pilot Officer D.J.P. Lee, later Air Marshal Sir David Lee, could not find the target village from the map. Eventually the village was attacked by Wapitis (Nos 27 and 60 Squadrons) and

Harts (Nos 11 and 39 Squadrons). On 13 August the Khan of Khotkai submitted and the Pretender to the Afghan throne was expelled.

The tactics employed in these operations were firstly to use leaflet drops, and a flight of three aircraft would make demonstration flights over the affected area. Contact would be maintained with local police posts using Aldis lamps and Popham panels. If all else failed and bombing was authorized, a typical attack would involve the use of 112 lb bombs. The example of Khotkai above is not unusual, in that the villages made difficult targets, being small and situated on steep hillsides. Both oblique and vertical photographs would be taken, and these would disclose the amount of damage inflicted; as has been noted, they were extremely useful in updating maps. Casualties would generally be higher among the tribesmen. In operations carried out in connection with the building of a road to Ghalani, government casualties amounted to nine killed and nine wounded, whereas tribesmen lost forty of their number, with fifty-two wounded. Aircraft were hit nineteen times and one was forced down to be burned by tribesmen. The crew, however, escaped.

The year ended with Squadron Leader Pryor's posting to command RAF Upavon in Wiltshire. His place was taken by Squadron Leader R.T.B. Houghton AFC on 1 December. He had commanded No. 11 (B) Squadron, equipped with Hawker Harts.

1934

Another famous name, Basil Embry, was at that time a flight lieutenant on the squadron, and he was posted to No. 1 (Indian) Wing as Air Staff Officer. He had been a flight commander at the Central Flying School and had taught instrument flying. He developed 'the hood' for aircraft in India so that the pilots on the North-West Frontier could be kept more up to date, using training facilities normally found only back at home. He also went to a great deal of trouble preparing officers at Kohat for promotion and specialization examinations. Airmen who served on the squadron at this time could well end up as senior officers. An air gunner named LAC Watkins eventually retired as a wing commander. He was an exceptionally good bomb aimer and rugby player.

The use of the landing ground at Razmak provides an interesting example of the hazards of flying from an airstrip 6,600 ft above sea level in a mountainous area. The landing strip had a slope of 1:20 and was some 500 yards long. Landings were made uphill, for the Wapitis did not have brakes, and take-offs were made downhill. The Wapiti could not take off uphill in a loaded condition, so the procedure was to taxi the aircraft to the top of the slope, whereupon the air gunner would leap out and take hold of the wingtip. This was necessary to turn the aircraft round, but since the aircraft had no brakes it would immediately begin to gather speed downhill. This called for a great deal of fitness and agility on the part of the air gunner, who had to make it to his cockpit as the pilot began to open the throttles. Any delay in reaching flying speed would mean that the pilot would not clear the fort immediately below the end of the strip. The return flight would be to Miranshah where Nos 27 and 60 Squadrons maintained a detached flight between them from their main base at Kohat. This detachment was maintained throughout the 1930s.

At the end of the year the squadron was to repeat the formation flight to and from Singapore that had been carried out by four Wapitis of No. 28 (AC) Squadron in January 1933. The aim of these exercises was to see if Singapore could be quickly reinforced in an emergency from the nearest RAF formation. A competition took place between units of No. 1 (India) Wing to see which sub-unit (flight) could prepare the best operation order for the formation flight there and back. In November 1934 it was B Flight of the squadron that won the competition. A single streamlined long-range fuel tank was fitted between the undercarriage legs, and the petrol was pumped up into the main tank, giving the aircraft a further two hours' endurance. To activate the wind-driven pump it was necessary to pull off a piece of string holding the vane [shades of Heath Robinson!]. Once activated, therefore, it could not be stopped, and if the pilot made a mistake by trying to top up the main tank before it was sufficiently empty there was a risk of a burst. There was a 'tele-level' fuel gauge on the tank, but this usually under-read the true contents.

The route to Singapore led by Flight Lieutenant A.E. Paish, with LAC Keen as his wireless operator, went via Ambala, Cawnpore, Gaya, Dacca, Akyab, Rangoon, Mergui and Alor Star. It was after the take-off from Alor Star on 4 December that Paish's aircraft suffered a severe petrol leak. Paish was covered with petrol, and both men risked being overcome by fumes. This was the first occasion recorded in the history of the squadron that aircrew had 'hit the silk', and both men baled out. Asked afterwards why he climbed out of his cockpit, only to get back in again, LAC Keen replied that he had forgotten his cigarettes. The three remaining aircraft circled overhead as the Wapiti dived into a mangrove swamp, when it disappeared from view. They then returned to Alor Star to organize a rescue. Since Paish was not fit to continue, Flying Officer Coulson took over the leadership of the formation, and the three Wapitis reached Seletar airfield safely. The flight of 3,315 miles had taken 32 hours 55 minutes flying time, spread over six days, at an average speed of 100 mph.

1935

The year 1935 is perhaps best remembered for the earthquake at Quetta and its tragic consequences in loss of life. A detailed account of this incident appears in this chapter in the history of No. 5 Squadron, and so has been omitted from this narrative.

In March there were changes at the top, and Air Marshal Sir John Steel was replaced by Air Marshal Sir Edgar Ludlow-Hewitt, who would later take on Bomber Command in the lead-up to the Second World War. He would witness some of the most extensive active operations in the history of the North-West Frontier during his 2½-year tour. It was during this month that Flying Officer Rutter, later Air Vice-Marshal Rutter, would leave the squadron. In August there was serious trouble in Mohmand country when sub-tribes tried to destroy the Gandab valley road. The Haji of Turangzai and his three sons were behind this attempt, and a lashkar of 1,900 tribesmen was assembled. When it was found that the tribesmen were reluctant to evacuate their villages, and bombing was authorized, practice bombs were used. These would do little harm unless it was a direct hit, but they did give off a spectacular white cloud of stannic chloride. This was the policy of the use of minimum force. In this instance it did not have the desired effect, and the practice bombs were followed up with two HE bombs. An hour and a half later these were followed by attacks on specified targets. It took four days to get the tribesmen to evacuate their villages. Then it was the turn of the Safi tribe, with warning leaflets being dropped on 21st August. When bombing commenced, some delayed-action fuses were used to dissuade villagers from returning once the area had been evacuated. On 31 August there was a three-squadron demonstration. The government's aim, by advancing further into Mohmand country, was to remove the influence the Haji had on the other tribes. When the campaign against the Haji ended, the squadron returned to routine training, by which time everyone was busy for the forthcoming exercise, which was the complete squadron reinforcement of Singapore, due to take place in January 1936.

1936

The squadron reinforcement exercise was in fact postponed until February. This time two Valentias of the bomber transport flight would accompany the squadron with much-needed spares and skeleton ground crews. Experience had already shown that landing grounds were few and far between on the Malay peninsula, and facilities were rudimentary, communications poor and meteorological facilities almost non-existent. The squadron departed Kohat on 7 February and the formation was made up as follows:

OC Squadron	Squadron Leader R.T.B. Houghton AFC with Cpl Ryder
A Flight	Flight Lieutenant H.G.Wheeler with LAC Turner

B Flight

Flying Officer I.W. Bray with LAC Duffy

Flying Officer J.B.P. Thomas with LAC Sanderson

Flight Lieutenant A.E. Paish with LAC Keen [+cigarettes]

Flying Officer A.D. Isemonger with Cpl Watkins

Flying Officer W.H. Forbes-Mitchell with LAC Slatter

Flying Officer E.B.C. Davies with LAC Davis

C Flight

Flight Lieutenant L.W. Cannon with LAC Ashmore

Flying Officer J.Y. Humphreys with LAC Cronin

Flying Officer A.O.D. Fox with Cpl Wood

Sergeant Pilot R.F. Hunter with Sergeant Pilot Holloway.

On this particular reinforcement exercise the squadron's historians praise the qualities of the Westland Wapiti. Recounting how Flying Officer Thomas's aircraft was attacked by a large vulture, they speak of the inherent strength of the biplane structure. The incident resulted in the knocking out of an interplane strut and the entanglement of the bird in the flying wires. Flying Officer Thomas had to make a forced landing, and ran into a wall before the aircraft tipped up on its nose.

On leaving Delhi, C Flight was forced down to 500 feet by thick low cloud. When the cloud thickened further some 25 miles SE of Algarh, the formation broke up and Flying Officer Fox had turned away from the formation. When he was some 120 miles SE of Delhi, near a place called Etah, he flew into a hill. Thomas was killed and his air gunner, Corporal Wood, was awarded the Albert Medal for attempting to pull Flying Officer Fox from the burning wreckage, but lost his hand from burns. Attempting to read the names of railway stations was one means of maintaining the course, but even the Valentias were forced down to a landing because of the weather. Ten of the twelve squadron aircraft reached Singapore safely, in spite of the sad death of Flying Officer Fox and Flying Officer Thomas's crash. In order to carry out training at the destination, four of the squadron's aircraft had to have the long-range tanks removed. Both pilots and air gunners attended lectures, carried out practice bombing on a motor boat and learned about the coastal defence of Singapore. On the return journey two of the pilots from C Flight and and Squadron Leader Houghton had to divert to Delhi to attend the court of inquiry following the death of Flying Officer Fox.

Pilot Officer F.L. Newall, a pilot on C Flight, described life and flying training at Kohat at this time. He was clearly impressed with the swimming pool, tennis courts and squash courts, and the large garden with trees providing welcome shade and flowers. He had a high airy room with bathroom and dressing-room behind. The airfield was outside the cantonment, and the flying hours in the hot-weather routine were from 06.00 hrs to 12.00 hrs, and during the cooler months from 08.30 hrs to 13.30 hrs. As a newcomer Newall had to reach an operational standard as soon as possible with a period of concentrated flying. Ten hours' flying had to be completed before being allowed to carry a passenger, then forty more hours before night-flying commenced. Flying practice to 16,000 ft without oxygen meant sitting in an aircraft before take-off dressed in a Sidcot suit, only to get roasted once on the ground again. There were cross-country flights, air firing from front and rear guns, both air to air and air to ground. Camera guns were followed by firing live ammunition in air-to-ground practices. There was also instrument-flying, and high emphasis was placed on vertical photography, both 'pinpoint' and 'line overlay'. Photographic reconnaissance of the Unadministered Territory was an important duty, and it was possible to build up a Tribal Directory covering almost every village, and even the ownership of individual houses. This was very useful for political officers. Newall's opinion was that the Wapiti had become dated, and spares were sometimes difficult to obtain, but that it was probably the best type ever produced for frontier work.

On 14 May Squadron Leader Silvester replaced Squadron Leader Houghton as the CO of the squadron. Houghton had been in post for 2½ years and Silvester had come from the Aircraft Depot to command only until October, when his tour in India was complete. On 16 October Squadron Leader R.H. Carter then became CO of No. 60 Squadron. There was a considerable turnover among the other officers on the squadron. Flight Lieutenant Isemonger returned to the United Kingdom and Flying Officer Bray took over A Flight, while Flight Lieutenant Cannon remained with C Flight. Flying Officer Eversfield went to Lahore and Flying Officer Foster became the Squadron Adjutant. Five officers and all the flight sergeants on the station were leaving, while eight new pilot officers arrived, coming from such stations as Bircham Newton and Upper Heyford.

The first Armament Training Camp to be held in India took place in November 1936 at Drigh Road, Karachi, where everyone lived under canvas. There was high-level bombing and dive-bombing, together with air firing. This took place over the sea off Manora Point. An armoured motor boat known as HMS *Centurion* was the target of practice bombs. The motor boat was scaled up to represent a battleship so that if a bomb fell within eight yards either side of the target it was regarded as a hit. The squadron obtained good scores.

In the early autumn, trouble flared up in Waziristan which would continue almost without a break until 1939. The Faqir of Ipi declared himself Champion of Islam and called for a jihad against the British. A number of factors had contributed to his quickly gaining influence, and the political authorities pressed the Tori Khel to control the Faqir. The elder maliks advised the authorities that they could control neither him nor their own young men, but they would allow an Army column into the Lower Khaisora to evict the Faqir. However, the Army would be opposed. The advance began on 25 November, with No. 27 Squadron supporting the Bannu Column, which met the Razmak Column on the 26th at Biche Kashkai, retiring to Damdil the following day. During the advance 24 government troops were killed and 107 wounded. Of the tribesmen 41 were killed and 31 were badly wounded. The squadrons involved were Nos 5 and 27. Although the Faqir was evicted he conducted an ongoing war from his various hiding places, and this war continued almost without a break until 1939. The seriousness of the situation required the take-over of the political and military control of Waziristan, and this took place on 29 November 1936, with the GOC Northern Command, General Sir John Coleridge GCB, CMG, DSO, in command. A proscribed area was declared, and to cover the Army's advance into it a road was constructed to break it up. This road would be built from Mirali to Biche Kashkai and Dreghundari, east of the Shinki defile. The area was constantly patrolled by the RAF squadrons, who used 20 lb or 112 lb bombs against sheep, cattle and men moving in the proscribed area. Attacks below 2,500 ft were not permitted, for the tribesmen were no mean marksmen. This did make it more difficult for pilots to hit their targets, and so in 1937 the ceiling was reduced to 2,500 ft.

The Faqir of Ipi was active again in December, having mustered a lashkar of 700 Maddha Khel, Afghans and Wazirs, and some Mahsuds. The tribes were exhorted to commit hostile acts. The problems of bombing enemy strongholds are illustrated by attempts to bomb the fort at Arsal Kot, which was 132 yards long by 66 yards wide. Bets were laid on who could hit such a target using the old course-setting bombsight, bombing from 4,000 ft. Flight Lieutenant Cannon led 'C' Flight in an attack on the last day of 1936. His air gunner, Corporal Cronin, was an exceptionally able bomb aimer, and the rest of the flight followed to deliver a pattern of 230 lb bombs around the base of a tower that lay in the north-west corner of the fort. The blast cut off the top two-thirds of the watch tower, and so Wing Commander Lees lost his bet that the tower would still be standing at the end of three days' bombing. The squadron accordingly earned the nickname No. 60 (Demolition) Squadron. The successful bombing of Arsal Kot deprived the Faqir of a firm base in the Shaktu valley, and he had to occupy caves in the area from which to continue attacks upon government forces.

1937

On 2 February 1937 the GOC-in-C was able to restore the area to political control, following the success of the Khaisora operations of 1936/7. Although these operations were described as a success, the Faqir of Ipi continued to incite outlaws and issue anti-government propaganda. On 7 February the assistant political agent of North Waziristan was killed in an ambush while taking moneys amounting to £2,400 to pay the tribal Khassadars. The Mahsud tribe as a whole were held responsible and fined 32,000 rupees, or £5,625, and bombs were dropped on two villages in the Kazha valley. On 26 February the Faqir of Ipi was back at Arsal Kot, plotting against the government. Supported by Din Faqir of the Bhittani tribe, a lashkar of 400 assembled at the fort, and on 8 March 1937 the 1st Indian Division had to be brought into Waziristan to contain the deteriorating situation. When the Tori Khels failed to get the Faqir evicted from their territory, an air demonstration took place on 6 April over the Shaktu valley. Not only were single aircraft patrols from dawn to dusk maintained by Nos 27 and 60 Squadrons, but bombs were dropped on villages to keep people out of them, and others were timed to go off at night. A great deal of night-flying was undertaken.

On 9 April a convoy of forty-nine lorries was ambushed in the Shakur Tangi gorge, involving the Khoni Khel and Abdur Rahman Khel. Forty-seven were killed, including seven British officers, with fifty wounded, whereas the tribesmen lost only sixteen, with twenty-six seriously wounded. One of No. 5 Squadron's Wapitis was forced down when the pilot suffered a wound in the head and had rounds through the petrol tank. By the end of April Miranshah resembled a busy airport when No. 28 Squadron moved up to assist with operations. To add to the troubles experienced by the squadrons at this time was the discovery of water in a consignment of petrol, which produced crashes and engine failures. With further attacks on convoys, piquets and posts, the GOC was forced to reassume military control of Waziristan on 22 April with the aim of advancing in the Khaisora valley and on Arsal Kot to evict and if possible capture the Faqir. The 1st (Indian) Division cleared the Khaisora valley at a cost of five killed and forty-four wounded, compared with 257 casualties among the tribesmen. A largely extended proscribed area around Arsal Kot was covered by Nos 27 and 60 Squadrons, including the Sham plains to the north-east of the village. The mighty precipices of the Saraghar range had to be covered, where tribesmen were seen running between caves along narrow tracks.

On 6 May a 2,400-strong lashkar, half of whom were Afghans, assembled in the Khaisora-Shaktu area. By the

11th that number had swollen to 4,000 with the lashkar then assembled on the Sham plain. The 1st Infantry Brigade entered the plain, and the tribesmen were seen to retire to the south-west. The Army then established a military presence in the area and called the new base camp 'Coronation Camp' in celebration of the Coronation of King George VI. The Valentias, under command of Flight Lieutenant A.B. Begg, began to supply the camp by air drop, but the air currents over the drop zone were so strong that the parachutes were carried 3,000 ft above the aircraft before finally coming to ground. The complex of underground caves that had been used by the Faqir and his party were demolished, requiring 1,900 lb of gun cotton. The proscription ended in most areas by 30 May, with total Army casualties for the period 25 November 1936 to 30 May 1937 being 164 dead, including fifteen British officers, and 431 wounded. The tribesmen lost 715 killed and 657 injured.

But this did not bring the fighting to an end. When a decision was taken to open up the Tori Khel and Mahsud country with new roads, government forces found themselves confronting the Bhittani tribe. Attacks were made in the Bannu Administrative District, which called for punitive measures. Air action formed part of these measures, which brought the situation under control in three weeks. Heavy bombing of the villages of hostile tribesmen played a major part. When the Faqir of Ipi recommenced his activities in mid-June, determined efforts were made to capture him. In this the Tochi and Waziristan Scouts did not succeed, but they did capture Arsal Khan, owner of Arsal Kot and the Faqir's host.

On a lighter note there were squadron celebrations on the promotion of Wing Commander Lees to group captain and acting group commander. 'Nunky' Lees was a very popular officer who was carried shoulder high to his bungalow after the celebration guest night. With an improvement in the security situation, No. 28 Squadron was able to return to Ambala, leaving just one flight at Miranshah. But then it was reported that the Faqir of Ipi was again ensconced in a new complex of five caves on the slopes of Prekari Sar, in Shabi Khel Mahsud country, twenty miles south of Mirali. On 3 August he moved again. The squadron played its part in keeping him on the move by bombing and demonstration flights. On 23 August, for example, thirty aircraft led by Flight Lieutenant Ubee, and known as 'Ubee's Armada', made a demonstration formation flight over Shawal and Bhittani country.

The Government was intent on disarming the tribes in its drive to pacify them. At the end of August the Western Mahsuds came to terms, and the Tori Khel submitted on 10 September. By this time the Faqir of Ipi had a new hideout west of Razmak, and an area around Gembakal was proscribed between 25 September and 8 October. No. 27 Squadron's detached flight at Miranshah, together with B Flight of No. 60 Squadron,

carried out operations in the area. Life was not easy at Manzai in 1937. Sited on a treeless desert plateau, it was the hottest forward base on the Frontier. In one particular week the temperature did not drop below 120ºF. All ranks were under canvas, and there were cases of heat exhaustion. In spite of this, operations continued against hostile tribes. The Bhittani tribe submitted in mid-November, and the Faqir was becoming more isolated, but the foregoing paragraphs tell of an ongoing war, with tribes submitting to government demands only to cause further trouble after a period of quiet.

By way of a change an early phase of mobilization plans was put into operation. No. 60 Squadron's planned role was to supply coastal defence flights around the coast of India. Long-range petrol tanks were obtained, together with special R/T and W/T long- and short-range sets. The word was that modern aircraft were on their way to India and the squadron could get Blenheims or Wellesleys. Since the Wapiti was heavy on the controls, the squadron needed aircraft with lighter controls to prepare pilots for new aircraft, and Hawker Harts were issued so that conversion training could begin on 24 September in anticipation of squadrons' re-equipment.

1938

It was policy for the reinforcement of Singapore to be carried out by one squadron from Kohat and one from Risalpur It was the turn of Nos 60 and 39 Squadrons to undertake this task in 1938. A reserve aircraft, pilot and air gunner would be provided by No. 27 Squadron, in this case Flight Lieutenant D. Newman. The squadron took off on 11 January, led by Squadron Leader J.H.T. Simpson, with Corporal D.H. Davis as his air gunner. The flights were as follows:

A Flight	Flight Lieutenant I.W. Bray
	Flying Officer F.R. Foster
	Pilot Officer J.H. Giles
B Flight	Flight Lieutenant D. Newman (No. 27 Squadron)
	Flying Officer W.R. Selkirk
	Pilot Officer R. Backwell-Smith
C Flight	Flight Lieutenant E.L.A. Walter
	Flying Officer F.L. Newall and Corporal Cronin
	Pilot Officer A.B. Olney and Corporal Everett
	Pilot Officer J.F. Grey and LAC Petch
Equipment Officer:	Pilot Officer C.R.B. Wigfall

The crews enjoyed mostly good weather and a trouble-free flight. A Valentia accompanied the flight with spares back-up. Indeed the only part of the flight that tested the pilots was the landing and take-off at Victoria Point. It was surrounded to the east and south-east by jungle-covered slopes that ran up to the edge of the airfield. When the wingtip tube of one of the aircraft was damaged on landing, it was possible to fashion a replacement from wood from the jungle. That it was possible for a resourceful rigger to carry out such a repair may remind the reader of the relative simplicity of construction of the Wapiti. The squadron arrived at Seletar, Singapore, on 15 January 1938, to be joined by No. 39 Squadron at Tengah on 28 January.

The reinforcement squadrons then took part in the Far East Combined Manoeuvres. These started on 2 January 1938, and eight squadrons, including No. 84 Squadron from Shaibah, took part. The manoeuvres were overseen by Air Commodore A.W. Tedder, the AOC Far East. Trenchard had worked hard during his time as Chief of the Air Staff to involve the RAF in the defence of Singapore. The Army and Navy were prepared to place their faith in huge 15 in. guns, which would be used to deter a seaborne Japanese invasion. Eight such guns were favoured, but Trenchard had argued that torpedo-bombers would provide the most effective means of destroying or disabling enemy warships or aircraft-carriers. The other two services argued that reinforcement by air would mean having a chain of staging posts across the Middle and Far East. A compromise was reached in 1926 that only three guns would be installed, while the other five guns would wait, pending further consideration. It would take two years to clear mangrove swamps to construct a runway and flying-boat slipway at Seletar, and the RAF's Far East Flight with Southamptons arrived in February 1928. It would not be until 1934, following Japanese aggression in Manchuria and China, that the Vildebeest torpedo-bombers of No. 100 Squadron would arrive in the colony. The irony is that when Singapore did fall to the Japanese in 1942, the enemy soldiers bicycled down the Malay peninsula to attack from the landward side, not from the sea. In war the boldest moves are often made when one side does what the other least expects it to do, like Lawrence of Arabia, who attacked Aqaba from the desert, when the Turkish guns were pointed out to sea.

On its return to Kohat the squadron was immediately involved in operations against its arch-enemy, the Faqir of Ipi, who was still in Mada Khel country. The usual warning of impending bombardment was given on 3 March. Aircraft from Kohat and Risalpur bombed Wucha Kazha, Sar Kalai, Stara Kazha and Sarrum. Wing Commander Oliver led the attack on Sar Kalai, and he went in low with LAC Fudge of No. 27 Squadron as his air gunner. Delayed-action 250 lb bombs were dropped, but there was particularly heavy rifle fire, which visibly damaged the wings and rudder. Although Oliver got his aircraft safely back to Miranshah, the undercarriage gave way on landing. The laughter at seeing the CO crash his

aircraft stopped when the battle damage to the aircraft was inspected. Fudge got a DFM for his part in the action. Thirty-four raids were carried out by the squadron against Sar Kalai, but the rest of March was quiet.

Personnel changes in the spring of 1938 were as follows:

Group Captain N.H. Bottomley posted to Home Establishment

Group Captain C.C. Darley posted to Command No. 1 (Indian) Wing, vice Group Captain Bottomley

Squadron Leader C.B. Hughes to command No. 60 Squadron

Flying Officer A.E. Saunders became Adjutant of No. 60 Squadron

Flying Officer Newall assumed command of C Flight, No. 60 Squadron

Flight Lieutenant Walter of No. 60 Squadron to Home Establishment

Flying Officer Young of No. 60 Squadron to Lahore as Station Adjutant

Pilot Officer G.H. Goodwin joined C Flight, No. 60 Squadron

Pilot Officer Dobson joined C Flight, No. 60 Squadron.

Squadron Leader Simpson's wife had become seriously ill while he was away in Singapore. It was therefore decided, on compassionate grounds, to post Squadron Leader Simpson to Home Establishment, and he became Senior Engineering Officer at No. 3 FTS South Cerney.

The Faqir of Ipi was still at large, but he was contained in Madda Khel country, which cut him off from much of Waziristan behind a long, high range of inaccessible mountains. That did not stop the Madda Khel joining in anti-government activity to frustrate the building of MT (motor transport) roads. The Faqir of Ipi was keen to see the Madda Khel taking action. The authorities did not want was to see a rise in tribal activity when RAF squadrons were being re-equipped with new aircraft and the international situation was deteriorating. All leave in India was cancelled, and four days of bombing was heavy on the Madda Khel village of the Sherani, in the headwaters of the Tochi river.

The squadron cooperated with Nos 27, 11 and 39 Squadrons, plus the bomber transport flight, in bombing Sherani. The bomber transport flight alone was able to drop 500 lb of bombs. The squadron's Wapitis were in a poor state through damage and a lack of spares, a situation that had deteriorated since 1937. Be that as it may, the attacks continued, and Flying Officer Newall managed to drop 1½ tons of bombs in four days. Only buildings on the periphery of the village remained intact, and five other villages were destroyed. Undaunted, the Madda Khel assembled a lashkar of 300 men in late May, and the squadron had to bomb at night

No. 60 Squadron at Miranshah in June 1938.

as well as by day to keep up the pressure. There was always the risk that pilots might stray into Afghan air space, which was a court martial offence. An account of one such raid taken verbatim from the squadron history is of Flying Officer Newall's personal experience:

I went off at 20.00 hrs with twelve 20 lb bombs and two parachute flares. We had not seen the sun much for about ten days and there was quite a haze. The moon was nearly full but not strong enough to show up the ground. I got to Miranshah at about 8,000 ft and tried to follow the Tochi river westwards. I rather lost myself, crossed it at right angles, then followed it along and got into some clouds coming up from the west. Dropped one parachute [i.e. flare] but was none the wiser where I was, so I might have dropped a bomb on Afghanistan, thereby causing a situation! So I flew back to try and pick up some landmark on the river; then tried to Datta Khel Fort and saw something like it. Clouds were still coming up so I decided the area was covered in cloud between eight and ten thousand feet, which was between 4/5,000 ft above the river and considerably less above the surrounding hills. I dropped the other flare and came home, landing at 23.00 hrs. We used the new airfield floodlight for the first time in India, instead of the oil flares.

These operations continued to the end of June 1938, when the Madda Khel submitted to government demands and evicted the Faqir of Ipi, who then moved

to Kharre. In July tribesmen attacked Bannu cantonment and city, setting fire to the bazaar; the Kohat road was blocked nightly and telephone wires cut; Miranshah was attacked on 8 July. When the Faqir left Kharre for the Mastoi valley, he was bombed in his new location.

In August medals were awarded to pilots and crews for their part in operations on the North-West Frontier:

Squadron Leader Embry – Distinguished Service Order
Flying Officers Dudgeon, Cryer and Beresford – Distinguished Flying Cross
Flight Lieutenant Newall, Flying Officer Foster, Flight Sergeant Panton and Corporal D. Davis – Mentioned in Dispatches

An additional clasp to the North-West Frontier Medal 1937–1939 was awarded to all those who took part in these operations.

There was some excitement for the squadron due to the Munich Crisis when an order was received for a move to Singapore. The squadron personnel were all packed up and mess bills were paid when the crisis passed. The movement order was cancelled at 20.30 hrs on 30 September. The Faqir never did give up his hostile acitivities, even though he had been offered free pardon by the Government of India. Throughout the Second World War the Madda Khel remained the most hostile of the tribes and continued to harbour the Faqir. With No. 60 Squadron moving to coastal defence duties, the new Indian Air Force took over the duties on the North-West

Frontier, thus relieving the RAF squadrons, which were being prepared for war. No. 60 Squadron left Kohat for Ambala on 2 March 1939, having completed 3,000 operational flying hours that year. The final paragraph from the squadron history sums up its contribution to keeping the peace during the inter-war years:

Thus ended the second phase of the history of No. 60 Squadron RAF. In nineteen years on the North-West Frontier the squadron had seen action in some degree practically every year, and it had taken part in five major campaigns to keep the King-Emperor's peace among the turbulent Frontier tribes. In that time, often working and flying at great pressure in extremes of heat and cold with outdated aircraft, members of Sixty had been awarded one Empire Gallantry Medal, converted to the George Cross, and twenty-seven other honours or awards.

NO. 70 SQUADRON

Usquam
(Anywhere)

AIRCRAFT
Vickers Victoria IV, V & VI
Vickers Valentia

1930

October   On the 31st Wing Commander Blount OBE, MC assumed command of the squadron.

November   Cross-country flights were flown on the 8th.

1931

January   Routine training activities.

February   More cross-country flights. [The record book only records the flights with the pilots who flew them.]

March   On the 16th Wing Commander Blount carried out tests with new parachute flares.

April   Executive operations [but the diary does not say where. One aircraft which landed in Quaradagh valley after a forced landing spent six days on the ground. The take-off run had been sufficiently cleared of boulders and stones to effect a take-off.]

June   A report on the hours flown that month by day was 340 hours and 12 hours by night. Stores carried during the month amounted to 12,831 lb, and the number of passengers was 366. Forced-landings were seven in number. The squadron transported HM King Faisal to Amman. Two days later he was deplaned at Baghdad West.

July   There were six forced landings during the month. The Command Training Officer visited the squadron to examine all pilots. There was an organizational change when the job of the adjutant was divided into two, with an operational adjutant and a disciplinary one. Flight Lieutenant Davies took over as the operational adjutant.

August   During the month there was one forced landing, and 16,820 lb of freight were carried, together with 647 passengers. There was a Trade Test Board held during the month. In the examination for LAC there were thirteen passes and eight failures. For AC1 there were four passes and one failure.

December   A flight was made by two Victorias to get stretcher cases from Bileh. This operation was carried out under conditions of extreme difficulty due to the waterlogged state of the ground.

1932

February   There were no active operations. A total of 148 passengers were carried and the hours flown were 314 by day and ten by night. Long-distance communications flights were made and the Squadron Armament Officer had to devise a simple carrier for dropping bombs.

April   Active operations comprised bombing raids on Raizan in the operational area of Kurdistan, operating from Hinaidi. 20 lb and Cooper bombs were dropped. Experimental loudspeaker equipment was carried in the Victorias and was used to have an affect on the disaffected. [The Adjutant had a sense of humour.]

1933

December   The initial equipment of C Flight was increased during the month to four Victorias. The total flying hours for the month were 357, which included 93 hours on a flight from the United Kingdom. Personnel and stores were carried to Shaibah for the Iraq Levies.

1934 and 1935

Operations were nil.

1936

October   On the 29th and 30th Al Fariq Bekkir Sidqi's military coup was accomplished. Jafar Pasha was murdered and Nuri-as-Sa'id, the Foreign Minister, with his wife and son and son's wife took refuge in the British Embassy. His Excellency the Ambassador became anxious about their safety and they were all secretly transferred to the British General Hospital in the evening. On the 31st at 02.30 hrs Squadron Leader G. Findlay DFC and Squadron Leader J. Bussey proceeded to the Sisters' Mess to collect Nuri and his family, and escorted them to the squadron hangars in the greatest secrecy. At 03.30 hrs a Valentia, piloted by Flight Lieutenant I. McL. Cameron, left for Egypt with the party, and the pilot took the precaution of proceeding southwards until well clear of Hinaidi. The aircraft refuelled at Landing Ground H3 to reach Heliopolis safely on the afternoon of the 31st.

December The squadron had flown 5,600 hours for the year, with a total of 3,608 flights. 7,141 passengers were carried.

1937

March On the 5th ten officers and ten airmen pilots successfully completed the conversion course on twin-engined aircraft with the expansion of the RAF. [That is taken to mean that the RAF's policy was to prepare pilots for a greater number of multi-engined aircraft into service.] The twenty pilots returned to their unit fully qualified as T/E [twin-engined] pilots.

May On the 24th at 21.00 hrs a warning order was received from the Air Ministry that one flight of No. 70 (Bomber/Transport) Squadron was wanted for service in India at very short notice. Two hours later an executive order was received that that duty was to be supply dropping, with evacuation of casualties. On the 25th at 16.45 hrs four aircraft left Hinaidi under the command of Squadron Leader J. Bussey *en route* for Karachi.

September On the 10th Wing Commander W.R. Ackland DFC, AFC was admitted to the RAF General Hospital at Hinaidi, and he was discharged on the 27th for the purpose of proceeding to the United Kingdom on absorption leave. On the 29th he left Alexandria in the Imperial Airways flying-boat 'Coutier'. On the 10th, while attempting a landing at Athens, the flying-boat crashed, killing Wing Commander Ackland. Wing Commander G. Findlay assumed command of the squadron.

October On the 8th the Unit HQ opened at Dhibban, the move of the squadron from Hinaidi having been completed. A detached flight of the squadron went to Manzai and Risalpur for operations on the North-West Frontier.

1939

March On the 1st Wing Commander J.W. Merer took over command of the squadron from Wing Commander Broughall MC, DFC, who left for Home Establishment on the 3rd.

April On the 5th a Valentia, conveying officers of the Blenheim delivery flight, who had been ferrying aircraft from Thorney Island to No. 55 Bomber Squadron.

May Transportation in May was to various destinations. There was the sad death of No. 566121

Sergeant Phillips R.C., a pilot/fitter II, who had been temporarily detached from No. 70 Squadron to Communications Flight, Habbaniya. He crashed on landing a Gordon aircraft. On his first attempt to land he struck the ground heavily, damaging an oleo leg. He took off again, and after a second circuit of the aerodrome he landed the aircraft satisfactorily, but the shock of landing forced the damaged oleo leg through the petrol tank, and the aircraft tipped over onto a wingtip after coming to rest. The immediate action was for the pilot to switch off the fuel cocks, but the aircraft suddenly burst into flames. Two passengers managed to scramble out and were taken to hospital with slight burns, but Sergeant Phillips was so badly burned that he died the following day.

June On the 2nd the funeral of Sergeant Phillips took place in the afternoon in the RAF cemetery, Habbaniya. The same month the pilot of a Gordon lost his way and landed in Turkey. The pilot was allowed to take off to return to Iraq but crashed short of petrol a few miles north of Mosul. The crew was unhurt.

August During the hot weather months (May to August) the health of the squadron was good, but there were some cases of sandfly fever. On the 21st at 14.00 hrs the War Plan was put into operation. The 23rd was mobilization day and the scheme was initiated and completed by the 26th. Deployment to Helwan began on the 27th at 07.00 hrs. [Helwan was the squadron's war station.]

September All RAF units in Egypt were placed on active service on the 4th. In view of the comparative obsolescence of the Valentia, the role of No. 70 Squadron, in the event of operations against Italy, was to be confined to night-bombing attacks on objectives in Libya, using advanced landing grounds in the Western Desert. This would be on an 'as required' basis, and the use of the landing grounds would be to extend the effective range. The aircraft were to be used singly, together with aircraft of No. 216 Squadron. The original intention in the War Plan had been to form a bomber/transport wing, with wing headquarters and No. 70 Squadron stationed at Helwan and No. 216 Squadron at Heliopolis. In the event No. 70 Squadron would be equipped with Wellingtons the following year to become a true bomber unit. It would not return to the transport role until its re-formation at Kabrit in May 1948. No. 216 Squadron was to remain a transport squadron, and is still in that role today, equipped with Tristars.

NO. 84 SQUADRON

Scorpiones pungunt
(Scorpions sting)

AIRCRAFT
Westland Wapiti
Vickers Vincent
Bristol Blenheim I

1930

January/February The operations record book is unreadable. Virtually all the pages for the first two months of the year have been double-typed.

July The rest of the month was occupied by overhauls, returning machines to the aircraft depot for repairs and collecting substitutes. From the 25th of the month to 5 August the squadron cricket team had won their round in the Basra District 'RAF' and 'Open' competitions, then proceeded to Hinaidi and played on ten consecutive days, losing both the semi-final rounds to Air Headquarters in the 'Open' and to C Depot in the 'RAF' Cup. During this period the highest temperatures were recorded all over the country, reaching 129 °F in Basra and 122°F in Baghdad and Shaibah. At the end of the month two Wapitis were allotted to the squadron to be fitted with floats.

August On the 15th these Wapitis arrived for experimental use in the Marsh country and the Hammar lakes.

September On the 24th, while landing at night, Flying Officer M.J. Ducray turned over violently in a Wapiti Mk IIA and was slightly injured. On the 29th the AOC, Sir Brooke Popham, paid a farewell visit to the units in the area. He presented the squadron with the Squadron Leader A.A.B. Thompson Air Gunnery Cup, which had been won in the annual classification shoot with an average for the squadron of 34%.

October From the 27th of the month to 11 October a composite flight of four aircraft flew to Syria for a liaison visit and to attend the Fête du Regiment of the 37th Air Regiment Aviation. The pilots were Squadron Leader H. Stewart, Flying Officer R.A.T. Stowell, Flying Officer J.S. Outhwaite and Sergeant Monk. [Reference to the history of No. 55 Squadron in this chapter discloses that Flying Officer Stowell had reached the rank of squadron leader by 1938 and was appointed squadron commander of that unit on 23 March.]

December Between the 8th and the 10th C Flight was equipped with Wapiti Mk II aircraft. Between the 17th and the 19th the three flights were detached to Busayiah for night reconnaissances carried out in the Al-Amghar district to familiarize pilots with tracks and landmarks.

1931

January On the 6th Squadron Leader Stewart, while attempting to land during night-flying by the light of Flying Officer Stowell's flare, crashed. His machine turned over and caught fire. His passenger, LAC Wood, was pulled out with minor burns but Squadron Leader Stewart was killed. The funeral was held Basra cemetary on the 6th of the month. Squadron Leader R.C. Hardstaff took over command of the squadron, vice Flight Lieutenant Drummond.

March The squadron took over its new area, which then took in the whole of Iraq south of latitude 32 deg. N. On the 24th two Wapitis flown to Basra were converted to floatplanes and training of pilots on floatplanes commenced.

July From the 13th to the 17th reconnaissance flights were carried out at Rumaitha amd Nasiriyah and Suqash-Shuyikh on account of reported demonstrations by tribesmen. In each case the district reconnoitred was reported quiet. On account of the General Strike (15 July), outbreaks in Basrah and Ashar. These places were put out of bounds. The Iraq Army garrison was dispatched to the affected area. This meant substitution of the normal Iraqi Army camp guard with RAF personnel. The RAF guard was withdrawn on the return of the native troops on the 22nd. On the 17th three Victorias conveying a party of Iraq police arrived from Hinaidi; two of these machines landed at Basra landing ground, the other landed at Shaibah. The police were then conveyed to Ashar by lorry. On the 28th an outbreak of chlolera in a ship in the port of Margil was notified by the local authorities. The necessary precautionary measures were taken and all personnel in Shaibah cantonment were innoculated. Restrictions were placed on the supply of certain foodstuffs and on the movements of native personnel. The long-distance Wapitis were received by the unit on the 28th.

September On the 3rd the long-distance Wapitis were tested on a flight to Mosul, occupying 8 hours, and maximum duration was 11 hours. Between the 17th and 19th the squadron won the Sassoon Bombing Cup competition at Hinaidi, obtaining an average of 48 yards from the centre of the target.

October There was an outbreak of rabies at the Armoured Car Section, Makina, on the 3rd, requiring more precautionary measures.

1932

January On the 7th the Under-Secretary of State for Air, Sir Philip Sassoon, visited various units both outbound and on the return during a visit to India.

June   On the 3rd assistance was given to a French Orient airliner that had been force-landed in a salt marsh 25 miles south-east of Shaibah, a spot unapproachable from the land. Machines dropped supplies and matting, which was spread over the soft earth, permitting the airliner to take off successfully. The same day the new transmitting station at Shaibah was opened.

September   Group Captain A.D. Cunningham CBE, Senior Air Staff Officer at Air Headquarters, arrived from Hinaidi on the 13th and was flown to various landing grounds in the Southern Desert during his few days' stay.

December   The squadron was involved in a survey of the Kuwait area from December 1932 to January 1933.

1933

January   The Secretary of State for Air, the Marquess of Londonderry, inspected the squadron on the 25th. Dual instruction was given on Wapiti floatplanes at No. 203 (FB) Squadron to all available pilots on the 31st. Total flying hours for January were 344.

February   On the 3rd Squadron Leader P.L. Plant proceeded to Paris on leave and resigned his commission while on leave and did not return to the squadron. Flight Lieutenant A.E. Arnold DFC assumed temporary command of the unit.

May   Squadron Leader S.F. Vincent arrived from Home Establishment on the 20th to assume command of the squadron.

July   Between the 19th and the 23rd B Flight flew to Sharjah to make demonstration flights in consequence of a message from Airways that there was slight trouble between the Sheikh and the Bedouins.

August to December   Routine squadron training. The total flying hours for 1933 were 5,323, which was the highest annual figure recorded since 1927.

1934

January   From the 2nd to the 10th A Flight, consisting of three Wapitis and three Vildebeests, which had been attached to the squadron for trials, carried out a long-distance flight to Egypt. On the return journey they flew non-stop Heliopolis–Hinaidi. On the 24th a cypher signal was received from AHQ ordering the remainder of the squadron that had not gone on the Singapore flight to stand by following reported trouble at Sharjah between the Sheikh of Ajam and Sharjah. All eight aircraft were ready by the 25th, with long-distance tanks, but when there were no further developments the squadron stood down.

February   The Singapore flight returned to Shaibah.

1935

May   Flying Officer J.H. Supple died in Sick Quarters, Makina, on the 28th from malignant malaria, and was buried at 18.00 hrs on the following day in the British Cemetery, Basra.

October   From the 9th to the 11th ten aircraft of the squadron had been engaged in a search for three Moths of the Bombay Flying Club, which had got lost on their way to Shaibah from Baghdad. Extensive search of the Southern Desert, in cooperation with aircraft of Nos 30, 55 and 70 Squadrons, bore fruit when the missing aircraft were located fifty miles north of Ansab by aircraft of B Flight of this squadron.

December   The squadron took delivery of dual Vincent aircraft from the Aircraft Depot prior to being equipped with this type. [Many of the months of 1935 are simply recorded in the ORB as 'nil entry'.]

1936

January   A search was carried out in a westerly direction on the 2nd for a French aircraft, F-ANRY, and nine squadron aircraft were involved. The search had extended 200 miles from Shaibah when a signal was received that the aircraft had been located in Egypt.

1937

January   Twelve Vincents left for Singapore under the command of Squadron Leader Fogarty and arrived according to schedule on the 24th less two aircraft, K.4113 and K.4119, which had suffered damage to the bottom starboard mainplanes at Cawnpore and Rangoon respectively. Coastal defence training and combined-operations exercises were carried out while at Singapore between 21 January and 5 February.

March   On the 12th Squadron Leader G.H.A. Stevens assumed command of the squadron, vice Squadron Leader Fogarty.

May   On the 18th Air Vice-Marshal C.L. Courtney CB, CBE, DSO visited and inspected the unit for the first time since taking over command of the British Forces in Iraq. He also presented the new squadron badge.

June   A search was carried out on the 2nd in the desert lying to the west and north of Shaibah for a car containing six Arabs, five of them members of an influential Basra family, which had been missing on a journey from Basra to Batha since 27 May. The car was found by aircraft of the squadron in the sand belt 60 miles from Shaibah on a bearing of 260 deg. The dead bodies of the occupants were found later by desert police some miles to the south of the car.

August   On the 18th four Vincents visited the French Air Force in Syria at Rayak and Palmyra.

1938

September   The squadron was mobilized on the 7th in view of the Munich Crisis. The ground echelon left Shaibah by special train for Habbaniya.

November   On the 15th Squadron Leader D.L. Thompson was posted from No. 9 FTS Hullavington to assume command of the squadron.

1939

February   On the 17th the squadron received its first Blenheim Mk I aircraft, and a Browning gun had superseded the Vickers as the front gun. A Vickers gas-operated gun mounted in a power-operated turret superseded the Lewis gun on a ring-type mounting.

June   By the 3rd the squadron had been fully re-equipped with Blenheim Mk I aircraft. On the 30th the officers of the squadron were:

Squadron Commander	Squadron Leader D.L. Thompson
Adjutant	Flying Officer M.J. Stevenson
Flight Commanders – A Flight	Flight Lieutenant O. Godfrey
– B Flight	Acting Flight Lieutenant R.A. Towgood
– C Flight	Acting Flight Lieutenant L.P. Cattell

[The number of officers being appointed to squadron posts in Acting rank only serves to emphasize that the rapid growth in the number of squadrons in the late 1930s brought accelerated promotion for junior officers. This is referred to at length in Chapter 9 on officers' careers.]

September   War is declared on the 3rd.

NO. 208 SQUADRON
Vigilant

1930

The record book begins with a summary of the flying hours over the past four years:

1926/7	155 hrs 10 mins
1927/8	331 hrs 45 mins
1928/9	752 hrs 45 mins
1929/30	856 hrs 30 mins.

A message was received from Command HQ complimenting the squadron on its work with the Army over the past four years. [No. 208 Squadron was an Army Cooperation Squadron.]

April   There was a change of command of the squadron. Squadron Leader V.S.E. Lindop relinquished command after three years and was posted to Headquarters Palestine and Transjordan for staff duty. Squadron Leader M. Moore OBE, psa, assumed command of the squadron on the 14th.

May   On the 31st the squadron was re-equipped with the Atlas aircraft powered by Jaguar IVE engines.

1931

March   During the month the squadron was engaged in the RAF Display. The unit won the inter-unit football championships, and the station athletics competition was won for the second year running. Finally the squadron won the Musketry Cup for the Middle East Command.

August   On the 5th Flight Lieutenant A.R. Jones and No. 365572 LAC Henry were killed in a flying accident at Armaza aerodrome.

October   On the 1st Flying Officer Abbott and Lieutenant-Colonel P.S. Ryan, commanding the 1st Battalion the Wiltshire Regiment, were killed in an accident on the aerodrome at Ismailia.

1932

January   On the 12th Flight Lieutenant F.J. O'Doherty and 355992 AC1 Mahoney D.J.N. were killed in a flying accident near the Pyramids. The recorded hours spent in the year 1931/2 on air cooperation training with the Army in Egypt was 789 hours.

AIRCRAFT
Bristol F2B
Armstrong Whitworth Atlas
Hawker Audax
Hawker Demon
Westand Lysander

April   On the 27th the squadron was inspected by Air Vice-Marshal Sir Cyril Newall CB, CMG, CBE, and he reported as follows:

I have to report that I have inspected No. 208 (Army Cooperation) Squadron, Heliopolis. The squadron is commanded by Squadron Leader M. Moore OBE, psa. The Air Marshal went on to congratulate the squadron, and he commented on the special letter from the GOC British Troops in Egypt for the work the squadron had done. It was a creditable performance. He also commented on the satisfactory organization for training and the very satisfactory administration in spite of the fact that the accommodation was old, yet clean and well kept.

1933
April   Squadron Leader Maurice Moore relinquished command of the squadron on the 29th to take up staff duties at HQ RAF Middle East. Squadron Leader John Whitworth Jones, ex-commander of No. 13 (Army Cooperation) Squadron, Netheravon, took over command of the squadron on the same date. On the 15th Pilot Officer W.A.W. Jameson and No. 365129 LAC Allaway were killed in a flying accident at Ghobet.

June   The squadron undertook desert convoy training.

1934
April   On the 18th two Audax aircraft arrived at the aircraft depot Aboukir, the first two aircraft of this type with which the unit was to be equipped. On the 24th the Chief of the Air Staff, Air Chief Marshal Sir Edward Ellington KCB, CMG, CBE, inspected the squadron at work.

November   On the 1st Squadron Leader A Hyde, formerly at the RAF Record Office, assumed command of the squadron.

1935
February   The RAF Middle East Air Display took place in the month, featuring Audax and Atlas aircraft. There were aerobatics, message dropping and picking up and a low-flying attack in the Atlas. Flying hours for the year 1935/6 – by day 4,806 hours and by night 117 hours. Total flying hours – 4,923, of which 1,168 hours were spent in Army Cooperation.

1936
September   A warning order signal was received on the 20th from the HQ British Troops, Egypt, stating: 'Two flights of No. 208 Squadron are to be prepared to move to Palestine at short notice if required. If sent, flights will be allotted to sub-divisions on arrival.' On the 23rd the signal was received, giving dates for the movement of the various parties to RAF Ramleh, where the squadron would come under the GOC British Forces in Palestine and Transjordan for operations and the Commanding Officer RAF Ramleh for administration and discipline. The move to Ramleh was completed by the 30th.

October   On the 6th Flying Officer Gilbert Smith with LAC Hulse as passenger went out on a reconnaissance in response to a message from the 1st Division that armed bands were forming on two hills between them, 6 km west of Bethlehem and Wadi Fukin. A band was located and 42 rounds from the front gun and 40 rounds from the rear gun were fired. The bands disappeared into the caves in the hillside and did not reappear. An aircraft was hit by bullets in the tail, rudder and top longeron.

1937
October   This month saw the squadron coming of age. A picnic was held and there were general festivities on the 21st.

1939
January   The squadron began to rearm with Lysander aircraft. The first of these was flown from HQ Middle East. This was followed by working up on the new aircraft.

September   The squadron moved from Mersah Matruh to Qasaba on the 1st, taking the place of No. 33 Squadron. The move was necessitated by the position of the HQ Armoured Division with which the squadron was to cooperate. On the 3rd war was declared with Germany. The officers of the squadron on the outbreak of war were as follows:

Squadron Commander	Squadron Leader Stanley
Adjutant	Flying Officer Burand
A Flight Commander	Acting Flight Lieutenant McDougall
B Flight Commander	Flight Lieutenant Legg
C Flight Commander	Acting Flight Lieutenant Pope
Officers	Flight Lieutenant, the Hon. Humphries
	Flight Lieutenant the Hon. Shipley
	Flying Officer Black
	Flying Officer Currie
	Flying Officer Webber
	Flying Officer Beavis
	Flying Officer Brown
	Pilot Officer Keen
	Pilot Officer Bartrum
	Pilot Officer Alvis
	Pilot Officer Hardiman.

Part II
The Anatomy

Chapter 5
Aircraft weapons and defence systems –
procurement and development

The aircraft industry from 1930 to 1939 – Owners and designers – Company developments – Test flying at Martlesham, Felixstowe and RAE Farnborough – Some notable flights of prototypes – Aircraft weapons – Bombing techniques – Aero engine development and radar

INTRODUCTION

The RAF experienced a troubled birth in the early 1920s as the Army and Royal Navy attempted to regain ownership of their air forces, previously known as the RFC and the RNAS. By the early 1930s the RAF may have become the established third service, but it faced a crisis of a different kind. This was an economic crisis precipitated by the Wall Street crash of 1929. International trade had suffered and there was uncertainty in the markets. What began in New York soon spread to Europe. Five million unemployed in Germany and the collapse of major German banks contributed to the success of the Nazis, who proposed a simplistic solution to the nation's problems through the rhetoric of Adolf Hitler, and politics polarized between the Communists and the Nazis. At home, unemployment had far surpassed the two million mark of 1929. The Labour Party under the leadership of Ramsay MacDonald was desperately trying to grapple with the economic crisis. Industry and trade were suffering, and no industry could be immune from the effects of the Depression.

In spite of the situation described above and Air Estimates under £17 million net, the aircraft industry was still engaged in reasonably profitable production. Included in the Estimates was the sum of £1.5 million for Research and Development, which gave the industry work producing new prototypes. Chapter 1 led with a listing of the aircraft inventory of the RAF in 1930. These were still largely left-overs from the Great War or developments of Great War types. Avro 504Ns were still the standard trainer of the RAF. There were reconditioned DH9As, some Fairey IIID seaplanes and Vickers Vimy bombers. The Gamecock fighter was of wooden construction and was only beginning to be displaced by the steel-framed Bristol Bulldog, and the DH9A was being replaced with the Wapiti, of mixed wood and metal construction. The Vickers Virginia, the lumbering bomber introduced in 1924, would remain in service until 1937. When Hawker produced its Hart light bomber it was an embarrassment for the Air Ministry to find that it was faster than the Bulldog fighter. To have cancelled the contract for the production of Bulldogs would not only have incurred financial penalties for the Air Ministry, it would have contributed to the level of unemployment. This was not the first time that an RAF light bomber was faster than contemporary fighters, but when one considers that the design of fighters and light bombers in the biplane era was remarkably similar, performance was also similar.

There was a widespread impression that French and German designs were technically ahead of British designs. Dornier, for example, had produced a giant twelve-engined flying-boat with a 158 ft wingspan and accommodation for seventy passengers in a roomy cabin. But against this Supermarine could claim to have produced the winners of two Schneider Trophy competitions, and de Havilland could justly claim that its Moth was the finest light trainer in the world. Then there was the Hawker Hornet fighter, which was at least 40 mph faster than the latest light bomber; and the Fairey IIIF, the replacement for the IIID, had aggregated 26,000 trouble-free miles of tropical flying. The British aircraft industry was certainly holding its own.

1930
A ROUND-UP OF THE BRITISH AIRCRAFT INDUSTRY

As the decade opened these were the major firms that comprised the aircraft industry (see next page for a list of designers and test pilots):

Dornier Do X flying-boat.

AIRCRAFT MANUFACTURERS, THEIR DESIGNERS AND TEST PILOTS

This is a ready reference of the names of best known designers, and test pilots whose names appear in the texts which follow, who were in the business of aircraft production in the 1930s.

Firms	Designers	Test Pilots
Armstrong Whitworth	John Lloyd	Campbell-Orde
Avro	Roy Chadwick	H.A. Brown
Blackburn	George Petty	'Dasher' Blake
Bristols – aircraft	Frank Barnwell	Cyril Uwins
Engines	Roy Fedden	
Faireys	Hollis Williams	Chris Staniland
Glosters	Folland	Gerry Sayer, George Carter
Handley-Page	Geroge Volkert	Harry England
Hawker	Sydney Camm	George Bulman
Martin Baker	Jimmy Martin	Val Baker
Saunders Roe	Henry Knowler	Frank Courtney
Shorts	Arthur Gouge	Lankester Parker
Supermarine	Reginald Mitchell	Jeffrey Quill
	Joe Smith	
Vickers	Reginald Pierson	'Mutt' Summers
	Dr Barnes Wallis	
Westland	Geoffrey Hill	Harald Penrose

Supermarine and Short The Supermarine works at the head of Southampton Water was busy working on the Southampton X with its stainless-steel hull, but the take-off could not match the standard duralumin-hulled Southampton, and this prompted Mitchell to increase the power and wing area. The company's test pilot, Henri Biard, was also testing the 92 ft span triple-Jaguar-powered high-wing monoplane Air Yacht. This had been ordered by the Hon. A.E. Guinness, who had hitherto used a three-engined Supermarine Solent flying-boat, which he used to commute between his castle in Ireland and England. The Air Yacht was seen as an advance upon the three-engined Blackburn Iris that was being delivered to the RAF, in that it was aerodynamically cleaner. Short was working on the Singapore II, which was uniquely powered by two pairs of tandem 480 hp Rolls-Royce XII engines. The power units were mounted midway up the inboard pairs of struts without additional supporting structure. This made it the cleanest machine of its type yet produced.

Saunders-Roe Saunders-Roe was busy at East Cowes with its new line of flying-boats designed by Henry Knowles. The small twin-engined amphibian *Cutty Sark* had finished its air trials, and six of these craft, with more powerful 120 hp Gipsy II engines, were being constructed. Saunders-Roe was hoping to reach a world market with these amphibians, and the New Zealand government had placed an order for one, due for delivery in March. In a corner of the workshops was the biplane contender for the AM Spec. F20/27 fighter aircraft. Since the Bulldog II had won the competition, this prototype had lain there, dusty and neglected. The company chief test pilot, Flight Lieutenant Stuart Scott, was to fly the 88 ft wingspan Severn-sesquiplane biplane flying-boat, powered by three 485 hp Bristol Jupiter IXs.

Handley Page Handley Page was in litigation with the Curtiss Corporation of the USA for infringement of patents. Curtiss had entered its Tanager aircraft in the Guggenheim Safe Aircraft Competition, and it featured wing slots designed to prevent aircraft from stalling, even at low speed. Curtiss claimed that it was merely using Handley Page slots for scientific tests, and the question of patent rights only became valid if the aircraft type was put into production. The HP Gugnunc was not entered for the competition, as it was declared that the aircraft had been imported illegally, and Handley Page's test pilot was prevented from dismantling the airframe for return home. It was declared that the complete aircraft was required as evidence. Be that as it may, the winner and runner-up in the competition were both fitted with the leading-edge slots. This episode illustrated the difficulty that the British companies had

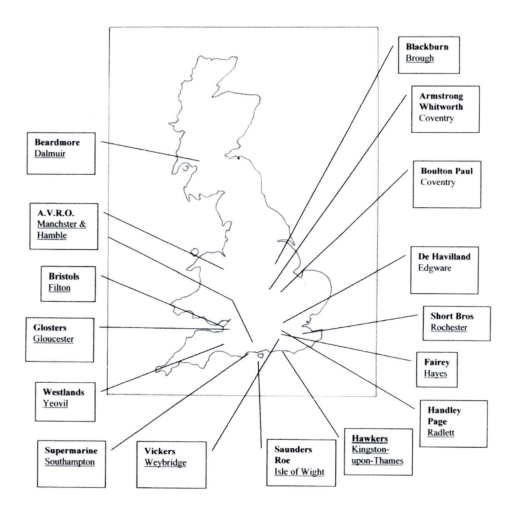

in competition with American ones, for the latter pooled their patents so that they shared the costs of proceedings. In the end both sides acknowledged that in litigation the main winners were the lawyers, and Curtiss acknowledged the infringement of patent in court and entered into a licensing agreement with Handley Page. So Handley Page could be content with the result, and was also able to pocket the cash from the sale of Cricklewood aerodrome. This site was soon covered with roads and houses as urban sprawl continued to follow the growth of light industry north of London. But since the workers still lived in Cricklewood, a daily bus service was provided for production workers and those working with prototypes at the Radlett works.

Beardmore   The map shows Beardmore as an aircraft producer at the end of the 1920s, but its aero department was closed and James Hamilton of the design department was taken on by Handley Page's chief designer, George Volkert. This small but vigorous Scotsman soon found himself working on the HP42 airliner. Another firm that had taken over the work of the

defunct Beardmore aviation department was Gloster which was building the Monospar Wing Company Ltd three-seat cabin monoplane.

Westland   Since Westland was busy at work on Wapitis for the RAF, the economic situation in the country demanded action to keep down costs, particularly since the industry was working in a global market at a time when international trade was being badly affected. Thus when the management asked employees to accept a 10% wage cut it was accepted, for all knew that there was precious little call for their skills in the labour market.

Blackburn   At Blackburn there was production testing of the Ripon ordered for the Fleet Air Arm. The Nautilus fleet spotting aircraft had been competing at Martlesham Heath with the Fairy Fleetwing and the Hawker naval version of the Hart. The company's chief test pilot, 'Dasher' Blake, was engaged in testing the Mk III Lincock fighter, which differed from the prototype in carrying two Vickers guns in troughs each side of the fuselage, and the Japanese and Chinese governments had each ordered two. The high-altitude Beagle bomber had not been taken up by the Air Ministry, although some testing did continue.

de Havilland de Havilland continued to construct aircraft predominantly for the civil airline market. That said, it was the company's Tiger Moth that would bring flying to so many people and contribute to the airmindedness of the nation. Flying schools and clubs were flourishing, and most clubs favoured the Moth. In the spring of 1930 the company decided to move its RAF flying school from Stag Lane to a large area of open fields that had been purchased at Hatfield, for the sky over Stag Lane had become too congested for both club and test flying. Soon afterwards the RAF gave a fairly large order for the new semi-metal Moth as a trainer. This was the de Havilland 60M, which had a fabric-covered fuselage structured with square-section steel tubular longerons and spacers of square or round section similar to the Hawker and Westland systems, combined with the welded-joint process that Avro adapted from Fokker. The maximum speed was 98 mph, with a coupé version that was 2 mph faster. The semi-metal Moth cost £675, the wooden version £595.

Hawker This company would go from strength to strength as the decade progressed. Its Hart light bomber spawned a number of derivatives, and fighters would include the Demon, Fury and Hurricane. The Harts were too fast to be intercepted in the 1930 Air Exercises, and by fitting a Kestrel V engine to the Hart its speed was increased to 182 mph. With a service ceiling equal to the Fury and somewhat greater than the Bulldog, this derivative became the Demon.

OTHER DEVELOPMENTS
The Cierva Autogiro

The Autogiro was a novel aircraft type. Like a helicopter it had a rotor and was designed to take off and land in very confined spaces. The helicopter flies forward by tilting the rotor slightly forward so that it gives both lift and forward motion. A tail rotor stops the fuselage spinning with the rotor. The Autogiro had a conventional engine with a front-mounted propeller providing forward thrust, while the rotor acted as a rotating wing that provided lift. This was an aircraft that could be of value to a battlefield commander for aerial reconnaissance and communications. On 13 February Señor Juan de la Cierva lectured to the Royal Aeronautical Society on the development of his invention.

It had recently been exhibited at the Aero Show at Olympia, and considerable interest was shown by both the Press and Movietone News. One of the mandatory magnetos failed and was illegally disconnected, but

Cierva assured those present that even if the remaining one failed the aircraft could be brought down safely. It was flown around followed by photographic Moths and landed in a 28 mph wind. The landing in the middle of the aerodrome may have seemed spectacular, but a Moth with wing slots made an equally good landing. The Autogiro could take off with a rotor speed of 85 rpm. It could be banked steeply like a conventional aircraft and could glide either at a fairly flat angle or a very steep one. The machine had a steep climbing angle although not as good as a conventional aircraft. The pilot, Flight Lieutenant Arthur Rawson, was witnessed making a steep landing near aircraft hangars. When between fifty to sixty yards from the hangars Rawson pulled back on the stick, the machine tilted back and the aircraft settled down a very steep path. On touching the ground the Autogiro came to a halt in two revolutions of the landing-wheels. The rotor hub brake was applied and the rotor soon stopped.

Although this was potentially of great value to the RAF, there were problems. Considerable judgement was required for a steep descent. If the wind was strong there was a risk that the spinning rotor might tilt the machine catastrophically sideways before the hub brake could take effect. At the slow speeds that the Autogiro could be flown, the controls were sluggish. A lot more work was going to be required before the machine was a practical proposition for the Air Ministry. Cierva had already written a handbook for potential licencees, entitled *Engineering Theory of the Autogiro*, and he was addressing the problem of calculating blade stresses. There was, however, a rival, and the Air Ministry had given a contract to Saunders-Roe to build the Isaaco-patented Helicogyre, which combined the rotor features of the Autogiro with an inferior rotor-tip-drive version of the Brennan helicopter.

1931
1931 PROTOTYPES
AM SPEC. S9/30 AND 7/31

Fairey and Blackburn were sticking to the tried and tested biplane with their latest machines for the AM Spec. S9/30. The Air Ministry was looking for a replacement for the Atlas in its AM Spec. 7/31. The specification was a post-issue for the cumbersome private venture Atlas Mk II with a Townend cowled Panther engine. On hearing of this, Hawker took one of its Hart light day-bombers from storage at RAF Kenley, K.1438, obtaining it on a loan agreement. In ten days it had been fitted with a message pick-up hook and the appropriate radio. The aircraft was fitted into the testing schedule at Martlesham in June (see Appendix H, p. 521). As a result of the trial, an ITP, or Instruction to Proceed, was issued, which authorized the production of drawings. The Hart became the Audax, adapted to AM Spec. 7/31.

AM SPEC. 7/30

There was much activity surrounding the issue of AM Spec. F7/30. Tenders were sent to Supermarine, Blackburn and Westland. It was to be a day/night-fighter with good all-round observation for the pilot, four guns, a speed not exceeding 250 mph, together with a greater climb and endurance than the Fury ($4\frac{1}{2}$ minutes to 10,000 ft). There had to be a landing speed of 50 mph, which meant that if it was going to be a monoplane it would have to have a large wingspan for sufficiently light wing loading. The completion of prototypes was set for 1933, to permit Rolls-Royce the time to develop its Goshawk engine. As it was, the specification was late in being issued, but it was not uncommon for the requirements to be issued a year after drafting. The Air Ministry wanted Bristol to take part in the competition, but was trying to persuade the directors to enter an aircraft as a private venture. Singling the company out in this way was probably due to the fact that it was doing well with its extensive engine and

Frank Barnwell.

airframe production. Be that as it may, the directors were unhappy about using an engine that was not 'in house' and designed by Roy Fedden.

The photographs opposite show the lengths that firms went to in meeting the specifications. Frank Barnwell designed a compact Goshawk-powered biplane with a cantilever lower wing connected to the thin top wing with conventional N-interplane struts, and the wingspan was a little more than 29 ft. Barnwell knew that it would have to be a biplane to get the low landing speeds, but he was more interested in a monoplane fighter. The Blackburn F3 design was very unconventional, and took the Air Ministry specification literally in providing the pilot with the all-round view, as long as it is remembered that he could not see directly below him, for the lower wing hid his view. It was not actually attached to the fuselage, and the upper wing was mounted midway up the fuselage. A fin attached the lower wing to the fuselage, which placed the wing so close to the ground that it left precious little room for the wide-track undercarriage wheels.

Westland had lost its test pilot, Openshaw, in a fatal crash that stressed the importance of pilot view from the cockpit. Devonport agreed with the test pilot, Harald Penrose, that the engine could be mounted behind the pilot, with a drive shaft forward to a tractor propeller. The result was a gull-winged aircraft with the pilot sitting well forward. Like Barnwell, Devonport would have preferred to design a monoplane, but the span would have been 40 ft to get within 8 mph of the low landing speed.

Mitchell at Supermarine went for a monoplane and found, as did the others, that it would mean a large wingspan. It had an anhedral root, which was necessary to raise the fuselage for propeller ground clearance yet low enough for the minimum height of the trousered undercarriage at the elbow.

Vickers was working on a fighter, the all-metal Jockey, which had been flown with root leading-edge slots, but as with the Westland Interceptor, these were useless in overcoming buffeting. A modified filler was about to be tried, together with the new rear fuselage of triangulated tubular trusses inside a monocoque skin designed by Barnes Wallis (later of 'Dam Busters' fame). This was to overcome earlier lack of torsional rigidity. The Vickers Type 161 COW-gun pusher fighter was at Martlesham for testing. The test pilots, who sat in front of the wings, were enthusiastic, but there was structural drag, added to which there were additional fins and the small four-bladed propeller was inefficient. Performance was well below requirement.

At Hawker, Tom Sopwith was intent on modifying the successful Hart for a variety of roles, and believed that the same policy should be applied to the Fury. The Hart and Fury variants could therefore be produced on the available jigging. This led Sydney Camm to investigate

The Westland F7/30.

The Supermarine F7/30 monoplane.

The Blackburn F3.

The Vickers Jockey.

The Gloster SS19.

the possibility of producing a super-Fury with lower drag and powered by the new Goshawk engine. Finally it has been recounted that Gloster was in dire straits but felt that the company was basically a designer of fighters. Henry Folland's view was that the SS18 could become the SS19 with six machine-guns, making it a better day/night-fighter than anything specified in AM Spec. F7/30. But the Gnatsnapper 3 with the Kestrel I evaporative cooling had proved too heavy for effective performance. The process of developing a fighter from the SS19, however, went ahead.

In conclusion, a study of the photographs and the description of Air Ministry requirements for a day/night-fighter at the beginning of the decade meant that the RAF did want the speed, rate of climb and firepower of a fighter, but given the low landing speed requirement, must have known that the result would be a biplane.

OTHER DEVELOPMENTS
Constraints upon expenditure

Money was always a problem, particularly during the Depression years of the early 1930s. The engine makers could not risk spending money on projects that were at the cutting edge of technology of the day. Development work on proved technologies such as the internal combustion engine was less risky. Profits in the industry were barely sufficient to cover costs, let alone plough money into equipment, and firms were working on the margins. If aircraft or engine makers went out of business there was little hope of keeping pace with the development of these technologies in competitor countries, and it would be more difficult to produce aircraft at home for the RAF. The Air Ministry was constrained by the limits set by the Air Estimates. The net total for 1931 was slightly up on the figure for 1930 (£17,850,000 to £18,100,000). There would be £6,529,000 for the supply of aircraft, seaplanes, engines and spares. While this was a reduction of £111,000 on the previous year, it was only a 2% drop in the industry's turnover, which had got off comparatively lightly given the economic situation. £170,000 less would be spent on airframes, though more spares for each would be produced.

Much was made in Volume I about Trenchard's policy of feeding contracts for prototypes to the various firms so that at least they might survive in a period of national belt tightening. Liability for the cost of prototypes was considered by the Committee on National Expenditure in its 1931 report on the matter. The committee did not quarrel with expenditure for research into aerodynamic problems but questioned whether or not it was the responsibility of the state to purchase aircraft that could be produced in quantity for the RAF. It was felt that it was up to individual firms to develop new types at their own risk. The Society of British Aircraft Constructors blamed those in the Treasury who were convinced that firms were conniving, through sub-contracting, to force up prices so that the nation was paying more than it should for its armaments. But the Air Ministry knew that without large production orders firms such as Parnall were surviving on sub-contract work. Such firms simply did not have the funds to design, build and test new prototypes in the hope of winning an Air Ministry competition. If a firm did not win the competition for an Air Ministry Specification there was always the next one, but there was a limit. After the Great War a number of aircraft firms went into making car bodies or some other such product. Gloster had to embark once again on non-aircraft work just to cover the company's overheads. Some of the hangars were sub-let for storing charabancs, for rearing pigs and growing mushrooms and to act as an indoor tennis court.

Government help was needed to develop aircraft and associated equipment that was, as yet, untested. Retractable undercarriages and variable-pitch propellers come to mind, but the Air Ministry technicians viewed these things as too futuristic and liable to go wrong. What was wanted was equipment that was simple and easy to maintain. But the conservatives did not have it all their own way. There were those who pressed for higher-performing machines, like the Hendon low-wing bomber, even though the prototype did crash on landing with defective directional control following an engine failure.

Consideration of gas turbine engines

It was not until the Second World War that Frank Whittle's jet engine would revolutionize the powering of aircraft, but other means of propulsion were being considered in the inter-war years. One such method was the contra-flow gas turbine engine. In 1926 Dr A.A. Griffith had expressed the basic principles in a report, No. H.1111, *An Aerodynamic Theory of Turbine Design*. He maintained that the turbine was superior to existing service engines and to projected compression-ignition (diesel) engines. The efficiency was higher and weight and bulk less. No external cooling was required and there would be a substantial decrease in fuel consumption. There would be no need for variable-pitch propellers, starting would present no difficulty and any fuel of suitable composition could be used without reference to anti-knock value or volatility. This sounded admirable, but there were unresolved problems of metallurgy associated with bearings and turbine blades operating in extremely high temperatures. The Engine Sub-committee of the Aircraft Research Committee did not support large expenditure on such a project given the existing amount of knowledge, and it was considered that the internal combustion engine would be superior for the foreseeable future. The committee did not close the door on the idea and recommended that Dr Griffith should build his multi-stage test rig so that flow, pressure and temperature distribution could be analysed in order to determine conditions under which a high efficiency of compression might be obtained, and to assess the efficiency of the unit when used as a high-pressure component of a turbine compresser of a 500 bhp installation. This was never carried out, and nothing more was done on gas turbines at the RAE until seven years later.

1932

The honouring of Mitchell

For his work on the Schneider Trophy floatplanes that won the competition outright in 1931, R.J. Mitchell was awarded the CBE. His work culminating in the Supermarine S6B undoubtedly contributed to the eventual success of the eight-gun fighter, the Spitfire. But at the same time as being honoured he was also disappointed that the government, for reasons of economy, had just cancelled a huge monoplane flying-boat, powered by six Rolls-Royce Buzzard engines. This would have been a forty-seat marine airliner capable of a speed of 145 mph. This was a pity, because it marked a great engineering advance, and the cantilever shoulder-wing gave it an extremely clean appearance despite the engines in raised nacelles above the wing and outboard balancing floats. *The Aeroplane*'s editor, C.G. Grey, criticized the government for its false economy, given the importance of air travel to a country with an empire to manage. The cancellation of the Supermarine discloses the vacillation and usual caution of civil servants who would prefer to go for the 'tried and tested' rather than something more imaginative and an advance in technology. The programme of exploratory structural testing carried out at the RAE, under the direction of Ian Gerard, was preferred. Here the strength factor was determined by calculation with that revealed by mechanical tests. An alternative was to use strain gauges like those developed at the Massachusetts Institute of

Technology by Professor J.S. Newall. Gerard did admit that there had been little experience in Britain of strain gauges on tests of large skin-stressed structures such as monocoque fuselages, hulls and metal-covered wings, but he hoped that it would soon be possible to design gauges meeting those special requirements. Until then the RAE would stay with the time-honoured measurement using scales, levels and dial indicators.

Direction-finding (DF) facilities

The Air Ministry was making intensive efforts to establish DF facilities – as far as finance would allow, that is! A Marconi Adcock 'anti-night-effect' direction station was established at Pulham in Norfolk. It took the form of a square with a 70 ft wooden tower at each corner and a vertically suspended aerial from which copper feeders led above ground to the receiver and radio-goniometer in a hut in the centre of the square, the diagonal of which bore particular relation to the 800- and 1,800-metre waveband. The Air Ministry arranged for a night flight to be made during which fourteen observations were made by an aircraft transmitting signals from known positions about 100 miles distant. Thus complete accuracy of the new direction finder could be confirmed. This new system eliminated entirely the 'night effect' experienced with wireless direction finding, even over much shorter distances. Britain had only two DF stations, whereas Germany had fourteen for her civil aviation, reminding us that Germany did not officially have an air force until 1935. Eight of these stations were suitable for night-flying aircraft because of freedom from beam deviation at sunset, night and dawn. Germany also had 1,085 miles of lighted airways with beacons every fifteen miles on iron posts 60–70 ft high. But if visibility was less than a mile the pilots of Lufthansa would fly blind at a safe height, using radio and DF.

Fairey Hendon.

The Air Estimates for 1932/3 – the effects upon the aircraft industry

The Air Estimates for 1932/3 were introduced to the House of Commons on 11 March. They had gone down by £1,494,500 to £1,702,700, but the worsening economic situation demanded cuts, which were accepted in all three services. The sum voted for Technical and Warlike stores went down by 4%, leaving a net total of £7,350,000, of which £2,657,000 was for the purchase of aircraft, a decrease of £791,000. £1,746,000 was available for the purchase of engines. Engine spares were down but other spares for aircraft, parachutes, etc. remained at the previous year's total of £900,000. In turn this meant that the 1923 expansion programme was stopped for another year: forty-two squadrons, of which five were cadre units and eight auxiliary.

Those firms in the aircraft industry that just wanted to sub-contract to stay alive just had to be grateful for small mercies. If a firm was not invited to submit a prototype, yet considered that it could impress the Air Ministry that it had a worthwhile project to meet a particular specification, then it might embark upon a PV (private venture). This was naturally risky, but there was no shortage of PV aircraft during the decade. For those firms that were invited to submit prototypes but were unsuccessful, then it could be argued that at least the firm's design staff had been enriched by the experience of working on the prototype. Things were little better for the successful firms, as some years might elapse before a squadron was re-equipped. It was not until the first quarter of 1932 that the Furies were filtering through to No. 25 Squadron at Hawkinge and No. 1 Squadron at Tangmere. At long last the Horsleys of No. 100 Squadron at Donibristle were being replaced with Vildebeests. Three bomber squadrons might be getting Gordons in place of their Fairey IIIFs, but No. 6 Squadron at Ismailia was still soldiering on with Bristol Fighters. At least things speeded up with the Hart variants, and Audaxes were replacing Atlases. At sea the Flycatcher was at last being phased out to be replaced with the Nimrod, the naval version of the Fury. There was nothing for the heavy-bomber squadrons, which had to soldier on with Hinaidis and Virginias.

New developments

Further examples of the Air Ministry holding back on new developments that would put the RAF in the lead can be found in landing flaps, leading-edge slots, variable-pitch propellers and retractable undercarriages. These were seen, not as an asset, but as items adding weight, cost and complexity, items that might have to be serviced, repaired or replaced by the humble RAF mechanic. Too often caution won the day. Gloster had not received Air Ministry support for its Hele-Shaw/ Beacham propeller, and so sold the manufacturing licence to the Japanese. Mr Tom Hamilton of Hamilton

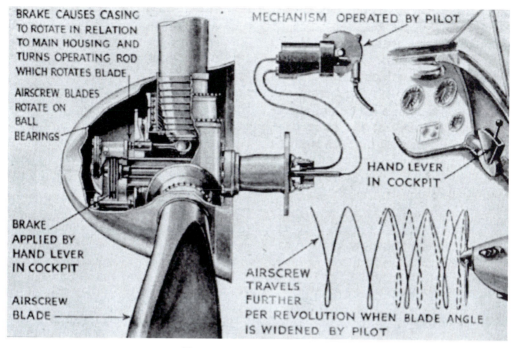

BRAKE CAUSES CASING TO ROTATE IN RELATION TO MAIN HOUSING AND TURNS OPERATING ROD WHICH ROTATES BLADE.

AIRSCREW BLADES ROTATE ON BALL BEARINGS

BRAKE APPLIED BY HAND LEVER IN COCKPIT

AIRSCREW BLADE

MECHANISM OPERATED BY PILOT

HAND LEVER IN COCKPIT

AIRSCREW TRAVELS FURTHER PER REVOLUTION WHEN BLADE ANGLE IS WIDENED BY PILOT

The variable-pitch airscrew.

Airscrews USA came to the United Kingdom to see a demonstration of this propeller. He took copious notes and showed considerable interest, not to obtain a licence but to patent his own propeller in the USA. The propeller had two positions, one for fine pitch for take-off, and coarse pitch for cruising. He got the backing of the US government and quickly developed his propeller. There were those in the USA like Robert Schlaifer, the Harvard author of *Development of Aircraft Engines*, who maintained that if there had not been a military demand for variable-pitch propellers, the idea would have been dropped. Charles Walker of de Havilland disagreed, claiming that a superabundance of horsepower would not get a heavily loaded aircraft out of the confines of an aerodrome.

Propellers designed for maximum efficiency up to about 130 mph did not suffer unduly on take-off, the weight per bhp being a factor governing take-off characteristics. But for a propeller that is at maximum efficiency at 180 mph will produce only half the relative thrust horsepower of that designed for 130 mph. In France the one-shot Ratier propeller was being developed. It could be pumped up to produce a fine pitch for take-off, and then the system was gradually leaked to provide a coarse pitch for cruising, when it would have to remain at coarse pitch for the remainder of the flight. This was a disadvantage, but the propeller was a less complex mechanism and gained the interest of both de Havilland and Fairey Aviation.

The Loss of a Heyford prototype and Vickers Jockey Aircraft

On 8 July the Heyford prototype was lost. It had external bomb racks fitted to bring the load up to that of the Fairey Hendon, which was also undergoing trials. It was obviously in trouble as soon as it took off, and it completed a slow circuit only to sink into the sand dunes on landing. A fire started and it was burned out. Fortunately the RAF crew escaped. Further testing would have to wait until the first production machine was ready. This happens if only one prototype is produced. Next to come to grief was the low-wing monoplane Vickers Jockey previously described in this chapter. Ever since the first flight in April 1930 there had been trouble with the Jockey. Barnes Wallis had stiffened the rear fuselage and it shook less, although some buffeting remained. The need for an expanding root fillet was not understood. A Townend ring and rear fairings to the engine cylinders had given a little improvement and increased the top speed. The aircraft had a tendency to top spin, and this was investigated in the RAE vertical wind tunnel. Changes were made to provide fuselage taper, a new rudder of increased chord with the balance removed and a longer tailplane to give a more effective elevator. Finally wheel spats were fitted. In spite of these modifications, when the Jockey was tested at Martlesham it went into a flat spin and the pilot had to bale out, fortunately landing safely. As a result of the Jockey crash the RAE and the NPL intensified research into flat spins. The problem seemed to be blanketing of vertical tail surfaces by the wake of the tailplane. This led to a recommendation that tailplanes should either be abaft the fin and rudder or above it.

1933

Introduction

The year began with the installation of Adolf Hitler as Chancellor of Germany. He would take the world to war in a little over six years. As a direct result the British government would initiate a succession of expansion plans that would give so much work to the aircraft construction industry that a shadow factory scheme would have to be introduced to ensure sufficient front-line aircraft and reserves were produced to meet the threat. For the time being there was an economic depression and a standstill on the modest 1923 expansion plan for the RAF. The failure of the Geneva Disarmament Conference might have been predicted, but it could only add to the uncertainty of having two Fascist dictators in Europe.

COMPANY DEVELOPMENTS

Short

The RAF had been testing the Singapore II for the preceding two years, yet there was no production contract. The company's Sarafand was still at Felixstowe, where it was regarded as something of a white elephant. By the beginning of 1933 the Short works were almost empty and the firm was reliant on building over 2,000 bus bodies to carry them over. This was equivalent to half the buses on the London streets. In spite of the large number of bus bodies the turnover was insufficient to make a large profit. The company, as with all aircraft builders, had high overheads in the design staff and experimental and laboratory facilities. However hard the company tried, overheads could barely be covered. As it turned out, Short was to have its busiest year since the 1918 Armistice. Handley Page had been asked by Imperial Airways to construct two more HP42 aircraft powered by Tiger II engines. But it was thought to be too costly to produce just two instead of a production run, so Handley Page quoted £42,000 for each aircraft, twice the price of the original machines. Oswald Short could produce a cheaper version by substituting an underslung fuselage for the hull of the four-engined Kent flying-boats. These two aircraft were to go into the London–Paris service.

Blackburn

Blackburn had redesigned its M1/30 bomber, a private venture, with a monocoque fuselage. It bore the maker's cypher B3 and it was flown by 'Dasher' Blake on 24 February, being delivered to Martlesham on the 14th of the month for performance testing. The combination of fuel tank and fuselage was criticized due to its vulnerability to gun fire, which might lead to an explosion of fuel. On the other hand it was agreed that a conventional fuel tank within a separated skin also presented a risk, whereas the Blackburn design had the advantage of in-built flotation. The Air Ministry agreed to purchase this machine, and took it on charge as K.3591. Meanwhile the Air Ministry had to come to a decision about the acceptability of the watertight fuselage-cum-tank as a matter of urgency, for it featured in Blackburn's entry for AM Spec. S15/33, the Shark torpedo-spotter-reconnaissance machine. The introduction of the S15/33 specification almost amalgamated the S9/30 and M1/30, with the Blackburn Shark as the chief contender, and the equivalent Gloster and Fairey machines had to be revised to make them competitive.

Gloster

Gloster continued with its work on the SS19. The SS19B had wheel spats, a Mercury VI engine and Townend ring. On preliminary evaluation at Martlesham this aircraft attained a speed of 212 mph at 14,500 ft. By uprating the engine to 570 hp the speed was raised to 215.5 mph at 16,500 ft, which was 41 mph faster than the Bulldog. She could climb to 20,000 ft in 11mins 43 secs and was ready to make an appearance in the F7/30 competition as the Gloster Gauntlet. The Air Ministry decided to place a contract for the Gauntlet, which was a two-bay biplane day/night-fighter. This was originally the SS18 built to AM Spec. F24/33 with the 640 hp Mercury VIS2 engine. The original idea of fitting six guns to the SS18 to make it a more attractive proposition seems to have been dropped, and it was only a two-gun fighter. The pilots may have loved flying it but it was already virtually obsolete!

The Gloster Gauntlet.

Fairey

Fairey had two aircraft that were so unlike that one wondered whether or not they were entered for the same competition to the same specifications. There was the S9/30 stainless-steel aircraft, complete and ready to go to the aerodrome. Two or three months behind was what Mr Fairey called the 'Greek' machine. He called in the chiefs of the FAA and showed them the S9/30 in the experimental shop. He pointed out that it might be what the Navy wanted but it was ten times more expensive to build than the private-venture 'Greek' machine. The latter, he pointed out, could do everything that the S9/30 could do. There were also production difficulties, and by the time the naval gentlemen left they had switched their

The 'Greek' machine, the future Swordfish.

interest to the aircraft that would cripple the Italian fleet on 11 November 1940 in Taranto harbour, and cripple the German battleship *Bismarck* in May 1941. It was the Swordfish. Fairey was also producing IIIFs for the FAA, powered by an Armstrong Siddeley Panther and given the naval name, the Seal. It was very similar in appearance to the Fairey Gordon ordered to meet AM Spec. 18/30. The Seal had Frise ailerons and a more shapely fin and rudder. To meet Spec. G4/31 Fairey had a PV aircraft that differed from the other biplanes in the competition in placing the pilot in the customary position just behind the wings with the gunner close behind. The pilot was seated high up, which gave him a reasonable view forward, but not as good as the competitors. The view to the rear was also good, but did not match the HP47. The AGM for Fairey Aviation Co. Ltd was held at the end of 1933. For Fairey the peak year had been 1932. The following year profits were down £67,900 to £116,682, and the dividend was 10% less tax. There had been less re-equipment of RAF squadrons with the firm's aircraft. An accident to the prototype and a delayed decision on another aircraft that had completed its tests in the summer of 1933 did not help matters. On the other hand foreign orders had reached a record due to the firm's ability to produce quickly and cheaply.

Westland and Vickers

Westland shared with Fairey the policy of turning out derivatives. Its Wallace aircraft were equipping the auxiliary squadrons to replace their Wapitis. In the experimental shop at Yeovil was the high-wing monoplane P7, being erected in skeleton form to AM Spec. G4/31. The near equivalent was the Vickers Vildebeest. Both aircraft had a position for the pilot just ahead of the wing, as required in the specification. The Vildebeest's derivative was the Vincent. The Vildebeest had flown in the spring of 1928 and went through several versions before the first production contract for nine in 1932. Thirty Mk IIs followed, and the Mk III had a redesigned rear cockpit for a third crew member. The Mk I version powered with a Pegasus engine was named the Vincent.

Handley Page

Handley Page also hoped to win a contract for a general-purpose aircraft to meet the Specification G4/31. The company was working on the HP47, a low-wing cantilever monoplane and uniformly tapered wing based on a single main spar and torsion nose with fabric-covered section aft except for the metal-skinned centre section.

de Havilland

de Havilland's 13th AGM revealed a gross profit of £104,629, of which £25,000 went into the reserves. The sale of the Stag Lane aerodrome did not go into the 1933 account. This meant that the purchase of the factory at Hatfield could not be shown, but there was no shortage of working capital.

1934
RESEARCH AND TESTING
Low-wing monoplanes

Research into aircraft and engines was actively pursued in all the major countries into such matters as turbulent flow, three-dimensional flow, velocity fields, supersonic velocities, rotating wings, rocket propulsion, etc. – the list was endless. Every manufacturer was, in 1934, testing aircraft aerodynamically in wind tunnels. Typical was the circular-section longitudinally corrugated spar that F. Duncanson had devised at Gloster. Folland, however, seemed to be more interested in biplanes, so Duncanson moved to Blackburn. The latter's interest in the spar was that it could make the wing capable of storing fuel, which would then not have to be kept in separate tanks. Alternatively the wings could act as a bouyancy chamber in naval aircraft if the latter were ditched. This led to designs of low-wing Duncanson-sparred monoplanes with a capacity of up to twenty persons. Experiments with a modified Blackburn Seagrave fuselage resulted in considerable weight saving, so important in an aircraft.

One can also see in this example the gradual move on the part of some designers and constructors from the biplane to the monoplane. The Air Ministry, although remaining cautious, had been interested in even faster twin-engined passenger-carrying aircraft, with an eye on Lockheed at Burbank, California. After some discussion with Frank Barnwell and Roy Fedden, together with Blackburn's forward thinking in making low-wing monoplanes, the Air Ministry held an inquiry on 10 May into the possibility of building a military version of the Blackburn HST8, and then the HST10, which was larger, with a retractable undercarriage, hydraulically operated landing flaps and powered with twin 365 hp Napier Rapiers. The Director of Technical Development did not, however, decide against them, so Blackburn went ahead with the HST10 as a private venture. This again illustrates the cautious approach by the Air Staff.

Barnwell was working on a low-wing all-metal aircraft that could attain 240 mph at 6,500 ft, powered by Bristol Mercury engines. When Lord Rothermere heard of it he expressed his intention of purchasing one for his private use at a cost of £18,500, not only to encourage businessmen to make more use of civil aviation but to impress upon the Air Ministry that such a high-speed transport used as a bomber would outclass the existing biplane fighters. Another reason for the Air Ministry's reluctance to proceed with high-speed monoplane aircraft would be the need to extend airfield runways and even to pave them at considerable cost.

Radio

Experimental work was going ahead in the use of 'micro-ray' or VHF radio services. The RAE, Marconi and Standard Telephones were all engaged in this work. The British and French air ministers were operating a service between Croydon, Lympne and St Inglevert, near Calais. Hitherto messages had had to go by land line, which meant that an aircraft would arrive at Croydon before news of its departure from France was received. It took a teleprinter only two minutes to convey flight information.

At Farnborough experiments were being made on the transmission and reception of marker signals to indicate the position where a pilot should flare the glide-path for landing. It was observed that a 'beating effect' occurred at times when VHF waves were received on the ground. N. Cox-Walker, who made these observations, obtained correlation between this phenomenon and an aircraft's presence in the neighbourhood of the receiving set. He was unaware, however, that the same effect had been reported two years earlier by GPO engineers.

The RAE had been working on a radio-controlled flying naval target using a Fairey III, known as the 'Fairey Queen'. Success in these experiments led to the transfer of the equipment to a Tiger Moth seaplane, to be named the 'Queen Bee'. It was successfully catapulted from ship and shore. When the wheels were refitted, the aircraft could taxi, take off, manoeuvre and land by radio control. Adoption by the Army and Navy followed, and it was only natural that there was immediate speculation that pilots would soon become redundant in both peace and war.

COMPANY DEVELOPMENTS

Saunders-Roe   Saunders-Roe was continuing with flight trials of the A27 on the Solent. This flying-boat would be successful in entering RAF service as the Saro London. It had made its maiden flight at the beginning of 1934 piloted by Stuart Scott. It was similar in many respects to the Saro Severn, having high-mounted, but relatively small, horn-balanced rudders. The London, however, used inset servo tabs instead of outrigger Flettners. Trials showed that the London was just as fast

as the four-engined Singapore III and had eight hours' endurance compared with six and a quarter hours' for the Singapore. With overload tanks the London managed thirteen and a half hours.

Short   At Short the first Singapore III flying-boats were nearing completion. Lankester Parker was testing the gull-winged 'Knuckleduster', or Short R.24, which had had the rudder area noticeably increased so that the flying-boat could be flown straight and level on a dead engine. This proved too heavy, and Parker had to resort to side-slipping, although there was some improvement with toe-in and balance increased. A shock absorber had to be fitted to the wing when the shock load on landing was transmitted from the floats to the wings. On one particular flight the fairing gave way on the gunner's cockpit, which gave rise to a sudden, startling tail-down change of trim. This could only be remedied by applying the throttle. Further trouble was encountered with the steam cooling of the Goshawk engines, but on 26 March Parker was ready to take her up to 15,000 ft at full load. He would go down in history as the first man to dive a monoplane flying-boat to its maximum speed of 200 mph. He had complied with the latest test flying requirements laid down in Air Publication 970. Later the stern frames were modified to incorporate a quarter-spherical tiltable cupola over the tail cockpit. This was a step towards gun turrets.

Gloster   It has been shown that Gloster was in trouble, and when the government approached firms for a reduction in the number of firms in the industry, in line with the shipping industry, it made sense to accept a take-over proposal by Hawker. Although this ended Gloster's independence, it did later regain something of its autonomy. The main problem was Folland's position as chief designer. He was still wedded to the biplane and felt that he would be subject to scrutiny by Sidney Camm at Hawker. Although he inspired loyalty from his staff, he had been a pre-Great War designer at the Royal Aircraft Factory, brought up on the SE5A. This may explain why he was living in the past, having a somewhat outdated view of good aircraft design. He seemed not to have many friends among other aircraft designers and was understandably frustrated. There was talk that his future could only lie in setting up his own company.

The new Gloster SS37 piloted by Gerry Sayer made its debut. For Folland this was the product of evolution from the time he was involved with the SE5A. The aircraft had a Gauntlet fuselage modified to take cantilever undercarriage legs and Dowty sprung wheels. It was later named the Gladiator and did see squadron service. It used the same 530 hp Mercury IV engine and was 6 mph faster than the Gauntlet, but touched down 10 mph more slowly. It was estimated that the Gladiator

The Gloster Gladiator.

was capable of over 250 mph, which was ideal for the F7/30 competition, armed with two fuselage-mounted guns and a drum-fed Lewis gun beneath each lower wing. Folland had taken the biplane fighter about as far as it could go.

Westland   There was trouble with the Autogiro. Earlier references to this novel machine disclosed problems with the rotor blades and the tendency of the aircraft to tip on its side. Westland was having trouble with its C.29 Autogiro, so Cierva came to Yeovil to test the machine once the Panther engine had been adjusted. It was tethered to the ground to make sure that it did not take off accidentally. When the clutch was engaged there was heavy swaying, which increased to the point where it was dangerous to increase the revolutions. To prevent the inverted control column lashing around the cabin it had to be secured centrally with a rope. There seemed to be no solution for this exaggeration of the hitherto accepted behaviour of previous Autogiros. Out-of-balance cyclic vibration of rotor blades and synchronous undercarriage response were a mystery. Usually the blades would be changed one by one. Even when more blades were made the result was the same, and so Cierva concluded that it was unsafe to fly, and it was abandoned, putting back the development of big rotor craft by several years.

The Yeovil firm must be congratulated for persevering with the unorthodox in speaking of the Pterodactyl and the Autogiro, particularly since neither saw squadron service with the RAF. The firm was producing both a single twin-gunned version of the former, the Mk V and Mk VI respectively. The Mk VI was built to AM Spec. F5/33, and had a pusher engine with the pilot enclosed in the front centre section. This afforded unobstructed fields of fire forward of the aircraft, and even backwards over the top wing. The intention was that both types would accompany the bombers, the pusher Mk VI Pterodactyls in the lead, with the tractor Mk Vs giving cover to the rear.

Geoffrey Hill also obtained a design study contract for a tailless tandem-engined flying-boat to AM Spec. R1/33 in collaboration with Saunders-Roe with its specialized knowledge in hull design. Tests carried out at the NPL water tank were promising, but an unforeseen problem arose with steering the craft on water in confined waters. In his design Hill had replaced the conventional rudder with a retractable swivelling outboard engine, but a flying-boat was no different from a ship trying to manoeuvre with little or no steerage way. Ocean liners need tugs for this purpose, and cross-channel ferries that rely on a very quick turn-round use bow thrusters, small propellers mounted transversely in the bow below the waterline. Other ideas from this visionary designer were for a twin-engined fighter and a high-speed bomber. Perhaps the most futuristic was the airliner with a 100 ft wingspan, with the passsengers accommodated in the wing. Hill was convinced that flying wings were the future answer if aircraft were to achieve supersonic speed.

As to more mundane matters, the Westland F7/30 and PV7 were flying with their enclosed cockpits, but not before several snags had been overcome on the fighter. On 15 March it was ready for taxiing, followed by the initial flight at Andover on the 23rd of the month after work on the brakes and cooling system. Once airborne, the pilot, who sat well forward between the gull wings, received severe buffeting unless he kept his head rigidly in the centre line, and he could only cruise gently before landing. This was the price that had to be paid for giving the pilot an excellent forward view. This was not the only problem, for the coolant temperatures were at their limit and it was found that the steam condensers could not cope with varying temperatures of differing flight and atmospheric conditions. It was too involved a system to be practical in service use. By the end of the month runs were being made over the speed course, in spite of engine limitations and cockpit buffeting, but the speed was disappointing. It was 30 mph below the estimated performance. The pilot's cockpit would have to be enclosed to protect him from the buffeting and to aid streamlining. This was still contrary to advice from pilots and the Air Staff that fighter pilots must fight from open cockpits, but all this was about to change. The enclosed cockpits on both the F7/30 and the PV7 gave comfort to the pilot, with an almost undiminished view. After adjustment to the ailerons the fighter was beautifully harmonized. The torsional problem with the wings of the PV7 had to be cured before the ailerons could be adjusted, and there were also problems with the horn-balanced rudder. Since the fighter was perfect in that respect it was decided to put a back-set hinged rudder on the PV7 and redesign the fin to suit. Fairey had encountered similar problems with its equivalent GP biplane when movement of the rudder was found to be impossibly heavy. Adding a servo tab only added to other problems.

Bristol   Bristol was having problems in attempting to complete its Type-123 biplane to meet AM Spec. F7/30 The cantilever one-piece lower wing had been mounted, complete with integral undercarriage. The double-skinned leading edge of the wing acted as cooling condensers, and these were connected to the honeycomb radiator under the fuselage, but the engine was still missing. The thin swept-back top wing had to be connected by struts. Barnwell was not happy, and eventually agreed to build his Type-132 low-winger as a private venture with a gull wing and Mercury engine. This was largely Roy Fedden's doing, as he was anxious for his radial engine to compete with the liquid-cooled engines of Rolls-Royce.

Martin Baker   A new name was about to be added to the aircraft industry in 1934. A determined Irishman, the sandy-haired Jimmy Martin, was about to be joined by Val Baker, who was the chief pilot at Airwork. Martin had been building a low-winger at Denham, and the famous flyer, Amy Mollison (née Johnson), had hoped to fly in it in 1929, to Australia. Unfortunately a lack of cash meant that he could not complete the aircraft, but he became established as a sub-contractor in metalwork and carried out repair work at the local flying club. He developed a 'Meccano system' of simplified tubular metal structuring, which he then applied to a fabric-covered two-seat cabin low-winger that was powered by a Javelin engine and was similar to the Miles Falcon. But would yet another small aircraft expensively made of metal compete with wooden ones? The answer lies in later sections, but many readers will be able to associate the company name with the construction of aircraft ejector seats once the Jet Age had begun.

OTHER DEVELOPMENTS
The genesis of the eight-gun monoplane fighter
At the Directorate of Operational Research in the Air Ministry was a new team of RAF pilots. These were men who were prepared to move forward from the biplane. The experience with AM Spec. 7/30 showed that if a monoplane was produced it would have to have a very large wing area in order to land in a short space. In the department was Squadron Leader Ralph Sorley, who had joined the RNAS when only sixteen, and his last post was testing aircraft at Martlesham. He argued for far greater firepower and engine power in a monoplane with the cleanest possible lines. He noticed that the design formula for twin-engined bombers gave them a speed very nearly equal to single-engined fighters, giving the fighter only a very small advantage in pursuit and interception. Assuming, therefore, that the enemy machine could be held in the gunsight for only a matter of seconds it must be possible to have the firepower to destroy an enemy machine in, say, a two-second burst.

There were two issues to be addressed. Which gun was the best suited to unleash the lethal burst, and secondly, how many guns could reasonably be mounted in an aircraft? The more guns a fighter carried the longer it would take to rearm during a turnaround between sorties. The choice of gun lay between the 0.303 in., the 0.5 in. and the 20 mm cannon. The Hispano-Suiza 20 mm cannon was greatly attracting the French and other European countries. It could fire armour-piercing shells, explosive or incendiary. The gun itself weighed 106 lb (48 kg) and a magazine of shells weighed 55 lb (25 kg). The 0.5 in. gun might have greater hitting power than the 0.303 in. gun, but little work had gone into its development and it was a heavy weapon with a low rate of fire. The best possibility of achieving the rate of fire would be to build up the density of 256 rounds in two seconds, i.e. each gun must fire 32 rounds per second. But with so many Vickers guns left over from the Great War, would the Air Ministry countenance the expenditure for eight new guns for each fighter produced at a time of financial stringency?

The question then was where the eight guns would be positioned on the aircraft. To mount them all within the fuselage would only add to the cross-sectional area when the fuselage should be as slim and streamlined as possible. Mounting the guns externally would add to drag. The monoplane wing, however, did provide enough space to mount all eight guns, four in each wing. In the meantime a mission of armament officers visited France, only to find that the 20 mm Hispano cannon was supersensitive to the rigidity of its mounting. They found a cannon designed to be mounted on the Hispano engine to fire through the propeller boss. The Poles had tried to mount a cannon beneath the wing, but these mountings were not sufficiently rigid. Tests at Martlesham showed that a 20 mm solid shell was very effective but the difficulties in mounting made it an unattractive proposition. The Germans, on the other hand, opted for fewer guns in their Me 109. There was a 3 cm cannon and two machine-guns firing through the propeller, each with a thousand rounds. This gave the Me 109 a heavier punch than either the Hurricane or the Spitfire. A direct hit from one or two of these exploding shells could destroy an aircraft, whereas the eight-gun fighter with its Brownings would need to obtain a lethal burst to be sure of a kill.

The concept of the eight-gun fighter then depended on trials with the 0.303 in. machine-gun. These proved sufficiently convincing to carry the day, permitting the Air Ministry to issue its Spec. 5/34, which called for a speed of not less than 275 mph at 15,000 ft, an endurance of 1½ hrs, a climb to 20,000 ft in 7½ mins and a service ceiling of 33,000 ft.

In-flight refuelling
In mid-August 1934 Sir Alan Cobham and Squadron Leader Helmore were practising in-flight refuelling

using an Airspeed Courier and Handley Page W10 bombers. They planned to fly non-stop to India, leaving on Friday 20 September, but the take-off was delayed by adverse weather over Malta, which prevented the tanker there from taking off. The next day they did get away and took on board 90 gallons, after which the tanker turned back to land at Ford, but a tailplane bracing bolt failed due to fatigue. The tanker struck the ground, instantly catching fire. Sadly the crew perished, unknown to Cobham at the time. But then he had trouble of his own while refuelling from the Malta tanker. The throttle linkage failed and the engine lost power. If the two men were to reach Malta in a long glide the undercarriage would have to be retracted. Eventually a belly landing was made to avoid nosing over, and the semi-protruding wheels prevented any great damage. The project may have failed in its aim to reach India non-stop, but it proved that in-flight refuelling was practicable in good weather.

Postscript
In closing the section on the year 1934 it is as well to remember that the massive expansion scheme for the RAF had just then been announced (see Chapter 2), but the man in the street was unaware of the perils facing the nation with the threat posed by the Fascist dictators. For him unemployment had fallen below two million and there was growing prosperity. The aircraft industry was going to have to meet the demands made upon it, and the 'shadow factories' would provide the extra aircraft and engines to equip the growing number of RAF squadrons. In the industry there were the dozen or so entirely separate pioneer firms, small enough for directors, designers, pilots and senior officials to know each other. They knew and frequently met officials from the Air Ministry, RAF and FAA administrators and their operational and armament specialists. This was a sound basis for expansion and bears comparison with the similar organizations in Nazi Germany.

1935
Introduction
The future looked brighter for the major aircraft companies. The index of production representing national prosperity was up above the post-war high just before the Wall Street Crash, and the cost of living had fallen. New industries were burgeoning, particularly north of London, new light industries such as radio and electrical appliances, and in the heavy industries such as chemicals, cars and lorries. But international trade was still depressed, which meant that firms had to place greater reliance on demand in the domestic market. This was part of Fairey's problem when there was a dearth of Air Ministry orders. The many firms in the French aircraft industry were compelled to organize themselves into four main groups. At home Miss Irene Ward, MP for

Wallsend, on her own initiative, set about forming an alliance of Anthony Fokker with Swan Hunter and Wigham Richards, in conjunction with Airspeed Ltd, to build Fokker and Douglas aircraft in vacant Tyneside shipyards. This was a policy of taking the work to the people, for it was not the policy of the aircraft manufacturers to set up shop on the Tyne. For that industry, help in the form of the RAF Expansion Scheme A would soon be making itself felt.

COMPANY DEVELOPMENTS
Fairey
At the AGM a profit was announced of £47,534, a reduction on the previous year of £69,148, and the dividend was reduced to 5%. Several reasons were cited, one of which was the inevitable change-over from wood to metal construction, which increased the development time of new types, and a long period of preparation was required for production runs. Secondly, fewer orders had been received from the Air Ministry. There had been a preliminary production order for one of the two new types, and Mr Fairey said that he hoped for a second, but there had been a delay in finishing the trials due to two accidents. A third reason was the purchase of the Heaton Chapel factory at Stockport so that production was no longer just confined to Hayes, and there was twice the area in the northern site. But this move was very dependent on Air Ministry support to take full advantage of the increase in productive capacity. Finally it was announced that the company would be busy on experimental work in 1936.

Westland
Westland was in some trouble. There had been a serious delay in fulfilling contracts for spares for the Wapitis in India, and the enclosed-cockpit version of Wapiti, the Wallace, was behind schedule because the hoods were incomplete. Bill Gibson, the production manager, was blamed, and after a meeting with Stuart Keep, the general manager, he resigned. Although Keep tried to take control, the company soon received a warning that unless a new workshop manager was appointed within twenty-one days, there would be a future loss of orders. Sir Ernest Petter asked his test pilot if he would like the job, but Penrose enjoyed the freedom of test flying too much and declined. Eventually John Fearn was appointed. He had come from managerial posts with BSA and knew nothing of aircraft, but he soon made up for his lack of knowledge and became an effective works manager.

The work on the Pterodactyl had come to an abrupt end once Captain Hill, the designer, had left to be a professor at London's University College. Herbert Mettam, a key man on Hill's staff, had resigned and joined A.V. Roe, and Petter had no wish to continue the aircraft's development. The torsional flexibility of the wing remained a problem, preventing more than a 200 mph dive with the stick fully forward. Wimperis, the Director of Scientific Research, agreed that the prototype Mk V should be sent to Farnborough for general investigation, but within seconds of take-off the coolant warning light flickered, at which time Penrose was 100 ft above houses. He instantly turned back as the engine seized, and he just skimmed the hedge on a downwind landing. An inspection revealed that the articulated undercarriage had gone full travel and knocked the radiator cock to the closed position. The machine was sent by lorry to Farnborough and was never flown again.

OTHER DEVELOPMENTS
Autogiro accident
This year marked the first fatal accident in England involving an Autogiro. Old Sarum had acquired one of these machines, which was being flown by Flying Officer L.W. Oliver. He disappeared into cloud at 2,000 ft, and when he reappeared he was diving towards the ground at 45 degrees, until he hit the ground. Cierva's draughtsman admitted that the C.30 should not be dived at top speed to steeper than 10 degrees. Thirty degrees was permissible at slow speeds. He told the coroner that there had been a similar accident to a French-designed machine, but it had been proved that the pilot had fainted. Harald Penrose of Westland had experienced diving an Autogiro, and was as certain as he could be that there was a critical speed beyond which the dive would increase uncontrollably, due to blade twist. There is no evidence to show that Oliver was aware of the risk of diving steeply, or if he did, he suffered a loss of orientation in cloud.

In-flight refuelling
Of interest in this context is Major Mayo's comment on in-flight refuelling. He had proposed the idea of a large aircraft carrying a smaller aircraft, 'piggy-back' style. On the approach to the destinations of the two aircraft, the smaller one could be launched to proceed independently to its separate destination, thus effecting a considerable saving of fuel. Mayo commented that in-flight refuelling was another method of dodging the problem of getting heavily loaded aircraft safely into the air. In-flight refuelling was only a fair-weather method. Catapulting could not be considered a satisfactory solution because of high cost, lack of mobility and the risk that in releasing an aircraft low down it could not land safely should an engine fail. Mayo's advocacy of the Composite was based on the idea that the power of both aircraft would combine to ensure a normal take-off.

THE GENESIS OF RADAR
The experience of the Great War had shown that the manned airship and bomber could inflict considerable

damage on economic targets as well as centres of population. In 1935 the idea of military airships dropping bombs was out of the question, but the manned bomber was faster and larger and carried a much greater bomb load. Furthermore, in the large-scale Air Defence Exercises held in 1934, well over half the bombers reached their targets unopposed, and so the Government decided to appoint a special committee, to be known as the Committee for the Scientific Survey of Air Defence (CSSAD). This committee was to investigate the possibility of utilizing the recent progress in scientific invention to counter air attacks. Sir Philip Sassoon named the members of the committee as H.T. Tizard, Rector of Imperial College (Chairman); A.V. Hill, Foulerton Research Professor of the Royal Society; H.E. Wimperis, the Director of Scientific Research, and P.M.S. Blackett, Professor of Physics at London University. The committee would invite other distinguished scientists to contribute evidence as the investigations proceeded if it was felt that the work would be facilitated.

Originally the investigation went into the possibility of developing what the popular Press called the 'death ray'. This was mentioned briefly in Volume I, and was the sort of idea that would give rise to speculation and popular excitement since it offered the prospect of being able to kill aircrews and destroy their aircraft by means of unseen rays. Tizard was therefore understandably anxious to eliminate this from the committee's

Robert Watson-Watt.

investigations if it was beyond the means of the current state of technology to create death rays. Wimperis was asked if he could find a scientist who could come up with an answer, and as a result, the 43-year-old Robert Watson-Watt was appointed. He passed the mathematical problem to his 28-year-old assistant at the radio research station at Slough, Arnold Wilkins. Both men deduced that producing a beam of sufficient power to harm human beings was not possible in the existing state of technology, but they felt that it would be possible to detect the presence of an aircraft from a distance.

Three years earlier engineers at the Post Office radio station between St Albans and Hatfield had found that reception was disturbed by reflections from aircraft taking off from the nearby de Havilland's airfield. It was also found that radio signals were reflected back from the ionized layer above the earth and it was possible to measure the elapsed time that occurred between the transmission of the signal and its reception back on the ground. If signals could be reflected from aircraft and the elapsed time measured it would be possible to determine the range to that aircraft. Watson-Watt submitted his report, and within the week a meeting was arranged between Air Marshal Dowding and Wimperis. Dowding was asked for £10,000 to develop the pulse/echo technique, but he was not going to commit the Air Ministry without a demonstration. Watson-Watt and Wilkins agreed and chose the powerful short-wave station at Daventry. Transmissions were sent and the power reflected from a Heyford bomber flying up and down at various known ranges was measured. When detection was achieved up to eight miles the money was granted.

Experiments were then carried out over the sea from a site at Orfordness, where three pairs of 75 ft lattice masts were installed, mounting aerials. To begin with, the detection range was seventeen miles, soon increased to forty miles by July 1935. It was necessary to show the map position of the plot and its height. Watson-Watt felt able to propose the building of a chain of warning stations around the coast to provide warning of attack and to direct the defending fighters to their targets. He proposed the building of a station at once, and if this was successful, to build a second to cover the Thames estuary, then a final chain to cover the east and south coasts of the country.

THE BIPLANE VERSUS THE MONOPLANE

The question of the biplane versus the monoplane was still engaging members of the aircraft industry as late as 1935. Geoffrey de Havilland spoke about the matter in a lecture to the RAeS on 15 April. De Havilland, of all the aircraft constructors, concentrated mainly on civil aircraft, when the maximum economy had to be combined with speed. He believed that biplanes were lighter whereas monoplanes were faster. Taking off with

a larger load was easier with a biplane, making it well suited for operation from poorer aerodromes and at great heights. In 2005 it is taken for granted that an airliner will take off from a paved runway, but airliners in the 1930s took off from grass, so the debate was relevant at the time. De Havilland commented that since the immediate post-war era civilian aircraft had evolved very differently from the military types. Then it was considered that the civilian air fleet of a country could be used for military purposes. Small aircraft used about the same amount of fuel to cover a given distance as a motor car, but were much faster and had surpassed the speed of their single-seat fighter ancestry, which had twice the power. Civil development aims at the utmost performance for every horsepower developed, whereas the military want performance regardless of the amount of power.

AIR MINISTRY SPECIFICATIONS
AM Spec. 5/34

Roy Fedden, Bristol's engine designer, was responsible for some successful radial engines and was naturally anxious that AM Spec. 5/34 admitted a radial-engined fighter. At that time both Supermarine and Hawker were working experimentally on designs, both using the new Rolls-Royce Merlin engine. Folland had gone for four guns mounted in the fuselage, with guns mounted below the lower wing. Both Sydney Camm at Hawker and Reginald Mitchell at Supermine had accepted and were working on the eight-gun fighter, of which the mock-ups were nearing completion.

Installation of the guns inside the wing was new, but if the guns fired inside the arc of the propeller, as they would do with fuselage-mounted guns, then a mechanical interrupter gear would have to be used. But if one was trying to achieve the highest density of fire in just two seconds the last thing one wanted was for the fire to be interrupted. On the other hand, guns could experience stoppages which, if the pilot could reach the gun, he might clear. Pilots since the Great War had been used to this, so moving the guns to the wings would be controversial. It was then pointed out that guns firing continuously might not be prone to stoppages, and with eight guns they wouldn't all jam at once. Then there was the question of how the guns were to be fired. Using a Bowden cable to actuate the trigger meant a time lag, which was no use if the pilot was trying to get in a lethal two-second burst, so Dunlop developed a new firing system whereby the pilot had only to press a button on the control column. Finally there was the problem of trajectory. If the guns were mounted in the wings the trajectory of each gun would run parallel and there would never be a concentration of fire. Guns in the wings would have to be pointed inwards so that there would be a concentration of fire at a predetermined point ahead of the aircraft. With a gun firing through the

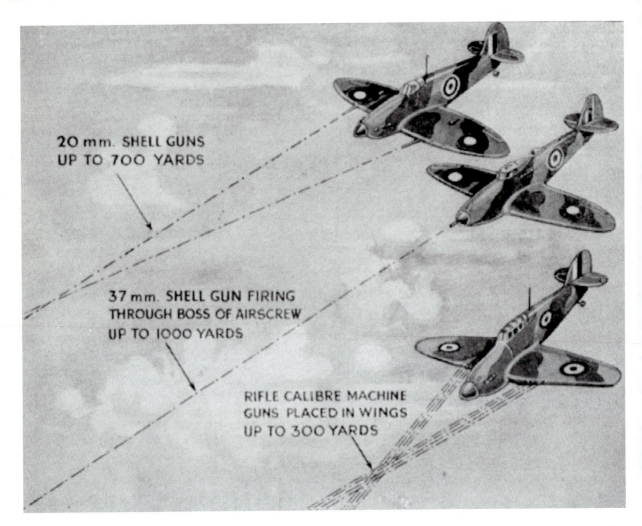

20 mm. SHELL GUNS
UP TO 700 YARDS

37 mm. SHELL GUN FIRING
THROUGH BOSS OF AIRSCREW
UP TO 1000 YARDS

RIFLE CALIBRE MACHINE
GUNS PLACED IN WINGS
UP TO 300 YARDS

propeller boss, as it did in the American Aircobra fighter, this would not be a problem (see diagram). What became known as 'Dowding's spread' was the setting of the guns to provide the concentration of fire at 400 yards ahead of the fighter aircraft. Experience in combat showed that the range to the target aircraft should be less than that.

AM Spec. G/41

The Vickers entrant for this AM Specification was the Type 287, private-venture monoplane with a wingspan of 74 ft 7 in. It made its maiden flight at Brooklands on 19 June with Vickers test pilot 'Mutt' Summers at the controls. During May Air Vice-Marshal Dowding and Air Commodore Verney had visited Martlesham to inspect the other seven contenders:

1. Vickers Type 253, semi-geodetic biplane.
2. Blackburn B7 biplane based on the Shark with Tiger IV engine.
3. HP47 monoplane.

4. Hawker PV4 with Pegasus IV (Hart derivative) engine.
5. Parnall biplane designed by Clarke with Pegasus III engine.
6. Fairey biplane with Tiger IV engine.
7. Westland PV7.

In spite of the crash with the Westland PV7 prototype, the Martlesham pilots and technical staff recommended it, but it was rejected by the Air Staff. The Vickers Type 253 was preferred, followed by the Fairey TSR II (not listed above), which had been considered suitable as a result of handling tests carried out in 1934. The HP47 was next, followed by the Blackburn B7. Accordingly an order was placed for 150 of the Vickers biplane, even though 'Mutt' Summers and the Vickers designer, Reg Pierson, much preferred the Type 287 monoplane, and eventually the Air Ministry was persuaded to cancel the order for the Type 253 and replace it with the Type 287.

1936

Introduction

When King George V carried out his Silver Jubilee inspection of the RAF at Mildenhall in June 1935 he was driven down lines of biplanes. He witnessed a biplane air force, and it is therefore significant that 1936 is perhaps best remembered for the unveiling of the prototype Spitfire and Hurricane. With the monoplane fighters and bombers that were to follow, the RAF would be transformed in three short years. The biplane Fury and Gauntlet, Heyford and Virginia would stay on for another two years, but would be gone by the outbreak of war. Only the FAA, which gained its independence from the RAF in 1938, would use biplanes as first-line aircraft when the country went to war, the most famous of them being the Swordfish. Operating biplanes over the ocean far from land-based fighters meant that their inferiority in speed and performance did not matter to the extent that it did for fighters operating over land. The Germans and Italians did not have aircraft carriers.

Fairey

At Fairey's AGM the shareholders found that the profit was £39,112 10s. 5d., compared with £47,534 2s. 4d. for the previous year. It is not clear whether that included the Belgian factory, where profits were taxed in that country, but Dick Fairey seemed unconcerned. He could announce that three types were going into production and orders for another type were in prospect. He nevertheless used the opportunity to take a sideswipe at the rumoured shadow factories, but that was understandable given the threat they might constitute to the established aircraft construction companies. He claimed that it would not be possible for the shadow factories outside the aircraft

Dick Fairey.

industry to produce aircraft without specialized equipment and a highly skilled workforce. Fairey was clearly trying to reassure his shareholders, but he had little need to worry given the enormous rate of expansion. The existing firms could not possibly have coped without the assistance of the non-established aircraft firms and the shadow factories. Certainly the purchase of the Heaton Chapel factory at Stockport had been a sound investment, and already 750 persons worked there.

Hawker

Hawker, too, had purchased more land. Brooklands was too small and congested, so an extensive arable area near the village of Langley had been purchased for the construction and testing of prototypes. The company's associated firm, Armstrong Whitworth, had also moved from a cramped location. The move from Whitley aerodrome was to the Coventry municipal aerodrome at Baginton, where an initial factory building 600 ft × 150 ft had been erected. There was every possibility of extending if the need arose, for the factory was right in the middle of a 1,100-acre site owned by Coventry Corporation.

THE SPITFIRE AND HURRICANE PROTOTYPES

The Hurricane

Although both aircraft were eight-gun monoplane fighters, in one respect the Hurricane was the last of the old. The rear fuselage consisted of fabric-covered stringers, whereas the Spitfire was of stressed-skin construction. On the orders of the Air Ministry the Hurricane prototype was delivered to Martlesham after only ten flights totalling eight hours, in spite of the fact that there was a run of teething troubles. Because of the urgency to fly the aircraft to Martlesham, such limited flying as was possible had to be restricted to brief periods of evaluation stability and control. Modifications to the sliding canopy, retractable undercarriage and engine installation had to be tested, for all were giving considerable trouble.

The first sliding canopy came off after the third flight and could not be opened at a speed above a rather slow climb. Using the hand-operated hydraulic pump, it was impossible to retract and lock the undercarriage; indeed, the pump was not engine driven. Then the engine started to develop serious mechanical faults, and because it had to be nursed, it was very difficult to test the suitability and control at speeds greater than level flight because the engine was limited to only 5% above the maximum permissible, nor was the aircraft spun or aerobatted.

It was almost in this parlous state that one of the finest fighters ever built by the British aircraft industry arrived at Martlesham, where the pilots reported on the ease of handling and good control at all speeds down to a stall. The Air Staff had set the requirement for a speed of 275

K.5083 Hurricane prototype flown by George Bulman.

mph for the new fighters, and the Hurricane had easily exceeded this figure, with a speed of 315 mph at 16,000 ft. That said, the unreliability of the new Merlin engine was a real problem, and there were at least three engine changes in the first two weeks. Defects included internal glycol leaks, causing rapid loss of coolant. This was the most serious problem. There was also distortion and ultimate cracking of the cylinder heads due to the much higher temperatures possible with this type of coolant. Completion of the Martlesham tests had to be postponed and the aircraft returned to Brooklands.

The response from Rolls-Royce was not encouraging. The company decided that the troubles could only be overcome by intensive flight development with redesigned cylinder heads. The Merlin I engines would not be available for production Hurricanes, and the modified Merlin IIs would not be ready until the autumn of 1937, some three months after the first production Hurricane was due off the production line. Finally, there was only a bare minimum of engines to keep the prototype flying.

The Spitfire

K.5054 was the elegant, polished, blue-grey prototype of the Spitfire that was flown by 'Mutt' Summers, the Vickers chief test pilot, at Eastleigh airport on 6 March. Reginald Mitchell, by then a very sick man, was there to watch. He was always in a state of tension when prototypes made their maiden flight, as he felt personally responsible for any death or injury that might befall the test pilots. Though suffering periodic bouts of pain, he continued to supervise the work in hand closely, and spent most of his time with his draughtsmen. Since Summers was very busy with the prototype Wellington, Jeffrey Quill took over the prototype Spitfire. Harald Penrose, Westland's chief test pilot, was privileged to fly the Spitfire several months after the first flight of the prototype. He recalled the experience:

I flew it at Martlesham, the first non-Vickers industrial pilot to do so. There was a rolling gait of the narrow undercarriage as I taxied out, the dropping wing and emphatic swing as the over-coarse fixed-pitch wooden propeller laboriously gripped the air, dragging the machine into a run faster and longer than anything I experienced. Longitudinal control felt excessively sensitive and because the undercarriage retraction pump was on the right I could not stop my left hand on the control column moving in sympathy, so the flight path violently oscillated until the thud of the legs locking into the wing recesses and the machine settled into a steady flight path. Suddenly a Gladiator appeared 1,000 ft above, its fixed cantilever undercarriage extended like an eagle's claws, offering the opportunity of a dog fight. I drew the stick back in the manner to which I had become accustomed, forgetting the lightness of the controls. A vice clamped my temples, my face muscles sagged and all was blackness. My pull on the stick relaxed instantly, but returning vision found the Spitfire almost vertical and the Gladiator a full 2,000 ft below.

In Penrose's opinion every pilot who flew the Spitfire recognized it as a winner. The prototype was 34 mph faster than the Hurricane, and both were faster than the Messerschmitt Bf 109 in its early version with a Kestrel engine and wooden propeller, though it was later tested with a Jumo engine. When a production order went out for 310 Spitfires to AM Spec. F16/36, German intelligence soon picked it up and there was increased pressure to speed up the trials between the Bf 109 and the Heinkel He 112. This was the largest order thus far received by Supermarine, but the firm's experience with the Schneider races and the production of metal flying-boat hulls held them in good stead. The Spitfire was an advanced metal monocoque structure, and expensive jigging and tooling would be required. The works' capacity was insufficient and extensive sub-contracting was called for.

OTHER PROTOTYPES
Battle prototype
The Fairey Battle prototype, K.4303, flew on 10 March piloted by Chris Staniland. The silver-painted low-wing monoplane had suffered the same delay as the Hurricane due to snags with the Merlin engine. This was a two-seat fighter bomber akin to the Bristol fighter. Such was the urgency of rearmament that the Air Ministry had decided to order 155 machines before the prototype had left the ground. The stipulation was that the speed must not be less than 195 mph at 15,000 ft. The prototype did achieve a speed of 263 mph but the figure was lower for production models. It handled very easily, if a little heavy on the controls, and was easy to land due to the cushioning effect of the broad low wing.

Battles under construction.

Whitley prototype
The Whitley prototype, K.4586, made its maiden flight one week after the Battle. This was at Baginton, Armstrong Whitworth's new airfield, and the test pilot was Campbell-Orde. This was another example of an aircraft ordered off the drawing-board, and eighty of these bombers had been ordered seven months before the maiden flight of K.4586. The bull-nosed, box-like fuselages and wings with their great box spars were already lining the erecting shops while the 795 hp Tiger

The Whitley.

K.5054 Spitfire prototype flown by 'Mutt' Summers.

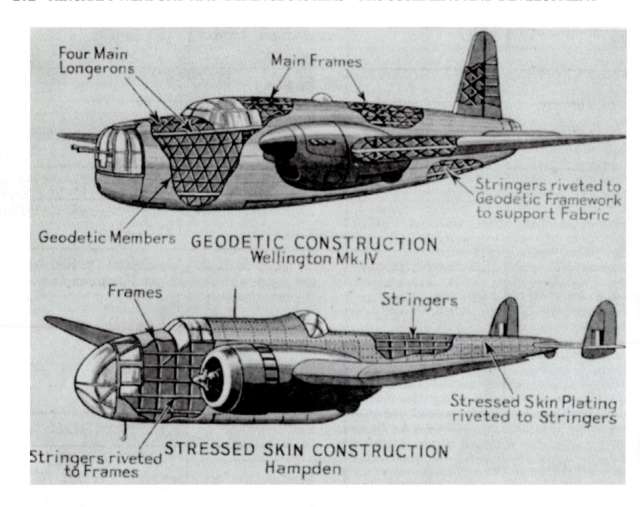

Four Main Longerons

Main Frames

Stringers riveted to Geodetic Framework to support Fabric

Geodetic Members

GEODETIC CONSTRUCTION
Wellington Mk.IV

Frames

Stringers

Stressed Skin Plating riveted to Stringers

Stringers riveted to Frames

STRESSED SKIN CONSTRUCTION
Hampden

The Wellington – prototype and production aircraft.

engines were being assembled. This gives some idea of the pressure on everyone in the aircraft industry to produce completed aircraft to a very tight schedule as the expansion scheme got under way. Lieutenant-Colonel Henry Disney had been appointed Director of Production in the department of the Air Member for Supply and Organization with effect from 31 March. His task was to coordinate all aircaft and engine manufacturing programmes, and to investigate hold-ups.

Wellington prototype

Built to AM Spec. B9/32, the Wellington bomber made its maiden flight on 15 May, flown by 'Mutt' Summers. The prototype K.4049 was unusual in its geodetic construction designed by Barnes Wallis to provide exceptional strength in its structural integrity. Trevor Westbrook was responsible for the construction of the fuselage, and both men accompanied Summers on the maiden flight. The diagram illustrates the difference between 'stressed-skin' and 'geodetic' construction.

The nose- and tail-gun positions had been faired with stringers and fabric. The aircraft climbed easily from Brooklands, and Summers experienced no difficulty in handling. There was some elevator overbalance and directional anomalies with a hunting rudder. This was a mid-wing monoplane, which permitted room in the fuselage for the bomb-bay beneath the wing. The geodetic trellis not only provided great strength, it was light. Compared with a monocoque skin it was like cutting out hundreds of diamond shapes from that skin, with all the saving in weight that that implied. The original specification was for a bomb weight of 1,000 lb with a range of 720 miles. The Wellington bomber had a bomb capacity of 4,500 lb and a range of 3,200 miles, cruising at 180 mph. The comparative photographs that follow show how different the prototype was from the production Wellington.

The Lysander

This Army Cooperation aircraft, the Lysander, prototype K.6127, also had its maiden flight on 15 May, piloted by Harald Penrose. The photograph, which is of the second prototype, K.6128, discloses its very unusual and distinctive appearance. It flew from the long-deserted airfield at Boscombe Down near Amesbury, only twelve months after the issue of the contract. Penrose got airborne in less than 150 yards and changed to coarse pitch. At 5,000 ft he was ready to try the controls. The response was good but the ailerons were a little heavy and there was a measure of longitudinal instability with the controls free. He then tried a stall with the tip and root slats fully extended and there was perfect control with the stick right back. He mentally added 20% to the stalling speed as he made his approach to Boscombe. He noticed that the control column was fully back to

The Westland Lysander.

maintain a slow enough speed, and he used a little engine to increase the slipstream over the elevators. As the aircraft touched down on its main wheels, the tailwheel was just off the ground. His report was favourable, but he warned of difficulties with tail trim. The wind tunnel tests, as so often was the case, had failed to predict precisely the handling characteristics once an aircraft was airborne. In this case it was the big change of downwash, and this necessitated several redesigns of the trimming gear to secure an exceptionally big negative tailplane angle for landing. That too had its danger.

The Defiant and Hotspur

The Defiant, like the Fairey Battle, was one of those aircraft that simply did not live up to expectations when committed to combat. Having decided that the new family of monoplane fighters would have four Browning machine-guns in each wing to concentrate the fire of eight guns in a lethal concentration, it was not certain that such a fighter would always succeed. The Air Staff accepted, therefore, that a fighter with a four-gun power-operated turret might be able to attack a bomber formation from a standing patrol. This was a different concept, and would mean that an enemy aircraft could be attacked without the fighter being pointed at the target aircraft. But it would also mean accepting a slightly reduced performance. With added fuel load and the weight of the gunner, the resulting aircraft would not have the same agility as the eight-gun fighter. This led to AM Spec. F9/35, and tenders were received from Boulton Paul (Defiant) and Hawker (Hotspur). In both cases the gunner was mounted above the pilot and the gunner had all-round fire capability provided the target aircraft was above the fighter. He could not engage an enemy aircraft that was below. To have added forward-firing guns so that the pilot would be able to engage an enemy that was out of the line of fire of the gunner would have added an unacceptable addition to the all-up weight of the aircraft. And so the pilot was reduced

Defiants.

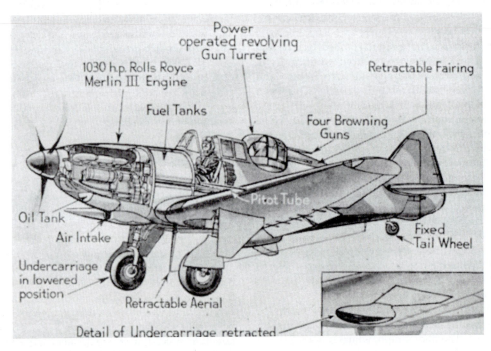

1030 h.p. Rolls Royce Merlin III Engine

Power operated revolving Gun Turret

Retractable Fairing

Fuel Tanks

Four Browning Guns

Oil Tank

Air Intake

Pitot Tube

Fixed Tail Wheel

Undercarriage in lowered position

Retractable Aerial

Detail of Undercarriage retracted

to placing his aircraft in such a position that the gunner could engage an enemy aircraft. In combat the turret came as a nasty shock to those German pilots who made the usual attack from behind. Needless to say, it did not take them very long to work out the best position from which to attack this type of fighter. The Defiant, which actually entered service, was soon withdrawn after suffering a high casualty rate.

OTHER DEVELOPMENTS
AM Spec. 10/35 – the mounting of the Hispano cannon

One of the characteristics of the Hurricane in which it was superior to the Spitfire was that it was a more stable gun platform, and it was decided to revive AM Spec. 10/35 and mount four 20 mm Hispano cannon in the wings of a Hurricane. A decisive result could therefore be achieved in two seconds because of the devastating effect of cannon shells upon a target aircraft. A further specification was issued, F.37/35, for a twin-engined, single-seat fighter armed with four cannon.

Research at the RAE

Research could not have been more important if the RAF and FAA were to keep abreast of the potential enemy. The change to metal-skinned construction was revolutionary and gave the RAE plenty of work on mathematical and experimental investigation into such matters as stress diffusion, box structures and sandwich construction. Much of this work fell on Dr D. Williams. There was a new 24 ft atmospheric wind tunnel that permitted full-scale investigation of air-cooled engines to provide adequate cooling with the least drag. Work also proceeded on honeycomb radiators for liquid cooling that would blend aerodynamically without loss of thermal efficiency. Given the growing size of bombers, the development of servo controls was being studied as part of the general problem of stability and control. Metallurgists were devising improved protection for magnesium fuel tanks against corrosion from water and leaded fuel. The engine department was investigating vibration of propellers and aircraft structures. The wireless section was examining the German Lorenz and American Hegenbeurger blind-landing systems, the effect of noise and temperature on radio communication and design of aerials and components. A new department had been created to look at ground camouflage, balloon barrages, ground defence schemes involving parachutes, cables, rockets and aerial mines released from aircraft. The armament department, headed by R. Purves, was devising fragmentation and incendiary bombs, release units and carriers, smoke-curtain generators, gun ancillary equipment, high-speed targets and researching on bomb shapes. Under the direction of P. Salmon, the drawing office was designing a large hydro-pneumatic catapult to launch the projected heavy bomber aircraft of 65,000 lb all-up weight. This hive of activity reminds one of the scenes from the James Bond films when 'Q' is demonstrating his new gadgets to 007.

1937

1937 PROTOTYPES
Blackburn Skua

Blackburn had been working on a two-seat dive-bomber, the B24, later known as the Skua. This was a low-wing monoplane powered by an 840 hp radial engine. As with all carrier aircraft, the wings folded for the movement on the lift and stowage below decks, and the Skua was 14 ft when folded. The aircraft was built to FAA Spec. 027/34 and was flush-riveted and Alclad-skinned, with the engine driving a three-bladed propeller. It had a buoyancy compartment below the

pilot's cockpit, with another behind the gunner's cockpit, and a watertight box between the main spars forward of the ailerons. The maiden flight by 'Dasher' Blake proved satisfactory, but the centre of gravity was near the aft position, and so longitudinal stability was marginal. Accordingly an extra bay was inserted so that the engine could be brought forward 2 ft 5 ins. The wingtip slots were found to be unnecessary, so were eliminated from production machines, of which 190 were built to Spec. 25/26. These had been ordered off the drawing-board in July 1936.

COMPANY DEVELOPMENTS
Gloster's new chief designer

Previous sections on Gloster dealt with Folland's position as chief designer and his unhappiness of being, in a sense, subordinate to Sydney Camm, who had designed the Hurricane. Folland's past reputation for being wedded to the biplane was bound to bring him into conflict with the designers in other companies who were working on the new designs that had to meet changing Air Ministry specifications requiring monoplanes. Sooner or later Folland would have to stand down, and when he did his place was taken by George Carter from the parent company, Hawker, where Camm had been one of his juniors. As he joined Gloster the shops were full of Gauntlets, of which 204 had been ordered, and Gladiators, the very last biplane fighter for the RAF. In the meantime Carter was in the process of completing design work on a twin-engined, two-seat fighter with a turret to meet AM Spec. F34/35.

Flying-boats

The three firms Short, Saunders-Roe and Supermarine were all working on flying-boats, and here again the biplane was being elbowed out by the monoplane. The Saro London and the Supermarine Stranraer had been built to AM Spec. R24/31, and they would be the last of the biplanes. The American Consolidated Company had produced the twin-engined, high-wing monoplane maritime reconnaissance flying-boat capable of attacking surface ships and submarines. This was the PBY known as the Catalina which would go into service with the RAF. Short was also busy working on a military version of its splendid Empire flying-boat, later named the Sunderland, which would prove to be one of the most successful additions to the RAF's maritime inventory, serving with distinction during the Second World War and the Korean War of 1950–3. The Sunderland would have both bow and stern turrets, with bombs stowed on rails amidships that could be winched outboard through side-hatches to be jettisoned. An admirable example is on display at the Imperial Museum, Duxford, near Cambridge.

The death of R.J. Mitchell

Supermarine's chief designer, Reginald Joseph Mitchell, lived long enough to see the product of his genius take to the air when 'Mutt' Summers flew the prototype Spitfire. Mitchell died on 11 June 1937 at the early age of 42 years. He had joined the company in 1916 and received his early training on flying-boats, which progressed to success with his floatplanes in the Schneider Trophy races. In all he was responsible for twenty-eight designs and their variants. Supermarine shared with the other companies the experience of having prototypes turned down by the Air Ministry, but Mitchell did have twenty-three designs accepted by the Air Ministry, of which fifteen were successful. Eight went into production and two were not completed. The surgical operation he underwent in 1933 was only

partially successful. He suffered increasing bouts of pain during the following three years, and when he underwent further surgery in March 1937 his disease was found to be incurable. He went to a Vienna clinic in April, but nothing could be done and he returned home at the end of May. He died three weeks later after a period of unconsciousness. On his death Joe Smith carried on the work to develop the Spitfire.

The four-engined bomber

The concept of the four-engined strategic bomber was a natural outcome, given the increasing power of engines and bomb-carrying capacity of aircraft where the bombs would be dropped from bays within the fuselage. The Americans had shown the destructive potential of the four-engined bomber as Boeing developed its forerunner of the famous B-17. At home Vickers Supermarine had plans for such a bomber, but had its hands full with the Wellington and the Spitfire. It would fall to Short, Avro and Handley Page to produce the British four-engined bomber. A left-over of the 1920s was the idea that a troop carrier like the Vernon could also carry bombs. The Handley Page Harrow was one such aircraft. This led to complexity in British design of bombers/troop carriers. AM Spec. B12/36 asked for a four-engined machine with accommodation for reserve crew and twenty-four fully equipped troops, which fundamentally affected structural design. AM Spec. P13/36, however, reduced the requirement for troop carrying to twelve troops with no reserve crew. The design of B12/36 meant that only 2,000 lb of armour-piercing bombs could be carried, whereas P13/36 could take two torpedoes. The bomb-bay of the former was divided into small compartments. The latter had uninterrupted bomb cells of maximum length and width. A further explanation for the complexity of design was the Air Ministry requirement to have airframes that could be readily dismantled into components that would fit RAF packing-case sizes that would in turn fit into standard railway wagons. All such components had also to be interchangeable. Then there was the need for short take-off and landing from grass airfields, for paved runways on most RAF airfields were still to come. Finally such aircraft must be able to remain afloat in a level attitude for several hours following a ditching. All-in-all the Air Ministry's demand was a pretty tall order.

Profitability of firms

Blackburn shared with the other firms a profitable year due to the expansion scheme taking effect. The firm's profits for the year were £120,480, with adequate general reserves, enabling a 12% dividend on ordinary shares. Bristol's profits were £295,008, and £100,000 was added to the general reserve. Coupled with the premium on £1,200,000 shares issued in July, this brought the reserve to £1,100,000. De Havilland had a profit of £71,709, but was £6,000 down on the previous year. In spite of this it maintained its 10% dividend, as the company now had doubled capital due to the recent issue of 600,000 shares at a pound. General aircraft had a profit of only £3,239 6s. 5d., but this was an improvement, given the set-back when the ST-18 Monospar was lost in the Timor Sea. On the other hand, staff were being doubled and the works would be fully employed during 1938 even if no further orders were accepted. Handley Page could not present its accounts because the Inland Revenue might appeal against a recent court decision that money received from patents was capital and not revenue. If no liability could be established, the general reserve would be £140,000 and the directors might consider another bonus issue to ordinary shareholders. Dick Fairey presided at the ninth AGM on 20 December and reported a profit of £248,178, enabling a dividend of 12½% to be paid. Fairey was then working with the Austin Motor Co. Ltd in making the Battle light bomber.

1938
1938 PROTOTYPES
Whirlwind prototype
The prototype Whirlwind, L.6844, made its first flight on 11 October. It had propellers that rotated in opposite directions, and Exactor throttles had been developed to control the engines. There was, however, a problem in that a large movement in the throttles might not result in any change of revolutions. This meant repriming the system by pulling back the lever and then pumping it back and forth. If engine power was required instantly in an emergency this was a real danger. At Boscombe Down, where the maiden flight was made, the take-off would be on grass from east to west. Then it was discovered that the engines were steaming. When, eventually, a take-off run was made, the throttles had to

be opened so that the aircraft could clear the fence. After half an hour in the air it was clear that there were problems with the controls. In tight turns the aircraft juddered, the tip slats extended with an unacceptable jerk, there was a nose-down tendency at speed and the engines ran too hot. Incandescent gases burned through an aileron push-rod and the aircraft went into a vicious starboard roll. It had to be flown home with both ailerons upturned, using rudder alone.

Bristol Beaufort prototype
On 15 October the Bristol Type 152 Beaufort twin-engined reconnaissance torpedo-bomber development of the Blenheim made its first flight at Filton, piloted by Cyril Uwins, only eleven weeks after Frank Barnwell's death. Seventy of these aircraft had already been ordered back in September 1936, and this was the first production machine. Special low-drag nacelles had been fitted, which had vertical flanking air exits, but since those retained too much heat they were replaced by normal gill cowling. But even then the engines were still too hot. Retractable undercarriages were by then the norm for new designs, but there were still teething troubles.

There were various ways in which the doors could come down, and if one leg came down before the other there could be asymmetrical drag. This was overcome by having the doors open up sideways. There was turbulence caused by the dorsal gun turret, and problems with the engine and oil cooling, all pointing to a far larger development time than at first envisaged.

Development of the Wellington
There were problems with the production version of the Wellington, which was a complete redesign of the prototype (see p. 212), and it incorporated features of the larger, more powerful Warwick. Two months' delay followed an early undercarriage failure and the installation of the Pegasus VII engines, and when it finally got airborne again it was found to be nose heavy in dives. Pierson was at loggerheads with the RAE over the possible cure, the latter proposing an inset hinge balance instead of servo tabs. Pierson then reverted to horn-balanced elevators, but in the end it was by trial and error that the situation improved, with small changes to the trim tabs and horn balance. There remained, however, a big nose-up change of trim when the flaps were lowered.

Saunders-Roe A.33 and S.36 Lerwick

In the autumn the Saunders-Roe A.33 and S.36 Lerwick were test flown. Frank Courtney, who had done much test flying in the 1920s, had reappeared from the USA and was given the task of test flying the A.33, which had been built to the same specifications as the Short Sunderland. The 90 ft wingspan flying-boat was launched on 10 October and underwent taxiing trials on the smooth surface of the River Medina. On the 14th Courtney felt ready to attempt a first flight, and it was taxied out to the Solent, where the sea was smoothest. The A.33 was 10,000 lb below the designed maximum of 41,500 lb for this test, and she eventually got airborne after some porpoising. This was due to wave impact on the wing sponsons. After several more flights Courtney was ready to try a take-off in somewhat heavier seas, but this time the porpoising was so bad that the flying-boat hit the water hard. The starboard inner section of the monospar failed, and the wing twisted so much that a propeller blade pierced the hull and sponson. The motor boat on stand-by rushed to the scene and towed the mangled A.33 back to the slipway at East Cowes. The damage was too great, and the Air Ministry decided not to have her reconstructed.

Saunders-Roe had little better luck with its Lerwick, which did not last long in operational service. It was built to AM Spec. R1/36. Although it had a deep hull it was a wet boat, and as the hull lifted up onto its step prior to take-off the bow wave sometimes impinged upon the propellers. A heavy swing to starboard could not be fully corrected by movement of the rudder, and the pilot had to throttle the starboard engine to correct the swing. When Courtney tried to fly it on a single engine the rudder was impossibly heavy, and a tendency to porpoise meant months modifying the step. Finally, as if the aforementioned problems were not bad enough, the Lerwick took so long to get airborne that the service load had to be restricted to 8,300 lb. Even with the supercharged Hercules II engines, the speed was a disappointing 215 mph against an estimate of 230.

OTHER DEVELOPMENTS
Aeronautical Inspection Department

The increased output of aircraft and engines under the expansion schemes meant more inspection. By 1938 there were 175 resident inspectors, and 6,000 other inspectors supervised the work of 1,600 approved firms. Their work had been made more complex because equipment development had been made more difficult at a time of revolutionary changes in design. This had put a great strain on the AID. But the inspectors had not been trained as engineers. Handley Page commented upon the need to have a large body of men in the industry trained as engineers. He further opined that the AID staff were amateurs in common with many in the

industry, and had in mind the SBAC scheme of scholarships to remedy the situation.

More on in-flight refuelling

Further to Alan Cobham's attempt at in-flight refuelling, there followed trials by Dick Atcherley with a civilian aircraft called Cumbria and a redundant AW.23 bomber/transport loaned by the Air Ministry as a tanker. The patents were owned by a company called Interair Ltd. The reel holding the pipeline was positioned beneath the pilot's cabin of the tanker. A weighted line from the tanker grappled a line trailing from the Cambria's stern and the pipeline was then winched in and the feed hose connected to the pipeline leading to the Cambria's tanks. On completion the two aircraft simply pulled away, breaking the connection.

The death of Frank Barnwell

Bristol's designer, Captain Frank Barnwell, was tragically killed in a 25 ft low-winger he had built for fun flying. While he may not have been first and foremost a pilot, he did his best to experience his own designs in the air, although Cyril Uwins and the Bristol directors did their best to prevent him. He was universally mourned. Originally trained as a naval architect, he felt the excitement of flying, and after a year in the USA he joined with his brother to form the Grampian Engineering and Motor Co. Ltd. However, they built aeroplanes that were not entirely successful. In March 1911 he joined the British and Colonial Aeroplane Co. He was a draughtsman of the old school, before mass production, and was extremely neat and methodical in everything he did. He worked his way up to become a world-famous designer, only to die when his aircraft stalled on take-off on 2 August.

Bomb aiming and bomb-carrying capacities

The methods of aiming and dropping bombs had come a long way since the Great War. In that conflict bombs were simply dropped over the side of the aircraft by one of the crew. Later bombs were placed in racks beneath the lower wings. It was crude, unscientific and very much hit and miss when it came to hitting the target. But the early bombs were dropped from low altitudes, and when flying was in its infancy, the morale effect was more important than causing actual damage. It was a fear of the unknown, and was marked in civilian populations that suffered the Zeppelin airship and Gotha bomber attacks, like the people of south-eastern towns of England. Trenchard overplayed the bomber threat in the inter-war years, and certainly endowed the bomber with offensive capabilities that it simply did not have. Even the air exercises held in the late 1920s were skewed in favour of the bomber. But in fact little had changed since the Great War. The bombs may not have been dropped by hand over the side of the aircraft, but

Bomb aimer.

only two crew members, as there had been in the old Bristol Fighter that saw service up until 1932.

What changed in the later 1930s was that bombs were mostly carried within a bomb-bay inside the fuselage. Also, a crew member would double as a gunner and bomb aimer. The tremendous increases in the power of aircraft engines meant that the bomb loads could be increased. The bomb aimer in the photograph has his thumb ready to release the bombs, and the aiming equipment made allowances for the aircraft's speed and the wind's strength and direction. The greater the altitude, the lower the threat from enemy fighters, but the lower the level of accuracy. Also there was always the possibility that cloud might obscure the target from view.

1939
1939 PROTOTYPES
Stirling prototype

It was unusual for Short's chief test pilot, Lankester Parker, to be test flying a landplane, but Short had won a contract to equip the RAF with a four-engined bomber. The cockpit was a very high perch. On the maiden flight Parker was accompanied by Squadron Leader Eric Moreton, who had been loaned from the RAF to assist with the test flying of the four-engined flying-boat, the Sunderland. Behind the two men sat George Cotton. He had to be prepared to lower the huge articulated undercarriage, a ten-minute job by hand if the power failed. They were gone for twenty minutes before

they were not aimed using any sort of aiming device, nor was it felt necessary to have any member of the aircraft crew trained in dropping bombs. The light bombers of the early 1930s were still biplanes with the bombs carried in racks beneath the lower wings. There were

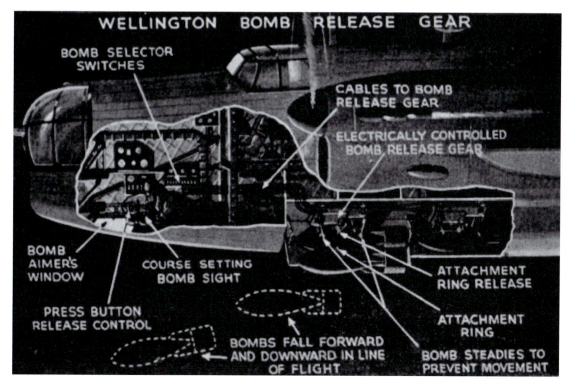

making an approach to land. Although it was a gentle landing the aircraft suddenly swung round on touchdown when the landing gear collapsed. The aircraft was thrown onto its nose and a wingtip, and the structure was so badly damaged that the prototype was a write-off. One of the brakes had seized. Aircraft were becoming heavier, and designers had no experience with the very large four-engined variety. Brake failure would not be expected to result in the write-off of a very large aircraft. Part of the problem lay in the Air Staff thinking on grass airfields. These were less conspicuous than airfields with paved runways, but it had to be recognized that aircraft were getting ever heavier, and unless tyre pressures were low (35 psi) the aircraft could become bogged down. But balloon tyres restricted the wheel diameter, and with it the brake-shoe area. It was not long before bomber airfields had paved runways.

The Whirlwind

In the Whirlwind the fuel cocks were opened hydraulically, using the pressure accumulator as the brakes. In common with the Stirling above, if an engine failed, hand pump operation would be necessary. The hydraulically operated large Fowler flap was linked with the radiator shutters, which closed except for a small gap when the flaps were in flight position and progressively opened with lowering flaps until a gated position, at which point the shutters were fully open. A problem occurred during taxiing when plumes of steam were seen. Sometimes temperatures were at danger level, and a stop had to be made to allow the system to cool down. The Whirlwind's controls were not right. Alterations were made to servo tab gear ratios and to the sealed leading edge of the ailerons. The slat venting had to be adjusted to prevent a jerk on opening, and a slight horn balance was added to the off-set rudder. The junction of the tailplane and fin was such that the breakdown of airflow caused severe shuddering when the aircraft was turned to starboard. An acorn-shaped fillet was eventually fitted, and with only slight buffeting in a hard turn the aircraft was acceptable. Then it was possible to examine the controls at higher speeds, up to a maximum dive when an increasing 'nose-down' trim could be felt. At the time no one was aware of the change in behaviour as an aircraft approached the speed of sound. What was being experienced was the beginning of Mach trouble, for the Whirlwind reached

430 mph in a dive, and it was feared that the aircraft would go out of control if dived faster than 445 mph.

Martin Baker MB2

The Martin Baker fighter was demonstrated by Val Baker at Heston on 26 May. This aircraft had received no previous publicity, yet it was dived at 400 mph from 10,000 ft, pulling out of the dive at 150 ft. It had been designed by the sandy-haired James Martin. After seeing the prototype Hurricane, Martin decided he could design a better fighter, but the Air Ministry showed no interest and Rolls-Royce was not prepared to loan an engine. Napier, however, was prepared to offer a Dagger engine, so Francis Francis, Martin's financial backer, was prepared to put up the money for a private venture. The design aimed at far easier maintenance than any other fighter. The steel fuselage frame had metal-covered panels that were instantly detachable. Arming the eight guns was far simpler, for the turn of a small handle caused the upper surface of the wing to open for access to the guns. These could be replaced in five minutes. The wingspan was only 34 ft, compared with 40 ft for the Hurricane, and it had a trousered undercarriage.

On its maiden flight, Baker was lucky to make an accident-free circuit. The rudder and miniature fin gave impossible directional characteristics. Before going to Martlesham a taller triangular fin and triangular rudder were designed and fitted, but the RAF pilots found its stalling speed too high and the elevator too sensitive. The ailerons were too light at slow speed and too heavy at high speed. The lateral stability was negligible and it was directionally unstable for small angles of yaw. Instead of banking naturally it tended to slew. Landings were not comfortable given the hard undercarriage and Martlesham's rough surface.

For all its shortcomings the MB2 was the best example of ease of maintenance, and recommendation was made to the Air Ministry that James Martin be given a contract for an improved fighter with a retractable undercarriage and Merlin engine. In the event this was designed with a Sabre engine, and changes were made to overcome the problems previously mentioned. What was probably the most remarkable aspect of the design was the unprecedented armament of six 20 mm cannon, each fed

with 200 rounds on a patented flat-feed system. It was seen as a possible successor to the Spitfire, but it was not to be.

The Saro Lerwick

In the 1938 section of this chapter the problems of porpoising were mentioned, and three of the production models were used for prototype trials to look into continued roll and yaw deficiencies and an elevator that was too heavy. A raised tailplane and auxiliary fins did not cure the problem, although a taller fin and rudder did improve the directional characteristics, but there was still lateral wallowing. When a stall was attempted there was a quick loss of height, but the flying-boat did not spin. With the flaps lowered a stall was even more uncomfortable. The machine was difficult to fly on one engine in spite of a bigger fin, and side-slipping was necessary. Furthermore if the tail turret rotated abeam the nose pitched down. The foregoing paints a picture of the Lerwick as a flying disaster, but the government's policy during the expansion scheme was to order from the drawing-board, such was the urgency to have maritime patrol aircraft in strength should war come. The submarine menace in the waters around the British Isles during the Great War was remembered, and there would be an urgent need to protect convoys in home waters. And so ten Lerwicks had been ordered at a unit cost of £55,000.

The PBY-4 Consolidated Catalina

The Air Ministry had to regard the Lerwick as a stop-gap, and it equipped just three squadrons and had gone by August 1942 when they left No. 422 Squadron. There was hope that the Blackburn B20 with Rolls-Royce Vulture engines and retracting hull bottom might replace the Lerwick, but Rolls-Royce was beset by development problems. Fortunately MAEE Felixstowe was testing the Consolidated PBY-4, which had been delivered to England by air. The flying-boat had flown from Botwood, Newfoundland, to MAEE, a distance of 2,450 miles, in 13½ hours. A statement from the Air Ministry made clear that it was necessary to keep abreast of design developments in other countries, but the Air Staff also had a replacement for the Lerwick in mind. Although 20 mph slower than the Saro machine, the

PBY-4 was a much better aircraft and was to prove a valuable addition to the inventory of Coastal Command during the war.

The Avro Manchester and Lancaster

It would not be too great an exaggeration to say that the world-famous Lancaster bomber resulted from a failed Manchester. The Manchester was a twin-engined bomber, of which some good examples were reaching squadrons, like the Wellington and the Blenheim, but problems with the Manchester resulted in a very short service life. Although it served on seven RAF squadrons, on five of them it only served for a matter of months. It entered service in November 1940 with No. 207 Squadron, but last saw service in June 1942. On 25 July 1939, after engine running and final flight clearance, Sam Brown and his assistant, Flight Lieutenant Bill Thorne, made a successful maiden flight, much to the relief of Roy Chadwick, the designer. The test pilot's primary task is to ensure that all three controls are working correctly, i.e. that the rudder, elevators and ailerons are responding to the control column and rudder bar. The control surfaces must be effective over the whole range of movement. Previous descriptions of prototype flying that appear in this chapter show that this was not often the case, and that controls had sometimes to be held in an extreme position just to maintain straight and level flight. The throttles had sometimes to be used to counteract a tendency to veer either to port or to starboard. Secondly, it was evident that wind-tunnel tests were not an accurate prediction of what would happen in the air. In the case of the Manchester the tail units were found not to give directional stability, and it was decided to put a third fin between the other two on the centre line of the aircraft. This proved to be inadequate, even though the wind-tunnel test had established the correct size of the tail units.

The second prototype had an increased span, and there was a feeling of enormous power in the two 1,760 hp Vulture engines. But a snag common to all twin-engined aircraft is that if one of the engines cuts on take-off at a slow speed, the aircraft suffers an uncontrollable swing, the outer wing lifts and the aircraft suffers a considerable loss of height. The effect was more marked in the Manchester because of the enormous power of the engines. Since the Vulture engines were still in the development stage, the risk of engine failure on take-off was always a possibility. When, later, the engine of the prototype Manchester failed on take-off, the aircraft dived into the ground just outside the airfield boundary, killing its pilot. Air Marshal Tedder and Sir Wilfred Freeman went to Avros just after the prototype had spun in. They found unhappiness about the aircraft and its engines, and Rolls-Royce was luke-warm about the Vultures. By taking off the wings and replacing them with ones which each mounted two Merlin engines, the Manchester became the Lancaster.

COMPANY BUSINESS
Handley Page

A very good example of how the expansion plans were affecting the established aircraft manufacturing companies can be seen on the occasion of the 30th Anniversary of Handley Page on 17 June 1939. An order for 200 Hampdens had just been received and the firm's founder celebrated the event with a feast for 4,500 employees in a huge marquee on the south coast. Eight trains had been ordered to convey them from London (Waterloo) to Southsea. On the 19th Frederick Handley Page again threw a party, this time for 400 guests invited to Grosvenor House. This liberal display of hospitality was in keeping with Handley Page, who would go to considerable lengths to 'sell' his company to the RAF. It was established company policy for the firm's chief test pilot to visit Martlesham and entertain the test pilots there. At the Grosvenor party the Marquess of Londonderry added his laudations, commenting that the RAF was the greatest factor in preserving peace and that turning the other cheek was no longer acceptable. Only by having the strongest armed forces could the British Empire speak with authority.

MISCELLANEOUS WEAPON SYSTEMS, RADIO AND OTHER DEVELOPMENTS

Introduction

This last section of Chapter 5 is intended for other, not previously mentioned, items of equipment with which the RAF went to war in 1939. Chapter 3 deals exhaustively with the thousand and one items that were made by a multitude of sub-contractors in the late 1930s, for the aircraft firms and shadow factories simply could not cope with the demands made upon them by the various expansion plans.

100-octane fuel

The higher the octane number of a fuel, the greater its resistance to detonation. This means that engines can be boosted before detonation occurs. Without 100-octane fuel the Hurricane and Spitfire would have been at a disadvantage in combat with the Messerschmitt Bf 109. When the two British fighters came into service only 87-octane fuel was available, which limited the Merlin engines to 3,000 rpm. With 100 octane the boost pressure could go from 6.25 psi to 12 psi, an increase of 300 bhp. The Air Ministry placed a contract with Esso for engine tests with its 100-octane fuel. The tests were conducted on Rolls-Royce and Bristol engines and proved satisfactory, but Esso did not have the thousands of gallons that would be needed in war. Just in time for the outbreak of the war in 1939 substantial quantities arrived from Dutch Shell. The 100-octane fuel was reserved for the Merlin, Tiger and Pegasus engines.

Radio

Radios were the business of Marconi. Fighters had used the TR9 high-frequency sets (HF), but they were often subject to interference. What was needed was very-high-frequency (VHF) sets. Development had been slow, and it was not until 1935 that it was sufficiently advanced for production to take place. Development was started in

Marconi R1155.

1937 for the TR1133 sets at the RAE, and the first of these sets were ready by August 1939, with trials starting in October, using the Spitfires of No. 66 Squadron, Duxford. As a result of the trials an improved version, the TR 1143, was put into production. Production delays meant that Fighter Command had to operate with HF and VHF sets for some time. The set with which the majority of RAF aircraft were equipped from mid-1940 onwards was the Marconi R1155. One major deficiency when the RAF went into war was that in VHF ground-to-air communications the Lysanders that were working with the Army had to use message pick-up hooks, as the Army Cooperation aircraft had done throughout the inter-war period.

Engines
Three engines that deserve mention are the Vulture, Merlin and Hercules engines. The Vulture represented a new generation of aero engine intended for the new four-engined heavy bomber then coming into service. The engine developed 1760 hp and had 24 cylinders, and was installed in the Avro Manchester. The problems with the Manchester have already been described, and an unreliable engine did not help. The four-engined Halifax was going to have the Merlin and later the Hercules. In the event the Vulture entered service in the Manchester. The Hercules XI engines developed 1,590 hp, and the Hercules 106 was still in service after the war with the Handley Page Hastings. The 1,650 hp Hercules XVI engine powered the Stirling four-engined bomber. The Merlin 1,000 hp 12-cylinder engine was being developed

in 1938, and the Spitfire I began with the Merlin II engine, which developed 1,030 hp; in the Mark XIII the 1,620 hp Merlin 32 was installed.

Cameras
Cameras had been used extensively during the inter-war years, and Chapter 4 recounts squadron operations where aircraft either produced mosaics or accompanied bombing raids to record the results of bombing raids on tribal villages. But further development was necessary, for only a few aircraft in 1939 could take pictures at night using parachute photoflash, and it was only just before the outbreak of war that Wellington bombers were fitted with 35 mm Leica cameras. Covert operations were called for to develop daylight photography, and reconnaissance flights were made over Germany in a civil Lockheed 12A. One of the things photographed was the German equivalent of the French fortifications, the Maginot Line, namely the Siegfried Line. Italian airfields in Tunisia were also photographed. These developments were the work of Wing Commander F. Sidney Cotton, the designer of the Sidcot Suit. For high-level reconnaissance the Spitfire was ideally suited, since it had the altitude necessary and could take pictures from 33,000 feet using an F.24 camera.

Radar
By the outbreak of war the chain of radar stations that girdled the coasts of Britain was fully operational. Air exercises had proved the reliability of the reports passed

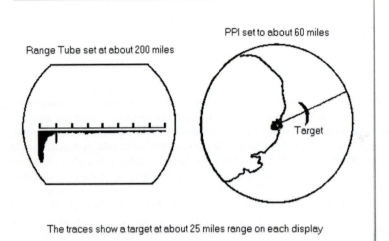

Range Tube set at about 200 miles

PPI set to about 60 miles

Target

The traces show a target at about 25 miles range on each display

Inside the station building the plotters had to establish whether the incoming aircraft were friendly of not, and IFF (Identification Friend or Foe) was used to verify this. A plan position indicator would establish the range and direction to the target. There were two cathode ray tubes in a cabinet, the one on the left giving the range and the one on the right the direction.

The radar map opposite shows the two levels of radar coverage designed to catch aircraft formations coming in at an altitude and those that would try coming in low. What is known as 'ground clutter' can disguise the presence of low-flying aircraft, but aircraft approaching the shores of the United Kingdom would be coming in over the sea. It will further be noticed that the radar coverage is not complete, but the gaps face away from the continent of Europe. The high-level radar facing France extended to many of the airfields occupied by the *Luftwaffe* in 1940.

The cabinet above houses the two displays. A later CHL array is illustrated on the right.

by the various radar stations to the fighter sector controllers, who spoke directly to the pilots of defending fighters. The photograph on the previous page is of an east coast CH station. The transmitter antennae were supported by the three masts in the foreground. The receivers were on the four towers in the distance.

Radar coverage of the United Kingdom, 3 September 1939.

Chapter 6
The RAF at Sea

The RAF manning of aircraft-carriers in the early 1930s – Disarmament policy as it affected the FAA – Naval air policy following the decision to rearm – The Abyssinian crisis and remilitarization of the Rhineland – Admiralty claims to control shore-based maritime aircraft – The formation of RAF Coastal Command – Employment of naval air forces; the Fleet Air Arm is transferred to the Admiralty – Naval response to the Munich Crisis

Introduction

The inter-service rivalry between the Admiralty and the Air Ministry in the period following the Great War had resulted in a government ruling that the RAF would be the sole aviation service. The Army would be allotted Army Cooperation squadrons, and although General Wilson hoped very much that the newborn RAF would be strangled at birth, the Army finally accepted that there was not to be a separate army air corps. It was not to be as straightforward for the Navy. The RAF would man, equip and exercise operational control of shore-based squadrons employed on maritime duties, but the arrangements for ship-borne flying units was not so clear cut. Operational control of FAA aircraft flights on aircraft-carriers and warships was to be exercised by fleet commanders, but the manning, servicing and equipment of FAA units was to be a joint Navy/RAF responsibility. Naval officers were permitted to fill some flying posts and were given an equivalent RAF rank while employed with the FAA. The details of the agreed arrangements between the two services are to be found in Chapter 6 of Volume I. The shared responsibility for running the FAA meant that there was always the possibility of friction between the two services, particularly when it came to the provision of aircraft produced to air specifications determined by the Air Ministry, albeit to meet Navy requirements. When the RAF expansion scheme got under way in 1934, a further cause of friction was to be the number of new units that would be added to the FAA inventory. Eventually the Admiralty was to take control of the FAA, but this would come at a time when the RAF was sufficiently well established to be able to lose its naval component without risking disbandment, as it would have done in the early 1920s.

THE RAF MANNING OF THE FLEET AIR ARM IN THE 1930s

The manning of aircraft-carriers' headquarter units by RAF personnel at the end of the decade are given at Appendix H. In 1938 the manning of the FAA became the responsibility of the Admiralty, but it was not possible to manage without RAF personnel until after the war had started. The following paragraphs give an insight into the operational and administrative matters that were of joint concern to both services in the 1930s, and could at times result in very complex arrangements, such as that for discipline of naval personnel on RAF courses or following disembarkation.

Provision of personnel for the Fleet Air Arm (AMO A.152 – 1.6.33)

The Air Council and Board of the Admiralty had examined the provision of personnel for the Fleet Air Arm with a view to building up a body of officers in the ranks of sub-lieutenant to commander in the Navy, and a body of officers in the ranks of flying officer to wing commander in the RAF, experienced in the work of the FAA. The aim was to have an equal division as between Air Force and naval pilots in carrier posts. FAA catapult posts were to be filled with naval officers. As regards posts outside the FAA but connected with its work, it was decided to regard as appropriate to naval officers two wing commander and two squadron leader posts at RAF shore establishments, and a post on the staff of the Rear Admiral (A), and to regard as appropriate to Air Force officers posts as fleet aviation officer on the staffs of the C-in-C Home and Mediterranean fleets. Further, two posts in the Air Ministry connected with work of the FAA would be filled by naval officers, and one post in the Naval Air Division, Admiralty, would be filled by an Air Force officer.

The order then went on to introduce certain modifications in the conditions of service of naval pilots in the FAA. Naval pilots serving in the FAA at this time were given the appropiate RAF rank equivalent to their naval rank. Promotion was given in the RAF rank to naval officers as follows:

To Flight Lieutenant	Between $3^{1}/_{2}$ and $5^{1}/_{2}$ years' seniority as a lieutenant.
To Squadron Leader	Between $2^{1}/_{2}$ and $4^{1}/_{2}$ years' seniority as a lieutenant-commander.
To Wing Commander	After 2 years' seniority as commander.

Provision was made for those naval officers who did not receive promotion within the zones listed above. These officers would revert permanently to naval service, but if they could be spared from naval duties in an emergency,

The spring of 1935, and a Baffin takes off from HMS *Eagle* during a fleet exercise.

they could be regarded as available for FAA duties. The question of giving such officers flying practice was not dealt with in this order.

Fleet Air Arm – naval and marine personnel temporarily under Air Force discipline – AMO 57/1933

The following order was based on an Admiralty Fleet Order 503 of 1933, and admirably illustrates the problem of which service was responsible for discipline during a period of detachment. Even though naval and marine personnel were borne on the books of one of HM ships at the time they were attached to the the RAF for regular periods of service, they were subject to the Air Force Act except when members of the Air Force unit in which they were serving were themselves subject to the Naval Discipline Act. The naval and marine officers who were detailed for service training at a RAF station were deemed to have been lent to the RAF and therefore subject to the Air Force Act. From the moment they left the dockyard, boat or ship in transit for a RAF station they came under the Air Force Act. This also applied to

passage by air in an RAF aircraft flying to an RAF aerodrome. If they crossed the coastline the Act would apply from the moment of crossing. On leaving an RAF seaplane base *en route* for a naval ship they ceased to come under the Act once they crossed the coastline. If a coastline was not crossed and they were flying in seaplanes from a seaplane base to a ship they would cease to be subject to the Act once they alighted alongside the ship.

This order was modified in the sense that, although naval and marine officers were deemed to have been lent to the RAF, they remained on ships' books. So, if it was possible, the Admiralty preferred that their personnel be tried and punished under the Naval Discipline Act even though they were, at the time of the alleged offence, lent to the RAF.

Fleet Air Arm – training of units; responsibility for returns of practices – AMO A90/1933

This order provided for the training of FAA units. They were to be trained in accordance with the syllabus of instruction issued from time to time by the Admiralty

A Hawker Osprey is catapult-launched from the cruiser HMS *Neptune* in 1934.

The hazards of carrier operations. HMS *Glorious* was conducting flying operations east of Gibraltar on 1 April 1931 when she ran into thick fog. A change of course was necessary to clear the fog so that her aircraft might be recovered, but she risked collision with her escorts. When a collision did occur, however, it was not with an escort but with the French liner *Florida*, which carried almost 700 passengers and crew.

Twenty-four passengers and crew died aboard the *Florida*, and one seaman was killed aboard the *Glorious*. Four Flycatchers also had to ditch as the fighters ran out of fuel.

after consultation with the Air Ministry. If the ships were embarked the responsibility rested with the ships' captains carrying the aircraft. This could include ships with catapult launchers. At home it was Coastal Area of the RAF that took responsibility for disembarked FAA flights. Such stations as Gosport and Lee-on-Solent would receive disembarked FAA flights, and the responsibility for training would pass from the Admiralty to the RAF, via the AOC Coastal Area. Abroad it was the responsibility of the AOC RAF Mediterranean to ensure that training of disembarked units was carried out. Hal Far and Kalafrana come to mind in this context.

Careful liaison was needed so that the receiving RAF station would know what training had been carried out while afloat. For this purpose returns of training and exercises carried out at sea had to be submitted by the captains of HM ships to the RAF and Admiralty and vice versa for training and exercises carried out by disembarked units so that ships' captains would be informed.

Exercises for personnel of RAF units – cooperation of HM ships – AMO A74/1936
In order that personnel of RAF units at the RAF stations at Gosport, Mount Batten, Pembroke Dock and

Donibristle, and pupils of the Air Navigation School at Manston, Kent, might have opportunities of estimating the course and speeds, and of reporting the positions of ships, HM ships on passage in waters within reach of those units were, when requested, and provided circumstances permitted, to cooperate with the Officers Commanding the RAF stations listed above. The Officers Commanding the RAF stations taking part in an exercise were instructed to inform participating ships of the wave frequency and call-signs of the aircraft taking part, the time at which the aircraft left for and returned from the exercise, and the number and type of aircraft taking part. The duration of the exercise should not exceed $1\frac{1}{2}$ hrs. A searchlight was to be trained on the aircraft when in sight from the ship and alterations of course were to be made every 7 to 12 minutes.

DISARMAMENT POLICY AS IT AFFECTED THE FAA
(Source: National Archives Document AIR 41/45)
Towards the end of 1929 a Five-Power Naval Conference was due to be held in London, to be followed by the General Disarmament Conference in Geneva. Any limitations to carrier tonnage agreed at the conference would affect the requirement for ship-borne aircraft. If this was increased the FAA would be absorbing a greater proportion of Britain's total air strength, which itself was subject to financial limitations and any limitations agreed at the disarmament conference. Every aircraft allotted to the FAA would, in these circumstances, mean one fewer for home defence.

From the Air Ministry's point of view, a reduction in carrier tonnage would relieve the situation. In the table below are the carrier tonnage limits agreed in the Washington Naval Treaty of 1922. Alongside are tonnage figures reached by the five powers by December 1929.

Before the conference the Admiralty had specified a requirement for 176 aircraft on carriers, with sixty-five aircraft to be carried aboard cruisers and capital ships. Using the Glorious class of carrier as a benchmark, with a complement of fifty-two aircraft, Britain would require 76,000 tons of carrier tonnage. The authorized limit could be safely lowered to 78,000 tons, giving it parity with the USA and corresponding proportional cuts in Japan, Italy and France. But the Air Ministry was

Country	Washington tonnage limit	December 1929 tonnage built or building
Great Britain	135,000	108,000 (6 carriers)
USA	135,000	78,000 (3 carriers)
Japan	81,000	61,000 (3 carriers)
France	60,000	21,000 (1 carrier)
Italy	60,000	Nil

NB: Originally the maximum individual carrier tonnage was 27,000, but in October 1925 Great Britain proposed 23,000 tons.

concerned that the Washington Treaty placed no limit on carriers of under 10,000 tons displacement. Thus a nation would be free to build any number of these smaller carriers, which could pose a serious threat to Britain's far-flung ocean trade routes. These views were expressed in a letter from the Secretary of State for Air to the Prime Minister on 17 December 1929. Then in January 1930 the Admiralty circulated a memorandum to the London Naval Conference recommending a new authorized limit of 125,000 carrier tonnage and made no reference to carriers under 10,000 tons. Needless to say, this would raise the requirement for carrier-borne aircraft, and the memorandum prompted the Secretary of State for Air, Lord Thompson, to write to the Prime Minister expressing his disappointment that the Admiralty was not seizing the opportunity to make really worthwhile reductions in carrier tonnage. Lord Thompson pointed out that if the higher limit was agreed, the increase in the establishment of carrier-borne aircraft would result in a reduction of home defence aircraft, and the ability of the RAF to defend Britain against air attack by land-based aircraft.

With the formation of a Labour government on 8 June 1929, Mr A.V. Alexander had become the First Lord at the Admiralty. His response to the stance taken by the Air Ministry with regard to carrier tonnage was to deny the assumptions made. He asserted that the FAA existed purely for naval needs and the strength of the FAA was fixed according to the requirements of the fleets and nothing else. The FAA was not part of the RAF and its aircraft were used for naval work paid for out of the Naval Vote. Furthermore, 70% of FAA personnel were naval officers and ratings.

This was to spark off a revival of the old controversy, which was almost inevitable given the shared responsibility for the FAA. In spite of Lord Thompson's objections, the Admiralty stuck to its 125,000-ton limit. Three old carriers were due for decommissioning, and the First Sea Lord, Admiral Sir Charles Madden, had in mind their replacement by three larger carriers, hence the higher Navy limit. This could raise the requirement for carrier-borne aircraft from 176 to 284, with sixty-five for capital ships, a total of 350 aircraft. The First Sea Lord had nevertheless to take into consideration the limitation placed on the total air strength of the nation within which naval requirements would have to be set, since the Geneva Disarmament Conference was to follow the London Naval Conference. If it was possible at Geneva to settle for parity with France, which had the most powerful European air force, a figure of 1,000 front-line aircraft might be agreed. But if 350 of these aircraft were to be with the FAA this would seriously compromise home defence requirements, let alone Britain's commitments abroad. To make matters worse, the Cabinet made a decision in December 1929 to put back yet again the completion of the 1923 Air Expansion

Scheme from 1935 to 1938, i.e. no major war for at least ten years. Lord Thompson therefore submitted that 100,000 tons would be quite sufficient to meet the Navy's requirements for accommodation and operation of its aircraft.

On 4 February 1930 the government published a memorandum summarizing the position to be taken by Britain at the conference. HMG considered that the aircraft tonnage figure should include all such vessels of 10,000 tons and under, and the total tonnage for the Royal Navy and the US Navy should be 100,000 tons, and not 135,000 tons as authorized under the Washington Treaty, with an adjustment in ratio for other nations. The maximum size of individual carriers should not exceed 25,000 tons, with the age extended from twenty to twenty-six years. In the event the London Conference, which was signed at St James's Palace on 22 April 1930, retained the 135,000-ton limit for carriers for both Britain and America. The Admiralty was free to expand the FAA, just as Thompson had feared, but in reality the government was hardly likely to sanction an immediate increase in carrier construction. The tonnage figure was an upper limit, and building up to that limit had to be affordable. Be that as it may, the Admiralty put forward a proposal to the Fighting Services Committee of the Cabinet in June 1930 for a revised development plan for the FAA. The Navy's requirement was for 241 aircraft by 1939, or 213 by 1936, in which year it was proposed to review the matter again. Given the state of the national economy, the Navy was wise not to press for the construction of a new carrier immediately, but rather thinking in terms of laying one down in 1936, unless foreign programmes rendered the earlier date necessary.

Disarmament quotas The Air Ministry had to estimate, not only the requirements for FAA and home defence, but also those for maritime aircraft at home and flying-boats and landplanes abroad in such places as the Sudan, Egypt, Mesopotamia, Aden, India and Singapore. These estimates would be needed as a basis for negotiations at the preparatory Disarmament Commission. In a review taken in July 1931, the Air Staff considered that the coastal defence requirements had been underestimated. Not since 1926 had there been an official programme of expansion of maritime aircraft. There was a tacit understanding that the number of flying-boats should be gradually increased to a total of seventy-two by 1936, but the number of landplanes and torpedo-bombers was not given. By 1931 the RAF had twelve flying-boats and twelve torpedo-bombers in the United Kingdom. Then there were twelve floatplanes, eight flying-boats and twelve torpedo-bombers abroad, a total of fifty-six aircraft. To give the UK parity with the French Air Force, a declared strength of forty flying-boats at home and thirty-five abroad, and 136 landplanes at home and 180 abroad was required. In February 1932

Britain's maritime air forces amounted to only:

UK	Abroad
16 flying-boats	8 flying-boats
	12 floatplanes
12 landplanes	12 landplanes
96 FAA aircraft	62 FAA aircraft

On 20 July 1931 the Cabinet reaffirmed that the proposed policy for planning was to be based on the assumption that there would be no major war for ten years, and with Europe in the grip of depression money for defence would not have a high priority. The fact remained that the Chiefs of Staff Committee, in reviewing Imperial defence policy, considered the cumulative effects that the 'Ten-Year Rule' had had on the state of Britain's defence forces, which were weak and unready, particularly in the Far East. The committee recommended the abandonment of the rule. In March 1932 the Committee of Imperial Defence agreed, but another eleven months were to pass before the Cabinet accepted that advice. By then there had been a change of government.

Clashes with the Admiralty With strength negotiations about to begin at the Disarmament Conference, the First Lord of the Admiralty issued a memorandum in which he asked for a minimum FAA strength of 400 aircraft by 1936. He added that the request 'represented the tactical requirements of the Fleet and was an absolute and not a relative factor'. Lord Londonderry, who had taken over as Secretary of State for Air in the new coalition government, not unexpectedly queried the entire paper. At a time when the USA and Japan were being asked to reduce their tonnage, the Admiralty request looked ill timed. The 400 FAA aircraft might be within the carrier capacity allowed to Britain in the naval treaty, but that capacity was not likely to be realized for many years. In the economic climate of the 1930s construction of carriers was out of the question, and would, in any case, be counter-productive in the disarmament talks if all the chief naval powers did the same. The Air Ministry wished to combine a global limitation figure for all categories of aircraft that would not be in excess of France, with parity in the metropolitan and immediately adjacent areas. On the other hand, the Admiralty wanted to be able to determine the number of aircraft it needed to meet operational needs. Naval strategy and tactics could not be subject to considerations of parity with France. Indeed, the Navy's view was symptomatic of the ongoing disagreement between the two services, but given the parlous state of the nation's finances, the demand for a large increase in FAA strength was not pressed. In any event there was no wish to prejudice the work of the disarmament conference.

Ratio of Navy to RAF officers in the FAA Another cause of friction between the two departments made a reappearance on 30 July 1932. This concerned the conditions of entry and promotion in the FAA. In 1924 it had been agreed that 70% of officers serving with the FAA should be naval officers, albeit with equivalent RAF rank titles, to ensure that over a period of time the Navy would acquire officers with valuable aviation experience. Certain matters that had been settled in conference were then, according to the Admiralty, denounced by an Air Ministry demand that the agreed 50% representation in the ranks of squadron leaders and wing commanders until 1936 should be made a permanent arrangement and extended down to flight lieutenants. The substitution of a 50:50 (Navy to RAF) ratio for the existing 70:30 ratio was quite unacceptable to the Admiralty. On 4 August Lord Londonderry replied to the First Lord's letter of 30 July, in which he refuted any suggestion that the Air Ministry's proposals were new or revolutionary. The Admiralty's counter-proposal that they should retain 70% of flight lieutenant posts was a clear breach of the agreed basis for the conference discussions. This basis had been arrived at by an Air Council letter of 1 March 1932, expressing a hope that the Admiralty would eliminate any continuance of the contention that the 70:30 ratio was a predetermined 'must', to which the Admiralty had replied on 7 April that it agreed to the problem being examined from a general policy point of view rather than the maintenance of any fixed ratio of naval officers in the FAA. Lord Londonderry went on to say that the whole matter stemmed from the Balfour Committee findings of 1923, when the Admiralty had claimed the upper limit (70%) that that finding had tentatively mentioned only as a possible figure. Ever since, the Air Ministry had claimed that this percentage was not a satisfactory basis for the manning of the FAA. It had been supported in its view by the Colwyn Committee in 1925, when it was recommended that the naval ratio be reduced to 30%, and in 1926 by Mr Baldwin, who appealed to the Admiralty in its own interests to agree to a lower rate. He had hoped, therefore, that the recent conference implied willingness to discuss the 70:30 ratio that had so long obstructed agreement between the two departments and the settlement of any permanent policy.

The Secretary of State for Air also mentioned in his letter other concessions by the Air Ministry since 1926, such as the granting of 50% of posts in all carriers and shore establishments, and the promotion of naval officers to the Air Force rank at much lower ages than their Air Force colleagues in the same units. The offer of 50% to the Air Force quota in the higher ranks only until 1936 was far too short a time. It must, said Lord Londonderry, be fixed over a period long enough to

A Fairey IIIF landed, port wing low, and headed for the edge of the flight deck of HMS *Hermes* on 22 June 1932 during flying operations off Wei-Hai-Wei . . .

and ended up in the drink. The plane-guard destroyer is seen bearing down on the ditched aircraft, a Mk IIIB S.1477, but it was not needed. The crew, Captain R.M. Giddy RM, and observer Lieutenant-Commander E.R. Dymott, were saved, but the aircraft sank.

allow the human individuals affected to work out their careers under it.

Further deliberations continued in the combined conference until December 1932, when settlement was reached on details of entry, promotion and length of service for naval officer pilots. It was also agreed that a limited number of RAF sergeant pilots would be employed in the RAF quota and that carrier posts should continue to be on a 50:50 ratio, but that there should be 100% allocation of naval pilots to all catapult flights in capital ships and cruisers.

NAVAL AIR POLICY FOLLOWING THE DECISION TO REARM

Introduction

Clearly the failure to agree on the details that would have resulted in meaningful disarmament on the part of the major powers at Geneva, together with Germany's

withdrawal from the League of Nations in October 1933, created a new situation. With disarmament giving way to rearmament, differences between the Admiralty and the Air Ministry over the management of the FAA could only increase. The Navy was now even more anxious to go ahead with its own plans for carrier construction and would not wish to be constantly at odds with the RAF over matters of personnel and provision of aircraft. With two Fascist dictators in power in Germany and Italy there was a new sense of urgency in repairing the weakened state of Britain's armed forces, and towards the end of 1933 the Admiralty submitted its plans for carrier construction to the Defence Requirements Priorities Sub-committee. The new large aircraft-carrier envisaged would require shore accommodation and training facilities for its aircraft. In addition to the existing programme strength, a further seventy-two aircraft would be required. Since the supply of aircraft was a matter for the Air Ministry, the Secretary of State for Air would become involved, but Lord Londonderry was away in India at the time the matter came to the attention of his department. Accordingly the Under-Secretary of State for Air, Sir Philip Sassoon, wrote to the First Lord on 11 January 1934, asking him to allow time for the implications from the air supply angle to be considered. The First Lord was not prepared to discuss the matter. The requirement for new aircraft was absolute, not relative. Both the USA and Japan were building carriers up to the naval treaty limits, and the Air Ministry was reminded, yet again, that the FAA was an essential part of the Royal Navy, not an integral part of the RAF.

When Lord Londonderry wrote to the Prime Minister on his return, he told Ramsay MacDonald that the current dispute was not the first difficulty he had experienced with both the Admiralty and the War Office. The latter expressed surprise, since differences had not surfaced in the Chiefs of Staff Sub-committee. What annoyed Londonderry was that a paper had been put before a Cabinet committee without first informing the Air Ministry. In the event the naval programme was approved, and note was taken that the building of a new aircraft-carrier would involve extra expenditure by the Air Ministry.

RAF AND NAVAL REQUIREMENTS CONSEQUENT UPON EXPANSION

Expansion of the armed forces to meet the growing threat from Nazi Germany was bound to create further tensions between the Admiralty and the Air Ministry. Since the Navy relied upon the RAF for the provision of land-based maritime patrol aircraft, the former would apply pressure for extra squadrons to provide protection for convoys and to patrol home waters. The Air Ministry, on the other hand, had to balance the requirement to build up the number of bomber and fighter squadrons with the need to satisfy the needs of the Navy. The expenditure of moneys for FAA units came from the Naval Vote, but that for RAF maritime patrol squadrons did not.

The 'Ten-Year Rule' had been applied by successive British governments since the early 1920s. In 1923 the government approved the modest expansion of the RAF to fifty-two home-based squadrons, but this expansion was to be implemented in stages. The economic situation in the early 1930s, as well as the pursuit of the policy of disarmament, had caused the government to 'put the brakes on'. With the change in the international situation the brakes were taken off, and the Defence Requirements Committee presented its report on 5 March 1934, recommending that the 1923 home air defence programme be completed as soon as possible. That plan had provided for an increase in bomber and fighter squadrons, not maritime squadrons. Another forty squadrons would be required to complete the air defence programme, but there would still remain an insufficiency in flying-boats for convoy protection, anti-submarine duties and maritime reconnaissance, not to mention extra fighter squadrons to protect home ports and cities in the north of England. This would mean twenty-five squadrons in addition to the forty already mentioned.

Interchangeability of FAA and home defence units

A ministerial committee considered the needs of Imperial defence. In Expansion Plan A (see Chapter 2) the FAA would get another 4½ squadrons, or nine flights, which would give the Navy 213 aircraft by 1939. This, however, would not give the Admiralty what it wanted in the short term, for it was recognized that the production potential of the aircraft industry and the country's finances could not meet the requirement for the extra twenty-five squadrons in the next five years. Accordingly a proposal was put before the Admiralty and the Air Ministry that home defence units of the RAF might be interchanged with FAA units in an emergency, and a recommendation was made that two or more squadrons from each of these forces be trained in a dual role. A ministerial sub-committee on the Allocation of Air Forces discussed the matter during July 1934 and came to a decision that, while FAA units might be used for home defence, the converse was not possible. Carrier-based aircraft are much heavier than their land-based counterparts. They have to be strengthened to be thrown down on a possibly heaving carrier deck, and the pilots must be specially trained for deck landings. But the Air Ministry disagreed in the belief that RAF pilots could be so trained to fly fighter and torpedo-aircraft on carriers. It was therefore agreed that units from both forces should be trained in the dual role.

The use of lower-deck ratings as pilots for the FAA

In March 1934 the Admiralty opened its claim for the entry of lower-deck rating pilots into the FAA. This would be akin to training RAF sergeants to become pilots. The Air Ministry was well aware that the manning of the FAA was a constant source of friction between the two services, and sought to tie in the training of home defence units in the dual role with any discussion of the entry of naval rating pilots. It was, by then, October, for the introduction of Expansion Scheme A had caused a postponement of the meeting of the inter-service conference to discuss these and other matters. On 12 November, the First Sea Lord, Sir Ernle Chatfield, replied to the Air Ministry, rejecting the proposal on the ground that the matter of FAA manning could be discussed in conjunction with a matter of national strategy. The Admiral wanted a meeting to discuss the dual role only. He regarded the existing arrangements for manning the FAA led to ineffiency. He singled out the attachment of junior RAF officers to the FAA, which was only for two years instead of the four years contemplated in the 1923 Balfour Committee report. Fleet training was suffering because of the greater turnover of RAF pilots attached to carriers, which in turn reduced their naval experience.

In his reply to the First Sea Lord, the Chief of the Air Staff, Air Chief Marshal Sir Edward Ellington, confined himself to the question of the dual role. He proposed that two or more squadrons from each force might carry out experiments in interchangeability during the summer of 1935. This came to nought, however, for in April that year, the Chiefs of Staff Sub-committee issued a statement to the effect that no FAA aircraft, though they were stationed in the United Kingdom, could in any way be counted as an integral part of the RAF metropolitan first-line strength. Henceforward, the FAA units were discounted in parity comparisons between the RAF and the *Luftwaffe*.

This still left the question of the employment of lower-deck rating pilots to be resolved. The Admiralty's dissatisfaction with the RAF manning of units of the FAA and the difficulty in recruiting naval officer pilots only served to sour relations between the two service departments. In a memo sent by the First Sea Lord to the Secretary of State for Air on 20 May 1935, it was made plain that the efforts to resolve the dispute had failed. With the ever-growing number of RAF squadrons needing to be manned, the Air Staff needed all the pilots they could get, but at the same time, by insisting that the manning of the FAA was the RAF's responsibility, they had a duty to find pilots for both RAF squadrons and naval flights. A more rapid turnover of pilots in service on carriers helped, but as has already been made clear, the Navy wanted tbem to remain with the Navy for longer, not shorter, periods, in order to gain the necessary experience at sea. The findings of the Balfour

Committee of 1923 found that the tours on carriers should be four years, which was even then too short a period for the Navy's liking. By 1935 the average tour of an RAF officer aboard a carrier had been reduced from four years to twenty-three months. Another objection to the existing arrangements, raised by the Admiralty at this time, was the reluctance of naval officers to volunteer for service with the FAA in having to serve two masters. If the Air Ministry objected to the employment of naval rating pilots, it only worsened the manning situation.

The Admiralty asked for the appointment of a Cabinet committee to enquire into the conditions arising out of the dual control of the Fleet Air Arm, but in June 1935 there was a change of Prime Minister and Secretary of State for Air. It would take some time for Stanley Baldwin and Sir Philip Cunliffe Lister to settle into their new posts, and the First Sea Lord's memo requesting the appointment of a Cabinet committee was not circulated to the Cabinet. In the meantime the Air Staff were preparing their answers should the matter be raised again in the future.

The interchangeability of aircraft and the manning controversy

The government's adherence to the 'Ten-Year Rule' meant that the plan to form and equip fifty-two home defence squadrons was subject to a completion date that was not 'set in concrete'. Economic depression had had its effect, as had the international goal of disarmament. Of course disarmament should not affect a nation's right to defend itself, and having home defence squadrons could hardly be counted as an addition to offensive capability. Planning was based on France being the major threat, unrealistic as that might be, and by 1934 only forty-two of the fifty-two squadrons had been provided. The Geneva Disarmament Conference ended without agreement, and with it went any hope of securing international agreement on arms limitation. The whole climate changed, and the threat changed from France to Germany. An additional thirty-three squadrons were approved, and the Air Ministry could hardly oppose expansion of the Fleet Air Arm.

There remained, however, the limitations imposed by the nation's finances and the capacity of the aircraft industry to produce the required aircraft as part of the five-year plan. Then there was the ongoing dissatisfaction on the part of the Admiralty with the system the RAF used to administer the FAA. From the government's point of view the expansion in the number of home defence squadrons could be achieved while still expanding the FAA by having aircraft that were interchangeable. Discussion took place in July 1934 in a Ministerial Sub-committee on the Allocation of Air Forces. It was decided that although FAA aircraft might be used for home defence the opposite was not possible.

Aircraft designed for operations from airfields would not have the strength for carrier operations, where aircraft had to be thrown hard onto a pitching deck. With regard to the provision of personnel for the FAA, the Air Ministry believed that a part of the home defence personnel could be adequately trained to provide a part of the complement of aircraft-carriers, in the fighter and torpedo squadrons. It was agreed that an experiment be conducted, using FAA aircraft for home defence, as well as using home defence personnel in the FAA.

The sub-committee also considered the question of manning and reserves. Regarding the question of RAF reserves, the members thought it better in parliamentary pronouncements to publish the increase in the number of first-line squadrons while hiding the fact that there was no war reserve backing. Hence the start of the 'window-dressing' policy that was the feature of so many of the subsequent expansion schemes. But this policy was no solution to the conditions peculiar to the Fleet Air Arm, with its mixture of naval and RAF personnel.

THE ABYSSINIAN CRISIS AND THE RE-MILITARIZATION OF THE RHINELAND

Mussolini's war in Abyssinia in October 1935 and Hitler's re-militarization of the Rhineland in March 1936 only served to pose a dual threat to Britain. Not only would home waters have to be defended, but the Mediterranean theatre had then to be added. The Royal Navy might have its own naval air component with the fleet, but it relied upon the support of land-based maritime patrol aircraft as well. Only a handful of flying-boats were available in home waters for coastal reconnaissance to monitor the movement of enemy surface units and submarines. Any further requirements for aircraft would have to be met from FAA resources. In Malta and Alexandria there were, again, a handful of flying-boats to cover the entire Mediterranean.

The Admiralty and the Air Ministry had then to consider the surface and submarine threat to British shipping in both theatres. Italy had not been constrained by the limits imposed upon Germany in the Treaty of Versailles, and was building battleships and submarines that could threaten British commerce from Gibraltar to Suez.

It was the situation in Germany, however, that was changing. The treaty limits imposed upon Germany were that no submarines nor warships of more than 10,000 tons displacement could be in their naval inventory, in the belief that Germany would be denied battleships. Undaunted, the German naval architects had produced designs for a heavy cruiser that carried a battleship's armament. Three had been built, and were nicknamed 'pocket battleships', namely the *Admiral Scheer*, the *Admiral Graf Spee* and the *Deutschland*, later renamed the *Admiral Lutzow*. (Following the scuttling of the *Graf Spee* off Montevideo on 17 December 1939, Hitler was not keen to see a warship named Germany being sent to the bottom.) In an attempt to limit the growth in Germany's navy, the Anglo-German Naval Agreement was signed on 18 June 1935, which permitted Germany to build up to 35% of the British fleet in each category of surface vessel, and 45% in submarine tonnage by 1942. These ratios were subject to certain transfer rights as between one category and another. This resulted in the laying of the two 26,000-ton battle cruisers *Scharnhorst* and *Gneisenau*. And when Hitler no longer felt constrained by international treaty, the battleships *Bismarck* and *Tirpitz* would be added to the inventory. An aircraft-carrier was laid but never completed.

The foregoing had its impact upon British defence requirements and upon the ongoing controversy between the Admiralty and the Air Ministry. On 24 July 1935 the Defence Requirements Committee submitted its report to the Cabinet, which reflected the gloomy international situation. A speeding-up of all three service programmes was recommended to put Britain in a reasonable state of war preparedness by early 1939, but the committee asked for more time to work out the precise details. The FAA was to get its 213 aircraft by 1937, to be increased to 277 by April 1939. The Admiralty felt that this was insufficient to counter the growing threat, and proposed 312 aircraft by 1939, and 504 by 1942.

ADMIRALTY CLAIMS TO CONTROL SHORE-BASED MARITIME AIRCRAFT
Introduction
In 1935 the Admiralty wanted not only the return of the FAA to the Royal Navy, but the control of all shore-based maritime patrol aircraft. This was to turn into a heated debate between the Air and naval staffs, which necessitated government intervention. In the end the Navy would get back the FAA but not the shore-based aircraft. The continued complaints by the Admiralty, that not enough was being done to protect the fleet and the merchant marine, were answered by the Air Ministry with the formation of Coastal Command in the major reorganization of the RAF in 1936. The debate between the two departments, often bordering on the acrimonious, is charted in the paragraphs that follow,

and shows that there was often more heat than light being shed by both sides in the determination to win the argument. Those charged with the task of arbitrating between the warring factions had to try to assess the best way of deploying the maritime air forces, in both operational and administrative terms, as well as achieving maximum economy.

The situation in 1935, and naval proposals
In 1935 there were four flying-boat squadrons in the United Kingdom available to work with naval forces. Additionally six landplane squadrons of the seventy-five that would be available for home defence under the expansion schemes could be trained to operate in support of naval forces. Four of these squadrons would be coastal general-purpose, and two would be coastal torpedo-bomber squadrons. At that time these units belonged to RAF Coastal Area. The squadrons could take part in an air counter-offensive or attack enemy vessels that approached British shores. The Admiralty was unhappy with the RAF's ad hoc policy for such a major commitment as air defence of home waters. On 9 October 1935 the First Sea Lord raised a request in the Defence Requirements Committee for the formation of mobile air units based on depot ships for the protection of trade routes, and said that the whole subject of the cooperation of shore-based aircraft should be discussed. For its part the Air Ministry was not prepared to say that such and such a squadron would always be available to assist in coastal defence, protecting trade routes and attacking enemy vessels, beyond saying that the principal duties of the ten squadrons already mentioned were maritime reconnaissance squadrons and would patrol in conjunction with naval forces. The Air Staff were reserving the right to deploy their forces to meet developing and actual threats to the British Isles. If that meant diverting maritime reconnaissance and torpedo-bomber squadrons temporarily to other duties, then that was a matter of judgement by an RAF commander.

Their Lordships were clearly unhappy with this arrangement, and on 30 October the Admiralty countered with an assessment of its own requirements for aircraft for war:

The naval staff realized that, for financial reasons, all these forces could not be provided in peacetime, but the requirements were regarded as reasonable. Of course,

Against Germany alone	Against Japan alone	Against Italy alone
1 medium carrier	2 medium carriers	1 medium carrier
(30 amphibians)	(60 amphibians)	(30 amphibians)
6 small carriers	7 small carriers	7 small carriers
(90 amphibians)	(105 amphibians)	(105 amphibians)
162 coastal aircraft	24 coastal aircraft	8 coastal aircraft

Their Lordships were also putting down a marker, for it was obvious that there was no way in which the RAF could provide these forces without seriously depleting the air effort in other roles. In the meantime the Admiralty would settle for:

1 medium carrier + 30 amphibians
4 small carriers + 60 amphibians
81 coastal aircraft at home, with 100% reserve
36 coastal aircraft at Singapore.

Aerodromes and other facilities at various places around the shores of the United Kingdom and in Malaya were also listed. It was noted that their primary purpose was not to attack surface raiders and submarines, but only to report their location, leaving it to surface vessels fitted with Asdic to carry out an actual attack.

The RAF response to naval proposals

On 4 January 1936 the Air Staff gave their response. The naval proposals were seen as a huge waste of national resources, for these naval aircraft would be purely defensive. It could not be understood why an aircraft capable of speeds in excess of 200 mph should be confined to reporting the presence of an enemy to friendly warships capable at best of a speed of some 20+ knots. Maritime aircraft could be equipped to deliver attacks directly against surface craft and submarines. Amphibians might be of use only to the Navy, when what was wanted was ubiquitous aircraft that would be interchangeable in other roles. These would be multi-engined aircraft with crews trained in navigation, reconnaissance and bombing. The Air Staff also argued that the best way of countering the surface and submarine threat was to attack ports and dockyards, i.e. offensive defence through strategic bombing sorties. This was not disputed by the Naval Staff.

It was clear that what the Navy wanted was complete control of the FAA and all shore-based Naval Cooperation aircraft. The Naval Staff had already downgraded the submarine threat, stating that the fitting of Asdic to its warships would render submarine attack against convoys unprofitable, and that any nation undertaking such warfare would soon desist. But the experience of anti-submarine warfare was gained in the Great War. If Asdic gave the advantage to the surface craft it was equally possible that improvements in submarine design and tactics could reduce the advantage gained. This was the grave mistake made by the French in building the Maginot Line, which was to state an intention to refight the static trench war when the Germans were busy developing the *Blitzkrieg* mobile war. The snorkel that permitted a submarine to cruise at surface speed while at periscope depth, and the employment of the multiple attack on convoys by submarines fighting in packs, are examples, but in 1936

the Admiralty wanted to win an argument. Their Lordships could equally well turn Trenchard's dictum on the RAF. The sea was indivisible, and that meant that all operations in pursuit of winning the war at sea were the business of the Navy. But then the Army could claim ownership of the Royal Marines, since they fought on land. Of course, there was no definitive way of settling these inter-service arguments, and successive governments had to urge the willing cooperation of all three services in winning the war.

Chiefs of Staff Sub-committee

Questions of affordability had to decide the issue, and the government had to avoid duplication and waste. The Chiefs of Staff Sub-committee was called upon to investigate the problem of protecting Britain's seaborne trade in time of war. The Admiralty and the Air Ministry were asked to put their ideas to the Joint Planning Committee. The terms of reference were to discuss:

1. How far the two services regarded an attack as a menace to the country's supplies of food and raw materials in time of war.
2. How such an attack could be countered.
3. What part the RAF should play in cooperation with both the other services in the protection of trade.

The Admiralty was insistent. The situation with regard to the provision of shore-based aircraft employed on Naval Cooperation work was unsatisfactory, and to make matters worse, the aircrews were all RAF, who only had contact with the Navy during the occasional exercises with the fleet. The RAF came back with the argument about flexibility in being able to deploy all its air assets to meet anticipated and actual threats, but the Navy used this to argue that RAF aircrews did not specialize in Naval Cooperation work. What was needed was a thorough understanding of naval tactics, and this would only come from specialists, not generalists. It was also pointed out that aircraft developed for naval work were constructed differently, and equipped for the role. For good measure the Admiralty complained that there were no common headquarters, no close liaison and no common doctrine.

Joint Planning Committee Report, 2 July 1936

The committee reported on the matters of trade defence and food supply in wartime on 2 July 1936. The submarine threat was compared with that which prevailed in the Great War, and the fact that Asdic had been invented had, in the minds of the committee members, greatly reduced that threat. An enemy would quickly realize that attacks by submarines on convoys would be unprofitable, leading to an abandonment of submarine warfare by a nation facing destroyers equipped with Asdic. There remained the threat from air attack and from heavy surface units. Attacks from the air could be made by a continental power in home waters using land-based bombers, and Italian bombers or torpedo-bombing aircraft could threaten convoys passing Malta, *en route* for Suez or Gibraltar, from the Italian mainland. To threaten convoys in mid-ocean a nation would need carrier-borne aircraft. Of the three most likely enemy nations, only Japan was developing carriers. There was a serious threat from surface units. A ship with cruiser speed like the pocket battleships and battle cruisers of the *Kriegsmarine* could, and did in the event, pose a serious threat to British seaborne trade. The Admiralty again pressed its case that naval operations involving both ships and aircraft must be carried out with naval assets, and the Air Staff argued again that aircraft and aircrews who were specialized exclusively in Naval Cooperation work represented a waste of resources, particularly at a time when there was no immediate threat to Britain's seaborne trade.

The report had not moved the debate on, as the two sides were as far apart as ever. The only area of agreement was over the RAF's role in the counter air offensive in attacking the enemy's warships and submarines in their bases. Another area of disagreement was over convoy protection in narrow waters. When merchant ships were attacked by submarines they were more secure in a convoy, when escorting destroyers could provide a protection screen. But when the threat was from aircraft it was better if ships were dispersed, since having found one ship in a convoy enemy aircrews did not have to go off hunting for others. Again the Navy played down this threat claiming that multiple pom-pom guns were very lethal. Predictably the Air Staff accused their opposite numbers in the Admiralty of overestimating the effects of ack-ack fire from ships and underestimating the effects of bombing. To sum up the Navy's case, the submarine threat was reduced, ship-mounted ack-ack fire was effective against attacking aircraft, and the threat of bombing attacks against ships was also downgraded. Naval cooperation aircraft belonging to the Royal Navy should be able to report a specific threat to merchant shipping for the appropriate surface vessels to deal with it. The Air Staff had to show that the RAF was still best fitted to provide all the land-based aircraft to protect convoys and merchant ships proceeding independently. It was essential to convince the Joint Planners that the Navy did not need specialized air units for Naval Cooperation. An Air Staff plan, said the Joint Planners, should show:

1. If any additional air bases were required.
2. The proportion of the metropolitan air striking force which should specifically be trained for the attack of enemy naval forces if and when required.
3. If it was considered unavoidable that aircraft must be specialized for a role ancillary to sea forces, and if so, how many should be specialized.

4. The best disposition of GR (General Reconnaissance) squadrons at home, to enable them to fulfil their alternative roles of trade defence, air reconnaissance or the general air offensive or a European war.

The First Sea Lord was not satisfied with these terms, and on 7 August 1936 he suggested that as it was not essential to the Joint Planners that the Chiefs of Staff should resolve immediately the points of disagreement, they should leave questions of principle aside and concentrate on the technical side of the subject. He countered by proposing the following terms of reference:

1. Prepare an estimate of the numbers and types of shore-based aircraft required to be specialized in a role ancillary to sea forces to assist in the protection of trade when at sea.
2. To report on aerodrome and base organization required for these aircraft, both in permanent occupation and for reinforcing air units in an emergency.
3. The above investigations to cover war with Germany, war with Japan and simultaneous wars on the assumption that we would remain on the defensive in the Far East until the war against Germany was won.
4. Due regard should be paid to the use of the flying-boats.

It goes without saying that the Chief of the Air Staff would reject No. 1 above, and he came back with his own suggested terms:

1. To examine the 'worst case' which might arise:
   (i)   In a war with Germany.
   (ii) In a war with Japan.
   (iii) In a war simultaneously with both, on the assumption that Britain would remain on the defensive in the East until the war with Germany was won.
2. To estimate the probable types, sources and scales of attacks which would be experienced on our trade routes in each of the above contingencies.
3. To estimate the size and type of the force required to meet such attacks.
4. To consider the most effective disposition of forces required in war under para. 3 in the foregoing paragraph, and to estimate what additional facilities should be provided in peace for this purpose.

This was agreed by the First Sea Lord on 14 October 1936, and the agreed terms of reference were passed to the Joint Planning Committee. But no sooner had the latter sat down to consider them than the Admiralty gave notice of a future requirement for 150 light reconnaissance aircraft and seventy-five armed merchant cruisers that they proposed to commission.

The Air Staff could only question the strain on the already overstretched aircraft industry in meeting the Admiralty proposal, which was passed to the Minister for Coordination on 30 October. The latter ruled the proposal be accepted as an increase in the FAA, for which provision would be made only to become effective on mobilization, without prejudice to any priority directed by the CID for other requirements by the Air Ministry. These 150 aircraft, if forthcoming, would need crews, and these would be trained and partially manned by the RAF. The Minister ruled that no decision as to the provision of personnel required should be made at this stage, but could be considered as part of the whole question of personnel when the Air Ministry was in a position to review their requirements completely. The Minister had not said 'Yes', neither had he said 'No', to the Admiralty's proposal. Instead he had deftly placed the matter on a 'back burner'.

Part I of the Joint Planners' Report, 15 December 1936

Part I of the Joint Planners' Report, dated 15 December 1936, dealt only with a war with Germany. Sir Thomas Inskip was anxious to hurry things along, and on 2 November he had asked for the most immediate threat (Part I) be reported on, leaving Parts II and III to a later date. The air threat to Britain's seaborne trade was best met by a counter air offensive. To counter the threat from German surface vessels, movements of these vessels in the North Sea would have to be monitored, and the Northern Blockade Patrol would have to be maintained. To counter the threat from submarines in restricted warfare, sea areas would need to be patrolled by A/S vessels, supported where necessary by aircraft. If the Germans engaged in unrestricted submarine warfare then ships would have to travel in convoy, in which case A/S vessels would act as escorts. The number of shore-based aircraft was estimated as follows:

1. For air reconnaissance in the North Sea (south of the line Firth of Forth to SW Norway) to be carried out twice daily. Total – 84 aircraft.
2. For Air Cooperation with the Northern Blockade Patrol. Total – 12 aircraft.
3. In the 'worst case' of unrestricted submarine and air attack at sea the convoy system would be inaugurated. One aircraft to be maintained continuously in the air during daylight hours with each convoy where attack was likely. Total – 165 aircraft.
4. For air reconnaissance from oversea Atlantic ports against any surface raiders which succeeded in

getting out, Britain would require 12 aircraft at each of the main ports of Halifax (Nova Scotia), Kingston (Jamaica), Gibraltar and Sierra Leone. Total – 48 aircraft.

There was thus a total of 261 shore-based aircraft based in the United Kingdom. It was agreed that the RAF airfields overlooking the North Sea coasts of England and Scotland were suitably located for reconnaissance over the North Sea. It was also noted that there were suitable airfields/seaplane bases to cooperate with convoys in the following sea areas:

1. Portland to Western Approaches. Total – 30 aircraft)
2. Western Approaches to Milford Haven. Total – 16 aircraft
3. Bristol to Milford Haven. Total – 6 aircraft
4. Milford Haven to Liverpool and Belfast. Total – 18 aircraft
5. Belfast to the Clyde and northabout to the Forth. Total – 51 aircraft
6. Scandinavian convoys. Total – 8 aircraft
7. Forth to the Thames. Total – 18 aircraft
8. Thames to Portland. Total – 18 aircraft

Prior to the adoption of convoys in any or all of these areas, the aircraft would provide cooperation with the anti-submarine surface patrol forces.

The question now was, could the RAF provide all of these aircraft in time of war without detriment to other tasks? At this time (December 1936) there were only ninety shore-based aircraft in Coastal Command. The Chiefs of Staff accepted these figures, but it remained to be seen how many of the new command's aircraft could be regarded as specializing on shipping protection duties. The Air Staff were not prepared to commit themselves to a figure at this stage, claiming that very much depended on the strategic needs of maritime aircraft when and if war came. In any case, Parts II and III of the Joint Planners' Report was still outstanding. Until then the Air Staff could remain non-committal. In any event the Air Ministry would not wish to provoke the Admiralty into renewing its demand for its own shore-based Naval Cooperation aircraft force. But these delaying tactics were all very well. In fact this inter-service rivalry was actually harming Coastal Command's readiness for war, since the training policy of the command could not be determined until the operational role was settled. Moreover, it was not only Coastal Command that needed maritime aircraft. Overseas commands would need flying-boats in places like Singapore, Gibraltar, Malta and Alexandria, not to mention Jamaica and Sierra Leone.

FORMATION OF RAF COASTAL COMMAND

The reorganization of the RAF as it affected maritime air capabilities

In 1936 major changes were made to the organization of the RAF at home. This is described in Chapter 2. The importance of the reorganization in the context of maritime air capability is that in creating a Coastal Command, alongside the Fighter and Bomber Commands, was that the former would have its own establishment of squadrons and aircraft that could be justified on the maritime defence of the British Isles. It also signalled to the Admiralty that the RAF was responsible for the provision of shore-based aircraft. Under Expansion Plan A provision had been made for squadrons with a total of sixty-four aircraft. Under Expansion Plan C, which had prompted the creation of Coastal Command, the new organization would have:

7 general-purpose squadrons, each of 18 aircraft – 126 aircraft

2 torpedo-bomber squadrons, each of 12 aircraft – 24 aircraft

6 flying-boat squadrons, each of 6 aircraft. Total aircraft – 36

Total aircraft – 186

This total would be reduced in time of war to 162 aircraft, since the two torpedo-bomber squadrons would be assigned to Bomber Command.

The new Coastal Command

Initially it had been proposed that the new command should have an AOC, not an AOC-in-C as had been agreed for Fighter and Bomber Commands. But the Admiralty needed to be convinced that it could be relied upon to provide the squadrons needed under the pressures of war, and after some thought the command status was upgraded to an AOC-in-C. The Admiralty hoped that the new organization would correspond to the naval commands, ie on a geographical and not a functional basis, but the Director of Organization at the Air Ministry had other ideas, and produced a functional plan. Doubts were expressed that a functional organization could relate to naval commands in time of war. As it was, Group HQ would not be able to operate both landplane reconnaissance aircraft and flying-boats simultaneously. Be that as it may, it was decided, in March 1936, that the functional groups should be maintained, but personnel shortages prevented the formation of three groups, and the flying-boat squadrons joined the GR and torpedo-bomber squadrons in No. 16 Group formed at Lee-on-Solent on 1 December 1936. At least No. 16 Group could deploy its squadrons on a geographical basis.

Air Marshal Sir Arthur Longmoor was appointed as the new AOC-in-C on 14 July 1936 (he had been AOC Coastal Area since 1 October 1934), but on 1 September he was replaced by Air Marshal P.B. Joubert de la Ferté. The plan produced by the Director of Organization was as follows:

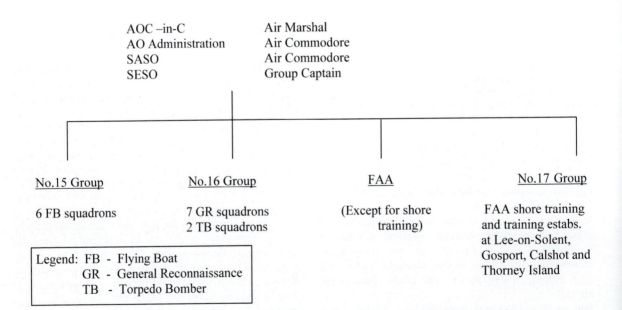

AOC –in-C	Air Marshal
AO Administration	Air Commodore
SASO	Air Commodore
SESO	Group Captain

| No.15 Group | No.16 Group | FAA | No.17 Group |
| 6 FB squadrons | 7 GR squadrons
2 TB squadrons | (Except for shore training) | FAA shore training and training estabs. at Lee-on-Solent, Gosport, Calshot and Thorney Island |

Legend: FB - Flying Boat
         GR - General Reconnaissance
         TB - Torpedo Bomber

Given the constraints imposed by manning, the revised organization was to place the flying-boat squadrons into No. 16 Group, so that it would then be possible to provide support for the Navy on a geographical basis:

No. 16 Group
3 GR squadrons of Ansons at Bircham Newton.
2 TB squadrons of Vildebeests at Donibristle.
5 FB squadrons of Londons, Singapores, Southamptons and Scapas at Calshot, Felixstowe, Mount Batten and Pembroke Dock.

Coastal Command's inventory of aircraft

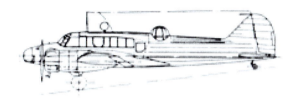

Anson.

Vildebeest.

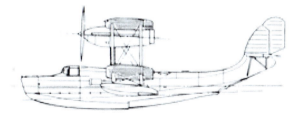

Scapa.

London.

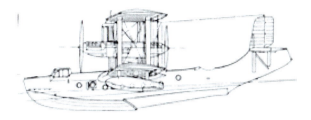

Singapore.

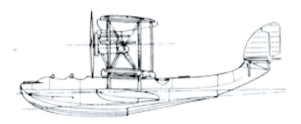

Southampton.

Note: only the Ansons are monoplanes; the Sunderlands, Catalinas and Hudsons are to come; and the last two will be American aircraft.

No. 17 Group This was the training group responsible for shore training of personnel going to No. 16 Group as well as to squadrons overseas. All three headquarters (Command and Nos 16 and 17 Groups) were co-located at Lee-on-Solent. The administration and training of the FAA units, however, came directly under Command HQ.

OPERATIONAL EXERCISES AND INCREASE IN STRENGTH, 1935–7

The programme of exercises and increase in strength, 1935–7 Reverting to the discussion about how well Coastal Command was able to meet the requirements of Naval Cooperation, it is instructive to see what the command's squadrons were doing in 1936. Very few exercises took place during 1935 and 1936. There was a lot of re-equipping going on, and the Abyssinian crisis affected the maritime squadrons. No. 210 Squadron was flying its Singapores out to the Far East between January and June to re-equip No. 205 Squadron. No. 209 Squadron was having trouble with its Iris V flying-boats and was re-equipping with the Perth, and the re-formed No. 230 Squadron was not operational on its Singapores until midsummer. The only squadrons available for operations during the first half of 1935 were Nos 201 and 204 Squadrons with flying-boats and No. 22 Squadron with torpedo-bombers. They took part in two fleet exercises with the 5th Submarine Flotilla and the Anti Submarine School, while No. 22 Squadron carried out some torpedo attacks on a target cruiser. The Abyssinian crisis resulted in the cancellation of exercises. Nos 204 and 210 Squadrons, rearmed respectively with the Scapa and Rangoon flying-boats, were dispatched in response to the Italian threat. No. 210 Squadron went to Gibraltar, Nos 204 and 230 Squadrons to Alexandria. In October No. 22 Squadron went to Malta. In addition to the patrols in connection with the Italian occupation of Abyssinia, the flying-boats cooperated in exercises with the Mediterranean Fleet. This major detachment continued in Mediterranean waters until the end of August 1936.

This left home waters with virtually no flying-boats. Nos 201 and 209 Squadrons were partially operational on a mixture of Singapores and Southamptons. Between them they carried out four shadowing exercises with the 1st Battle Squadron, and two exercises with the 3rd Submarine Flotilla and the Portland Anti-Submarine School. The three flying-boat squadrons returned home from the Mediterranean in September 1936, but No. 230 Squadron was immediately dispatched to the Far East, and No. 210 Squadron came out of the line to re-equip with Singapore boats. The torpedo-bomber squadron returned later in the year. Thus only Nos 201, 204 and 209 Squadrons were available for exercises during the last quarter of 1936. In October an extensive fleet reconnaissance and night shadowing exercise was carried out by them in the North Sea, and in this they were joined on the last day of operations by the first of the GR landplane squadrons, No. 48 with Ansons. This squadron was formed at the end of 1935 and was originally equipped with Saro Clouds before getting the Ansons, at which time it was stationed at Manston, where the aircraft were used for GR training courses. During the remaining two months of 1936 the three flying-boat squadrons only took part in shadowing exercises with single units of the 1st Battle Squadron and one A/S Patrol exercise with submarines.

Between the last months of 1936 and mid-1937 the newly established Coastal Command received some welcome increases in strength with an additional torpedo-bomber squadron and a new flying-boat squadron (Nos 42 and 228), the latter having a mixture of a London, a Scapa and three Singapores, and the land-based GR Anson squadrons were forming in rapid succession. Of these, No. 206 appeared in the autumn of 1936, followed by Nos 220 and 269 Squadrons at the end of the year and Nos 224, 217 and 233 Squadrons during the first half of 1937. All were Anson GR squadrons. Re-equipment to the latest types of flying-boat was proceeding, and by March 1937 both Nos 201 and 203 Squadrons had Londons and the first Stranraer had gone to No. 228 Squadron.

Coastal Command was then in a much better position to provide the Naval Cooperation required by the Admiralty. The exercises during 1937 were more numerous and diverse in character. There were two full-scale exercises, one being trade protection and the other coastal defence exercises. There were seven fleet exercises, three in night operations and six torpedo and bombing exercises. Four exercises were carried out with the submarine flotillas and two with the Portland Anti-Submarine School with additional ship and submarine recognition exercises, and several anti-submarine exercises were carried out with submarines from Gibraltar. Between August and December, three of the flying-boat squadrons (Nos 204, 209 and 210) were detached to the Western Mediterranean, where they were employed on 'anti-piracy' patrols under the Nyon Agreement during the Spanish Civil War. This agreement provided for French and British anti-submarine patrols in the Mediterranean, and showed what Britain and France could do if the two governments acted together and with resolve.

Vacillation in deciding Coastal Command's role in war
It took all of 1936 for the new scheme of internal organization to be completed. In fact the Command Staff, at Lee-on-Solent, did not officially come into place until 1 January 1937. They had to consider the Joint Planners' figure for a home-based maritime force of 261 aircraft when the command had at that time only ninety aircraft. Although it was a significant increase on the figure for a year earlier, there was still no definite role in war assigned to these units. An Air Staff paper written at the end of 1935 stated that the primary role of the shore-based units was coastal defence, involving reconnaissance for the fleet, patrols offshore, the attack on enemy ships and general cooperation with naval forces, but it then went on to say that if the air threat to the British Isles exceeded the seaborne threat, the GR and torpedo-bomber squadrons were to assist with the counter air offensive against targets in enemy territory. Furthermore a large proportion of the maritime force might have to be deployed overseas, as happened in the Abyssinian crisis.

Germany was the likely enemy, and the command's units would have to shadow enemy surface craft and submarines by day and night, and be prepared to attack them. At that time there were no radio detection finders (RDF) to help track the movement of enemy aircraft, but the flying-boat squadrons would be required to keep a watch over certain enemy ports and naval bases. The torpedo-bomber squadrons would be required either to reinforce Bomber Command or to act as a striking force against enemy surface ships. This stance was confirmed in an Air Staff paper, dated 7 December 1936, slightly in advance of Part I of the Joint Planners' Report. They took the view that it would be wasteful if the general reconnaissance of the North Sea was to be met by planning for each of the individual requirements, as opposed to being regarded and planned as a combined requirement. For example, two daily sweeps of the

North Sea southward of the line Firth of Forth to South Norway fulfilled both the requirement of trade defence and some of the other roles. It was even suggested that bombers proceeding to or returning from attacks on targets in enemy territory could carry out reconnaissance as they passed over the southern North Sea. In conclusion the Air Staff did not dispute that a certain minimum number of aircraft would be required for trade defence. What they did dispute was that they should be used exclusively for this purpose.

On 22 December 1936 Air Marshal Joubert de la Ferté, the AOC-in-C of Coastal Command, gave his view on the responsibilities of his command. He believed that the most immediate threat would be from the German Air Force, in which case the primary task would be to support Bomber and Fighter Commands, but it was conceded that it would be necessary to assign some units to protect sea communications in narrow waters from the German naval threat. If the threat came from an enemy beyond the effective air range of home-based squadrons, then overseas reinforcement would have to be considered. This was not likely to calm the fears of the Naval Staff, who could be forgiven for thinking that Naval Cooperation came way down the list of priorities. Indeed the Air Ministry appeared to be at odds with Joubert. The Department of Naval Cooperation (DONC) produced a minute, dated 1 March 1937, in which it pointed out that neither participation in a general air offensive nor the provision of overseas reinforcements was a duty that should be undertaken before Britain's sea communications had been assured and the threat of seaborne attack removed. Perhaps Joubert's assessment of the enemy threat can be partly understood given the relatively small size of the German surface fleet, whose heaviest units consisted of three pocket battleships and two battle cruisers. (The battleships *Bismarck* and *Tirpitz* would come later.) It was probable that the German Naval Staff would not wish this small force to come into action with heavy units of the Royal Navy in home waters. Admiral Raeder's Z Plan, providing for a much larger fleet with aircraft-carriers, was not due for completion until 1945. It was unfortunate for him that Hitler started the war too soon. It would be probable that the Germans would attack Britain's seaborne trade, using her larger warships as surface raiders operating far from home waters, and this is precisely what happened. Avoiding contact with heavy units of the Royal Navy was paramount, which explains the use of camouflage, radio silence and resupply in mid-ocean from supply ships like the *Altmark*, which sustained the *Admiral Graf Spee* in the South Atlantic. Although the *Graf Spee* was eventually cornered in Montevideo, resulting in her being scuttled in December 1939, it should not be forgotten that her sister ship, the *Admiral Scheer*, was loose in three oceans without being cornered, and returned to Germany safely in April 1941, having sunk sixteen ships. It is an example of great ingenuity and seamanship that the *Scheer* did not put into any port and maintenance was carried out in mid-ocean, when, for example, the bilges were pumped out, causing the ship to tilt, so that the barnacles could be removed from that part of the hull normally below the waterline.

It is not so easy to understand Joubert's thinking in relation to the U-boat threat. The sinking of the battleship *Royal Oak* on 14 October 1939 in the supposed safety of the Scapa Flow naval base in the Orkneys by the U.47 showed how serious a threat the U-boat could be and proved to be. Clearly Joubert wanted to keep his options open, but as has been pointed out, the training policy of the command could not be settled until the roles of the various squadrons were decided. Operating over the sea requires skills not required in attacking targets on land. Vast expanses of water must be criss-crossed systematically to ensure that enemy surface units and submarines do not go undetected. This required patient yet often tedious and fruitless hours peering through binoculars, not to mention the navigational skills required. These are greater since there will be no landmarks as points of reference. As things stood, aircrews trained to these standards would also have to be trained in other roles.

The clear-sighted appreciation of DONC staff did not carry sufficient weight, and on 25 March 1937 the Air Ministry's instructions were a compromise. It was said that Coastal Command in war might be employed in:

1. Cooperation with Bomber Command in the main strategic air offensive.
2. Cooperation with naval forces and such Army forces as are allocated to coast defence in countering enemy attacks on Britain's coast and sea communications.

The relative importance of these two roles will vary in different campaigns, and it is not possible to state definitely whether or not one or the other is the primary role, as a combination of both may be necessary. Units of Coastal Command must therefore be trained in both roles.

In spite of all the minutes, memos and reports, little had changed, except, that is, the size of the force at Joubert's disposal. The Admiralty's claim to ownership of the shore-based squadrons was rejected, and the policy just described remained in force until the remaining parts of the Joint Planners' Report were completed and approved by the Committee of Imperial Defence. Only then was it possible to determine the precise war roles of the squadrons of Coastal Command.

EMPLOYMENT OF NAVAL AIR FORCES AGAINST SUBMARINES AND WARSHIPS

(Source National Archives document AIR/41/45)

ANTI-SUBMARINE WARFARE

The forgotten lessons of the 1914–18 war Convoy escort Squadron Leader J.K. Waugh DSC gave a lecture at the RAF Staff College during its fourth course, in which he drew lessons from the 1914–18 war and his service in the RNAS and the RAF. 'The effectiveness of air escort and patrol should be judged by the tonnage of ships sunk or damaged in the patrol area/convoy,' he said, 'and not by the number of submarines sighted or sunk.' Since submarine commanders might well be deterred from surfacing in the presence of aircraft, a lack of sighting might be regarded as evidence of effectiveness. Indeed, the absence of air cover in a day or part of a day often resulted in ships being attacked in an otherwise trouble-free area. From April 1917 there were 312 ships torpedoed in convoy. Of these only two were torpedoed when the convoy was under air escort. Two aircraft could provide optimum air cover: one would scout ahead and on the bows of the convoy up to a distance of five miles, while the second aircraft would cover the rear to ensure that the convoy was not being trailed.

The bombing of submarines The lesson from the Great War was that relatively heavy bombs of high explosive to weight ratio were essential for attacks on submarines. Ideally this would be the 500 pounder, which could only be carried by a few wartime aircraft. In general use was the 230 lb bomb fused to explode at a depth of approximately forty feet and effective against submarines on the surface and to a depth of sixty feet. Of 236 air attacks against submarines during the last two years of the Great War, only ten resulted in sinkings and fifteen in damage. Pilots too often made the mistake of dropping the entire bomb load on the swirl of water left when the submarine dived, in the hope of securing a lucky hit, instead of waiting for about half an hour, when the submarine commander might risk surfacing. In cases where attacks on submarines were withheld, there was evidence that delayed attacks were successful.

Tactics If ships were proceeding independently then air patrols should be mounted on navigational focal points. With ships sailing in convoy it was just as important for aircraft to direct surface escorts to attack a submarine as it was for the aircraft to carry out the attack. The lowest priority should be accorded to the employment of aircraft in searching for and attacking submarines proceeding to and from their operational areas. Squadron Leader Waugh finished his lecture to the staff college by emphasizing the importance of air and sea forces collaborating closely to combat the submarine menace.

Naval Staff policy on anti-submarine warfare The advice given above does not appear in any staff policy, appreciation and instruction on anti-submarine warfare. Only the general point was made that aircraft could assist in reporting the presence of submarines well ahead of the fleet. On 29 June 1931 the Naval Staff submitted a paper on the submarine menace to the Committee of Imperial Defence. The heavy losses suffered by the Allies during the Great War to the U-boat were enumerated. It was said that the Navy had limited resources to counter the submarine. The value of Asdic was questioned, since the apparatus must be in the hands of well-trained personnel, and the sea state and speed of the vessel must both be moderate. Moreover, there were a limited number of vessels fitted with Asdic, and experience of the Great War showed that an average of twenty-three separate convoys could be at sea in the Atlantic alone, and so the Asdic protection for convoys would be very small. The discussion on p. 237 discloses a change of opinion when, in 1936, the Joint Planners were claiming that Asdic would render submarine attacks on convoys unprofitable, resulting in the abandonment of submarine warfare.

With regard to the effectiveness of aircraft in sinking submarines, it was stated that of 188 U-boats destroyed only seven were sunk by aircraft. It was felt that little had materially changed in the thirteen years since the Armistice in this respect, but it was conceded that the range of aircraft had increased to enhance their reconnaissance capability. Aircrews could see submarines below the surface where ships' crews could not, but it was seen as the role of the maritime patrol aircraft, not to attack, but to direct Asdic vessels to the location of a submarine. This will explain the Naval Staff's insistence, already mentioned in this chapter, that Naval Cooperation aircraft should only report the whereabouts of enemy submarines and surface warships. The Air Staff believed that aircraft had the capability to deliver an attack. But there was a lack of priority given to anti-submarine warfare training of RAF crews, and slow progress was made in developing an anti-submarine bomb. One, which was in limited production in 1934, was quite unproved against a realistic target.

ANTI-SHIPPING WARFARE

The Air Staff's stance on attacking warships
The Air Staff had a view about attacking and destroying warships from the air. In 1935 the decks of warships were being armoured. The trajectory of shells fired in the Great War was flat, which meant that warships would need side armour only. By the Second World War the trajectory of shells was plunging. Unfortunately the battlecruiser HMS *Hood* was too busy showing the British flag to the world, and the Admiralty never got around to armouring the decks. Tragically the sixth salvo

from the *Bismarck* early on 24 May 1941 caused an explosion that sent the *Hood* to the bottom within minutes, and all but three of her crew perished. For the Air Staff this posed the question of how to penetrate deck armour. It was believed that it would be necessary to drop bombs from 10,000 feet to be sure of penetration. From 10,000 feet cloud could obscure the target, and even without cloud, precision bombing would require new bomb-sights. The alternative was to bomb in clusters from either a formation of bombers or a single aircraft using a bomb distributor, or a combination of both.

Alternatively bombs could be released from dive-bombers, which would attack at an angle of 45°. This would overcome the problem of all but very low cloud obscuring the target. The bombs would be released from between 1,000 and 1,500 feet, so achieving accuracy would not present so great a problem. The problems associated with this type of bombing were the necessity to develop specialist dive-bombers like the German Ju 87 Stuka and the improbability of penetrating the deck armour from a low altitude.

Aerial torpedo attacks meant that the attacking aircraft would have to approach the target warship at wave-top height and fly straight and level immediately before the torpedo was launched. If the aircraft launched the torpedo too high the missile would enter the water at too great an angle, causing it to dive below the hull of the target ship. This angle was therefore critical, and in the accompanying photograph is seen a Blackburn Shark, which was loaned to the Torpedo Development Unit for trials on a new torpedo. The difference between an angle of 2° and 4¹/₂° was all-important. Torpedo-bombers were not new, having been used in the Great War, but new torpedoes of greater destructive power were being

developed. The drawbacks with this type of attack were that the attacking aircraft would have to fly straight and level before the attack, rendering them particularly vulnerable to ack-ack fire, and the addition of bulges onto the hulls of warships that could absorb much of the force of the explosion.

The Naval Staff view

The Naval Staff reversed the order of importance of the three types of attack. This may be understood in the development of torpedo bombing in the FAA and the fact that the Navy did not possess either high-level or dive-bombers. Nor did the Naval Staff credit Britain's potential adversaries with having the defensive armour possessed by Royal Navy warships. Both schools of thought used trial experiments to bolster their arguments, and there was an exchange of letters on the subject between the Secretary of State for Air and the First Lord of the Admiralty during March 1936. Lord Swinton maintained that the effectiveness of naval ack-ack fire had not been proved, since trials had only involved the use of towed targets and the Queen Bee pilotless target aircraft, which could not be flown above 85 mph when modern aircraft could exceed 200 mph. It was doubtful, he said, if targets could be hit during the very short time that the aircraft were flying straight and level.

As regards the effects of bombs dropped on warships, experiments had been carried out with 250 lb bombs, but not 500 lb bombs. A dummy 500 lb bomb was found to have penetrated deck armour, but that did not disclose the destructive effect after penetration The First Lord replied that two 500 lb bombs had been placed inside a vessel in positions to which they could have expected to penetrate and the explosions did remarkably little damage. The war of words continued, with the Navy wishing to prove that even high-level bombers would be vulnerable to ack-ack fire, that armour-piercing bombs would not inflict serious damage on armoured warships and that dive-bombers would be particularly vulnerable to the new multiple pom-poms. Predictably the RAF took a different view, and Lord Swinton suggested that instead of theorizing it would be better to conduct real live trials.

Whenever the vulnerability of battleships was discussed, the Admiralty would go onto the defensive. Never would it be admitted that the battleship had had its day, which would prove to be the case in the Second World War. Their Lordships held that advances in shipboard ack-ack would enable the battleship to perform its primary function, but events proved the opposite. Air bombing and/or torpedo attacks would seal the fate of the *Bismarck* and *Tirpitz*, the *Repulse* and *Prince of Wales*, Japanese battleships in the closing stages of the Second World War, the battleships of the US Pacific Fleet in Pearl Harbor and the Italian fleet in

A Blackburn Shark Mk I
torpedo/spotter/reconnaissance aircraft K.4350, an aircraft from HMS *Courageous*. Here it is on loan to the Torpedo Development Unit at Gosport to determine the best angle for launching a Mk VIII torpedo.

Taranto Harbour. Fleet actions accounted only for HMS *Hood* and the *Scharnhorst*. Be that as it may, the Admiralty in 1935 declared, 'In the Main Fleet the capital ship remains the essential element upon which the whole structure of our naval strategy depends.'

During the Abyssinian crisis in 1935 British naval units were withdrawn from Malta, and the fleet at Alexandria was therefore exposed. Was the Navy afraid of air attack by Italian aircraft? Questions were asked in Parliament and the Press about the vulnerability of capital ships, and when the building of two new capital ships was proposed in the 1936 Defence White Paper, the Prime Minister felt obliged to have the matter again investigated. The Navy would show that advances in shipboard ack-ack and the addition of deck armour would suffice to protect battleships. In this the Admiralty received support from an unexpected quarter. Sir John Salmond, the retired Chief of the Air Staff, felt that a considerable number of direct hits would be required to sink a battleship and that an attack would have to be made from a great height to ensure penetration. Lord Trenchard had no definite opinion on the matter but said that the mere advent of airpower had restricted the freedom of movement and harbouring of naval vessels in a number of ways. He did not believe that capital ships were indispensable, and felt that money would be better spent on aircraft, cruisers, destroyers, submarines and motor boats. Ellington for the RAF took a contrary view to that of the Naval Staff. A sub-committee of the CID took a mass of conflicting evidence before making its report on 30 July 1936. Members of the sub committee were not persuaded by the arguments of air enthusiasts, who were not very impressive under cross-examination, and so the battleship was saved.

All-in-all the whole debate over the future of the FAA and shore-based maritime aircraft was characterized by an all-pervading inter-service rivalry, which again and again would require government intervention. The RAF's retention of all shore-based maritime aircraft was assured, but the junior service would lose the other battle. The FAA would return to the Navy.

THE FLEET AIR ARM IS TRANSFERRED TO THE ADMIRALTY

Introduction

In 1923 the Balfour government had declared in favour of a unified single air service. Volume I described in detail the sometimes acrimonious battles between the Admiralty and the Air Ministry for ownership and direction of the Fleet Air Arm. The Air Ministry view prevailed, and the RAF air and ground crews manned carrier-borne flights of fighter and reconnaissance units, and flew aircraft catapulted from warships. The RAF also operated, equipped and manned shore-based

squadrons employed on maritime operations. The RAF demand in the early 1920s that it should be the only service to provide aeroplanes in war prevailed because a cost-conscious government wished to avoid duplication of flying training effort and the design, development and production of aircraft. In 1923 the cost savings were a major consideration, but Air Marshal Trenchard knew that the hiving off of Army Cooperation squadrons to the Army and the Fleet Air Arm to the Navy would leave an unviable rump that would spell the end of the RAF.

During the 1920s and early 1930s the compromise worked out between Trenchard and Keyes permitted naval personnel to fill a number of posts in maritime air units, both ashore and afloat. The Admiralty retained the right to deploy air units afloat that were part of the fleet. Ashore, air units employed on maritime operations were deployed by RAF commanders. With the 'Ten-Year Rule' in place, a major conflict involving British armed forces remained a remote possibility, and the Trenchard-Keyes agreement might have sufficed indefinitely had it not been for a change in the international situation. By 1934 the RAF was about to begin its major expansion to meet the new and growing threat from Germany. If the Admiralty made a fresh attempt to reclaim the FAA and was successful it would no longer spell the end of the RAF.

THE TRANSFER OF THE FAA TO THE ADMIRALTY
Fresh attempts to modify the Trenchard-Keyes agreement

With expansion in the air, the Admiralty made approaches to the Air Ministry in 1934 for an easing of the manning situation in naval air units by training a number of naval ratings as pilots. Since this was not part of the agreement, the Air Ministry turned it down. So the First Lord then made approaches direct to the Prime Minister, and when these did not bear fruit he enlisted the help of the Defence Coordinator, Inskip, and in May 1936 the Prime Minister, Baldwin, agreed to the investigation of the whole question of FAA manning and reserves. The Air Minister, Lord Swinton, agreed, provided the long-established manning arrangement remained unchanged. For his part, Lord Weir, who had been involved in securing the 1923 agreement, was very unhappy at the prospect of renewed naval/air wars over the FAA.

The 1936 Inskip Report

In his report in November 1936, Inskip gave it as his opinion that the period of service of RAF pilots in the FAA should be increased from two to four years. This would be to relieve the manning situation, and he accepted an offer from Lord Swinton for a trial entry of between twelve and fifteen naval rating pilots. This in itself would not solve the problem of building up a 10% reserve, and the report gave no ruling on this point. But then Inskip went beyond his brief by suggesting that the efficiency of the FAA was being subordinated to the Trenchard-Keyes agreement. Now that expansion was planned, the degree of collaboration required between the two services for the working of the agreement was increasing to the point where smooth working was at risk. It became increasingly clear that the constitution of the FAA would have to be reviewed, and Inskip wrote to the Prime Minister suggesting an inquiry, for their Lordships were becoming increasingly restive. But on hearing that the position of the FAA was yet again to be reviewed, Lord Weir protested to Baldwin, for it was his belief that the two services must simply learn to work together in the existing system.

Sir Samuel Hoare becomes First Lord of the Admiralty

Sir Samuel Hoare, who had been the Air Minister at the time of the Balfour Report, rejoined the government as the First Lord of the Admiralty. His First Sea Lord, Admiral Sir Ernle Chatfield, wrote to Hoare expressing the view that the FAA constitution devised in 1923 had outgrown its usefulness. Chatfield believed that the Navy's efficiency was being seriously impaired, and there had to be a complete and immediate change in the administration, organization and control of the naval air service. Chatfield circulated a letter to the Prime Minister, Swinton and Inskip to that effect. The Air Minister was prepared to accept the request that the RAF accept thirty-four ratings at the earliest possible date for aircrew training. Hoare also backed up Chatfield's letter with one of his own. In it he referred to the battles he had waged in the early 1920s to maintain the integrity of the RAF at a time when the survival of that service was under threat. Now that the RAF was firmly established he believed that a great deal of inter-departmental controversy could be avoided if the FAA went to the Admiralty. But, importantly, he could not agree to the RAF losing coastal air command with its land-based aircraft.

Weir threatens resignation

The Admiralty then followed up the exchange of letters with a vocal campaign in Parliament. The Navy wanted administrative control of the FAA and shore-based aircraft. This was just the moment when the Prime Minister was preoccupied with the Abdication crisis, but Hoare still managed to persuade Baldwin to initiate an inquiry. The First Lord had been pressing for the earliest consideration of the Navy's case, which included the defence of shipping by shore-based aircraft. Inskip nominated himself, together with Halifax (Lord President of the Council) and Oliver Stanley (President of the Board of Trade) as the three Cabinet ministers who would conduct the inquiry, and Swinton was asked if he was in agreement with this proposal in a letter from the

Prime Minister. Swinton then showed Baldwin's letter to Lord Weir, who promptly threatened resignation. Weir had been intimately involved in the formation of the Royal Air Force, and Swinton was loath to lose his 'unique experience and constant help'. Swinton told the Prime Minister of Weir's threatened resignation, but told Inskip that the resignation had already occurred. Inskip then regretted not having invited Weir to take part in the inquiry, and offered the excuse that he wanted someone with a fresh mind and outlook, by which he meant Cabinet ministers who did not have a vested interest in the outcome. This left the Prime Minister with the problem of proceeding with the inquiry without losing Weir's services, and he came up with a compromise. There would not be a committee of inquiry with formal terms of reference, but Inskip would sit alone with the Chiefs of Staff. Weir's withdrawal of his threat of resignation was announced to Parliament on 11 March.

The Inskip report

Inskip consulted not only the Chiefs of Staff, but also Churchill and Hankey. Churchill supported the Navy's claim, but Hankey felt that the RAF would be able to concede the Navy's claim for the transfer of the FAA provided the Air Ministry retained the squadrons of Coastal Command. Of course the Admiralty would need to be sure that it got the support it needed in time of war. On 21 July the report was submitted to Neville Chamberlain, who had succeeded Baldwin as Prime Minister. Inskip had already accepted the advice that he had been given, and recommended that the Admiralty should have operational and administrative control of the FAA, but that the shore-based aircraft of Coastal Command should remain with the RAF. It was felt, that given the degree of service cooperation achieved by 1937, the RAF would do its best to meet the Navy's needs. If the Admiralty had been given the shore-based aircraft there would be an understandable desire to cover every sea area in time of war and protect every convoy, which would lock up a very large number of aircraft. Given the flexibility of the application of airpower, the RAF would allocate aircraft to meet perceived threats to the naval units, the merchant marine and trade generally, i.e. the RAF would make more economical use of the maritime aircraft at its disposal. The Admiralty had complained that insufficient specialized training was given to units of Coastal Command, but Inskip held that this could be remedied by closer liaison between the two services, and he closed his report by giving his opinion that matters of acute controversy affecting the two services could not be settled absolutely. Common sense had to prevail to answer questions of degree and proportion. The science and the art of flying would remain to be fostered by the RAF, which was the primary air arm, and the transfer of the FAA to the Admiralty could succeed, given goodwill and determination on both sides. Inskip's view would be vindicated on the outbreak of war, given the cooperation between the Navy and the RAF in bringing about the sinking of the German battleship *Bismarck* in May 1941. Reconnaissance Spitfires and Catalinas of the RAF spotted the *Bismarck* and *Prinz Eugen* 'breaking out' into the North Atlantic, and Swordfish of the FAA disabled the battleship prior to its sinking by heavy units of the Royal Navy.

Cabinet approval

The Chief of the Air Staff, Air Chief Marshal Sir Edward Ellington, seems not to have seen an advance copy of Inskip's report that went to the Prime Minister. When Trenchard met Ellington at a Buckingham Palace garden party, the latter was quite unperturbed, believing that the transfer of the FAA to the Admiralty was still under consideration and that the Cabinet would be convinced by the Air Staff's case. Trenchard is reported to have rebuked the CAS, saying, 'Do you never leave your office, Ellington? The thing's over. It's been decided over your head, which is well buried in the sand as usual!' Ellington then had less than a month to serve, thus ending this most unusual career for an officer who rose to head an air service. The CAS had never exercised operational command of aircraft in war, having spent his entire career on staff duties.

The Times called the transfer a 'judgement of Solomon which gives each claimant a part only of what it demanded'. It was felt that Inskip had satisfied neither service. Indeed Inskip himself said as much to Weir when he sent him an advance copy of his report. Be that as it may, the Cabinet approved the transfer on 29 July, by which time Mr Duff Cooper had succeeded Hoare as First Lord. Duff Cooper's first reaction was that the Admiralty had not got what it hoped for in the matter of shore-based aircraft, but Inskip had told Weir that his report was never going to please everyone. Hoare, who had then become Home Secretary, reminded everyone that the 1923 compromise was always something of an experiment, which would some day have to be reconsidered. Since the number of aircraft that would be transferred to the Navy would not exceed 500, as against 2,000 operational RAF front-line aircraft, it could hardly be described as the creation of an air force under the Admiralty. He said that the Air Ministry would gain financially and that the interests of economy would be observed.

The transfer

The Prime Minister announced the transfer of the FAA to the Admiralty to the House of Commons on 30 July 1937. The Admiralty and the Air Ministry were to work out a scheme for the implementation of the transfer by stages. But although both services did their best to facilitate the detailed arrangements, problems that were mainly administrative meant that the transfer was not completed until May 1939. Even then RAF aircrews were still at sea on the outbreak of war, for the RAF could not compel RAF personnel to transfer to the Royal Navy. There was therefore an acute shortage of trained naval personnel to man the FAA. There was also a lack of suitable naval aircraft, but it is a fitting postscript to this section to reflect that the aircraft that crippled the Italian fleet at Taranto on 11 November 1940 and disabled the *Bismarck* in May 1941 were neither Seafires nor Blackburn Skuas or Rocs, but the old 'stringbags', the Swordfish biplanes.

Transfer of Fleet Air Arm equipment to the Admiralty

The following Air Ministry Order gave effect to the transfer of responsibility from the Air Ministry to the Admiralty in respect of equipment. The order reflects the many detailed arrangements that had to be made, and also the provisional nature of some of them:

A161 Transfer of Fleet Air Arm Equipment other than Airframes and Engines to the Admiralty – Financial and Accounting Procedure (882732/39 – 27.4.39)

I, GENERAL ARRANGEMENTS

1. The general responsibility for the administration of the Fleet Air Arm will pass to the Admiralty at a date to be promulgated later. Responsibility for the provision, storage receipt and issue of equipment, other than airframes and engines, for the Fleet Air Arm units both at home and overseas will, however, be taken over by the Admiralty with effect from 1st May, 1939, except in the case of the Mediterranean Command and at Singapore, the effective dates for which will be promulgated later. Maintenance, including modifications of equipment at stations where no naval facilities exist, will be carried out by the Air Ministry on an agency basis.

2. In addition to Fleet Air Arm units, it is probable that the following RAF stations at home will eventually be transferred to Admiralty control:

Lee-on-Solent
Worthy Down
Donibristle
Ford
Southampton
Lympne

Pending further instructions, demands for equipment required for Fleet Air Arm purposes at these stations are, on 1st May 1939, to be made on the appropriate Admiralty supply depot.

3. In addition to the above, it is probable that accommodation at certain RAF stations at home will

be made available for units of the Fleet Air Arm disembarked from HM ships. Any such stations will remain under RAF control. Accommodation for disembarked Fleet Air Arm aircraft will continue to be provided at RAF stations abroad for the time being.

4. An RN store depot has been established at Coventry for the storage and maintenance of Fleet Air Arm equipment other than armament (including explosives), flying clothing and parachutes. Armament and flying clothing will be dealt with by the naval armament depot at Priddy's Hard, Portsmouth, and the Victualling Yard, Gosport, respectively. Parachutes will continue to be held by an RAF maintenance unit for the time being, storage, repairs, etc. being carried out as an agency service. Transfer of stocks from RAF maintenance units to the RN Store Depot at Coventry commenced on 1st February 1939. From 1st May 1939, the appropriate Admiralty supply depot will undertake supply to all stations for the maintenance of Fleet Air Arm units.

NAVAL RESPONSE TO THE MUNICH CRISIS OF SEPTEMBER 1938 IN THE MATTER OF FAA EQUIPMENT AND DEPLOYMENTS

Source Letter: C-in-C Home Fleet aboard HMS *Rodney*
(Reference: 2211/HF 001120, dated 15 November 1938)

Introduction

The C-in-C Home Fleet Admiral Forbes laid before the Admiralty his views about the deployment and equipment of the FAA in the event of a conflict, and referred to the draft memo on FAA Tactics and Equipment. He was concerned about the threat to aircraft-carriers from surface units, and said that throughout 1939 the *Kreigsmarine* would have only two battle cruisers, the *Scharnhorst* and *Gneisenau*, but no battleships. (This threat proved somewhat prophetic, since these two battle cruisers were to sink the Royal Navy carrier *Glorious* during the Norwegian campaign in 1940.) Forbes believed that the battleships, which were to be named *Bismarck* and *Tirpitz*, would not go into service until September to December 1940, the same time that the Royal Navy battleships *Prince of Wales* and *King George V* would enter service. He then went on to refer to the two planned German aircraft-carriers, which in the event did not materialize. These were planned to have forty aircraft apiece.

SECRET

Functions of the Fleet Aircraft

In the Draft Memo on the Tactics and Equipment of the FAA paragraph 4 dealt with the functions of fleet aircraft. These would be (a) Strategical to provide the fleet with deep and continuous reconnaissance, and (b) Tactical, which meant the attainment of air superiority and its maintenance during the battle. In paragraph 6 detailed considerations which have led to these conclusions on which the provision of aircraft must be based, were summarized as follows:

1. Reconnaissance   This may involve 100% aircraft carried, conferring the initiative on the fleet and will often be essential to the success of any operation.
2. Spotting   This is probably the essential function in battle.
3. Fighting   This is essential in battle to ensure spotting continues and to deny enemy spotting. Fighting will have little value against air attack except against shadowing aircraft.
4. Striking   AA armaments render daylight attacks on a fleet not in action uneconomical as compared with attacks on carriers.
5. Tactics   Early and successful attack against carriers will ensure maximum of air superiority with its far-reaching advantages. Early attack on the enemy battle fleet is uneconomical and not commensurate with the possible sacrifice of ultimate air superiority.

With regard to the two headings Striking and Tactics above, the operating of a carrier in a column of capital ships or cruisers is now being practised in the Home Fleet, and there is no reason why it should not be done by an enemy, thus weakening the widely held principle that the enemy aircraft-carriers should be the objective of the air striking force. Further, throughout 1939 and for some time in 1940 Germany will have no aircraft-carriers and Italy has none (except the *Miraglia*), and none are projected. It is therefore considered that in a European war the most likely role of the fleet aircraft would be that of a striking force to slow down the enemy and force action.

As regards reconnaissance it is agreed that there is no overstating the importance of this function, and provided that action can be forced there is no doubt as to the effectiveness of spotting. It is agreed that fighting is required only to deny air spotting to the enemy, to defend our spotters and to circumscribe the activities of enemy air shadowing aircraft.

The types of FAA aircraft in carriers

According to paragraph 56 of the pamphlet, 'Air Requirements in War' dated September 1938, it appears that three types of aircraft are under development (night shadowing aircraft not considered:

1. Torpedo-bomber reconnaissance (TBR)
2. Spotter fighter (SF)
3. Fleet fighter (FF)

The SF is said to be suitable reconnaissance and/or active observation and spotting in the face of fighter opposition, but I gather is not as good a fighter as the FF. I am at a loss to understand how the function of spotting and fighting can be carried out at the same time; the pilot, the observer and the air gunner would be quite differently employed in each case. It is considered that the TBR should be used for the functions of reconnaissance, which includes action observation, striking and spotting, and that the FF, which will presumably be the best fighter that can be produced, should be used for fighting.

I am unaware whether the Skua, which has lately been under trial in the *Courageous*, is the FF which is being developed, but it has not so far proved successful for use in a carrier. There is no reason from the navigational point of view why SF fighters should not be used. They are not required by their functions to fight far from the fleet, and the homing beacon is sufficiently reliable to ensure their return to the carrier. The decision as to whether they should be one- or two-seater should depend entirely on their fighting capabilities, but in the meantime it is most desirable that the *Courageous* and the *Furious* should be armed with Gladiators.

Numbers of types of aircraft to be carried in Aircraft Carriers

In Appendix IIIA of the pamphlet 'Air Requirements for War' for the equipment of three carriers with the Home Fleet it is proposed that on board there should be 51 × TBR, 30 × FS and 18 × FF. From paragraph 19 of the pamphlet 9 × FS are required for action observation, leaving 21 (+ 10 carried in ships), so it is inferred that some of these are required as fighters. It is considered that the proportion of aircraft, viz. 48 out of 99, which cannot carry a bomb or torpedo load if required is much too large as it must be remembered that none of these 48 aircraft will be used until action is actually joined between the enemy main force and our own. In other words none of these 48 aircraft help to bring the enemy to action. It is recommended that the proportion of fighters should be 1:3 TBRs. The best equipment for a *Victorious* or *Furious* type of carrier is considered to be 24 TBRs and 9 FFs, and for the *Courageous* there should be 36 TBRs and 12 FFs, the TBRs being used for spotting.

Signed – Admiral Forbes

SECRET

Minutes recorded on the subject matter of the C-in-C's SECRET letter of
15 November 1938 (as above)

Conditions applicable to a European war only are considered (in the C-in-C's letter), whereas allocation of aircraft has been considered for employment in any fleet theatre, and it would be unwise to design or allocate aircraft for special purposes or areas. There should be a common doctrine on the matter of obtaining air superiority. The principle has been confused with a tactical issue as to whether (enemy) aircraft-carriers or battle fleet should be the first objective of fleet aircraft. It is up to respective C-in-Cs but the simplest method is to destroy the enemy aircraft-carriers. If none are present then active offence against aircraft can only be pursued by aircraft.

It is imperative now to follow one common policy in regard to design and allocation of aircraft, for the United Kingdom has no practical war experience in the operation of modern aircraft with a fleet, and the results of peacetime exercises can be misleading. Therefore without the proof of war any one opinion may be as good as another. It is considered, without wishing to stifle criticism or constant review of material and methods that for the economic and every other point of view we require a period to consolidate the FAA.

Additional notes on the minutes above

There is no exact information available as to the equipment of German aircraft-carriers. The USA and Japan already have a larger proportion of fighters than the 1:2 we are proposing for fleet carriers, and the relative power of fighters is increasing. The draft memorandum on FAA tactics and equipment was written $2\frac{1}{2}$–3 years ago before the recent RDF (radio detection finding) and multi-gun fighter developments commenced. Putting carriers among capital ships affords them protection, but does not alter the principle to obtain air superiority at an early stage. SF aircraft can be used for reconnaissance and for action observation and in facing fighter opposition when temporarily forced to cease spotting or action observation. It has never been suggested that any aircraft can spot and fight simultaneously, but they do need strong defensive armament in case enemy fighters break through.

A TBR cannot be designed at present which could hope to live for long in the face of an attack by a modern fighter aircraft – i.e. ten seconds in every twenty minutes. The Skua was designed four years ago by Blackburn to combine the functions of fighting and dive-bombing. This was a mistake since the functions are incompatible, and the dive-bomber functions will not again be combined with fighting, but if the Skua was good aerodynamically at least it has a reasonable endurance, which the Gladiator has not. The Blackburn Roc, a two-seat fighter, and the Fairey Fulmar, a two-seat front-gun fighter, are also on order. The latter was not designed initially as a fighter and the former is an experimental type. The relative merits of the two types can only be gauged by tactical or gunnery trials.

The two-seat fighter is necessary for accompanying striking forces to their objective, a tactic which RDF may make necessary and which has been confirmed by practice in Spain and China. The modern eight-gun fighter is so large and heavy (if it is given suitable endurance for FAA work) that little reduction in performance entailed should be investigated in calling for the next fighter designs. The Fulmar is unnecessarily large since it was designed as a light bomber and it was forced on us:

a) Because of delays in the Skua and Roc.
b) Because we had no prototype following up the Skua and the Roc.

It is intended for the present to equip *Courageous* and *Furious* with Sea Gladiators as soon as they are available in spite of the fact that their endurance is only 2½ hours as compared with 5 hours with the Skua and Roc. The proportion of striking aircraft here referred to is higher than that in the USA and Japan now, and anti-aircraft, fighter and RDF developments may decrease attacking power very materially in the next three years, i.e. before the SF can materialize. It is not correct to suggest that the SF cannot be used until action is joined. It can be used as much as TBRs for reconnaissance. Since there is no proof of war, allocation of the aircraft must be related to enemy armament and allocation, i.e. the proportion of 66% of TSRs and 33% of FFs is considered correct for fleet carriers in normal circumstances, and 100% TSRs for trade-route carriers.

When fleet carriers are detached from the main theatre of operations 100% TSRs may often be desirable. Similarly certain operations can be envisaged both in the North Sea and the Mediterranean in which 100% fighters would be desirable, but it is not financially possible to provide for every alternative. It was concluded that the proportion of fighters to other types will be affected by the need for the latter to be protected, otherwise their operations will be severely handicapped.

STATE OF THE FLEET AIR ARM IN THE EVENT OF WAR
Source: Admiralty document dated 1/4/39

MOST SECRET

1. Owing to the shortage of observers and air gunners it will only be possible to man aircraft for *Ark Royal, Glorious* and *Eagle* catapult ships and training by accepting a reduction from 12 to 8 observers per TSR squadron in carriers and a maximum of one observer per carrier.
2. The Air Ministry has been asked to form first-line squadrons for *Courageous, Furious* and *Hermes*, but have so far refused to provide for carriers in reserve owing to their own shortage of maintenance ratings. These squadrons are required not later than April in order to continue the training of pilots on completion of courses and could not be used in war for some time after their formation, even if observers and air gunners were available to man them fully.
3. If squadrons for *Furious* and *Hermes* were formed by 1 April it would only be possible to man them for first-

line service by June provided casualties to observers and air gunners had not substantially exceeded peace rates. It would in fact be necessary to conserve our reduced first-line strength as much as possible during the whole of 1939 owing to shortage of war reserves of aircraft as well as of flying personnel. It will be necessary to inform C-in-Cs accordingly, and in view of the untrained state of personnel for commissioning carriers after the outbreak of war, it will be most undesirable to throw them into the fray until they have been allowed to 'work up' for at least six weeks in good weather conditions.

4. Assuming this conservation of our strength, it should be possible to equip and man squadrons for working up in *Courageous* and *Albatross* by about October 1939. If, after this date our position rapidly improved until, early in 1940, the full FAA would be able to commence carrying out its war functions properly provided the necessary maintenance personnel and aircraft production are allocated to the Navy. In this matter we are entirely in the hands of the Air Ministry, with no CID decision in regard to priority.
5. Homing Beacons (without which distant reconnaissance will imply the breaking of wireless silence to 'home aircraft') are only fitted in *Ark Royal* and *Courageous*. *Glorious* should be fitted by 1 April with a set dispatched to the Mediterranean at the request of the C-in-C Mediterranean. But *Eagle, Furious* and *Hermes* will not be fitted during 1939 unless special steps are taken, although the equipment is available now.
6. Night deck landing equipment (which would be reasonably safe for use in war in the vicinity of the enemy) is fitted in *Ark Royal* (a not entirely satisfactory set), and will be fitted in *Glorious* and *Courageous* by April 1939. It should be possible to provide equipment for *Furious* and *Hermes* by June 1939 but special steps would have to taken to provide for and equip the *Eagle*.
7. It may be considered desirable to commission *Courageous* and *Hermes* on the outbreak of war and use the former for deck landing training and reallocate *Ark Royal*'s aircraft as follows:

	TSR	FF
Ark Royal	18	12
Furious	16	6
Hermes	8	-

Allocating 50% IR TSRs to any carrier operating on the trade routes.

Signed   D.N.A.D.
30.12.38

MOST SECRET

Chapter 7
RAF Stations, Airfields and Other Establishments

The location of airfields and other establishments, an overview – The 1930s transformation – The cost of airfields – The realignment of 1939 – The construction and layout of airfields – The airfields, seaplane bases and miscellaneous units by region of the United Kingdom and overseas

Introduction

Volume I went into great detail about the layout and location of airfields, both at home and abroad during the First World War and up to and including 1929. The rapid release of airfields and landing grounds during the period 1919 to 1923 was also charted, and it is all the more remarkable that a new airfield should be opened at a time when so many were being closed. This was RAF Duxford, near Cambridge, positioned to provide fighter defence of the Midlands.

The airfields in the United Kingdom during the 1920s were positioned to provide fighter defence of the home base, bomber airfields and airfields/seaplane bases for maritime defence, together with airfields on the coast that could accept fleet aircraft when aircraft carriers were in port or on decommissioning or refit. It will be remembered that the RAF was at this time responsible for manning fleet-based aircraft, together with a growing number of Navy personnel. Such airfields as Leuchars and Calshot come to mind. The coastal airfields for land-based aircraft came under Coastal Area, other airfields came under Inland Area until the reorganization of 1925 when a command known as the Air Defence of Great Britain was formed under the expansion plan which would take the RAF to fifty-two home-based squadrons. This command was divided into two areas, Fighting Area and Bombing Area. Throughout the 1920s, however, the airfields that existed at the time of the reorganization housed the existing and new squadrons. A number of airfields had been taken out of Care and Maintenance (C & M).

Abroad the airfields were not categorized as fighter or bomber. The airfields in Egypt were intended to provide a reserve of aircraft in case the need arose, Trenchard's 'Clapham Junction' of the Middle East. Other airfields, such as those in India, Aden, Iraq and the Sudan, were the bases and landing grounds for squadrons employed on air control operations. The RAF stations at Kalafrana, Malta and Basrah in Iraq were used for maritime operations and fleet-based aircraft from carriers in the Mediterranean Fleet also landed in Malta. All of this was to change in the 1930's. The failure of the disarmament talks in Geneva and the rise of Nazism in Germany injected a sense of urgency into defence planning and if more squadrons were going to be needed the existing RAF airfields were not going to be enough.

FROM 1930 TO 1939

The expansion plan of 1923 had always been subject to the 'Ten-Year Rule'. The rise to fifty-two home-based squadrons in peacetime would always attract the attention of 'cash-strapped' governments and excite the pacifists, particularly in the Labour Party. However, it must be said that the short-lived Labour administrations had not dismantled the expansion plan, a policy made easier to defend to the 'left' of the Party when no date for completion of the plan had been set. In terms of the number of airfields required, it was possible to accommodate the number of squadrons re-formed during the 1920s on existing stations, the bombers going to stations like Worthy Down, Manston and Upper Heyford and the fighters to Kenley, Duxford and Hawkinge. But the expansion plan announced in July 1934 was of a different order. In some cases it was possible to reactivate airfields but many new airfields were required. On the outbreak of war in September 1939 there was a mix of airfields, seaplane bases and other establishments, namely:

1. Those built during the Great War.
2. Former RNAS airfields and seaplane bases taken over by the RAF in 1918.
3. Municipal airports taken over by the RAF in 1939.
4. Reactivated former Great War airfields.
5. New airfields.
6. Relief landing grounds.

The regional maps that accompany the airfield histories show the airfields and other establishments taken into use between 1930 and 1939, and emphasize the rapid growth of the RAF during the 1930s. But they disguise the fact that a still far greater number had been planned and were nearing completion, like Coltishall, which opened soon after the commencement of hostilities, while others, particularly those required by the US VIIIth Air Force, were opened year by year until 1944. By the outbreak of war some airfields still had that Great War look, stations like Netheravon, Old Sarum and lastly Manston, where the officers' mess was still of the old design and was only replaced by a new mess building shortly before the station closed in 1999. Others like Waddington had had a 'make-over', while the rest of the 1930s crop were built in a standardized layout with buildings to match.

The standardized layout of the 1930s airfields meant that it was easy to find one's way around a station that was not a man's parent station. The aircraft hangars, usually in an arc, were sited closest to the aircraft movement area. Behind the hangars came the technical buildings, including the armoury, signals, safety equipment, workshops, general engineering and motor transport. Then there would be the administrative buildings, such as the stores, education section, gymnasium, airmen's barrack blocks and mess. Finally the buildings that would be furthest from the airfield, by the camp entrance, would be the main guardroom and station headquarters (SHQ) where the station commander and station warrant officer had their offices, together with the accounts and personnel departments. The officers' and sergeants' messes, churches, married quarters and the NAAFI could be across the road, running past the camp main entrance, but this differed from station to station. Finally, the bomb dump would be sited on the edge of the perimeter track furthest from human habitation. The plans of Manston and Linton-on-Ouse make clear the difference in layout.

LOCATION OF AIRFIELDS AND OTHER ESTABLISHMENTS – AN OVERVIEW

It must not be imagined that the areas of the United Kingdom furthest from the continent, such as the North-West and Wales, would witness the smallest amount of growth. While there were only twenty-seven airfields in this region in 1939, that number had risen to 115 by 1945. The training, maintenance, aircraft storage and experimental units were positioned well away from the expected areas of conflict, for which Wales and the North-West were well suited. On the other hand, East Anglia, with its proximity to the continent, had only four active military airfields before the Expansion Plan of 1934. First World War airfields that were reactivated in this region were Marham and Wyton.

With new monoplane bombers in prospect, longer take-off runs would be required. The new airfields would have to have the necessary acreage, and so reactivated airfields of Great War vintage needed extra land to permit bombers with a full bomb load to get airborne. Catapult take-offs were considered as an alternative, but the launchers were vulnerable to attack and that ruled them out. Heavily laden bombers needed at least 1,000 yards to get airborne, but acquiring the necessary land in an agricultural region was not going to be well received by the farming community. The situation of long-range bomber airfields was determined by the proximity to Germany, the expected enemy, and airfields in Yorkshire would ensure the greatest penetration. Lincolnshire and East Anglia would have the medium and light bombers.

In the South-West there were three municipal airports at Bristol, Exeter and Plymouth, and three aircraft manufacturers operated airfields at Yeovil, Filton and Yate, but on the military side, even after the implementation of the Expansion Plan, there were only two flying-boat bases and thirteen military airfields, of which a number were only grass airfields. But all this was to change with the coming of the war. Not only were the Germans in occupation of the Channel Islands, but the U-boat threat in the Western Approaches would add substantially to the maritime commitments.

In spite of its proximity to the continent, the South-East and southern England had fared little better, and economies were called for with the infamous 'Geddes Axe' of 1922, and by the end of the decade there were just eleven stations in the region. These included the fighter stations at Hawkinge and Tangmere, two bomber stations at Worthy Down and Andover, experimental flying at Farnborough, air armament at Eastchurch, Army Cooperation at Odiham, technical training at Manston and naval aviation at Gosport and Lee-on-Solent. Aircraft production was centred on Rochester (Short Brothers), with Avro, Fairey, Saunders and Supermarine on the Solent. Several aero club airfields had sprouted, and civil aviation had grown to the extent that airfields were built at Shoreham, Eastleigh and Portsmouth. Indeed it was to be the civil airfields that often accommodated the Reserve training schools. Thorney Island was a new station, Odiham was upgraded from a landing ground for summer camps to a full-blown RAF station, and Detling and Ford were reactivated. The Expansion Plan meant, not just extra airfields, but more business for the aircraft industry, and new factories were opened at Hamble, Portsmouth and Eastleigh. The Cowes plant was expanded and Supermarine's Woolston works were rebuilt. At the outbreak of war the number of military airfields had grown to sixteen. Thirteen of these were of Great War origin and only two had paved runways. The RAF promptly requisitioned ten civil aerodromes. In 1938 the Fleet Air Arm gained its independence, and naval air stations were quickly established in the south of Hampshire and West Sussex.

In East Anglia there were fifteen active airfields, which by 1945 had risen to 107. Even Newmarket racecourse was pressed into service, with squadron personnel being accommodated in the Grandstand. However, at the beginning of the 1930s there were only four active military airfields in the region. The perceived threat in the 1920s was from France, not that anyone actually believed that the French would attack the UK. Rather the French Air Force was merely a yardstick, being the largest continental air force at the time. It seems a little odd that East Anglia should have had so few airfields, being in the front line, so to speak. Bircham Newton housed bombers and Duxford the fighters. This left the two experimental stations, for landplanes at Martlesham and seaplanes at Felixstowe. Following the loss of the R101 in 1930, which resulted in the abandonment of the British airship programme, the airship station at Cardington was reduced to producing barrage balloons.

THE DOUBLE TRANSFORMATION
(Source: National Archives, AIR41/8)

Introduction
The RAF underwent a double transformation in the years 1934–9. The change, as compared with 1923, when the first expansion scheme was approved, was of course still more marked. The modernization of the RAF's equipment was more evident in 1934, for by then types of aircraft far exceeded in size and performance those that were in service when the first expansion began. The second transformation was in the way the familiar face of England would be changed. England, not Britain as a whole, was where there were the greatest additions to the RAF's real estate, that is the country south of the Tweed and east of the River Severn.

The stations of 1923
To look at a map of Eastern England in 1930 and in 1939 shows how great the transformation was. In 1923 the RAF had no aerodromes for operational squadrons in that part of the country, with the exception of Duxford, Newton and Bircham Newton. Some other airfields were projected in the 1923 expansion plan. On 30 November 1923, the Committee of Imperial Defence advised that the thirty-five bombing squadrons contemplated in the plan were to be located mainly in Oxfordshire, Gloucestershire, Hampshire and Wiltshire. There were to be three aerodromes in Norfolk and one in Suffolk. The seventeen fighter squadrons were to be in the south, with no station north of Duxford.

The stations of 1934
In 1934 the scene had changed a little. The direction the RAF was facing was still south, and not east. By that time the Air Defence of Great Britain had been organized in three areas – two 'bombing' and one 'fighting'. It is significant that the Bombing Areas were Western and Central; there was no Eastern Area. The Western Area had its bomber squadrons at Andover, Boscombe Down and Worthy Down. It had two squadrons 'out of area', namely at Manston in Kent and Aldergrove in Ulster, but these were non-regular Special Reserve squadrons, and being in the nature of 'militia units' were necessarily located in the districts from which they were recruited. The Central Area stations were mainly in Oxfordshire, at Upper Heyford and Bicester, but it had two squadrons at Bircham Newton and one at Abingdon in Berkshire. There were also three Special Reserve squadrons administered by this area. They were located at Filton and Hucknall.

Besides the five Special Reserve squadrons, there were also eight squadrons of the Auxiliary Air Force, at that time all bomber units. These were administered by a separate group, No. 1 Air Defence Group. Each was a territorial air unit of a county or a city. London had two squadrons, with one for Edinburgh, Glasgow, Middlesex and Warwick, Durham and Yorkshire, and each had its HQ in the locality with which it was situated. All these units were allocated a 'war station' to which they would proceed on mobilization.

In contrast with the two Bombing Areas, the Air Defence Group, the Fighting Area, had its squadrons based around London. They were located at North Weald and Hornchurch in Essex, Biggin Hill and Hawkinge in Kent, Kenley in Surrey, Tangmere in Sussex and Northolt in Middlesex. The only aerodrome not in these counties was Duxford in Cambridgeshire. Duxford, Hawkinge and Northolt each accommodated one squadron, and the other five stations each had two.

The implication of the siting
The siting of the bomber squadrons in 1934, facing south, and not east, shows that the Air Ministry did not have a military threat from Germany in mind. The neutrality of the Low Countries could be assumed, but an offensive against Germany would have to be launched from bases in Yorkshire, Lincolnshire, Norfolk and Suffolk. Yet in 1934 there was only one station, Bircham Newton, in these four counties. The Auxiliary Air Force aerodrome at Thornaby, the RAF Cadet College Cranwell and the experimental stations of Felixstowe and Martlesham were not operational stations. For the purposes of air warfare these four counties constituted almost a demilitarized zone. Once the threat from Nazi Germany emerged, there was going to have to be an awful lot of airfield construction.

VOTE 4 OF THE AIR ESTIMATES
Rapid growth in expenditure
One has only to study the Air Estimates for the years 1935 to 1939 to appreciate the rate of expansion in airfield construction that went hand-in-hand with the growth in the construction of aircraft and the training of aircrews and technical and administrative personnel. Few people would read them for entertainment; only the officials who prepared them really understood them. It was Vote 4 of the Air Estimates that provided for works and buildings. One could also follow the rate of expansion in the other Votes, such as Vote 3 for the construction of aircraft, engines, arms and other equipment for the RAF. The cost of material grew from £8.5 million in the Estimates for 1933/4 to £143,500,000 in the Estimates for 1939/40 (including the Supplementary Estimate of July 1939).

The Estimates of 1935/6 were the first to reflect the government's decision in July 1934 to embark on the expansion of the RAF with Scheme A (see Chapter 2).

There was not much effect on Vote 4 in that financial year, the increase being less than £1.5 million. In the Estimates for 1936/7 the provision in the Vote was £2.5 million greater than that made in 1935, but still the sum taken for works and buildings was only £6.25 million, a comparatively moderate figure under the circumstances. It had to be increased, however, before the end of the financial year. In March 1937 the Supplementary Estimate raised the total of Vote 4 to about £9.5 million. Nearly double that amount was provided in the Estimates for 1937/8, when the Vote accounted for £18.5 million. In the next Estimates for 1938/9 the starting Vote 4 was £16.33 million, but this amounted to twice the increase in the Supplementary Estimates of July 1938 and February 1939, by which time the final figure was £30.75 million. A still larger sum was found necessary for the estimates of 1939/40, when the provision under Vote 4 was £49 million, increased to £65 million by a Supplementary Estimate of July 1939. Expenditure on Vote 4 alone was, by the outbreak of war, more than three times as large as the cost of the entire air service in 1934. That was £20,165,000.

Aircraft storage
This was a tell-tale item in Vote 4. The rapid expansion in aircraft production capacity, following the introduction of the 'shadow factory' scheme, meant a corresponding increase in the output of aircraft. These were destined, not only for the increased number of RAF squadrons, but also for storage. In planning for a major war the Air Ministry had to calculate the losses in aircraft due to enemy action in the first few weeks of conflict, as well as losses over a longer period, should a war become one of attrition. During the 1920s and early 1930s reserve equipment, including aircraft, were stored in the odd corners of operational stations. But once the expansion began, the provision for aircraft storage was an important item in Vote 4. In the Estimates for the year 1936/7 there was provision of £400,000, rising to £6 million in the 1937/8 Estimates. The expenditure of £8.75 million in the year 1938/9 was put under the heading of 'reserve storage'. In the first year of the war the figure had risen to £17,300,000.

Major works services
Subhead B of Vote 4 lists the annual expenditure on major works services, station by station for individual items of, and exceeding, £2,500. A perusal of Vote 4B reveals what new stations are being built and what old ones are being enlarged or reconditioned. For the financial year 1935/6, provision was made for a large number of building programmes, most of them towards the eastern side of England:

Financial Year	County	Station	Remarks
1935/6	Norfolk	Marham	approaching completion
	Suffolk	Mildenhall	approaching completion
		Thelwell	
		Stradishall	
	Lincolnshire	Waddington	
		Manby	
	Yorkshire	Church Fenton	
	Beds/Bucks border	Cranfield	
	Berkshire	Harwell	
1936/7	Yorkshire	Dishforth	
		Driffield	
		Leconfield	
	Lincolnshire	Hemswell	
		Scampton	
	Huntingdonshire	Upwood	a good jumping-off point for the North Sea
		Wyton	a good jumping-off point for the North Sea
	Essex	Debden	
1937/8	Norfolk	Watton	
		West Raynham	
	Hertfordshire	Bassingbourne	
	Rutland	Cottesmore	
	Yorkshire	Finningley	
	Suffolk	Wattisham	

Financial Year	County	Station	Remarks
1939/40	Norfolk	Coltishall	and two other unnamed stations
	Yorkshire	Leeming	
		Topcliffe	
	Lincolnshire	Binbrook	
		Kirton-in-Lindsey	
	Hertfordshire	Hatfield	
		Woodhouse	
	Nottinghamshire	Newton	

Cost Particulars of cost shown against each entry in the Estimates are not the same. Almost invariably the costs are greater than before. The best estimate for building a new station would be a third to half a million pounds; the final estimate might well approach £750,000. The building of an aerodrome was always a financial Rake's Progress. Some stations cost far more than £1 million, but these would not be operational stations. They were the large training schools, maintenance units and stores depots. The following appear in the Estimates for 1937/8 and 1938/9:

Cosford, Carlisle, St Athan, Quedgley, Hartlebury, Yatesbury, Locking, Heywood, Stafford, Wroughton, Chilmark

The maintenance units in Carlisle, Quedgley, Hartlebury, Heywood and Stafford each had a floor space of 854,000 sq. ft, which compares with the 729,000 and 447,000 sq. ft of the pre-1934 storage depots like Ruislip and Milton. The estimated cost of the five new depots ranged from £1,230,000 to £1,450,000 each. St Athan, which housed a large training school of technical training and two maintenance units, cost nearly £2 million.

THE REALIGNMENT OF 1939

(The RAF stations by commands are listed in Appendix J.)
Many of the new stations were still under construction in the autumn of 1939, but the number already completed was sufficient for the needs of the RAF force in the early months of the war. The alignment had come by that time. The alignment of 1939 was very different from what it was in 1934. The old Air Defence of Great Britain had been broken up into Bomber, Fighter and Coastal Commands. Of the five groups of Bomber Command, four were now definitely facing east:

No. 1 Group – stations in Oxfordshire, Berkshire and Wiltshire
Nos 2 and 3 Groups – stations in Norfolk (8 squadrons), Suffolk (7 squadrons), Huntingdon (4 squadrons) and Buckinghamshire (2 squadrons)
No. 4 Group – stations in Yorkshire (10 squadrons)
No. 5 Group – stations in Lincolnshire (6 squadrons), Rutland (2 squadrons) and Hertfordshire (2 squadrons).

The fighter stations were still mainly in the south-east of England, and more especially on the periphery of the Greater London area. Though less pronounced than in Bomber Command, there was still in Fighter Command a turning away to face a peril from the east, as well as a south-easterly direction. On the periphery of London the fighter stations were:

Kent – Biggin Hill and Hawkinge (squadrons at Hawkinge would move to Northolt on mobilization)
Surrey – Kenley
Essex – Hornchurch and North Weald
Middlesex – Northolt
Cambridgeshire – Duxford
Hampshire – Tangmere was an outer bastion

To these were added stations in the north and the east. In this context it is pointed out that the Auxiliary Air Force squadrons, which had been bomber in 1934, had become fighter in 1939.

Lincolnshire – Digby
Northamptonshire – Wittering
Essex – Debden
Cambridgeshire – Sywell
Yorkshire – Church Fenton and Catterick

Auxiliary Air Force:

Glasgow – Abbotsinch
Edinburgh – Turnhouse
Durham – Usworth

The German menace The new alignment was clear and significant. Before 1934 the idea that Britain should have to wage another war with Germany was far from the nation's thoughts. But as soon as the German menace became clear it also become an obsession. People spoke of the 'next war' as a war against Germany and none other than Germany. Be that as it may, even as the expansion of the RAF gathered pace, those in polite society could not bring themselves to grasp the fact that the RAF stations facing east would provide the springboard from which British flyers would set out to bomb Germany. Such things were simply not said. In the House of Commons on 27 July 1938, Mr Fred Montague interjected a supplementary question stemming from a previous question referring to a Civil Air Service (House of Commons Debates, Vol. 338, Columns 3100 to 3101). He asked, 'If it will be possible in 1940 to carry 40 passengers to Berlin would it also be possible to carry 40 bombs?' The House was shocked. There were cries of 'Withdraw!'. Later Mr Montague made the usual personal explanation and withdrew the question. He later admitted that his question had been open to serious misunderstanding. The matter was then allowed to drop.

A DECADE'S PROGRESS
Acquisition of sites

The construction before zero hour of such a rampart of air bases as that raised close to the North Sea was a notable achievement. But this was hardly more than a beginning, for the growth in the number of airfields and satellite airfields dwarfed what had been achieved before the outbreak of war. Before 1934 there had been fifty-two aerodromes in the possession of the RAF in the United Kingdom. This figure was quoted in the Secretary of State's memorandum accompanying the Air Estimates for 1937/8. That number had increased to eighty-nine by May 1938.

The rate of growth can be seen by the number of site acquisitions during this period:

Year	No. of sites with which action was taken to acquire each year	Remarks
1934	5	
1935	17	
1936	18	Plus 3 auxiliary Air Force aerodromes taken over
1937	12	Plus 22 civil aerodromes RAVR schools
1938	27	Plus 1 AAF and 14 civil aerodromes for RAFVR
1939	63	Plus 10 civil aerodromes for RAFVR
1940	126	
1941	106	
1942	91	Plus 20 Advanced Landing Grounds
1943	3	Plus 2 Advanced Landing Grounds

The sites acquired were not just for the RAF once war with Japan had commenced, for that brought in the 8th US Army Air Force.

Satellite aerodrome system

There were 111 satellite aerodromes in addition to 432 stations by 1944. No such aerodromes existed when the expansion began in 1934. They were first suggested at a War Organization Committee on 12 March 1936. It was recommended that:

1. Such aerodromes should be acquired and constructed in peacetime.
2. Civil aerodromes should be used as far as possible to provide satellites, and where civil aerodromes existed, proposals for meeting the needs of each station individually, together with estimates of cost, should be prepared.
3. Such aerodromes should conform as nearly as possible in size to the current service requirements of operational stations and should be located within a distance of five miles for fighters and ten miles for bombers.

The question of the provision of satellite aerodromes was discussed at an Expansion Progress Meeting of 5 October 1937, when approval was given in principle to proposals put forward by the Air Member for Supply and Organization, which were that fifty-six satellite landing grounds were estimated to be required for the purposes of Expansion Scheme F to be provided, as follows:

1. Eleven civil aerodromes that were suitably situated should be used.
2. Two further civil aerodromes should be made available by small extensions.
3. The balance of forty-three should be obtained by the purchasing of suitable land, grassing it and letting it as pasture. Ten sites had already been found and thirty-three more were to be located. The average cost of the sites was estimated at £23,000 each.

The last of the recommendations for the satellite airfields made on 12 March 1936 was departed from at a later date, and many of the satellites were at a greater distance than five or ten miles from the parent airfield. Some stations had two satellites. The geographical index lists seventeen that were doubly insured: Carlisle, Church Lawford, Cranwell, Derby, Finningley, Hemswell, Hucknall, Kenley, Kidlington, Lossiemouth, Montrose, Netheravon, Newton, South Cerney, Tangmere, Ternhill and Watchfield. They were all stations for operational training, advanced flying units and flying training schools.

Two stations were trebly insured: these were Wheaton Aston and Little Rissington. The former was an Operational Training Unit with satellites at Bridleway Gate, Perton and Patten Hill. Little Rissington was an Advanced Flying School with satellites at Chipping Norton, Windrush and Akerman Street. Seventy-one other stations each had one satellite, and there was no need for any satellites in areas sprinkled with operational aerodromes.

THE INCREASED ELABORATION

Objections to the selection of sites for airfields   In comparing the earlier with the later years one must remember that a change almost as great at that which accompanied the development of Britain's aeronautical equipment after 1934 was to be noted also in the ground establishments. These were far larger and more elaborate at the end of the expansion than they had been at the beginning. Even before the war began it was recognized that the accommodation that had sufficed previously was no longer adequate. It was for that reason that very little use was made of the aerodromes left from the Great War and abandoned after it but still remaining in a passable condition. A few of them were reconditioned and taken back into use again, but these were the exceptions. In a memo accompanying the Air Estimates of 1938/9, the Secretary of State made clear that they were not suitable for modern requirements. Previously the average airfield had only an apron of tarmac in front of the hangars. There were no metalled runways and arrangements for aircraft dispersal were primitive. But when the question of laying down paved runways on grass airfields was considered the fear was expressed that it would be extremely difficult to camouflage, and at an EPM dated 21 February 1939 the matter was deferred, but only a month later the question of camouflage was discounted, and on 13 March it was decided to lay paved runways at fighter stations. With the increase in weight and power of aircraft coming into service, bad weather could easily put a grass airfield out of action.

Once it was apparent to the general public that airfields were being paved, objections were raised. It was not just the runways, but there were the taxiways that went round the airfield perimeter and dispersals. A lot of good pasturage and tillage country was going to be affected in, for example, Norfolk and Lincolnshire, and it was inevitable that there would be a conflict of interest. Both food production and defence were of national importance. Farmers and landowners who found that the Air Ministry was encroaching on their property were naturally vocal in their protests. In the House of Commons on 21 June 1939, Mr Williams alleged that the very best agricultural land in the country was being appropriated when there were other areas that were equally suitable. There were other objectors, like the long-shoremen and yachtsmen, who feared the siting of a bombing and gunnery range on their strip of the coast. Disturbance of game was another problem, and a strong objection was raised when a bombing range near Chesil Beach, Dorset, was seen as a threat to a colony of swans. There were all sorts of obstacles to be overcome, and when the search for airfields ventured into areas not previously associated with warlike preparations, then protest could be expected. But it was a different matter before 1938. Then the government's principle was 'business as usual'; but if that was a good rule for industry then why not agriculture? After the German menace became clear, there was a change of attitude, with a growing acceptance that sacrifices needed to be made.

Sir Philip Sassoon's statement   Sir Philip Sassoon referred to some of the difficulties outlined above when he introduced the Air Estimates on 15 March 1937. He made the following points:

1. There were a limited number of suitable sites that conformed to military requirements.
2. Airfields had to be sufficiently far apart to avoid congestion in the air. (This was not always possible, for example in a peninsula like Cornwall, with St Mawgan and St Eval.)
3. They had to be on well-drained land or on land that could be drained without undue expense.
4. There had to be room for suitable forced-landing grounds in the area. (Gone were the 1920s when aircraft could put down in a field, for in 1937 aircraft had a greater all-up weight and landing speed.)
5. The meteorological conditions were reasonably good: too much rain could lead to soggy ground.

He said that the Aerodrome Board had an extremely difficult task in finding suitable sites conforming to all the above conditions and free from objections from people in the locality. Birds had been driven away from their sanctuaries where it had been hoped to preserve them, and he stressed that it was not the intention to destroy them. The Air Ministry dealt with all objections in the most sympathetic way possible, and he was finding that local landowners and farmers were meeting the Ministry in the right spirit.

Acquisition of airfield sites   The procedure for the acquisition of land for airfields and landing grounds was a cumbrous one, and there was a good deal of delay in many instances before possession could be obtained under the Defence Act. Another delay was caused when clearance rights and easements had to be acquired under the Military Lands Acts, which were somewhat restrictive. If public rights of way had to be closed or diverted, the procedure necessary for this purpose might take nine to ten months. There was also a very considerable time-lag in the making of bye-laws for coastal ranges. The question of obtaining fresh legislation to expedite the acquisition of land or rights was considered at an EPM of 15 June 1939, when it was decided to seek the necessary statutory powers and also to expedite the departmental procedures. The outbreak of war two and a half months later, and the consequent availability of the powers under the Defence of the Realm Act, made it unnecessary to obtain legislation for the purposes in question.

The Airfield Board   Sir Philip Sassoon had referred to the difficulties facing the Aerodrome Board (subsequently changed to the Airfield Board) in finding suitable sites for airfields. Particulars of the composition and work of this body were given in a report submitted to the Select Committee on National Expenditure on 3 September 1943. It was shown that the Board came into existence in June 1934. The first President was Air Vice-Marshal Longcroft, who had retired from the RAF in 1929. He had been a pilot and a landowner for thirty years, and could therefore appreciate problems of land acquisition from both points of view. He was assisted by another senior officer and three other members, all with flying experience. Of these one was a considerable landowner, another a civil engineer and a third had experience of airfield work in civil aviation. Additionally the services of civil engineers and land officers from the Directorate of Works were available to the board when making local surveys. The Admiralty was also represented from 1939, since RAF airfields had been acquired once the Fleet Air Arm was restored in its entirety to the Navy. Naval requirements would probably be dictated by the position of an airfield relative to ports where aircraft-carriers would fly off their carrier-borne aircraft on return to home waters.

The board did not initiate enquiries for new airfield sites but set out to find them when asked to do so by the Director-General of Organization at the Air Ministry. The latter notified the president of the board of the number of types of airfields required and the areas in which they would have to be located. An officer of the board then made a preliminary survey, and when a site, or sites (*prima facie*) were deemed to be suitable the president of the board would submit a report to the Director-General of Organization. The latter then reported to the Director-General of Works, who reported in greater detail upon the proposed requisition, and the final selection was made in the light of such a report and the comments of the appropriate Air Ministry Branches and other government departments concerned, such as those dealing with agriculture and civil aviation. Once approved, the site was requisitioned by the Lands

Branch, as were the sites of the ancillary buildings of an airfield. It was often the case in the airfields built in the 1930s that they were standardized in their layout, with the officers' and sergeants' messes and airmen's accommodation sometimes being sited across a main road from the airfield itself. The married quarters could be some way from the main camp entrance. The taking of land usually resulted in some loss of food crops, but this was kept as low as possible by cooperation with the County War Agricultural Executive Committee.

The Airfield Board was not concerned with the selection of sites for stations that did not need airfields, such as recruit depots, technical training schools, initial training wings, certain maintenance units, barrage balloon depots, wireless stations and bombing ranges. Sites for such units were proposed by the user directorate, and the approving authority was the Director-General of Organization. In the 1943 report it was said that the Airfield Board carried out its work with 'unadvertised efficiency' that concealed the magnitude of the task performed.

Troglodytic airfields   Putting airfield buildings, storage depots and bomb storage underground was considered by the Air Ministry between the wars. It had been tried at Manston in the Great War, but the experiment was not followed up. In a note dated 30 April 1935 the Air Staff recorded their conclusions regarding the possible building of troglodyte airfields. The note referred to the policy being adopted for airfields at that time, which was to build splinter-proof hangars. The increased protection that underground storage would provide would only be for a direct hit. Protection would have to be provided against high-explosive bombs, gas or incendiaries, and protection against bombs would also cover the other two risks. Against a semi-armour-piercing 500 lb bomb the roof of the hangar would have to be no less than 25 ft below the surface, accessed by lift or inclined taxiway. Lifts would have the following operational disadvantages:

1. Liability to derangement due both to accident and to bomb damage.
2. Contamination by gas.
3. Delay in getting aircraft to the surface.
4. Dependent on power supply.

Inclined approaches would have the following operational disadvantages:

1. The possibility of gas or damage that would immobilize the aircraft in the hangar.
2. Assuming a steep gradient of 1:15, the approach would have to have 300 yards to take aircraft down to a 65 ft level.
3. Delay in getting aircraft from the hangar.

The note went on to say that from only an operational point of view underground hangars would produce delay in bringing aircraft into action. The aircraft might also be incarcerated and there would be a fire risk. Then there were the other buildings to consider, which served the needs of combat aircraft, such as bomb dumps, workshops, armouries and fuel dumps. An operational airfield was highly complex, and the cost of placing all essential facilities underground would be enormous. Underground aircraft storage would cost four times as much as surface storage. The Air Staff felt that splinter-proof hangars were still the best solution, and since only aircraft that were being serviced were in a hangar, the serviceable ones could be dispersed around the airfield perimeter or on satellite airfields. During the Battle of Britain, flying clubs were used for dispersing fighter squadrons when base airfields came under sustained enemy attack.

Other sites where underground storage might be considered were aircraft storage depots and bomb dumps. If underground sites were used for the storage of reserve aircraft there would be the increased fire risk, when dispersal and camouflage would be cheaper and as effective. Bomb dumps were more obvious candidates for underground storage, but as it happened, the Chilmark, Box (Wiltshire) and Fauld (Staffs.) bomb depots used quarries, which provided natural cover since it was possible to tunnel into pre-existing slopes. The Air Staff note concluded that splinter-proof hangars on airfields, and dispersal and camouflage, were the most cost-effective way of protecting assets, and that, in any event, the delay in getting aircraft out of underground hangars would not be acceptable operationally.

THE CONSTRUCTION AND LAYOUT OF AIRFIELDS

AIRFIELD LAYOUT IN THE 1920s

Little had changed in the layout of airfields by the end of the 1920s. They were much the same as they had been at

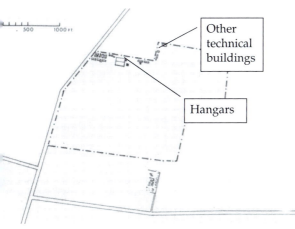

Simple grass airfield.

Bessoneaux hangars.

the end of the Great War. Even bombing aircraft had a relatively low all-up weight and landing speed, and so did not need particularly long runways and could land on grass without too much fear of sinking into the ground. Unless there was some local restriction, aircraft could land and take off directly into the wind. There was no radio-controlled approach to the airfield requiring a manned air traffic control tower, only a watch office to which returning or visiting aircraft pilots could report on landing. Airfields, or more accurately RAF stations, would have hangars for aircraft servicing and workshops for armament and signals. A domestic site with officers', sergeants' and airmen's messes and sleeping accommodation would be sited slightly away from the flying and servicing areas. A bomb dump would be sited furthest from all habitation, on the airfield periphery.

DEVELOPMENT OF RAF AIRFIELDS IN THE 1930s

The airfields built in the 1930s were built to a standardized pattern. Local conditions might dictate variations on this basic layout. It has been made clear already that the landing and take-off speeds and all-up weight of aircraft during the inter-war years did not call for paved runways. Although the layout of the station buildings changed from that of the early 1920s, it was not until just before the outbreak of war that paved runways came in. This matter was dealt with in a previous section, the worry being that it would be very difficult to camouflage, but with the coming of the heavy four-engined bomber, grass airfields would be unusable in bad weather when the ground might be soft or waterlogged.

The layout of the airfield built in the expansion period was as follows:

1. The hangars would most often be sited in a crescent shape, closest to the airfield, i.e. aircraft movement area, including runways and taxiways. Aircraft would be taken into the hangars for servicing. Around the airfield perimeter would be dispersals for squadron aircraft. The bomb dump would be at a point on the perimeter as far as possible away from the working and domestic accommodation.

2. Behind the hangars would be the technical support buildings, including station workshops, armoury, signals, parachutes, safety equipment, photographic and station equipment.

3. Furthest from the airfield would be the administrative buildings, including accounts, personnel, churches, NAAFI, etc. Most often the accounts and personnel departments would be housed in the station headquarters building. The Commanding Officer, the Station Adjutant, the Officer Commanding the Administrative Wing, and the Station Warrant Officer would also have their offices in the SHQ. Closest to the main road and the camp entrance would be the station guardroom, with facilities for holding airmen under arrest.

4. Depending upon local circumstances, the domestic accommodation might be on the same side of the public road serving the station or it might be across

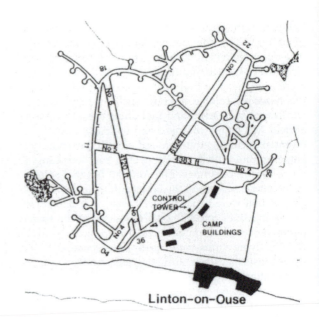

Linton-on-Ouse

the public road. This would include the officers' mess, sergeants' mess, airmen's mess and barrack blocks, and the officers' and airmen's married quarters. The airmen's mess and barrack blocks were mostly on the main site.

As the caption states the runways did not begin to appear until shortly before the outbreak of war, but the layout of the station remained the same.

The diagram above is of Linton-on-Ouse in Yorkshire, and illustrates the aircraft dispersals for squadron aircraft and the numbering of runways from 1 to 6, giving pilots one that would be facing into the wind. The longest runway would most probably be that which faced the prevailing wind, i.e. either No. 1 or No. 4.

The photograph, page 263, illustrates an airfield that has been built with the then new C-Type hangars typical of the expansion period of the late 1930s, with the aircraft sitting on the grass and not on concrete aprons. These are the Battles of No. 105 Squadron at Harwell. This was one of the seven Battle squadrons to go to France at the outbreak of war in 1939. The designers of the hangar allowed for offices for administrative and other staff along the front of the building at both ground-floor and first-floor level. From them one has a good view of what is going on in the hangar, as well as aircraft or other movements around the airfield. The author enjoyed office space on the first floor of the West Hangar at Catterick when the airfield was used for fire and ground defence training.

The next diagram shows the detailed layout of the station site of another expansion airfield, that of Little Rissington in the Cotswolds. A flying training school like Little Rissington would be sited well away from potential conflict, should war occur with Germany.

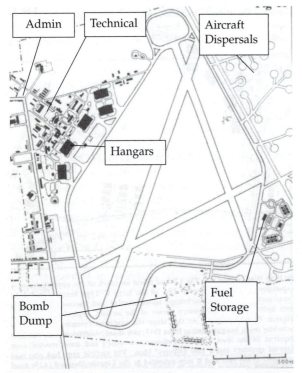

A three-runway airfield of the type that appeared in the 1940s and permitted an approach in any one of six compass headings, depending upon wind direction.

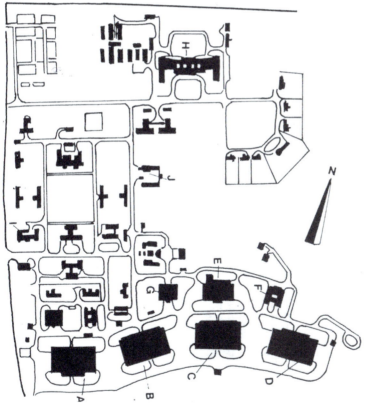

KEY TO BUILDINGS

A. Aircraft storage
B. Aircraft servicing
C. Aircraft servicing
D. Flying training school
E. Aircraft repair shed
F. Workshops
G. Main stores
H. Officers Mess
I. Segeants Mess
J. Motor Transport Section
K. Main parade square flanked by the airmen's mess on its northern edge and airmen's barrack blocks on the other three sides of the square.

Note: The buildings to the left or west of the officers' Mess building would be for the large number of trainee pilots. Only the Officers on the permanent staff would be accommodated in the main building.

Little Rissington opened in August 1938.

Earlier mention was made of the objections raised by farmers and communities to the siting of military airfields in their locality. The Air Ministry was conscious of this and went so far as to invite the Council for the Preservation of Rural England and the Fine Arts Commission to advise upon the design of military aerodromes in the expansion period, so that they were, as far as possible, aesthetically attractive and would not harm the countryside. Sir Edwin Lutyens was invited to submit a design for the officers' mess, and these may be found all over eastern England on stations built in the 1930s. They say that the RAF is like one large family, and

An expansion period officers' mess.

when one moved from, say, Debden to Swinderby to live in a building of identical design, one felt immediately at home simply because everything was where one expected it to be. These were graceful buildings, and as has been said before, were like hotels in the facilities they provided. Indeed, after RAF Middleton St George became Tyne Tees Airport, the officers' mess became a hotel. In the case of Little Rissington station, buildings were constructed in the local stone to blend in with the surroundings.

AIRFIELDS BY GEOGRAPHICAL AREA

How to read the Maps

The maps that preface each section are designed to show those airfields, seaplane bases and miscellaneous units in all areas as they were at the beginning of the decade (1930), compared with the outbreak of war:

Units in *italics*: In RAF use throughout the decade 1930–9, designated with a black circle, e.g.

Units in normal type: In RAF use by 3 September 1939, designated with a white circle, e.g.

In this way it illustrates the enormous expansion in the number of airfields in the run-up to war. It is almost the reverse of the situation shown by corresponding maps in Volume I, which illustrated the dramatic rundown of the RAF between 1919 and 1923. The list of units is not complete but concentrates instead on stations that housed operational squadrons and flying training schools. In one or two cases, where a station or airfield was in use at the beginning of the decade but was closed before the outbreak of war, such a unit has an asterisk against its name.

The stations, seaplane bases and miscellaneous units listed mostly show squadron movements, which illustrate the frequent unit moves consequent upon expansion of the RAF during the late 1930s. Most squadrons re-formed at this time were taken from one of the flights of an existing squadron, then, in many cases moved as soon as accommodation at a newly opened RAF station was available. It is very difficult to keep up with squadron movements at this time, and the whereabouts of war stations and scatter airfields, which were notified to units, made for even more squadron movements on the outbreak of war. The purpose of the scatter airfields was to prevent the enemy from mounting a pre-emptive strike upon the RAF's bomber force when enemy intelligence would almost certainly have known the whereabouts of individual units on their home stations.

AIRFIELDS IN GREATER LONDON
ACTON LONDON, W OF LONDON

Acton had been an active airfield during the Great War but was closed in 1920. In 1937 only a hangar remained. This was used by various companies, and it was known as the Alliance hangar, having been used by the company of that name for building aircraft. In 1937 it was occupied by No. 1 (MT) Storage Sub-unit RAF. With the coming of the Second World War the hangar was requisitioned by the Ministry of Aircraft Production.

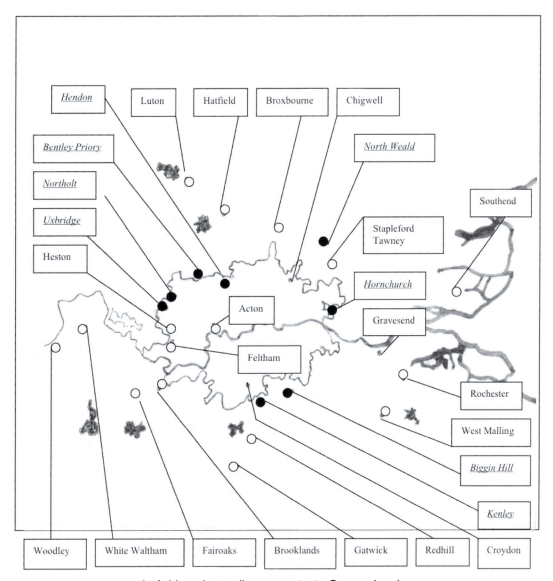

Airfields and miscellaneous units in Greater London.

BENTLEY PRIORY (STANMORE PARK) MIDDLESEX, NW OF STANMORE

The grounds of Bentley Priory housed a small community of Austin Canons, probably founded in pre-Norman times. From then until 1926 the priory changed ownership and occupation when the priory estate was split up, and the lot that included the priory itself and some forty acres was sold to the Air Ministry for about £25,000. The HQ Inland Area, part of the Air Defence of Great Britain, moved from Uxbridge to Bentley Priory on 26 May 1926, where it remained until 1936, when it was renamed HQ Flying Training Command and moved out to Shropshire as HQ Fighter Command moved in from Hillingdon House on 14 July. It was from here that Air

Marshal Dowding commanded the thirty-nine squadrons, mainly of Hurricanes and Spitfires, which were to fight the Battle of Britain.

BIGGIN HILL KENT, N OF BIGGIN HILL AND WESTERHAM

In 1927 Biggin Hill had been in constant use since its opening ten years earlier. Then No. 56 Squadron left for North Weald, and in 1929 the departure of the Vimys of the Night-Flying Flight left the station empty. Then began an extensive building programme. On the northern perimeter a new technical site was constructed. The station was completed with the construction of hangars, administrative offices, barrack blocks and workshops.

Nos 23 and 32 Squadrons, equipped respectively with Demons and Bulldogs, moved in, and a new unit, the Anti-Aircraft Cooperation Flight, was formed to give training to the growing number of AA sites in the London area. When No. 23 Squadron moved to Northolt on 21 December 1936, No. 32 Squadron, with its Gauntlets, remained in sole occupation until the arrival of the Gauntlets of No. 79 Squadron. In 1938 No. 601 (County of London) Auxiliary Squadron's Gauntlets joined with those of the two resident squadrons for the Munich Crisis. When the crisis passed, Biggin's two squadrons were re-equipped with Hurricanes. Meanwhile the station buildings were camouflaged, air raid shelters were dug and trees were planted in an attempt to disguise the aerodrome. A tarmac runway measuring 4,800 feet by 150 feet was also constructed. Two days before the outbreak of war the married quarters were evacuated, the families being moved to alternative accommodation. No. 3 Squadron, which had been at the station since May, moved to its war station at Croydon, to be replaced by No. 601 Squadron. Two days later the station was at war.

BROOKLANDS (WEYBRIDGE) SURREY, SW OF WEYBRIDGE

By the end of the 1920s Brooklands had long been associated with aircraft production and club flying. In October 1935 the prototype Hawker Hurricane K.5083 arrived at Brooklands from the factory at Kingston, and Bulman test flew the prototype for the first time on 6 November. On 15 June 1936 'Mutt' Summers made the first flight of the prototype Wellington bomber K.4049 from Brooklands. The airfield was used for test flying of production aircraft during the Second World War.

BROXBOURNE (WEYBRIDGE) SW OF WEYBRIDGE

Broxbourne began life on 13 November 1930 as a small aerodrome straddling the Hertfordshire and Essex county boundaries. During the 1930s the airfield was used by flying clubs and other organizations, and the facilities were expanded. The clubhouse was enlarged to include sleeping accommodation, and additional hangars and workshops were built and the flying field enlarged, making Broxbourne one of the finest privately owned airfields of the pre-war period. In 1938 the Civil Air Guard established a unit there, and by the end of the year 202 members were undergoing instruction. The Herts and Essex Aero Club had twenty-four aircraft with thirteen instructors and fifty ground staff. On the outbreak of war Broxbourne was taken over by the government and was used as a maintenance and repair base for light aircraft. Many of the club's light aircraft were unsuitable and were left to rot.

CHIGWELL ESSEX, NW OF ROMFORD

On 16 May 1938 RAF Chigwell became the recruiting centre for No. 909 Balloon Unit when it opened. On 4 August No. 4 Balloon Centre was established on the station, but Chigwell is best remembered as the station having the Central Test Board, assessing airmen for ground trades.

CROYDON (WADDEN) SURREY, SW OF CROYDON

Croydon was associated with flying from 1915 as both a military and a civilian airfield. The RAF in fact left Croydon in 1920, and it grew to become the main airport for London. Throughout the 1930s Croydon became the place where many famous fliers left on record-breaking and pioneering flights. With the approach of war it was noted that the defence of Croydon consisted of one Army subaltern, six men and a gun. During the Munich Crisis a few trenches were dug, but nothing more. Civil airlines continued to operate right up to the outbreak of war, the last Lufthansa flight being dispersed to Whitchurch and Exeter. The transition from a civil to a military airfield continued on Friday 1 September, when all the remaining civilian aircraft were flown out. The following day, the Gladiators of No. 615 (County of Surrey) Squadron flew in under the command of Squadron Leader A.V. Harvey. These were dispersed to the north of Roundshow Recreation Ground. These were followed that day by No. 3 Squadron's Hurricanes from Biggin Hill, and they moved into the two southern hangars previously used by Sabena, KLM and Air France. The build-up on that Saturday, 2 September, was completed by the arrival of the Hurricanes of No. 17 Squadron, making Croydon a three-squadron fighter station when war was declared.

FAIROAKS SURREY, N OF WOKING

Fairoaks became active as a result of the expansion schemes to train pilots for the RAF. Hangars and offices were constructed in the north-west corner of the airfield site near the A319, and Universal Air Services, which had the contract for instruction, opened for business on 1 October 1937 as No. 18 E & RFTS. Initially Tiger Moths were used, supplemented by Battles and Harts. On the outbreak of war this unit and No. 19 E & RFTS from Gatwick were combined to become an EFTS.

FELTHAM (HANWORTH PARK) MIDDLESEX, SW OF LONDON

The airfield was built to the south of Feltham and the north-west of Hanworth. It came by several names, such as the London Air Park, Hanworth Park and plain Feltham aerodrome. During the Great War it had been an aircraft acceptance park. In 1929 National Flying Services Ltd started work on the aerodrome so that flying could begin. The old manor house became a hotel and flying club premises. This building was an island in the middle of the airfield, surrounded by 50 ft trees. The roadway to the hotel had to be set flush with the grass so that aircraft crossing it did not suffer from broken undercarriages. The airfield was grass, giving two runways, SE–NW 1,000 yards, and just under 900 yards in the NS, NE–SW and EW directions. Flying Training Ltd, a subsidiary of Blackburn, operated No. 5 E & RFTS, which occupied a hangar on the north side of the airfield, the unit forming on 1 June 1935. It operated Blackburn B2s, Hart trainers, an Avro Anson and a Fairey Battle. Old wooden railway sleepers, laid to cover a culvert, caused trouble for the Battle, which broke through the sleepers. The London Air Park Flying Club joined the Civil Air Guard scheme. The pupil pilots wore a flying overall in RAF blue with silver buttons embossed CAG, and paid five shillings an hour for instruction, with the balance being paid by HMG. The pilots of No. 5 E & RFTS undertook some night-flying, which was complicated by the lack of a flare-path. Instead, a floodlight in the corner of the landing area, with a shadow bar, was used. Sheep that were held in a corner of the airfield were used to keep the grass short. On the day war was declared No. 5 E & RFTS became No. 5 EFTS, and all civil flying ceased.

GATWICK SURREY, 28 MILES S OF LONDON

Gatwick was first licensed as an aerodrome on 1 August 1930. The owner, Home Counties Aircraft Services, was soon experiencing financial difficulties, and sold the aerodrome to Redwing Aircraft Company in May 1932. That ownership did not last long, and the following year Gatwick again changed hands when Airports Ltd became the new owner. Throughout this period Surrey Aero Club operated from the airfield. By 1936 the airport was ready and the terminal building was connected to a new railway station by an underground passageway. This was very modern for its day. British Airways Ltd moved its operations from Stapleford Abbotts to Gatwick, but this proved not to be a good move, and after the airport became waterlogged the airline moved to Heston in February 1937. In the October, No. 19 E & RFTS was formed, operating Tiger Moths and Hawker Harts housed in No. 1 Hangar. The unit was then provided with an operations block, parachute store, machine-gun butts and buildings to house staff and pupils. RAFVR pilots were also trained by the school. On 25 June 1938 a large crowd came to Gatwick to see Battles, Blenheims, Whitleys, Lysanders and No. 3 Squadron Hurricanes perform in an air display organized by the *Daily Express*. In September 1938 Airports Ltd was given a contract to train direct-entry officers at No. 19 E & RFTS. To carry out this task a further twelve instructors, a Bellman hangar and sixteen Miles Magisters were obtained. On 1 September 1939 all reservists were called up. No. 19 E & RFTS was one of the schools that ceased to operate, its aircraft and ground crews being transferred to No. 18 EFTS at Fairoaks.

GRAVESEND (CHALK) KENT, E OF GRAVESEND

Gravesend Airport officially opened on 12 October, sited just north of Chalk village. The resident flying club was Gravesend School of Flying, which was run on service lines and gave instruction up to commercial pilot standard. The Dutch airline, KLM, came to use the airport and was well pleased, encouraging others, and Gravesend came to be styled 'London East'. Since Croydon could often be closed due to fog, Gravesend became a diversion airfield for Deutsche Lufthansa, Sabena and Swissair. These airlines did not, however, make the airport a base, as had been hoped by the managing director, Herbert Gooding. The RAF's first use of the airfield occurred when three Hawker Audaxes and an Atlas used it as a base during exercises. Percival aircraft had used the site for sales and servicing, but the company's success meant that it outgrew Gravesend and moved to Luton. Essex Aero Ltd moved in, specializing in tuning and converting aircraft, but in 1937 the site was taken over by Airports Ltd, the company that operated from Gatwick. But the airport was still found to be unprofitable and was offered for sale to Gravesend Council to serve as a municipal airport. A sum could not be agreed and the Air Ministry stepped in to purchase the airfield for use as a training school under the rearmament programme. The result was the formation of No. 20 E & RFTS, and a contract was signed permitting the training of Royal Navy pilots. On the outbreak of war civil flying ceased, No. 20 E & RFTS moved and the airfield was requisitioned by the Air Ministry to become a satellite for Biggin Hill.

HATFIELD CHISWICK, E OF ST ALBANS

De Havilland had outgrown its premises at Stag Lane, moving to Hatfield in the early 1930s. Initially the company moved only a flying school to Hatfield, but a new factory and offices had been built on the airfield boundary by 1934. The flying school used DH9s to give refresher training to members of the RAF Reserve. Aircraft on approach and landing had to contend with a 75 ft aircraft factory chimney on the east side of the airfield, with 200 ft radio masts to the west. During the expansion period the flying school became No. 1 E & RFTS, and at the outbreak of war this unit became No. 1 EFTS.

HENDON MIDDLESEX, BETWEEN EDGWARE AND HENDON

Hendon's association with flying goes back to 1909. Throughout the Great War and afterwards it was an active airfield, and during the post-war period was renowned for the RAF Pageants/Displays. In 1925 the airfield was sold to the RAF. In July 1933 No. 24 (Communications) Squadron arrived from Northolt. This squadron provided aircraft for Air and staff officers to visit RAF stations on inspections and routine visits. It was also possible for staff officers at the Air Ministry to maintain competence as pilots during their 'deskbound' period. From time to time members of the Royal Family were flown in aircraft of the squadron. Two more Auxiliary squadrons were formed at Hendon during the 1930s: No. 604 (County of Middlesex) Squadron on 17 March 1930, remaining there until September 1939; and No. 611 (West Lancashire) Squadron on 10 February 1936, moving to Liverpool two months later. Nos 600, 601 and 604 Squadrons had been formed as bomber squadrons but changed to fighters in 1934. No. 600 Squadron went to Kenley in September 1938 and No. 601 Squadron to Biggin in 1939. When No. 604 Squadron moved to North Weald in September 1939, no operational aircraft were on the station on the outbreak of war.

HESTON MIDDLESEX, NE OF HEATHROW AIRPORT

Heston aerodrome opened officially on 6 July 1929 under the control of Airwork Ltd. Some of the hangars were built for the display of aircraft for sale. Heston was the first aerodrome in Britain to feature an all-concrete apron and hangar, and the first to have a Customs post, established in 1931. With floodlights night-flying became a regular feature. Throughout the 1930s Heston became firmly established as an airport. The main hangar was completed in 1935, and a new Customs and Immigration building was opened in 1938. In that year the Secretary of State for Air purchased Heston with the intention of extending the airfield, but this did not happen. In the September Neville Chamberlain came into Heston with his famous piece of paper declaring 'Peace in Our Time'. At the outbreak of war the RAF requisitioned the airfield and it became a satellite of Northolt in No. 11 Group, Fighter Command. It later came to house the Heston Flight, which became the Photographic Development Unit under Sidney Cotton.

HIGH WYCOMBE BUCKINGHAMSHIRE, JUST OFF THE A40 AT HIGH WYCOMBE

When Bomber Command was formed on 14 July 1936 it was located at Uxbridge, before moving to the thickly wooded site in the Chilterns in 1939. Building started with eighty specialists and 800 workmen laying some six million multi-coloured, sand-faced bricks. The site of ninety acres was close to Booker aerodrome, and the building received 200 tons of reinforcement. The evacuation and moundings covered 28,800 cu. yds, and 8,800 yards of reinforced concrete were used.

HORNCHURCH (SUTTON'S FARM) ESSEX, BETWEEN HORNCHURCH AND RAINHAM

This Great War airfield was reactivated on 1 April 1928 and was then officially titled Sutton's Farm, to be renamed exactly two months later as RAF Hornchurch. No. 111 Squadron was the first to arrive, commanded by Squadron Leader Keith Park MC, DFC, who was later to be AOC No. 11 Group, Fighter Command, during the Battle of Britain. Hornchurch would be one of his airfields. In 1930 it became a two-squadron station when No. 54 Squadron was re-formed on 15 January, equipped with Siskin IIIAs. When No. 111 Squadron moved out on 12 July 1934, it was replaced by No. 65 Squadron, which re-formed on the station on 1 August, equipped with Demons. The following year saw a third fighter squadron being based at Hornchurch when No. 74 Squadron arrived from the Middle East. By 1936 all three squadrons were equipped with Gauntlets. On the formation of Fighter Command that year, Hornchurch became part of No. 11 Group, and was to be a Sector HQ during the Battle of Britain. In 1938 Nos 54 and 65 Squadrons were equipped with the Gladiator, the last of the RAF's biplane fighters, and then, in March, No. 54 Squadron received the Spitfire. In August defence exercises were held between Eastland and Westland, and VIP visitors were eager to see the new Spitfires under exercise conditions. On 11 August No. 54 Squadron moved to Rochford to practise the evacuation of Hornchurch in the event of German bombing. By the end of August all of Hornchurch's buildings had been camouflaged, and regulars and reservists recalled. From 1 September the operations room was continuously manned.

KENLEY SURREY, S OF CROYDON

Kenley was one of the few Great War stations that was retained in the post-war RAF, and it was home to fighter squadrons throughout the 1920s. No. 23 Squadron arrived from Henlow on 6 February 1927. Douglas Bader joined No. 23 Squadron in August 1930, and in 1931, while on a flying visit to Woodley aerodrome, Reading, he crashed his Gloster Gamecock while undertaking low-level aerobatics, losing his legs in the accident. On 17 September 1932 No. 23 Squadron moved to Biggin Hill, followed on the 21st by No. 32 Squadron, leaving Kenley without any flying units, which allowed some reconstruction to take place. When the work was complete in 1934 it was possible for Nos 3 and 17 Squadrons to be transferred from Upavon. On 3 September 1936 No. 46 Squadron was re-formed at Kenley, equipped with Gauntlets, and moved to Digby on 15 November 1937. On 3 March that year No. 80 Squadron was re-formed, again with Gauntlets, and in the following week moved to Henlow. Another Kenley formation was No. 615 Squadron, and that unit moved to Old Sarum at the end of August 1938, only to return a week later. In October 1938 No. 600 Squadron's Demons came and went. In 1939 Nos 3 and 17 Squadrons moved out to permit the laying of concrete runways, but No. 615 Squadron was able to keep on flying and did not move out until the last day of peace. Constable, Hart and Co. carried out the site work, which included a considerable extension of the runway. Three pairs of hangars were demolished to allow the perimeter track and runway to be laid. There were then two runways, NW–SE and NE–SW, twelve aircraft pens, each accepting four aircraft on dispersal, fuel storage for 35,000 gallons of aviation spirit and 2,500 gallons of oil, together with storage for $1^{1}/_{2}$ million rounds of ammunition.

LUTON BEDFORDSHIRE, SW OF LUTON
The site was first used by the Percival Aircraft Company, which moved from Gravesend in October 1936. The official opening of this grass airfield was on 16 July 1938. Luton was used to house No. 24 EFTS on the outbreak of war.

NORTHOLT MIDDLESEX, W OF LONDON ON THE A40
Northolt was another of the few Great War stations to be retained in the post-war RAF, and it was licensed as a joint civil/RAF field. No. 24 Communications Squadron moved in on 15 January 1927 to join No. 41 Squadron. No. 24 Squadron's role was not simply to provide pilots on the staff of the Air Ministry with flying practice, but also to fly high-ranking officials and military personnel on duty around Britain. On occasion this included members of the Royal Family, some of whom learned to fly at Northolt, Squadron Leader D.S. Don having taught Prince George, the Duke of Kent. In July 1933 No. 24 Squadron moved to Hendon. The following year No. 111 Squadron's Bulldogs arrived from Hornchurch, and in 1925 the London University Air Squadron was equipped with Tutors and Harts and accommodated at Northolt and Kensington. The Commanding Officer of the UAS was also in charge of the Station Flight. In the October No. 41 Squadron ended its twelve-year stay on the station when it proceeded to Aden during the Italo-Abyssinian War. On 1 May Northolt was confirmed as a fighter station, and it became a No. 11 Group airfield in Fighter Command on 1 May 1936. In December 1936 No. 23 Squadron with Hawker Demons joined No. 111 Squadron, but stayed only until 16 May 1938, when it left for Wittering. No. 213 Squadron also had a brief stay, re-forming at the station on 8 March 1937 with Gloster Gauntlets, moving to Church Fenton on 1 July. In January 1938 No. 111 Squadron was the first fighter unit to receive the Hawker Hurricane. Sadly the introduction of this most successful eight-gun fighter was not without incident. On 1 February Flying Officer Bocquet was killed when his aircraft, L.1556, was seen to dive straight into the ground between Hillingdon and Ickenham. On 19 March, Hurricane L.1551 force-landed at Colnbrook. Two days later L.1549 crashed on approach to land. Into 1939, and there were two crashes on 17 January, and as training continued there were further crashes. As war approached, a further C-Type hipped hangar was built, together with five H-Type barrack blocks in the south-eastern corner of the airfield. The laying of two paved runways, each of 2,400 ft, made Northolt one of the few RAF airfields to be so equipped on the outbreak of war.

NORTH WEALD ESSEX, W OF CHIPPING ONGAR
North Weald had been an active airfield, but it had lain dormant. Reconstruction began in 1926, and the station reopened on 27 September 1927 under Wing Commander A.G.R. Garrod. While it remained a grass airfield, the accommodation and facilities were much improved. In 1932 the two resident squadrons, Nos 29 and 56, were re-equipped with Bristol Bulldogs. Later that year both these squadrons joined in the Hendon Air Display. The station commander at this time was Wing Commander Sholto-Douglas MC, DFC. In March 1935 No. 29 Squadron received the Hawker Demon in time for the Abyssinian crisis, and the squadron moved to Egypt on 4 October. B Flight of No. 56 Squadron became the nucleus of No. 151 Squadron, which formed on 4 August 1936 under the command of Squadron Leader W.V. Hyde. No. 29 Squadron returned to North Weald from the Middle East the following month, and in July 1937 its Gauntlets were replaced with Gladiators. At the end of July No. 64 Squadron arrived with its Demon fighters, but returned to Martlesham after only two weeks. Before No. 29 Squadron moved to Debden in November 1937, there was sadly a mid-air collision over the airfield on 30 September between two Demons, and both pilots were killed. The squadron moved to Debden on 22 November. Meanwhile No. 56 Squadron was being re-equipped with Hurricanes, but No. 151 Squadron would have to wait until November 1938. During the period of the Munich Crisis, No. 604 (County of Middlesex) Auxiliary Squadron moved to the station. There was a record public attendance for Empire Air Day, when 16,000 people came to the station, reflecting the growing public interest and awareness of the work of the RAF. In May 1939 No. 17 Squadron was moved to North Weald, exchanging its Gauntlet IIs for Hurricane Is the following month. The day before war was declared, No. 604 Squadron, which had been detached to the station during the Munich Crisis, moved in to take up its war station. One of the squadron's Blenheim I pilots was Pilot Officer John Cunningham, who with his gunner, Jimmy Rawnsley, were later to be the top-scoring night-fighter team.

REDHILL SURREY, SE OF REIGATE
The first military use of this airfield was in 1937, when No. 15 E & RFTS was formed. It was operated by British Air Transport, and Magisters and Harts were used for training. On the outbreak of war the school was redesignated No. 15 EFTS, retaining the Magisters for training.

ROCHESTER KENT, SE OF ROCHESTER
Short Brothers needed an airfield for test flying landplanes, and until 1933 civil types were flown from

Lympne or Gravesend and military types from Martlesham. In 1933 Rochester Council purchased land between the Rochester–Maidstone and Chatham roads. This was for the purpose of constructing a municipal airport on the 105-acre site. On 22 November 1933 Rochester Council took the decision to lease the land on the understanding that it would be available for use as an airport keeping open private and public landing rights. The council supervised the work of levelling the ground, using unemployed men, and Short Brothers moved in before any hangars were erected. Short's first four-engined biplane airliner, the *Scylla,* had to be constructed in the open. The site was developed to include engineering shops, test facilities and offices. On 9 June 1934 air services were established from Rochester when Short began a service from the airfield to Southend. The flight lasted twelve minutes and cost eight shillings single or twelve shillings return. This was a very quick way to get from Kent to Essex in the days before the M25 was constructed. The RAF presence began on 1 April 1938 with the formation of No. 23 E & RFTS in No. 26 Group, under the command of Flight Lieutenant R. Chambers. When in 1938 the school was expanded to train pilots for the Fleet Air Arm, a second hangar and administrative block were built. On the naval side there were sixteen instructors, and the Avro 504N was still being used for instruction until replaced by Tutors, and then Magisters. Intermediate and advanced training was given on Audaxes and Harts. Nos 23 and 24 E & RFTSs were merged to become No. 24 EFTS at Sydenham on 3 September 1939.

SOUTHEND (ROCHFORD) ESSEX, 2 MILES N OF SOUTHEND-ON-SEA

Rochford was not included among the airfields to be retained by the RAF after the Great War, and after brief use for pleasure flying the land was returned to agriculture. It was not until the early 1930s that the potential for civil aviation interested local government, and Southend Corporation bought the land for the construction of Southend Municipal Airport, which was officially opened on 18 September 1935. The Under-Secretary of State for Air, Sir Philip Sassoon, arrived for the opening in his DH 85 Leopard Moth. The airport was managed by Southend Flying Club, which operated a Leopard Moth and five Cadets. Many privately owned aircraft were attracted to the airport. The airfield was known as Rochford, and also as Holt Farm, but became Southend on the opening of the airport. During the expansion period the airfield was used by the RAF as an Auxiliary Air Force camp, and in 1937 two Auxiliary squadrons came to camp. Meanwhile No. 34 E & RFTS was formed and was operated by Air Hire Ltd with an establishment of Tiger Moths. On the outbreak of war the Elementary and Reserve Flying Training School closed and the Air Ministry requisitioned the airfield.

The airfield was renamed RAF Rochford and was designated Hornchurch's satellite.

STAPLEFORD TAWNEY ESSEX, NE OF LONDON BETWEEN CHIGWELL AND ONGAR

Following two years during which the airfield remained dormant, it was reopened by the RAF in 1938 to house No. 21 E & RFTS. The school was operated by Reid and Sigrist Ltd to train RAFVR pilots. Tiger Moths were used for basic training, and Harts, Hinds and Audaxes for advanced training. One of these trainee pilots was 'Johnnie' Johnson, who was to receive no fewer than five British decorations for gallantry, and a similar number of foreign awards. On the outbreak of war No. 21 E & RFTS moved out and the airfield was prepared to accept operational aircraft.

WEST MALLING (KINGS HILL) KENT, 5 MILES W OF MAIDSTONE

West Malling opened as a private landing ground in 1930, and was home to the Maidstone School of Flying, but began life as a 2nd Class landing ground during the Great War, when it was known as Kings Hill. The site covered an area of forty-seven acres (650 yd × 380 yd) $1\frac{1}{2}$ miles from West Malling station in wooded surroundings. In 1931 Kent Aeronautical Services began air services from the aerodrome, using modified SE5As and a Sopwith Dove. In 1932 the airfield became Maidstone Airport, a registered company. Operations were carried out by Malling Aviation with a collection of aircraft. Malling Aviation purchased the airport in 1935 and renamed it Malling Aero Club. VIPs who visited West Malling included Alan Cobham and Amy Johnson. On the outbreak of war the RAF took over the airfield.

WHITE WALTHAM MAIDENHEAD, SW OF MAIDENHEAD

Opened on 16 November 1935, the airfield opened as the second de Havilland School of Flying. The school was formed to carry out *ab initio* training for pupil pilots and elementary and advanced training for officers and NCOs under the command of the Superintendent of Reserve HQ, RAF Reserve, Hendon. During the expansion period the school became No. 13 E & RFTS on 18 November 1935, to be renamed No. 13 EFTS on the outbreak of war.

WOODLEY (READING) BERKSHIRE, E OF READING

No. 8 E & RFTS was at Woodley from the mid-1930s, and in 1939 the unit became No. 8 EFTS. During the late 1930s some 680 pilots and 100 navigators had been trained at the Reserve Flying Training School.

UXBRIDGE MIDDLESEX, SE OF UXBRIDGE

The present RAF station at Uxbridge comprises the house and land known as Hillingdon House and its estate. The RFC came to the station in December 1917 with its Armament School, which passed into RAF service on 1 April 1918. By 1930 a list of units, too long to mention, had come and gone. Two units stand out, however, and they remained at Uxbridge. They are the RAF Depot and the RAF Central Band. The main task of Uxbridge during the inter-war years was the training and the forming of the characters of the young men of the service, and the name of the station was synonymous with RAF sport. Administrative changes took place in the early 1930s, and in January 1933 the Central Band was transferred from the control of HQ Inland Area to HQ No. 21 Group, while the RAF Officers' Hospital made the opposite move. A year later all Uxbridge units (excluding the Air Defence Great Britain and HQ Fighting Area) were passed to the direct control of HQ Inland Area when No. 21 Group was disbanded. The expansion schemes of the mid-1930s had considerable impact on the RAF Depot. During the years 1931–4 the Depot had received just over 3,000 recruits, but the number jumped to 8,500 for the year 1935 alone. In May of that year the intake was 338 recruits, but by August it had risen to 1,279. Changes in the command structure were made in 1936, when Air Defence of Great Britain (ADGB) was replaced with functional commands. In April, HQ Fighting Area became HQ (11) Fighter Group and HQ ADGB became HQ Bomber Command, which was still at Hillingdon House. HQ Inland Area was renamed HQ Training Command, and Uxbridge units administered by HQ Inland Area were transferred to the newly formed No. 24 (Training) Group. Also in 1936 the Central Dental Laboratory was established at Uxbridge. In spite of all these organizational changes, recruit training still went on. From April 1936 until August 1939 the average intake was 600 recruits per month, and a new sub-depot had to be opened at Henlow to take the strain. This was made necessary by a new Air Ministry requirement that each recruit should have 60 sq. ft per man. It is probable that all recruits went firstly to Uxbridge for initial training, then on to Henlow to complete their course; the latter was officially named No. 2 RAF Depot with effect from 1 September 1937. The RAF Anti-Gas School had been established on the station earlier that year. With the imminence of war, ten sub-depots were opened for recruits between July and October 1938, and on 26 September No. 1 Mobilization Pool was opened ready to receive reservists at Uxbridge the following day, but the signing of the Munich Agreement delayed the 'call-up'. As war approached, however, other measures were put in hand. On 1 May the School of Administration was set up, while the Anti-Gas School moved to Rollestone camp in Wiltshire. On 23 August the School of PT closed, to reopen just a month later on 29 September 1939. No. 1 Personnel Transit Centre was opened, and on 25 August the personnel of No. 2 Base Unit and other unspecified units

began to arrive. On 27 August the short-service officers' courses were moved to Grantham, and on the next day HQ Bomber Command moved to Iver. The order to mobilize was received on 1 September, and on the following day the Central Trade Test Board was established on the station. On the day war was declared the Central Attestation Section was opened.

AIRFIELDS, SEAPLANE BASES AND MISCELLANEOUS UNITS IN SOUTH-WEST ENGLAND

ALTON BARNES WILTSHIRE, 4 MILES NW OF UPAVON
The first use of Alton Barnes was by the Central Flying School in the mid 1930s, and it was one of a number of landing grounds in Wiltshire. There was nothing on the airfield beside a windsock, for it was used only by embryo instructors practising circuits away from the busier main base at Upavon. Finding the airfield from Upavon was made easy with a white horse cut into the side of Mill Hill, easily visible on the approach. When the Avro 504Ns were replaced with Tutors in 1937, the latter remained in service until late 1941.

ASTON DOWN GLOUCESTERSHIRE, 1½ MILES SE OF CHALFORD ON A419
The first use of this site was as an aircraft storage unit, which had eight large, dome-roofed storage hangars dispersed around the airfield. It was opened as No. 7 ASU on 12 October 1938, and renamed No. 20 Maintenance Unit on the 17th. Aircraft started to arrive during February 1939, and on 6 September that year, twelve Wellingtons of No. 214 Squadron arrived from Feltwell without warning, having received dispersal orders, but left the next day. The unit was then occupied with the preparation of Blenheims for Yugoslavia and Romania. Fighter Command took an interest in Aston Down and used it as No. 12 Group Pool from 23 August 1939. Blenheims, Harvards and Gladiators were used to give intermediate training to pilots posted to No. 12 Group squadrons. The numbers of pilots under training soon exceeded the capacity of the station to accommodate the officers, who were then billeted in the George Hotel, Nailsworth. The officers were given four meals a day for six shillings (30p in today's money). In the following month Fighter Command took over the airfield and No. 20 MU remained as a lodger unit.

BARNSTAPLE DEVON, 3 MILES W OF BARNSTAPLE
North Devon Airport was opened at Barnstaple on 13 June 1934, and services were started to the Bristol Channel island of Lundy using a DH Dragon. By summer up to ten flights a day were being made, and the company (Boyd and Nash) gradually increased the scope of its services, which were extended to Cardiff and Plymouth using Short Scions. In 1938 the company

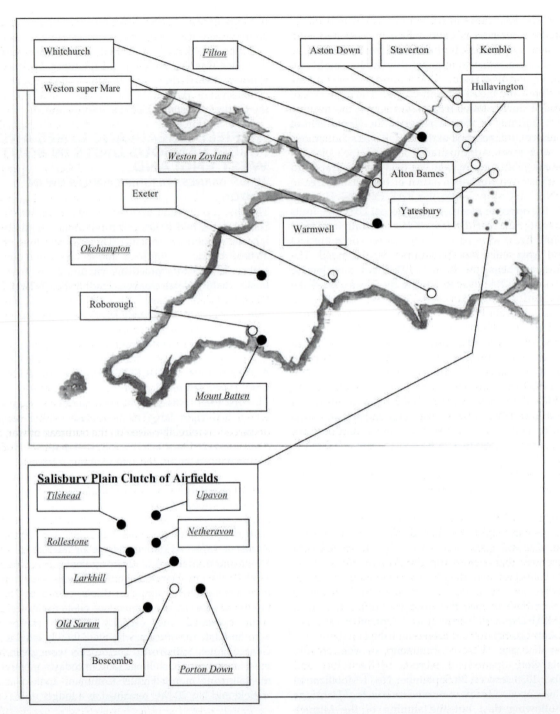

undertook Civil Air Guard training, and on 8 May 1939 Western Airways called in at North Devon Airport on flights between Manchester and Penzance. The airfield was requisitioned by the Air Ministry on the outbreak of war, when passenger services were suspended and the Scions were used for Army Cooperation flights. The airfield was closed to flying on the development of Chivenor, and used only for dispersing aircraft.

BOSCOMBE DOWN WILTSHIRE, 1½ MILES SE OF AMESBURY

This Great War airfield was closed in 1919, not to reopen until 1930. Virginias of No. 9 Squadron arrived from Manston in November of that year, to be joined by the Hinaidis of No. 10 Squadron in April 1931. The two squadrons occupied Boscombe Down until No. 9 Squadron moved to Andover on 15 October 1935. In

February 1937 the station moved over to Coastal Command, when two Anson (GR) squadrons moved in just after No. 10 Squadron had departed for Dishforth. But the station returned to Bomber Command and No. 4 Group, No. 217 Squadron departing for Tangmere on 7 June 1937 and No. 224 Squadron for Thornaby on 9 July. In April 1938 the station was again transferred, this time to No. 1 Group. The two resident squadrons on the outbreak of war were Nos 88 and 218, with Battles, but they went immediately to France, and the Aeroplane and Armament Experimental Establishment took up residence, having been moved from Martlesham Heath, where the unit was vulnerable to enemy attack.

CALSHOT HAMPSHIRE (MARINE), 2 MILES SE OF FAWLEY

Calshot as a military seaplane base dates right back to 1913, taking its name from Calshot Castle. The base survived the closures after the Great War, having been taken over by the RAF in 1918. The station became well known in the late 1920s in connection with the work of the High-Speed Flight and the Schneider Trophy races. Work went on from 1927 until 1931, when Great Britain won the contest outright. Until the formation of No. 240 Squadron in March 1937 the only resident unit was No. 201 Squadron, equipped with Southamptons, then Londons. During the Munich Crisis the two squadrons moved to their war stations while Calshot prepared for war. Civilian bathing huts were removed from the Spit, and machine-gun posts and trenches were added to the list of tasks to be undertaken. Both Nos 201 and 240 Squadrons left on the outbreak of war, leaving only the Flying-boat Training Squadron on strength.

EXETER DEVON, 1 MILE E OF CLYST HONITON

Exeter Airport was built to the east of the city on the road to Honiton, and opened on 31 May 1937. Jersey Airways commenced flights from the Channel Islands in June, which connected with the Plymouth to Bristol schedules of Railway Air Services. The Air Minister, Sir Kingsley Wood, officially opened Exeter Airport on 30 July 1938 on completion of the terminal building. The Straight Organization ran the aerodrome and the aero club. The Corporation gained the contract to operate No. 37 E & RFTS with Tiger Moths. It was intended that this unit would train reservists, but since it was not formed until 3 July 1939 the E & RFTS was overtaken by events, and was closed down at the outbreak of war. Exeter then became a sub-station for the National Air Communications organization.

FILTON GLOUCESTERSHIRE (NEW AVON), 4 MILES N OF BRISTOL ALONGSIDE THE A38

Filton's association with flying dates back to 1910, when the British and Colonial Aeroplane Co. Ltd was formed, and during the Great War the airfield was used for military flying. Although activity was much reduced after the war, the company was awarded a contract to run a Reserve School for the RAF, which was opened on 15 May 1923. Then on 14 June 1929 No. 501 (County of Gloucester) Squadron was formed, equipped with Avro 504Ns, followed by a DH9A in March 1930. Work on alteration to existing buildings and the erection of new accommodation for one regular and one cadre squadron began on the RAF site, which was on the north side of the airfield. In 1937 the Reserve School became No. 2 E & RFTS, but was still operated by the Bristol company for the Air Ministry. A ferry flight had to be formed at Filton in January 1939 to cope with the output of Blenheims, and this was titled No. 2 Ferry Pilots' Pool. When No. 501 Squadron became a fighter unit at the end of 1938, it was embodied into the RAF for the duration of the emergency.

GUERNSEY CHANNEL ISLANDS, 3 MILES WSW OF ST PETER'S PORT

On 1 May 1939 Guernsey Airport was opened by Sir Kingsley Wood, the Secretary of State for Air, and Guernsey Airways began services to Alderney, Jersey, Southampton and London on the 5th. In August a Care and Maintenance party arrived from No. 16 Group, Coastal Command, since the airfield had already been earmarked on a forward base for Anson squadrons expected to patrol the English Channel once war was declared. Civil flying ceased on the outbreak of war, and a period of military activity followed until the airfield was evacuated before the arrival of the *Luftwaffe*.

HULLAVINGTON WILTSHIRE, 5 MILES N OF CHIPPENHAM

A flying training station and attached storage unit at Hullavington was included in the 1936 Air Estimates, which included a vote of £146,000 as the first stage of an expected total cost of £347,000 for its construction. The station was opened on 14 June 1937 with permanent domestic and technical accommodation on the main site constructed from the attractive local stone. No. 9 FTS arrived from Thornaby on 10 July with Hart (T) and Hart Specials, but these biplanes were soon supplemented by the comparatively advanced Anson, on which training commenced in March 1938. On 8 July 1938 No. 9 MU formed at the station, but was administered by Kemble. To avoid confusion with No. 9 FTS it was decided to renumber the maintenance unit as No. 10 MU in February 1939. Its initial usage was the storage of MT vehicles. There was insufficient hangar space, and Harvard aircraft had to be stored in the open by picketing. On 1 September 1939 the mobilization orders resulted in the arrival of ten Blenheims of No. 114 Squadron on deployment from Wyton, and with that Hullavington entered the Second World War.

KEMBLE GLOUCESTERSHIRE, 4 MILES SW OF CIRENCESTER ON THE A429

No. 5 MU was formed at RAF Kemble on 22 June 1938 as an aircraft storage unit. It was then a brand-new airfield straddling the Fosse Way and had three large hangars, but plans were already in hand to expand. The MU absorbed the personnel and equipment of the MU at Waddington in February 1939.

LARKHILL WILTSHIRE, 4 MILES NW OF AMESBURY

The airfield at Larkhill was one of the oldest in British aviation, but did not become an RAF station until January 1936. It had been used for Army Cooperation exercises on Salisbury Plain during the inter-war years. The ground was rough and the facilities were few, but there were not many problems associated with this sort of flying. The station was therefore host to visiting squadrons and did not receive its first permanent unit until 2 June 1940.

MOUNT BATTEN (CATTEWATER) DEVON, I MILE S OF PLYMOUTH ACROSS THE SOUND

This was another station that dated back to the earliest days of flying, being a natural seaplane base in the Great War. The name was changed from Cattewater to Mountbatten on 1 October 1929. No. 209 Squadron was formed there in 1930, equipped with Blackburn Iris flying-boats. No. 204 Squadron's Sunderlands arrived in June 1939, and it shared the station with the Shark floatplanes of No. 2 AACU, which provided aircraft training at the gunnery school. On the outbreak of war No. 204 Squadron had six operational flying-boats, and operational patrols were made in the Western Approaches on the second day of the war.

NETHERAVON WILTSHIRE, 6 MILES N OF AMESBURY, OFF THE A345

Netheravon survived the rundown after the Great War and was numbered No. 1 FTS. In the gradual expansion in the mid-1920s the station was tasked to train pilots for the Fleet Air Arm. The station was also home to operational squadrons such as Nos 33 and 99 until the station was transferred to No. 23 Group on 1 April 1935 and No. 6 FTS was re-formed there, equipped with variants of the Hart/Audax and the Tutor. Having been equipped with Ansons this FTS then moved to Little Rissington in August 1936, and was immediately replaced by No. 1 FTS. In the immediate pre-war years Netheravon operated as an advanced flying school, still working with Fleet Air Arm trainees. Harvard aircraft were introduced to the FTS in early 1939, and together with Hawker biplanes No. 1 FTS entered the war.

OKEHAMPTON (FOLLY GATE) DEVON, I½ MILES NW OF OKEHAMPTON ON THE A386

Okehampton was established as an airfield for Army Cooperation aircraft in 1928. Every year the large flat field at Folly Gate was in use during the period May to September when the artillery practice camps on Dartmoor ranges were under canvas. Nos 13 and 16 Squadrons equipped initially with Bristol F2Bs, followed by Atlas and Audax aircraft operated from the field. In the summer of 1938 the Audaxes of No. 16 Squadron were replaced with Lysanders. Throughout this period there were no airfield facilities at Folly Gate. Okehampton remained unused at the outbreak of war until No. 16 Squadron arrived with Lysanders from Cambridge, fresh from the war in France.

OLD SARUM (FORD FARM) WILTSHIRE, 2 MILES N OF SALISBURY

Like Netheravon, Old Sarum was saved from the closures of the early 1920s and became associated with Army Cooperation. From 1924 several squadrons, which included Nos 13, 16 and 59, were in residence. No. 16 Squadron was still at Old Sarum in 1939 with its Lysanders. The School of Army Cooperation had Hectors, Lysanders, Blenheims and Ansons on strength at the outbreak of war, but the airfield was not really suitable for the operation of Blenheims.

ROBOROUGH PLYMOUTH, 3½ MILES NE OF PLYMOUTH OFF THE A386

The field was first used for flying in the autumn of 1923, and although used by a variety of organizations there were not enough customers, and the airfield was closed. When, some years later, the airfield was used by the Plymouth and District Aero Club, the Corporation was persuaded to open a civic airfield. The Roborough polo ground and adjoining fields were purchased, and the aerodrome was opened on 15 July 1931, when the Great Western Railway started an air service to Cardiff in April 1932. The RAF used Roborough for communications and the occasional air exercise from 1935 onwards, and in June 1939 No. 15 Group Communications Flight formed at the station.

ROLLESTONE WILTSHIRE, I MILE E OF SHREWTON VILLAGE

Throughout the 1920s Rollestone had been associated with balloon training. In 1932 the balloon storage hangars of the Bessoneaux type, which were easily damaged in the wind, were replaced by a large double shed capable of holding two inflated balloons. The unit was named No. 2 Balloon Training Unit, which was transferred from No. 22 Group to No. 24 Group, Training Command, in December 1936. The unit moved to Cardington on 1 February 1939. In the following June, with the building of additional accommodation, the camp was reopened as the RAF Anti-Gas School, providing training for specialist RAF personnel and all unit and flight commanders throughout the war.

STAVERTON GLOUCESTERSHIRE, 3 MILES NE OF GLOUCESTER

An airstrip was opened at Down Hatherley by the Cotswolds Aero Club in September 1932, but when proposals were put forward for a public aerodrome on the site it proved impossible to extend the field. A site was therefore chosen on the other side of the Cheltenham–Gloucester road, then the A40. The Cheltenham and Gloucester Councils finally agreed to the joint purchase of 160 acres in March 1934, and work started on the site the following November. On 18 November 1936 an operating licence was received, and Railway Air Services started an air service on its Bristol–Birmingham route. The Air Ministry became interested in the site with the RAF expansion plan, and agreement was reached for the use of the airfield for twelve years for training purposes, as long as the RAF extended the airfield and provided night-flying equipment. Buildings were erected for No. 31 E & RFTS, which formed on 29 September 1938 with Tiger Moths, and was operated by Surrey Flying Services. In May 1939 the Airwork Civil School of Air Navigation also moved in to Staverton. The school provided elementary training for RAF observers, using Dragon Rapides. Rotol Ltd also established a flight test department on the airfield, and on 17 April a Wellesley arrived, to be the first of ninety aircraft used for Rotol trials during the war. The Airwork organization became No. 6 Civil Air Navigation School on 6 August, and with the war imminent, No. 31 E & RFTS was closed. The airport was officially renamed RAF Staverton on 10 September 1939.

TILSHEAD WILTSHIRE, I MILE W OF TILSHEAD VILLAGE

From 1925 Tilshead was used by Army Cooperation squadrons during annual manoeuvres on Salisbury Plain. During these manoeuvres a small ground party would erect tents on the edge of the landing ground and await the arrival of aircraft used for artillery spotting and reconnaissance. To begin with, Bristol Fighters were used, to be followed by Atlases, Audaxes, Hectors and Lysanders. A flight of No. 16 Squadron was detached to Tilshead for a month in June 1931 and August 1932, but usually detachments were for a much shorter period. Since the airfield was not to be used during the war it was obstructed. The obstructions were cleared to permit the dispersal of aircraft of units returning from France, for there was a serious lack of landing-grounds at this time.

UPAVON WILTSHIRE, I½ MILES SE OF UPAVON VILLAGE

It was a strange place to build an airfield, on top of a hill, with a sharp escarpment on the northern side and a drop to the Avon valley in the west. The result was turbulence, even on good days, but the airfield survived and became the Central Flying School. When the station was transferred to the newly formed No. 3 Group in 1926, the CFS was transferred to Wittering. Until 1934 Nos 3 and 17 Squadrons were the resident units, and for three years they operated as the only night-fighter squadrons in the RAF. When these units moved to Kenley in May 1934, the station became a shore base for FAA units. But this situation did not last long, for Upavon was transferred to No. 23 (Training) Group, Inland Area. The FAA units moved to Gosport and the CFS returned to the station. The Avro 504 was finally retired and replaced by the Avro Tutor. Hart (T) and Fury aircraft were added, and Ansons were included on the station inventory for twin-engined training until replaced by Oxfords in November 1937. With the rapid growth of Elementary and Reserve Flying Training Schools, there was a need for the Upavon staff to categorize the civilian instructors who taught at these schools. Even as late as 1938 the station retained its 1914–18 wooden huts, although the original hangars had been replaced. Accordingly work was commenced on station improvements. In the first phase some married quarters, a single C-Type hangar, barrack blocks, workshops and airmen's dining hall were added. The CFS Refresher Flight was given the task of writing *Pilots' Notes* as a separate volume, for in the past aircraft handling notes were simply added to the technical manual for each type. By the end of 1938 the *Notes* were proving their worth, although squadrons were still receiving aircraft for which their pilots were totally unprepared. A decision was therefore made to send new aircraft to the CFS so that handling notes could be prepared to a standard format. On 5 May 1938 His Majesty King George VI visited the station in his Airspeed Envoy, when he inspected a line-up of CFS aircraft. With the approach of war there was pressure for the four training flights to increase output, and this resulted in a reduction of the length of the course from ten to nine weeks and an increase in student strength from forty to fifty per intake. On completion of the C-Type hangar in April 1939, the very varied collection of CFS aircraft could be housed in it. On the outbreak of war the training aircraft were dispersed around the perimeter and guarded by armed RAF personnel, for Upavon was a difficult station to secure.

WARMWELL (WOODSFORD) DORSET, 3½ MILES SE OF DORCHESTER

Gunnery practice was carried out in the 1920s and early 1930s during a camp held each summer at a landing ground. But following the RAF expansion this was not a satisfactory way of coping with the increased number of units required to undertake gunnery practice. And so armament practice camps were set up near gunnery and bombing ranges with permanent staff and accommodation for squadron detachments. One of these ranges was on the Chesil Bank, and a site at Woodford, eight miles NE of Weymouth, was chosen. Opened on 1 May 1937, it was the home of No. 6 APC. A station flight was established in July 1937, with Tutor and Wallace target tugs. The first units to use the APC were Nos 206 and 220 Squadrons, which took part in a coastal defence exercise. Soon FTSs were attending camps, in addition to operational squadrons. On 1 April 1938 the unit was renamed No. 6 Armament Training School, coming under No. 25 Group. In order not to confuse the airfield's name with Avro's factory airfield at Woodford in Manchester, it was decided to rename it after the nearby village of Warmwell in July 1938. On mobilization the Ansons of No. 217 Squadron arrived at Warmwell to patrol the English Channel until St Eval was ready in October 1939. No. 6 ATS was expanded on 2 September with a mixed collection of aircraft, including Seals, Sidestrands and Harrows, and was renamed No. 10 AOS, but changed shortly afterwards to No. 10 Bombing and Gunnery School.

WESTON-SUPER-MARE SOMERSET, 1¹/₂ MILES SE OF WESTON-SUPER-MARE ALONGSIDE THE A371

Work on Weston Airport began during February 1936. It was sited between the Great Western line and the A371, and work was sufficiently advanced to commence services on 25 May. This was the Plymouth–Cardiff–Weston–Bristol service run by Railway Air Services. The services through Weston were expanded, and in October 1938 Western Airways began the first scheduled night services in the UK. Also in 1938 the RAF opened a School of Technical Training at Locking, one mile to the east of the airport, and arrangements were made by the Air Ministry to locate a Station Flight at the airport for communications and staff training. In 1939 No. 39 E & RFTS was opened at Weston, operated by the Straight Corporation, owner of Western Airways. The unit's aircraft were Magisters and Harts, and it opened on 3 July, but was soon disbanded on the outbreak of war, in common with other E & RFTSs, to provide aircraft for the EFTSs. The operating company was then tasked to undertake navigation training and No. 5 Civil Air Navigation School was formed on 1 September.

WESTON ZOYLAND SOMERSET, 4 MILES SE OF BRIDGEWATER

From the 1920s a large anti-aircraft gunnery school was established at Weston Zoyland and the Air Ministry arranged for a large field to the east of the village to be used by Horsleys of No. 100 Squadron for a summer camp in 1926. Due to the successful cooperation between the squadron and the gunners, these camps became an annual affair. In 1929 the Night-Flying Flight, Biggin Hill, took over and was renamed the Anti-Aircraft Cooperation Flight, continuing the summer camps until 1936. The landing-ground was opened up each May and the summer was spent under canvas. In February 1938

the unit was again renamed, to become No. 1 Anti-Aircraft Cooperation Unit, and A Flight, with its Wallaces, towed targets up and down the ranges. In 1939 Henleys replaced the Wallaces. On the outbreak of war Watchet remained as an anti-aircraft camp.

WHITCHURCH SOMERSET, 2 MILES S OF BRISTOL

In 1928 the Bristol and Wessex Aeroplane Club decided to establish a small airfield at Whitchurch since Filton was becoming overcrowded. With the help of the local council a site two miles west of Whitchurch village was chosen, necessitating the purchase of two farms in 1929, so that work could begin on clearing and levelling the ground. Whitchurch was officially opened on 31 May 1930 as Bristol Airport, in a formal ceremony performed by HRH Prince Albert, Duke of York. For the first five years of its life the airport was operated by the club, enabling a number of small airlines to run summer services from 1932, but development was slow and in 1935 Bristol City Council became responsible for airport development. The Reserve School at Filton used the aerodrome as an RLG, but in December 1938 No. 33 E & RFTS, operated by Chamier Gilbert Lodge Co. Ltd, was established at Whitchurch, operating twelve Tiger Moths. Harts and Battles were brought in for the annual training of Reservists during 1939. Considerable improvements were made to the airport, which then had a large tarmac apron, a direction-finding beacon and runway lighting, and a large hangar was erected to house the Reserve School. When Imperial and British Airways was tasked to produce a war dispersal plan, requiring the evacuation of Croydon and Heston, Whitchurch attracted its attention. At the end of 1939 sixty large passenger aircraft were assembled there in what was called A Base. The airport was requisitioned by the Air Ministry on the outbreak of war, and No. 33 E & RFTS was disbanded, leaving Whitchurch free for national communications schedules to operate services to French destinations during the autumn of 1939.

YATESBURY WILTSHIRE, 4 MILES E OF CALNE

When Yatesbury was closed in 1929 it did not see service again until 1935, when the Bristol Aeroplane Company was given a contract for a second Reserve Training School. The company purchased 290 acres of the old Great War Yatesbury airfield, and the two Great War hangars were refurbished, together with the landing-ground and the building of a new administrative block, hospital, MT section and boiler-house. The new school opened on 6 January 1936, but because of the severe winter weather, Yatesbury was not ready and operations had to begin at Filton. When operations returned to Yatesbury, the pupils were billeted in local farmhouses until the beginning of April, when the new accommodation was complete. On 1 February 1938 the Bristol School was redesignated No. 10 E & RFTS, and came under No. 26 (Training) Group. At first Tiger Moths were used for primary training, and these were supplemented by Hart variants for advanced training. A further contract was secured for the training of navigation, and No. 2 Civil Air Navigation School was opened in the September. Then plans were made for the training of ground radio operators, and construction was put in hand for a large hutted camp alongside the airfield. On 13 October 1938 No. 2 Electrical and Wireless School was formed.

AIRFIELDS AND MISCELLANEOUS UNITS IN THE COTSWOLDS AND CENTRAL MIDLANDS

ABINGDON OXFORDSHIRE, 5 MILES SW OF OXFORD, I MILE NW OF ABINGDON TOWN

Abingdon was planned in 1925 and was intended to be a simple airfield, with only fifty-one buildings listed, which included four hangars. Construction did not commence until 1929, and the station opened on 1 September 1932 as a station in the Wessex Bombing Area.

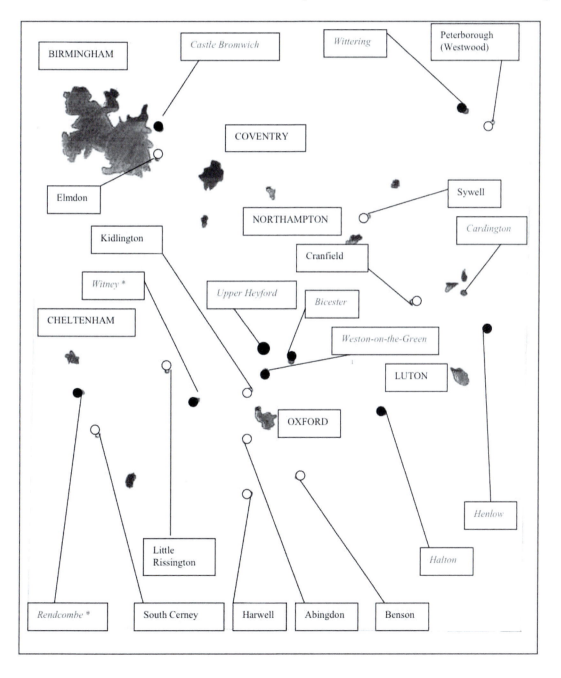

Fairey Gordons were the first aircraft to arrive. These aircraft were single-engined biplane bombers of No. 40 Squadron, which moved from Upper Heyford, having completed a period of armament training at Catfoss. The squadron remained at Abingdon until 1939. On opening, the station flight was equipped with an Atlas, Avro 504N and a DH Moth. Oxford University Air Squadron moved in on 3 November. In November 1933 the station came under Central Area, and on 1 June the following year the Gordons were joined by the Harts of No. 15 Squadron when that squadron was re-formed. This was the squadron that had been the armament-testing unit at Martlesham Heath. As evidence of the expansion plan gathering pace, more buildings were completed in January 1936, and C Flight of No. 40 Squadron became the nucleus of No. 104 Squadron, and a flight of No. 15 Squadron became the nucleus of No. 98 Squadron, equipped with Hinds. On Empire Air Day 1936 the station received over 2,000 visitors, who paid one shilling for entrance. They were treated to the sight of a Heyford, Overstrand, Bulldog, Moth and a stripped Tutor flying with two Hinds. In the following year the number of visitors rose to 6,000. On 3 May 1937 No. 40 Squadron gave birth to No. 62 Squadron, which later went to Cranfield. When No. 15 Squadron gave birth to No. 52 Squadron on 18 January 1937, it was necessary for it to move to Upwood on 1 March to relieve an overcrowded station, and the Tutors of the Cambridge University Air Squadron came in. Over the Christmas period 1937/8 the station hosted the Ospreys and Nimrods of No. 802 Squadron of the Fleet Air Arm, which then returned to HMS *Glorious*. The re-formation of squadrons continued to affect the station, as the number rose rapidly. On 3 March No. 185 Squadron was formed from B Flight of No. 40 Squadron. In June 1938 No. 15 Squadron was equipped with Battles, which also equipped No. 40 Squadron. Other Battles arrived for No. 106 Squadron, and this and No. 18 Squadron moved to Thornaby in August and September. Nos 15 and 40 Squadrons were placed on operational readiness during the Munich Crisis of September 1938. Although war did not come until a year later, the Abingdon Battles practised their role in the Advanced Air Striking Force. On 2 September 1939 the camouflaged Battles flew to France, setting off at 10.00 hrs, and that night civil aircraft arrived on the station to transport the ground personnel across the Channel.

BAGINTON (COVENTRY AIRPORT) 4 MILES SE OF COVENTRY

From 1935 Baginton was used by Armstrong Whitworth for the production of Whitley bombers until March 1939. No. 1 Camouflage Unit formed here on the outbreak of war.

BENSON 13 MILES SE OF OXFORD

Building commenced in 1937 and the station was given four C-Type hangars ready for occupation in early 1939. The first units to be stationed here were Nos 103 and 150 Squadrons, equipped with Battles. In common with other Battle squadrons in service, these two squadrons were scheduled to go to France should hostilities break out. Indeed, they joined the Advanced Air Striking Force on 2 September. The Whitleys of Nos 97 and 166 Squadrons were supposed to move into Benson, but the grass airfield made it unsuitable, and so Nos 52 and 63 Squadrons' Battles came instead. The Whitleys went to Abingdon.

BICESTER 1½ MILES NE OF THE TOWN

This Great War airfield was resurrected in 1925. In the late 1920s Bicester was home to the Hawker Horsleys of No. 100 Squadron, but on 4 November 1930 the Hawker Harts of No. 33 Squadron arrived to stay for a few weeks before moving on to Upper Heyford. On 1 December 1934 the Sidestrands of No. 101 Squadron moved in from Andover. That year the expansion began, and Bicester was treated to some major improvements, including two C-Type hangars, which did not replace but supplemented the existing hangarage. Then there were the E-Type barrack blocks that could accommodate an NCO and ninety-six airmen, a watch office and a tower. By 1939 nine barrack blocks, and nine airmen's married quarter units and six officers' married quarters had been added. No. 48 (GR) Squadron was formed at Bicester on 25 November 1935, but then moved directly to Manston. The station was transferred to No. 1 Group, Bomber Command, on 17 August 1936, and a station headquarters was established on 21 September. No. 144 Squadron was formed from C Flight of No. 101 Squadron, and moved to Hemswell on 8 February 1937. A Flight of No. 101 Squadron was temporally equipped with Hawker Hinds until the Blenheim Is arrived in May 1937, and the squadron was fully equipped in June 1938. Before the outbreak of war two squadrons of Battles, Nos 12 and 142, came to the station before departing for France as part of the Advanced Air Striking Force on 2 September 1939.

BRIZE NORTON 6 MILES SW OF WITNEY

Building work began at Brize in 1935. There might have been problems with flooding, given the flat nature of the land and a high water table. An earlier section of this chapter refers to problems confronting the Airfield Board in choosing and recommending sites for airfields to the Director-General of Organization. The name, too, presented a problem. In most cases the name given to an RAF station was determined by the proximity of the main camp gate to the nearest town or village. But to call the station Carterton risked it being confused with Cardington. This had once caused confusion between Scopwick and Shotwick, so the former was renamed Digby and the latter Sealand. The first unit to move into Brize was No. 2 FTS on 13 August 1937, with a mixture of Harts, Audaxes and Furies. Then, commencing on 22 February 1938, the Oxford began to replace the biplanes for pilot training. Other buildings were added, including 'lamella' hangars to accommodate No. 6 MU in the south-east corner of the airfield. This was a No. 41 Group unit, which opened on 10 October 1938. In March 1939 the Harvard Is arrived, much to the annoyance of the local populace. The aircraft propellers put up a most awful whine, having something to do with the tip speed. Indeed, the author can recall the time he attended an annual ATC camp at Moreton-in-the-Marsh in 1952, when the noise of the Harvards was enough to shatter the eardrums. By the time war the war started, Weston-on-the-Green was an active satellite of Brize Norton. No. 101 Squadron's Blenheims were scattered at Brize, and the resident FTS was equipped with Harvards and Oxfords.

CARDINGTON 3 MILES SOUTH-EAST OF BEDFORD

In 1930 Cardington was already famous for being home to the airship and the government-sponsored R101, which was to meet a tragic end when it crashed into a hillside close to Beauvais in northern France on 5 October 1930. Although its rival, the private-venture R100, was successful in its flight to Canada, the loss of the R101 spelt the end for big airship design in Britain, and Cardington's primary role. Although the Royal Airship Works remained in name only until 1938, without the airship work the station was placed on Care and Maintenance. Then, in 1933, No. 2 Aircraft Storage Unit was established, supplying aircraft to the RAF until 1938. A station headquarters was formed on 15 December 1936, by which time the Royal Airship Works had become the Balloon Development Establishment, and on 9 January 1937 No. 1 Balloon Training Unit was formed to train barrage balloon handlers to control the barrages and ground equipment. When the ASU left, the BDE was renamed the Balloon Development Unit. In September 1937, No. 2 RAF Depot arrived from Henlow to give basic recruit training. In 1939 the station passed from Training Command to Balloon Command, and the Recruit Depot became a lodger unit of Training Command.

CASTLE BROMWICH 4 MILES ENE OF BIRMINGHAM

The links that Castle Bromwich had with aviation go back to 1911. In 1930, No. 605 (County of Warwick) Auxiliary Air Force Squadron was re-equipped with Wapitis. The airfield was also used by Railway Air Services, and the Great Western Railway ran flights from there to Cardiff. In April 1934 the Midland and Scottish Air Ferries introduced a service to Liverpool. No. 605 Squadron went on to replace its Wapitis with Harts, and then Hinds. Early in 1937 a big 'make-over' of the station was announced, and the Auxiliaries got a new HQ building, while the station acquired a new C-Type

hangar. The station was then required to house No. 14 ERFTS to train pilots of the RAFVR, to be followed by a unit of the Civil Air Guard, which remained at Castle Bromwich after No. 14 ERFTS had moved to Elmdom in 1939. No. 605 Squadron was then informed that it would become a fighter squadron. In May 1939 the scheduled air services were switched to Birmingham, and at the outbreak of war No. 605 Squadron moved to Tangmere, to be replaced by an assortment of ground units. Castle Bromwich was also famous for producing Spitfires during the war, and 33,919 test flights were made from the station.

CRANFIELD 8 MILES SW OF BEDFORD

A station headquarters was opened on 1 June 1937, and exactly one month later so was the airfield. It came under No. 1 Group, Bomber Command, and No. 108 Squadron, equipped with Hinds, came from Farnborough on 7 July, and the next day the Hinds of No. 82 Squadron arrived from Andover. When No. 62 Squadron arrived on 12 July, it gave the station a complement of thirty-six Hind aircraft. No. 62 Squadron was then equipped with Blenheim Is in February 1938 before the unit's departure for the Far East and Tengah in the following August. No. 108 Squadron had to go to Bassingbourne for re-equipment with Blenheims, and the squadron departed on 2 May 1938. No. 82 Squadron was also equipped with Blenheim Is, and they departed for Watton on 22 August 1938. Two days later the Anson Is and Battles of No. 207 Squadron arrived from Cottesmore. This unit was disbanded on 19 April 1940. Finally before the outbreak of war, No. 35 Squadron arrived from Cottesmore with Anson Is on 25 August.

ELMDON 7 MILES ESE OF BIRMINGHAM

The airport at Elmdon served Birmingham and was officially opened by HRH Duchess of Kent on 8 January 1939. From 1 May No. 44 E & RFTS was operated by Airwork Ltd. The unit was established with Hawker Hinds. On the outbreak of war Nos 14 and 44 E & RFTS amalgamated to become No. 14 EFTS, which was established on 7 September 1939, a unit in No. 53 Group.

HALTON 2 MILES N OF WENDOVER

Halton remains one of the oldest of RAF stations. Today (2007) it is the RAFs recruit training depot, but the station is most famous for its association with apprentice training, started in the period immediately after the Great War to be the bedrock of Trenchard's peacetime air force. With the 1930s expansion, extra buildings were constructed to house a growing number of apprentices. Halton was also home to an RAF hospital, which was opened in 1927, and in 1935, the RAF Pathological Laboratory, which had moved from Finchley in 1925, and was renamed the Institute of Pathology and Tropical Medicine. A fourth unit at Halton was the Medical

Training Establishment. (For further details of the Apprentice Training Scheme see Chapter 8.)

HARWELL 5 MILES S OF ABINGDON

In April 1935 it was decided to turn a night landing ground into a bomber station, and construction commenced in June. *The Times* reported that 200 acres had been acquired for £11,650, and it was handed over to the RAF in February 1937 ready for the arrival of No. 226 Squadron's Audaxes, which arrived on 16 April 1937. Later that month No. 105 Squadron re-formed at Harwell, also with Audaxes. Both squadrons used these Army Cooperation aircraft, due to the shortage of bombers. Indeed this was the value of all the Hart derivatives in the early to mid-1930s, in that Hawkers could produce them relatively cheaply to help the Air Ministry to keep units up to a nominal strength until the monoplanes came off the production lines. The total bomber squadron complement of the station was raised to three with the arrival of No. 107 Squadron's Hinds on 14 June. On 18 August 1937 the first of the Battles arrived to equip No. 105 Squadron. King George VI and the Chief of the Air Staff, Air Chief Marshal Sir Cyril Newall, visited Harwell on 9 May 1938, to be met by the AOC-in-C, Bomber Command, Sir Edgar Ludlow-Hewitt. In August Blenheims arrived for No. 107 Squadron. Both Nos 105 and 226 Squadrons had Battle Is, and since these squadrons had been selected to join the Advanced Air Striking Force on mobilization, it was decided to exchange these aircraft for Cottesmore's Battle IIs of Nos 35 and 207 Squadrons. (The Air Ministry wanted the Battles earmarked to go to France to have the Merlin II engines.) In the winter of 1938/9 the airfield became a quagmire, and netting and cinders were tried but to no avail. In May 1939 No. 107 Squadron's Blenheims went to Wattisham, and on 2 September the Harwell Battles left for France.

HENLOW 5 MILES NNW OF HITCHIN

It was Henlow's airmen who pulled the ill-fated R101 from its shed in October 1930 for its flight to India, and it was the same men who lined the streets of Bedford for the funeral of some of those who died in the disaster at Beauvais, in France. Henlow may also be remembered for one of its famous pupils who went on to design the jet engine, Flying Officer Frank Whittle. Whittle joined the engineering course in August 1932, and shortly afterwards he went to Cambridge for a two-year graduate course. With the expansion under way, there was a growing need for ground technicians, and the Home Aircraft Depot became a school for airframe riggers. No. 1 Wing trained machine-tool operators and Fitter I tradesmen, and Nos 2 and 3 Wings trained flight riggers and flight mechanics. With the growth in the number of trainees it became necessary to erect new accommodation in the north-west of the station. On 15 March 1937 No. 80 Squadron had to move temporarily to Henlow from Kenley, pending re-equipment with the

Gladiator, such was the bottleneck in accommodation brought on by the rate of expansion. From Henlow No. 80 Squadron moved on to Debden. In January 1937 training was extended to MT drivers, followed by training in cookery. To relieve the pressure on the RAF Depot, an initial training unit (ITU) was set up to introduce over 1,000 men to life in the RAF. By this time the pressure was on Henlow, and the domestic accommodation was insufficient to cater for the station's needs. New trainees had to sleep in tents until the ITU was moved to Cardington, where huts had been erected. By 1938 there were 5,000 trainees at Henlow and the station's repair role had gone. Henlow then comprised the Parachute Training Unit, the RAF School of Aeronautical Engineering, three training wings, the MT Training School and the Pilotless Aircraft Section. The plan for the station's future was that, in war, it should revert to its repair role, and in September 1938 a large part of the training wings moved to St Athan in South Wales. This allowed for the establishment of No. 2 Mobilization Pool, which would undertake repair, and in October 1938 the Home Aircraft Depot became No. 13 MU in the reorganization of supply. No. 1 Training Wing then moved to Halton in Buckinghamshire.

KIDLINGTON 6 MILES NW OF OXFORD

Kidlington came into RAF use in 1938 with the opening of No. 26 E & RFTS on 24 June. It was equipped with Audaxes and Hinds until the unit closed on the outbreak of war. Kidlington then acted as Abingdon's satellite.

LITTLE RISSINGTON 4 MILES S OF STOW-ON-THE-WOLD

This station was very much a Cotswold creation, and the characteristic stone of the area was used in some of the buildings. It sat on a 750 ft plateau, looking down on the beautiful houses in the village from which it took its name. Between 20 and 25 August 1938 No. 6 SFTS moved from Netheravon, bringing with it Harts and Audaxes. Furies and Ansons would be added later, together with Harvards in June 1939. The station also housed No. 8 MU, handling Spitfires and Wellingtons from October 1938, and on the day war broke out there were 268 aircraft in storage. It was then that No. 215 Squadron's Wellingtons scattered to the station. No. 6 SFTS had an Intermediate Squadron that took pilots from elementary training and raised them to a standard where they could proceed to operational training units, hence the mix of training aircraft. Operational training could be on bomber, fighter, reconnaissance or transport types.

PETERBOROUGH (WESTWOOD) 2 MILES NW OF THE CITY

No. 7 SFTS formed at Peterborough on 2 December 1935, equipped with seventeen Hawker Harts, to be joined the following February by Avro Tutors, Furies and Audaxes.

The first course for trainees pilots began on January 1936. The Advanced Training Squadron took the trainees through applied flying techniques, which included formation flying and tactics, together with weapon training. Four multi-engined training Oxfords arrived on the station in the New Year of 1937. Just before the outbreak of war, between May and July 1939, the station was at half strength and could afford to take on pilot training for the Fleet Air Arm.

SOUTH CERNEY 3 MILES SE OF CIRENCESTER

South Cerney was built in 1936/7 to house No. 3 SFTS. The move of this flying training school had become necessary because its previous location in Lincolnshire had put the training aircraft in airspace populated by operational aircraft. The urgency given to the move was such that when the advanced party arrived to take over the station on 16 August 1937, only one aircraft shed was ready to accommodate the Audax trainers. This was room to house only the aircraft of the Intermediate Training Squadron, and the aircraft of the Advanced Training Squadron had to remain in the open until the remaining hangars were erected. In the summer of 1937, as one course ended at Grantham, the new course would begin at South Cerney. A hangar fire on 3 October 1937 did not help the situation. Fortunately only one Audax was damaged, but it did nothing to relieve the accommodation shortage. At this time the station was training on biplanes, and it was not until 14 June 1938 that the first Oxford arrived and training on monoplanes could commence. Three days later more Oxfords began to arrive, and the re-equipment was sufficient by the end of the following month for No. 24 Course to commence on 25 July. By the end of September re-equipment of the training squadrons was complete, and advanced flying training on Oxfords continued until the end of the war in 1945.

SYWELL 6 MILES NE OF NORTHAMPTON

Sywell was one of those civil airfields to which the RAF came by way of contracted-out elementary flying training. On 10 June 1935 pilot training began on DH60s, then Tiger Moths. In April 1937 Hart Variants were added for RAFVR pilot training, and three Ansons arrived for the training of air observers and air gunners. When the E & RFTS schools were disbanded on the outbreak of war, *ab initio* pilot training was undertaken by No. 6 EFTS with twenty-five Tiger Moths and sixteen flying instructors, the observer and navigator training switching to No. 8 Civil Air Navigation School. No. 6 EFTS lost its civilian status when the flying instructors were called up for RAF service.

UPPER HEYFORD 5 MILES NW OF BICESTER

Upper Heyford had reopened as a bomber station on 12 October 1927. At the beginning of the 1930s the station housed two bomber squadrons, No. 99 with Hinaidis and No. 10 with the older Hyderabads. The first Hinaidis did not reach No. 10 Squadron until 9 December 1930. On 1 April the following year No. 40 Squadron arrived with Fairey Gordons, and No. 10 Squadron moved to Boscombe Down. On 20 October 1931 No. 18 Squadron was re-formed and equipped with Hawker Harts, the re-equipment being complete by the end of March 1932. On 5 September No. 57 Squadron, also with Harts, came to Upper Heyford, and No. 40 Squadron then left for Abingdon when space was made available in October 1932. No. 99 Squadron had to keep its Hyderabads until 14 November 1933, when the first Heyfords to enter service arrived. These strange-looking aircraft provided the crew with a real test of agility to get to their crew positions, for the fuselage was attached to the upper wing, and access was gained by stepping onto the lower wing and then climbing a narrow ladder up into the fuselage. When the pilot and gunner finally got into their lofty seats, they at least had a fine view of the local countryside. A year after this re-equipment, No. 99 Squadron moved to Mildenhall, which made room at Upper Heyford for No. 33 Squadron from Bicester. With the reorganization of the RAF in 1936, the station found itself in No. 1 Group. No. 57 Squadron was repeatedly plundered as new squadrons were formed. No. 113 Squadron formed on 18 May 1937, only to go to Grantham in August. In January 1938 the Long-Range Development Flight was formed and equipped with five specially modified Vickers Wellesleys, and in April 1938 No. 57 Squadron began training on the Blenheim Is. In the following months No. 18 Squadron also received this light bomber, and when No. 34 Squadron arrived from Lympne the station could boast three Blenheim squadrons. But in January 1939 No. 34 Squadron moved to Watton. As war approached, the two Blenheim I squadrons that remained were earmarked for a role within No. 70 Wing, the Air Component of the British Expeditionary Force, to provide aerial reconnaissance for the British Army in France.

WESTON-ON-THE-GREEN 3¹/₂ MILES SW OF BICESTER

The use of Weston-on-the-Green dates back to the Great War. On 27 July 1918 No. 28 Training Depot formed at the airfield, but was closed shortly after the war's end. Units either passed through or came to disband, and then all activity ceased. It is believed to have remained in the RAF's hands, but the field was turned over to grazing. Just before the outbreak of war in 1939 it became a satellite of Brize Norton. When war was imminent the 'scatter' plan was initiated, and No. 90 Squadron brought its Blenheims to Weston. It can lay claim to have been the first airfield in Oxfordshire to have received the attention of the *Luftwaffe*, when bombs were dropped on 9 August 1940.

WITTERING

From the A1, which passes the airfield, the land slopes upwards to a plateau so that one cannot observe aircraft movements from the road. This was always a source of annoyance to the author, who passed daily on his way to Stamford School in the 1940s and could not get a glimpse of aerial activity. The station was first called Stamford, which was put on Care and Maintenance at the end of the Great War, but with the modest expansion plan announced in 1923, Wittering was resurrected to house the Central Flying School, which was moved from Upavon. On 14 May 1938 No. 11 FTS left, since it was the policy to move training to the West Midlands, the Cotswolds and the North-West, leaving the Eastern Counties for the location of operational squadrons. Wittering was to become a fighter station, and two days later No. 23 Squadron came from Northolt with Demons, to be re-equipped with Blenheim Is in December 1938. On 18 May 1938 No. 213 Squadron arrived from Church Fenton with Gauntlet IIs, and in June the following year converted to Hurricane Is.

AIRFIELDS, SEAPLANE BASES AND MISCELLANEOUS UNITS IN CENTRAL-SOUTH AND SOUTH-EAST ENGLAND

ANDOVER   2¹/₂ MILES W OF ANDOVER ON THE A303

This station, opened in the Great War, was one of the few in the south-east to be saved in the rapid rundown of the RAF following the Armistice. It was formed as a station on 1 April 1925 and came under Wessex Bombing Area in 1926. As the station moved into the 1930s it had two bombing squadrons, No. 101 with Sidestrands and No. 12 with Harts. As a result of the Wessex Area bombing trials, the Air Pilotage School was re-formed on the station on 5 May 1933. In the October the Wessex Bombing Area was split into two, and Andover, Boscombe Down and Worthy Down came under the new Western Area. On 1 December 1934 No. 101 Squadron moved to Bicester, and in January of the following year the Air Navigation School was formed. Two days later the Harts of No. 142 Squadron flew in from Netheravon, where the squadron had been re-formed. Thus, with two Hart squadrons on the station these aircraft settled into the hangars vacated by No. 101 Squadron, but in October of that year both Nos 12 and 142 Squadrons were on their way to the Middle East in response to the Abyssinian crisis, not to return to Andover until the following year. In their absence two heavy-bomber squadrons moved into the station. These were Nos 9 and 214 Squadrons with Virginia Xs. The year 1936 saw more changes, with the introduction of the new command structure in the RAF, and on 1 May Western Area became No. 3 (Bomber) Group. Meanwhile the Air Navigation School moved to Manston and additional brick-built

accommodation was constructed. This was doubly necessary when Nos 103 and 107 Squadrons were re-formed at the station with Hind day-bombers. In January 1937 No. 3 Group moved its HQ to Mildenhall, and No. 2 Group, responsible for the light bombers, moved from Abingdon. Accordingly the heavy bombers moved out, No. 9 to Aldergrove and No. 214 to Scampton. No. 103 Squadron went to Usworth and No. 107 Squadron to Old Sarum, leaving the original occupants in occupation, namely Nos 12 and 142 Squadrons. Together with the Staff College, these units were the residents of the station, and in February and March 1938 the two squadrons were re-equipped with Battles, and the aircrews had to learn to cope with retractable undercarriages and variable-pitch propellers. When No. 2 Group HQ moved to Wyton, Andover found itself for a while under No. 1 Group. The Munich Crisis brought preparations for airfield defence and dispersal, involving the siting of gun positions and the digging of slit trenches. In July 1938 HQ Maintenance Command moved to Andover, beginning a long association with the station. With the expectation of war, Nos 12 and 142 Squadrons were formed into No. 76 Bomber Wing. The Munich Crisis passed but preparations for war continued. With the expansion of Maintenance Command, No. 40 Group formed on the station, while No. 41 Group took up residence in buildings on the Weyhill Road, Andover. In May 1939 Andover was transferred from Bomber to Fighter Command, and the two Battle squadrons moved out to be replaced by Hectors and Blenheims of No. 59 Squadron, the operating unit of No. 51 (AC) Wing. On the day war was declared, HQ No. 42 Group was formed on the station, the Staff College closed and No. 51 (AC) Wing was warned to stand by for operations in France.

BEKESBOURNE   KENT, 4 MILES SE OF CANTERBURY

Bekesbourne had been an active fighter station in the Great War, but when the RAF relinquished it in 1919 the airfield became Canterbury Aerodrome. During the 1930s the Kent Flying Club was active at Bekesbourne, and a section of the Civil Guard was established there in 1938. On the outbreak of war in 1939 the airfield was closed, although it saw brief service as a forward landing-ground for aircraft operating across to France. The airfield was finally abandoned after the Dunkirk evacuation.

DETLING   KENT, 4 MILES NE OF MAIDSTONE ON THE A249

Like Bekesbourne, Detling had been another active fighter station in the Great War, but after the war the airfield was returned to farmland, only to be reopened under the 1934 expansion. The standard technical and domestic sites were built by Binbury Manor, and the grass airfield was extended to provide a 1,400 yd

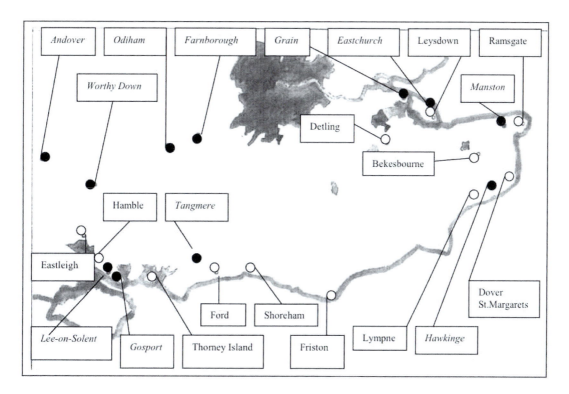

NE–SW runway. The station was reopened on 14 September 1938 in No. 6 (Auxiliary) Group of Bomber Command. No. 500 (County of Kent) Squadron was then moved from Manston on 28 September, equipped with Hinds. Another transfer occurred on 1 November when Detling was placed under No. 16 Group of Coastal Command, and No. 500 Squadron was accordingly equipped with Ansons in March 1939. The unit became a general reconnaissance squadron, and the Auxiliaries had to become accustomed to two engines and a retractable undercarriage. The Ansons were proudly shown off on Empire Day, and on the outbreak of war were employed on convoy escort duties.

DOVER (ST MARGARETS) KENT, SWINGATE

The clutch of stations surrounding Dover had been active during the Great War, but were not reactivated during the Second World War. Only the site at Dover St Margarets was used from 1938 for the erection of one of the latticed towers of the operational chain of home radar stations that remained in operation until after the war had ended.

EASTCHURCH ISLE OF SHEPPEY, 1½ MILES S OF EASTCHURCH VILLAGE

Eastchurch dates back to before the Great War, and was active during and after that war. In 1930 this well-established station housed No. 33 Squadron and the Armament and Gunnery School. In January 1932 this was renamed the Air Armament School and was joined

by the Coastal Defence Cooperation Flight, a lodger unit of No. 22 Group. When this unit moved to Gosport in the May, the AAS expanded. With the formation of a separate Armament Group on 1 February 1936, Eastchurch became the Group HQ. In November 1936 a station flight of aircraft was formed to enable staff officers to travel to inspect the armament practice camps. On 1 November 1937 the Air Armament School was renamed No. 1 AAS, allowing for the formation of No. 2 AAS in July 1938. Then, on 15 August 1938, No. 1 AAS was moved to RAF Manby. That same day No. 21 Squadron arrived from Lympne to convert from Hinds to Blenheims. A fortnight later the Ansons of No 48 Squadron arrived from Manston, from a training role to one of general reconnaissance. In November 1938 Eastchurch was transferred to No. 16 Group, Coastal Command, and so No. 21 Squadron and No. 1 AAS became lodger units. In March 1939 No. 21 Squadron moved to Watton and No. 48 Squadron went to its war station at Thorney Island. Then No. 2 AAS moved to Pembrey, which temporarily left Eastchurch without any units, and two days before the outbreak of war the station was placed on Care and Maintenance. It was not long, however, before the station was again operational.

EASTLEIGH HAMPSHIRE, 1½ MILES S OF EASTLEIGH TOWN ON THE A335

Eastleigh was another station that predated the Great War and saw service in that war. The station was closed in 1920. Not until 1929 did Eastleigh look like becoming an airfield again when the Southampton authorities looked for a site for a municipal airport. Work was put in hand, and the official opening took place in November 1932. Jersey Airways and Railway Air Services operated services from Eastleigh during the mid-1930s, and then the Air Ministry negotiated with Southampton Corporation for the use of part of the airfield by the Fleet Air Arm. In July 1935 the Audaxes of Nos 4 and 13 Squadrons held a summer camp there. Wooden buildings and Bessoneaux hangars were erected for the ground crews looking after the squadron aircraft disembarked from aircraft-carriers, and RAF Eastleigh became RAF Southampton on 1 August 1936. With the worsening international situation, the original three-year agreement, which limited the use of the airfield to twenty weeks a year, was reviewed, and the restrictions on use were dropped. RAF squadrons, such as those taking part in Spitshead Review in May 1937, were also able to use the facilities, and the airfield was open to the public during Empire Air Day. In April 1938 the Air Ministry became responsible for air traffic facilities, and Supermarine was busy assembling Spitfires in Hangars 1 and 2. Another name change came on 1 July 1939, when the airfield was commissioned as HMS *Raven*, having been transferred from the Air Ministry to the Admiralty.

FARNBOROUGH HAMPSHIRE, 2 MILES NW OF ALDERSHOT ON THE A325

No British airfield can be more famous than Farnborough. Its part in the formation of the RAF is well charted, and in July 1918 the Royal Aircraft Factory was renamed the Royal Aircraft Establishment, which was then set upon the road of research. At the end of the decade the facilities at the RAE were improved, including a seaplane test tank and wind tunnel enabling full-scale tests on both aircraft and engines. Considerable practical test work was carried out on flight refuelling between 1931 and 1938. Pressurized flying suits and breathing equipment were developed as part of the trials in 1936, using a Bristol 138A monoplane, and Squadron Leader F.R.D. Swain gained a new World Altitude Record of 49,967 feet during a two-hour flight. When the Italians gained a new world record, Flight Lieutenant M.J. Adams regained the record by reaching an altitude of 53,937 feet. On 10 July 1936 the station was transferred to No. 24 Group. During the next two years No. 4 Squadron ended its long stay at Farnborough and moved to Odiham. No. 53 (AC) Squadron, a specialist night reconnaissance unit, moved in, but it too moved to Odiham. No. 1 Anti-Aircraft Unit (AACU) moved in from Biggin Hill, and two new Wallace-equipped flights were formed. On 1 June 1938 the station reverted to No. 22 Group. The two Wallace flights moved around according to the requirements of the armament practice camps, and during the winter of 1938/9 pilots of the AACU were converting to the latest target tower, the

Henley. Farnborough entered the war with the RAE and the School of Photography as a lodger unit.

FORD WEST SUSSEX, 2¹/₂ MILES W OF LITTLEHAMPTON ON THE A2024

This Great War station was closed in 1920, and flying did not return until 1930, when DW Aviation renovated two of the hangars to produce biplanes. That plan came to nought, and the Ford Motor Company leased the airfield from July 1931 as a maintenance base for the sales of its trimotor aircraft. With the demise of the Ford operation in 1934, Sir Alan Cobham made the airfield his HQ, and he established Flight Refuelling Ltd for development work, using the AW 23 and HP 51 prototype bomber transports. He later prepared two Harrows for refuelling trials, aimed at getting the Short C flying-boats across the Atlantic non-stop. In 1936 the Air Ministry acquired the airfield, and £109,000 was allowed in the Air Estimates for the building of a hutted camp and hangars, and additional land was purchased to the east of the original airfield. The station officially opened on 1 December 1937, in No. 17 (Training) Group of Coastal Command, and the School of Naval Cooperation moved from Lee-on-Solent equipped with Sharks and Swordfish. When the Fleet Air Arm gained its independence from the RAF in 1938, Ford was transferred to the Admiralty, commissioned as HMS *Peregrine*, and the training unit was renamed the RN Observer School. Thus Ford as an RAF station in the 1930s had a very short life, although the FAA withdrew after the devastating raid of 18 August 1940. Ford then returned to the RAF and No. 11 Group of Fighter Command on 30 September 1940.

FRISTON EAST SUSSEX, 4¹/₂ MILES W OF EASTBOURNE OFF THE A259

This private landing ground was used by Hawker Audax Army Cooperation machines of Nos 2 and 4 Squadrons for exercises with an Army brigade during August and September 1936, and may have been used by Auxiliary Air Force camps, but then lay dormant until designated a Fighter Command ELG during the summer of 1940.

GOSPORT HAMPSHIRE, 4 MILES W OF PORTSMOUTH OFF THE A32

This Great War airfield was retained after the Armistice as a torpedo school. Various other units came and went during the 1920s, but it was not until 1930 that improvements were made to the accommodation. Permanent hangars began to replace the wooden sheds on the eastern boundary, and new barrack blocks enabled the men to move out of the two dreary forts in April 1930. Training then included Army and Naval Cooperation, telegraphist and air gunner training, torpedo and deck landing. In May 1932 the Coast

Defence Cooperation Flight arrived from Eastchurch with Fairey IIIFs, only to be renamed the Coast Defence Training Flight. Three months later two more of these flights were formed at Gosport, and they were numbered one to three. In April 1933 the FAA flights, which had always been numbered in the 400 series, were now amalgamated into squadrons that were logically numbered in the 800 series, e.g. Nos 442 and 449 Flights became No. 821 Squadron. In October 1934 two of the training flights went to Lee-on-Solent. These were the Army and Navy Cooperation and Telegraphist Air Gunner Training Flights. This left the Torpedo Training Flight, the Torpedo Experimental Flight and the Deck-Landing Flight at Gosport. In April 1935 the Gosport Base officially became RAF Station Gosport, and the aforementioned Coast Defence Training Flights were amalgamated to become the Coast Defence Development Unit, but this unit was disbanded in December 1936, leaving only No. 1 Coast Artillery Cooperation Flight in operation; No. 17 Group then moved to the station and was joined by No. 2 AACU, equipped with Blackburn Skuas. As war broke out Gosport was home to HQ No. 17 Group, No. 1 AACU, No. 2 AACU, Storage Unit and Torpedo Section.

HAMBLE HAMPSHIRE, 4 MILES SE OF SOUTHAMPTON

Although Hamble is best remembered for aircraft production, notably by the Fairey and Avro companies, it was also home to Reserve Air Force units in the 1930s. Under an Air Ministry rationalization plan the Reserve School became No. 3 E & RFTS in April 1935. Civilian registered aircraft were retained for training purposes by Air Service Training Ltd, who ran the school, and during 1935 used twelve Avro Tutors and seventeen Avro Cadets. A total of 8,828 flying hours were devoted to RAF training that year. When the school undertook navigation training in 1937, two Cutty Sark amphibians and some redundant civil air transports were pressed into service. Further expansion in 1938 of the school's activities included advanced training with Hinds and Battles and Army Cooperation training. When VR training ceased on the outbreak of war, the unit was redesignated No. 3 EFTS, equipped with thirty-two Cadets and two Link trainers, and in training personnel there were twenty-nine qualified flying instructors (QFIs) and eight ground instructors.

HAWKINGE KENT, 2 MILES N OF FOLKESTONE ON THE A260

This active Great War airfield was retained as a fighter station in the peacetime RAF. From 1930 Hawkinge was used for Auxiliary and Reserve squadron summer camps, and from 1931 to 1933 a rebuilding programme was put in hand. This included the construction of married quarters, NAAFI, an education block, two

airmen's barrack blocks, officers' and sergeants' messes and an airmen's dining hall. The work was virtually completed when there was a setback. On 7 August 1933 No. 4 Hangar, which housed six Blackburn Darts, was set ablaze and completely gutted. The fire had been started following an accident involving a Horsley of No. 504 Squadron. This aircraft was on the approach to the airfield when the engine suddenly lost power. The pilot could not avoid the hangar, which was directly in his path, and managed to put the aircraft down on the roof. He and his crewman managed to scramble clear, but the escaping fuel caught fire with the resultant loss described. On 3 November 1935 No. 2 (AC) Squadron moved from Manston to Hawkinge. An SHQ was formed and the station transferred to No. 22 Group of Inland Area. The Audaxes of this unit were soon involved in almost non-stop Army Cooperation work. During the Munich Crisis the station buildings were darkened with camouflage paint, the defence scheme activated and No. 25 Squadron moved to its war station. Meanwhile No. 2 Squadron, which by then had changed to Hectors, was busy converting again, this time to Lysanders. When the crisis passed, No. 25 Squadron returned from its war station and began converting to Blenheims. Once equipped with the night-fighter version it was decided to move the squadron to Northolt since Hawkinge was too small a grass airfield for operating such aircraft as the Blenheim if the grass was wet. This move took place on 22 August 1939. No. 2 Squadron made its planned move to France shortly after the outbreak of war and the station was transferred to Training Command as No. 3 Recruit Training Pool. In 1940, however, the station was to revert to Fighter Command.

LEE-ON-SOLENT HAMPSHIRE, 2½ MILES NW OF GOSPORT

Lee-on-Solent was active during the Great War and was retained in the much-reduced peacetime RAF. The station was very active during the 1920s, with units in a variety of roles. One such unit was the Schools' Cooperation Flight, which completed conversion to Fairey IIIFs in February 1930, followed by the reborn Floatplane Training Flight in June 1931. On 18 January 1932 No. 10 Group was disbanded and HQ Coastal Area moved from Central London to the station. When more land was purchased behind the seaplane hangars, work started on the construction of an aerodrome complete with administrative and technical buildings and new barrack blocks. On completion of construction the airfield was taken over from the AMWD (Air Ministry Works Department) on 25 October 1934, and two Queen Bee drones, destined for HMS *Achilles*, were the first to land. The School of Naval Cooperation was then reorganized, involving some of the Gosport units. Since A Flight at Lee-on-Solent was then to undertake seaplane and landplane training, three Moths and six Fairey IIIFs were absorbed from its opposite number at Gosport. B Flight at Lee-on-Solent would undertake naval observer training, and for this purpose the flight was formed from No. 2 (Training) Flight. Then Gosport's B Flight, with its five Faireys, five Seals and a Blackburn Ripon, became C Flight at Lee-on-Solent and undertook telegraphist air gunner training. Finally, on 15 July 1935 D Flight was formed to train air observers' mates. These training commitments put Lee-on-Solent under pressure, and it was to decided to move the Ospreys of Nos 407 and 444 Flights to Mount Batten in June 1935. Then the old Coastal Area that had been around since the Great War became Coastal Command in July 1936, and the Group HQs of No. 16 (Reconnaissance) Group and No. 17 (Training) Group were formed at the station in the December, and No. 1 Gunnery Cooperation Flight became No. 2 AACU. It was not long before the School of Naval Cooperation was again reorganized, and the new training flights had between eight and ten Blackburn Sharks on strength. On 1 January 1938 the school went to Ford. This left the SHQ Lee-on-Solent to administer the remaining diverse units on the station and a number of FAA squadrons. There was the addition of more technical and domestic accommodation on the station, including a ten-bay C-Type hangar. When No. 18 Group was formed at the station it meant that three Group HQs were sharing the station with operational and training units. The cramped situation did not last long, however, for HQ No. 16 Group moved to Chatham, while HQ No. 18 Group went to Donibristle, leaving HQ No. 17 Group to share the station with Command HQ, the Communications Flight, the Floatplane Training Flight, which moved from Calshot in April 1938, the Fleet Requirements Unit, Storage Unit and No. 2 AACU. In March 1939 HQ No. 15 Group formed on the station. With the absorption of the FAA into the Royal Navy, Lee-on-Solent was one of the stations transferred to the Admiralty, and it was commissioned as HMS *Daedalus* on 24 May 1939, which had been the title given to Cranwell before it became the RAF Cadet College. This meant moving out all the purely RAF formations, and so HQ No. 15 Group went to Plymouth in June 1939, while HQ No. 17 Group moved to nearby Gosport. Lee-on-Solent then became home to the Flag Officer (Air) Home having under command familiar ex-RAF stations that had become naval shore stations, namely Donibristle (HMS *Merlin*), Eastleigh (HMS *Raven*), Worthy Down (HMS *Kestrel*) and Ford (HMS *Peregrine*). Additionally under command was Bermuda (HMS *Malabar*). HQ Coastal Command moved out on 7 August 1939.

LEYSDOWN ISLE OF SHEPPEY, ½ MILE SE OF LEYSDOWN-ON-SEA ON MINOR ROAD

The Pilots and Observers' Aerial Gunnery and Aerial Fighting School (SE) rapidly ran down and was closed in 1919, but Leysdown remained open to administer ranges used by aircraft from Eastchurch. The grass landing-strips were kept clear for emergency landings by aircraft using the ranges, and this situation continued throughout the Second World War.

LYMPNE KENT, 2½ MILES W OF HYTHE ON THE B2067

It was not until 1936, with RAF expansion in mind, that the RAF returned to this Great War airfield. Lympne had been used for summer camps by Nos 600 and 601 Auxiliary Squadrons. On 28 October 1936 the airfield was reactivated as a temporary No. 1 (Bomber) Group station, and on 3 November, Hind day-bombers of Nos 21 and 34 Squadrons flew in and a SHQ was formed. Although the old Great War sheds had gone, the remaining Belfast hangars were still usable, and temporary living accommodation was provided for personnel. It had been intended to transfer the station to No. 2 (Bomber) Group, but in December 1937 this was deferred as the Hinds flew off, No. 34 squadron to Upper Heyford on 12 July 1938, and No. 21 Squadron to Eastchurch on 15 August, reducing Lympne to Care and Maintenance on 1 October. In spite of Lympne's excellent forward position it was not reopened as a fighter station but as a No. 24 Group School of Clerks Accounting in Training Command on 17 October. This was rectified on 24 May 1939, when Lympne was transferred to Fighter Command, only to be transferred to the Admiralty as HMS *Buzzard* on 1 July.

MANSTON KENT, 2 MILES W OF RAMSGATE OFF THE A253

Manston had uninterrupted RNAS/RFC/RAF service from 1915, and by January 1930 was a No. 23 Group station. That month AW Atlases arrived to replace the Virginias of No. 9 Squadron that had gone to Boscombe Down, but these very large bombers were again seen over Manston when No. 500 (County of Kent) Squadron was formed on 1 March 1931. The mayors of Margate and Ramsgate christened the first Virginia X to arrive the 'Isle of Thanet', in a ceremony on 4 June. This squadron, manned partly by Regulars and partly by Reservists, soon attracted local volunteers, and by mid-1932 the unit had six Virginias and two Avro 504 training aircraft. On 1 October 1932 the station was transferred to No. 22 Group, Inland Area, and the first Empire Day, held in May 1934, attracted 6,000 people to Manston. Two months later Nos 500, 501 and 503 Squadrons gathered at Manston to provide an Auxiliary bomber force for Southland in the annual air exercises. These Auxiliary squadrons joined with Regular squadrons on Salisbury Plain to oppose the fighters of Northland from Biggin Hill and North Weald. On 1 July 1935 the training school for technical tradesmen became No. 3 S of TT. On the flying side No. 2 Squadron departed for Hawkinge, and the Air Pilotage School (Andover) was combined with the Navigation School (Calshott) at Manston in January 1936, and the combined school became the School of Air Navigation. The School used, among other aircraft, the Saro Cloud amphibian. New huts were erected and other buildings converted into billets to house the growing number of station personnel. Also in January 1936 No. 500 Squadron changed its aircraft from Virginias to Harts, thus becoming a light-bomber squadron. When the RAF Reserve was reorganized that year, No. 500 Squadron became an Auxiliary Air Force squadron. The flying unit responsible for providing aircraft for the School of Air Navigation was No. 48 Squadron, and its Clouds, which had not lived up to expectations, were replaced with Anson Is. This was the first RAF aircraft to have a retractable undercarriage. This took 172 turns of a handle to raise or lower it. Although nominally a coastal reconnaissance unit, during its first two years at Manston No. 48 Squadron was able to fulfil its training role as well as carrying out night-flying for the Air Defence Experimental Establishment at Biggin Hill. Only when the School of Air Navigation was equipped with its own aircraft was No. 48 Squadron able to take up its reconnaissance role, and it moved to Eastchurch in September 1938. At the time of the Munich Crisis the number of people at Manston was so great that 700 persons had to live in tents. Like many other stations in the UK at this time, trenches were being dug, aircraft and buildings were being camouflaged, gun positions sited and bomb and ammunition dumps set up. The pressure on accommodation meant that the summer camp for No. 616 Squadron had to be cut short. When general mobilization was ordered on 1 September, the courses run by No. 3 S of TT had to be dispersed, the School of Air Navigation was moved to RAF St Athan and for a few days the station was under Care and Maintenance. It was not long, however, before operational units flew in, and Manston would become heavily involved in the Battle of Britain that was to follow.

ODIHAM HAMPSHIRE, 6¹/₂ MILES ESE OF BASINGSTOKE ALONGSIDE THE A32

During the 1920s Odiham had been used as a landing-ground for summer camp exercises with the Army, but with the RAF expansion of the mid-1930s Odiham was a natural site for a permanent airfield, and a further 150 acres were purchased by the Air Ministry to add to the landing-ground. The firm Lindsey Parkinson Ltd began clearance of the site in 1934 to prepare Odiham to take three squadrons of Army Cooperation aircraft. The three C-Type hangars were complemented by the usual H Blocks and technical and administrative buildings, the whole lot costing £315,000, and RAF Odiham joined No. 22 Group on 3 December 1936. It was the home of No. 50 Army Cooperation Wing. By the middle of February 1937 Nos 4 and 13 Squadrons had completed their move

to the station, and in May, Hectors replaced the Audaxes. The engine of the Hector, the 805 hp Napier Dagger IIIMS, was temperamental, giving a great deal of trouble during the annual round of exercises with the Aldershot Command. These exercises involved reconnaissance, ground strafing, artillery spotting and photography. On 18 October 1937 the station was officially opened by the German Secretary of State for Air, General Erhard Milch. This was the first time this honour had been afforded to a *Luftwaffe* officer, and it was certainly an interesting choice given the worsening international situation with Germany, the expected enemy. On 8 April 1938 No. 53 Squadron arrived, bringing the strength up to the planned three squadrons. In January 1939 it was No. 53 Squadron that received the twin-engined Blenheim IV bombers instead of Lysanders that equipped Nos 4 and 13 Squadrons. The waterlogging of the airfield, which had accompanied the arrival of these two squadrons in 1937, resulted in Odiham becoming one of the first airfields with concrete runways, and these were ready by the spring of 1939. By the end of June No. 53 Squadron had completed conversion to the Blenheim, and in August the entire No. 50 (AC) Wing took part in a mobilization exercise, which then became the real thing on the 23rd of the month. Nos 4 and 13 Squadrons' Lysanders had already been earmarked for service with the British Expeditionary Force, and were ready to go on the outbreak of war.

RAMSGATE KENT, 1¹/₂ MILES N OF RAMSGATE TOWN

Three RAF squadrons held their summer camps at Ramsgate Airport during August 1937, and the resident aero club took part in the Civil Air Guard scheme during 1938. The airport was closed on the outbreak of war but was soon back in use as a 'scatter' airfield until permanently obstructed after the Battle of Britain.

ROCHFORD ESSEX, 2 MILES S OF SOUTHEND OFF THE B1013

This very active Great War airfield was closed in 1920 and the land released for agriculture. The site was returned to flying in 1933 when Southend Council purchased the field to bring it up to licensed aerodrome standard. By the time the airport was officially opened in September 1935, the two resident airlines were losing money. When they withdrew, only the flying club and private owners remained, and the airport had to rely on flying displays and rallies for income. During the summer of 1937 No. 602 Squadron's Hinds were flown down to Rochford from Glasgow for their annual camp, and were followed by No. 607 (County of Durham) Squadron. The squadron's Demon two-seat fighters were inspected by Air Marshal Sir Hugh Dowding, AOC-in-C Fighter Command. No. 34 E & RFTS was formed at the airport early in 1939 as a unit in the Volunteer Reserve, operated by Air Hire Ltd. Tiger

Moths, Harts and a few Ansons were used until No. 50 Group closed the unit down on 1 September 1939, the aircraft going to the other FTSs. On 11 August 1939 No. 54 Squadron took part in a practice evacuation of Hornchurch, when its aircraft were flown to Rochford, for it was to become a forward satellite airfield.

SHOREHAM WEST SUSSEX, I MILE NW OF SHOREHAM-BY-SEA

Shoreham's use as an airfield dates back to 1911, and it was active during the Great War. In December 1921 the airfield was closed and returned to grazing, but in the early 1930s the local authorities of Brighton, Hove and Worthing got together with a local airport in mind, and an airport committee was formed. After purchase of further land, construction went ahead and the airport terminal building was opened on 13 June 1936. With RAF expansion in mind there was an increased need for pilot-training facilities, and the Martin School of Air Navigation received a contract for training pilots of the RAF Volunteer Reserve, the School being designated No. 16 E & RFTS. Initially the school was equipped with service Tiger Moths, and later Harts, Hinds and a few Battles. In May 1938 navigation training for bomber pilots was also moved to Shoreham, when the Martin school used Rapide and Dragon biplanes for practical training exercises on a twelve-week course. Then the Air Ministry policy had changed to the effect that bomber crews would have an observer (trained) navigator instead of a pilot who had received specialist navigation training. This work, however, did not remain at Shoreham, since the Air Ministry was not satisfied with the efficiency of Martin's training, and the contract was transferred to Airwork at Staverton, although VR pilot training continued until 1 September 1939, when the E & RFTSs were closed and the aircraft transferred to the EFTSs. In the meantime Shoreham was busy as an international airport until the outbreak of war, when the airfield was requisitioned by the Air Ministry as an advanced airfield in the Kenley Sector of No. 11 Group, Fighter Command.

TANGMERE WEST SUSSEX, 3 MILES E OF CHICHESTER, S OF THE A27 (T)

This active Great War airfield was closed in 1920, but the Air Ministry retained the land and buildings. On 1 June 1925 Tangmere was reactivated and the Coastal Area Storage Unit was opened. A station HQ was formed on 23 November 1926 and the airfield was activated. The station became known for its tropical routine, a day that began at 07.30 hrs and ended at 13.00 hrs, and there was friendly rivalry between the two resident squadrons, Nos 1 and 43. Work on a station uplift was completed in 1930. In May 1931 the 'Fighting Cocks' (No. 43 Squadron) received the Hawker Fury, and No. 1 Squadron, still with its Siskins, could only look on

enviously. With both squadrons showing off at the Hendon Air Display, Tangmere acquired a formidable reputation as a fighter base, and Auxiliary squadrons vied with each other for the privilege of holding their summer camps on the station. In 1937 Nos 72 and 87 Fighter Squadrons were formed in March, followed by No. 233 Squadron in the May, equipped with GR Ansons. When Nos 72 and 87 Squadrons moved out to Church Fenton and Debden respectively in June, another Anson squadron, No. 217, flew in from Boscombe Down. More building work took place, which included barrack blocks and married quarters. In 1938 an asphalt perimeter track was laid and the airfield extended eastwards to increase the maximum take-off run to 4,500 feet. During the Munich Crisis of 1938 the hangars were camouflaged, air raid shelters were constructed and the Furies were painted brown and dark green. As the crisis passed, No. 1 Squadron got Hurricanes in the October and No. 43 Squadron in the November. No. 605 Squadron joined the two resident squadrons on 27 August 1939, for Tangmere was its war station. This unit had six Hurricanes and ten Gladiators, and was there to replace No. 1 Squadron, which was earmarked for service in France.

THORNEY ISLAND HAMPSHIRE, 2 MILES S OF EMSWORTH

When a Hawker Fury crashed in a field close to St Nicholas's Church in September 1933, the accident investigation team reported the potential of the area to the Air Ministry. With the expansion scheme under way, a five-squadron airfield was planned, and a 1,450-acre site was cleared to make way for six C-Type hangars, which, together with the technical and administrative buildings, covered an area north and east of the approach road to West Thorney village. It was not until the end of 1937 that the major construction work was complete, the deadline of August for the station opening having been passed. The station finally opened on 3 February 1938, a station in No. 16 Group of Coastal Command. The following day witnessed the arrival of the Vildebeest III/IVs of No. 22 Squadron that flew in from Donibristle, followed by No. 42 Squadron, which then constituted the whole of the home-based strike force. The station then transferred to No. 17 (Training) Group, and the School of General Reconnaissance was formed there to teach over-sea navigation to embryo GR pilots. The first two courses were transferred from Manston's School of Air Navigation. The Thorney school's Ospreys, Nimrods and Sharks were replaced by Ansons for the flying phases of the courses, which produced an annual turnout of 200 pilots. The King paid an official visit to the station on 9 May 1938. During the Munich Crisis No. 42 Squadron was dispatched to Thornaby, its war station. No. 22 Squadron's aircraft were armed with torpedoes and parked inside sandbagged dispersals. On 1 November 1938 Thorney Island returned to No. 16 Group, which meant that the School of General Reconnaissance became a No. 17 Group lodger unit. No. 42 Squadron moved to its new station at Bircham Newton on 12 August 1939, and was replaced by No. 48 Squadron. On the outbreak of war the Ansons and Vildebeests from Thorney Island began patrolling for U-boats over the Channel.

WORTHY DOWN HAMPSHIRE, 3 MILES N OF WINCHESTER ON THE A34 (T)

After the Great War this airfield was saved from closure, and by 1930 was home to Nos 7 and 58 Squadrons. An eighteen-month building programme had included permanent barrack blocks and a new church, which was dedicated by the Bishop of Winchester on 19 January 1930. For four weeks in 1932 efforts were made to level and drain the airfield, necessitating the detachment of the two resident squadrons to Catfoss, and the work continued into the following year. In November 1932 Worthy Down's squadrons ferried Victorias to the Middle East, the crews returning by boat just in time for Christmas. In 1934 Flight Lieutenant A McKee flew a special Valentia to Iraq. It would have served as an in-flight refuelling tanker for a projected non-stop flight to India by Sir Alan Cobham, but sadly the latter's Airspeed Courier lost the pin to the throttle in flight due to vibration, and the attempt had to be abandoned at Malta. In the same year urgent War Office material had to be flown to Marseilles, and this task was undertaken by two Virginias of No. 58 Squadron. In April 1935 the ponderous and stately Virginias of No. 7 Squadron were pensioned off, to be replaced by Heyford IIs. This unusual-looking bomber had the fuselage attached to the upper wing, providing the crew with a lofty perch. On 1 October 1935 No. 7 Squadron's B Flight became No. 102 Squadron, and A Flight of No. 58 Squadron became No. 215 Squadron. These last named went to Upper Heyford on 14 January 1936. With the formation of Bomber Command on 14 July that year the allocation of bombing squadrons to Groups was either as light or heavy bombers. This would account for the movement of squadrons from one station to another at this time. Accordingly, in August No. 49 Squadron, equipped with Hinds, arrived from Bircham Newton, and Nos 7 and 102 Squadrons departed for Finningley. Next to arrive at Worthy Down were Nos 35 and 207 Squadrons' Gordons from the Sudan, having ended their commitment to the Abyssinian crisis. With Gordons and Hinds on the station, it could be transferred to No. 2 Group. The station's resident squadrons then began a series of armament camps and exercises at Aldergrove, Leuchars and West Freugh. On 17 August 1937 the Fairey Gordon units began to re-equip. No. 35 Squadron was up to strength in Wellesleys by mid-September, followed by No. 207 Squadron. For many pilots variable-pitch

propellers, pneumatic brakes and retractable undercarriages were a new experience, and they had to cope with a large wingspan, which made taxiing very difficult, not to mention undercarriages that could collapse without warning. On 15 April 1938 Worthy Down was transferred to Coastal Command and the Wellesleys went to Cottesmore, and the Hinds of No. 49 Squadron to Scampton. With Worthy Down in No. 17 (Training) Group, the Ansons of Nos 206 and 233 Squadrons arrived on attachment in early July for exercises with HMS *Centurion*. These units were followed by a succession of FAA units equipped with such aircraft as Sharks, Nimrods, Skuas, Ospreys and Gladiators. With the return of the FAA to the Admiralty, Worthy Down was formally transferred from the RAF to the Royal Navy on 24 May 1939, when it was commissioned as HMS *Kestrel*.

AIRFIELDS, SEAPLANE BASES AND MISCELLANEOUS UNITS IN EAST ANGLIA

ALCONBURY BY THE A14 NW OF HUNTINGDON

Land was first acquired as a satellite airfield on a site north of Alconbury village in 1938, and No. 63 Squadron's Battles were dispersed there from Upwood on 17/18 May. The crews were accommodated under canvas as the squadron practised operating from its main base, having been earmarked to join the Advanced Air Striking Force in France on mobilization for war.

BASSINGBOURNE 4 MILES N OF ROYSTON

The station opened in March 1938 and was to have the Hinds of Nos 104 and 108 Squadrons, even while four C-Type hangars were being erected. During May and June of that year the two resident squadrons were re-equipped with Blenheim Is, which became training units in September 1939. With war imminent the hangars were covered with brown nets before receiving camouflage paint.

BIRCHAM NEWTON ON THE B1153 S OF DOCKING

On 9 November 1929 No. 207 Squadron returned to Bircham Newton from Eastchurch, having been formed on 1 February 1920 at Bircham before going to Turkey in 1922. The squadron then flew Fairey IIIFs, to be replaced by Gordons in 1932, which were a common sight over East Anglia. On 1 October 1933 the Wessex Bombing Area was divided into a Central and a Western Area. Bircham Newton was then part of Central Area and was home to Nos 33, 35 and 207 Squadrons. On the formation of Bomber Command in 1935, these two Areas became No. 3 Group on 1 May 1936. When the Gordons left the station two new squadrons, Nos 21 and 34, formed at the station in December 1935, but both these units left for Abbotsinch in July the following year. In January 1936

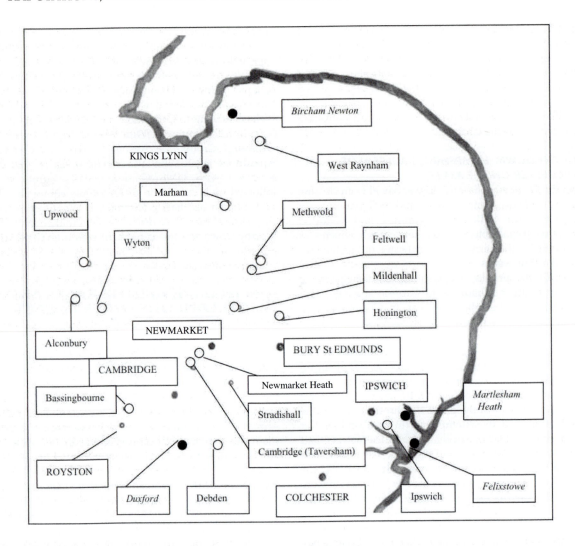

the Hawker Hinds of No. 18 Squadron arrived. This was during the early expansion period, when it was common practice to take a flight of a squadron to form the nucleus of a newly formed squadron, and on 10 February, C Flight departed to form the nucleus of No. 49 Squadron at Worthy Down. After so many years as a bomber station, Bircham Newton was transferred to No. 16 Group of Coastal Command on 10 August 1936, by which time the Ansons of No. 206 Squadron had arrived from Manston, to be joined on 17 August by No. 220 Squadron. Since the station then housed two Coastal Command units, three C-Type hangars were constructed to replace the wooden sheds built in 1916. In the summer of 1936 the North Norfolk coast was used for anti-aircraft gunnery training, which involved the Westland Wallaces brought to the station for target towing, and on 18 August 1939 No. 42 Squadron arrived, equipped with Vildebeest bombers. With the commencement of hostilities No. 206 Squadron's Ansons were used for inshore convoy protection.

CAMBRIDGE (TAVERSHAM) E OF CAMBRIDGE ON THE A45

Home, in the 1930s, to No. 22 E & RFTS with Hart Variants. At weekends Volunteer Reserve training crews flew Battles. Also No. 7 Squadron Whitleys were frequent visitors to the station. Once Marshall was established at Taversham it became a repair base for RAF aircraft.

DEBDEN 3 MILES SE OF SAFFRON WALDEN

Debden originated as one of the expansion-scheme stations of the 1930s. When a Bristol Bulldog had to force-land in 1934 in the area occupied later by the station, this was a determining factor in its location. The station was officially opened on 22 April 1937 to house No. 87 Squadron, newly equipped with Gladiators. Since Debden had been designed to house three squadrons, Nos 73 and 80 Squadrons soon arrived, also equipped with Gladiators, to join No. 87 Squadron. In November No. 29 Squadron, flying Hawker Demons, came to

Debden to replace No. 73 Squadron, which went to Digby. On 30 April 1938 No. 80 Squadron was on its way to the Middle East, and eventually to the war in the Western Desert. To replace No 80 Squadron No. 85 Squadron was re-formed at Debden from A Flight of No. 87 Squadron. During the final months of peace Nos 85 and 87 Squadrons were equipped with Hurricanes, while No. 29 Squadron converted to Blenheims. On the outbreak of war it was Debden's Hurricanes that went off to France with the Advanced Air Striking Force.

DUXFORD 7 MILES NE OF ROYSTON
During September 1931 No. 19 Squadron was re-equipped with Bulldogs. It was the resident fighter squadron, which shared the use of the station with Cambridge University Air Squadron, flying the highly visible yellow Avro Tutors. In January 1935 No. 19 Squadron changed from Bulldogs to Gloster Gauntlets, and on 20 July the following year No. 66 Squadron was re-formed at Duxford, also equipped with Gauntlets. The Meteorological Flight, equipped with Bulldogs, then Gauntlets, was based at Duxford until moving to Mildenhall in November 1936. At the outbreak of the Second World War No. 611 Squadron was at Duxford before being moved to Digby. No. 19 Squadron was the first in the RAF to equip with the Spitfire in 1938.

FELIXSTOWE E OF FELIXSTOWE TOWN
Felixstowe had long been the home of the Marine Aircraft Experimental Establishment by 1930, and during the decade before the outbreak of the Second World War was to test and evaluate the Perth, Iris, Stranraer, London, Scapa and Sunderland flying-boats. Unlike the landplanes being test flown at nearby Martlesham, the flying-boats had to be tested for seaworthiness as well as airworthiness. The 'piggy-back' composite Maia and Mercury aircraft carried out separation exercises over the estuary. The idea of flying two aircraft to two destinations to save the fuel of the

The 'piggy-back' Maia and Mercury composite aircraft.

upper aircraft until it was ready to 'peel off' to its own destination seemed to be a 1930s fashion, for the Great Western Railway would drop or slip the rear coaches of express trains as they approached intermediate stations, and so the front part of the train did not need to stop. Felixstowe was also the base for the flying-boats of No. 209 Squadron on and off between 1 May 1935 and 22 August 1939. On the outbreak of war it was felt that Felixstowe, like Martlesham, was too exposed to enemy attack, and the MAEE moved to Rhu, near Helensburgh on the Clyde.

FELTWELL TO THE LEFT OF THE B1112 FROM FELTWELL VILLAGE
The station opened in April 1937, and on the 19th of that month No. 214 Squadron's Harrows arrived from Scampton. On the 26th of the month B Flight was detached to become the nucleus of the re-formed No. 37 Squadron. On 6 May 1939 both squadrons received Wellington Is. On 27 August 1939 No. 37 Squadron was mobilized and No. 214 Squadron placed on reserve, moving to Methwold. Feltwell was then ready for war.

HONINGTON 3 MILES E OF THE A134 S OF THETFORD
Building of this station commenced in 1935, and it officially opened as a No. 3 Group station on 3 May 1937. The first unit to arrive was No. 77 Squadron, equipped with Audaxes and Wellesleys, in the July. Then came No. 102 Squadron with Heyfords. No. 77 Squadron had been re-formed at RAF Finningley from B Flight of No. 102 Squadron, which in turn had been re-formed from B Flight of No. 7 Squadron at Worthy Down in October 1935. In July 1938 both squadrons left Honington for Driffield, to be replaced by the Harrows of No. 75 Squadron. When this squadron re-equipped with Wellingtons in July 1939, it moved to Bassingbourne in the September. No. 9 Squadron, also equipped with Wellington Is, moved in from Sradishall on 15 July 1939.

IPSWICH SE OF IPSWICH
Ipswich was opened by HRH the Prince of Wales on 26 June 1930 to become the home of Suffolk Aero Club. In October 1938 the Civil Air Guard began flying from the airfield. In 1939 No. 4 Elementary and Reserve Flying Training School was established at Ipswich to train Volunteer Reserve Pilots. Since the airfield was nominated to be a satellite for Wattisham, Blenheim IVs were dispersed there on 2 September 1939, to return to base if required for operations.

MARHAM 10 MILES E OF DOWNHAM MARKET
Marham had opened as Narborough in August 1915, and worked in a variety of roles before closure when the Great War ended. On 1 April 1937 the station reopened as a two-squadron bomber station. On 5 May the Fairey

Hendons of No. 38 Squadron arrived. These were the only Hendons in the RAF. When 115 Squadron was re-formed on the station on 15 June 1937 from B Flight of No. 38 Squadron, Hendons briefly equipped that squadron too. In November 1938 No. 38 Squadron began to re-equip with Wellington 1s and Wellington 1As at the outbreak of war. No. 115 Squadron first re-equipped with Harrows, before moving on to Wellington 1s and 1As.

MARTLESHAM THE A1093 CROSSES THE SITE

By 1930 Martlesham was well established as the Aeroplane and Armament Experimental Establishment, comprising the two resident squadrons, No. 15 Squadron testing armaments and No. 22 Squadron testing both military and civilian aircraft. Much armament testing was carried out using DH9s. The A & AEE also had a Parachute Section until this unit moved to Henlow. Appendix H lists the civilian and military aircraft tested between 1 January 1930 and 3 September 1939. When the Empire Air Day was introduced by the RAF in 1936 to allow the public to see its men and machines at close quarters, Martlesham was an obvious choice. The 1936 event took place on 25 May Also that year the Wellesley, Battle, Hurricane, Spitfire, Lysander and Blenheim arrived for testing. The first production Spitfire, K.9787, arrived for testing until July 1938. On 12 September 1936 No. 64 Squadron arrived with Hawker Demons, but moved on to Church Fenton on 18 May 1938. Security had to be stepped up following the Munich Crisis but was relaxed to allow the staging of the Empire Air Day on 20 May 1939. When war came, Martlesham was too close to the expected area of operations, and the A & AEE was moved to Boscombe Down on 1 September 1939.

METHWOLD N OF BRANDON

Methwold was prepared before the outbreak of war as a satellite to Feltwell, and the first squadron to be dispersed here on mobilization was No. 37 Squadron, equipped with Wellington Is.

MILDENHALL NW OF MILDENHALL ON THE A1101

Known locally as Beck's Row, Mildenhall opened on 16 October 1934. The first resident squadron was No. 99, whose nine Heyfords arrived on 14 November. As was the usual practice during the expansion period, No. 99 Squadron detached its B Flight to become No. 38 Squadron. In late 1936 a few Fairey Hendons were issued to No. 38 Squadron, but these aircraft were underpowered, with deep wing-root sections to accommodate the bombs. A trousered undercarriage further reduced its speed. A badly positioned nose turret and only a Scarff ring for rear defence made these poor bombing aircraft, and they did not equip any other squadrons. The year 1937 was very busy for the station. No. 4 Group was formed there on 1 April, followed by No.

5 Group in July. For the second time No. 99 Squadron detached its B Flight to form the basis of No. 149 Squadron, also equipped with Heyfords. On 14 June No. 211 Squadron was formed but left for Grantham on 2 September. There was great excitement during the Munich Crisis when everyone expected the station to go to war. The few months of peace were sufficient to see No. 99 Squadron, and then No. 149 Squadron, re-equipped with Wellington Is. Before war broke out the Wellingtons of both squadrons were able to make long-distance flights over France to assess the range of these new bombing aircraft. The station was mobilized on 1 September when German forces entered Poland, and No. 99 Squadron flew off to its war station at Newmarket Heath. Meanwhile No. 149 Squadron was dispersed around the airfield with bombs ready for action, and all was quiet, on the surface, as war was declared on the Sunday.

NEWMARKET HEATH ROWLEY MILE, W OF NEWMARKET

Two days before war began, No. 99 Squadron's Wellingtons flew in from Mildenhall, the air and ground crews being accommodated in the Grandstand, but the squadron was not to see action until 14 December 1939. Newmarket was the war station for Mildenhall and was to remain so until February 1945. By the summer of that year the RAF had gone.

STRADISHALL 7 MILES NE OF HAVERHILL

Stradishall opened on 3 February 1938 under the command of Group Captain J.H. Herring DSO, MC. On 10 March the station was ready for No. 9 Squadron's Heyford IIIs and No. 148 Squadron's Wellesleys. The latter was to re-equip with Heyford IIIs and Ansons in November 1938. Air Ministry policy had provided that the Wellesleys be confined to the Middle Eastern theatre. Late in that year the building of runways commenced, and both squadrons re-equipped with Wellingtons early in 1939. On 15 July No. 9 Squadron departed for Honington, to be replaced by the Wellingtons and Ansons of No. 75 Squadron on 15 August 1939.

UPWOOD 2 MILES SW OF RAMSEY

The first aircraft to arrive at RAF Upwood, which opened in January 1937, were the RAFs new light bombers, the Fairey Battles. They were issued to No. 63 Squadron to replace that unit's Hinds and Audaxes. No. 52 Squadron was the other resident squadron, which received its Battles at the end of 1937 to replace its Hinds. Although twice as fast as the Hinds, the Battles could not reach Germany from a UK base and would only be of use in attacking targets in Germany from forward bases on the continent. Even then they were under-powered, lacked manoeuvrability, were poorly armed and were an unfit ground attack aircraft. Battles were assigned to the Advanced Air Striking Force sent to France on the outbreak of war, though in the event the two Upwood squadrons did not go to France, but became training units of No. 6 Group.

WEST RAYNHAM 2 MILES FROM WEST RAYNHAM VILLAGE

Opened in 1939, the station's first unit was No. 101 Squadron, equipped with Blenheims, which arrived in May. The station was not initially an operational station, but the main training unit in No. 2 Group, and that is how West Raynham started the war.

WEYBOURNE 3 MILES W OF SHERINGHAM

Anti-aircraft gunnery practices were carried out on the new ranges on the north Norfolk coast from the summer of 1936, and Wallace biplanes from Bircham Newton towed targets for the gunners. It was at Weybourne that the catapult-launched, radio-controlled Queen Bee target aircraft were used for gunnery practice from 6 June 1939. The unit responsible was X Flight of No. 1 Anti-Aircraft Cooperation Unit. Technically, therefore, Weybourne was an airfield, since these radio-controlled aircraft were launched from the site and could land either on the sea or back on land.

WYTON NE OF HUNTINGDON AT THE JUNCTION OF THE A141/B1090

Wyton has a long history, dating back to 1916, when RFC pilots were trained to fly on what was then a small airfield. The aerodrome buildings were erected on the west side of the airfield. During the inter-war years Alan Cobham's Flying Circus made use of the field. Construction of the new aerodrome began at the end of 1935, the hangars being sited on the south side. RAF Wyton was opened in July 1936 before the hangars were ready for occupation, and the Hinds of No. 139 Squadron, which re-formed on 3 September 1936, had to be accommodated in one of the old wooden sheds. Unfortunately the roof sagged, and once opened the doors could not be closed again, and the Hinds had to be picketed until No. 1 Hangar was ready in the November. In the following month No. 114 Squadron re-formed at the station, and on 1 March 1937 Wyton came under No. 2 Group, just as the first Blenheims began to arrive. When the Blenheim conversion programme slipped. No. 114 Squadron, having given up its Hinds, had to accept Audaxes as an interim measure. Both squadrons were re-equipped with Blenheim IVs before the outbreak of war.

AIRFIELDS AND SEAPLANE BASES IN WALES AND NORTH-WEST ENGLAND

COSFORD I MILE NW OF ALBRIGHTON

Cosford began life in 1938 when No. 2 School of Technical Training opened in the August. The school's task was to train technical tradesmen to service all the aircraft on order for the rapidly expanding air force. The school was to train over 70,000 airframe and engine mechanics and armourers. On completion of the first C-Type hangar, it was occupied by No. 90 MU, which was formed on 15 March 1939. The first aircraft to be received by the MU was Anson No. 5055. No. 90 MU was to go on to store and issue Spitfires, Battles and Blenheims. The unit actually supplied Blenheims to the Romanian government, and Gloster Gauntlets to the Finns.

HAWARDEN 3 MILES SW OF CHESTER

Government-sponsored shadow factories were inaugurated by the British government to ensure a steady flow of airframes and engines, made to proved designs. to replace losses in time of war, leaving the parent factories to develop new designs. The site for these shadow factories had to be near, but not too near, centres of population that could provide a pool of labour. A site three miles south-west of Chester met this criterion. The land adjacent to the factory had been an RLG for RAF Sealand, and this became the factory airfield. Wellingtons were to be built from parts made mainly in Weybridge. Work commenced on the construction of the Hawarden factory in November 1937, and it was possible to place a contract for 750 Wellingtons in May 1939. L.7770, the first of the batch, made its maiden flight on 2 August. Wellington assembly continued throughout the war, and by the end of hostilities 5,540 had been produced

HOOTON PARK I MILE SE OF EASTHAM

Hooton Park was designated the official airport for Liverpool in 1930, but Speke, on the opposite bank of the Mersey, was much more suitable as a site for an airport serving a major city. While Hooton continued to be used for commercial flying, it was also home to No. 610 (County of Chester) Squadron, formed at Hendon on 10 February 1936 as a light-bomber unit, which moved to Hooton on 16 April. Equipped with Harts and Hinds, the unit remained in the bombing role until converting to Hurricanes in September 1939. On 9 October that year No. 16 Group took the station under its wing.

KINGSTOWN CUMBRIA, 2 MILES N OF CARLISLE

Kingstown started life as a municipal airport in 1933 and was ideally situated for flights to and from the Isle of Man, yet in its first years it experienced only light aircraft use. From June 1935 Kingstown was home to the Border Flying Club, and in September 1939 the club's aircraft were impressed into RAF service. In June of that year No. 38 E & RFTS of the RAFVR was established, and extra hangars and other buildings were erected to accommodate the unit. During July and August 1939 Henleys of No. 1 AACU were sent to Kingstown for exercises.

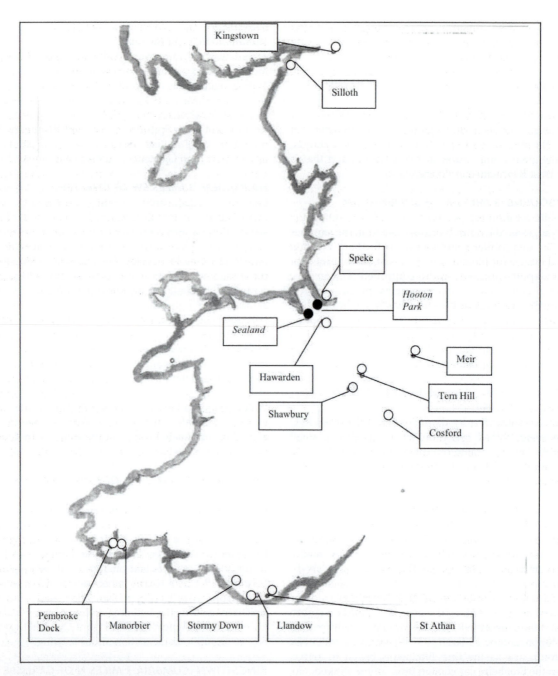

LLANDOW THE B4270 CROSSES THE SITE

RAF use was dated back to 1937, when No. 614 Squadron formed at Llandow with Hinds and Hectors, but the squadron moved to Pengam Moors in September 1939. The station reopened as an aircraft storage unit on 1 April 1940.

MANORBIER 1 MILE E OF MANORBIER

Manorbier was used solely for target towing and radio-controlled flying, and was opened in the mid-1930s. During the summer of 1937 B Flight of No. 1 AACU was at Manorbier, and annual practice camps continued in 1938 and 1939, when a pilotless aircraft unit became permanently available for the local training of ack-ack gunners.

MEIR STAFFS., 2 MILES E OF LONGTON

Meir opened as an airport on 18 May 1934, but its close proximity to Stoke-on-Trent reduced the scope for development. Railway Air Services used Meir as part of its Croydon–Belfast–Glasgow service from 12 August 1935. While the North Staffordshire Aero Club maintained a few aircraft at Meir, the bulk of the flying was attributable to the work of No. 28 E & RFTS, operating Tiger Moths and Hawker Harts. It was not until 12 February 1940 that No. 1 Flying Practice Unit arrived at Meir.

PEMBROKE DOCK CLOSE TO THE TOWN CENTRE
The station opened on 1 January 1930, but its first resident unit, No. 210 Squadron with Southampton IIs, did not arrive until 1 June 1931. No. 230 Squadron with Singapore IIIs formed at Pembroke Dock on 1 December 1934. Until a hangar was completed in September 1935, all maintenance work was carried out on a floating dock. No. 210 Squadron had been to Gibraltar before returning to Pembroke Dock, and at the outbreak of war was equipped with Sunderlands. By this time No. 230 Squadron was stationed in the Far East and had been replaced with the Sunderlands of No. 228 Squadron.

PENRHOS 3 MILES W OF PWLLHELI
Penrhos opened on 1 February 1937 as No. 5 Armament Training Camp, equipped with six Wallaces. The targets were positioned on the foreshore, with patrol boats out to sea to ensure that the sea area was kept clear of other vessels. The first training course was postponed to 3 April as the targets had been swept away in heavy seas. During 1938 and 1939 aircraft from several flying training schools were attached for monthly periods. On 28 May 1938, 11,000 spectators attended an air show at Penrhos on the occasion of Empire Air Day. In September 1939 Penrhos became home to No. 9 Air Observers' School.

ST ATHAN 7 MILES W OF BARRY
RAF St Athan opened in February 1939 as No. 4 School of Technical Training, and No. 19 MU formed in the March as an aircraft storage unit which had 280 aircraft on charge by January 1940, mainly Battles and Hurricanes.

RAF SEALAND 1 MILE NE OF QUEENSFERRY
Sealand's history as a military airfield goes back to the Great War. In 1930 the RAF Packing Depot had then only recently arrived from Ascot. The depot dismantled and packed aircraft in crates for shipment overseas. It was the expansion schemes of the 1930s that resulted in the station's growth, and Hart, Audax and Fury aircraft were used by No. 5 FTS flying from Sealand. No. 3 Aircraft Storage Unit was formed there on 2 December 1935 and joined the Packing Depot on the South Camp site. Although some of the buildings were of standard RAF design, others were peculiar to Sealand. The barrack blocks on RAF stations were normally two-storeyed, but at Sealand they had three-storeys. The hangars were a mixture of Belfast, C and L Types. War broke out before plans to overcome the serious shortfall of pilots could be implemented.

SHAWBURY ON THE B5063 ADJACENT TO SHAWBURY VILLAGE
The history of Shawbury as a military airfield dates back to 1917, but the airfield closed in 1920 following the ending of hostilities and the rapid rundown of the RAF. It did not reopen until February 1938. In 1935 the Air Ministry was looking for airfield sites in the relatively safe areas of western and north-western England, which would be furthest from likely areas of conflict, and where aircraft construction, storage and repair would take place, as well as aircrew training. Shawbury would be ideal for a flying training school and maintenance unit, and No. 27 MU formed at Shawbury on 1 February 1938. This unit stored and overhauled most of the RAF's combat aircraft of the day, with up to 324 aircraft on charge shortly after the outbreak of the Second World War. On 14 May 1938 No. 11 FTS arrived from Wittering with an assortment of aircraft, including Audaxes, Gauntlets, Tutors and Hart trainers.

SILLOTH CUMBRIA, 1 MILE NE OF SILLOTH TOWN
Silloth opened on 5 June 1939 as a station in Maintenance Command, but it was realized that, given its location, it would be an ideal situation for teaching general reconnaissance, and the station was transferred to Coastal Command. This meant that No. 22 Maintenance Unit that took up residence at Silloth was at a station of another command. In these circumstances No. 22 MU had to be classified as a lodger unit. The Coastal Command Group Pool formed on 1 November 1939.

SPEKE MERSEYSIDE, 7 MILES SE OF LIVERPOOL CITY CENTRE
Liverpool City Corporation bought the Speke estate in 1928, setting aside 400 acres for the development of an airport. Initially a Liverpool–Manchester–Birmingham–Croydon service was subsidized by the four municipal corporations, but was not a success. An unsubsidized service was then inaugurated from Liverpool to Blackpool and on to Isle of Man. The operator was the Blackpool and West Coast Air Service, and the firm had the use of an old farmhouse as a terminal. A hangar was erected to house the aircraft, and farm buildings became stores and workshops. These temporary arrangements were made more formal when a 'public use' licence was issued in 1933. Customs facilities were also provided, and an air pageant was staged to mark the official opening on 1 July 1933, in which an RAF display team took part. Speke was well established as a commercial airfield when the RAF arrived in May 1936. No. 611 (West Lancashire) Squadron had been formed at Hendon, and came to Speke with Hawker Hinds and Harts in the light-bomber role, but converted to the fighter role on 1 January 1939. Spitfires were received in May, and No. 611 Squadron went to Duxford, its war station, on 13 August. The airport was requisitioned in

September 1939, and Nos 61 and 144 Squadrons came to Speke under the 'scatter' scheme designed to protect the bomber force from surprise attack.

STORMY DOWN 2 MILES NE OF PORTHCAWL

Stormy Down was built pre-war to house No. 9 Armament Training Station, and was renamed No. 7 Air Observers' School on 1 September 1939, and then No. 7 Bombing and Gunnery School. The original name of Porthcawl was dropped in favour of Stormy Down early in 1940.

TERN HILL SALOP, ON THE A41 1 MILE S OF THE JUNCTION WITH THE A53

Tern Hill had been a Great War station that closed in 1922, but the expansion plan of 1934 resulted in former airfields being considered for reactivation. The site was

requisitioned in 1935, but hundreds of rabbit warrens had to be dealt with before the ground could be drained, levelled and sown with grass. The official opening was on 1 January 1936, and the resident unit was No. 10 FTS, equipped with Harts, Audaxes and Tutors. These aircraft were used for advanced training of pilots who had gained their wings at an E & RFTS. The airfield was also destined to house an aircraft storage unit, and the contractors had to construct one C-Type hangar and two D-Type hangars on the south-east side of the airfield. This was in addition to three C-Type hangars on the main site. There was therefore fevered activity, and the airmen had to sleep in the hangars until the barrack blocks were ready. The work completed, No. 4 ASU opened on 1 June 1937 for the handling and storage of Swordfish, Lysanders and Wellingtons. The unit was

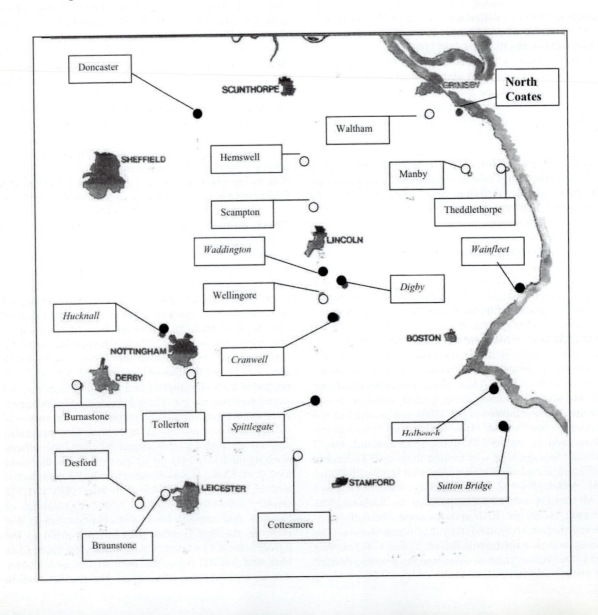

renamed No. 24 MU, and at the outbreak of war stored 354 aircraft of different types.

AIRFIELDS AND MISCELLANEOUS UNITS OF LINCOLNSHIRE AND THE EAST MIDLANDS

BRAUNSTONE (LEICESTER) BETWEEN THE A50 AND A47 W OF LEICESTER

Braunstone was originally opened as Leicester airport on 13 July 1935. There was a club house and hangar leased to the Leicestershire Aero Club, flying Moths and Puss Moths. Future development of the eastern side of the airfield was planned, but these plans did not come to fruition and at the outbreak of war the airfield was used as a satellite of No. 7 EFTS at Desford.

BURNASTON SW OF DERBY JUST SOUTH OF THE VILLAGE OF BURNASTON

Burnaston officially opened on Saturday 17 June 1939 as Derby's municipal airport. The site was already an airfield, and housed the RAF Volunteer Reserve Training Centre, which was formed in September 1938. On 29 September 1938 No. 30 E & RFTS was formed. At the outbreak of war No. 27 E & RFTS arrived from Tollerton to become No. 30 EFTS.

COTTESMORE 10 MILES NW OF STAMFORD

Work began on Cottesmore airfield in 1935. The domestic and technical buildings were sited immediately to the north of Cottesmore village and west of Ermine Street. The official opening was on 11 March 1938, as a station in No. 2 Group of Bomber Command. Work was still going on to ready the station when Nos 35 and 207 Squadrons arrived from Worthy Down. No. 35 Squadron, which came to Cottesmore with Battles, left for Cranfield on 25 August 1939 with Battles and Ansons. No. 207 Squadron also left Cottesmore for Cranfield, having replaced its Wellesleys with Battles and Ansons; and in came the Hampdens of No. 185 Squadron from Thornaby. At the outbreak of war a Hereford and four Ansons had been added. The station was then transferred to No. 5 Group. Ground defence of the aerodrome was originally the responsibility of the local Army units until a rifle squadron of 250 airmen was formed. (By 1942 the RAF had its own indigenous defence force, entitled the RAF Regiment.)

CRANWELL LINCOLNSHIRE, NW OF SLEAFORD BETWEEN THE A17 (T) AND THE B1429

This internationally famed airfield, since 1920 the Officer Training School of the RAF, dates back to 1915, when the RNAS began work constructing wooden huts for the personnel of HMS *Daedalus*, with its kite balloons, airships and aeroplanes. But the RAF acquired the site when RNAS shore-based units were absorbed into the new service in 1918. Air Marshal Trenchard was looking for a home for his new cadet college that was far enough away from the 'fleshpots' of London, and the RAF Cadet College opened at Cranwell on 5 February 1920. During the 1920s the cadet courses became well established, and began turning out officers who would rise to the highest ranks of the service. During this period Cranwell also housed apprentices, who were trained there pending completion of accommodation at Halton. As the decade came to a close, the Electrical and Wireless School was established on 6 August 1929, training both air and ground wireless operators. Finally there was a Royal Air Force Hospital at Cranwell from 1922 to 1940 to serve the local stations. During the 1930s the expansion plans for the RAF brought other units to the station, such as the School of Store Accounting and Storekeeping, formed in July 1934, and renamed the Equipment Training School from October 1936. Then there was the a Supplies Depot from October 1936 and the School of Clerks Accountancy from May 1939. From December 1938 Cranwell was also the Headquarters of No. 21 Group of Training Command. When the Second World War broke out the college was closed, not to be officially reopened until April 1947, although Cranwell remained in the flying training role during the period of hostilities.

DESFORD LEICESTERSHIRE, S OF DESFORD BETWEEN THE A47 (T) AND THE B582

Desford was a small grass airfield opened in 1935 as a civilian-manned E & RFTS. Desford was very close to the city of Leicester, and at the outbreak of war in 1939 became the home of No. 7 EFTS, equipped with Tiger Moths.

DIGBY LINCOLNSHIRE, W OF THE B1191 FROM SCOPWICK VILLAGE

Digby was originally named Scopwick, for it was usual to name an RAF airfield or station after the village closest to the main camp entrance, although for a variety of reasons that was not always possible. However, when Scopwick became confused with Shotwick near Chester, it was decided to choose the village of Digby in place of Scopwick, and RAF Shotwick became Sealand. Digby had been a satellite for HMS *Daedalus* (Cranwell) during the Great War. In the 1920s it became a flying training school, latterly No. 2 FTS, which was disbanded in December 1933, when Digby again became a satellite for Cranwell. After a ten-month gap No. 2 FTS was re-formed with Hawker Furies and Harts and the basic trainer, the Avro Tutor. The original hangars were demolished during the period 1935/6, and barrack blocks were built for the airmen. On 7 September 1937 No. 2 FTS moved to Brize Norton, and Digby became a fighter station when, two months after the departure of the trainers, came the Gloster Gauntlets of No. 46 Squadron and Gladiators of No. 73 Squadron. In August 1939 both squadrons were equipped with Hurricanes, and on the 27th of that month the two squadrons were joined by No. 504 (County of Nottingham) Squadron's Hurricanes. All three were prepared for fighter defence and convoy patrols.

DONCASTER YORKSHIRE, ON THE A638 SW OF THE RACECOURSE

Doncaster had been associated with flying even before the Great War, and the racecourse itself was an active airfield during that war, but it was given up as surplus to requirements in 1919. Crilly Airways began a service from Doncaster to Croydon in 1935, but the racecourse could not also be used as an airfield for what was to become Doncaster Airport, and a site was chosen to the south-west. Although bounded on all sides by roads and railways, the site still became an airport in 1939. On 1 November 1938 No. 616 (South Yorkshire) Squadron of the Auxiliary Air Force was formed as a bomber unit. The RAF took over Doncaster in 1939 with war imminent, and it was declared a 'scatter' station, with a decoy airfield at Armthorpe, north-east of the racecourse.

HEMSWELL (HARPSWELL) APPROXIMATELY 13 MILES N OF LINCOLN

Named Harpswell during the Great War, after the hamlet at the southern end of the airfield, it was used as a training airfield for pilots and observers going on night-flying operations, but when No. 199 TS disbanded in 1919 the airfield was closed. In 1930 the site was again surveyed for use by the expanding RAF, and it was to be one of the earliest of the bomber bases of the expansion plans. This new bomber airfield was built on Hemswell cliff and opened in January 1937 as a station in Bomber Command's No. 5 Group. The two resident squadrons were Nos 61 and 144. No. 144 Squadron, equipped with Anson I aircraft, arrived at Hemswell on 9 February and converted to Audaxes the following month, and then to Blenheim Is in the August. No. 61 Squadron was re-formed at Hemswell on 8 March 1937, equipped with Audaxes, and then Anson Is. The last aircraft that had equipped No. 61 Squadron was the Camel fighter when the squadron was disbanded at Rochford in 1919. In 1939 both squadrons were equipped with Hampdens that took part in the earliest bombing raids of the Second World War.

HOLBEACH LINCOLNSHIRE, ON THE MUD FLATS OF THE WASH NEAR HOLBEACH ST MATTHEW

Holbeach opened as a bombing and gunnery range in 1928 and still serves as such today.

HUCKNALL NOTTINGHAMSHIRE, ON THE OUTSKIRTS OF HUCKNALL, S OF THE B6009

In the latter half of the 1920s No. 504 (County of Nottingham) Squadron had been formed at Hucknall as a cadre unit of the Special Reserve, converting to an Auxiliary squadron in May 1936 in the day-bomber role.

It was equipped with the Hawker Horsley, then the Westland Wallace, and later the Hawker Hind, but on 31 October 1938 No. 504 Squadron re-equipped with Hurricanes, then moved to Digby in August 1939. Earlier in December 1934 Rolls-Royce took over two of the hangars for engine test flying, and among other engines developed there was the famous Merlin engine, which equipped the Spitfire. The expansion period saw Nos 98 and 104 Squadrons coming to Hucknall from Abingdon on 21 August 1936 with Hinds, but these aircraft proved to be a little troublesome, with several suffering forced landings. Flying Officer Dawson had to bring K6721 down on a hill near Pinxton, Notts while Flying Officer Plant managed to overturn K.6718 in a field at Broxstowe, and Pilot Officer Grindon had to force-land K.6719 at Gunthorpe. On 2 May 1938 No. 104 Squadron departed for Bassingbourne, to be equipped with Blenheim Is. In June 1938 No. 98 Squadron was re-equipped with Battles. Although Hucknall was an airfield in Fighter Command at the outbreak of the war, the resident units were No. 98 with its Battles and No. 1 (RAF) Ferry Pilots' Pool, which was in Maintenance Command. The station never did receive fighters, and remained in the training role throughout the Second World War.

MANBY LINCOLNSHIRE, E OF LOUTH

Construction work on the airfield began in 1936. It was decided to use Manby for experiments with a wind-break to use in cross-wind landings, and a wind-break 50 feet high and 500 yards long was erected across the landing area while work on the station continued. This device was completed in April 1937, and practice landings were made with a Battle, a Whitley and a Blenheim. The screen proved a success in the strong east-coast offshore winds. As Manby neared completionm trials with the screen were moved to Rollestone camp, Wiltshire but the project was abandoned since none of the RAF Commands seemed to think that there was the need for such a screen. The airfield opened in August 1938 with brick-built accommodation on the eastern side of the airfield. The hangars comprised three C-Type (hipped) seven-bay hangars and two aircraft repair sheds. When the station opened it was in No. 25 Group of Flying Training Command, and home to No. 1 Air Armament School. Courses for armament officers began when the station took over the bombing and gunnery range at Theddlethorpe. Courses extended to include bomb aimers, air gunners and armourers, using a variety of aircraft, which included Wellingtons, Hinds, Battles and Wallaces.

NORTH COATES S OF GRIMSBY BETWEEN HORSESHOE POINT AND NORTH COATES POINT

The airfield at North Coates had been used operationally by maritime patrol aircraft during the Great War, but was abandoned soon after the Armistice. Since the east coast of Lincolnshire was perfect for armament training, the Air Ministry bought eighty-eight acres of the Great War site in 1927 for annual summer armament practice camps. It continued providing annual camps for bomber squadrons until 1934. Then it was decided to upgrade the site into a permanent airfield, and so a station was opened in 1935 as No. 2 Armament Training Camp. In January 1936 the Air Observers' School was formed, and these two units were merged into No. 2 Air Armament School in 1937. Another name change came in March 1938, when it became No. 1 Air Observers' School, flying Battles, which remained at North Coates until the outbreak of war, when the school went to North Wales as part of Coastal Command. The school did not become RAF North Coates until war had started.

SCAMPTON N OF LINCOLN BETWEEN THE A15 AND THE B1398

Scampton was known as Brattlebury when it opened as an airfield in November 1916. It was both a training and an operational station, but was not included among the stations to be retained in the post-war RAF, and closed in 1919. With the expansion under way in the 1930s the site of the Great War airfield was surveyed and the land was repurchased to be a grass airfield. Some land to the south of the original airfield was included in the purchase, which then put Aisthorpe House, occupied by a Mr Fieldsend, on the airfield boundary and in the flight path of incoming aircraft. On the night of 31 August/1 September 1937 the No. 9 Squadron pilot of a Heyford struck Aisthorpe House while attempting a landing. Fortunately no one was killed. The new station had an arc of C-Type hangars that occupied the south-east corner of the airfield. Initially the men were accommodated in tents until the barrack blocks and messes were ready. The official opening of the station was 27 August 1936 in No. 3 Group. In the October the first flying units arrived. No. 9 Squadron came from Aldergrove, Northern Ireland, on the first of the month, newly equipped with Heyford IIIs. No. 214 Squadron came from Andover, although some of its Virginias were detached to Aldergrove at the time. In January 1937 No. 214 Squadron was re-equipped with Harrows, but then left Scampton for Feltwell on 12 April 1937. Two months later No. 148 Squadron was re-formed at Scampton, equipped with the Audax and Wellesley, and in March 1938 both Nos 9 and 148 Squadrons left for Stradishall, to be replaced by Nos 49 and 83 Squadrons on 14 March. Both units were equipped with Hinds, to be re-equipped with Hampdens. Four days earlier the station had been transferred to No. 5 Group. With both squadrons each having sixteen aircraft and construction work complete, the station was ready for war.

SPITTLEGATE GRANTHAM, E OF GRANTHAM ADJACENT TO THE A52

Spittlegate had been a training airfield during the Great War and was retained after the Armistice. In the early 1920s it was both a day-bomber and flying training station, but when Nos 39 and 100 Squadrons left, only No. 3 FTS remained in residence until the summer of 1937, when the airfield transferred to No. 5 Group of Bomber Command. The first units to arrive in the new role were No. 113 Squadron with Hinds from Upper Heyford and No. 211 Squadron with Hinds and Audaxes from Mildenhall. When both these units moved to Egypt in April and May 1938, they were immediately replaced by two Battle squadrons, Nos 106 and 185. It became clear that the station was too small to support two bomber squadrons, and Spittlegate reverted to the training role. In October 1938 No. 12 FTS was formed on the station. At the outbreak of war in September 1939 the flying school had Harts, Ansons and Audaxes on strength, with 927 personnel.

SUTTON BRIDGE HOLBEACH, E OF KINGS LYNN

Sutton Bridge was first used as a temporary armament practice camp in 1926 for use by fighter squadrons and advanced flying training units. Sutton Bridge was in the Fen Country, and was named after the bridge that crossed over the A17 road, so that the landing-ground was in Norfolk and the domestic site was in Lincolnshire. The site was close to the Wash, which is ideally suited to firing and bombing ranges. From 1926 to 1936 only tented accommodation was available during the summer camp season, but even in the summer the men found the tents cold. Bulldogs, Siskins and Harts were the main visitors to Sutton Bridge, which became an RAF station in 1936, when a limited number of married quarters were built. The armament training camp became No. 3 Armament Training Station but had to move to a safer area on the outbreak of war.

THEDDLETHORPE LINCOLNSHIRE, N OF MABLETHORPE

Theddlethorpe opened in 1935 as a bombing and gunnery range.

TOLLERTON NOTTINGHAM, N OF TOLLERTON VILLAGE OFF THE A52

The airfield was officially opened on 19 June 1930 by the Minister for Aviation, Sir Sefton Brancker, and had been leased to National Flying Services. Then Nottingham Flying Club moved in in September 1931. In 1937 the Civil Air Guard was formed, and a school opened with about fifty pupils. An RAFVR training school, No. 27 E & RFTS, was also formed on 24 June 1938, equipped with Magisters, Ansons and Harts. In 1938 the training school expanded, and a map room, parachute room, canteen, office block, Bellman hangar and a cinema for showing training films were added. Field Aircraft Services Ltd of Croydon, which ran a repair and servicing organization, erected a large factory hangar on the west side of the airfield. On the outbreak of war the flying club and Civil

Air Guard unit were closed and No. 27 E & RFTS disbanded. The field was handed over to the Air Ministry, and Tollerton became a 'scatter' airfield.

WADDINGTON LINCOLNSHIRE, S OF LINCOLN BETWEEN THE A607 AND THE A15

Waddington had seen service as a flying school during the Great War. Sited on the Lincolnshire Heights five miles south of Lincoln, the station was retained after the Armistice but was closed as an active airfield until 1926, when it became the base for No. 503 Bombing Squadron. This unit, redesignated the County of Lincoln Squadron, changed its Fawns for Hyderabads in February 1929, and was a night-bomber squadron until 1935, when it was re-equipped with Wallaces and reverted to a day-bomber squadron. A major rebuilding programme was put in hand in the mid-1930s, and No. 110 (B) Squadron re-formed at the station in 1937 with Hawker Hinds. This was followed by Nos 50 (B) and 88 (B) Squadrons in May and June respectively. June also saw No. 44 Squadron arrive with Hinds, having re-formed at Wyton in March. The following month No. 88 Squadron moved to Boscombe Down. In the December No. 44 Squadron became the first unit to be equipped with Blenheim Is. Next to move was No. 503 Squadron, which moved to Doncaster, only to be disbanded and re-formed as No. 616 (South Yorkshire) Squadron. Last to move before the outbreak of war was No. 110 Squadron, which re-equipped with Blenheims and moved to Wattisham in May 1939.

WAINFLEET SW OF SKEGNESS

Wainfleet opened in August 1918 as a gunnery and bombing range on the site of an old artillery range that had been in use since the 1890s. Wainfleet was used during the war by bombing units, including the 'Dambusters' Squadron, No. 617.

WALTHAM LINCOLNSHIRE, S OF GRIMSBY JUST W OF THE A16

Grimsby's civil aerodrome was a large field in the 1930s, equipped with a clubhouse and two wooden hangars used for minor repairs. Rather like Leicester Airport today, it was only used for light aircraft. In June 1938 No. 25 E & RFTS was established at Waltham. This school was operated by the Herts and Essex Aero Club, and flew with Tiger Moths, Magisters and Hind trainers. The school was disbanded on the outbreak of war, but the airfield went on to be used by bombing units during hostilities.

WELLINGORE LINCOLNSHIRE, SA OF THE VILLAGE OF WELLINGORE

Owing to the congestion that could arise in the skies above the Lincoln Escarpment, relief landing-grounds (RLGs) were essential. There was South Carlton, Brattlebury (Scampton), Harpswell, Waddington and Leadenham, not to mention the training aircraft doing circuits around Cranwell. Temple Bruer and Wellingore were large fields that could be used by Cranwell until June 1940, when it became an RLG for Digby.

AIRFIELDS AND SEAPLANE BASES OF YORKSHIRE

BEVERLEY N OF KINGSTON-UPON-HULL

Flying ceased at Beverley after the Great War, but part of the site remained with the RAF, and during the 1930s a radio section operated from the airfield, and the RAF's first radio-telephone sets were tested through Beverley in 1938. During the Second World War Beverley was used by the Army.

CATTERICK S OF CATTERICK BETWEEN THE MAIN A1 ROAD AND THE RIVER SWALE

Catterick had been a Great War flying station, but there was very little activity after the Armistice until No. 26 Squadron was re-formed with Atlas aircraft as an Army Cooperation squadron on 11 October 1927. The station came under Army Cooperation Command, and in July 1936 the unit was re-equipped with Audaxes. Further buildings were added as part of the expansion schemes, including two C-Type hangars, a fire-tender shelter near the watch tower, airmen's and officers' married quarters, workshops for three squadrons, MT shed and operations room. No. 41 Fighter Squadron joined No. 26 Squadron in September 1936. In August 1937 Hawker Hectors replaced the Audaxes on No. 26 Squadron until the spring of 1939, when the unit had Lysanders. In October 1937 No. 41 Squadron changed to the Hawker Fury II, and to the Spitfire in early 1939. During August 1939 a detachment of No. 64 Squadron was followed by No. 609 Squadron's Spitfires from Yeadon. In September 1939 Catterick became a sector station in No. 13 Group, Fighter Command.

CHURCH FENTON NW OF SELBY ON THE SOUTH SIDE OF THE B1223

Church Fenton opened as a grass airfield in June 1937, and two fighter squadrons came to the station, No. 72 Squadron, which arrived from Tangmere on 1 June, and No. 213 Squadron with Gauntlets, which arrived from Northolt on 1 July. In May 1938 No. 213 Squadron left for Wittering, to be replaced by the Demons of No. 64 Squadron. Shortly after the squadrons arrived, the Demons were exchanged for Blenheim IFs. Until the outbreak of war there were two fighter squadrons at Church Fenton, and in September 1939 the station was transferred to No. 13 Group of Fighter Command.

DISHFORTH RIPON, E OF RIPON AND THE A1

Dishforth opened in September 1936, but with much of its permanent accommodation still to be completed. An

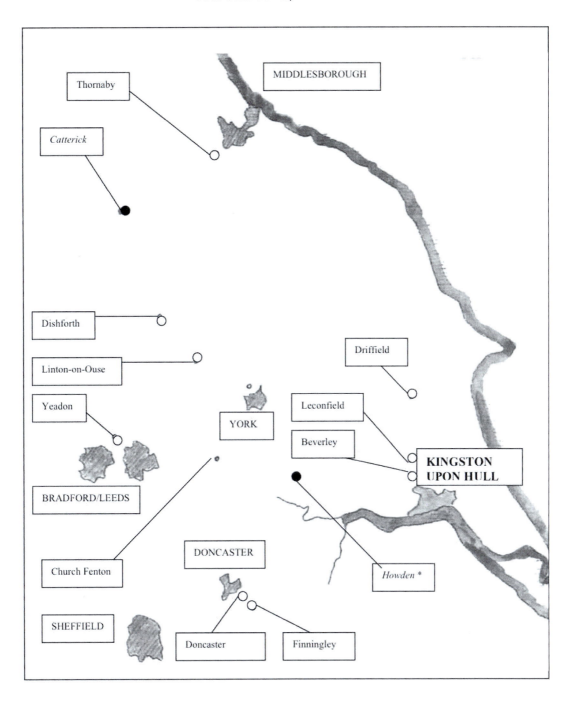

arc of five C-Type hangars was situated on the south-east boundary close to North Hill Farm. These were to accommodate the Heyfords of No. 10 Squadron, which flew in from Boscombe Down in January 1937. This unit was the first to be equipped with the Whitley Mk Is. No. 78 Squadron was next to arrive, also with Heyfords, and also to be equipped with Whitleys. Both squadrons were able to carry out day formation flying before war broke out.

DONCASTER SW OF THE RACECOURSE ON THE A638

During the inter-war years Doncaster was used as a civil airfield, and in 1939 it was designated a 'scatter' airfield.

DRIFFIELD W OF GREAT DRIFFIELD BETWEEN THE A166 AND THE A163

Driffield had been a Great War airfield, and was surveyed in the early 1930s for possible reactivation. It was found suitable and work began at the end of 1935, one of fourteen airfields planned for the North-East. It had five C-Type hangars on the eastern side of the airfield, with brick-built messes and administrative buildings behind. The official opening of the station was on 30 July 1936, and Group Captain Murliss-Green commanded this No. 3 Group bomber station. Two months later Nos 58 and 215 Squadrons' Virginias arrived from Worthy Down, and were soon embarked on a course of night-flying. In March the following year, B Flight of No. 58 Squadron was detached, to become No. 51 Squadron, and both these units were then moved to Boscombe Down. No. 215 Squadron also had its B Flight detached, to become No. 75 Squadron, initially equipped with Virginias and Ansons, but then Harrows. On 29 June the station was transferred to No. 4 Group. In July 1938 No. 75 Squadron was moved to Honington, to be replaced by No. 102 Squadron. No. 215 Squadron then followed No. 75 Squadron to Honington, and No. 77 Squadron's Wellesleys moved to Driffield. Nos 102 and 77 Squadrons were then re-equipped with Whitleys during the winter months of 1938, and these two squadrons were among the first to fly on operational missions in the Second World War.

FINNINGLEY SE OF DONCASTER TO W OF FINNINGLEY VILLAGE

The cost of the compulsory purchase of land for Finningley airfield in September 1935 was £11,584 for the necessary 433 acres of farmland. The crops had to be speedily harvested so that the land could be sown with the special grass required to take bombers. Behind an arc of five C-Type hangars in the north-west corner of the site was the brick-built accommodation, made to the standard pattern that characterizes all stations of the period. The first commanding officer was Wing Commander Gallehawk, who took up his post in August 1936, just in time to witness the arrival of No. 102 Squadron, shortly followed by No. 7 Squadron. The station, with a strength of thirty-five officers and 350 men, opened on 3 September 1936. It was not long before both squadrons gave birth to two more squadrons. On 12 April 1937 No. 76 was re-formed from B Flight of No. 7 Squadron, equipped with Wellesleys, and on 14 June, No. 77 Squadron was re-formed from B Flight, No. 102 Squadron, equipped with Audaxes. In July both Nos 77 and 102 Squadrons left for Honington. The Whitley was, in 1938, classed as a heavy night-bomber, and these aircraft equipped No. 7 Squadron in the spring of that year. Although there was a massed formation of Finningley's bombers for the Empire Air Day, to the delight of the local people, the Munich Crisis brought a sombre note. The aircraft had their squadron numbers painted over as units were brought to a state of war readiness – NM for No. 76 Squadron and LT for No. 7 Squadron. Both these units were re-equipped with

Hampden Is and Anson Is in the spring of 1939. The Gauntlets of No. 616 Squadron Auxiliary Air Force were detached to Finningley, but moved to Leconfield, their war station, shortly after the outbreak of war. In September 1939 Finningley was transferred to No. 5 Group.

HOWDEN N OF GOOLE OFF THE B1228

Howden had been steeped in the history of the Great War as an airship station, but following the Armistice in 1918 it had been run down, and then, with the revival of the airship programme in the 1920s, had been brought back to life. The Airship Guarantee Company used the site to build the R100, but with the loss of the R101 over France on 5 October 1930 the British airship programme was abandoned, and by the mid-1930s the huge hangar that had accommodated the R100 was dismantled and sold for scrap.

LECONFIELD N OF BEVERLEY ON THE E SIDE OF THE A164 AT LECONFIELD VILLAGE

Leconfield opened on 3 December 1936, a bomber station in No. 3 Group. The main railway line from Beverley to Great Driffield formed the eastern boundary, and to the west was the A164. To the west of the landing area was an arc of C-Type hangars that fronted the workshops, messes and living accommodation. The first unit to arrive was No. 97 Squadron with Heyfords. These arrived from Boscombe Down on 7 January 1937, to be followed by the Heyfords of No. 166 Squadron two weeks later. In June the station was transferred to No. 4 Group. In that month both squadrons became involved in observer (navigator) training, running twelve-month courses for direct-entry personnel. In March 1939 both squadrons then became Group Pool squadrons, and converted to Whitleys before moving to Abingdon in September. After a period of inactivity Leconfield was taken over by No. 13 Group, Fighter Command, in October 1939.

LINTON-ON-OUSE NW OF YORK OFF THE A19

Linton-on-Ouse was officially opened on 13 May 1937, firstly as the HQ for No. 4 Group, and then, after construction was almost complete, it also became a bomber base. This is an example of one of the earlier bomber airfields constructed in the mid-1930s north of Linton-on-Ouse and the River Ouse. An arc of five C-Type hangars, backed by technical buildings and administrative buildings, was situated on the south-east side of the airfield. The first occupants were Nos 51 and 58 Squadrons' Whitleys, which arrived from Boscombe Down in April 1938. These two squadrons were to be the first to penetrate German airspace when they dropped propaganda leaflets during the first few days of the war. For one month, between April and May 1939, No. 58 Squadron was equipped with Heyford IIIs.

THORNABY W OF MIDDLESBOROUGH ADJACENT TO THE A1045

Thornaby was built prior to the Expansion period, one of the first to be opened after the Great War. It had very few facilities, was situated to the west of Thornaby and bounded on the east by Stainsby Beck. The technical and other buildings were situated in the north-western corner of the airfield, and to the south-west was Thornaby Wood, with Stainsby Wood to the south-east. On 17 March 1930 No. 608 (North Riding) Squadron of the Auxiliary Air Force was formed here as a light-bomber squadron. It was equipped with Wapitis, which arrived in June. No. 224 Squadron arrived from Tangmere on 26 March 1938 with Anson Is, and No. 233 Squadron, also with Anson Is, arrived on 9 July. Although No. 224 Squadron moved temporarily to Eastleigh in January 1938, it returned to Thornaby in the March. Both squadrons then departed for Leuchars on 1 September. Next month Nos 606 and 185 Squadrons arrived with their Battles. Both these squadrons came and went during the following months, finally moving to Cottesmore. In September 1939 the airfield was transferred to No. 18 Group of Coastal Command.

YEADON NE OF YEADON ON THE A658

Yeadon was officially opened as Leeds/Bradford Municipal Airport on 17 October 1931, but with unrest in Europe an RAF presence was established upon the formation of No. 609 (West Riding) Squadron of the Auxiliary Air Force on 10 February 1936. It was a light-bomber squadron with Hawker Harts, later Hinds, and temporary hangars were constructed in the north-west corner of the field. Then in 1938 a Civil Air Guard unit was formed, and there was a huge increase in flying training. In December 1938 No. 609 Squadron was redesignated a fighter squadron, and with its Spitfires, moved to its war station at Catterick on 27 August 1939. With the outbreak of war the airfield was requisitioned by the RAF as a fighter station in No. 13 Group.

YORK N OF YORK BETWEEN THE A19 AND THE B1363

York was officially opened for civil flying on 4 July 1936, and was controlled by Yorkshire Aviation Services Ltd. At the outbreak of war in September 1939 the club's airfield, as well as its aircraft, was requisitioned by the RAF. Its initial wartime role was as a relief landing-ground and dispersal site for Linton-on-Ouse.

AIRFIELDS AND SEAPLANE BASES OF SCOTLAND AND NORTHERN IRELAND

ABBOTSINCH 5 MILES WEST OF GLASGOW CITY

An RAF station HQ was formed at Abbotsinch on 1 July 1936, a unit under the command of No. 6 Auxiliary Group of Bomber Command. No. 602 had been operating from the station since 1933, when it had airport status, and the squadron had re-equipped with Hawker Hinds. On 1 January 1937 the station was transferred to Coastal Command and No. 269 Squadron was posted in with Ansons from Bircham Newton to undertake in-shore patrols. On 2 May 1938 Nos 602 and 603 Squadrons flew over Ibrox Stadium in salute when it was officially opened by King George VI. Shortly before war began No. 602 Squadron was sent to Grangemouth with its new Spitfires.

ACKLINGTON 3 MILES NE OF FELTON

Acklington was the main fighter base in the North-East of England, housing Spitfires, Hurricanes, and Gladiators, though not, of course, all at the same time. It was built on the site of a Great War landing-ground known as Southfields, and was opened as No. 7 Armament Training School. A change of name followed on 15 November 1938 to No. 2 Air Observers School, which was reminiscent of the Great War, when changes of title were made to service establishments in rapid succession. The school moved to Warmwell in Dorset on the outbreak of war. The airfield then became a satellite of Usworth until the fighters arrived.

ALDERGROVE 4 MILES S OF ANTRIM

The history of this airfield dates back to the Great War, and it is one of the few that survived the rundown after 1919. Although it was officially closed that year, it was reactivated for air exercises. It was also used by No. 2 Squadron when the latter was standing by to counter possible trouble in Ulster. When No. 502 Squadron was formed in 1925 as an Auxiliary bomber squadron, the station came into permanent RAF use, and remains so to this day, even if the site is shared by Belfast Airport. In October 1935 No. 502 Squadron became a day-bomber squadron with Wallaces and Hinds. No. 9 Squadron's Virginias visited the station in January 1936, but it was then re-equipped with Heyford IIIs before moving on to Scampton on 1 October 1936. Aldergrove was often used for camps and exercises by first-line squadrons and flying training schools. No. 2 Armament Training Camp formed at Aldergrove in March 1936, and a Meteorological Flight equipped with Bulldogs started work in the October of that year. The Armament Camp became No. 2 Armament Training Station (ATS), which combined with No. 1 ATS on 17 April 1939 to become No. 3 Bombing and Gunnery School on 1 November 1939.

ALNESS 1 MILE S OF ALNESS

Alness was first used as a mooring area for flying-boats, and there was a slipway for beaching aircraft. Before the Second World War flying-boats would call there, as for example, when No. 201 Squadron's Londons stayed for a week in October 1938. Singapores and Stranraers of

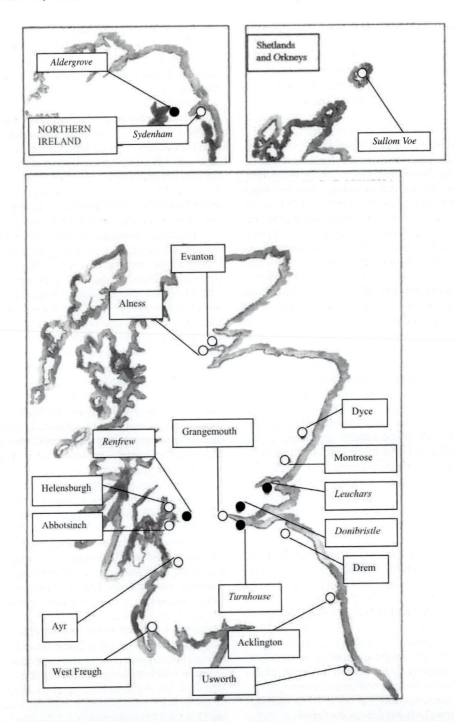

No. 209 Squadron Felixstowe also paid a visit. In August 1939 No. 240 Squadron arrived from Calshot before taking up its war station at Sullom Voe two months after the war began.

DONIBRISTLE 2 MILES E OF ROSYTHE

This sheltered airfield was in constant service use from 1917 until 1959. The RNAS had used it as a place where

shipborne aircraft could be stored and repaired. When the RAF took over control of Donibristle in 1918, it stayed in its previous role as a Fleet Aircraft Repair Depot. With aircraft-carriers berthed at nearby Rosyth, the depot was in a convenient location. Although it was put on a Care and Maintenance basis in 1921, it was reactivated in 1925 as a shore base for disembarked carrier flights. On 30 November 1930, No. 100 Squadron arrived from Bicester with its Horsleys, so that torpedo delivery could be practised in the sheltered waters of the Forth. Then in December 1933, the squadron re-equipped with Vildebeests before being redeployed to the Far East. This made room for No. 22 Squadron, which was re-formed on 1 May 1934 equipped with Vildebeests.

DREM 2 MILES S OF DIRLETON
Drem had been a Great War airfield, but remained unused after the war ended until September 1933. Then it became a refuelling point during a coastal defence exercise. Then another dormant period passed before the arrival of No. 13 FTS early in 1939, equipped with Oxfords, Harts and Audaxes. When war came the FTS had to make way for Spitfires because Drem was well positioned to provide fighter defence for the Scottish Lowlands.

DYCE 6 MILES NW OF ABERDEEN
Dyce started life as a civil airport linking it with Thurso, Wick and the Orkneys. Services were extended to Edinburgh, the Shetlands and Norway. The company was Allied Airways. On 1 June 1937, No. 612 Squadron was formed on the airfield, equipped with Hectors employed in Army Cooperation work, but the role was changed in July 1939 to a general reconnaissance role, and the aircraft were changed to Ansons.

EVANTON 1 MILE NE OF EVANTON
On 16 August 1937, No. 8 Armament Training Camp was formed at Evanton, a unit of Training Command, and the buildings had previously belonged to Coastal Command. The small airfield had been used by the FAA for aircraft being disembarked from aircraft-carriers of the fleet. Some examples were Nos 800, 801, 820 and 821 Squadrons. The airfield was also visited by Nos 7 and 99 Squadrons, and the trainees of Nos 6 and 8 FTSs spent some time here on courses.

GRANGEMOUTH JUST SE OF THE TOWN
It was the former RAF Chief of the Air Staff, Marshal of the Royal Air Force Viscount Trenchard, who opened Grangemouth on 1 May 1939 as the Central Scotland Airport. On that day RAF use began, with the opening of No. 35 E & RFTS, equipped with Tiger Moths and Harts. Then No. 10 Civilian Air Navigation School opened, with Ansons. Administered by Scottish Aviation, these units had a short life with the closure of the E & RFTS and the absorption of the Air Navigation School into No. 1 AONS at Prestwick. In the month that the war opened and in succeeding months Grangemouth was associated with fighter movements.

HELENSBURGH ¹/₂ MILE S OF RHU
On the outbreak of war the Marine Aircraft Experimental Establishment moved from Felixstowe,

where it had been throughout the inter-war years. Its move to Helensburgh would take it well away from likely combat zones, and work on flying-boats and depth charges continued. In August 1945 the MAEE was returned to Felixstowe.

LEUCHARS 5 MILES NW OF ST ANDREWS
Scotland certainly had its share of military airfields that date back to the earliest days of flying. Leuchars is one of them, for the Royal Engineers experimented with balloons on the field in 1911. During the 1920s the station was used for aircraft that had been disembarked from aircraft-carriers, and a base training squadron for FAA aircraft was formed in 1932. In February 1935 this unit became No. 1 Flying Training School, with jurisdiction over the Tentsmuir Ranges. Flying instruction was given to RN officers on Ospreys, Seals, Tutors, Nimrods and Harts. In August 1938 No. 1 FTS moved to Netheravon, and Leuchars joined Coastal Command. With the arrival of Nos 224 and 233 Squadrons' Anson Is on 1 September 1938, the station became operational for the first time. Soon both squadrons re-equipped with Hudsons, and on the second day of the war one of No. 224 Squadron's Hudsons attacked a Dornier 18 over the North Sea.

MONTROSE 1 MILE N OF MONTROSE
Montrose is the oldest military airfield in Scotland. The hangars on the airfield were of various types, reflecting the different stages of the airfield's development, and they date back to 1912. In January 1913 No. 2 Squadron came to the airfield, which was active during the Great War as a training station or as a base for forming squadrons. When the war ended the airfield was abandoned and was not reactivated until 1 January 1936. £18,600 was paid for the land, and No. 5 FTS was established, giving *ab initio* training to forty-eight trainees. Having laid dormant for so long, it required much levelling and turfing before the Hart and Audax aircraft could operate. The war had begun before the Master monoplane trainer came to replace the biplanes.

PRESTWICK 1 MILE N OF PRESTWICK
No. 12 E & RFTS was formed at Prestwick on the date of the official opening and was operated by Scottish Aviation Ltd using Harts and Tiger Moths. On the outbreak of war this unit became No. 12 EFTS.

RENFREW STRATHCLYDE
Renfrew's use as an airfield changed from military to civil and back to military over a number of years. It was used during the Great War and lay dormant after it. In 1925 No. 602 Squadron was formed here, and the following year the Scottish Flying Club opened. The DH9s and Fawns of the squadron were replaced by Wapitis in 1929, but then the unit was moved to Abbotsinch in January 1933. Back in civilian use for the

An expansion airfield – the newly completed RAF Finningley in 1936 with its resident squadron, No. 102 Squadron, equipped with Heyford IIs and IIIs. This unit suffered a peacetime disaster when seven of the squadron's aircraft, en route from Northern Ireland, encountered fog and severe icing conditions. Only one aircraft reached Finningley. Three force-landed and three crashed. One crew abandoned their aircraft and six men were casualties, three of them fatal.

remainder of the 1930s, the RAF did not return to Renfrew until 6 November 1940, with the arrival of No. 309 Squadron.

SULLOM VOE 25 MILES N OF LERWICK

Sullom Voe was set up in 1939 to be able to cover the gap between Norway and Iceland, so that if enemy surface units tried to break out into the North Atlantic they might be detected. Indeed, this was to be the case with the German pocket battleships, battle cruisers and battleships (*Graf Spee*, *Admiral Scheer*, *Deutschland*, *Scharnhorst* and *Bismarck*) that for a time acted as a grave threat to the British merchant fleet in the early war years. The first aircraft to come to the moorings at Sullom Voe were the Sunderlands of No. 201 Squadron, which arrived from Calshot on 9 August 1939. The squadron aircraft patrolled until 6 November, and were then replaced by the Londons of No. 240 Squadron.

SYDENHAM 2 MILES NE OF BELFAST

In 1933 the land beside Harland and Wolff's shipyard was converted into an aerodrome, but the land was considered too soft to cope with passenger traffic. Harland and Wolff improved the landing ground as part of the rearmament programme, and Sydenham was officially opened on 16 March 1938. On 1 January 1939 No. 24 E & RFTS was opened, with Short Brothers as the operating company. Pupils were trained on Tiger Moths and Magisters before moving on to Harts and Demons. In 1940 the airport was taken over by the RAF.

TURNHOUSE 5 MILES W OF EDINBURGH

Turnhouse was active during the Great War. After the war the station became the base for No. 603 Squadron, formed there in 1925. On 24 October 1938 the squadron became a fighter unit with Gladiators, and then Spitfires. On 4 August 1936 No. 83 Squadron re-formed here and moved on to Scampton in February 1938. In September 1939 Turnhouse became a sector station in No. 13 Group.

USWORTH 2 MILES SW OF BOLDON

Usworth was in military use during the Great War, but was not activated again until the 1930s. On 17 March 1930 No. 607 Squadron was formed, but it was two years before the squadron personnel could occupy the site. This was an Auxiliary day-bomber unit, and it received its Wapitis in December 1932. Demons replaced the Wapitis in September 1936, and the unit was redesignated a fighter squadron. In December 1938 the squadron converted to the Gladiator I, and the squadron went to war with this aircraft. From 26 February 1937 No. 103 Squadron operated from Usworth with Hinds, and then Battles, and moved on to Abingdon on 2 September 1938. G Flight of No. 1 AACU was at Usworth from 1 February 1939 until May of that year.

WEST FREUGH 5 MILES SE OF STRANRAER

Building work began at West Freugh in August 1936 for a camp and ranges. Early problems were encountered in Luce Bay, where the bombing targets were situated, as the 6 ft piles driven into the sand failed to withstand the wind and the tide. This meant that when No. 4 Armament Training Camp opened on 1 January 1937, it was not until the end of April that the targets were ready. The improved targets were mounted on three towers constructed from steel plates and girders. A number of units came and went, and on 1 April 1938 the unit was renamed No. 4 Armament Training Camp. Heyfords came to the ranges for training air observers in bombing and firing. Another change of name, to No. 4 Air Observers' School, came in 1939, and Battles were added to the establishment. On 1 November 1939 the unit was again renamed, to No. 4 Bombing and Gunnery School.

AIRFIELDS OVERSEAS

ABU SUEIR EGYPT

Abu Sueir is perhaps best remembered as the home of No. 4 FTS. In the early days of the RAF, Trenchard regarded Egypt as the 'Clapham Junction' of the Middle East, from where squadrons could be deployed in an emergency, and it was very useful if men who were serving abroad could be trained to fly without having to return to the United Kingdom. On occasion Army officers were trained and transferred to the RAF. A bomber squadron, No. 214, briefly stayed at Abu Sueir in 1920. In August 1938 work began on buildings for the storage and maintenance of aircraft. This would be

No. 102 MU, which was opened in the November. Abu Sueir did not become a RAF station proper until the day before the outbreak of war, when No. 4 FTS moved to Habbaniya.

DRIGH ROAD INDIA

Otherwise known as the Karachi Depot, Drigh Road was where the RAF squadrons operating on the North-West Frontier would come for repaired or replacement aircraft. The unit also assembled aircraft that had arrived at Karachi by sea, such as the DH9As and Wapitis. It was not a base for squadrons, although No. 31 Squadron was forced to take refuge there after the Quetta earthquake in 1935. It was not until the Second World War that the scope of its facilities was extended to cover the maintenance and supply of aircraft in Burma and Malaya.

GIBRALTAR

There is no doubt of Gibraltar's strategic importance standing at the western entrance to the Mediterranean, where it could monitor the movement of enemy vessels, particularly submarines. The use of the colony for military air operations goes back to the Great War. The RAF station, with paved runways, eventually took the name of 'North Front' in 1942, but in the early days landplanes took off from the racecourse and seaplanes from the harbour. One of the main problems for aircraft

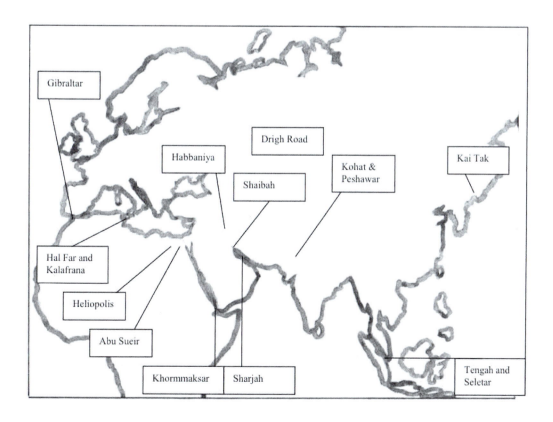

using Gibraltar was the air turbulence around the famous 'Rock'. The Navy had used the facilities for flying floatplanes like the Short 184, and when the Great War ended and the squadrons were handed over to the RAF, these were disbanded as part of the post-war rundown. Only the FAA used the racecourse, for disembarked aircraft from carriers or warships. In the 1930s RAF flying-boats would pass through, and the Rangoons and Singapores of No. 210 Squadron were attached from Pembroke Dock from 28 September 1935 to 7 August 1936. It was planned that No. 202 Squadron would move from Kalafrana, Malta, to Gibraltar in the event of war, and so early in 1939 the London IIs paid a visit in preparation for the move.

HABBANIYA IRAQ
A clause of the Anglo-Iraqi Treaty permitted the British a base west of the Euphrates, and work began in 1934 to build a station at Dhibban, later changed to Habbaniya. It was first formed as an RAF station in March 1937, but it had been used as an airfield since 19 October 1936, when No. 30 Squadron arrived, equipped with the Hawker Hardy. This squadron moved to Ismailia a week before the outbreak of the Second World War. During the same period the Vincents of No. 55 Squadron and the Valentias of No. 70 Squadron were based at the station. These units again moved on with the outbreak of war, making way for No. 4 FTS, which had for so many years been based at Abu Sueir. The FTS was equipped with Oxfords, Harts, Gordons and an Anson.

HAL FAR MALTA
RAF Station Hal Far was opened on 31 March 1929, and a station flight was formed shortly afterwards consisting of Fairey IIIFs. Most of the use during the early 1930s was by disembarked carrier flights from Nos 802 Squadron (Nimrods), 812 Squadron (Ripons) and 823 Squadron (Fairey IIIFs and Seals).

In May 1935 there was a spectacular display of night formation flying by illuminated aircraft of No. 812 Squadron and aerobatics by two Avro Tutors. When the Abyssinian crisis arose in late 1935, twelve Demons arrived at Hal Far to become No. 74 Squadron, and these were joined by Vildebeests of No. 22 Squadron, which were prepared, if called upon, to attack units of the Italian fleet. With the end of the crisis these squadrons returned to the UK and Hal Far returned to the role of receiving disembarked units of the FAA. It will be remembered from Chapter 6 that the FAA came under RAF control until 1938, when it returned to the Navy. By this time Swordfish aircraft were being disembarked. No. 3 Anti-Aircraft Cooperation Unit was formed at the station on 1 March 1937, equipped with de Havilland Queen Bees. Just before the outbreak of hostilities in 1939 No. 3 AACU was designated an operational unit and

absorbed the Station Flight into its establishment. A spotter detachment for coastal defence cooperation was formed in July 1938, equipped with one Fairey Seal, which was attached to the Station Flight.

HELIOPOLIS EGYPT
Military flying at Heliopolis dates back to the Great War, and after the war two bomber squadrons were stationed there. No. 216 Squadron began a twenty-one year stay in 1925. On 1 March 1928 Heliopolis became an RAF station, and in 1931 the station provided personnel to assist with mooring the *Graf Zeppelin* airship when it paid a visit to Almaza. Also in 1931, No. 216 Squadron, which had been carrying passengers and mail, was designated a bomber-transport squadron with its Victoria aircraft. Immediately before the war a number of Fleet Air Arm units paid visits to the station. No. 64 Squadron was re-formed here on 1 March 1936, and equipped with Demons before departing the following month for Ismailia. No. 208 Squadron, which had been re-formed at Ismailia, came to the station on 18 April 1936, and numerous detachments were made from this before the squadron went briefly to Mersa Matruh in September 1938, returning to the station on 13 October. The squadron was then equipped with Lysanders I and II, and left again in early 1939 for Mersa Matruh and other stations before finally returning to Heliopolis in November 1939. The number of Blenheims passing through the station *en route* for India was such that it was necessary to set up a Blenheim Servicing Flight.

KAI TAK HONG KONG
On 10 March 1927 Kai Tak was taken over by the RAF, mainly for the use of the FAA. Much work remained to be done even after its opening, including the building of a slipway and seawall for the flying-boats. No. 442 Flight was the permanent unit, equipped with Fairey IIIFs. In September 1928 four Southampton flying-boats of the Far East Flight arrived in the harbour for a short stay before returning to Singapore. When No. 442 Fleet Reconnaissance Flight returned to the UK, leaving the colony in August 1930, no permanent flying unit remained. Until 1 April 1935, the establishment had been titled the 'RAF Base Kai Tak'. On that date it became formally RAF Station, Kai Tak. At about that time a Marine Craft section was established, giving service to and working with the flying-boats. Then a Station Flight was formed with Hawker Horsleys previously belonging to No. 36 Squadron in Singapore. Another responsibility was the small number of Walrus and Swordfish aircraft that made reconnaissance flights over Japanese ships supporting their forces advancing into China. There was a need to improve the facilities, but Japanese occupation of the colony in 1941 brought an end to such plans.

KALAFRANA MALTA

Kalafrana had been active during the Great War, and on 1 April 1918 it was handed over by the Admiralty to the RAF. The inter-war years began with the station becoming a self-accounting site with a resident unit, No. 481 Flight. Carrier-borne aircraft also disembarked to the station. On 1 January 1929 No. 481 Flight became No. 202 Squadron, equipped with Fairey IIIDs. The squadron set off on an Eastern Mediterranean cruise in July 1931. During the 1930s the station was known as RAF Base Kalafrana. An assortment of British and French seaplanes called in to the station, and three of No. 203 Squadron's Rangoons staged through on their way to Basrah in February 1931. On 15 July 1936 four catapult flights were using Kalafrana as a base. These were Nos 701, 705, 711 and 713 Flights of the FAA. Anti-piracy patrols were mounted from the station using Singapores of No 209 Squadron, which was detached from Felixstowe from 22 to 30 September 1937. These patrols were organized for the benefit of British shipping during the Spanish Civil War. No. 202 Squadron took over this task with its London IIs, and the station began the task of repairing and overhauling these aircraft. On the outbreak of war No. 202 Squadron moved to Gibraltar.

KHORMAKSAR ADEN

Khormaksar had been busy during the 1920s, when its resident squadron, No. 8, was actively involved in internal security operations against dissident tribesmen. This continued into the 1930s, with No. 8 Squadron being alone until the arrival of Nos 12 and 41 Squadrons in October 1935 during the Abyssinian crisis. In March 1939 the colony acquired its own Protectorate Defence Force, with Sea Gladiators, sensing the possibility of opposition from the Italians in Somaliland. Then No. 8 Squadron was equipped with Blenheims to add to its Vincents. On the outbreak of war No. 8 Squadron continued with its punitive raids against dissident villages.

KOHAT NORTH-WEST FRONTIER

Kohat had been busy hosting units operating along the North-West Frontier. The station enjoyed exceptional facilities, such as a swimming pool, tennis courts and a golf course. These were shared with the local Army units and the resident squadron, No. 60. In the very hot weather the squadron personnel would go to a hill depot, where conditions were a little cooler. In the spring of 1930 the old warhorse, the DH9A, was at last retired, to be replaced by the Wapiti. Throughout the 1930s the operations against dissident tribesmen continued (see Chapter 4).

PESHAWAR NORTH-WEST FRONTIER

This airfield was very active during the 1920s. (The term 'airfield' is used because it did not officially become an RAF station until 1940. The word 'station' will, however, be used) It was actively engaged in the Kabul rescue in 1929 since it is very close to Afghanistan, being not much more than thirty miles from the Khyber Pass. In the early 1930s No. 20 Squadron was involved in the operations against the 'Red Shirts (see Chapter 4 – No. 20 Squadron). The squadron's role was to fly aerial reconnaissance flights and monitor movement of people in and around the villages. Re-equipment of the squadron with Wapitis was not complete until January 1932. At long last the Bristol F2B was to be pensioned off! Apart from the air-control operations, No. 20 Squadron was engaged in the relief operations following the earthquake at Quetta. In December 1935 the Wapiti was replaced with the Hawker Audax aircraft. In May 1939 No. 20 Squadron pilots collected four Hawker Hinds from Drigh Road, Karachi, for onward delivery to the Afghan Air Force. Before they were handed over, the pilots demonstrated message snatching and supply dropping. In August 1939 No. 20 Squadron moved to Miranshah.

SHAIBAH IRAQ

Shaibah was very active during the 1920s, but apart from air-control duties, the 1930s were very quiet. No. 84 Squadron remained the resident RAF unit and administered the station (see Chapter 4 for operational commitments of No. 84 Squadron).

SHARJAH TRUCIAL STATES

Sharjah was used as an airfield as early as the early 1930s. In July 1932 HMG signed an agreement with the local sheikh for the use of the airfield by Imperial Airways. Imperial had had to adopt a more southerly route when an agreement with Persia to use her air space had expired. By 1933 No. 70 Squadron's Victorias and Nos 55 and 84 Squadrons' Wapitis were routing through Sharjah. Operational RAF aircraft did not use the airfield until 1940.

SELETAR SINGAPORE

The origins of this airfield date back to 1921, when HMG decided to build a naval base in Singapore. Construction began in 1926. Singapore did not have a civil airport, and permission was obtained for civil aircraft to use the airfield. No. 205 Squadron with Southampton II flying-boats was re-formed on 8 January 1929 and situated in the harbour nearby. This unit had been formed from the flying-boats that had belonged to the Far East Flight and had been flown, by stages, from Felixstowe. On 1 January 1930 RAF Base Singapore was officially opened, and in the following December No. 36 Squadron arrived with Hawker Horsley torpedo-bombers. The first squadron task was to make survey flights over the Malay peninsula to search for potential landing-grounds. Then it was tasked to bomb rebels in Burma. In

December 1933 the headquarters of Far East Command was established at Seletar, and on 6 January No. 100 Squadron arrived from Donibristle, equipped with the Vildebeest II, bringing the station strength up to three squadrons. In December 1935 a training commitment arose with the formation of the Straits Settlement Volunteer Air Force, equipped with Harts, Audaxes and Tutors. No. 230 Squadron, equipped with Singapore IIIs, arrived from Pembroke Dock on 8 January 1937, which gave Seletar two flying-boat squadrons. In June 1938 No. 230 Squadron was re-equipped with Sunderland I flying-boats. When war was declared in 1939 it did not greatly affect the units in the Far East. That would all change with the Japanese attack on Pearl Harbor on 7 December 1941.

TENGAH SINGAPORE

When Japanese forces invaded Manchuria in 1932 and moved down into China, there was concern about the security of Singapore and Malaya, and defence measures were put in train. But it was not until 1937 that contractors began to clear the site, and cutting down the rubber and coconut trees delayed completion of the airfield, which comprised the station buildings and a 2,500 ft landing-strip. On 5 August 1939 Wing Commander McFarlane became the first station commander. Nos 11 and 39 Squadrons arrived from India, equipped with Blenheim Is, but left for Kallang in September, to be replaced by Nos 34 and 62 Squadrons, which became Tengah's first resident units.

Chapter 8
Support Services – Technical and Supply

Introduction – Repair and maintenance in early 1930s – Repair and maintenance in response to expansion – Increased recruitment and training of maintenance personnel – Fitter training – Technical tradesmen – Organization of maintenance and supply – The formation of a Technical Branch – The Halton Apprentices – Constitution of the Stores Branch – Supply at station level

Introduction

Chapter 8 of Volume I dealt with the Apprentice Scheme and the technical support given to flying operations on an RAF station. On the supply side the basics of equipment administration at station level were explained. Two things stand out in a study of the RAF in the 1920s: firstly, that the repair and maintenance facilities had only to provide for a small metropolitan air force, with additional repair and supply depots situated in the various theatres overseas; secondly, that the lack of the sophistication of aircraft at that time meant that specialist career technical officers were not required. Trenchard's air force was a pilot's air force, where officers were expected to fly and where airmen of the technical trades worked under the direction of a squadron pilot who had the appropriate specialist suffix to his title to enable him to oversee the work. Officers who had to oversee the engineering work of the squadron would have attended a course at the Home Aircraft Depot at Henlow. This would hardly turn them into experts in engine overhaul or the rigging of an aircraft, but the Apprentice Scheme was designed to provide the peacetime air force with skilled technical tradesmen who could be relied upon to carry out their work with the minimum of oversight. These Halton 'brats', as they were affectionately known, would also be the firm base upon which the RAF would be built in a time of rapid expansion.

As the RAF entered the 1930s, the situation had hardly changed from that of the previous decade. The government still applied the Ten-Year Rule, which did not envisage a major war for at least ten years, this figure being carried forward from year to year. Secondly, the modest expansion scheme announced by the government in 1923 did not specify a completion date, so that it could be delayed to suit political and economic circumstances of the time. In the period 1930 to 1932 the country was in the grip of an economic depression of exceptional severity, and was also committed to the pursuit of international disarmament at the Geneva Conference. The repair and maintenance facilities of the RAF were adequate until the expansion began, and even then it was not until the last moment that the provision of these facilities to a greatly expanded service was considered and measures were put in hand to remedy a lack of them.

The expansion schemes that began to be activated in 1934 were lettered A to M, and have been described in detail in Chapters 2 and 3. In short, it was necessary to provide for:

1. Front-line squadrons to meet the air threat to the British Isles and the Empire, and to carry the war to the enemy.
2. Sufficient reserves to meet wastage rates in a war of attrition.
3. The repair and maintenance of aircraft both at home and overseas.

REPAIR AND MAINTENANCE IN THE EARLY 1930s

It was anticipated that in peacetime the wastage rate would be between 16 and 20% of front-line strength per annum, rising to between 40 and 50% in the event of a major war. At home there was the Home Aircraft Depot at Henlow, where aircraft could be repaired and where tradesmen could be trained, not only for the Metropolitan Air Force but for overseas theatres. Abroad, repair and maintenance was almost entirely a service responsibility. There were supply depots like Lahore, and repair and assembly facilities like those at Drigh Road, Karachi, where crated aircraft from the UK were assembled and flight tested before collection by squadrons. These facilities were adequate at that time, and it is interesting that the expansion plans that were put into effect, beginning in 1934, dramatically increased the number of front-line squadrons and aircraft in reserve without a corresponding increase of the capacity to repair and maintain these aircraft.

The Home Aircraft Depot, Henlow
(Source: AMWO – A60/32)

The Home Aircraft Depot in 1930 was administered by HQ No. 21 Group of Inland Area. The Air Ministry's Director of Equipment dealt directly with the Commanding Officer Home Aircraft Depot (HAD) on questions relating to:

1. Output of engines and airframes.
2. Development of special items of ground and workshop equipment, as required from time to time by the service.

3. The requirements of the Depot in works services and telephones affecting the Depot's functions.
4. Allotment of airframes and engines.
5. Write-off and disposal of airframes and engines.
6. Test and issue of parachutes.
7. Supply of technical stores.
8. Allotment and control of mechanical transport.

All other matters were the responsibility of the Air Officer Commanding Inland Area (through the CO, No. 21 Group), subject to the following procedure in regard to the items mentioned.

The establishment of the Home Aircraft Depot

In the event of mobilization the service would need to mobilize an Expeditionary Force Depot (EFD), which would have to be manned entirely by the HAD. The establishment of the HAD. would have to be twice that of the EFD and it would have to be organized in such a way that the work of the HAD was not disrupted on mobilization. There would also have to be included in the establishment of the HAD an additional allowance for the manning of those functions peculiar to it, namely the Engineering Officers' Course and the parachute-testing unit.

The functions of the Home Aircraft Depot

The general functions of the HAD were to be based on the productive requirements of the EFD. This would mean organizing the workshops to provide 'flow production'. The organization and administration of the depot had to give due consideration to mobility. The technical personnel would need to familiarize themselves with the types of aircraft and engines that would accompany the expeditionary force, and the intake of these items would be limited, as far as possible, to the expeditionary types. This would include a sufficient number of airframes and engines of the latest types that might be used to equip expeditionary force squadrons. This 'special' intake would be limited so as not to interfere with flow production. The CO of the HAD was required to submit half-yearly reports to the Air Ministry on 1 January and 1 July, indicating the anticipated output of the depot in airframes and engines during the six months that were to follow. He would also have to account for any variation between the anticipated and actual output on a Form 1284.

The Home Aircraft Depot in 1938

By 1938 it was realized that additional steps must be taken to provide trained men of all trades for maintenance duties in the RAF under the expansion programme, and that the whole of overseas maintenance depended on the availability of personnel at the home depots. Accordingly the Air Member for Supply and Organization (AMSO) asked what the requirements

would be for accommodation at the training units. This was to meet Expansion Scheme K up to April 1939. On receiving this information he concluded that a considerable expansion of ground training facilities was necessary. Even then it would take several years before deficiencies in certain trades were made up. By mid-1939 the new repair depots that could provide training facilities, at Sealand and St Athan, would be ready but would not be working to capacity until mid-1940. Henlow had been unable to shed its training role and return to repair due to the escalating training needs consequent upon the expansion. It should have reverted to a depot by 1937 at the latest. In March 1938 it was clear that even the opening of training schools at Sealand and St Athan would not permit the re-establishment of Henlow as a repair depot. Ground training accommodation had not been extended since the inception of Expansion Scheme C, and the training facilities at Henlow and Manston were simply insufficient.

To increase the total ground training capacity it was decided to establish a new technical school with three training wings at Weston-Super-Mare for the instruction of Fitters III as an alternative to Manston, and to erect hutted accommodation for 1,000 trainees at Henlow. Looking back, one can see that moving training from Manston was to take a sensible precaution. Its proximity to the coast of northern France made it a prime target for the *Luftwaffe* in the Battle of Britain, and the airfield was at times so badly cratered that it was unusable.

THE ORGANIZATION OF REPAIR AND MAINTENANCE IN RESPONSE TO EXPANSION

Introduction

With only eighteen months to go before the outbreak of war there was no repair depot or properly planned system of repair. With the rapid expansion of the service, British industry was too busy with the production of new aircraft and weapons, which left no spare capacity to expand repair facilities. At home civilian firms could be contracted to undertake work for the Air Ministry, but overseas repair work was almost an entirely service responsibility. What was needed was the creation of an efficient repair organization at home and a pool of fully trained men from which overseas depots could draw.

Civilian versus service manning of repair depots

If the HAD was to be re-established as a depot, it raised the question, should it be civilian or service manned? If the needs of overseas depots were to be met then it made sense to have the depot service manned, but there was an acute shortage of service technical staff at this time. Another argument in favour of a service-manned depot was the necessity to provide RAF working parties, whose task it was to install into aircraft any equipment not incorporated before delivery and to incorporate certain modifications. If these working parties were not available, the aircraft would have to be returned to the factory, with consequent delay and expense. On the other hand a service-manned depot was more expensive to run than one that was civilian manned, and it was hoped that the Sealand and St Athan depots would suffice. Meanwhile the Director of Aircraft Production was looking to see if there was any spare industrial capacity that could be used for repair work. He preferred a civilian organization, since the service depots would be primarily engaged in training servicemen rather than acting as production units. The Air Member for Research and Development (AMRD) foresaw difficulty in staffing civilian repair depots, and pointed out that personnel, once trained, could not be held. On the other hand service manning of the proposed repair depots might result in manpower shortages on RAF stations, so the Secretary of State for Air suggested that service units situated near industrial areas might relieve any resulting RAF manpower shortage by employing civilians. To counter this suggestion it was pointed out that the provision of service transport to collect civilians would present problems.

On 15 March 1938 the Secretary of State announced a plan to overcome the bottleneck of skilled repair and maintenance personnel. The Cabinet had just accepted the accelerated Scheme K, and a resolution of this problem became ever more urgent. Selected firms engaged in Expansion Plan production could erect shops alongside factories to be used for the repair of aircraft. Firms could, in fact, repair their own products and thus allow service personnel to concentrate on maintenance rather than repair. In spite of this proposal, nothing was done. There was hope that Henlow could soon return to its depot function, for it was still acting as a school of technical training. Six months passed and the two training schools that were supposed to take on the technical training had not opened. No forecast could be obtained for the completion of the RAF stations at St Athan and Weston-super-Mare. This led AMSO to conclude that the building of a front-line air force to rival the *Luftwaffe* was nothing but a façade. The question of repair depots was one of many items essential for the maintenance of the RAF that was lacking.

Three service depots were approved, at Sealand, St Athan and Henlow. The proposals for civilian depots was not approved, but it was agreed that, on completion of the Expansion Programme, the shadow factories might take on repair work. Then the Munich Crisis of September 1938 led the AMSO to raise the question of civilian-manned repair depots yet again, but after discussion it was considered that only one was possible

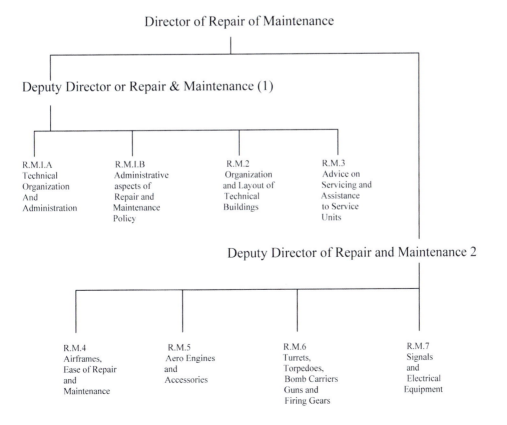

at that time. A site at Preston was looked at, and at the Expansion Progress Meeting (EPM) No. 138 it was finally agreed to establish a civilian-manned repair depot at Warrington (Burtonwood). By the time the work started on the Warrington depot in November 1938 it had been decided to return to the original plan, of having three civilian-manned depots, and machine-tools for three depots were ordered without delay (EPM No. 140). But there was a difference of opinion over whether or not two larger depots would be preferable to three smaller ones. The Director of Supply and Maintenance believed that each depot should be capable of repairing 500 aircraft annually, but would take further advice.

At this very late stage, with war imminent, the construction, layout and functioning of the civilian repair depots was still undecided, and the Air Council sought advice from such persons as Sir Malcolm McAlpine as to the construction of these depots. At last it was possible to decide upon the second site, at Abbotsinch, with a third depot at Stoke (EPM No. 161). It was by then 27 June 1939, with war only two months away, yet the policy with regard to managerial staffing, industrial relations and the running of the depots had not been decided. One thought was for large engineering firms to run the depots on an agency basis, where demand for their products was likely to diminish with time. When war came, however, no firm policy had been decided.

INCREASED RECRUITMENT AND TRAINING OF MAINTENANCE PERSONNEL
Introduction
Thus far the discussion has centred upon the argument over civilian versus service manning, and the policy for running of the civilian repair depots. Of equal importance was the recruitment of technical tradesmen into the RAF. The Apprentice Schools started in the early 1920s had recruited boys into a variety of trades. They came into the service for a career, and some of them reached Air rank. Alongside the apprentices were the direct-entry tradesmen, who were trained at such stations as Manston, again in a variety of technical trades. Recruitment to personnel establishments in the 1920s had not been a problem, but come the expansion, shortages began to appear. It would be possible to meet growing manpower needs by recruiting apprentices over and above the peacetime intakes, as well as boosting the number of direct-entry recruits. This did not, however, alter the fact that all were coming from the same national pool of available manpower, and the Army and Navy were 'fishing in the same pool'.

Fitters and Mates
An example of the shortages that were arising in 1935 is that of the trade of Fitter II. Men in these trades were needed to man the ever-rising number of RAF squadrons. As a temporary measure the trades of Flight Rigger and Flight Mechanic were introduced. These men would fill airacraftmen posts in flights and would be supervised by skilled rigger and fitter NCOs. They had to have engineering or mechanical training on enlistment. Initially these men would be trained as Mates. The best in each course would then be selected for a further eight months' training, at the end of which they would be able to service airframes and engines. At the same time it was decided to increase the intake of apprentices in excess of immediate requirements.

From 1934 to 1937 the squadrons functioned on one of two systems:

1. Fitter I – Fitter II – Mate
2. Flight Mechanic – Flight Rigger (supervised by skilled fitter and rigger NCOs)

The problem with employing unskilled Mates in the flights of operational squadrons was the advent of aircraft of greater power, speed and complexity. The employment of these men had begun in 1932, and at command level this was seen to be dangerous. To reduce the reliance on unskilled technicians, efforts were made to entice back ex-servicemen (EPM 8). The results were encouraging, and the numbers of men who returned to the service gradually increased, but in the summer of 1935, the lack of accommodation at the RAF Depot, Uxbridge, created a bottleneck. The old trade of Aircrafthand and Mate was kept as low as possible, but every available fitter was taken. Some 1,700 applications had been received from Boy Apprentices by early October, but the numbers had to restricted to the accommodation available at the Apprentice schools.

A change of policy in favour of medium bombers, as opposed to light bombers, increased the requirement for fitters from 15,792 to 17,236, to be recruited by 1 April 1939. This necessitated an increased recruitment during 1936 and 1937 for the trade of Flight Mechanic and Flight Rigger at the rate of 650 a year. The total requirement for these trades was estimated to be 8,613 by 1 April 1939. When the number of skilled men being recruited in 1937 was down on the previous year, it became more important to the RAF to train men in the technical trades from scratch. On its own, No. 1 School of Technical Training at Halton could not cope, and the construction of the new school at Cosford did not begin until November 1937.

With the HAD Henlow still acting in 1938 as a technical training school, it is of interest to look at the training that was being given in February 1938 to airmen converting to the trade of Fitter I. The following is an extract taken from the notebook of No. 564484 LAC Wake of the 63rd Entry.

Page 316 shows a test page that LAC Wake had to sit regarding the operation and boosting of an aircraft engine. From the three notebooks maintained by this airmen, the range of technical knowledge required of a Fitter I may be assessed. Subject matter included:

1. Small tools, pipework, drills and lathes, case hardening, blacksmithing and metals.
2. Motor transport – gearboxes, clutches, propeller shafts, steering, etc.
3. Contact breakers, magnetos.
4. Revolution indicators, roller and ball bearings.
5. Lubricants, physical and chemical testing of lubricants.
6. Balancing of engines, single- and multiple-cylinder engines, engine boosting and supercharging, aviation fuels.
7. Electric motors, magnetism and electricity, spark plugs, screening and bonding.
8. Controls in a pilot's cockpit.

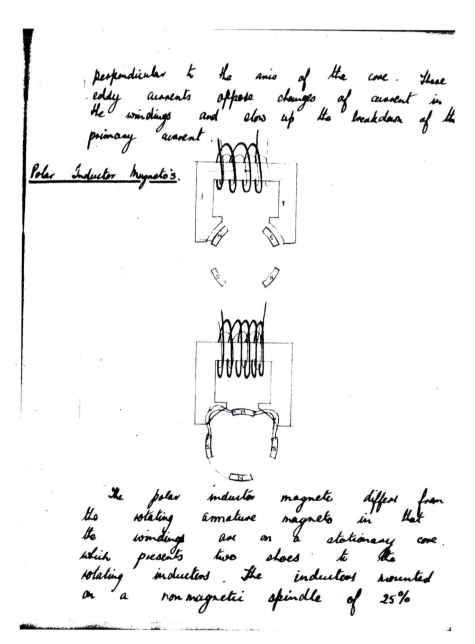

A page from the course notes of No. 564484 LAC Wake, 63rd Entry, RAF Henlow, 1938.

FITTER I CONVERSION COURSE

No.2 Technical Education Progress ~~Report~~ TEST – 67th Entry

1. What do you understand by Turbulence ?
   Explain how and why it is important.

2. To which class of magnetos does the Watford belong ?
   Explain how and why the rotor of this magneto differs from
   the polar inductor type as manufactured by the B.T.H.
   firm, for example.

3. Explain the terms :- Zero Boost, Rated Boost, Rated or
   International Power, Maximum Power Rating.

4. Explain fully, why a "Maximum Boost for Taking-Off" has
   to be allowed on a supercharged engine and why must the
   time be limited during which this boost pressure is
   permitted.

5. Sketch the apparatus used for testing a boost gauge and
   name the parts of the apparatus.
   A test was carried out on a boost gauge, when the barometric
   pressure of the day was 29". The gauge was exhausted to
   read - 2.25 lbs/sq.in. The difference in the height of
   the mercury in the legs of the U-tube was 3.25"
   Was the gauge reading correct ? If not, what was the error ?
   Would you pass this gauge as fit for service?

6. The dimensions given for a hole were $2 \begin{array}{c} + 0.00075" \\ - 0.00025" \end{array}$

   The dimnesions of the pin to fit the hole were $\begin{array}{c} + 0.0015 \\ 2 + 0.0010 \end{array}$

   State the maximum and minimum interference allowed on this
   fit and the tolerance on the hole and on the pin.

7. What are the constituents of the exhaust gases from an
   aero engine ? If the engine were running on a rich
   mixture, which of these gases would you find in larger
   quantities than if the engine were receiving the correct
   mixture ?

   Why and when is an engine given a rich mixture ?

------ooooOooooo---------

Royal Air Force Station,
   Henlow.

February 1938.

Two more schemes for increasing the recruitment and training of technical personnel demonstrate the lengths to which the Air Ministry was prepared to go in an attempt to 'square the circle'. One was a proposal by the Air Member for Personnel at the end of 1937 to recruit Group II tradesmen from the elementary schools, but that met with the objection that such trainees would require special treatment. The second proposal was that airmen might be trained at the aircraft contractors' works. All but Handley Page agreed to cooperate, the latter requiring certain relaxations. Courses were arranged for between twelve and twenty men at a time, and Commands were required to release these men for training, with a consequent reduction in squadron effort.

A summary of the technical recruitment conundrum
The more complex the RAF's aircraft became the less did it make sense to employ Mates, and by April 1938 it was found that Aircrafthands could do the work of Mates and the Mate system was abandoned. Perhaps this was symptomatic of the circle that could not be squared. The Air Ministry found itself in an almost impossible situation, for the following reasons:

1. Aircraft were becoming ever more complex, requiring skilled, not semi-skilled or unskilled technicians to maintain them.
2. Accommodation at the schools of technical training was a factor limiting recruitment over a given period.
3. The opening of new training schools was late in coming.
4. The successive expansion schemes were giving rise to a growing number of RAF squadrons.
5. The policy change putting the emphasis on medium as opposed to light bombers.

The preceding paragraphs show how many schemes were considered in the desperate attempt to keep a growing air force in the air. Some may seem to have been far fetched, like the proposal to take young men from elementary schools. At the time of the Munich Crisis no stone was left unturned. To relieve the accommodation shortages, hutted camps, temporary accommodation and even holiday camps were considered for housing trainees, but the Air Ministry decided that a third training school was required, in addition to Weston-Super-Mare and St Athan. As it happens, there was competition between the three services to acquire holiday camp accommodation once the war began.

DIRECT-ENTRY TECHNICAL TRADESMEN/WOMEN, 1935 TO 1940
The Expansion Plan of 1934 provided for an intake of 27,000 other ranks, and the trade structure was rearranged to allow for the growing complexity of aircraft. The new entries of 1934 were first and foremost direct-entry tradesmen. The intakes of apprentices and boy entrants of that year would not pass out until 1937. The direct-entry technical tradesmen were all volunteers. Trenchard had built 'a village on the foundations of a castle'. The whole idea in 1919 was that the RAF could be capable of expansion without diluting the quality. On the firm basis of technical tradesmen, trained on successive apprentice intakes, the Air Staff

knew that these NCOs could be promoted to take up supervisory duties on the growing number of squadrons, depots and training schools. In the years 1920 to 1934, RAF tradesmen could expect little promotion, and it was 'dead men's shoes' that they hoped to fill. It might take a tradesman twelve years to make the rank of corporal, remaining in that rank until retirement. In the early days vacancies for the rank of corporal would be filled from within the unit. If there was not a suitable applicant on the unit, application would have to be made to the Air Officer Commanding.

As the recruits flooded in, a shortage of accommodation, both domestic and training, began to manifest itself. New recruit training depots had to be opened when Uxbridge could no longer cope. There were long queues for everything – food, medical injections and pay in particular. At Orpington, Cardington, West Kirby and Squires Gate recruiting depots were opened to ease the situation.

An all-purpose trade was ACH (GD), or Aircraft Hand (General Duties), which provided men for a variety of tasks that could be undertaken by those who had no particular speciality. Airmen who helped launch and retrieve flying-boats at the School of Naval Cooperation would be ACH (GD). In the summer such men might sunbathe while awaiting the return of the aircraft. In winter the bitter cold would penetrate their protective clothing, and an issue of Navy rum was the order of the day. Aircrafthands were not necessarily of a low educational standard, and those with ability might remuster to another trade.

The training schools were so busy with new recruits that tradesmen on squadrons would have to attend manufacturers' courses. The increased specializations required corresponding servicing equipment. Five new Group 1 trades were introduced in 1938:

1. Fitter 2 Airframe
2. Fitter 2 Engine
3. Fitter Armourer
4. Instrument Fitter
5. Wireless Fitter

These courses lasted for approximately a year, but under pressure of war they were reduced in length. A course at RAF Innsworth was reduced to four months.

Auxiliary squadron airmen (AAF)
The Auxiliary squadrons were an important element of the RAF in reserve. Being a territorial organization, these units were maintained by County Joint Associations. Squadrons were named after counties and cities. The AAF was open to all trades, and men attended on selected evenings. There was a nucleus of approximately forty Regular officers and airmen, and they organized the training sessions during weekdays, as well as

weekend training and annual camps. All Auxiliary airmen had to be British subjects, and joined, initially, for four years, and could re-engage for one, two, three or four years at a time. They could opt out by giving three months' notice and pay up to a maximum of £5, but they were liable for call-up in the event of an emergency. When they went to annual camp the Auxiliary airmen were integrated into the routine of the station. The prime purpose was to give the men aircraft-operating experience under normal squadron routine. After the Munich Crisis the men were put on a war footing, which permitted the squadrons to go to war retaining their territorial identity.

Womens Auxiliary Air Force

One way of relieving the shortage of manpower in the technical trades was to use womanpower. With the formation of the Women's Auxiliary Air Force (WAAF) on 28 June 1939, the RAF companies of the Auxiliary Territorial Service (ATS) were invited to join the WAAF. Women who joined the RAF companies were recruited with a view to training them as photographers, draughtswomen, tracers and aircrafthands, working as waitresses, cleaners, messengers, fabric workers, etc. In the event, this recruitment was not pursued by the RAF companies. They were, however, assessed for officer and NCO qualities, obviously with an expansion of women's service in time of war. With the mobilization of the WAAF on 28 August 1939, recruitment of women began into the trades of telephonist, teleprinter operator, radar plotter, MT driver, clerk, equipment assistant, cook and mess staff. That was only the beginning. Eventually the women's trade structure was almost as large as that of the men, and they moved into the technical trades working as groundcrew.

Conscription

As a consequence of the Munich Crisis the Air Member for Personnel tried to raise the intake of recruits to 1,000 a week, but this figure was not achieved. The country had to accept that conscription was inevitable, and the Military Training Bill was passed early in 1939. Except for those in the 'reserved' occupations, men were liable for call-up but could express a preference for one of the three services, subject to there being vacancies. By 13 June 1939 there were between 25,000 and 26,000 men who wanted to join the RAF, but there were only 12,000 vacancies. Be that as it may, there was still a shortage of trained men in the squadrons, and the AMSO, anxious not to return to a dilution of standards, was asked to

consider the possibility of the further civilianization of RAF establishments. As war grew ever closer, the personnel requirement rose to a total intake of 45,000 against an original figure of 26,000, and entry was up to 900 a week. It was decided to withdraw men from courses in certain trades where 75% of the course had been completed, to free training accommodation. Also, the Grade I medical standard was relaxed, but these measures did not produce the numbers required. Only the outbreak of war did that. By 22 September 1939 7,000 men had been accepted, and the intake was expected to reach 14,000 by the end of the month. October was expected to produce a further 10,000 recruits, but the number of skilled men accepted for training far exceeded the training places available. It was better, however, to have secured their services, even if there were insufficient training places immediately available. At least the Reservists called up were reducing the dilution of the Fitter grades. The instrument trades were the worst off, and female instrument repairers were being trained at West Drayton to relieve the manning situation.

Finally the recruitment of Fitter apprentices provides an interesting insight into the thinking of those trying to grapple with the manning situation at the beginning of the war. The intake of these apprentices was reduced from 2,000 to 500 in order to free the training accommodation for older skilled men at RAF Halton. The rationale for this move was that, on the basis of a three-year war, by the time the apprentices graduated they would not be effective early enough to be of value. Further reductions in apprentice numbers were planned for 1940 and 1941. Accelerating the training of apprentices to reduce the time that they were in occupation of training accommodation at Halton was not a realistic option, but a plan to put them into productive work in factories was.

THE ORGANIZATION OF MAINTENANCE AND SUPPLY

Introduction

The organization of maintenance and supply in the early 1930s was that carried over from the previous decade. At home the supply depots were in the same position as the Home Aircraft Depot, in that they came under the administrative control of Inland Area but reported direct to the Air Ministry. The following table shows to which directorate at the Air Ministry these establishments reported:

Unit	Group	Area	Directorate of Air Ministry controlling unit or establishment
No. 1 Stores Packing Depot, Kidbrooke	21	Inland	Directorate of Equipment
School of Stores Accounting and Storekeeping	22	Inland	Deputy-Directorate of Manning
No. 2 Stores (Ammunition) Depot, Altrincham	21	Inland	Directorate of Equipment
No. 3 Stores Depot, Milton	21	Inland	Directorate of Equipment
No. 4 Stores Depot, Ruislip	21	Inland	Directorate of Equipment
Packing Depot, Sealand	23	Inland	Directorate of Equipment
RAF Record Office, Ruislip	21	Inland	Deputy-Directorate of Manning

In 1936 the RAF underwent a major change in organization with the formation of Commands to replace the Areas. Since the various depots were serving the needs of units in all Areas it made sense to have the operational control centralized in the hands of Air Ministry directorates. The supply depots that had previously come under Inland Area for the purposes of domestic administration then came under the new Training Command. With the rapid growth of the RAF, however, it no longer made sense to have the divided responsibility of operational control coming under a directorate of the Air Ministry and domestic administration coming under Training Command. It was not simply the size of the RAF that made this arrangement impracticable, it would become impossible in wartime. Added to the RAF at home there were the overseas commands and any expeditionary force to think of. The time had come to put the operational and administrative control of the whole of the maintenance and supply organization together in one new command.

THE INCEPTION OF MAINTENANCE COMMAND

In September 1937 the Director of Organization prepared a Note for the consideration of the Air Council of the advisability of forming a command to control the maintenance units of the RAF. It was proposed that the new command should have responsibility for:

1. Salvage and repair.
2. Equipment storage.
3. Supply.

The Note then went on to consider the basis of the organization of the new command, i.e. should it be geographical or functional? There would be a variety of maintenance units involved in providing a service under the three heads listed above, and it would become uneconomical to have all types of maintenance unit in each geographical area. The areas supplied by different types of maintenance unit would have to overlap. The conclusion was that it would be impracticable to organize the new command on a geographical basis.

The Note therefore proposed that the new command be divided into four functional Groups:

1. A repair and salvage Group comprising the aircraft depots and any other workshop units that might become necessary.
2. An ammunition and fuel Group comprising the ammunition depots, ammunition parks, fuel and oil reserves and distribution depots.
3. An equipment Group comprising the equipment depots.
4. An aircraft, mechanical transport and marine craft Group comprising all the Aircraft Storage Units and the Packing Depot.

The proposals contained in the Director of Organization's Note were considered at an Expansion Progress Meeting of the Secretary of State for Air on 21 September 1937. After some discussion it was decided that:

1. The formation by gradual stages of a maintenance organization consisting of a number of Groups to control the various maintenance units. It was not decided whether or not there should be one controlling authority, and a decision was deferred on this matter.
2. The officers commanding the Groups would be Equipment Branch officers, and the commander of the controlling authority would be an officer of the General Duties Branch.
3. The Groups would be functionally organized and the controlling authority would be outside the Air Ministry.
4. The AMSO should work out the various stages by which the new Maintenance organization should be put into effect.

It was six months before the necessary arrangements were put into effect, and on 1 July 1938, Air Vice-Marshal J.S.T. Bradley took over the administrative and technical responsibilities from Training Command and the Directorate of Equipment respectively. It had been decided that all the groups would come under one command, and this was to be Maintenance Command, with its headquarters at RAF Andover. This took effect on 7 August 1938.

The groups within Maintenance Command

The groups within Maintenance Command were more or less what had been proposed at the meeting of 21 September, and were as follows:

1. No. 40 Group – Equipment Estimating for, custody and distribution of all categories of equipment to home units and equipment overseas. Maintenance of reserve MT vehicles and MT allotment.
2. No. 41 Group – Aircraft The maintenance of all aircraft reserves; their allotment and delivery to home units and shipment overseas.
3. No. 42 Group – Ammunition and Fuel Supply of ammunition, oxygen, aviation and MT fuel and oil to all home units and shipment of oil and ammunition overseas.
4. No. 43 Group – Repair The repair of all types of equipment and the salvage of aircraft beyond the capacity of units to repair.

Early teething troubles with Maintenance Command

By the end of 1938 the Command and Group Headquarters were still greatly understaffed. Another problem was that a proportion of the civilian employees were RAF Reservists and liable for call-up in the event of mobilization, added to which there was a lack of housing for civilian employees, as the maintenance units (MUs) were often in sparsely inhabited districts. In No. 40 Group there was a lack of planned accommodation, and stocks of equipment had to be dispersed for security reasons. This made it exceedingly difficult to distribute the equipment on demand from units. The most serious deficiency, which quickly became apparent, was the lack of technical spares, particularly for the latest types of aircraft. Many aircraft types had several variants that had different parts, and these were not always interchangeable. Some items of equipment were coming from the contractors minus some parts. Then there was the problem of storing service vehicles held in reserve for possible mobilization. Some 8,000 motor vehicles were affected.

The Air Ministry had estimated that, in the event of war, the workload measured in terms of stock issues would increase between seven and eight times. This only emphasized the need for careful and complete preparations for war, but since Maintenance Command had only just been formed there were too many problems, as described above, to be overcome in getting the command 'up and running' to deal with the business of maintenance and supply in war. The problems encountered by No. 41 Group in 1938 and 1939 were caused by the lack of staff at Group Headquarters. The overloaded staff at Andover and sometimes the staff at the Air Ministry were having to do the work that properly belonged to No. 41 Group. At the aircraft storage units there was a shortage of staff, and by March 1939 the aircraft in store were not being properly maintained.

No. 42 Group was better off in terms of stocks and distribution, but here again there was a lack of staff at Group Headquarters. There were problems at the ammunition storage depots due to the slow and piecemeal work on the construction of underground storage. Accordingly there were a large number of contractors' employees in these storage areas who were not vetted for security purposes, and this posed a threat to high-explosive munitions. The supply of fuel and oil was the one area that remained under Air Ministry control, since the service was an agency one performed entirely by the oil companies.

The work of No. 43 Group had not been set in train by the summer of 1939, and the lack of salvage and repair sources was a very serious gap in the nation's defences. The problems with getting a repair organization into operation has been discussed in detail in the preceding sections of this chapter.

THE FUNCTIONING OF THE GROUPS OF MAINTENANCE COMMAND

Introduction

The allocation of responsibility between Maintenance Command and its constituent groups differed from the other RAF commands at home. As much administrative and executive work as possible was carried out at group level. Specialists were also mainly to be found at Group Headquarters, but since these, with the exception of No. 40 Group, were co-located with Command HQ at Andover, the necessary specialist advice was always 'just round the corner'. No. 40 Group HQ was initially located at Andover, but was moved to Abingdon, which was not that far distant. For the purpose of supply, ammunition, oxygen, fuel and equipment, the country was divided into a number of subsidiary supply areas, each of which was allocated a supplying unit. The size of the supply areas varied according to intensity of consumption and the distance over which supply was economical. Flexibility and security were obtained by giving each distribution area an overload capacity and by transferring units from one area to an adjoining one to meet changes in load concentrations.

No. 40 Group (Equipment)

No. 40 Group was formed at Andover on 1 January 1939, and moved to Abingdon on 31 August of that year. Each depot in the Group was to hold a complete range of equipment for distribution by road convoys to link up all consuming units in each supply area. The aim was that, should war come, consuming units could be supplied within forty-eight hours of the submission of the demand. By the time war came, six depots were in being. They were not yet Universal Equipment Depots (UED) that would be able to issue equipment on a geographical basis. The first of these was not ready until December 1939. The UEDs were backed up by a number of smaller maintenance units with varying items of stores.

No. 41 Group (Aircraft)

Group Headquarters was formed at Andover on 1 January 1939, but it was not until 3 April that it gained executive control of its constituent units. The Aircraft Storage Units (ASUs) were to receive, maintain and issue aircraft to RAF units at home and, via the Packing Depot at Sealand, to units overseas. No. 41 Group HQ administered the ASUs and the packing depot.

Under peacetime conditions the ASUs only held the reserve aircraft behind the initial equipment and immediate reserve aircraft with which flying units were supplied. Aircraft for re-equipment or to replace wastage were, as far as possible, delivered direct to units from the factories at which they were manufactured, the equipping of aircraft being completed after they had arrived on the station. The intention was, however, that in time of war the aircraft would be delivered to flying units fitted with the full scale of operational equipment. There were approximately 2,500 aircraft in store at the end of August 1939, which included all the reserve aircraft for the RAF commands and the Fleet Air Arm. Two packing depots and twenty-four ASUs had been planned as part of the expansion scheme, with each ASU possessing a capacity to store 400 aircraft. On the outbreak of war, of eleven ASUs that had been formed, nine were functioning. There was one packing depot. The allotment of aircraft to units at the outbreak of war was carried out by the Air Ministry, but it had been planned to transfer the task to No. 41 Group HQ as soon as sufficient personnel could be provided and trained. Delivery of aircraft from the factories to the ASUs was carried out by ferry pilots, often female pilots, like the famous Amy Johnson. The aircraft allotted to the squadrons were collected by the consignee.

No. 42 Group (Ammunition and Fuel)

No. 42 Group HQ formed at Andover on 17 April 1939 and assumed executive control of its units on 15 June, catering for fuel, oxygen and ammunition supplies. It differed from storage in the other groups in that, for the holding and supply of fuel and oxygen, the RAF relied upon large industrial concerns to hold stocks, firms like Shell and Esso. This worked on an agency basis, and Maintenance Command controlled a part of the resources of these companies.

Five ammunition depots were planned, but owing to the special storage requirements for holding incendiary

bombs it was planned to hold these items at just three of them. Storage had to be underground, owing to the destructive power of so many munitions packed close together. To have spaced them out on the surface would have required a huge area of land. The ideal would have been a lot of smaller ammunition dumps, but it was difficult enough to find storage, and it would only have added to the problems of security. Disused mines and quarries made ideal sites for ammunition storage. The stores with a high-explosive content were stored in concrete chambers. The less-explosive materials like pyrotechnics (flares) were stored in small semi-underground buildings that were lightly covered with earth and turfed over. Under peacetime conditions it was planned to distribute the ammunition direct from the depots to the consumers. In war six or seven Air Ammunition Parks were to be established in the neighbourhood of the operational units, holding one week's stock of war consumption rates for the units they served. Disribution from the depots to the parks was to be by rail, and from the parks to the consuming units using transport provided by the latter.

The supply of oxygen for HP breathing apparatus was on an agency basis. There were to be eleven drying and compressing plants suitably located to serve consuming units and contracted to produce oxygen, which was to be delivered in large transport cylinders, from which flying units could recharge the aircraft containers. In peacetime the arrangement was that the deliveries were made direct from the plants to consuming units, but in war the delivery would be from air ammunition parks unless the oxygen plant was nearer.

The supply of fuel and oil had, throughout the inter-war years, been obtained directly from the oil companies under a scheme of standing contracts. But in war there was a need for reserves to be held in service fuel dumps. These were situated within the ocean terminals of the oil companies. Come the Munich Crisis, however, and it was felt that additional reserve stocks should be held in places well away from the areas of England most likely to be subjected to enemy attack. Another reason was that oil imported from the USA would go into a port on the west coast of the British Isles. The Reserve and Distribution Fuel Depots were of large capacity and underground, built on the west coast. There were to be a number of smaller depots serving the bomber airfields. Finally, the supply system would be enhanced with the construction of two factories owned by the Air Ministry for the production of containers and the mechanical filling of the containers with fuel and oil.

No. 43 Group (Repair)

The Repair Group HQ had not been formed when war commenced. Up until 1938 the aircraft industry had carried out the repair of aircraft for the RAF. This matter was well aired in the early part of this chapter, and it had become clear that the aircraft industry, even with the shadow factories, had no spare capacity to undertake repair. Given the other calls on industry and the lack of trained manpower, either civilian or service that could be spared to carry out repairs, it was going to be difficult for the RAF to achieve self-sufficiency. In March 1939 it was agreed that there should be:

1. Three Service Repair Depots:

   (a) No. 13 MU Henlow
   (b) No. 30 MU Sealand
   (c) No. 32 MU St Athan

2. Three Civilian Repair Depots:

   (a) No. 34 MU Abbotsinch
   (b) No. 47 MU Burtonwood
   (c) No. ?   MU probably at Stoke

The three service depots were each to have an establishment of 1,500, and their primary purpose was to provide, on mobilization, personnel for aircraft depots for field and advanced air striking forces, a war salvage organization and aircraft storage units for the erection of reserve aircraft. It was expected that the service depots would undertake some 25% of the repair to airframes, aero engines, motor transport and aircraft equipment. The salvage of aircraft would be undertaken by six regional salvage centres. The other 75% of repairs would fall to the Abbotsinch, Burtonwood and, if and when opened, Stoke depots. If necessary the establishments of the repair depots could be raised and treble shift patterns introduced.

On the outbreak of war no repair work had been carried out by the repair organization. Firstly, No. 43 Group had not been formed, and only No. 13 MU, of the service-manned units, was in being. As for the civilian-manned depots, only at Burtonwood had construction work begun. Such repair as was being undertaken fell to aircraft parent and fringe firms. But then there was a discussion about a possible change of policy. On 10 August 1939 it was agreed that, of the three civilian depots, one should be operated by RAF personnel, and the other by a civilian firm on an agency basis. A decision on the manning of the third depot would be taken in the light of experience with the first two. But the debate about what to do was to be overtaken by events. The Secretary of State for Air asked Lord Nuffield, the Chairman of Morris Motors Ltd,if he would be prepared to take over the Burtonwood depot, then under construction, as well as the proposed depot at Stoke. He was being asked to be responsible for the management of the Burtonwood depot and informed that if he accepted responsibility for the Stoke depot he could develop it as he wished. Lord Nuffield attached certain

conditions to his acceptance, and, instead of Stoke, he proposed Cowley, where there was an abundance of the right type of labour.

In the event, only the Burtonwood depot went ahead under the RAF scheme, but Mr Boden, Deputy Chairman of the Nuffield organization, was unhappy about running the repair depot in the way that the Air Ministry envisaged. He could not manage it as a commercial concern, and plans for the depot were too far advanced to change it. He would give help and advice, but the RAF would man it, as originally planned, and the Morris organization would provide a manager. It was a great blow to the efforts being made to enlist the help of industry in this way that Mr Boden died of heart failure on 6 March 1940.

MAINTENANCE OF AIRCRAFT

On 1 February 1939 the Air Council issued a letter on the matter of restructuring the repair organization and the modification of technical administration at operational stations:

1. Repair depots Repair depots would undertake major repairs and salvage, and would provide working parties for the embodiment of difficult modifications at units.
2. Operational stations Squadron servicing parties were to undertake major inspections of aircraft, minor repairs and the embodiment of modifications within their capacity. At flight level minor inspections of initial equipment and aircraft were to be undertaken. Station workshops were to be responsible for the work of allied tradesmen and to repair mechanical transport.

War was to come seven months later, and stations were still in the process of reorganizing their maintenance. It was not an easy task, for there was a shortage of skilled men and there was not a technical branch of specialist engineering officers to supervise their work (see next paragraph). What the reorganization did achieve was to take away from flying units the responsibility for major repairs and complete overhauls. It also curtailed the functions of station workshops. Finally, it more correctly utilized the varying skills of tradesmen. For example, all supervisory work was carried out by Group I tradesmen, and flights were manned by Group II tradesmen.

INTRODUCTION OF THE TECHNICAL BRANCH

Policy in the 1920s and the 1930s
The point has already been made earlier in this chapter that the Air Force in the 1920s was Trenchard's Air Force, an air force where officers were expected to fly. Given the relative simplicity of aircraft design, officers who had

Maintenance abroad: No. 203 Squadron, Basrah, Iraq – inspection of a Kestrel engine of a Singapore III, May 1938.

attended a short course could supervise the technical tradesmen on the squadrons. The suffix after a pilot's name indicated his speciality in engineering, armament, signals or photography. This policy continued throughout the 1930s, in spite of the growing complexity of aircraft, but it remained a pilot's air force with officers of the General Duties Branch, which could take officers up to the highest ranks of the service. The only modification to this policy was the commissioning of officers from the ranks where they had learned and practised technical skills. Such officers were filling junior officer posts on stations working in a technical capacity. A few reached the rank of squadron leader.

The policy change of 1939

It was not until the early months of 1939 that the Air Council approved proposals for the direct entry of engineers from industry and the universities, and agreed to the creation of a Technical Branch of the RAF. This was followed by a Press release of 1 August 1939. A month later the country was at war and so the policy had to be implemented in difficult circumstances. There would be recruits coming forward to man the branch from outside

the service, but in the meantime it was necessary to take existing permanent specialist GD officers, officers granted GD commissions immediately before the war, existing commissioned engineer officers, signals and armament officers and airmen commissioned for engineer duties.

APPRENTICE AND BOY ENTRANT TRAINING

Halton Entries in the early 1930s
(For apprentice entries see Appendix K)
The economic depression that afflicted the nation in the early 1930s did not leave Halton unscathed. The School of Technical Training was organized on a two-wing rather than a three-wing basis. The reduction in the intakes of apprentices permitted a reduction in the number of instructors. This appeared in the Estimates for 1932/3. Those not re-engaging at the end of their twelve-year engagements could elect to serve for four years on the Reserve with a gratuity of £100. Dual training was introduced, whereby apprentices received instruction in both airframes and engines. This lasted until 1938, when aircraft were becoming more complex in design, and it was then necessary to return to separate specializations.

On 17 December 1931 Air Marshal Sir Geoffrey Salmond attended the passing-out parade of the 19th Entry. From an intake of 382 apprentices, fifty passed out as LACs, 269 as AC1s, and sixty-one as AC2s, with two failures. This prompted the Commanding Officer to say that, in his opinion, their standard of training was not quite up to that of previous intakes.

During the depression years the RAF continued to contract, and with it there was a contraction in the size of intakes. Between 1931 and 1934 the total of apprentices from the 23rd Entry to 30th Entry was only 2,320. From May 1932 No. 4 Wing was closed down and did not reappear until January 1936, when the expansion scheme was well under way. The 31st and 32nd Entries totalled 1,500, and in August 1936 it was possible to form No. 3 Wing, making four Apprentice Wings. In July 1937 No. 5 (A) Wing was formed, and the following August it became an Airmen's Wing. The apprentices on that wing were either transferred to other apprentice wings or to RAF Cosford.

Arrival of Apprentices at Halton
For apprentices entering the RAF in 1931 an entrance examination would have to be passed. On arrival at Wendover they would have to be met by an officer carrying the regulation yellow cane walking-stick. He would be wearing a white shirt, not the blue-grey of today, and would have trousers with turn-ups. The recruits would be taken up to the camp in a truck with solid tyres, and on arrival would be taken to their

barrack block, a multi-storeyed building. The large barrack-room that would be their home had two rows of beds, each with a box for personal kit. A metal locker was fastened to the wall above each bed and there were five blankets and two sheets, which had to be built into a square pack when the bed was made up. The following morning the recruits would be medically examined, and failure would result in being sent home. Those who had passed the medical would then be given the King's Shilling and a service number. An interview followed in the order of merit achieved in the entrance examination. This interview determined to which technical course the recruit would be assigned, and the uniform worn would signify the apprentice's course. A light blue band was worn around the hat, and a coloured disc, appropriate to the course joined, was worn behind the hat badge. Finally, there was the customary four-bladed brass propeller on the left sleeve.

Training of Apprentice Riggers

The initial basic training for an Apprenctice Rigger in 1931 would be carried out on Siskins, Harts, Bulldogs and Avro 504Ks. The maintenance of flying-boats was carried out on Short Mussels. Rigging an aircraft involved dismantling and erecting mainplanes, adjusting the tension on the wires that went between the interplane struts to obtain the correct dihedral, incidence and stagger. Later on the apprentice learned to start various engines, swing a propeller and fill in the documentation, the Form 700, which recorded work carried out on an aircraft. Theoretical and practical aspects of metallurgy were studied, together with the inspection and maintenance of aircraft, major and minor repairs, fabric covering, doping and repairs to mainplanes and control surfaces.

Pass-out of the 22nd Entry

The pass-out of the 22nd Entry in August 1933 was inspected by Lord Trenchard. From a total of 481 apprentices there were those who:

1. had purchased their discharge   8
2. were unlikely to become efficient   21
3. were discharged on medical grounds   9
4. were put back to a junior entry   12

Ninety per cent had been classified as either a Leading Aircraftman (69) or AC1s. This was the highest pass in the history of Halton.

THE EXPANSION AS IT AFFECTED APPRENTICE AND BOY ENTRANT TRAINING, 1935–1939
Introduction of boy entrants

The expansion that began in 1934 took the annual entry figure of apprentices from 550 to over 1,000, and a new class, that of Boy Entrant, was added for the trades of armourer, wireless operator and photographer. The level of education and mechanical knowledge was lower than that for an apprentice. Boy entrants invited for interview came predominantly from those who had failed the entrance examination for apprentice. Their training lasted for a year and they engaged for a shorter period of service than the apprentices. Approximately 4,000 boys were entered for training between 1934 and 1939.

Working on Bulldogs.

Growth in Intakes

At Halton eight new barrack-blocks were built for Paine Wing in response to expansion. In January 1935 the intake of the 31st Entry increased to 550 apprentices, the 32nd Entry to 916 and the 34th Entry in August 1936 took the figures to 1,250. The RAF in 1936 needed 2,500 pilots and 22,000 airmen to be trained in less than two years. The pass-out results for the 28th Entry were good. A new system of revision had been introduced. Revision was conducted in a separate section of the workshops under specially selected instructors. Dress regulations were changed in September 1936. Blue collars and ties replaced the tunics that had buttoned up to the neck, and breeches and puttees were replaced with slacks. Gone were the bell-type greatcoats which matched the 'winged' breeches, and gone, also, were the nickle-plated crested-knob canes. In 1937 the newspapers and aviation weeklies announced the recruitment needs. Wanted were 1,500 well-educated boys of secondary school standard to become apprentice fitters, wireless operator mechanics, instrument makers, fitter armourers or clerks. For boy entrance wireless operators, armourers or photographers were required. On top of this there was a requirement for 11,000 direct-entry personnel in a variety of ground trades.

Workshop training

With the growing complexity of aircraft it was no longer possible in a three-year course to teach both airframes and engines, and these items became subject to two separate courses. The problem of skill training has already been mentioned in relation to staffing squadrons and repair depots, and this skill shortage was having its impact on workshop training at Halton. There was a lack of new aircraft that could be worked on, and instructors experienced on these latest types. The skills required to keep biplanes in the air were not those that would help in removing or assembling the wings of a Battle or a Wellington. The apprentice still learned the basic skills of a craftsman. Workshop training at Halton involved basic metalwork such as banging of anvils, using cold chisels and heat-treating all types of steels and light alloys, and apprentices had to be able to manufacture an item out of steel. Carpentry was still useful for working on aircraft that contained wood in their construction, like the Anson, or the rear end of a Hurricane, but had no application to a stressed-skin, all-metal Spitfire. It was not until early in 1939 that the RAF's latest fighter put in an appearance at Halton. Workshop training was complemented by an aerodrome course where apprentices learned how to handle aircraft on the flight line of a flying unit, starting engines of all kinds, swinging propellers. Theoretical and practical instruction was given on hydraulics, and the working of control systems and undercarriages was taught.

Training of apprentices for the FAA

RAF Halton became involved in the transfer of the Fleet Air Arm to the Admiralty. It was agreed that, from May 1939, the Admiralty would provide the full manpower required to work on ship-borne aircraft. Volume I of this inter-war history described in detail the manning of the FAA flights, when the RAF provided both pilots and ground crews. The RAF manning of these flights was to cease, but RAF Halton would help with training, and did so from 1938 until 1942. The new naval apprentices had to pass an entrance examination similar to that for RN artificers. The successful ones first joined No. 4 Wing at Halton in September 1938. RAF apprentices were asked if they wished to exchange their blue uniforms for navy blue, and transfers took place in January and June 1939. By the outbreak of war, 459 naval apprentices were under training in No. 4 Wing, made up of direct naval entrants and RAF transfers. These trainees were then transferred to No. 1 Wing, which became known officially as the Naval Wing, under the command of Captain P.H. McCartan RN. In order to speed up the passing-out of naval apprentices, sports afternoons and drill sessions and other non-essentials were dropped from the programme. This permitted the 35th and 36th Entries to pass out together in December 1939. The last naval apprentices of the 42nd Entry passed out from Halton on 29 July 1942.

A last glimpse of life at RAF Halton in the late 1930s may seem somewhat amusing. Over 1,000 apprentices were required to form lines on the grassed area close to the station cinema. They were meant to look like a plantation of young trees and were photographed from a circling Avro Tutor. These aerial photographs, which presumably were meant to come into the possession of German intelligence, were to convey an area of woodland, not an airfield. The author would be pleased to know if there is any evidence that *Luftwaffe* pilots were taken in by this subterfuge.

SUPPLY

(Source: AMWOs 428/30 and RAF Equipment Regulations)

CONSTITUTION OF A STORES BRANCH
Introduction

The Air Council approved the constitution of a Stores Branch following an inquiry into the officer requirements initiated in 1928. The existing system meant that stores officers found the rate of promotion very slow, particularly the able ones, and officers could not advance in rank commensurate with their age and ability. The way the branch was structured, it would have been too costly simply to upgrade the posts.

The Air Council was looking for officers who wished to make the new branch their career. This would mean officers capable of reaching the highest ranks of the service, having high administrative capacity and wide experience. They should be capable, not simply of managing a supply organization in peacetime, but of adapting it to meet the varying needs of war. Finally the career should be sufficiently attractive to retain in service men of good education and ability.

Proposed structure
The plan was to emulate the General Duties Branch and not fill all the posts with career officers. The short-service commission provided the GD Branch with officers to fill the junior posts. The supply branch would differ in this respect. A large proportion of junior posts were to be filled by men who did not intend making a career of the Supply Branch:

1. Warrant Officer storekeepers could fill junior staff posts, which would enhance career prospects for the airmen in the stores trades.
2. A large number of flight lieutenant/flying officer posts at home, and to a lesser degree abroad, could be filled by retired officers serving under civil service conditions. Retired officers of any branch could apply, as well as those from the Army and Royal Navy.
3. A large number of flight lieutenant/flying officer posts could be filled by granting commissions to warrant officers of any trade. Such officers would not ordinarily expect promotion beyond the rank of flight lieutenant.

Note: The civilian stores officers and commissioned warrant officers were to be given a three-month course in stores duties.

As a result of the steps just described, the remaining flight lieutenant/flying officer posts could be filled by career officers whose prospects for promotion would be greatly enhanced. To further improve career prospects for these officers, a number of supply posts were to be upgraded to squadron leader, wing commander and group captain over a number of years. This would mean that every career officer could expect to be promoted to the rank of flight lieutenant. Every career flight lieutenant could expect to reach the rank of squadron leader. A majority of squadron leaders could expect to reach the rank of wing commander, but a substantial minority of wing commanders could expect to be promoted to the rank of group captain.

Entry to the Branch as a career
The entry to the Supply Branch as a career would be made by competitive examination sat by applicants from civilian life. They would have been men between the ages of 23 and 25 years, preferably with business experience. Exceptionally, Cranwell cadets who had become physically unfit for flying could be considered, as could a young career officer of the GD Branch. It was then envisaged that, at a later date, airmen of Group IV who had entered service as an apprentice clerk, attained the rank of corporal and reached the age of 25 years could be considered for entry to the Stores Branch as a career.

Careful consideration was given to the effect that this restructuring of the Stores Branch would have on those officers then serving in the branch. The process was to be spread over a number of years, and the Air Council did not contemplate having to retire officers prematurely. In 1930, when this order was published, a modest expansion had been under way for a number of years, and as serving officers retired in accordance with their existing conditions of service, vacancies would naturally occur in the junior posts both for career officers and for officers not seeking a permanent career.

SUPPLY ON RAF STATIONS
(Source: AP 830)
Introduction
The detailed regulations for the administration and accounting for stores was contained in Air Publication 830. The following was not regarded as RAF equipment:

1. Medical and dental stores.
2. Foodstuffs.
3. Station plant (as defined in the AP 830) and other works stores.
4. Meteorological stores.
5. Stationary, forms, office machinery and publications.

Accounting for equipment
The regulations relating to equipment accounts did not apply to units serving on the North-West Frontier of India. For accounting purposes equipment was divided into three classes:

1. Class A stores Stores that were to be held on inventory and would be large and/or expensive, such as aircraft or motor vehicles. These items would each have their own accountable items on an inventory.
2. Class B Stores All other stores that needed to be accounted for and were accordingly held on inventory.
3. Class C Stores These were items, liquids and solids, that would be consumed in use, e.g. polish, soap, paint.

It was the job of the Senior Equipment Officer (SEO) to demand, receive, hold in store and issue equipment to units on a station. It was the job of the Accountant Officer to maintain paper records of these transactions. Normally stores accounting was the responsibility of an officer of the Accounts Branch, but it could fall to an officer of the Stores Branch.

Centralization of storekeeping

At stations where more than one unit was located, only one stores and one accounting section was to be maintained. Stocks required for one unit were not to be stored separately from stocks of similar articles required by another unit on the station. All commissioned and non-commissioned personnel of the stores branch/storekeeping trade were to come under the SEO unless the establishment of units on the station provided for stores personnel on the strength of those units. A barrack or station warden would always come under the control of the SEO. Barrack stores were there to equip buildings on the station, including messes and married quarters.

Demand, issues and receipts of equipment

In demanding equipment, demand vouchers had to be for items for which there was an establishment. In other words, units on a station could not demand whatever equipment they pleased. It had to be shown that units could not perform their function without it. The number of approved items was also shown in establishments for units, messes and married quarters. If a demand for equipment was in excess of establishment, the voucher had to be signed by the Commanding Officer, for those items of equipment that were held in stores depots. Sometimes items of equipment that had a service nomenclature might be needed urgently when a demand through the normal service channels would result in an unacceptable delay. In these cases a Casual Purchase Order could be raised for a non-service equivalent obtainable locally, e.g. a spare part for the CO's car. For those items that were not held in stores depots there was the Local Purchase Order. Both Casual and Local Purchase expenditure was limited by the provisions of the AP 830 (Volume I).

Having demanded equipment from the appropriate stores depot, it was the responsibility of the Senior Equipment Officer for storage. This was subject to regulations that ensured that it was kept secure, did not deteriorate and that the appropriate fire precautions were observed. Periodic stocktaking checks were to be carried out and any surpluses and deficiencies recorded. Items issued to squadrons and flights on the station were held on inventory, in which case the responsibilities of the SEO mentioned above would pass to the inventory holder. The SEO would of course be on hand to give advice on storage to inventory holders. It was not permitted for a unit to pass equipment to another unit on the station. Such transfers, if approved, had to go through the station stores.

An interesting example of the responsibility for holding, accounting for and maintaining equipment was to be found in the parachute. Parachutes were issued to units for onward issue to pilots and crew members of aircraft, provided that they were members of that unit. If an officer or airman was attached on temporary duty to another station, for example a flying course, he would take his parachute with him. If the detachment did not involve flying he would return his parachute to store. Also, he would not take his parachute with him if he attended a course of instruction at the Central Flying School. If an officer or airman was posted to another unit for flying duties, his new unit would be responsible for issuing him with a parachute. The primary responsibility for the care and maintenance of a parachute lay with the individual to whom it was issued. The general responsibility for the care and maintenance of parachutes lay with the unit commander, who was to ensure that the proper storage facilities were made available.

Losses, deficiencies or damage to equipment

When it came to deficiencies or damage, it had to be decided whether blame would be apportioned to units or individuals. For items of crockery or glassware it was accepted that, with the best will in the world, there would be breakages, and holders of mess and married quarter inventories had a crockery and glass allowance. An anecdote is called for at this stage: a brother officer of the author, who was at that time stationed at RAF Felixstowe, told of a recent task he had been given by the station adjutant of investigating unusual losses of breakable items in a sergeant's married quarter. This officer visited this married quarter, and on entering the house heard a great deal of commotion coming from an upstairs bedroom. He told the author that he witnessed a pillow being thrown from a bedroom onto the landing, where it did not flop but hopped half-way down the staircase. This gave substance to the defence that the sergeant had offered, that a poltergeist was attracted to his younger daughter. The officer returned to the adjutant stating that he wanted no further part in the investigation. This officer was sober when he recounted the event, so the reader might wish to draw his or her own conclusions.

Poltergeists aside, if blame or neglect was not in question, the CO could authorize the 'write-off' of the items of equipment that had been lost or damaged. Collective charges could only be made in the case of barrack damages, otherwise the individual would be charged with the assessed amount of the loss or damage. Airmen paid through deductions from their pay ledger. Officers were required to pay either in cash or by cheque. There is the story of an officer who was found responsible by a court of inquiry for the loss of an aircraft due to negligence, and who retorted, in exasperation, that if that was the feeling of the court they would have to put it on his mess bill. Losses due to what was called 'fair wear and tear' were not charged. Losses or damage occasioned by civilian employees, which could not be attributed to an individual, could be written-off by the CO as a charge against public funds. If a deficient article, recorded as a loss, was subsequently found, then a refund could be authorized.

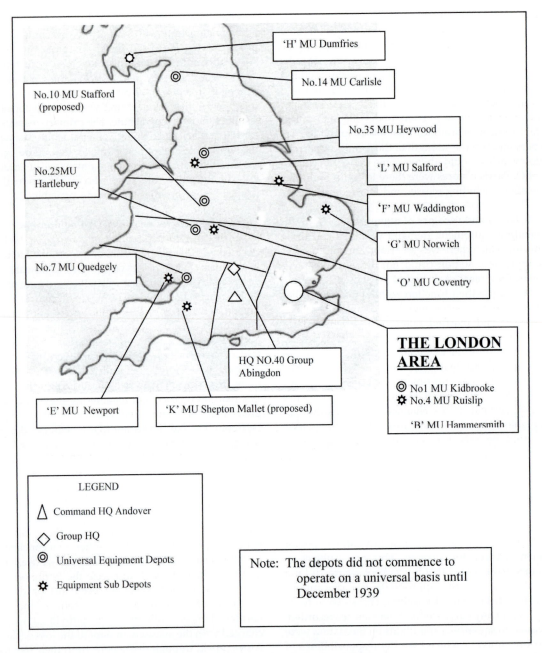

'H' MU Dumfries

No.14 MU Carlisle

No.10 MU Stafford
(proposed)

No.35 MU Heywood

'L' MU Salford

No.25MU
Hartlebury

'F' MU Waddington

'G' MU Norwich

No.7 MU Quedgely

'O' MU Coventry

**THE LONDON
AREA**

◎ No1 MU Kidbrooke
✿ No.4 MU Ruislip

'B' MU Hammersmith

HQ NO.40 Group
Abingdon

'E' MU Newport

'K' MU Shepton Mallet (proposed)

LEGEND

△ Command HQ Andover

◇ Group HQ

◎ Universal Equipment Depots

✿ Equipment Sub Depots

Note: The depots did not commence to
operate on a universal basis until
December 1939

Universal equipment depots and supply areas.

Finally, the regulations regarding the receipt, holding and issue of petrol, oils and lubricants (POL) are considered. Fuel is an attractive substance to a thief, and regular checks were required in equipment regulations. The fuel storage tanks had to be dipped and the fuel levels compared to the recorded issues to squadrons for filling the tanks of aircraft and to MT drivers. The aviation fuel known today as AVGAS could be used in MT vehicles. AVTUR only came into use with the introduction of jet and turbo-prop aircraft. So in the 1930s all aircraft fuel was usable in MT vehicles. Equipment regulations decreed that fuel removed from an aircraft after a crash could not be used for flying purposes. Fuel removed from an aircraft that had crashed into the sea was filtered and transferred to MT bulk fuel installations. When aviation fuel was removed from aircraft for reasons other than a crash, its subsequent use would be at the discretion of the CO. If it was to be used for flying purposes the CO had to be satisfied that it was not contaminated.

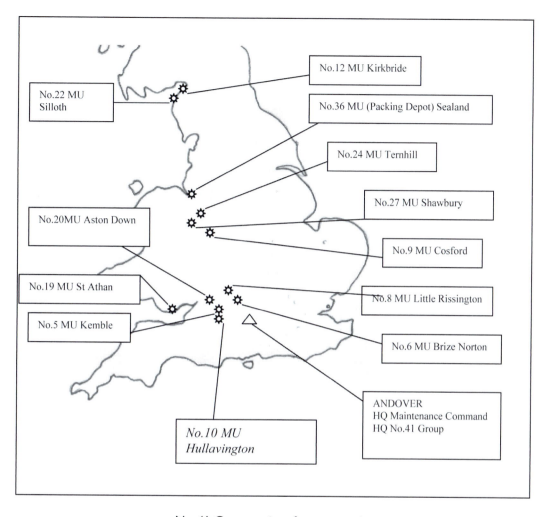

No. 41 Group – aircraft storage units.

Chapter 9
Personnel

The establishment of personnel, 1934–9 – The Auxiliary Air Force – The Air Force Volunteer Reserve – The Civil Air Guard – The Commonwealth Air Training Scheme – The Women's Auxiliary Air Force – The Observer Corps – Officers' careers – Airmen's careers – Pay and allowances – Uniform – Social life in the service

Introduction

The organizers of the expansion of 1934–9 built on existing foundations when it came to providing the personnel for the enlarged force. These were the foundations built by Trenchard, who was determined to create a highly professional air-minded force. But there was always the understanding that not all officers could reach the highest ranks of the service. The short-service commissioned officers, together with airman pilots, provided a body of flying personnel who would man the squadrons but would not be aspiring to high rank, which had the further advantage of providing a reserve to be used in time of emergency. Then there were the Auxiliary and Special Reserve squadrons, which provided a further pool of trained personnel that could be added to the Regular service in time of war.

This arrangement worked very well in the 1920s, but the failure of disarmament in 1932 was followed by the expansion schemes. What was feared was that too rapid an expansion would result in a dilution of the quality nurtured during the Trenchard years. This chapter will chart the succession of schemes whereby the needs of a rapidly expanding flying service could be met. Gradually the RAF delved deeper and deeper into the pool of manpower available in the country without resorting to compulsory service. In 1934, when the expansion began, compulsory service, with all its concomitants, was right out of the question. The nucleus of the RAF in 1934 was composed of Regular career officers and airmen. The temporary element consisted of the short-service personnel who gathered around the nucleus destined, after the due period of service, to form part of the Reserve. Then there was the non-Regular air force, the Auxiliary Air Force, corresponding to the Territorial Army and, like the TA, this was intended to merge with the Regulars on embodiment. The RAF Volunteer Reserve (RAFVR), which was to follow, corresponded in some respects with the Royal Naval Volunteer Reserve. The RAF that went to war in 1939 was a fusion of these four elements. So integral and complete was the amalgamation that the distinctions between the component parts in peacetime ceased to be discernible. The work that had to be done, the perils that were faced and the renown that was won, were all shared by Regular, Reservist, Auxiliary and Volunteer alike.

ESTABLISHMENTS OF OFFICERS AND AIRMEN
The short-service system

It has already been explained that not all officers could reach the highest ranks of the service. There had to be a body of flying personnel who could man the squadrons for a number of years and would then have a Reserve commitment for a number of years following the completion of Regular service. Casualties in air warfare would be high, and the wastage had to be catered for in the flying branch of the service. A missing bomber means the loss of one aircraft, but quite possibly the loss of six or eight men. A reserve of aircraft was, if anything, less important than a trained Reserve. The solution of the problem thus presented was a revolutionary one, so far as filling the bulk of the commissioned ranks of the service. There had long been in operation a system of short service for other ranks of the Army, but it had not been applicable to officers. In 1919 it was decided to institute short-service commissions in the RAF. Officers so commissioned served for a few years, four or five at first, six at a later date, on the active list, followed by renewable periods of Reserve service. It was at an Expansion Progress Meeting (EPM) of 11 January 1939 that the period of short-service commissions was increased from four to six years, subject to Treasury approval, which was granted. This was followed in the 1930s by the introduction of medium-service commissions of ten years. The short-service officers were trained, at first, by RAF instructors at the flying training schools. In 1935 the system was changed when the elementary instruction was entrusted to civilian flying schools. The schools received from the Air Ministry a fee for each entrant trained. The short-service system was completely successful, and it solved the problem of manning the commissioned ranks of the service. The short-service officers formed, at any given time, the bulk of the officers of the RAF, which was, therefore, a short-service force. The flyers were birds of passage.

Tradesmen of the RAF

In filling the non-commissioned ranks of the service, the problem presented was a different one. The core of it was the provision of specialized mechanics. Aircrews had also to be considered, but the question related mainly to the recruitment of the highly skilled tradesmen needed for the aircraft and engines of the force. The best policy was to catch the recruit young and train him specially for the work that he would have to do, which in certain respects had no real counterpart in civilian life. A school for apprentices was opened at RAF Halton, near Wendover in Buckinghamshire, shortly after the end of the Great War, and the training is described in great detail in Volume I.

The growth of the RAF from 1934 to 1939

The RAF recruited some 31,000 officers and men in 1934. It had been more or less stabilized at about the same strength for some years. The vote of money in the Annual Air Estimates, approved by Parliament, limited the establishment of personnel. In 1935 this vote reflected the beginnings of the expansion. This was a modest addition of 2,000 personnel to the 1934 establishment, but as the expansion gathered pace so did the establishments. The figure of 33,000 personnel was increased to 50,000 in the Estimates for the year 1936/7 and to 55,000, 70,000 and 83,000 in the following three years. During the period 1935 to 1938 some 4,500 pilots and 40,000 airmen and boys were taken into the RAF, an annual average of 1,500 pilots and 30,000 airmen and boys. This may be compared with a typical pre-expansion entry of 300 pilots and 1,600 airmen. As war approached, the Vote for 1938/9 had had twice to be increased, taking the establishment to 96,000 in July 1938 and to 102,000 in February 1939. The Estimates for 1939/40 provided for 118,000 officers and men, which was increased to 150,000 in a Supplementary Estimate of July 1939. The actual strength of the RAF on 1 September 1939 was approximately 118,000, behind which stood Reserves totalling about 45,000. The strength was thus, all told, five times as great at the close of the expansion as it had been at the beginning.

THE AUXILIARY AIR FORCE

Meanwhile the Auxiliary Air Force was also increasing in stature. The history of the force was a curious one. It was created in 1924 along with the Special Reserve and Air Force Reserve Act of that year. The two forces were modelled on the Territorial Army and the Special Reserve of the Army (formerly a militia). The Special Reserve squadrons, the name of which was later changed to 'cadre' squadrons, contained a higher proportion of Regular personnel (about one-third) than Auxiliary squadrons. The Special Reserve squadrons were eventually absorbed into the Auxiliary Air Force.

Under the Act of 1924 the members of both forces could be called out to serve within the British islands in defence of the Realm against actual or apprehended attack. Service within the British Isles was defined as 'any flight of which the points of departure and intended return are within the British Islands or the associated territorial waters'. This was ruled, notwithstanding that the flight might in its course extend beyond these limits.

Otherwise, as Mr William Leach, the Under-Secretary of State for Air, stated in the House of Commons on 21 May 1924, he was moving the Second Reading of a Bill that gave the State no power to send any men abroad. The Auxiliary squadrons were, at first, bomber squadrons, in which case a parachute drop from a stricken bomber aircraft could place an Auxiliary airman in enemy-held territory. These units became fighter units before the outbreak of war.

Comparative qualities of Regular and non-Regular units

The irregular air units were originally conceived as a home-defence air force, but were not very highly rated as such. The Air Staff, in completing the number of first-line aircraft needed to give Britain parity with France in 1932, reckoned 127 non-Regular aircraft as the equivalent of only forty-three Regular aircraft. This is a proportion of non-Regular to Regular aircraft of 3:1 (Sir John Salmond's Memorandum of 31 December 1931, CPO10(32)). It comes as no surprise that the Auxiliaries did not share this view of their capabilities. Indeed, it would have been very bad for their morale if they had done so. They did not have an inferiority complex – very much the opposite. In fact some of the squadrons were inclined to look down on the Regulars, very much as the Army's cavalry did on the infantry. Poetic justice would have expected such pride to end in a fall. There was no fall. The Auxiliary Air Force was as good in action as it thought it was. Shooting down enemy aircraft, as the Auxiliaries did over the Firth of Forth in October 1939, was an excellent way to lose amateur status. This was followed by excellent work in the Battle of Britain. The Auxiliaries needed lessons from no one. There had been eight Auxiliary squadrons in 1934, but twenty by 1939. The four Special Reserve squadrons, Nos 500, 501, 501 and 504, were converted to Auxiliary squadrons (see Appendix B). Just before the outbreak of war a number of balloon squadrons was added to the strength of the Auxiliary Air Force, adding significantly to the strength in personnel. The numbers of personnel speak for themselves. On 1 October 1939 there were 23,000 officers and men in the Auxiliaries, where there had been little over a 1,000 at the beginning of 1934. Some 600 belonged to the flying squadrons and some 18,400 to the balloon squadrons.

THE AIR FORCE RESERVE

The Reserve was fed by a stream of officers and airmen who served for a few years with the Regular Air Force and then returned to civilian life with the obligation to return to the Active List when needed. In the meantime they were to carry out their regulated periods of training. This system worked well until the expansion began in 1934. It depended on a steady flow of men, year in, year out, but that flow was interrupted after

1934, when it became the practice to retain on the Active List personnel whose time would normally have expired. This caused a slackening of the rate of replenishment and was of much concern to the Air Ministry.

Provision may be made for the building-up of a reserve of aircraft to cover wastage in war, but the same attention may not be paid to wastage of personnel. This matter was, however, well understood in the Air Ministry. In a Memorandum submitted to the Cabinet on 25 October 1938, the Secretary of State for Air, Sir Kingsley Wood, said that the limiting factor in mobilizing squadrons at the beginning of 1940 would be aircrews and not aircraft. He let it be known that efforts would be concentrated on providing an adequate reserve of trained pilots behind the fighter squadrons. The aim was to match the number of reserve fighter aircraft with pilots, both Regular and Reserve. Paragraph 44 of a Cabinet Paper 218 (38), entitled 'Relative air strengths and proposals for the improvements in this country's position', touched on this matter. In para. 53 of the same paper, Sir Kingsley emphasized that the problem of personnel, in relation to the very large scale of wastage which might occur in modern warfare, would then become of increasing importance.

THE ROYAL AIR FORCE VOLUNTEER RESERVE

Initial proposals

One of the measures, designed to solve the problem of the provision of a sufficient reserve of pilots, had already been taken. This was the Royal Air Force Volunteer Reserve (RAFVR). Air Commodore Tedder, the Director of Training at the Air Ministry, took up the idea with enthusiasm when it was suggested to him. The proposal that the RAFVR was to have town centres and aerodrome centres was ultimately adopted, and was put forward in a memorandum by Mr W.L. Scott of Secretariat Branch S7 to the Air Member for Personnel on 20 February 1936 (Air Ministry File S37628). Tedder added a minute to the file, giving general support to the proposals, but he was unable to concur with all of them. Mr Scott had envisaged a freely associated body of volunteers who were to have a discipline and tradition quite different from that of the Regular service. Tedder felt that while this might be based on experience of the two older services, it would be inappropriate for the RAF. Any wide distinction between the Regulars and the Reserves would create a most serious weakness, affecting the efficiency of the service as a whole. Tedder believed that the new Reserve must be built up into a Citizen Air Force as a real second line of defence, 'Citizen units behind the Regular units'. Each would have its own squadron and flight commanders controlling their own training.

In the event, the RAFVR did not develop in this way. It remained fluid, not segmented into units of its own. It was common ground among the directors who discussed this question that the RAFVR should not be connected with the Auxiliary Air Force, which, like the Territorial Army, depended on a territorial association. The RAF felt that the TA depended upon the support of the country gentry, which was a moribund connection. Tedder preferred an association with big commercial and industrial concerns, and the keynote that was struck was essentially a democratic one. It was to the young men of the cities that the RAFVR appealed, and that was the intention. There was to be no class distinction, and the Air Ministry wanted the new force to appeal to the whole middle class in the widest sense of that term. That meant the output of the public and secondary schools. So as not to distinguish between an officer and airman class, men would be recruited on a common basis as airman pilot or observer. Promotion to commissioned rank would follow at a later date, and be determined by a display of leadership qualities. This was all contained in an Air Ministry letter, S32768, dated 19 June 1936, and sent to the Treasury. There remained the question of what title to give to the new service, and after much debate, which included such names as 'Citizen Air Force', ' Royal Volunteer Air Force', ' Civil Division of the Royal Air Force' and the ' Royal Air Force Volunteer Reserve', the last of these was adopted.

The start of the RAFVR

All necessary approvals having been obtained, the new scheme was announced by the Air Ministry at the end of August 1936. His Majesty, it was stated, had approved the constitution of the RAFVR, and the organization of the pilots' section of it would be proceeded with at once. Those accepted would be men who had no previous experience with the RAF, and they would be taught to fly in their spare time. They would have to attend an annual flying course for a period of fifteen days. All entries would be in the rank of airman pilot, but with the opportunity of promotion to commissioned rank. Air Ministry Order A201, dated 27 August 1936, provided for members of the Air Force Reserve, who had entered from civil life, to be able to transfer to the RAFVR.

A start was made with training in April 1937. The first centres to be used were the thirteen civil flying schools at which the elementary flying training of short-service entrants of the Regular Air Force, as well as refresher courses for the ordinary Reserve, was undertaken. The Secretary of State for Air, in submitting the Air Estimates for 1937/8, expressed a hope in an accompanying memorandum that no fewer than 800 pilots would be entered in the RAFVR in 1937. That hope was fulfilled, and in a further memorandum accompanying the Estimates for the following year, the Secretary of State was able to record that over 1,000 pilots had joined the new service. In 1937 twenty-one Aerodrome Centres were already in operation, with a further twelve to be opened. Medical and Equipment Branches had already been formed during 1938, and a section would be formed to provide crews for aircraft, i.e. observers, wireless operators and air gunners. By the time the Estimates, presented on 25 February 1939, had been published, sections for the administrative, as well as medical and equipment officers, and for aircrews and ground trades, had been added. By that time the pilot strength of the RAFVR had increased to over 2,500. The target figure of 800 a year set in 1936 had been reached with a comfortable margin.

THE RAFVR IN 1939
Aerodrome centres
By May 1939 twenty-five aerodrome centres had been opened and twenty-three were to open in 1939/40. By September 1939 there were forty-two aerodrome centres in operation. London was the greatest recruiting centre and had the largest share of them, and there were eight centres spread out around its perimeter:

London	Bristol	Birmingham	Manchester
Gatwick	Filton	Castle Bromwich	Barton
Gravesend	Weston-super-Mare	Elmdon	Ringway
Hatfield	Whitchurch		
Hanworth			
Redhill			
Stapleford Abbotts			
White Waltham			
Woking			

Twenty-seven other towns each had one aerodrome centre. There were one or two curious juxtapositions as a result of firms venturing into unaccustomed fields. The aerodrome centre at West Hartlepool, for instance, was operated by Southsea and Isle of Wight Aviation Ltd, and the Gloucester and Cheltenham centre by the Surrey Flying Services Ltd.

Local training
The main weakness of the scheme was one that was inherent in any system of training designed not to interfere with the trainee's ordinary work. Spare-time instruction was necessarily rather slow-motion instruction, yet speed was the essence of the contract. Attention was drawn to this weakness in a memorandum distributed to members of the Cabinet by the Secretary of State for Air on 25 October 1938. He pointed out that the training of VR crews, and especially of observers and wireless operators, was a difficult problem. Although it was acknowledged that the Reservists were enthusiastic, the training was limited to periodical attendance at town centres during the week and aerodromes at weekends, with a period of fourteen days' training each year. With the best will in the world the training was taking four times as long as it would for a conscript. Sir Kingsley Wood was preparing a new training scheme for those joining the RAFVR. Initially they would undergo a short period of continuous training, after which they would receive an inducement in the form of a bonus and a retaining fee thereafter. Details of this proposal appear in Cabinet Paper 218 (38) para. 54, dated 25 October 1938. The scheme referred to was one under which entrants would perform six months of continuous training on enlistment.

The effect of compulsory service on the RAFVR
It could only be a voluntary scheme as long as compulsory service was not in force. Hence the necessity for inducements. The position was different once the Military Training Act had become law. When the Act received the Royal Assent on 26 May 1939, the Air Ministry was in a position to make initial training compulsory, and an Air Ministry Order No. 252/39 dated 5 July 1939 was issued to this effect. The position changed again on 1 September 1939, when the Royal Air Force Reserve, including the Volunteer Reserve, was called up for permanent service by Royal Proclamation, and all of the Reservists came under the same regulations as the Regulars. Air Ministry Order A388-39, dated 16 September 1939, was issued to that effect. The Volunteer Reservists were all immediately mobilized, but there were not sufficient training facilities for all of them, and many had to be employed on ground duties until training places at the flying training schools became available. At an EPM held on 14 of November 1939 the Air Member for Personnel blamed this on the course of the war, which increased the load on the resources of the RAF's flying training organization. In these circumstances the VR personnel would be employed on any duties required.

THE CIVIL AIR GUARD
Yet another organization was added to the Auxiliary Air Force, the RAF Reserve and the Volunteer Reserve as the Air Ministry dipped yet further into the nation's pool of manpower. In July 1938 it was announced that a Civil Air Guard was to be formed. It was stated that the object was to provide a body of men and women whose

knowledge of flying would be of assistance to the RAF in time of emergency or who would perform any other services in connection with aviation that might be required. It was controlled by a body of commissioners presided over by Lord Londonderry. It was a purely civilian organization, and no person undertook a Reserve liability in any of the three services. In the matter of flying training, the RAFVR relied mainly upon the services of the civil flying schools, which were already engaged in *ab initio* instruction to the short-service entrants. The facilities afforded by the light aeroplane and other flying clubs had not been utilized up to this point, but with the introduction of the Civil Air Guard, this resource too was tapped in the service of the nation. The Air Ministry agreed to pay civil flying clubs certain grants-in-aid if they would form sections for the Civil Air Guard and would undertake to charge pupil pilots favourable rates for training to pilot standard.

The short history of the Civil Air Guard

Sir Kingsley Wood referred to the Civil Air Guard when he introduced the Air Estimates on 9 March 1939. He said that it would provide a reserve which in time of emergency would be able to serve in the RAF or to give help in other ways. He told the House of Commoms that the guard possessed some 1,400 members in possession of 'A' licences and 3,800 who were undergoing flying training. The holders of 'A' licences had been divided into three groups according to their qualifications for different types of service:

Group 1   Those who could serve as pilots.
Group 2   Those who could serve as instructors, air observers, wireless operators and air gunners.
Group 3   Men and women who might be suitable for employment as ferry pilots, as ambulance pilots and for communication duties.

The classification by groups, as listed above, was approved at an Expansion Progress Meeting of 23 November 1938. Certain selected volunteers would receive more advanced training than the rest, and members who were unlikely to qualify for any of these classes were encouraged to undertake other forms of national service. One of the advantages of this scheme was that it utilized the facilities provided by the flying clubs throughout the country for the training of pilots and other aircrew categories, thus lightening the load of the flying schools. Returning to the House of Commons debate, Kingsley Wood made it clear that those in Groups 1 and 2 would be of definite value to the RAF and that those in Group 3 would also be of use.

The Civil Air Guard did not survive the outbreak of war. On 29 August the commissioners announced that

the *ab initio* training for applicants over 32 years of age would cease. The upper age limit had been 50 years. It was expected that those guard members who were not already involved in training would wish to offer themselves for other forms of voluntary service. Many did, in fact, do so, either by transferring to the RAFVR or by joining the Air Transport Auxiliary, which was organized for the ferrying of aircraft for the RAF.

COMMONWEALTH AIR TRAINING SCHEME

It cannot be known with any certainty whether the provision made in the various ways described above would have solved the problem of the manning of the RAF during the protracted war that followed. That some supplementary measures were thought to be necessary is evident from the three steps that were taken by the government, two of them after the outbreak of war and the other just before it. The first two were the organization of the Commonwealth Air Training Scheme and the Air Training Corps. The third was the formation of the WAAF, or Women's Auxiliary Air Force. Between them these three measures, especially the first, would ensure that the needs of the RAF in personnel would be amply met. There was never any difficulty on this score, and the quality of the output of the training establishments may be contrasted with that of the *Luftwaffe* in the later stages of the war, when the Germans were recruiting men of a distinctly inferior type.

Sir Kingsley Wood made a statement in the House of Commons on 10 October 1939 on the Commonwealth Air Training Scheme to inform the House that the governments of Canada, Australia and New Zealand had received 'an outline of the arrangements for the rapid expansion, on a cooperation basis, of the training organization of pilots, observers and air gunners required'. First would be the considerable enlargement, followed by the maintenance on an enlarged basis, of the air forces of the respective countries. Training schools would be established and maintained in each of these Dominions. The Union of South Africa preferred to make separate arrangements, but pledged to make her training as complete as possible and to expand her air force to the fullest extent of her resources.

The advanced training would be concentrated in the main in Canada. Sir Kingsley had made it clear that the task was one of great magnitude, resulting in a large increase in the number of training schools. He hoped that the scheme would provide, in addition to the training output of UK training schools, a sufficient output of pilots, observers and air gunners to meet the needs of the cooperating air forces in time of war in overwhelming strength. The aim was achieved. The supply became so copious that by the end of the war supply outstripped demand. On 18 July 1944 the Air

Ministry announced that a proportion of young men who had been accepted for aircrew duties in the RAF and who were awaiting entry to training would be made available to the Ministry of Labour and National Service or service in the Army in connection with the prosecution of the war. It was explained that the increased superiority over the enemy achieved by the Dominion and Allied Air Forces had resulted in a much lower casualty rate than that anticipated. The Commonwealth Air Training Scheme and the Air Training Corps were inaugurated only after the war had begun. The recruits to the RAF from overseas did not come simply as a result of the Commonwealth Air Training Scheme. Substantial numbers of young men from the Dominions and Colonies had been coming throughout the expansion period. Some of them had already received flying training before coming to the United Kingdom, and could be posted straight to a service squadron. Others were merely boarded before departure, and received flying training on arrival.

WOMEN'S AUXILIARY AIR FORCE
Introduction
To these new arrivals was added another force, the Women's Auxiliary Air Force, which came into existence only a couple of months before war began. Except for the members of the Princess Mary's RAF Nursing Service, the RAF had been completely devoid of members of the fair sex since the Women's Royal Air Force was disbanded in 1920. In July 1938 the Auxiliary Territorial Service was established by the War Office, and the original intention was that it should serve the needs of the Air Force, as well as the Army, and thirty-five ATS companies were allotted to the RAF.

Formation of the Women's Auxiliary Air Force (WAAF)
On 9 March 1939 Sir Kingsley Wood made a statement in the House of Commons regarding proposals made to the Air Ministry in November 1938 by Lady Londonderry. She had suggested the formation of a women's flying school and a technical training school, with the provision of women pilots for ferry work in mind, but by that time the Air Ministry had decided to continue to associate the RAF with the War Office scheme for the Auxiliary Territorial Service. In a reply to Lady Londonderry, it was pointed out that women could enter Class II of the Civil Air Guard for pilot training. Then, in June 1939, a separate women's organization for the RAF was established and provided for in the Supplementary Estimates presented on 11 July 1939. A sum of £15,000 was taken under Vote 7 of the estimates for the expenses of the WAAF. In the Annual Estimates presented on 27 February 1939, only £3,800 had been taken for the ATS. Such was the beginning of a service that was to grow in five years to a strength very nearly as great as the RAF itself, including the Reserves, at the beginning of the war.

By September 1939, 230 officers and 7,460 airwomen had been enrolled in the WAAF. In September 1944 that number had grown to 170,000. The scope of the duties of the force had been enlarged, moreover, to an extent that no pre-war forecast had ventured to suggest. Originally employed on domestic duties regarded as suitable for women, the members' services were utilized, as time went on, in work that had hitherto been considered only fit for men. Short of serving as combatants, they came very close, turning their hand to almost every kind of work in the RAF. Beyond all question they rendered invaluable service in freeing men for the other duties, and thus relieved the pressure on manpower, especially strained as the war progressed, and women's service became increasingly global.

THE ROYAL OBSERVER CORPS
Mention must be made of a body that, although not part of the RAF, Army or Royal Navy, was a vital element in Britain's system of defence against air attack. This was the Observer Corps, whose duties were to identify any aircraft that crossed the British coast and to pass on the information to enable the machinery of interception to be brought into operation without delay. Before radio location was developed, the observers' warnings were the first to be received of the approach of possible raiders. Even when a network of radar stations had been established, the observers still had the indispensable duty to perform of distinguishing between friend and foe. A large number of men, drawn from all ranks and callings, had been well trained for this duty by the time war began. They were all civilians and all volunteers. Some were full-time workers who were paid £3 for a 48-hour week. They were mainly part-time employees, and they received 1s. 3d. an hour towards their expenses.

At first members of the Observer Corps were recruited locally and controlled by the Home Office, being administered through the Chief Constables of the counties. The operational control was assigned to the AOC-in-C Fighter Command. The corps rendered valuable service in the Battle of Britain. In September 1940 the Secretary of State for Air, Sir Archibald Sinclair, sent the corps a message in which he said, 'By your vigilance and faithful devotion to duty you are making an indispensable contribution to the achievements of our fighter pilots. Their victories are your victories too.' A little later the King was pleased to approve the addition of the word 'Royal' to the title of the corps. The members continued to render valuable service to the RAF throughout the war. Some observers were trained to work with the Navy as 'aircraft identifiers' with the rank of petty officer in connection with the invasion of the continent.

OFFICERS' CAREERS

Introduction

(Source: AMO 237, 241/1930)

The decade began with an Air Ministry offer to selected short-service commissioned officers to be appointed to permanent commissions, and medium-service in the General Duties Branch (see Volume I, Chapter 9 for medium-service commissions). Those officers recommended for appointment were asked whether they wanted to be considered for a permanent commission, medium-service commission, or either of the two, without guarantee that their choice could be met. Para. 4 of the order (see source above) stipulates that applicants must be fully qualified pilots and physically fit. There are two points to be made here. The first is that the term 'general duties' meant that pilots were required to supervise the specialities of engineering, signals and armament. Short courses qualified them to undertake the responsibilities on squadrons. It was, of course, a matter of pilot first and specialization afterwards. Air Marshal Trenchard had only then retired from the post of Chief of the Air Staff after ten years in the job. Up to the period of expansion the policy followed that which applied in the 1920s. By and large it was a pilot's air force, but one that recognized, little by little, that a service of growing complexity needed officers who would not necessarily be able to fly an aeroplane, but who should specialize in the job in hand. Trenchard had bequeathed his air force as a 'cottage built on the foundations of a castle', but one that could be expanded to meet the needs of war. But too fast an expansion risked dilution of the service. Of course only the career officer was concerned with his progress up the ladder to the top. The vast majority of officers coming into the service in the mid- to late 1930s were in the service on a part-time basis, or perhaps only for the duration of hostilities. Cranwell would provide the career officers and Halton the career airmen, but would they be in sufficient numbers to cope with expansion? Four factors played in the minds of the Air Member for Personnel and his staff. With the onset of the expansion the policy with regard to the careers of officers had to change, in particular:

1. There was a need to retain officers in the service whose release date was due.
2. In 1936 there would be a major reorganization of the RAF at home. The new commands created a need for commanders at command and group level and the staff officers to man the various headquarters.
3. The large number of stations being opened in the expansion period needed officers of the rank of group captain or wing commander to command, and the appropriate number of officers in the rank of wing commander and squadron leader to manage the various sub-units on the station.
4. The rapid growth in the number of squadrons.

A second point relates to physical fitness. Flying Officer Douglas Bader had lost both his legs in a flying accident in 1930, and since he was able to walk again on artificial legs, he was offered employment in a ground job in the RAF, which would mean his being able to remain in the service that he loved. But given Bader's personality, it was 'flying or nothing'. If he could not fly he would leave the service, which he did. But when war came in 1939, the needs of the moment meant setting aside the normal rules that applied in peacetime. Provided Bader could satisfy the flying instructors at the Central Flying School that he could fly an aircraft safely, he could rejoin the service. The author remembers having a conversation with a colleague one night in the mess regarding 'characters' in the service. Not unkindly, he said that the RAF liked 'grey' men and tolerated eccentrics. By that he meant that it needed officers who conformed to the requirements of the RAF in attitude, behaviour and loyalty to the service, yet needed those who stood out as different from the rest. He had in mind 'Johnny' Johnson, Bert Harris and Douglas Bader.

The growth in the number of squadrons was achieved by taking a flight from an existing squadron to form the nucleus of the new squadron. There would be a need to replace the flight from the depleted squadron and the formation of new flights in the new squadrons. Squadrons were normally commanded by a squadron leader, with flight lieutenants as flight commanders. Of course, no matter what method was used to expand the number of squadrons, there would be a need for X numbers of extra officers in the appropriate ranks. Then there were the growing number of maintenance units, repair and supply depots and the concomitant need for support services, such as medical and dental, provost and legal. The extracts from Air Ministry Orders that follow will give the reader some idea of how the Air Staff set about meeting the personnel needs of the expansion.

MEASURES INTRODUCED IN THE YEARS 1934/5

AMO A18/1934 Promotion to Flight Lieutenant

AMO A20/1934 Appointment of Warrant Officers, Accountant, to commissioned rank in the Accountant Branch

The first of these orders provided for officers of the rank of flying officer to be promoted to the rank of flight lieutenant on a time basis in the General Duties and Accounts Branches to match that of officers in the Medical and Dental Branches. The appropriate promotion examination would have to be passed, but the new arrangement would not apply to officers seconded or attached from the Navy or the Army. The pressing needs, both for more flying instructors and to retain existing instructors, received a knock-on effect from this time-promotion scheme. There would no longer be any need for separated flying officer and flight lieutenant flying instructor posts. Previously a flying instructor in the rank of flying officer would have to be posted on promotion to flight lieutenant. The second order, which followed the constitution of an Accounts Branch, permitted Warrant Officers, Accountant, to be granted permanent commissions. There would be a vacancy for one such officer every two years in areas or commands of the RAF.

AMO A190/1934 Personnel measures required to meet the Expansion Progamme

Three provisions of this order applied to commissioned personnel. The first applied to an increased entry of short-service officers, and No. 2 FTS at RAF Digby was to be reopened in October 1934 to cater for the increased throughput. Secondly, there would be an increased entry to medium-service, and additional appointments would be offered to short-service commissioned officers. Finally, there would be an increase in the establishment of permanent officers. This would be a strictly limited increase of permanent officers of the General Duties Branch, which would be dictated by the capacity of the service to provide a satisfactory career. It should be remembered that the expansion then taking place was to be prepared for a war with Germany. If this did not happen, then there could be a reduction in the size of the service, and if it did happen and Britain won that war, there would be an exodus from the service as there had been after the Great War.

AMO A19/1935 Personnel measures required to meet the Expansion Programme

The Air Ministry Order that follows is a further illustration of the urgent need to retain officers in the service following the expansion. The order applies to officers serving on short-service and medium-service commissions, described in detail in Volume I. It also applies to officers of the General Duties Branch who were employed in a number of roles prior to the introduction of specialist branches.

The following special measures, in addition to those announced in AMO A190/34, will be taken to meet the increased requirements of personnel consequent upon the decision of HM Government to expand the Air Force:

1. *Extension of service of certain short-service officers from five to six years* Extension of service in the rank of flying officer to complete six years on the active list, followed by four years on the reserve, may be granted to short-service officers commissioned prior to 1 April 1932 (and therefore entered for five years' active list followed by four years' reserve service) who volunteer and are recommended therefore. The gratuity in respect of the sixth year of active service will be £100. Applications from officers who were of four years' service or over on 1 January 1935 should

be forwarded immediately. Applications from officers who were of three years' service but under four years on 1 January 1935, or will be of that service on 1 January 1936, should be forwarded so as to reach the Air Ministry by 1 April 1935 or 1936 as the case may be.

2. *Extension of service of medium-service officers* Extension of service to complete eleven years on the active list, followed by four years' service in the reserve, may be granted to medium-service officers due to transfer to reserve prior to 1 April 1937, who volunteer and are recommended therefore. The gratuity in respect of the 11th year of active list service will be £100. Applications from officers due to transfer prior to 1 April 1936 should be forwarded immediately; applications from those due to transfer to reserve on or after that date and prior to 1 April 1937, should be forwarded so as to reach the Air Ministry by 1 October 1935.

3. *Extension of service of squadron leaders and flight lieutenants of the General Duties Branch* The service of a limited number of officers of the ranks of squadron leader and flight lieutenant will be extended to ages 48 and 45 respectively. The selection of officers will be made periodically by the Air Council and applications from individual officers are not required. The names of officers selected for extension will be published in Air Ministry Orders at least six months before they reach the retiring age of their rank or complete twenty years' service, if later. A squadron leader or a flight lieutenant may be placed on the retired list at any time during his extended service if the Air Council consider that his further retention is not desirable.

AMO A302/1935 RETURN OF RETIRED, RESERVE AND EX-OFFICERS TO THE SERVICE

This order provided for retired, reserve and ex-officers to return to the RAF in certain posts under civilian conditions of service. These would be mainly specialist and administrative, including such positions as unit adjutants or personnel posts. This was designed to permit officers on the active list to be posted to other duties, e.g. on the growing number of squadrons. The terms of service would permit the replacement of these officers by those on the active list once the period of expansion had passed, and the posts being filled by these civilian officers would continue to be shown in unit establishments as service posts. To give these civilian officers powers of command and discipline under the Air Force Act they would be granted 'pro forma' commissions in the RAF Reserve in the rank of flight lieutenant, with honorary rank corresponding to any higher rank to which they might be entitled if on the retired list.

AMO A202/1935 EXTENSION OF SERVICE OF FLIGHT LIEUTENANTS OF THE STORES AND ACCOUNTANT BRANCHES

This order refers to the extension of service of selected flight lieutenants. The periods of extension would be determined on a case-by-case basis up to a maximum of 50 years of age. Officers who have their periods of service extended would be eligible for promotion under normal rules, but such officers may be placed on the retired list at any time during the period of extended service if the Air Council consider further retention is not desirable.

MEASURES INTRODUCED IN 1939

Two further measures introduced in March 1939 are indicative of the steps being taken to ensure that there would be enough officers to man the vastly expanded service.

AMO A59/1939 Conditions of Service for Short-Service Officers of the Equipment Branch

Short-service commissions had been introduced as a temporary measure, which meant four years of active service followed by six years on the reserve. Six months' training in the rank of acting pilot officer was given to prepare such officers for employment in the branch. They would then be given the rank of pilot officer on probation. After eighteen months they would be promoted to the rank of flying officer if recommended. There would be a limited number of appointments to permanent commissions from suitable applicants.

AMO A58/1939 Promotion to the acting rank of Flight Lieutenant in the General Duties Branch

Reference has already been made to the problems created by the rapid increase in the number of RAF squadrons. Appendix J lists the squadrons that were both formed and re-formed between 1934 and 1939. This order applied to junior officers of the General Duties Branch who were being required to fill the posts of flight commander under the expansion scheme. Flying officers were no longer required to complete one year's service in that rank before becoming eligible for promotion to the rank of acting flight lieutenant. Pilot officers and flying officers who filled flight commander vacancies or filled posts for flight lieutenant (flying) in squadrons armed with heavy bombers or flying-boats became eligible for the grant of the rank of acting flight lieutenant. Pay increases were awarded as appropriate to reflect the new rank and responsibility. It was affirmed that the grant of acting rank would not apply to any other types of post. It would be the exception if an acting flight lieutenant was required to fill a squadron leader (flying) post, and when it happened the officer would retain the acting rank. The order applied to all permanent and short-service officers of the General Duties Branch, as well as officers holding temporary commissions while seconded to the RAF from the Army. Acting rank would not, in these circumstances, count for seniority of service in the substantive rank.

In conclusion it is evident that the service was anxious to provide meaningful careers for officers in the various branches. Since the days were passing where every officer was a pilot first and specialist afterwards, it was necessary formally to constitute officer branches with their own terms of service. Thus in 1934 an Accountant Branch and a Medical Branch were officially constituted, followed by a Dental Branch in 1935. Finally the term 'medium-service' was abandoned in 1939, for it no longer denoted eligibility for a different rate of gratuity from that issuable to short-service commissioned officers.

RAF Branches in 1935

1. General Duties
2. Stores
3. Accounts
4. Dental
5. Chaplain
6. Legal
7. Medical
8. Miscellaneous:
   (a) Provost Marshal
   (b) Commissioned Engineer
   (c) Commissioned Signals Officer
   (d) Commissioned Armament Officer
9. RAF Educational Service (non-commissioned)
10. PM RAF Nursing Service

AIRMEN'S CAREERS

(Sources: AMO A364/1932 and A195/1934)

The trade structure

As the decade unfolded, so too did technological progress. More sophisticated aircraft meant greater demands upon the technical services of the RAF. The creation of a technical branch for officers was one answer, restructuring the airmen's trade groups was another. Then came the expansion. Not only did the RAF need airmen with new skills, it needed them in ever greater numbers. The expansion that began in 1934 meant another 2,500 pilots and 27,000 other ranks. The trade groups were restructured to cater for the greater numbers and the advances in technology. On 1 January 1934 there were 25,170 airmen in the service, so that would mean more than doubling the strength. There would be five trade groups and a small additional one to comprise the airmen of the medical and dental trades and musicians. Recruits to the service were enlisted through either the apprentice or direct-entry schemes. There would be a greater recruitment of the former, but it would be 1937 by the time airmen apprentices were to pass out.

The trades listed on the next page are those that were in place by 1938, but are detailed so that sense can be made of the measures taken by the Air Council to recruit men into these trades and to provide for reasonable careers:

Group I

Blacksmith and Welder	Fitter MT
Coppersmith and sheet metal worker	Fitter (torpedo)
Draughtsman	Instrument maker
Duty pilot	Instrument repairer, Grade I
Electrician, Grade I	Link trainer instructor
Engine Driver (fitter)	Link trainer instructor (visual)
Fitter I	Machine-tool setter and operator
Fitter II (airframe)	Metal rigger
Fitter II (engine)	Metal worker
Fitter (aero engine)	Radio mechanic
Fitter (armourer, bombs)	Wireless mechanic
Fitter (armourer, guns)	Wireless operator mechanic
Fitter (marine)	Wireless and electrical mechanic

Group II

Acetylene welder	Grinder
Armoured car crew	MT Mechanic
Armourer (bombs)	Meteorologist
Armourer (guns)	Miller
Balloon operator	Pattern maker (architectural)
Blacksmith	Photographer
Bricklayer	Plumber
Carpenter	Radio operator
Coppersmith	Sheet metal worker
Electrician, Grade II	Steel erector
Electrician (wireman)	Turner
Flight mechanic (airframe)	Wireless operator
Flight mechanic (engine)	

The Group II trade of meteorologist had been civilianized.

Group III

Balloon fabric worker	Fabric worker
Balloon rigger	Hydrogen worker
Balloon rigger/fabric worker	Motor boat crew
Concreter	Parachute repairer
Cook and butcher	PAC operator
Drainlayer	Shoemaker
Driver, winch (balloon)	Tailor

Group IV

Clerk, accounting	Clerk (special duties)
Clerk, pay accounting	Equipment assistant
Clerk, equipment and accounting	Radio telephony operator
Clerk, general duties	Teleprinter operator

Group V

Aircrafthand	Maintenance assistance
Aircrafthand (under trade training)	Messing duties
Armament assistant	Motor cyclist
Barber	Musician
Batman	Parachute packer
Driver MT	Physical training instructor
Ground gunner	Pigeon keepers
Ground observer	Service police
Groundsman	Telephone operator
Machine-gun instructor	Torpedoman

Group M

Dental clerk orderly	Mental nursing orderly
Dental mechanic	Nursing orderly
Dental orderly under training	Operating room assistant

Dispenser	Radiographer
Laboratory assistant	Sanitary assistant
Masseur	Special treatment orderly
Medical orderly under training	Trained nurse

Aircrew	Air gunner	Radio operator (air)
	Air observer	Wireless operator (air gunner)
	Airman pilot	

The trade descriptions in themselves give a detailed picture of the technical complexity of the RAF by the outbreak of war. RAF personnel were manning landplanes, flying-boats, motor boats, station technical and administrative flights, station medical centres and hospitals. One aircraft that had disappeared from the service inventory was the airship. The only lighter-than-air-craft were the barrage balloons. With the loss of the R101 in October 1930, the British airship programme was abandoned, even though the Germans and Americans persisted throughout the 1930s. Then there were the RAF tradesmen serving aboard Royal Naval aircraft-carriers. Even though the Fleet Air Arm was transferred to the Admiralty before the outbreak of war, it took some time before the Navy could entirely replace the RAF tradesmen with men of its own. On board they were having to be practised in repair methods in very confined spaces, and the drills required to get the aircraft quickly on deck and below deck as the situation demanded.

AMO 364/1932

The airmen's trade groups described in Chapter 9 of Volume I were those that were needed in a small peacetime air force that flew wood-and-fabric biplanes. As the RAF entered the 1930s, all-metal construction was creeping in, like the Hinaidi bomber, and more reliable aero engines were resulting in diminished frequency of overhauls. A634/32, which was published before the expansion, is a recognition of the need to provide technical airmen for working in both wood and metal. The largest class of skilled men were fitters, aero, and riggers, and the Air Ministry was anxious, not only to improve their skill, but to improve also their promotion prospects and the marketability of their skills on leaving the service. Entry to these trades and possibilities of re-engagement were to be strictly regulated so that the numbers would be commensurate with the work to be done and the need for enough airmen in supervisory positions. The introduction of Fitters and Mates into the service is described in Chapter 8. This permitted the employment of technical airmen as assistants who would not have direct responsibility for the safety of aircraft, but who could nevertheless undertake work under supervision. The work of the fitter and rigger would be combined in a new trade description of Fitter Grade II, and conversion courses were open to a limited

number of fitters and riggers. Aircraft apprentices who entered Halton after 1 January 1932 as trainee fitters, aero, and metal riggers would be trained in the new trade to qualify as Fitters II. Fitters could also be trained as airmen pilots, indeed there is an account in the squadron histories in Chapter 4 of a fitter/pilot flying a Fairey Gordon.

AMO A195/1934

This order refers to the aforementioned order. It mentions the need to have in the service the right number of technical airmen with good promotion prospects. In 1934 the emphasis was on recruiting direct-entry men, who passed through a much shorter training course than apprentices. These men were recruited as Aircrafthand GD and trained as Fitter's Mates on a five-week course. At the end of that course those who had done well in the examination could undergo a further eight months' training to become Flight Riggers or Flight Mechanic. There was no difficulty in obtaining recruits who were all volunteers. The problem was no longer the one that prevailed throughout the 1920s, when, in a small service, men would have to wait years for promotion. For example, a man might be promoted to corporal within twelve years and then spend the next twelve years to pensionable age in that rank. But in the period 1935 to 1940 squadrons were being opened almost every month, and the worry was whether there would be sufficient men of experience to supervise the new entrants. In spite of this, medical and educational standards were not lowered on entry, and many men were turned down. But on the outbreak of war these standards had to be lowered, if only slightly. Promotion came first to the cadre of highly trained ex-Apprentices and direct entrants to Group 1 trades. The old hands and the new ones had to get to grips with the new generation of monoplane aircraft, of variable-pitch propellers, hydraulic and pneumatic systems and stressed-skin construction. Some had to go on manufacturers' courses to learn the new skills. In 1938 new Group 1 trades were added to the trades listed above.

It was decided to recruit airmen for Trade Groups I, II, III and V from the following sources:

1. Aircraft Apprentice entries (Group I trades of fitter, fitter armourer, wireless operator mechanic and instrument maker).

2. Boy entrants (Group II trades of armourer, wireless operator and photographer).
3. Skilled men entered directly from civil life (Group I and II trades not provided for under 1 or 2 above or 4 below).
4. Airmen selected from aircrafthands (Group III and Group V trades and the Group II trade of rigger (airship).

The order provides that if the number of men required in a particular trade is so small that an adequate career on a service basis is impracticable, then a policy of civilianization will be adopted. This was to apply to the trade of draughtsman and moulder, while the trade of carpenter (boat builder) was merged into the Group II trade of carpenter. Promotion in the various trades was important. This had been a problem in most of the inter-war years, when a man could serve for almost all of his service without promotion. Promotion zones would be created so that suitably qualified and able men could expect to be promoted. Thus, if a man has not been promoted by the time that he passed out of the promotion zone for his trade, he would not normally be considered for promotion unless he had given exceptionally valuable service. A review of establishments showed that both downgrading and upgrading would be required if airmen of the appropriate experience and standing were to be allotted correctly to posts that required them. An example was to be found in the establishment of wireless operator mechanics. This was being overhauled with a view to the transference to the less skilled trade of wireless operator of as many posts as possible, consistent with efficient provision for wireless and electrical maintenance. Arrangements were being made to improve the standard of training of wireless operators. For non-apprentice trades, recruitment was to be made from skilled men in civilian life for a period of nine years' regular service. Re-engagement was allowed for to permit men to reach a pensionable age and for suitable men to attain the higher NCO ranks. An example of recruitment to non-apprentice trades in Group I was that of fitter (torpedo), machine-tool setter and operator and metal worker. The latter was by then a merger of the trades of blacksmith and welder, coppersmith and metal worker. The apprentices in Group I trades would provide fitters (armourers), instrument makers and wireless operator mechanics.

The boy entrants were to be recruited for a period of nine years' service from the age of 18 years from among those of a high standard of education. This was because the majority of air observers would be recruited from their ranks. This matter is dealt with in AMO A196/1934. The trades in Group II that would be filled by the class of boy entrants were armourer, wireless operator and photographer.

The non-technical trades were partially civilianized, such as those of cook and butcher, where such men were employed, for example, in officers' messes at home, whereas such men required for service with operational units overseas would need to be servicemen. These Group III trades were recruited entirely by selection from aircrafthands in Group V who would be required to pass the appropriate trade test before being accepted as Group III tradesmen. Fabric workers in this group would be in greater demand, since it was found that doping of aircraft could be performed at RAF stations without specially heated and ventilated doping rooms – without, therefore, the necessity of returning aircraft to repair depots. This also applied to the repair of parachutes. The consequent necessity for an increase in the establishment of fabric workers on stations enhanced the career prospects of these men.

The establishments of men in the Group IV trades, the medical, dental and musicians trades, were still under consideration when AMO A195/1934 was published. For the Group V trades airmen were to be enlisted for a period of seven years' regular service, with an allowance for extensions of service beyond that period, except in the case of those remustered to a trade or selected for the special employments. The extensions of service were as far as possible limited to the numbers required to re-engage for pension, and to fill the NCO and warrant officer ranks. During the first eighteen months' service such airmen could be selected for training in one of the trades in Group III, for it was known that for airmen to remain in Group V would mean that they would have less favourable careers. The regulations for entry to, and advancement in, the various trade groups were sufficiently flexible for those of ability to remuster to higher trade groups. That flexibility was extended to the possibility of commissioning from warrant officer or non-commissioned rank:

1. Airmen pilots could be commissioned as General Duties Branch officers.
2. Warrant officers of the engineer, signals or armament specialities could also be appointed to branch commissions.
3. Warrant officers of trades other than engineer, signals, armament or accountant, could be appointed to commissions in the Stores Branch.
4. Warrant officers in the accountant speciality could be commissioned as officers in the Accounts Branch.

AMO A196/1934 Air Observers

Previous reference was made to the provision of air observers. The existing system was to employ air gunners on a part-time basis, but this did not meet the fighting requirements of the service, given the growing complexity of the work of squadrons and the organization of crews in multi-engined aircraft. The Air

Council decided that the new aircrew category of Air Observer would be introduced. The air observers would then replace the existing full-time gunner, and save in flying-boat squadrons, two-seat fighter squadrons and, to an extent, in Army Cooperation squadrons, the part-time air gunner would disappear. In the Fleet Air Arm, observers would continue to be provided from naval personnel. The service was looking for airmen of a good type and educational standard, whose service could extend for as long a period as possible. They were to be of an adequate rank and experience and should be adequately trained, stated the AMO, and drawn from the following trades in the approximate proportions as shown below:

	%
Fitter (armourer)	8
Armourer	16
Wireless operator mechanic	16
Wireless operator	40
Photographer	7
Fitter (including rigger)	9
Instrument maker	4

It was reasoned that these were the trades most closely connected with the work of squadrons in the air, which would assist them in becoming efficient when airborne. This they would do on half-observer, half-trade basis. Those from the apprentice trades would fill 37% of air observer posts, the remainder would come from the three trades of armourer, wireless operator and photographer. These in turn were to be recruited from the new class of boy entrants. For training as air observers, airmen would have had to have seven years' man service.

Aircraftman Bennett to Squadron Leader Bennett

In Volume I the case study of an officer, Squadron Leader Whistler, was used as an illustration of an officer's career in the 1920s. In this volume an airman has been chosen. Aircraftman Frank Bennett joined the service in 1935 and went on to serve in India, rising eventually to the rank of squadron leader. Frank joined the RAF on 4 April 1935 reporting to the reception centre at West Drayton. He did three months' drill at the RAF Depot Uxbridge under the tender loving care of his drill NCO, Corporal Rawson, before moving on to the Isle of Sheppey for an armament fitter's course. His first posting was to the station armoury at RAF Cranwell. It was by this time 1937, and he suddenly found himself on the boat to India on a posting to Risalpur on the North-West Frontier. He then moved to Kohat before being posted to Iraq, all in the same year, so 1937 was a busy one for him. At Habbaniya, the new main RAF base in the country, Frank served on No. 70 (B/T) Squadron, where he was employed as an air gunner. He recalls the time when the

No. 520867 AC1 Frank Bennett.

squadron transported a tented field hospital to a site between the Tigris and Euphrates, when all they had if they were feeling unwell in the turbulence was 2 lb sugar bags in lieu of the normal-issue sick bags. He remembers taking part in the parade to mark the Coronation of King George VI and a trip to Cairo on the occasion of the marriage of King Farouk and Queen Farida. The occasion is fixed in the memory because all ranks were given twenty-four hours in the capital and treated to free beer. Frank also tells of a friend, 'Lofty' Reeves, a wireless operator/mechanic who applied for a flying course at Abu Sueir but failed the course because he was too tall! Was this a tall story?

Frank had an unusually short tour in India, for by 20 December 1938 he was back in the United Kingdom on a refresher fitter/armourers' course at RAF Church Fenton. Leaving a station overseas to return to the United Kingdom was always celebrated by a 'Boat Party' before returning on a troop ship, on this occasion the SS *Nevasa*. The illustrations speak for themselves.

SS *Nevasa*, British India Steamship Company –
9,213 tons.

Frank was eventually commissioned. His experience
with weapons made him an ideal recruit for the RAF
Regiment, formed in 1942, when he rose to the rank of
squadron leader later in the war.

PAY AND ALLOWANCES

Introduction

The pay and allowances for all ranks at the beginning of
the decade reflect the dire economic circumstances of the
time. Officers and men could not be asked to accept cuts
in their pay and allowances except as part of an overall
'belt tightening'. An Air Ministry Order A35 dated 2
March 1931 called for the necessity for public economy
in the prevailing financial crisis. Air Officers
Commanding and Commanding Officers were being
asked to do everything possible to effect economies, and
no particular suggestions were made. Everything was to
be looked at, keeping in mind obligations already made
under contract and in keeping good faith, subject only to
three overriding factors:

1. The safe flying of aircraft must not be endangered in
   any way.
2. The national security must not be impaired.
3. There must not be a loss of efficiency disproportionate
   to the savings it was hoped to achieve, for this would
   be false economy.

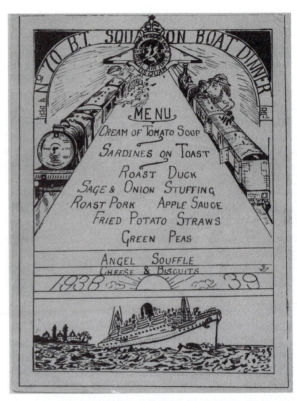

On the menu at Frank's boat party.

PAY
Officers' pay
(Source: AMO A218/1934)

The pay of officers was revised on 30 August 1934, and
was based on the cost-of-living index, which represented
a reduction of $9^{1}/_{2}$% from standard rates. The order
brought the new rates into effect from 1 September, and
stated that until the state of the nation's finances
permitted the issue of the full consolidated rates, the
current rates then in force, authorized in an earlier order
of the year, would continue in issue. A selection of the
consolidated daily rates promulgated in the order will
serve to show the comparison between ranks and
branches.

Rank	GD Branch			Stores Branch			Accountant Branch			Medical Branch		
	£	s	d	£	s	d	£	s	d	£	s	d
Pilot Officer	0	14	6	0	11	10	0	13	6	—		
Flying Officer	0	18	2	0	13	6	0	17	2	1	1	8
Flight Lieutenant	1	3	6	1	0	10	1	0	10	1	3	6
after 4 years in	—											
substantive rank				1	2	8	1	2	8	1	7	2
Squadron Leader	1	10	10	1	9	0	1	9	0	1	15	4

Rank	GD Branch			Stores Branch			Accountant Branch			Medical Branch		
Wing Commander	1	16	2	1	13	6	1	13	6	2	9	10
after 6 years in												
substantive rank	2	1	8	1	18	0	1	18	0	2	17	0
Group Captain	2	9	10	2	5	4	2	5	4	3	3	4
Air Commodore	2	18	4	—			—			3	12	4
Air Vice Marshal	4	10	6	—			—			4	10	6
Air Marshal	5	8	8	—			—			—		
Air Chief Marshal	6	6	8	—			—			—		

AIRMEN'S PAY

(Source: AMO A132/1934)

The airmen's daily rates are shown for the five trade groups described earlier in the chapter.

Rank	Group I		Group II		Group III		Group IV		Group V	
	s	d	s	d	s	d	s	d	s	d
Aircraftman 2nd Class	3	10	3	7	3	4	3	4	2	$10^{1}/_{2}$
1st Class	4	$4^{1}/_{2}$	4	$3^{1}/_{2}$	3	10	3	$10^{1}/_{2}$	3	2
Leading Aircraftman	5	6	5	1	4	$3^{1}/_{2}$	4	6	3	10
over 6 years	6	1	5	8	4	11	5	1	4	$5^{1}/_{2}$
Corporal	7	$7^{1}/_{2}$	6	7	5	$6^{1}/_{2}$	5	8	4	9
over 6 years	8	3	7	2	6	$2^{1}/_{2}$	6	3	5	5
Sergeant	9	6	8	6	6	9	7	0	6	3
over 6 years	10	3	9	3	7	$7^{1}/_{2}$	7	9	7	$1^{1}/_{2}$
Sergeant (pilot)	12	6	11	6	9	9	10	0	—	
Flight Sergeant	11	6	10	0	8	3	8	6	7	9
Flight Sergeant (pilot)	15	0	13	6	11	9	12	0	—	
Warrant Officer 2nd Class	13	0	11	6	10	0	10	6	10	0
Warrant Officer	14	0	12	6	11	0	11	6	11	0
over 6 years	17	3	15	0	13	9	14	0	13	9

PRINCESS MARY'S RAF NURSING SERVICE – REVISION OF EMOLUMENTS (AMO A190/31)

All rates per annum	*Minimum*				*Increment*				*Maximum*			
	Old rate		New Rate		Old rate		New Rate		Old rate		New Rate	
	£	s	£	s	£	s	£	s	£	s	£	s
Staff Nurse	65	0	62	18	2	10	2	9	70	0	67	16
Sister	75	0	72	12	5	0*	4	17*	110	0	106	11
Senior Sister	110	0	106	11	5	0*	4	17*	120	0	116	5
Matron	130	0	125	16	10	0	9	16	200	0	194	8

* increments are biennial

ALLOWANCES
Quarterly clothing allowances 1931 – non-commissioned personnel (AMO A176/31)

The rates of quarterly clothing allowance that applied to non-commissioned personnel from 1 October were a cut from the previous rates in common with all pay and allowances during this period. Notice also the provision made for RAF personnel working on aircraft carriers.

	WO Class I F.Sgt, Sgt	WO Class II,	Cpls, ACs and Apprentices
Home (including aircraft-carriers in home waters)	39s 0d	35s 3d	34s 0d
Motor boats on the coast at home	41s 0d	37s 0d	35s 6d
Egypt, Palestine and Transjordan, Mediterranean and China	35s 6d	33s 9d	32s 9d
Iraq and Persian Gulf	37s 3d	35s 6d	34s 6d
Sudan and Aden	35s 3d	34s 0d	33s 0d
Malaya	36s 0d	34s 6d	33s 6d
Aircraftmen in other than Home Waters	36s 0d	33s 3d	32s 3d

Marriage Allowance – Rates and Dates of Payment in 1930
(Source: AMWO 86/1930)

1. With reference to KR & ACI para. 3350, the index figure for the cost of living as at 1 January, 1930 published by the Ministry of Labour, is 66. Marriage Allowance for the year commencing on the first Thursday in April 1930 will therefore remain as for the preceding year at the following rates:

(i) For a Weekly Rate

Wife	7s 0d
Wife and 1 child	13s 0d
2 children	17s 0d
3 children	19s 0d
4 children	20s.6d
5 children	22s 0d
6 children	23s 0d
7 children	24s 0d
and each additional child	1s 0d

(ii) For children, where no allowance is admissible for a Wife

1st child	6s 0d a week
2nd child	4s 0d
3rd child	2s 0d
4th child	1s 6d
5th child	1s 0d
6th child	1s 0d
7th child	1s 0d
and for each additional child	1s 0d

Rations at Home Stations during February, 1930
(Source: AMWO 84/1930)

1. The following rates and values will be used for the purpose of ration accounting, sales on repayment, issue of allowances, etc., during the month of February 1930.
2. *Ration entitlement, value* – The total value of the ration is 12.2339d., made up as follows:

(i) Issues in kind	6.2d.*
(ii) Cash equivalent allowance	3.0239d.
(iii) Commuted ration allowance	3.0d.

* Includes the cost of one issue of preserved meat a month and a quarter of a ration a week of biscuit, in place of meat and bread respectively.

3. *Ration in kind,* — (i)   The average prices a lb of the components of the ration issued in kind, including departmental expenses, are as follows:

	Pence a lb
Bread	1.41
Biscuit	3.31
Flour (when issued in lieu of bread)	1.88
Beef (frozen)	5.67
Meat (preserved)	8.71
Tea	11.17
Sugar	2.31
Salt	0.28

These prices are to be used for the valuation of rations in Form 1475.

(ii) When mutton is issued under the special conditions which have been notified separately, the actual contract price, or the RASC price (including departmental expenses at $2\frac{1}{2}$ per cent.) is to be used for accounting in Form 1475.

4. *Cash equivalent allowance.* — (i) Bacon, cheese, margarine and jam are commuted items, a cash equivalent allowance being given in lieu in accordance with para. 7 (i) (a), chapter 1, of Air Publication 112. Supplies of these items through the NAAFI will be invoiced by them at the rates stated below at *A*, and at the end of the month the requisite adjustments will be made in respect of cheese and margarine at the prices shown under *B*:

	A	*B*
Bacon	1s. $1\frac{1}{4}$d. a lb	123s. 8d. a cwt.
Cheese	10d. a lb	93s. 3d. a cwt.
Margarine	5d. a lb	44s. 6d. a cwt.
Jam	$4\frac{3}{4}$d. a lb	$4\frac{3}{4}$d. a lb

  (ii) The price for jam is on the basis of equal supply of the various kinds. In practice, it may not be possible for the responsible officer to demand equal quantities of each kind, and he is therefore to order, alternatively, either single fruit or mixed jam.

  (iii) Supplies drawn on the last day of the month for consumption on the first day of the following month will be charged for at the prices in force on the first day of the following month, and will be charged to the account for that month. Such purposes will be limited, normally, to supplies for one day, but if the first day of the month should fall on a Sunday or on a public holiday, the same principle will apply. This rule applies to purchases at retail prices as well as at contract prices.

5. *Cash equivalent allowance issued to an individual.* – When the cash equivalent allowance, the rate to be taken is 3.0d.

6. *Ration allowance, lower rate.* – When ration allowance is issued under para. 32, chapter 1, of Air Publication 112, the rate applicable will be 12.1d (including commuted ration and cash equivalent allowance, but excluding extra cost of issue of preserved meat and biscuit).

7. *Issues of bread and meat on repayment to army and airforce personnel.* – The prices to be charged for bread and meat issued on repayment under para. 46, chapter 1 of Air Publication 112, the following prices will be charged:

Bread	$1\frac{1}{2}$d. a lb)	Inclusive of departmental
*Beef (frozen)	6.0d. a lb)	expenses.

* When supply is obtained under local contract at appreciably higher prices, or when fresh meat, or mutton, is issued, the actual cost to the Royal Air Force, plus $\frac{1}{4}$d. a lb, is to be charged.

8. *Sales on repayment to civilian employees, etc.,* — When ration items are issued on repayment to individuals under para. 43, chapter 1 of Air Publication 112, the following prices will be charged:

Beef (frozen)	$9\frac{1}{4}$d. a lb
Bread	9d. for 4 lb
Tea	2s. 5d. a lb
Sugar	$2\frac{3}{4}$d. a lb
Salt	$1\frac{1}{2}$d. a lb

9. *Attachments.* – The rate to be charged for rations issued to army personnel attached to air force units will be 12.23d.

UNIFORM
All ranks
The uniform for officers in the 1930s differed little from that worn in the 1920s, and the full range of clothing is shown in Appendix L. Volume I dealt in detail with the matter of uniform. The major change in uniform was to come in 1936. Before this the tunic, which was worn by airmen up to the rank of corporal, was buttoned up to the neck. This had been a heavy and hairy wool tunic that could be very uncomfortable, particularly in hot weather. Gone also were the baggy breeches and puttees, pictured earlier in this chapter worn by AC1 Bennett. A tunic with collar and tie was introduced, and the shirts were blue with soft or semi-stiff collars. Everyone then wore trousers, even on formal parades. Before 1936 only a peaked cap was worn on the head. The side-cap, or forage-cap, which had been introduced to the service by Sykes, was brought back. The very formal ceremonial dress worn by officers did not survive the Second World War. The imitation flying-helmet, pictured in Appendix L, survives only as part of the dress of members of the RAF Central Band. The wearing of a moustache was optional, but the RAF never followed the example of the Senior Service by permitting the wearing of beards.

THE OLD
This is, in fact, Lawrence of Arabia in the guise of Aircraftman Shaw.

THE NEW
For aircraftmen collar and tie are now the order of the day.

The following two illustrations are of changes introduced in the early and mid-1930s to officers' uniform. The mess dress is called 'mess dress' and 'mess undress'. For more formal occasions the white waistcoat is worn, and for the less formal, such as a routine dining-in night, the blue waistcoat was worn, hence the term 'undress'. With this in mind the author cannot resist one of his little anecdotal stories. As a retired member of the RAF Regiment he knew of the honour bestowed on the corps when it was permitted to mount the guard on the Tower of London. It was the custom for the Officer of the Guard to wear his mess kit to dinner, and this young Regiment officer wore his blue waistcoat. Then he was summoned to Buckingham Palace to dine with members of the Royal Family. The Duke of Edinburgh saw what the officer was wearing and asked on what occasions be wore his white waistcoat, to which the officer replied that it was worn only on special occasions!

AMO A311/34 Dress for Officers of the Royal Air Force – approved changes in Mess Dress and Full Dress

The shoulder-straps that previously carried the rank were removed and the rank was above the cuff and made of gold-wire lace. The silk facings of the jacket were replaced by ribbed silk and the cut of the jacket was slightly more pointed. The flying-badge was a gold-embroidered miniature. At that time there were no navigators – only pilots and observers – and these two aircrew categories were permitted to have the appropriate flying-badge on the mess dress. A white waistcoat was introduced for mess dress, and this had a roll collar with three buttons. The overalls were of a looser cut, and officers of the rank of flight lieutenant to group captain had a stripe of gold lace down the seam. Air officers had a wider stripe of pale blue balladine silk. With mess undress the officer wore a cloth waistcoat in blue, and the overalls with the gold stripe were not worn. The mess-dress cap that was formerly worn by officers of the rank of wing commander and below was abolished and replaced with service-dress caps. For mess dress a stiff-fronted shirt was worn with Wellington boots. These were worn right up to the time that the author was in the service, and he can remember the change-over to a soft black patent leather shoe with mess dress. Officers who were entitled to wear a device on the shoulder straps, e.g. Personal ADC to the King, were in future to wear such a device on a plain shoulder-strap.

Mess dress.

AMO A230/1933 Tropical Full Dress

Introduced in 1933, tropical full dress was approved by HM The King for wear by officers in commands overseas. The dress comprised a head-dress, tunic, overalls, boots, gloves, shirt, sword, belt and slings. The provision of tropical full dress was optional, for it goes without saying that it was a costly purchase.

The white Wolseley helmet had a black patent leather chin strap, and the RAF flash was borne on the left-hand side of the helmet. Air Officers Commanding wore a plume of cock's feathers of the same shade as the plume for full-dress head-dress (home pattern). The plume was fixed to a gilt ornament screwed to the top of the helmet. On the tunic the pilot's badge, which was the same as that for full dress (home pattern) was detachable, as were the shoulder-straps, which bore the rank braid and the medal mountings. The material used for the tunic was white, of fine drill. The Wellington boots and white gloves were as used with full dress (home pattern). The sword belt was worn under the tunic, and the sword, scabbard and sword knot were the same as those approved for full dress (home pattern).

Tropical full dress.

Fitting of R/T receivers to flying helmets

The following is of interest since it shows the progressive transition to the use of R/T and W/T in aircraft. The flying caps issued in 1930 did not have earphones as an integral part of the cap. This was still the time when pilots flew in open cockpits, and the rush of wind could make it very difficult to hear with an ill-fitting cap. To modify the cap was a job that could be done in station workshops by following these instructions.

AMO A207 Receivers, Telephone – Instructions for fitting to Caps, Flying (1930 Pattern), (Stores Ref. 22C/51)

1. The undermentioned new type of fitting has been introduced for use with the 1930-pattern flying cap.

Stores Ref. 10A/2266. Caps, earpiece	1
Stores Ref. 10A/2265 Earpieces, receiver, securing	1
Stores Ref. 10A/7350 Rings, earpiece, with locking spring	1

2. Helmet telephone fittings (Stores Ref. 10A/2664) are hereby declared obsolescent and are not to be fitted to 1930-pattern flying caps. These fittings will in future be known as Type A Flying caps. Caps already fitted with Type A fittings will continue to be used as long as the caps are serviceable.

3. It is of the utmost importance for the successful reception of R/T or W/T signals in the air that the telephone receivers are correctly fitted in the flying cap. The instructions below are therefore to be carefully followed, and the wearer fitted individually, care being taken to ensure that a cap of the correct size to suit the wearer is selected and that the sides fit closely to the face, to prevent wind and noise passing between the cap and cheek.

4. The cap is to be fitted to the head of the individual and the marking of the hole centres carried out while the cap is in position. Reference is made to the diagram accompanying this order.

5. The sequence of fitting operations is as follows:

    (i)   Mark off centre hole to suit the wearer.

    (ii)   Cut or punch a hole 1″ diameter right through the cap, i.e. through outer leather, inner leather (if fitted), sponge rubber, and chamois lining, concentric with the centre mark already made.

    (iii) Enlarge the hole in the outer leather to $2^3/_{16}$″ diameter.

    (iv) Stitch the ring, earpiece, securing (Stores Ref. 10A/7350), to outer leather with flange inside. The same stitches are to secure the inner leather*.

    (v)   Buttonhole stitch round the edge of the 1″ hole, stitching the chamois to the inner leather, the stitches to pass through the edge of the sponge rubber.

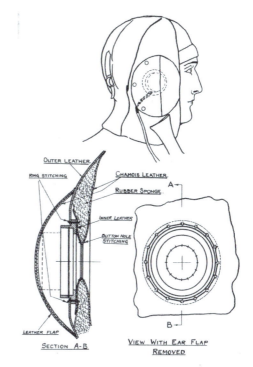

    (vi) Insert telephone earpieces in the securing rings, and affix the leather flap** and stitch press-button in position.

Notes: * Present issues of flying caps (Stores Ref. 22C/51) are not with the inner leather, which may be provided locally if desired. On the other hand the modification may be carried out without this leather.

** The provision of leather flaps to cover the telephone earpieces as shown in the accompanying diagram, is being arranged, and notification will be made when they are available at No. 1 Stores Depot. In the meantime they are to be produced locally.

The new uniform introduced in 1936, forage caps *et al.*

Forage caps, even on parade!

Flying clothing

Flying-clothing had to protect the wearer against the cold weather at altitude. Pilots and air gunners alike flew in open cockpits. This was the case with light

bombers, which had a pilot in the front cockpit and an air gunner in the rear. The Hart, Audax and Hardy were the last of a breed and were gradually phased out as war approached. The Virginia heavy bomber was in front-line service until 1937, and had 'fighting tops', with air gunners situated in open cockpits in the upper wing. The flying-suit needed in these circumstances was as seen in the photograph:

The flying suit issued in the 1930s was called the Sidcot suit. Douglas Bader describes how he waddled across to the aeroplane for his first flight at Cranwell in 1928. His stride was inhibited as his parachute banged against his buttocks. The new breed of aircraft – fighter, bomber and flying-boat – had enclosed cockpits and powered turrets for nose and tail gunners. Pilots of Spitfires and Hurricanes flew in their service dress and shoes, with just a Mae West. Bomber crews wore boots and leather flying-jackets. It was important not simply to feel comfortable, particularly on a long flight, as operating navigational and wireless equipment meant having flying clothing that was not cumbersome. Some bomber crews also wore overalls; there was no golden rule. When war came the service dress, which was cumbersome in flight, was replaced by the battledress, which became standard wear by all aircrew.

SOCIAL LIFE IN THE RAF

The social relationship between officers and airmen was determined to a large extent by the messing arrangements. Officers lived in the officers' mess, which served as a social base for all officers, including those who lived in married quarters on the station. It was almost like a hotel with bars, sitting rooms and bedrooms. The warrant officers and senior NCOs lived in the sergeants' mess, and junior NCOs and aircraftmen lived in barrack-block accommodation. The corporals did, however, have their status recognized by relaxing in a corporals' club, and they would occupy their own private room in the barrack block. When Air Marshal Trenchard became Chief of the Air Staff he had that unique opportunity of shaping the new service's institutions, but he chose to copy the two sister services by segregating the commissioned and non-commissioned ranks.

Although the lives of officers and airmen were spent socially apart, there were opportunities for both to meet, particularly on sporting occasions. Indeed, sport was always and remains a very important facet of a serviceman's life. The other opportunity was at work. Here the relationship between commissioned and non-commissioned personnel was different from the other two services, particularly the Army. The officer would have considerable respect for the airmen. A pilot put his faith in the technical airmen who serviced his aeroplane, and his life was very much in their hands. The latter would have marketable skills very much in demand in civilian life, unlike the infantryman in the Army.

Mess life

Paul Tunbridge, in his history of RAF Halton, describes the social life of officers who served on the apprentice wings. They had few administrative duties but had to keep their keep their aircrew status, which meant flying for four hours a month. They would take an aircraft to attend a sports meeting or receptions at another station. Promotion for these officers, he reported, was almost unheard of, and flight lieutenants could spend as long as twelve years in the rank. There were separate dining arrangements for senior and junior officers. Personal calling-cards were printed in black copperplate, and officers would leave them on a silver tray in the mess to indicate that one was about to call. This was followed by calling on the station commander in his quarter, for every officer was expected to make himself known in a purely social setting, to meet the station commander's lady. There were around eighty officers living in mess, where they dined in full mess kit. After dinner it was custom to play mess games. Those outside the service might think of these as a bit childish when officers would toboggan down the double-width stairway on a dinner gong, but no one had his arm twisted to take part. At weekends they could relax in their dinner jackets. Drinks were ordered through mess waiters, who served them in the ante room, service parlance for a lounge. Woe betide an officer who did not attend social functions with the appropriate frequency. In the 1930s gentlemen addressed each other by their surname. The author was surprised to find an elderly officer at RAF St Athan still maintaining this custom as late as 1956.

The educational and social background of officers and airmen was different, being determined to a great extent by the more marked class differences in the 1930s than exist today. Since the potential officer would probably have gone to a public or state grammar school, he would have had the opportunity of joining the Officers' Training Unit (OTU) at school. (This organization became the Combined Cadet Force after the Second World War.) At OTU, the officer would have been encouraged to join the armed forces. In the 1920s Trenchard added the universities to the institutions helping to prepare air-minded young men for a life in the RAF. Thus the officer in the 1920s would have been socially and educationally differentiated from the airmen under his command. But this was to change in the late 1930s. With the rapid expansion in the number of RAF squadrons would come the growing need for pilots. Volunteers were not hard to find, and those who were physically fit enough and could satisfy the recruitment officers that they were of an acceptable educational standard were accepted for training. Only when the recruits were under training did those who exhibited leadership qualities get selected for training as an officer. Of course, the Cranwell officer entries were still maintained in the 1930s for the career officer, but the expansion of the RAF meant a much larger number of officers were being recruited from outside the public and grammar schools. The result was that the officer corps was to comprise a greater social mix.

It used to be said of the RAF between the two world wars that it was the 'best flying club in the world'. Officers lived a life where the station and its mess were the centre of their lives. Indeed, junior officers were not expected to get married in their twenties since it might detract from their professional development. And when one did get married one had to get the permission of the Commanding Officer. An Air Ministry Weekly Order of 1932 says it all!

A15/32 Junior Officers living in Mess

Junior Officers are required to be living-in dining members of the Officers' Mess and thus acquire the knowledge of the service which comes from mixing with his fellows in mess life. Permission to become a non-dining member will not be granted to an officer until he has completed three years' service or attained the age of 25 years.

Cinema entertainment

Cinemas were an important part of service life, since most flying stations were deep in the countryside, like Bircham Newton, which was seventeen miles from anywhere and another seventeen miles from everywhere. Personnel on some stations were luckier, like those at Upwood A thirty-minute walk would take one into Ramsey, and a public house was only ten minutes away. Most had to walk, for few, even among the officers, could afford to own a car. The following 1930 Air Ministry Order describes the arrangements made for the entertainment of service personnel before the days of television. The order lays down the charges that could be met by the taxpayer, and those that would have to be met from station funds for clubs, messes, etc.

A164 – Use of Service Buildings as Cinemas (77169/30)

1. Service buildings may be used for the purpose of cinematograph entertainments conducted by units, provided that their use for public purposes, whenever required, is nor interfered with. Maintenance of buildings so used will be a public charge, but any expenditure on adaptation and subsequent reinstatement will be borne by the unit concerned, unless in special circumstances Air Ministry sanction is given for the cost to be defrayed from public funds.
2. With effect from 1 January, 1931, the rent payable for the use of the building will be 10 per cent of the net profits arising from the entertainments, except that (i) at Uxbridge and other stations where the general public is admitted, a commercial rent will be payable; and (ii) where entertainments are held in airmen's accommodation, e.g. dining room, institute, etc., no charge for rent will be made.
3. The provision and maintenance of seats will be a public charge, but no refund will be made of expenditure incurred by units on these services.
4. Apparatus will not be provided or maintained at public expense. Where it has already been so provided, refund will not be required, but the cost of replacements for such apparatus will not be a public charge.
5. All expenses in connection with the hire of films, insurance of non-public property, wages of attendants and other running costs, will be defrayed from non-public funds.

Airmen's social life

Officers and sergeants had their messes, and even corporals had their club. Social life for an airman centred on his barrack block or the NAAFI. If a man left the station without a car or a motor-cycle he wouldn't get far. He would have to be back on the station by 23.59 hrs. An apprentice had to be in even earlier, at 21.00 hrs. The buses to either Tring or Aylesbury were infrequent, and with only four hours between ceasing work and the return to camp, an apprentice did not have much time to socialize. In organizing his free time, the apprentice lived a more directed social life. Halton's Debating Society produced comic operas, and in 1930, *Flight* magazine remarked on the life and vigour of the show with the orchestra of twenty-five apprentices. As for sex, the official attitude to relations with women may be found

in Paragraph 11 of the Rules for Boy Entrants and Apprentices. Boys were forbidden to associate with females, and this rule even applied to those who, before leaving Halton, might have reached the age of twenty. When an apprentice of the 36th Entry passed the guardroom in the company of a female he was challenged by the service policeman. He was almost charged with being cheeky to an NCO when he declared that he was not with a female, but his sister, who happened to be working in the NAAFI.

Sport was important for all ranks. Douglas Bader excelled at cricket and rugby. Officers would play squash and airmen soccer. Going to another station for a match was not only enjoyable in itself, it also gave airmen a chance to get off the station. Others, who were not actually competing, would go to give support to the station team. Sport was inter-station, inter-command and even inter-service. Air Ministry Orders would give details of fixtures.

Stanley Humphrey, in his book, *Press on Regardless*, describes the life of an airman he calls 'Ginger', both at home and overseas. After his initial recruit training at Uxbridge, Ginger went to Manston on a Fitter Mates course. He recalls the Virginia taking off at 45 mph before it floated around at less than 100 mph. One could get airborne if the 'blood book' was signed. Thence to RAF Lee-on-Solent to work on aircraft that served the needs of the fleet. He was posted to India on 18 October 1935, but the posting was cancelled due to the Abyssinian crisis. Then the dress changed in 1936, and shoes replaced boots for leaving camp and the carrying of a cane was abolished. (The photograph of AC1 Bennett shown earlier in this chapter shows the cane.) On 6 December 1936 his posting went ahead. The voyage to India was on HMS *Dorsetshire*, and the men slept in hammocks. In the evening one played tombola, the only gambling game permitted in the forces. When the ship put into Port Said all personnel were told that this would be the last opportunity to post a letter that would reach home by Christmas. Once into the Red Sea, khaki drill uniform was ordered. Ginger's draft was destined for stations on the North-West Frontier, Ambala, Kohat and Risalpur. Ginger himself went to Risalpur. By this time his warmer clothes were in his 'deep-sea' luggage, and khaki drill was no good for the Frontier in January. Since the tour overseas was then five years, some of the men arriving on the frontier had already spent two years in Iraq. He was taken up for a flight in a Hart by the station commander. Both men had their 'goolie' chits, an insurance policy in case one was shot down by hostile tribesmen who might want to cut off parts of one's anatomy. A financial reward was offered for the safe return of the airman, but Ginger could not understand why an officer's goolies were worth twice as much as those of an airman. Each bed in the airmen's accommodation had a mat called a 'dhuri', which was impregnated with something to stop the insects crawling up his legs in bed. Then there were the large, black, hairy spiders and a deadly snake called a Silver Krait. There was a station cinema, but most films were about two years old. On sports day everyone was expected to contribute something, so Ginger helped organize the tug-of-war.

Work began at 06.30 hrs when the air was dense enough to provide lift for the aircraft. Breakfast was not eaten until 08.00 hrs, then it was back to work until 11.00 hrs. By this time the shade temperature was 100°F, and it was still 90°F at night. These conditions were so taxing that it was necessary for all ranks to take to the hills for rest at the Hill Depot, 8,000 feet up, where life was more bearable. Ginger did well in the trade tests and education tests, which qualified him to return to the United Kingdom to attend a Fitter, Group 1, course back at Manston. He recalls hearing of the abdication of King Edward VIII while on the boat back to Britain. He and his colleagues who had been in India had been away from women for so long that they had fallen into the habit of swearing. If a man wanted to marry he had to have the permission of the Commanding Officer, and marriage allowance, the princely sum of 26s. 3d., did not start until a man was 26 years of age. A friend of Ginger would have £3 a week between himself and his girlfriend, and Ginger had to persuade him to wait until he was an LAC. It is of interest to note that a Divorce Reform Bill had been passed, and one of the clauses of the bill put a three-year limit before desertion could be established. The five-year tour abroad had to be reduced to three-years, depending on the climate.

On completion of his course Ginger had to complete his overseas tour, and he was posted to No. 84 Squadron, Shaibah. It was welcome to sandfly fever, malaria, scorpions and the Shaibah sh—s. There were no wireless sets in the airmen's bungalows as they would have been incapable of receiving programmes from home, so news came via the W/T Section. Finally he remembers the Medical Officer being a golf fanatic, who proposed making a green out of flints and sand, 'puddled' and allowed to dry. A nine-hole course was built and gave the men an important outlet for their energies. *Rhapsody in Blue* and *Stardust* were top of the pops at this time.

Chapter 10
Air Doctrine, the Air Ministry and Command

Introduction – Strategic bombing doctrine – Western air plans – Air exercises 1932 and 1933 – Requirements for a bomber –
Bomber tactics – Fighter tactics and fighter defence of the UK – Strategic maritime doctrine – Comparative performance and
capability – The air commanders

Introduction

The Strategic Air Doctrine of the RAF, which was inherited by Air Chief Marshal Sir John Salmond in 1930, was very much a product of the Trenchard years. It was firmly understood by the Air Staff that should a major war come then the RAF would immediately take the war to the enemy with a bomber force that would prove decisive in breaking an enemy's will and ability to win. The modest expansion plan of 1923 was to lift the strength of the Metropolitan Air Force to fifty-two squadrons. Of these, thirty-five squadrons would be bomber and seventeen fighter. The emphasis was clearly on the importance of the bomber. During the 1920s the expansion to fifty-two squadrons proceeded very slowly, for the Ten-Year Rule was in operation, which meant that the country did not expect to be involved in a major war for at least ten years. This period was simply rolled forward year on year unless or until it was decided that circumstances in international relations called for a reappraisal, as they did in 1934, following Hitler's rise to power. The growth in the number of RAF squadrons at the beginning of the decade slowed due to the economic depression, necessitating cuts in public expenditure, and the desire by the government not to be seen to be rearming when negotiations were going on at the Disarmament Conference at Geneva. From 1923 onwards the Metropolitan Air Force was called the Home Defence Force, since it was intended to convey a message of non-belligerence. This disguised the bias in favour of bomber squadrons, since it was argued that the surest way of defending the country was to take the war to the enemy.

When the expansion of the RAF began in earnest in 1934 and the shadow factories came into play to rearm at an unprecedented rate, changes were made in the Air Ministry, which are discussed in this chapter, and which were necessary to manage the expansion. What did not change, however, was the basic doctrine, which saw the bomber playing the leading role in a future war. The air exercises of the late 1920s were undoubtedly skewed in favour of offence, and the Air Staff saw no need to change the policy. What will be discussed in this chapter is the blind unquestioned assumption that the bomber would always get through to the target. Little attempt was made to ask how many would get though and what effect the bombing would have if they did. Bomber tactics were not evaluated, nor was the destructive power or the reliability of the bombs, 'left-overs' from the Great War, put to the test until very late in the day.

STRATEGIC BOMBING DOCTRINE
Formulating a doctrine

During the 1920s strategic bombing had three aims in order of importance:

1. Bombing would have a morale effect that would sap the will of an enemy to continue fighting.
2. Attacks upon economic and strategic military targets would reduce the means by which an enemy could prosecute a war.
3. Attacks could be made on an enemy's military forces in the field. The Air Staff were obliged to consider that an enemy would have the same intentions in the air, and therefore a fighter defence would be required.

In a private letter from Sir Maurice Hankey to Trenchard, dated 28 April 1928, the former stated his belief that the morale effect of bombing had been overstated and that the claims made by Trenchard were 'an abuse of language'. (Volume I, Appendix Q, refers). He added that, given the range of bombers of the period, it would be relatively easy for a continental power to move its vital factories out of range of British bombers. Even allowing for the improvements in performance, he did not believe that in the foreseeable future the RAF could deliver a 'knockout' blow. Even within the range of British bombers an enemy would scatter and camouflage its essential factories and military facilities. Hankey cited cases of bombing in the Great War, which had little effect on Germany's ability to wage war, and added that Field Marshal Haig had played down the effectiveness of bombing attacks on enemy communications.

In spite of these criticisms, the Air Staff in the early to mid-1930s did not shift from their view that the strategic bombing offensive was the primary means of winning the war, although it was no longer claimed that the RAF could win a war alone. As the threat from Nazi Germany became ever more menacing in the late 1930s, the Air Staff had to review their strategic bombing policy, given the state of the bombing force at their disposal. This showed that the RAF lacked bombers with the performance and hitting power to achieve the objectives outlined above. Moreover the squadrons were being re-formed at such a rate that there were few experienced pilots to go round. Little had been done to test the effectiveness of bombs and the ability of bombers to fight their way to a target, to find a target in all weathers or to measure the effectiveness of bomber tactics. Finally there were no operational conversion units to train aircrews in the business of bombing. The Prime Minister, Mr Baldwin, might declare that 'the bomber will always get through', but this was a very questionable presumption.

Among other things this chapter seeks to discuss the inadequacies of Bomber Command as Britain went to war in 1939. At the Air Ministry Plans Department was John Slessor, who was attempting to devise attack plans that were achievable, and passing these to Bomber Command, where Sir Edgar Ludlow-Hewitt, as C-in-C, had the task of preparing his aircrews for bombing missions and for writing the necessary operational orders that could be issued promptly if and when hostilities commenced. These plans were known as the Western Air Plans. Accurate intelligence would be vital to know the whereabouts of the various squadrons of the *Luftwaffe* and the location of industrial targets that would be vital to Germany if the war was going to last for any appreciable period. Given the expected bomber losses in a future war, reserves of aircraft would be extremely important, as would the replacement of aircrews killed or injured in action. Indeed, this point also did not escape Hankey in his warnings about a protracted air war, for he said that it would not be long before the RAF lost many of its experienced aircrews and

would be relying more and more on young men thrown into battle following the shortest possible period of training.

WESTERN AIR PLANS

The Prime Minister, speaking in the House of Commons in the autumn of 1938, said that as far as the RAF was concerned the country should be able to meet the following objectives 'within a reasonable period'. They were:

1. Protection of this country.
2. Preservation of the trade routes.
3. Defence of British territories overseas.
4. Cooperation in the defence of the territories of our allies in case of war.

To meet these objectives the RAF had Fighter and Coastal Command, together with RAF commands overseas and an expeditionary force earmarked to achieve Objective 4. No mention is made of attacks upon the enemy, because these are implicit in a policy of offensive defence. The plans for Bomber Command in a war were the responsibility of John Slessor at the Air Ministry, who drew up thirteen (later sixteen) Western Air Plans, which were passed down to Bomber Command so that operational orders could be produced and the necessary crew training put in hand. An increase in staff, under the direction of Group Captain Don, was authorized for Bomber Command HQ so that the necessary military appreciations could be carried out:

THE WESTERN AIR PLANS

Index Number		Subject
WA1	(a)	Attack on the German air striking force, its organization and the aircraft industry.
	(b)	Attack on certain aerodromes within range.
WA2		Reconnaissance in cooperation with the Navy in home waters.
WA3		Convoy protection in cooperation with the Navy.
WA4		Attack on German military, rail and other communications.
	(a)	Attack on rail and road communications during the concentration period in West Germany.
	(b)	Attack to delay German invasion of southern Holland, Belgium and France.
WA5	(a)	Attack on German industry.
	(b)	The Ruhr Plan and attack on the military communications of Western Germany.
WA6 (WA5c)		The Oil Plan.
WA7	(a)	Attack on Wilhelmshaven in cooperation with the Navy.
	(b)	Attack on Wilhelmshaven with air forces alone.
WA8		Attack on war stores.
WA9		Attack on the Kiel Canal.
WA10		Attack on enemy shipping.
WA11		Attack on forests.
WA12		Attack on the German fleet at sea.
WA13		Attack on administrative centres in Germany.
WA14		Dropping leaflets.
WA15		Attack on enemy shipping with magnetic mines, in cooperation with the Navy.
WA16		Attack with mines on German canals .

For the purposes of this discussion, only four were given priority before the Munich Crisis:

WA1 The attack on the German air striking force and its maintenance organization.

WA4 The attack on German military, rail, canal and road communications:
  a. During the period of the concentration of the armies, and
  b. To delay a German invasion of the Low Countries and France.

WA5 The attack on the German war industry, including the supply of oil, with priority to that in the Ruhr, Rhineland and the Saar.

WA6 The attack on the German aircraft industry. (This was later added to WA1, and a new WA6 was issued, called the 'Oil Plan'.)

WA1 WA1 was considered the best attack plan to reduce the severity of air attacks on Britain. The problem was knowing which airfields to attack, for the Germans were very good at changing the whereabouts of their bombers. Even if the airfields could be located, one could never be sure which units occupied them. Hitting the factories was another option, but unless they were all destroyed in a 'knockout blow' the ability to replace lost aircraft could continue indefinitely. Then there were the deficiencies in Bomber Command already discussed in this chapter. The more one looked at this particular attack plan, the more unrealistic it became. By the time of Munich this plan had been virtually abandoned.

WA4 The Air Staff and the Army General Staff held different opinions about WA4. The Army felt that it would be better for RAF bombers to concentrate on attacking bridges, viaducts and railway cuttings, while the Air Staff favoured attacks on locomotive sheds, junctions and railway stations. Observers of the Spanish Civil War and the war in China, involving Japanese forces, would support the Air Staff view. When one thinks of the success of Lawrence in cutting off vital supplies to the Turkish forces in the Arabian peninsula, it must be borne in mind that there was one main railway line to cut. In western Europe the density of the railway network was such that it would be very difficult to stop, totally, the movement of men and supplies.

WA5 Attacks on the Ruhr seemed, then, to be more promising than the two plans discussed above. Ludlow Hewitt, the C-in-C of Bomber Command, requested a 'reasoned statement' showing the best targets to go for in their order of importance. Power and coking plants were listed, and it was estimated that it would take 3,000 sorties and involve the loss of 176 aircraft to destroy all

nineteen power stations and twenty-six coking plants. The Air Staff believed this to be too optimistic, arguing that these locations had to be found, in all weathers, and subjected to very accurate bombing. At this time the RAF did not have four-engined heavy bombers, and so it would mean using Whitleys, Wellingtons and Hampdens, hence the large number of sorties to deliver the requisite bomb load. The Air Targets Sub-Committee felt that more damage could be done in fewer than 3,000 sorties if the Mohne and Sorpe dams were attacked, together with the canal system and aqueducts that connected the Ruhr with northern Germany. Today many people in Britain know about the famous Dam Buster raids by No. 617 Squadron carried out under the leadership of Wing Commander Guy Gibson, and that it took a specially designed bouncing bomb to attack these two dams in 1943. Dr Barnes-Wallis, who had designed these bombs, proved that only bombs that were exploded under the water at the base of the dam would produce the destructive force necessary to shatter the masonry. It therefore makes it doubly interesting that these dams were singled out for attack by bombers with a far smaller bomb load than that possessed by the Lancaster armed with conventional bombs. Be that as it may, it was considered that if such attacks were coupled with attacks on the principal railway workshops and repair depots, the German industrial system could be paralysed for many months. Together they were known as WA5 (a) and WA5 (b).

To achieve a 'knockout blow' Britain would need to deliver these attacks on the outbreak of war, but even if squadrons of Bomber Command were based in France, the bombers at Ludlow Hewitt's disposal simply did not have the hitting power to inflict the damage on the scale required, and the *Luftwaffe* was not just going to sit there and let the RAF paralyse German industry. What the Air Staff were proposing was classic Trenchard doctrine. Would the bomber crews have been trained to use their defensive armament to ensure that a sufficient number of bombers reached their targets intact, or would the bombers need fighter escort, assuming the fighters had the range? And if the attacks were to be mounted from French airfields there would have to be an enormous supply of spares, ammunition and fuel to sustain the attacks, even over as short a period as a month. Anything longer would not be a knockout blow, but would be bordering on a war of attrition.

Ludlow Hewitt was anxious to preserve his bomber force until it was truly ready for a strategic bombing campaign, and preferred to restrict his crews to dropping propaganda leaflets over Germany, which would have the secondary advantage of practising his crews in flying over enemy territory at night (WA14). Air Marshal 'Bomber' Harris was later to remark, somewhat wryly, that all that was achieved was to supply the German population with toilet paper for the duration of the war.

Before one judges the RAF too critically over these seemingly innocuous leaflet raids, it must be said that it was the government that was putting the restraining hand on Bomber Command. On the outbreak of war the government required the RAF to strike at purely military targets. This point has already been discussed in this chapter. Distinguishing, let alone hitting, purely military targets was difficult in the extreme. In the recent Iraqi wars, using laser-guided weapons, there has been collateral damage to civilian areas for which the Americans have had to apologize on more than one occasion. Slessor at Plans was anxious to know what might be the reaction of the German government and public to RAF bombing attacks, and on 24 October 1938 he wrote a minute to the Deputy Director of Intelligence. It read as follows:

1. In the selection of targets for the preparation of war plans, one of the overriding factors appears to be the political reactions arising from the psychological effect on the population of air bombardment.

2. The effect produced might vary in different districts. For example, at Hamburg, which has many trading interests in common with Great Britain and is believed to be the focus of anti-Nazi feeling, air bombardment might arouse sentiments of national patriotism which it would be in our interest to avoid. On the other hand, the pacifist tendencies of the Communists in the Ruhr might be increased under the stress of sustained raids, causing a loss in production of vital importance to our war aim.

3. It would be of great advantage to the Plans Branch if you could appreciate the probable effects of bombing attacks on different parts of Germany. It is suggested that, if your information regarding the political tendencies of various communities in Germany is insufficient for a full appreciation of this important factor, the Foreign Office might be approached for their views on the subject.

Neither the Foreign Office, nor the British Embassy in Berlin nor the Air Attachés could help. It seemed that there was no part of Germany where the population could be relied upon to react to bombing in a way that would be of benefit to Britain.

To summarize the stance adopted by the British government in the immediate pre-war period towards the bombing of targets in Germany, the following factors are relevant:

1. The policy of appeasement, which had driven the relationship with Mussolini, was pursued in the hope that the Italian dictator would not, after his African adventure, continue to try to build an African empire. To have taken military action against Italy in 1935 would risk throwing Mussolini into the arms of

Hitler, which is precisely what happened. This created the Rome–Berlin Axis. The Air Staff would not wish to see added to the German air threat the threat of Italian airpower in the Mediterranean.

2. The policy of appeasement in relation to Hitler was pursued in the vain hope that the German dictator's territorial ambitions could be accommodated without recourse to war. When this proved an illusion, the government still nursed the hope that restraint on bombing that might kill civilians, together with leaflet raids, might persuade the German people, if not their Fuhrer, that the war should be immediately brought to an end.

3. If the policy outlined in para. 2 above failed, bombing attacks should be limited to purely military targets. If industrial areas were to be attacked, the procedures adopted in air-control operations could be applied to targets in, say, the Ruhr, i.e. the population could be warned that if hostilities were not ended, they could expect bombing to commence on a specified date.

In the final analysis, this chapter has sought to show that, no matter what military operations the government wanted Bomber Command to perform, there were not the aircraft to carry on a strategic bombing campaign that would be decisive in the coming war. Crew training was not sufficiently advanced nor was there the technical means of reaching and accurately bombing military and industrial targets. Fortunately there was foresight in planning the introduction of the four-engined heavy bomber, which would contribute to the eventual winning of the war.

The question then arose: how was a bomber force to get to its target largely intact? There were three possibilities:

1. Bombers that had no defensive armament could carry a greater load of bombs due to the saving in weight of the gunners and their guns. But such bombers would have to rely on speed to evade fighter interception. They might also fly at greater altitudes, but only if bombing accuracy was sacrificed.

2. Bombers could carry defensive armament, but this would be at the expense of bomb load. Such bombers would probably not be as fast as the undefended bomber and would have to rely on the defensive armament to drive off attacking fighters. Bombers flying in close formation would protect each other with the interlocking fire of their guns.

3. Bomber formations could be provided with a protective fighter screen, but to be sure of maintaining the protection to the target, such fighters would have to have the range of the bomber and a speed to match that of the defending fighters.

It was the job of the Air Staff to issue Air Ministry

specifications to the aircraft industry for the aircraft that they wanted to equip their squadrons operating in the different roles, e.g. fighter, day- or night-bomber, anti-submarine, maritime reconnaissance, etc. One would have expected that the tactics that such aircraft would employ in combat would have to be evaluated so that the appropriate specifications could be issued. This chapter will explore this matter and show that aircraft were produced that could not carry out the tasks assigned to them, or were inadequate because they were inferior in performance to those of a potential enemy. Such was the pace of rearmament by the late 1930s that aircraft were being ordered 'off the drawing-board'. Others were obsolete by the time they reached squadron service, like the Fairey Battle, and the thinking that went into the specifications for the Boulton Paul Defiant resulted in a fighter that was simply not a match for those of the enemy.

AIR EXERCISES, 1932 AND 1933
Introduction
Before moving on to discuss the nature of the strategic offensive and the formulation of strategic doctrine in detail, the outcome of the first three air exercises is considered. The object of these exercises was to test the air defences of the United Kingdom. At this time the RAF had biplanes with speeds not exceeding 200 mph. In all cases the bombs were carried externally, adding extra drag. The light bombers had fixed, forward-firing Vickers guns and a Lewis gun in the rear, and the fighters also had fixed, forward-firing guns. The quantum leap in aircraft design had still to come, and in many respects the air exercises differed little from those of the late 1920s. Since Germany had not, in the period 1930 to 1933, become the major air threat to Britain, the performance of French aircraft remained the yardstick.

1932 Air Exercises
The AOC-in-C Air Defence of Great Britain, Air Marshal Sir W.G.H. Salmond, wrote in his report of the exercise, 'It was my original intention to hold full-scale home defence exercises during 1932, with London as the objective for the "enemy" force. As it is known, however, political considerations ruled out the use of any portions of London for this purpose.' Due to widespread Press coverage of the 1931 exercise, the public were beginning to feel that, in any future war, the capital could expect to be heavily bombed. Both pro- and anti-war factions would use the exercises to prove their points, the pro-war lobby insisting that Britain needed to rearm decisively to avoid defeat, and the antis saying that the best way of keeping the country safe was to go for universal disarmament. The exercise that year was being staged while the Geneva Disarmament Talks were in progress.

A lesson learned from a previous year was that the exercise must be strictly controlled. The stated objective of the exercise was:

1. To gain experience in the employment of interceptor squadrons.
2. To test the value of an aircraft observation patrol to supplement the intelligence available for the defence commander.
3. To try out the possibility of fighters intercepting bombers at night without the aid of searchlights.

The two forces were Northland and Southland. Northland, under the command of Air Vice-Marshal F.W. Bowhill, had twelve fighter squadrons, while fourteen squadrons of bombers comprised Southland's force, under the command of Air Vice-Marshal Sir T.I. Webb-Bowen. Since the intention was to test the air defence system, the exercise was confined to a small area. This meant that the bombers had to fly a set course to ensure that they entered the area where the air defences were set up. There were day and night raids. By day the attacking forces were of squadron strength, and of these attacks nine were not intercepted, twenty were intercepted on the way to the target, and eight were intercepted on the way out. This would mean that the target was successfully bombed on seventeen occasions. Clearly the target area would have received many hits, but in the raids that were successfully intercepted the bomber force would have suffered casualties, and it is doubtful whether the bombers could have kept up the pressure for very long without reinforcements. It may therefore be concluded that bombers did get through, but at a cost. The night attacks bore no fruit for the defenders without the aid of searchlights. In his report of the exercise, Bowhill was not willing to state that his fighters had achieved a great success against Webb-Bowen's bombers. He then stated that night-bombers could be intercepted without searchlights, but that there was insufficient evidence to judge whether or not reconnaissance aircraft were of any assistance in detecting incoming bombers. Balloon barrages would be necessary, as well as standing patrols. These were fighters that were already airborne, and hoped to intercept the raiding aircraft. The alternative was to scramble the necessary squadrons from their airfield dispersal areas, but without radar, which was still to come, standing patrols were the best hope of catching the enemy formations. Webb-Bowen's conclusions were that the exercise disclosed weaknesses in his bomber force, and new tactics were needed, such as cloud-flying, which would increase the chances of reaching the target undetected, with target location at night possibly necessitating illumination of the objective. Also there was a need for selection of objectives, particularly for night-bomber aircraft. Interestingly his findings were not related to the exercise objectives, but more likely the weaknesses of which Webb-Bowen spoke were those that he had already identified before the exercise. When Geoffrey Salmond submitted his overall report, as C-in-

C ADGB, he did mention cloud-flying, but not the need for target markers or the importance of good intelligence in selecting objectives for attack.

1933 Air Exercises

It was Northland and Southland again in the 1933 Air Exercise. Southland's base was in theory located across the English Channel, while Northland's base was a rectangular zone of approximately one thousand square miles around London. Northland was a developed nation depending on exports to pay for essential imports, and Southland had attempted to embargo its adversary. Northland had an air force of twelve fighter squadrons and a fairly extensive ground control system, including observers and searchlights, but no anti-aircraft guns. For the first time in the air exercises the targets were military and industrial targets. There were no actual targets to attack; instead a general area was designated where these hypothetical targets were situated.

Forty-seven raids were carried out by day-bombers and seventy-nine by night-bombers. The interception rate was measured and the fighters were deemed to have been successful. Two-thirds of the daytime raids were intercepted, and three-quarters of the night raids. Safety reasons precluded mock combats, which made it difficult to assess casualties. Nevertheless the Air Staff concluded that if the bombers maintained their formations they could not be prevented from reaching their targets, and so they were given a fighting value of 2, as against the fighters, whose value was 1. The Air Staff could not, of course, have it both ways, and if the prospects for the bomber were that good, those for air defence must be correspondingly small.

Whatever the Air Staff felt about the ability of bombers like the Heyford, Hinaidi, Virginia and Sidestrand to withstand attacks by Bulldogs and Furies, continuing evaluation of performance and tactics would be required, for technology rarely stands still. This was part of the problem, for throughout the 1920s little had changed in performance, save marginal increases in speed. There were still just the Vickers and Lewis guns for armament, and open cockpits with bombs of Great War vintage, dropped from external racks. As the 1930s progressed, a massive increase in the killing power of fighters would force a rethink. The following sections discuss the requirements for a bomber and the tactics employed by both fighters and bombers.

REQUIREMENTS FOR A BOMBER

The day/night-bomber

If a day-bomber required heavy defensive armament while the night-bomber required speed, a combination of the two roles in one aircraft would result in a compromise general-purpose bomber aircraft. This blurring of operational requirements served to act as a restraint in the 1920s, when the aircraft industry was in a precarious state. It would have been a bold company indeed to have ignored Air Ministry specifications, and firms anxious to obtain production orders would give the Air Ministry what it wanted. There was too little money to research new technologies that might have given the Air Staff something new to consider, although firms did, from time to time, produce private-venture prototypes and hoped to sell new designs to the RAF. A good example of this would be Fairey Aviation importing the rights to produce the American Curtiss engine, which was installed in the Fox light bomber. This made the Fox faster than the fighters of the day. The day-bomber had to be large enough to house gun positions but small enough not to be prone to excessive blind spots, and had to be manoeuvrable in formation. On the other hand, as explained in the introduction, a bomber could dispense with defensive armament and rely on speed to evade interception. The high-speed bomber also had the advantage that there would be no need to consider cooperation and communication between a bomber pilot and air gunners on board. Fewer air gunners would also mean fewer personnel to train. But if a high-speed bomber was to be able to outrun fighters it would have to carry a lighter bomb load. The Air Staff tended to favour the heavy bomber.

Defensive armament

If a bomber was to carry defensive armament, the design of the aircraft would have to be spelt out in the specifications to incorporate gun positions, such as nose, tail, dorsal, ventral and beam. Then there was a need to consider whether or not there should be underbelly armour to protect the aircraft from attack from below if there was no gun in the ventral position. Armouring an aircraft would mean sacrificing speed and manoeuvrability due to the increase in weight. The alternative of providing fighter escorts for bomber formations was rejected by Trenchard, who was loathe to divert scarce resources for the production of such aircraft, and so in the 1920s the Air Staff had to produce specifications for bombers that could defend themselves. The Virginia bomber, for example, had nose and tail positions, as well as 'fighting tops', or gun positions in the upper surfaces of the top wings. Two or three air gunners might be found in a heavy bomber, but the light bombers

| Nose position | Dorsal position | Ventral position |

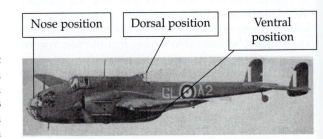

had a crew of only two, with the gunner behind the pilot. What was lacking in the specifications that went to the aircraft industry in the later 1920s was that the latter did not produce aircraft that combined performance and manoeuvrability with defensive armament and bomb load. Since the Air Staff had gone for compromise and sought a general-purpose bomber it was necessary to combine all these features in one airframe.

Engine power and airframe design

The bombers of the early 1930s did not have the engine power to carry the weight of bombs and defensive armament and at the same time impart speed and manoeuvrability to give the aircraft a good chance of reaching the target with the formation largely intact. The attitude of the Air Staff to all-metal designs appears to have been ambivalent at best, due to the expense and delay in production that would ensue. The aircraft engines were simply not powerful enough to carry the defensive armament necessary for the bomber to fight its way through to the target nor to carry a heavier, all-metal airframe.

Bombs

If the bomber got to a position that the bombs could be dropped, insufficient attention was paid by the Air Staff to the quality of the bombs held in the RAF's inventory, the height from which the bombs would be dropped and the destructive power of bombs as a ratio of their weight. Some of the blame may be laid at Trenchard's door. He had placed the morale effect of bombing ahead of the destructive effect. Thus the fact that the bomb exploded with a loud noise that would frighten the defenders and the civilian population mattered, but it did little to spur efforts to investigate the destructive effects of bombs. The research into the development and improvement of bombs was desultory, and the fundamental question of how to inflict the maximum material damage on an enemy was not addressed. As late as 1939 the quality of the RAF's stock of bombs was, according to John Terraine, generally speaking, awful. They often failed to explode, and when they did, they produced negligible results. H.R Allen held that approximately 20% of British bombs dropped during the Second World War either failed to detonate or produced negligible results due to the 1:4 charge to weight ratio.

Target acquisition

Little work was carried out during the inter-war years to enable a bomber aircraft to reach the target. For example, there was no unit formed to develop bombing techniques at a time when great strides were being made in aircraft design and engine power and reliability. In the Great War most bombing missions were carried out in fine weather. During peace or war, flying in bad weather was extremely hazardous. The service ceiling of bombers at that time was such that the ground remained visible and navigation was determined by reference to landmarks. If the weather was bad the mission was cancelled. The Great War revealed the need for scientific and technical development in navigation and bomb-sighting equipment if the missions were to stand any chance of being accomplished in a future war, yet little was done. The Bomber Command readiness reports for the years leading up to the Second World War bore this out. They disclosed the inability of bomber crews to reach even the general vicinity of the target. The trouble was that during the inter-war years there was no need to improve navigation and bombing for operational purposes. The navigational aids and bombsights had been sufficient for air control in the outposts of the Empire. In places RAF pilots flying over the desert had only to follow furrows ploughed in the sand. Even navigation training in the United Kingdom was carried out over countryside near the base airfield with which trainees were familiar.

BOMBER TACTICS

Doctrine may be formulated using the following sources:

1. War games.
2. Reports of full scale manoeuvres and squadron exercises.
3. The experience gained in combat.

Annual air exercises, which were held in the late 1920s, merely confirmed pre-existing notions of doctrine. The Air Staff placed the greatest emphasis on the offensive yet paid little attention to devising and testing the necessary bombing tactics. The stated aim of the annual air exercises was to test the air defences of Great Britain, and the reports of exercises held in the 1930s disclose a predisposition still to err on the side of the bomber. In considering the strategic bombing offensive in the late 1930s, Ludlow Hewitt was anxious to test bombing tactics and the effectiveness and destructive power of British bombs, but at some point the quality of the enemy's fighters and fighter pilots, as well as the tactics that they might employ, had to be taken into account. It was not sufficient simply to apply a mirror image in believing that the enemy would do to RAF bomber formations what Fighter Command would do to formations of German bombers. The two could not be compared. In the late 1930s Air Marshal Dowding was to develop a radar-based fighter control system that was unrivalled in Europe.

Questions relating to the bomber offensive

The Air Staff needed to address two problems if the bomber force was to be effective in war. The first was to ensure that a bomber formation could reach the general target area intact, and secondly, having reached the target area, they had to consider how the attack was to be delivered. Advanced flying training covered formation flying and methods of bombing, but the tactics were not submitted to realistic testing. Formation-flying ensured that aircraft stayed together so that the full weight of bombs from all aircraft in the formation would be dropped on the target. Enemy fighters could be expected to intercept and attack from any direction, but most likely from behind. The answer lay either in having bombers that flew at great altitude and speed to evade interception, or to provide the bombers with defensive armament. The greater the number of guns, the greater the weight of guns, and air gunners and bomb load would have to be sacrificed. Alternatively engine power could be increased to carry defensive armament without sacrificing bomb load. Since the provision of fighter escorts was not part of Air Staff thinking, a bomber formation would have to defend itself by means of their interlocking fire. The diagram shows the arcs of fire of one Wellington bomber, and these could be combined with the other bombers in the formation to provide the interlocking arcs of fire.

Bomber formations

The question then arose as to the best bomber formations to use to ensure that the target was reached without heavy loss. Opinions on these matters were often aired in the RUSI journal by RAF officers like Air Commodore Samson and Flight Lieutenant Yool, who gave their views in consideration of the tactical formations that bombers should adopt. The problem for all those entering into the debate in the 1930s was that they had to go back to the Great War to cite examples of the strategic employment of bombers. But things had moved on in terms of aircraft speed, defensive armament and bomb-carrying capacity, so that combat experience from 1918 was of less and less relevance. In the early 1930s the Japanese had bombed targets in China, but they were not confronting an adversary capable of mounting an aerial defence. In the late 1930s there was the immediate experience of the Spanish Civil War from which to draw

lessons, but it was here that the *Blitzkrieg* form of warfare was being developed, and this did not provide lessons in the employment of strategic bombers. Indeed, the Germans never did develop a four-engined heavy bomber to rival the Lancaster and American B-17 Flying Fortress.

So this left Air Commodore Samson, Flight Lieutenant Yool and others to refer to the national air exercises of the period or to consider the effectiveness of bomber formations in the abstract. Samson was forced to admit that there was very little data to act as a guide and that few practical trials had been carried out. He believed that the bomber had greater gun power than the fighter and that the speed of the individual bomber was nearly that of the fighter. Yool also believed that the bomber formation would provide a formidable proposition for the fighter. In formation, however, the bomber would not be able to manoeuvre to the same extent, and its speed would be lower. In view of the development of the eight-gun fighters like the Spitfire and Hurricane, it is clear that any ideas about the relative speeds and firepower of the fighter and bomber were being overtaken by events. The maximum speed of the Messerschmitt Bf 109B was 292 mph, and its service ceiling was initially 26,575 ft, rising to 41,000 ft in later versions. The maximum speed of the earlier versions of the Wellington bomber was between 235 and 256 mph, with a service ceiling of 22,000 ft. In view of the superior performance of the fighter in the late 1930s, the bomber could always manoeuvre to avoid a successful fighter attack, but then Samson was right to assert that manoeuvring to avoid fighter attack would slow down the bomber stream and delay arrival over the target. This meant, also, that the bombers would be forced to rely on their combined defensive armament. The thinking that went into the concept of the Flying Fortress in the United States at this time was that bombers flying in close formation would be able to put up such a curtain of interlocking firepower that few defending fighters would successfully penetrate it. In the event, the German Fw 190F was able to inflict unsustainable losses on American bomber formations in the daylight raids over Nazi-occupied Europe during the Second World War, and it became necessary to provide close fighter support in the form of long-range fighters like the Mustang, Lightning and Thunderbolt.

With the benefit of hindsight we can see that the Air Staff were wrong in believing that defensive firepower alone was the best solution in protecting the formation, but then, hindsight is an exact science.

Further consideration in 1938 of bomber formations

In 1938 Air Marshal Sir Edgar Ludlow Hewitt had become C-in-C Bomber Command, and he was concerned about the lack of preparedness of his command for a war against the *Luftwaffe*. On 27 January

1938 a meeting took place of the Air Fighting Committee, and Hewitt called for investigation and experimentation into different aspects of the bomber offensive. Again the matter of the bomber formation cropped up. It was pointed out that bombers will not always fly in good weather, and keeping formation in cloud or at night, together with the tactics of evasion of anti-aircraft fire and enemy fighters, needed to be worked out and practised. Smaller, more manoeuvrable formations of three aircraft would be the most practical in anything but good weather, but this was just the sort of assumption that needed to be tested. Another matter that worried the Air Marshal was attacks by enemy aircraft outside the effective range of the bombers' defensive armament. This would be unlikely to happen with fighters that had wing-mounted guns turned inwards to provide a lethal density of fire at a predetermined distance ahead of the aircraft, such as the Spitfire or the Hurricane, which needed to close with the enemy before the pilot opened fire. Be that as it may, Hewitt wanted theories to be tested. It may give the reader some idea of the unpreparedness of Bomber Command for war when these matters were being worked out at a time when new bomber types were rolling off the production lines. Air Ministry specifications should be issued to the aircraft industry after the operational requirements have been determined. It was left to Hewitt's Senior Air Staff Officer, Air Vice-Marshal D.S. Evill, to contact the Air Fighting Development Establishment (AFDE). It was agreed that the AFDE would cooperate, and No. 90 (Bomber) Squadron was assigned to work with the unit. No. 90 Squadron was equipped with Blenheim Is and based at RAF Bicester. Evill asked if it was possible to determine:

1. The best defensive formation for each of the bomber types.
2. The problems associated with taking evasive action.
3. The best methods of achieving fire control and supporting fire.

Hewitt added:

4. The relative vulnerability of aircraft at night.
5. The best method of reporting the position of the enemy, their numbers and aircraft types to other members of the crew.
6. Difficulties encountered in communications between crew members.
7. Problems associated with aiming.
8. Distances at which recognition was possible in various degrees of visibility.

The period of attachment of No. 90 Squadron to the AFDE was from 22 June to 26 July 1938. The AFDE fighters carried out beam attacks, attacks from astern

A. frontal attack
B. stern chase
C. beam attacks

and from below while climbing. It is of interest to note the findings of the AFDE in relation to the Blenheim bomber. It was concluded that the nose gun was of little value, that the rear gunner had a limited field of fire due to the fin and rudder, tailplane and the fuselage creating blind areas. This made the Blenheim susceptible to attacks from below, and it was decided that as a temporary expedient a Hampden bomber, with its ventral gun, could be added to a Blenheim bomber formation. Of course it would not take long for the enemy to realize the significance of the presence of the Hampden, which would then be singled out for attack. It was the same with the Defiant fighter, which had a power-operated turret behind the pilot. It did not take long for the enemy to work out that an attack from below would be in the turret gunner's blind spot. The element of surprise in both instances was soon lost.

Experimentation in defensive tactics by the bombers included:

1. The rotating three: three aircraft in the formation continually change position so as not to present stable targets.
2. Skidding: the bomber is skewed in flight to render it an unstable target.

The object of both manoeuvres was to avoid presenting a stable target to the enemy.

Methods of bombing

In March 1938 the Air Staff sent the Bombing Policy Sub-Committee of the Bombing Committee what they considered the best methods of bombing, as illustrated below.

High-level bombing could give the formation the advantage of cloud cover, but in the air exercises of 1938

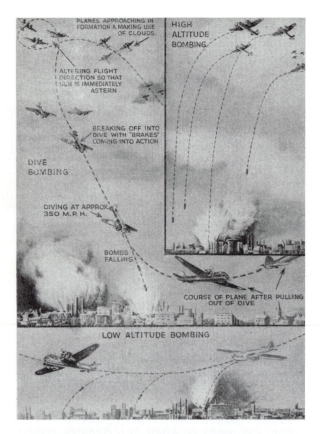

the bombing error was so great that it was concluded that areas, and not precise targets, would be the subject of high-level bombing. The latter were those targets that required a direct hit. The area targets were deemed to be a zone or group of sub-targets of near-equal importance. For low-level bombing the bomb release would be from 200 to 300 ft. No bombsight would be used save a datum line on the windscreen. The bomb would be aimed by either the pilot or the observer.

Selection of targets

The Air Staff accorded priorities in the selection of targets in war. Not unsurprisingly, the first priority was to attack the enemy's morale or will to win. Indeed, when war was declared, among the first missions of Bomber Command was to drop propaganda leaflets on enemy cities. Economic and industrial targets came next, followed by attacks on the enemy's armed forces. Refer to p. 356 for the War Plans of the RAF in the event of hostilities being declared.

POLICY WITH REGARD TO THE SELECTION OF SITES FOR BOMBER AIRFIELDS
(National Archive document AIR41/8)
Introduction
The foregoing sections have discussed the strategy and tactics of bombers in a future war. This section accepts

that the enemy would be Germany. The bomber squadrons in the 1920s had been situated at Worthy Down, Andover, Upper Heyford, Manston and Bircham Newton. Except for Bircham Newton the stations were facing south, not east. The thinking that went into the decisions as to which squadrons would go where, are discussed below, but they clearly reflect the need to be able to take the war to the enemy from secure bases. Methods of achieving security and the resistance put up by local communities to the siting of bomber stations is discussed in Chapter 7.

The location of bomber squadrons in the United Kingdom
Under Scheme C it was decided to locate the heavy bombers in Yorkshire and East Anglia, the medium bombers in Lincolnshire and the light bombers behind the fighter zone in Oxfordshire, Bedfordshire and Huntingdonshire. A major consideration was to avoid, as far as possible, the need to pass RAF bombing aircraft across the fighter zone at night. In a minute dated 9 March 1938, the Director of Organization, Air Vice-Marshal C.A. Portal, stated that a few of the medium bombers had been located in East Anglia. When Scheme F was substituted for Scheme C, no change was then made, but at the beginning of 1938 the distribution of squadrons was reconsidered for the purposes of that scheme, regard being paid, also, to the introduction of Scheme K. In a letter dated 4 February 1938, Ludlow-Hewitt submitted an important paper to the Air Ministry. It bore the title, 'An appreciation of the correct disposition of Bomber Command in the light of War Plans'. In para. 6 of this paper it was proposed that aircraft with the shortest range, such as the Blenheims and Battles, should be located at the airfields closest to the western frontier of Germany. He was referring to airfields in East Anglia and Kent. The heavier, longer-range bombers would be located at more distant airfields. The airfields in Kent were unavailable as they housed fighter squadrons. He therefore proposed that the light bombers be located further inland, but that on mobilization they would be moved forward into Kent or to the continent. This would leave the airfields in Yorkshire, Lincolnshire, East Midlands and Oxfordshire to house the heavier, longer-range aircraft. It was conceded that the airfields in Yorkshire and Lincolnshire were furthest away from the frontier of Germany but that penetration into Germany would be achieved by routing the medium and heavy bombers across the north of Holland. The East Midlands area was particularly suitable as a base for long-range aircraft operating by either the northern or southern routes. The Oxfordshire area it, was added, was well protected but awkwardly situated, insomuch as aircraft operating from it would have to make a considerable detour to avoid the congested London area. This Oxfordshire area was

considered suitable for the medium-bomber squadrons, which could move either to Kent or the continent on the outbreak of war.

The distribution proposed by Bomber Command had to vary slightly due to difficulties in accommodation. Heavy-bomber stations had been built in East Anglia, and the medium-bomber squadrons would have been over-hangared if located there, while the old medium-bomber stations in the East Midlands would be under-hangared for the heavy bombers. Portal, in his minute of 9 March 1938, mentioned in the previous paragraph, summed up the position, saying that the bomber stations had been laid down and built to meet a definite plan. The war tasks that the Air Staff had given to Bomber Command had led them to suggest a better layout, but they were unfortunately nearly three years too late. In any case the disadvantages under which Bomber Command had to work would only have to last a few years until the Battles and Blenheims in the two East Anglian groups were replaced with the heavy types. For the time being it was decided that the bomber squadrons should be located as follows:

Hampdens	Yorkshire
Whitleys	Lincolnshire
Harrows	Norfolk and Suffolk
Wellingtons	Norfolk and Suffolk
Some Blenheims	Norfolk and Suffolk
Other Blenheims	East Midlands
Battles	Oxfordshire

In the Air Ministry letter, dated 28 August 1938, approving this layout, it was stated that the necessity to move the Battle squadrons of No. 1 Group in Oxfordshire forward on the outbreak of war was recognized and that gun protection against hostile air attack would be provided for aerodromes in East Anglia. Whether the Battle squadrons would move forward to the continent would depend on conversations with the French and arrangements with the War Office. The whole discussion at that time, the distribution of squadrons and the changes subsequently approved, all took it for granted that the enemy would be Germany.

Conclusions regarding strategic bombing doctrine

It is clear from the foregoing discussion that the Air Staff carried over into the 1930s the Trenchard doctrine of offensive defence, and the expansion programme begun in 1923 gave prominence to the bomber. This doctrine was not questioned throughout the 1930s, in which case one might have expected the bombers, their crews and the bombs to be capable of fulfilling operational expectations. In fact bombers were being built in the mid- to late 1930s that had inadequacies, The Battle and Blenheim have been mentioned in this respect, and we

find the Air Officer Commanding-in-Chief of Bomber Command asking pertinent questions about RAF's bombing tactics and policy as late as 1938, when they should have been asked much earlier. When war came, only the Battle light bombers were sent forward into battle, if one will forgive the pun, and they were simply no match for the enemy. The medium and heavy bombers fared little better in striking military targets. Causing terror among the German civilian population was not contemplated as long as there was a chance that Hitler might reconsider Germany's situation. Hitler did not change his mind, and when the phoney war ended and the German forces stood on the Channel coast, it was principally up to Fighter Command to save the country from invasion.

THE FIGHTER DEFENCES OF THE UNITED KINGDOM

A consideration of fighter tactics

It will be helpful at this stage to consider the tactics that an enemy might employ against an RAF bomber formation. Since the AFDE was a British service establishment, the diagrams displayed are ones depicting attacks by RAF fighters against the expected enemy, Nazi Germany. The *Luftwaffe*'s latest fighter in 1938 was the Messerschmitt 109 in all its existing

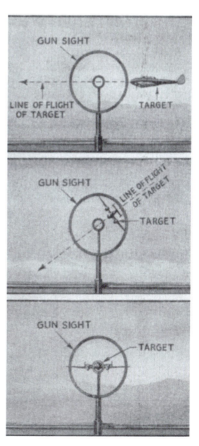

versions at that time. The performance of the Me 109 was similar in most respects to the Spitfire and the Hurricane then coming into squadron service. The following diagrams illustrate the skill required of the fighter pilot if he is to be fairly sure of a kill. If the target aircraft is crossing directly across the fighter's flight path then maximum deflection will be required. This will apply with a beam attack. Attacking obliquely from either above or below will require a partially deflected shot, whereas a stern chase or an aircraft on collision course will require no aim-off. Clearly, then, a stern chase will make the fighter pilot's job easier, but if the bombers execute a rotating three or skidding, as mentioned earlier, the fighter pilot will have difficulty in getting the target aircraft in his sights for long enough to deliver the two-second burst needed to deliver a lethal volume of fire (see Chapter 5).

The diagram below illustrates an enemy aircraft flying into the line of sight obliquely. It also illustrates the convergence of the fire, from the guns in either wing, at a predetermined distance in front of the fighter. Not only has the fighter pilot to take account of deflection, but the range to the target is critical if the pilot is to achieve a lethal density.

Seen in this light the bomber pilot stands a fair chance of getting to the target unscathed. Defensive fire from the bombers will also complicate matters for the fighter pilot, who will have to take evasive action, and he may find it extremely difficult to keep the target aircraft in his sights. The fighter interceptor does not rely for effectiveness simply on the skill of the fighter pilot. These aircraft have four qualities, namely speed, climb, armament and manoeuvrability. As a generality the RAF placed the greatest importance in armament, followed by speed, climb and manoeuvrability. The *Luftwaffe* put speed at the top of the list, followed by climb, armament and manoeuvrability, whereas the Italians laid the stress on manoeuvrability, followed by climb, speed and armament. Of course much would depend on the precise aircraft type being met in combat, which means that

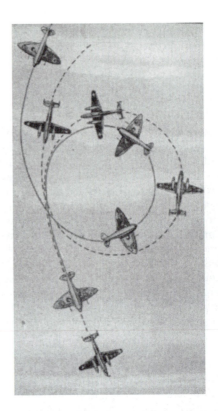

bomber crews had to have good aircraft recognition skills and knowledge of the enemy types that would be met in combat.

All four attributes of a fighter were necessary, but at different times. Speed was vital in making an interception, particularly if warning of the approach of an enemy formation was late in coming. This was where the RAF scored in the Battle of Britain, because radar was used to detect the approach of the enemy, and the fighters could be aloft waiting for them. Armament was the main attribute of the Spitfire and Hurricane in having four machine-guns in each wing. On the other hand manoeuvrability could be a vital quality once contact had been made with the enemy. The pilot of a very agile machine that had engaged in a stern chase would try to get inside his adversary until he was on his tail.

Theory and practice

Theory is of course one thing, and practice can be another. In their excellent account of how the pilots of Fighter Command were trained and fought in the Battle of Britain (*Spitfire Ace*, Channel 4 Books) Davidson and Taylor give first-hand accounts of a number of young men who went to battle against the *Luftwaffe* in 1940, their preparedness for combat and their first experience in meeting the enemy. Without exception, none was given any instruction of how to actually shoot down an enemy aircraft. The officers they describe came into the

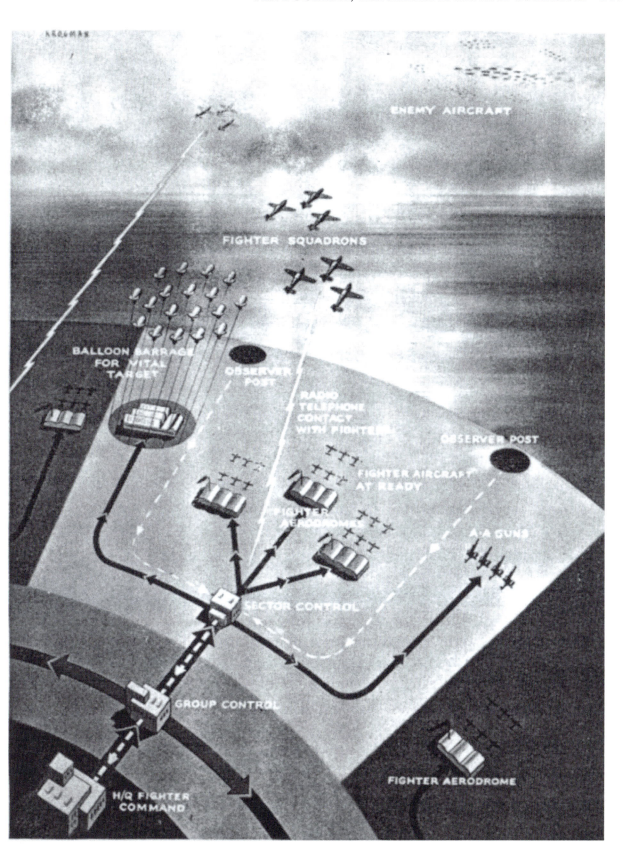

RAF either through Cranwell, the Volunteer Reserve or the Auxiliary Air Force, and they came in for a variety of reasons, but nearly always it was a love of flying, not to fight in a war. George Unwin came in through desperation because he needed work. He remembers that combat skills were absent from the training programme as they were for Cranwell cadets. What he learned about firing his guns was either at practice camp or from an experienced pilot on the squadron. At the end of Chapter 1 of Volume I of this history, the experience of fighter pilots in the Great War was described. Those who lived longest were those who could resist opening fire at long range but could wait until they were sure of hitting the target aircraft. When trainee pilots did fire at a practice drogue towed behind another aircraft no one seemed to mind if you scored a hit or a miss. Even the ability to fly the aeroplane, let alone fire its guns, was not taught in a dual-seat trainer. Tom Neil says that he went straight from biplanes to the Spitfire. All the training he got was to sit in a hangar with a Spitfire on trestles and a blindfold round his eyes while he felt around for all the knobs, levers and switches he would use in the air. This took half a day, after which he was told to get in his aeroplane and fly it. And George Unwin again recalls that one learned combat for the first time in combat. The RAF rule book of fighter tactics was thrown out, and squadrons made up their own rules of engagement. All the business of flying in Vics of three, like the unfortunate Wellington crews who tried it found out, only invited the risk of collision if all aircraft did not turn together or in a prearranged manoeuvre. In Unwin's squadron the only rule was to get in quick and get out equally quickly. These examples make it perhaps easy to scoff at the contribution made by staff officers in the period before the commencement of hostilities, who try to work out the best way to fight with the various aircraft in their different roles. Because the advice and training given to pilots in peacetime may turn out to be at fault, it does not make it wrong to plan. After all, the whole fighter control system that enabled these pilots to meet the enemy on the best possible terms was due to the sheer hard work that went into the development of the radar-based fighter-control system under the direction of Air Marshal Dowding and his staff.

The organization of Britain's fighter defences

Fighter Command was established in 1936 following the major organizational changes to the Metropolitan Air Force. Its headquarters were at Bentley Priory, Stanmore. Here was established an operations room from which the fighter defences of the entire United Kingdom could be controlled. The country was then divided into Fighter Groups, each with its own Air Officer Commanding:

1. No. 10 Group covering the South-West and South Wales.

2. No. 11 Group covering the South and South-East.
3. No. 12 Group covering the middle of the country up as far as Liverpool and Hull.
4. No. 13 Group covering the North of England and all of Scotland.

Each fighter group also had its own operations room, which would control the defensive battle over its area. The group's operational area was further divided into Sectors and it was from the Sector Operations Rooms that the fighter controllers could talk directly to the fighter squadrons, once airborne. The whole organization was to be fed with radar sightings of approaching enemy formations, at both high and low level. This was to be supplemented by observers of the Royal Observer Corps. Ground defences included heavy anti-aircraft guns and balloon barrages over vital targets.

The reorganization of the RAF commands in 1936 meant that Fighter, Bomber and Coastal Commands, each commanded by an AOC-in-C, were distinct entities with responsibility, through the Chief of the Air Staff, to the Air Council. Dowding, as the AOC-in-C Fighter Command, was left to organize the fighter defence of the United Kingdom between 1936 and the outbreak of hostilities. As with the other commands, the siting of airfields and the deployment of squadrons to these airfields was a matter for the AOC-in-C. During those critical years it would be Fighter, and not Bomber, Command that was most ready for war. With the introduction of the eight-gun fighter was added the bullet-proof windscreens, the integration of the RDF units with the communications and control orgnanization, and the recruitment and training of a sufficient number of observers. The diagram on page 367 shows that integrated nature of the organization from the Group Headquarters down to the Sector Operations Rooms, which had direct radio contact with the aircraft in their sector to direct them onto incoming enemy formations. Notice that the arrow points backwards from Group Operations Room to Fighter Command operations, emphasizing that it was the group and not the command in control of the operations. Notice also that the observers on the ground talked directly to the fighter controllers in the sector operations rooms, because it was the latter who talked to the pilots.

Although it was, in the event, to be No. 11 Group that bore the brunt of the battle, at the time the defence arrangements were put into place the *Luftwaffe* was not in occupation of the north coast of France. If German aircraft were to attack from bases in Germany they would have to skirt round the Benelux countries, which it was assumed would remain neutral, and attack across the North Sea. It could be assumed that Britain would fight alongside France, and therefore German aircraft would have to fight their way across France to approach Britain from the south-east.

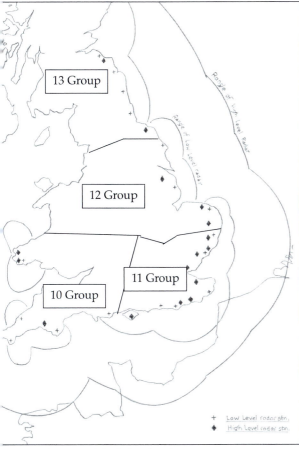

Low- and high-level radar coverage.

when, in a future war, the enemy's homeland would be attacked to break his will to win and to destroy his military and economic targets. The opposite happened. Only after securing the home base could the bomber offensive begin in earnest. The first successful battle fought by the RAF when war came was a defensive one. Having secured the home base the offensive could then go ahead, as it did with the '1,000-bomber' raids that commenced in 1942, beginning with Cologne. A quote from Dowding himself makes the point.

> The best defence of the country is the fear of the fighter. If we are strong in fighters we should probably never be attacked in force. If we are moderately strong we shall probably be attacked and the attacks will gradually be brought to a standstill . . . If we are weak in fighter strength, the attacks will not be brought to a standstill and the productive capacity of the country will be virtually destroyed.

Having the right equipment and personnel is vital to the winning of battles, but so also is leadership. These two men were to be the adversaries in the battle that was to come. One might argue that the true adversaries were the commanders of German air fleets, like Sperle and

Reichmarschall Hermann Goering Air Minister, Commander-in-Chief of the *Luftwaffe* and Minister of the Four-Year-Plan

One can imagine the amount of work involved laying all the land-lines from the RDF stations and observer posts before the war. The importance of fighter control using information received from the RDF stations cannot be overstated. Without them it would have been necessary for Fighter Command to mount standing patrols, as the RFC had to do in the Great War. This is where aircraft have to be airborne at all times to prevent surprise attacks. This entails pilots flying, often fruitlessly, hours on end, in the skies above England so as to be in a position to attack immediately on seeing the enemy. Not only is this a waste of fuel, it can mean that the enemy is sighted just at the moment when the defending aircraft are running out of fuel.

THE ADVERSARIES
A CONSIDERATION OF TWO OPPOSING COMMANDERS – AIR MARSHAL DOWDING VERSUS REICHMARSCHALL GÖRING
Introduction
In a sense the Trenchard dictum with which the Air Staff kept faith throughout the inter-war years was to be stood on its head. This was the doctrine of offensive defence

Air Chief Marshal
Sir Hugh Dowding
Air Officer
Commanding-in-
Chief RAF Fighter
Command from
July 1936 to
November 1940

Kesselring, who commanded *Luftlotten* II and III, but this is to misunderstand the nature of the working of Fascist regimes. If the Air Minister in Britain had commanded the RAF in battle, Sir Kingsley Wood would have been attired in uniform, getting involved in strategic and even tactical decisions, perhaps even overriding decisions made by the Chief of the Air Staff, Sir Cyril Newall. But the conduct of operations of fighter groups was a matter for their group commanders. Dowding had put the defensive organization in place, and it was his job to ensure that the right men were in the right places, like Air Vice-Marshal Keith Park (11 Group) and Air Vice-Marshal Trafford Leigh-Mallory (12 Group).

A comparison of the two men's career development is illustrative. The following is the career path of Dowding, and it is typical of RAF commanders of the period:

Air Chief Marshal Sir Hugh Dowding – b. 24/4/1882, d. 15/2/1970

Promotions		*Appointments*
18 Aug 1900	2nd Lieuenant RA	
8 May 1902	Lieutenant RA	
18 Aug 1913	Captain RA	
5 Aug 1914	Flying Officer RFC	training RFC
6 Oct 1914		No. 6 Squadron in France
18 Nov 1914		GSO3, HQ RFC (Staff position)
4 Mar 1915	Temporary Major	OC No. 9 Squadron, France
26 Mar 1915		OC Wireless Experimental Establishment
		No. 9 Squadron Brooklands
23 Jul 1915		OC No. 16 Squadron, France
22 Jan 1916	Temporary Lieutenant-Colonel	No. 7 Wing, RAF Farnborough
18 Jun 1916		OC No. 9 Wing, France
1 Jan 1917	Temporary Colonel	Southern Group, Salisbury
23 Jun 1917	Temporary Brigadier-General	
1 Aug 1919	Permanent Commission as a Group Captain	
18 Oct 1919		OC No. 16 Group
29 Feb 1920		OC No. 1 Group, Kenley
1 Jan 1922	Air Commodore	
27 Feb 1923		Chief Staff Officer, HQ Inland Area, Uxbridge
19 Sep 1924		Chief Staff Officer, HQ Iraq Command
27 May 1926		Director of Training, Air Ministry
1 Jan 1929	Air Vice-Marshal	
7 Sep 1929		AOC Transjordan and Palestine
4 Jan 1930		AOC Fighting Area (Fighters)
1 Sep 1930		Air Member for Supply and Research
1 Jan 1933	Air Marshal	
14 Jan 1935		Air Member for Research and Development
14 Jul 1936		AOC-in-C Fighter Command
1 Jan 1937	Air Chief Marshal	

This shows clearly the mix of command and staff positions following each promotion, and therefore the wealth of experience, not in simply fighting a war but in scientific development, organization and supply. No such career path can be mapped out for Hermann Goering. He went from First World War squadron commander to Air Minister via the Nazi Party. He was one of those who fell under Hitler's spell from the beginning, and after the Nazis came to power he connived with Heinrich Himmler, the leader of the SS, to liquidate the SA leadership in the infamous 'Night of the Long Knives' on 30 June/1 July 1934. Röhm had coveted the Ministership for War and a special place for his SA in the future of Germany. With Röhm gone, a rival for power had been removed in what was nothing more than state-sponsored murder. Since Hitler and his subordinates ran the regime by giving jobs to cronies, often irrespective of ability, Goering could, given his air force past, claim the *Luftwaffe* as a natural right to the spoils. And when in post he did not have to prove himself by being either an inspired leader or diligent in his duties. If he turned up at the Air Ministry it was because it suited him, not because he was supposed to be in charge. A man with absolutely no staff or command training would equally be a poor judge of whom to appoint to the various positions of responsibility in the corridors of power. On the death of General Wever, when there might have been some hope that the *Luftwaffe* would be equipped with the right aeroplanes, there was some in-fighting. Albert Kesselring was not an effective chief-of-staff. Hans-Jürgen Stumpff and Hans Jeschonnek proved to be little better. Jeschonnek was also under Hitler's spell, which did not help matters, for Hitler always kept lines of responsibility purposely ill defined so that his subordinates were always squabbling with each other. If Jeschonnek believed that the Fuhrer was a great military leader he was pinning his hopes on a man who had even less military experience than Goering. Ernst Udet was a Great War fighter pilot and a post-war barnstormer, but did that equip him to be the head of the *Luftwaffe*'s technical departments, as well as the Office of Air Armament, where he controlled research and development? He was a Goering appointee, with twenty-six separate departments under his control, yet he possessed neither technical nor engineering skills. More power struggles were to come, and Udet would eventually be driven to suicide.

There is an awful lot more evidence of the incompetent leadership of the *Luftwaffe*, both in the period before the war and afterwards. This short dissertation is intended to show only that there was no comparison with the pool of talent that a senior RAF commander could draw upon. Dowding could appoint as his group commanders officers of the highest calibre. The man who would eventually bear the brunt of the battle in 1940 would be Keith Park, who would regularly visit his squadrons in his personal Hurricane, OK1. Dowding was more aloof, and carried the nickname 'Stuffy', but did not need to be so close to his airmen, given able leadership under his command. This is not to say that Dowding did not care about his pilots, for he reportedly called them his 'chicks'. Nor is it true to say that there were not differences in opinion on the best way to fight the battle when it came. It has been said that Dowding would not arbitrate in disputes between his subordinates when Park was left to fight the enemy squadron by squadron, whereas Leigh-Mallory, AOC 12 Group, believed in assembling, airborne, three wings of fighters before committing them to action.

Before leaving this discussion it can be said, in the *Luftwaffe*'s defence, that having been officially formed in 1935, there was precious little time for subordinate commanders to acquire staff skills. That said, the far-sighted General von Seekt at the beginning of the 1920s incorporated into his Army staff, officers with military aviation experience, since the Versailles Treaty forbade Germany to have an air force. It remains true that this was an unequal contest in the terms described.

STRATEGIC MARITIME DOCTRINE
Introduction
With the approach of war in 1939, the RAF and Royal Navy faced the same threat at sea as that faced in 1914–18, namely unrestricted submarine warfare. The German surface fleet was small, but posed a threat in home waters and the North Atlantic. The Germans had one aircraft-carrier under construction, but it was never completed. In the Mediterranean there was a sizeable Italian surface fleet of battleships and modern cruisers, destroyers and submarines. In the Far East there was a potential threat from Japan, a significant naval power with battleships and aircraft-carriers.

In 1936 the RAF had been reorganized, and Coastal Command was responsible for maritime air operations. In 1938 the Fleet Air Arm was returned to the Royal Navy, but it was decided that the Admiralty would not get the maritime air forces that operated from land bases, only those air units that were an integral part of the various fleets. This included carrier-borne aircraft and aircraft operating from warships equipped with the means of launching them and, if possible, retrieving them.

Doctrine is in part determined by capability. One thing that distinguished maritime air forces in the late 1930s and those of the Great War was the increased range, endurance and firepower of flying-boats and landplanes assigned to Coastal Command. In Volume I there is a map which shows the location of air bases around the shores of the United Kingdom in November 1918. They stretched from the Hebrides right around to the North Sea Coast, and it is amazing just how many there were. The range and speed of the Great War types were such that only a great density of overlapping patrol areas would do. Apart from a few flying-boats like those of the Felixstowe class, which operated over the North Sea and in the Western Approaches, the other airfields had either DH4s or 9s. There were also airships that operated from mooring-out stations. The new breed of monoplane flying-boats like the Sunderland and Catalina had the ability to operate far from land, and with the cooperation of the United States after 1941 it became possible for flying-boats to cover the entire North Atlantic.

STRATEGIC CONSIDERATIONS

The RAF shared with the Fleet Air Arm the overall task of keeping open the sea lanes and defeating the enemy naval forces that threatened both merchant and naval shipping. This involved the following types of operation:

Anti-submarine warfare.
Anti-shipping strikes.
Minelaying and mine clearance.
Convoy escort.
Maritime reconnaissance.
Air-sea rescue.

The Fleet Air Arm would be responsible for air operations associated with the fleet at sea normally out of the range of landplanes, or where close protection of naval vessels was paramount. Convoy escort could be shared. There were only so many aircraft-carriers, and it was going to be impossible for all convoys in war to be accompanied. In mid-ocean only units of the Fleet Air Arm could provide protection to the fleet or convoy, but with long-range maritime aircraft it would be possible for these aircraft to escort a convoy to the limit of their range.

OPERATIONAL THEATRES
Home
The sea areas that would need the attention of Coastal Command in a war would be:

The North Sea and English Channel.
The Western Approaches to the English Channel and the Bristol Channel.
The Irish Sea to cover the approaches to Liverpool.

When it was clear that the enemy was most likely to be Nazi Germany, then it would be necessary to cover the seas along the coast of Norway and outwards towards the Denmark/Iceland gap, the Denmark/Faeroes gap and the sea area between the Faeroes and the Orkney Islands. This would be to prevent the breakout into the North Atlantic of major enemy surface units from their bases in Germany.

The North Atlantic
The necessity to keep open the shipping lanes across the North Atlantic would be extremely important in all circumstances, particularly from Canadian ports. In the late 1930s there was no prospect of providing air cover for shipping across the entire North Atlantic. Merchant or naval ships would have to be provided with the protection of destroyers and units of the Fleet Air Arm if available.

The Bay of Biscay
In the late 1930s the rapid collapse of France was not envisaged, and it was fair to assume that the Bay of Biscay, which must be crossed to reach Gibraltar and the Mediterranean, would be covered by units of the French Air Force. It was not envisaged that the Atlantic coast ports of France would house German U-boats.

The Mediterranean and Suez
With British air bases in Gibraltar, Malta and Egypt, it would be possible for land-based aircraft to cover much of the Mediterranean and the sea approaches to Gibraltar at one end and to the Suez Canal at the other. Here the threat would be the Italian Navy.

The Indian Ocean and the Far East
The defence of Singapore had been considered even before Trenchard's retirement. Was it to be massive guns that would fend off an attack by Japan on Singapore or units of the RAF? In fact torpedo-bombers were sent to defend the colony from an attack from the sea. In the event it was the attacking Japanese land forces and not naval forces that took Singapore. Japanese soldiers actually rode on bicycles as they made their way down the Malay peninsula.

THE AIRCRAFT
The commitments of Coastal Command and the land-based maritime aircraft of RAF commands overseas would be determined by the perceived threat to the sea areas listed above. When the war began there were not enough maritime aircraft to meet all the commitments, but the quality of the new aircraft, with the exception of the Saro Lerwick, meant that they were certainly up to the job. They were:

1. The Short Sunderland long-range maritime reconnaissance, anti-submarine flying-boat.
2. Consolidated Catalina long-range maritime reconnaissance, anti-submarine flying-boat.
3. Lockheed Hudson Medium-range maritime reconnaissance.
4. Avro Anson Short-range maritime reconnaissance, anti-submarine/anti-shipping.
5. Bristol Beaufort Anti-shipping and general reconnaissance aircraft.

6. Supermarine Stranraer General reconnaissance flying-boat.
7. Saro London General reconnaissance flying-boat
8. Saro Lerwick General reconnaissance.
9. Vickers Vildebeest Torpedo-bomber.

According to requirements for specific operations, reconnaissance might be carried out by other aircraft. By the outbreak of war in 1939, the Catalina and the Beaufort had then to reach squadron service. The precise order of battle of Coastal Command units on 3 September 1939 is to be found at the end of Chapter 3. The map below shows the surface threat. Enemy submarines could be expected to follow roughly the same routes, but could also risk a passage through the English Channel. Coastal Command had the task of protecting Allied shipping from both the surface and the submarine threat. Clearly the long-range flying-boats would have to be based on the south-west and west coasts of Britain to cover the Western Approaches and the Atlantic sea lanes into Liverpool. At the commencement of the war Mount Batten near Plymouth

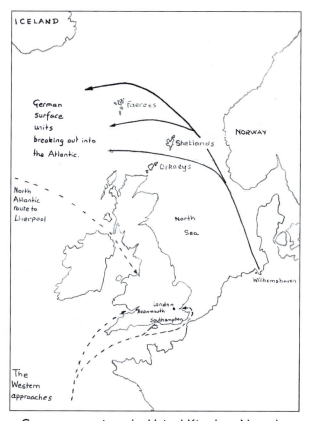

Convoy routes into the United Kingdom. Note the threat of a breakout of heavy surface units of the *Kreigsmarine* from their bases in Germany to the North Atlantic.

and Pembroke Dock in west Wales were the obvious bases for the Sunderlands. Other flying-boats could be situated in the Shetlands to cover any possible breakout of German naval units into the North Atlantic. The shorter-range Ansons could cover the North Sea.

Requirements of maritime aircraft
The surface and submarine threat to British and Allied naval shipping called for aircraft that could counter both threats through reconnaissance, and if required carry out attacks upon enemy naval units. Sometimes there was simply a requirement to reconnoitre and not to carry out an attack on the enemy, i.e. to report back so that the appropriate naval units could be tasked to intercept and destroy the enemy. There was also a commitment to rescue aircrews from the sea. These were the days before helicopters, and so flying-boats could put down on water in an emergency, assuming the sea state would permit a landing. If that was not possible, a flying-boat or landplane could drop life-rafts and food and water. There would be a considerable threat from the air over the North Sea and English Channel, which would mean defensive armament. For those flying-boats operating far out into the Atlantic the air threat would be minimal. Since neither Italy nor Germany was known to possess aircraft-carriers there was no way in which the potential enemy could present an air threat over the ocean. Wireless communications would be vital since the prompt reporting of the whereabouts of enemy naval units would enable the appropriate submarine or surface vessels to proceed to intercept.

Maritime aircraft would need to cover vast areas of the ocean, and so it would be wasteful of resources for more than one aircraft to reconnoitre a particular shipping area at a time. There would be no question, for example, of flying-boats operating in formation, as bombers did, to provide mutual protection. But good defensive armament was vital to ensure that attacking aircraft could be beaten off. Much the same applied overseas. One major difference in countering the threat from Japan, as opposed to Germany and Italy, was that the former had several aircraft-carriers. In the Mediterranean medium- to long-range maritime patrol aircraft would be needed in Gibraltar, Malta and Alexandria to keep open the sea lanes from the Bay of Biscay, through the Straits of Gibraltar and on to Suez. When war did come, a reconnaissance Spitfire might be used, since it would have the speed and service ceiling to outrun enemy fighters if it was intercepted. Extra fuel would take the place of ammunition. One other important attribute of a maritime reconnaissance aircraft is endurance, as opposed to simple range. An aircraft's range tells one how far it can go to reach a target and have enough fuel to return safely. The crew of an aircraft searching a vast sea area probably have little idea exactly where the enemy is. What is wanted is endurance, not

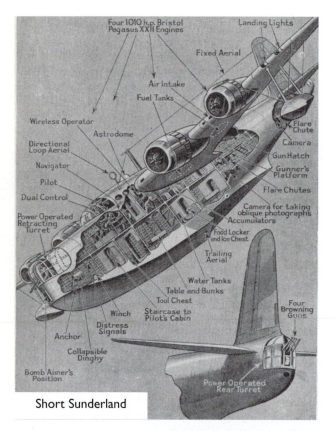

Short Sunderland

aircraft was to meet the operational tasks outlined above. Clearly the Sunderland had the range, endurance, equipment, bombs and defensive armament to deal with almost any eventuality. This aircraft was to prove very effective against submarines.

COMPARATIVE PERFORMANCE AND CAPABILITY

A comparison of performance and capabilities of the bombers and fighters of the *Luftwaffe* and the RAF will also give a clue to the actual, as opposed to the perceived, threat to this country in the event of war. The threat from the *Luftwaffe* in the late 1930s is described in Chapters 2 and 3, and it is clear that the Germans did not have the aircraft to fight a strategic war against the British Isles. They did have an air force that could give close air support to the land forces, and fighters capable of defending German territory or occupied territory. They had only one long-range, four-engined maritime aircraft, the Fw Condor, but no long-range flying-boats. At sea they had floatplanes on their warships but these were useful only for reconnaissance purposes, and they possessed no aircraft-carriers. (The Arado floatplanes were used in the Aegean for reconnaissance, and a Blohm und Voss flying-boat came into service operating, for example, in Romania.) In other words, Germany could deploy its air force to advance a land war, which would be fine as long as military campaigns were being fought on the continent, but if the war extended to the British Isles or into the Mediterranean the Germans would have problems without the requisite maritime air forces and surface naval units. The following figures are given for four main types in service on each side before the commencement of war:

range, that is the ability to stay airborne as long as possible. That means having accommodation where individual crew members can sleep and eat, i.e. a galley and bunks. The illustration of a Short Sunderland is worth close study and will show how well equipped this

Royal Air Force

Spitfire I

Max Speed: 355–62 mph
Service Ceiling: 32,000 ft
Range: 395 miles
Armament: 8 X 0.303 in. Brownings

Hurricane I

Max Speed: 318 mph
Service Ceiling: 36,000 ft
Range: 460 miles

Luftwaffe

Me Bf109 E

Max Speed: 348-54 mph
Service Ceiling: 34,450 ft
Range: 365–460 miles
Armament: 2 X 7.92 mm guns above engine, 2 guns in wings

Messerschmitt Bf 110

Max Speed: 349 mph
Service Ceiling: 32,800 ft
Range: 528 miles at 304 mph

Armament: 8 X 0.303 in. Brownings

Wellington IC

Max Speed: 235 mph
Service Ceiling: 22,000 ft
Range: 1,200 miles with 4,500 lb bombs
      2,550 miles with 1,000 lb bombs
Armament: 2 X 0.303 in. guns in nose/tail
      2 X 0.303 in. guns in beam positions

Blenheim

Max Speed: 266 mph
Service Ceiling: 31,500 ft
Range: 920 miles with 1,000 lb bombs
Armament: 1 X 0.303 in.gun in port wing and
    one in dorsal turret

Armament: 2 X 20 mm cannon
      4 X 7.92 mm guns in nose
      1 X 7.92 mm gun rear cockpit racks for 4 X
      551 lb bombs

He 111P-6

Max Speed: 242 mph at 16,400 ft
Service Ceiling: c. 25,590 ft
Range: 745 miles max bomb load - 4,410 lb
Armament: 1 X 7.92 mm gun in nose, dorsal and ventral

Ju 87B-2

Max Speed: 242mph
Service Ceiling: 26,250 ft
Range: 373 miles with 940 lb bombs
Armament: 2 X 7.92 mm guns in wings
      1 X 7.92 mm gun rear cockpit

The four RAF and four *Luftwaffe* aircraft are representative of the inventory of both air forces as they went into the war in 1939, i.e. two fighters, one medium/heavy bomber and one light/dive-bomber. The three single-engined fighters were fairly evenly matched, but the twin-engined Me 110 was very heavily armed with exceptional range for a fighter. The actual combat experience with these aircraft in the first year of the war is considered to have ascertained how much of a threat they really were. Their fortunes changed throughout the war as the types underwent development. The data quoted for each aircraft did in fact vary, even with one mark, so the figures must be treated as representative.

Messerschmitt Bf 109

This was undoubtedly an exceptionally good fighter, and more than equal to any of its adversaries in the pre-war and wartime days. Save for the Spitfire, which it outnumbered, the Me 109 could outmanoeuvre, outclimb and outpace contemporary fighters. It was small and cheap to produce. It could be regarded as a threat to the RAF in the lead-up to war, especially as it had proved itself in the Spanish Civil War. But with a combat range of a maximum of 460 miles, it could not escort the He 111 on long-range bombing missions that confronted fighter opposition.

Me 110

The *Reichluftfahrtministerium* issued a requirement in 1934 for this two-engined fighter, known as the 'destroyer'. It was to be capable, like other single-engined fighters, of fighting other aircraft with its firepower to make up for its lack of manoeuvrability. The range of this fighter would mean that it could act as a bomber escort penetrating deep into enemy territory. It was not tested in the Spanish Civil War as were the other three aircraft shown. It performed well in the Polish campaign and the battle for the Low Countries and France, but when it came up against the Spitfire and Hurricane it was no match, and these bomber escorts had themselves to be escorted by Me 109s.

Heinkel 111

Flight performance of this medium bomber was improved during the Spanish Civil War. However, the success of the early elliptical-winged version misled the *Luftwaffe* into believing that nothing could withstand fleets of He 111s. But the aircraft was designed in the mid-1930s, when it outpaced the biplane fighters of the day, and so did not need much defensive armament. It was not until the Battle of Britain that it came up against the serious opposition of the eight-gun fighter. Then the main thing in its favour was that it was strong and could struggle back to base when badly damaged. Accordingly it needed close fighter escort, but as the previous paragraph makes clear, its close-escort fighter, the Me 110, itself needed fighter support, so it all depended on the Me 109. The result was the weight of more defensive guns and gunners. If the same bomb load was to be carried it meant more powerful engines. The He III became a lumbering, heavily defended aircraft by 1942/3, a far cry from the fast medium bomber of 1937. Rather than introduce a replacement, German industry continued to churn out the He III in ever-increasing versions, even 'bolting' two together to make into a glider tug. When the Germans stopped building them, the Spanish continued until 1956. As a matter of interest it was the Spanish Air Force that was able to loan its He 111s to the film company that made the epic film *The Battle of Britain* in the 1960s. It had a range of *c.*750 miles, less than the RAF's Wellingtons and half that of the four-engined Lancaster. To penetrate only as far as London in any numbers, the German fighters would need to give close fighter support, and unless the *Luftwaffe* could occupy airfields as close as possible to Britain, i.e. in northern France, the Me 109 would not have the range. Assuming Britain's fighter defences were in fighting order, all in all the He 111 was never going to be able to fight a sustained strategic bombing campaign.

Ju 87 (Stuka)

There is no doubt that this dive-bomber was a very effective weapon in the Spanish Civil War as a close-support weapon, but in common with the He III and Me 110, it was no match for the Spitfire and Hurricane. The *Blitzkrieg* form of warfare developed by Richthofen in Spain was effective in the Polish campaign in 1939 and the battles for the Low Countries and France in 1940, but the *Luftwaffe* first attacked the enemy's airfields, significantly reducing the threat of fighter opposition. These tactics were fine until the *Wehrmacht* reached the English Channel, but the *Blitzkrieg* could not recommence until the Germans had established a bridgehead in southern England. Crossing the Channel was essential if the Ju 87 was to come into its own again, but that presumed that the British fighter force had been defeated. The Ju 87s were used in the Battle of Britain but were not of any great value in the air battle over Kent and the Home Counties.

Spitfire and Hurricane

The data shown on p. 374 put these two aircraft in the same category. Although it is always said that it was the Spitfire and not the Hurricane that could outmanoeuvre the Me 109, it was the latter that accounted for more enemy aircraft shot down in the Battle of Britain. The Hurricane provided a much better gun platform and, having a fabric-covered rear fuselage, could be repaired more quickly following battle damage. Both aircraft, in a defensive battle and with a radar-based fighter control system in place, would acquit themselves well against all four of the previously mentioned aircraft. In a defensive battle these two fighters would be over home territory, and if pilots baled out, they would not become prisoners of war. They would also be able to remain for longer in contact with the enemy, because they would engage them with nearly full fuel tanks.

Wellington

The Wellington was of geodetic construction, which is exceptionally strong. It carried a good defensive armament and had a range that would take it to Berlin from airfields in eastern England with a bomb load equivalent to that of the He III. Of course there were four-engined bombers to be added to the RAF inventory with even greater range and bomb-carrying capacity, but in the lead-up to the war Britain already had a strategic bomber in the shape of the Wellington. It did start out with a low service ceiling of 22,200 feet, although this was improved upon in later marks. Its low speed compared to the German types, and low service ceiling, would make it vulnerable in a hostile environment. Add to this the unpreparedness of Bomber Command for war, as already described in this chapter, and one could not be sure how effective the Wellington would have been when up against determined fighter opposition. As it happens, the combat operations undertaken by Wellingtons in the first few weeks of war were largely a failure, but as part of the combined Anglo-American bomber force undertaking the 1,000-bomber raids over enemy occupied territory they acquitted themselves well.

Bristol Blenheim

This light bomber was lightly armed and had a modest range. It was also built as a fighter with the appropriate armament (Blenheim IF).With a high service ceiling it could more easily stay out of trouble, and had a reputation for being a fast new bomber, which excited a lot of foreign interest, and there were exports to Romania, Greece, Turkey, Lithuania and Yugoslavia.

CONCLUSION

Of course hindsight is an exact science, and the historian has the advantage of knowing how these aircraft actually performed in war. In the mid- to late 1930s the Air Staff had the task of advising the government of the best means of securing this country against air attack. This they did on the perceived threat. This section looks at whether or not Great Britain faced near or certain defeat by Germany in the years 1939/40. With regard to the strategic air threat the *Luftwaffe* simply did not have the means to mount a prolonged strategic air war against Britain, whether by landplanes or seaplanes. It had a tactical air force that could support a rapidly moving land campaign until the army reached the English

Channel. As to the RAF mounting a strategic campaign in 1939/40, one might have expected an air force brought up on Trenchard's doctrine of the strategic air war to be ready in all respects to fight such a war at the commencement of hostilities. Bomber Command's AOC-in-C did not believe they were ready as late as 1938. The Air Staff did not envisage a rapid French collapse, forcing Britain onto the defensive, but in the event Britain's defences were not found wanting.

THE AIR COMMANDERS

(The Members of the Air Council and Commanders of RAF formations in the 1930s are shown in Appendix M.)

Introduction

In Volume I the point was made that the RAF's senior commanders had all, without exception, been steeped in military or naval tradition. Their only experience of war in the air was the four years of the Great War, and all of them had learned to fly only immediately before the war. Some of them, like Sir Edward Ellington, had no operational combat experience in the air, commanding only a 'desk'; others, like Sir John Salmond, had such operational experience. Trenchard had commanded a strategic bomber force in France, and from that experience was to make claims for the strategic employment of airpower that had hardly been proved in a few months of 1918. Trenchard was, in a sense, obliged to make overblown claims for the offensive employment of airpower because he was fighting a life-and-death struggle with the Army and the Navy to stop the RAF being dismembered and returned to its sister services, whence the RAF had come. He had to show that only an air force was uniquely equipped to fight an air war that might be carried out in isolation, i.e. against enemy industrial and economic targets and communications well away from the land battle. Sometimes he got carried away with his ideas and was in danger of angering the other service heads by appearing to suggest that a war could be won with airpower alone. Sir Maurice Hankey had to be bring Trenchard down to earth by explaining, in a personal letter, that the experience of the Great War showed only too clearly the limitations in employment of airpower, while acknowledging the importance of the RAF in contributing to the winning of a war in conjunction with its sister services.

With Trenchard's retirement little changed in the overall view of the Air Staff, and the 1930s started in an atmosphere of hope that the world might disarm, a forlorn hope as it turned out. The policy of the 1923 expansion to fifty-two squadrons, of which a majority was to be bomber, only emphasized the uncritical view that the bomber would always get through and that bombers could fight their way through to the target, which, if true, held out little hope for Britain if ever an aerial armada should attack the British Isles. With the

failure of the disarmament talks in Geneva and the growing threat from Nazi Germany, it is of interest to note how the various air commanders reacted to both events and the part they played in preparing the RAF for war in 1939. The following list of commanders is not exhaustive, but it includes, firstly, the three Chiefs of the Air Staff in the 1930s, followed by other commanders, both at command and staff level, who had an influence on outcomes. The names of Air Marshals Dowding and Ludlow Hewitt have not been included, since the part that they played in preparing Fighter Command and Bomber Commands, respectively, for war has already been discussed in this chapter.

Sir John Salmond – Chief of the Air Staff, 1930 to 1933

Whereas his predecessor, Hugh Trenchard, had held the post of CAS for ten years, Salmond was to hold it for only three, which was to be the norm. Trenchard's tenure in office was exceptional, given the need for the development of the brand-new service in the face of great opposition from the Army and the Navy. Salmond had worked with Trenchard on his staff and was given independent command of all land and air forces in Iraq, followed by command of the Air Defence of Great

Sir John Salmond.

Britain. He was an experienced operational air force commander and pilot, and by 1930 was the natural choice to take over. But he did so at a bad time, and in three short years was to make little impact on the further development of the RAF. This was not his fault. The country was in the depth of the Depression, when resources were very scarce, and he was in no position to spend money on more squadrons or new aircraft. In any event the last thing the British government wanted, as the negotiators went to Geneva to plan to disarm, was their CAS planning major developments in air armament. Among the proposals being considered at Geneva were the abolition of bombing, at a time when RAF aircraft were daily bombing tribesmen on the North-West Frontier, and the abolition of all military aircraft. Salmond could only try to prove the impracticality of what was proposed at the conference. The RAF would have been forced to dispense entirely with the policy of offensive defence which underpinned everything Trenchard and the Air Staff had professed throughout the 1920s. He therefore retired on 31 March 1933 without having achieved anything of great significance, for even though Britain won the Schneider Trophy in perpetuity in 1931, it was thanks to a private benefactor, not the Air Ministry.

Sir Edward Ellington – Chief of the Air Staff, 1933 to 1937

Sir Edward Ellington's career was discussed at some length in Volume I, for it disclosed a career spent mostly behind a desk. Even as AOC in Iraq and India he had no experience whatsoever in commanding aircraft in combat, and he never served on a squadron, let alone commanded one. His command experience was therefore only in Air rank. The operations that he oversaw were therefore entirely of an air-control nature, yet he became CAS at a time when a threat was developing from Germany, which was rearming with the latest types of aircraft. In Iraq and India there was no air threat. It was not expected that Ellington would get the top job, for Geoffrey Salmond was tipped to take over when illness, followed by his death, sadly ruled him out. Ellington therefore took over at a time when the expansion schemes for the RAF were just being initiated. From what has been said of him he was not likely to be the most able of men to command at such an important time. He was, however, supported by men of great talent, whose names are to follow, and Ellington himself had been one of the initial founders of the RAF, working alongside Trenchard to create the new service.

His first reaction on being given the go-ahead for expansion was to plead for it not to be too rapid. He had inherited an air force of no more than 30,000 personnel and aircraft that were long out of date. After so many lean years it was difficult to comprehend the effects on

Sir Edward Ellington.

the service of the expansion plans that would take the Metropolitan Air Force from forty-eight squadrons to a force of seventy-five in the first scheme, Scheme A. It was no use his expanding the RAF with obsolete aircraft, and as new types of aircraft were introduced he had the problem of meeting the training needs of the service, for both aircrews and technical tradesmen. The training facilities available to Ellington at this time were simply not going to be sufficient to meet the demand. Fortunately the creation of the Auxiliary Air Force had gone some way to providing a reserve of pilots.

Ellington, like his predecessors, still clung to the belief that the fighter could not successfully defend the country against the bomber, and the ratio of bombers to fighters was fixed at 5:2. He did plan for the replacement of all the biplane light bombers with medium bombers, and the specifications were laid down for the building of the four-engined heavy bombers that were to be so important in the strategic bombing campaign of the Second World War. The Hurricane and the Spitfire received the go-ahead under his command, and he set in train the air defence arrangements for the British Isles. He also began the building of all the extra RAF stations that would be required, presided over the introduction of the shadow factory scheme, introduced the new RAF command structure in 1936, approved the introduction of the RAF Volunteer Reserve and made plans to purchase aircraft from the USA. All in all, Ellington accomplished a great deal in a short time. He was, however, well supported by his Air Staff and the Secretary of State for Air, Lord Swinton. What he did not do was to save the FAA from being returned to the Admiralty in 1937. This episode provides an example of how Ellington had spent too long behind a desk, when Trenchard berated him for so doing, complaining that he had his head buried in the sand and that the final decision had been made over his, Ellington's, head. But it is doubtful that his intervention would have changed the outcome.

One obvious glaring failure, which was not Ellington's alone, was to develop a strategic bombing doctrine based upon proper trial and experiment. It is one of the enduring mysteries of the whole inter-war period that a service so wedded to the supremacy of the bomber never, either at command or staff level, seriously questioned or tested the practicalities of strategic bombing. Ellington did not change this uncritical acceptance of bombing doctrine, and it was Sir Edgar Ludlow-Hewitt who would find Bomber Command so unprepared for war when it came.

Sir Cyril Newall – Chief of the Air Staff, 1937 to 1940

Having led No. 41 Wing in France in the Great War, Cyril Newall had experience of attacking targets of military importance in Germany. When No. 41 Wing became VIII Brigade in February 1918, his force carried out fifty-seven attacks on Germany. When VIII Brigade was expanded into the Independent Bombing Force, he became Trenchard's deputy. No other officer in the post-war RAF could therefore claim to understand better the effects of strategic bombing. With service at Halton and the Air Ministry's Directorate of Operations and Intelligence, and command experience as AOC Middle East, he was well qualified to become Deputy Chief of the Air Staff. When the expansion began he was the Air Member for Supply and Organization, so that when he took over from Ellington in September 1937 he could appreciate what work needed still to be done to prepare the RAF for war. By supporting Expansion Scheme J (see Chapter 2), he was exhibiting his belief that the bomber force was the basis of all strategy, and the counter-offensive was the best way of defending Britain. This was classic Trenchard, but hardly surprising given his Great War experience. The 'knockout blow' was a serious proposition, but would require a bombing force capable of delivering it, a force of heavy bombers that would not come on stream until after Newall's retirement. This point was appreciated by Sir Thomas Inskip, the Minister for the Coordination of Defence, who could turn the argument around and say that it would be the Germans who would be in a position to deliver such a blow. Newall could not have it both ways. If the RAF could do it, then why not the *Luftwaffe*? Partly out of financial considerations, but also realism, Inskip preferred to concentrate on fighter production. The Cabinet supported him, and against the advice of Swinton, Newall and the Air Staff, Scheme K gave greater emphasis to fighters.

After Munich, with war seeming imminent, Newall had to consider whether or not to concentrate on bringing the existing forces to readiness or to continue with the expansion schemes. Newall preferred the former course of action, but this would not stop the expansion, and Scheme L was proposed by the Air Ministry. This was initially resisted by Inskip and the Chancellor because of the expense involved. However, Newall realized that the RAF was not ready to fight a strategic war at that stage, but that efforts must not be relaxed to achieve the force levels required to strike against Germany as soon as this could be realized. He had already approved the order to build three heavy bombers off the drawing-board, and was meanwhile talking to the French, since Britain was committed to sending an expeditionary force, land and air, to the continent when war came. Newall was doing his best to

Sir Cyril Newall.

overcome the shortcomings of the past and hoped that time could be bought for the RAF to be ready. Ludlow-Hewitt was keeping up the pressure to remedy the shortcomings in Bomber Command and Dowding was doing the same for Fighter Command. The rest, as they say, is history, and Newall handed over to Portal in October 1940, by which time Hitler had postponed Operation Sealion, the invasion of Britain.

Sir Charles Portal

As a distinguished Great War pilot and post-war flying instructor at Cranwell, Portal went on to develop his experience and skills in the inter-war years. By 1935 he was the youngest air commodore in the RAF, and he commanded the British forces in Aden at the time of the Abyssinian crisis. He had studied at the Imperial Defence College and served in the Plans Branch of the Air Ministry. As Director of Organization in 1937 he was intimately involved in the rapid expansion of the service. His responsibilities included the finding of sites for new airfields, forming new squadrons with aircraft and crews and the setting up of the new Maintenance Command in July 1938. He then joined the Air Council as Air Member for Personnel in February 1939, where he presided over the inauguration of the Empire Training Scheme, the creation of the Women's Auxiliary Air Force, the establishment of the Directorate of Manning and the formation of a specialized Technical Branch. This is a list of formidable achievements, which would have secured

any officer's place in history, but his work was far from being over. He was appointed C-in-C Bomber Command in March 1940 in succession to Sir Edward Ludlow-Hewitt, by which time it was widely acknowledged that his new command was not by any means ready to take the war to the enemy. Before being appointed CAS in October of that year he could do little more than limit, as far as possible, the losses to the squadrons under his command, so as to conserve strength for the future.

Sir John Slessor

In his book *The Central Blue*, Slessor recalls the host of problems which came to lie on his desk in the Plans Branch in the immediate pre-war years. His previous career from Great War pilot to the CFS and inter-war squadron air service led on to flying training and a short spell as a junior staff officer at the Air Ministry before commanding No. 4 Squadron at Farnborough. Later in

Sir Charles Portal.

Sir John Slessor.

the 1920s Slessor returned to the Air Ministry in the Directorate of Operations and Intelligence. At the end of the decade he was to work with the Army, both at the School of Army Cooperation and at the Army Staff College at Camberley. After a period in India he returned in 1937, in the rank of group captain, to the post of Deputy to the Director of Plans, and then Director. It was in this post that he was to be intimately involved in the RAF's preparedness for war.

Slessor admits that, in the inter-war years, the Air Staff underestimated the technical difficulties of modern air bombardment. So much unquestioning faith had been pinned on the ability of the bombing force to bring about a satisfactory outcome for Britain in a future war. Yet too little had been done to improve target acquisition, fighting towards the target at night or in bad weather and long-range navigation. Moreover, the bombing aircraft of 1936 were still biplanes with the bombs slung below the wings, little advanced from the bombers of the Great War with which Slessor had been familiar.

The Plans Department did draw attention to the need for research and experiment in such matters as tactics, the types of bombs to be used and the vulnerability to bombing of different targets such as warships. For a department that was tasked with preparing plans for the employment of the bomber force in war, Slessor admits that he and his colleagues had no practical experience of what a bomber could achieve in a modern war, and as late as November 1938 it was necessary to ask for the appointment of a panel of experts from the various Air Ministry staffs to advise the planners.

The *Luftwaffe* was asking the same questions about bombing policy, such as finding and hitting targets at night, but in the event their successes in Spain, Poland, the Low Countries and France were largely achieved through dive-bombing, when obtaining accuracy and target acquisition were not major problems. The RAF would not get a Bomber Development Unit until 1939, by which time Slessor had realized, particularly through Ludlow-Hewitt's experiences as C-in-C Bomber Command, that the bombing force would not be ready for war that year. The latter had stressed the need for the operational training of his crews, especially in long-range navigation and bad-weather flying. Slessor had to think in terms of conserving the bomber force until it was better equipped to take the war to the enemy.

Slessor's plans were also affected by the government's policy with regard to international law in the matter of bombing. This involved distinguishing between purely military and civilian targets and those that were not clearly one or the other. To bomb military targets when collateral damage might be caused to areas of civilian habitation could invite savage reprisals. When it was difficult enough to find the target, particularly in bad weather or at night, the probability of bombs falling

wide of the mark would limit the number of enemy targets that could be included in the plans. Were the civilians constructing aircraft legitimate military targets but the civilians supplying materials to the factory not? These considerations only complicated matters, when the government was anxious not to provoke retaliation against the civil population in the event of war. At one point Slessor considered adopting the policy used in air-control operations, namely to issue a warning to tribesmen who were not complying with the requests of the government that they could expect bombing to commence at a specified time. Such a policy applied to the workers of the Ruhr, for example, could permit the German government to evacuate the civilian population before factories producing armaments were bombed. But this was to misunderstand the nature of a Fascist regime operating a corporate economy, when the nation, both servicemen and civilians, was mobilized to one end. Slessor had conversations with the American aviator Colonel Lindbergh on the evening of 22 September 1938 that were reported to the CAS the following day. Lindbergh had toured Europe and witnessed, first hand, German production methods. He had great admiration for German workmanship and their magnificent spirit, and advised that war with Germany should be avoided at almost any cost. He was, of course, in agreement with Chamberlain's appeasement policy. The problem for Slessor was to assess how much credence could be placed upon this report, given that the Germans might have been putting on a show for propaganda purposes.

In the final months of peace following the Munich Crisis, Slessor had to concentrate on the necessary defensive precautions to meet and mitigate the effects of German bombing of Britain. On the outbreak of war he was posted to the USA on special duty in the rank of air commodore. He would become CAS in 1951.

Sir Arthur Harris

Arthur Harris appeared in Volume I on a number of occasions, particularly with reference to his experiments in bombing, using the transport aircraft at his disposal on No. 45 Squadron, while serving in Iraq in the 1920s. He also served as OC No. 58 Squadron, Worthy Down, before his promotion to wing commander. After a spell as a student at the Army Staff College, he was back to the Middle East as Senior Air Staff Officer, then on to a flying-boat course at Calshot in October 1932, before commanding a flying-boat squadron. Perhaps late in the day he found himself on staff duties in the Air Ministry from July 1933 to until June 1937, first as Deputy Director of Operations and Intelligence, and then as Deputy Director of Plans. He was then involved in important policy issues that would affect the RAF's readiness for war, notably concerning new aircraft types. He was the RAF member of the Chiefs-of-Staff Joint Planning

Sir Arthur Harris.

produce aircraft at the rate necessary to keep pace with German rearmament.

Lord Swinton wanted to have people he knew in positions of responsibility to oversee the huge RAF expansion, which was, by then, well under way. He had been Colonial Secretary and knew of Freeman's work in Palestine and Newall's from Iraq. As Commandant of the Staff College, Freeman had been entitled to sit on Swinton's Parity sub-committee, and there was about to be some reorganization in the Air Council to take account of the urgency of rearmament, given the deteriorating international situation. Hugh Dowding was the Air Member for Research and Development (AMRD), concentrating on the development of the new aircraft technology, and Cyril Newall was appointed the Air Member for Supply and Organization (AMSO) with responsibility for production. On 1 April 1936 Freeman was appointed as AMRD when Dowding became AOC-in-C Fighter Command.

Following the deliberations of the Bombing Committee, Freeman pressed the Air Staff to place orders for the new monoplane heavy bombers directly from the drawing-board. The urgency of the situation

Committee that drew up the various war plans. In this he was helped by his having worked with the Navy and the Army. After a brief spell as AOC No. 4 Bomber Group, he went back to the Middle East before the outbreak of war. He is, of course, best remembered for his role as C-in-C Bomber Command during the Second World War, when he ordered the controversial bombing of Dresden.

Sir Wilfred Freeman

There is no doubt that Wilfred Freeman made significant contributions to the preparedness of the RAF for war in 1939 and for its offensive capability thereafter. He had been a station commander at RAF Leuchars, a staff officer, AOC Palestine and Commandant of the RAF Staff College at a time when he was going through a divorce from his first wife. Divorce was a serious business in those days, particularly if third parties were involved, and Freeman was prepared to leave the service when fate intervened. In June 1935, Baldwin succeeded Ramsay MacDonald as Prime Minister, and appointed Sir Philip Cunliffe Lister (later Lord Swinton) to the post of Secretary of State for Air. He was faced with the daunting task of re-equipping the service with the new monoplane fighters and bombers in the knowledge that the aircraft industry simply did not have the capacity to

Sir Wilfred Freeman.

was such that the RAF could not afford the luxury of testing new types before placing orders, and the go-ahead was given for 200 Manchesters (later to be developed into the Lancaster), 200 Stirlings and 100 Halifaxes. This decision alone would have the most profound consequences for the RAF in prosecuting the strategic air war against Germany. He was also responsible for sanctioning the production of the all-wooden Mosquito against considerable opposition. Another reorganization in August 1938 saw the combination of development and production in one post, and Freeman was appointed Air Member for Development and Production on the first of the month. Exceptionally he was given the authority to talk directly to the Treasury. He oversaw the production of the Spitfire and the Hurricane and the construction of the radar system. He also gave support to Frank Whittle in developing the jet engine.

Sir Arthur Tedder

Arthur Tedder made his greatest contribution to the Allied successes in the Middle East during the Second World War. In the early 1930s he did much to improve the training of pupils at the Air Armament School, Eastchurch, where he was CO. He was then appointed to be Director of Training, and his name appears in Chapter 2 in relation to pilot training, where he exploited the potential of civilian flying schools, which supplemented the work of the four flying training schools in the United Kingdom. He ensured that standards of flying training were maintained by the Central Flying School. In 1936 he was posted as AOC Far East, where he did much to improve the airfields in the Malay peninsula. On his return home in 1938 he worked in research and development under Sir Wilfred Freeman. Probably his greatest asset was his ability to work with commanders of other British and Allied services, such as Generals Montgomery and Eisenhower, even though he was often critical of Montgomery's methods.

Sir Arthur Tedder (Photo via Chaz Bowyer).

Other commanders

There are other commanders who worked hard during the 1930s, and the author hopes the reader will forgive any omissions. Those selected for inclusion in this section are those who played the most significant part in the preparedness of the RAF for war.

Chapter 11
The Royal Air Force and Government

Air estimates – Disarmament talks – Exchanges in Parliament over the conduct of rearmament – Parliamentary criticisms of the management of the Air Ministry – Changes of Prime Minister and Secretaries of State for Air – The Munich Crisis

Introduction

The years 1930 to 1939 are remarkable for two reasons. Firstly, there was a National government comprising the main political parties in the House of Commons for the whole period, and secondly, the period started off with the world economy in recession, sparked off by the Wall Street Crash. The German economy was in such dire straits that five million of the workforce were unemployed, and it was the inability of successive Centre Left coalition governments to agree on the unpopular measures necessary to combat the recession that helped Hitler into power. Of course other factors played their part, but the state of the economy did not help. In Britain, also, unemployment was high, and the government was faced with having to cut benefits to the unemployed in an effort to cut public spending. It was either that or raise taxes; both were deeply unpopular measures. In the end benefits were cut, but by 10%, which was not as much as previously planned. Public salaries were also cut, but it hurt an able seaman more than an admiral, a 25% cut as against a 7% cut, and there was a fleet mutiny at Invergordon when sailors refused to carry out their duties.

The RAF was also to suffer when the government was not prepared to fund the preparation, training and entry of the High-Speed Flight for the 1931 Schneider Trophy Race due to take place at Calshot that year. The competition open to seaplanes had been won twice in succession by the RAF team. The rules of the competition were that the country that won the races three times in succession would win the trophy in perpetuity. The government knew this, but felt that it could not make an exception, given that virtually the whole nation was being asked to tighten its belt. Fortunately a benefactor came forward in the shape of Lady Houston, and Britain's entry was safe.

As the decade unfolded, the economy was to pick up, but in the period 1930 to 1934, when the worst of the recession was being felt, the RAF was not expanding and had to make do by effecting economies. But when the expansion schemes were commenced in late 1934, the dramatic increase in the production of aircraft, works services in building airfields and recruitment to the RAF, both regular and reservists, had the effect of reducing unemployment and increasing tax revenues from previously unemployed workers.

The decade began with Ramsay MacDonald as Prime Minister of a Labour government, and when his government fell on 24 August 1931, King George made what some regarded as a controversial decision by reappointing MacDonald as Prime Minister. Most of his party sat in opposition, and there were Conservatives and Liberals in the Cabinet, but this was a National government, and was to remain so until 1945. Baldwin, the Conservative leader, was content to work in a MacDonald cabinet, for the serious economic situation in the country demanded consensual action, not opposition.

The interaction of the RAF and the government will be dealt with by calendar years. The changes in the posts of Prime Minister, Secretary of State for Air and Chief of Air Staff are shown on the next page.

1930
The Air Estimates 1930/1

The White Paper was signed by Lord Thomson. The gross estimate was £20,923,000, and a net of £17,850,000, an improvement of £890,000. Much of the paper was devoted to airships and to the R100 and R101, the 'capitalist' and 'socialist' airships, as they were known. They were both cited as satisfactory experiments. Lord Thomson reported that both airships were stable and easy to control, but he was incorrect in stating that the R101's diesel engines were the first to power an aircraft. He had not been informed about the Typhoon-engined Aldershot bomber, which flew in 1927. In the debate that followed, he said that the main feature of the 1930 programme was the consolidation of existing units of the Home Defence Force. Britain would have a breathing space in which to watch development of the new spirit that informed specific international instruments such as the Treaty for the Renunciation of War. The opposition found little consolation that the RAF then totalled seventy regular squadrons, including the equivalent of twelve squadrons in the FAA, plus twelve non-Regular squadrons.

GOVERNMENTS AND SECRETARIES OF STATE IN THE 1930s

	Government and Prime Minister	Secretary of State for Air	Chief of the Air Staff
1930	Ramsay MacDonald, Labour government	Lord Thomson	Air Marshal Sir John Salmond
		Lord Amulree on death of Lord Thomson in R101 disaster, 14/10/30	
1931	Labour government falls, 24/8/31. Ramsay MacDonald	Lord Londonderry, August 1931	
1932	remains as head of a National government		
1933			Air Chief Marshal Sir Edward Ellington,
1934			22/5/33
1935	Stanley Baldwin takes over as Prime Minister of the National government, June 1935	Sir Philip Cunliffe-Lister (later Lord Swinton), July 1935	
1936			
1937	Stanley Baldwin retires, May 1937 Neville Chamberlain becomes Prime Minister of the National govt		Marshal of the Royal Air Force Sir Cyril Newall, 1/9/37
1938		Rt Hon. Sir Kingsley Wood PC, May 1938	
1939			

Appointment of a new Secretary of State for Air

Following the death of Lord Thomson in the tragic circumstances of the crash of the R101, Lord Amulree was appointed as the Secretary of State for Air on 14 October. This was a strange appointment, since he knew no one in the aircraft industry and had not shown any previous active interest in flying. He was, however, a leading lawyer and therefore more likely to be a dispassionate judge than an enthusiastic amateur. There was no immediate successor to Sir Sefton Brancker as Director of Civil Aviation when he also died in the R101.

1931

Appointment of Secretary to the Air Ministry

Mr C.L. Bullock replaced Sir Walter Nicholson as the Secretary to the Air Ministry on 20 January. He was 50 years old, formerly of the Green Howards, the RFC and the RAF. He had shown great ability and tact in dealing with the Indian government, which wanted its nationals to run the Imperial air routes from Karachi to Rangoon and had opposed Imperial Airways in its choice of aircraft.

Debate on the RAF

In March a debate ensued in Parliament about the state of the RAF, Lord Thomson speaking in the House of Lords and the Under-Secretary of State in the House of Commons. Lord Thomson referred to the 1923 Expansion Plan, which provided for the formation of a Home Defence Force of fifty-two squadrons, with no date set for completion of the plan. There were in 1931 only thirty-nine squadrons, with 452 aircraft. Thirteen of these were non-Regular or Auxiliary, and could only be called up in time of war. Adding three further squadrons in the financial year was not inconsistent with pursuing a policy of disarmament. He said that Britain was not in a race for air armaments, for a major war remained only a remote possibility. Britain was fifth among the air powers of the world, and her air strength was distributed thinly bearing in mind the commitment of defence of the outposts of Empire. He promised that five squadrons of obsolete Bristol Fighters would be replaced by new types in the year. And only a few DH9As remained in service. No wooden aircraft had been ordered, and only a few of composite construction. It was pointed out to the members that the term 'all-metal' did not apply to wing fabric, and that research was continuing on the possibilities of metal skinning to simplify repair and maintenance. Finally it was explained that the life of metal-structured airframes was double that of the wooden airframe of 1927.

The Marquess of Douglas and Clydesdale, in a maiden speech, advertised the value of the Auxiliary squadrons, in which he was a flight lieutenant. Sir Philip Sassoon also paid tribute to the Auxiliary Air Force and pressed for the formation of Auxiliary seaplane squadrons. He maintained that the requirements for air defence were no less than seven years previously, and that it was unwise to rely upon superior efficiency to make up for numerical inferiority. John Sorensen, a Labour member, countered with an amendment to reduce the RAF to 32,000 personnel of all ranks, exclusive of those serving in India, to which Captain Balfour replied that if the amendment was carried it would add 30,000 to the number of unemployed. Other Labour members spoke of the barbarity of war, but the amendment was defeated by 248 votes to 12. Despite Labour's caution on expenditure, it did not prevent a Conservative vote of censure on the government for extravagance.

Dissolution of Parliament

The King dissolved Parliament on 8 October. And MacDonald argued for a free hand in re-establishing the country's economy. In the election that followed, all the Conservative candidates canvassed as 'National' candidates, as did a number from the Labour and Liberal parties, but the bulk of the Labour Party remained staunchly Labour, and when a National government was formed, they went into opposition. Several candidates used aircraft for publicity, including MacDonald. His pilot who flew him across country was Gloster's liaison officer, Wing Commander Don.

1932

Disarmament Commission

The Disarmament Conference was sitting in Geneva, and the British government supported the establishment of a Disarmament Commission, the abolition of gas and chemical warfare and submarines. The establishment of a commission was seen as important since, if the conference got bogged down in irreconcilable wrangling over detail, the commission would represent an ongoing attempt to achieve international agreement on disarmament. This meant that defence had to be emphasized at the expense of attack capabilities to reduce the temptation to resort to armed conflict.

Following the air exercises, which began on 18 July, Stanley Baldwin was moved to say that the 'man in the street' must realize that no power on earth could prevent him from being bombed. He continued, 'There are two national instincts that make for the preservation of the race, the reproduction of the species and fighting for its safety.' He believed that the highest duty of statesmanship was to remove the causes of war. He knew that, until the Great War, civilian populations were largely exempt from the perils of war. But now the threat of aerial bombardment had changed that perception,

and the threat would be present in the first five minutes of the war. In Nuremberg the authorities had opened a school for the training of the civilian population in defensive measures against massed air attacks. HM Government did not pretend that it was not taking similar precautions, which would take several years to put into place.

1933

Air Estimates for 1933

The Air Estimates for 1933 were presented in the usual White Paper, with the government ever anxious to appear to be supporting disarmament, and the modest Home Defence Force, the product of the 1923 Expansion Scheme, was to be held in suspense for another year. The gross was £19,638,000, that is £64,100 less than the previous year, but the net figure was slightly up on the previous year, after deducting the FAA grant. RAF strength remained at sixty-two Regular squadrons and twenty-seven FAA flights. The customary debate followed on 14 March, and one newspaper reported that the Commons was paying proper attention to a debate on the Air Estimates, and the House generally was becoming more air minded, many members having given time to the subject. Winston Churchill expressed the hope that the House did not believe that the RAF existed only to fight locusts and drop nothing but blankets. He said that there was the same kind of hopelessness in dealing with air problems as there was with unemployment, the currency or questions of the economy. He was concerned that the step-by-step disarmament by Britain and France while German aviation remained constant would mean that Britain would have to stand side-by-side with France to counter aggression. He much preferred larger air estimates, so that Britain could choose her own course of action rather than shackle herself to the European ideal of giving up arms. He added,

> I consider that an adequate air force is almost complete protection, not against injury and annoyance, but against destruction. I cannot understand why the government does not inculcate these truths widely. To have no adequate air force in the present state of the world is to compromise the foundations of national freedom and independence. I regret to hear the Under-Secretary of State say that the Ten-Year programme has been suspended for another year. I am sorry to hear him boast that the government has not laid a single new unit this year. Such ideas are increasingly stultified by the march of events, and we should be well advised to concentrate upon air defences with greater vigour. The air which gives the invader access to the heart of our country is also a bridge uniting us to the most distant parts of the Empire. The sea no longer gives complete security for our island development.

With that he left the Chamber of the House of Commons. In contrast there was a feeling that Mr Baldwin's recent speech had caused alarm without giving guidance.

During a debate on the Foreign Office vote on the Civil Air Estimates, Captain Harold Balfour said that he regarded the danger from Russia, not from Germany, as the more important. No European country bordering on Russia was going to agree to any great measure of disarmament until the menace of Russian airpower was dealt with. Stalin had fallen out with Trotsky on the matter of the imminence of world revolution. The former regarded the consolidation of the Socialist state in Russia as more important than carrying the Bolshevik revolution to the world. Stalin saw Russia as the sole Socialist state surrounded by hostile Capitalist or non-Socialist states, and the necessity for strong armed forces to protect the Soviet Union was vital. Captain Balfour pointed particularly to the four-engined Tupolev long-range bomber, of which he had counted 158 at the May Day celebrations.

1934

The Secretary of State visits the RAF abroad

On 29 January *The Times* announced the arrival in Rome of the Secretary of State for Air, Lord Londonderry, who was expected to meet Mussolini to discuss facilities for Imperial Airways' services *en route* to the East. He was using the opportunity of the presence in Rome of Colonel Shelmerdine and Mr Lloyd Tailor of Imperial Airways. From Rome the Secretary of State continued on a 16,000-mile tour of RAF stations in Egypt, Palestine, Transjordan, Iraq and India. He visited every station and unit in India by air and car, and was impressed with the economy of air control and the efficient coordination of RAF and Army units.

Disarmament

The government had modified its views on disarmament, as revealed in a White Paper (Cmnd 4498) issued on 31 January. It was agreed that the arms of a kind permitted in one state could not indefinitely be denied to another state, and that the choice before Europe was that agreement must be reached with a convention either abandoning certain classes of weapons by the most heavily armed forces or that those powers must at least undertake not to increase their present armaments. The White Paper made reference to the amendment moved by the German delegation at Geneva proposing total abolition of military and naval aircraft, without, however, making specific provision for civil aviation. Hitler had never made a secret of his rejection of the Versailles Treaty limitations on the size and composition of the German armed forces. If Germany had no air force it was logical to argue that, to obtain parity with the other powers, the latter would have to abolish their military and naval aircraft. Of course Hitler

knew that neither France nor Britain would contemplate abolition, and it was only a question of time before Germany's acquisition of an air force would have to be faced, and, if it happened, accepted as a *fait accompli*, which is where this paragraph began. HM Government therefore suggested that if the Disarmament Commission had not decided on abolition at the end of two years, all countries should be entitled to possess military aircraft. Countries would therefore reduce or increase force levels by stages over a period of eight years to attain by the end of the convention the figures in the table previously agreed or such figures as might be agreed.

Hitler's reaction was entirely predictable. He pronounced that the Geneva Conference would reach no agreement on armament reduction, whether on the British Memorandum or any alternative. Goering asserted that Germany required an air force of at least 30–40% of the combined strength of her neighbours France, Belgium, Czechoslovakia and Poland. That would amount to between 900 and 1,200 aircraft, which would make the RAF insignificant. Anthony Eden had been to Berlin, Rome and Paris on a mission to achieve agreement on force levels. If agreement was not possible, he said that it would indicate a lack of trust. France's lack of security would remain a stumbling block, and HM Government recognized that if the Disarmament Conference failed, then every country would have to review its armaments, and Britain more than others because she had disarmed so much already.

Air Estimates 1934/5

The Air Estimates grossed £20,165,000. The addition was the equivalent of six squadrons. At the end of the financial year the Home Defence Force would be forty-six squadrons, but its fighting strength would be forty-five, since No. 100 Squadron's Vildebeests had been transferred to the Far East Command. There would be an extra flying-boat squadron and the FAA, by the Naval Vote, gained two flights of catapult seaplanes. The total money available was £2,810,000 for aeroplanes and £1,940,000 for engines.

On 8 March there was an Air Debate, and Members of the House of Commons showed a proper appreciation of airpower. The *Aeroplane* reported that no debate on any service estimates had been so largely attended for many years. Winston Churchill pleaded for a continued effort to secure an international convention, yet admitted that Britain would never be justified in trusting her safety to such agreements. He did not propose war to prevent Germany from breaking the Treaty of Versailles, but pointed out that it was no longer a democracy. Hitler was not constrained by a democratic parliament nor a constitutional system. Baldwin agreed that the great peril from the air was the probable attempt by an aggressor at an immediate knockout blow, which would be an unlikely outcome if there was equality in the air. He restated his view that the bomber would always get through, and he ended his speech with this sentence: 'I say that if all our efforts fail and it is not possible to obtain this equality, then any government of this country, a National government more than any, and this government in particular, will see to it that in air strength and airpower this country shall no longer be in a position inferior to any country within striking distance of our shores.'

A Ministry of Defence

There was discontent in some quarters with the services being controlled by three separate service ministries. In the House of Lords, Major-General Lord Hutchinson, a former Liberal Chief Whip, proposed a Ministry of Defence, believing that it was not a matter for soldiers and sailors, but embraced the activities of the nation. In a future war, conscription of every form of national life would be necessary. Lord Londonderry then reminded the House that the idea of an MoD had been turned down in 1922 by a committee chaired by Lord Weir, again in 1924 by the Sub-committee of Imperial Defence chaired by Lord Salisbury, and more recently in 1931 by the May Committee on National Expenditure. Londonderry's answer was to point out that the Committee of Imperial Defence drew together the three services and was well suited to the British Constitution. The CID catered for the three services, the needs of Empire and the ancillary services. This was something that, by implication, an MoD could not do.

When the Commons debated Imperial defence, this matter came up again. Clement Attlee argued that the RAF had emerged to a position of great importance, but met tremendous resistance built up by tradition and prestige. His recommendation was for one Cabinet minister with overall responsibility for the three services instead of three service ministers. There would be a Defence Staff representing all three services, but separated from them. This staff would deal with broad matters of Imperial defence and strategy, the involvement in national life and the representation of the country in all international discussions in security and disarmament. The Prime Minister, in reply, echoed Lord Londonderry's speech in the Lords. Defence planning already involved all three services in the meetings of the Chiefs of Staff. He said that policy had to be related to Britain's position as a world power and a European power, and to the whole of Imperial unity. Churchill seemed to agree with Attlee that a Minister of Defence was a natural outcome. As he saw it, each of the three services was preparing to meet a different aggressor. The Navy was concerned with the Pacific theatre and Britain's links with Australia and New Zealand. The Army was behaving like a glorified police force on the North-West Frontier, containing barbarous tribes, while

the RAF was measuring its strength against Nazi Germany. New technologies of war demanded the unified direction of the war, which would certainly prove more economical. Churchill said that the Germans created a 'weapon office' to coordinate organization, strategic and scientific matters, and supply would certainly improve if a Ministry of Defence evolved from the present situation, and a unified Defence Service should be a goal. Baldwin had listened to practically the whole debate, although he was not moved to meet the aspirations of those who wanted to change, but Churchill was right. An MoD would come, but not until after the Second World War.

Chamberlain's Bristol speech, October 1934

Early in October 1934 Neville Chamberlain made a speech in Bristol. He sought to reassure the Conservative Party that the government had made a proper investigation of Empire defence, and plans were such that they could be altered as conditions changed. He explained the publicity given to the RAF because attack from the air would affect everyone, whereas attacks by navies and armies would not do so to the same extent. The government must not, however, be in such a hurry to ensure adequate air defence that it neglected to supply the right type of aircraft and supplies to meet different threats. An aircraft must be thoroughly tested and suited to its role. Multi-role aircraft like the Hart could not be fully effective. What was needed was specialized types of fighter, general-purpose aircraft, bomber aircraft, etc., that would put Britain ahead of the USA and Germany, although there was no intention of emulating either country by returning to airships.

1935

Anglo-French collaboration

A meeting took place at the beginning of February between Sir John Simon as Secretary of State for Foreign Affairs, the French Prime Minister, Pierre Flandin, and his predecessor, Georges Laval, the Foreign Minister. There had to be a collateral examination of methods of keeping the peace in Europe. A statement from the Foreign Office referred to special dangers to peace created by modern developments in the air, which had impressed the two governments. There had to be reciprocal regional arrangements whereby the French Air Force and the RAF would render immediate assistance in the event of an unprovoked attack on either of them. Moreover, such an arrangement would act as a deterrent, and both governments resolved to invite Italy, Belgium and Germany to join such an arrangement.

On 9 February *The Times* reported Germany's view. Germany lay centrally between France and Russia and could be threatened from both east and west. A rigid Western European Air Convention would not provide a sufficient safeguard of security, for in the view of the

German government, Russia was acting in close cooperation with France. Ramsay MacDonald favoured a Royal Commission on Armaments. He had in mind the prohibition of private manufacture and trade in arms and munitions of war. By nationalizing the armaments industries, governments could exert greater control. Be that as it may, MacDonald did not prevent the official purchase from the USA of a Northrop light bomber.

The Air Estimates, 1935/6
Knowledge of German air strength came too late to affect the Air Estimates for the financial year 1935/6. Goering had already got 20,000 men and 1,888 aircraft under command, to which 200 were being added by the month. This made the increase in the gross Estimate of £3,685,500 alarmingly small. The government had had to tread the thin line between the payment of lip service to disarmament and the meeting of the growing threat from Nazi Germany. With the expansion scheme in place the RAF urgently needed pilots to fly the growing number of aircraft, and the mechanics to service them. The Under-Secretary of State for Air, Sir Philip Sassoon, recognized that no matter what he did he would be criticized for moving either too fast or too slowly, and he said that Britain ranked fifth in the terms of front-line strength. France was still the strongest airpower in Europe, having 1,650 front-line aircraft, but it was believed that Russia had more than 2,000. The US government at this time was being attacked for the alleged inferiority of American aircraft to European designs. Sir Philip said that this would nullify any superiority the USA might have in her numbers of front-line aircraft. On the other hand the British Press had reported on the remarkable qualities of American aircraft and of the inability of the available British military types even to keep pace with American commercial machines. In similar vein the French Press had attacked the quality of French military aircraft, so there were obvious jitters among the powers that they were falling behind in the air arms race. Sir Philip went on to announce the addition of eleven new squadrons to the Home Defence Force and three flights to the FAA, so there would be fifty-four Home Defence squadrons and thirteen Auxiliary squadrons by the end of 1935, just twenty-one squadrons short of the new total for Home Defence of seventy-five squadrons. This put front-line strength of Regular squadrons at 890 aircraft, with 130 aircraft in non-Regular units. These figures would rise to 1,170 in 1935 and 1,310 in 1936.

Winston Churchill was well known for being the lone voice in Parliament in the 1930s, warning members of the dangerous threat posed by Nazi Germany, and the Press rounded on him over his speech in the debate on the 1935/6 Estimates. This threat from both Stalinist Russia and Hitler's Germany still seemed unreal to the general public. British insularity reigned supreme, and

Neville Chamberlain, who would shortly become Prime Minister, reflected this national reluctance to countenance another major European war with his appeasement of the Dictators. Except in the usually depressed areas of South Wales and the North, life was getting better. Mass production ensured a range of consumer goods at affordable prices. A suit of clothes could be bought for £2 10s., and food was cheap. If one did not own a small car one might be able to afford a second-hand motor-cycle. Important international events, such as the Spanish Civil War, Paraguay leaving the leaving the League of Nations and Germany introducing compulsory military service, hardly registered in the mind of the 'man in the street'. Yet the air arms race had begun, which would take Britain up to the outbreak of the Second World War.

HM Government announces the revised Expansion Scheme for the RAF
On 22 May Lord Londonderry in the House of Lords, and Stanley Baldwin in the House of Commons, announced the revised schemes for expansion of the RAF (details of all the expansion schemes can be found in Chapters 2 and 3). Given the rate of expansion, Lord Londonderry stressed the risks that must be taken with the money available to the government, because such was the pace of technological advance, aircraft were already obsolete from the time they were adopted by the Air Ministry. Baldwin wanted the Commons to know that there would be no profiteering. He also reflected on the fact that Russia was still in the League of Nations, Germany had left but he hoped it would return, the USA was still out, and Japan had left, unlikely to return. This could only serve to reinforce the feeling that Britain had to live in an uncertain world with an uncertain future.

Action to be taken in the face of aggression
The League of Nations worked well enough to keep the peace in the 1920s when only small countries were involved, but when Japan invaded Manchuria, and Italy invaded Abyssinia, there were bound to be problems. The League of Nations as a body had no armed forces at its disposal to enforce resolutions, and that applies to the United Nations today. Member countries are invited to send troops. With the USA not participating in the League of Nations, it left Britain, France and the Soviet Union as the only major powers who could use force. Clearly Stalin was preoccupied with establishing Socialism in the USSR, leaving only Britain and France. Economic sanctions were the only other way of forcing compliance with League of Nations' resolutions, but these could be a blunt weapon, hurting mostly the civil population and not the errant government. At the Labour Party Conference in the October there was a split between the National Executive and those opposed to

both sanctions and rearmament. Ernest Bevin was one of those who believed that sanctions could lead to war, and George Lansbury resigned as Party Leader because he disagreed with the official resolution. Clement Attlee was elected in his place.

The 1935 General Election

The opposition to rearmament was such that Baldwin felt the need for the nation's backing, or otherwise, in a general election. He won, with 432 seats for the National government against 180 seats for the Opposition. Ramsay MacDonald continued as Lord President, with Neville Chamberlain as the Chancellor of the Exchequer, and Sir Philip Cunliffe Lister was reappointed as the Secretary of State for Air. Following his ennoblement, he became Lord Swinton, and Sir Philip Sassoon remained as Under-Secretary of State for Air. Churchill might have expected to be called back into government as War Minister, but it was not to be. Perhaps his dire warnings about Hitler's intentions sounded too bellicose, for hopes still lingered that Hitler could be won over.

1936

The remilitarization of the Rhineland

Hopes for peace in Europe suffered a further setback when Hitler ordered the remilitarization of that part of Germany that straddled the River Rhine and lay to the west up to the French border. The Treaty of Versailles forbade the stationing of German troops in the Rhineland precisely because France wished there to be a 'buffer zone' between German forces and those of France. On 7 March German forces moved into the area, and the opportunity was taken to show off the *Luftwaffe*. German air units occupied the civil aerodromes of Cologne, Dusseldorf, Mannheim and Frankfurt. The outcry from France was entirely predictable, and Hitler came forward with a nine-point plan ranging from taking the Versailles Treaty out of the Covenant of the League, through non-aggression pacts with Germany's eastern neighbours, to a return to the League of Nations if the matter of Germany's colonies was amicably discussed. This was typical of Hitler, who was very good at appearing to be very reasonable when, in reality, he had his own agenda, which he would pursue when it suited him. Britain and France had a choice in acting militarily or seeking some accommodation with Germany's *fait accompli*. France could take some comfort in her fortified defence works, known as the Maginot Line, which stretched along the entire border with Germany, while HM Government, whose territory was not so closely threatened, could take the view that Germany was only stationing troops on its own territory, a right that any nation should expect to enjoy. Whichever view is taken about the inaction of both governments, the fact remains that nothing was done to oblige Hitler to withdraw his forces from the Rhineland. Instead, the

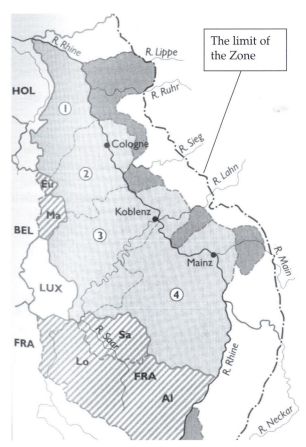

The Rhineland – the demilitarized zone.

two governments turned their attention to the civil war in Spain and the question of non-intervention.

The Supplementary Estimates

With the rate of expansion gathering pace, Supplementary Air Estimates were required. These were introduced by Sir Thomas Inskip, Minister for the Coordination of Defence, with a figure of £13,262,000. Inskip made the point that had expansion taken place any earlier the RAF would have been out of date for any emergency that they might have had to face in the future. Churchill said that such statements would be a surprise for the RAF but amounted to a new excuse for miscalculating the relative strengths of it and the *Luftwaffe*. He said that while the British people were on holiday and dreaming of the Coronation, Goering was busy fashioning a tremendous fighting machine. He asked the government that the intermediate stages between peacetime and the inevitable war be proclaimed a state of emergency in view of the increasing dangers gathering around the British people. This was greeted with silence, and the Estimates were passed.

Dismissal of Sir Christopher Bullock

Sir Christopher Bullock, the Permanent Secretary to the Air Ministry, was dismissed by the Prime Minister after a special government committee had investigated discussions alleged to have taken place between Sir Christopher and representatives of Imperial Airways. There was no question of corruption, and a White Paper made it clear that his activities had not influenced negotiations for a projected contract between Departments of State and Imperial Airways, nor had he bartered honours in return for personal advancement. He had endeavoured to secure the best terms for the government, resulting in a very satisfactory agreement with the company. But it was also known that he might leave the Civil Service for a career in commerce and business. He had lunched with Sir Eric Geddes, seeking an appointment as a government director of Imperial Airways, but the latter felt that Bullock's aspirations were hopeless. In 1934 the government was negotiating a contract for the carriage of first-class Empire mail, and Bullock thought it opportune for an honour to be conferred on Sir Eric, chairman of the company, for his services. Bullock put it to Lord Londonderry, who then asked Geddes whether an honour would be acceptable, and Bullock took that as his authority to seek an answer, which was that an honour would be welcome. When the Birthday Honours list was published, Geddes' name was not on it, and the angry chairman let it be known that if the government wanted Imperial Airways to carry the Royal Mail they could forget it. Then rumours began to circulate that Bullock would replace Geddes as chairman. On 11 June Bullock dined with George Woods Humphery, Imperial's managing director. Bullock referred to Geddes' indisposition, and told Humphery that with him as chairman and the latter as deputy chairman and managing director, the two men would represent a good working combination. The report that resulted in Bullock's dismissal referred to the Code of Conduct of Civil Servants. Bullock's mistake was to use public negotiations as a means of advancing his own personal, private interests. This marked the end of Sir Christopher Bullock as a public figure, and he was replaced by Sir Donald Banks KCB, DSO, MC, formerly Director-General of the Post Office.

1937

The Air Estimates, 1937/8

The net figure for the Estimates was £56,500,000, some £17,500,000 greater than the figure for the previous year. For the first time the RAF would get more than the Army. The gross figure included the Air Force grant to the Navy for the FAA, various appropriations and a projected armament loan. Sir Philip Sassoon was, as always, brilliant in his presentation of the Estimates. Having memorized them, he spoke without notes and emphasized the unparalleled rate of expansion of the

British armed forces in peacetime, all with voluntary effort. This was in contrast to Nazi Germany with its direction of labour in a regimented society. Production would be expedited by reducing the number of types of aircraft and making as few modifications as possible. Both Air Ministry and main contractors were doing their best to widen production by sub-contracting. The shadow factory scheme was a practical policy to give Britain war potential and reinforced production without interfering with normal industry. The government persuaded firms taking part in the expansion scheme to make large extensions to their factories and plant by permitting them to claim compensation if, on completion of expansion, they found themselves with surplus capacity. This would take into account any excess profits made.

Neville Chamberlain becomes Prime Minister

On 27 May Mr Baldwin resigned as Prime Minister in favour of Mr Neville Chamberlain, who then held the post of Chancellor of the Exchequer. Baldwin had presided during a turbulent period in Britain's history following the rise of the Fascist dictators, and was doubtless glad to hand over the baton. The Downing Street secretaries had become concerned over his health. He was, after all, 68 years of age and his hearing was going. He had the air of a pipe-smoking, stolid country gentleman of moderate

Mr Stanley Baldwin.

outlook and dependability, and this carried conviction with the public. Neville Chamberlain, on the other hand, was brusque in manner, with a harsh voice, was an able administrator and showed great will-power, yet his name would always be associated with the appeasement of the dictators. This may be partly understood because of his unfamiliarity with foreigners. Others have suggested that he was naïve in believing that one could ever trust Hitler. He had shown no interest in aviation and he did not have an aeronautical record, as far as can be ascertained. Anthony Eden remained at the Foreign Office, and Sir Thomas Inskip continued in the role of Minister for the Coordination of Defence. Leslie Hore-Belisha moved to the War Office, and Sir John Simon succeeded Chamberlain as the Chancellor of the Exchequer. The Department of Civil Aviation was divorced from the Air Ministry, and Sir Francis Shelmerdine was appointed as its director-general.

Debate on national defence

By one of those quirks of Parliamentary procedure a debate on national defence resulted from a consideration of the Civil Estimates, with special reference to the salary of Sir Thomas Inskip. It was a tangled debate, raising many pertinent points, but sometimes Inskip's replies to questions were only in the form of generalized assurances lest state secrets be divulged. A great deal had been done with air raid precautions, and the whole country had been divided into zones. When financial responsibility was agreed these plans could take effect. The government majority on this occasion was 165. In spite of the speed of German rearmament, Sir Thomas Inskip came down against Scheme J on the grounds that the economy and financial position were not equal to it. He accepted only Air Staff proposals for an increased number of fighters. Sir John Slessor, as Head of Plans at the Air Ministry for three and a half years prior to the war, made the comment that 'multiplying fighters is the usual refuge of someone who is ignorant of airpower', but admits that in the event Inskip was right. The latter did agree in principle to some increase in the striking force subject to various involved conditions about reserves and war potentials, but just before going on their Christmas holiday in 1937 the Cabinet rejected Scheme J and the Air Staff were told to think again. The Air Staff came up with an emasculated version of Scheme J, i.e. Scheme K.

Slessor believed that the principle of non-interference with the flow of normal trade still continued to bring comfort to our governors during the Christmas recess. They disregarded what the enemy was doing by saying in early 1938 that the three fighting services should not be allowed to spend more than £1,600 million over the five years 1937–41, a little over an average of £300 million a year, even though it was known that the Germans were spending £1,000 million in warlike preparations. Slessor concludes that the Air Staff during

the period 1937–9 cannot be accused of failing to warn the government of the perils of not providing parity with Germany in the air.

1938

Foreign policy as it affected the RAF

Chamberlain and Eden, the Foreign Secretary, were not at one over foreign policy. Mussolini's invasion of Abyssinia had only resulted in economic sanctions against Italy for the fear that any harsher punishment would throw the two dictators together, which is precisely what did happen with the formation of the Rome–Berlin Axis. The problem for Britain, with her vast Empire commitments, was keeping open the sea lanes from Gibraltar to Suez. Since Mussolini had declared the Mediterranean the '*mare nostrum*', the strengths of the Italian Navy and Army had to be weighed in the balance of advantage that the Axis powers might have against Anglo-French forces. Chamberlain felt that appeasing Mussolini would detach him from an alliance with Hitler. Eden disagreed, saying that it would only encourage Hitler in his several territorial demands in Europe in the late 1930s, which is precisely what happened. Chamberlain demanded Cabinet support for his appeasement policy on pain of his own resignation, but Eden resigned instead, followed by his under-secretary, Lord Cranborne. Lord Halifax followed Eden as Foreign Secretary.

Another problem facing the British government in trying to separate Mussolini from Hitler was their two countries' involvement in the Spanish Civil War. Both had sent troops and aircraft to assist the Nationalist forces led by General Mola, while Stalin gave some logistical support to the Republican government in Madrid. Those with left-wing sympathies could also be found fighting for the Republic in the International Brigade, and there were some anarchists too. For all their outward show, the Italian forces did not perform particularly well, and the war was causing grave damage to the Italian economy. On the other hand the German Condor Legion was learning valuable tactical lessons in what would prove to be the success of the *Blitzkrieg* war against Poland, the Low Countries and France in 1939 and 1940 (see Chapters 2 and 3). For the French and British governments there was little that could be done to influence the outcome of the war, but as more and more of Spain came under Nationalist control both countries had eventually to decide which of the warring factions represented the official government of Spain. Following the death of General Mola in an aircraft accident, General Franco assumed overall command of the Nationalist forces, and the British government would have to consider what the General might do to Gibraltar. The loss of Gibraltar would have had incalculable consequences for the British prosecution of the air war in the Mediterranean in securing the sea lane to Malta and

Suez. In the event Franco did not join the Axis. His countrymen had been at war for three years and were not ready for involvement in a European war. Nor did Franco relish the loss of the Canary Islands, which could have been taken by the Allies to prosecute the war in the Atlantic.

The Air Estimates, 1938/9

Lieutenant-Colonel Muirhead introduced the Air Estimates for 1938/9 on 15 March. These had grown to six times the 1934 figure. The gross figure was £103,500,000. Expenditure on Technical and Warlike Stores was £66,734,000, up £18,500,000 from the previous year. Allowing for yet further expansion, the Estimates also allowed for a Supplementary Estimate if required. There would be 1,750 aircraft by March 1939. At the time of the Estimates there were 123 squadrons at home and twenty-six squadrons overseas. The FAA had forty flights. The Naval Estimates, which followed the debate on the Air Estimates, allowed for £5,718,000 for an expanding FAA which passed from Air Ministry to Admiralty control. Between April 1935 and March 1938 some 4,500 pilots and 40,000 airmen and boys had entered the RAF, together with 430 cadet pilots from the Dominions. Manufacturing manpower had increased from 30,000 in 1935 to 90,000 at the beginning of 1938. Muirhead referred to the need to keep a balance between the speed of production and being up to date. Gun supply was satisfactory and power-operated turrets were a notable step forward. Indeed, because of the increasing importance of armament developments, the responsible government department now had its own director.

Muirhead turned to the contractual position. Some 63% of prices had been settled and 12% further quotations had not been accepted. These two categories embraced 75% of the contracts and covered half the expansion in aircraft ordered. In another 12% of contracts, batch costing had been resorted to instead of fixed prices. He reported that one important case had been settled by arbitration, and progress was being made in negotiation on all outstanding cases.

Mr Montague, who had been Secretary of State for Air under Lord Thomson, demanded a full investigation into the military side of the Air Ministry. Whatever the arguments might be about the virtue of using force, and he believed that the country realized the necessity for military preparations, he attacked the aircraft industry for profiting from the expansion. Gross profit figures for some of the major constructors were:

Armstrong Siddeley	£133.000
Bristol	£86,000
Fairey	£188,000
Hawker Aircraft	£154,000
Hawker Siddeley	£750,000
Vickers	£243,000

Handley Page had a 50% dividend and 100% bonus shares. Montague argued that, should war come, the aircraft industry should be nationalized. In the debate that followed, Lieutenant-Commander Fletcher, Labour Member for Nuneaton, moved an amendment that the House of Commons was not satisfied with the existing arrangements for production. Mr Garrow Jones, Labour, seconded the motion and challenged the Minister to deny that front-line German air strength was 50% greater than that of Great Britain. He was particularly worried about the vulnerability of Britain's shipping in the narrow waters around the British Isles, reminding the House that Britain had lost more than 3,000 ships in the Great War, which amounted to about half the Merchant Navy. He also advocated government control of the aircraft industry, with a really capable minister in charge of the Air Ministry. Sir Stafford Cripps, Labour MP for Bristol, backed both MPs, but the amendment was defeated by 253 to 139.

On 24 March the Prime Minister made an announcement to the effect that a greater effort must be made to increase and accelerate the rearmament programme, especially for the RAF and anti-aircraft defences (ack-ack). Ack-ack guns and ammunition would be a priority, and air raid precautions would be speeded up. Ten squadrons of barrage balloons had been organized for the London area, and 80% of the balloons and all the winches had been delivered. As for the protection of merchant shipping, Chamberlain said that there was little experience of air cooperation, and whether or not a convoy system would be instituted would have to be decided if and when war came.

RAF interest in the Lockheed Electra

Interest was aroused in the Lockheed Electra following its employment as a civil airliner. It had a high landing speed, which could prove difficult in trying to land in poor visibility. One of these aircraft overshot and went through the boundary fence when the pilot was attempting to land through a thick overcast. This did not deter the Air Ministry, who had seen that a military version might be a useful addition to the RAF inventory. A commission was set up comprising Air Commodore Arthur Harris, Air Commodore Jimmy Weir, Commander Casper John, Squadron Leader Horrex and Freddie Roworth of the A & AEE, Martlesham. When the party left for the United States, Earl Winterton told Parliament that they had gone to make exploratory enquiries, especially about an early date for delivery. The commission would also explore the capacity and potentiality for production of these aircraft in Canada. This was enough to get Montague to his feet demanding to know why difficulties with labour, skill and materials were not a problem in America, Canada or Germany but seemed insuperable in Britain. Earl Winterton replied that any plan to build aircraft in Canada was not a reflection of Britain's ability to do the same.

Formation of a Supplies Committee

On 29 April the Air Ministry announced the formation of a Supplies Committee, to be chaired by Earl Winterton, to place orders and arrange an extension of existing works or the creation of new ones. The new plan was prepared by the Air Ministry after consultation with representatives of the aircraft industry, with the aim of increasing output almost immediately. Provision had been made for the formation of extra squadrons, an increase in the strength of other squadrons and for an increase in personnel in all ranks. Members of the committee were:

Air Marshal Sir Wilfred Freeman	Air Member for Research and Development
Air Vice-Marshal W.L. Welsh	Air Member for Supply and Organization
Air Vice-Marshal R.E.C. Peirce	Deputy Chief of the Air Stafford House College
Mr A.H. Self	Second Deputy Under-Secretary of State
Mr E. Bridges	Treasury
Mr H. Russell	Secretary

Warning from the Chief of Air Staff to the Secretary of State for Air

In April the Chief of the Air Staff sent a minute to the Secretary of State for Air with a warning about Germany's capacity to wage a long war, if not to deliver a knockout blow against the United Kingdom. The CAS wrote:

I feel strongly that the time for mincing words is past and that the Air Staff should state their view of the situation plainly. Their view is that unless the Cabinet are prepared to incur at the very least the full expenditure required for Scheme L, and possibly more, we must accept a position of permanent inferiority to Germany in the air. In that event we must be prepared to accede to any German demand without a struggle, since in the event of war our financial and economic strength that the present financial limitations are designed to secure will be of no use to us because we shall not survive a knockout blow. No one can say with absolute certainty that a nation can be knocked out from the air, because no one has yet attempted it. There can be no doubt, however, that Germany and Italy believe it possible, as there can be no other explanation for piling up armaments to a level that they could not hope to maintain in a long war. When, as I firmly believe, the issue is that of the survival of British civilization, we cannot afford to take so great a chance for the sake of £60 or £100 million.

We were certainly wrong about Germany's inability to sustain a long war – and in that we are not alone. We may have been wrong about the knockout blow; I still do not believe anyone is justified in saying that we were *certainly* wrong there. Right or wrong, that was our view and it was our duty to express it. And at least no one should judge the men of 1938 without understanding that that was the atmosphere in which decisions were made, or accuse the Air Ministry of failing to warn the government of the consequences of their continued refusal to face the country with the necessary burdens of rearmament.

The contents of the above minute may be compared with the views of Sir John Slessor. He believed that the Air Staff had become obsessed with the perils of the situation that the country faced in 1938, and were depressed with the apparent impossibility of arousing the government or the nation to the reality of those perils. It was not simply that the government frustrated the Air Staff with an obsession with Britain's economic limitations and the obstinate devotion to the principle of non-interference with the normal flow of trade. He asked if the Air Staff were blameless. Did they set their sights high enough, soon enough? There was none of the 'Dreadnought for Dreadnought' (battleships) that preceded the Great War. In its place Oxford undergraduates were debating peace. There was no appetite for war among the public nor was there a belief in the inevitability of war. Even the Prime Minister reflected the feeling of insularity when, on 27 September 1938, he referred to the Czechoslovakian crisis as 'a quarrel in a far-away country between people of whom we know nothing'. Slessor commented that the Prime Minister might have added, 'which we are selfish and stupid enough to believe is no concern of ours'.

Further Parliamentary criticisms of the Air Ministry

On 12 May the salaries of Air Ministry personnel were debated, and Sir Hugh Seely moved for a reduction of £100. This is parliamentary language for criticism. Sir Hugh pointed to the 8,000 German aircraft, of which 3,500 were front-line and would rise to 6,000 within the year. Under the latest scheme Britain would have 2,700 front-line aircraft in two years, and he reminded the House that when MPs inspected the Hurricane in June 1936 they were told that 340 or more would be completed by 1938. Sir Hugh then asked the Minister if he would deny that only twenty-eight were actually equipping front-line fighter squadrons. As for the Spitfire, he asked if the Minister would deny that only one was in existence. He went on to describe superfluity in certain types of aircraft, gun turrets and engines. Because of the unbusinesslike methods of the Air

Ministry, Seely proposed a Ministry of Supply. In particular he pointed to the number of overdrafts of firms that were not being paid on time for the products and services required by the expansion scheme. He criticized training, which he said had fallen behind. Operational training was practically non-existent, and bombing accuracy was worse than it had been before the expansion began, due to difficulties with new aircraft and the non-arrival of essential ancillary goods. Instrument and bad-weather flying had suffered, and armament training was held up because of an almost complete lack of gun turrets.

Earl Winterton and the Supplies Committee were blamed for the situation described above. One opinion was that he had not been in post long enough to master his brief, but he defended the Air Ministry by saying that delays in aircraft production were not always the fault of the Air Staff. The whole country had demanded disarmament, but was now demanding rearmament. The expansion scheme was not a panicky measure but a natural extension and acceleration of a rapidly growing Air Force. He ventured to suggest that relations between the Air Ministry and industry were close, and in a swipe at Winston Churchill he said that, even if the Archangel Gabriel was in charge the expansion scheme, 'It would not satisfy the Honourable Member for Epping'.

In the House of Lords, Lord Weir reminded Members that he had been responsible for the supply of aircraft in war, and he did not believe that it was wise to have a production department in the Air Ministry telling the aircraft industry how best to produce aircraft. With the change-over from biplane to monoplane designs, the introduction of power-operated gun turrets and installing bombs in bomb-bays meant that no one knew for sure the best production methods to adopt, and lessons were being learned every day in the factories. It was the duty of the Air Ministry to make preparations for war by such means as the shadow-factory scheme. Lord Londonderry pledged his support for Lord Swinton, the Air Minister, in planning the further expansion of the RAF, and said that he had personal experience of being a scapegoat. He believed that Lord Swinton should not be held to blame for delays in production. The criticisms were nevertheless wounding, and on 13 May he resigned, followed by Lord Weir and Colonel Muirhead the following day.

Sir Kingsley Wood becomes Air Minister

Lord Swinton's post was taken by the Rt Hon. Sir Kingsley Wood PC, who had been successful in all the positions he had held since his election to Parliament in December 1918. His last post before becoming Secretary of State for Air was as Postmaster-General from 1931 to 1935. Captain Harold Balfour was appointed as his under-secretary, after resigning his directorship of British Airways Ltd.

Sir Kingsley Wood.

The change in management did not stop the attacks by Parliamentary opponents. A fortnight after the change-over, Mr Hugh Dalton (Labour) went on the offensive. He wanted an independent inquiry into the management of the Air Ministry, given, as he put it, the growing public concern about the state of Britain's air defences. He was quite specific in his attack on RAF officers and officials at the Air Ministry. Except for Captain Balfour he claimed that no member of the Air Council had engineering qualifications, nor had any member of the Air Council done blind flying, navigated an aeroplane or fired a gun in the air. The new Air Minister had been brought in from the Post Office and his under-secretary from the Ministry of Agriculture, and neither man had any practical knowledge of air matters. Dalton then accused the higher elechons of the Air Ministry, where, he alleged, there was a lack of up-to-date knowledge of the vital problems. Turning his attention to the Department of Supply and Organization, he said it that was evident from many quarters that it was in a mess, and this was due to its director, Air Vice-Marshal Welsh, not being 'on top of his job'. As for the AID, Colonel Disney was credited with knowledge of telephone and wireless but not aircraft production muddles. Dalton finished by saying that there was a state of friction and jealousy between Air Ministry departments amounting almost to war.

This was a highly personalized attack upon individuals, and might have been expected from members of the Labour Party, which at that time had a pacifist wing. Chamberlain, in reply, did not deny that there had been delays and disappointments in the programme, which had to be altered and expanded from time to time. The problems stemmed from advances in technology, and the Prime Minister singled out the development of the all-metal aeroplane, the variable-pitch airscrew and new engines of unprecedented efficiency. His grasp of detail showed how well briefed he was when he came to the Dispatch Box. He went on to compare the production of a Ford V-8 engine, which had 1,700 parts, with a modern bomber, which had 11,000 parts in the engine alone, with 70,000 parts in the airframe, which required between 5,000 and 7,000 separate drawings. In rebutting the suggestion that RAF pilots could not navigate, the Prime Minister cited the case of the pilot of a Hurricane that had flown from Edinburgh to Northolt in forty-eight minutes, steering a correct course using instruments alone. But this still did not satisfy Churchill, who asserted that the Air Ministry and the War Office were absolutely incompetent to produce the great flow of weapons then required from British industry. He did not, however, press for an inquiry because he did not believe that it would help Sir Kingsley, so recently installed as the Secretary of State for Air.

Sir Kingsley's answer to these attacks upon the competence of members of the Air Ministry was to say that it was ridiculous to believe that there were serious breakdowns within the staff. He regretted the attack upon such a distinguished officer as Air Vice-Marshal Welsh, and hoped that the House would disregard comments made by Members that would imply that he was not an effective leader. Sir Kingsley did agree that special consideration must be given to supply questions, and he proposed to enlist the help of industrial experts. Lord Nuffield had already responded, and with Oliver Bowden, his vice-chairman, would help in the direction most needed, namely the provision of airframes. The vote at the end of the debate produced a majority for the government of 185. The House accepted that an inquiry into the efficiency of the Air Ministry at that time would hinder rather than help.

Separation of civil aviation from the Air Ministry

Civil aviation features prominently in Volume I of this inter-war encyclopedia. At the beginning of the 1920s there was little to distinguish between civil and military aircraft design, and it was asserted that the civil air fleet of a country could be used for bombing, i.e. with little adaptation would be needed to fit airliners for this purpose. Also during this period most civil airline pilots had been military pilots and flew in their retired ranks. In contrast, this volume has excluded almost all references to civil aviation. Civil and military aircraft design called for different qualities, such as fuel economy and comfort in airliners. Military and civil aviation grew apart to the point of separation, and on 23 August an Order in Council created a Licensing Authority for home airlines. Members of this authority were:

Chairman	A.M. Trustram Eve KC
	Major-General Sir Frederick Sykes*
	Mr F.R. Davenport

* Sir Frederick Sykes had been the Controller-General of Civil Aviation in the early 1920s, and for a very brief period the second Chief of the Air Staff.

To secure a licence, airlines had to submit all relevant information about the need and possibilities of proposed routes, details of the company's finances and description of proposed type of aircraft. The licence cost only £10, but it did involve firms in the chore of submitting multi-returns of activities.

THE MUNICH CRISIS

The Munich Crisis has been comprehensively covered in so many military and political histories of the period, and it illustrates the high point of the appeasement of the Fascist dictators following the rape of Czechoslovakia and the false hope of lasting peace in Europe. It also illustrates the sincere belief of a very English insular Prime Minister that any country's leader would respond to the voice of reason. It was only after the failure of Chamberlain's intervention on behalf of the government of Czechoslovakia that he realized that Hitler could not be trusted not to make further territorial demands in Europe. As far as this history is concerned, the extra twelve months from September 1938 to the outbreak of war was vital in building up Britain's strength in the air. At the time of the crisis there was partial mobilization, buildings were camouflaged, air raid shelters dug and sandbags filled with sand.

Preparations for war continued for war during the last few months of peace, but building up the strength in numbers does not, of itself, tell us that Britain was in a better position to meet German aggression in the air. Did the RAF have the right aircraft to fight the projected war in the air? These matters are discussed in Chapter 10 on strategic doctrine. The debate in the Commons, following Chamberlain's return from his meetings with Hitler, disclosed the feeling, particularly among leading Conservatives, that Czechoslovakia had been badly let down by giving in to Hitler's demands that the Sudetenland Germans and the Czech land they occupied

Sandbags and shelters!

Peace in our time!

should become part of the Third Reich. The Prime Minister's popularity fell, but the vote on the Munich agreement was 366 for and 144 against. Senior Conservatives who dissociated themselves from the agreement included Winston Churchill, Duncan Sandys, Anthony Eden, Robert Boothby and Harold Macmillan. Clement Attlee claimed, 'A gallant and democratic people has been handed over to a ruthless despotism.'

Meeting of the Air Member for Research and Development

Sir Wilfred Freeman's role and the changes made in the organization of the Air Ministry to cope with the demands of expansion at this time can be found in Chapter 10. As a member of the Air Council he had direct access to the Cabinet. On 30 September Freeman anticipated an immediate declaration of war over Czechoslovakia. On learning that Mr Chamberlain had returned from meeting Hitler with the now famous piece of paper, he held a meeting in his office that evening, where it was agreed that 'peace in our time' would give the RAF a few more months to get ready for war. Freeman therefore asked the Cabinet for a decision on timing. Should the RAF plan for a war in 1939 or continue with Scheme L, due for completion in March

1940? The Cabinet response was to decide to raise the first-line targets under Scheme L and to sanction industrial capacity for a so-called 'war potential' programme. This envisaged production of 1,700 aircraft in the first twelve months of a war beginning in October 1939 and for a wartime capacity of 2,000 aircraft a month by the end of 1941, for the government could not agree to wartime levels of production in peacetime. Right up to the outbreak of war in September 1939 there was a substantial gap between the peacetime programme (Scheme M) and the war potential programme.

When Hitler seized the rump of Czechoslovakia in March 1939 the Cabinet finally lost any illusions about the dictator's intentions, and seeing the vital importance of the work of Freeman's department, the Cabinet gave him the unprecedented privilege of dealing directly with the Treasury.

1939

Introduction

In spite of Chamberlain's brave words about 'peace in our time', the last year of peace began with the growing feeling about the inevitability of war. France had acquiesced in Britain's acceptance of Hitler's demands to annex the Sudetenland, and Chamberlain had had to return to meet Hitler again, this time at Bad Godesburg on 22 September, when the German dictator dismissed partition boundaries previously agreed and demanded the immediate occupation of a greater area of Czechoslovakia. This was conceded provided that it took place under international supervision. Once Chamberlain realized that, in spite of his best efforts, he had not succeeded in curbing Hitler's appetite for territorial expansion, Poland would be next.

With the benefit of hindsight, it is clear that had Hitler been stopped when the Rhineland was remilitarized things might have been different, and the country was in far greater danger from German attack in 1938 than it hd been in 1936. Undaunted, Chamberlain continued to try to find a peaceful solution, and he pledged the determination of the National government to continue, with all possible means, to eradicate all differences that would make for war. The military strength of Great Britain would be a decisive factor in the preservation of peace, which meant proceeding with all speed on the latest expansion plan. Indeed, in the Statement on Defence presented by the Prime Minister in the Commons on 15 February, the highest financial allocation ever was made to the three armed services. In 1937 the sum totalled £262 million, rising to £388 million in 1938 and £523 million in 1939. Parliament was asked to vote £66,561,000 for the air services after deducting appropriations in aid and other receipts from the gross of £220,626,700.

The Debate on Defence, 20/2/39

The Debate on Defence opened on 20 February. Sir John Simon spoke at length in support of the government, and Hugh Dalton spoke on behalf of the Labour Party. Simon spoke in support of the aircraft industry, claiming that inordinate profits were not being made, and moved the second reading of the Defence Loans Bill. Dalton criticized the high limit on government borrowing and the coordination of defence by questioning the wisdom of appointing a sailor to this task. One by one the protagonists on both sides 'caught the speaker's eye'. The leading dissidents from the Conservative benches had already been named, and Mr Hugh Dalton was emerging as the chief spokesman of the Labour Party. Mr Pethwick Lawrence, a one-time supporter of the Suffragettes, continued in support of Dalton, and moved an amendment regretting the necessity for an unprecedented defence programme, and he too spoke of the need for better coordination of the service departments and the elimination of excess profits. Sir Archibald Sinclair spoke in similar vein, defining the case for a Ministry of Supply. It was evident that the Opposition knew that rapid rearmament had to take place, and was therefore reduced to sniping at the way the public's money was being spent. With regard to excess profits being made by the contractors, Sir Kingsley Wood explained that if reasonable prices could not obtained, they would be fixed by arbitration. UK costs were lower than in the USA for corresponding service types of aircraft. He added that accumulated and accumulating knowledge of the cost and performance of each firm's previous contracts were known.

What worried the aircraft industry was getting the Air Ministry to ensure adequate backing for the supply of raw materials of every possible kind, ready availability of hand-tools and sufficient time for an extended clerical staff unaccustomed to aviation to order the wide-ranging necessities of every contract. The building of engines and airframes in the shadow factories by motor-car men was bound to throw up problems, but the aircraft firms were providing every assistance. When Lord Nuffield's Birmingham factory was switched from building Battles to Spitfires the jigging had to be changed, but orders for the already outmoded Battles had slumped, and the Austin factory at Longbridge could cope with the reduced demand. In spite of the continuing criticisms of the way rearmament was being managed, virtually the entire House of Commons could see that war was imminent, and the Estimates were accepted. The new provisions would take the RAF from 1,750 aircraft to 2,370 during 1939, together with an overseas strength of 500 aircraft and completion of expansion of the FAA.

The end of the Spanish Civil War

On 27 February the Prime Minister made the following announcement to the House of Commons:

> His Majesty's Government have given very careful consideration to the position in Spain and to the action they should take in light of all the information at their disposal. In these circumstances they have decided to inform General Franco of their decision to recognize his Government as the Government of Spain and formal action has been taken in this sense today.

Like it or not, a third Fascist dictator was being recognized in Europe, but short of intervening in the internal affairs of another state, HMG had no choice but to accept the accomplished victory of the Nationalist forces in the civil war. It nevertheless came as a relief to the British government that General Franco had declared the independence of Spain. Had Franco joined the Axis powers, the shift in the balance of military power in Europe could have proved catastrophic.

What was of greater significance for the RAF was the *Luftwaffe*'s involvement in the civil war, with the development of the *Blitzkrieg* form of warfare. As it happened, in the swiftly won German campaigns of the coming war the *Blitzkrieg* came to an abrupt halt once Hitler's men reached the English Channel. The *Luftwaffe* was not prepared for a radar-based defence system and the Hurricane and Spitfire fighting over home ground.

Postscript

The Labour government of Great Britain began the decade of the 1930s with a commitment to disarmament and the fact of a severe economic depression that would, in any event, have placed strict limits on defence spending. The 'Ten-Year Rule' about the possibility of a major war in Europe involving Great Britain was carried over from the 1920s, as was the modest expansion plan for the RAF begun in 1923. There followed a combination of factors that dramatically changed the defence stance of Great Britain. The first was the formation of a National government, with the National Liberals and Conservatives supporting the government, and the Labour Party, with its pacifist wing, largely going into opposition. The second was the failure of disarmament talks at Geneva, which meant that European powers had to reassess the effectiveness of alliances that might or might not be relied upon to provide mutual support in the event of the commission of acts of aggression. The final factor was the rise of the Fascist dictators, principally Adolf Hitler, which threatened peace in Europe in such a way that rearmament on a massive scale was vital to ensure national security. HMG always got the support it needed from both Houses of Parliament, with a vocal minority criticizing the way in which rearmament was being carried out. Winston Churchill was a constant and very vocal critic of the government in the 1930s, but was not given office until the outbreak of war. His inclusion in the government at an earlier stage might have had the effect of silencing him, but he might not have sat very comfortably in a Chamberlain Cabinet.

The successive Chiefs of the Air Staff had the support of the National government, and the necessary changes to the organization of the Air Ministry were made to cope with the rapid rate of rearmament involving the shadow factories. Looking back, one can say that, from the beginning of the expansion in 1934 to the outbreak of war and beyond, the resources of the nation and the Commonwealth were brought into play in time to meet the German threat. It was, nevertheless, vital to have the tacit support of the United States in the period before Pearl Harbor. After that the material support of the USA was to prove decisive in winning the war that ended in 1945.

On the declaration of war on 3 September 1939, a War Cabinet (see below) was formed. It is of interest to note that the politician who had done more than any in the 1930s to warn Parliament of the threat posed by Nazi Germany, Mr Winston Churchill, was back in the Cabinet, as First Lord of the Admiralty, the post which he had held at the outbreak of the Great War, and which prompted the message dispatched to units of the fleet, 'Winston's back!' Things had come full circle, but it was not long before Winston accepted the heavy burden of Prime Minister in 1940.

THE WAR CABINET FORMED ON THE OUTBREAK OF WAR, 3 SEPTEMBER 1939

Prime Minster
Mr Neville Chamberlain

Chancellor of the Exchequer
Sir John Simon

Secretary of State for Foreign Affairs
Lord Halifax

Minister for the Coordination of Defence
Admiral of the Fleet, Lord Chatfield

First Lord of the Admiralty
Mr Winston Churchill

Secretary for War
Mr Hore-Belisha

Secretary for Air
Sir Kingsley Wood

Lord Privy Seal
Sir Samuel Hoare

Minister Without Portfolio
Lord Hankey

SERVICE COMMANDERS
Chief of the Imperial General Staff
General Sir E. Ironside

British Commander-in-Chief of British Forces in the Field
Lord Gort VC

Commander-in-Chief of the Home Forces
General Sir Walker Kirke

First Sea Lord
Admiral of the Fleet Sir Dudley Pound

Chief of the Air Staff
Marshal of the Royal Air Force Sir Cyril Newall

Appendix A
Aircraft Technical Specifications

PART I – AIRCRAFT IN OPERATIONAL SQUADRON SERVICE BETWEEN 1 JANUARY 1930 AND 3 SEPTEMBER 1939 (EXCLUDING NO. 24 (COMMUNICATIONS) SQUADRON

PART II – NON-SQUADRON TRAINING AIRCRAFT, HIGH-ALTITUDE, HIGH-SPEED AND LONG-DISTANCE AIRCRAFT OF THE SAME PERIOD

Notes:
1. The information shown relates to a representative mark/version of the type.
2. Details of test flying and development are to be found in Chapter 5.
3. Aircraft by squadrons are shown in Appendix B.

PART I
SQUADRON AIRCRAFT
1. Armstrong Whitworth Atlas
2. Armstrong Whitworth Siskin
3. Armstrong Whitworth Whitley
4. Avro Anson
5. Blackburn Iris
6. Blackburn Perth
7. Boulton Paul Overstand
8. Bristol Blenheim
9. Bristol Bulldog
10. Bristol F2B
11. DH9A
12. Fairey IIIF
13. Fairey Battle
14. Fairey Fox
15. Fairey Gordon
16. Fairey Hendon
17. Gloster Gauntlet
18. Gloster Gladiator
19. Handley Page Hampden
20. Handley Page Harrow
21. Handley Page Heyford
22. Handley Page Hinaidi
23. Handley Page Hyderabad
24. Hawker Audax
25. Hawker Demon
26. Hawker Fury
27. Hawker Hardy
28. Hawker Hart
29. Hawker Hector
30. Hawker Hind
31. Hawker Horsley
32. Hawker Hurricane
33. Lockheed Hudson
34. Saro A7
35. Saro Cloud
36. Saro Lerwick
37. Saro London
38. Short R24
39. Short Rangoon
40. Short Singapore
41. Short Sunderland
42. Supermarine Scapa
43. Supermarine Spitfire
44. Supermarine Southampton
45. Supermarine Stranraer
46. Vickers Valentia
47. Vickers Victoria
48. Vickers Vildebeest
49. Vickers Vincent
50. Vickers Virginia
51. Vickers Wellesley
52. Vickers Wellington
53. Westland Lysander
54. Westland Wallace
55. Westland Wapiti

AIRCRAFT SPECIFICATION: (1)
ARMSTRONG WHITWORTH ATLAS

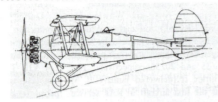

Span: 39 ft 6.5 in.
Length: 28 ft 6.5 in.
Wing area: 391 sq. ft
Weights: Empty, 2,550 lb
　　　　　Loaded, 4,020 lb
Power plant: One 450 hp Armstrong
　　　　　Siddeley Jaguar IVC

Armament/Bomb load: One fixed forward-firing Vickers machine-gun; one trainable
Lewis gun on scarff ring; four 112 lb bombs below wings

Performance
Max. speed: 142.5 mph at sea level
　　　　　124 mph at 15,000 ft
Climb rate: 5.5 min to 5,000 ft
　　　　　28 min to 15,000 ft
Endurance: 3.25 hr
Range: 480 miles
Service ceiling: 6,800 ft

Air Ministry Specifications:
Design Specification - 33/26 Prototype J8675
Production contract – 11/28 Production prototype J9951
Dual Control Trainer – 12/28 Prototype J8792
Army Co-operation Dual Control – 9/31 Prototype K2514

History
The prototype Atlas J.8675 made its first flight on 10 May 1925, and continued in production until 1933. Of a total of 446 aircraft built, 175 were dual-control trainers. The Atlas was the first to enter RAF service specifically designed as an Army-Cooperation aircraft. The Trenchard memorandum, setting out the shape of the peacetime RAF, provided for squadrons that would be earmarked for work with the Army in support of land operations. Hot-weather trials were conducted with No. 5 Squadron at Peshawar in 1927, since it was planned to use the aircraft to work with the Indian Army. These trials are described in Volume I, Chapter 4, and showed that the supercharged engine was unsuitable for use in hot climates. Both at home and overseas the Atlas proved to be a rugged and reliable aircraft. Work entailed spotting for the artillery, signalling results by radio, photographic reconnaissance, supply dropping, ground attack with bombs and machine-guns and message retrieval using a retractable hook pivoted on

the undercarriage spreader bar. The first squadron to be equipped was No. 26 Squadron at Catterick in October 1927. They then replaced Bristol Fighters on No. 208 Squadron in Egypt in 1930. They were also used as station communications aircraft and with the School of Photography. Eventually the Atlas was replaced in service by the Hawker Audax.

AIRCRAFT SPECIFICATION: (2)
AMSTRONG WHITWORTH SISKIN IIIA

Span: 33 ft 1 in.
Length: 23 ft 0 in.
Wing area: 296.0 sq. ft
Weights: Empty – 1,830 lb;
　　　　　loaded – 2,735 lb
Power plant: One 325 hp Armstrong
　　　　　Siddeley Jaguar III
Armament/Bomb load: Twin fixed synchronized Vickers guns.

Performance
Max. speed: 134 mph at 6,500 ft; 128 mph at 15,000 ft
Climb: 5 min to 6,500 ft; 8.5 min to 10,000 ft; 16.5 min to 15,000 ft
Service ceiling: 20,500 ft

History
Together with the Gloster Grebe, the Armstrong Whitworth Siskin was the first of the post-war fighters to reach squadron service as a replacement for the Sopwith Snipes of Great War vintage. There had been earlier versions of the AW Siskin, such as the Siddeley Siskin of 1919, but it was the Siskin III and IIIA that equipped RAF squadrons. The prototype Siskin III, J.6853, flew on 7 May 1923. It was all-metal and the first to have 'Vee' interplane struts. The first production aircraft, J.6981, which flew on 24 March 1924, followed the placing of contracts by the Air Ministry in 1923. From a total of 62 aircraft built for the RAF, 32 were built as two-seat trainers. No. 41 Squadron at Northolt received its Siskin IIIs in May 1924, and No. 11 Squadron at Duxford in the following June, to be replaced by IIIAs in 1927. These were the only two squadrons to be equipped with the IIIs, which could be identified by greater dihedral on the upper wing and the extension of the fin below the fuselage. What really distinguished the IIIA was its superior

performance at altitude, having a supercharged Jaguar IVS engine, and the prototype flew for the first time on 21 October 1925. Besides Armstrong Whitworth, Blackburn, Bristol, Gloster and Vickers produced the IIIAs, bringing the total to 343, to equip eleven squadrons. No. 56 Squadron was the last to operate the Siskin, until October 1932.

AIRCRAFT SPECIFICATION: (3)
ARMSTRONG WHITWORTH For Mk I WHITLEY

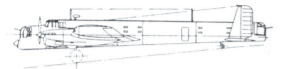

Span: 84 ft
Length: 69 ft
Wing area: 1,232 sq. ft
Weights: Empty: 14.275 lb
        Loaded: 21,660 lb
Power plant: Two 810 hp Armstrong Siddeley, Tiger IX

Armament/Bomb load
Four 0.303 in. Brownings in power-operated tail turret and one 0.303 in. gun in the nose turret.
Maximum bomb load – 7,000 lb

Performance
Max. speed: 184 mph at 7,000 ft
Cruising speed: 135 mph
Service ceiling: 16,000 ft
Range: 1,250 miles

History
The Air Ministry Specification was issued in July 1934. The Whitley's predecessor was the AW23 bomber transport, but unlike the latter, which had a low wing, the Whitley was a mid-wing monoplane. Following its maiden flight on 17 March 1936, the prototype K.4586 made its first public appearance in the New Types Park at the RAF Display, Hendon. The Air Ministry had chosen this aircraft to equip heavy-bomber squadrons, and in August 1935 a contract was placed for 80 aircraft. The first production **Mk I** (K.7183) was powered with the Tiger IX radial engines, and early production models had no wing dihedral, unlike later models. The **Mk II** version, which was delivered to the RAF in January 1938, was the first aircraft in RAF service with two-stage superchargers. The **Mk III**, delivered in August 1938, differed from all other variants in that it had a 'dustbin' ventral turret. The **Mk IV** version changed to a Rolls-Royce Merlin and sported a power-operated Nash and Thompson turret mounting Browning guns. This made it the first British bomber to be so heavily armoured. The major production version was the **Mk V**, with delivery commencing in 1939.

The Whitley I first entered service with No. 10 Squadron

at Dishforth, Yorkshire. With the Wellington and Hampden it was one of the mainstays of Bomber Command in the early years. Unlike the other two, however, the Whitley was used from the start as a night-bomber. It began the war dropping leaflets over Germany, known by the code-name 'Nickel'. There were six squadrons of Whitleys on the outbreak of war in No. 4 Group of Bomber Command. The remaining squadrons were with No. 6 Training Group.

AIRCRAFT SPECIFICATION: (4)
AVRO ANSON

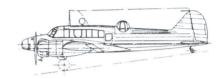

Figures for Mk I
Span: 56 ft 6 in.
Length: 42 ft 3 in.
Wing area: 410 sq. ft
Weights: Empty: 5,375 lb
        Loaded: 8,000 lb
Power plant: 2 x 350 hp Armstrong Siddeley Cheetah IX

Armament/Bomb load:
1 x 0.303 in. fixed gun forward
1 x 0.303 in. gun in turret
Bomb load: 360 lb

Performance
Max. speed: 173 mph at 7,000 ft
Cruising speed: 158 mph
Range: 790 miles
Service ceiling: 17,000 ft

Air Ministry Specifications: 18/35

History
This versatile aircraft spent 32 years in the service of the RAF, acting in the reconnaissance, training and light transport roles. It was a military development of the Avro 652 civilian six-passenger commercial aircraft used by Imperial Airways. The Air Ministry accepted the Anson design from the drawing-board in September 1934, and a prototype (K.4771) made its maiden flight at Woodford in Cheshire on 24 March 1935. It had a manually operated dorsal turret and the cabin windows were square and not round as in the civilian version. It was famous for needing 120 turns of a crank to raise the undercarriage.

Trials were conducted at the Coast Defence Development Unit in May 1935, pitting the Anson against the de Havilland Dragon Rapide, and in a fleet exercise held off the east coast the Anson demonstrated its superior range and endurance. In July 1935 an initial contract for 174 aircraft was awarded against Air Ministry Specification 18/35, which covered the production version with 38 modifications. The first production-version Anson I had larger cabin windows than the prototype, but the Cheetah IX engine specified for the production model did not become available until 1936. The first squadron to be equipped with the aircraft was No. 48 at Manston, and by the outbreak of war there were 760 Ansons in service, including 300 machines that were mainly in Coastal Command. Some Anson squadrons of Coastal Command were equipped with the Lockheed Hudson.

AIRCRAFT SPECIFICATION: (5)
BLACKBURN IRIS

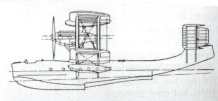

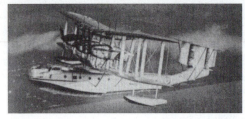

Span: 97 ft
Length: 67 ft 4¹/₂ in.
Wing area: 2,461 sq. ft
Weights: Empty: 19,301 lb
           Loaded: 29,000 lb
Power plant: 3 x Rolls-Royce
           Condor IIIB

Armament/Bomb load
1 x 0.303 in. gun in bows, midships and tail positions
Bomb load: 2,200 lb

Performance
Max. speed: 118 mph at sea level
Range: 470 miles
Endurance: 4.9 hr
Service ceiling: 10,000 ft

Air Ministry Specifications:

History
The Blackburn Iris saw RAF service from 1930 to 1934, at which time it was the largest aircraft in the RAF's inventory. It equipped only No. 209 Squadron, which was re-formed at RAF Mount Batten, Plymouth, in January 1930. It had three tractor engines mounted mid-way between the wings so that the arcs of the propellers were well clear of the water. Apart from building small single-seat flying-boats, this was Blackburn's first attempt to build a large, multi-engined, multi-crewed aircraft. The Iris I made its maiden flight in September 1926, and was powered by Rolls-Royce Condor engines. The hull was made of wood, whereas the Mk II had a new metal hull. The Iris Mk IIs were very active, featuring in the 1927 Baltic Cruise of British flying-boats, taking on board the Secretary of State for Air, Sir Samuel Hoare.

Another Iris boat took part in the search for the submarine H47, which had sunk off Plymouth, and when Sir Philip Sassoon made his 17,000-mile round trip in 1928 on an inspection of India, an Iris II took him on the greater part of that journey. Then there was the flight made by an Iris III, which made an 11-hour flight from Stornoway to Reykjavik, Iceland, on the occasion of the 1,000th Anniversary of the Icelandic Parliament. The final Iris III (S.1593) mounted a 37 mm COW gun in an enlarged bow cockpit. When the Iris boats S.1263, S.1264 and S.1593 were fitted with the more powerful Buzzard engines they became the Iris V. Aircraft S.1593 may be regarded as the prototype Blackburn Perth.

AIRCRAFT SPECIFICATION: (6)
BLACKBURN PERTH

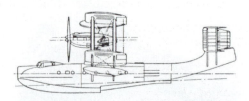

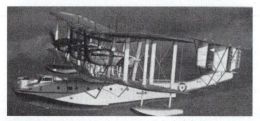

Span: 97 ft
Length: 70 ft
Wing area: 2,461 sq. ft
Weights: Empty: 20,927 lb
           Loaded: 32,500 lb
Power plant: 3 x 825 hp Rolls-Royce Buzzard II MS

Armament/Bomb load:
1 x 37 mm automatic gun;
1 x 0.303 in. gun in bows
1 x 0.303 in. gun amidships
1 x 0.303 in. gun in tail
Bomb load: 2,200 lb

Performance
Max. speed: 132 mph at sea level
Range: Max. – 1,500 miles
         Normal – 898 miles
Service ceiling: 11,500 ft

Air Ministry Specifications: 20/32

History
As the narrative on the Blackburn Iris shows, the Perth succeeded the Iris in more ways than one. The side elevation drawings disclose remarkable similar silhouettes. They shared the same Rolls-Royce Buzzard engines; indeed, the Iris V S.1593 was the prototype Perth. But there were important differences. There was a closed cockpit for the pilots, a navigation compartment with chart table, a wireless cabin, berths and a galley. We are not told who did the cooking! Besides the two pilots there was a navigator, wireless operator, engineer/ gunner and gunner.

The Perth was the largest and fastest RAF flying-boat in the biplane era. Like the Iris it had a 37 mm automatic gun mounted in the bows, which fired 1½ lb shells at the rate of 100 rounds per minute. This was in addition to the normal defensive armament of three machine-guns. The four Perths equipped No. 209 Squadron based at Mount Batten, Plymouth, and then at Felixstowe in Suffolk. They exercised mainly in the Irish Sea, often on exercises with the fleet. The Perth's only appearance at the RAF Display was in 1934, when it joined four other maritime aircraft to take off from Felixstowe to fly past the crowd in procession. Between October 1934 and July 1935 the Perths had to be withdrawn from service due to problems with the tail assembly. The prototype Scapa and Knuckleduster boats had to stand in while the problems were rectified. The Perth was withdrawn from service in 1936.

AIRCRAFT SPECIFICATION: (7)
BOULTON PAUL OVERSTRAND

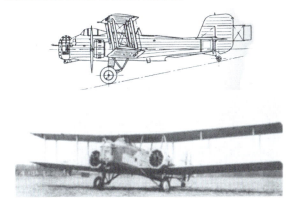

Span: 72 ft
Length: 46 ft
Wing area: 980 sq. ft
Weights: Empty: 7,936 lb
　　　　　Loaded: 12,000 lb
Power plant: 2 x 580 mph Bristol
　　　　　Pegasus II M3

Armament/Bomb load
3 x 0.303 in. in nose turret, mid-upper and ventral positions.

Performance
Max. speed: 153 mph at 6,500 ft
Range: 545 miles
Service ceiling: 22,500 ft

Air Ministry Specifications: 29/33, 23/34

History
No. 101 Squadron was destined to be the only RAF unit to be equipped with the Boulton Paul Sidestrand and its successor, the Overstrand. The squadron was the pioneer medium-bomber squadron, and its aircraft combined bomb load and range with the speed and agility of a single-engined bomber. Of these Bicester-based aircraft the Overstrand had the more powerful Bristol Pegasus engines. She also sported a revolving enclosed nose turret, an enclosed and heated cockpit for the crew and a large protective windshield for the mid-upper gunner. The power-operated front turret was a great success and improved the accuracy of the front gunner five-fold in air-to-air firing.

Twenty-four production aircraft were built at Boulton Paul's Norwich factory, but these were to be the last. As the remaining Overstrands were being delivered, the company had relocated to Wolverhampton. They made three appearances at the RAF Display in 1935, 1936 and 1937, but were then replaced in front-line service by the Blenheim.

AIRCRAFT SPECIFICATION: (8)
BRISTOL BLENHEIM

Figures for Mk I light bomber

Span: 56 ft 4 in.
Length: 39 ft 9 in.
Wing area: 469 sq. ft
Weights: Empty: 8,100 lb
　　　　　Loaded: 12,500 lb
Power plant: 2 x 840 hp Bristol
　　　　　Mercury VIII

Armament/Bomb load
1 x 0.303 in. machine-gun
　in port wing and one
　in dorsal turret
Bomb load: 1,000 lb

Performance
Max. speed: 260 mph at 15,000 ft
Cruising speed: 200 mph
Endurance: 5 hr
Range: 920 miles
Service ceiling: 25,500 ft

Air Ministry Specifications: 28/35

History
The Blenheim's performance was such that it could outpace contemporary fighters, and it is not surprising, therefore, that the Mk I version was built as a light bomber and a fighter. This was the Mk IF. The difference was in the armament. The armament for the light-bomber version is shown above. The fighter version had four 0.303 in. Browning machine-guns in a tray beneath the fuselage. The Blenheim was an enormous technical advance on the Hind biplane that it replaced.

This aircraft was ordered off the drawing-board, and the first contract for 150 was placed in August 1935. The first Blenheim (K.7033) prototype flew on 25 June 1936, and the first production aircraft left the factory in November that year. The first RAF squadron to receive the Blenheim was No. 114 at Wyton in March 1937. The brakes must have been a little fierce on this first batch, for one of the squadron pilots succeeded in performing a ground loop with one machine, and wrote it off.

By the outbreak of war there were 301 Blenheim Mk Is. in squadron service in the UK. The aircraft overseas were also Mk Is, and there were 99 in the Mediterranean , 70 in Iraq, 53 in India and 21 in Aden. When it was realized that, in combat, the fighter version would not be a match for aircraft like the Me 109, it was consigned to the night-fighting role.

AIRCRAFT SPECIFICATION: (9)
BRISTOL BULLDOG II/IIA

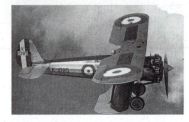

Span: 33 ft 11 in.
Length: 25 ft 2 in.
Wing area: 306.6sq. ft
Weights: Empty – 2,412 lb
       Take-off – 3,503 lb
Power plant: One 490 hp Bristol Jupiter VIIF Radial piston engine
Armament/Bomb load:
Two 0.303 in. Fixed machine-guns

Performance
Max. speed: 174 mph at 10,000 ft
Climb rate: 14 min 30 sec to 20,000 ft
Range: 275 miles
Service ceiling: 27,000 ft

Air Ministry Specifications: F9/26

History
The Bulldog was built to AM Specification F9/26, and the prototype flew on 17 May 1927, to be followed by the prototype Mk II, J.9480, on 21 January 1928. The Bulldog was chosen to replace the Siskin on RAF fighter squadrons after an Air Ministry competition involving the Hawfinch, Starling, Goldfinch and Partridge. Bulldogs entered service with No. 3 Squadron at Upavon in May 1929, and appeared in the Hendon Air Display that summer. By 1932 nine squadrons were equipped with this aircraft, and in 1935 No. 3 Squadron's Bulldogs were sent to the Sudan during the Abyssinian crisis. In spite of it being a spectacular aerobatic aircraft, it was not as fast as the RAF's light bombers of the early 1930s, and having comprised 70% of the RAF's fighter strength during the inter-war years it was replaced by the Gladiator in 1937, having been declared obsolete. 312 Bulldogs were supplied to the RAF, being Mk IIs and IIAs.

The IIA had certain refinements, including a redesigned oil system, a tailwheel to replace the skid, Bendix wheel-brakes and a modified fin.

AIRCRAFT SPECIFICATION: (10)
BRISTOL F2B

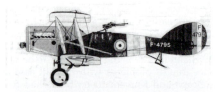

Span: 39 ft 3 in.
Length: 25 ft 10 in.
Wing area: 405.6 sq. ft
Weights: Take-off weight – 2,848 lb
Power plant: One 275 hp Rolls-Royce
       Falcon III water-cooled V Type
Armament/Bomb load: Two or three 0.303 in. machine-guns (One fixed and one trainable) and up to twelve 20 lb bombs

Performance
Max. speed: 123 mph at 5,000 ft
Endurance: 3 hr 0 min
Service ceiling: 18,000 ft

History
Of all F.S. Barnwell's designs the Bristol Fighter was the most successful. The aircraft originated as theR2A, which had a centrally mounted forward-firing Vickers gun and a single Lewis gun mounted on a Scarff ring in the rear cockpit. Deliveries began in December 1916 with No. 48 Squadron in France. They were operated as previous two-seaters, with the observer's Lewis gun being the primary weapon, but losses were heavy. Once the aircraft was flown as a front-gun fighter, the Bristol Fighter was an immediate success. With many hundreds more Bristol Fighters on order, the F2B version had wider-span tailplanes, modified lower centre-sections and an even better view from the front cockpit. It was this version that went on to serve with such distinction , not only during the First World War, but on air policing duties throughout the Empire during the 1920s. By the spring of 1918 the 'Brisfit',as it had been nicknamed, had established a formidable reputation, and enemy fighters could be relied upon not to attack more than two Brisfits at a time. Under wartime contracts more than 5,250 Bristol Fighters were ordered, and 3,101 are known to have been accepted by the RFC/RAF units by November 1918. The Americans also bought this design, but fitted unsuitable 400 hp Liberty 12 engines, which made their aircraft a failure.

The British version had the very successful Falcon engines, but the supply of these engines could not keep up with the demand, and other engines had to be considered, of which the Sunbeam Arab was the most widely used. They served in all wartime theatres, with squadrons on the Western Front, in Palestine and Italy, and No. 111 Squadron used them to transport Colonel T.E. Lawrence between General Allenby's Headquarters and the Arab guerrilla forces. The Bristol Fighter remained in post-war service until 1932, but in the air policing role it did not meet air opposition, and together with its stable-mate, the DH9A, it can be more accurately described as a general-purpose aircraft.

AIRCRAFT SPECIFICATION: (11)
AIRCO DH9A

Span: 45 ft 11 in.
Length: 30 ft 3 in.
Wing area: 487.0 sq ft
Weights: Empty – 2,800 lb ; max. take-off 4,645 lb
Power plant: One 420 hp Packard Liberty 12Vee – 12 Piston engine
Armament/Bomb load: One fixed forward-firing 0.303 in. Vickers machine-gun and one or two 0.303 in. Lewis guns on Scarff ring in rear cockpit; external pylons with provision for 660 lb of bombs

Performance
Max. speed: 123 mph
Endurance: 5 hr 15 min
Service ceiling: 16,750 ft

History
The DH9A, or Ninak, as it was fondly called, was the workhorse of the inter-war years in India and the Middle East in the air policing role. While classified as a general-purpose aircraft in the 1920s, overseas the Ninak started life as a bomber during the Great War, and continued as such in light-bomber squadrons at home. It was a refined version of the DH9 fitted with a 400 hp American Liberty engine, 3,000 of these engines having been ordered from the USA in 1917. Although only 1,050 of these engines reached the UK, there was a sufficient number to power the Ninaks constructed during the war. The larger engine meant bigger wings than those of the DH9. The fuselage was redesigned and a large frontal radiator fitted. By the time of the Armistice four squadrons in France had these aircraft, but since two of

these squadrons received their Ninaks in November 1918 the aircraft saw little operational service. After the war the Ninak remained in service, nearly 2,500 being built by a dozen British manufacturers, but predominantly Westland and de Havilland. These aircraft began to be replaced in the late 1920s by the Wapiti, and it continued only in the training role until 1931.

AIRCRAFT SPECIFICATION: (12)
FAIREY IIIF LANDPLANE
Note: the Fairey IIIF Floatplane details are not shown separately. Only the photograph is shown below.

Span: 45 ft 9 in.
Length: 36 ft 85/8 in.
Wing area: 438.5 sq. ft

Weights: Empty – 3,890 lb; Loaded – 6,041 lb
Power plant: One 455 hp Napier Lion XIA

Armament/Bomb load: One Vickers, one Lewis gun; bomb load – 500 lb
Performance
Max. speed: 120 mph at 10,000 ft
Climb: 6 min to 5,000 ft

Range: 400 miles with 80 galls 1,520 miles with 237 galls and no bombs

History
The prototype Fairey IIIF (N.198) flew on 19 March 1926, and was built to Air Ministry Spec. 19/24. Like the IIID, it was both a floatplane and a landplane, but had a much more streamlined appearance. Chapter 4 discloses its first operational use, with No. 47 Squadron in the Sudan and

then No. 8 Squadron in Aden and No. 14 Squadron in Palestine, in which case, as with the DH9A, Bristol Fighter and Wapiti, the term 'General-Purpose' was applied to the landplane. A three-seat reconnaissance version was built for the Fleet Air Arm. Production ended in 1932, with 560 having been built, of which 215 were of the Mk IV variety in use with the RAF. Air Commodore C.R. Samson led four Fairey IIIFs from Cairo to the Cape in March 1927 (Serial Nos 1141–4). These flights continued in 1928 and 1929, and in the early 1930s IIIFs flew to West Africa and took part in a joint reinforcement exercise with the South African Air Force, when over 9,000 route miles were flown by five of these aircraft. The Fairey IIIF floatplanes equipped No. 202 Squadron, Kalafrana, Malta (see photograph), when they replaced the IIIDs, and remained there until the Scapa flying-boats came into service. In the United Kingdom the IIIF was used both as a bomber and a communications aircraft. In December 1927 No. 207 Squadron, Eastchurch, received IIIFs in place of the ageing DH9As. Eventually they were replaced by the Fairey Gordon, a derivative of the IIIF. Two Fairey IIIFs, Serial Nos J.9061 and K.1115, were part of the No. 24 Squadron at Hendon used for VIP communications when time was of the essence. HRH the Prince of Wales flew in one during the 1930 Air Defence exercises, and was intercepted by Siskins. On another occasion Lord Londonderry flew to the 1932 Disarmament Conference in Geneva in one of these aircraft, which has been described as bad judgement, given that it was a military plane.

AIRCRAFT SPECIFICATION: (13)
FAIREY BATTLE

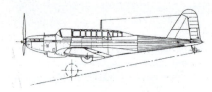

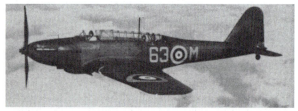

Span: 54 ft
Length: 42 ft 1³/₄ in.
Wing area: 422 sq. ft
Weights: Empty: 6,647 lb
        Loaded: 10,792 lb
Power plant: 1 x 1,030 hp Rolls-Royce
        Merlin I, II, III or V

Armament/Bomb load:
1 x 0.303 in. Browning gun forward and 1 x Vickers gun aft.
Bomb load: 1,000 lb

Performance
Max. speed: 241 mph at 13,000 ft
Cruising speed: 204 mph

Range: 795 miles
Service ceiling: 23,500 ft

Air Ministry Specifications: P7/32   P23/35   P32/36

History
The rapidly expanding RAF of the late 1930s needed a monoplane replacement for the biplane light bombers like the Hart and the Hind, which could only carry half the bomb load of the Battle. Sadly this aircraft did not live up to expectations. One entire group of Bomber Command was equipped with a bomber that lacked the power and defensive armament to look after itself in combat with fast monoplane fighters. By 1939 the Battle was already obsolescent, but since there was no suitable light bomber to replace it on the outbreak of war, it continued in first-line service until September 1940. By that time Battles had suffered grievously in the battle for the Low Countries, when German forces swept into Belgium and Holland.

The Air Ministry specification was issued in April 1933, and the first Battle prototype flew on 10 March 1936. This was K.4303, which later appeared in the New and Experimental Types Park at the RAF Display the same year. It went into production to AM Spec. 23/35, following an order to build 155 machines. With the introduction of the shadow factory scheme, the Austin Motor Company added to the productive capacity of Fairey's Stockport factory under AM Spec. 32/36. Out of a total of 2,200 Battles built, Austins had turned out 1,029 machines at Longbridge by October 1940.

Battles entered squadron service in May 1937, going firstly to No. 63 Squadron, Upwood, Huntingdonshire. They went on to equip about 15 squadrons of Bomber Command, and there were over 1,000 in front-line service on the outbreak of the Second World War.

AIRCRAFT SPECIFICATION: (14)
FAIREY FOX

Span: 37 ft 8 in.
Length: 28 ft 3 in.
Wing area: 324.5 sq. ft

Weights: Empty-2,609 lb; Loaded – 4170 lb
Power plant: One 240 hp Curtiss D-12 Felix
Armament/Bomb load: One Vickers gun forward + one Lewis gun aft. Bomb load: 460 lb

Performance
Max. speed: 156.6 mph at sea level; 150 mph at 10,000 ft.
Climb: 1.8 min to 2,000 ft, 39.75 min to 19,000 ft
Range: 500 miles at 130 mph
Service ceiling: 19,3000 ft

History
The original Fox prototype flew on 3 January 1925, and in August that year a demonstration in front of Air Chief Marshal Trenchard so impressed the Chief of the Air Staff that he promptly ordered a squadron of Foxes. This was to be No. 12 Squadron, which received the aircraft to replace its Fawns, but in spite of this aircraft's superb performance, financial economies meant that only 28 were built for the RAF. The Fox was 50 mph faster than the Fawns and could outpace the fighters of the day. In the Air Defence Exercises of 1928 the Fox evaded all fighter defences. The secret of the aircraft's success was its clean aerodynamic shape. With the radiators being mounted in the wings, the bulky front end of aircraft like the Fawn and DH9A was replaced by a streamlined nose, and the Scarff ring was replaced by a high-speed mounting to reduce drag. With the Curtiss D12 engine to power the Fox, a top speed of 156 mph was achievable. When the Rolls-Royce Kestrel IIA replaced the Curtiss engine, the aircraft was designated IA. The first production Fox flew on 10 December 1925, built to Air Ministry Spec. 21/25, and the Fox IA to Spec. 1/27. The Mark II was entered for the competition for a new light bomber to Spec. 12/26, but Fairey lost to Hawker with its new Hart light bomber. Although the Fox had a short life on only one squadron, Fairey showed that a streamlined appearance could be achieved with a water-cooled engine, and much impetus was given to British designers of the period.

AIRCRAFT SPECIFICATION: (15)
FAIREY GORDON

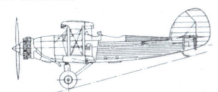

Figures for Mk I
Span: 45 ft 9 in.
Length: 36 ft 8⅝ in.

Wing area: 438.5 sq. ft
Weights: Empty: 3,500 lb
Loaded: 5,906 lb
Power plant: 1 x 525 hp Armstrong Siddeley Panther IIA

Armament/Bomb load
1 x Vickers gun forward
1 x Lewis gun aft
Bomb load: 500 lb

Performance
Max. speed: 145 mph at 3,000 ft
Cruising speed: 110 mph
Range: 600 miles
Service ceiling: 17,000 ft

Air Ministry Specifications: 18/30 14/33

History
Fairey IIIF Mk IVM, J.9154, was fitted with a radial engine, and made its first flight on 17 April 1929. It was then submitted for trials with No. 207 Squadron. J.9154 was fitted with a Jaguar engine, later exchanged for a Panther, which was to become standard on production Gordons. The Fairey IIIF was being developed into the Gordon, but the first definitive Gordon prototype was the converted IIIF Mk IVB, K.1697, which made its first flight on 3 March 1931, and was initially given the designation Fairey IIIF Mk V, but was then named the Gordon. It had an improved performance and a much better take-off when fully loaded. The order for quantity production was to AM Spec. 18/30. Those produced to AM Spec. 14/33 were designated Gordon Mk II. These had a modified rear fuselage, Frise ailerons and a tail assembly similar to that of the Fleet Air Arm version of the Gordon, the Seal. All the Gordon Mk IIs were shipped overseas. Out of a total of 272 Gordons built, 75 machines were converted Mk IIIs. In 1931, No. 40 Squadron at Upper Heyford was the first to receive the Gordon, and in the Middle East it was at last possible to pension off the Bristol Fighters of No. 6 Squadron.

At home No. 207 Squadron's Gordons were withdrawn in November 1937, but overseas both Gordon land- and seaplanes of No. 47 Squadron remained in service until December 1939. They were operationally deployed in 1935 in response to the Abyssinian crisis, and Nos 35 and 207 Squadrons were sent to the Middle East as part of a general reinforcement. In 1938 nine Gordons were lost in operations over Palestine. They served as target tugs at Air Armament schools, served with No. 4FTS at Abu Sueir and made a heroic defence of Habbaniya during the Iraqi rebellion in May 1941.

AIRCRAFT SPECIFICATION: (16)
FAIREY HENDON

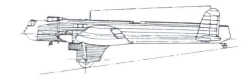

Span: 101 ft 9 in.
Length: 60 ft 9 in.

Wing area: 1,446 sq. ft
Weights: Empty:12,773 lb
Loaded: 20,000 lb
Power plant: 2 x 600 hp Rolls-Royce Kestrel VI

Armament/Bomb load
1 x Lewis gun in nose, midship and tail positions
Bomb load: 2,660 lb

Performance
Max. speed: 155 mph at 15,000 ft
Cruising speed: 133 mph at 15,000 ft
Range: 1,360 miles
Service ceiling: 21,500 ft

Air Ministry Specifications: B19/27 20/34

History
The Fairey Hendon entered RAF sercvice in November 1936 with No. 38 Squadron at Mildenhall in Suffolk. Although it was the first all-metal, low-wing cantilever monoplane in the RAF, marking a new advance in bomber design, it did not survive to see active service.The Hendon was replaced by the Wellington bomber in January 1939. The Air Ministry specfication was issued as early as 1927, and the Handley Page prototype, K.1695, first flew on 25 November 1930. Following an accident the prototype had its Bristol Jupiter engines replaced by the Rolls-Royce Kestrel IIIS. At that time it was called simply a Fairey night-bomber, and did not bear the name 'Hendon' until 1934. In that year it was on display in the New and Experimental Park at the RAF Display, where it attracted much attention at a time when biplanes still equipped most RAF squadrons.

The production of this heavy night-bomber was to AM Spec. 20/34, and between September 1936 and March 1937 fourteen were built. A later contract for 62 Hendons was cancelled. The Hendon II had more powerful Kestrel VI engines, an enclosed cockpit for the pilot and a nose turret in place of the open front gunner's cockpit. The fitting of three-bladed Fairey-Reed metal propellers was a further refinement.

AIRCRAFT SPECIFICATION: (17)
GLOSTER GAUNTLET

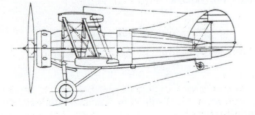

Span: 32 ft 9.5 in.
Length: 26 ft 2 in.
Wing area: 315 sq. ft
Weights: Empty: 2,775 lb
Loaded: 3,970 lb
Power plant: 1 x 645 hp Bristol Mercury VIS2

Armament/Bomb load
Two synchronized Vickers guns mounted in sides of the fuselage.

Performance
Max. speed: 230 mph at 15,800 ft
Range: 460 miles
Service ceiling: 33,500 ft

Air Ministry Specifications: 20/27 & 24/33

History
The Gloster Gauntlet was to be the last open-cockpit fighter of the RAF, and it equipped No. 19 Squadron at Duxford in May 1935. It would be replaced by a completely new generation of fighters two years later, the eight-gun monoplane Spitfire. So it was very much a question of 'out with the old and in with the new'. Fourteen squadrons of Fighter Command were equipped with the Gauntlet, but it left first-line service in June 1939, when No. 17 Squadron, North Weald, was equipped with Hurricanes. Only a few Gauntlets remained in two squadrons, No. 616 Auxiliary Air Force at Leconfield and No. 6 Squadron in Palestine.

The prototype Gauntlet was J.9125, which was ready to be shown off at the 1933 SBAC Display. It was designated the SS19B, a day- and night-fighter, and was itself derived from earlier designs, the SS18 and 19. All shared the same airframe, which was powered by a variety of engines. The SS18 fighter was built to AM Spec. F20/27, and the prototype flew in January 1929. When the SS19B performed well in its acceptance trials the Air Ministry ordered twenty-four of these aircraft, which were built to Spec. 24/33 and powered by the Bristol Mercury IVS2 engine, which was then uprated from 530 to 645 hp. These were followed by 104 Gauntlet IIs in April 1935, and a further 100 were ordered in September of that year. The Gauntlet IIs differed from the Mk I in having a new type of fuselage and wing spar structure. This followed the purchase of Gloster by Hawker Aircraft Ltd with the rationalization of production techniques. Some of the later Gauntlets had Fairey three-blade fixed-pitch propellers instead of the original two-bladed wooden type. The Gauntlet was, from 1935 to 1937, the fastest fighter in RAF service. It also had the distinction of being the first fighter to intercept another aircraft while directed by ground radar.

AIRCRAFT SPECIFICATION: (18)
GLOSTER GLADIATOR

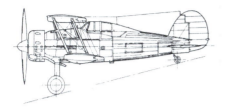

Span: 32 ft 3 in.
Length: 27 ft 5 in.
Wing area: 323 sq. ft
Weights: Empty: 3,450 lb
Loaded: 4,750 lb
Power plant: 1 x 840 hp Bristol Mercury IX

Armament/Bomb load
Four x 0.303 in. Brownings, two in sides of fuselage and two below the lower wings

Performance
Max. speed: 253 mph at 14,500 ft
Cruising speed: 210 mph
Endurance: 2 hr
Service ceiling: 33,000 ft

Air Ministry Specifications: F7/30 & 14/35

History
While the Gauntlet was the last RAF biplane open-cockpit fighter, the Gladiator was the last biplane fighter. The prototype K.5200 first flew on 12 September 1935, with the designation SS37. This aircraft had been built as a private venture, but was submitted for Air Ministry consideration to meet AM Spec. 7/30. It was in competition with other Goshawk-powered aircraft made by Westland, Supermarine and Blackburn. When it was decided not to proceed with the Goshawk engines in fighters, the specification was changed to 14/35, and the order went to Gloster for the Gladiator. The initial contract was for 23 machines. A further 202 were ordered between 1935 and 1937, and production continued with 280 Mk II machines between 1938 and 1940. By this time 490 Gladiators had been delivered to the RAF. It was unusual in combining a closed cockpit with biplane construction. The production aircraft differed from the prototype in having the later Mercury engine. From the 71st production aircraft the two Vickers and two Lewis guns had

been replaced by four 0.303 in. Brownings. The Mk IIs were powered by the Bristol Mercury VIII engines with Fairey-Reed three-bladed propellers.

The first Gladiators entered service with No. 72 Squadron in February 1937, and by September of the following year there were 96 of these aircraft in Fighter Command. As the Second World War progressed, it was inevitable that biplanes would be phased out, but Gladiators did see active service overseas, the most memorable time of which was probably the defence of Malta by just three aircraft, Faith, Hope and Charity.

AIRCRAFT SPECIFICATION: (19)
HANDLEY PAGE HAMPDEN

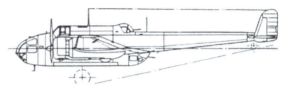

Figures for Mk I
Span: 69 ft 2 in.
Length: 53 ft 7 in.
Wing area: 668 sq. ft
Weights: Empty: 11,780 lb
Loaded: 18,756 lb
Power plant: 2 x 1,000 hp Bristol, Pegasus XVIII

Armament/Bomb load
One fixed, one portable 0.303 in. gun forward and twin 0.303 in. guns in dorsal and ventral positions
Bomb load max: 4,000 lb
Torpedo-bomber version carried one 18 in. torpedo and 1,000 lb external bomb load.

Performance
Max. speed: 245 mph at 13,800 ft
Cruising speed: 212 mph
Range: with 2,000 lb bombs – 1,885 miles
With 4,000 lb bombs - 1,200miles
Service ceiling: 19,000 miles

Air Ministry Specifications: B9/32 30/36

History
The Hampden was a medium bomber, which, unlike its contemporaries, the Wellington and the Whitley, did not have power-operated turrets. It was, however, more manoeuvrable and the fastest of the three. Indeed it was almost as fast as the Blenheim while carrying twice the

bomb load almost twice as far. The Hampden was the last of the twin-engined monoplane bombers to enter service with Bomber Command during the Expansion period. It was built to AM Spec. B.9/32, issued in September of that year. The prototype, K.4240, first flew on 21 June 1936, and was later displayed in the New Types Park at the Hendon Display. The photograph shows how slender was the tail, earning the aircraft the nickname 'Flying Panhandle'. It had leading-edge HP slats, which gave it a low landing speed of 73 mph. In August 1936 a production order was placed to AM Spec. 30/36 for 180 Hampdens, and the first production prototype, L.4032, incorporated a number of refinements. These included a streamlined perspex moulding in place of the square-cut nose of the original, a repositioning of the rear guns and a change to 1,000 hp Pegasus XVIII engines. Sadly it did not live up to expectations. The defensive armament was wholly inadequate, the crew conditions cramped and the fixed forward gun of little or no use. The rear guns had limited arcs of fire and there were significant blind areas. The Hereford, which was a variant of the Hampden, did not see operational service, for it was used instead as a bomber-crew trainer.

AIRCRAFT SPECIFICATION: (20)
HANDLEY-PAGE HARROW

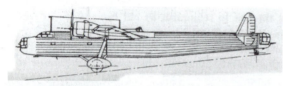

Figures for Mk II
Span: 88 ft 5 in.
Length: 82 ft 2 in.
Wing area: 1,090 sq. ft
Weights: Empty: 13,600 lb
    Loaded: 23,000 lb
Power plant: 2 x 925 hp Bristol Pegasus XX

Armament/Bomb load
Single 0.303 in. gun in nose, dorsal and ventral turrets and twin guns in tail power-operated turret.
Bomb load 3,500 lb

Performance
Max. speed: 190 mph at 19,000 ft
Cruising speed: 163 mph at 15,000 ft
Range: 880 miles
Service ceiling: 22,800 ft

Air Ministry Specifications

History
Like the Fairey Hendon and the Handley Page Heyford, the Harrow was one of the new generation of bombers that

were introduced to RAF service during the Expansion period but never actually saw operational service. When the Harrow bomber was finally withdrawn from service in December 1939, a number of machines were converted for use as military transports. This was the role for which it was originally conceived. The Harrow transports did see active service with No. 271 Squadron right up to the last few months of the Second World War. In September 1944, for example, Harrows were used to help evacuate casualties after the ill-fated Arnhem airborne operation. The transports had the turrets removed and faired over and the nose was reshaped to reduce drag. This version could carry 20 troops or other personnel or an equivalent load of freight. The Harrow has been originally designed as a transport and was adapted to become a bomber. Although not used operationally, it did give valuable service in training bomber crews to handle the new monoplane bombers.

AIRCRAFT SPECIFICATION: (21)
HANDLEY-PAGE HEYFORD

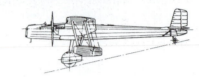

Figures for Mk1A
Span: 75 ft
Length: 58 ft
Wing area: 1,470 sq. ft
Weights: Empty: 9,200 lb
    Loaded: 16,900 lb
Power plant: 2 x 575 hp Rolls-Royce Kestrel IIIS

Armament/Bomb load
Three Lewis guns in nose, midship and ventral dustbins
Bomb load: 2,000 lb

Performance
Max. speed: 142 mph at 13,000 ft
Range: 920 miles with 1,600 lb bombs
Service ceiling: 21,000 ft

Air Ministry Specifications:
19/27   23/32

History
It was unusual, to say the least, that a biplane should have the fuselage attached to the upper wing. This did have the advantage of facilitating the rapid rearming of the bomber, since the lower wing was closer to the ground. The bombs were stowed in a thickened centre section of the lower wing. The Heyford was designed to AM Spec. 19/27, and the

prototype, J.9130, flew for the first time on 12 June 1930. The aircraft was ordered in quantity to AM Spec. 23/32, and the first production Heyford, K.3489, flew in June 1933. A total of 124 aircraft were delivered to the RAF before production ended in July 1936. From March 1935 production changed to the Mk II, of which 16 were built. Finally the Mk III appeared in September 1935. Seventy Mk IIIs were produced to AM Spec. 23/32.

The first Heyford Mk Is were delivered to No. 10 Squadron at Boscombe Down in August 1934, and the Mk II version joined No. 7 Squadron at Worthy Down in April 1935. In both cases the Vincent Virginia was replaced. The main production version was the Mk III, and this was delivered to No. 38 Squadron, Mildenhall, in September 1935.

Sadly it was not in battle that the Heyford would achieve notoriety. Seven aircraft of No. 102 Squadron were returning to Finningley from Aldergrove on 13 December 1936. As they climbed to cross the Pennines, ice began to form on the wings, and four were lost following accidents. This was Bomber Command's worst peacetime training disaster.

Hyderabad conversions. The two features that distinguished the two aircraft were that the Bristol Jupiter radials replaced the Lion engines, and the Hinaidi was built from metal, not wood. And so with better performance the Hinaidi could carry a greater bomb load. Only one new-build Mk I was produced by Handley Page, and this featured a 2.5% sweep-back of the outer wing panels. It was not until two years later that the first all-metal Mk II prototype was flown, on 8 February 1929, and this had a more pronounced wing sweep-back to counter a tendency to nose heaviness. In October 1929 No. 99 Squadron at Upper Heyford received the first Hinaidis, and these remained in service for four years until replaced by the Heyford, but the former continued to fly with the Special Reserve until 1935. In February 1928 Air Ministry Spec. C20/27 called for a troop carrier, and Handley Page responded with the Chitral, later to be named the Clive (both names have Indian connotations). The Clive was a Hinaidi development, and could carry twenty-three troops. Built in wood, then in metal, the Clive served in India with the Heavy Transport Flight based at Lahore.

AIRCRAFT SPECIFICATION: (22)
HANDLEY PAGE HINAIDI

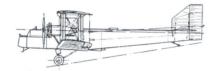

Span: 75 ft 0 in.
Length: 59 ft 2 in.
Wing area: 1,471.0 sq. ft
Weights: Empty 5,040 lb; Loaded 14,500 lb
Power plant: Two 450 hp Bristol Jupiter VIII
Armament/Bomb load: Three Lewis guns in nose, midships and ventral positions.
Bomb load: 1,568 lb

Performance
Max. speed: 122.5 mph at sea level; 115 mph at 10,000 ft
Cruising speed: 75 mph
Initial Climb rate: 495 ft/min; 16 min to 6,560 ft with 1,448 lb bombs
Range: 850miles

Service ceiling: 14,900 ft

History
The Handley Page Hinaidi was a heavy night-bomber that was derived from the Hyderabad, the two aircraft showing great resemblance. Indeed, the prototype Hinaidi, J.7745, was a converted Hyderabad and made its maiden flight on 26 March 1927. Even the first eleven Mk I Hinaidis were

AIRCRAFT SPECIFICATION: (23)
HANDLEY PAGE HYDERABAD

Span: 75 ft 0 in.
Length: 59 ft 2 in.
Wing area: 1,471.0 sq. ft
Weights: Empty- 8,910 lb;
        Loaded- 13,590 lb
Power plant: Two 450 hp Napier Lion II or 500 hp Lion V
Armament/Bomb load:
Three Lewis guns in nose, midships and ventral positions; bomb load: 1,100 lb

Performance
Max. speed: 109 mph at sea level
Cruising speed:
Initial Climb rate: 495 ft/min climb to 6,500 ft in 16 min
Range: 500 miles
Service ceiling: 14,000 ft

Air Ministry Specifications 31/22

History
The Handley Page Hyderabad was built as a heavy night-bomber, developed from the W8 commercial airliner. The prototype, J.6994, made its first flight in October 1923, built

to Air Ministry Spec. 31/22. The first production model, J.7738, was flown in December 1925, and was the last heavy bomber of the RAF to be built of wood. Only one Hyderabad, J.8813, was built to incorporate the HP leading-edge wing-slats. The first of these aircraft went to No. 99 Squadron at Bircham Newton in December 1925 to replace the single-engined Avro Aldershots, which had been in service for only a year. Air Ministry policy had changed to the effect that heavy bombers should not in future have to rely on a single engine. If a forced landing was made, a single-engined bomber would probably have to be dismantled unless a very long take-off run was possible. No. 10 Squadron at Upper Heyford was next to receive Hyderabads, but not until January 1928. Two cadre squadrons of the Special Reserve were selected in 1929 for re-equipment with these aircraft. These were No. 503 Squadron at Waddington, which had Fairey Fawns, and No. 502 Squadron at Aldergrove, Northern Ireland, which had Vickers Vimys. In all, 44 Hyderabads were built for the RAF.

AIRCRAFT SPECIFICATION: (24)
HAWKER AUDAX

Span: 37 ft 3 in.
Length: 29 ft 7 in.
Wing area: 348 sq. ft
Weights: Empty: 2,946 lb
            Loaded: 4,381 lb
Power plant: 1 x 530 hp Rolls-Royce Kestrel 1B

Armament/Bomb load
1 synchronized Vickers gun forward and 1 x Lewis gun aft.

Performance
Max. speed: 170 mph at 2,380 ft
            157 mph at 13,120 ft
Endurance: 3 hr 35 min
Service ceiling: 21,000 ft

Air Ministry Specifications:
7/31

History
The Audax was an adaption of the Hawker Hart to equip the Army Cooperation squadrons and units of the North-West Frontier (NWF). Produced to AM Spec. 7/31, the prototype was K.1438. This Hart variant could be distinguished by a message pick-up hook pivoted on the undercarriage spreader bar and by long exhaust pipes. The Audax was chosen to replace the Armstrong Whitworth

Atlas and to re-equip two Wapiti squadrons on the NWF. The first production Audax flew on 29 December 1931. By then it was the practice to distribute the production of Hart variants among the aircraft industry. Gloster, Avro, Westland and Bristol joined the parent company to produce the Audax. The large numbers produced exceeded the requirements of the Army Cooperation squadrons, and Audaxes were used as trainers in the newly formed FTSs and as an interim equipment in the growing number of bomber squadrons awaiting the Battle, Wellesley and Blenheim.

The first squadron to receive the Audax was No. 4 Squadron at Farnborough in December 1931, and it was not until 1937 that the Hector replaced the Audax on Army Cooperation squadrons. Abroad they did see active service in the early stages of the war with No. 237 (Rhodesia) Squadron, and at RAF Habbaniya during the 1941 Iraqi rebellion.

AIRCRAFT SPECIFICATION: (25)
HAWKER DEMON

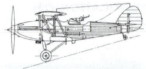

Span: 37 ft 3 in.
Length: 29 ft 7 in.
Wing area: 348 sq. ft
Weights: Empty: 3,067 lb 3,336 lb (Turret)
            Loaded: 4,464 lb 4,668 lb (Turret)
Power plant: 1 x 525 hp Rolls-Royce Kestrel IIS or 585 hp Kestrel V (DR)

Armament/Bomb load
Twin synchronized 0.303 in. guns
forward and one Lewis gun aft
Light bombs under wings in army
support role

Performance with Kestrel IIS
Max. speed: 182 mph at 16,400 ft
            155 mph at 3,280 ft
Service ceiling: 28,580 ft with Kestrel V
MaxSpeed: 202 mph at 15,000 ft
Service ceiling: 28,580 ft

Air Ministry Specifications: 15/30 6/32

History
The fighter variant of the Hawker Hart was the Demon, which had an after-turret to accommodate a gunner. There had not been a two-seat fighter introduced to the RAF since the Great War. The prototype was J.9933, built to AM

Spec.15/30, and was a converted Hart day-bomber with a fully supercharged Kestrel engine, twin forward-firing guns and an after-turret. Initially they equipped a flight of No. 23 Squadron, a Bulldog unit, as an experiment. This proved to be a success, and the entire squadron converted to the Demon in April 1933. Production of the Demon to AM Spec. 6/32 went ahead with the 525 hp Kestrel IIS engine, and then with the 585 hp Kestrel V. The parent company built 128 machines, and a further 106 were produced at the new Boulton and Paul factory at Wolverhampton, bringing the total Demon output to 234 aircraft. From October 1936 the Wolverhampton Demons were fitted with the Frazer-Nash hydraulic turret with a 'lobster-back' to protect the rear gunner from the slipstream. The production of Demons was the result of Air Ministry policy of obtaining greater front-line strength as quickly as possible, even if it meant retaining obsolescent biplanes. Demon squadrons were deployed in the Abyssinian crisis, and they were still in front-line service at the time of the Munich Crisis, but they had gone by the outbreak of war. They were replaced mostly by Blenheim IFs.

AIRCRAFT SPECIFICATION: (26)
HAWKER FURY

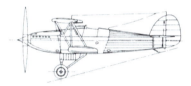

Span: 30 ft
Length: 26 ft 8.5 in.
Wing area: 252 sq. ft
Weights: Empty: 2,623 lb
Loaded: 3,490 lb

Power plant: 1 x 525 hp. Rolls-Royce Kestrel IIS

Armament Bomb load
2 synchronized Vickers guns

Performance
Max. speed: 207 mph at 14,000 ft
Range: 305 miles
Service ceiling: 28,000 ft

Air Ministry Specifications: 13/30

History
Those who flew the Fury knew how light and sensitive the fighter was on the controls. It had a fast rate of climb and was unsurpassed for aerobatic prowess. It was the first fighter in squadron service to exceed 200 mph in level flight.

In competitive trials with the Fairey Firefly IIM the Fury was declared the winner. The service requirement had been changed, and speed and rate of climb were then of greater importance than endurance.

The first Fury, K.1926, made its maiden flight at Brooklands on 25 March 1931. One hundred and thirteen Furies were built to AM Spec. 13/30. No. 43 Squadron at Tangmere was the first to be fully equipped with the Fury I in 1931 to replace the Siskins. Furies became the 'star turn' at the Hendon displays, with aircraft tied together while undertaking aerobatic manoeuvres. No. 1 Squadron formed at Tangmere with Furies in February 1932, the same month that No. 25 Squadron replaced its Siskins with the same. It was No. 25 Squadron that won every RAF fighter challenge during the years 1933–5.

The Fury remained in first-line service until 1938, when it was replaced on Nos 1 and 43 Squadrons by the Hurricane. The Fury I was also used as an advanced trainer at the various FTSs, as well as at the RAF College Cranwell.

AIRCRAFT SPECIFICATION: (27)
HAWKER HARDY

Span: 37 ft 3 in.
Length: 29 ft 7 in.
Wing area: 348 sq. ft
Weights: Empty: 3195 lb
Loaded: 5,005 lb
Power plant: 1 x 530 hp Rolls-Royce Kestrel IB or Kestrel X

Armament/Bomb load
1 synchronized Vickers and 1 Lewis gun aft Two supply containers or 500 lb bomb load under wings

Performance
Max. speed: 161 mph at sea level
Range: 380 miles
Service ceiling: 17,000 ft

Air Ministry Specifications: G23/33

History
The Hardy was yet another Hart derivative. It bore a general resemblance to the Audax, but since it was to be employed as a general-purpose aircraft in the Middle East it was equipped for more than Army Cooperation work. The prototype, K.3013, was a converted Hart built to AM Spec. G23/33. In addition to the usual message pick-up hook, it

had supply containers under the wings. Ever mindful of the harsh treatment meted out to tyres when landing on rough desert strips, later Hardy aircraft had 'doughnut' mainwheel tyres.

Production began in 1936, and 47 machines were built exclusively in the Gloster factory. The Hardy first entered service with No. 30 Squadron, Mosul, in April 1935, replacing the Wapiti. In 1938 the squadron's aircraft were replaced with Blenheims, and the Hardys were transferred to No. 6 Squadron, where they were used in the Palestine disturbances by cooperating with the 16th Infantry Brigade. They remained operational until replaced by Lysanders. The Hardy equipped No. 237 Squadron, which used it in action against the Italians in East Africa.

AIRCRAFT SPECIFICATION: (28)
HAWKER HART

Span: 37 ft 3 in.
Length: 29 ft 4 in.
Wing area: 348 sq. ft
Weights: Empty: 2,530 lb
Loaded: 4,554 lb
Power plant: 1 x 525 hp Rolls-Royce Kestrel IB or 510 hp Kestrel X (DR)

Armament/Bomb load
1 synchronized Vickers forward
1 Lewis gun aft
Bomb load 500 lb

Performance
Max. speed: 184 mph
172 mph at 10,000 ft
Cruising speed:
Range: 430 miles
Service ceiling: 21,320 ft

Air Ministry Specifications: 12/26 9/29

History
Hawker submitted the Hart to the Air Ministry to meet AM Spec. 12/26, and it was chosen as the new standard light day-bomber after being in competition with the DH Hound and the Avro Antelope. The prototype, J.9052, made its maiden flight in June 1928, and the production of 15 development aircraft to AM Spec. 9/29 permitted the equipment of No. 33 Squadron at Eastchurch. The production total was in fact 459 machines. The Hart (India) variants served on the North-West Frontier and had extra cooling vents on the engine to cope with tropical conditions. Ninety (Special) variants operated mainly in Kenya, Palestine, Aden and Egypt, and were interim equipment on Nos 17 and 40 Squadrons at home. A few were in use as communication aircraft on No. 24 Squadron.

They were fast, manoeuvrable aircraft that outmatched the Bulldog and Siskin fighters in the 1930 Air Exercises. This was not a new phenomenon, for the Fairey Fox light-bomber was also faster than the opposing fighters in the air exercises of the late 1920s. Between 1930 and 1936 Harts equipped eight regular home-based squadrons, and from 1933 they were used by ten Auxiliary squadrons, where they remained until 1938. They replaced the Wapiti in India and were deployed to the Middle East during the Abyssinian crisis. At the 1935 Royal Jubilee Display, 45 Harts and 36 Audaxes flew past the saluting base. Not surprisingly, people began to call the RAF the 'Hawker Air Force'. The Hart was eventually superseded by the Hawker Hind.

AIRCRAFT SPECIFICATION: (29)
HAWKER HECTOR

Span: 36 ft 11³/₈ in.
Length: 29 ft 9.75 in.
Wing area: 346 sq. ft
Weights: Empty: 3,389 lb
Loaded: 4,910 lb
Power plant: 1 x 805 hp Napier Dagger IIIMS

Armament/Bomb load
1 synchronized Vickers gun forward and 1 Lewis gun aft 2 x 112 lb bombs or supply containers below wings

Performance
Max. speed: 187 mph at 6,500 ft
171 mph at 16,400 ft
Range: 300 miles
Service ceiling: 24,000 ft

Air Ministry Specifications:

History
The Hector was the last of the Hart variants to remain in RAF service. It was designed as a replacement for the Audax, but differed in two respects from the other Hart

variants. One has only to look at the photograph to see that the usual streamlined nose has been replaced by a more rectangular shape. This is because the usual Kestrel engine has been replaced by a 24-cylinder, air-cooled, in-line Dagger engine, with the cylinders arranged like a letter 'H'. Secondly, the usual sweep-back of the upper wing has gone. The wings on the Hector were straight to compensate for the change in the centre of gravity resulting from the introduction of the Dagger engine. The original design in what was first called the Dagger Hart did have a sweep-back on the upper wing. The first production Hector, K.3719, flew on 14 February 1936, and the Air Ministry placed an initial production order for 78 machines, later increasing it by 100 in May of that year. It was decided that all the production Hectors should be carried out by Westland of Yeovil, and the final production aircraft was delivered in December 1937.

Nos 4 and 13 Squadrons at Odiham were first to be equipped with the Hector, and they appeared in the last RAF Hendon Display. In all, they equipped six Army Cooperation squadrons and five squadrons of the Auxiliary Air Force. The squadrons were eventually equipped with the Lysander, except Nos 53 and 59 Squadrons, which received the Blenheim Mk IVs for night reconnaissance and Army support.

AIRCRAFT SPECIFICATION: (30) HAWKER HIND

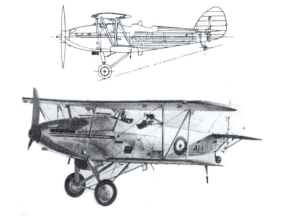

Span: 37 ft 3 in.
Length: 29 ft 7 in.
Wing area: 348 sq. ft
Weights: Empty: 3,195 lb
Loaded: 4,657 lb
Power plant: 1 x 640 hp Rolls-Royce Kestrel V

Armament/Bomb load
1 synchronized 0.303 Vickers gun forward. 1 Lewis gun aft. Bomb load: 500 lb

Performance
Max. speed: 186 mph at 16,400 ft
Range: 430 miles
Service ceiling: 26,400 ft

Air Ministry Specifications: G7/34

History
The Hind was a derivative of the Hart light day-bomber. It equipped light-bomber squadrons at a time when expansion was taking place. The new monoplanes, like the Battle and the Blenheim, were not then in quantity production to equip the growing number of squadrons, and so the Hind constituted an interim equipment. The prototype, K.2915, first flew on 12 September 1934, and was designed in response to AM Spec. G5/34. The principal difference between it and the Hart was the fully supercharged Kestrel V engine, the cut-away rear cockpit, a tailwheel instead of a tailskid, and various other refinements.

The Hind went to No. 21 Squadron at Bircham Newton in December 1935, and over the following year the remaining Hart squadrons were re-equipped with this aircraft. By mid-1937 there were twenty-six squadrons of Hinds in Nos 1 and 2 Groups of Bomber Command. In addition there were thirteen Auxiliary squadrons at home, and Nos 113 and 211 Squadrons overseas all equipped with this light day-bomber. Bomber Command had replaced all its Hinds by the time of the Munich Crisis in 1938, and the Auxiliary squadrons followed thereafter.

AIRCRAFT SPECIFICATION: (31) HAWKER HORSLEY

Span: 56 ft 5.75 in.
Length: 38 ft 10 in.
Wing area: 693.0sq. ft
Weights: Empty- 4,760 lb; take-off- 7,800 lb
Power plant: One 665 hp Rolls-Royce Condor IIIA in-line piston engine
Armament/Bomb load: Two 0.303 in. machine-guns, one fixed and one trainable and up to 1,500 lb of bombs or one 18in torpedo

Performance
Max. speed:125 mph at 6,000 ft
Climb: to 15,000 ft in 23 min
Endurance: 10 hr 0 min
Service ceiling: 14,000 ft

Air Ministry Specification 24/25

History

The Hawker Horsley day bomber was designed to Air Ministry Spec.26/23 and the prototype J7511 flew in 1925 and was named after T.O.M. Sopwith's residence at East Horsley, Surrey. Production began in July 1926 and ended in November 1931 during which time 133 were built for the RAF. The MkI and MkII versions were day bombers and a torpedo bomber version was built to Air Ministry Spec.24/25 first flown in May 1927. Forty-eight torpedo bombers in all were built. Early production models were built in wood, then wood/metal and finally all-metal. In the day bombing role the Horsley replaced the Fawns of No.100 Squadron in August 1926 followed by No.11 Squadron in January 1927. The torpedo bomber version went to the newly re-formed No.36 Squadron at Donibristle, Scotland in October 1928 and in 1930 the Squadron, with its all-metal Horsleys became the first land based torpedo squadron to be based overseas when it moved to Singapore. The Horsley is also remembered for a long-haul flight when Flight Lieutenant C.R.Carr with Flight Lieutenant L.E.M. Gillman as his navigator left Cranwell in Serial No. J.8607 for a non-stop flight to India only to be forced down in the Persian Gulf after completing 3,420 miles in 34½ hours The Horsley ceased to be employed as a bomber in March 1930 when Hawker Harts replaced the former on No.33 Squadron, Eastchurch. The torpedo bombers of Nos.100 & 36 Squadrons were phased out in 1932 and 1935 respectively. No.504 (County of Nottingham) Special Reserve Squadron at Hucknall retained its Horsleys until March 1934 and they saw out their days as target towing aircraft at Kai Tak, Hong Kong until February 1937.

AIRCRAFT SPECIFICATION: (32)
HAWKER HURRICANE

Figures for Mk.I
Span: 40 ft
Length: 3 ft 5 in.
Wing area: 257.5sq. ft
Weights: Empty: 4,670 lb
        Loaded: 6,600 lb

Power plant: 1 x 1,030 hp Rolls-Royce Merlin II or III

Armament/Bomb load
8 x 0.303 in. Browning guns in the wings

Performance
Max. speed: 316 mph at 17,500 ft
Service ceiling: 33,200 ft

Air Ministry Specifications:

History

Like the Spitfire, the Hurricane was to be equipped with eight Browning machine-guns mounted in the wings. In both aircraft this was a significant increase in fire power and a shift from the usual positioning of fixed forward firing machine-guns. In January 1934 it was decided not to use the Goshawk engine but the new Rolls-Royce PV12 engine, later famously known as the Merlin, again like the Spitfire. In one important respect, however, the two aircraft differed. While both aircraft had metal stressed-skin wings the Hurricane retained the fabric covered fuselage of its Hawker predecessors going back to the 1920s.

The first prototype was K5083 which made its maiden flight on 6 November 1935. The Board of Directors were impressed enough with its performance to prepare to produce 1,000 machines even before receiving an Air Ministry contract. The latter was not long coming and an initial order for 600 machines was placed. The first production machine, L1547, differed from the prototype in having a 1,030 hp Merlin II engine, a modified cockpit canopy and exhaust pipes and redesigned undercarriage fairings.

One could fill a book with the design developments and war time history of this most famous fighter aircraft. It may not have been as manoeuvrable and fast as the Spitfire but it provided a more stable gun platform and was responsible for shooting down more enemy aircraft than all the other air and ground defences put together.

AIRCRAFT SPECIFICATION: (33)
LOCKHEED HUDSON

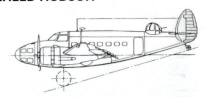

Span: 65 ft 6 in.
Length: 44 ft 4 in.
Wing area: 551sq. ft
Weights: Empty: 12,000 lb
        Loaded: 17,500 lb
Power plant: 2 x 900 hp Wright Cyclone R –1820-G 102A

Armament/Bomb load

Twin fixed 0.303 in. gun forward
Twin 0.303 in. guns in dorsal
Turret an 1 x 0.303 in. gun in ventral position. Provision for 2 x 0.303 in. guns in beam positions. Bomb load; 750 lb

Performance
Max. speed: 222 mph at 7,900 ft
Cruising speed: 170 mph
Range: 1,370 miles
Endurance: 6 hr
Service ceiling: 27,000 ft

Air Ministry Specifications:

History
The Lockheed Hudson was the first American built aircraft to serve with the RAF in World War II and eventually replaced the much shorter range Avro Ansons. The Hudson was a military version of the Lockheed 14 Super Electra airliner and was ordered for the RAF by the British Purchasing Commission in the USA in June 1938. The initial order for 200 aircraft caused something of a storm in Britain since many believed that it was wrong for the RAF to use any other than home designed and built aircraft. Be that as it may the Hudsons were effective in harrying U-boats from the air. The original intention was to use them as navigation trainers but the RAF was critically short of maritime patrol aircraft when the war began.

Some of the original order for 200 aircraft were diverted to Canada for service with the RAF but orders for the Mk.IIs were in hand. The Mk.I Hudson entered service with No.224 Squadron in May 1939 to replace the Anson and, by the outbreak of war, had been joined by No.233 Squadron at Leuchars while a third squadron, No.220, was converting from Ansons at Thornaby.

AIRCRAFT SPECIFICATION: (34)
SARO A7

Span: 88 ft
Length: 64 ft 6 in.
Wing area: 1,557 sq. ft

Weights: Empty: 14,800 lb
Normal loaded: 22,000 lb
Max.Overload tested: 25,750 lb

Power plant: 3 X 490 hp Bristol Jupiter XIFP

Armament/Bomb load
3 X 0.303 in. Lewis guns in bow, dorsal and tail postns.
4 X 500,520 or 550 lb bombs or
8 X 230 lb bombs

Performance
Max. speed: 126 mph
Cruising speed: 96 mph at 22,000 lb
Endurance: 6 hr
Service ceiling: 8,930 ft
Absolute ceiling estimated: 10,800 ft

History
Built to AM Spec R.4/27 called for a large, multi-engined metal-hulled flying boat for maritime patrol duties. The Saunders Roe patented method of hull construction involved longitudinal corrugations which dispensed with the need for riveted stringers. Work on the A7 began in July 1927 and construction was almost complete by late 1929. The launch date, according to MAEE records, was 10 July 1931. Company trials were carried out by Stuart Scott and the prototype N.240 then went to MAEE Felixstowe for trials. The flying boat was found to be under elevatored and very heavy on the rudders. These defects were remedied at Cowes. A proving cruise was planned for N240 which left Felixstowe for Mount Batten en route for Aboukir 15 August 1931 returning on 16 September. Corrosion was found to be minimal and the hull structure was found to be generally intact but there were problems to the elevators, rib failures in the top mainplane, dazzle from the forward decking which tended to give the pilot and co-pilot a blinding headache and various panels dropped off at frequent intervals. The Air Ministry took the view that the many defects of the flying boat made it unacceptable and no production orders were forthcoming. The A.7 was abandoned in favour of the R.24/31 which incorporated some of the broad design features of the A7 though it was considerably stronger. The A7 went into service with No.209 Squadron for maritime patrol duties as an interim measure in February 1932 but was withdrawn in the July.

AIRCRAFT SPECIFICATION: (35)
SARO CLOUD

Span: 64 ft
Length: 48 ft 8 in.
Wing area: 650sq. ft
Weights: Empty: 6,800 lb
Loaded: 9,500 ft
Power plant: 2 x 340 hp Armstrong Siddeley Serval (Double Mongoose)

Armament/Bomb load
Provision for gun mountings in bow and aft compartments and 4 x 50 lb practice bombs beneath the wings

Performance
Max. speed: 118 mph
Cruising speed: 95 mph
Range: 380 miles
Service ceiling: 9,430 ft

Air Ministry Specifications: 15/32

History
Like its civil counterpart the Saro Cutty Sark, the Cloud was built both as a flying boat and an amphibian. The RAF placed an order for the Cloud built to A.M.Spec.15/32. This amphibian could be used for the instruction of flying boat pilots before moving on to bigger boats as well as providing a flying classroom for navigators. The high wing and spacious cabin offered plenty of room for chart tables and a good view below. The Cloud first entered service with B Flight of the Seaplane Training Squadron, Calshot in August 1933. 'A' Flight had the Sea Tutor floatplanes where pilots would qualify before passing to B Flight for instruction on the Cloud. Finally pilots would pass to the Southampton before being posted to a squadron.

The School of Air Pilotage at Andover was also equipped with the Cloud and in January 1936 No. 48 Squadron at Manston received these amphibians, which were replaced by Ansons a few months later. Only sixteen Clouds were built the last being delivered in January 1935.

AIRCRAFT SPECIFICATION: (36)
SARO LERWICK

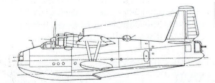

Figures for MkI
Span: 80 ft 10 in.
Length: 63 ft 7.5 in.
Wing area: 845sq. ft
Weights: Loaded: 28,500 lb (normal)
Loaded: 33,200 lb (max)

Power plant: 2 x 1,375 hp Bristol Hercules II or IV

Armament/Bomb load
One Vickers guns in bow turret, twin Browning guns in dorsal turret and four Brownings in tail turret.
Bomb load: 4 x 500 lb or 8 x250 lb or equivalent weight in depth charges

Performance
Max. speed: 213 mph
Cruising speed: 165 mph
Range: 1540 miles
Service ceiling: 14,000 ft

Air Ministry Specifications: R1/36

History
The Lerwick was not a success. Handling characteristics were poor and there are no records of this flying boat scoring any successes against enemy shipping or submarines in the early part of World War II. The Lerwick served for less than three years before being withdrawn from service. Twenty one Lerwicks were built to A.M.Spec. R1/36 the last being delivered in June 1941. No.240 Squadron at Calshot received Nos.L7250 and L7251 in July 1939 but these aircraft were totally inadequate and were withdrawn. Although Lerwicks did equip No. 209 Squadron at Oban in December 1939 it was found to have unpleasant handling characteristics. The aircraft suffered from lateral instability and a viscous stall resulting in several accidents. They did not handle well on water and the serviceability rates were poor. Constant modifications did not cure the problems and the boats were finally withdrawn in October 1942.

AIRCRAFT SPECIFICATION: (37)
SARO LONDON

Figures are for the Mk.II
Span: 80 ft
Length: 56 ft 9.5 in.
Wing area: 14,255sq. ft
Weights: Empty 12,800 lb
Loaded 19,300 lb
Power plant: Two 1055 hp Bristol Pegasus X
Armament/Bomb load
3 X Lewis Guns in bows and midships. Bomb load 2,000 lb or equivalent in depth charges

Performance
Max. speed: 155 mph @ 6,250
Cruising speed: 106 mph
Endurance: 5.2 hr
Range Max. – 1740 miles
          Normal 1,100 miles
Service ceiling: 18,000 ft

Air Ministry Specifications: R24/31 R3/35

History
The Saro London prototype, K3560, built to A.M.Spec.R24/31 first flew in 1934 and in March 1935 the Air Ministry placed an order for the London Mk.I, the first ten of which had the Pegasus III engine. Tests were carried out at Felixstowe, following receipt of AM Spec.R3/35., which resulted in the installation of the Pegasus X engine fitted with circular cowlings and four-blade propellers. Starting with the eleventh production aircraft this was the London Mk.II. The final Saro London left the Cowes works on May 1938.

The London replaced the Southampton boats on No.201 Squadron in April 1936 and the Scapa boats in the October on No.204 Squadron at Mount Batten in Plymouth. Overseas the London boats went to No.202 Squadron in Malta in October 1937 but these were moved to Gibraltar on the outbreak of war.

From December 1937 to May 1938 five London boats made an historic 30,000 mile flight from Mount Batten to New South Wales for which special long-range fuel tanks were fitted. These increased the maximum range from 1,740 to 2,600 miles. The Londons were also engaged in active patrols in the Mediterranean during the Spanish Civil War. They were finally superseded on No.202 Squadron by Catalinas.

AIRCRAFT SPECIFICATION: (38)
SHORT R24

Span: 90 ft
Length: 63 ft 3 in.
Wing area: 1,147 sq. ft
Weights: Empty: 11,720 lb
          All-up Weight: 18,500 lb
Power plant: 2 X Steam-cooled Rolls-Royce Goshawk engines

Armament/Bomb load
3 X 0.303 in. Lewis in the bow, midships and aft all mounted on Scarff rings. Bombs on underwing racks

Performance
Max. speed: 150 mph
Range: 1,040 miles
Service ceiling: 15,500 ft

History
Nicknamed the 'Knuckleduster, the Short R/24/31 was its AM Spec., which called for a twin-engined general purpose flying boat, capable of flying on one engine and suitable for long-range patrols with a crew of five. The specification also called for an aircraft that was easy to maintain and a recommendation was made that it be constructed in Alclad with longitudinal corrugations instead of riveted-on stringers. Three prototypes were ordered and Saro and Supermarine submitted designs for biplanes with Pegasus engines. The Short Brothers prototype received their request for a more ambitious monoplane design with experimental Rolls-Royce Goshawk steam-cooled engines. The cranked wing was designed to place the airscrews well clear of the spray on take-off. Construction began in early 1933 and the serial number K.3574 was assigned to it. The pilot and navigator sat side by side in an enclosed cockpit. The front gunner was also a bomb aimer. The maiden flight was made 29 November 1933 but early trials disclosed problems with the rudders and major modifications had to be made to the tail unit. Later the flying boat was successfully dived at speeds of over 200 mph. This was the first time this had been done to a military flying boat by the contractor's test pilot. After being found fit by the pilots of the MAEE Felixstowe it went to No.209 Squadron, along with the Stranraer and London prototypes to deputise for squadron's Perth boats which were temporarily out of commission. It was these other two prototypes which won production contracts and the 'Knuckleduster' was later retired to become an instructional airframe at the training school at RAF Cosford.

AIRCRAFT SPECIFICATION: (39)
SHORT RANGOON

Span: 93 ft
Length: 66 ft 9.5 in.
Wing area: 1,828sq. ft
Weights: Empty:14,000 lb
          Loaded: 22,500 lb

Power plant: 3 x 540 hp Bristol Jupiter IXF

Armament/Bomb load
1 x Lewis gun in bows and two amdiships.
Bomb laod: 1,000 lb

Performance
Max. speed: 115 mph at 1,000 ft
Cruising speed: 92 mph
Range: 650 miles max
Endurance: 4.4 hr at 115 mph
            7.7 hr at 92 mph
Service ceiling: 12,000 ft

Air Ministry Specifications: R18/29 22/36

History
The Rangoon was a military adaptation of the Short Calcutta, a commercial flying boat used from 1928 on the India and Africa services. Their all-metal hulls proved very reliable and their operational success clearly impressed the Air Ministry resulting in the issue of A.M.Spec.R18/29 was issued. Shorts came up with the prototype, S1433, which made its maiden flight on 24th September 1930. To turn the Calcutta into the Rangoon, Shorts added a Scarff ring in the bows, two gun positions amidships and provision for bomb carrying. There were fresh water tanks, cooking facilities and berths for off-duty crew. The feature that was particularly attractive to the Air Ministry was the all-metal hull, which could restrict the effects of prolonged exposure at the moorings furthermore it could take off and land on two of its three engines.

In April 1931 these boats joined No.203 Squadron at Basra to replace the Southamptons. Three of the six flying boats were flown out from Felixstowe where the delivery flight had started on 6 February 1931. Re-equipment of the squadron was completed in ten weeks. There they assisted the Royal Navy in protecting British interests in the Persian Gulf and made a memorable cruise to Australia in 1934 to mark the 150 Anniversary celebrations. They remained with No.203 Squadron until July 1935 when they were flown to the United Kingdom to equip No.210 Squadron. They were replaced in service by the Short Singapore.

AIRCRAFT SPECIFICATION: (40)
SHORT SINGAPORE

Span: 90 ft
Length: 64 ft 2 in.
Wing area: 1,834sq. ft
Weights: Empty: 20,364 lb
            Loaded: 32,390 lb
Power plant: 2 x Rolls-Royce Kestrel IX
Tractor engines
2 x Rolls-Royce Kestrel VII Pusher engines

Armament/Bomb load
1 x Lewis gun in bow, midships and tail positions
Bomb load: 2,200 lb

Performance
Max. speed: 136 mph at 5,000 ft
Range: 1,235 miles at 104 mph (without bombs) or 863 miles (full bomb load)
Endurance: 6.25 hr
Service ceiling: 15,000 ft

Air Ministry Specifications: R3/33

History
The Singapore I design originated in 1926 and was powered by Rolls Royce H10 engines. One aircraft was loaned by the Air Ministry to Sir Alan Cobham for his memorable 23,000 mile flight around Africa in 1927–8. When the Mk III appeared it entered service with the RAF during 1934. Thirty-seven aircraft were produced and it first went to 210 Squadron at Pembroke Dock. In 1935 they joined 205 Squadron in Singapore and during the Spanish Civil War they flew with Nos 209 and 210 Squadrons based in Malta to protect British shipping. At the outbreak of WWII 19 Singapores were still in service.

AIRCRAFT SPECIFICATION: (41)
SHORT SUNDERLAND

Span: 112 ft 9.5 in.
Length: 85 ft 4 in.
Wing area: 1,487sq. ft
Weights: Empty: 37,000 lb
            Loaded: 60,000 lb
Power plant: 4 x 1,200 hp Pratt & Whitney Twin Wasp R-1830

Armament/Bomb load
2 x 0.303 in. guns in nose turret.
4 x 0.303 in. guns in tail turret.
2 x .50 guns in beam positions.
Bomb load 2,000 lb (some aircraft had 4 x 0.303 in. guns in bows)
Performance
Max. speed: 213 mph at 5,000 ft
Range: 2,980 miles at 134 mph
Endurance: 13.5 hr
Service ceiling: 17,900 ft

Air Ministry Specifications: R2/33   R22/36

History
The Sunderland is probably one of the most famous flying boats, designed in the inter-war years, to operate with conspicuous success during World War II. They were also to figure prominently in the Korean War between 1950 and 1952 as part of the Far East Flying Boat Wing. Indeed this brief description of the Sunderland could never do justice to its pre-eminence in maritime operations. The Sunderland was a derivative of the 'C'Class Empire flying boats to meet the requirements of R2/33. This called for a four-engined monoplane to replace the biplane boats that had been in RAF service ever since the Great War. It was in competition with the Saro R2/33 with four Perseus engines but this met with an accident leaving the Sunderland as the sole contestant. The prototype, K4774, made its maiden flight on 16 October 1937 and was the first flying boat to feature a power-operated turret. The initial contract for 21 boats to A.M.Spec. 22/36 was placed in March 1936 and the first to enter RAF service in June 1938 went to No.230 Squadron in Singapore and No.210 Squadron, Pembroke Dock in West Wales. In both cases the Singapore was replaced by a machine of much superior performance and strong defensive armament which earned the Sunderland the

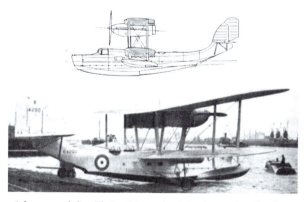

nickname of the 'Flying Porcupine' At the outbreak of war there were three Sunderland squadrons in Coastal Command, totalling 27 aircraft.

AIRCRAFT SPECIFICATION: (42)
SUPERMARINE SCAPA
Figures for Mk.I
Span: 75 ft
Length: 53 ft
Wing area: 1,300sq. ft
Weights: Empty: 10,010 lb
　　　　　　Loaded: 16.040 lb

Power plant: 2 x 525 hp Rolls-Royce Kestrel III MS
Armament/Bomb load
3 x Lewis guns in bow and midships. Bomb load: 1,000 lb

Performance
Max. speed: 141.5 mph at 3,280 ft
Cruising speed: 123 mph
Range: 1,100 miles
Service ceiling: 15,480 ft

Air Ministry Specifications: R20/31 19/33

History
The Scapa was, in effect, a completely re-engined and modernised version of the Southampton. Indeed, when the Scapa first flew on 8 July 1932 it was designated Southampton Mk.IV. It was not until October 1933 that the name was changed to Scapa. The overall dimensions and basic layout remained the same but detailed changes were extensive. Reference to Annex A-43 may be of interest in making a comparison. The Scapa cockpit was closed; there were twin fins and rudders instead of three; the wings and hull were all metal unlike the wooden wings of the Southampton. The Scapa was made much more aerodynamically efficient. For example, the Rolls-Royce Kestrels were neatly cowled and faired into the upper wing instead of the complex array of bracing struts which held the twin Lion engines of the Southampton in position. Increases internal capacity was obtained by redesigning the hull with straighter sides.

The prototype Scapa was S1648, designed to meet A.M.Spec.R20/31 and the production machines were built to A.M.Spec. 19/33. Fourteen of these aircraft were built and delivery was completed in July 1936. This aircraft was chosen to equip No.202 Squadron at Kalafrana, Malta and together with the Scapas of No. 204 Squadron at Aboukir and Alexandria, flew on anti submarine patrols in the Mediterranean during the Spanish Civil War. Their mission was to protect neutral shipping. The Scapas of No,204 Squadron had been flown to the Middle East during the Abbyssinian crisis and they returned to Mount Batten in August 1936. The Scapas of these two squadrons were replaced   by Londons during 1937 and the Singapores replaced those of No.240 Squadron at Calshot in December 1938.

AIRCRAFT SPECIFICATION: (43)
SUPERMARINE SOUTHAMPTON II

Span: 75 ft 0 in.
Length: 51 ft 1in
Wing area: 1,449.0sq. ft
Weights: Empty - 9,000 lb; loaded – 15,200 lb
Power plant: Two 502 hp Napier Lion VA

Armament/Bomb load:
Three Lewis guns in bow and
Midships; bomb load 1,100 lb

Performance
Max. speed: 108 mph at sea level
Cruising speed: 83 mph
Initial Climb rate: 610 ft/min
Range: (normal) 770 miles; (maximum) 930 miles
Service ceiling: 14,000 ft

History
The Felixstowe flying boats were the mainstay of the Naval Air Service in the Great War with the F2A and F3 boats. The Felixstowe F5 which followed remained in squadron service until the Southampton boats replaced them. The prototype Southampton N218 was derived from the civil Swan and was built to Air Ministry Spec.R18/24. The MkIs had wings with straight leading edges and wooden hulls. The first, of an order of six, made its maiden flight on 10 March 1925. Then followed an order for eighteen MkIs and forty-two MkIIs, the latter had duralumin hulls and uprated Lion V engines. Southamptons built from 1927 onwards features sweep back in the outer-wing panels. By the end of 1933 when production ceased, the RAF had received 66 of these aircraft. All boats that had been built with wooden hulls were reassembled with all-metal ones. Southamptons first went into service with No.480 (Coastal Reconnaissance) Flight at Calshot. During their service with the RAF some memorable long distance flights were made. These included a 10,000 mile cruise around the British Isles in 1925, a 7,000 mile return flight to Egypt from Plymouth in 1926, a 19,500 mile return flight by No.205 Squadron from Singapore to Nicobar and the Adaman Islands in 1929 and the 27,000 mile cruise by the Far East Flight (later titled No.205 Squadron) from Felixstowe, leaving on 14 October 1927, for Singapore and Hong Kong. The latter was led by Group Captain Henry Cave-Brown-Cave. In December 1936 the last Southampton boats in service were with No.201 Squadron at Calshot where they were replaced by London flying boats.

AIRCRAFT SPECIFICATION: (44)
SUPERMARINE SPITFIRE

Figures for Mk.I
Span: 36 ft 10 in.
Length: 29 ft 11 in.
Wing area: 242sq. ft
Weights: Empty: 5,332 lb
　　　　　　 Loaded: 5,784 lb
Power plant: 1 x 1,030 hp Rolls Royce Merlin II or III

Armament/Bomb load
8 x 0.303 in. Browning guns in wings

Performance
Max. speed: 355 mph at 19,000 ft
Service ceiling: 32,000 ft

Air Ministry Specifications: F7/30 F5/34 F37/34

History
Even those with no interest in the history of aviation can have failed to have heard of the Spitfire. R.J.Mitchell, who produced the floatplanes that won the Schneider Trophy outright in 1931, was to create this masterpiece. It shared much with the Hurricane in having a Merlin engine, closed cockpit, retractable undercarriage and eight .303 in. Brownings. Where it differed was in having an all-metal monocoque fuselage and elliptical wings.

Initially Mitchell's design to meet A.M.Spec.F7/30 was the Goshawk powered prototype, K2890, which had a fixed undercarriage, open cockpit and cranked inverted wings. Mitchell was dissatisfied with this aircraft which did not meet the requirements of A.M.Spec. 7/30 and embarked on a private venture design still with the Rolls-Royce Goshawk engine. Then came A.M.Spec. F5/34 calling for an 8 gun fighter and this at a time when Rolls-Royce had just produced the Merlin engine. The new engine would be 1,000 hp with a very high power/output ratio. Therefore A.M.Spec F37/34 catered for both the new engine and the eight Browning guns. The prototype, K5054, made its maiden flight on 5 March 1936 and in June the Air Ministry ordered 310 aircraft to be delivered by March 1939. Production of the Mk.I began in 1937 and this was fitted with the Merlin II in place of the Merlin 'C' engine. The early production models had tail wheels and not skids and ejectors in the place of flush exhausts. The Mk.Is had only four Browning guns but this was increased to eight in the Mark.IA. In February 1939 a Spitfire was experimentally fitted with two 20 mm. Guns to become the Mk.IB. The first delivery of the Spitfire went to No.19 Squadron at Duxford in June 1938

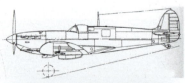

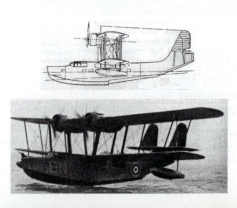

AIRCRAFT SPECIFICATION: (45)
SUPERMARINE STRANRAER
Span: 85 ft
Length: 54 ft 10 in.
Wing area: 1,457sq. ft
Weights: Empty: 11,250 lb
Loaded: 19,000 lb
Power plant: 2 x 980 hp Bristol Pegasus X

Armament/Bomb load
1 x Lewis gun in nose, midship and tail positions
Bomb load: 1,160 lb

Performance
Max. speed: 165 mph at 6,000 ft
Cruising speed: 137 mph
Range: 1,315 miles at 132 mph
1,615 miles at 103 mph
Endurance: 7.75 hr
Service ceiling: 18,500 ft

Air Ministry Specifications: 17/35

History
The Stranraer was the last of a long line of biplane flying boats and was designed by J.R.Mitchell, who was also responsible for the Spitfire. The Stranraer, was so named in August 1935 and, like the Scapa which preceded it, was firstly designated a Southampton, this time a Mk.V. The prototype, K3973, had Pegasus IIIM radial engines whereas the Pegasus X was fitted to the production aircraft. The two-blade wooden propellers of the prototype were also discarded for the Fairey three-blade metal propellers. The Stranraer was a bigger boat than the Scapa. There was an extra bay in the wings, a lengthened hull and a gun position in the tail. The Air Ministry placed the contract for 17 aircraft in August 1935 to A.M.Spec.17/35 but an order for an extra six, placed in May 1936, was cancelled.

The Stranraer first entered service with No.228 Squadron at Pembroke Dock in April 1937. Although they exercised over the Mediterranean in September 1938, these aircraft were not based overseas. At the outbreak of war fifteen Stranraer boats were still in service. They operated from their 'war station' in Scotland with No.209 Squadron and from June 1940 with No.240 Squadron. They were finally withdrawn from front-line service in April 1941.

AIRCRAFT SPECIFICATION: (46)
VICKERS VALENTIA
Span: 87 ft 4 in.
Length: 59 ft 6 in.
Wing area: 2,178sq. ft
Weights: Empty: 10,944 lb
Loaded: 19,500 lb
Power plant: 2 x 650 hp Bristol Pegasus III3 or IIM3

Armament/Bomb load
Up to 2,200 lb in racks beneath the wings.

Performance
Max. speed: 120 mph at 5,000 ft
Cruising speed: 117 mph
Range: 800 miles
Service ceiling: 16,250 ft

Air Ministry Specifications:

History
The Valentia was developed from the earlier Victoria troop transports. Many Valentias were in fact converted Victoria Mk.V or VIs. When it came to external appearance it is significant that the Valentia could be most easily distinguished from the Victoria Mk.VI in having a castoring tail wheel.(Compare side elevation view above with that in the following Annex) 54 Valentias were converted Victorias to which were added 28 new-builds. The initial sixteen aircraft were ordered by the Air Ministry in July 1933. A further order for six aircraft was placed in September 1934 with another six in May 1935.

In the Middle East the Valentias of Nos. 70 and 216 Squadrons were the theatre transports. In India the Valentias served with the Bomber Transport Flight in Lahore from 1935 and fully equipped No.31 Squadron from April 1939. This aircraft did sterling work in the Middle east in the transport role and were joined by Bombays in October 1939. In the bombing role the Valentia was fitted with a gun position in the nose, which also included a bomb aimer's position. A mid upper position was also added. This was a 'field' modification introduced at the time of the Abyssinian crisis when all RAF units in the Middle East were mobilised and reinforced. The Valentias in India made a notable contribution to the relief of the Chitral Column and supported the Army's campaign against the rebel tribesmen in Waziristan. One aircraft, K4632, used four loudspeakers for passing information or issuing warnings to tribesmen. Valentias were finally retired from RAF service overseas in July 1944 with the departure of aircraft No.K3600 from the Iraq Communications Flight.

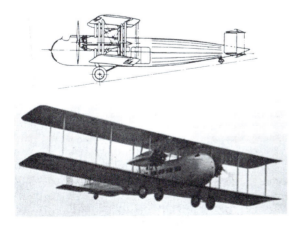

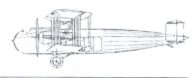

AIRCRAFT SPECIFICATION: (47)
VICKERS VICTORIA Mk.V
Span: 87 ft 4 in.
Length: 59 ft 6 in.
Wing area: 2,179.0sq. ft
Weights: Empty -10,030 lb;
Loaded – 17,760 lb
Power plant: Two 570 hp Napier Lion
Armament/Bomb load: Nil - troop transport

Performance
Max. speed: 110 mph at sea level
Climb: 11 min to 4,920 ft
Range: 770miles
Service ceiling: 16,200 ft

History
The Victoria was designed to Air Ministry Spec.5/20 as a replacement for the Vernon. On 22 August 1922 the first prototype, J6860, was flown followed by a second, J6861. These prototypes Mks I & II, had dihedral only on the bottom wing with the engines mounted on the lower wing, the production Mk IIIs did not. It was not until 1926 that the first Mk III was built and forty six had been produced by March 1928. By fitting HP slats and substituting metal outer wings to thirteen Mk.IIIs they became Mk IVs. One newly built Mk.IV, J9250, had Jupiter radials fitted in 1927. This aircraft served on No.70 Squadron and was later fitted with Pegasus engines. In common with other types produced during the 1920s there was a transition to all-metal construction and Air Ministry Specs 7/29 and 6/31 resulted in the all-metal Victoria Mk V. Thirty-seven Mk Vs were built and were delivered to the RAF between September 1929 and September 1933. These all featured all-moving fins and rudders and Lion XIBs replaced Lion II engines. The final Mark was the VI which differed from the later Valentia by the inclusion of a tail skid in place of a tail wheel. The Victoria entered service in February 1926 with No. 70 Squadron in Iraq followed by No.216 Squadron in the July. Both squadrons changed their Victorias for Valentias in 1935. Victorias participated in the Kabul rescue of December 1928 described in Chapter 3, this operation being the first major airlift in history. These aircraft also engaged in long distance training flights and were used for troop reinforcement during outbreaks of trouble as occurred in Cyprus in 1932. Only a handful of Victorias flew in the United Kingdom. One notable example was the use by the Central Flying School for training pilots in blind-flying techniques.

AIRCRAFT SPECIFICATION: (48)
VICKERS VILDEBEEST
Span: 49 ft
Length: 37 ft 8 in.
Wing area: 728sq. ft
Weights: Empty: 4,724 lb
Loaded: 8,500 lb
Power plant: 1 x 825 hp Bristol Perseus VIII

Armament/Bomb load
1 x Vickers gun forward'
1 x Lewis gun aft
1 x 18" MkIV torpedo of
1,870 lb or 1,000 lb of bombs

Performance
Max. speed: 150 mph
Range: 630 miles
Service ceiling: 19,000 ft

Air Ministry Specifications:

History
The Vickers Vildebeest was the replacement for the Horsley torpedo bomber and the prototype, N230, flew in April 1928. It appeared in the 1932 RAF Display with an uncowled Pegasus engine instead of the Bristol Jupiter engine originally fitted. The Mk.I Vildebeests were first delivered to No.100 Squadron in November 1932. The Mk.II & III versions soon followed. The Mk.II featured the Pegasus IIM3 engine and it was this version which was sent to the Far East when No.100 Squadron moved from Donibristle in Scotland to Singapore in December 1933. The Mk.III version had a permanent third seat and modified rear cockpit. A final contract for 18 Mk.IV Vildebeest aircraft was placed in December 1936. This version was powered by a Perseus sleeve-valve engine in a long-chord cowling driving a three-blade Rotol propeller. One hundred Vildebeests remained in service in September 1939.

On the outbreak of war in 1939 Coastal Command had no other torpedo bomber, than the Vildebeest, in front-line service. Until April 1940 this aircraft had to fly all in-shore patrols around the coasts of the United Kingdom. The Beaufort which would replace it had been delayed in production. The situation was even more serious in the Far East where Australian built Beauforts were awaited and the Vildebeest units suffered heavy losses in combat with the Japanese. In Java, Vildebeests of No.36 Squadrons fought on until March 1942.

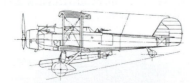

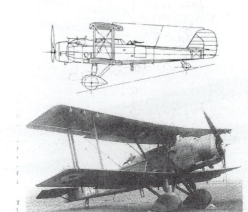

AIRCRAFT SPECIFICATION: (49)
VICKERS VINCENT

Span: 49 ft
Length: 36 ft 8 in.
Wing area: 728sq. ft
Weights: Empty: 4,229 lb
        Loaded: 8,100 lb
Power plant: 1 x 635 hp Bristol Pegasus IIM3

Armament/Bomb load
1 x Vickers gun forward
1 x Lewis Gun aft
Bomb load: 1,100 lb

Performance
Max. speed: 142 mph at 4,290 ft
Range: 625 miles (normal)
       1,250 miles (max)
Service ceiling: 19,000 ft

Air Ministry Specifications:

History
In 1934 the Air Ministry recognised the need for an aircraft to replace the Wapiti and Fairey IIIF working as general purpose aircraft carrying out air control operations in places like Iraq, Aden and the Sudan. A modified Vildebeest, Serial No.S1714 had carried out extensive trials in the Middle East to see if this would fit the bill. Where the torpedo usually sat it was found that a fuel tank could be fitted to increase the range of the aircraft to 1,250miles. It was decided to call this aircraft the Vincent and the prototype, K2945, was actually a converted Vildebeest II. A message pick-up hook was fitted for Army co-operation duties, together with other equipment necessary for the aircraft to cope in hot climatic conditions.

Between July 1934 and October 1936, 197 Vincents were produced. No.84 Squadron, Shaibah was re-equipped in December 1934 in and No.8 Squadron, Khormaksar in Aden. From July 1936 the Gordons of No.47 Squadron in the Sudan began to get the Vincent but No.55 Squadron in Iraq had to wait until February 1937. By then the Vincent had become one of the key aircraft in the Middle Eastern theatre and No.8 Squadron still had this aircraft as late as March 1942.

AIRCRAFT SPECIFICATION: (50)
VICKERS VIRGINIA X
Span: 87 ft 8 in.

Length: 62 ft 2.75 in.
Wing area: 2,178.0sq. ft
Weights: Empty – 9,650 lb;
        Loaded: 17,600 lb
Power plant: Two 580 hp Napier Lion VB
Armament/Bomb load: One Lewis gun in nose, twin Lewis guns in tail; bomb load – 3000 lb usually comprising nine 112 lb bombs internally and a combination of 550,250,112 and 20 lb bombs carried externally.

Performance
Max. speed: 98 mph at sea level 108 mph at 5,000 ft
Climb: 14 min to 5,000 ft
Range: 985 miles
Service ceiling: 9,400 ft

History
The Vickers Virginia took over the role of RAF heavy bomber from the Vimy during 1924/5 and remained in service until 1937. During that time ten Marks were introduced to incorporate a number of modifications. The Mk I was built to Air Ministry Spec.1/21 and the prototype, J6856, flew at Brooklands on 24 November 1922. On 6 June 1924 a Virginia Mk III prototype, J6992, was delivered to No.7 Squadron at Bircham Newton. Thereafter issues were made to Nos. 7, 9 and 58 Squadrons between 1924 and 1928 through the various Marks up to Mark X and can be seen by reference to the appropriate squadron numbers in Appendix B. The prototype had Napier Lion engines in rectangular nacelles mounted on the lower wings but production Virginias had oval nacelles raised above the lower wings. Raising the engines above the lower wing also occurred on the Vernon and Victoria. The Marks III to V maintained the feature of the prototype in having dihedral on the lower wings only. From the Mark VI onwards the nose was redesigned and lengthened and there was sweep-back of the wings. The Marks IX and X both had gun positions in the tail but perhaps the most interesting features, shown in the photograph, are the 'fighting tops' on the Mark VIII, J6856, of No.9 Squadron. Enclosed power operated turrets were still to come but this was intended to provide defensive fire from attack from above and behind. Finally the Mark X was of all-metal construction with fabric covering. By the time production ended in December 1932 the RAF had received 124 Virginias. Of these fifty were new build Mark Xs. No.7 Squadron was first to receive Virginias with automatic pilots which helped the squadron to win the Lawrence Minot bombing trophy eight times. The Virginias of No.51 Squadron were still in Bomber Command's order of battle in February 1938 the month they left the service.

AIRCRAFT SPECIFICATION: (51)
VICKERS WELLESLEY

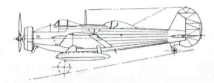

Span: 74 ft 7 in.
Length: 39 ft 3 in.
Wing area: 630sq. ft
Weights: Empty: 6,369 lb
Loaded: 12,500 lb
Power plant: 1 x 925 hp Bristol Pegasus XX

Armament/Bomb load
1 x Vickers gun forward
1x Vickers K gun aft.
Bomb load: 2,000 lb max

Performance
Max. speed: 206 mph at 19,680 ft
Cruising speed: 160 mph
Range: 1,335 miles
Service ceiling: 26,100 ft

Air Ministry Specifications: G4/31 22/35

History
The Wellesley was the first RAF aircraft to employ geodetric construction, a well known feature of the Wellington bomber which was to follow. The prototype, K7556, was built as a private venture which first flew on 19 June 1935. In spite of the loss of this aircraft in an accident the Air Ministry ordered 96 aircraft to Spec.22/35 and a total of 176 Wellesleys were built.

This aircraft entered service with No.76 Squadron at Finningley in Yorkshire in April 1937 and although it equipped five other squadrons the Wellesley had been replaced by the Whitley, Battle and Hampden by April 1939. The resultant surplus of Wellesleys at home saw them being transferred overseas replacing the Vincents on Nos. 45,47 and 223 Squadrons before the outbreak of war.

The Wellesley has its place in history for the breaking of the World's Long-distance Record with the RAF's Long-range Development Flight. On 5 November 1938 three Wellesleys L2638, L2639 and L2680, led by Squadron Leader R Kellett, took off from Ismailia, Egypt to fly non-stop to Darwin, Australia. L2639 did not quite make it but the two remaining aircraft reached Darwin on 7 November having flown 7,162 miles in 48 hours with the help of extra fuel tanks.

AIRCRAFT SPECIFICATION: (52)
VICKERS WELLINGTON

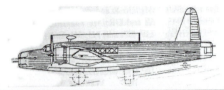

Span: 86 ft 2 in.
Length: 64 ft 7 in.
Wing area: 840sq. ft
Weights: Empty: 18,556 lb
Loaded: 28,500 lb
Power plant: 2 x 1,000 hp Bristol Pegasus XVIII

Armament/Bomb load
2 x 0.303 in gun in nose and tail
2 x 0.303 in guns, manually operated in beam positions
Bomb load: 4,500 lb (max)

Performance
Max. speed: 235 mph at 15,500 ft
Range: 1,200 miles with 4,500 lb Bomb load
2,550 miles with 1,000 lb
Service ceiling: 18,000 ft

Air Ministry Specifications: B9/32   29/36

History
Nicknamed the 'Wimpey' the Wellington was the second aircraft to feature geodetic construction and was designed by Dr. Barnes-Wallis, who had been an airship designer and was to design the 'dam busting' bombs dropped by Lancaster bombers in 1943. The prototype Wellington bomber, K4049, built to A.M.Spec. B9/32 made its maiden flight on 15th June 1936. The sleek lines of the Wellington attracted much attention at the RAF Display, Hendon in 1936. Although the prototype was lost in a crash the Air Ministry went ahead in August 1936 with an initial order for 180 Mk.I aircraft to A.M.Spec. 29/36. The first production aircraft, L4212, which made its first flight on 23 December 1937, differed from the production aircraft which followed in that it had the Pegasus X engines. Those which followed had the Pegasus XVIIIs. The original Wellington had the Stranraer tail but this was replaced by the characteristic tall fin and rudder. The tailwheel was made to retract and in the Mk.Ias the Vickers nose and tail turrets were replaced by the Nash and Thompson variety. In the Mk.IC the ventral turret was replaced by beam guns.

To speed up production of Wellingtons on the approach of war a Chester factory was added to the parent company's plant at Weybridge. Yet another factory was opened at Squire's Gate, Blackpool and, by the outbreak of war, it was possible for Bomber Command to put eight squadrons of Wellingtons on the line.

AIRCRAFT SPECIFICATION: (53)
WESTLAND LYSANDER

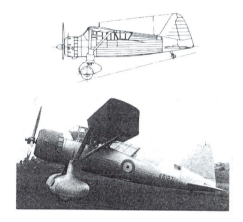

AIRCRAFT SPECIFICATION: (54)
WESTLAND WALLACE

Figures for Mk I
Span: 50 ft
Length: 30 ft 6 in.
Wing area: 260sq. ft
Weights: Empty: 4,065 lb
            Loaded: 5,920 lb
Power plant: 1 x 890 hp Bristol Mercury XII

Armament/Bomb load
2 x fixed 0.303 in. guns forward
1 or 2 x manually operated 0.303 in guns in rear cockpit
Six light bombs

Performance
Max. speed: 219 mph at 10,000 ft
Range: 600 miles
Service ceiling: 26,000 ft

Air Ministry Specifications: A39/34   36/36

History

The Lysander, affectionately known as the 'Lizzie,' replaced the Hawker Hector on Army co-operation squadrons. The prototype, K6128, made its maiden flight on 15 June 1936 and was designed to A.M.Spec.A39/34. The first production contract was placed in September 1936 to A.M.Spec.36/36 and the Lysander first entered service with No.16 Squadron, Old Sarum in May 1938.

Their function was to spot the fall of shot of artillery pieces and carry out battlefield reconnaissance, but they were vulnerable in a fast moving air war and five Lysanders were shot down during the Battle of France in June 1940. They were remarkable aircraft, nonetheless, and with their short take-off and landing capability, were very useful when it came to getting Allied agents into and out of enemy occupied Europe. They were eventually replaced in the Army co-operation role by Tomahawks and Mustangs but they continued to serve as target tugs and on air/sea rescue duties.

Figures for MkII
Span: 46 ft 5 in.
Length: 34 ft 2 in.
Wing area: 488sq. ft
Weights: Empty: 3,840 lb
            Loaded: 5,750 lb
Power plant: 1 x 665 hp Bristol Pegasus IV

Armament/Bomb load
1 x fixed Vickers gun forward
1 x Lewis gun aft Bomb load: 580 lb

Performance
Max. speed: 158 mph at 15,000 ft
Cruising speed: 135 mph
Range: 470 miles
Service ceiling: 24,100 ft

Air Ministry Specifications: 19/32 G31/35

History

The Wallace was a private venture build by Westland. The idea was to build on the success and experience gained in the construction of more than 500 Wapitis. In common with other aircraft companies at the time it was usual to designate a derivative by allocating a later Mark. No. to a prototype. Hence the Wapiti Mk.VII became the Westland Wallace. The Wallace prototype, K3488, featured a lengthened fuselage, a spatted undercarriage with wheel brakes and a Pegasus IIM3 engine. The Air Ministry then ordered twelve Wapitis to be converted to this standard and they were named Wallace Mk.Is.

The Wallace was never used in front-line day bomber squadrons, going instead to the Special Reserve and Auxiliary squadrons and was retired from bomber duties in May 1937. This aircraft was, however, to remain in service for a further six years with armament practice camps, air observer schools etc.,

In response to A.M. Spec.G31/35 Westlands produced the Wallace MkII with the more powerful Pegasus IV engine. This had an enclosed canopy for both pilot and observer/gunner. This protected the gunner from the slipstream and improved his aim. A few Wallace IIs did equip bomber squadrons but they were destined to operate in various training roles. The last of these aircraft did not finally retire from RAF service until 1943.

AIRCRAFT SPECIFICATION: (55) WESTLAND WAPITI IIA

Span: 46 ft 5 in.
Length: 31 ft 8 in.
Wing area: 488.0sq. ft
Weights: Empty – 3,810 lb;
    Loaded – 5,400 lb
Power plant: One 550 hp Bristol Jupiter VIII or VIIIF
Armament/Bomb load: One fixed forward firing Vickers gun + one Lewis gun aft; bomb load 580 lb

Performance
Max. speed: 135 mph at 5,000 ft
Cruising speed: 110 mph
Initial Climb rate: 1,140 ft/min 9.5 min to 10,000 ft
Range: 360miles
Service ceiling: 18,800 ft

History
The Wapiti was the workhorse of the RAF in India and Iraq during the inter war years. In 1928 the RAF began to re-equip squadrons which had for years used another workhorse, the DH9A, No.84 Squadron at Shaibah being the first to receive the Mk Is in June of that year. A number of the components from the DH9A were used for the Wapiti. The prototype J8495 first flew on 7 March 1927 and the Mk I had a 420 hp Jupiter VI engine. By 1933 twenty squadrons had been equipped with this aircraft, eleven regular and nine Auxiliary and Special Reserve. No.55 Squadron, Iraq flew Wapitis until 1937 whilst on the North West Frontier the Wapiti equipped eight squadrons which had previously used DH9As and Bristol Fighters. During the 1930s the Wapitis were progressively replaced with Harts and Audaxes but No.5 Squadron soldiered on with their Wapitis until June 1940 before getting Harts. These aircraft were just as busy training or with the auxiliary and reserve units. Again they replaced DH9As on the auxiliary day bomber squadrons, except No.602 Squadron at Renfrew where they replaced Fairey Fawns. It was not until 1937 that the Auxiliary Air Force gave up its Wapitis but not before these aircraft belonging to Nos.600, 601, 604 and 605 Squadrons gave impressive formation flying demonstrations at the annual RAF Hendon Display. Four hundred and sixty Wapitis in all were delivered to the RAF. The Mk II was of composite construction and the IIA was the first all-metal version with an uprated Jupiter VIII engine. The Wapiti V was designed for Army co-operation work and the VI was a dual control trainer with a Jupiter XIF engine. It was these aircraft that mostly went to the reserve and auxiliary units. Finally there were the Wapiti IAs, J9095 and 9096 of No.24 Squadron at Northolt in 1928. They were used by HRH the Prince of Wales, Prince Edward, when flying on official visits.

PART II – Non Squadron Aircraft
SQUADRON AIRCRAFT
56. Airspeed Oxford
57. Avro 504N
58. Avro Tutor
59. Bristol Type 138A
60. De Havilland Tiger Moth
61. De Havilland Dragon Rapide/Dominie
62. De Havilland 86 Express
63. De Havilland Leopard Moth
64. Hawker Hart Trainer
65. Hawker Henley
66. Hawker Hind Trainer
67. Hawker Tomtit
68. Miles Nighthawk
69. Miles Magister I
70. Miles Mentor
71. North American Harvard
72. Fairey Postal
73. Supermarine 6B
74. Vega Gull

AIRCRAFT SPECIFICATION: (56)
AIRSPEED OXFORD

Span: 53 ft 4 in.
Length: 34 ft 6 in.
Wing area: 348sq. ft
Weights: Empty: 5,380 lb
            Loaded: 7,600 lb
Power plant: Two 375 hp Armstrong Siddeley Cheetah X

Performance
Max. speed: 188 mph
Service ceiling: 19,000 ft

Air Ministry Specifications:

History
The Oxford was the first twin-engined advance trainer to enter service with the RAF. This aircraft was the military version of the Airspeed Envoy and the prototype, L4534 flew on 19 June 1937. The Air Ministry placed an initial production contract for 136 aircraft and they were produced in the Airspeed factory in Portsmouth as well the de Havilland factory in Hatfield. The wartime contracts also involved production by the shadow factories of Standard and Percival.

The original Oxford Is had the Armstrong Whitworth turret fitted as they were intended for all aspects of aircrew training including gunnery. These aircraft continued in the training role until 1954 with the closing of 10 FTS at Pershore.

AIRCRAFT SPECIFICATION: (57)
AVRO 504 N

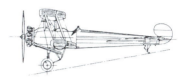

Span: 36 ft
Length: 28 ft 6 in.
Wing area: 320sq. ft
Weights: Empty: 1,584 lb
            Loaded: 2,240 lb
Power plant: 1 x 180 hp Armstrong Siddeley Lynx IVC

Performance
Max. speed: 100 mph
Cruising speed: 85 mph
Range: 250 miles
Endurance: 3 hr
Service ceiling: 14,600 ft

History
The Avro 504N was the first training aircraft to be adopted by the service after the Great War. It was the successor to the Avro 504K and was powered by an Armstrong Siddeley Lynx engine and became known as the Lynx- Avro. It was used by the university air squadrons and the flying training schools until superseded by the Avro Tutor in 1932/3. Trials were carried out with different engines and the first to be fitted with the Lynx engine were three converted 504Ks, serial numbers E9265,E9266 and F2575. Then the first 504N prototype, J733, was fitted with a Bristol Lucifer engine. The other prototype, J750, was fitted with a Lynx engine.

Production of the 504N began in 1927. Early examples had tapered ailerons and wooden fuselages. In the later production models the wings had rectangular frise ailerons and fuselages of welded tubular steel construction. The 504Ns went into service with auxiliary squadrons, No. 24 Squadron, RAF Kenley and with the flying training schools. Most of the trainee pilots of the period will have had their first experience of flying in a Lynx-Avro. The Central Flying Shool at RAF Wittering used these aircraft in developing blind flying techniques with 'E' Flight. Hoods that came forward to cover the pilot gave the latter only the sight of his instruments

In the Hendon displays of 1935/36 and 37, Avro 504Ns gave displays of 'crazy flying' When they were phased out of service many of them were sold to joy riding companies where many a member of the public got his or her first experience of flying.

AIRCRAFT SPECIFICATION: (58)
AVRO TUTOR

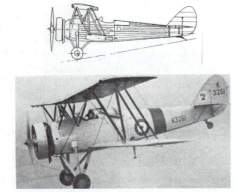

Span: 34 ft
Length: 26 ft 6 in.
Wing area: 300sq. ft
Weights: Empty: 1,800 lb
            Loaded: 2,458 lb
Power plant: 215 – 240 hp Armstrong Siddeley Lynx IVC

Performance
Max. speed: 122 mph
Cruising speed: 105 mph
Endurance: 2.75 hr
Service ceiling: 16,200h ft

Air Ministry Specifications: 3/30   18/31

History
The tradition of using Avros for flying training was maintained when the Avro Tutor replaced the Avro 504N in the flying training schools in 1932. The early batch of aircraft built to AM Spec. 3/30 had five cylinder Siddeley Mongoose engines but in the later Tutors the Siddeley Lynx seven cylinder engines were used. The Mongoose trainer entered service in 1930 but as part of competitive trials to find the best training aircraft before entering service with the flying training schools. They ended up in the Air Navigation School at Andover in 1935 before being withdrawn in 1937. The production Tutors were built to AM Spec. 18/31 and 394 were constructed for the RAF. Fourteen of these aircraft were fitted with floats and named Sea Tutors. Production of the Tutors ceased in May 1936.

First deliveries of the Tutor were to the Central Flying School (CFS) and these featured in the 1933 Hendon Display. The top surfaces of the upper wings were painted with red and white stripes for easy recognition by spectators when flying inverted. The RAF College Cranwell and No.5 FTS received their Tutors in 1933. At No.3 FTS the Tutor replaced the Tiger Moth. Soon all flying training schools had these aircraft as standard equipment. They were also used with Station Flights and the Auxiliary Air Force. A navigation trainer was also produced.

AIRCRAFT SPECIFICATION: (59)
BRISTOL TYPE 138A

Span: 66 ft
Length: 44 ft
Wing area: 568sq. ft
Weights: Empty: 4,391 lb
            Loaded: 5,340 lb
Power plant: 1 x 460 mph Bristol Pegasus PE VIS with two-stage supercharger and four-blade fixed-pitch wooden propeller.

Performance
Max. speed: 177 mph at 45,000 ft
                123 mph at sea level
Climb rate: 62 min to 50,000 ft

Air Ministry Specifications:

History
The Air Ministry required a high altitude research aircraft capable of reaching a height of 50,000 ft and a Ministry Specification was put out if 1934. The aircraft had to be light and a fixed undercarriage was fitted thus dispensing with the need for weighty retractable gear. A large span was required with high aspect ratio wings since the aircraft would be operating in the upper reaches of the atmosphere where there is reduced lift. Wooden construction also helped to lighten the load.

Bristol answered the call with the Type 138A and the aircraft. K.4879, made its maiden flight with the company's chief test pilot, Captain Cyril Uwins, on 11 May 1936. The first high altitude attempt was made by Squadron Leader F.R.D. Swain when he took the aircraft up to 49,967 ft, virtually what was asked for in the Specification. This broke the previous altitude record giving Swain the new record for heavier-than-air craft.

This prompted a second attempt and K4879 underwent some modifications. Smaller wheels were fitted (see photograph) and the brakes were removed. A finer pitch propeller was fitted and the Bristol Pegasus engine was overhauled and reconditioned. On 30 June 1937 the second attempt was made, this time with Flight Lieutenant M.J.Adam at the controls. Taking off from RAE Farnborough, as Swain had done, Adam embarked on a sortie which lasted 2½ hours. During the ascent his canopy fractured but his pressure suit saved him from injury and he eventually reached an altitude of 53,937 ft thus regaining the record . Both pilots were awarded the Air Force Cross for their achievements.

AIRCRAFT SPECIFICATION: (60)
DE HAVILLAND TIGER MOTH

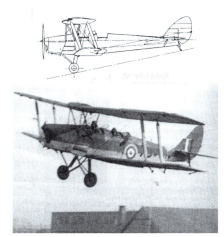

Span: 29 ft 4 in.
Length: 23 ft
Wing area: 239sq. ft
Weights: Empty::1,115 lb
              Loaded: 1,770 lb
Power plant: 1 x 130 hp Gypsy Major

Performance
Max. speed: 109 mph at 1,000 ft
Cruising speed: 93 mph
Range: 302 miles
Endurance: 3 hr
Service ceiling: 13,600 ft

Air Ministry Specifications: 23/31 26/33

History
The Tiger Moth must be amongst the most famous training aircraft in the world and it served for over 15 years with the RAF until being replaced by the Percival Prentice and the de Havilland Chipmunk. The Tiger Moth II was a development with the Gipsy Major but differed in having staggered and swept back wings. By inverting the engine the view forward for the Pilot was much improved. It was fully aerobatic up to a weight of 1,750 lb and suitable for blind flying instruction.

The A.M. Specification for this aircraft was 23/32 and the prototype flew on 26 October 1931. The initial production version was the Mk.I and it had 120 hp Gypsy III engines. This was followed by the Tiger Moth Mk.II built to A.M.Spec. 26/33 powered by 130 hp Gypsy Major engine which became the standard power plant. The original Tiger Moths did not have the anti-spin strakes on the tail. These were a war time innovation. By the outbreak of war over 1,000 of these aircraft had been delivered. They were mostly with the ERFTSs for ab-initio flying training. Trainee pilots then went on to FTSs.

AIRCRAFT SPECIFICATION: (61)
DE HAVILLAND 89/89M RAPIDE/DOMINIE

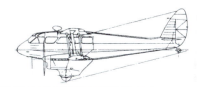

Span: 48 ft
Length: 34 ft 6in
Wing area: 336sq. ft
Weights: All up: 5,500 lb

Power plant: 2 X 200 hp de Havilland Gypsy Six

Armament/Bomb load
As described in text

Performance
Max. speed: 157 mph
Cruising speed: 132 mph
Range: 578 miles
Service ceiling: 19,500 ft

Air Ministry Specifications: G18/35

History
The prototype Rapide was flown at Hatfield by H.S.Broad on April 17 1934 and went into service with Hillman Airways and Railway Air Services Ltd. Other airlines followed and the aircraft was modified in 1937 to be designated the DH98A when small trailing edge flaps were fitted under the lower mainplane outboard of the nacelles. AM.Spec. G18/35 called for a general reconnaissance aircraft for maritime duties and the Rapide was fitted with a MkV Vickers gun on the starboard side of the nose, a bomb bay for two 100 lb bombs and four 20 lb bombs and one MkIII Lewis gun DH patented mounting on top of the rear fuselage. Extra cabin windows were fitted with a long curved dorsal fin. This prototype, K4227,was designated DH89M but it was passed over for the Avro Anson. The work was not in vain, however because three DH89Ms were purchased by the Spanish government in December 1935 for police duties in Morocco. Back home a standard Rapide K.5070, joined No.24 Communications Squadron as a VIP transport for members of the Air Council from March 1935 until October 1944. The Rapide DH89B became the Dominie Mk.I navigation and W/T trainer for the RAF and some went into service with the FAA.

AIRCRAFT SPECIFICATION: (62)
DE HAVILLAND 86A EXPRESS

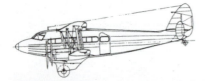

Span: 64 ft 6in
Length: 46 ft 1in
Wing area: 641sq. ft
Weights: single pilot version all up: 5,520 lb

Power plant: Four 200 hp de Havilland Gypsy Six series I or 205 hp Gypsy Six series II

Performance with Gypsy Six I
Max. speed: 166 mph
Cruising speed: 142 mph
Range: 760 miles
Service ceiling: 17,400 ft

Air Ministry Specifications:

History
The prototype flew at Stag Lane on 14 January 1934 piloted by H.S.Broad and it received its Certificate of Airworthiness at Martlesham Heath on 30 January. The aircraft carried passengers and mail and was flown by a single pilot in the nose with a wireless operator/navigator seated behind him. It went into service with Imperial Airways on the Croydon to Singapore and Australian service. Various other modifications and refinements were made and these airliners went into service both at home and in Australia. They came into RAF service in 1938 when four were acquired, two going to No.24 Communications Squadron where they served from October 1937 to March 1943. The other two were used as flying classrooms for navigator and wireless operator training. On the outbreak of war a further batch of civil DH86s and DH86Bs were impressed for ferrying supplies to the British Army in France. The photograph is of a DH86B L.8037, which was used for W/T training.

AIRCRAFT SPECIFICATION: (63)
DE HAVILLAND LEOPARD MOTH DH85/85A

Span: 37 ft 6in
Length: 24 ft 6in
Wing area: 206sq. ft
Weights: all up: 2,225 lb

Power plant: DH85 – One 130 hp
Gypsy Major
DH85A – One 230 hp
Gypsy Six R

Performance
Max. speed: 137 mph
Cruising speed: 119 mph
Range: 715 miles
Service ceiling: 21,500 ft

History
No fewer than 60 Leopard Moths were sold overseas and 44 were impressed into RAF service at the outbreak of the war for communications duties. Some were used by the Air Transport Auxiliary and several of these aircraft formed part of the Delhi Communications Flight whilst others served in Southern Rhodesia. The DH85A had a considerably more powerful engine than the DH85 ie., a 230 hp DH Gypsy Six R compared with a 130 hp Gypsy Major. These aircraft were manufactured at the de Havilland Hatfield works. The type went into service with No. 24 Communications Squadron from September 1939 until April 1940.

AIRCRAFT SPECIFICATION: (64)
HAWKER HART TRAINER

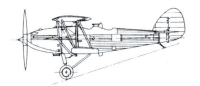

Span: 37 ft 4 in.
Length: 29 ft 4 in.
Wing area: 349.5sq. ft
Weights: Empty: 3,020 lb
          Loaded: 4,150 lb
Power plant: 1 x 525 hp Rolls-Royce
Kestrel IIB or 510 hp
Kestrel X or X(DR)

Performance
Max. speed: 165 mph at 3,000 ft
Cruising speed: 145 mph
Endurance: 2.9 hr
Service ceiling: 22,800 ft

Air Ministry Specifications: 8/32

History
Given that the Hart single engined day bomber had several derivatives there was clearly a need for a Hart trainer version for which a case was made in 1932. The prototype trainer, K1996, was a dual control aircraft with the instructor in the rear cockpit. The gunner's scarff ring was removed from the rear cockpit. The later Hart trainers can easily be recognised by the long exhaust pipes which extended below the lower ring. (see photo.)

K.1996 made its first flight on 20 April 1932 and was followed by two pre-production aircraft, K2474 and K2475. The first production trainers were built to A.M.Spec.8/32 and in June 1933 Hart trainers superseded the Atlas trainer at the RAF College, Cranwell and the dual controlled Siskins which had equipped Nos.25 and 43 Squadrons. The Auxiliary Air Force also received Hart trainers.

Hawkers had just finished 56 machines when, in 1935, the Air Ministry issued further contracts, to Vickers for 114 aircraft and to Armstrong Whitworth for 303. In addition to the 473 machines thus produced, approximately 60 day bombers went to the training schools, such was the growing demand for pilots. Many RAF pilots who flew in the war had gained their wings on Hart trainers between 1935 and 1939.

AIRCRAFT SPECIFICATION: (65)
HAWKER HENLEY

Span: 47 ft 1.5 in.
Length: 36 ft 5 in.
Wing area: 342sq. ft
Weights: Empty: 6,010 lb
          Loaded: 8,480 lb
Power plant: 1 x 1,030 hp Rolls
Royce Merlin II or III

Performance
Max. speed: 272 mph (with air-to-air drogue) at 17,500 ft
Cruising speed: 235 mph at 15,000 ft; (with ground-to-air gunnery drogue) 200 mph
Range: 900 miles
Service ceiling: 27,000 ft

Air Ministry Specifications:

History
The Air Ministry Specification called for a high-speed monoplane light bomber and with all their experience in producing single-engined day bombers Hawkers rose to the challenge in competition with a Fairey monoplane. To facilitate quantity production it was decided to use the same outer wing sections undercarriage and tail surfaces as the Hurricane and the Henley prototype flew at Brooklands on 10 March 1937. It made its debut at that year's RAF Display by which time the RAF had changed its mind about light bomber requirements. So it was decided to convert the Henley for target towing duties to replace the ageing Gordon and Wallace target tugs. Given the speed of the new fighters and light bombers the Henley was able to provide more realistic training conditions. The Henleys were produced at Hucclecote and the initial contract was for 350 machines, later reduced to 200 in number in May 1937, when resources were needed to increase Hurricane production. The Henley target tugs entered service with No.1 Anti Aircraft Co-operation Unit at Farnborough. Henleys remained in service until April 1945.

AIRCRAFT SPECIFICATION: (66)
HAWKER HIND TRAINER

Span: 37 ft 3 in.
Length: 29 ft 7 in.
Wing area: 348sq. ft
Weights: These differed from Hind SEDB in that the armaments were removed
Power plant: 1 x 640 hp Rolls-Royce Kestrel V

Performance
Max. speed: 186 mph at 16,400 ft
Range: 430 miles
Service ceiling: 26,400 ft

History
Hawker Hind trainers were produced by converting bombers in much the same way as the Hart trainers. General Aircraft Limited carried out the conversion of 144 Hinds to make them dual control aircraft; twenty of which were new build as trainers. Hind trainers played an important role in flying training schools from 1937 and there were still 145 of the trainers on strength at the outbreak of war.

AIRCRAFT SPECIFICATION: (67)
HAWKER TOMTIT

Span: 28 ft 6 in.
Length: 23 ft 8 in.
Wing area: 238sq. ft

Weights: Empty: 1,100 lb
Loaded: 1,750 lb
Power plant: 1 x 150 mph Armstrong Siddeley Mongoose IIIC

Performance
Max. speed: 124 mph at 1,000 ft
102 mph at 10,000 ft
Range: 350 miles
Service ceiling: 19,500 ft

History
By the end of the 1920s there was a need to replace the ageing Avro 504K. The new trainer was to be built around the Armstrong Siddeley Mongoose engine and of all-metal construction. The Tomtit first flew in November 1928. The other contender for acceptance as the RAF's new trainer was the Mongoose powered Avro trainer, the forerunner of the Tutor. The Tomtit had Handley-Page automatic leading edge slots fitted to the upper wing to reduce the stalling speed and a blind flying hood was attached to the rear cockpit. The cockpits were well clear of the wings to facilitate rapid exit by parachute in case of emergency.

Between 1928 and 1931 twenty-five Tomtits were produced for the RAF. No.3 FTS and the Central Flying School had this aircraft on charge and some equipped No.24 Squadron at Northolt where the Prince of Wales flew one of these aircraft from time to time. The Tomtit left RAF service in 1935.

AIRCRAFT SPECIFICATION: (68)
MILES NIGHTHAWK

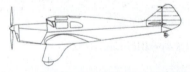

Span: 35 ft
Length: 25 ft
Wing area: 181sq. ft
Weights: empty: 1,650 lb all up: 2,400 lb
Power plant: 200 hp de Havilland Gypsy Six

Performance
Max. speed: 180 mph
Cruising speed: 160 mph

Air Ministry Specifications: 24/36

History
This aircraft first flew on 18 December 1935 with Mr F.G. Miles at the controls. Built initially as a private venture the Miles company had to find the money for two sets of blind flying instruments. Its primary role was to be night flying,

instrument flying, navigation and radio instruction. It could also be used as a three-seat communications aircraft. The Air Ministry became interested and awarded a development contract to AM.Spec 24/36. Under the contract the aircraft had to be spun with a wide range of C.G. which almost resulted in the test pilot becoming air sick after six consecutive spins. Spinning tests continued with the Martlesham test pilots at the controls. These tests were exhaustive with Wing Commander Stent and Flight Lieutenant Moir at the controls. Stent had to bale out when full control movements and full throttle failed to bring the aircraft out of the spin. After a rebuild the Nighthawk went into service as a communications aircraft and served with No.24 Communications Squadrons from July 1937 until September 1938.

AIRCRAFT SPECIFICATION: (69)
MILES MAGISTER

Span: 33 ft 10 in.
Length: 25 ft 3 in.
Wing area: 176 sq. ft
Weights: Empty: 1,286 lb
              Loaded: 1,900 lb
Power plant: 1 x 130 hp De Havilland Gypsy Major I

Performance
Max. speed: 142 mph at 1,000 ft
Cruising speed: 123 mph
Range: 367miles
Service ceiling: 16,500 ft

Air Ministry Specifications: T40/36 37/37

History
The Magister was the first monoplane trainer to be used by the FTSs and was introduced to the CFS in September 1937. Its design went against the trends of the late 1930s in that it was of all-wooden construction. The Magister met the requirements of A.M.Spec. T40/36 which called for a monoplane in keeping with the new types entering service under the expansion scheme. It was faster than the biplane

equivalents yet had a modest landing speed of only 42 mph. It was fully aerobatic and introduced trainee pilots to the new trailing-edge split flaps.

Production of the Magister was to A.M.Spec. 37/37 and 1230 machines had been built by 1941. By 1938 the Magisters had increased rudder area to assist in spin recovery. It served with the Elementary Flying Training Schools during the war but without the spats as originally fitted. This simplified maintenance. After the war many surplus RAF Magisters were sold on the civil market. Civil clubs and flying schools operated them as the Hawk trainer Mk.III.

The Magister I served on No.24 Communications Squadron from June 1938 until 1940

AIRCRAFT SPECIFICATION: (70)
MILES MENTOR

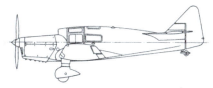

Span: 34 ft 9½ in
Length: 26 ft 1½ in
Wing area: 181sq. ft
Weights: empty – 1,978 lb
              all up – 2,710 lb
Power plant: 200 hp de Havilland Gypsy Six

Performance
Max. speed: 156 mph
Rate of Climb: 780 ft/min
Service ceiling: 13,800 ft

Air Ministry Specifications: 38/37

History
As a result of the handling trials on the Nighthawk, a production order was placed by the Air Ministry to their Spec. AM 38/37. Modifications to the aircraft, which was made of wood, completely altered and worsened the handling characteristics and the it was renamed the Mentor. The duties required of this aircraft were very similar to the Nighthawk. The prototype made its maiden flight on 5 January 1938 with W Skinner at the controls. As already explained its handing was very heavy and sluggish but after official trials, it was regarded as satisfactory for RAF service for which 45 were built. The Mentor served on No.24

Communications Squadron from October 1938 until August 1944.

AIRCRAFT SPECIFICATION: (71)
NORTH AMERICAN HARVARD

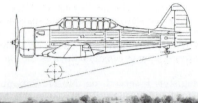

Span: 42 ft 10.25 in.
Length: 28 ft 11⁷⁄₈ in.
Wing area: 253sq. ft
Weights: Empty: 4,158 lb
Loaded: 5,250 lb
Power plant: 1 x 550 hp Pratt & Whitney Wasp R-1340-49

Performance
Max. speed: 205 mph at 5,000 ft
Cruising speed: 170 mph
Range: 750 miles
Endurance: 3.9 hr
Service ceiling: 23,000 ft

History
The Harvard was one of the longest serving pilot training aircraft in the RAF. It was first delivered to the RAF in December 1938 and remained in service with the flying training schools until 1955. Even later it was still serving with the University Air Squadrons of Home Command and some saw service in operations in Kenya during the Mau Mau emergency. The Harvard I was the British version of the US Army Air Corps BC1. and 400 were supplied to the service. Later as many as 5,135 would go into service with British flying schools. The Mk.II had the characteristic triangular fin and rudder. Structural changes were also made when the steel tube fabric covered fuselage of the Mk.I was replaced by a light alloy monocoque in the rear fuselage except the Mk.IIA which had a plywood rear fuselage. One of the less endearing characteristics of the Harvard, was the high-pitched whine of the propeller. This was enough to waken the dead and was caused by the direct drive airscrew which gave the propeller a very high tip speed.

AIRCRAFT SPECIFICATION: (72)
FAIREY POSTAL

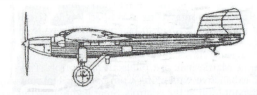

Span: 82 ft
Length: 48 ft 6 in.
Wing area: 900sq. ft
Weights: 15,500 lb

Power plant: One 570 hp Napier Lion XIA

Performance
Cruising speed: 110 mph
Range: over 5,000 miles
Take-off run for record flight was 1,600 yards

History
Following the failure of the Hawker Horsley in 1927 to gain the World Long Distance record for Britain, the Air Ministry made the decision to purchase an aircraft for this purpose. The Fairey Postal was chosen having long-span cantilever wings and a large fuel capacity of over 1,000 gallons which gave the aircraft a range of over 5,000 miles. Two of these aircraft were constructed and the first, J9479, made its initial flight at Northolt in November 1928 and in April 1929 Squadron Leader A.G. Jones-Williams with Flight Lieutenant N.H. Jenkins made the first non-stop flight from England to India. The aircraft left Cranwell on 24 April and landed at Karachi on 26 April after a flight of 4,130 miles with a flying time of 50 hr 37 min. Strong headwinds prevented the two men from reaching the intended destination of Bangalore. As it was only eight gallons of fuel remained on landing at Karachi and the distance record remained unbroken. A second attempt was made to South Africa but J.9479 crashed in Tunisia killing both occupants.

AIRCRAFT SPECIFICATION: (73)
SUPERMARINE S6 -6B

Span: 30 ft
Length: 28 ft 10 in.
Wing area: 145sq. ft

Weights: Empty- 4,560 lb
Loaded – 6,066 lb

Power plant: One 1,900 hp Rolls-Royce 'R' in the S6 and the 2,300 hp in the S6B.

Performance
Max. speed: 407 mph in 1931
Alighting Speed: 95 mph.

History
The RAF High-Speed Flight was formed at Felixstowe in April 1929 in readiness for the 1929 Schneider Trophy contest. The S6s were destined for this contest, the S6Bs for the one held in 1931. The first of the S6s were delivered five weeks before the race. Two Gloster VI seaplanes (N249 and N250) were also delivered to the Flight but were withdrawn from the race owing to problems with the engines and were used as training aircraft. The notable development was the replacement of the Napier Lion engines with the Rolls-Royce engines which were specially developed for racing. The S6 had a 1,900 hp engine, the S6B one of 2,300 hp. The water-cooling radiators of the S6B occupied almost the entire wing surfaces and the upper parts of the floats and oil cooling ducts lined the fuselage. Britain, having won the 1927 Schneider Trophy contest, was the venue for the one in 1929 and since Britain also won the 1929 contest that in 1931 was also held in the UK. (there were no contests in 1928 and 1930). Since, therefore, Britain won the contest on three consecutive occasions the rules of the competition meant that this country held the trophy in perpetuity. N247 was flown by Flying Officer Waghorn in the 1929 contest and he was declared the winner with an average speed of 328 mph. Flying Officer Atcherley gained the World speed record in N248 flying at 332 and 331 mph over the 50km and 100km courses respectively. On 12 September Squadron Leader Orlebar AFC raised the World speed record to 357.7 mph in N247. When these two S6 Seaplanes were fitted with larger floats they were designated S6A. The economic situation in Britain was such that the government was not prepared to

fund the 1931 contest at Spithead but due to the generosity of Lady Houston the funds were found and S6B Nos.S1595 and S1596 with larger floats and the 2,300 hp engines were the two team aircraft. Flight Lieutenant J.N. Boothman in S1595 won the contest averaging 340.08 mph. On 29 September Flight Lieutenant G.H. Stainforth achieved a World speed record with a speed of 407.5 mph. This made the Supermarine S6B the first aircraft in the world to fly at a speed in excess of 400 mph.

AIRCRAFT SPECIFICATION: (74)
VEGA GULL

Span: 39 ft 6 in.
Length: 25 ft 4 in.
Wing area:
Weights: loaded: 3,250 lb

Power plant: de Havilland Gypsy Six II

Performance
Max. speed: 174 mph
Range: 660 miles
Service ceiling: 16,000 ft

Air Ministry Specifications: 26/38

History
The Percival company built the Vega Gull which was developed from an earlier Gull and first appeared in 1935. Built to AM Spec.26/38, as a communications aircraft, it went into service with No.24 Communications Squadron in November1938 where it remained until October 1942. The first six went to No.24 Squadron with a further six going to other RAF units. This was the Vega Gull III and received the serial numbers P1749 – 54 and P5988 – 93. The Percival Proctor which went into RAF service was a direct derivative of the Vega Gull and the side elevation shown above is of a Proctor.

Appendix B
RAF Squadron Histories – Aircraft and Locations 1918 to 1939

SQUADRON LOCATIONS AND AIRCRAFT, 1918–39

No. 1 Squadron to No. 616 Squadron

(Note: Only those squadrons are listed that were in existence and service on 11 November 1918 or were formed or re-formed on or before 3 September 1939 and were still in service on the latter date.

F = Formed
RF = Re-formed
DB = Disbanded
Det/Dets = Detachment/s
(1/23) = Indicates month and year when aircraft ceased to be operational with that unit.

No. 1 SQUADRON   MOTTO: In omnibus princeps (First in all things)

Month/Yr	Location	Aircraft Type	Remarks
11/11/18	Bouvincourt	SE5A (2/19)	from 26/10/18
18/11/18	to Le Hameau	SE5A (2/19)	
3/3/19	to London (Colney)	SE5A (2/19)	as cadre
19/9/19	to Uxbridge	SE5A (2/19)	as cadre
21/1/20	Re-established at Risalpur	Snipe (11/26)	
1/4/20	Redesignated No. 1 Sqn		
11/5/20	to Bangalore	Snipe (11/26)	
20/4/21	to Hinaidi	Snipe (11/26)	Det Sulaimania
4/23		Nighthawk (9/23)	
1/11/26	DB		
1/2/27	RF Tangmere		
2/27		Siskin IIIA (2/32)	
2/32		Fury I (11/38)	
2/37		Gladiator I (3/37)	
10/38		Hurricane I (4/41)	

No. 2 SQUADRON   MOTTO: Hereward

Month/Yr	Location	Aircraft Type	Remarks
11/11/18	Genech	AW FK8 (2/19)	
14/2/19	to Bicester		As cadre
9/19	to Weston-on-Green		
20/1/20	DB		
1/2/20	Re-formed at Oranmore		
2/20		Bristol F2B (1/30)	det Castlebar, Fermoy, No. 105 Sqn renumbered
7/20	to Fermoy		det Oranmore
13/2/22	to Digby		
2/6/22	to Aldergrove		
29/9/22	to Farnborough		det Aldergrove
17/9/23	to Andover		
31/3/24	to Manston		
20/4/27	en route to China		via HMS *Hermes*
31/5/27	to Shanghai Racecourse		
13/9/27	en route to UK		via HMS *Hermes*
27/10/27	to Manston		
12/29		Atlas (6/33)	
5/33		Audax (11/37)	
30/11/35	to Hawkinge		
11/37		Hector (9/38)	
7/38		Lysander I (2/40)	

No. 3 SQUADRON   MOTTO: Tertius primus erit (The third shall be first)

Month/Yr	Location	Aircraft Type	Remarks
11/11/18	Inchy	Camel (2/19)	
15/2/19	to Wye		as cadre
2/5/19	to Swingate Down		
15/10/19	to Croydon		
27/10/19	to Uxbridge		
21/1/20	Re-established at Ambala		intially identified as 'A' Sqn
22/3/20	to Bangalore		

Month/Yr	Location	Aircraft Type	Remarks
1/4/20			'A' Sqn redesignated No. 3 Sqn
6/20		Snipe (3/21)	
1/4/21	to Ambala		
30/9/21	DB		
1/10/21	RF Leuchars		
10/21		DH9A (3 Seater) (10/22)	
1/22		Walrus (4/23)	
8/11/22	to Gosport		
1/4/23	DB		
1/4/24	RF Manston		
4/24		Snipe (8/25)	
30/4/24	to Upavon		
5/25		Woodcock II (8/28)	
8/28		Gamecock I (6/29)	
6/29		Bulldog II/IIA (7/37)	
10/5/34	to Kenley		
18/10/35	to Port Sudan		
22/10/35	to Khartoum		
22/1/36	to Port Sudan		
28/8/36	to Kenley		
3/37		Gladiator I (3/38)	
3/38		Hurricane I (7/38)	
7/38		Gladiator I (7/39)	
1/5/39	to Biggin Hill		
5/39		Hurricane I (4/41)	
2/9/39	to Croydon		

No. 4 SQUADRON   MOTTO: In futurum videre (to see into the future)

Month/Yr	Location	Aircraft Type	Remarks
11/11/18	Linselles	RE8 (2/19)	
16/11/18	to Ascq		
3/12/18	to Linselles		
13/2/19	to Northolt		as cadre
20/9/19	to Uxbridge		
30/4/20	to Farnborough		re-established
			dets Stonehenge, Aldergrove and Baldonnel
4/20		Bristol F2 B (10/29)	
26/9/22	en route to Turkey		via HMS *Ark Royal* and HMS *Argus*
11/10/22	to Kilya Bay		
11/12/22	to Kilid el Bahr		
5/9/23	en route to UK		
18/9/23	to Farnborough		
10/29		Atlas (2/32)	
12/31		Audax (7/37)	
16/2/37	to Odiham		
5/37		Hector (1/39)	
12/38		Lysander II (9/40)	

No. 5 SQUADRON   MOTTO: Frangus non flectas (thou mayst break but shall not bend me)

Month/Yr	Location	Aircraft Type	Remarks
11/11/18	Aulnoy	RE 8 (9/19)	
27/11/18	to Cognelée		
7/12/18	to Elsenborn		
21/12/18	to Hangelar		
3/19		Bristol F2 B (10/19)	
19/9/19	to Bicester		
9/10/19			reduced to cadre
20/1/20	DB		
1/4/20	RF Quetta	No. 48 Sqn renumbered	
			det Loralai
4/20		Bristol F2 B (5/31)	
26/10/22	to Ambala		det Saugor
10/3/24	to Dardoni		
22/1/25	to Kohat		dets Tank, Miranshah and Jhelum
15/10/25	to Risalpur		dets Quetta, Miranshah Hassani Abdel and Jhelum
15/12/28	to Quetta		dets Risalpur and Drigh Road
16/5/30	to Kohat		det Miranshah
15/5/31	to Quetta		dets Secunderabad, Poona,
	Jubbulpore, Ford Sandeman		
5/31		Wapiti (6/40)	
9/6/35	to Drigh Road		as cadre
31/7/35	re-established		
1/8/35	to Risalpur		
15/10/35	to Chaklala		dets Julalpore, Lahore, Risalpur, Kohat and Miranshah

Month/Yr	Location	Aircraft Type	Remarks
6/3/37	to Miranshah		
20/4/37	to Risalpur		dets Miranshah and Chaklala
8/11/37	to Chaklala		dets Miranshah
23/4/38	to Risalpur		dets Arawali,Kohat,Miranshah
	Ford Sandeman, Hakimpet		
	and Sialkot		

No. 6 SQUADRON   MOTTO: Oculi exercitus (The eyes of the army)

Month/Yr	Location	Aircraft Type	Remarks
11/11/18	Gondecourt	RE8 (7/20)	
16/11/18	to Pecq		
6/12/18	to Gerpinnes		
2/19		Bristol F2 B (4/19)	
19/3/19	to Sart		
14/4/19	en route to Middle		
	East via Marseilles		
16/7/19	to Basrah		
6/9/19	to Baghdad West	dets Bushire, Abu Kemal	
	and Annah		
7/20		Bristol F2 B (6/32)	dets Samawah,Hillah. Kirkuk
	Mosul and Sulaimania		
9/10/22	to Hinaidi		
19/5/24	to Mosul		
20/10/26	to Hinaidi		
28/10/29	to Ismailia		dets Semakh, Ramleh,Haifa
	& Qasaba		
6/31		Gordon (10/35)	
9/35		Hart (1/38)	
10/35		Demon (11/36)	
29/5/36	to Ramleh		det Semakh
19/11/36	to Ismaila		
22/11/37	to Ramleh		
1/38		Hardy (4/40)	
8/39		Gauntlet I & II (4/40)	
9/39		Lysander I (12/39)	

No. 7 SQUADRON   MOTTO: Per diem,per noctem (By day and by night)

Month/Yr	Location	Aircraft Type	Remarks
11/11/18	Menin	RE 8 (10/19)	
15/11/18	to Stacegham		
25/11/18	to Peronnes		
26/11/18	to Fort Cognelee		
6/12/18	to Elsenborn		
15/12/18	to Bickendorf		
20/12/18	to Spich		
11/5/19	to Bucheim		
7/8/19	to Heumar		
21/9/19	to Old Sarum		
9/10/19	reduced to a cadre		
27/10/19	to Eastleigh		
19/11/19	to Farnborough		
31/12/19	DB		
1/6/23	RF Bircham Newton	from D Flt 100 Sqn	
6/23		Vimy(4/27)	
5/24		Virginia III (5/25}	
9/24		Virginia II (2/27)	
9/24		Virginia IV (6/25)	
1/25		Virginia V (5/26)	
6/25		Virginia VI (8/26)	
3/27		Virginia VII (1/33)	
7/4/27	to Worthy Down		
9/27		Virginia IX (8/33)	
11/28		Virginia X (4/38)	
4/35		Heyford II (4/38)	
4/36		Heyford III (4/38)	
3/9/36	to Finningley		
4/37		Wellesley (4/38)	
3/38		Whitley II (12/38)	
11/38		Whitley III (5/39)	
4/39		Hampden (4/40)	
1/9/39	to Doncaster		

No. 8 SQUADRON   MOTTO: Uspiam et passim (Everywhere unbounded)

Month/Yr	Location	Aircraft Type	Remarks
11/11/18	Malincourt	AWFK 8 (12/18)	
16/11/18	to La Bellevue		
12/18		Bristol F2B (7/19	

Month/Yr	Location	Aircraft Type	Remarks
11/5/19	to Sart		
28/7/19	to Duxford		
20/1/20	DB		
18/10/20	RF Helwan		
10/20		DH9A (Jun 28)	
11/12/20	to Suez		
23/2/21	to Basrah		
4/3/21	to Baghdad West		
29/12/21	to Hinaidi		
27/2/27	to Khormaksar		
1/28		Fairey IIIF (3/35)	
2/35		Vincent (11/40)	
10/35		Demon	Oct 35 – 1 Flt only
			det Burao
4/39		Blenheim (10/41)	dets Riyan, Berbera & Sheikh Othman

No. 9 SQUADRON   MOTTO: Per noctum volamus (Through the night we fly)

Month/Yr	Location	Aircraft Type	Remarks
11/11/18	Tarcienne	RE 8 (5/19)	
11/12/18	to Fort Cognelée		
19/12/18	to Clavier		
3/1/19	to Ludendorf		
2/19		Bristol F2B (7/19)	
30/7/19	to Castle Bromwich		
31/12/19	DB		
4/24		Vimy (10/25)	
30/4/24	to Manston		
9/24		Virginia IV (3/27)	
1/25		Virginia V (5/26)	
6/25		Virginia VI (4/27)	
7/26		Virginia VII (6/30)	
1/27		Virginia VIII (3/27)	
7/27		Virginia IX (2/32)	
1/29		Virginia X (4/36)	
26/11/30	to Boscombe Down		
15/10/35	to Andover		
15/1/36	to Aldergrove		
3/36		Heyford III (5/39)	
1/10/36	to Scampton		
10/3/38	to Stradishall		
1/39		Wellington I (12/39)	
15/7/39	to Honington		
9/39		Wellington I (9/40)	det Lossiemouth

No. 10 SQUADRON   MOTTO: Rem acu tangere (To hit the mark)

Month/Yr	Location	Aircraft Type	Remarks
11/11/18	Stacegham	AWFK 8 (2/19)	
15/11/18	to Menin		
1/12/18	to Reckem		
17/2/19	to Ford Junction	as cadre	
15/10/19	to Croydon		
31/12/19	DB		
3/1/28	RF Upper Heyford		
1/28		Hyderabad (11/31)	
12/30		Hinaidi (9/32)	
1/4/31	to Boscombe Down		
9/32		Virginia X (1/35)	
8/34		Heyford IA (1/36)	
11/35		Heyford III (6/37)	
25/1/37	to Dishforth		
3/37		Whitley I (6/39)	
5/39		Whitley IV (5/40)	dets Villeneuve & Kinloss

No. 11 SQUADRON   MOTTO: Ociores acrioresque (Swifter and keener than eagles)

Month/Yr	Location	Aircraft Type	Remarks
11/11/18	Béthencourt	Bristol F2B (10/19)	
18/11/18	to Aulnoy		
19/12/18	to Nivelles		
20/5/19	to Spich		
3/9/19	to Scopwick		
9/10/19			reduced to cadre
31/12/19	DB		
15/1/23	RF Andover		
1/23		DH9A (4/24)	
16/9/23	to Bircham Newton		
4/24		Fawn (5/27)	
31/5/24	to Netheravon		

Month/Yr	Location	Aircraft Type	Remarks
11/26		Horsley (11/28)	
10/28		Wapiti (8/32)	
29/12/28	en route to India		
22/1/29	to Risalpur		det Miranshah
2/32		Hart (7/39)	fets Gilgit, Arawali & Miranshah
7/39		Blenheim I (1/41)	
7/8/39	to Tengah		

No. 12 SQUADRON   MOTTO: (Leads the field)

11/11/18	Estourmel	RE 8 (7/19)	
		Bristol F2 B (7/22)	
29/11/18	to Clavier		
19/12/18	to Duren		
5/5/19	to Heumar		
17/11/20	to Bickendorf		
27/7/22	DB		
1/4/23	RF Northolt		
4/23		DH9A (3/24)	
24/3/24	to Andover		
3/24		Fawn (12/26)	
6/26		Fox (1/31)	
1/31		Hart (10/36)	
4/10/35	en route to Aden		
20/10/35	to Khormaksar		
18/5/36	to Robat		
28/7/36	to Khormaksar		
11/8/36	en route to UK		
29/8/36	to Andover		
10/36		Hind (2/38)	
2/38		Battle (11/40)	
9/5/39	to Bicester		
2/9/39	to Berry-au-Bac		

No. 13 SQUADRON   MOTTO: Ajuvamus tuendo (We assist by watching)

11/11/18	Carnières	RE 8 (3/19)	
1/12/18	to Vert Galand		
19/1/19	to St Omer		
27/3/19	to Sedgeford		as cadre
31/12/19	DB		
30/5/24	RF Kenley		
4/24		Bristol F2B (1/38)	
30/5/24	to Andover		
8/27		Atlas (7/32)	
23/9/29	to Netheravon		
5/32		Audax (5/37)	
3/5/35	to Old Sarum		
5/37		Hector (2/39)	
1/39		Lysander II (1/41)	

No. 14 SQUADRON   MOTTO: I spread my wings and keep my promise

11/11/18	Mikra Bay	RE 8 (11/18)	
9/12/18	en route to UK		
1/1/19	to Tangmere	as cadre	
2/2/19	DB		
1/1/20	RF Ramleh		No.111 Sqn renumbered
2/20		Bristol F2B (2/36)	dets Amman, Damascus, Aleppo, Mafraq & Beersheba
6/24		DH9A (3/30)	
15/2/26	to Amman		
11/29		Fairy IIIF (9/32)	
7/32		Gordon (4/38)	
3/38		Wellesley (12/40)	
24/8/39	to Ismailia		

No. 15 SQUADRON   MOTTO: Aim Sure

11/11/18	Selvigny (Ferme Guilleman)	RE 8 (2/19)	
2/12/19	to Fowlmere		as cadre
31/12/19	DB		
20/3/24	RF Martlesham		as A & AE Trials Unit Heath
3/24		DH9A (10/26)	
10/26		Horseley (5/34)	
31/5/34	DB		note that equipment was largely notional and would have been that operated in the event of mobilisation.

Month/Yr	Location	Aircraft Type	Remarks
1/6/34	RF Abingdon		
6/34		Hart (6/36)	
3/36		Hind (7/38)	
6/38		Battle (12/39)	
2/9/38	to Betheniville		

No. 16 SQUADRON MOTTO: Operta aperta (Hidden things are revealed)

Month/Yr	Location	Aircraft Type	Remarks
11/11/18	Auchy	RE8 (219)	
14/2/19	to Fowlmere		as cadre
31/12/19	DB		
1/4/24	RF Old Sarum		Co-op Sqn of School of Army Co-operation redesignated
4/24		Bristol F2 B (3/31)	
1/31		Atlas (1/34)	
12/33		Audax (10/38)	
5/38		Lysander I (4/39)	
4/39		Lysander II (11/40)	

No. 17 SQUADRON MOTTO: Excellere contende (Strive to excel)

Month/Yr	Location	Aircraft Type	Remarks
11/11/18	Amberkoj	DH9 (11/19)	Flts at Philipopolis, Mustapha Pasha, Mikra Bay & Batum
12/18		Camel (11/19)	
28/1/19	to San Stephano		dets Kars & Tiflis
14/11/19	DB		
1/4/24	RF Hawkinge		
4/24		Snipe (3/26)	
3/26		Woodcock II (1/28)	
14/10/26	to Upavon		
1/28		Gamecock I (9/28)	
9/28		Siskin IIIA (10/29)	
10/29		Bulldog II/IIA (8/36)	
23/5/39	to North Weald		
6/39		Hurricane I (2/41)	
2/9/39	to Croydon		

No. 18 SQUADRON MOTTO: Animo et Fide (With courage and faith)

Month/Yr	Location	Aircraft Type	Remarks
11/11/18	La Brayelle	DH9A (8/19)	
28/11/18	to Maubeuge		
24/1/19	to Bickendorf		
1/5/19	to Merheim		
9/9/19	to Weston-on-the-Green		as cadre
31/12/19	DB		
20/10/31	RF Upper Heyford		
10/31		Hart (5/39)	
7/1/36	to Bircham Newton		
4/36		Hind (5/39)	
7/9/36	to Upper Heyford		
5/39		Blenheim (5/40)	

No. 19 SQUADRON MOTTO: Possunt quia posse videntur (They can because they think they can)

Month/Yr	Location	Aircraft Type	Remarks
11/11/18	Abscon	Dolphin (1/19)	
9/2/19	to Genech		
18/2/19	to Ternhill		as cadre
31/12/19	DB		
1/4/23	RF Duxford		one Flight only, attached to No. 2 FTS
4/23		Snipe (12/24)	brought up to strength
1/6/24			
12/24		Grebe II (4/28)	
3/28		Siskin IIIA (9/31)	
9/31		Bulldog IIA (1/35)	
1/35		Gauntlet I (3/39)	
9/36		Gauntlet II (2/39)	
8/38		Spitfire I (12/40)	

No. 20 SQUADRON MOTTO: Facta non verba (Deeds not words)

Month/Yr	Location	Aircraft Type	Remarks
11/11/18	Iris Farm	Bristol F2B (5/19)	
3/12/18	to Ossogne		
30/4/19	en route to India		
16/6/19	to Risalpur		
7/19		Bristol F2 B (3/32)	dets Tank & Sorarogha
21/719	to Parachinar		dets Risalpur & Bannu
2/9/19	to Bannu		det Tank
18/7/20	to Parachinar		det Tank

Month/Yr	Location	Aircraft Type	Remarks
5/11/20	to Tank		
20/4/21	to Parachinar		
17/10/21	to Ambala		
24/10/22	to Quetta		det Loralai
5/1/25	to Peshawar		det Miranshah
22/5/25	to Kohat		dets Miranshah
12/10/25	to Peshawar		dets Miranshah, Quetta & Manzai
1/32		Wapiti (12/35)	dets Miranshah, Hassani Abdel, Jhelum & Quetta
12/35		Audax (12/41)	
2/12/36	to Peshawar		dets Risalpur, Hassani Abdel & Arawali
7/1/37	to Miranshah		
14/8/37	to Peshawar		det Miranshah
13/5/38	to Miranshah		
20/5/39	to Peshahwar		dets Miranshah, Kohat & Prarachinar
29/8/39	to Miranshah		dets Manzai & Peshawar

No. 21 SQUADRON   MOTTO: Viribus vincimus (By strength we conquer)

11/11/18	Froidmont	RE 8 (2/19)	
16/11/18	to Sweveghem		
18/12/18	to Coucou		
14/2/19	To Fowlmere		as cadre
1/10/19	DB		
3/12/35	RF Bircham Newton		nucleus from 82 Sqn
12/35		Hind (8/38)	
25/7/36	to Abbotsinch		
3/11/36	to Lympne		
15/8/38	to Eastchurch		
8/38		Blenheim I (9/39)	
2/3/39	to Watton		
9/39		Blenheim IV (3/42)	dets Bassingbourne, Horsham St Faith & Bodney

No. 22 SQUADRON   MOTTO: Preux et audacieux (Valiant and brave)

11/11/18	Aniche	Bristol F2B (8/19)	
17/11/18	to Aulnoye		
22/11/18	to Wiheries		
20/12/18	to Nivelles		
21/5/19	to Spich		
31/8/19	to Ford Junction		as cadre
31/12/19	DB		
24/7/23	RF Martlesham		as A & AE Trials Unit Heath
7/23		DH9A (10/26)	
10/26		Horsley (5/34)	
1/5/34	DB		Note: equipment was largely notional and would have been that operated in the event of mobilisation
1/5/34	RF Donibristle		
5/34		Vildebeeste I (10/35)	
5/35		Vildebeeste III (2/40)	
10/10/35	to Hal Far		
29/8/36	to Donibristle		
10/3/38	to Thorney Island		
3/38		Vildebeeste IV (2/40)	
9/39		Vildebeeste I (11/39)	

No. 23 SQUADRON   MOTTO: Semper Aggressus (Always having attacked)

11/11/18	Bertry East	Dolphin (3/19)	
3/12/18	to Clermont		
15/3/19	to Waddington		as cadre
31/12/19	DB		
1/7/25	RF Henlow		
7/25		Snipe (4/26)	
4/26		Gamecock I (9/31)	
6/2/27	to Kenley		
7/31		Bulldog IIA (4/33)	
7/31		Hart Fighter (7/32)	
7/32		Demon (12/38)	
17/9/32	to Biggin Hill		
21/12/36	to Northolt		
16/5/38	to Wittering		
12/38		Blenheim IF (4/41)	

No. 24 SQUADRON   MOTTO: In omnia parati (ready in all things)

11/11/18	to Bisseghem	SE5A (1/19)	
16/11/18	to Ennetières		

Month/Yr	Location	Aircraft Type	Remarks
12/2/19	to London Colney		as cadre
19/9/19	to Uxbridge		
1/2/20	re-established at Kenley from the Air Council Inspection Squadron		
2/20		Bristol F2B (7/30)	
7/20		DH9A (6/27)	
15/1/27	to Northolt		
1/27		Avro 504N	
1/27		Moth (7/33)	
6/28		Wapiti (/30)	
7/28		Fairey IIIF (/33)	
7/30		Tomtit (/33)	
11/31		Tutor (10/32)	
1/33		Hart C (7/41)	
6/33		Tiger Moth (6/38)	
10/7/33	to Hendon		
7/33		Audax (2/38)	
3/35		Dragon Rapide /Dominie (10/44)	
7/37		Nighthawk (9/38)	
10/37		DH86 Express (3/43)	
6/38		Magister I (/40)	
6/38		Anson I (6/38)	
10/38		Mentor (8/44)	
11/38		Vega Gull (10/42)	
9/39		Leopard Moth (4/40)	

No. 25 SQUADRON   MOTTO: Feriens tego (Striking I defend)

Month/Yr	Location	Aircraft Type	Remarks
11/11/18	La Brayelle	DH9A (10/19)	
29/11/18	to Maubeuge		
26/5/19	to Bickendorf		
7/7/19	to Merheim		
6/9/19	to South Carlton		
9/10/19		reduced to a cadre	
3/12/19	to Scopwick		
31/1/20	DB		
26/4/20	RF Hawkinge		
4/20		Snipe (10/24)	
28/9/22	en route to Turkey		
11/10/22	to San Stephano		
22/9/23	en route to UK		
3/10/23	to Hawkinge		
10/24		Grebe II (7/29)	
5/29		Siskin IIIA (3/32)	
2/32		Fury I (/37)	
11/36		Fury II (10/37)	
10/37		Demon (6/38)	
6/38		Gladiator I (2/39)	
26/9/38	to Northolt		
12/10/38	to Hawkinge		
12/38		Blenheim IF (1/41)	
22/8/39	to Northolt		

No. 26 SQUADRON   MOTTO: 'N wagter in die Lug (A guard in the sky)

Month/Yr	Location	Aircraft Type	Remarks
11/10/27	RF Catterick		
10/27		Atlas (9/33)	
7/33		Audax (9/37)	
8/37		Hector (5/39)	
2/29		Lysander III (11/40)	

No. 27 SQUADRON   MOTTO: Quam celerrime ad astra (With all speed to the stars)

Month/Yr	Location	Aircraft Type	Remarks
11/11/18	Villers-les-Cagnicourt		
28/11/18	to Bavay	DH 9(3/19)	
18/3/19	to Scopwick		as cadre
22/1/20	DB		
1/4/20	RF Mianwali		No. 99 Sqn renumbered
4/20		DH9A (5/30)	
14/4/20	to Risalpur		dets Tank & Dardoni
14/12/22	to Dardoni		
20/4/23	to Rislapur		dets Dardoni, Miranshah & Arawali
26/5/25	to Peshawar		
12/10/25	to Risalpur		det Miranshah
17/12/28	to Kohat		
4/30		Wapiti (11/40)	dets Manzai, Miranshah, Juhu, Arawali, Gilgit & St Thomas Mount

Month/Yr	Location	Aircraft Type	Remarks
No. 28 SQUADRON	**MOTTO: Quicquid agas age (Whatsoever you may do,do)**		
11/11/18	Sarcedo	Camel (2/19)	
10/3/19	to Yatesbury		as cadre
29/3/19	to Leighterton		
20/10/19	to Eastleigh		
20/1/20	DB		
1/4/20	RF Ambala		No. 114 Sqn renumbered
4/20		Bristol F2B (9/31)	
15/10/21	to Kohat		dets Dardoni, & Tank
15/4/22	to Parachinar		
10/10/22	to Kohat		
12/12/22	to Dardoni		
17/3/23			to Tank
19/4/23	to Peshawar and Tank		dets Dardoni, Hassani, Abdel
5/1/25	to Quetta		det Poona
15/12/26	to Ambala		dets Poona, Bangalore, Deolali Secunderabad, Jubbulpore, Saugor & Miranshah
13/8/30	to Risalpur		
1/12/30	to Ambala		
9/31		Wapiti (7/36)	dets Jhelum, Delhi, Peshawar, Mhow & Jullundur
6/36		Audax (12/41)	det Delhi)
23/4/37	to Manzai		det Miranshah
6/7/37	to Ambala		dets Delhi, Juhu & Miranshah
3/3/39	to Kohat		dets Miranshah,Peshawar, Arawali Manzai, Risalpur, Quetta, Drigh Rd, Dum Dum, Fort Sandemen, Jhelum, Jullundur & Sialkot
No. 29 SQUADRON	**MOTTO: Impiger at acer (Energetic and keen)**		
11/11/18	Marcke	SE 5A (8/19)	
26/11/18	to Nivelles		
19/12/18	to Bickendorf		
11/8/19	to Spittlegate		as cadre
31/12/19	DB		
1/4/23	RF Duxford		
4/23		Snipe (1/25)	
1/25		Grebe II (3/28)	
3/28		Siskin IIIA (6/32)	
1/4/28	to North Weald		
6/32		Bulldog IIA (4/35)	
3/35		Demon (3/36)	
31/10/35	to Amiriya		
3/36		Gordon (8/36)	
20/7/36	to Helwan		
6/8/36	to Aboukir		
12/9/36	to North Weald		
10/36		Demon (Turret) 12/38	
22/11/37	to Debden		
12/38		Blenheim IF (2/41)	det Martlesham Heath
No. 30 SQUADRON	**MOTTO:Ventre a terre (All out)**		
11/11/18	Kifri	Martinsyde G100 (2/19)	Flt at Baquba dets Hamadan and Zinjan
23/11/18	to Baquba		Flts at Kifri,Kazvin,Baghdad & Bushire
1/19		SE 5A (2/19)	
2/4/19	to Baghdad		
9/4/19			reduced to a cadre
1/2/20			re-established at Baghdad West from No. 63 Sqn
2/20		RE 8 (1/21)	dets Mosul, Kazvin, Bushire, Ramadi & Samawah
1/21		DH 9A(9/29)	
3/12/22	to Hinaidi		det Kirkuk
11/4/27	to Kirkuk		dets Hinaidi & Sulaimania
27/10/27	to Hinaidi		
4/29		Wapiti (8/35)	
23/10/29	to Mosul		
4/35		Hardy (4/38)	
19/10/36	to Dhibban		
1/38		Blenheim I (3/41)	
25/8/39	to Ismailia		det El Daba
No. 31 SQUADRON	**MOTTO: In caelum indicum primus (First into Indian skies)**		
11/11/18	Risalpur & Lahore	BE 2E (2/20)	dets Bannu, Tank, Khanpur, Dera Ismail Khan, Dera Ghazi Khan
6/19		Bristol F2B (4/31)	dets Bannu, Tank & Kohat
15/4/20	to Mhow		

Month/Yr	Location	Aircraft Type	Remarks
26/11/20	to Cawnpore		
31/10/21	to Peshawar		dets Tank & Dardoni
17/4/23	to Dardoni		
13/3/24	to Ambala		dets Quetta
15/12/26	to Quetta		dets Jubbulpore,Mhow, Fort Dandeman & Loralai
2/31		Wapiti (8/39)	dets Fort Sandeman, Secunderabad, Hakimpet & Mhow
8/6/35	to Drigh Road		as cadre
1/8/35			re-established. Dets Quetta, Hakimpet, Jubbulpore, Fort Sandeman, Poona & Risalpur
27/10/38	to Lahore & Risalpur		dets Fort Sandeman, Jubbulpore, Ambala
4/39		Valentia (8/41)	

No. 32 SQUADRON   MOTTO: Adeste comites (Rally round comrades)

Month/Yr	Location	Aircraft Type	Remarks
11/11/18	La Brayelle	SE 5A(3/19)	
16/1/18	to Le Hameau		
18/1/19	to Serny		
5/3/19	to Tangmere		as cadre
8/10/19	to Croydon		
31/12/19	DB		
1/4/23	RF Kenley		
4/23		Snipe (12/24)	
11/24		Grebe II (1/27)	
9/26		Gamecock (I (4/28)	
4/28		Siskin III (1/31)	
1/31		Bulldog IIA (7/36)	
21/9/32	to Biggin Hill		
7/36		Gauntlet II (10/38)	
10/38		Hurricane I (7/41)	

No. 33 SQUADRON   MOTTO: Loyalty

Month/Yr	Location	Aircraft Type	Remarks
11/11/18	Kirton-in-Lindsey	Avro 504K (6/19)	dets Scampton & Elsham
2/6/19	to Harpswell		
13/6/19	DB		
1/3/29	RF Netheravon		
3/29		Horsley (3/30)	
14/9/29	to Eastchurch		
2/30		Hart (2/38)	
5/11/30	to Bicester		
27/11/34	to Upper Heyford		
4/11/35	en route to Egypt		
25/10/35	to Mersa Matruh		det Ramleh
13/7/36	to Amman		det Ramleh
10/8/36	to Gaza		
14/11/36	to Ismailia		
2/38		Gladiator I (6/40)	det Ramleh
29/9/38	to Heliopolis		det Ramleh
3/10/38	to Ismailia		
21/10/38	to Ramleh		dets Lydda & Amman
24/4/39	to Helwan		
25/5/39	to Ismailia		dets El Daba & Qasaba
5/8/39	to Qasaba		
1/9/39	to Mersah Matruh		

No. 34 SQUADRON   MOTTO: Lupus vult, lupus volat (Wolf wishes, wolf flies)

Month/Yr	Location	Aircraft Type	Remarks
11/11/18	San Luca	Bristol F2 B (7/18)	
16/11/18	to Villaverla		
28/2/19	to Caldiero		
3/5/19	to Old Sarum		as cadre
15/10/19	DB		
3/12/35	RF Bircham Newton		nucleus from No. 18 sqn
1/36		Hind (7/38)	
30/7/36	to Abbotsinch		
3/11/36	to Lympne		
12/7/38	to Upper Heyford		
7/38		Blenheim I (11/41)	
2/3/39	to Watton		
12/8/39	en route to Far East to Tengah		

Month/Yr	Location	Aircraft Type	Remarks
No. 35 SQUADRON	**MOTTO: Uno animo agimus (We act with one accord)**		
11/11/18	to Grand Fayt	Bristol F2B (1/19)	
13/11/18	to Elincourt		
29/11/18	to La Bellevue		
19/1/19	to Ste-Maries-Vappel		as cadre
3/3/19	to Netheravon		
26/6/19	DB		
1/3/29	RF Bircham Newton		
3/29		DH 9A (1/30)	
11/29		Fairey IIIF (9/32)	
7/32		Gordon (8/36)	
4/10/35			en route to Middle East
18/10/35	to Ed Damer		
7/4/36	to Gebeit		
14/8/36			en route to UK
26/8/36	to Worthy Down		
11/36		Gordon (9/37)	
7/37		Wellesley (5/38)	
4/38		Battle (2/40)	
20/4/38	to Cottesmore		
7/39		Anson I (4/40)	
25/8/39	to Cranfield		

Month/Yr	Location	Aircraft Type	Remarks
No. 36 SQUADRON	**MOTTO: Rajawali raja langit (Eagle king of the sky)**		
11/11/18	Hylton/Usworth	Bristol F2B	dets Seaton Carew & Ashington
13/6/19	DB		
9/10/28	RF Donibristle		Coastal Defence Torpedo Flt redesignated
10/28		Horsley (7/35)	
14/10/30	to Far East by sea		via Leuchars
14/11/30	to Seletar		
7/35		Vildebeeste III (3/42)	dets Kota, Bahru, Gong Kedak & Kuantan

Month/Yr	Location	Aircraft Type	Remarks
No. 37 SQUADRON	**MOTTO: Wise without eyes**		
11/11/18	Stow Maries	Camel (7/19)	det Goldhanger
17/3//19	to Biggin Hill	Snipe (7/19)	
1/7/19	DB		renumbered as No. 39 Sqn
26/4/37	RF Feltwell		from B Flt. No. 214 Sqn
4/37		Harrow (6/39)	
5/39		Wellington I (11/39)	

Month/Yr	Location	Aircraft Type	Remarks
No. 38 SQUADRON	**MOTTO: Ante lucem (Before the dawn)**		
11/11/18	Harlebeck	FE2b (1/19)	
16/12/18	to Serny		
14/2/19	to Hawkinge		as cadre
4/7/19	DB		
16/9/35	RF Mildenhall		nucleus from B Flt. No. 99 Sqn
9/35		Heyford III (6/37)	
11/36		Hendon II (1/39)	
5/5/37	to Marham		
11/38		Wellington I (4/40)	
9/39		Wellington IA (6/40)	

Month/Yr	Location	Aircraft Type	Remarks
No. 39 SQUADRON	**MOTTO: Die Noctuque (By day and night)**		
11/11/18	North Weald	Bristol F2B (11/18)	
16/11/18	DB		deployment to Bavichore abandoned before completion
1/7/19	RF Biggin Hill		No. 37 Sqn renumbered
7/19		Snipe (10/19)	
14/10/19			reduced to a cadre
20/12/19	to Uxbridge		
12/4/20	to Kenley		
12/3/21	to Spittlegate		re-established
4/21		DH9A (11/28)	
12/1/28	to Bircham Newton		
29/12/28	en route to India		
22/1/29	to Risalpur		
3/29		Wapiti (12/31)	dets Miranshah, Gilgit & Peshawar
11/31		Hart (7/39)	dets Jhelum, Delhi, Gilgit & Miranshah
6/39		Blenheim I (1/41)	
12/8/39	to Tengah		

Month/Yr	Location	Aircraft Type	Remarks

No. 40 SQUADRON   MOTTO: Hostem coelo expellere (To drive the enemy from the sky)

Month/Yr	Location	Aircraft Type	Remarks
11/11/18	Aniche	SE 5A (2/19)	
29/12/18	to Orcq		
13/2/19	to Tangmere		as cadre
4/7/19	DB		
1/4/31	RF Upper Heyford		
4/31		Gordon (11/35)	
8/10/32	to Abingdon		
11/35		Hart (Special) (3/36)	
3/36		Hind (8/38)	
7/38		Battle (12/29)	
2/9/39	to Béthenville		

No. 41 SQUADRON   MOTTO: Seek and Destroy

Month/Yr	Location	Aircraft Type	Remarks
11/11/18	Halluin	SE5A (2/19)	
10/2/19	to Tangmere		as cadre
8/10/19	to Croydon		
31/12/19	DB		
1/4/23	RF Northolt		
4/23		Snipe (5/24)	
5/24		Siskin III (3/27)	
3/27		Siskin IIIA (11/31)	
10/31		Bulldog IIA (8/34)	
7/34		Demon (10/37)	
4/10/35	en route to Aden		
20/10/35	to Khormaksar		
18/3/36	to Sheikh Othman		
11/8/36	en route to the UK		
25/9/36	to Catterick		
10/37		Fury II (1/39)	
1/39	`	Spitfire I (11/40)	

No. 42 SQUADRON   MOTTO: Fortiter in re (Bravely in action)

Month/Yr	Location	Aircraft Type	Remarks
11/11/18	Ascq	RE 8 (2/19)	
14/11/18	to Marquain		
26/11/18	to Aulnoy		
11/12/18	to Saultain		
30/12/18	to Abscon		
18/2/19	to Netheravon		as cadre
26/6/19	DB		
14/12/36	RF Donibristle		from B Flt. No. 22 sqn
12/36		Vildebeeste III (12/37)	
1/37		Vildebeeste I (3/37)	
3/37		Vildebeeste IV (4/40)	
11/3/38	to Thorney Island & Gosport		dets Eastleigh, Lee-on-Solent, Tangmere
28/9/38	to Thornaby		
11/10/38	to Thorney Island		
18/8/39	to Bircham Newton		
9/39		Vildebeeste III (4/40)	

No. 43 SQUADRON   MOTTO: Gloria finis (Glory in the end)

Month/Yr	Location	Aircraft Type	Remarks
11/11/18	Bouvincourt	Snipe (9/19)	
15/11/18	to Bisseghem		
26/11/18	to Fort Cognelée		
19/12/18	to Bickendorf		
12/8/19	to Eil		
25/8/19	to Spittlegate		
28/9/19			reduced to a cadre
31/12/19	DB		
1/7/25	RF Henlow		
7/25		Snipe (5/26)	
4/26		Gamecock I (6/28)	
12/12/26	to Tangmere		
6/28		Siskin IIIA (5/31)	
5/31		Fury I (1/39)	
12/38		Hurricane I (4/41)	

No. 44 SQUADRON   MOTTO: Fulmina regis justa (The King's thunderbolts are righteous)

Month/Yr	Location	Aircraft Type	Remarks
11/11/18	Hainault Farm	Camel (6/19)	
1/7/19	to North Weald Basset		as cadre
31/12/19	DB		
8/3/37	RF Wyton		

Month/Yr	Location	Aircraft Type	Remarks
3/37		Hind (12/37)	
18/3/37	to Andover		
16/6/37	to Waddington		
12/37		Blenheim I (2/39)	
2/39		Anson I (6/39)	
2/39		Hampden (12/41)	det Lossiemouth

No. 45 SQUADRON   MOTTO: Per Ardua surgo (Through difficulties I arise)

Month/Yr	Location	Aircraft Type	Remarks
11/11/18	Bettoncourt	Camel (1/19)	
10/18		Snipe (1/19)	
21/11/18	to Izel-le-Hameau		
19/1/19	to Liettres		
17/2/19	to Rendcombe		as cadre
15/10/19	to Eastleigh		
31/12/19	DB		
1/4/21			RF Helwan
4/21		DH 9A (7/21)	
11/7/21	to Almaza		
7/21		Vimy (2/22)	
2/22		Vernon (1/27)	
14/3/22	to Basrah		
14/4/22	to Baghdad West		
16/5/22	to Hinaidi		
17/1/27	to Helwan		as cadre
25/4/27			re-established at Heliopolis
4/27		DH 9A (9/29)	
21/10/27	to Helwan		det Ramleh
8/29		Fairey IIIF	dets Amman, Gaza, Ismailia, Hinaidi Mosul, Shaibah & Eastleigh
9/35		Hart (1/36)	
11/35		Vincent (12/37)	
1/36		Gordon (12/36)	Eastleigh det of the squadron became nucleus of 223 Sqn
11/37		Wellesley (6/39)	
3/1/39	to Ismailia		
6/39		Blenheim I (2/41)	
4/8/39	to Fuka		

No. 46 SQUADRON   MOTTO: We rise to conquer

Month/Yr	Location	Aircraft Type	Remarks
11/11/18	Busigny	Camel 2/19)	
16/11/18	to Baizieux		
10/2/19	to Rendcomb		as cadre
31/12/19	DB		
3/9/36	RF Kenley		from B Flt. No. 17 Sqn
9/36		Gauntlet II (3/39)	
15/11/37	to Digby		
3/39		Hurricane I (5/41)	

No. 47 SQUADRON   MOTTO: Nili nomen roboris omen (The name of the Nile is an omen of our strength)

Month/Yr	Location	Aircraft Type	Remarks
11/11/18	Yanesh	AW FK8 (1/19)	Flts @ Mikra Bay, Kukush,Snevche
		DH 9 (10/19)	Hadzi, Junas, Kirec, Kalabac, Hajdarli, Amberkoj, dets Thasos, Florina, Mudros,Gmuldjina & Dedeagatch
14/2/19	to Amberkoj		
24/4/19	to Novorossisk		
4/6/19	to Ekaterinodar		Flts @ Velikoknyajaskaya, Zimovniki, Kotelnikovo, Gniloaksaiskaya & Beketovka
8/19		DH 9A (10/19)	
9/19		Camel (10/19)	
7/10/19	to Beketovka		
20/10/19	DB		redesignated asNos.11,12 & 13 sqns Russian 7th Division
1/2/20	RF Helwan		No. 206 Sqn renumbered
2/20		DH 9 (9/20)	det Khartoum
6/20		DH 9A (6/28)	
21/10/27	to Khartoum		
12/27		Fairey IIIF (1/33)	
1/33		Gordon (12/39)	
7/36		Vincent (8/40)	
6/39		Wellesley (3/43)	det Kapoeta

Month/Yr	Location	Aircraft Type	Remarks
No. 48 SQUADRON	**MOTTO: Forte et fidele (Bravely and faithfully)**		
11/11/18	Reckem	Bristol F2B (5/19)	
17/11/18	to Nivelles		
19/12/18	to Bickendorf		
26/5/19	en route to India		
27/6/19	to Quetta		
8/19		Bristol F2B (4/20)	det Loralai
1/4/20	DB		renumbered as No. 5 Sqn
25/11/35	RF Bicester		from 'C'Flt No. 101Sqn
16/12/35	to Manston		
1/36		Clouds (6/36)	'B'Flt Seaplane Training Squadron attached from Calshot 17/1 -6/36
6/1/36			'X'Flt, School of Air Navigation attached until 1/9/38
3/36		Anson I (12/41)	
1/9/38	to Eastchurch		
28/9/38	to Thorney Island		
10/10/38	to Eastchurch		
4/8/39	to Manston		
13/8/39	to Eastchurch		
25/8/39	to Thorney Island		dets Bircham Newton, Detling, Guernsey, & Carew Cheriton
No. 49 SQUADRON	**MOTTO: Cave Canem (Beware of the dog)**		
11/11/18	Villers-lès-Cagnicourt	DH 9 (7/19)	
24/11/18	to Bavai		
29/5/19	to Bickendorf		
18/7/19	DB		
10/2/36	RF Bircham Newton		from 'C'Flt No. 18 Sqn
2/36		Hind (12/38)	
8/8/36	to Worthy Down		
14/3/38	to Scampton		
9/38		Hampden (4/42)	det Kinloss
No. 50 SQUADRON	**MOTTO: From defence to attack**		
11/11/18	Bekesbourne	Camel (6/19)	
13/6/19	DB		
3/5/37	RF Waddington		
5/37		Hind (1/39)	
12/38		Hampden (4/42)	dets Lossiemouth, Wick & Kinloss
No. 51 SQUADRON	**MOTTO: Swift and sure**		
11/11/18	Marham	Camel (6/19)	dets Mattishal & Tydd St Mary
14/5/19	to Suttons Farm		
13/6/19	DB		
15/3/37	RF Driffield		from 'B'Flt No. 58 Sqn
3/37		Virginia X (2/38)	
24/3/37	to Boscombe Down		
3/37		Anson I (2/38)	
2/38		Whitley II (12/39)	
20/4/38	to Linton-on-Ouse		
8/38		Whitley III (3/40)	
No. 52 SQUADRON	**MOTTO: Sudore quam sanguine (By sweat other than through blood)**		
11/11/18	Aulnoy	RE 8 (2/19)	
16/11/19	to Linselles		
23/11/18	to Aulnoy		
18/2/19	to Netheravon		as cadre
28/6/19	to Lopcombe Corner		
23/10/19	DB		
18/1/37	RF Abingdon		from 'B'Flt No. 15 Sqn
1/37		Hind (12/37)	
1/3/37	to Upwood		
11/37		Battle (4/40)	
2/39		Anson I (4/40)	det Alconbury
No. 53 SQUADRON	**MOTTO: United in Effort**		
11/11/18	Sweveghem	RE8 (4/19)	
16/11/18	to Seclin		
28/11/18	to Laneffe		
15/3/19	to Old Sarum		as cadre
25/10/19	DB		
28/6/37	RF Farnborough		
6/37		Hector (3/39)	
8/4/38	to Odiham		
1/39		Blenheim IV (8/41)	

Month/Yr	Location	Aircraft Type	Remarks
No. 54 SQUADRON	**MOTTO:** Audax omnia perpeti (Boldness to endure anything)		
11/11/18	Merchin	Camel (2/19)	
17/2/19	to Yatesbury		as cadre
25/10/19	DB		
15/1/30	RF Hornchurch		
1/30		Siskin IIIA (12/30)	
4/30		Bulldog IIA (9/36)	
8/36		Gauntlet II (5/37)	
4/37		Gladiator (4/39)	
3/39		Spitfire I (2/41)	

No. 55 SQUADRON	**MOTTO:** Nil nos tremefacit (Nothing shakes us)		
11/11/18	Azelot	DH 4 (1/19)	
16/11/18	to Le Planty		
2/12/18	to André-aux-Bois		
1/2/19	to Renfrew		as cadre
1/1/20	to Shotwick		
22/1/20	DB		
1/2/20	RF Suez		No. 142 Sqn renumbered
2/20		DH 9 (9/20)	det Ramleh
6/20		DH 9A (2/30)	
8/7/20	en route to Turkey		
12/7/20	to Maltepe		
3/9/20	en route to Basra		vis HMS *Ark Royal*
23/9/20	to Basra		
30/9/20	to Baghdad West		dets Bushire & Mosul
20/3/21	to Mosul		
19/5/24	to Hinaidi		
2/30		Wapiti (3/37)	
2/37		Vincent (5/39)	
14/9/37	to Dhibban/Habbaniyah		
3/39		Blenheim I (12/40)	
25/8/39	to Ismailia		

No. 56 SQUADRON	**MOTTO:** Quid si coelum ruat (What if heaven falls)		
11/11/18	La Targette	SE 5A (2/19)	
22/11/18	to Béthencourt		
14/2/19	to Narborough		as cadre
30/12/19	to Bircham Newton		
22/1/20	DB		
1/2/20	RF Aboukir		No. 80 Sqn renumbered
2/20		Snipe (9/22)	det San Stephano (Remained until 8/23)
23/9/22	DB		
1/11/22	RF Hawkinge		
11/22		Snipe (11/24)	
7/5/23	to Biggin Hill		
9/24		Grebe II (9/27)	
9/27		Siskin IIIA (10/32)	
12/10/27	to North Weald		
10/32		Bulldog IIA (5/36)	
5/36		Gauntlet II (7/37)	
7/37		Gladiator I (5/38)	
4/38		Hurricane I (2/41)	

No. 57 SQUADRON	**MOTTO:** Corpus non animum muto (I change my body not my spirit)		
11/11/18	Beauvois	DH4 (5/19)	
22/11/18	to Vert Galand		
24/11/18	to Le Casteau		det Spa
12/12/18	to Spa		dets La Louveterie & Franc Waret
7/1/19	to Morville		
2/19		DH 9A (7/19)	dets Sart, Maisoncelle, Nivelles & Marquise
4/8/19	to South Carlton		as cadre
31/12/19	DB		
20/10/31	RF Netheravon		
11/31		Hart (5/36)	
5/9/32	to Upper Heyford		
5/36		Hind (5/38)	
3/38		Blenheim I (5/40)	

No. 58 SQUADRON	**MOTTO:** Alis nocturnis (On the wings of the night)		
11/11/18	Provin	HP0/400 (1/20)	
12/4/19	en route to Egypt		via Marseilles
2/5/19	to Heliopolis		
7/19		Vimy (1/20)	

Month/Yr	Location	Aircraft Type	Remarks
1/2/20	DB		renumbered as No. 70 Sqn
1/4/24	RF Worthy Down		
4/24		Vimy (5/25)	
12/24		Virginia V (11/26)	
3/25		Virginia III (4/26)	
7/25		Virginia VI (5/27)	
8/26		Virginia VII (12/30)	
4/27		Virginia IX (4/34)	
1/28		Virginia X (1/38)	
13/1/36	to Upper Heyford		
3/9/36	to Driffield		
2/37		Anson I (11/37)	
24/3/37	to Boscombe Down		
10/37		Whitley I (4/38)	
10/37		Whitley II (7/39)	
20/4/38	to Linton-on-Ouse		
4/39		Heyford III (5/39)	
5/39		Whitley III (4/40)	dets Reims & Boscombe Down

No. 59 SQUADRON   MOTTO: Ab uno disce omnes (From one learn all)

Month/Yr	Location	Aircraft Type	Remarks
11/11/18	Caudry	Bristol F2 B (8/19)	
29/11/18	to Gerpinnes		
14/3/19	to Bickendorf		
3/5/19	to Duren		
4/8/19	DB		
28/6/37	RF Old Sarum		
6/37		Hector (9/39)	
5/39		Blenheim IV (8/41)	
11/5/39	to Andover		

No. 60 SQUADRON   MOTTO: Per ardua ad aethera tendo (I strive through difficulties to the sky)

Month/Yr	Location	Aircraft Type	Remarks
11/11/18	Quiévy	SE 5A (1/19)	
23/11/18	to Inchy		
17/2/19	to Narborough		as cadre
1/1/20	to Bircham Newton		
22/1/20	DB		
1/4/20	RF Risalpur		No. 97 Sqn renumbered
4/20		DH10/10A (4/23)	dets Mianwali, Rajkot, Juhu, Tank, Karachi and Dardoni
3/23		DH 9A (5/30)	dets Hassani Abdel, Dardoni, Quetta, Arawali, Delhi & Miranshah
29/5/25	to Peshawar		dets Quetta & Drigh Road
15/10/25	to Kohat		dets Risalpur,Drigh Road, Quetta, Arawali & Miranshah
3/30		Wapiti (7/39)	dets Miranshah, Delhi,Seletar, Drigh Road Arawali, Manzai,Gilgit, Kanpur & Dum Dum
3/3/39			to Ambala
3/39		Blenheim I (2/42)	dets Dum Dum,St Thomas Mount, Juhu, Drigh Road, Sharjah & Peshawar

No. 61 SQUADRON   MOTTO: Per purum tonantes (Thundering through the clear sky)

Month/Yr	Location	Aircraft Type	Remarks
11/11/18	Rochford	Camel (6/19)	
13/6/19	DB		
8/3/37	RF Hemswell		
3/37		Audax (4/37)	
3/37		Anson I (2/38)	
1/38		Blenheim I (3/39)	det Wick

No. 62 SQUADRON   MOTTO: Insperato (Unexpectedly)

Month/Yr	Location	Aircraft Type	Remarks
11/11/18	Villers-lès-Cagnicourt	Bristol F2 B (7/19)	
18/11/18	to Aulnoye		
		B-27	
14/12/18	to Bouge		
20/12/18	to Nivelles		
2/5/19	to Spich		
31/7/19	DB		
3/5/37	RF Abingdon		From 'B'Flt No. 40 Sqn
5/37		Hind (3/38)	
12/7/37	to Cranfield		
2/38		Blenheim I (1/42)	
12/8/39	en route to the Far East		to Tengah

Month/Yr	Location	Aircraft Type	Remarks

No. 63 SQUADRON   MOTTO: Pone nos ad hostem (Follow us to find the enemy)

Month/Yr	Location	Aircraft Type	Remarks
11/11/18	Tikrit	Martinsyde G102 (8/19)	
12/11/18	to Samara		dets Mosul & Ramadi
17/2/19	to Baghdad		dets Ramadi, Kazvin, Bushire, Kerman shah, Mosul & Kirkuk
2/19		SE 5A (4/19)	
5/19		Camel (9/19)	
29/2/20	DB		used to re-establish No. 30 Sqn
15/2/37	RF Andover		from 'B'Flt No. 12 Sqn
2/37		Hind (4/37)	
3/3/37	to Upwood		
3/37		Audax (8/37)	
5/37		Battle (4/40)	
3/39		Anson I (4/40)	

No. 64 SQUADRON   MOTTO: Tenax propositi (Firmness of purpose)

Month/Yr	Location	Aircraft Type	Remarks
11/11/18	Aniche	SE 5A (2/19)	
22/11/18	to Saultain		
4/12/18	to Froidmont		
14/2/19	to Narborough		as cadre
31/12/19	DB		
1/3/36	RF Heliopolis		nucleus from Nos. 6 & 208 Sqns via No. 29 Sqn
3/36		Demon (12/38)	
9/4/36	to Ismailia		
1/8/36	to Aboukir		
16/8/36	en route to the UK		
12/9/36	to Martlesham Heath		
18/5/38	to Church Fenton		
12/38		Blenheim IF (4/40)	
7/8/39	to Duxford		
12/8/39	to Sutton Bridge		
24/8/39	to Church Fenton		dets Leconfield, Catterick & Evanton

No. 65 SQUADRON   MOTTO: Vi et armis (By force of arms)

Month/Yr	Location	Aircraft Type	Remarks
11/11/18	Bisseghem	Camel (2/19)	
12/2/19	to Yatesbury	as cadre	
25/10/19	DB		
1/8/34	RF Hornchurch		
8/34		Demon (7/36)	
7/36		Gauntlet II (6/37)	
6/37		Gladiator I (4/39)	
3/39		Spitfire I (4/41)	

No. 66 SQUADRON   MOTTO: Cavete praemonui (Beware, I have given a warning)

Month/Yr	Location	Aircraft Type	Remarks
11/11/18	San Pietro-in-Gu	Camel 3/19)	
10/3/19	to Yatesbury		as cadre
29/3/19	to Leighterton		
25/10/19	DB		
20/7/36	RF Duxford		from 'C'Flt No. 19 Sqn
7/36		Gauntlet II (12/38)	
10/38		Spitfire I (11/40)	

No. 70 SQUADRON   MOTTO: Usquam (Anywhere)

Month/Yr	Location	Aircraft Type	Remarks
11/11/18	Menin	Camel (3/19)	
25/11/18	to Fort Cognelée		
7/12/18	to Elsenborn		
18/12/18	to Bickendorf		
1/19		Snipe (9/19)	
27/8/19	to Spittlegate		
28/9/19			reduced to a cadre
22/1/20	DB		
1/2/20	RF Heliopolis		No. 58 Sqn renumbered
2/20		HP 0/400 (4/20)	
2/20		Vimy (11/22)	
16/1/22	to Baghdad West		
11/22		Vernon (12/26)	
31/5/22	to Hinaidi		
1/24		Victoria I (3/26)	
2/26		Victoria III (6/34)	
11/28		Victoria IV (5/34)	
4/30		Victoria V (8/35)	
7/31		Victoria VI (11/35)	
11/35		Valentia (10/40)	
16/10/37	to Dhibban/ Habbaniya		
30/8/39	to Helwan		det Habbaniyah

Month/Yr	Location	Aircraft Type	Remarks
No. 72 SQUADRON	**MOTTO: Swift**		
11/11/18	Baghdad	Bristol M1 C (2/19)	Flts @ Mirjana, Samarra dets Hamadan,
		SE 5A (2/19)	Tikrit, Baku, Kazvin & Zinjan
		SPAD S.VII (1/19)	
		Martinsyde G.100 (11/18)	
25/11/18			Squadron re-united at Baghdad
1/2/19			reduced to a cadre
22/9/19	DB		
22/2/37	RF Tangmere		nucleus from No. 1 Sqn
3/37		Gladiator I (5/39)	
1/6/37	to Church Fenton		
4/39		Spitfire I (4/41)	
No. 73 SQUADRON	**MOTTO: Tutor et Ultor (Protector and avenger)**		
11/11/18	Malincourt	Camel (2/19)	
15/11/18	to Baizieux		
10/2/19	to Yatesbury		as cadre
2/7/19	DB		
15/3/37	RF Mildenhall		
3/37		Fury II (7/37)	
12/6/37	to Debden		
6/37		Gladiator I (7/38)	
9/11/37	to Digby		
7/38		Hurricane I (1/42)	
No. 74 SQUADRON	**MOTTO: I fear no man**		
11/11/18	Cuerne	SE 5A (2/19)	
17/11/18	to Froidmont		
30/11/18	to Halluin		
10/2/19	to Lopcombe Corner		as cadre
3/7/19	DB		
1/9/35	RF Hornchurch		initially referred to as "the Demon Flights"
3/9/35			established on board HMT *Neuralia* en
			route to Malta
9/35		Demon (4/37)	
11/9/35	to Hal Far		
21/9/36	to Hornchurch		
3/37		Gauntlet II (2/39)	
2/39		Spitfire I (9/40)	
No. 75 SQUADRON	**MOTTO: Ake ake kia kaka (Maori – For ever and ever be strong)**		
11/11/18	Elmswell	Avro 504 K (NF) (6/19)	dets Harling Road & Hadleigh
22/5/19	to North Weald Basset		
13/6/19	DB		
15/3/37	RF Driffield		from 'B'Flt No. 215 Sqn
3/37		Virginia X (9/37)	
3/37		Anson I (11/37)	
9/37		Harrow(7/39)	
11/7/38	to Honington		
3/39		Anson I (10/39)	
7/39		Wellington I (4/40)	
13/7/39	to Stradishall		
No. 76 SQUADRON	**MOTTO: Resolute**		
11/11/18	Ripon	Avro 504 K (NF)	(5/19) dets Copmanthorpe, Helperby and Catterick
18/3/19	to Helperby		dets Copmanthorpe and Catterick
30/5/19	to Tadcaster		as cadre
13/6/19	DB		
12/4/37	RF Finningley		from 'B'Flt No. 7 Sqn
4/37		Wellesley (4/39)	
3/39		Hampden (4/40)	
5/39		Anson I (4/40)	
No. 77 SQUADRON	**MOTTO: Esse potius quam videri (To be rather than seen)**		
11/11/18	Penstone	Avro 504K (NF) (6/19)	det Whiteburn
13/6/19	DB		
14/6/37	RF Finningley		from 'B'Flt No. 102 Sqn
6/37		Audax (11/37)	
7/7/37	to Honington		
11/37		Wellesley (11/38)	
25/7/38	to Driffield		
11/38		Whitley III (10/39)	
9/39		Whitley V (10/42)	dets Villeneuve & Kinloss

Month/Yr	Location	Aircraft Type	Remarks
No. 78 SQUADRON	**MOTTO: Nemo non paratus (Nobody unprepared}**		
11/11/18	Suttons Farm	Camel (7/19)	det Biggin Hill
		Snipe (7/19)	
1/7/19			reduced to a cadre
31/12/19	DB		
1/11/36	RF Boscombe Down		from 'B'Flt No. 10 sqn
11/36		Heyford III (10/37)	
1/2/37	to Dishforth		
7/37		Whitley I (12/39)	
6/39		Whitley IVA (6/40)	det Ternhill
8/39		Whitley V (3/42)	det Linton-on-Ouse
No. 79 SQUADRON	**MOTTO: Nil nobis obstare potest (Nothing can stop us)**		
11/11/18	Reckem	Dolphin (7/19)	
26/11/18	to Nivelles		
20/12/18	to Bickendorf		
15/7/19	DB		
22/3/37	RF Biggin Hill		From 'B'Flt No. 32 Sqn
3/37		Gauntlet II (11/38)	
11/38		Hurricane I (7/41)	
No. 80 SQUADRON	**MOTTO: Strike true**		
11/11/18	Flaumont	Camel (12/18)	
12/11/18	to Grand Fayt		
3/12/18	to Strée A		
12/18		Snipe (2/20)	
3/19	to Clermont		
26/5/19	en route to Egypt		via Marseilles
10/6/19	to Aboukir		
1/2/20	DB		renumbered as No. 56 sqn
8/3/37	RF Kenley		from 'B' Flt No. 17 Sqn
3/37		Gauntlet II (5/37)	
15/3/37	to Henlow		
5/37		Gladiator I (11/40)	
9/6/37	to Debden		
30/4/38	en route to Egypt		
10/5/38	to Ismailia		det Ramleh
24/9/38	to Amiriya		
9/10/38	to Ismailia		
16/1/39	to Helwan		
21/4/39	to Amiriya		
19/5/39	to Helwan		det Amiriya
15/7/39	to Amiriya		
No. 81 SQUADRON	**MOTTO: Non solum nobis (Not for us alone)**		
25/11/18	RF Upper Heyford		also designated as No. 1 Sqn Canadian Air Force
11/18		Dolphin (4/19)	
2/5/19	to Shoreham		
5/19		SE 5A (1/20)	
28/1/20	DB		
No. 82 SQUADRON	**MOTTO: Super omnia ubique (Over all things everywhere)**		
11/11/18	Menin	AW FK8 (2/19)	
19/11/18	to Bertangles		
15/2/19	to Shoreham		as cadre
5/19	to Tangmere		
4/7/19	DB		
14/6/37	RF Andover		from 'B'Flt No. 142 Sqn
6/37		Hind (3/38)	
8/7/37	to Cranfield		
3/38		Blenheim I (9/39)	
22/8/39	to Watton		
8/39		Blenheim IV (3/42)	dets Odiham, Lossiemouth, Tangmere & Luqa
No. 83 SQUADRON	**MOTTO: Strike to Defend**		
11/11/18	Estrées-en-Chausée	FE 2B (2/19)	
13/12/18	to Serny		
14/2/19	to Hawkinge		as cadre
9/19	to Lympne		
15/10/19	to Croydon		
31/12/19	DB		
4/8/36	RF Turnhouse		
8/36		Hind (12/38)	

Month/Yr	Location	Aircraft Type	Remarks
14/3/38	to Scampton		
11/38		Hampden (1/42)	det Lossiemouth

No. 84 SQUADRON   MOTTO: Scipiones pungunt (Scorpions sting)

Month/Yr	Location	Aircraft Type	Remarks
11/11/18	Bertry West	SE5A (8/19)	
3/12/18	to Thuilles		
13/5/19	to Bickendorf		
6/7/19	to Eil		
12/8/19	to Tangmere		as cadre
8/10/19	to Croydon		
1/20	to Kenley		
30/1/20	DB		
13/8/20	RF Baghdad West		
8/20		DH 9A (1/29)	
20/9/20	to Shaibah		dets Baghdad West, Nasiriyah, Bushire,
6/28		Wapiti (1/35)	
12/34		Vincent (6/39)	
2/39		Blenheim I (4/41)	det Sharjah

No. 85 SQUADRON   MOTTO: Noctu diuque venamur (We hunt by day and night)

Month/Yr	Location	Aircraft Type	Remarks
11/11/18	Phallempin	SE 5A (2/29)	
7/12/18	to Ascq		
19/2/19	to Lopcombe Corner		as cadre
3/7/19	DB		
1/6/38	RF Debden		from 'A'Flt No. 87 Sqn
6/38		Gladiator(4/41)	
9/38		Hurricane (4/41)	
18/10/38	to Aldergrove		
4/11/38	to Debden		

No. 87 SQUADRON   MOTTO: Maximus me metuit (The most powerful fear me)

Month/Yr	Location	Aircraft Type	Remarks
11/11/18	Boussieres	Dolphin (2/19)	
9/2/19	to Ternhill		as cadre
24/6/19	DB		
15/3/37	RF Tangmere		nucleus from No. 54 Sqn
3/37		Fury II (6/37)	
7/6/37	to Debden		
6/37		Gladiator I (8/38)	
7/38		Hurricane I (9/42)	

No. 88 SQUADRON   MOTTO: En garde (Be on your guard)

Month/Yr	Location	Aircraft Type	Remarks
11/11/18	Bersée	Bristol F2B (8/19)	
18/11/18	to Aulnoy		
13/12/18	to Dour		
14/12/18	to Franc Waret		
18/12/18	to Nivelles		
10/8/19	DB		
7/6/37	RF Waddington		nucleus from No. 110 Sqn
6/37		Hind (12/37)	
17/7/37	to Boscombe Down		
12/37		Battle (4/41)	

No. 90 SQUADRON   MOTTO: Celer (Swift)

Month/Yr	Location	Aircraft Type	Remarks
11/11/18	Buckminster	Avro 504K (NF) (6/19)	dets Stamford & Leadenham
13/6/19	DB		
15/3/37	RF Bicester		from 'A'Flt No. 101 Sqn
3/37		Hind (6/37)	
5/37		Blenheim I (4/39)	
3/39		Blenheim IV (4/40)	
10/5/39	to West Raynham		
13/8/39	to Penrhos		
27/8/39	to West Raynham		
3/9/39	to Bircham Newton		

No. 91 SQUADRON   MOTTO: We seek alone

Month/Yr	Location	Aircraft Type	Remarks
11/11/18	Kenley	Dolphin 7/19	
7/3/19	to Lopcombe Corner		
3/7/19	DB		

No. 92 SQUADRON   MOTTO: Aut pugna aut morere (Either fight or die)

Month/Yr	Location	Aircraft Type	Remarks
11/11/18	Bertry East	SE 5A (8/19)	
3/12/18	to Thuilles		
14/6/19	to Eil		
7/8/19)	DB		

Month/Yr	Location	Aircraft Type	Remarks
No. 93 SQUADRON MOTTO: Ad arma parati (Ready for Battle)			
11/11/18	Port Meadow	Dolphin (11/18)	
21/11/18	DB		
No. 94 SQUADRON MOTTO: Avenge			
11/11/18	Senlis-le-Sec	SE 5A (1/19)	
19/11/18	to Izel-le-Hameau		
17/1/19			reduced to a cadre
30/6/19	DB		
26/3/39	RF Khormaksar		
3/39		Gladiator I (4/40)	
3/39		Gladiator II (6/41)	
2/5/39	to Sheihh Othman		dets Berebera, Laferug & Little Aden
No. 95 SQUADRON MOTTO: Trans mare exivi (I went out over the sea)			
11/11/18	Kenley	(for Buzzard)	nucleus from Nos.21,28,30 and 51 TDS
20/11/18	DB		
No. 96 SQUADRON MOTTO: Nocturni obambulamus (We prowl by night)			
11/11/18	Wyton	Salamander (12/18)	nucleus from Nos.2,32,38 & 46 TDS
9/12/18	DB		
No. 97 SQUADRON MOTTO: Achieve your aim			
11/11/18	Xaffévillers	HP 0/400 (3/19)	
17/11/18	to St-Inglevert		
4/3/19	to Ford Junction		
4/19		DH 10 (3/20)	
19/7/19	en route to India		dets Lahore, Risalpur & Mianwali
23/8/19	to Allahabad		dets Mianwali,Karachi, Juhu & Rajkot
15/11/19	to Lahore		
28/3/20	to Risalpur		
1/4/20			renumbered No. 60 Sqn
16/9/35	RF Catfoss		from 'B'Flt No. 10 Sqn
9/35		Heyford IA (1/36)	
26/9/35	to Boscombe Down		
11/35		Heyford III (2/39)	
7/1/37	to Leconfield		
2/39		Anson I (4/40)	
2/39		Whitley II (4/40)	
2/39		Whitley III (4/40)	
No. 98 SQUADRON MOTTO: Never failing			
11/11/18	Abscon	DH 9 (3/19)	
27/12/18	to Marquain		
19/1/19	to Alquines		
28/3/19	to Shotwick		as cadre
24/6/19	DB		
17/2/36	RF Abingdon		from'C'Flt No. 15 Sqn
2/36		Hind (6/38)	
21/8/36	to Hucknall		
6/38		Battle 7/41)	dets Weston Zoyland,Upwood, & Bassingbourne
No. 99 SQUADRON MOTTO: Quisque tenax (Each tenacious)			
11/11/18	Azelot	DH 9 (11/18)	
9/18		DH 9A (3/20)	
16/11/18	to Auxi-le-Chateau		
29/11/18	to St-André-aux-Bois		
12/12/18	to Aulnoy		
14/5/19	en route to India		via Marseilles
15/6/19	to Ambala		
26/9/19	to Mianwali		det Ambala
1/4/20	DB		renumbered as No. 27 Sqn
1/4/24	RF Netheravon		
4/24		Vimy (12/24)	
31/5/24	to Bircham Newton		
8/24		Aldershot (12/25)	
12/25		Hyderabad(1/31)	
5/1/28	to Upper Heyford		
10/29		Hinaidi (12/33)	
12/33		Heyford (11/38)	
15/11/34	to Mildenhall		
10/38		Wellington I (12/39)	
1/9/39	to Newmarket		
9/39		Wellington IA (4/40)	

Month/Yr	Location	Aircraft Type	Remarks
No. 100 SQUADRON	**MOTTO: Sarang tebuan jangan dijolok (Malay - Never stir up a hornet's nest)**		
11/11/18	Xaffévillers	HP 0/400 (9/19)	
25/11/18	to Ligescourt		dets St-Inglevert & Quilen
16/6/19	to St-Inglevert		
12/9/19	to Baldonnel		as cadre
1/2/20			re-established (Absorbed cadre of No. 141 Sqn
2/20		DH 9A (6/21)	
2/20		Bristol F2 B (3/22)	dets Castlebar & Oranmore
4/2/22	to Spittlegate		
2/22		DH 9A (5/24)	
2/22		Avro 504K (5/24)	
2/22		Vimy (5/24)	
5/24	to Eastchurch		
5/24		Fawn (12/26)	
7/24	to Spittlegate		
8/26		Horsley (4/33)	
10/1/28	to Bicester		
3/11/30	to Donibristle		
11/32		Vildebeeste I (9/33)	
8/33		Vildebeeste II (1/41)	
7/12/33	en route to the Far East		
6/1/34	to Seletar		
12/37		Vildebeeste III (2/42)	
No. 101 SQUADRON	**MOTTO: Mens agitat (Mind over matter)**		
11/11/18	Hancourt	FE 2B (3/19)	
12/11/18	to Catillon		
29/11/18	to Strée		
13/12118	to Morville		
12/3/19	to Laneffe		as cadre
18/3/19	to Filton		
11/10/19	to Eastleigh		
31/12/19	DB		
21/3/28	RF Bircham Newton		
4/28		Sidestrand (7/36)	
12/10/29	to Andover		
1/12/34	to Bicester		
1/35		Overstrand (8/38)	
6/38		Blenheim I (4/39)	
4/39		Blenheim IV (7/41)	
9/5/39	to West Raynham		dets Manston & Brize Norton
No. 102 SQUADRON	**MOTTO: Tentate et perficite (Attempt and accomplish)**		
11/11/18	Bevillers	FE 2B (3/19)	
14/12/18	to Serny		
26/3/19	to Lympne		as cadre
3/7/19	DB		
1/10/35	RF Worthy Down		from 'B'Flt No. 7 Sqn
10/35		Heyford II & III (11/38)	
3/9/36	to Finningley		
7/7/37	to Honington		
11/7/38	to Driffield		
10/38		Whitley III (1/40)	det Villeneuve
No. 103 SQUADRON	**MOTTO: Nili me tangere (Touch me not)**		
11/11/18	Ronchin	DH 9 (3/19)	
26/1/19	to Maisoncelle		
28/3/19	to Shotwick		as cadre
1/10/19	DB		
10/8/36	RF Andover		
8/36		Hind (8/38)	
26/2/37	to Usworth		
7/38		Battle (10/40)	
2/9/38	to Abingdon		
1/4/39	to Benson		
2/9/39	to Challerange		
No. 104 SQUADRON	**MOTTO: Strike hard**		
11/11/18	Azelot	DH 9 (2/19)	
20/11/18	to Maisoncelle		
11/18		DH 10 (2/19)	
1/2/19	to Turnhouse		
3/3/19	to Crail		as cadre
30/6/19	DB		

Month/Yr	Location	Aircraft Type	Remarks
7/1/36	RF Abingdon		from 'C'Flt No. 40 Sqn
7/36		Hind (5/38)	
21/8/36	to Hucknall		
2/5/38	to Bassingbourne		
5/38		Blenheim I (4/40)	
5/39		Anson I (4/40)	

No. 105 SQUADRON   MOTTO: Fortis in proeliis (Valiant in battles)

11/11/18`	Omagh	RE 8 (12/19)	dets Oranmore & Castlebar
12/18		Bristol F2B (2/20)	
28/1/19	to Oranmore		dets Castlebar, the Curragh, Tallaght & Fermoy
1/2/20	DB		renumbered as No. 2 Sqn
12/4/37	RF Upper Heyford		from 'B'Flt No. 18 Sqn
26/4/37	to Harwell		
4/37		Audax (10/37)	
8/37		Battle (5/40)	
2/9/39	to Reims		

No. 106 SQUADRON   MOTTO: Pro libertate (For liberty)

11/11/18	Fermoy	RE 8 (1/19)	
1/19		Bristol F2B (10/19)	dets Birr & Oranmore
8/10/19	DB		
1/6/38	RF Abingdon		from 'A'Flt No. 15 Sqn
6/38		Hind (7/38)	
7/38		Battle (5/39)	
1/9/38	to Thornaby		
26/9/38	to Grantham		
14/10/38	to Thornaby		
5/39		Anson I (9/39)	
5/39		Hampden (3/42)	det Evanton
1/9/39	to Cottesmore		

No. 107 SQUADRON   MOTTO: Nous y serons (We shall be there)

11/11/18	Moislains	DH 9 (3/19)	
18/11/18	to Bavay		
13/12/18	to Franc Waret		
20/12/18	to Nivelles		
4/1/19	to Maubeuge		
18/3/19	to Hounslow		as cadre
13/8/19	DB		
10/8/36	RF Andover		
9/36		Hind (9/38)	
16/2/37	to Old Sarum		
15/6/37	to Harwell		
8/38		Blenheim I (6/39)	
3/5/39	to Wattisham		
5/39		Blenheim IV (2/42)	dets Lossiemouth, Newmarket, Ipswich, Swanton Morley, Hunsdon & Horsham St Faith

No. 108 SQUADRON   MOTTO: Viribus contractis (With gathering strength)

11/11/18	Bisseghem	DH 9 (2/19)	
16/11/18	to Gondecourt		
16/2/19	to Lympne		as cadre
3/7/19	DB		
4/1/37	RF Upper Heyford		from 'B'Flt No. 57 Sqn
1/37		Hind (6/38)	
18//2/37	to Farnborough		
7/7/37	to Cranfield		
2/5/38	to Bassingbourn		
6/38		Blenheim I (4/40)	
5/39		Anson I (4/40)	

No. 110 SQUADRON   MOTTO: Nec timeo nec sperno (I neither fear nor despise)

11/11/18	Bettoncourt	DH 9A (8/19)	
20/11/18	to Auxi-le-Chateau		
30/11/18	to Maisoncelle		
3/7/19	to Marquise		
27/8/19	DB		
18/5/37	RF Waddington		
5/37		Hind (1/38)	
1/38		Blenheim I (9/39)	
11/5/39	to Wattisham		

Month/Yr	Location	Aircraft Type	Remarks
6/39		Blenheim IV (6/42)	dets Lossiemouth, Horsham St Faith, Manston, Lindholme, Ipswich, Luqa, Martlesham Heath, Brize Norton & Swanton Morley

No. 111 SQUADRON   MOTTO: Adstantes (Standing by)

11/11/18	Qantara		
1/19		Bristol F2B (2/20)	
6/2/19	to Ramleh		dets Damascus & Aleppo
1/2/20	DB		renumbered as No. 14 Sqn
1/10/23	RF Duxford		
10/23		Grebe II (1/25)	
4/24		Snipe (1/25)	
6/24		Siskin II (11/26)	
9/26		Siskin IIIA (2/31)	
1/31		Bulldog IIA (6/36)	
12/7/34	to Northolt		
6/36		Gauntlet I & II (1/38)	
12/37		Hurricane I (4/41)	

No. 112 SQUADRON   MOTTO: Swift in destruction

11/11/18	Throwley	Camel (6/19)	
/19		Snipe (6/19)	
13/6/19	DB		
16/5/39			RF on board HMS *Argus*
26/5/39	to Helwan		
6/39		Gladiator I & II (6/41)	dets Port Sudan, Summit & Erkowit

No. 113 SQUADRON   MOTTO: Velox et vindex (Swift to vengeance)

11/11/18	Sarona	RE 8 (2/20)	dets El Affule & Haifa
18/11/18	to Qantara		
16/2/19	to Ismailia		
2/19		BE 2E (12/19)	
1/2/20	DB		renumbered as No. 208 sqn
18/5/37	RF Upper Heyford		
5/37		Hind (6/39)	
31/8/37	to Grantham		
30/4/38	en route to Egypt		
11/5/38	to Heliopolis		
29/9/38	to Mersah Matruh		
11/10/38	to Heliopolis		
21/4/39	to El Daba		
21/5/39	to Heliopolis		
6/39		Blenheim I (4/40)	

No. 114 SQUADRON   MOTTO: With speed I strike

11/11/18	Lahore	BE 2C (10/19)	det Jubbulpore
		BE 2E (4/20)	
26/3/19	To Quetta		dets Lahore & Cawnpore
20/5/19	to Lahore		dets Quetta, Cawnpore & Kohat
16/6/19	to Quetta		dets Bannu & Loralai
2/10/19	to Ambala		
10/19		Bristol F2B (4/20)	det Agra
1/4/20	DB		renumbered as No. 28 Sqn
1/12/36	RF Wyton		
12/36		Hind (3/37)	
3/37		Audax (4/37)	
3/37		Blenheim I (5/39)	
5/39		Blenheim IV (9/42)	

No. 115 SQUADRON   MOTTO: Despite the elements

11/11/18	St-Inglevert	HP 0/400 (3/19)	
4/3/19	to Ford Junction		as cadre
18/10/19	DB		
15/6/37	RF Marham		fom 'B'Flt No. 38 Sqn
6/37		Hendon II (8/37)	
6/37		Harrow (6/39)	
3/39		Wellington I (10/39)	
9/39		Wellington IA (8/40)	det Kinloss

No. 116 SQUADRON   MOTTO: Precision in defence

11/11/18	Feltham	HP 0/400 (11/18)	
20/11/18	DB		

Month/Yr	Location	Aircraft Type	Remarks
No. 117 SQUADRON	**MOTTO: It shall be done**		
11/11/18	Norwich	DH 9 (10/19)	
30/11/18	to Wyton		
23/3/19	to Tallaght		
24/4/19	to Gormanston		
6/10/19	DB		absorbed by No. 141 Sqn
No. 119 SQUADRON	**MOTTO: By night by day**		
11/11/18	Wyton	Various aircraft	
9/18		DH 9 (12/18)	
6/12/18	DB		
No. 120 SQUADRON	**MOTTO: Endurance**		
1/11/18	Bracebridge Heath	Various aircraft	
23/11/18	to Wyton		
11/18		DH 9 (10/19)	
20/2/19	to Hawkinge		
17/7/19	to Lympne		
21/10/19	DB		
No. 122 SQUADRON	**MOTTO: Victuri volamus (We fly to conquer)**		
11/11/18	Upper Heyford	DH 10	
20/11/18	DB		
No. 123 SQUADRON			
20/11/18	RF Upper Heyford		also designated No. 2 Sqn
	Canadian Air Force		
11/18		DH 9A (2/20)	
31/3/19	to Shoreham		
5/2/20	DB		
No. 132 SQUADRON	**MOTTO: Cave leopardum (Beware the leopard)**		
11/11/18	Castle Bromwich	Various aircraft	
23/12/18	DB		
No. 138 SQUADRON	**MOTTO: For freedom**		
11/11/18	Chingford	Bristol F2 B (2/19)	
1/2/19	DB		
No. 139 SQUADRON	**MOTTO: Si placer necamus (We destroy at will)**		
11/11/18	Arcade	Bristol F2 B (2/19)	
14/11/18	to Grossa		
30/1/19	to Caldiero		
25/2/19	to Blandford		as cadre
7/3/19	DB		
3/9/36	RF Wyton		
9/36		Hind (7/37)	
7/37		Blenheim I (9/39)	
7/39		Blenheim IV (12/41)	
No. 141 SQUADRON	**MOTTO: Caedimus noctu (We slay by night)**		
11/11/18	Biggin Hill	Bristol F2 B (2/20)	
1/3/19	to Tallaght		dets the Curragh & Birr
14/12/19	to Baldonnel		dets Gormanston & Birr
1/2/20	DB		absorbed into No. 100 Sqn
No. 142 SQUADRON	**MOTTO: Determination**		
11/11/18	Ramleh		dets Damascus & Haifa
25/11/18	to Qantara		
1/19		DH 9 (2/20)	
16/2/19	to Suez		
1/2/20	DB		renumbered as No. 55 Sqn
1/6/34	RF Netheravon		
6/34		Hart (11/36)	
3/1/35	to Andover		
3/10/35	en route to the Middle East		
13/10/35	to Aboukir		
26/10/35	to Mersa Matruh		det Helwan
3/8/36	to Ismailia		
5/11/36	to Aboukir		
20/11/36	en route to the UK		
3/12/36	to Andover		
1/37		Hind (4/38)	
3/38		Battle (11/40)	

Month/Yr	Location	Aircraft Type	Remarks
9/5/39	to Bicester		
2/9/39	to Barry-au-Bac		

No. 143 SQUADRON   MOTTO: Vincere et vivere (To conquer is to live)

Month/Yr	Location	Aircraft Type	Remarks
11/11/18	Detling	Camel (10/19)	
6/19		Snipe (10/19)	
31/10/19	DB		

No. 144 SQUADRON   MOTTO: Who shall stop us

Month/Yr	Location	Aircraft Type	Remarks
11/11/18	Mikra Bay	DH 9 (12/18)	dets Mudros & Amberkoj
4/12/18	en route to the UK		
16/12/18	to Ford Junction		as cadre
4/2/19	DB		
11/1/37	RF Bicester		from 'B'Flt No. 101 sqn
1/37		Overstrand (2/37)	
2/37		Anson I (9/37)	
9/2/37	to Hemswell		
3/37		Audax (9/37)	
8/37		Blenheim I (4/39)	
3/39		Hampden (3/43)	

No. 145 SQUADRON   MOTTO: Diu noctuque pugnamus (We fight by day and night)

Month/Yr	Location	Aircraft Type	Remarks
11/11/18	Qantara	SE 5A (2/19)	
8/2/19			reduced to a cadre
16/2/19	to Suez		
6/9/19	DB		

No. 148 SQUADRON   MOTTO: Trusty

Month/Yr	Location	Aircraft Type	Remarks
11/11/18	Erre	FE 2B (2/19)	
9/12/18	to Serny		
17/2/19	to Tangmere		as cadre
4/7/19	DB		
7/6/37	RF Scampton		nucleus from No. 9 Sqn
6/37		Audax (7/37)	
6/37		Wellesley (11/38)	
10/3/38	to Stradishall		
11/38		Heyford III (3/39)	
3/39		Wellington I (4/40)	
4/39		Anson I (4/40)	

No. 149 SQUADRON   MOTTO: Fortis nocte (Bold at night)

Month/Yr	Location	Aircraft Type	Remarks
11/11/18	Ste-Marguerite	FE 2B (8/19)	
26/11/18	to Fort Cognelée		
24/12/18	to Bickendorf		
26/3/19	to Tallaght		as cadre
1/8/19	DB		
12/4/37	RF Mildenhall		from 'B'Flt No. 99 Sqn
4/37		Heyford III ((5/37)	
5/37		Heyford IA (3/39)	
1/39		Wellington I (12/39)	
9/39		Wellington IA (6/40)	

No. 150 SQUADRON   MOTTO: Always ahead (Greek script)

Month/Yr	Location	Aircraft Type	Remarks
11/11/18	Mikra Bay	Bristol M1C (1/19)	dets Kiree, Gumuljina & Dedeagatch
		SE 5A (2/19)	
		Camel (2/19)	
		BE 12A (12/18)	
		BE 2E (1/19)	
12/18		AW FK8 (1/19)	
15/3/19			reduced to a cadre
11/6/19	to San Stephano		
18/9/19	DB		
8/8/38	RF Boscombe Down		
8/38		Battle (9/40)	
3/4/39	to Benson		
2/9/39	to Chellerange		

No. 151 SQUADRON   MOTTO: Foy pour devoir (Fidelity unto duty)

Month/Yr	Location	Aircraft Type	Remarks
11/11/18	Bancourt	Camel 2/19	
5/12/18	to Liettres		
21/2/19	to Gullane		as cadre
10/9/19	DB		
4/8/36	RF North Weald		from 'B'Flt No. 56 Sqn
8/36		Gauntlet II (3/39)	
12/38		Hurricane I (6/41)	dets Martlesham Heath

Month/Yr	Location	Aircraft Type	Remarks
No. 152 SQUADRON	**MOTTO: Faithful ally**		
11/11/18	Carvin	Camel (2/19)	
29/11/18	to Liettres		
21/2/19	to Gullane	as cadre	
30/6/19	DB		
No. 153 SQUADRON	**MOTTO: Noctividus (Seeing by night)**		
11/11/18	Hainault Farm	Camel (6/19)	
13/6/19	DB		
No. 155 SQUADRON	**MOTTO: Eternal vigilance**		
11/11/18	Chingford	DH 9A (12/18)	
7/12/18	DB		
No. 156 SQUADRON	**MOTTO: We light the way**		
11/11/18	Wyton	DH 9A (11/18)	
9/12/18	DB		
No. 157 SQUADRON	**MOTTO: Our cannon speak our thoughts**		
11/11/18	Upper Heyford	Salamander (2/19)	
1/2/19	DB		
No. 158 SQUADRON	**MOTTO: Strength in unity**		
11/11/18	Upper Heyford	for Salamander	
20/11/18	DB		
No. 166 SQUADRON	**MOTTO: Tenacity**		
11/11/18	Bircham Newton	HP V/1500 (5/19)	
31/5/19	DB		
1/11/36	RF Boscombe Down		from 'B'Flt No. 97 Sqn
11/36		Heyford III (9/39)	
20/1/37	to Leconfield		
6/39		Whitley I (2/40)	dets Benson & Boscombe Down
No. 167 SQUADRON	**MOTTO: Ubique sine mora (Everywhere without delay)**		
11/11/18	Bircham Newton	HP V/1500 (5/19)	
21/5/19	DB		
No. 185 SQUADRON	**MOTTO: Ara fejn hu (Maltese - Look where it is)**		
11/11/18	East Fortune	Cuckoo (4/19)	
9/4/19			reduced to a cadre
14/4/19	DB		listed as a cadre until 6/11/19 when it was DB retrospectively.
1/3/38	Abingdon		from 'B' Flt No. 40 Sqn
3/38		Hind (7/38)	
6/38		Battle (6/39)	det Thornaby
1/9/38	to Thornaby		
27/9/38	to Grantham		
15/10/38	to Thornaby		
6/39		Hampden (4/40)	
8/39		Hereford (4/40)	
8/39		Anson I (4/40)	
24/8/39	to Cottesmore		
No. 186 SQUADRON	**MOTTO: Nil**		
31/12/18	Formed on board HMS *Argus*		
17/2/19	to Gosport		
6/19		Cuckoo (2/20)	
1/2/20	DB		renumbered as No. 210 Sqn
No. 201 SQUADRON	**MOTTO: Hic et ubique (Here and everywhere)**		
11/11/18	La Targette	Camel (1/19)	
22/11/18	to Béthencourt		
5/2/19			reduced to a cadre
17/2/19	to Lake Down		
2/9/19	to Eastleigh		
31/12/19	DB		
1/1/29	RF Calshot		No. 490 Flt renumbered
1/29		Southampton II (12/36)	
4/36		London I (6/38)	
1/38		London II (4/40)	
29/9/38	to Invergordon		
7/10/38	to Calshot		
9/8/39	to Sullom Voe		

Month/Yr	Location	Aircraft Type	Remarks
No. 202 SQUADRON	**MOTTO: Semper vigilate (Be always vigilant)**		
11/11/18	Bergues	DH 4 (3/19)	
25/11/18	to Varssenaere		
27/3/19	to Driffield		as cadre
12/19	to Spittlegate		
22/1/20	DB		
9/4/20	RF Alexandria		from 'A'Flt No. 267 Sqn
4/20		Short 184 (5/21)	
16/5/21	DB		
1/1/29	RF Kalafrana		No. 481 Flt renumbered
1/29		Fairey IIID (9/30)	
7/30		Fairey IIIF (8/35)	
5/35		Scapa (11/37)	
9/37)		London II (6/41)	
No. 203 SQUADRON	**MOTTO: Occidens oriensque (West and east)**		
11/11/18	Bruille	Camel (3/19)	
24/11/18	to Auberchicourt		
22/12/18	to Orcq		
18/1/19	to Boisdinghem		
27/3/19	to Waddington		as cadre
12/19	to Scopwick		
21/1/20	DB		
1/3/20	RF Leuchars		
3/20		Camel (8/22)	
8/22		Nightjar (4/23)	
18/9/22	en route to Turkey		via HMS *Argus*
27/9/22	to Kilya Bay		
19/12/22	en route to UK		via HMS *Argus*
4/1/23	to Leuchars		
1/4/23	DB		split into Nos. 401 & 402 Flts
1/1/29	RF Mount Batten		No. 482 Flt renumbered
1/29		Southampton II (4/31)	
28/2/29	en route to Persian Gulf		
14/3/29	to Basrah		
3/29		Fairey IIIF (4/29)	
3/31			det Felixstowe for Rangoon (9/35)
8/35			det Pembroke dock for Singapore III (3/40)
26/9/35	to Isthmus		
24/8/36	to Basra		
2/9/39	to Isthmus		
No. 204 SQUADRON	**MOTTO: Praedam mari quaero (I seek my prey in the sea)**		
11/11/18	Heule	Camel (2/19)	
11/2/19	to Waddington		as cadre
31/12/19	DB		
1/2/29	RF Mount Batten		
2/29		Southampton II (10/35)	
8/35		Scapa (1/37)	
27/9/35	to Aboukir		
22/10/35	to Alexandria		
5/8/36	to Mount Batten		
10/36		London I & II (7/39)	
6/39		Sunderland I (9/43)	
No. 205 SQUADRON	**MOTTO: Pertama di - Malaya (First in Malaya)**		
11/11/18	Moislains	DH 9A (3/19)	
27/11/18	to Maubeuge		
12/1/19	to La Louveterie		
21/3/19	to Hucknall		as cadre
12/19	to Scopwick		
22/1/20	DB		
15/4/20	RF Leuchars		
4/20		Panther (4/23)	
11/11/18	DB		became Nos.440,441 & 442 Flts
8/1/29	RF Seletar		from Far East Flight
1/29		Southampton II (2/36)	
4/35		Singapore III (10/41)	
No. 206 SQUADRON	**MOTTO: Nihil nos effugit (Naught escapes us)**		
11/11/18	Linselles	DH 9 (1/20)	
26/11/18	to Nivelles		

Month/Yr	Location	Aircraft Type	Remarks
20/12/18	to Bickendorf		
27/5/19	to Maubeuge		
7/6/19	en route to Egypt		via Marseilles
19/6/19	to Heliopolis		
27/6/19	to Helwan		
1/2/20	DB		renumbered as No. 47 Sqn
15/6/36	RF Manston		from 'C'Flt No. 48 Sqn
6/36		Anson I (6/40)	
1/8/36	to Bircham Newton		

No. 207 SQUADRON   MOTTO: Semper paratus (Always prepared)

Month/Yr	Location	Aircraft Type	Remarks
11/11/18	Estrées-en-Chaussée	HP 0/400 (8/19)	
1/12/18	to Carvin		
1/1/19	to Merheim		
10/5/19	to Hangelar		
22/8/19	to Tangmere		as cadre
8/10/19	to Croydon		
10/1/20	to Kenley		
16/1/20	to Uxbridge		
20/1/20	DB		
1/2/20	RF Bircham Newton		nucleus from No. 274 Sqn
4/21		DH 9A (1/28)	
29/9/22	en route to Turkey		
11/10/22	to San Stephano		
22/9/23	en route to the UK		
3/10/23	to Eastchurch		
12/27		Fairey IIIF (9/32)	
9/11/29	to Bircham Newton		
8/32		Gordon (4/36)	
28/10/36	to Ed Damer		
6/4/36	to Gebeit		
4/36		Vincent (7/36)	
29/8/36	to Worthy Down		
8/36		Gordon (11/37)	
9/37		Wellesley (4/38)	
20/4/38	to Cottesmore		
4/38		Battle (4/40)	
7/39		Anson I (4/40)	
24/8/39	to Cranfield		

No. 208 SQUADRON   MOTTO: Vigilant

Month/Yr	Location	Aircraft Type	Remarks
11/11/18	Maretz	Camel (11/18)	
11/18		Snipe (11/19)	
3/12/18	to Strée B		
23/5/19	to Heumar		
7/8/19	to Eil		
9/9/19	to Netheravon		
7/11/19	DB		
1/2/20	RF Ismailia		No. 113 sqn renumbered
2/20		RE 8(11/20)	det Ramleh
10/20		Bristol F2B (5/30)	
28/9/22	to San Stephano		
26/9/23	to Ismailia		
27/10/27	to Heliopolis		det Ramleh
5/30		Atlas (8/35)	
4/34		Audax (1/39)	
9/35		Demon (3/36)	'D' Flt only dets Mersah Matruh & Amiriya
24/1/36	to Mersah Matruh		
18/4/36	to Heliopolis		dets Ramleh, Fayid, Helwan, Burrumbul, Mersah Matruh & Aboukir
28/9/38	to Mersah Matruh		
13/10/38	to Heliopolis		
1/39		Lysander I & II (5/42)	
26/2/39	to Mersah Matruh		
16/3/39	to Heliopolis		
7/8/39	to Mersah Matruh		
1/9/39	to Qasaba		

No. 209 SQUADRON   MOTTO: Might and Main

Month/Yr	Location	Aircraft Type	Remarks
11/11/18	Bruille	Camel 2/19	
22/11/18	to Saultain		
11/12/18	to Froidmont		
14/2/19	to Scopwick		as cadre

Month/Yr	Location	Aircraft Type	Remarks
24/6/19	DB		
15/1/30	RF Mount Batten		
2/30		Iris III (12/32)	
2/32		Saro A7(7/32)	
6/32		Iris V (6/34)	
8/32		Singapore II (11/32)	
2/33		Southampton II (6/34)	
1/34		Perth (12/34)	
10/34		Southampton II (11/34)	
10/34		London I (11/34)	
1/35		Southampton II (2/35)	
1/35		London I (2/36)	
2/35		Stranraer (9/35)	
4/35		Short R.24/31 (9/35)	
1/5/35	to Felixstowe		
7/35		Perth (5/36)	
1/36		Southampton II (7/36)	
2/36		Singapore III (3/39)	
22/9/37	to Kalafrana		
31/9/37	to Arzeu		
17/12/37	to Felixstowe		
29/9/38	to Invergordon		
8/10/38	to Felixstowe		
12/38		Stranraer (4/40)	
22/5/39	to Stranraer		
17/6/39	to Felixstowe		
12/8/39	to Invergordon		
22/8/39	to Felixstowe		
30/8/39	to Invergordon		det Falmouth

No. 210 SQUADRON   MOTTO: Yn y nwyfre yn hedfan (Hovering in the heavens)

Month/Yr	Location	Aircraft Type	Remarks
11/11/18	Boussieres	Camel (2/19)	
17/2/19	to Scopwick		as cadre
24/6/19	DB		
1/2/20	RF Gosport		No. 186 Sqn renumbered
2/20		Cuckoo (4/23)	
1/4/23	DB		renumbered as Nos.460 & 461 Flts
1/3/31	RF Felixstowe		
5/31		Southampton II (8/35)	
15/6/31	to Pembroke Dock		
11/34		Singapore III (4/35)	ferried to No. 205 Sqn
7/35		Singapore III (8/35)	ferried to No. 203 sqn
8/35		Rangoon (9/36)	from No. 203 sqn
28/9/35	to Gibraltar		
10/35		London II (11/35)	
10/35		Stranraer (11/35)	
7/8/36	to Pembroke Dock		
8/36		Singapore III (11/38)	
22/9/37	to Arzeu		
18/12/37	to Pembroke Dock		
6/38		Sunderland I (4/41)	
29/9/38	to Tayport		
8/10/38	to Pembroke Dock		

No. 211 SQUADRON   MOTTO: Toujours a propos (Always at the right moment)

Month/Yr	Location	Aircraft Type	Remarks
11/11/18	Iris Farm	DH 9 (3/19)	
3/12/18	to Thuilles		
15/3/19	to Wyton		as cadre
24/6/19	DB		
24/6/37	RF Mildenhall		
7/37		Audax (10/37)	
8/37		Hind (5/39)	
2/9/37	to Grantham		
12/5/38	to Helwan		
18/7/38	to Ramleh		det Semakh
29/9/38	to Helwan		
31/1/39	to Ismailia		
4/39		Blenheim I (11/41)	det El Daba
10/8/39	to El Daba		det Qotafiyah

No. 212 SQUADRON   MOTTO: Amari ad astra (From the sea to the stars)

Month/Yr	Location	Aircraft Type	Remarks
11/11/18	Great Yarmouth	DH 4 (1/19)	
		DH 9A (2/20)	
		DH 9 (2/20)	
		Camel (1/19)	

Month/Yr	Location	Aircraft Type	Remarks
7/3/19	to Swingate Down		
9/2/20	DB		

No. 213 SQUADRON   MOTTO: Irritatus lacessit crabro (The hornet attacks when roused)

11/11/18	Bergues	Camel (3/19)	
27/11/18	to Stalhille		
19/3/19	to Scopwick		as cadre
31/12/19	DB		
8/3/37	RF Northolt		from 'A' Flt No. 111 Sqn
3/37		Gauntlet II (3/39)	
1/7/37	to Church Fenton		
18/5/38	to Wittering		
1/39		Hurricane I (3/42)	

No. 214 SQUADRON   MOTTO: Ultra in umbris (Avenging in the shadows)

11/11/18	Chemy	HP 0/400 (2/20)	
4/7/19	to Abu Sueir		
1/2/20	DB		absorbed into No. 216 Squadron
16/9/35	RR Boscombe Down		from 'B' Flt No. 9 Sqn
9/35		Virginia X (4/37)	
15/10/35	to Andover		det Aldergrove
1/10/36	to Scampton		
1/37		Harrow (6/39)	
19/4/37	to Feltwell		
5/39		Wellington I (5/40)	
3/9/39	to Methwold		
9/39		Wellington IA (9/40)	

No. 215 SQUADRON   MOTTO: Surgite nox adeste (Arise, night is at hand)

11/11/18	Xaffévillers	HP 0/400 (2/19)	
21/11/18	to Alquines		
2/2/19	to Ford Junction		as cadre
18/10/19	DB		
1/10/35	RF Worthy Down		from 'C' Flt No. 58 Sqn
10/35		Virginia X (9/37)	
14/1/36	to Upper Heyford		
3/9/36	to Driffield		
2/37		Anson I (11/37)	
8/37		Harrow (12/39)	
25/7/38	to Honington		
7/39		Wellington I (4/40)	

No. 216 SQUADRON   MOTTO: CCXVI dona ferens (216 bearing gifts)

11/11/18	Rovilles-aux-Chenes	HP 0/400 (10/21)	
17/11/18	to Quilen		
14/12/18	to Marquise		
3/7/19	to Qantara		
7/20	to Abu Sueir		
8/20		DH10 (6/22)	
15/4/21	to Heliopolis		
6/22		Vimy (1/26)	
12/25		Victoria II (10/26)	
7/26		Victoria III (4/35)	
2/29		Victoria V (8/34)	
4/29		Victoria IV (4/31)	
4/33		Victoria VI (11/35)	
2/35		Valentia (9/41)	det Eastleigh

No. 217 SQUADRON   MOTTO: Woe to the enemy

11/11/18	Crochte	DH 4 (3/19)	
25/11/18	to Varssenaere		
29/3/19	to Driffield		as cadre
19/10/19	DB		
15/3/37	RF Boscombe Down		
3/37		Anson I (12/40)	
7/37	to Tangmere		
16/8/37	to Bicester		
13/9/37	to Tangmere		
28/9/38	to Warmwell		
10/10/38	to Tangmere		
25/8/39	to Warmwell		

Month/Yr	Location	Aircraft Type	Remarks
No. 218 SQUADRON	**MOTTO: In Time**		
11/11/18	Reumont	DH 9 (2/19)	
16/11/18	to Vert Galand		
11/2/19	to Hucknall		as cadre
24/6/19	DB		
16/3/36	RF Upper Heyford		from 'C' Flt No. 57 Sqn
3/36		Hart (3/38)	
1/38		Battle (5/40)	
22/4/38	to Boscombe Down		
2/9/39	to Auberives-sur-Suippes		
No. 219 SQUADRON	**MOTTO: From Dusk till Dawn**		
11/11/18	Westgate/Manston	DH 9 (6/19)	Seaplanes Nos.406 & 442 Flights
		Camel (6/19)	at Westgate. Landplanes Nos. 470,
		Short 184 (2/20)	555 & 556 Flts at Manston
		Fairey IIIB (2/20)	
7/2/20	DB		
No. 220 SQUADRON	**MOTTO: We observe unseen (Greek script)**		
11/11/18	Imbros	DH 4 (1/19)	
		DH 9 (1/19)	
		Camel (1/19)	
2/19	to Mudros		as cadre
21/5/19	DB		
17/8/36	RF Bircham Newton		nucleus from No. 206 Sqn
8/36		Anson I (12/39)	
21/8/39	to Thornaby		
9/39		Hudson I,III & VI (6/42)	dets St Eval & Wick
No. 221 SQUADRON	**MOTTO: From sea to sea**		
11/11/18	Mudros	DH 9 (9/19)	assets absorbed by No. 222 Sqn
12/18			re-established
29/12/18	en route to South Russia		via HMS *Riviera* & HMS *Empress*
5/1/19	to Batum		
10/1/19	to Baku		
15/1/19	to Petrovsk Kaskar		dets Chechen & Lagan
4/19		DH 9A (9/19)	
18/8/19			began evacuation
1/9/19	DB		
No. 222 SQUADRON	**MOTTO: Pambili Bo (Zulu)**		
11/11/18	Mudros	DH 9 (2/19)	dets Amberkoj & Dedeagatch
		DH 4 (2/19)	
		Camel (2/19)	
15/11/18	to San Stephano		
23/11/18	to Mudros		
27/2/19	DB		
No. 223 SQUADRON	**MOTTO: Alae defendunt Africam (Wings defend Africa)**		
11/11/18	Mudros	DH 4 (5/19)	
		DH 9 (5/19)	
16/5/19	DB		
15/12/36	RF Nairobi		from Flt of No. 45 Sqn
12/36		Gordon (2/37)	
2/37		Vincent (7/38)	
6/38		Wellesley (4/41)	det Summit
No. 224 SQUADRON	**MOTTO: Fedele all'amico (Italian – Faithful to a friend)**		
11/11/18	Pizzone	DH4 (4/19)	
		DH 9 (4/19)	
15/4/19	DB		
1/2/37	RF Manston		from 'C' Flt No. 48 Sqn
2/37		Anson I (7/39)	
15/2/37	to Boscombe Down		
9/7/37	to Thornaby		
17/1/38	to Eastleigh		dets Montrose & Gosport
26/3/38	to Thornaby		
1/9/38	to Leuchars		
5/39		Hudson I (5/41)	det Aldergrove
No. 225 SQUADRON	**MOTTO: We guide the sword**		
11/11/18	Pizzone	Camel (12/18)	
18/12/18	DB		

Month/Yr	Location	Aircraft Type	Remarks
No. 226 SQUADRON MOTTO: Non sibi sed patriae (For country not for self)			
11/11/18	to Taranto	DH 4 (11/18)	
		DH 9 (11/18)	
		Camel (11/18)	
18/12/18	DB		
15/3/37	RF Upper Heyford		fom 'B' Flt No. 57 Sqn
3/37		Audax (11/37)	
16/4/37	to Harwell		
10/37		Battle (5/41)	
2/9/39	to Reims		dets Perpignan/La Salanque
No. 227 SQUADRON			
11/11/18	Pizzone	DH 4 (12/18)	
		DH 9 (12/18)	
9/12/18	DB		without ever having become fully established
No. 228 SQUADRON MOTTO:Auxilium a caelo (Help from the sky)			
11/11/18	Great Yarmouth	Felixstowe F.2A (3/19)	
		Curtiss H12/16 (/19)	
30/4/19	to Brough		as cadre
5/6/19	to Killinghome		
30/6/19	DB		
15/12/36	RF Pembroke Dock		
2/37		Scapa (8/38)	
2/37		London I (9/38)	
4/37		Stranraer (4/39)	
4/37		Singapaore III (9/37)	
29/9/38	to Invergordon		
11/38		Sunderland I (8/41)	
5/6/39	to Alexandria		
No. 229 SQUADRON MOTTO: Be bold			
11/11/18	Great Yarmouth	Short 184 (3/19)	
		Short 320 (3/19)	
		Fairey IIIC (3/19)	
3/3/19	to Killinghome		as cadre
31/12/19	DB		
No. 230 SQUADRON MOTTO: Kita chari jauh (Malay - We seek far)			
11/11/18	Felixstowe	Felixstowe F.2A (3/19)	
		Curtiss H16 (3/19)	
		Camel (12/18)	det Butley
		Felixstowe F.3 (3/19)	
		Short 184 (3/19)	
		Fairey IIIB/C (3/19)	
13/3/19			reduced to a cadre
31/12/19			re-established from No. 4 (Communications) Sqn
1/20		Felixstowe F.3 (9/21)	
1/20		Fairey IIIC (6/21)	
1/20		Felixstowe F.2A (4/23)	
1/20		Felixstowe F.5 (4/23)	
7/5/22	to Calshot		
1/4/23	DB		renumbered as No. 480 Flt
1/12/34	RF Pembroke Dock		
4/35		Singapore III (12/38)	
23/9/35	en route for Egypt		
24/10/35	to Alexandria		
24/11/35	to Lake Timsah		
1/12/35	to Alexandria		
30/7/36	en route to the UK		
3/8/36	to Pembroke Dock		
14/10/36	en route to Far East		
8/1/37	to Seletar		
6/38		Sunderland I (1/43)	dets Trincomalee, Colombo, Penang & Koggala
No. 231 SQUADRON			
11/11/18	Felixstowe	Felixstowe F.2A (3/19)	
		Felixstowe F.3 (3/19)	
		Felixstowe F.5 (3/19)	
13/3/19			reduced to a cadre
7/7/19	DB		

Month/Yr	Location	Aircraft Type	Remarks
No. 232 SQUADRON	**MOTTO: Strike**		
11/11/18	Felixstowe	Felixstowe F.2A (1/19)	
		Felixstowe F.3 (1/19)	
5/1/19	DB		redesignated as No. 4 (Communicatioms) Sqn

No. 233 SQUADRON	**MOTTO: Fortis et fidelis (Strong and faithful)**		
11/11/18	Dover Harbour &	DH 9 (3/19)	
	Guston Road	Camel (11/18)	det walmer
		Short 184 (5/19)	
1/19		DH 4 (5/19)	
15/5/19	DB		
18/5/37	RF Upper Heyford		
5/37		Anson I (12/39)	
9/7/37	to Thornaby		
1/9/38	to Leuchars		
28/9/38	to Montrose		
10/10/38	to Leuchars		
8/39		Hudson I (6/41)	

No. 234 SQUADRON	**MOTTO: Ignem mortemque despuimus (We spit fire and death)**		
11/11/18	Trescoe	Curtiss H.12 (5/19)	
		Short 184 (5/19)	
		Felixstowe F.3 (5/19)	
15/5/19	DB		

No. 235 SQUADRON	**MOTTO: Jaculamur humi (We strike them to the ground)**		
11/11/18	Newlyn	Short 184 (2/19)	
22/2/19	DB		

No. 236 SQUADRON	**MOTTO: Speculati nuntiate (Having watched, bring word)**		
11/11/18	Mullion	DH 6 (3/19)	
		DH 9 (5/19)	
31/5/19	DB		

No. 237 SQUADRON	**MOTTO: Primum agmen in caelo (The vanguard is in the sky)**		
11/11/18	Cattewater	Short 184 (5/19)	
15/5/19	DB		

No. 238 SQUADRON	**MOTTO: Ad finem (To the end)**		
11/11/18	Cattewater	Curtiss H.16 (/19)	
		Short 184 (5/19)	
		Felixstowe F.2A (5/19)	
		Felixstowe F.3 (5/19)	dets Holy Island, Killinghome & Calshot
15/5/19			reduced to a cadre
20/3/22	DB		

No. 239 SQUADRON	**MOTTO: Exploramus (We seek out)**		
11/11/18	Torquay	Short 184 (5/19)	
31/5/19	DB		

No. 240 SQUADRON	**MOTTO: Sjo-Vordur Lopt-Vordur (Guardian of the sea, guardian of the sky)**		
11/11/18	Calshot	Short 320 (5/19)	
		Felixstowe F.2A (5/19)	
		Campania (5/19)	
		Short 184 (5/19)	
		Curtiss H.12 (/19)	
15/5/19	DB		
30/3/37	RF Calshot		ex 'C' Flt, Seaplane Training Squadron
3/37		Scapa (1/39)	
11/38		Singapore III (7/39)	
7/39		Lerwick I (9/39)	
7/39		London II (7/40)	
12/8/39	to Invergordon		det Falmouth

No. 241 SQUADRON	**MOTTO: Find and Forewarn**		
11/11/18	Portland	DH 6 (1/19)	
		Short 184 (6/19)	
		Campania (6/19)	
		Wight Converted (6/19)	det Chickerall
18/6/19	DB		

Month/Yr	Location	Aircraft Type	Remarks

No. 242 SQUADRON   MOTTO: Toujours pret (Always ready)

11/11/18	Newhaven	Short 184 (5/19)	
		DH 6 (1/19)	
		Campania (11/18)	det Telscombe Cliffs
15/5/19	DB		

No. 243 SQUADRON   MOTTO: Swift in pursuit

11/11/18	Cherbourg	Short 184 (5/19)	
		Wight Converted	
15/3/19	DB		

No. 244 SQUADRON

11/11/18	Bangor	DH 6 (1/19)	dets Tallaght, Llangefni & Luce Bay
22/1/19	DB		

No. 245 SQUADRON   MOTTO: Fugo non fugio (I put to flight, I do not flee)

11/11/18	Fishguard	Short 184 (5/19)	
10/5/19	DB		

No. 246 SQUADRON

11/11/18	Seaton Carew	Kangaroo (11/18)	
		Short 184 (3/19)	
15/3/19	DB		

No. 247 SQUADRON   MOTTO: Rise from the East

11/11/18	Felixstowe	Felixstowe F.2A (1/19)	
		Felixstowe F.3 (1/19)	
22/1/19	DB		

No. 248 SQUADRON   MOTTO: Il faut en finir (It is necessary to make an end of it)

11/11/18	Hornsea	Sopwith Baby (11/18)	
		Short 184 (3/19)	
		Short 320 (3/20)	det North Coates
10/3/19	DB		

No. 249 SQUADRON   MOTTO: Pugnis et cacibus (With fists and heels)

11/11/18	Dundee	Sopwith Baby (11/18)	
		Hamble Baby (11/18)	
3/3/19	to Killinghome	Short 184 (3/19)	as cadre
8/10/19	DB		

No. 250 SQUADRON   MOTTO: Close to the sun

11/11/18	Padstow	DH 6 (5/19)	
		DH 9 (1/19)	det Westward Ho
31/5/19	DB		

No. 251 SQUADRON   MOTTO: However wind blows

11/11/18	Hornsea	DH 6 (5/19)	dets Atwick, Greenland Top, West Ayton
		DH 9 (1/19)	Owthorpe, Seaton Carew & Redcar
31/1/19	to Killinghome		as cadre
30/6/19	DB		

No. 252 SQUADRON   MOTTO: With or on

11/11/18	Tynemouth	DH 6 (1/19)	dets Cramlington, Seaton Carew
	& Redcar		
31/1/19	to Killinghome		as cadre
30/6/19	DB		

No. 253 SQUADRON   MOTTO: Come one, come all

11/11/18	Bembridge	Hamble Baby (5/19)	dets Barding & Chickerall
		Short 184 (5/19)	
		Campania (5/19)	
		DH 6 (1/19)	
31/5/19	DB		

No. 254 SQUADRON   MOTTO: Fljuga vakta ok ljosta (Norse - To fly, to watch and to strike)

11/11/18	Prawle Point	DH 6 (2/19)	det Mullion
		DH 9 (2/19)	
22/2/19	DB		

No. 255 SQUADRON   MOTTO: Ad auroram (To the break of dawn)

11/11/8	Pembroke	DH 6 (1/19)	dets Llangefni & Luce Bay
14/1/19	DB		

Month/Yr	Location	Aircraft Type	Remarks

No. 256 SQUADRON   MOTTO: Addimus vim viribus (Strength to strength)

11/11/18	Seahouses	DH 6 (1/19)	dets New Haggerston, Rennington
			Cairncross & Ashington
11/18		Kangaroo (1/19)	
31/1/19	to Killinghome		as cadre
30/6/19	DB		

No. 257 SQUADRON   MOTTO: Thay myay gvee shin shwe hti (Burmese - Death or glory)

11/11/18	Dundee	Felixstowe F.2A (4/19)	
		Curtiss H.16 (/18)	
4/19			reduced to a cadre
30/6/19	DB		

No. 258 SQUADRON   MOTTO: In medias re (Into the middle of things)

11/11/18	Luce Bay	DH 6 (3/19)	
		Fairey IIIA (3/19)	
5/3/19	DB		

No. 260 SQUADRON   MOTTO: Celer et fortis (Swift and strong)

11/11/18	Westward Ho	DH 6 (2/19)	
		DH 9 (2/19)	
22/2/19	DB		

No. 263 SQUADRON   MOTTO: Ex ungue leonem (From his claws one knows the lion)

11/11/18	Otranto	Sopwith Baby (5/19)	det Santa Maria di Leucca
		Hamble Baby (5/19)	
		Short 184 (5/19)	
		Short 320 (5/19)	
		Felixstowe F.3 (5/19)	
11/18	to Taranto		
16/5/19	DB		

No. 264 SQUADRON   MOTTO: We defy

11/11/18	Suda Bay	Short 184 (12/18)	det Siros
12/18			reduced to a cadre, personnel withdrawn
			to Malta
1/3/19	DB		

No. 266 SQUADRON   MOTTO: Hlabezulu (The stabber of the sky)

11/11/18	Mudros	Short 184 (3/19)	det Skyros
		Short 320 (3/19)	
10/3/19	to Petrovsk Port		det Chechen
1/9/19	DB		

No. 267 SQUADRON   MOTTO: Sine mora (Without delay)

11/11/18	Kalafrana	Short 184 (10/21)	det Alexandria
		Felixstowe F.2A (2/23)	
		Felixstowe F.3 (6/21)	
12/20		Fairey IIID (8/23)	dets HMS *Ark Royal* & Kilya Bay
1/8/23	DB		redesignated as 481 Flt

No. 268 SQUADRON   MOTTO: Adjidaumo (Chippeway Indian - Tail in the air)

11/11/18	Kalafrana	Short 184 (10/19)	
		Short 320 (10/19)	
11/10/19	DB		

No. 269 SQUADRON   MOTTO: Omnia videmus (We see all things)

11/11/18	Port Said	BE 2E (3/19)	
		Short 184 (11/19)	
12/18		DH 9 (3/19)	
15/9/19	to Alexandria		
15/11/19	DB		absorbed by No. 267 Sqn
7/12/36	RF Bircham Newton		from 'C' Flt No. 220 Sqn
12/36		Anson I (6/40)	
30/12/36	to Abbotsinch		
17/1/38	to Eastleigh		
24/3/38	to Abbotsinch		
29/9/38	to Thornaby		
6/10/38	to Abbotsinch		
25/8/39	to Montrose		

Month/Yr	Location	Aircraft Type	Remarks

No. 270 SQUADRON

11/11/18	Alexandria	Short 184 (9/19)	
		Sopwith Baby (4/19)	
		Felixstowe F.3 (9/19)	
		DH 9 (/19)	
15/9/19	DB		merged into No. 269 sqn

No. 271 SQUADRON   MOTTO: Death and Life

11/11/18	Taranto	Short 184 (12/18)	det Otranto
		Felixstowe F.3 (12/18)	
9/12/18	DB		

No. 272 SQUADRON   MOTTO: On, on!

11/11/18	Macrihanish	DH 6 (3/19)	
		Fairey IIIA (3/19)	
5/3/19	DB		

No. 273 SQUADRON

11/11/18	Burgh Castle	DH 4 (3/19)	dets Covehithe, Westgate & Manston
		DH 9 (3/19)	
		Camel (3/19)	
14/3/19			reduced to a cadre
6/19	to Great Yarmouth		
5/7/19	DB		
1/8/39	RF China Bay		
8/39		Seal (3/42)	
		Vildebeeste III (3/42)	det Ratmalana

No. 274 SQUADRON   MOTTO: Supero (I overcome)

15/6/19	F Bircham Newton		nucleus from No. 5 (Communications) Sqn
6/19		HP V/1500 (1/20)	
20/1/20	DB		

No. 500 SQUADRON   County of Kent   MOTTO: Quo fata vocent (Whither the fates may call)

16/3/31	F Manston		as a Special Reserve Squadron
3/31		Virginia X (1/36)	
1/36		Hart (5/37)	
25/5/36			transferred to AAF
2/37		Hind (3/39)	
28/9/38	to Detling		
3/39		Anson I (4/4I)	
30/7/39	to Warmwell		
13/8/39	to Detling		

No. 501 SQUADRON   City of Bristol 1930–6
County of Gloucester 1936–57 MOTTO: Nil time (Fear nothing)

14/6/29	F Filton		as a Special Reserve Squadron
3/30		DH 9A (11/30)	
9/30		Wapiti (3/33)	
1/33		Wallace (7/36)	
1/5/36			transferred to AAF
7/36		Hart (3/38)	
3/38		Hind (3/39)	
3/39		Hurricane I (5/41)	

No. 502 SQUADRON   Ulster   MOTTO: Nihil timeo (I fear nothing)

15/5/25	F Aldergove		as a Special Reserve Squadron
6/25		Vimy (7/28)	
7/28		Hyderabad (2/32)	
12/31		Virginia X (10/35)	
10/35		Wallace (4/37)	
4/37		Hind (4/39)	
1/7/37			transferred to AAF
1/39		Anson I (10/40)	det Hooton Park

No. 503 SQUADRON   County of Lincoln

5/10/26	F Waddington		as a Special Reserve Squadron
10/26		Fawn (6/29)	
2/29		Hyderabad (1/34)	
10/33		Hinaidi (11/35)	
8/35		Wallace (7/36)	
1/5/36			transferred to AAF
6/36		Hart (11/38)	
6/38		Hind (11/38)	
1/11/38	DB		moved to Doncaster and renumbered 616 Sqn

Month/Yr	Location	Aircraft Type	Remarks

No. 504 SQUADRON   County of Nottingham   MOTTO: Vindicat in ventis (It avenges in the wind)

Month/Yr	Location	Aircraft Type	Remarks
26/3/28	F Hucknall		as a Special Reserve Squadron
10/29		Horsley (3/34)	
3/34		Wallace I (5/37)	
3/36		Wallace II (5/37)	
18/5/36			transferred to AAF
5/37		Hind (11/38)	
11/38		Gauntlet II (8/39)	
5/39		Hurricane I (7/41)	
27/8/39	to Digby		

No. 600 SQUADRON   City of London   MOTTO: Praeter sescentos (More than 600)

Month/Yr	Location	Aircraft Type	Remarks
14/10/25	F Northolt		
10/25		DH 9A (10/29)	
18/1/27	to Hendon		
8/29		Wapiti (1/35)	
1/35		Hart (5/37)	
2/37		Demon (4/39)	
1/10/38	to Kenley		
4/10/38	to Hendon		
1/39		Blenheim IF (10/41)	
25/8/39	to Northolt		

No. 601 SQUADRON   County of London

Month/Yr	Location	Aircraft Type	Remarks
14/10/25	F Northolt		
6/26		DH 9A (10/30)	
18/1/27	to Hendon		
11/29		Wapiti (6/33)	
2/33		Hart (8/37)	
8/37		Demon (12/38)	
12/38		Gauntlet II (3/39)	
1/39		Blenheim IF (2/40)	
2/9/39	to Biggin Hill		

No. 602 SQUADRON   City of Glasgow   MOTTO: Cave leonem cruciatum (Beware the tormented lion)

Month/Yr	Location	Aircraft Type	Remarks
12/9/25	F Renfrew		
10/25		DH 9A (1/28)	
9/27		Fawn (10/29)	
7/29		Wapiti (4/34)	
20/1/33	to Abbotsinch		
2/34		Hart (6/36)	
6/36		Hind (11/38)	
11/38		Hector (1/39)	
1/39		Gauntlet II (5/39)	
5/39		Spitfire I (6/41)	

No. 603 SQUADRON   City of Edinburgh   MOTTO: Gin ye daur (If you dare)

Month/Yr	Location	Aircraft Type	Remarks
14/10/25	F Turnhouse		
10/25		DH 9A (5/30)	
3/30		Wapiti (3/34)	
2/34		Hart (2/38)	
2/38		Hind (3/39)	
3/39		Gladiator II (10/39)	
9/39		Spitfire I (11/40)	

No. 604 SQUADRON   County of Middlesex   MOTTO: Si vis pacem, para bellum (If you want peace, prepare for war)

Month/Yr	Location	Aircraft Type	Remarks
17/3/30	F Hendon		
4/30		DH 9A (10/30)	
9/30		Wapiti IIA (/34)	
9/34		Hart (6/35)	
6/35		Demon (1/39)	
1/39		Blenheim I (5/41)	
2/9/39	to North Weald		det Martlesham Heath

No. 605 SQUADRON   County of Warwick   MOTTO: Nunquam dormio (I never sleep)

Month/Yr	Location	Aircraft Type	Remarks
5/10/26	F Castle Bromwich		
10/26		DH 9A (7/30)	
4/30		Wapiti IIA (11/34)	
2/34		Hart (9/36)	
8/36		Hind (1/39)	
4/39		Gladiator I (11/39)	
6/39		Hurricane I (12/40)	
27/8/39	to Tangmere		

Month/Yr	Location	Aircraft Type	Remarks

No. 607 SQUADRON   County of Durham

17/3/30	F Usworth		
12/32		Wapiti IIA (1/37)	
9/36		Demon (8/39)	
12/38		Gladiator I (5/40)	

No. 608 SQUADRON   County of York - North Riding (North Riding from May 1937)   MOTTO: Omnibus ungulis (With all talons)

17/3/30	F Thornaby		
6/30		Wapiti IIA (1/37)	
1/37		Demon (3/39)	
3/39		Anson I (5/41)	

No. 609 SQUADRON   West Riding   MOTTO: Tally Ho

10/2/36	F Yeadon		
5/36		Hart (1/38)	
1/38		Hind (8/39)	
8/39		Spitfire I (5/41)	
27/8/39	to Catterick		

No. 610 SQUADRON   County of Chester   MOTTO: Alifero tollitur axe ceres (Ceres rising in a winged car)

102/36	F Hendon		
16/4/36	to Hooton Park		
5/36		Hart (5/38)	
5/38		Hind (9/39)	
9/39		Hurricane I (9/39)	
9/39		Spitfire I (2/41)	

No. 611 SQUADRON   West Lancashire   MOTTO: Beware, beware

10/2/36	F Hendon		
1/4/36	to Liverpool		
6/5/36	to Speke		
6/36		Hart (4/38)	
4/38		Hind (5/39)	
5/39		Spitfire (9/40)	
13/8/39	to Duxford		

No. 612 SQUADRON   County of Aberdeen   MOTTO: Vigilando custodimus (We stand guard by vigilance)

1/6/37	F Dyce		
12/37		Hector (11/39)	
6/39		Anson I (1/41)	dets Stornaway & Wick

No. 613 SQUADRON   City of Manchester   MOTTO: Semper parati (Always ready)

1/3/39	F Ringway		
4/39		Hind (4/40)	

No. 614 SQUADRON   County of Glamorgan   MOTTO: Codaf I geislo (Welsh - I rise and search)

1/6/37	F Pengam Moors		
6/37		Hind (1/38)	
4/38		Hector (2/40)	
7/39		Lysander II (7/41)	

No. 615 SQUADRON   County of Surrey   MOTTO: Conjunctis viribus (By our united force)

1/6/37	F Kenley		
11/37		Audax (3/38)	
11/37		Hector (2/39)	
		B-69	
12/38		Gauntlet II (9/39)	
6/39		Gladiator I (10/39)	
2/9/39	to Croydon		

No. 616 SQUADRON   South Yorkshire   MOTTO: Nulla rosa sine spina (No rose without a thorn)

1/11/38	F Doncaster		from No. 503 Sqn
11/38		Hind I (1/39)	
1/39		Gauntlet II (12/39)	
5/39		Battle (11/39)	

Appendix C

Pilot Training Courses at RAF Elementary and Reserve Flying Training Schools – United Kingdom – 31 August 1939

E&RFTS & Date formed	Pilot training Courses			RAF Regular	Operating Company	Remarks
	RAF Reserve	RAFVR Ab Initio	Advanced			
No.1 Hatfield 1.5.23	1.5.23	1.4.37	30.6.39	1.8.35	De Havilland	Moved from Stag Lane to Hatfield in May 1930
No.2 Filton 23.5.23	23.5.23	1.4.37	x	1.8.35	Bristol Aeroplane Co.Ltd	
No.3 Hamble 31.7.23	31.7.23	1.8.37	27.6.39	1.8.35	Air Service	Originally opened at Coventry. Was operated by Beardmores. Moved Hamble 4/31
No.4 Brough 21.5.24	21.5.24	1.8.37	21.6.39	1.8.35	Blackburn Aircraft Co.	Was operated by the North Sea Aeriel & General Co.Ltd until 1938
No.5 Hanworth 10.6.35	10.6.35	1.4.37	30.6.39	10.6.35	Flying Training Ltd	
No.6 Sywell 10.6.35	10.6.35	1.4.37	x	10.6.35	Brooklands Aviation Ltd.	
No.7 Desford 25.11.35	25.11.35	1.4.37	x	25.11.35	Reid & Sigrist Ltd	
No.8 Reading 25.1.35	25.11.35	1.4.37	6.7.39	25.11.35	Phillips & Powis Ltd.	
No.9 Ansty 6.1.36	6.1.36	1.4.37	13.7.39	6.1.36	Air Service Training Ltd.	
No.10 Yatesbury 6.1.36	6.1.36	-	-	6.1.36	Bristol Aeroplane Co.Ltd	

E&RFTS & Date formed	Pilot training Courses				Operating Company	Remarks
	RAF Reserve	RAFVR Ab Initio	Advanced	RAF Regular		
No.11 Perth 27.1.36	27.1.36	1.4.37	30.3.39	27.1.36	Airwork Ltd	
No.12 Prestwick 6.1.36	17.2.36	1.4.37	1.6.39	17.2.36	Scottish Aviation Ltd	
No.13 White Waltham 18.11.35	18.11.35	1.4.37	x	18.11.35	De Havilland Aircraft Co.Ltd	
No.14 Castle Bromwich 1.7.37	-	1.7.37	-	-	Airwork Ltd	
No.15 Redhill 1.7.37	-	1.7.37	6.7.39	-	British Air Transport Ltd	
No.16 Shoreham 1.7.37	-	1.7.37	9.1.39	-	Brooklands Aviation Ltd	
No.17 Barton & Ringway 1.10.37	-	1.10.37	x	-	Airwork Ltd	
No.18 Fairoaks 1.10.37	-	1.10.37	21.7.39	-	General Aircraft Ltd	
No.19 Gatwick 1.10.37	-	1.10.37	21.7.39	6.10.38	Airports Ltd	
No.20 Gravesend 1.10.37	-	1.10.37	13.7.39	-	Airports Ltd	Commenced F.A.A. 'ab initio' training on 6.3.39
No.21 Stapleford Abbots 1.1.38	-	1.10.37	13.7.39	-	Airports Ltd	

E&RFTS & Date formed	Pilot training Courses				Operating Company	Remarks
	RAF Reserve	RAFVR Ab Initio	Advanced	RAF Regular		
No.22 Cambridge 1.2.38	-	1.2.38	1.7.39	27.3.39	Marshalls Flying School Ltd	
No.23 Rochester 1.4.38	-	1.4.38	x	-	Short Bros.Ltd	Commenced 'ab initio' training on 25.6.38
No.24 Sydenham 1.1.39	-	1.1.39	x	-	Short.Bros.Ltd	
No.25 Grimsby 24.6.38	-	24.6.39	x	-	Herts & Essex Aero Club	
No.26 Oxford 24.6.38	-	24.6.38	x	-	Marshalls Flying Schools Ltd.	
No.27 Tollerton 24.6.38	-	24.6.38	1.7.39	-	Nottingham Airports Ltd	
No.28 Meir 1.8.38	-	1.8.38	x	-	Reid & Sigrist Ltd	
No.29 Luton 1.8.38	-	1.8.38	x	-	Birkett Air Service Ltd	
No.30 Derby 29.9.38	-	29.9.38	x	27.3.39	Air Schools Ltd	Commenced extended 'ab initio' courses 1.1.39 This was included in the Regular courses on 27.3.39
No.31 Gloucester 29.9.39	-	29.9.39	x	-	Surrey Flying Services Ltd.	
No.32 West Hartlepool 15.4.39	-	15.4.39	x	-	Portsmouth Southsea & Isle of Wight Aviation Ltd.	
No.33 Whitchurch 3.12.38	-	3.12.38	x	-	Channier, Gilbert Lodge & Co.Ltd	

E&RFTS & Date formed	RAF Reserve	Pilot training Courses		RAF Regular	Operating Company	Remarks
		RAFVR Ab Initio	Advanced			
No.34 Southend 1.1.39	-	1.3.39	x	-	Air Hire Ltd.	
No.35 Grangemouth 1.5.39	-	1.5.39	x	-	Scottish Aviation Ltd	
No.36 Sherburn	-	-	-	-	Blackburn Aviation Ltd	Was in the process of opening on the outbreak of war.
No.37 Exeter 3.7.39	-	-	-	-	Straight Corporation Ltd	RAFVR Trg only
No.38 Carlisle 1.7.39	-	1.7.39	x	-	Border Flying Club Ltd.	
No.39 Weston-Super-Mare 3.7.39	-	3.7.39	x	-	Straight Corporation Ltd	
No.40 Norwich 15.8.39	-	15.8.39	x	-	Air Contractors Ltd	
No.41 Dyce	-	-	-	-	Aberdeen Flying School Ltd	Was in the process of opening on the outbreak of war.
No.42 Blackpool 1.8.39	-	1.8.39	x	-	Reid & Sigrist Ltd	
No.43 Newcastle 1.6.39	-	1.6.39	x	-	Newcastle on Tyne Aero Club	
No.44 Sledon 1.5.39	-	1.5.39	x	-	Airwork Ltd	
No.45 Ipswich 3.7.39	-	3.7.39	x	-	Straight Corporation Ltd	

E&RFTS & Date formed	Pilot training Courses				Operating Company	Remarks
	RAF Reserve	RAFVR Ab Initio	Advanced	RAF Regular		
No.46 Portsmouth 1.8.39	-	1.8.39	x	-	Portsmouth, Southsea & Isle of Wight Aviation Ltd	
No.47 Doncaster 15.7.39	-	15.7.39	x	-	Nottingham Airport Ltd	
No.48 Baginton	-	-	-	-	Air Service Training Ltd	In process of opening on outbreak of war
No.49 Preston	-	-	-	-	-	In process of opening on outbreak of war
No.50 Marlow	-	-	-	-	Whetton Aviation Ltd	In process of opening on outbreak of war
No.51 Abbotsinch	-	-	-	-	Scottish Aviation Ltd	In process of opening on outbreak of war
No.52 York	-	-	-	-	-	In process of opening on outbreak of war
No.53 Kenley 22.8.39	-	22.8.39	x	-	British Air Transport Ltd	

NOTES

1. Other schools were to be opened at Yeadon and Southampton on the outbreak of war.

2. RAF Reserve courses were refresher courses.

3. RAF Regular pilots' courses comprised of:
    a. Short Service Commission personnel
    b. University candidates for permanent commissions
    c. Airmen pilots
    d. RAF Reserve personnel undertaking a year's full time training course.

4. RAF VR Advanced training courses were due to be carried out at all schools prior to the outbreak of war in Battles but many had not received any aircraft when war broke out.

5. On the outbreak of war all but nineteen of these schools were closed down. The surviving E&RFTSs retained only their elementary aircraft and undertook the elementary training of RAF personnel.

Appendix D

Non-Pilot Aircrew Training at RAF Elementary and Reserve Flying Training Schools – United Kingdom – 31 August 1939

E&RFTS & Date formed	Non pilot training Courses		Operating Company	Remarks
	RAF Regular Navigation Trg	RAFVR		
No.1 Hatfield 1.5.23	-	28.4.39	De Havilland	Moved from Stag Lane to Hatfield in May 1930
No.2 Filton 23.5.23	-	20.6.39	Bristol Aeroplane Co.Ltd	
No.3 Hamble 31.7.23	23.5.38	20.6.39	Air Service Training Ltd	Originally opened at Coventry. operated by Beardmores Moved to Hamble 4/31
No.4 Brough 21.5.24	-	13.6.39	Blackburn Aircraft Co.	Was operated by the North Sea Aeriel & General Co.Ltd until 1938
No.5 Hanworth 10.6.35	-	20.6.39	Flying Training Ltd	
No.6 Sywell 10.6.35	9.1.39	20.6.39	Brooklands Aviation Ltd.	
No.7 Desford 25.11.35	15.8.38	27.6.39	Reid & Sigrist Ltd	
No.8 Reading 25.1.35	-	3.8.39	Phillips & Powis Ltd.	
No.9 Ansty 6.1.36	5.8.38	27.6.39	Air Service Training Ltd.	
No.10 Yatesbury 6.1.36	26.9.38	-	Bristol Aeroplane Co.Ltd	
No.11 Perth 27.1.36	9.1.39	10.7.39	Airwork Ltd	
No.12 Prestwick 6.1.36	15.8.38*	10.7.39	Scottish Aviation Ltd	*3 Courses of Direct Entry Observers transferred to Grangemouth 26.6.38

E&RFTS & Date formed	Non pilot training Courses		Operating Company	Remarks
	RAF Regular Navigation Trg	RAFVR		
No.13 White Waltham 18.11.35	-	10.7.39	De Havilland Aircraft Co.Ltd	
No.14 Castle Bromwich 1.7.37	-	10.7.39	Airwork Ltd	
No.15 Redhill 1.7.37	-	1.8.39	British Air Transport Ltd	
No.16 Shoreham 1.7.37	23.5.38*	3.7.39	Brooklands Aviation Ltd	* This training was carried out by the Martin Navigation Ltd. using Shoreham aerodrome. Terminated on 13.5.39 and transferred to Gloucester.
No.17 Barton & Ringway 1.10.37	-	1.7.39	Airwork Ltd	
No.18 Fairoaks 1.10.37	-	1.7.39	General Aircraft Ltd	
No.19 Gatwick 1.10.37	-	8.7.39	Airports Ltd	
No.20 Gravesend 1.10.37	-	1.7.39	Airports Ltd	
No.21 Stapleford Abbots 1.1.38	-	8.7.39	Reid & Sigrist Ltd	
No.22 Cambridge 1.2.38	-	1.7.39	Marshalls Flying School Ltd	
No.23 Rochester 1.4.38	-	x	Short Bros.Ltd	
No.24 Sydenham 1.1.39	-	3.8.39	Short.Bros.Ltd	

E&RFTS & Date formed	Non pilot training Courses		Operating Company	Remarks
	RAF Regular Navigation Trg	RAFVR		
No.25 Grimsby 24.6.38	-	3.8.39	Herts & Essex Aero Club	
No.26 Oxford 24.6.38	-	11.8.38	Marshalls Flying Schools Ltd.	
No.27 Tollerton 24.6.38	-	6.7.39	Nottingham Airports Ltd	
No.28 Meir 1.8.38	-	x	Reid & Sigrist Ltd	
No.29 Luton 1.8.38	-	1.8.39	Birkett Air Service Ltd	
No.30 Derby 29.9.38	-	x	Air Schools Ltd	
No.31 Gloucester 29.9.39	-	x	Surrey Flying Services Ltd.	
No.32 West Hartlepool 15.4.39	-	x	Portsmouth Southsea & Isle of Wight Aviation Ltd.	
No.33 Whitchurch 3.12.38	-	11.8.39	Channier, Gilbert Lodge & Co.Ltd	
No.34 Southend 1.1.39	-	1.6.39	Air Hire Ltd.	
No.35 Grangemouth 1.5.39	26.6.39*	x	Scottish Aviation Ltd	*Training of 3 Courses of Direct Entry Observer training from Prestwick on 26.8.39
No.36 Sherburn	-	-	Blackburn Aviation Ltd	Was in the process of opening on the outbreak of war.
No.37 Exeter 3.7.39	-	3.7.39	Straight Corporation Ltd	

NOTE: RAFVR Observer Training was carried out on Ansons.

Appendix E
Administrative Arrangements for the 1931 Schneider Trophy Competition

The source for this appendix is Air Ministry Weekly Orders N363 (101645/31) dated 4 August 1931

N363 – Schneider Trophy Contest, 1931

1. In connection with the Schneider Trophy Contest on 12th September next, the War Office has kindly placed part of Gilkicker Fort at the disposal of officers of the Royal Air Force, civil servants in the employ of the Air Council, and friends. Gilkicker Fort is situated on the sea coast, south of Gosport and opposite Ryde, and since the course to be flown passes over it, it forms an admirable view-point.

2. (a) The accommodation allotted to officers of the Royal Air Force is for 850 spectators, and also a limited number of tickets are also available for civil servants in the employ of the Air Council. In order to meet the cost of certain essentials within the fort to adapt it for the purpose , it will be necessary to make a charge of 1s. [5p] a head for admittance.

 (b) Arrangements have been made for the provision of the buffet at which light luncheons, refreshments and drinks can be obtained at moderate prices.

 (c) No arrangements are being made for the provision of chairs within the fort, since the slope of the glacis provides adequate room for sitting down. Spectators are therefore advised to bring rugs, shooting sticks, etc.

 (d) There will be no further charge for admittance on succeeding days in the event of the contest being postponed.

3. The Royal Engineers are arranging for a car park about 300 yards to the north of the fort. The charge per car will be 2/6d. [12$\frac{1}{2}$p] which will cover the cost of admission to the park on any subsequent day should the contest be postponed. Motor bicycles will be admitted free. Tickets for the car park , including those for motor cycles, must be obtained from the Air Ministry beforehand.

4. Spectators arriving by train are advised to book to Portsmouth Harbour Station, crossing to Gosport by ferry. Motor buses will be running from Gosport to within a very short distance of Gilkicker Fort. Spectators arriving by road are advised to travel via Fareham and Alverstoke. Spectators referred to in this paragraph will not receive railway warrants or subsistence allowance.

5. The foreshore between Fort Monckton and Stokes Bay, which is War Office property, will be reserved for the use of sailors, soldiers and airmen in uniform, members of the Observer Corps wearing their badges, and friends who accompany them. Admittance will be free.

6. (a) Since the number of officers and friends that can be admitted to Gilkicker Fort is limited to 850, tickets of admission at 1s. each will be allocated, if required, to commands in the following proportion:

Inland area	315
Air Defence of Great Britain	210
Coastal area	104
Cranwell	55
Halton	30
Staff College	20
Imperial Defence College	12
Oxford University Air Squadron	24
Cambridge University Air Squadron	26
Air Ministry	44
Held in reserve for Dominion officers and special guests	10

 No officer may bring more than one guest.

 (b) If any Command requires more than its quota of tickets, as shown above, application for the number required may be made in case a surplus should be available after the demands of other commands have been met.

 (c) Officers using the fort need not wear uniform.

7. A strictly limited number of tickets will be available for civil servants serving at outstations, applications from whom should be forwarded to the Air Ministry (S.2) through the usual channels by 26th August, 1931. No civil servant may bring more than one guest, and the nominal lists submitted should state whether the applicants require one or two tickets. A.Os C will ensure that the provisions of this paragraph are brought to the notice of all civil servants within their command.

8. (a) To facilitate the arrival of officers and airmen to view the contest, the arrangements are being made to accommodate 58 service aircraft from all commands at Gosport aerodrome. Accommodation for eight of these aircraft can be found in hangars, and the crews of these eight aircraft can be

accommodated on the station. The remaining 50 aircraft will have to be pegged out on the aerodrome and the crews will be required to make their own arrangements locally in regard to messing, sleeping accommodation etc., Visiting aircraft are to bring their own pickets with them and the crews will be held responsible for pegging out aircraft on the aerodrome. All aircraft are definitely to land at Gosport not later than 11.00 hr on Saturday 12th September, 1931

(b) Personnel (both crew and passengers) flying to Gosport for the purpose of the contest will be considered as 'on duty', but it must be clearly understood that, owing to the Government's decision that the contest shall cause no extra expense to public funds, no claim for subsistence or other expense will be allowed.

(c) The allotment of visiting aircraft to Commands is as follows:

	Aircraft with Accommodation	Aircraft without Accommodation
Inland area	4	21
Air Defence of Great Britain	3	16
Coastal area	1	4
Cranwell		4
Halton		2
Staff College		1
Oxford University Air Squadron		1
Cambridge University Air Squadron		1

Any command requiring more than the above quota may make application for the number required in case surplus accommodation should be available after the demands of other commands have been met.

9. A.Os.C and C.Os will notify the Air Ministry (O.1) not later than 28th August, 1931:

(a) The number of aeroplanes, by type, which will arrive at Gosport and will be

(b) accommodated in the hangars.

(c) The number of officers and airmen arriving by air for whom accommodation will be required at Gosport station.

(d) The number of aeroplanes, by types, which will arrive at Gosport and be pegged out in the open.

(e) The number of tickets for Gilkicker Fort required under the provisions of para. 6.

(f) The number of tickets for motor cars and motor bicycles required by RAF Officers under the provisions of para. 3 and forward to the Air Ministry (S.2.).

(g) Nominal lists of civil servants under the provisions of paras. 3 and 7.

Appendix F
Detailed Order of Battle of the Royal Air Force at Home and Overseas on 3 September 1939

The order of battle is shown by role only for home and overseas units.

METROPOLITAN AIR FORCE

STATION	HEAVY-BOMBER SQUADRONS
Feltwell	37 Squadron (Wellington I)
Honington	9 Squadron (Wellington IA)
Honington	215 Squadron (Wellington I)
Marham	38 Squadron (Wellington I)
Marham	115 Squadron (Wellington I)
Methwold	214 Squadron (Wellington I)
Mildenhall	149 Squadron (Wellington I)
Newmarket	99 Squadron (Wellington I)

MEDIUM & LIGHT-BOMBER SQUADRONS	
Upper Heyford	18 Squadron (Blenheim I)
Upper Heyford	57 Squadron (Blenheim I)
Wattisham	107 Squadron (Blenheim IV)
Wattisham	110 Squadron (Blenheim IV)
Watton	21 Squadron (Blenheim I)
Watton	82 Squadron (Blenheim IV)
West Raynham	101 Squadron (Blenheim IV)
Wyton	114 Squadron (Blenheim IV)
Wyton	139 Squadron (Blenheim IV)

Dishforth	10 Squadron (Whitley IV)
Driffield	58 Squadron (Whitley III)
Driffield	77 Squadron (Whitley V)
Driffield	102 Squadron (Whitley III)
Linton-on-Ouse	51 Squadron (Whitley III)

Hemswell	61 Squadron (Hampden)
Hemswell	144 Squadron (Hampden)
Scampton	49 Squadron (Hampden)
Scampton	83 Squadron (Hamden)
Waddington	44 Squadron (Hampden)
Waddington	50 Squadron (Hampden)

Boscombe Down	88 Squadron (Battle)

Bassingbourne	108 Squadron (Anson I)

STATION	FIGHTER SQUADRONS
Abbotsinch	602 Squadron (Spitfire I)
Catterick	41 Squadron (Spitfire I)
Catterick	609 Squadron (Spitfire I)
Church Fenton	72 Squadron (Spitfire I)
Duxford	19 Squadron (Spitfire I)
Duxford	66 Squadron (Spitfire I)
Duxford	611 Squadron (Spitfire I)
Hornchurch	54 Squadron (Spitfire I)
Hornchurch	65 Squadron (Spitfire I)
Hornchurch	74 Squadron (Spitfire I)
Turnhouse	603 Squadron (Spitfire I)

Biggin Hill	32 Squadron (Hurricane I)
Biggin Hill	79 Squadron (Hurricane I)
Croydon	3 Squadron (Hurricane I)
Croydon	17 Squadron (Hurricane I)
Debden	85 Squadron (Hurricane I)
Debden	87 Squadron (Hurricane I)
Digby	46 Squadron (Hurricane I)
Digby	73 Squadron (Hurricane I)
Digby	504 Squadron (Hurricane I)
Filton	501 Squadron (Hurricane I)
Hooton Park	610 Squadron (Hurricane I)
Northolt	111 Squadron (Hurricane I)
North Weald	56 Squadron (Hurricane I)
North Weald	151 Squadron (Hurricane I)
Tangmere	1 Squadron (Hurricane I)
Tangmere	43 Squadron (Hurricane I)
Tangmere	605 Squadron (Hurricane I)
Wittering	213 Squadron (Hurricane I)

Biggin Hill	601 Squadron (Blenheim IF)
Martlesham	64 Squadron (Blenheim IF)
Northolt	25 Squadron (Blenheim IF)
Northolt	600 Squadron (Blenheim IF)
North Weald	604 Squadron (Blenheim I)
Wittering	23 Squadron (Blenheim IF)
Croydon	615 Squadron (Gladiator II)
Usworth	607 Squadron (Gladiator I)
Doncaster	616 Squadron (Battle)

	MARITIME RECONNAISSANCE
Aldergrove	502 Squadron (Anson I)
Dyce	612 Squadron (Anson I)
Detling	500 Squadron (Anson I)
Montrose	269 Squadron (Anson I)
Thornaby	608 Squadron (Anson I)
Warmwell	217 Squadron (Anson I)

Invergordon	240 Squadron (London II)
Sullom Voe	201 Squadron (London II)
Leuchars	224 Squadron (Hudson I)
	233 Squadron (Hudson I)
Thornaby	220 Squadron (Hudson I/III/IV)

Mountbatten	204 Squadron (Sunderland I)
Pembroke Dock	210 Squadron (Sunderland I)
Invergordon	209 Squadron (Stranraer)

ARMY COOPERATION AND TACTICAL RECONNAISSANCE

Andover	59 Squadron (Blenheim IV)
Catterick	26 Squadron (Lysander III)
Cranfield	207 Squadron (Anson I)
Hawkinge	2 Squadron (Lysander I)
Odiham	53 Squadron (Blenheim IV)
Odiham	4 Squadron (Lysander II)
Odiham	13 Squadron (Lysander II)
Old Sarum	16 Squadron (Lysander II)
Pengam Moors	614 Squadron (Lysander II)
Ringway	613 Squadron (Hector)

ANTI-SHIPPING/SUBMARINE TORPEDO-BOMBER

Bircham Newton	42 Squadron (Vildebeest III)
Thorney Island	22 Squadron (Vildebeest I & IV)
Debden	29 Squadron (Blenheim IF)
Honington	9 Squadron (Wellington IA)
Bircham Newton	206 Squadron (Anson I)
Thorney Island	48 Squadron (Anson I)

TRANSPORT & COMMUNICATION

Hendon	24 Squadron (Various aircraft)

TRAINING UNITS

Bassingbourn	104 Squadron (Anson I)
Bircham Newton	90 Squadron (Blenheim I)
Cottesmore	185 Squadron (Anson I)
Cranfield	35 Squadron (Anson I)
Dishforth	78 Squadron (Whitley V)
Finningley	7 Squadron (Hampden)
Finningley	76 Squadron (Anson I)
Hucknall	98 Squadron (Battle)
Leconfield	97 Squadron (Whitley III)
Leconfield	166 Squadron (Whitley I)
Stradishall	75 Squadron (Wellington I)
Stradishall	148 Squadron (Anson I)
Thornaby	106 Squadron (Hampden)
Upwood	52 Squadron (Anson I)
Upwood	63 Squadron (Anson I)

ADVANCED AIR FORCE STRIKING FORCE – FRANCE

LIGHT BOMBERS (ALL BATTLE SQUADRONS)

Auberives sur Suippes	218 Squadron
Berry-au-Bac	12 Squadron
	142 Squadron
Betheniville	15 Squadron
	40 Squadron
Challerange	103 Squadron
	150 Squadron
Reims	105 Squadron
	226 Squadron

ROYAL AIR FORCE SQUADRONS OVERSEAS

STATION/THEATRE	AIR CONTROL
Khartoum (Sudan)	47 Squadron (Wellesley)
Ambala (India)	60 Squadron (Blenheim I)
Ismailia (Egypt)	30 Squadron (Blenheim I)
Khormaksar (Aden)	8 Squadron (Blenheim I)
Shaibah (Iraq)	84 Squadron (Blenheim I)
Tengah (Singapore)	39 Squadron (Blenheim I)
Kohat (India)	27 Squadron (Wapiti)
Kohat (India)	28 Squadron (Audax)
Miranshah (India)	20 Squadron (Audax)

	FIGHTER
Amiriya (Iraq)	80 Squadron (Gladiator I)
Helwan (Egypt)	112 Squadron (Gladiator I & II)
Sheikh Othman (Aden)	94 Squadron (Gladiator II)

STATION/THEATRE	BOMBER/TRANSPORT
Heliopolis (Egypt)	216 Squadron (Valentia)
Helwan (Egypt)	70 Squadron (Valentia)
Lahore (India)	31 Squadron (Valentia)

	DAY/LIGHT-BOMBER
El Daba (Egypt)	211 Squadron (Blenheim I)
Fuka (Egypt)	45 Squadron (Blenheim I)
Heliopolis (Egypt)	113 Squadron (Blenheim I)
Ismailia (Egypt)	55 Squadron (Blenheim I)
Tengah (Singapore)	11 Squadron (Blenheim I)
"	34 Squadron (Blenheim I)
Ismailia (Egypt)	14 Squadron (Wellesley)
Fort Sandeman (India)	5 Squadron (Wapiti)

TORPEDO-BOMBER

China Bay (Ceylon)	273 Squadron (Vildebeest III/Seal)
Seletar (Singapore)	36 Squadron (Vildebeest III)
Seletar (Singapore)	100 Squadron (Vildebeest III)

MARITIME RECONNAISSANCE/PATROL

Ismuth (Iraq)	203 Squadron (Singapore III)
Seletar (Singapore)	205 Squadron (Singapore III)
Kalafrana (Malta)	202 Squadron (London II)

Alexandria (Egypt)	228 Squadron (Sunderland I)
Seletar (Singapore)	230 Squadron (Sunderland I)
Tengah (Singapore)	62 Squadron (Blanheim I)
	En route…

TACTICAL RECONNAISSANCE

Qasaba (Egypt)	208 Squadron (Lysander I & II)

C/P

Mersah Matruh (Egypt) Ramleh	33 Squadron (Gladiator I)

Appendix G
Aircraft, Military and Civil, tested from 1930 to 1939
Martlesham Heath

NOTE
1. Aircraft are listed by manufacturer in alphabetical order.
2. Military and civil aircraft can be distinguished by their letters/numbers, e.g. Military: F.3492 (N denotes a naval aircraft) or civil: G-EAOX.
3. The letters MH in remarks column stand for Martlesham Heath.
4. The letters PV stand for Private Venture.

Aircraft	Serial No.	Month	Remarks
1930			
ABC Robin AN.17	G-AAID	Jun	S/seat light plane for C of A trials
Armstrong Whitworth Aries	J.9037	Apr	2-seat Army Cooperation aircraft for evaluation
Armstrong Whitworth Atlas	J.8792	May	Trainer version for evaluation
	G-ABDY	Sep	Civil demonstrator C of A
	G-EBYF	-	Civil demonstrator. Trials A/C
Armstrong Whitworth XVI	S.1591	Nov	S/seat interceptor. Evaluation trials
Avro Avian 616 IVa	VH-HAC	August	S/seat version for overseas buyer
Avro Tutor 621	K.1230	May	Performance trials
	K.1237	July	A/S Mongoose IIIc motor trials
	K.1797	Oct	Service trials for standard aircraft
Blackburn Lincock III	G-AALH	Feb	Metal version of original aircraft Performance
Blackburn Ripon II T5A	S.1270	Jan	Developed Mk I for evaluation
T5B Mk IIA	S.1272	Feb	Production aircraft for testing
T5B Mk IIC	S.1468	Mar	Mk IIA modified for service testing
T5B	S.1424	Jul	Production aircraft service trials
T5E Mk.III	S.1272	Oct	Further modifications aircraft
	S.1272	Dec	Revised upper mainplane tests
Bristol Type 109	G-EBZK	Sep	C of A trials
Bristol Bulldog IIA	K.1603	May	DTD trials aircraft
Comper Swift CLA 7	G-AARX	Aug	Further trials of civil aircraft
de Havilland 77 Interceptor	J.9771	Sep	S/seat interceptor information
de Havilland 80A Puss Moth	K.1824	Jun	Investigation trials aircraft. Wing failure
de Havilland 86	G-ACPL	Jan	C of A trials aircraft
Fairey S9/30	-	May	Evaluation of stainless-steel frame
Fairey Fox IIM (G-ABFG)	S.1325	Mar	Extended trials for Fleet Air Arm
Fairey IIIF Mk IV CR	J.9154	Aug	Service trials as a day-bomber
Gloster SS.18.B	J.9125	Feb	Re-engined aircraft for evaluation
Gloster SS.19	J.9125	Oct	Re-engined with Jupiter motor
Gloster AS.31 Survey	G-AADO	Jan	Further C of A trials
Gloster Gnatsnapper Mk I SS35	N.227	Mar	Developed Mk I with Jaguar radial
	N.254	Apr	2nd prototype with Mercury III
Mk II	N.254	Aug	New tailplane and Jaguar VIII motor
Handley Page HP.38 Heyford	J.9130	Mar	Heavy night-bomber performance trials
Handley Page Clive II		Aug	Metal version of Mk I evaluation
Handley Page Hare	J.8622	Sep	Engine trials
Hawker Hart Mk I	J.9933	All year	Extended performance trials
	K.1416	Jun	Service trials

Aircraft	Serial No.	Month	Remarks
Hawker Hoopee	N.237	Nov	Re-engined aircraft with Jaguar III
Hawker Horsley	J.8606	Apr	Handling trials
	S.1235	Aug	All-metal torpedo-bomber for performance
Mk II	S.1236	Aug	All-metal bomber for performance trials
Hawker Hornet	J.9682	Jun	Trials as Fury prototype, and Yugoslav sales tour
Hawker Norn HN1	-	Aug	S/S fleet fighter for trials
Hawker Osprey	J.9052	Sep	Hart prototype as Osprey prototype
Hawker Tomtit	G-AASI	Feb	Civil version of RAF trainer
Hawker F.20/27 Interceptor	J.9123	Jul	Original aircraft re-engined. Mishap
Henderson HSF 1	G-EBVF	Mar	6-seat civil aircraft for C of A trials
Hendy 302	G-AAVT	-	2-seat cabin monoplane for C of A tests
Parnall Elf I	G-AALH	May	2-seat biplane for C of A trials
Robinson Redwing I	G-AAUO	-	2-seat for club use C of A
Seagrave Meteor	G-AAXP	Jun	4-seat civil monoplane. Fuel trouble during C of A
		Oct	Further tests for C of A
Spartan Arrow	G-AAWY	May	2-seat civil biplane. C of A performance trials
Vickers Vannock 195 Mk II	J.9131	Mar	Heavy-bomber performance trials
Vickers Type 151 Jockey	J.9122	Apr	Evaluation trials for interceptor
Vickers Type 132 Vildebeest I	G-ADGE	Feb	Private venture torpedo bomber for performance trials
	S.1707	Apr	Service trials with same
Vickers Type 177	None	Feb	Shipboard fighter trials and performance tests. Forced landing at MH
Vickers Type 204 Vildebeest	0 – 1	Aug	PV. 2nd prototype Evaluation
Vickers Virginia Mk X	J.7275	Apr	Lion engined. Armament tests
	J.7421	Oct	Jupiter IX engine. Performance trials
Westland Wapiti Mk IIA	J.9328	Aug	Revised Mk II as production aircraft Performance
	J.9247	Sep	Standard aircraft performance trials
	K.1129	Sep	Long-range trials
Mk I	J.9102	Jul	Oil pump trials. Ballast tests

1931

Aircraft	Serial No.	Month	Remarks
Armstrong Atlas I	K.1540	Apr	Trials aircraft
	G-ABIV	Apr	Clean-up civil version for trials
	G-ABKE	Mar	Clean-up civil version for range tests
Armstrong Whitworth Siskin III	J.7161	Mar	Experimental cockpit heating
	J.9236	Apr	2-seat trainer fighter trials
Armstrong Whitworth XVI	A – 2	Jun	PV fighter. Official trials
Arrow Active I	G-ABIX	Jun	Civil aerobatic biplane. C of A tests
Avro 618 Ten	K.2682	Apr	Evaluation as RAF communications aircraft
Avro 620/Cierva C.19/111 Ex G-ABCM	K.1948	Mar	Rotating-wing Autogiro for evaluation
Avro Tutor Type 621	K.1237	Jul	Handling trials. Mongoose IIIC
Avro 627 Mailplane	G-ABJM	Aug	C of A performance trials
Blackburn Beagle	N.236	Mar	Re-engined with Jupiter XF. Performance trials
Blackburn CA 18 Seagrave I	G-ABFP	Feb	Original Seagrave aircraft. C of A trials
Boulton & Paul P.32	J.9950	Mar	Night-bomber handling trials
Bristol Bulldog IIIA	R – 5	Apr	Developed Mk IIA for testing
Bristol Type 119. Later K.2873	R – 3	Jul	General-purpose PV aircraft for evaluation
de Havilland 60T Tiger Moth	E – 5	Apr	2-seat elementary trainer for evaluation
Later G-ABNJ	G-ABPH	Jun	2nd prototype for evaluation

Aircraft	Serial No.	Month	Remarks
de Havilland 82	E – 6	Aug	Trials and handling aircraft
de Havilland 82 Tiger Moth	E – 6	Sep	Full service aircraft for performance trials
x 82A G-ABPH	K.4242	Oct	Shortened wing struts. Performance trials
Fairey Flycatcher	S.1286	Mar	Service aircraft for testing
Fairy Gordon	K.1697	Aug	2nd prototype for full handling trials
Fairey long-range Monoplane II	K.1991	Apr	Fuel tests
Gloster SS19	J.9125	May	Armament trials with 6 guns
Gloster SS19A	J.9125	Nov	Lewis gun removed. Night-flying tests
Gloster Gnatsnapper III	N.,227	Jun	Rebuild with R-R Kestrel IIS moto
Handley Page Hare	J.8622	Jun	Engine trials
Handley Page Heyford	K.3489	Apr	Non-standard aircraft for trials
Handley Page H.P.42	G-AAGX	Apr	C of A trials
Hawker Fury I	K.1926	May	Production aircraft for trials
	K.1927	May	Production aircraft for trials
	K.1928	May	Production aircraft for trials
Hawker Fury IA Yugoslavia	NFI	Aug	Export aircraft for trials
Hawker Hart	K.1416	Jan	Dive-bombing trials
	None	Jun	A/S Panther engine. Evaluation
India Hart	K.2083	May	Special aircraft for tropical duties
	K1438	Jun	Hart modified to Audax standards
	J.9933	Aug	Hart re-engined with Kestrel IIS
	J.9937	Nov	Further aircraft with same equipment
Hawker Osprey 19/30	S.1677	Jun	First Osprey roper. Performance trials
Hawker Horsley	S.1452	Jan	Target-towing trials
Monospar Wing Co.ST.3	G-AAHP	-	3-seat civil aircraft for performance tests
Saro A.19 Cloud	K.2681	Aug	Amphibian trainer. Evaluated in conjunction with MAEE Felixstowe
Saro A.21 Windhover	G-ABJP	Jan	Return visit of the amphibian. Performance tests
Short Cunard Amphibian	N.229	June	Tested in conjunction with MAEE Felixstowe
Vickers Type 161 COW gun J.9566		Sep	Pusher, biplane interceptor wth COW fighter gun. Performance and armament trials
Vickers Type 1732 Vellore II	G-AASW	May	Development of Vellore I. Performance trials
Vickers Type 173 Vellore III	K.2133 Ex G-ABKC	Aug	Twin-engined mailplane. Remained as station 'hack' after evaluation
Vickers Type 195 Vannock II	J.9131	Jun	Rebuild of Type 150. Kestrel III motors
Vickers Jockey Type 151	J.9122	May	Modified aircraft with Jupiter VIIF motor
Vickers Vespa VI Type 210	G-ABIL	Mar	C of A authentication for tour of China. Later World Altitude Record, 43,976 ft
Vickers Victora MkV Type 169	K.2340	Nov	Jupiter-engined aircraft for service trial
Vickers Vildebeest	N230	Jun	Service trials and performance trials
Westland F29/27 COW gun fighter	J.9565	May	S/S interceptor with COW gun. Performance and armament trials
Westland PV3 Later G-ACAZ	-	Mar	PV torpedo-bomber. First aircraft and K.4048 to fly over mount Everest
Westland Pterodactyl Mk IV	K.1947	Sep	Tailless 2-seat cabin research monoplane. Gypsy III motor
Westland PV6. Wapiti V	G-AAWA	Jul	General-purpose biplane evaluation. Later used on Mt Everest flight
Wapiti IIA	K.1380	-	Fitted with new elevators. Performance trials
Westland Wapiti MK VII	K.3488	Sep	Rebuild of PV6. Later Wallace. Performance
Westland Wallace II	K.3562	Oct	Wapiti to Wallace standard

Aircraft	Serial No.	Month	Remarks
1932			
Airspeed Ferry S.4. 'Youth'	G-ABSI	April	Certification as 10-seat airliner of Britain II'
Arrow Active II	G-ABVE	Mar	Developed Mk I C of A performance trials
Armstrong Whitworth AV.XV	G-ABPI	Jul	Certification as 17-seat airliner. Atlanta
Armstrong Whitworth AW XVI	G-ABKF	Sep	S/S PV interceptor. Engine trials
		Nov	Maintenance trials
Avro 621 Tutor	K – 4	Jan	Original design revised for evaluation
	G-AARZ	Aug	Further aircraft for evaluation
	K.1797	Nov	Service trials
	K.1237	Nov	Full performance trials
Avro Type 626 Prefect	-	Sep	Service and C of A performance trials
Blackburn B.2	G-ABUW	May	Elementary trainer for C of A trials
Blackburn CA.15C biplane	G-ABKW	Aug	Evaluated with Blackburn Mono to Air Min. specifications. Brake troubles
Blackburn CA.15C monoplane	G-ABKV	Aug	Evaluated with above. Performance
Blackburn Nautilas	N.234	Apr	Used as MH communications aircraft
Blackburn Ripon Mk IIC	S.1670	Apr	Production aircraft for testing
Bristol Bulldog IIIA	R – 5	Mar	Prototype re-engined Mercury IVS2
Bristol Type 118A	K.2873	Aug	Modified Type 118 for testing
Bristol Type 120. Later K.3587	R – 6	May	Development of 118 armament trials
Chance Vought V66E Corsair	K.3561	Jun	American dive-bomber for evaluation
de Havilland 60G III Moth Major	-	Sep	Development of 60G. C of A performance trials
de Havilland 83 Fox Moth	-	Jul	Small 4-seat aircraft for civil C of A
de Havilland 84 Dragon Later G-ACAN	E – 9	Feb	6-seat airliner for C of A performance tests
Fairey Night-Bomber 20/34	K.1695	May	Heavy night-bomber evaluation. Later Hendon
Fairey Seal	S.1325	Aug	Rebuild of IIIF Mk VI FAA trials
	K.3477	Oct	1st production aircraft for performance tests
General Aircraft Ltd Monospar ST.4	G-ABUZ	Jun	4-seat twin-engined monoplane for civil certification
Gloster FS.36 TSR 38	S.1705	Apr	2-seat fleet spotter. Evaluation
Gloster TC.33 Transport	J.9832	Oct	4-engine troop transport for performance test
Handley Page HP.36 Hinaidi II	J.9478	Jun	Developed Mk I performance trials
Handley Page HP.43	J.9833	May	Large 3-engine troop transport. Performance
Handley Page Heyford Mk II	K.3503	Jun	Developed Mk I with enclosed cockpit
Hawker Audax I	K.1995	May	First Audax proper. Performance tests
Hawker Demon	K.9933	Jun	2-seat fighter version of the Hart. Performance
Hawker Fury. Norway	401	Sep	Panther-IIIa-engined export fighter
Hawker Hart	K.2083	Feb	Engine trials with Kestrel V. Later Station Flight aircraft
Hawker Hart	146	Aug	First aircraft for Estonia
Hawker Hart Trainer	K.1996	May	1st prototype of Audax. Performance trials
	K.3146	Jun	Full standard aircraft. Performance trials
Hawker Nimrod I	S.1577	Mar	Propeller trials
	K2823	Aug	Mk II prototype. Full performance trials
Hawker Dantrop	201	Sep	Horsley for Royal Danish Naval Service
Heinkel HE 64C. Later K.3596	G-ACBS	Jul	German aircraft for flap and slotted-wing performance trials
Percival Gull PIA Mk II	-	Apr	Javelin-engined prototype for performance
PIB Mk II	-	Jul	Gipsy-Major-engined aircraft for performance
Percival Gull Four P.I	G-ABUR	Mar	1st civil prototype for C of A trials
Short Valetta	G-AAJY	Jul	Large civil monoplane for C of A
Spartan Cruiser I	G-ABTY	May	Light civil airliner for C of A trials

Aircraft	Serial No.	Month	Remarks
Vickers Type 151 Jockey I	J.9122	Jun	Continued trials. Crashed in spinning
Vickers Type 163	0 – 2	Feb	4-engined bomber trials. Performance
Vickers 195, Vannock Mk II	J.9131	Sep	Developed 150 and 163. Further evaluation bomber trials
Vickers Type 207	S.1641	Jun	Torpedo-bombing performance trials
Vickers Vannox	0 – 2	Nov	Further modified aircraft. Performance tests
Vickers Type 173 Vellore IV	K.2133	April	2nd aircraft. Performance trials
Vickers Victoria V	K.2340	Feb	Prototype Mk VI aircraft. Pegasus test-bed
	K.2807	May	Modified wing structure tests
Vickers Vildebeest I	S.1707	Sep	Handling and type trials
Westland Hill Pterodactyl Mk V	K.2770	Dec	2-seat tailless interceptor. Performance
Westland Wapiti Mk I	J.9084	Oct	Drop trials
Mk IIA	K.1129	Aug	Windscreen trials
Mk IIA	K.2262	Feb	Jupiter VIIIF and propeller trials
de Havilland 82A Tiger Moth	K.2576	Jan	Performance trials
	K.2579	Jan	Spinning trials

The following Martlesham aircraft took part in the 1932 Hendon Display:

Armstrong Whitworth Atlas G-ABIV
Blackburn Biplane G-ABKW
Boulton & Paul P.32 J.9950
Bristol Bulldog Mk IIIA R – 5
Bristol Type 120 R – 6
DH Tiger Moth K.2579
Fairey Hendon K.1695
Gloster TC.33 J.9832
Handley Page Heyford K.3503
Hawker Hart K.2083
Short Valetta G-AAJY
Vickers Jockey J.9122
Vickers Vildebeest S.1707
Westland Wallace K.3562

1933

Aircraft	Serial No.	Month	Remarks
Airspeed Courier AS.5	G-ABKN	Jun	Light civil cabin monoplane for C of A
	K-4047	Aug	Trials for service communications aircraft
Armstrong Whitworth AW.XVI	A – 2	Aug	Re-engined aircraft with Panther VII. Performance
Avro 621 Tutor	K.3189	Nov	Standard aircraft with modified controls
	E.59	Aug	Trials for Greek Air Force aircraft
Avro 626/637	G-ABJG	Mar	2-seat frontier patrol aircraft. Performance
Boulton & Paul Overstrand	J.8175	All year	Armament trials
Boulton & Paul P.64	ABYK	Sep	Performance trials. Crashed at MH Mailplane
Blackburn TSR	B – 6	Nov	PV 2/3-seat torpedo-aircraft. Performance
Blackburn Baffin	K.3546	Dec	1st production aircraft for testing
	K.3589	Apr	Acceptance trials. Pegasus motor
Blackburn M.1/30	S.1640	Jan	Fleet acceptance trials. Crashed
Blackburn M.1/30A	B – 3	Mar	Revised M.1/30 for evaluation
	K.3591	May	Above on RAF charge for tests
		Oct	Control systems trials. Ditching trials at Felixstowe
Blackburn Ripon	B – 4	Feb	Evaluated with Tiger motor
	B – 5	Feb	Evaluated with Pegasus motor
Blackburn Seagrave	-	Mar	Performance trials with civil aircraft

Aircraft	Serial No.	Month	Remarks
Blackburn Monoplane	G-ABKV	Apr	Comparison trials with above
Bristol Bulldog Mk IIA Mod.	K.3512	May	Developed IIA for trials
Mk IIIA	R – 5	Mar	Performance trials. Crashed at MH
	R – 7	Jul	Replacement aircraft to continue trials
Bristol Type 120	K.3587	Mar	Armament trials
de Havilland 82A Tiger Moth II	G-ACDA	Mar	Service version for trials
	K.2583	Nov	Mass-balanced aileron trials
de Havilland 85 Leopard Moth	G-ACHD	May	Civil C of A certification
Fairey IIIF Mk III	S.1847	Jun	Dual-control aircraft for FAA trials
Fairey Fox I (G-ACXO)	J.7950	May	Trials aircraft with Felix motor
Fairey Fox III Trainer	G-ACKH	Aug	Trainer version of Fox III. Performance
Fairey G.4/31 Mk I	-	Feb	TSR a/c for evaluation
Mk II	K.3905	Jul	2nd aircraft with Tiger motor. Performance
General Aircraft Light Monospar	G-ACCI	May	Performance trials on civil aircraft. Monospar
Gloster SS.19B Gauntlet	J.9165	Jun	Final development of SS.18. Propeller tests
Gloster TSR 38	S.1705	Mar	2nd visit for evaluation trials
Handley-Page Heyford Mk II	K.3489	Feb	1st Production aircraft for acceptance
Hawker Audax (India)	K.4850	Mar	Gloster-built aircraft for testing
	K.3067	Jun	Fitted with Vickers K gun armament
(Persia)	401	Aug	Fitted with Pratt & Whitney motor
Hawker Demon	K.9933	Oct	Developed aircraft with Frazer-Nash turret
Hawker Fury Persia	203	Mar	Pratt & Whitney Hornet-engined aircraft for Persian Air Force
Hawker Fury II	K.1935	Jun	Trials aircraft for specification draft
Hawker High-Speed Fury	K.3586	Aug	Developed Fury. Full performance test
Hawker Hart	K.2434	Dec	Test-bed for Napier Dagger I motor
	K.2969	Jul	Vickers-built aircraft for testing
	K.2967	Jul	Ballistic test aircraft
Hawker Hart Trainer (Interim)	K.2475	Feb	Dual-control trainer for trials
	K.3146	Jul	Production aircraft for trials
Hawker Hind	K.2915	Mar	Ex-Hart tested with Kestrel V
Hawker Nimrod (Intermediate)	K.2823	Feb	Mk II prototype. Swept-wing performance test
Hawker Osprey I	K.2776	Mar	Handling trials with enlarged rudder
Miles M.1 Satyr	G-ABVG	Feb	C of A trials
Spartan Clipper	G-ACEG	-	2-seat civil monoplane for C of A trials
Spartan Cruiser II	G-ACBM	-	Feeder airliner for C of A trials
Supermarine Seagull V	K.4797	Mar	Amphibian flying-boat for trials
Vickers Valentia Type 264	K.3599	Jun	Performance trials as trooper
	K.2344	Sep	Dunlop brake trials
Vickers Vannock II Type 255	J.9131	Mar	Rebuilt aircraft with lengthened wing
Vickers Type 259 Viastra X	G-ACCC	Apr	Civil aircraft for C of A certification
	VH-UOO	Jun	Tested for Australian use
Vickers Victoria V	K.2807	Aug	Performance trials and tailless wheel tests
	K.2808	Oct	Performance trials. Experimental aircraft
Vickers Vildebeest Type 244	S.1707	Mar	Trials with modified aircraft
	S.1715	Jun	Evaluated as night-bomber
	K.2816	Jun	Trials and development aircraft
	K.2819	Jun	Fitted Pegasus 11M3 and variable-pitch propellers
Westland Wallace	K.3562	Mar	Type test and performance trials
	K.3573	Dec	Rebuilt Wapiti J.9084 performance tests
	K.3673	Dec	Performance trials
Westland Wapiti	G-ACBR	Apr	Prototype Wapiti with rear cabin

Aircraft	Serial No.	Month	Remarks
1934			
Airspeed Envoy AS.6	G-ACMT	Sep	Civil C of A certification
Armstrong Whitworth 19.A.3	K.5606	Apr	Torpedo-bomber evaluation trials
Armstrong Whitworth AW 35	G-ACCD	Aug	Civil demonstrator performance trials
Avro 636	A – 14	Jun	2-seat fighter trainer trials
Avro 641 Coomodore	G-ACNT	-	Civil certification of cabin biplane
Avro 642	G-ACFU	Jan	C of A performance trials
Avro 671 Cierva C.30A Rota I	K.4230	Apr	Autogiro for full performance trials
Avro Tutor	K.1797	Feb	Fitted with Dowty wheels
	K.3189	Dec	Fitted with metal wings
Boulton & Paul P.71.A	G-ACOX	Mar	Airliner for C of A trials
Boulton & Paul Overstrand	J.9186	Jan	Extended armament trials
Blackburn G.4/31	B – 7	Feb	Revised aircraft for evaluation trials
Blackburn Baffin II	S.1665	Apr	DTD trials aircraft
Blackburn Shark I	K.4295	Sep	Torpedo-bomber for FAA trials
	K.4389	Sep	Torpedo-bomber for FAA trials
Boeing 24TD. Later NC 11369	NC257Y	-	Weighed in at MH for Air Race
British Aircraft Company Eagle	G-ACRG	Mar	Civil monoplane for C of A trials
Comper Kite	G-ACME	Jul	Civil monoplane for C of A trials
Comper Streak	G-ACNC	May	Civil monoplane for C of A trials
Comper Mouse	G-ACIX	May	Civil monoplane for C of A trials
de Havilland 60T Tiger Moth	K.2593	Apr	Cockpit heating trials
de Havilland 82A Tiger Moth	K.4242	Sep	Full performance trials
de Havilland 86	E2/G-ACPL	Aug	10-seat civil biplane C of A tests
	VH-USF	Dec	Crash investigation tests
de Havilland 87 Hornet Moth	E.6/G-ADIE	Jul	C of A and performance trials
de Havilland 89 Dragon Rapide	E – 4	May	C of A of twin-engined airliner. Speed restrictions at MH owing to panels damage by airflow
de Havilland TK.I	E3/G-ACKT	Sep	Light civil aircraft for C of A
Douglas DC.2 'Ulver'	PH-AJU	-	Weighed in for Air Race
Fairey Hendon	K.1695	Apr	Comparison trials with Heyford
Fairey TSR 2	K.4190	Mar	Revised TSR 1 for further trials
Gloster Gauntlet I	-	Dec	Standard aircraft fitted with Mercury VI
Gloster SS.37	G – 37	Nov	Rebuilt Gauntlet to F.7/30 spec.
Handley Page HP.47	K.2773	May	GP aircraft for trials. Twisted fuselage reported during MH trials
Heinkel 70	G-ADZE	May	High-speed German aircraft used by R-R for Kestrel engine trials
Hawker Audax	K.5163	Mar	Avro-built aircraft for trials
Hawker Audax (Persia)		May	Export aircraft with Pegasus radial motor
Hawker Fury (Persia)	203	Oct	Export aircraft with Mercury radial motor
Hawker Fury (Portugal)	50	Jun	Export aircraft with Kestrel 11S motor
Hawker Hardy	K.3013	Oct	Modified Hart for new specification
Hawker Hart I	K.2434	Feb	Trials aircraft. Dagger II motor
	K.2466	Jan	Dive-bombing trials
Hawker Hart (Swedish)	1301	Jan	Export aircraft with Pegasus radial motor
Hawker Hart Trainer	K.3743	Jul	Trials aircraft
	K.3012	Apr	Trials aircraft. To Canada
	K.3153	Sep	Trainer aircraft trials
Hawker Hind	K.2915	May	Light bomber derived from Hart. Performance
Hawker Nimrod II	K.2909	Feb	Developed Mk I stainless-steel frame
Hawker Osprey (Sweden)	2401	Oct	Mercury-engined aircraft for Sweden
Miles M.3A Falcon Major	U.3/G-ACTM	Apr	Performance trials on civil aircraft

Aircraft	Serial No.	Month	Remarks
Miles M.2F Hawk Major	G-ACTD	Jul	Performance trials on civil aircraft
Northrop 2E	K.5053	Jun	American dive-bomber for evaluation
Parnall Heck.3308	Class B	Apr	Civil aircraft for performance trials
Percival Gull Six P.3	G-ADEP	Apr	Improved Gull 4. C of A performance trials
Percival Mew Gull I	G-ACND	May	S/seat racing aircraft C of A trials
Short Scion I	G-ACJI	Jan	Small feeder airliner. Performance trials
Short Scylla	G-ACJJ	Apr	Large civil airliner. Certification
Supermarine F.7/30. Type 224	K.2890	Mar	Interceptor performance trials
Vickers Type 252 Vildebeest XI	-	Jul	Developed aircraft. Evaluation trials
Vickers Type 253	K.2771	Aug	Evaluation of 2-seat GP biplane
Vickers Type 266 Vincent	S.1714	Jan	Rebuild of Vildebeest. Trials aircraft
	K.4105	Mar	Further trials aircraft
Vickers Valentia	K.3599	May	Propeller trials and brakes
	K.3603	Dec	Handling trials. C of G tests
Vickers Type 212 Vellox	G-ABKY	Apr	10-seat airliner C of A certification
Vickers Victoria VI	K.3168	Jan	Fuel system tests
Vickers Virginia III	J.7130	Jan	Armament and engine trials
Westland F.7/30	K.2891	May	Evaluation of s/seat interceptor
Westland Wallace	K.3488	Feb	Gunner's cockpit trials
(ex K.2245)	K.4010	Oct	Handling trials

1935

Aircraft	Serial No.	Month	Remarks
Airspeed Convertible Envoy	-	Feb	Standard Envoy for military use
Airspeed Envoy	G-ACVI	Mar	Wolseley-engined aircraft. Flown to South Africa by Sqn Ldr E. Hilton
Armstrong Whitworth 23	K.3585	Jun	Troop carrier for evaluation
Armstrong Whitworth AW Scimitar	405	Aug	Export aircraft for Norway Performance tests
	407	Nov	Further aircraft for performance tests
	G-ACCD	Sep	Civil demonstrator for trials
Avro C.30 Rota I	K.4230	Feb	Autogiro for Army Cooperation trials
	K.4239	Apr	Performance trials
	K.4775	Nov	Handling trials
Avro 652 'Avalon'	G-ACRM	Mar	Feeder civil airliner. C of A tests
Avro 652A Anson	K.4771	Apr	Extensive trials for maritime aircraft
Avro 621 Tutor	K.3308	Dec	Extended performance trials
Blackburn B.7	B – 7	May	Evaluation and performance trials
Blackburn Baffin II	S.1665	Jun	Ripon aircraft to Baffin standard. Performance
Blackburn T9A Shark II	K.5607	Dec	1st production aircraft. Performance tests
	K.4295	Jul	Strengthened airframe tests
Boulton & Paul P.75 Overstrand	K.4546	Oct	1st production aircraft for service trials
Bristol 130. Bombay	K.3583	Mar	Troop carrier for performance trials
Bristol 142 'Britain First'	R – 12 G-ADCZ	Jun	Civil high-performance aircraft for trials
British Aircraft Co. No. 3 Cupid	G-ADLR	Aug	Light plane for performance trials
British Aircraft Co. Swallow II	-	May	2-seat club and touring aircraft. Performance
De Bruyre Snark	G-ADDL	Apr	Thick-wing-section performance tests
de Havilland 86A. Later 86A. SU-ABV	E – 2	-	Modified airliner for evaluation
de Havilland 88 Comet ex-G–ACSS	K.5084	Aug	Service trials. Undercarriage failure. Winner of Melbourne Air Race
de Havilland 89M	K.4772	Apr	Militay version of airliner. Performance
de Havilland 90 Dragonfly	-	Jun	5-seat light airliner. C of A tests

Aircraft	Serial No.	Month	Remarks
de Havilland TK.2	E.3/G-ADNO	May	Racing aircraft. Range and performance tests
Fairey G.4/31 Mk.II	K.3905	Jan	Rebuild of Mk I. Performance trials
Fairey Swordfish	K.4190	Mar	Original aircraft as production aircraft
Fairey S.9/30	S.1706	Jul	Spotter for Fleet use. Performance tests
Gloster Gauntlet I	K.4081	Jan	Handling and performance tests
	K.4082	Jan	Production aircraft tests
	J.9125	Jun	Prototype for production tests
Gloster Gladiator G.37	K.5200	May	Cleaned-up prototype. Evaluation
		Oct	Propeller trials
Gloster TSR 38	S.1705	Jun	Further performance trials
General Aircraft ST.25	-	Sep	Evaluation of 5-seat airliner. Monospar Jubilee
Handley Page 51	J.9833	Mar	Bomber transport for performance trials
Handley Page Hereford II	K.4029	May	Service trials
Heston Type I Phoenix	G-ADAD	Aug	5-seat civil monoplane C of A
Hawker Audax (India)	K.4850	Mar	Trials aircraft
Hawker Audax (Nisr Iraq)	-	Apr	Export aircraft with Pegasus radial
Hawker Audax I	K.5163	Feb	Avro-built aircraft for trials
	K.7380	Jul	Avro-built aircraft for trials
Hawker Demon	J.9933	Mar	Prototype Hart and Demon with turret
Mk II	K.3764	Jul	Evaluated Turret Demon. Armament
Mk I	K.5684	Sep	Evaluated Turret Demon. Armament
	K.4496	All year	Frazer-Nash turret trials
Hawker Fury Special	-	Mar	Lorraine-engined aircraft. Export
Hawker Fury II	K.7263	Aug	Engine trials with developed aircraft
Hawker Fury (Persia)	203	Feb	Export aircraft with Mercury radial
Hawker G.4/31 PV	K.6926	Jun	General-purpose aircraft for trials
Hawker G.7/34	K.2915	May	General-purpose aircraft for trials
	K.4636	Jun	Handling and performance trials
Hawker GPDB IPV 4	K.6926	Jun	PV dive-bomber for trials
Hawker Hardy I	K.5919	May	Developed aircraft for desert tests
Hawker Hart	K.2434	Apr	Napier Dagger test-bed. Engine tests
	K.3036	Mar	Rolls-Royce test-bed. Engine trials
Hawker Hartebeest	801	Jul	Performance trials on aircraft for South Africa
Hawker Nimrod Intermediate	K.2823	Dec	Standard aircraft with swept wing
Hawker PV3	IPV 3	Oct	Experimental day/night-fighter
Martin Baker MB.I	G-ADCS	-	2-seat light civil aircraft for trials
Miles M4A Merlin	U.8/G-ADFE	Aug	General-purpose biplane for trials
Percival Mew Gull Mk II P.6	G-AEKL	Jun	Redesign of racing aircraft. C of A certification
Percival Vega Gull III	L.7272	Apr	Service light communication aircraft
	G-AEAB	-	Performance trials
	G-AFIE	-	Handling trials
Short Scion II	G-ACUE	-	Developed Mk I for performance trials
Spartan Cruiser III	G-ACYK	Jun	Revised Mk II with cleaned-up lines
Supermarine Walrus	K.5772	Feb	Developed Seagull for service trials
Vickers Type 212 Vellox	G-ABKY	Jan	Further trials of civil airliner
Vickers Vildebeest Mk.III	K.4164	Dec	Mk IV prototype trials
Westland PV7	PV7	May	General-purpose aircraft for test. Crashed
Westland Wallace Mk II	K.3488	Apr	Handling trials of Mk II aircraft
	K.4346	Feb	Weighing and handling trials

During the year the following aircraft were evaluated in comparison trials.

Armstrong Whitworth AW.19)
Bristol 120)
Fairey G.4/31)
Handley Page HP.47)
Hawker PV4) None of these aircraft were ordered into quantity production.
Parnall G.4/31)
Vickers 253)
Westland PV7)

1936

Aeronca C.3	G-AEFT	May	Small civil aircraft of American
	G-ADSO	May	design for C of A performance trials
Armstrong Whitworth AW 38 Whitley	K.4586	Aug	Prototype monoplane bomber. Performance trials
Avro 652A Anson I	K.6152	Oct	1st production aircraft for service trials
	K.6228	Nov	Turret trials. Armament tests
	K.6157	May	Trials aircraft
Avro Tutor II	K.3308	Jul	Special aircraft. Double-bay wings. Performance
Avro Rota	K.4232	Sep	Civet-engined Autogiro. Performance tests
	K.4236	May	Handling trials
Blackburn Shark Mk II	K.5607	Jan	Performance trials on 1st production aircraft
Mk III	K.4882	Feb	3rd production aircraft with Pegasus
		Jun	Return visit for cockpit canopy
British Aircraft Co. No. 4 Double Eagle	G-ADVV	Jul	6-seat civil aircraft for C of A tests
	G-AEIN	Jul	Alternative-engined version C of A
Bristol 142M Blenheim I	K.7033	Apr	3-seat bomber for performance tests
CLW Curlew	G-ADYU	Nov	Civil aircraft performance trials
de Havilland 86B ex-G-ADYL	L.8037	Oct	Modified DH 86 for service tests
	G-ADYH	Dec	Rudder and aileron trials
de Havilland 87B Hornet Moth	P.6785	Feb	Communication aircraft for performance tests
	G-ADMS	Feb	Type test for civil aircraft
de Havilland 89 Dragon Rapide	G-ADWZ	Mar	Modified 60th production aircraft. Weight trials for new all-up load
de Havilland 90 Dragonfly	-	-	Type test of modified aircraft
Fairey Battle	K.4303	Nov	Prototype light-bomber trials
Fairey Seafox	K.4305	Aug	Light fleet aircraft. Service trials
General Aircraft Co. Monospar	G-AECB	Jun	Civil airliner C of A trials. ST.18 Croydon
Gloster Gauntlet I	K.4103	Aug	Flaps and oil cooler tests
	K.4101	Aug	Low-pressure tyres for test
	K.4094	Jul	Trial Browning gun installation
	K.4093	Nov	Tested with Mercury VIS
	K.5271	Aug	Evaluated as Mk II. To Finland
Hawker Audax (Egypt)	K.400	May	Panther-engined aircraft
Hawker Fury Series II (Spain)	4 – 1	Jun	Export aircraft
Hawker Fury II	K.8232	May	Built by General Aircraft
Hawker Fury Series II (Yugoslavia)	-	Oct	Export aircraft for performance trials
Hawker F.36/34 Hurricane	K.5083	Apr	S/seat interceptor for trials
	L.1547	Oct	Trials, aircraft re-engined
	L.1669	Aug	Service trials of production aircraft
	K.5083	Oct	Merlin C engine trials
Hawker Hart (T) (Singapore)	K.6426	Mar	C of G trials
Hawker Hector 14/35	K.3719	Jul	Prototype Army Cooperation aircraft
Hawker Hind	K.4636	Jan	Light bomber service trials

Aircraft	Serial No.	Month	Remarks
Handley Page Harrow HP.54	K.6933	Dec	Performance and handling trials later G-AFRG
Handley Page HP 52	K.4240	Jul	Medium bomber for performance tests
Hillson Praga HA 12	G-AEEU	May	2nd prototype civil aircraft C of A, Czech design
	G-AEPN	Sep	Civil aircraft C of A, Czech design
Lockheed 10	G-AEPN	Sep	American airliner evaluated
Miles Falcon M.3	K.5924	Jun	Civil monoplane for service test
Miles Hawk Major	K.8626	Feb	Civil monoplane for service test
Miles Mk II Whitney Straight	G-AECT	May	Civil aircraft for C of A certification
Parnall Heck IIC	K.8853	Mar	Armament trials aircraft
Short Scion Senior	G-AECU	Jul	4-engined development of Scion. C of A certification tests
Supermarine Spitfire	K.5054	Sep	Prototype aircraft for handling tests
Vickers Type 279 Venom	PVO-10	May	S/seat interceptor for trial
Vickers B.9/32 Type 271	K.4059	Apr	Prototype bomber trials. Crashed
Vickers G.4/31 Type 287 Wellesley I	K.7556	Mar	Monoplane bomber for evaluation
Westland Lysander Mk I	K.6127	Jul	Army Cooperation aircraft evaluation tests
	K.6128	Jul	2nd prototype for handling

For the next three years the lists of aircraft are in slightly different format. As numbers became greater, they were divided into their respective sections – performance and armament testing.

1937
PERFORMANCE-TESTING SECTION

Aircraft	Serial No.	Aircraft	Serial No.
Airspeed Envoy (King's Flight Aircraft)	G-AEXX	Miles Mentor	L.4392
Airspeed Oxford I	L-4534	Miles Nighthawk	L.6846
Armstrong Whitworth Whitley I	K.7183	Moss Brothers MAI	G-AEST
	K.4587	Parnall Heck II	K.8853
Avro Anson	K.4771	Percival Mew Gull X2	G-AFAA
British Aircraft Double Eagle	ZS.AIY	Percival Q.6	G-AEYE
Blackburn Shark II	K.8902	Vickers B.9/32	K.4049
Blackburn Skua 0.27/34	K.5178	Vickers Vannox III B19/27	-
Blackburn Monoplane	K.4241	Vickers PV F.5/34 Venom	0–10
Boulton-Paul Defiant	K.8310	Vickers Viastra	L.6102
Bristol Blenheim (DC)	K.7034	Vickers Vildebeest I	K.2819
Bristol Bolingbroke	K.7072	Vickers Vildebeest IV	K.6408
Bristol Bombay	K.7072		K.8087
CW Cygnet	G-AEMA	Vickers Wellesley I	K.7713
de Havilland 85A	G-ADUE		K.7756
de Havilland 86B	G-AUDH		K.7729
	G-AENR	Vickers Wellington I	L.4212
de Havilland TK.4	G-AETK		K.4049
de Havilland 93 Don	L.2387	Westland Lysander I	K.6128
	L.2391		
de Havilland 91 Albatross	G-AEVV		
de Havilland 94 Moth Minor	G-AFSD		
Fairey Battle	K.7558		
Fairey Hendon	K.5085		
	K.5086		
Fairey Seal	K.4779		
Fairey Swordfish	K.5660		
Forster Wickner Wicko	G-AEZZ		
Gloster Gauntlet II	K.5271		

Gloster Gladiator	K.7964
Handley-Page Harrow	K.6933
Handley-Page Hampden	K.4240
Hawker Demon I (Turret)	K.4496
Hawker Hardy	K.5919
Hawker Hector	K.8090
Hawker Hind (Portuguese)	
Hawker Hind	K.4636
	K.6770
Hawker Hurricane	K.5083
Hawker Nimrod	K.2823
Hawker P.4/34 Henley	K.5115
Miles Kestrel M.9	N.3300
Miles Magister	L.5912
	L.5933
	L.5934

ARMAMENT-TESTING SECTION

Boulton & Paul Overstrand	K.8175	Handley Page Heyford Mk I	K.4029
Bristol 120	K.3587	Mk II	K.3503
Bristol Bulldog IIA	K.1691	Mk III	K.6902
Dewoitine 510 (French)	L4670	Hawker Hart	K.2967
Fairey P.4/34	K.7555		K.2968
Fairey Battle	K.7577		K.2740
Gloster Gladiator	K.7919	Hawker Hind	K.2915
	K.7939	Supermarine F.7/30	K.2890
	K.7922	Supermarine Spitfire	K.5054
	K.5200	Vickers Valentia	K.3603
Handley Page Harrow	K.6934	Vickers Vildebeest	S.1715
Mk II	K.6983	Vickers Virginia X	J.7130

GENERAL-DUTIES AIRCRAFT

Avro Tutor	K.6116	de Havilland 82A Tiger Moth	K.4281
	K.3308	Gloster Gauntlet	K.4103
Avro Rota I (Autogiro)	K.4232	Hawker Fury II	K.1935
Bristol Bulldog IIA	K.4189	Hawker Osprey IV	K.5742
de Havilland Moth 60M	K.1227	Parnall G.4/31	K.2772

1938
PERFORMANCE-TESTING SECTION

Airspeed Oxford I	L.4534	Fairey Battle	K.7558
Armstrong Whitworth Ensign	G-ADSR		K.9281
Armstrong Whitworth Whitley II	K.7217		L.4935
I	K.7183	Fairey Seal	K.4203
II	K.7208	Fairey Swordfish	K.5660
Avro Anson I	L.7928	General Aircraft Monospar	K.8307
	L.6231	Gloster Gladiator	K.8039
Boulton-Paul Defiant I	K.8310		K.8049
Blackburn Shark	K.4882		K.7964
Blackburn Skua	K.5179	Gloster Gladiator (Portuguese)	-
Bristol Beaufort	L.2867	Handley Page Hampden I	K.4240
	L.4441		L.4032
Bristol Blenheim I	K.7034		L.4033
	L6594		L.4035
	L.1424		L.4037

Bristol Blenheim	K.7109	Handley Page Harrow	K.6934
	K.7168	Handley Page Heyford II	K.3503
	L.6595	Hawker Turret Demon I	K.4496
Bristol Bolingbroke	K.7072	Hawker Hardy	K.5919
Bristol Bombay	L.3583	Hawker Hart	K.3031
Bristol Type 146	K.5119	Hawker Henley	K.5115
CW Cygnet	G-AEMA	Hawker Hind (Iran)	601
de Havilland Albatross 'Faraday'	G-AEVV	Hawker Hind	K.4635
'Frobisher'	G-AFDI	Hawker Hind Mk Trainer	K.5387
De Havilland Don I	L.2388	Hawker Nimrod	K.2823
	L.2391	Hawker Hurricane	L.1547
Fairey Albacore	L.7074	Heston Aircraft T.1/37	L.7706
	L.7075	Hillson Praga	G-AEYL
Lockheed 14	G-AFGN	Supermarine Spitfire	K.9787
Martin Baker MB.2	G-AEZD		K.9788
Martin Baker Interceptor	P.9594	Tipsy 'B'	G-AFGF
Miles Magister	L.5933	Vickers Vildbeest I	K.2819
	L.6905	Vickers Vildbeest IV RNZAF	K.6408
	L.8168	Vickers Wellesley I	K.7729
Miles Master I	N.7510	Vickers Wellesley	K.7724
Miles Mentor	L.4392		K.7740
Miles Nighthawk	L.6846	Vickers Wellington I	L.4212
North American Harvard I	N.7000	Westland Lysander I	K.6127
Phillips & Powis PV Trainer	U – 5	Westland Lysander I	K.6128
Percival Q	G-AEYE		L.4673
	VH-ABL		L.4674
Short M.4 (Half-scale Stirling)	S.31	Westland Whirlwind	L.6844

ARMAMENT-TESTING SECTION

Airspeed Oxford I	L.4540		
Airspeed Oxford I	L.4543	Hawker Demon	K.3764
Armstrong Whitworth Whitley	K.7183	Hawker Fury	K.2082
Boulton-Paul Overstrand I	K.8175		K.2876
Boulton-Paul Defiant I	K.8310	Hawker Hardy	K3013
Blackburn Skua	K.5178	Hawker Hart	K.2967
Bristol Blenheim	K.7034		K.2968
	K.7044		K.1416
	L.1113	Hawker Henley	L.3243
	L.1201		L.3247
	K.7150	Hawker Hind	K.2915
	L.1253	Hawker Hurricane I	K.5083
	L.1424		L.1562
Bristol 148.A.39/34	K.6551		L.1574
Dewointine 510 (French)	L.4670		L.1695
Fairey Battle	K.9281		L.1696
	K.9223	Parnell Heck IIC	K.8853
	K.9231	Supermanrine Spitfire I	K.5054
	K.7577		K.6788
	K.9221	Vickers Valentia	K.3603
	K.7682	Vickers Vildebeest I	S.1715
	K.9227	IV	K.8087
Fairey P.4/34	K.7555	Vickers Virginia X	K.7130
Gloster Gladiator	K.7919	Vickers Wellesley I	K.7556
Handley Page Harrow II	K.7031		K.7791
Handley Page Heyford	K.4029	Vickers Wellington I	L.4212
	K.3503	Westland Wallace II	K.3673

GENERAL-DUTIES SECTION

Avro Tutor	K.3308	Hawker Fury II	K.1935
	K.6116	Hawker Hardy	K.5919
Bristol Bulldog	K.4189	Hawker Hind Trainer	K.4636
de Havilland Moth II 82A	K.4281	Parnall Heck IIC	K.8853
Gloster Gauntlet	K.4103	Vickers Vildebeest II	K.2819

EXPERIMENTAL COOPERATION FLIGHT
(the radio-location aircraft experimental unit)

Avro Anson	K.8758	Fairey Battle	K.9230
	K.6260	Miles Magister	L.8168
Fairey Battle I	K.9207	de Havilland 60M Moth	K.1876
	K.9208	Handley Page Harrow	K.7021

1939
(1 January to 1 September, when A & AEE moved from Martlesham Heath to Boscombe Down)

PERFORMANCE-TESTING SECTION

Airspeed Oxford I	L.4560	Handley Page Hampden I	L.4033
Armstrong Whitworth Whitley	K.7208		L.4035
	K.9836		L.4032
Armstrong Whitworth Ensign	G-ADSW	Handley-Page Hereford I	L.7271
'Eddystone'		Hawker Hardy I	K.5919
Avro Anson	K.8758	Hawker Hart	K.2968
	K.6260	Hawker Henley	L.3243
	N.4871	Hawker Hurricane	L.1547
Avro Tutor	K.6116		L.1696
Blackburn Skua	K.5178		L.1702
	L.2871	Heston Aircraft T.1/37	L.7706
	L.2888	Hendy Heck IIC	K.8853
Blackburn Roc	L.3058	Lockheed Hudson I	N.7205
	L.3059		N.7207
	L.3057		N.7208
Blackburn Botha	L.6104	Miles Magister	K.8168
Bristol Blenheim	L.6594	Miles Mentor	L.4393
	L.6622	Monospar ST.25 Jubilee	K.8307
	L.6623	North American Harvard I	N.7000
	L.6624		N.7001
	L.6625		N.7013
	L.6626	Phillips & Powis M.18	U - 2
	L.6627	Parnall T.1/37	J - 1
Bristol Bombay	K.3583	Reid & Sigrist Snargasher RS.1	G-AEOD
	L.5808	Seversky	NX.2586
Bristol Beaufort	L.4441	Supermarine Spitfire	K.9788
Fairey Battle	K.7605		K.9787
	K.9281		K.9793
	L.4935		K.5054
	K.9207	Vickers Vildebeest	K.2819
	K.9208	Vickers Wellington	L.4221
	K.9230		L.4223
	K.7577		L.4212
	L.8662		L.4213
	L.8689		L.4302
Fairey Swordfish	L.9776		L.4335

| Handley Page Harrow | K.7021 | Westland Lysander | L.4673 |
| | K.6934 | | |

ARMAMENT-TESTING SECTION

Armstrong Whitworth Whitley	K.7183	Handley-Page Harrow	K.6934
Avro Anson	K.6152	Hawker Demon	K.3764
Avro Tutor	K.6116	Hawker Fury	K.2082
Blackburn Skua	L.2868		K.2876
Blackburn Roc	L.3058	Hawker Hardy	K.3013
	L.3069	Hawker Hart	K.2968
Bristol Blenheim I	L.1201		K.1416
	K.7044	Hawker Henley	L.3247
	L.1495	Hawker Hind	K.2915
	L.1253	Hawker Hurricane	L.1574
de Havilland Moth	K.4281		L.1695
Fairey Battle	K.9221	Lockheed Hudson I	N.7206
	K.2931	North American Harvard I	N.7001
	K.9223	Supermarine Spitfire I	L.1007
Fairey Fantome/Feroc	L.7045	Vickers Valentia	K.3603
General Aircraft Monospar	L.4671	Vickers Virginia X	J.7130
Gloster Gladiator	K.7964	Vickers Wellington	L.4212
	K.6129		L.4221
Handley Page Hampden	L.4035	Westland Lysander	L.4739

In the last year of A & AEE at Martlesham Heath, large numbers of aircraft of one type visited the the unit for various tests, thereby cutting the time needed to completely evaluate an aircraft type.

Appendix H
Pilots on the Strength of Fighter, Fleet Spotter and Reconnaissance Flights of the Fleet Air Arm

NOTE: These personnel manning data are for units of the Fleet Air Arm in 1939, the year after the FAA was transferred to the Admiralty. Most of the officers were Royal Navy or Royal Marine officers who carried RAF ranks, which was the arrangement brought into force in the 1920s under the joint service agreement: that the FAA should be manned by RN/RM and RAF officers, the former being given RAF equivalent ranks. It shows the extent of naval manning of FAA units by this time.

HMS *Courageous* No. 800 (Fleet Fighter) Squadron – Southampton – Coastal Command

Flight Lieutenants:
G.N. Terry (Lt RN)
F.D.G. Bird (Lt RM)

Flying Officers:
J.C.M. Harman (Lt RN)
K.V.V. Spurway (Lt RN)
D.W. Balden
G.E.D. Finch-Noyes (Lt RN)
E.W.T. Taylor (acting Lt RN)
J.A. Rooper (Sub Lt RN)

Pilot Officers:
H.F.R. Bradbury
R.F. Aitken

HMS *Furious* No. 801 (Fleet Fighter) Squadron – Southampton – Coastal Command

Squadron Leader:
G.K. Fairtlough

Flight Lieutenants:
G.P. Seymour Price
J.M. Bruen (Lt RN)

Flying Officers:
R.H.P. Carver (Sub Lt RN)

HMS *Glorious* No. 802 (Fleet Fighter) Squadron – Hal Far – Mediterranean
Squadron Leaders:
J.P.G. Bryant (Lt Cdr RN)

Flight Lieutenants:
R.J.W. Nott (Lt RN)
J.F. Marmont (Lt RN)
N.B.R. Bromley

Flying Officers:
C.P. Campbell-Horsfall (Lt RN)
O.J.R. Nicolls (Lt RN)
R.L. Strange (Lt RN)
R.L. Smith
J.R.I. Bell
H.J. Garlick
W.L.LeC. Barnes (Sub Lt RN)

HMS *Courageous* No. 810 (Torpedo Spotter Reconnaissance) Squadron – Gosport – Coastal Command
Squadron Leaders:
N.R.M. Skene

Flight Lieutenants:
F.W. Brown (Capt RM)

Flying Officers:
A.P. Boddam-Whetham (Sub Lt RN)
A.S. Kennard (Sub Lt RN)
P.D. Gick (Lt RN)
D.F. Godfrey-Faussett (Sub Lt RN)
N.R. Corbet-Milward (Acting Lt RN)
W.A.L. Davis
A.A. Pardoe (Sub Lt RN)
A.W. Stewart (Acting Lt RN)

HMS *Furious* No. 811 (Torpedo Spotter Reconnaissance) Squadron – Gosport – Coastal Command

Squadron Leaders:
E.G.F Price (Lt Cdr RN)

Flight Lieutenants:
S.L.G. Evans (Lt RN)

Flying Officers:
W.A.A. de Freitas (Acting Flt Lt)
E.N. Stidolph
G.H.C. O'Rorke (Sub Lt RN)

HMS *Glorious*   No. 812 (Torpedo Spotter Reconnaissance) Squadron – Hal Far – Mediterranean

Squadron Leaders:
J.D.C. Little (Lt Cdr RN)

Flight Lieutenants:
A.D. Murray

Flying Officers:
W.A.H. Playfair (Lt RN)
R.W. Clifford (Lt RN)
F.M.A. Torrens-Spence (Lt RN)
J.H. Barnes (Lt RN)
G. Starkey (Lt RN)
E.B. Baker-Falkner (Sub Lt RN)
H.E.J.P.T. Parker (Sub Lt RN)
J.J.E. Coats
K.B. Gurr (Lt RN)

HMS *Eagle*   No. 813 (Torpedo Spotter Reconnaissance) Squadron – Far East

Squadron Leaders:
N. Kennedy (Lt Cdr RN)

Flight Lieutenants:
R.M. Smeaton (Lt RN)
P.M. Gregory (Lt RN)
P.N. Medd (Lt RN)

Flying Officers:
C.S. Cooper
D.O.F. Lumsden
F.G.R. Thomas
J. Compton

HMS *Courageous*   No. 820 (Torpedo Spotter Reconnaissance) Squadron – Gosport – Coastal Command

Squadron Leaders:
A.C.G. Erman (Lt Cdr RN)

Flight Lieutenants:
J. Dalyell-Stead (Lt RN)

Flying Officers:
P.G. Sugden (Lt RN)
R.N. Everett (Lt RN)
M.R. North (Acting Lt RN)
T.S. Rivett-Carnac
R.S. Hankey (Acting Lt RN)
D.V.W. Francis
B.E. Boulding (Sub Lt RN)
N.M. Hearle (Lt RN)

H.de G. Hunter (Sub Lt RN)

HMS *Courageous*   No. 821 (Torpedo Spotter Reconnaissance) Squadron – Gosport – Coastal Command

Squadron Leaders:
N.E. Morrison

Flight Lieutenants:
A.G. Leatham (Lt RN)
A.W.J. Clark

Flying Officers:
J.H. Stenning (Lt RN)
B. Willoughby (Lt RN)
A.H. Abrams (Lt RN)
J.Greenhalgh

HMS *Furious*   No. 822 (Torpedo Spotter Reconnaissance) Squadron – Coastal Command

Squadron Leaders:
K. Williamson (Lt Cdr RN)

Flight Lieutenants:
A.F. Hall (Lt RN)
C.F. Herington

Flying Officers:
D.A.S. Wright (Sub Lt RN)
J.A.C. Karran

HMS *Glorious*   No. 823 (Torpedo Spotter Reconnaissance) Squadron – Hal Far – Mediterranean

Squadron Leaders:
R.A.Kilroy (Lt.Cdr.RN)

Flight Lieutenants:
G.F.L. Scott
J.L. Hallewell (Lt RN)
J.R. Jeudwine
D.H.S. Rusher
P.W. Compton (Lt RN)

Flying Officers:
A.R.H. Barton (Lt RN)
J.C. Reed (Lt RN)
R.H. Furlong (Lt RN)
E.L. Wurtele
J.R. Fishwick
R.W. Slater (Lt RN)
A.J.G. Lydekker (Acting Lt RN)

Warrant Officer:
C.A. Denne

HMS *Eagle*   No. 824 (Torpedo Spotter Reconnaissance) Squadron – Far East

Squadron Leaders:
R.G. Forbes

Flight Lieutenants:
G.A.L. Woods (Lt RN)

Flying Officers:
G.W.L.A. Bayly (Lt RN)
O. Patch (Lt RM)
M.R.F. Lemon (Lt RN)
M.R. Maund (Acting Lt RN)
F.O. Dickson
B.J. Sandeman
A.N. Young (Sub Lt RN)

HMS *Glorious*   No. 825 (Torpedo Spotter Reconnaissance) Squadron – Hal Far – Mediterranean

Squadron Leaders:
J.W. Hale (Lt Cdr RN)

Flight Lieutenants:
A.S. Whitworth (Lt RN)

Flying Officers:
G.B. Bateman (Lt RN)
E.L. Williamson (Lt RN)
G.W.B. Smith (Acting Lt RN)
R.W.V. Hamilton (Lt RN)
J. Rankin

Appendix I
RAF Stations by Commands, 1938, and Forming/Re-forming of Squadrons on Stations

Bomber Command Stations	Fighter Command Stations
Abingdon	Abbotsinch
Andover	Aldergrove
Benson	Bentley Priory
Bicester	Biggin Hill
Boscombe Down	Catterick
Castle Bromwich	Chigwell (balloon)
Cranfield	Church Fenton
Driffield	Croydon
Feltwell	Debden
Filton	Detling
Finningley	Digby
Grantham	Duxford
Leconfield	Hawkinge
Linton-on-Ouse	Hendon
Harwell	Heston
Heyford	Hook (balloon)
Hooton Park	Hornchurch
Hucknall	Kenley
Lincoln	Lympne
Marham	Northolt
Mildenhall	North Weald
Norwich	Odiham
Scampton	Old Sarum
Speke	Stanmore (balloon)
Stradishall	Tangmere
Upwood	Tavistock Place
Waddington	Thornaby
Worthy Down	Turnhouse
Yeadon	Usworth
	West Freugh
	Wittering

Stations under construction	Station under construction
Bassingbourne	Kirton in Lindsey
Binbrook	
Bulkington	
Coltishall	
Cottesmore	
Doncaster	
Ely Hospital	
Hatfield Woodhouse	
Hemswell	
Honington	
Horsham St Faith	
Langham	

Leeming
Middle Wallop
Newton
Topcliffe
Wattisham
Watton
West Raynham
Wyton

Coastal Command Stations	**Training Command Stations**
Aberdeen	Acklington
Bawdsey	Altrincham
Bircham Newton	Brize Norton
Calshot	Buntingsdale Hall
Donibristle	Cardington
Eastchurch	Cardiff
Eastleigh	Catfoss
Evanton	Cirencester
Felixstowe	Cranwell
Ford	Farnborough
Gosport	Great Rissington
Lee-on-Solent	Halton
Leuchars	Henlow
Leysdown	Hullavington
Manston	Manby
Martlesham	Netheravon
Montrose	North Coates Fitties
Mount Batten	Pembrey
Orfordness	Pembroke
Pulham	Penrhos
Thorney Island	Peterborough
Wick	Porthcawl
	Rolleston

Maintenance Command Stations

Brook Green	Sealand
Chilmark	Shawbury
Ickenham	South Cerney
Kemble	Sutton Bridge
Kidbrooke (balloon)	Tern Hill
Milton	Upavon
Minchinhampton	Uxbridge
Wembley	West Drayton

The following Maintenance Units were lodger units on stations of other commands

Brize Norton	Shawbury
Great Rissington	Tern Hill
Hullavington	
Sealand	

Stations under construction

Carlisle	Moreton-in-the-Marsh
Cosford	Quedgley
Fauld	St Athan
Hartlebury	Silloth
Kirkbride	Wroughton
Lancashire Depot	Yatesbury

RAF squadrons formed or re-formed during the expansion years

Date	Squadron	Formed or Re-formed F or RF	Station	Aircraft
1934				
1 May	No. 22 Squadron	RF	Donibristle	Vildebeest I
1 Jun	No. 15 Squadron	RF	Abingdon	Hart
1 Jun	No. 142 Squadron	RF	Netheravon	Hart
1 Aug	No. 65 Squadron	RF	Hornchurch	Demon
1 Dec	No. 230 Squadron	RF	Pembroke Dock	Singapore III
1935				
1 Sep	No. 74 Squadron	RF	Hornchurch	Demon
16 Sep	No. 38 Squadron	RF	Mildenhall	Heyford III
16 Sep	No. 97 Squadron	RF	Catfoss	Heyford 1A
16 Sep	No. 214 Squadron	RF	Boscombe Down	Virginia X
1 Oct	No. 102 Squadron	RF	Worthy Down	Heyford II & III
1 Oct	No. 215 Squadron	RF	Worthy Down	Virginia X
25 Nov	No. 48 Squadron	RF	Bicester/Manston	Cloud
3 Dec	No. 21 Squadron	RF	Bircham Newton	Hind
3 Dec	No. 34 Squadron	RF	Bircham Newton	Hind
1936				
7 Jan	No. 104 Squadron	RF	Abingdon	Hind
10 Feb	No. 49 Squadron	RF	Bircham Newton	Hind
10 Feb	No. 609 Squadron	F	Yeadon	Hart
10 Feb	No. 610 Squadron	F	Hendon to Hooton Park	Hart
10 Feb	No. 611 Squadron	F	Hendon to Speke	Hart
17 Feb	No. 98 Squadron	RF	Abingdon	Hind
1 Mar	No. 64 Squadron	RF	Heliopolis	Demon
16 Mar	No. 218 Squadron	RF	Upper Heyford	Hart
15 Jun	No. 206 Squadron	RF	Manston	Anson I
20 Jul	No. 66 Squadron	RF	Duxford	Gauntlet II
4 Aug	No. 83 Squadron	RF	Turnhouse	Hind
10 Aug	No. 103 Squadron	RF	Andover	Hind
10 Aug	No. 107 Squadron	RF	Andover	Hind
17 Aug	No. 220 Squadron	RF	Bircham Newton	Anson I
3 Sep	No. 46 Squadron	RF	Kenley	Gauntlet II
3 Sep	No. 139 Squadron	RF	Wyton	Hind
1 Nov	No. 78 Squadron	RF	Boscombe Down	Heyford III
1 Nov	No. 166 Squadron	RF	Boscombe Down	Heyford III
1 Dec	No. 114 Squadron	RF	Wyton	Hind
7 Dec	No. 269 Squadron	RF	Bircham Newton	Anson I

14 Dec	No. 42 Squadron	RF	Donibristle	Vildebeest III
15 Dec	No. 223 Squadron	RF	Nairobi	Gordon
15 Dec	No. 228 Squadron	RF	Pembroke Dock	Scapa

1937

4 Jan	No. 108 Squadron	RF	Upper Heyford	Hind
11 Jan	No. 144 Squadron	RF	Bicester	Overstrand
18 Jan	No. 52 Squadron	RF	Abingdon	Hind
1 Feb	No. 224 Squadron	RF	Manston	Anson I
15 Feb	No. 63 Squadron	RF	Andover	Hind
22 Feb	No. 72 Squadron	RF	Tangmere	Gladiator I
8 Mar	No. 44 Squadron	RF	Wyton	Hind
8 Mar	No. 61 Squadron	RF	Hemswell	Audax
8 Mar	No. 80 Squadron	RF	Kenley	Gauntlet II
8 Mar	No. 213 Squadron	RF	Northolt	Gauntlet II
15 Mar	No. 51 Squadron	RF	Driffield	Virginia X
15 Mar	No. 73 Squadron	RF	Mildenhall	Fury II
15 Mar	No. 75 Squadron	RF	Driffield	Virginia X
15 Mar	No. 87 Squadron	RF	Tangmere	Fury II
15 Mar	No. 90 Squadron	RF	Bicester	Hind
15 Mar	No. 217 Squadron	RF	Boscombe Down	Anson I
15 Mar	No. 226 Squadron	RF	Upper Heyford	Audax
22 Mar	No. 79 Squadron	RF	Biggin Hill	Gauntlet II
30 Mar	No. 240 Squadron	RF	Calshot	Scapa
12 Apr	No. 76 Squadron	RF	Finningley	Wellesley
12 Apr	No. 105 Squadron	RF	Upper Heyford	Audax
12 Apr	No. 149 Squadron	RF	Mildenhall	Heyford III
26 Apr	No. 37 Squadron	RF	Feltwell	Harrow
3 May	No. 50 Squadron	RF	Waddington	Hind
18 May	No. 110 squadron	RF	Waddington	Hind
18 May	No. 113 Squadron	RF	Upper Heyford	Hind
1 Jun	No. 612 squadron	F	Dyce	Hector
1 Jun	No. 614 Squadron	F	Pengam Moors	Hind
1 Jun	No. 615 Squadron	F	Kenley	Audax
7 Jun	No. 88 Squadron	RF	Waddington	Hind
7 Jun	No. 148 Squadron	RF	Scampton	Audax
14 Jun	No. 77 Squadron	RF	Finningley	Audax
14 Jun	No. 82 Squadron	RF	Andover	Hind
15 Jun	No. 115 Squadron	RF	Marham	Hendon II
24 Jun	No. 211 Squadron	RF	Mildenhall	Audax
28 Jun	No. 53 Squadron	RF	Farnborough	Hector
28 Jun	No. 59 Squadron	RF	Old Sarum	Hector

1938

1 Mar	No. 185 Squadron	RF	Abingdon	Hind
1 Jun	No. 85 Squadron	RF	Debden	Gladiator
1 Jun	No. 106 Squadron	RF	Abingdon	Hind
4 Aug	No. 151 Squadron	RF	North Weald	Gauntlet II
8 Aug	No. 150 Squadron	RF	Boscombe Down	Battle
1 Nov	No. 616 Squadron	F	Doncaster	Hind I

1939

1 Mar	No. 613 Squadron	F	Ringway	Hind
26 Mar	No. 94 Squadron	RF	Khormaksar	Gladiator I
16 May	No.112 Squadron	RF	HMS *Argus*/Helwan	Gladiator I & II
1 Aug	No. 273 Squadron	RF	China Bay	Seal

Appendix J
RAF Apprentice Entries During the 1930s

Entry No.	Highest and Lowest Service Numbers		Arrival Date	Annual Totals
21	564049	564576	Jan 1930	
22	564577	565056	Sep 1930	1008
23	565057	565458	Jan 1931	
24	565459	565843	Sep 1931	787
25	564844	566009	Jan 1932	
26	566010	566241	Sep 1932	398
27	566242	566458	Jan 1933	
28	566463	566702	Sep 1933	457
29	566707	566956	Jan 1934	
30	566959	567346	Aug 1934	638
31	567348	567892	Jan 1935	
32	567893	568813	Aug 1935	1466
33	568814	569665	Jan 1936	
34	569668	570749	Aug 1936	1934
35	570756	571604	Jan 1937	
36	571605	572851	Aug 1937	2096
37	572855	573688	Jan 1938	
38	573691	574991	Aug 1938	2135
39	574992	576080	Jan 1939	
40	576084	577461	Aug 1939	2135

The numbers of entrants fell during the Depression years to an all-time low in 1932, only to rise dramatically in the first complete year of the expansion in 1935. The total annual intakes for 1940 and 1941, however, drop to 926 and 267 respectively, reflecting the fact that the Second World War had commenced and that the RAF expansion had reached the level necessary to take the country into war. In any event, the length of the Apprentice course could not materially affect manning levels until well into the war. As it was, the nation's manpower was being fully tapped through conscription, and women were being trained in the technical trades.

Appendix K
RAF Officers' Uniforms

Full Dress

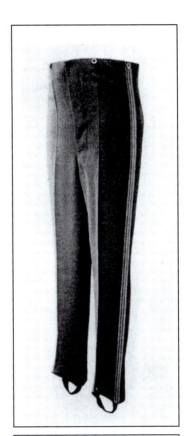

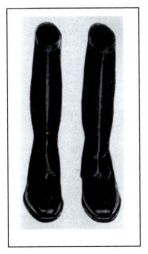

Helmet front

Ceremonial Helmet side

Service Dress

Service Dress Jacket

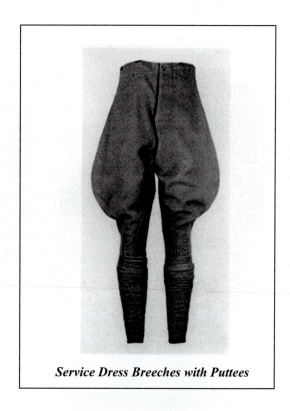

Service Dress Breeches with Puttees

Service Dress Boots

Air Officers' Peak

Service Dress Cap – Pilot Officer to Wing Commander

Group Captain's Peak

Service Dress *continued*

Full uniform greatcoat

Service Dress Greatcoat

Raincoat

Service Dress with Webbing

Mess Dress

Mess Kit Jacket

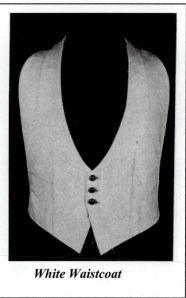

White Waistcoat

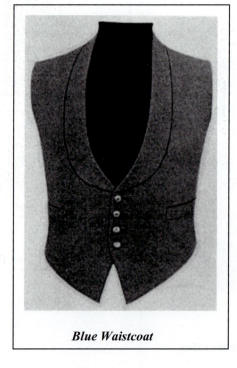

Blue Waistcoat

Tropical Dress

Tropical Service Dress Jacket

Pith Helmet

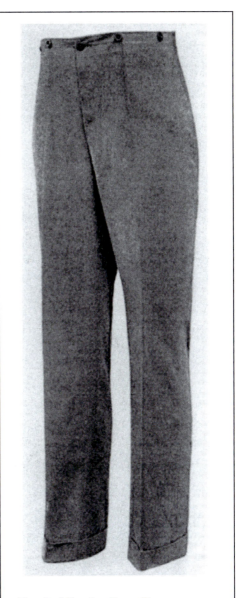

Tropical Service Dress Trousers

Appendix L
Members of the Air Council in the 1930s

31 March 1930

Secretary of State for Air – Brigadier-General the Rt Hon. the Lord Thomson PC, CBE, DSO, psc

Under-Secretary of State for Air – F. Montague Esq., MP

Chief of the Air Staff – Air Chief Marshal Sir John Salmond KCB, CMG, CVO, DSO

Air Member for Personnel – Air Vice-Marshal T.I. Webb-Bowen CB, CMG

Air Member for Supply and Research – Air Marshal Sir John F.A. Higgins KCB, KBE, DSO, AFC

Deputy Chief of the Air Staff – Air Vice-Marshal C.L.N. Newall CB, CMG, AM (Additional Member)

Secretary – Sir Walter F. Nicholson KCB

31 March 1931

Secretary of State for Air – The Rt Hon. the Lord Amulree PC, GBE, KC

Under-Secretary of State for Air – F. Montague Esq, MP

Chief of the Air Staff – Air Chief Marshal Sir John Salmond KCB, CMG, CVO, DSO, LLD

Air Member for Personnel – Air Vice-Marshal T.I. Webb-Bowen CB, CMG

Air Member for Supply and Research – Air Vice-Marshal H.C.T. Dowding CB, CMG,

Secretary – C.Ll. Bullock Esq., CB, CBE

31 March 1932

Secretary of State for Air – The Most Hon. the Marquess of Londonderry KG, MVO

Under-Secretary of State for Air – Major the Rt Hon. Sir Philip A.G.D. Sassoon Bart, GBE, CMG, MP

Chief of the Air Staff – Air Chief Marshal Sir John Salmond GCB, CMG, CVO, DSO, LLD

Air Member for Personnel – Air Marshal Sir Edward L. Ellington KCB, CMG, CBE, psc, ADC

Air Member for Supply and Research – Air Vice-Marshal H.C.T. Dowding CB, CMG

Secretary – C.Ll. Bullock Esq., CB, CBE

31 March 1933

Secretary of State for Air – The Most Hon. the Marquess of Londonderry KG, MVO

Under-Secretary of State for Air – Major the Rt Hon. Sir Philip A.G.D. Sassoon Bart, GBE, CMG, MP

Chief of the Air Staff – Marshal of the RAF Sir John Salmond GCB, CMG, CVO, DSO, LLD

Air Member for Personnel – Air Chief Marshal Sir Edward L. Ellington KCB, CMG, CBE, psc, ADC

Air Member for Supply and Research – Air Marshal H.C.T. Dowding CB, CMG, psc

Secretary – Sir Christopher Ll. Bullock KCB, CBE

31 March 1934

Secretary of State for Air – The Most Hon. the Marquess of Londonderry KG, MVO

Under-Secretary of State for Air – Major the Rt Hon. Sir Philip A.G.D. Sassoon Bart, GBE, CMG, MP

Chief of the Air Staff – Air Chief Marshal Sir Edward L. Ellington KCB, CMG, CBE, psc

Air Member for Personnel – Air Vice-Marshal F.W. Bowhill CMG, DSO

Air Member for Supply and Research – Air Marshal Sir Hugh C.T. Dowding KCB, CMG, psc

Secretary – Sir Christopher Ll. Bullock KCB, CBE

31 March 1935

Secretary of State for Air – The Most Hon. the Marquess of Londonderry KG, MVO

Under-Secretary of State for Air – Major the Rt Hon. Sir Philip A.G.D. Sassoon Bart, GBE, CMG, MP

Chief of the Air Staff – Air Chief Marshal Sir Edward L. Ellington KCB, CMG, CBE, psc

Air Member for Personnel – Air Vice-Marshal F.W. Bowhill CMG, DSO

Air Member for Research and Development – Air Marshal Sir Hugh C.T. Dowding KCB, CMG, psc

Air Member for Supply and Organization – Air Vice-Marshal C.L.N. Newall CB, CMG, CBE, AM

Secretary - Sir Christopher Ll. Bullock KCB, CBE

31 March 1936

Secretary of State for Air – The Rt Hon. the Viscount Swinton GBE, MC

Under-Secretary of State for Air – Major the Rt Hon. Sir Philip A.G.D. Sassoon Bart, GBE, CMG, MP

Chief of the Air Staff – Air Chief Marshal Sir Edward L. Ellington KCB, CMG, CBE, psc

Air Member for Personnel – Air Vice-Marshal F.W. Bowhill CMG, DSO

Air Member for Supply and Research – Air Marshal Sir Hugh C.T. Dowding KCB, CMG, psc

Air Member for Supply and Organization – Air Marshal Sir Cyril L.N. Newall KCB, CMG, CBE, AM

Secretary – Sir Christopher Ll. Bullock KCB, CBE

31 March 1937

Secretary of State for Air – The Rt Hon. the Viscount Swinton GBE, MC

Under-Secretary of State for Air – Major the Rt Hon. Sir Philip A.G.D. Sassoon Bart, GBE, CMG, MP

Chief of the Air Staff – Marshal of the RAF Sir Edward L. Ellington KCB, CMG, CBE, psc

Air Member for Personnel – Air Marshal Sir Frederick W. Bowhill KCB, CMG, DSO

Air Member for Research and Development – Air Marshal W.R. Freeman CB, DSO, MC, psc

Air Member for Supply and Organization – Air Marshal Sir Cyril L.N. Newall KCB, CMG, CBE, AM

Secretary – Colonel Sir Donald Banks KCB, DSO, MC

31 March 1938

Secretary of State for Air – The Rt Hon. the Viscount Swinton GBE, MC

Chancellor of the Duchy of Lancaster, Deputy to the S of S – The Rt Hon. the Earl Winterton MP

Under-Secretary of State for Air – Lieutenant-Colonel A.J. Muirhead MC, MP

Chief of the Air Staff – Air Chief Marshal Sir Cyril L.N. Newall KCB, CMG, CBE, AM

Air Member for Personnel – Air Marshal G.S. Mitchell KCB, DSO, MC, AFC

Air Member for Research and Development – Air Marshal Sir Wilfred R. Freeman CB, DSO, MC, psc

Air Member for Supply and Organization – Air Vice-Marshal Sir Cyril W.L. Welsh CB, DFC, AFC

Secretary – Colonel Sir Donald Banks KCB, DSO, MC

31 March 1939

Secretary of State for Air – The Rt Hon. Sir Kingsley Wood MP

Parliamentary Under-Secretary of State for Air – Captain H.H. Balfour MC, MP

Chief of the Air Staff – Air Chief Marshal Sir Cyril L.N. Newall KCB, CMG, CBE, AM

Air Member for Personnel – Air Vice-Marshal C.F.A. Portal CB, DSO, MC

Air Member for Development and Production – Air Marshal Sir Wilfred R. Freeman CB, DSO, MC, psc

Air Member for Supply and Organization – Air Vice-Marshal Sir Cyril W.L. Welsh CB, DFC, AFC

Director-General of Production – E.J.H. Lemon OBE, MIMechE, Minst T

Permanent Under-Secretary – Colonel Sir Donald Banks KCB, DSO, MC (at this time on a mission to Australia and New Zealand)

First Deputy Under-Secretary of State – Sir Arthur Street KBE, CB, CMG, CIE, MC

Bibliography

The remarks below are those of the author, who wishes to explain the value of the source books in compiling this encyclopedia.

PUBLICATIONS

Hyde, Montgomery, *British Air Policy between the Wars*, London, Heinemann

Very good on relations between governments and the RAF, Air Estimates, the unfolding international scenario from 1919 and inter-service rivalry.

Bowyer, Chas, *RAF Operations 1918 to 1939*, London, William Kimber

Factual accounts of operations. Places squadrons and personnel in context.

James John, *The Paladins, a social history of the RAF up to the outbreak of World War II*, Macdonald & Co. Ltd

The inspiration for the compilation of this encyclopedia.

Taylor, John W.R., *Pictorial History of the RAF, Volume I 1918–1939*, Ian Allan

A wealth of photographs, each of which tells a story.

Various, 'Action Stations' series, Various publishers

This series of publications covers RAF airfields and miscellaneous establishments in the entire United Kingdom and a selection of bases overseas. Chapter 7 of this encyclopedia was based almost exclusively on these works.

Jefford, Wing Commander C.G., MBE, RAF, *RAF Squadrons*, Airlife Publishing Ltd

This book was invaluable in compiling Appendix B.

Penrose, Harald, *British Aviation – the adventuring years 1920 to 1929*, Putnam Press

——, *British Aviation – widening horizons 1930 to 1934*, HMSO

——, *British Aviation – ominous skies 1935 to 1939*, HMSO

All three works are excellent, not only in charting the development of aircraft and the aircraft industry, but in weaving in political, international and economic events that served as a backdrop to the period.

Slessor, MRAF Sir John, *The Central Blue*, Cassell and Company Ltd

Good on contribution of senior RAF officers to the development of British airpower.

Thetford, Owen, *Aircraft of the Royal Air Force since 1918*, Putnam Press

Invaluable for compiling Appendix A.

Kinsey, Gordon, *Martlesham Heath*, Terence Dalton, Lavenham, Suffolk

This was invaluable in compiling the data for Appendix G.

Together with source material from the National Archives, Kew, and the RAF Museum, Hendon. All sources are quoted in the text to which they refer.

Index